UNIVERSITY OF NORTHUMBRIA
AT NEWCASTLE LIBRARY
WITHDRAWN

Houseman's Law of Life Assurance

Fourteenth edition

Houseman's Law of Life Assurance

Fourteenth edition

Robert Surridge
Solicitor, Chief Counsel, Friends Life

Brian Murphy
Chartered Financial Planner, Financial Planning Manager, AXA Wealth

Noleen John
Solicitor, Consultant, Norton Rose

With contribution from:

Colin Griffin
Senior Pensions Technical Analyst, AXA Wealth
Chapter 16: The Tax Framework for Registered Pension Schemes

Bloomsbury Professional

Bloomsbury Professional Ltd, Maxwelton House, 41–43 Boltro Road, Haywards Heath, West Sussex, RH16 1BJ

Bloomsbury Professional is an imprint of Bloomsbury Publishing Plc

A CIP Catalogue record for this book is available from the British Library.

ISBN 14 978 1 84766 748 9

Typeset by Phoenix Photosetting, Chatham, Kent
Printed and bound by CPI Group (UK) Ltd, Croydon, CR0 4YY

Preface

As ever in producing this edition of *Houseman* we have tried to cover the areas we think a practitioner needs to be aware of in detail where possible and by sign-posting where that would be beyond the scope of this work.

We find ourselves once again publishing this book at a time of change from a regulatory perspective. There have already been changes at the European level, including the creation of the European Insurance and Occupational Pensions Authority (EIOPA). EIOPA will have a significant role to play in the introduction of the Solvency II Directive. In the UK changes are proposed which will see the FSA's current role in relation to insurers being shared between the Prudential Regulation Authority (PRA) and the Financial Conduct Authority (FCA). At the time of writing it is proposed that the UK changes be in place by 2013 at which time parts of Solvency II may also be in place. We anticipate that the next edition of this book will cover Solvency II in further detail by which point it is hoped that its final shape will be clearer. Other significant changes in the pipeline include the implementation of the Retail Distribution Review which again should be much clearer in the next edition. We still await a slowing down in the pace of change!

We would like to thank all of those people whose patience and understanding has enabled this book to be rewritten including, in particular, AXA Wealth, Friends Life and Norton Rose. Robert would like to thank his colleagues in the Friends Life legal department for their helpful suggestions and input. He would like to dedicate his contribution to his mother Marion and to the memory of his father Richard. Brian would like to thank Colin Griffin of AXA Wealth for all his work on the sections of the book concerned with the pensions regime and Brian Fisher of Friends Life for his assistance with the long-term care section. In addition to a general thanks to her colleagues at Norton Rose Noleen would like to thank in particular Laura Hodgson and Simon Baker and her secretary Coral Mendez.

This book is based on our understanding of the laws of England and Wales on 1 September 2011. Any views expressed by the editors are personal views and should not be regarded as views of our respective employers.

Noleen John
Robert Surridge
Brian Murphy
November 2011

Contents

Table of Statutes

Table of Statutory Instruments

Table of Cases

T

Introduction

The authors feel that before launching into the more detailed areas concerning the law relating to life assurance a basic overview of the way life companies and life funds are taxed would be useful to the reader.

General Overview of the Taxation of Life Assurance Companies

Whilst a life company has a single corporation tax assessment, each class of business it conducts has to be looked at separately as there are different tax rules for each class. All of the company's income, gains and expenditure have to be apportioned to each class in order to calculate the overall tax liability.

Unlike most companies – which are taxed on their accounting profits – life companies are currently largely taxed on the results in their annual FSA returns, although this is expected to change from 2013 to an accounts basis.

For a diagrammatic summary of life company taxation, and how it interacts with the taxation of policyholders, see below.

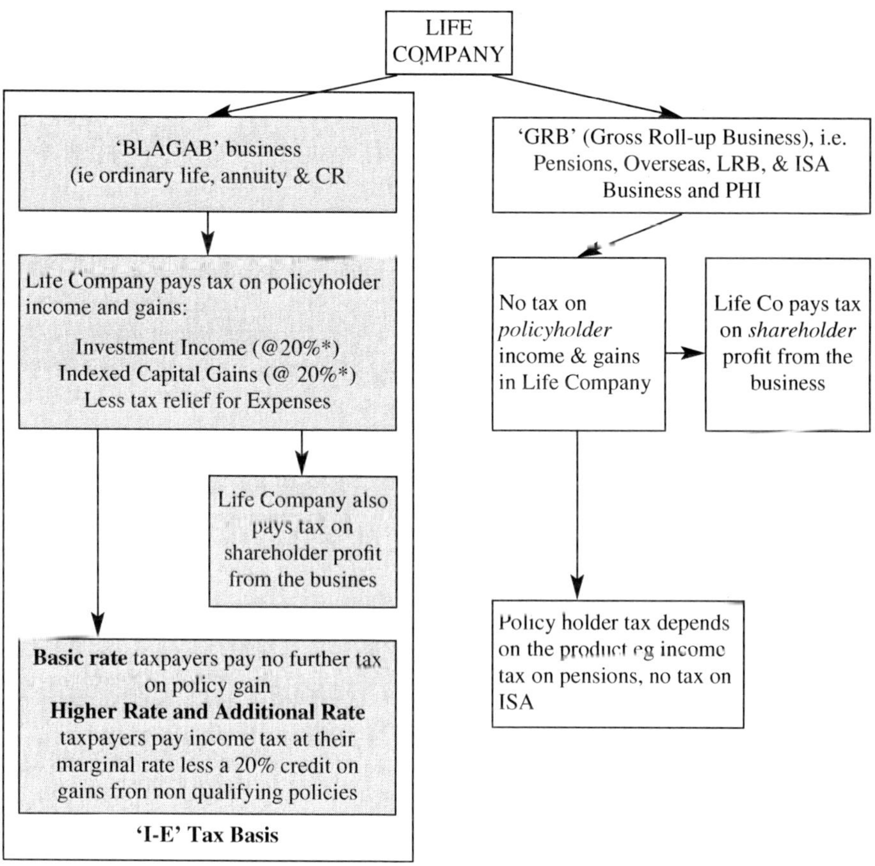

Definitions of each class of business and how they are taxed

Basic Life Assurance & General Annuity Business ('BLAGAB') – includes Capital Redemption Business

This is business that does not fall into any of the other classes below and is (generally) directly written life policies. It is taxed on the so called 'I-E' basis – that is investment income and capital gains less expenses and commission. The tax rate is currently 20%. The first slice of I-E profits equal to the shareholder profits from the business are taxed additionally at the difference between the main corporation tax rate (26% for FY2011) and the 20% rate.

Where there are excess expenses or capital losses, these are carried forward. Most of the world taxes life insurance only on the shareholder profits – the so called 'gross roll up' or GRU system and this may be considered in the UK.

Gross Roll-up Business ('GRB')

Shareholder profits from this business are taxable at the main corporation tax rate. Losses are carried forward. GRB includes the following sub-categories of business:

Pension Business ('PB')

This is business in respect of policies issued in connection with UK registered pension schemes (including reinsurance). Details of the way these funds are taxed are given in the section headed **Taxation of Pension Business Funds**. Losses on PB from years prior to 2007 can only be set against the PB proportion of any GRB profit.

Overseas Life Assurance Business ('OLAB')

This is policies (including reinsurance) effected by policyholders who are not residing in the UK. It is subject to strict rules concerning certification of residence when the policy is taken out and changes in residence thereafter. Policyholder income and gains are exempt from tax.

Life Reinsurance Business ('LRB')

This is reinsurance business that is not OLAB or PB. For business accepted (ie the reinsurer), policyholder income and gains are exempt from tax. The cedant company is taxed on the investment return being earned by the reinsurer. These rules were brought in as an anti avoidance measure and can be unfair and capricious in their application. The LRB rules do not apply to reinsurance between UK members of the same tax group or to pure risk business.

ISA business

Policyholder income and gains are exempt from tax. Until 5 April 2004, the 10% tax credits on UK dividends could be recovered.

Permanent Health Insurance ('PHI') business

PHI is not currently part of GRB but is expected to be amalgamated into GRB from 2013. Policyholder income and gains are exempt from tax.

Protection business

Protection business (for example, term assurance or whole-of-life business with little or no investment component) is currently part of BLAGAB but will instead become part of GRB for protection business written on or after 1 January 2013.

TAXATION OF POLICYHOLDER FUNDS

Taxation of Life Funds

Life Funds (ie not pension business) are taxed on their investment income and gains as follows:

Income

Dividends from UK companies ('franked investment income') – no further tax on 'net' dividend received.

All other investment income (and sundry income such as underwriting commission) – 20%. Foreign tax suffered at source on overseas dividends can generally be offset against the UK tax liability on them.

Gains

Realised Capital Gains on equities and equity derivatives – 20% of the RPI indexed gain.

Realised **and Unrealised** gains on unit trusts/OEIC holdings – 20% but spread over seven years if the unit trust/OEIC is equity-based.

Realised **and Unrealised** gains on fixed interest securities and their derivatives – 20%.

For unit-linked business, the above rates are charged in the unit price. However, to preserve equity amongst policyholders, companies also make a deduction for tax on **unrealised** capital gains – although this is at a rate lower than the full 20% to allow for the fact that the tax is not payable to HMRC until the investments are sold.

The life company gets tax relief on expenses and commission relating to Life Funds. Where these expenses relate to the acquisition of new business (as opposed to the administration of existing business), the tax relief is spread over seven years. For unit-linked business, the benefit of this tax relief is usually passed on through a lower management charge.

Taxation of Pension Business Funds

All investment income and gains belonging to policyholders are free of UK tax but it is not possible to reclaim the notional 10% tax credits arising from UK dividend income. Any foreign tax suffered at source on overseas dividends is deducted from the policyholder funds.

CHAPTER 1

The contract of life assurance

SUMMARY

SECTION 1 NATURE OF THE CONTRACT

1.1 A contract has been defined by *Anson* as 'an agreement enforceable at law made between two or more persons by which rights are acquired by one or more to certain acts or forbearance on the part of the other or others'. *Chitty* defines a contract as 'a promise or set of promises which the law will enforce'.

Contracts of Insurance, like other contracts, satisfy these criteria but a more descriptive definition is required in order to more accurately describe the particular nature of a life assurance contract. There is no statutory definition of the term 'contract of insurance' even though it is used in defining the basis on which insurers are regulated in the UK. An attempt at a definition of life assurance contracts was made in *Prudential Insurance Company v Inland Revenue Commissioners*[1] by Channel J. The fundamental requirement for a contract of

1 [1904] 2 KB 658.

insurance is the payment of money (or another benefit) on the happening of an uncertain event. In addition, to be a life assurance contract the contingency insured against must relate to death or survival. Further examination of what constituted a life assurance contract occurred in *Fuji Finance Inc v Aetna Insurance Co*[1] where the fact that the amount payable on death was the same as that payable on surrender did not prevent the contract being one of life assurance. See **1.69** et seq for further consideration of this case.

1.2 A practical definition might be that a life assurance contract is one whereby one party (the insurer) undertakes for a consideration (the premium) to pay money (the sum assured) to or for the benefit of the other party (the assured) upon the happening of a specified event, where the object of the assured is to provide a sum for himself or others at some future date, or for others in the event of his death or survival[2].

This may not be comprehensive today because of the variety and complexity of products which are available. For example, it probably does not contemplate the fact that many life assurance policies are essentially wholly designed for investment purposes. It should, however, suffice as a working statement. The 'Regulated Activities Order'[3] defines what constitutes 'long-term business'. 'Long-term business' is wider than just 'life assurance'.

Other definitions relating to life assurance are set out in various statutes. For example, section 7 of the Policies of Assurance Act 1867 defines a 'policy of assurance' as 'any instrument by which the payment of moneys by or out of the funds of an assurance company on the happening of any contingency depending on the duration of human life is assured or secured'. Section 2 of the Life Assurance Companies (Payment into Court) Act 1896 defines 'life policy' as including 'any policy not foreign to the business of life assurance'. The Financial Services Authority (FSA) has avoided a definition of an insurance contract (although it has expressed its view in the Perimeter Guidance Manual (PERG) on some of the borderline issues for non-life business (eg warranty cover)). The FSA Rules also use the term 'life policy' for conduct of business purposes but the definition is of limited usefulness because it excludes the most obvious and straightforward life assurance policies (ie pure protection contracts, such as term insurance). The definition is notable because it includes personal pension schemes where the contribution is paid to a life office. For a UK authorised life company, any pension scheme it establishes and incorporates into a life assurance contract[4] must itself contain some element of insurance (eg provision of an

1 [1997] Ch 173.

2 See the definition in *Prudential Insurance Co v IRC* [1904] 2 KB 658 at 663–664, per Channel J, which was cited by Templeman J in *Dept of Trade and Industry v St Christopher Motorists Association Ltd* [1974] 1 All ER 395, although criticised by Buckley LJ in *Gould v Curtis* [1913] 3 KB 84 because of its failure to cover a life policy containing endowment provisions. See also *Medical Defence Union v Dept of Trade* [1980] Ch 82 in which it was held that one of the necessary elements of a contract of insurance is that the assured becomes entitled to money or its equivalent on the occurrence of some event.

3 SI 2001/544, Sch I, Part II.

4 See INSPRU 1.5.13.

annuity or benefits payable on death). Alternatively a UK life assurer may make its products available to trustees of other pension schemes by providing a trustee investment plan (TIP).

It is also important to note that life assurance contracts, unlike most other forms of insurance, are not essentially contracts of indemnity, which means that unless the contract provides otherwise, the amount payable is not limited to a loss suffered or incurred.

Although life assurance contracts have certain incidents peculiar to themselves, they are in most respects subject to the principles which apply to contracts generally. It is appropriate, therefore, to consider some general principles of the law of contract together with special reference to matters relating to life policies.

SECTION 2 FORMATION OF THE CONTRACT

A Formation

1.3 There are three main elements in the formation of a valid contract. First, there must be an intention to contract. Second, there should be agreement, achieved through an offer and acceptance of mutually understood terms. Third, unless the contract is made in the form of a deed (for differing ways of execution see Section 6), there must be consideration.

In addition, in the formation of a contract, the parties must possess the capacity to enter into the contract and the object must not be illegal.

These various elements will now be considered.

1 Intention

1.4 There is no contract unless the parties intend to be bound. Intention to be bound, or the lack of it, may be inferred from the circumstances or the subject matter. Generally, in domestic or social situations, there would need to be evidence of clear intention to be bound before the courts would hold that a contract had been formed[1]. If, for example, two friends agree to have dinner together they would not normally regard such an agreement as legally binding. There is no contract between them.

On the other hand, in commercial agreements the parties will be presumed to have intended to enter into a contract. This presumption may, however, be rebutted and, indeed, the parties to an agreement may go further and expressly state that they do not intend the agreement to be legally binding[2]. This is often encountered in respect of what are termed 'comfort letters' or in pre-contractual negotiations in what are sometimes referred to as 'heads of agreement'. There is

1 *Balfour v Balfour* [1919] 2 KB 571. However, the later cases of *Merritt v Merritt* [1970] 1 WLR 1211 and *Pettitt v Pettitt* [1970] AC 777 indicated possible limits to this doctrine.

2 *Rose & Frank Co v J R Crompton & Bros Ltd* [1925] AC 445.

generally little doubt in the business of life assurance whether or not the parties have intended to contract.

2 *Offer and acceptance*

1.5 An offer must be something more than a mere declaration of intention. It must consist of a definite promise to be bound provided that certain specified terms are accepted. The offeror must complete his part in the formation of the contract by declaring his willingness to undertake an obligation upon certain conditions. The offer may be expressed orally or in writing or by conduct.

An offer need not be made only to one person but may be made to the public at large.

> *Carlill v Carbolic Smoke Ball Co*[1]
>
> The defendants were the proprietors of a medical preparation called 'The Carbolic Smoke Ball' and they issued an advertisement offering to pay £100 to any person who succumbed to influenza after having used one of their smoke balls in accordance with certain directions. The advertisement stated that they had deposited a sum of £1,000 with their banks 'to show their sincerity'. The plaintiff, relying on the advertisement, bought and used the smoke ball as directed but caught influenza. She sued for the £100. It was held that there was a binding contract. It was possible for an offer to be made 'to all the world' with the contract being made with that limited portion of the public who come forward and accept the offer. In addition, the deposit of £1000 indicated an intention to be bound.

Carlill was followed in *Bowerman v Association of British Travel Agents Ltd*[2] where a package holiday was cancelled due to the insolvency of the tour operator, who was a member of the defendant association, the Association of British Travel Agents (ABTA). A notice in the tour operator's premises included the statement that in the event of the financial failure of an ABTA member before the beginning of the holiday, 'ABTA arranges for you to be reimbursed the money you have paid for your holiday'. A majority in the Court of Appeal held that these words constituted an offer as they would reasonably be regarded as such and so were capable of being accepted by doing business with an ABTA member.

A distinction may be drawn between an offer and an 'invitation to treat'. The latter is an attempt to induce offers and is not normally an offer itself. For example, advertisements by way of circulars or catalogues of goods for sale would be regarded as merely invitations for someone to make an offer and not, as in the *Carlill* case, an offer to be accepted simply by replying.

This distinction could be relevant to life assurance business, as the use by a life office of non-medical proposal or application forms would not, without more, it is contended, be regarded as an offer 'to all the world' but an invitation to treat, inducing proposers to make an offer. Therefore, whilst there might be commer-

1 [1893] 1 QB 256.
2 [1995] New LJ 1815.

cial pressures on an office to accept such a 'simplified' proposal, the life office may still decline the offer. However, if the life office advertises (as is often the case for contracts sold by direct marketing) guaranteed acceptance if certain conditions are satisfied, then this would probably constitute an offer and not an invitation to treat. This is even more likely where the life office has personalised the 'offer'. In such circumstances, provided the prospective policyholder complies with the terms of the advert, he is entitled to accept the offer unless it is withdrawn, and that fact is communicated to him before acceptance. Acceptance in such cases would normally be by means of completion (and return) of an application form included in or with the advert which includes either a direct debit instruction or a promise to pay the premiums. However, to avoid doubt, the life office should make clear its intention when wording proposal forms.

1.6 For an acceptance to be effective in law the parties must have agreed upon all the material terms of the contract they wish to make. It is not a requirement that absolutely every term be agreed upon. Sometimes the law may be able to imply a term but if this is not the case then a contract will not have arisen. There must be a 'consensus ad idem' (agreement as to the same thing) as to these terms (ie there must be either an express agreement or a reasonable inference from the circumstances that the parties had tacitly agreed). A qualified acceptance operates as a rejection of the offer, though it may itself constitute a counter-offer which the original offeror may then accept or reject[1].

Even if the offer is acceptable to the offeree, agreement between the parties is not complete until acceptance of the offer has been communicated to the offeror. The offer may be withdrawn at any time before acceptance is communicated. Withdrawal of the acceptance must reach the offeror before acceptance (normally when acceptance is communicated to the offeror but see the 'postal rule' mentioned at **1.9**). The method of communication, unless prescribed in the offer, will depend upon the nature of the offer and the circumstances in which it is made[2]. Generally speaking, the prescribed method of acceptance must be adhered to[3] and the offeror is entitled to specify by what method the offeree is to signify and communicate acceptance.

3 *Contractual process in establishing a life assurance policy*

1.7 Clearly, the detail will differ between offices but the usual practice in the formation of a contract of life assurance is for the proposer to make an offer by completing a printed proposal (or application) form which will set out the amount of benefits required and the premium payable. The proposal form would usually only constitute an invitation to treat. It is advisable to state in the

1 *Lark v Outhwaite* [1991] 2 Lloyd's Rep 132, which found that a contract of insurance was created where there had been an unqualified acceptance by one party of an offer made by the other.

2 See *Entores Ltd v Miles Far East Corp* [1955] 2 QB 327 for a useful discussion on forms of communication.

3 *Beta Computers (Europe) v Adobe Systems Europe* [1996] SLT 604.

proposal form that the applicant is applying for a contract on the life office's standard terms and conditions. The life office will consider the proposal and, where relevant, any medical reports and information. If the office is then prepared to issue a policy, it may send a letter, sometimes referred to as a 'letter of acceptance'. Whether this constitutes acceptance normally depends on whether it introduces any new terms or requirements (eg it could include a term that acceptance is dependent on payment of the first premium in which case the act of payment would constitute acceptance). As regular premiums are often now paid by direct debit it is not necessarily the case that acceptance would be deferred in this way.

If the letter from the life office states that it will grant a policy not on its standard terms but subject to additional requirements (eg additional premium or exclusion from cover) then the letter will in fact in most cases be a counter-offer, and the proposer would accept the counter-offer by complying with the conditions and, if so stated, by making payment of the first premium.

> *Canning v Farquhar*[1]
>
> C applied for life assurance on the usual type of proposal form. The office notified him that his proposal had been accepted at a stated premium, but that no insurance would take effect until the first premium was paid. Before he paid the premium C fell over a cliff and was seriously injured. The premium was then tendered, but refused and then C died. It was held by the Court of Appeal that the life office was not liable because (a) the proposal and the notification of 'acceptance' were not intended by the parties to constitute a binding contract, but were merely part of the preliminary negotiations; and (b) there would have been no binding contract, since the 'acceptance' contained a new term not previously mentioned (namely, the amount of the premiums) and therefore was in reality a counter-offer which could not be considered as continuing after the risk had changed, since the statements made in the proposal as to good health were no longer true.

The modern practice, particularly in relation to unit-linked investment contracts, is for acceptance to take place by issue of the policy (with or without a letter indicating the date risk is assumed by the life office). If there is no such letter the relevant details will be recorded in a schedule to the policy issued. It is important that this is clear for unit-linked contracts as the policy will specify the date premium received is allocated to units (ie notionally used to buy units in an underlying fund).

1.8 The negotiations which precede the issue of a life policy will vary greatly, depending upon the circumstances of each case, and can become quite protracted. Because of this, it is sometimes difficult to determine the precise point at which agreement is complete and a binding contract formed.

The offer and acceptance require a level of mutual agreement by the parties. However, the courts will not require the parties to reach separate agreement on all the terms, provided there is agreement on essential ones such as the type of policy, assured and life assured, period of cover, sum assured, premium and

1 (1886) 16 QBD 727.

mode of payment. Where there is no specific agreement on terms, the law may be able to imply a term into the contract. It will also normally be assumed that the proposer impliedly offers to contract on the life office's usual terms and conditions[1] and in many cases the proposal form contains express reference to this effect.

The case of *Rust v Abbey Life Assurance Co Ltd* held that the mere issuing of the policy constituted acceptance as the proposal stated that the policy issued was to be on the insurer's standard terms and conditions. The Association of British Insurers (ABI) Statement of Long-Term Insurance Practice recommended[2] that 'the proposal form (or a supporting document) should include a statement that a copy of the completed proposal form or of the completed proposal conditions is available on request'. This is still considered to be good practice.

1.9 Mere communication of acceptance will not result in a binding contract unless it corresponds with the offer. This principle is important in cases where the proposer and the life office are at cross-purposes. In such cases there is no contract and the proposer may recover any premiums paid in the mistaken belief that a contract of insurance had been formed[3]. But where one party contends that they are not in agreement with the other, they may be prevented from arguing that they never meant to accept the terms put forward by the other party if, objectively, their conduct is that of one who accepts the terms offered to them and certain other conditions are satisfied. Where it is stipulated that the offer from the life office must be accepted by payment of the first premium, then acceptance is by the act of payment and no further communication to the life office is required in order to create a binding contract.

The moment of completion of a contract and the moment of commencement of the risk (which are not necessarily the same) are matters of intention to be ascertained from the documents used or from the conduct of the parties or from both. So, for example, the parties could have agreed a condition precedent that risk will not attach until payment of the first premium.

An offer may be withdrawn at any time before acceptance. It cannot be withdrawn after acceptance. Withdrawal does not take effect until notice of it reaches the offeree or his agent[4].

Note should be made of the postal rules, namely that a postal acceptance takes effect when the letter of acceptance is posted. Therefore, a postal acceptance prevails over a withdrawal of the offer which was posted before the acceptance but which has not yet reached the offeree when the acceptance was posted[18].

The parties may, pending completion of the contract, enter into an interim contract in the form of a 'cover note'. Although this practice is quite common in the

1 *General Accident Insurance Corp v Cronk* (1901) 17 TLR 233.

2 A statement of practice originally agreed between the Life Officers' Association, the Association of Scottish Life Offices and the Department of Trade for the conduct of life assurance business and subsequently the Association of British Insurers.

3 *Johnston v Prudential Assurance Co* [1946] IAC Rep 59, and *Batty v Pearl Assurance Co Ltd* [1937] IAC Rep 12.

4 *Byrne & Co v Leon Van Tienhoven & Co* (1880) 5 CPD 344.

5 *Adams v Lindsell* (1818) 1B & Ald 681.

case of other forms of insurance, it is not so common amongst life offices. Many life offices do enter into interim cover arrangements, pending consideration of the proposal. Sometimes this is limited to fatal accident cover and is usually subject to relatively modest monetary limits. Very often the cover will be provided free of charge. If the office is not prepared to accept the proposal at ordinary rates, the interim contract comes to an end.

Rights to cancel life policies may arise for specified periods after they have been entered into under the cancellation rules in the FSA's Conduct of Business Sourcebooks[1].

4 *Consideration*

1.10 A promise not made by deed is not enforceable unless it is made for valuable consideration, which has been defined[2] as consisting:

> 'either in some right, interest, profit or benefit accruing to the one party or in some forbearance, detriment, loss or responsibility given, suffered or undertaken by the other'.

The promise it is sought to enforce must have been made in return for the doing, or forbearing from doing, something; or giving something (including a promise) of some value in the eyes of the law. Sir Frederick Pollock summarised the position in *Dunlop Pneumatic Tyre Co Ltd v Selfridge & Co Ltd*[3]:

> 'An act or forbearance of one party, or the promise thereof, is the price for which the promise of the other is bought, and the promise thus given for value is enforceable.'

In many modern contracts a bargain is struck by the exchange of promises. Thus, A orders goods on credit from B. From the moment of agreement both are bound, for where there are mutual promises the consideration for the promise by one party may consist of the promise of the other party.

In the case of life assurance policies the consideration which passes from the policyholder will be the premium(s) he pays, whilst the consideration given by the life office is the promise to pay the benefit stated in the policy on the happening of the event insured against.

Although consideration must be of some value, generally speaking the law is not concerned as to its adequacy[4]; this is a matter to be decided on by the parties themselves as part of the bargain. This principle is recognised and broadly preserved in the Unfair Terms in Consumer Contracts Regulations 1999[5]. The consideration must relate to the bargain, so that a promise by one party to do

1 COBS and ICOBS, see further Chapter 5.
2 *Currie v Misa* (1895) LR 10 Exch 153.
3 [1915] AC 847.
4 *Thomas v Thomas* (1842) 2 QB 851. It is also excluded from the scope of the Unfair Contract Terms Directive 93/13/EEC, see further Section 4.
5 SI 1999/2083, reg 6(2)(b).

something which he is already under a general obligation, or an obligation to the other party, to do, is no consideration for a promise by the other party.

1.11 The general position is that a person claiming to enforce a contract must show that *he* has made some promise in consideration of the defendant's promise, or that some benefit or advantage has accrued to the other party *from him*, or that *he* has done, forborne or suffered something which was the consideration for the other's promise. 'Consideration must move from the promisee'[1], and an action to enforce a contract must be brought by the person from whom the consideration moved, and not a third party. This is subject to the possible effects of the Contracts (Rights of Third Parties) Act 1999. If its provisions have not been excluded a third party is not prevented from enforcing a term by the fact that no consideration has moved from him. The third party's right to enforce the promise has been described as a quasi exception to the rule that consideration must move from the promisor. If the Act is excluded, then if A contracts with B to pay money to C, C cannot sue on the promise, because he had not done or suffered anything in return for A's promise. In the case of *Price v Easton*, A was promised by the defendant that if A did certain work for him he would pay a sum of money to the plaintiff. A did the work but the defendant did not pay. The court held that the plaintiff could not sue. The contract between A and B is however enforceable, and A may sue B for damages. The damages will probably be nominal in most cases, however, and so A may prefer to bring an action for specific performance for the defendant to fulfil his contractual obligations to pay B[2].

There has been much discussion[3] about whether the inability of the third party to sue, in the circumstances outlined above, rests on the principle that consideration must move from the promisee or on the doctrine of privity of contract – which holds that only a party to a contract may bring an action on it (subject to the Contracts (Rights of Third Parties) Act 1999). The distinction, drawn by Lord Haldane in the *Dunlop* case, has been challenged by some learned authors as being no more than two sides of the same principle, and accepted by others as a true and important difference. In practice, the English courts have had no difficulty in reaching conclusions on the facts before them and it is likely that the debate is no more than academic.

In some cases the contract will create a trust in favour of C, in which case C can enforce the trust in equity, although not the contract as such. As stated above, the Contracts (Rights of Third Parties) Act 1999 will permit a third party to enforce rights which are for his benefit and for this reason the Act is often excluded by life assurance contracts.

5 *Capacity to contract*

1.12 The capacity of certain classes of persons to bind themselves by contract is restricted by law.

1 *Price v Easton* (1833) 4 B & Ad 433; *Tweddle v Atkinson* (1861) 1 B & S 393.
2 *Beswick v Beswick* [1968] AC 58.
3 See *Chitty on Contracts* (28th edn).

(a) Infants or minors

1.13 The general rule at common law is that a contract made by an infant or minor (these terms both mean a person under the age of 18 in English law)[1] is voidable at his option, although it is binding on the other party. However, 'voidable' had two meanings in this context:

(i) some contracts were valid and binding on a minor unless repudiated by him before or within a reasonable time after attaining his majority;

(ii) others were not binding on the minor unless ratified by him when he attained his majority.

Two types of transaction were treated as exceptional; beneficial contracts of service, which were regarded as valid, and contracts for necessaries, which imposed liability on the minor.

These common law rules were affected in two important respects by the Infants' Relief Act 1874, which provided that:

(1) three kinds of contract should be absolutely void, namely contracts of loan, contracts for goods (other than necessaries) and accounts stated (an admission of a sum of money due from one person to another where neither is under a duty to account to the other); and

(2) it was no longer possible to ratify at majority those contracts which formerly were not binding on the infant unless he had ratified them.

The 1874 Act was repealed by the Minors' Contracts Act 1987 and as such the 1874 Act will not apply to any contracts made after 9 June 1987. The effect of the repeal of the 1874 Act is that contracts of loan, contracts for goods other than necessaries and contracts for accounts stated entered into by a minor made after 9 June 1987 will be subject to the common law rules. As regards ratification, the position now is that a minor, on attaining the age of majority, can ratify contracts that are unenforceable against him or voidable at his option.

1.14 An accident insurance policy has been held to be a contract beneficial to a minor[2]; moreover, it is possible to argue that, if a minor's financial and other social circumstances were appropriate, a life assurance or pension policy could be a 'necessary'. But the situations when either could arise are remote and, for minors, life assurance contracts will generally be voidable contracts (ie contracts of continuing obligation valid and binding on the infant unless he repudiates them during his minority or within a reasonable time of attaining his majority).

Thus, a minor may propose for and accept a policy of life assurance, which would be a contract voidable at his option[3]. This applies whatever the minor's

1 Family Law Reform Act 1969, ss 1 and 12.
2 *Clements v London and North-Western Rly* [1894] 2 QB 482.
3 *Ritchie v Salvation Army Assoc Soc Ltd* [1930] IAC Rep 31.

age but, in practice, most life offices will need to be satisfied that the child is old enough to know what he is doing – to render less likely the policy being avoided later and to counter accusations of improper selling.

When income tax relief was available on premiums payable towards qualifying life policies the Inland Revenue contended that no child of 'tender years' (which they interpreted as including a child of less than 12 years of age) was capable of 'making' a contract for the purposes of section 19(2) of the Income and Corporation Taxes Act 1970. As a result, many life offices were prepared to issue policies to children as young as 12 and take the risk of the contract being subsequently avoided by the minor. In view of the requirements for suitability and client understanding of risk as set out in the Conduct of Business Rules of the FSA it must be unlikely that policies would now be issued to children of such a young age.

When minors propose for life assurance, it is sometimes suggested that a parent should complete and sign the proposal form for the infant, thereby, it is argued, making up for the want of capacity of the child. There is, however, no basis in law for this – signature by a parent does not validate the contract, as the parent is unable to authorise something which the infant cannot do himself. (The parent's signature may, of course, be of some significance in ensuring that the infant is not entering into a transaction beyond his means or if the form imposes obligations on the parent.)

1.15 In the context of voidable life policies issued to minors, two questions remain to be considered:

(1) If the policy continues and premiums are paid, can the infant deal with the policy (eg by mortgage, sale, surrender or assignment) during his minority?

(2) If the infant repudiates the contract during minority, or on attaining full age, can he claim a refund of premiums?

It is, generally, unsafe for the life office to deal with the infant in connection with the policy. The infant would not be able to give the office a valid discharge to a surrender or other payment until he had attained his majority. Although the point has never been judicially decided in this country so far as life policies are concerned, there is a line of cases on other types of contracts which supports the proposition that if the infant has derived any intermediate advantage from a voidable contract, he cannot get back what he has paid. The authority is *Steinberg v Scala (Leeds) Ltd*[1], and based on the principles enunciated in that case it is contended that if the infant has derived the benefit of life cover from the life policy then he should receive no return of premiums.

In *Steinberg* it was said that the right of recovery does not turn on whether the infant has derived *any* substantial benefit from the contract. As Younger LJ put

1 [1923] 2 Ch 452; a case involving the purchase of shares in which the minor could not recover the purchase moneys even though no dividends has been received. See also *Ritchie v Salvation Army Assurance* [1930] IAC Rep 31.

it: 'The question is not: has the infant derived any real advantage? But: Has the consideration wholly failed?' Thus in *Steinberg*, the minor applied for and was allotted shares in a company and paid the amounts due on allotment and on first call, and subsequently repudiated whilst still under age. Since the infant had obtained the consideration for which she had bargained it was irrelevant that what she had obtained might be valueless.

On the basis of dicta in that case, it is likely that premiums would not be recoverable even under life policies which did not provide 'life cover' in the normal sense but merely expressed payment on death before the age of 16 or 18 as a return of the premiums paid. There is, however, still a risk in connection with unit-linked contracts, such as bonds or whole of life policies with a low sum assured/high investment content. For this reason many life offices, if they are prepared to deal with a minor in such circumstances, will allow investment in low volatility funds and will not permit dealings with the policy until the minor attains majority. However, it is likely that cases will need to be viewed on a case by case basis to prevent a challenge being upheld by the Financial Ombudsman Service (FOS).

By statute, an infant may be a member of a friendly society, whatever his age, but if he is under the age of 16 his parent or guardian should execute all instruments and other documents[1].

(b) Scotland

1.16 In Scotland it is understood that the Age of Legal Capacity (Scotland) Act 1991 abolished the previous two-tiered system of pupils and minors. Now children aged 16 or over have full legal capacity. However, those aged under 18 have a period after attaining the age of majority in which to apply to the court for prejudicial transactions to be set aside. Prejudicial transactions being transactions which an adult exercising reasonable prudence would not have entered into in the circumstances and which has caused, or is likely to cause, substantial prejudice to that person. Furthermore, the Act introduced a procedure whereby the court can ratify transactions entered into by minors aged 16 and 17.

(c) Married women

1.17 At common law a married woman could not contract for her own benefit, but under the Married Women's Property Act 1882 (and, in Scotland, under the Married Women's Property (Scotland) Act 1920) she was enabled to do so with regard to her separate property.

Under section 11 of the 1882 Act a married woman in England was specifically empowered to effect a policy on her own life or on the life of her husband for her own benefit. It was, however, not until 1980 that a similar power was given to married women in Scotland by the Married Women's Policies of Assurance (Scotland) (Amendment) Act 1980.

1 Friendly Societies Act 1974, s 60(1) and (2).

(d) Enemy aliens and financial sanctions

1.18 British subjects cannot, in ordinary circumstances, contract with enemy aliens. If before the outbreak of war an alien, who thereupon becomes an enemy alien, has already acquired an interest in an English life policy, his interest is not destroyed by the outbreak of war, but is merely suspended until peace is made; but in the cases of both the first and second world wars, there was special legislation and such interests were in most cases vested in the Custodian of Enemy Property. Similar restrictions applied also, for example, in the original Gulf War and the Iraq war where there were sanctions to freeze the assets of all the residents of Iraq. Financial sanctions can, and have more recently, been imposed in relation to specified individuals. Financial sanctions are normally statutory instruments made in respect of a particular situation arising as a result of EU or UN obligations. The sanctions seek to prevent funds being made available to a sanctions target and to prevent the effect of the sanctions being circumvented or avoided. The terms of sanctions are normally very wide and they apply to UK resident/incorporated companies and their overseas branches. The FSA was disappointed by the results of its thematic review in this general area in 2009 and has issued a consultation paper, CP11/12 on 22 June 2011, entitled *Financial Crime: a guide for firms*. Financial sanctions are covered in Chapter 8 of the draft guide (see also FSA Handbook rules in SYSC 3.2.6.R). There can be significant penalties for breach of sanction orders and if a company's key personnel are complicit in the commission of an offence, they can be imprisoned or fined.

There is also the possibility of directions under the Counter Terrorism Act 2008, to support the work of the Financial Action Task Force. The Act gave the Treasury the power to issue directions to financial sector firms which includes insurers. In high level terms, directions can impose requirements in relation to due diligence, monitoring and reporting and can restrict or prohibit business dealings. Unless already revoked, directions cease to have effect a year from the day that they are issued. The penalty for failure to comply can be a fine imposed by the FSA or Office of Fair Trading (OFT) or a criminal prosecution, with a maximum term of two years and an unlimited fine. No offence is committed if a firm took all reasonable steps and exercised all due diligence to ensure the requirement would be complied with.

The interaction with money laundering and, in particular, notification and tipping off offences where the money laundering legislation applies (eg where there is suspicion of a crime) also needs to be considered (see Chapter 5).

(e) Mentally disordered persons

1.19 Generally speaking, a contract made by a person of unsound mind is binding upon him if his disability was not known to the person contracting with him. However, the contract is voidable if his disability was known to the other party[1]. The burden is on the disabled person to show that his disability prevented

1 *Imperial Loan Co Ltd v Stone* [1892] 1 QB 599.

him from understanding the particular transaction, and that the other party knew of this. In certain cases the property and affairs of a mental patient are, on application, placed under the management of the Court of Protection. The person then has no capacity to personally contract although he may still contract through a receiver provided the receiver has the requisite powers. Unlike most powers of attorney which contain a general power to act, a Court of Protection order specifically sets out what the receiver's powers are.

(f) Corporations

1.20 A company or society which is incorporated is a legal person and has an existence distinct from its members.

The powers of a corporation to contract are to be ascertained as follows:

If incorporated by Royal charter	Generally speaking, they have absolute power as for an individual person
If incorporated by Special Act of Parliament	Powers defined or necessarily implied by the special Act
If incorporated under the Companies Acts	Powers within its memorandum of association and the Companies Acts

As a result of the abolition, by the Companies Act 2006, of the ultra vires rule from 1 October 2009, unless a company has a specific restriction in the Objects clause of its memorandum of association, its Objects will be unrestricted and it should therefore be able to carry any commercial activity (see section 39 of the Companies Act 2006). Even if it does have a restriction in its constitution, a third party can still benefit from section 40 which provides that a person dealing with the company in good faith is entitled to assume that the power of the directors to bind the company or authorise others to do so, is deemed to be free from any limitation under its constitution.

A company or corporation may contract in the same way as an individual; a company is only required to execute a document as a deed in those cases where an individual would also be required to do so (eg an enforceable gratuitous promise). A proposal for life assurance or a discharge for the policy monies or a surrender may accordingly be signed on behalf of a company or corporation by any person acting under its authority, whether express or implied.

(g) Unincorporated associations

1.21 These are associations of persons which have not been incorporated but which are not partnerships as the members of such associations do not carry on a business or profession in common, with a view to profit.

As *Chitty* put it[33]:

1 *Chitty on Contracts* (28th edn) Vol 1, 9–069.

'An unincorporated association is not a legal person and therefore cannot sue or be sued[1] unless such course is authorised by express or implied statutory provisions, as in the case of a trade union[2] ... Nor can a contract be made so as to bind all persons who from time to time become members of such an association[3]. But a contract purportedly made by or with an incorporated association is not necessarily a nullity. If the person or persons who actually made the contract had no authority to contract on behalf of the members they may be held to have contracted personally[4]. On the other hand, if they had the authority, express or implied, of all or some of the members of the association to contract on their behalf, the contract can be enforced by or against those members as co-principals to the contract by the ordinary rules of agency'[5].

(h) Partners

1.22 Every partner normally has the capacity to contract for the partnership within the scope of the partnership business.

Where a firm takes out a life policy, it is preferable to issue the policy in the names of the individual partners, coupled if desired with the name of the firm (eg A, B and C trading as Z & Co), rather than it being effected by one partner on behalf of the partnership or simply in the name of the partnership as otherwise problems may arise when personnel leave or join the firm. A conventional partnership is not (in England) a legal entity and the title to a policy effected on behalf of a partnership could remain vested in the persons effecting the contract, unless and until the title is transferred to new owners by assignment or by operation of law. However, a great deal can depend on how the partnership is constituted and what mechanisms are in place when partners join, leave or die. Unless stated to the contrary in the partnership deed, a partnership comes to an end on the occurrence of one of these events. In Scotland a partnership is a legal entity but not normally a body corporate and theoretically a firm could take out a life policy simply in the name of the partnership.

Limited liability partnerships under the Limited Liability Partnerships Act 2000 are body corporates with separate legal personality. Their constitution will be governed by an incorporation document and not the general law of partnership.

6 *Legality of object*

1.23 A contract that is illegal is treated as if it had not been made at all. It is void ab initio and no remedy is available to either party. A contract is illegal if it is prohibited at common law on grounds of public policy or if its formation is in

1 *London Association for Protection of Trade v Greenlands Ltd* [1916] 2 AC 15; *Steele v Gourley* (1886) 3 TLR 118, 119; affirmed (1887) 3 TLR 772.
2 Trade Union and Labour Relations (Consolidation) Act 1992, s 10(1)(a).
3 See *Walker v Sur* [1914] 2 KB 930; *Jarrot v Ackerley* (1915) 85 LJ Ch 135.
4 *Bradely Egg Farm v Clifford* [1943] 2 All ER 378.
5 See further *Chitty on Contracts*.

contravention of a statute or opposed to its general interest. Thus, for example, if a company carries on the business of life assurance, without authorisation to do so, as currently required by the Financial Services and Markets Act 2000, then the policies it issues during the period it is unauthorised are illegal and void, as the object of the statute is to prohibit companies from doing business until authorised[1]. Similarly, the Life Assurance Act 1774 prohibits the making of insurances on lives without insurable interest, and policies made contrary to the provisions of the 1774 Act are therefore 'null and void'[2]. If an insurance contract is illegal, the general rule is that once it is entered into the insured can recover neither the policy moneys nor the premiums paid (but see further Chapter 2).

If a contract is on the face of it illegal then, if its illegality is not pleaded in defence to an action, it is the duty of the courts to take cognisance of it and refuse to enforce the contract[3]. Any bargain not to dispute a claim arising under a contract which is illegal and void is itself void.

However, the rule that there should be no benefit from a criminal act did not prevent the enforcement of a life insurance policy held by an assignee so far as it was necessary to protect the actual interest of the assignee. Such was the case in *Davitt v Titcumb*[4] where an endowment policy was taken out on the lives of two people and payable on the first death. The policy was subsequently assigned to the building society on the terms that if the policy paid out, then the proceeds would be used to pay off the mortgage. When one of the lives assured murdered the other, the building society were properly entitled to receive the proceeds of the policy. The murderer, the defendant, argued that he was entitled to a share in the proceeds of the house. However, because only the deceased's estate could force the building society to use the proceeds of the policy to pay off the mortgage, the defendant being unable to by reason of 'ex turpi causa non oritur actio' (a right of action does not arise out of an evil cause), it necessarily followed that the policy proceeds, as applied by the building society, belonged solely to the deceased's estate.

B The proposal

1 *The proposal form*

1.24 A form of proposal is not a legally required preliminary to a contract of life assurance. However, in practice, where the contract in question con-

1 See *Bedford Insurance Co Ltd v Instituto de Resseguros do Brasil* [1984] 3 All ER 766 and *Phoenix General Insurance Co Greece SA v Administration Asiguraliror de Stat* [1987] 2 All ER 152, where the Court of Appeal held that the statutory prohibition on unauthorised insurance business is not limited to effecting contracts of insurance but extends to carrying out unauthorised insurance business (eg mere paying of claims may be caught). (It follows that although the prohibition is imposed unilaterally on unauthorised insurers, unauthorised insurance contracts are illegal and void and therefore unenforceable not just by the insurer but also by the insured).

2 *Harse v Pearl Assurance Co* [1904] 1 KB 558.

3 *Gedge v Royal Exchange Assurance Corp* [1900] 2 QB 214.

4 [1989] 3 All ER 417.

tains more than a nominal amount of life cover, a prospective policyholder is usually required to give various details, such as his occupation, height, weight, medical and family history, whether he engages in hazardous pursuits and whether any previous proposal for life assurance has been declined or accepted only at an increased premium. The completed proposal form is usually incorporated into the policy. Under the ABI's Statement of Long-Term Insurance Practice a life office was required to include specific questions in its proposal forms relating to any matter which it had commonly found to be material to risks of the relevant class of insurance. This will now be expected by the FSA in order to treat a customer fairly. It is also the approach proposed by the Law Commissions for changes to the law on non-disclosure and misrepresentation, see **2.48**.

The proposal form usually contains an authority to refer to any doctor who has attended the proposer. This aspect is governed by the Access to Medical Reports Act 1988, which lays down clear rules on when information can be released, inter alia, to life offices for insurance purposes. As such, a life office may have access to any medical report relating to a prospective policyholder (if he consents to such an application by the life office). The life office must inform the individual that he has the right to withhold consent and to have access to the report before it is supplied to the life office or within six months thereafter. It must also inform him that he has the right to withhold consent after he has had access to the report or to amend anything in it which he considers to be incorrect or misleading and that in certain circumstances (as described below) the doctor is not obliged to let the individual see the report (or any part of it).

The individual would normally give his consent in the proposal form, and he may request access to the completed report before it is supplied to the life office. If he does the life office must inform the doctor of that request and at the same time notify the individual that it has asked the doctor for a report. Both of these notifications must state that the doctor is not to give the report to the life office unless the individual has had access to it and consented to its being supplied, either as prepared, or as amended by the doctor. If the doctor refuses to amend the report the individual may attach a document setting out his objections. In addition the notification must include the information that if 21 days elapse from the life office application for the report without the individual having contacted the doctor in respect of it, the report may then be supplied.

In the event that the individual does request to see the medical report before it is passed to the life office, the doctor may delete parts of the report if he believes that the report would be likely to cause serious harm to the physical or mental health of the individual or would indicate the intentions of the doctor in respect of the individual. The exemption also applies if it is likely to reveal information about another person or reveal the identity of another person who has supplied information to the doctor about that individual unless that person has consented or is a 'health professional'. If the doctor wishes to rely on these exemptions he must inform the individual of that fact and he is not to supply the report to the life office unless the individual consents. If the exemptions apply the individual would still be entitled to see the remainder of the report which is not affected. Clearly, from a practical point of view, if the life office does not receive a report then it is very unlikely to be prepared to issue a policy.

2 *Joint life policies*

1.25 Life assurance contracts may be issued to more than one person, normally but not necessarily on a joint life basis. Joint life policies can be specified to pay on either the first or last death. Some life offices may have recorded such policies as being issued jointly or alternatively if that were not the intention as tenants in common on a specified basis (such that no interest in the policy would pass by survivorship). Many merely state the policyholders/owners as the named individuals without an additional wording. The conventional thinking in respect of such policies was to regard them as jointly owned (as there is a presumption of a joint tenancy when no words of severance are used). This meant that on the death of the first policyholder their interest would pass to any surviving policyholder(s).

The law has been thrown into disarray somewhat in cases where the parties' intention has not been recorded by the case of *Murphy v Murphy*[1]. In that case a husband and wife had taken out a policy on a joint life death basis. The policy did not specify how the joint interest was to be held. The case concerned the right to make an order under the Inheritance (Provision for Family and Dependants Act) 1975. If the policy was held under a joint tenancy immediately before the first death it could have been the subject of such an order. The issue for the Court of Appeal was one of interpretation of the policy as to whether the policyholders had a joint interest or each held separate rights to the death benefit. The court held that although there was no evidence in relation to the circumstances surrounding the policy, the plain inference was that it was to be held solely for the survivor and that each had a separate interest which was not defeasible by a notice of severance. The court came to this view by looking behind the policy itself and by analogy with other forms of insurance where policyholders have separate interests and protect those separate interests by the same policy. In the authors' view such policyholders have a separate interest because they do not have insurable interest in the other person's loss. As a husband and wife each have an unlimited insurable interest in each other's lives, it is not clear whether the analogy is apt to cover this situation. Also, it is arguably not consistent with the fact that an assignment of the policy can only be made in relation to the whole policy and not just part (as here the death benefit).

The Court of Appeal did appear to accept that in the case of an endowment, it would ordinarily be intended that the benefit payable on maturity would be available for them jointly. This produces the very unsatisfactory position of the same policy wording, creating different types of interest dependent on the type of policy or the purposes for which it is used. From the life office's perspective this makes it very difficult to ascertain whether or not (as often happens on divorce) the owners can sever the joint tenancy on which they believe they have been holding the policy.

Following *Murphy v Murphy* it is not clear whether unit-linked policies should be treated as endowments (ie because there is some savings element). In any event, to avoid confusion life offices may want to amend their policy documen-

1 2004 1 FCR.

tation to make clear that the policy is issued to joint policyholders (and all rights under it are held by them) as joint tenants.

1.26 The proposal form is customarily incorporated into the policy by reference. The ABI Statement of Long-Term Insurance Practice (see **2.44**) set out certain matters which should be included in proposal forms. Insurers were advised to draw attention to the consequences of failure to disclose all material facts (ie that it could affect the payment of benefits) explaining that these are facts which an insurer would regard as likely to influence the assessment and acceptance of a proposal. Particular matters which have commonly been found to be material to particular risks should be the subject of clear questions in the proposal form, and life offices should avoid asking questions which would require knowledge beyond that which the proposer could reasonably be expected to possess and which would not be practicable for him to obtain. The proposal form or a supporting document should also include a statement that a copy of the completed proposal form and of the policy conditions is available on request.

The proposal form may also include a declaration to the effect that the proposal, and sometimes statements made to the insurer's doctor (where, for instance, the individual has agreed to be consulted by the insurer's doctor as opposed to his own doctor), or by the proposer's medical attendant, shall be the basis of the contract. In the case of *Dawsons v Bonnin*[1] it was held that a warranty resulted from a provision in the policy that statements in the proposal form should be the basis of the contract. Such a statement is inconsistent with paragraph 1(b) of the ABI Statement of Long-Term Insurance Practice that the proposal form must not contain any provision which converts any statement of fact, whether past or present, made by the proposer, into a warranty. There was an exception where the warranty related to the life to be assured under a life of another contract, and there was also an exception which permits the life office to require specific warranties to be given about matters which are material to the risk to be insured. The Law Commissions have proposed amendments in this area to prevent basis of the contract clauses having such effect and this is reflected in the Consumer Insurance (Disclosure and Representations) Bill which was introduced in to the House of Lords for its first reading in May 2011. The Bill also deals with other issues the Law Commissions were looking at in relation to the law on non-disclosure and this representation in insurance contracts[2] (see Chapter 2).

In the case of a proposal for a sum assured which is large in relation to the life office's average sum assured per policy or the proposer's apparent circumstances, the office might ask for supporting 'financial' information (often termed 'financial underwriting') to ensure that the sum assured proposed:

(1) is consistent with the insurable interest;

(2) relates to the proposer's demonstrated needs; and

(3) is within the means of the proposer to pay for it.

1 [1922] 2 AC 413.
2 Scoping paper, January 2006.

Furthermore, it is possible that proof of identity, required in accordance with money laundering obligations, may be requested in the proposal form (see Chapter 5 for further discussion on money laundering requirements).

1.27 Where a new policy is issued in substitution for a former one, the contract for the new policy should be based on a new proposal form, but if the life office waives full replies to the questions in the new proposal form, the new policy should be based on the declarations in the proposal forms for both old and new policies.

Where the proposal is for an assurance on the life of another person, the questions as to family and medical history are normally answered by the life to be assured, who is not a party to the contract, and the person effecting the assurance would normally declare that the answers are correct to the best of his knowledge and belief, although it would also be permissible with a life of another contract to require that the statements made shall form the basis of the contract. The proposer may also be required to declare that he has an insurable interest, and sometimes to give details. He may also be asked to provide consents relating to sensitive (eg information on health) and/or processing of information outside the EEA for the purposes of the Data Protection Act 1998.

Although an agent (eg an attorney) may sign a form of proposal on behalf of the proposer, his signature will not ordinarily be acceptable to the life office in any case where information on the subject of health is required. Care should be taken that the person signing a proposal for a child's deferred assurance or any other policy on the life of the child, offered by a Friendly Society, is one who is in a position to know the state of health of the child.

Where the proposal form contains an agreement (expressly or impliedly) by the proposer to accept the usual form of policy of the life office, and in any particular case the life office wishes to vary that form, the life office must communicate this to the proposer. If, for example, the usual form of policy covers death from aviation, death from that cause cannot be excluded unless the life office has contracted on that basis by excluding that risk, such communication to the proposer being a counter-offer subject to acceptance by the policyholder.

In some instances the proposer may communicate information to the insurer other than via the proposal form. In *Ayrey v British Legal*[1] the proposer communicated orally to the company's agent and it was held that this was reasonable for the proposer to do. Life offices may therefore seek to include provisions in their proposal forms which deal with how material information is communicated to them (eg excluding communication to agents). (See also Chapter 4.)

3 *Proof of age and name*

1.28 It is desirable that proof of age should be furnished when a life assurance policy is effected. If there is any inaccuracy in the age stated, the terms of the contract can then be suitably amended (or the contract may not be proceeded

1 [1918] 1 KB 137.

with). In the case of an annuity, proof of age must be furnished before any payment of annuity is made.

If the assured mis-states his age it is likely that the insurer will adjust the sum assured instead of avoiding the policy, but if he does neither and accepts further premiums after he has discovered the true age he will be fully liable under the policy[1].

Age is usually proved by production of a birth certificate (ie an official certified copy of an entry in an official register of births but not a photocopy). Under the Births and Deaths Registration Act 1953, a certified copy of any entry is admissible as evidence of the facts properly recorded therein. In cases where the birth is not registered or a birth certificate is not obtainable the best available evidence should be sought, supported, if thought necessary, by a statutory declaration.

Apart from setting the correct premium level, age can also be important in establishing the identity of the deceased as the life assured under the contract.

If there has been a change of name since registration of birth, it should be evidenced as follows:

(1) If a change on marriage, by a marriage certificate.

(2) If a change on adoption, by an adoption certificate. Where the adoption certificate contains a record of the date of birth it is itself also sufficient evidence of age[2].

(3) If a voluntary change, by deed poll, or by an office, copy of the deed poll where the original deed is enrolled at the Central Office of the Supreme Court.

A surname is, however, a name of repute, and any person may, without any deed poll or advertisement, assume any surname he pleases. In such a case the life office should require evidence of identity in the form of a certificate by a responsible person, supported, if thought necessary, by statutory declaration.

A company may change its name, and if it does so the change should be evidenced by production of the appropriate certificate issued by the Registrar of Companies.

C 'Cooling-off' and cancellation

1.29 The FSA's conduct of business rules (COBS and ICOBS) provide cancellation rights which are a requirement of the Consolidated Life Directive and are generally 30 days for long-term insurance contracts. Whilst it is uncertain whether the existence of such rights prevents the contract from being formed from the outset, it is generally thought that the contract is in place but may terminate early in exercise of the right. Although the right is expressed to fully

1 *Hemmings v Sceptre Life* [1905] 1 Ch 365.
2 Adoption Act 1958, s 20.

unwind the contract, it allows for investment shortfall and issue of the contract triggers other rights (eg in relation to distance contracts) (see further Chapter 5).

SECTION 3 E-COMMERCE

A E-commerce and life assurance contracts

1.30 There are a number of relevant questions from an e-commerce perspective. The first is the ability of a provider to use the internet to sell online within the EU. The second is the law applicable to that operation and any resulting contract. The third is the legal disclosure and other requirements to the customer (eg both in relation to the provider and the process for contracting online). Finally providers need to consider the effect of digital signatures both in relation to their customers and intermediaries. This Chapter deals with the issues relevant to contract formation (see Chapter 5 for marketing and sales-related issues). In order to do so it is necessary to give a brief overview of the relevant e-commerce regulation. There are two relevant EU Directives: the E Commerce Directive and the Electronic Signatures Directive. The E-Commerce Directive[1] was implemented by the Electronic Commerce (EC Directive) Regulations 2002[2]. Implementation of the directive in the UK by the Electronic Commerce Regulations is only part of the picture, for FSA regulated firms the directive was implemented via a new part of the FSA Handbook, the Electronic Commerce Sourcebook, the relevant provisions of which have now been replaced by COBS and ICOBS rules.

The directive is a harmonisation directive seeking to provide a basic framework of mutual recognition for businesses advertising online or providing goods and services online[3] within the EU[4]. Its aim was to require online facilities established in one member state to have to comply only with the laws of their home state. This area of mutual recognition of laws is called the co-ordinated field. There are, however, a number of exclusions from the co-ordinated field, the most relevant ones being consumer protection measures established by the home state to comply with EU requirements[5]. The directive also does not affect the choice of law to govern the contract or issues of jurisdiction. However, subject to these exclusions and the requirements of existing EU single market directives, online providers should be able to operate from their home state in the same way as they do for their domestic customers. The directive requires disclosure of information (eg details of the provider) both generally to consumers and in relation to the process for contracting online.

The Digital Signatures Directive[6] was implemented in the UK by the Electronic Communications Act 2000 and the Electronic Signatures Regulations

1 2002/311/EC.
2 2002/13, 2002/1775, 2002/1776, 2002/2015 and 2002/2157.
3 Not merely by exchange of email.
4 The area is extended by a separate provision to the EFTA countries.
5 Tax, data protection and copyright issues are also excluded.
6 (99/93/EC).

2002[1]. They created an environment which enabled recognition of online contracts and the use of digital signatures[2].

B Formation of e-commerce contracts

1.31 The question of how to categorise 'invitations to treat', offers, counter-offers and acceptance, in the area of life assurance may be more complicated where all or part of the transaction is concluded electronically or at a distance. A contract can be formed electronically, except where there are specific provisions requiring writing, etc (and even in such cases the position is arguable, see below).

From a contract formation perspective the first step in the e-commerce process is often a website. Websites are probably analogous to advertisements, price lists, circulars and displays of goods in supermarkets and constitute invitations to treat. Indeed most businesses will take steps to make it clear that their websites are invitations to treat. A popular method of reinforcing that websites are invitations to treat is for the business to state that they will not be bound until the customer's offer is accepted by the business, often by issue of an email confirmation.

To seek to avoid potential problems, the provider should clearly set out the procedure to be followed for a binding contract to come into existence so that customers have clear knowledge that the provider does not intend to be bound until that procedure is completed. The E-Commerce Directive (and, from a UK perspective where the provider is established in the UK, COBS and ICOBS[3]) require UK providers to provide an explanation of the different steps required for completing a contract electronically so that the parties can give their full and informed consent. Therefore, the provider should explain clearly how the contract comes into being by electronic means. All this must be provided before the contract comes into force. The provider must include information on the different stages involved in the contract, and, for example, whether the contract will be filed (not common in the UK), and whether it will be accessible. The procedure for correcting errors prior to placing the order must also be made clear. The terms and conditions of the contract must be made available in a way which allows the customer to store and reproduce them, for example, by enabling him to print out the relevant documentation.

Receipt of orders must be acknowledged without undue delay and by electronic means and providers must indicate any codes of conduct to which they are subject and information on how those codes can be consulted electronically.

Section 8 of the Electronic Communications Act 2000 gives powers for orders to be made by statutory instrument, to 'remove restrictions in other legislation which prevent the use of electronic communication in place of paper, and to enable the use of electronic communications to be regulated where it is already

1 SI 2002/318.
2 See also section 8 authorising secondary legislation to remove legal obstacles.
3 COBS 5.2.6 and ICOBS 3.2.6.

allowed'. It is not possible to make an order unless the Minister in question is satisfied that it will be possible to produce a record of anything that is done by virtue of the authorisation which is no less satisfactory than by any other means. In addition, a person cannot be required to abandon paper-based transactions unless he has previously chosen to do so. The intention is that the Minister's powers should be used selectively to offer the alternative of electronic contracting to those who choose to contract in this manner.

C Where is the contract formed

1.32 The place where the contract is formed can be crucial in e-commerce transactions. The provider and/or the customer may easily find themselves subject to different legal and taxation systems.

There is some doubt under English law as to which one of two approaches to contract formation applies to e-commerce. Receipt by the purchaser of the provider's acceptance is one test whereas the other is when the provider sends his acceptance (the so-called 'postal' rule which may have effect in an analogous way for e-commerce transactions). Generally speaking, the internet is a continuous communications medium so this would tend to indicate that the actual receipt of the acceptance is the important factor. This provides further arguments for the inclusion of clear statements in the terms and conditions as to how offer and acceptance is to be communicated, sent and received.

Under Article 11 of the E-Commerce Directive[1] the provider is obliged without undue delay to send the consumer acknowledgement of receipt of an order by electronic means. The order acknowledgement is deemed to be received when the party to whom it is addressed is able to access it. Unfortunately, the directive does not state at what stage the contract is formed. Therefore, the place and time of contract formation will depend on national private international law provisions.

The place where the contract is formed will, in the absence of express provision, be likely to be where the purchaser is located. For life insurance contracts under the Consolidated Life Directive, the law of the contract (which should determine issues of contract formation) is based on habitual residence of the policyholder. Ordinarily, the law of the member state in which the policyholder has their habitual residence will be the law of the contract, unless the policyholder chooses the law of the member state of which he is a national. Alternatively, member states may permit (and the UK has permitted) a free choice of law, subject to mandatory rules of the member state of habitual residence.

D Digital signatures

1.33 One particular risk which is brought into focus by the internet is that the 'purchaser' will seek to repudiate the contract by, for example, claiming that

1 2002/311/EC.

someone else was using his credit card number. A so-called 'digital signature' can offer protection to the provider in these circumstances.

The traditional function of a signature is to authenticate the document on which it appears. Except where the signature can be established to be a forgery, the signatory generally has an uphill struggle in subsequently denying the contract, or its provisions. Although it is rare for an actual signature to be a legal requirement on any type of contract, there is obviously a desire to seek to replicate, so far as is possible, a verifiable alternative to the handwritten signature for online transactions. Such transactions are not normally amenable to the traditional concept of a written signature. The development of digital signature technology has been mainly driven by the banking sector, but it clearly also has potential applications to the life insurance industry.

1.34 A digital signature can establish the identity of the person entering into the contract. An additional benefit is that a digital signature can definitively establish the time of such signature in a way which cannot be replicated by a 'physical' signature where a false date can be added or a date inserted at a different time to the time of the actual signature.

1.35 Although this book is not the place to examine the underlying technology, some reference to the basic concepts is useful. The ability to create digital signatures currently relies on the technology of cryptography and in particular the technology of public and private keys. A message which has been encrypted with the individual's or organisation's private key can be decrypted only with the public key which is appropriate to that private key.

1.36 The two methods of authenticating 'signed' communications are either by the recipient directly or by third parties acting as referees/arbiters. The second method potentially overcomes the significant problem that the sending party could deliberately reveal its private key in circumstances where it wished to repudiate authorship of its own genuine digital signatures. Providers can incorporate as part of their digital signature scheme a 'trusted third party' who acts as an arbiter to settle disputes between senders and receivers. This person would therefore have some similarity with the functions undertaken by notaries.

E Electronic Signature Directive

1.37 Although doubts exist with regard to the use of electronic signatures as a replacement for handwritten signatures on documents, the directive clearly envisages the recognition and use of 'electronic signatures' in the sphere of e-commerce in the EU for the purposes of data authentication. There is a distinction in the directive between simple 'electronic signatures' and 'advanced electronic signatures'. The latter are guaranteed under the directive to be legally effective and admissible in legal proceedings whereas the former only qualify for certain purposes and can be denied recognition on certain grounds.

> 'Advanced electronic signatures' must be created by a 'secure signature-creation device', as defined, and:

'(a) satisfy the legal requirements of a signature in relation to data in electronic form in the same manner as a handwritten signature satisfies those requirements in relation to paper-based data; and

(b) are admissible as evidence in legal proceedings'.

The essential features of an 'advanced electronic signature' are that it is uniquely linked to and capable of identifying the signatory. It must be created using means that the signatory can maintain under his sole control and be linked to the data to which it relates, in such a manner, that any subsequent change in data is detectable. Advanced electronic signatures must also be based on a 'qualified certificate' provided by a certification service provider. Article 5(2) provides, essentially, that a non-advanced electronic signature is not to be denied legal effectiveness or admissibility solely on the grounds that it does not meet any of the criteria for an advanced electronic signature.

1.38 The Electronic Communications Act 2000 implemented the Electronic Signature Directive[1]. Section 7 of the Act makes it clear that all types of electronic signatures, whether or not approved providers are involved and irrespective of the jurisdiction where they were issued, will be legally admissible in court. Subsection 7(1) confirms the admissibility of electronic signatures where they are incorporated into the communication or logically associated with it. It will be for the court to decide in any individual case whether a signature has been used correctly and what weight should be given to it. Subsection 7(2) sets out what is meant by an electronic signature. Essentially this is 'anything in electronic form ... for the purpose of being used in establishing the authenticity of the communication or data, the integrity of the communication or data, or both'. It is, therefore, something associated with an electronic document which performs similar functions to those of a manual signature, so it can be used to provide the recipient with confirmation that the communication really is from the person it purports to be from, or to provide confirmation that it has not been tampered with. Subsection 7(3) sets out how the electronic signatures are to be certified.

E Bringing contractual terms to the attention of the consumer

1.39 Providers in the world of e-commerce will generally wish to ensure that a set of standard terms and conditions apply to all transactions. A problem which is common to conventional providers but which is highlighted in online trading, is how to bring standard terms to the attention of the consumer before the contract is concluded and to incorporate them into an online contract. Websites can be labyrinthine and it will not always be easy for a provider to prove that the consumer was aware of all relevant terms and conditions.

The approach which seems to be commonly adopted, is to require the customer to read through the applicable terms and conditions and to signify his acceptance to them before proceeding. The provider will generally require that

1 1999/93/EC.

the customer 'clicks' on a relevant box to indicate his acceptance of terms. Of course, he may choose not to read them but proceed anyway (in much the same way as a conventionally concluded contract) but the provider must make reasonably sufficient efforts to bring terms to the attention of the customer and it is likely, that this approach would satisfy this. This is not going so far as requiring the customer to attach his digital signature in each case which is likely to be viewed as being unduly burdensome.

Exclusion clauses and clauses limiting liability should in particular be highlighted and brought to the customer's attention. The E-Commerce Directive also requires that the customer be able to print out the required information, together with the terms and conditions and the details of their order.

An alternative approach is to provide hypertext links to a page of 'legal information' but if it is possible to proceed to order or apply without this page necessarily appearing as part of the process, then there must be an increased likelihood that this would not be construed by the courts as sufficient notice. However, it may be that for some products or services, especially those with a relatively low value (eg books or compact discs) that this is viewed as an acceptable risk whereas for others it is not.

E-commerce is by its nature best suited to standardised products and processes. In the area of life assurance complete e-trading has in the main been limited to protection type contracts where a case does not require individual underwriting. In such cases policy terms may also not be as complicated as for investment contracts and may therefore work better for this purpose (ie drawing the customer's attention to them).

F The Distance Selling of Financial Services Directive

1.40 The distance selling of financial services to retail customers is now covered by rules adopted to implement the EU Directive on this subject[1]. As regards FSA-regulated financial services the rules are to be found in the FSA's conduct of business rules (See COBS 5.1 and ICOBS 3.1). The Treasury implemented other aspects in the Distance Marketing Regulations[2].

The purpose of the directive was to harmonise the basis on which contracts were sold at a distance to retail customers (ie without face-to-face contact at any stage of the process). It sets minimum standards for the provision of information before a contract is concluded, provides for cancellation rights, and includes provisions to protect consumers in relation to misuse of payment cards and unsolicited communications.

The FSA rules relating to the provision of information apply where a sale is conducted at a distance as part of an organised initiative and not under an 'initial' (in the sense of a framework) services agreement (see Chapters 4 and 5). The idea is to ensure that the consumer is fully informed before he is committed to the

1 2002/65/EC
2 SI 2004/2095.

contract. In practice this means that a person contracting at a distance should have received very detailed contractual information 'in a durable' medium and had an opportunity to review it before he is bound.

SECTION 4 UNFAIR CONTRACT TERMS

A The Unfair Contract Terms Directive

1.41 The Unfair Contract Terms Directive[1] was implemented into English law on 1 January 1995 by the Unfair Terms in Consumer Contracts Regulations[2] (although the regulations did not apply to contracts concluded before 1 July 1995). The directive's provisions should not be confused with the Unfair Contract Terms Act 1977 (UCTA), which applies only to exemption clauses. This directive potentially applies to *all* terms of a contract other than its core terms (eg description of subject matter and adequacy of price).

The Department of Trade and Industry (DTI) issued a consultative document on implementation of the directive in January 1994. In September 1994 a further consultative document and revised draft regulations were issued. The 1994 regulations were revoked and replaced in very similar terms by the Unfair Terms in Consumer Contracts Regulations 1999 which commenced in October 1999[3].

On 5 May 2005, the FSA issued a 'statement of good practice' in relation to unfair terms in consumer contracts. This sets out the FSA's views in relation, in particular, to terms in a contract which allow the supplier of financial services to make changes. This statement refers to draft ABI guidance which was finalised and issued in May 2006. The ABI guidance is specifically directed at reviewable rate insurance contracts and it includes model wording for critical illness policies and Key Features documents. The ABI guidance also explains that the ABI had consulted with and achieved some buy-in from both the FSA and the FOS in relation to the approach adopted. Firms also need to bear in mind the need to treat their customers fairly and contract terms, including those not subject to the regulations, will need to be operated fairly in practice. The FSA's Unfair Contract Terms Regulatory Guide (See FSA Handbook) explains the FSA's role and policy in relation to the regulations.

B Exclusions

1.42 Regulation 6(2)(a) and (b) effectively exclude from the requirement of fairness, terms which define the main subject matter of the contract or which relate to the question of adequacy of the price (also referred to as 'core terms') in so far as those terms are in plain, intelligible language. A recital to the directive also excludes terms in insurance contracts which define or circumscribe the risk.

1 EC 93/13.
2 SI 1994/3159.
3 SI 1999/2083.

However, this was not adopted in the regulations, as it is viewed as only one example of main subject matter exemption.

In the case of *Director General of Fair Trading v First National Bank plc*[1] the Court of Appeal took a restrictive interpretation of the exclusion of 'core terms' on the basis that otherwise 'almost any provision containing any part of the bargain would be capable of falling within the reach of regulation 3(2) (the equivalent regulation under the 1994 regulations)'. However, the more recent Abbey National case held that overdraft charges which could be applied if a bank account were to become overdrawn, were part of the core terms, even if 'contingent' at the outset of the contract. These cases are discussed further at **1.47**.

The regulations also do not apply to:

(1) Contractual terms which are incorporated in order to comply with, or which reflect, mandatory statutory or regulatory provisions and the provisions or principles of international conventions to which member states or the community are a party.

(2) By implication, contracts which are not for the supply of goods or services.

C Unfair terms

1.43 The directive provides that:

> 'A contractual term which has not been individually negotiated shall be regarded as unfair if, contrary to the requirement of good faith, it causes a significant imbalance in the parties' rights and obligations arising under the contract, to the detriment of the consumer[2].'

From this it is clear that the directive applies to terms (note it applies to individual terms rather than contracts in their entirety) which have not been individually negotiated, in contracts between a seller/supplier and a consumer. The regulations define consumer as 'a natural person who, in contracts covered by these Regulations, is acting for purposes which are outside his trade, business or profession[3]'. A seller or supplier, conversely, is someone acting in the course of his trade, business or profession. Clearly, insurance companies will be dealing in the course of their business. When a person is dealing as a consumer is straightforward in most cases but there are potentially difficult situations. For example, it is open to question how far someone is acting for purposes outside his business if he acts as a trustee of an occupational pension scheme, particularly if he is an employer representative of a small scheme.

The regulations specifically provide that a term shall always be regarded as not having been individually negotiated where it has been drafted in advance and the consumer has therefore not been able to influence its substance[4]. This would

1 [2002] 1 All ER 97.
2 EC 93/13.
3 Regulation 3.
4 Regulation 5(2).

appear to apply to almost all insurance contracts where at least some, if not all, of the terms will be in a standard printed form and any negotiation will be likely to have been in relation to price.

1.44 It can be seen from the definition of unfair terms above that it appears to have three limbs:

(1) It (the individual term) is contrary to the requirement of *good faith.*

(2) It causes *a significant imbalance in the party's rights* and obligations arising under the contract.

(3) Such imbalance is to the *detriment of* the consumer.

The requirement of good faith in contracts is not something with which English lawyers, unlike many of their European counterparts, are familiar. There is, of course, the overriding obligation of utmost good faith (uberrima fides) in insurance contracts but that is predominantly concerned with pre-contractual disclosure of information material to the decision to accept business. There is a list of terms which may be regarded prima facie as unfair in Schedule 2 to the regulations (see **1.46**). There is no longer a specific schedule setting out guidance regarding factors relevant to an assessment of good faith as there was in the 1994 regulations. The essence of the matter, in most cases appears, therefore, to be fairness in relation to a consumer's interests. Hence, where a consumer takes out a contract to cover a particular loss, then it is presumably not dealing equitably with his legitimate interests for the insurer to include a term which results in the insurer avoiding paying at all, or paying less than the sum insured, whether as an abuse of stronger bargaining position or a technicality. Conversely, it is arguable that, where powers in a contract exercisable at the discretion of the insurer are expressly subject to a requirement of reasonableness, that the objectivity of the requirement of reasonableness is indicative of the insurer dealing fairly and equitably with the consumer's legitimate interests, particularly where such powers have been disclosed to the consumer before he became bound by the contract. An alternative approach may be to make terms or discretions subject to an obligation on the insurer to only exercise a power or discretion if it is consistent with the insurer's duty to treat its customers fairly.

The second limb of the definition of unfair terms is difficult in insurance contracts with consumers where an inequality of bargaining power will almost always exist. That imbalance is not caused by the term, so presumably for the term to cause an imbalance to the detriment of the consumer it would need to produce an effect that is unreasonable (because the consumer would not expect a term of that nature and/or it was not disclosed to him prior to conclusion of the contract). The requirement of detriment to the consumer is also a somewhat uncertain requirement, as the term is not defined in the directive or the regulations. The requirement of detriment is familiar in issues of contractual consideration or equitable estoppel, in the sense of a financial loss to the innocent party or arranging affairs in an irrevocable way. It is also possible that it would extend to loss of opportunity. It is particularly difficult to apply the concept of detriment where a term (eg price/rate review clause) may have either a positive or a negative impact. However, it would appear from the FSA's statement of good practice, that it regards a potential detriment as sufficient to challenge a term. This is arguably supported by the *First National Bank*[1] case which did not appear to attach much significance to the requirement of detriment.

1.45 The *First National Bank* case concerned a clause providing for interest on a debt to continue to accrue after judgment in case of default. The court held that despite this term relating to the payment of interest on a debt, it was an ancillary, not a core term. It was therefore subject to the regulations. In fact having applied the regulations the court found the term to be fair. There is dicta in this case which is relied upon by the FSA to say that premium review clauses are not core terms and therefore are subject to the regulations. This point is not conceded in relation to premium review clauses in insurance contracts in the ABI guidance. From the point of view of the judgment, it would not appear too difficult to distinguish a term applying only in the event of a potential future default from a term which provides that the price from the outset is variable, dependant on the effect of specified parameters. In reality much will turn on the circumstances of the case (eg whether the reviewable nature of a policy and the specified parameters are made sufficiently clear to the consumer).

Although the Court of Appeal statements on core terms in the *First National Bank* case may therefore strictly be obiter, as far as consideration of premium review clauses in insurance contracts are concerned, they are still worth reading. The case is also useful in explaining the concepts of good faith and 'significant imbalance' in this context, as follows:

> 'The requirement of good faith in this context is one of fair and open dealing. Openness requires that the terms should be expressed fully, clearly and legibly, containing no concealed pitfalls or traps. Appropriate prominence should be given to terms which might operate disadvantageously to the customer, Fair dealing requires that a supplier should not whether deliberately or unconsciously take advantage of the consumer's necessity, indigence, lack of experience, unfamiliarity with the subject matter of the contract, weak bargaining position or any other factor listed in or analogous to those listed in Schedule 2 of the regulations[2].'

The case of *OFT v Abbey National plc and others*[3] involved a challenge to the OFT's view of what constituted a core term under the regulations. According to regulation 6(2), the regulations do not apply the test of fairness to terms which relate to 'the definition of the main subject matter of the contract nor to the adequacy of the price and remuneration on the one hand, as against the services or goods supplied in exchange on the other'. This is subject to the proviso that such terms are in plain intelligible language. In an insurance context, it is argued that terms setting out the price (and if it is variable, the fact and extent of the variability) and the benefits covered by the contract should be core terms. This has been disputed by the FSA based on dicta in the *First National Bank* case. The

1 [2002] 1 All ER 97.
2 [2002] 1 All ER 97 at 108.
3 [2009] UKSC 6.

Abbey National case related to overdraft charges on a bank account. These were set out in the bank's terms for its current accounts but would not apply until an account was in an overdrawn position. It was argued that such terms were ancillary to the main subject matter of the contract, it appears because they were contingent charges. The Supreme Court, reversing the Court of Appeal decision, found that it should not be dissecting the bank's offering to customers in this way in order to establish what were the 'more essential' terms of the contract. The court preferred to look at the bargain struck as a package (ie interest in credit, charges and/or interest in debit). The court also made the point that it was not necessary for core terms to have been individually negotiated so as to form part of the essential bargain between the parties.

D Potentially unfair terms

1.46 The definition of 'unfair terms' does not help to identify definitively or clearly terms which are unfair. Fortunately, the regulations provide an indicative, non-exhaustive list of terms which may be regarded as unfair[1].

Terms will be regarded as unfair which have the object or effect of:

(a) excluding or limiting the legal liability of a seller or supplier in the event of the death of a consumer or personal injury to the latter resulting from an act or omission of that seller or supplier;

(b) inappropriately excluding or limiting the legal rights of the consumer vis-à-vis the seller or supplier or another party in the event of total or partial non-performance or inadequate performance by the seller or supplier of any of the contractual obligations, including the option of offsetting a debt owed to the seller or supplier against any claim which the consumer may have against him;

(c) making an agreement binding on the consumer whereas the provision of services by the seller or supplier is subject to a condition whose realisation depends on his own will alone;

(d) permitting the seller or supplier to retain such sums paid by the consumer where the latter decides not to conclude or perform the contract without providing for the consumer to receive compensation of an equivalent amount from the seller or supplier, where the latter is the party cancelling the contract;

(e) requiring any consumer who fails to fulfil his obligations to pay a disproportionately high sum in compensation;

(f) authorising the seller or supplier to dissolve the contract on a discretionary basis where the same facility is not granted to the consumer or permitting the seller or supplier to retain the sums paid for services not yet supplied by him where it is the seller or supplier who himself dissolves the contract;

1 See art 3(3), the Annex and Sch 2 to the Regulations.

(g) enabling the seller or supplier to terminate a contract of indeterminate duration without reasonable notice except where there are serious grounds for doing so;

(h) automatically extending a contract of fixed duration where the consumer does not indicate otherwise, when the deadline fixed for the consumer to express this desire not to extend the contract is unreasonably early;

(i) *irrevocably* binding the consumer to terms with which he had no real opportunity of becoming acquainted before the conclusion of the contract;

(j) *enabling the seller or supplier to alter the terms of the contract unilaterally without a valid reason which is specified in the contract*;

(k) *enabling the seller or supplier to alter unilaterally without a valid reason any characteristics of the product or services to be provided*;

(l) providing for the price of goods to be determined at the time of delivery or allowing a seller of goods or supplier of services to increase their price without in both cases giving the consumer the corresponding right to cancel the contract if the final price is too high in relation to the price agreed when the contract was concluded;

(m) giving the seller or supplier the right to determine whether the goods or services supplied are in conformity with the contract or *giving him the exclusive right to interpret any term of the contract*;

(n) limiting the seller's or supplier's obligation to respect commitments undertaken by his agents *or making his commitments subject to compliance with a particular formality*;

(o) obliging the consumer to fulfil all his obligations where the seller or supplier does not perform his;

(p) giving the seller or supplier the possibility of transferring his rights and obligations under the contract where this may serve to reduce the guarantees for the consumer without the latter's agreement; or

(q) excluding or hindering the consumer's right to take legal action or exercise any other legal remedy, particularly by requiring the consumer to take disputes *exclusively* to arbitration not covered by legal provision, unduly restricting the evidence available to him or imposing on him a burden of proof which according to the applicable law should lie with another party to the contract.

1.47 The scope of some of these indicative terms was expressly limited in the directive and some of these exceptions are relevant to life offices. In particular, the right to terminate a non-fixed term contract, or to vary charges on financial services contracts or to vary the terms of contracts of indeterminate duration where reasonable notification is given to the consumer and where the consumer is free to dissolve the contract. The directive provided as follows:

> '(a) Subparagraph (g) is without hindrance to terms by which a supplier of financial services reserves the right to terminate unilaterally a contract of indeterminate duration without notice where there is a valid reason, provided that the supplier is required to inform the other contracting party or parties thereof immediately.
>
> (b) Subparagraph (j) is without hindrance to terms under which a supplier of financial services reserves the right to alter the rate of interest payable by the consumer or due to the latter, or the amount of other charges for financial services without notice where there is a valid reason, provided that the supplier is required to inform the other contracting party or parties thereof at the earliest opportunity and that the latter are free to dissolve the contract immediately.
>
> (c) Subparagraph (j) is also without hindrance to terms under which a seller or supplier reserves the right to alter unilaterally the conditions of a contract of indeterminate duration, provided that he is required to inform the consumer with reasonable notice and that the consumer is free to dissolve the contract'[1]

These provisions form part of the paragraph 2 of the Schedule 2 to the 1999 regulations.

Paragraph (b) above should permit variation for an undisclosed but valid reason even if it is not specified in the contract, provided the conditions as to notice and the consumer being free to dissolve the contract are complied with. Similarly, for most life contracts without a term, paragraph (c) should permit termination on reasonable notice where the consumer is free to dissolve the contract. However, it is worth looking at the FSA's description of these provisions in its statement of good practice. The FSA describes them as factors making it 'less likely' that the terms will be unfair. From a legal perspective this seems slightly at odds with the wording of the underlying provision. However, it would appear that both the FSA and the FOS are keen for the reason and parameters around any ability to make changes to a contract to be specified in the contract itself.

In relation to the term 'free to dissolve the contract' the FSA statement confirms that a consumer may be free to dissolve the contract even if that involves a loss of opportunity. Free to dissolve should therefore mean 'without having to make a payment or give prior notice', but the OFT appears to take a wider view which could exclude any potential detriment to the consumer in having entered into the contract[2]. Any extension of the words 'free to dissolve', beyond having the contractual right to exit without paying a penalty would appear to add a gloss on the underlying requirement, which in the absence of any cases on the point, seems to be unjustified. It should also be noted that the FSA has accepted undertakings that rely on the concept of free to resolve (see **1.52**). The issue of loss of opportunity may, however, fall within treating customers fairly (TCF) issues (eg ability to get new cover, etc) and firms will need to consider reliance on any contractual term in this context.

1 Sch 2, para 2(b).

2 See OFT Guidance September 2008.

E Clear disclosure

1.48 A recurrent theme running through the examples in the schedule of the regulations is that if the reason for a particular term is valid, is disclosed to the consumer at the earliest opportunity, or the consumer has the right to dissolve the contract when they are notified of a change, then the term should generally be fair. This is coupled with, and to a certain extent exemplified by, the requirement in the directive and the regulations that all written terms be drafted in *plain, intelligible language*. Where there is doubt about the meaning of a term, the interpretation most favourable to the consumer shall prevail. It should be noted that the requirement of 'plain, intelligible language' also applies to terms dealing with the main subject matter of the contract, as this is a condition of the core terms exemption.

The European aspect of this should also be noted. If a policyholder is resident in another member state and the law of that country applies (which it normally would) then, unless there was a choice of law available in that country, the requirement may well be for the terms to be in, for example, plain, intelligible Polish.

F Relevance to life contracts

1.49 Clauses in life contracts that might be caught by the examples in Schedule 2 are:

(a) terms excluding liability – limitation clauses or exemption clauses not related to the nature of the risk or arguably the main risk (ie not covered by the main subject matter exemption);

(b) terms requiring payment of disproportionate amounts for failure to fulfil obligations – early surrender penalties;

(c) clauses irrevocably binding the consumer to terms which were unavailable – this could apply to all terms of an insurer's standard contract which do not circumscribe the risk. It is arguable where cancellation rights exist and the policyholder receives the policy within that period, that the consumer is not irrevocably bound until the end of the cancellation period. There is also an argument that the right to inspect a copy of the contract is a real opportunity for the consumer to get a copy of the policy before he even completes the proposal form;

(d) power of unilateral variation – any power of alteration which is discretionary (subject to what has been said above in relation to altering rates of interest and charges in financial services contracts without notice for a valid reason);

(e) power to change charges – any terms allowing charges or fees to be increased without allowing the consumer a right to cancel – could be caught. However, there is an exemption in paragraph 2(d) of Schedule 2 which permits indexation of charges provided the basis is explicitly described;

(f) terms requiring formalities – imposing time limits (for example on claims), requirements of notification in a particular form (eg writing) without a valid reason.

The issue which has attracted the most attention to date is that of reviewable premium contracts. The FSA appears to accept that such contracts have a value in terms of affordability and flexibility in the marketplace and are not intrinsically unfair. The FSA's focus seems to be to ensure that there is a valid (ideally specified) reason for the clause permitting change and that the customer is given adequate notice and explanation, so that any changes do not come as a nasty shock to them. This involves being very specific about why and how such changes are made. So, for example, a clause permitting the company to decide relevant factors at its discretion will not satisfy the requirements. Similarly, a non-exhaustive list of factors to be taken into account at the company's discretion will not, in the FSA's view, satisfy the requirement[1].

Generally, in assessing whether a reason is valid, the more the trigger for change is outside the control of the company, the more likely it is to be accepted (eg legal or regulatory changes). Contracts with third parties (eg reassurers) will not automatically benefit from being outside the company's control. The FSA indicates that the reasonableness of the reassurance contract itself would need to be reviewed. A term that only allows a change which is proportionate to the underlying reason for the change is also more likely to be fair than one where there is an element of discretion.

In relation to reviewable contracts, the FSA states that a term should not allow a firm to recoup its investment losses prior to the review, to increase profitability, to loss lead or to increase premiums at all if its records do not enable it to prove the basis of the original premium. The FSA is also keen that review clauses do not give the company the discretion to decide when to carry out the review (or indeed not to carry one out).

The ABI guidance includes a statement from the FOS (1.2.5) about the FOS's attitude. This states that the FOS will take both the FSA and ABI papers into account and will look at how fairly terms are applied in practice. The ABI paper is also useful because it contains model contract wordings for critical illness policies which all parties to the consultation have seen. The model approach is to explain why reviewable premiums are offered (eg affordability/potentially less than guaranteed rates) and why the premium might change, (eg because medical advances may affect the insurer's expectation of future claims). The trigger for the change is stated to be the company's view of the specified assumptions at the review date being different from that it took at the outset. The ABI example gives a de minimis change (x%) which will not lead to a change in premiums. It also states that the company will apply the method it uses to calculate premiums in a fair and reasonable way. It is worth noting, that it does not seek to include a formula to actually calculate the increase. The ABI approach also makes clear (if it is true), that there is no maximum amount of increase. It had been suggested

1 See PPP Lifetime Care Undertaking.

that specifying a maximum would be necessary to make such clauses fair but that is not the position adopted by the ABI.

1.50 As stated above, the FSA does not appear to be keen on the exceptions in Schedule 2 (see **1.47**) and prefers to see the reason for a power to vary a contract specified in the contract. This can cause issues for unit-linked insurance contracts. Most unit-linked insurance contracts benefit from a beneficial solvency regime (originally 0% but now under Solvency I, 25% of expenses, see INSPRU 1.1.88). This is available provided the investment and expense risk is borne by the policyholder. This therefore means that insurers wishing to retain such treatment (which realistically they need to as the alternative is to hold a need 1% margin, the costs of which, if passed on to the customer would make the product unviable) to retain the ability to pass on all expenses, whatever they might be, or to cap them for periods of up to five years and vary them thereafter. When the original unfair contract terms regulations were implemented many insurers amended their policies to make this ability to vary (normally the Annual Management Charge (AMC)) clearer. At almost the same time as the original regulations were implemented, the Key Features document and illustration requirements were introduced. These specified (and the FSA's rules continue to specify) that the policy may not return as much as expected due to the fact that the charges could change. The FSA, however, has sought to challenge such products (see the Skandia undertaking) because insurers have not specified in their contracts the reason for retaining the ability to vary the AMC (ie the need to retain the solvency treatment and charging structure of the products). The Skandia undertaking is unfortunate, (and may be a result of the way Skandia's products are structured), in that by imposing a requirement of reasonableness on the expenses, it appears to cut across the discretion that life offices are required to retain by the FSA Handbook rules in INSPRU 1.1.88 in order to retain the solvency treatment of the product. Other life offices have been challenged by the FSA but have argued, in part based on the INSPRU 1.1.188 requirement and the contractual disclosure of the fact that charges could vary, that the term permitting variation of the AMC is not unfair under the regulations. There are a number of reasons why this is arguable but much will depend on the disclosures made to the policyholder. First, there are arguments that the contracts sold had variable charges from the outset and therefore the term is a core term. This is consistent with the *Abbey National* case referred to above. There is also an argument that as INSPRU 1.1.88 implements terms of the Consolidated Life Directive it is a mandatory term for this type of product and so the regulations do not apply at all. Even if the regulations do apply, consumers cannot get a 'nasty shock' as the power to vary and the fact that it may affect their return are disclosed. Similarly, the exemptions from the Unfair Contract Terms Directive (see **1.47**), allow changes either where there is a valid reason (ie change to charges on financial services contracts) or where the consumer is given reasonable notice and is free to dissolve the contract. As a result of the Skandia undertaking some life offices have added an explicit reason for the power to vary AMC (eg to retain the existing solvency treatment), or have made it explicit that penalties will not apply if the power is exercised (so the consumer is aware that they are free to dissolve) and/or have amended the power to say that any change will be proportionate (but not limited to reasonable expenses). Another alternative could be to cap the fees for a fixed period and review them at specified intervals.

G Representative actions – function of Director General

1.51 In the original consultative document the Department of Trade and Industry (DTI) indicated that, based on the strict wording of the directive, it would not be implementing the provisions in the directive[1] allowing representative actions. However, consumers' representative bodies are understood to have complained and comments were also received from independent solicitors to the effect that action to implement Article 7 of the directive was required. It should also be borne in mind that, in relation to non-UK resident policyholders, other member states will have implemented this provision.

A compromise was suggested in the second consultative document. The result is found in regulations 10 to 15. The Director General of Fair Trading is under a duty to consider complaints about unfair terms (unless they are frivolous or vexatious). If he finds them to be unfair, he may, if he considers it appropriate, then apply to the court for an injunction to restrict their use. The Director General must give reasons for his decision to apply or not to apply, as the case may be, for an injunction in relation to any complaint he is required to consider[2]. The court may grant an injunction on such terms as it sees fit, including prohibiting continued use of unfair terms in consumer contracts by sellers or suppliers or recommended by associations of sellers or suppliers[3]. Alternatively, a 'qualifying body' as set out in Schedule 1, may agree to consider a complaint that a contractual term is unfair in place of the Director General. This now includes the FSA by virtue of the amending regulations issued in 2001. These provisions should increase the likelihood of terms being challenged and, indeed, of their use being prevented. It should also increase the profile of the directive's provisions as the Director General is empowered to arrange for the dissemination of information and advice to the public and all persons likely to be affected by the regulations.

The FSA also states that in deciding whether to take enforcement action (eg an injunction), it will consider any undertakings from the firm about the way the term is operated in practice. Whilst the courts are always the final arbiters, life offices may be able to get a high level of certainty by giving the FSA such an undertaking. Undertakings are published by the FSA and can be useful in forming a view on similar terms.

H Examples of undertakings

1.52 Firms need to monitor undertakings given to the FSA and the OFT in connection with unfair contract terms issues. Although the undertakings given

1 Article 7.
2 Regulation 10.
3 Regulation 12.

by insurance companies are likely to be the most relevant, undertakings given by other entities can also highlight general issues of unfairness. The insurance specific undertakings include certain themes, for example, the meaning of a 'valid reason', terms being used to unfairly put responsibility on the customer, the imposition of formalities, the retention of a right to interpret a term, and the use of language which is not 'plain and intelligible'. Examples of cases relating to ambiguous rights to vary contracts include *Woolwich/Barclays* and *Intelligent Finance* where the term allowed 'any valid reason'. Similarly in the Skandia undertaking, 'Skandia reserves the right to vary this charge' (but see **1.50**). There are also cases which highlight the fact that the customer needs to be free to dissolve, so in the *Brittanic Assurance* case, a withdrawal fee applied. Interestingly the Jarvis Investment management undertaking provides a combination of a number of points. In that case a power to vary was amended so as to permit variation for 'any valid reason' with certain valid reasons specified in the contract. The point which seems to have made this case different to other uses of the term 'any valid reason', is that the term also provided that an exit charge could only be applied if the reason for the variation was one of those specified in the contract (see also the Sippdeal undertaking). Undertakings relating to potential unfairness or imbalance include payment protection insurance (PPI), single premium policies in relation to surrender values if the underlying loans were paid off early, warranties for uninterrupted service and unauthorised use of passwords (Sippdeal) and making the customer liable for fraud of third parties where the customer has not been negligent (London Capital Group).

Examples of language which have been held not to be 'plain and intelligible' include endorsement, bona fide, holder of value, discontinue (Tunbridge Wells) consequential loss (UK insurance) and indemnify (Abbey Life). Terms imposing conditions to claims (eg timing and reporting losses) are more commonly a feature of general insurance contracts. One further point to note is in relation to wordings in application forms that state that the customer has read and understood the supplier's terms and conditions. The undertaking from the On-line partnership agreed to amend such a term to say:

> 'This is our standard client agreement upon which we intend to rely. For your own benefit and protection you should read these terms carefully before signing then. If you do not understand any point please ask for further information.'

As a result of this undertaking some life offices have opted for a shorter wording whereby the customer states that they have received the terms (if correct) and that they understand that it is important that they read them as they set out the terms on which the life office intends to rely.

I Blue pencil test?

1.53 Assuming that a term is found to be unfair, the effect is that the term in question is not binding on the consumer[1]. There is no power to rewrite or restrict

1 Regulation 8(1).

the term and the remainder of the contract will continue to bind the parties 'if capable of continuing' without the unfair term(s). Thus the effect of the remaining terms of the contract may be entirely different without the offending term, but if they are capable of existence, even with that different meaning, they will continue. It remains to be seen how the courts will exercise this power in practice. It is suggested that clauses within a contract itself (ie severability) permitting changes to a contract to render a potentially unfair clause fair, would not themselves be fair. Although arguable, this does not seem consistent with the intention of the parties or the need to interpret a contract in such a way as to make it workable. The FSA does not appear opposed to such severability clauses provided that they are narrowly drafted (ie the discretion of the provider is not too wide).

J Treating customers fairly

1.54 It is worth noting that although the directive does not apply to contracts made before 1 July 1995, insurers with such contracts are still subject to the FSA's Principles and in particular the need to treat customer's fairly. The FSA makes clear in its statement that even if terms (such as review clauses) were held to be 'core terms' and therefore excluded from the regulations, they would still be subject to the need to apply the terms fairly, and the same rationale would apply to existing contracts.

K UCTA 1977

1.55 As has been seen, the directive's provisions are wider (ie applying to all terms and to insurance companies) than UCTA. The intention is, however, that for non-insurance contracts, the regime will run alongside that of UCTA and will not qualify or restrict any rights under that Act. Insurance contracts remain exempt from the provisions of UCTA.

SECTION 5 LAW OF CONTRACT

1.56 The question of which law applies to a contract of life assurance is of practical importance in view of the increasingly international nature of much of the business transacted. Many life offices maintain branches or employ agents in a number of countries and issue policies to persons resident or carrying on business in the country in which the branch is situated or where the agent carries on business.

A contract of life assurance is governed by its proper law and many life policies will expressly state the country whose law has, through the contractual process, been chosen to govern the contract. The parties' choice of which system of law shall apply may depend upon where the proposer has his habitual residence, especially when selling in the EU.

The Second Life Directive harmonised the law applicable to life contracts in the EU. The general scheme of that harmonisation is that the law of the contract is the law of the member state in which the policyholder has his habitual residence or is a national at the time the contract is effected, unless in that state a choice to the contrary can be and is made. This was implemented in the UK by changes to both the Insurance Companies Act 1982 and the Contracts (Applicable Law) Act 1990. The latter Act had incorporated the Rome Convention[1] into English law. The Insurance Companies Act 1982 provisions were replaced by the Financial Services and Markets Act 2000 (Law Applicable to Contracts of Insurance) Regulations 2001[2].

The Rome Convention was replaced by the Rome I Regulation[3]. This is directly applicable in the UK and must be applied by courts in the EU. As the regulation permits member states to exercise certain options regarding choice of law, the UK introduced, with effect from 17 December 2009, the Financial Services and Markets Act 2000 (Law Applicable to Contracts of Insurance) Regulations 2009[4]. Regulation 4 of these regulations provides that where, applying the rules in Article 7(3) (a) (b) or (e) of the Rome I Regulation, the law of the contract would be a law of the UK, then the parties may choose another law provided that choice complies with Article 3, Article 6 and Articles 9 to 22 of the Rome I Regulation. In relation to life assurance Articles 7(3) (a) and (b), which cover where the risk is situated and the policyholder's state of habitual residence respectively, would both produce the same effect (ie the law of the member state where the policyholder is habitually resident). Where this is the UK, this should permit a choice provided that choice is consistent with the other Articles listed and subject to mandatory rules provided for by those Articles.

Article 3 is the main choice of law section and provides for a free choice of law . However where there are 'other elements relevant to the situation' at the time of the choice which are located in another country, the provisions of the law of that country which cannot be derogated from will also apply[5]. Where the choice of law is not that of a member state, Article 3 also provides[6] for community laws implemented into the law of member states not to be derogated from. Article 6 relates to consumer contracts but provides that the parties have a discretion to choose a law other than that of the consumer's habitual residence, provided that such a choice does not deprive the consumer of protections that cannot be derogated from under the law of the country where he is habitually resident. Article 9 provides a description of 'mandatory provisions' as those regarded by the relevant country as crucial to protect its public interests, such as political, social or economic organisation. Nothing in the Regulation restricts the application of the overriding mandatory provisions of the law of the forum. There do not appear to be relevant restrictions in Articles 10 to 22 that would prevent a choice

1 Which excluded this issue.
2 SI 2001/2635.
3 Rome I Regulation [593/2008].
4 SI 2009/2075.
5 Article 6(2).
6 Article 3(5).

of law. Article 19 defines the habitual residence of companies and individuals acting in the course of business and Article 22 provides that where there is more than one country within a member state, each is treated as a separate state for these purposes. The net effect of all of these provisions appears to be that the position is unchanged by the adoption of the Rome I Regulation, so that where the UK would be the law of the contract for any insurance contract (ie where the policyholder is habitually resident in the UK at the outset), it will still, subject to applicable mandatory rules, be possible to have a free choice of law.

Where the law chosen is not that of a member state, mandatory EU provisions will also apply (eg Unfair Contract Terms Directive provisions). The Second Life directive introduced the concept of 'mandatory rules' for insurance contracts, essentially rules which cannot be derogated from, irrespective of the law of the contract. They would, normally, therefore apply where the policyholder and the insurance company are in different member states. The two situations in which they can apply are:

(1) where the law of the contract is not that of the member state of the commitment (ie where the policyholder is habitually resident) and the law of that member state provides for mandatory rules to apply where that member states law is not chosen as the law of the contract; and

(2) where they are part of the law of the forum (ie the country in which a court case is being heard and that law is not the law of the contract).

The DTI formerly published an extensive list of mandatory rules for UK purposes. The FSA's approach is to specify that parts of its rules apply to EEA insurers but not to include a list other provisions of the law applicable to insurers. EU insurers do not in practice seem to receive notice of the UK mandatory rules. It is therefore not clear whether the requirement of insurable interest would be a mandatory rule if the UK were the member state of commitment or if a case came before the English courts. This question has particular reference to the use of beneficiary clauses, a practice which is common in many other member states. The question was raised with the DTI whether UK insurers would be able to provide contracts which include a beneficiary clause to residents of other member states where such clauses are valid. The DTI's view was that where the law of the contract was English law, the provisions (section 1 of the Life Assurance Act 1774) would apply, but that where it was not, they could only apply if the policyholder sued in the English courts. This would be on the basis that it is possible that the provisions would be held to be part of the procedural rules of the forum. In the authors' opinion it would seem odd if a contract with a foreign policyholder, which, according to the law of the contract could contain a beneficiary clause, could not be enforced in the English courts. It would be helpful if there were guidance in relation to the provisions that might constitute mandatory rules in the U.K.

It should also be noted that the Brussels Regulation[1] which replaced the Brussels Convention on Jurisdiction and Judgments, prevents an insurer from

1 Brussels Regulation [44/2001], Articles 12–13.

including in its proposal forms or policy documentation a choice of law which would enable the insured to be sued other than in the courts of the member state in which the insured is domiciled. In relation to subsequent disputes, the parties may be able to come to a different agreement or the insured may be able to make a different choice.

SECTION 6 THE POLICY

A Form of the contract – the policy document

1 Policies in writing

1.57 It is important to distinguish the contract from its physical manifestation, the policy document. The policy document will not necessarily contain all the terms of the contract. Some may be contained in the proposal or other document and others may be implied by law.

The common law does not require a contract of insurance to be in any particular form or, indeed, to be in writing at all[1]. It was widely believed, however, that section 100 of the Stamp Act 1891 required a life assurance policy to be issued, as by that section any person who received or took the credit for any premium on any life insurance and did not within one month make out and execute a duly stamped policy of insurance incurred a penalty. It has been argued[2], on the other hand, that the Act does not require any such contract of insurance to be expressed in a policy as a condition precedent to the validity of the contract; it is concerned with the stamping of policies in being. However, section 100, which was concerned with the penalty for not making out a policy or making a policy not duly stamped, has been repealed by section 173(3) of the Finance Act 1989 and as such, section 173 abolishes stamp duty on policies of life insurance. In order for the policy to be a 'qualifying policy' for income tax purposes the contract must be in writing (see further Chapter 13). In any event, it is now the general practice to issue policy documents.

Section 4 of the Policies of Assurance Act 1867[3] requires that the policy should specify the principal place or places of business at which notices of assignment may be given.

2 Form of policy and schedule

1.58 The policy is the document prepared by the life office to express the terms of the contract which has already been made, and with which it must conform. In earlier times the policy was usually prepared in advance so that it could be handed over in exchange for the first premium. Under modern practice,

1 *London Life Insurance Co v Wright* (1881) 5 SCR 466.
2 MacGillvray on Insurance Law (9th edn, 1997) p 111, paras 3–4, note 9.
3 See Appendix 2.

however, the proposer is very likely to pay or agree to pay the premium before they receive the policy document and to agree expressly (in the proposal form) or impliedly, to accept a policy on the life office's standard terms and conditions[1]. The life office must issue a policy which is in accordance with its marketing literature and the proposal form. The proposer need not otherwise accept it. As it is drafted by the life office, in case of any ambiguity, the policy terms will be construed against the interests of the life office pursuant to the contra proferentum rule.

A life policy may be issued either under hand or under seal, but must be executed in accordance with the constitution or regulations of the life office. The general modern practice is to use two documents or one document which is in two parts, one document or part for terms of general application with a second document or part being a schedule for insertion of items specific to the assured. The schedule includes the policy number, the name of the assured and the life assured, the nature and amount of the benefit, when and to whom it is payable, and the amounts of the premium and when they are payable. The general conditions and provisions attaching to the policy usually form part of the first document or part mentioned, and may include provisions as to payment of claims, days of grace for payment of premiums, protection against forfeiture, surrenders, loans (although if more than the possibility of obtaining a loan is expressed then the policy may then be subject to consumer credit legislation), and conversions to paid up assurance and suicide (see Section B below for further information).

3 *Segments*

1.59 The advent of unit-linked life assurance business led to the introduction of policies issued in 'clusters' or 'segments', so that when the assured proposes for a contract of assurance he receives, in return for a given premium, not one policy but a number of policies of equal value – each one issued in return for an equal fraction of the total premium payable. Life policies issued as 'segments' offer opportunities for tax planning as it is possible to encash whole segments. The general practice is for one document to be issued as the principal 'contract of assurance' together with a number of separate schedules of benefits which expressly incorporate the individual contracts by reference. This was originally achieved by having a separate piece of paper for each 'segment' which was rather artificial and probably unnecessary. As a consequence, the practice is dying out and it is usual for one schedule to evidence a specified series of policies on identical terms.

4 *Group or master policies*

1.60 Where a company contracts to grant assurances or annuities in respect of all (or defined categories of) employees of a particular employer, whether in connection with a pension scheme or otherwise, it is common practice to issue a

1 *General Accident Insurance Corp v Cronk* (1901) 17 TLR 233.

series of individual policies in the form set out in a master policy in respect of each employee or for a group policy to be held subject to the terms of a trust. Some policies are also issued directly to the employer to cover its liability to employees (eg to pay specified amounts on death).

The use of group policies is not confined to cases where the members of the group are bound together by common employment. They may, for instance, be members of an association, customers of a credit card company or hire-purchase trader or parents of the pupils of a school where either an appropriate agency or trust arrangement exists.

B Common terms and conditions of a life assurance policy

1.61 Although life assurance policies differ from office to office and from policy to policy, it may be useful to briefly describe some of the common terms and conditions found in life assurance policies. Obviously, not all of the following apply to all policies. Some policies such as term assurance policies will only have the basic provisions as described below (perhaps (i) to (viii)) whereas more sophisticated policies will have additional features. As mentioned above in Section A, specific personal details relating to the assured or life assured are often set out in a schedule although again for the simpler types of policy all the terms and conditions may well be in the same document. Example terms and provisions are set out below. It is likely that (i) to (viii) below will be in virtually all life policies.

(i) Name of assured and of life assured[1].

(ii) Policy date.

(iii) Policy number.

(iv) Sum assured – amount payable on death or maturity (as relevant).

(v) Event upon which sum assured is payable – death of sole life assured, death of first life assured (joint lives (first death) contract), death of last life assured (joint lives (last survivor) contract) or survival to the maturity date (where relevant).

(vi) Premium payments – amount, frequency, method of payment, consequences of non-payment.

(vii) Method of reinstating or reviving policies which have lapsed.

(viii) How notice is to be given to the life office including principal place of business of life office (for example, to give notice of assignment)[2].

(ix) Details regarding surrender values (where relevant) and how this will be calculated (will differ considerably between unit-linked and with-profits policies).

1 Life Assurance Act 1774, s 2.
2 Policies of Assurance Act 1867, s 1.

(x) Options to alter sum assured/premium/life assured.

(xi) Options to convert policy into a different type, for example, from term assurance to endowment.

(xii) Options to effect further assurance with no further health evidence, for example, on the birth or adoption of a child.

(xiii) Option to issue replacement policy on, for example, surrender of, or reduction in, sum assured under, the original policy.

(xiv) Option to increase sum assured where an inheritance tax liability can be shown to have increased, for example as a result of a change in legislation or through an increase in the value of the estate.

(xv) Option to increase sum assured on evidence of increase in value of assured's interest in a business.

(xvi) Waiver of contribution benefit (also known as premium waiver benefit). For an additional premium regular premiums may be suspended if the life assured is unable to pay them due to illness, etc.

(xvii) Accidental death benefit – sum assured is increased where death is due to an accident (as defined).

(xviii) Investment provisions/fund rules – as many life insurance products are almost wholly or at least partially investment-based there will be provisions relating to the underlying investment funds. This may well include the division of the fund into notional units, how units are valued, calculation of 'bid' and 'offer' prices, ability to close funds and make new funds available, where expenses are paid from, creation and cancellation of units, charges relating to investment management, rights to defer allocation or redemption of units, etc. In every case it should also be explained that the division of the fund into units is notional and the policyholder has no proprietary rights to the underlying investments.

C The policy and extrinsic evidence

1 General rules of construction

1.62 Where a contract is recorded in writing, the terms of the writing alone will normally be referred to in order to ascertain the rights and obligations of the parties: and the policy is the normal evidence of the contract of life assurance. The construction of policies is underpinned by certain basic rules which are outlined as follows: words are given their ordinary meanings (with reference to previous judicial authority as appropriate); a businesslike interpretation will be applied; unreasonable results should be avoided; ordinary meanings will be displaced if it can be established that they have a different technical legal meaning; the usage in that trade is different or the context requires a different meaning; the application of the 'ejusdem generis' rule whereby if certain words of a certain type are followed by general words, the general words are intended to describe only other things of the same type as those set out in the particular words[1].

Preliminary statements and documents, such as marketing literature, Key Features documents, quotations and proposal forms, which are part of the negotiations, form no part of the contract unless they are incorporated in the policy by reference or otherwise, in which case they are read as part of the policy. They cannot normally be referred to in construing the policy; although this rule is subject to many exceptions. A mere reference to the proposal in the policy is not in itself an incorporation of it in the contract. There must be something else to show that it is referred to as part of the contract and not merely by way of recital.

The statements made by a life office in any marketing literature or other advertisement will normally only be incorporated into the contract by express reference. If the statements are regarded as representations which induced the contract, they may afford grounds for rescission of the contract and return of premiums, but it would be rare for them to be read as part of the contract between the parties. The court may award damages under section 2(1) of the Misrepresentation Act 1967, which states that:

> 'Where a person has entered into a contract after a misrepresentation has been made to him by another party thereto and as a result thereof has suffered loss, then, if the person making the misrepresentation would be liable to damages in respect thereof had the misrepresentation been made fraudulently, that person shall be so liable notwithstanding that the misrepresentation was not made fraudulently, unless he proves that he had reasonable grounds to believe and did believe up to the time the contract was made, that the facts represented were true.'

Contrary to common law[2] but not equity[3], therefore, the life office will be liable for misrepresentations unless it can prove that it had reasonable grounds to believe, and did believe up to the time that the contract was made, that the facts represented were true. Companies are required by the FSA's rules relating to financial promotions to retain a record of the basis of any such statements. The life office will, furthermore, normally be liable for the representations made by its agents. It might technically be possible to exclude liability for non-contractual misrepresentations but it would be difficult in most cases to reconcile this with the duty to treat customers fairly (FSA Principle 6).

2 *Parol evidence*

1.63 There is a presumption that the policy document contains all the terms of the contract – the 'parol evidence' rule[4]. Also, where the words of the policy possess a clear meaning then it is not required to look elsewhere for an alternative meaning[5]. For these two reasons the basic rule is that extrinsic evidence is inadmissible.

1 See further *MacGillivray on Insurance Law* (9th edn, 1997) p 264, 11–1 to 11–19.
2 *Anderson v Fitzgerald* (1853) 4 HL Cas 484.
3 Eg *Redgrave v Hurd* (1882) 20 Ch D 1.
4 *Horncastle v Equitable Life Assurance Society* (1906) 22 TLR 735.
5 *Shore v Wilson* (1842) 9 Cl & F 355.

Evidence extrinsic to the policy may, however in certain circumstances, be admissible (in the absence of an express stipulation to the contrary in the policy) and some more common examples are set out below:

(1) To show that the statements form part of the contract and that the policy does not truly set out the full terms of the agreement between the parties. The court will then need to refer to what passed during the preliminary negotiations, including any relevant documents, and may order rectification of the policy in order to represent the true contract between the parties.

Sun Life Assurance Co of Canada v Jervis[1]

The life office sent to J a proposal form with a document called an 'Illustration', showing how the suggested policy would apply in his case. The 'Illustration' contained figures filled in by the agent. The wording of the proposal form was such that it could be completed only by a person who had read the 'Illustration'. Held, that the latter formed part of the contract and the policy should be rectified accordingly.

(2) To show the existence of a collateral agreement outside the terms of the policy which does not vary those terms but which represents a supplementary part of the bargain[2]. This supplemental agreement must be strictly collateral to the policy contract; statements as to practice or probable benefits to be derived from the insurance may be merely expressions of expectation or belief and will not then be construed as promises forming part of the contract.

Thiselton v Commercial Union Assurance Co Ltd[3]

The assured effected a policy on the basis of a prospectus which contained the following provision: 'Loans are granted upon security of the society's policies at 4.5%, except when the loan amounts to £200 or more when the rate is only 4%'. Mr Thiselton sought to compel the society to lend to him at the rates quoted. Held, that although the existence of some agreement outside the policy could not be denied, such agreement must be strictly collateral and the *statement of practice* as to loans was not collateral.

(3) To explain words which may not be obvious, such as technical or foreign words or abbreviations or shorthand.

(4) To show the intention of the parties where there is a patent ambiguity in the policy or where there is, on investigation of the circumstances, a latent ambiguity.

Where there is ambiguity or inconsistency in the policy, the court may apply various principles in an attempt to give effect to the contractual intention of the

1 [1943] 2 All ER 425; see also *Anstey v British Natural Premium Life* (1908) TLR 871.

2 *Bowtle v Salvation Army Assurance Society* (1927) IAC Rep 47.

3 [1926] Ch 888.

parties. For example, an earlier clause would generally take priority over a later one, although great caution must be exercised in this respect as much will depend on the wording and structure of the policy. Also, written wordings would tend to be given precedence over the printed clause with which they were inconsistent. It would seem that where the parties have deleted printed provisions this should be a factor in the court deciding what the parties intended[1] and this may be enhanced by the parties in some way authenticating the deletion, for example by initialling. Also of relevance is the contra proferentum rule which means that the ambiguity in a policy is construed against the party which prepared it. In most cases this will be the insurer but could be the insured where, for example, the proposal form is incorporated into the policy and the ambiguity relates to the insured's answers. Note should also be made here of the Unfair Terms in Consumer Contracts Regulations 1999, which are considered in Section 4.

3 *Rectification*

1.64 If either party to the contract establishes that the policy document does not set out the full or correct terms of the agreement between them, then he is entitled to have the policy rectified so that it expresses their true agreement[2]. However, there is a presumption that a policy contains the complete and final contract between the parties and so a strong burden of proof lies on the party seeking rectification to show clearly that agreement was reached as to the terms of the contract to be set out in the policy and that the policy fails to record their agreement[3].

It is sometimes stated that mistake is not generally a ground for rectification of a policy unless the mistake is 'mutual'[4]. Such phraseology can be misleading in that for both parties to make the same mistake would not only be coincidental but an arbitrary basis for rectification. Perhaps a more accurate description is that both parties must have understood the agreement between them to be something other than is mistakenly recorded in the policy issued by the life office[5]. The unilateral error of one party usually affords no grounds for rectification. Thus in *Royal Liver Friendly Society v Shearer*[6], a Friendly Society claimed rectification of its policy on the ground that in drafting the proposed form of policy the Society's officials had made a mistake in reading their own table of benefits set out in the Society's rules. Rectification was refused because there was no mistake on the part of the assured who got the policy he asked for.

In one case[7], not involving insurance, however, it was held that rectification would be allowed where there was a mistake on the part of one of the parties

1 *Punjab National Bank v de Boinville* (1992) 1 WLR 1138.
2 *Collett v Morrison* (1851) 9 Hare 162.
3 *Parsons v Bignold* (1846) 15 LJ Ch 379.
4 *Slack v Hancock* (1912) 107 LT 14.
5 *Fowler v Scottish Equitable Life Insurance Society and Ritchie* (1858) 28 LJ Ch 225.
6 [1930] 1 AC (NI) Rep 73.
7 *Thomas Bates & Son Ltd v Wyndham's (Lingerie) Ltd* [1981] 1 All ER 1077.

only. Rectification would be allowed in such cases provided it could be shown that (1) one party erroneously believed that the document sought to be rectified contained a particular term or provision; (2) the other party was aware of the omission and that it was due to a mistake; (3) the other party had failed to draw the mistake to his attention; and (4) the mistake must be one calculated to benefit the other person. If those requirements were satisfied the court might regard it as inequitable to allow the other party to resist rectification to give effect to the mistaken party's intention on the ground that the mistake was not, at the time of the execution of the document, a mutual mistake.

It should be noted that under the Unfair Terms in Consumer Contract Regulations, a policyholder may argue that contractual terms which have not been individually negotiated shall be regarded as unfair and therefore deleted, if, contrary to the requirement of good faith, they cause a significant imbalance in the parties' rights and obligations arising under the contract to the detriment of the policyholder. For further discussion of this area, See Section 4.

D Residence and occupation

1.65 Where a policy is intended to provide a significant level of cover it will normally include provisions relating to residence and hazardous occupations. Persons who at the time when they effect a policy have no intention of going abroad to live in a country where there is an undue health risk or risk of political disturbance are usually granted policies free from any restrictions as to residence. In other cases, the policies may become free of such restriction after, say, five years provided the life assured has not been outside the 'free limits' during that period.

Where a policy free from restriction, on grounds of residence or occupation, cannot be granted at the ordinary rates of premium because:

(1) the proposer is resident or is likely to reside in a country where there is an undue health risk or risk of political disturbance; or

(2) the proposer is, or is likely to be, engaged in some especially hazardous occupation;

the additional risk may be treated in one of the following ways:

(a) by provision that the policy shall be void if the additional risk shall be incurred unless covered by payment of an additional premium;

(b) by the issue of a policy free from restriction at an increased annual premium, to be paid whether the additional risk be in fact incurred or not; or

(c) by the exclusion from the cover under the policy of death from the additional risk.

Living in a country with undue health risks or engaging in a hazardous occupation may well affect the duration of life, even though death does not directly arise from it. The insertion in a policy of a condition equivalent to a warranty (method (a) above) is, however, very burdensome and the avoidance of a policy for breach of the condition may operate harshly, especially if the breach is trifling or due to some emergency. Method (c) is difficult to operate in practice. If the circumstances permit, method (b), an unrestricted policy being issued and a temporary or permanent extra premium being paid to cover the extra risk, is considered the better way of dealing with the issue.

It is usual to cover, without extra premium, ordinary flying risk on recognised air routes, but extra premium is often required for flying personnel in the armed forces. For civilian lives, life offices normally cover war risks, but extra premium is sometimes required for members of the armed forces.

Where applications are received from persons resident or domiciled abroad, care needs to be exercised by the insurer. In some jurisdictions it is illegal to contract with foreign insurers. From the life office's viewpoint, the complicating factors relating to governing law, claims, position of agents and intermediaries has led many companies to conclude that such business if undertaken on an ad hoc basis is simply not worth the risk.

E Stamps on policies

1.66 Stamp duty is no longer chargeable under the heading 'Policy of Life Insurance' in Schedule 1 to the Stamp Act 1891[1]. Furthermore, there is no stamp duty on annuity-certain policies (whether the policy is under hand or under seal ie executed by deed) or sinking fund or capital redemption policies.

F Glossary: some types of life policies and associated terminology

1.67 Life offices may be divided into:

(1) *mutuals* – in which the effecting of a policy conveys membership of the company and the whole of whose distributable surplus or 'profit' belongs to the with-profit policyholders; and

(2) *proprietary companies* – which are limited by shares and which are established and carried on wholly or mainly for the purpose of providing profits for the shareholders (despite the fact that a major part of any distributable surplus is allocated in the form of bonuses to with-profit policyholders).

Contracts of great variety are now made. Set out below is a reference guide to the types of policies which are issued. The descriptions set out below are not necessarily mutually exclusive, so it is possible to have, for example, a whole life, last survivor policy.

1 Finance Act 1989, s 173(1)(a).

Type of policy	*How or when the benefit is payable*
Whole life assurance	At death whenever it occurs. Premiums normally payable for whole life.
Endowment assurance	On survival to a specified date or on death before that date. (Often used as a mortgage repayment vehicle.)
Pure endowment	On survival to a specified date but not otherwise.
Temporary assurance (term assurance)	At death only if it occurs before a specified date. A surrender value would not be payable.
Convertible temporary assurance	At death only if it occurs before a specified date with an option to convert to a whole life or endowment assurance.
Joint life (first death) assurance	At the death of the first to die of two or more lives.
Joint lives (first death) endowment assurance	On survival of the lives assured to a specified date or at the earlier failure of the joint life of two or more lives.
Last survivor assurance	At the death of the last survivor of two or more lives.
Last survivor endowment assurance	On survival to a specified date or at the earlier death of the last survivor of two or more lives.
Contingent survivorship assurance	On failure of one life during the continuance of another.
Child's deferred assurance	At death after (usually) age 21 (or some are from 18 to 25) with options at the age chosen.
Family income policy	On death if that should occur during a specified term from the issue of the policy – a fixed periodical instalment is payable until the end of that term.
Mortgage protection policy	A form of temporary assurance designed to cover the principal outstanding under a mortgage (usually decreasing in line with repayment of the capital sum).
With-profits policy	A contract (usually endowment assurance) entitled to participate in the profits made and distributed by the life office. (See below for further details.)
Without-profits policy	A contract which is not entitled to participate in the profits of the life office.

Type of policy	*How or when the benefit is payable*
Accidental death policy	Benefits only payable if death occurs as a result of an accident and involving some external factor. May also be an additional feature under a whole life, endowment or term assurance and so would have the effect of an addition to the standard sum assured.
Unit-linked (or just 'linked') assurance	A contract where the benefits payable are determined by reference to the value of or income from, investment funds specifically designed for insurance policies unit trusts, open-ended investment companies, or by reference to fluctuations in, or in an index of, the value of any property. The policyholder receives, or is 'allocated', notional 'units' in return for his premium the underlying fund being divided up into units of equal value. The number of units depends on the value of those units at the time of allocation which will fluctuate in accordance with underlying investment values.
'Ten plus' policy (essentially a marketing name, so will be known by other names as well)	This is basically a ten-year endowment, or whole life policy under which premiums must be paid for a minimum of ten years (if there are to be no adverse income tax results). At the end of ten years the policyholder has the option:
	(1) to cease paying premiums and take the policy benefits; (2) to cease paying premiums and to let the capital sum continue to be invested in the insurance company's funds; (3) to continue paying full premiums for a further selected period – usually ten years, and to withdraw part of the value of the policy each year as an 'income' which can be varied from year to year to suit the policyholder's requirements. This income will be free of tax in the hands of the policyholder
Issue risk policy	An insurance effected by a person who, for example, holds a reversionary interest under a trust or who will suffer loss by the birth of a child or children, for example, to the life tenant. Sometimes effected as a contract of indemnity.

Type of policy	*How or when the benefit is payable*
Whole of life dread disease/critical illness benefit	On death or on diagnosis of a disease or critical illness or disability specified within the policy document (possibly subject to conditions regarding survival after diagnosis).
Investment bonds (also known as single premium bonds)	Whole life policies which are almost entirely investment-oriented (see **1.69**).
Trustee Investment policy/plan	Investment contract issued to trustees of an occupational or personal pension scheme. Whole of life or providing an annuity are standard
Broker bonds	An investment bond where one of the unit-linked funds available to the policy is managed by an IFA, or their associate and generally branded with the IFA's name.
Life of another policy	Assured and life assured are different persons. Assured must have an insurable interest in the life assured. Benefits will be payable on the death of the life assured. Policy may be whole life, endowment or temporary.
Capital redemption assurance	Benefits payable at a specified date, not dependent on life, but still classified as long-term business.
Annuities	
Immediate annuity	Annuity payable during life commencing on completion of contract.
Deferred annuity	Annuity payable during life commencing at a future date. If the annuitant dies in the period prior to the vesting date the life office will normally refund the premiums paid.
Reversionary annuity	Annuity payable during life commencing at the death of a specified person.
Guaranteed annuity	An annuity with a proviso that it shall continue for a stated number of years at least, irrespective of whether the annuitant dies in the meantime.
Joint lives and survivor annuity	Annuity payable during the joint lifetime and the life of the survivors or survivor of two or more lives.

Type of policy	*How or when the benefit is payable*
Temporary annuity	Annuity payments cease at the end of a fixed term, or on the death of the annuitant, whichever happens first. May be on a joint first lives or last survivor or guaranteed basis.
Personal pensions	Replaced retirement annuity contracts and are normally investment contracts offering the customer the option of an annuity when they take retirement benefits.
Stakeholder pensions	Similar to personal pensions but simplified and with restricted charges.

1 With-profits

1.68 As future rates of mortality, interest and expense cannot be accurately forecast, it is not possible to fix a premium which on average will exactly cover the risk and therefore a margin is allowed by the life office. This margin should over time give rise to a surplus in the long-term business fund, which is revealed at the periodical valuations of the office's assets and liabilities. The long-term business fund may also be subdivided into several different funds. In the case of a proprietary company, a part of the surplus is available to pay dividends to shareholders; the balance of the surplus, or the whole of it in the case of a mutual office, can be allotted or distributed to the with-profit policyholders in the form of some benefit additional to the sum assured. The additional benefit usually takes the form of a 'reversionary bonus' payable with the sum assured, but may be in the form of a cash payment or of a reduction in the future premiums. In addition, on maturity of a policy (or on death) there may be a 'terminal bonus'. If there is a surrender of the policy before maturity or death an 'interim bonus' may be payable. The life office will not usually distribute the whole surplus but will retain some for the purpose of 'smoothing' bonus levels over the investment period. The amount distributed is at the discretion of the life office in consultation with the actuary.

The management and operation of with-profits funds are now subject to very detailed FSA requirements. These are explained in Chapter 6.

2 'Bonds' and Fuji v Aetna

1.69 'Bonds' offered by insurance companies are generally life assurances or capital redemption assurances (from non-UK companies) purchased with a single premium, the benefits under which are defined by reference to notional units. The underlying fund may consist of fixed interest investments, equities, real property, unit trusts, open-ended investment companies or a combination of some or more of these and the amount of additional life cover (in relation to the investment value if such a bond) is usually very modest. It is usually expressed as a percentage of the total value of units at the time of death. For example, 101% of the value of units.

Note should be made of the important decision in *Fuji Finance Inc v Aetna Life Insurance Ltd*[1] which raised some important issues for the life industry and which involved consideration of the legal issues relating to bonds. In 1986 Fuji, a Panamanian company, took out a single premium policy for a premium of £50,000. The life assured was an experienced investor and the central figure behind Fuji. Sums, which were calculated by reference to the amount and value of units allocated to the policy, were payable on the death of the life assured or the earlier surrender of the policy. The policy enabled the policyholder to switch units allocated to his policy between several funds effectively with the benefit of hindsight. As a result of such switching of the units, by June 1992 the policy was valued at over £1m. The insurance company, Aetna Life, then changed its switching procedures.

Fuji claimed this was repudiatory breach of contract and surrendered the policy. The surrender proceeds of £1,110,758 were paid. Fuji claimed damages for breach of contract. The insurance company denied committing any breach. One of its defences was that the policy as a life policy was null and void under section 1 of the Life Assurance Act 1774 (for lack of insurance interest). Another was that it was in breach of section 16(1) of the Insurance Companies Act 1982.

The policy could be surrendered at any time for a cash sum equal to the value of units held at surrender but if surrender occurred within the first five years, a modest discontinuance charge reduced the amount payable. The central decision at first instance, was that a purported insurance contract, where the same sum was payable on the death of the life assured as would be payable on demand before death, was not a contract of insurance on the life of a person within section 1 of the Life Assurance Act 1774, it therefore did not constitute insurance business for the purpose of section 16 of the Insurance Companies Act 1982 (section 16 required insurance companies to restrict their activities to insurance business or connected activities). Indeed, Sir Donald Nicholls V-C went on to say that it could not be that the presence of a minor and insignificant element of insurance sufficed to turn a contract, otherwise of a different nature, into a contract of insurance. Therefore, the 1774 Act did not apply to such contracts. If the policy was not a contract of insurance, it could not have been issued under section 16(1) of the Insurance Companies Act 1982, which restricted the business of an insurance company to insurance. However, he stated that Parliament did not, thereby, intend that a contract made by an insurance company in breach of section 16 should be unlawful and unenforceable. The intended remedy for a default lay in the powers of intervention conferred on the Secretary of State.

The conclusion reached, which was obviously of serious concern to the life assurance industry, was that single premium insurance bonds which offer little or no life cover, were not insurance contracts. This raised the ominous issue of insurers having a considerable number of non-insurance contracts on their books. In most cases neither the insurer nor the policyholder would want the contract to cease. However, the public policy issues of permitting insurers to retain a large number of contracts which were not technically insurance contracts, would have had to have been considered. Another possible spectre related to tax-

1 [1994] Ch 173; [1995] Ch 122; [1994] 4 All ER 1025.

ation treatment. If such policies were not insurance policies, how would they be taxed? If they are not insurance policies they would appear to be unauthorised collective investment schemes. It would, however, be very rare for the Inland Revenue to act retrospectively. Historically, they have taken action from the date of pronouncement of any change of stance.

1.70 Fortunately for the life industry, the Court of Appeal overruled the High Court decision. The contract was a life assurance policy under the 1774 Act and so, Fuji was subject to the limitation set out in section 3. Morritt LJ did not consider that the fact that no greater sum was payable on death than on surrender was important, provided that the event on which benefits were payable was sufficiently life/death related. In this case a benefit was payable on the death of the life assured. The timing of death was uncertain and it was that uncertainty and the fact that the policyholder could not stop the policy paying out, as a result of death occurring, that rendered the policy one of life insurance. The judge also thought that the effect of the discontinuance charge (ie it did not apply on death only on surrender) could have been relevant, had he not already decided that the contract was a life assurance contract. The court did not accept that insurance needed to be the 'principal object' of the contract.

As a result, the question of whether the effect of section 16 of the Insurance Companies Act 1982 was that the contract was unenforceable against the insurance company no longer required consideration. It was a life assurance contract and hence within section 16. However, the Court of Appeal still considered the point, although of course, their comments are strictly 'obiter'. Morritt LJ agreed with the Vice Chancellor. The purpose of section 16 was only to limit the scope of an insurance company's undertakings and it was not a necessary implication that every contract entered into outside that scope was thereby invalidated. The fact that there were no criminal sanctions for breach of section 16 reinforced that view. Sir Ralph Gibson disagreed. His opinion was that such contracts were void and unenforceable.

The Court of Appeal decision was not ultimately appealed to the House of Lords. The position therefore seems to be that insurance contracts which offer little or no life cover in addition to the investment value of the contract can nevertheless be life assurance contracts. It is not the quantum of the additional amount payable on death that seems to be important, rather the fact that death is a trigger for the payment of the policy value.

SECTION 7 THE PREMIUM

A Non Discriminatory premia

1. Gender based premium factors

1.71 UK insurers have until recently been free to use a variety of factors including gender for rating purposes. In the context of life assurance, gender based premia have meant that women generally pay more for annuities but less for life assurance because they are, on average statistically likely to live longer than men. The power to do this was contained in section 45 of the Sex Discrimination Act 1975. This section was amended, with effect from 6th April 2008, to reflect requirements of the EU Gender Directive[1]. This prevents discrimination by insurers refusing to offer cover to a person based on their sex and discrimination in relation to pregnancy or maternity. However, the directive included a potential derogation, adopted by the UK, to permit gender to be used as a factor in risk based premia. The derogation required the use of gender to be proportionate to actuarially assessed, published (and regularly updated) data. The Sex Discrimination Act provision was replaced by the Equality Act 2010 with effect from 1 October 2010[2]. However, the basis of the derogation in the Gender Directive was at the same time being challenged, in the *Test Achats* case[3] in the European Court of Justice (ECJ), by a Belgian consumer's association . The Advocate General's opinion in the case, issued in September 2010, was fairly detailed. She did not accept the argument that the use of gender, based on objectively verified statistical data, was consistent with the EU's Charter of Fundamental Rights which had been incorporated into the EU Treaty by the Treaty of Lisbon. This inconsistency lead the Advocate General to decide that the derogation in the Gender Directive was therefore unlawful, despite the fact that it had been agreed by the Commission and the Parliament. She proposed a three year transitional period, after which the use of gender based factors to determine premiums or benefits (even on existing contracts) would become unlawful. The full court of the ECJ gave its decision on 1 March 2011. The basis of its decision was slightly different to that of the Advocate General and potentially less problematic for the Commission and the Parliament who had included the derogation in the Gender Directive. The basis of the court's decision was that the derogation had a built in review date (after five years) and that as that derogation could not persist indefinitely (as to do so would be incompatible with the Charter), the court would make an order to prevent the derogation applying after that time. The court therefore ordered that the derogation (Article 5(2) of the Gender Directive) is invalid with effect from 21 December 2012.

2. What are the implications of this ruling?

The result of the ECJ decision is that a transitional period has been allowed until 21 December 2012. After this date all insurance pricing must become unisex. The transitional period may of course present short term opportunities for those who can, for example, purchase annuities under the existing regime or delay the purchase of annuities until 21 December 2012.

The judgment is quite short and unfortunately it does leave some questions unanswered (ie it is not actually clear what the effect of the removal of the carve-out from 21 December 2012 is on existing contracts). Contracts entered into

1 SI 2004/113/EC.

2 Schedule 3, Part 5.

3 *Association Belges des Consumateurs Test Achats and others v Conseil des Ministres* C236/09.

before the Gender Directive came into effect should generally be safe from the ruling's effect as the Gender Directive only applied to new contracts made after it was implemented (6 April 2008 in the UK). For contracts entered into after 6 April 2008 and before 21 December 2012, it seems likely that they will be exempt from the new unisex requirements (provided they have complied with the requirements of the carve out (eg in the UK differences in premiums or benefits are proportionate to published actuarial and statistical data and do not relate to pregnancy or childbirth). The UK Government's view, expressed in a Ministerial statement,[1] is that the judgment should only apply to new contracts concluded after the prohibition comes into effect on 21 December 2012. The UK Government intends to remove the current exemption from the Equality Act 2010 early in 2012. It also intends to press the Commission to issue guidance on the interpretation of the judgment.

However, there are still some areas of uncertainty in relation to existing contracts which provide for the purchase of future benefits or reviews to be carried out on the insurer's standard terms. One such area is the purchase of pensions annuities. There are technical legal arguments for insured pension contracts, that the purchase of the annuity is part of the existing contract (and not a new contract). This is because most insurers are normally contractually committed to an annuity at their 'standard rates' should the policyholder choose to take it up. However, if the obligation to provide an annuity arises after the end of the transitional period, the insurer's standard rates should then be unisex rates. Insurers may be able to argue that annuities provided under contracts entered into prior to the Gender Directive's implementation should be subject to non-unisex standard rates. Although legally this is arguable, in practice it may be a difficult argument to run as it could permit non unisex rates to be available on retirements taking place in 15 or 20 years time. It is therefore possible that after the end of the transitional period, even annuities provided under pre 2008 contracts may need to be on unisex rates.

It seems likely that the effect of the judgment will be to cause insurers to increase the cost of annuities for men. Insurers are therefore in the difficult position, that although the majority of annuities may be provided to men, they cannot discriminate in terms of who annuities are offered to and so cannot control their mix of male/female business. They will therefore presumably need to assume a level of female annuities which will push the price of male annuities up towards the current female rates.

3. *Proposed EU Equality Directive*

One of the results of the judgment, particularly for life products, seems likely to be greater emphasis on the health of the life assured and this has caused some people to question whether there should be a relaxation of the ABI rules on the use of genetic testing. In any event, it seems that insurers may need to find other factors on which to base their assessment of risk. One of the other potential drivers of risk may be the socio-economic position of the life assured. In recent

1 By Mark Hoban, 30 June 2011.

years so called 'postcode underwriting' has allowed insurers to make assumptions about longevity. This could result in those lower down the socio-economic ladder ending up with a worse deal for life assurance although perhaps not for annuities.

However, it is worth considering the basis of the ECJ's decision and the current proposals for an EU Equality Directive, which would prohibit discrimination on grounds of religion or belief, disability, age or sexual orientation. The basis of the ECJ decision in *Test Achats* is that the Charter of Fundamental Rights, which is enforceable against member state governments and EU institutions, prevents discrimination on such grounds. The specified grounds include age, disability and social origin as follows:

> 'Any discrimination based on any ground such as sex, race, colour, ethnic or social origin, genetic features, language, religion or belief, political or any other opinion, membership of a national minority, property, birth, disability, age or sexual orientation shall be prohibited (Article 21(1)).'

The Charter also provides that everyone is equal before the law[1]. As currently drafted, this proposed directive contains a provision which would deem the use of life or health factors in risk based premia not to be discrimination where their use is a 'determining factor' in the assessment of risk and they are based on relevant actuarial principles, statistical data or medical knowledge. Following the logic of the *Test Achats* case, pricing based upon these characteristics could also be considered to be incompatible with EU law and it seems possible this provision could be removed from the directive. This is a particular concern for life and health insurance as regards age and disability. It seems certain that the debate on this directive, will include discussion of how insurance can operate if it cannot take into account age and disability. It is to be hoped that a solution can be found to avoid extending the gender problems to other areas.

B First premium

1.72 The consideration required from the assured, in return for the life office's obligations under the contract of life insurance, is the premium or the promise to pay premiums. Premiums may be periodic or single. Periodic premiums may be annual or of greater frequency. Very often they are payable monthly. They may be payable throughout the life of the assured, or may cease at the expiration of a fixed number of years or the death of the assured, whichever occurs first. It is not unusual for whole life policies (ie providing cover for the whole of life) to provide for premiums to cease at the age of 85 or 90.

A policy may be effected at an annual premium payable by instalments, in which case any instalment for the year not already paid at the time of claim is deducted from the policy proceeds.

There is no principle of law which requires a premium to be paid before a contract of insurance is concluded. In circumstances where a policy is issued and

1 (Article 20).

cover commences prior to the payment of premium, it is probable that the life office would be able to deduct the first premium from any claim moneys which become payable. A contract cannot, however, be concluded unless there is agreement as to the amount of premium and the method of payment.

It is still quite common for the life office to provide that the cover will not commence until the premium has been paid even though premiums are usually paid by direct debit or by cheque. It should be noted that payment by cheque is merely conditional payment and policies often refer to payment or receipt of cleared funds. Where payment is to be made by direct debit it is often no longer a requirement that the first premium has been received. Where the assured has engaged an intermediary to arrange the policy for him, payment of the premium to the intermediary (other than a tied agent) will not amount to payment to the life office[1]. Where payment of the premium has been made to the intermediary, then the intermediary will hold that money subject to the FSA Client Money provisions under which the intermediary must in accordance with the regulations, inter alia:

(1) keep client money separate from its own money in a client account with, in most cases, an approved bank;

(2) pay the client money into the account as soon as is reasonably possible;

(3) hold the client money as a fiduciary for the client; and

(4) generally pay interest on the client money.

C Early cancellation of policies

1.73 For various reasons, someone buying a policy may not at the time appreciate fully the terms of the contract he is entering into. He may later find that the policy is not what he intended to buy and in some cases that it is not suited to his needs. Alternatively, he may have been subject to high pressure sales techniques. The right to cancel is now contained in the FSA's conduct of business Sourcebooks COBS and ICOBS. These are considered in Chapter 5.

D Renewal premiums and days of grace

1.74 Where a life policy is issued at an annual or other periodic premium, the assured has a right to continue the policy from time to time on payment of the premium. Life assurance therefore differs from most classes of general insurance. There has been considerable judicial disagreement as to whether annual premium life policies are insurances for one year with an irrevocable order to renew upon payment of the agreed renewal premium or an insurance for the whole of the assured's life subject to defeasance upon non-payment of the

1 See Chapter 4 for further discussion of the role of the intermediary and agent.

renewal premium at the times stated[1]. It would appear that the latter view is probably the one which has the support of most judicial authority. In any event, the precise terms of the policy may clarify the position as it is not now usual to see any reference to renewal or renewal premia. The question can be important in terms of ascertaining the effect of death during any days of grace.

As a general rule, days of grace are allowed for payment of the renewal premium. The position in the event of the death of the life assured during the days of grace and before payment of the premium, must be ascertained from the policy and/or from the regulations of the life office. The life policy may expressly provide that cover continues during the days of grace even before payment of the premium, in which case the position is clear. Most policies for whole life assurance, endowment assurance and similar risks contain further provisions to define the position which arises if the renewal premium remains unpaid after the expiry of the days of grace.

The term of the days of grace and the conditions attached to them will be strictly construed. Time is of the essence in the matter and equity will give no relief against lapse for non-payment, for the assured and the life office are not on an equal footing. The assured has the right to renew but the life office cannot compel payment.

> *Rowan v Atlas Assurance Co Ltd*[2]
>
> S effected a policy at an annual premium with 30 days of grace. The renewal premium was not paid within the days of grace. The company voluntarily applied the cash value of the reversionary bonus attached to the policy so as to keep the policy alive for a fractional period. Held, that the calculation of that period by the company could not be questioned and no further days of grace would run from its expiry.
>
> *McKenna v City Life Assurance Co*[3]
>
> A policy was effected at a quarterly premium and contained the following condition: 'Any policy which has acquired a surrender value will not immediately lapse if a renewal premium be not paid within the days of grace, but will be kept in force for twelve calendar months from the date upon which the last premium became due'. Held that a tender of overdue premium must be made within twelve calendar months of the renewal date. A tender after that time, but within twelve calendar months of the expiry of the days of grace, was too late, and the policy had lapsed.

The assured is not entitled to rely on the receipt of a renewal notice or other reminder[4] as a warning that a premium is about to become due, and absence of such a notice is no excuse for non-payment.

1 See *Pritchard v The Merchants' and Tradesmen's Mutual Life Assurance Society* (1858) 3 CB (NS) 622; *Stuart v Freeman* [1903] 1 KB 47.
2 (1928) 72 Sol Jo 285.
3 [1919] 2 KB 491.
4 *Windus v Tredegar* (1866) 15 LT 108, HL.

1.75 Tender of payment without acceptance may suffice to keep the policy in force.

Farquharson v Pearl Assurance Co Ltd[1]

A policy allowed 30 days of grace for payment of premiums. It was mortgaged by the assured, and during the days of grace the mortgagee, being aware of financial difficulties of the assured, called at the district office of the company and offered to pay the premium. The offer was declined and the district manager said he was arranging for the assured to pay. The premium was not paid during the days of grace, and on the death of the assured the company denied liability on the ground that the policy had lapsed. Held, that the company could not be heard to say that the premium had not been tendered by a person authorised by the assured, since the mortgage deed signed by him contained a provision that the mortgagee might pay the premium. The company accordingly was liable.

The life office may extend the period during which payment of the premium may be made[2] or may waive any of the conditions precedent to the continuance of the risk, and although a policy has lapsed, the office may be held to have revived the assurance upon the same terms if they have led the assured to believe that they have reassumed the risk.

Stuart v Freeman[3]

An own-life policy allowed 30 days of grace for payment of the premium. The assured assigned the policy and the life office agreed orally with the assignee that if the assured did not pay the premium within the 30 days the assignee could pay it upon the following day. Held, that as between the life office and the assignee the policy must be read as if there were 31 days of grace.

I Non-forfeiture provisions

1.76 Policies often contain a provision intended to preserve the cover, or some part of it, in some cases for a limited period, if the premium is not paid by the end of the days of grace. The provisions vary with different offices, and reference should be made to the policy. The following are brief descriptions of some of these variations:

(1) The assurance is held in force so long as any surrender value exceeds the overdue premiums and any revival charges (an extra charge that would be made in the event of reinstatement), which are charged against the policy.

(2) The assurance is held in force for (say) one year and then converted to a paid-up policy of such a reduced amount as any surrender value will permit.

1 [1937] 3 All ER 124.

2 This will normally be subject, where appropriate, to the rules for qualifying policies. See further Chapter 12.

3 [1903] 1 KB 47.

(3) The surrender value is used as a single premium for a temporary assurance for the full sum assured for such a period as it will cover.

(4) The assurance is converted at the end of the days of grace to the paid-up value of the policy at that date.

Of course, the policy could instead lapse without value and where the policy has no surrender value, this would normally be the case. Non-payment of premium may not cause a policy to be forfeited if the requirement is waived by the life office. This may arise through a subsequent demand for, or acceptance of, the premium in circumstances which would lead the assured to believe the life office is treating the policy as subsisting. However, the mere acceptance of the premium after forfeiture, is not in itself conclusive. It will depend essentially on the terms on which the waiver is given by the life office.

Some non-forfeiture conditions, it has been argued, may cause the policy to be regarded as a consumer credit agreement for the purposes of the Consumer Credit Act 1974. It is submitted that these should not be deemed consumer credit agreements because the contract that the policyholder has with the life office has not, in the majority of cases, been taken out for the extension 'of credit or any other form of financial accommodation' (within the meaning of section 9(1) of the 1974 Act) and the 'credit' that arises is merely incidental to the parties' contractual arrangements. Therefore as the main purpose of the transaction is not the provision of credit, it being merely a part of the arrangements for reinstatement should premiums not be paid on time, it is argued that the contract is not subject to the 1974 Act[1].

In practice it does not appear that the contrary view, that the ambit of consumer credit agreements is sufficiently wide to catch such arrangements has been promulgated. In connection with the Consumer Credit Act 1974, the position of premium payments by credit cards is increasingly common. Section 75 of the 1974 Act is noteworthy in that the insured will, where the section applies, have concurrent remedies against the credit card company for breach of contract or misrepresentation. Unless agreed otherwise, the credit card company is entitled to be indemnified by the insurer if it has to meet a claim by the insured[2].

2 *Reinstatement and revival*

1.77 When a policy has lapsed the life office may be prepared to reinstate it. Provision is usually made for revival of the policy within a specified time and the fulfilment of certain conditions. Technically, a new contract will be made as a result of reinstatement. The life office may require further health and lifestyle evidence and the premium level may have changed and/or an extra premium for reinstatement may be required. Some or all of these requirements may be waived and prima facie would be waived by acceptance of the previously agreed

1 *Pott's Executors v IRC* [1951] 1 All ER 76; *Re HPC Productions Ltd* [1962] 1 All ER 37.
2 Section 75(2).

premium after the expiry of the days of grace. The life office may also be prepared to reinstate the policy outside such time limits with or without imposing any further requirements. For qualification purposes HMRC will treat reinstatements as the continuation of the original policy provided it occurs within 13 months of the due date for payment of the last premium to be paid (see Chapter 13).

SECTION 8 DEEDS

A Overview

1.78 For various reasons, deeds are relevant to, and frequently encountered in, the transaction of life assurance business. Knowledge of the basic features will, therefore, be helpful to the practitioner in the law of life assurance. This section provides a brief explanation of deeds generally.

A *deed* is (usually) an instrument whereby property is transferred or an obligation is undertaken, but its purpose may be merely declaratory (ie it sets out the rights, existing or future, of the parties mentioned in it). Under the Law of Property Act 1925 a deed was required to be a written document, signed, sealed and delivered. The law relating to deeds and their execution has been amended and is now contained within the Law of Property (Miscellaneous Provisions) Act 1989 (LP(MP)A). Prior to this Act, it was not necessary, even though it was usually the case, for the parties' signatures to be witnessed. The LP(MP)A now makes this a requirement of a properly executed deed[1]. The requirement of writing impliedly remains[2]. The requirement of sealing for the valid execution of a deed by an individual was abolished[3].

An *indenture* was formerly a deed executed in duplicate with both copies written on the same parchment or paper which was then cut in an irregular or tooth like manner, so that the edges of each part were indented. The exact fit of the two parts was proof that the parts were genuine.

A *deed poll* was formerly a deed with a smooth or polled edge, not executed in duplicate.

The term *indenture* now simply denotes a deed to which there is more than one party and a *deed poll* is a deed to which there is only one party, though more persons than one may join in expressing the same intention.

The terms deed poll and indenture are not commonly used today (although the deed poll has made something of a comeback in the sphere of personal pension schemes not established by way of trust). A deed is now usually simply referred to as a deed or described by reference to the nature of transaction (eg a conveyance, settlement, assignment, mortgage, appointment of trustees, etc).

1 Section 1(3)(a).
2 Section 1(1)(a).
3 Section 1(1)(b).

1.79 The date stated as the date of the deed ought to be the date on which it becomes operative. Where, however, there are several parties in places distant from one another, the document may be executed by different parties on different dates. The deed will only be effective from the date of the last person to execute the deed unless the deed is completed in escrow, eg it is not to be delivered until a future date or until some condition has been fulfilled.

B Execution

1.80 Section 1 of the LP(MP)A sets out the requirements for the execution of deeds:

(1) Section 1(2) of the LP(MP)A, which applies both to individuals and corporations, states that the instrument must make it clear on its face that it is intended to be a deed, and must be validly executed. Describing the instrument as a deed would satisfy this requirement as would expressing itself to be executed as a deed.

(2) Section 1(3)(a) of the LP(MP)A sets out the requirements for the execution of deeds specifically relating to individuals. The requirement of sealing has now gone and so deeds are validly executed by an individual if they are 'signed and delivered'.

1 Companies

1.81 It is no longer necessary for companies to have a common seal[1]. However, it remains for the company to choose whether to execute a deed by affixing its common seal or to utilise the method set out in section 44 of the Companies Act 2006. This provides that a document is validly executed if it is signed on behalf of the company by two authorised signatories or one director in the presence of a witness who attests the signature.

It should also be noted that section 44(5) provides that a document, which purports to be executed in this way in favour of a purchaser in good faith and for value, should be deemed to have been duly executed by the company, no matter what is provided for in the company's constitution.

Where a company is in liquidation, the liquidator has power to do all acts and execute in the name of and on behalf of the company all deeds and other documents and for that purpose to use the company seal where necessary[2].

2 Attorneys

1.82 The donee of a power of attorney may execute a deed in and with his own name and signature but it is preferable that he should use the formula 'AB

1 Companies Act 2006, s 45.
2 Insolvency Act 1986, Sch 4, Part III.

by his attorney CD'. Furthermore, Schedule 1, paragraph 6 of the LP(MP)A amends section 1 of the Powers of Attorney Act 1971 such that an instrument creating a power of attorney no longer needs to be 'signed and sealed', but now needs to be 'executed as a deed by' the donor of the power, if it is an ordinary power of attorney, and by the donor and the attorney if it is an enduring power of attorney. The standard form of enduring power of attorney requires execution as a deed (see also **1.95–1.97**).

3 The attestation of signatures

1.83 Section 1(3)(a) of the LP(MP)A makes it a requirement that the signature on a deed must be attested by a witness present at the time of signing. Furthermore, if the deed is not actually signed by a party it must be signed at his direction and in his presence with two witnesses attesting the signature. Circumstances where this may arise could be where the party is physically unable to sign the deed.

4 The delivery

1.84 A deed is binding on the maker of it if it has been signed, or possibly sealed in the case of a company, and delivered. Delivery does not mean handing over to the other side, it means an act done so as to evince an intention to be bound. When it has been fully executed but is awaiting the fulfilment of some condition it is called an *escrow*. After such fulfilment (and after delivery) it will become absolute.

5 Alterations in deeds

1.85 In the absence of evidence to the contrary, alterations in deeds are presumed to have been made before execution. Any material alteration should, however, be mentioned in the attestation clause and all alterations should be initialled by the parties.

SECTION 9 POWERS OF ATTORNEY

A Ordinary and enduring powers

1.86 A power of attorney is a deed by which one person (the donor or appointor) gives another person (the donee or attorney) authority to act for the donor either generally (which is the usual case) or only for specified matters. It is, therefore, a statutory species of agency arrangement. A power of attorney is often executed, for instance, when the donor is about to go abroad. The law regarding powers of attorney was altered and codified by the Powers of Attorney Act 1971 (which came into force on 1 October 1971) and the Enduring Powers of Attorney Act 1985 (which came into force on 10 March 1986). All powers of attorney must be made by deed. A donor who is unable to execute an enduring power of attorney because of some physical disability may direct another person to execute it on his behalf in the presence of two attesting witnesses. A person suffering from a mental disorder cannot confer a power of attorney. However, in such cases, an application can be made to the Court of Protection for the court to make an order giving directions as to how the affairs of that person should be carried out. Such directions will be specific and (unlike a general power of attorney) contain no general discretion on behalf of the 'receiver' to whom the powers will be given.

The contents of a power of attorney may be proved by production of the original document or by a photocopy. The copy must contain a certificate to the effect that the document or the page is a true and complete copy; the certificate must be signed by the donor, or by a solicitor or a member of the Stock Exchange. Photocopies of facsimiles are acceptable if certified.

A power of attorney expressed to be irrevocable and given to secure either a proprietary interest of the donee or the performance of an obligation owed to the donee cannot be revoked by the donor without the donee's consent so long as the donee has that interest or that obligation remains undischarged, and is not revoked by the donor's death, incapacity or bankruptcy, or by its winding up or dissolution where the donor is a company[1].

Powers not given as security may be revoked at any time by the appointor, and will be revoked by his death, unsoundness of mind, or bankruptcy. Section 5 of the Powers of Attorney Act 1971 gives protection to the attorney and to purchasers from him without notice of revocation. An attorney who acts in pursuance of a power without knowledge of its revocation incurs no liability to the donor or to any other person. A purchaser without notice of revocation will get as good title as if the power had not been revoked. If the purchase is made after the date (if any) on which the power is expressed to expire he will, of course, have notice of revocation. If the purchase is completed within 12 months of the date that the power came into force, the lack of knowledge of the purchaser will be conclusively presumed in favour of persons dealing with him. If the transaction is completed more than 12 months after the power comes into force, the purchaser can prove his lack of notice by making a statutory declaration that he did not at the material time know of the revocation. This declaration must be made before, or within three months after, the relevant purchase. 'Purchaser' and 'purchase' have the meanings assigned to them by section 205(1)(xxi) of the Law of Property Act 1925, so that a purchaser is one who acquires an interest for money or money's worth and includes a mortgagee.

1.87 The Powers of Attorney Act 1971 includes a short form of general power in Schedule 1 under which the authority extends to anything which can lawfully be done through an attorney[2]. This provision does not apply to any functions the donor may have as a trustee or personal representative[3]. The statutory form is as follows:

1 1971 Act, s 4.
2 1971 Act, s 10(1).
3 1971 Act, s 10(2).

THIS GENERAL POWER OF ATTORNEY is made this

day of (*year*) by of

I appoint CD of

AB [*or* CD of and EF of jointly *or* [*jointly and severally*] to be my attorney[s] in accordance with section 10 of the Powers of Attorney Act 1971.

IN WITNESS etc.

If more than one attorney is appointed, their authority may be joint, or joint and several, as the deed may specify.

The attorney may execute documents with his own signature (and as a deed if required) by the authority of the appointor[1]. The execution should include a reference to the power.

Until the Enduring Powers of Attorney Act 1985 (EPA 1985) every power of attorney was automatically revoked if the donor became mentally incapable. An enduring power of attorney may continue even if the donor becomes mentally incapable[2]. The EPA 1985 does not affect the position of ordinary powers of attorney and these can still be granted. However, whilst with an ordinary power of attorney the attorney may never know, or have consented, to his appointment, with an enduring power, the attorney is required to execute the deed as well as the donor. This, in effect, ensures that the attorney is aware and consents to his appointment.

Whilst the donor remains mentally capable the enduring power of attorney operates as an ordinary power of attorney. Once the attorney has reason to believe that the donor has become, or is becoming, mentally incapable he must make an application to the Court of Protection to register the power of attorney[3]. Until he does so all his powers are suspended[4] except as is set out in section 1(2). Once the court has registered the power, the attorney's powers are restored. Care should be taken by the life office to ensure that the attorney has the requisite powers to act for the donor.

The statutory form of enduring power of attorney is contained within the Enduring Powers of Attorney (Prescribed Form) Regulations 1990[5], and must be used. Failure to use the prescribed form will mean that the power of attorney will not take effect as an enduring power of attorney. The power may be effective as an ordinary power of attorney which would, in the ordinary way, be revoked in the event of the donor subsequently becoming mentally incapable. There is a case to support this view which held that an enduring power of attorney which was ineffective as such because of an inconsistency with section 11(1) was nevertheless capable of taking effect as an ordinary power[6].

1 1971 Act, s 7(1).
2 EPA 1985, s 1(1).
3 EPA 1985, s 4(2) and the Court of Protection (Enduring Powers of Attorney) Rules 2001.
4 Section 1(1)(b) and (c).
5 SI 1990/1376.
6 *X v (1)Y, (2) Z sub nom E* (2000) 1 FLR 882; [2000] 3 All ER 1004; (2000) 3 WLR 1974.

B Benefits and gifts

1 Ordinary powers of attorney

1.88 Unless expressly stated the attorney cannot make gifts to himself or to others. It is submitted that no such express provision exists with the short form of power in the 1971 Act.

2 Enduring powers of attorney

1.89 Section 3(4) of the Enduring Powers of Attorney Act 1985 provides that an attorney may provide for persons if the donor might be expected to provide for those persons' needs, and when benefitting those persons the attorney may do whatever the donor might be expected to do to meet the needs of those persons. The class of persons that may benefit includes the attorney.

There is also a limited power, by operation of section 3(5) of the EPA 1985, to make gifts under an enduring power of attorney, and the attorney can make gifts to himself, although this will be subject to any restrictions or conditions contained in the power of attorney. The Act allows gifts to be made 'of a seasonal nature or at a time, or on an anniversary, of a birth or marriage, to persons (including himself) who are related to or connected with the donor'[1], and 'to any charity to whom the donor made or might be expected to make gifts'[2].

When considering making gifts the attorney must consider whether or not it is of an unreasonable value taking into account all the circumstances and in particular the size of the donor's estate. A question which frequently arises in connection with life assurance transactions is whether an attorney can declare a trust of a life assurance policy. Although a universally agreed definition of a trust has been difficult to achieve it is clear that a trust is something more than a gift. However, it should be noted that in *In Re the Estate of Marjorie Langdon Cameron Deceased*[3] it was held that a gift made by an attorney under a testator's enduring power of attorney superseded a bequest by will by the process of ad emption. The gift involved an educational trust for the benefit of the son.

Where the attorney wishes to benefit either himself or others otherwise than in accordance with section 3(4) and (5) of the EPA 1985, he may apply to the Court of Protection, which has jurisdiction under section 8(2)(e) to authorise such benefits, subject to any restrictions contained within the power of attorney itself.

A life office dealing with the attorney must satisfy itself that the power is validly executed, that the time, if any, to which it is limited has not expired, and that the transaction with which the office is concerned is within the authority conferred by the deed. It will have to satisfy itself that: it has no notice of revocation; or, if it is dealing with a purchaser who derives title from an attorney, that the purchase was completed within 12 months of the power coming into opera-

1 Section 3(5)(a).
2 Section 3(5)(b).
3 TLR 2/4/99; [1999] 2 All ER 924; (1999) 3 WLR 394.

tion; or, if it was not, that the original purchaser has made the prescribed statutory declaration or that the power had not been revoked; or, if it has, that the purchaser's lack of knowledge is proved by some other method.

SECTION 10 CUSTODY OF DOCUMENTS

1.90 On a claim, loan or surrender the life office may retain any documents of title which affect only the policy. It does not seem that the life office is entitled to insist on the practice, for the claimant might need the documents for other purposes, for example to defend a hostile claim against him. Objection is, however, seldom raised.

Where a document (1) affects property in addition to a policy, or (2) declares trusts, it should not be retained by the life office but, in the case of (2) especially it often is although in most cases the life office would take a copy, note it on its records and return the original. The life office normally retains a right to production of the original title documents in the event of a claim. Such documents include trusts, deeds appointing trustees, deeds of assignment, etc.

It is convenient in practice for a life office, during the currency of a policy, to accept custody of documents of title relating to transactions such as assignments or mortgages. The documents will in any event usually be required before payment under the policy is made, and if any transfer of title can be proved to the satisfaction of the life office, a step towards the ultimate full proof of title is taken to the advantage of all concerned. No life office can, however, be compelled to adopt the practice.

CHAPTER 2

Insurance law issues

SUMMARY

SECTION 1 INSURABLE INTEREST

A Nature of insurable interest

1 General

2.1 A contract of insurance is a contract for the payment of a sum of money, or for some corresponding benefit, to become due on the happening of an uncertain event of a character adverse to the interest of the person effecting the insurance (see **1.1**). Where a person makes a bet he hopes to make a profit, but where he makes an insurance, he seeks to cover a possible loss. This distinction is important in considering the law relating to insurable interest.

Under the common law of England, though not of Scotland, the courts would enforce a wager on the duration of a human life; and so insurance companies did not refuse to issue policies to persons who had no interest in the lives to be insured.

2 The Life Assurance Act 1774

2.2 It was found, however, that insurances on lives or other events, in which the assured had no interest, involved undesirable gambling, and by the Life Assurance Act 1774, commonly called the Gambling Act, which is still in force (see Appendix 2), it was provided:

(1) That no life insurance should be made unless the person effecting the assurance had an interest in the life assured, and that any life insurance made

without such interest 'shall be null and void to all intents and purpose whatsoever'. Although not referred to as such in the Act itself, this has become known as the requirement for 'insurable interest'.

(2) That there should be inserted in the policy the name of the person or persons interested in it.

(3) That no greater sum should be recovered than the amount or value of the interest of the assured.

The 1774 Act, despite its title, does not apply only to life assurance contracts, but to all insurances other than those 'bona fide made ... on ships, goods or merchandises'. However, by construction of the 1774 Act all forms of indemnity insurance fall outside its scope[1] so the Act is effectively limited to insurances which pay a specified sum on the happening of the insured event. The 1774 Act does apply to accidental death policies and the case of *Feasey v Sun Life Assurance Company of Canada and another*[2] confirms this.

3 Life assurance is not essentially a contract of indemnity

2.3 It is a well-known principle of marine, fire and other risks, that any claim must be by way of indemnity only (ie recovery is limited to the loss suffered).

In the case of life policies on the lives of third parties, it would be quite possible to transact life insurance by way of indemnity and, indeed, when the Life Assurance Act 1774 was passed life assurance was thought to be a contract of indemnity, like most other forms of insurance. It was not until 1854 that the courts decided that apart from by express agreement, life assurance was not a contract of indemnity; and that if there is a recognised insurable interest at the time of the contract, the policy remains valid although the insurable interest has ceased before the time of claim.

Dalby v India and London Life Assurance Co[3]

The Anchor Life Office, having issued policies to the Rev John Wright on the life of the Duke of Cambridge for £3,000, reassured £1,000 with the India and London Life Office. The principal policies were surrendered, but Anchor continued the reassurance. The reassuring office resisted a claim, made by Dalby as trustee for the Anchor Life, on the ground of lack of insurable interest. It was held that the Life Assurance Act 1774 required an interest only at the date of the contract and that the policy was valid.

The requirement for the interest only having to exist at the time of effecting the policy is also evident from the wording of section 1 itself which states that the

1 *Mark Rowlands Ltd v Berni Inns Ltd* [1985] QB 211.
2 [2003] EWCA Civ 885.
3 (1854) 15 CB 365.

policy 'shall be made' by a person having an insurable interest, (ie there is no ongoing requirement for such an interest to subsist).

The Life Assurance Act 1774 did not define insurable interest, and its nature and extent must be ascertained principally from case law. It is worth considering the *Feasey Case* which involved a reinsurance by a P&I Club Steamship Mutual (Steamship) of liabilities it was exposed to in relation to death or specified illness of employees of a member of the P&I Club. Steamship was liable under its rules for this type of damage but the policy was issued for a fixed sum rather than the amount it would have to pay out under its rules. Steamship had previously reinsured this liability under a liability policy but had chosen, for purely administrative reasons, to reinsure it in the way described. As the policy was for a fixed sum, the 1774 Act applied and Sun Life of Canada contended that the reinsurance was not supported by insurable interest. It was also claimed in the alternative that Steamship was seeking to claim more than the value of any insurable interests it had, and that it was not entitled to do so by virtue of section 3 of the 1774 Act. The Court of Appeal emphasised that the courts would 'always lean in favour of an insurable interest, if possible'[1]. In this case Steamship would suffer a loss in the event that injury, which was covered by its membership rules, was sustained by a relevant employee. That was a legal obligation and the question was whether it was capable of pecuniary evaluation. The court quoted from McGillvray on Insurance Law (2003)[2] which defined a pecuniary interest as one capable of valuation by a court. The court stated that it was very difficult to define insurable interest in words which will apply in all situations. Lord Justice Waller, delivering the leading judgment in the Court of Appeal, set out four groups of situations where this could be the case. In the second of these groups, Group 2, fall cases where the court has defined the subject matter as the life of a particular person where a pecuniary loss flows from the death of that person. He stated that post *Dalby*, a fixed sum was sufficient to create an insurable interest (rather than the amount of the actual loss) provided that it did not exceed the maximum which might have flowed from the legal obligation at the outset of the policy. The court effectively held that Steamship had such an insurable interest.

As regards section 3 of the 1774 Act, the court stated[3]:

> 'Once appreciated that value must be assessed at the time the policy is entered into, and once appreciated that the assured is entitled to place such value on his interests as reflects the worse-case scenario, I do not think that Sun Life have even begun to demonstrate that Steamship are seeking to recover an amount in excess of the value of the interest as at the date of the policy'.

The court also made the point that just because the loss could have been covered by a liability policy did not mean it could not be covered by an accidental injury/life policy.

1 See *Stock v Inglis* [1884] 12 QBD 564.
2 At paragraph 65.
3 At paragraph 107.

4 *Nature of insurable interest*

2.4 Most life assurances are made by persons on their own lives[1] or on the life of their spouse (or civil partner). In such instances an insurable interest is presumed and section 3 of the 1774 Act will not apply[2]. Apart from these presumed interests the insurable interest must be a pecuniary interest[3], capable of valuation in monetary terms, which will result from the death. It must also be founded on an obligation or liability[4], or the loss or diminution of any right of property which would be recognised at law or in equity. A moral obligation or a mere expectation, however probable, is not sufficient.

In the absence of specific enquiry by the life office, it is not necessary to disclose the nature of the insurable interest, unless (exceptionally) it is a material fact. Some companies as a matter of practice require to know the nature of the interest; others content themselves with a declaration in the proposal that the person effecting the insurance has an insurable interest, and an increasing amount do not require even that.

5 *Amount of interest*

2.5 Section 3 of the Life Assurance Act 1774 provides that no greater sum shall be recovered from the insurer or insurers than the amount or value of the interest of the assured. The sum assured at the outset must be supported by an insurable interest of equivalent amount. Where the assured has effected more than one policy on the life, the total sum he can recover under all the policies will not be greater than the value of his interest at the time the policies were effected[5]. To this extent a life policy may include an element of indemnity.

A person has an unlimited insurable interest in his own life. A man has an unlimited interest in the life of his wife, and a woman in the life of her husband and similarly for civil partnerships[6]. In other cases, as has been seen in the *Feasey* case above, the courts have not been inclined to limit the amount which may be recovered to the equivalent of an indemnity. Partly this is because the precise amount in many cases is virtually impossible in practice to ascertain. The approach which appears to have been adopted, is that provided the cover requested is not grossly out of proportion to the actual value of the interest, then cover will be permissible. Where, for example, a policy is effected by a creditor (and he pays the premiums) on the life of a debtor, the creditor may claim under the policy, and in addition obtain payment of the debt from the executors of the debtor. The rationale for this is that there has been a risk that his debt would not be paid.

1 *Gould v Curtis* [1913] 3 KB 84 and *Wainwright v Bland* (1835) 1 Mood & R 481.
2 *Griffiths v Fleming* [1909] 1 KB 805, *Reed v Royal Exchange* (1795) Peake Ad Cas and the Married Women's Property Act 1882, s 11.
3 *Halford v Kymer* (1830) 10 B & C 724.
4 *Tidswell v Ankerstein* (1792) Peake NPC 151.
5 *Hebdon v West* (1863) 3 B & S 579.
6 Section 253 of the Civil Partnership Act 2004 extends the presumed categories of natural affection to civil partners.

6 Names of persons interested

2.6 Section 2 of the Life Assurance Act 1774 provides that there shall be inserted in the policy the name or names of the person or persons interested in the policy for whose use, or benefit, or on whose account, the insurance is effected. The court has been prepared to go behind the policy and, if satisfied that no interest exists, to declare the policy void where it is taken out on an own life basis for someone else.

> *Wainwright v Bland*[1]
>
> A policy had been effected by A on her own life at the suggestion of W with whom she lived. A paid the premiums with money provided by W. The jury decided that the policy was in reality effected by W, that he merely used A's name, providing the money himself and meaning to acquire the benefit of the policy for himself in some way and that W was someone who had no interest in A's life. It was held that W could not recover.

Payment of premiums towards a life policy by some person other than the assured is not conclusive to show that the policy was effected on behalf of that person, even though that person does in the event, obtain the benefit of the policy[2].

If the proposal is incorporated in the policy by reference, it is probably sufficient if the name of the person interested appears in the proposal. Also the words of section 2 have not, in practice, been construed too widely. Thus, they do not include all of those who are intended to benefit from the life policy by receiving the moneys payable. One of the main objects of life assurance is to enable a person, whenever death occurs, to have moneys to dispose of at death and a policy effected to this end is for the person's own benefit and account and therefore not outside the 1774 Act, even though he intends to bequeath the moneys from the policy to others. Section 2 has not been taken to mean, therefore, that, where a policy is payable to the life assured's executors or administrators, the names of the personal representatives, or the persons who will benefit under the will or intestacy, should be inserted in the policy.

Similarly, where a policy is effected by trustees, the names of the beneficiaries under the trust are not in practice specified (despite possible technical arguments to the contrary)[3]. A policy may also be effected in trust under the Married Women's Property Act 1882, although at the date of the policy the beneficiaries may not all be ascertained or even in existence.

During the 1960s concern arose that group life policies were illegal and voidable because they did not comply with section 2, in that the beneficiaries' names did not appear in them. Although this view was challenged by some, the matter was put beyond doubt by a change in the law in 1973. Section 50 of the Insurance Companies Amendment Act 1973 (which was not repealed by the Insurance

1 (1835) 1 Mood & R 481.
2 *Shilling v Accidental Death Insurance Co* (1857) 2 H & N 42.
3 *Collett v Morrison* (1851) 9 Hare 162.

Companies Acts of 1974, 1981 or 1982) provided that section 2 of the Life Assurance Act 1774 shall not invalidate a policy for the benefit of unnamed persons falling within a specified class or description, if the class or description is stated in the policy with sufficient particularity to make it possible to establish the identity of all persons who at any given time are entitled to benefit under the policy. The section applies to policies effected either before or after the passing of the Act[1].

7 *Policy assigned immediately after issue*

2.7 Any person may insure his own life provided the policy is bona fide and, at the time, for his benefit. There is nothing to prevent him from assigning the policy to someone else, even though at the time when he effected the policy he had the intention of doing so[2].

Where, for example, a proposer wishes to provide for another person, he can effect a policy and assign it to the beneficiary or to trustees for the benefit of a beneficiary. Where the beneficiary is only to be the wife or child of the proposer, the use of the Married Women's Property Act 1882 (see Chapter 9) to create a trust is simpler. Where the beneficiary is outside the class of persons within the Act it is of course still possible for the policy to be made subject to a trust (see Chapter 9).

An assignment cannot be used to defeat the statute where the insurance is really made by the beneficiary, for example, where there was a binding obligation to assign any policy which is issued to a person with no insurable interest. The court would go behind the wording of the policy to ascertain the true principal in the transaction[3].

Furthermore, in the *M'Farlane v Royal London Friendly Society* case it was stated that '... if ab initio the policy effected in the name of A is really and substantially intended for the benefit of B and B only' then this was 'within the evil and mischief intended to be met by the statute'. See, however, Modern practice at **2.25**.

8 *Spes successionis*

2.8 A spes succession is the hope or expectation of succeeding to property. It may be a most likely event as in the case of one of the next of kin succeeding by intestacy to the estate of a mentally disordered person who has not made a will and is most unlikely ever to have the capacity to do so. A spes is not, however, an interest known to the law and is not a ground of insurable interest[4]. For this

1 *Siu Yin Kwan v Eastern Insurance Co Ltd* [1994] 1 All ER 213, where it was held that the fact that the principal's name had not been inserted in the contract did not make the policy unlawful by virtue of the Life Assurance Act 1774, s 2.

2 *M'Farlane v Royal London Friendly Society* (1886) 2 TLR 755.

3 *Shilling v Accidental Death Insurance Co* (1857) 2 H & N 42.

4 A spes confers no interest at all, either vested or contingent, but only an expectation of an interest: *Clowes v Hilliard* (1816) 4 Ch D 413 at 416.

reason a person who expects to be the residuary legatee under a will has no insurable interest to effect an insurance on the life of the testator to cover the probable amount of inheritance tax which will be payable out of his legacy. The recipient of a gift inter vivos (during lifetime) has, however, an interest known to the law and may protect himself by effecting a policy against any amount of inheritance tax payable on the death of the person who made the gift[1].

Similarly, a person with a contingent right would also have an insurable interest. For example, in *Law v London Indisputable Life Policy Co*[2] a son received a legacy contingent on attaining age 30. This interest was purchased by his father and it was held that the father thereby had an insurable interest in the life of his son. If the son had died before reaching 30, the value of the father's interest would have been nil.

B Particular cases of insurable interest

1 A man and his own life

2.9 Although a person has an unlimited insurable interest in his or her own life, for the purposes of establishing insurable interest, a life office might, however, refuse to issue a policy where either the cover or premium is out of proportion to the means of the proposer. Such a policy involves a consideration quite distinct from the ordinary mortality risk and has a bearing on what is known as 'moral hazard'. If, for example, an individual with little or no capital and low income were to propose for, say, £500,000 of life cover, being a high amount of cover in relation to his income, then the life office should satisfy itself of the need for, or the ability to pay for, a policy of that amount.

2 Husband and wife, civil partners

2.10 The interest of a husband in the life of his wife is presumed and it is not necessary to give any evidence as to the amount[3].

It was established as long ago as 1795 that a wife has a similar insurable interest in the life of her husband to any amount.

> *Reed v Royal Exchange Assurance Co*[4]
>
> A wife insured the life of her husband. It was held that she was entitled to the sum assured and that it was not necessary to show an interest: per Lord Kenyon CJ: 'It must be presumed that every wife has an interest in the life of her husband'.

Civil partners will now have the same unlimited interest in each other's lives[5].

1 See generally Inheritance Tax Act 1984, s 3A.
2 (1855) 1 K&J 223.
3 *Griffiths v Fleming* [1909] 1 KB 805.
4 (1795) Peake Add Cas 70.
5 Civil Partnership Act 2006

3 Parent and child

2.11 A child, merely as such, has no insurable interest in the life of his parent. In Scotland because a parent used to have the right to be supported by his child[1] the parent had an insurable interest in the life of the child. This obligation was abolished by section 1(3) of the Family Law (Scotland) Act 1985.

> *Howard v Refuge Friendly Society*[2]
>
> A son insured the life of his father in which he had no pecuniary interest. Premiums were paid by the son for some time but then he gave notice to the Society that he would not pay any more and claimed a return of the premiums already paid. It was held that the son had no insurable interest in his father's life, the policies were 'wagering policies' and the premiums could not be recovered.

Similarly, a parent has, by relationship alone, no insurable interest in the life of his child.

> *Halford v Kymer*[3]
>
> A father effected a life policy in his own name on the life of his son in order to provide against the death of his son before he reached 21. It was held that, as the father had no pecuniary interest in the life assured on the event insured against, he had no insurable interest and the policy was void under the Life Assurance Act 1774.

The parent will have no insurable interest either in respect of money paid for education and maintenance or otherwise.

A person who fosters a child does not, by statute, have an insurable interest in the life of the child[4]. Under section 37(2) of the Adoption Act 1976, a person who maintains a 'protected child', within the meaning of section 32 of that Act (as amended), is deemed, for the purposes of the Life Assurance Act 1774, to have no interest in the life of the child. Accordingly, an insurance taken out on the life of a protected child by a person who maintains that child is void unless an independent insurable interest exists.

4 Debtor and creditor

2.12 A creditor or a surety has an insurable interest in the life of the debtor[5] to the extent of the debt and accrued interest, but if the debt is statute-barred when the policy is effected it is not thought that insurable interest would exist at that time. The position is clearly different if the debt is not statute barred at the time of effecting the policy on the principle established in *Dalby v India and London Life Assurance Co*. However, future interest and other costs of servicing

1 *Carmichael v Carmichael's Executrix* (1919) SC (Ct of Sess) 636.
2 (1886) 54 LT 644.
3 (1830) 10 B & C 724.
4 Children Act 1989, s 66(5), Sch 8, para 11.
5 *Von Lindenau v Desborough* (1828) 3 C & P 353.

the debt could not be included in setting the sum assured as at the time of insurance these would be mere expectancies. If the debt is to be paid by two or more persons jointly, it will support a good insurable interest for a policy on the life of each of them for the whole amount. Co-sureties and joint debtors also have an insurable interest in each other's lives[1]. A debtor has, however, no insurable interest in the life of the creditor as he would suffer no loss on the death of the creditor even though the creditor may have made a voluntary promise that the debt shall not be enforced during his life. On the other hand a binding promise not to enforce a debt during the life of the creditor would therefore give the debtor a legal interest in the creditor's life[2].

5 *Employer and employee*

2.13 Strictly speaking an employer has an insurable interest in the life of his employee, but only to the extent of the value of services agreed to be rendered. An employee has an insurable interest in the life of his employer (if an individual), but only to the extent of his remuneration for the agreed period of service, if his contract is to serve the employer for a fixed term, or the agreed period of notice in other cases. However, in practice this may not accurately represent the employer's or employee's interest. In law, the additional amount of interest beyond the notice period is based on an expectancy and not a legal right and probably cannot therefore be technically supported[3]. Nevertheless, the concept of 'key man' insurance has evolved and this is considered at **2.14**.

> *Simcock v Scottish Imperial Co*[4]
>
> An employer insured the life of his employee by two policies for £250 each. A claim under one policy was paid, but under the other it was defended on the ground of lack of insurable interest. Held that the limit of insurable interest was the value of service for the period of notice and so the employer could only recover under the one policy.
>
> *Hebdon v West*[5]
>
> H became indebted to a bank of which P was the managing director. P agreed verbally with H that the bank would employ H for seven years at a salary of £600 per annum; and that the debt would not be enforced during P's lifetime. H insured P's life. Held, that H had an interest under the agreement to the extent of the salary for the remaining term of employment, although an oral agreement for service for seven years was not then enforceable by reason of the Statute of Frauds. Held further, however, that H had no interest in respect of P's promise not to enforce the debt due to the bank. The promise was without consideration and the mere expectation of the debt being allowed to remain outstanding during P's lifetime did not create an insurable interest.

1 *Branford v Saunders* (1877) 25 WLR 650.
2 *Hebdon v West* (1863) 3 B & S 579.
3 However, see the case of *Marcel Beller Ltd v Hayden* [1978] QB 694 at 697 where such an interest was accepted without questions.
4 (1902) 10 SLT 286.
5 (1863) 3 B & S 579.

6 Keyman insurance – company or other employer on life of director or manager

2.14 The case of *Simcock* possibly suggested that a company has an insurable interest in the lives of 'key-men' (now often called 'key-persons'), ie directors or principal executives, the loss of any of whose special services would involve the company in reduced profit and the cost of finding a suitable successor and that this extended beyond the strict confines of the contract of service[1]. In such cases, the extent of the insurable interest would be the anticipated loss of profit, not the amount of remuneration, as in the case of employer and employee discussed above. A company has no insurable interest in the life of a director merely by virtue of his office. However, it may well be that there are technical objections to key man insurance in that that there is not necessarily a loss of profit, etc, so the insurance is therefore based merely on an expectancy. In practice life offices are nevertheless generally prepared to issue key man insurance subject to receiving satisfactory evidence of projected loss of profits and any costs and expenses which would be incurred as a result of the death.

7 Pension scheme trustees and employee

2.15 Where an employee has an enforceable right to death benefits provided by the employer under a pension scheme, the required funds may be provided by a policy of life assurance effected in the name of the trustees. Insurable interest arises from the legal obligation to make the payment under the pension scheme.

8 Partners and co-directors

2.16 The relationship of partner or director does not of itself give rise, inter se, to an insurable interest. However, partners would have an insurable interest in the life of a co-partner if the partnership deed provided that, on his death, they shall purchase from his personal representatives his share of the goodwill or other partnership assets. In many such cases it is doubtful whether the survivors would suffer a pecuniary loss merely on account of that obligation, except to the extent of the expense incurred in raising the sum required. However, most life offices are in practice prepared to issue policies to the full amount of any such partnership obligation.

Similar principles apply to co-directors of a private limited company where a 'buy and sell' agreement (see Chapter 16) is included in the Articles of Association or has been entered into subsequently by the directors, requiring the shares of a deceased or retiring director to be purchased, by the remaining directors. If appropriately worded, such agreement or arrangement creates the pecuniary liability, as between the directors, upon which the insurable interest would be based. As an alternative to a binding 'buy and sell' agreement the parties may enter into a 'cross option' (or 'double option') agreement. It should be noted that such an option arrangement would not create a legal obligation upon which an

1 See also Chapter 16 for more detail on this subject.

insurable interest must be based (albeit that this may be the most efficient type of arrangement for inheritance tax purposes and is therefore often used in practice).

9 Trustees

2.17 Trustees of a settlement do not as such have an insurable interest in the life of any beneficiary, but in many cases inheritance tax will be payable on the death of a beneficiary who had an interest in possession in the settlement. In that case the trustees, who are accountable for the tax, have an insurable interest in the life of the beneficiary up to the probable amount of the tax, and may effect a life policy to cover this liability. Trustees of a voluntary settlement may have an insurable interest in the life of the settlor during the seven years following the date of the settlement up to the amount of any inheritance tax for which they will be accountable on his death.

Another proposition which has been advanced is that the trustees may be viewed as agents of the beneficiaries. Trustees do not benefit personally (as trustees) from the insurance (although they may benefit as beneficiaries). However, the question remains that if there are a number of beneficiaries, some beneficiaries will not necessarily have an insurable interest in the life of the beneficiary whose life is being insured. Conversely the proposition is much stronger in the case of an absolute trust for a single beneficiary.

Whatever the strict legal position, many life offices are prepared to issue policies to trustees, even where an insurable interest may not strictly exist, often on the basis of a declaration of insurable interest. This is especially the case for investment orientated policies with nominal life cover.

10 Mortgagees

2.18 A policy to provide security for a mortgage may be effected by the mortgagor and assigned to the mortgagee. Here no question of insurable interest arises. But the mortgagee, like any other creditor, has an interest in the life of the mortgagor and can effect a policy on his life and pay the premiums himself. If he does so he is entitled both to the policy and the mortgage debt. Where, however, the premiums are paid by the borrower or charged to him, the lender must account to the borrower for any money received under the policy.

11 Engaged couples/cohabitees

2.19 Unlike the position with spouses and civil partnerships, no insurable interest exists purely as a result of these relationships, although the position was different for engaged couples when breach of promise to marry was actionable. This was abolished by the Law Reform (Miscellaneous Provisions) Act 1970. However, frequently the persons in such a relationship will be jointly liable to, for example, a bank or building society for borrowings. In such cases the death of one may well result in a liability falling on the survivor as a result of which an insurable interest can arise.

In practice, many life offices are nevertheless prepared to issue policies even where no such joint liability exists. In respect of cohabitees the Scottish Law Commission have recommended that cohabiting couples have an interest in each other's lives[1].

12 Divorcees

2.20 Although the marriage no longer exists and so the unlimited insurable interest has thereby ceased, it is very likely that there will be other pecuniary rights and liabilities which arise as a result of financial claims arising out of the divorce or associated court orders. The most common example is the obligation on a husband to pay maintenance. The ex-wife may wish to protect her position by insuring her ex-husband's life. Such an interest will, of course, be limited by, for example, the amount of the maintenance payments and life expectancies.

C Policies unsupported by a good insurable interest

1 Effect of policy

2.21 Section 1 of the Life Assurance Act 1774 provides that a policy effected without insurable interest shall from the outset be 'null and void to all intents and purposes whatsoever'. Section 2 provides that failure to insert the names of interested parties in the policy renders it illegal.

The Act does not impose any punishment and the making of such an insurance is not a statutory crime. The fact that the insurance company is not obliged to pay out was possibly thought to be sufficient deterrent.

Lack of insurable interest is a defence which the life office may plead in resisting a claim. If it does not plead the lack of insurable interest but relies on some other defence, it is the duty of the court to take cognisance of the illegality of the policy and refuse to enforce the contract[2]. A practice note issued in connection with *Mercantile Credit Co Ltd v Hamblin*[3], reads as follows:

> 'Where it occurs to counsel, however belatedly, that an agreement may be void for illegality, it is his duty, however embarrassing, to invite the court's attention to the matter and prevent the court from enforcing an illegal transaction.'

The court, however, will always lean in favour of an insurable interest, for after the company has received the premium the objection is usually technical and has no real merit between the company and the assured[4].

Where the life office waives the defence of lack of insurable interest and pays the policy moneys, the rights of property in those moneys will be determined

1 Law Commission (No 1350, Report on Family Law, para 16.41).
2 *Gedge v Royal Exchange Insurance Corp* [1900] 2 QB 214.
3 [1964] 1 All ER 680n.
4 *Stock v Inglis* (1882) 12 QBD 564, per Brett MR.

irrespective of the statute. In the Australian case of *Carter Bros v Renouf*[1] it was held that section 2 of the Life Assurance Act 1774 does no more than make the policy void between the insurance company and the insured, and that, if the company does not choose to rely on the defence that the contract does not comply with section 2, and pays under the policy, the question 'who is entitled to the money?' must be decided as if the statute did not exist. The Australian court followed the English case of *Worthington v Curtis*[2] in which a father effected (for his own benefit under a separate agreement) a policy on the life of, and in the name of, his son, in whose life he had no insurable interest. It was thus illegal, under section 1 of the Act, and also under section 2 because the father's name did not appear on the policy. The son died intestate and the father took out letters of administration. The insurers paid the sum to him as the son's personal representative. The son's creditors claimed that the sum paid was part of the son's estate. It was held by the Court of Appeal that the defence of want of insurable interest was available only to the insurance company and since they had waived it and had paid the policy moneys to the father he was entitled to apply the money to his own use. A similar view was taken by the Court of Appeal in another case[3] where a father effected in his own name without insurable interest a policy on the life of his son and the insurance company paid the sum assured to the father's assignees, in effect as an ex gratia payment. A similar rule apparently applies in Scotland[4]. However, this view is not universally accepted. *Worthington v Curtis* has been criticised[5]. The reason for such criticism is mainly based on the fact that this would appear not to be recognising the illegality of the contract. A more modern example of the effect of lack of insurable interest is the case of *Fuji Finance v Aetna* which is examined in more detail at **1.69**. Essentially, the policy in issue in that case, a life assurance bond, offered no greater benefits on death than on surrender. It was decided that this did not prevent the policy from being a contract of insurance within section 1 of the Life Assurance Act 1774. As a result, as Fuji Finance had no insurable interest in the life assured, the policy was technically 'null and void' under that Act which prevented Fuji Finance from pursuing a breach of contract claim resulting from changes made to the policy. In that case the life company had complied with the policy terms up to the point at which the changes were made.

2 *Admission of insurable interest*

2.22 A life office is sometimes requested to endorse a policy with an admission that it is satisfied that a good insurable interest has been shown. The parties cannot contract out of the statute and it does not appear that such an endorsement would bind the life office[6].

1 (1962) 36 ALJR 67.
2 (1875) 1 Ch D 419.
3 *A-G v Murray* [1904] 1 KB 165.
4 *Hadden v Bryden* (1899) 1 F (Ct of Sess) 710; 36 SLR 524.
5 *Fitzsimmons v City of Glasgow FS* [1933] IAC Rep 24 and *McMeaken v Prudential Assurance Co* [1936] IAC Rep 21.
6 *Anctil v Manufacturers' Life Insurance Co* [1899] AC 604.

3 Deferred assurances

2.23 If a parent has effected a deferred assurance on the life of a child, and does not vest the policy in the child as soon as the life risk commences, it would seem that the policy is technically unenforceable for lack of insurable interest.

4 Consequences of lack of insurable interest

2.24 As stated above, the 1774 Act does not prescribe any penalties for its infringement. Money paid under an illegal contract cannot generally be recovered. Therefore, technically it would appear that neither the sum assured nor the premiums paid will be recoverable. However, this may not be the position where the parties are not equally at fault in relation to the illegality (in 'pari delicto'). In such circumstances, if the person seeking to recover under an illegal contract was unaware of the illegality, he is entitled to recover the money provided he has not got what he bargained for.

> *Harse v Pearl Life Assurance Co*[1]
>
> H effected policies which were void for lack of insurable interest. He relied on the representation of the agent (of the company) that the policies were valid. Held, that as the agent had acted innocently, the parties were equally to blame and that the proposer could not recover the premiums.

This was an (innocent) misrepresentation of the law by the agent. It has been postulated that the decision would have been different had it been a misrepresentation of fact. Now that the long held principle that monies paid under a mistake of law cannot be recovered has been eroded by the case of *Kleinwort Benson Ltd v Lincoln City Council*[2], it may be that *Harse* would be decided differently today.

Where the life office has acted in such a way that its conduct can be said to have 'introduced the element of fraud, duress, oppression, or difference in the position of the parties which created a fiduciary relationship so as to make it inequitable for [it] to insist on the bargain' (Collins MR in *Harse v Pearl Life Assurance Co* at 563), the assured will not be in pari delicto and recovery of premiums will be possible (eg where the assured was induced to enter into the contract by fraudulent misrepresentation as to the legality of the policy made by the company's agent).

> *Hughes v Liverpool Victoria Legal Friendly Society*[3]
>
> T effected five policies on the lives of others, but subsequently allowed them to lapse and burnt them. Later, an agent of the company persuaded H to pay overdue premiums and keep up the policies, giving her duplicate policies for the purpose, and fraudulently representing that they would be valid. She had no insurable interest. Held, that the premiums could be recovered.

1 [1904] 1 KB 558.

2 TLR 30/10/98; ILR 4/11/98; (1998) 4 All ER 513; (1998) 3 WLR 1095; (1998) Lloyd's Rep Bank 387; (1999) LGR 1.

3 [1916] 2 KB 482.

British Workman's and General Assurance Co Ltd v Cunliffe[1]

The respondent insured the life of his brother-in-law in which he had no insurable interest. The policy was effected through the insurer's agent who fraudulently represented to the respondent that the policy would be valid. The respondent subsequently discovered that the contract was invalid and demanded the return of the premiums. As the representation was made by someone knowledgeable in insurance matters to a person ignorant of the true position, the premiums could be recovered.

D Modern practice

2.25 This book is concerned with the law of life assurance and its practical application and not speculation about what the law ought to be. But a section on insurable interest would, in the authors' opinion, be incomplete if there were not some reference to the way in which the subject is viewed and approached in practice by life offices today.

The Life Assurance Act 1774 was introduced to curb the widespread eighteenth century practice of ' mischievous' gambling which had developed by way of the indiscriminate effecting of insurance policies on the lives of public figures, or the chances of public events. It is not clear whether the Act was passed to protect life insurers, their shareholders, policyholders or the general public from these abuses. But it has been suggested that whilst a statute such as this might have been essential in the commercial and social conditions prevailing in the eighteenth century, it is inappropriate more than two hundred years on, as it must be extremely unlikely that, if the Act were repealed, life offices would be willing to issue 'gaming' contracts now.

Moreover, the argument runs, not only is the 1774 Act unnecessary today, it is indeed a constraint on the business which life offices could write, as many insurers find the provisions of the statute and the case law which has developed around it most unsatisfactory as a framework for the transaction of life assurance in modern conditions and the demands made for life assurance cover in contemporary society. The law of insurable interest is therefore often viewed as a technical prohibition preventing the issue of policies in circumstances in which life offices would be willing, subject to safeguards, to grant policies which in no sense could be regarded as 'gaming'. At the time of writing the Law Commission has made recommendations which it is hoped might be adopted (see **2.47**).

In terms of the way insurable interest is approached in practice, although insurers may not contract out of the 1774 Act they are sometimes prepared to issue policies where the assured has no insurable interest recognised by the law in the life to be assured, provided that the office is satisfied that there is a good reason for the proposed life cover and all parties signify their awareness of the nature of the transaction and the sum to be assured. Alternatively, and presumably in order to avoid any claim of having induced third parties into an illegal contract (which might enable them to seek a return of premi-

1 (1902) 18 TLR 502 CA; see also *Tofts v Pearl Life Ass Co* [1915] 1 KB 189.

ums), life offices rely upon an undertaking or statement in the proposal form that such interest exists.

Such policies are, however, strictly, 'null and void' or more accurately in practice, voidable. It would hardly be sound business practice in these cases for the life office to resist a claim on the grounds of lack of insurable interest (although *Fuji v Aetna* is a partial exception), but the fact that the practice of issuing such policies has developed is perhaps some comment on a statute that (at least in its current form) has outlived its usefulness.

There are other considerations for a life office in conducting business where an insurable interest does not exist. If it is openly permitting such business then it is potentially acting in breach of INSPRU 1.5.13 (restriction of business to insurance and activities directly arising). In addition, if such business is not insurance business then it raises a question concerning the taxation status of such business.

These issues were discussed in connection with lack of insurable interest in *Fuji v Aetna.* See **1.69** et seq.

SECTION 2 UTMOST GOOD FAITH AND NON-DISCLOSURE

A Uberrima fides

2.26 The general rule in contract law is that the parties to a contract need not furnish each other with information which if known might possibly influence their judgment. The rule does not justify misrepresentation but mere silence is not misrepresentation[1]. Failure to disclose a material fact which might influence the mind of the other party does not give a right to avoid the contract[2]. Subject to the growing body of consumer protection law, the maxim 'caveat emptor' applies to contracts generally. The buyer must make such enquiries as he may think prudent.

However, a number of important exceptions to this general rule have been established for various classes of contract in order to redress what has been regarded by the courts and Parliament as an imbalance in the relative bargaining positions of the parties. One such exception applies to all contracts of insurance, for here the party seeking to cover the risk has information as to the nature of the risk with which the insurer is not and cannot be acquainted, unless it is disclosed. The law will not allow the proposer, by non-disclosure of material information, to lead the insurer to make a bargain which the insurer would not entertain in the light of fuller knowledge of the risk. Each contracting party must, therefore, observe the utmost good faith. There must on both sides be what is known as uberrima fides[3].

1 *Hands v Simpson, Fawcett & Co Ltd* (1928) 44 TLR 295.

2 *Keates v Cadogan* (1851) 10 CB 591; *Fletcher v Krell* (1872) 42 LJQB 55.

3 *Carter v Boehm* (1766) 3 Burr 1905. See also *London Assurance v Mansel* (1879) 11 Ch D 363, which made it clear that the principle applied to all classes of insurance.

In *Carter v Boehm*, Lord Mansfield said:

> 'Insurance is a contract of speculation. The special facts, upon which the contingent chance is to be computed, lie most commonly in the knowledge of the assured only; the underwriter trusts to his representation, and proceeds upon confidence that he does not keep back any circumstances in his knowledge, to mislead the underwriter into a belief that the circumstance does not exist. The keeping back such circumstance is a fraud, and therefore the policy is void. Although the suppression should happen through mistake, without any fraudulent intention, yet still the underwriter is deceived and the policy is void; because the risque run is really different from the risque understood and intended to be run at the time of the agreement… . Good faith forbids either party, by concealing what he privately knows, to draw the other into a bargain from his ignorance of the fact, and his believing the contrary.'

Over a hundred years later the Court of Appeal reiterated[1] the substance of this justification of the doctrine and emphasised that it would be inequitable for the insured to demand a competitive premium while he has the 'means of knowledge as to the risk, and the insurer has not the means or the same means' (see also **8.9** re codification of this requirement). However, it should also be borne in mind that changes to the law in this area are currently proposed (see **2.48**). The duty of good faith requires that representations made by the insurer as well as by the proposer as to all matters relevant to the contract shall be accurate.

B The duty to disclose and materiality

2.27 It is the duty of the proposer voluntarily to disclose without misrepresentation all material facts known to him or which he ought to have known if he had made reasonable enquiries. As the proposer will often not appreciate what is a material fact this is a very onerous obligation.

In *Rozanes v Bowen*[2] it was said:

> 'It has been for centuries in England the law in connection with insurance of all sorts, marine, fire, life … that, as the underwriter knows nothing and the man who comes to him to insure knows everything, it is the duty of the assured … to make a full disclosure to the underwriters *without being asked* for all the material circumstances.' (Emphasis added)

2.28 All facts and circumstances which are material to the risk must be disclosed by the proposer to the insurer. The proposer cannot withhold material information merely because no specific question on the point is asked in the proposal form or in the medical examination. But he may be justified in inferring from the fact that the question is not asked that the information withheld was not regarded by the office as material[3]. Where, for example, the proposer is required

1 *Seaton v Burnand* [1899] 1 QB 782.
2 (1928) 32 Ll L Rep 98.
3 *Schoolman v Hall* [1951] 1 Lloyd's Rep 139, *Roberts v Plaisted* [1989] 2 Lloyd's Rep 341.

to state whether his parents or grandparents have suffered from certain illnesses, the proposer will know that the life office regards this information as material, but he may well be justified in assuming that to the life office it is immaterial whether or not brothers or sisters have suffered from those illnesses. But generally, it is no excuse for non-disclosure of a material fact, for the proposer to say that he omitted to disclose it through carelessness or mistake, or that he did not regard it as material[1].

In some cases the proposer will, for various reasons, omit to answer a question. It cannot be said that the insurer did not regard this information as material but if the insurer does not then reject the proposal the insurer is likely to be viewed as having waived such information.

Provisions contained in the proposal form are clearly also relevant here. The questions in the proposal form may either expand or restrict the proposer's duty of disclosure. It is common for proposal forms to contain (in what is often termed the 'Declaration') an indication as to whether the proposer is being asked to disclose information, even if not specifically covered by the actual questions contained in the proposal form. *Hair v The Prudential Assurance Co Ltd*[2] is an example of a case where such a declaration was deemed not to require the disclosure of material information beyond that specifically asked for. However, in many cases proposal forms will end with a general question requesting any other material information.

In order for a policy to be repudiated on the ground of non-disclosure, an inaccurate statement must be one of fact and not of opinion. Statements of opinion which in the event turn out not to be well-founded are not actionable if the opinion was given in good faith[3]. As a general rule, however, unless otherwise stated, an answer to a question in a proposal form will be construed as relating to the facts themselves and not to the proposer's knowledge or opinion of them[4].

The material facts which the proposer is required to disclose are all those circumstances which would influence a prudent insurer[5] in determining whether it will take the risk, at what premium and on what conditions. Other statements of the test of materiality refer to a 'reasonable insurer' but there is probably little significance in this difference[6]. The test is therefore an objective one, but note the requirement for the non-disclosure to have induced the contract (see **2.29** and **2.33**).

2.29 The question as to what is and what is not a material fact was considered in the case of *Pan Atlantic Insurance Co Ltd v Pine Top Insurance Co Ltd*[7]; see also *St Paul Fire and Marine Ins Co v McConnell Dowell*[8], which although con-

1 *Bates v Hewitt* (1867) LR 2 QB 595.
2 [1983] Lloyd's Rep 667.
3 *Anderson v Pacific Fire and Marine Insurance Co* (1872) LR7 CP 65.
4 *Zurich General Accident and Liability Insurance Co v Leven* 1940 SC 406.
5 *Lambert v Co-operative Insurance Society Ltd* [1975] 2 Lloyd's Rep 485.
6 *Mutual Life Insurance of New York v Ontario Metal Products Co* [1925] AC 344.
7 [1995] 1 AC 501 HL.
8 [1995] 2 Lloyd's Rep 116.

cerned with marine insurance was considered to be equally applicable to non-marine cases. Essentially, it was decided that it was sufficient for a fact to be material if it had an influence on the mind of the insurer. It did not have to be a decisive influence. This has been criticised by some commentators essentially on the basis that this represented a very low level of influence on the 'hypothetical prudent insurer'. However, as the House of Lords decided that the non-disclosure must also have induced the particular insurer to accept the risk the overall position in practice, particularly for consumer contracts which do not normally contain warranties (see **2.36**), is probably not that different to there being a requirement that there must be a decisive influence on a hypothetical prudent insurer.

It is irrelevant that the proposer does not consider that a particular fact or set of facts is material; if it is material it must be disclosed despite his opinion.

Godfrey v Brittanic Assurance Co Ltd[1]

Clause 5 of the proposal form read 'Have you suffered from any illness or accident or received medical advice or treatment with or without an operation? If so give particulars and state name of medical attendant and the date, nature and duration of the illness for which he was consulted'. The insured disclosed that he had had an accident to his hand but not that he had been sent by his own doctor to a hospital for a suspected kidney ailment nor that he had suffered from pharyngitis. He died of nephritis. Held, that he knew he had been sent to hospital for a check on his kidneys and that his health had been generally bad for two years. It was conceded that he had honestly thought these details not material. Nevertheless he was under a duty to disclose to the company every material circumstance known to him, not only of which he had actual knowledge but of which he ought to have known. Every circumstance was material which would influence the judgment of a prudent underwriter; the opinion of the insured whether a fact was material was irrelevant. The company was entitled to repudiate the contract.

British Equitable Insurance Co v Great Western Railway[2]

The proposer consulted a specialist who informed him that he had a dangerous kidney condition. This was not disclosed in a life assurance proposal on the basis that his general practitioner had told him that the specialist was wrong. The Court of Appeal held that he should have disclosed the specialist's prognosis which was ultimately shown to be correct.

It is for the court to rule as a matter of law whether a particular fact is capable of being material and to give directions as to the test to be applied, but the decision ultimately is one of fact, depending on the circumstances.

2.30 The Association of British Insurers (ABI) Statement of Long-Term Insurance Practice (see **2.44**) provided, for instance, that if the proposal form calls for the disclosure of material facts, a statement should be included in the

1 [1963] 2 Lloyd's Rep 515.
2 (1869) 20 LT 422.

declaration, or prominently displayed elsewhere on the form or in the document of which it forms part:

> '(a) drawing attention to the consequences of failure to disclose all material facts and explaining that these are facts that an insurer would regard as likely to influence the assessment and acceptance of a proposal; and
>
> (b) warning that if the signatory is in doubt about whether certain facts are material, these facts should be disclosed.'

The Statement also provided that those matters which insurers have commonly found to be material should be the subject of clear questions in proposal forms, and that insurers should avoid asking questions which would require knowledge beyond that which the signatory could reasonably be expected to possess.

2.31 The law also provides that a proposer cannot disclose what he does not know, and he cannot be expected to disclose matters, immaterial in themselves, which if further examined might lead to information which is material. As Fletcher Moulton LJ stated in *Joel v Law Union and Crown Insurance Co*[1]:

> 'The duty is a duty to disclose and you cannot disclose what you do not know. The obligation to disclose, therefore, necessarily depends upon the knowledge you possess.'

It is interesting in this context to consider the effects, if any, of the Data Protection Acts of 1984 and 1998 and of the Access to Medical Reports Act 1988, under which the proposer now has more extensive rights to information about his health than was hitherto the case. However, it is not clear that as a result he will be deemed to know the information in question. Also, such information (eg medical details) may still not be revealed to the proposer on the basis that its revelation could prove harmful to him. Although concerned with household contents insurance the case of *Economides v Commercial Union Assurance Co plc*[2] indicates that the proposer is under no duty to make further detailed enquiries.

The standard to be displayed by the proposer in considering whether a fact should be disclosed is the objective one of the reasonable man. So, for example, in *Fowkes v Manchester & London Life Assurance and Loan Association*[3] the fact that the proposer had gout (which might have been ascertainable to an experienced medical practitioner) could not be inferred to a reasonable man. This can be contrasted with the case of *Godfrey* above where the proposer should have appreciated that he was possessed of knowledge which he should have disclosed.

It is also clear from *Carter v Boehm,* that the proposer need not mention what the insurer already knows or what he ought to know or what he waives being informed about. For example, in *Ayrey v British Legal & United Provident Assurance Co Ltd*[4], the proposal form contained an agreement that if information which should have been disclosed was withheld then the contract would be void.

1 [1908] 2 KB 863.
2 [1997] 3 WLR 1066.
3 (1862) 3 F & F 440.
4 [1918] 1 KB 136.

The proposer did not disclose in the proposal form that he was in the Royal Navy Reserve, although he had told the district manager of the insurer. Premiums were paid to and accepted by the district manager. It was held that the district manager's knowledge was equivalent to knowledge by the insurer and acceptance of premiums amounted to a waiver of the breach of agreement in the proposal form. The contract was therefore valid. This case should be contrasted with *Malhi* at **2.34**.

In practice, if a proposer is in any doubt about disclosing information the best course of action would be to do so. Indeed, as stated at **2.30**, insurers were required to include this instruction in proposal forms under the Statement of Long-Term Insurance Practice.

2.32 The duty to disclose extends beyond the time of proposal and 'acceptance' of the proposal by the company until the contract is binding on both parties[1]. It is common in life assurance to include a statement in the proposal which provides that the life office shall not become bound until receipt of the first premium, and to include a continuing condition that the information supplied is still accurate at the time the policy is issued. It is therefore clear that the period during which disclosure is required extends up until a legally binding contract comes into existence so that any new or changed material facts affecting the terms upon which the policy is issued must be communicated to the office right up to the moment of receipt of the premium. However, it is crucial to examine the proposal and policy wordings in each case to see if there is a contract in place before the first premium is paid.

> *Looker v Law Union and Rock Insurance Co*[2]
>
> L made a proposal for a policy on his life and received a 'letter of acceptance' stating that the policy would be issued on the payment of the first premium, if the health of the life assured remained meanwhile unaffected, and reserving the right to alter or withdraw the acceptance. Before payment of the premium he became ill. A friend posted L's cheque for the premium but L died from the illness. Held, that the representatives of L could not recover as there was a duty to inform the insurers of any material change in the nature of the risk.

It is possible for a policy to lapse and for the assured to request that it is reinstated. In this case the duty of full disclosure revives. In practice the life office may ask the proposer to complete either a further full proposal form or an abridged version.

C Inducement and avoidance

2.33 To avoid a contract for non-disclosure of a material fact, the life office has to show that it has been *induced* by the non-disclosure to enter into the policy

1 *Banque Financière de la Cité SA v Westgate Insurance Co Ltd* [1990] 2 All ER 947, where is was held that an insurer is under a pre-contractual duty of disclosure to his insured but only in respect of matters which are material to the risk or to the recoverability of the claim. Breach of such a duty could not sound in damages, whether in contract or tort, but merely lead to the return of premiums.

2 [1928] 1 KB 554.

on the relevant terms[1]. This is assuming that the fact in question has been shown to be *material*. In cases of doubt it is possible for expert evidence to be admitted[2].

Avoidance results in the office being able to recover any sums paid by it as moneys paid out under a mistake of fact – for if the life office had known of the non-disclosure at the time, no benefits need have been paid. Similarly, premiums paid are returnable on the principle that there has been a failure of consideration. However, if there has been wilful or fraudulent non-disclosure there is no obligation to return the premiums[3]. But if the life office continues to accept premiums in respect of the policy with knowledge of the true facts, it cannot afterwards repudiate liability on the ground of non-disclosure.

The onus of proving on a balance of probabilities that there has been non-disclosure of a material fact is on the life office. The insurer will therefore have to show that the material information existed at the time of contract, that it was known to the insured, it was not disclosed and the life office was thereby induced into entering into the contract.

Joel v Law Union and Crown Insurance Co[4]

It was alleged by the office that the assured had not disclosed the facts that she had suffered from nervous depression after 'flu and had been attended by a specialist. The office adduced as supporting evidence the printed form containing questions which the medical examiner had put to her 'with any necessary explanation'. The answers given by the assured were filled in and a declaration that they were true was signed by her. In answer to the question 'What medical men have you consulted?', two doctors' names were entered but not that of the specialist. The medical examiner that had put the questions was not called as a witness. Held, that there was no evidence of non-disclosure. The printed form did not prove non-disclosure because it was not clear what questions or explanations had been put by the medical examiner. The insured therefore received the benefit of the doubt in this case.

2.34 Knowledge gained by a life office concerning a policyholder may be imputed to the life office in respect of other policies taken out by the policyholder, however, it is necessary to look at the circumstances in which the information is received by the life office and as such imputed knowledge may not arise unless the information is received by a person authorised and able to appreciate its significance. So it was held by the majority in:

Malhi v Abbey Life Assurance Co Ltd[5]

Mr Malhi (the deceased) and M took out a joint lives first death policy in May 1984 which lapsed and was reinstated in October 1985. On reinstating the policy the company relied upon the earlier declaration of health. Subsequently in 1986 a joint application for an endowment policy was made and declined by the company's underwriters following a report detailing the deceased's alcoholism.

1 *Pan Atlantic Insurance Co Ltd v Pine Top Insurance Co Ltd* [1995] 1 AC 501 HL.
2 *Reynolds v Phoenix Assurance Co Ltd* [1978] 2 Lloyd's Rep 440.
3 *Feise v Parkinson* (1812) 4 Taunt 640.
4 [1908] 2 KB 863.
5 [1996] LRLR 237.

The first policy was disclaimed on the deceased's death on grounds of non-disclosure, the deceased having been suffering from alcoholism prior to April 1984 and having contracted malaria prior to October 1985. It was established, inter alia, that it was impracticable for the underwriters, and there was no duty on them, to check earlier applications/policies. The majority of the Court of Appeal held that the information received in 1986 concerning the deceased was not received by a person authorised and able to appreciate its significance and therefore there was no imputed knowledge to the company to establish a waiver by election of its right to forfeit for non-disclosure.

The case has been criticised as being unduly lenient to the life office and there must be some doubt as to whether the decision in *Malhi* will continue to represent the law in the future taking into account the huge growth in information retrieval systems so that not only information in an insurer's own records may be imputed to him, but information generally available.

D Indisputable policies

2.35 If a policy is expressed to be 'indisputable', the life office cannot raise any question of non-disclosure, except where the policy was procured by fraud on the part of the contracting party; this is so even if there is no express exception of fraud in the policy[1]. An 'indisputable' clause would not prevent the insurer from raising the question of illegality, eg for lack of insurable interest[2]. It has also been held that it does not prevent an insurer from avoiding liability for negligent misrepresentation unless negligence is expressly mentioned in the exclusion clause or the clause does not otherwise make sense[3].

E Warranties

2.36 A contract of insurance can be made on the understanding that it shall be enforceable only if certain facts have been truly stated. Such a contract is based on a warranty (or more correctly a condition precedent to the risk), and it is not necessary for the insurer to show whether the matter warranted is or is not material to the risk, for the object of making it the subject of a warranty is to provide that the contract shall stand or fall by it. The insurer is therefore relieved from having to prove the materiality of statements made by the proposer.

If, for example, it is warranted that the assured has not suffered from a certain disease, and he has in fact suffered from it, although he did not know its nature, the life office is automatically discharged from further liability under the policy[4]. If it is a condition that the assured shall not reside in a certain country or under-

1 *Anstey v British Natural Premium Life* (1908) 24 TLR 871.
2 *Anctil v Manufacturers' Life Insurance Co* [1899] AC 604.
3 *Toomey v Eagle Star (No 2)* [1995] 2 Lloyd's Rep 88.
4 See *Bank of Nova Scotia v Hellenic Mutual War Risks Association (Bermuda) Ltd 'The Good Luck'* [1992] 2 Lloyd's Rep 540.

take a certain occupation, breach of the condition has the effect that the life office is discharged from liability from when the warranty ceases to be true, quite irrespective of the question whether the residence or occupation had any effect on the risk.

Where the proposal form includes a provision to the effect that the truth of the answers shall form the 'basis of the contract' (known as a 'basis clause'), this means that the proposer warrants the accuracy of his answers and if it transpires that any of these are false, this will be a breach of warranty entitling the life office to be discharged from all liability under the policy even though the statements were made in good faith and even if they are not material[1]. This also has the slightly odd effect of a crucial policy term being found outside the provisions of the policy document. Such provisions have been criticised both judicially and by academics. They were contrary to the ABI Statement of Long-Term Insurance Practice (see **2.44**) which prohibited a life office from using a proposal form or issuing a policy if that document contained: 'any provision converting the statements as to past or present fact in the proposal form into warranties except where the warranty relates to a statement of fact concerning the life to be assured under a life of another policy' (eg 'basis of the contract'). However, a life office is still able to require specific warranties to be given about matters which are material to the risk to be insured.

Modern life office practice tends towards the use of a form of proposal where the proposer is asked to give replies to the best of his knowledge and belief. In such circumstances it is not always clear exactly what (if anything) is warranted, and it will be for the court to decide if necessary. If the proposer only warrants that his answers were in accordance with his knowledge and honest belief, then if he gives replies which are not in fact accurate, but so far as he knew and believed were correct, the policy will stand. The life office cannot be discharged from liability unless it can be shown that the proposer did not know or hold such a belief at all. The same applies if the proposer himself qualifies his replies by saying that they are given to the best of his knowledge and belief. Courts are generally reluctant to construe answers given by the assured as anything other than the belief of the assured[2] unless the proposal is clearly to this effect. However, if the proposal is not clear the proposer would be well advised to qualify his answers to this effect[3].

Anstey v British Natural Premium Life Association Ltd[4]

The proposer, who had had a miscarriage some 10 years before making the proposal, answered questions as follows: Q. 'Have you had any local or other disease, personal injury, illness or infirmity?' A. 'No'. Q. 'If you have had any illness or infirmity, have you fully recovered from it?' A. 'Had none'. The Court of Appeal considered that the answers were not untrue, since the miscarriage was not an illness or infirmity.

1 The use of such warranties in relation to non-material facts is contrary to The Statement of Long-Term Insurance Practice.

2 *Delahaye v British Empire Mutual* (1897) 13 TLR 245.

3 *Wheelton v Hardisty* 1857 8 & B 232.

4 [1908] 24 TLR 871.

Kumar v Life Assurance Co of India[1]

K gave birth to a child by Caesarian section in hospital in February 1966. She was advised against becoming pregnant again for the next two years. She therefore consulted a doctor at a family planning clinic and was prescribed an oral contraceptive. The doctor asked her if she had ever had an operation. She answered 'No', but later mentioned the Caesarian section. In October 1966 K took out a life policy. The questions and answers in her proposal form included: Q. Have you consulted a medical practitioner within the last 5 years? A. No. Q. Did you ever have any operation, accident or injury? If so, give details. A. No. Q. Have you ever been in any hospital, asylum, or sanatorium for a check up, observation, treatment or an operation? If so, give details. A. No (only delivery).

The proposal form contained a declaration that her answers were true in every particular and that she had not withheld any information and that she agreed that the declaration and proposal should form the basis of the contract.

K took an oral contraceptive but she became pregnant and died in June 1968 after an operation for a ruptured ectopic pregnancy. The insurance company contended that K's answers were not true in every particular in that she had had a Caesarian section and had consulted a doctor at the family planning clinic, and that they were entitled to rescind the policy.

Held, that for the visit to the doctor at the family planning clinic to be a consultation within the meaning of the question the visit must be shown to be for a purpose material to the effecting of a life policy. 'Going on the pill' without any pre-existing health factor being involved was irrelevant. But there was here a pre-existing health factor and some risk, in the event of further pregnancy. The question about consulting a doctor was therefore answered incorrectly. The doctor had said in evidence that women from the East often did not consider a Caesarian section an operation but merely as part and parcel of having a baby. Nevertheless, her answer to the question about operations was held to be incorrect. The insurance company was entitled to avoid the policy.

2.37 If the answers to the questions in the proposal form are inconsistent or otherwise unsatisfactory the insurer must make further enquiries; otherwise it will be deemed to have waived its rights. If the space for the answer is left blank, there is no misrepresentation or breach of warranty, unless the circumstances indicate that leaving the space blank implies a negative answer to the question. There may, however, be non-disclosure of material information[2].

Where the proposer is medically examined by the life office's medical officer, or other doctor appointed by them, his replies to the doctor's questions must be correct to the best of his knowledge and belief. However, if they are, like the answers in the proposal form, made the 'basis of the contract' and therefore a warranty, the life office may be discharged from liability if they are not accurate, even if they are honestly believed by the proposer to be true. However, it should be noted that basis (of the contract) clauses were effectively banned by the ABI Statement of Long-Term Insurance Practice (see **2.44**) and should be abolished by the changes proposed by the Law Commissions (see **2.51**).

1 (1973) 117 Sol Jo 833.
2 *Roberts v Avon Insurance Co Ltd* [1956] 2 Lloyd's Rep 240.

The replies of private friends and medical referees are not usually, under modern practice, made the subject of warranty, so that the policy will not be voided by inaccurate replies by them unless there is an element of collusive fraud.

In the case of a life-of-another policy the non-disclosure or misrepresentation of the life to be assured does not discharge liability unless (a) the life assured is acting as agent of the assured, or (b) the truth of the life assured's statements are warranted or made the basis of the contract[1]. That said, however, it is the usual practice today for the proposer and life assured of a life-of-another policy to give answers 'to the best of their knowledge and belief' so it will be for the court to decide what might have been warranted.

F Waiver of breach of warranty

2.38 Where there is a breach of warranty the life office will be automatically discharged from any further liability for claims under the contract, although certain ongoing obligations may survive the breach. The effect of breach operate outside the election of the life office. This was established in the case of *Bank of Nova Scotia v Hellenic Mutual War Risks Association (Bermuda) Ltd (The Good Luck)* which considered the effect of section 33 of the Marine Insurance Act (MIA). Lord Goff stated that 'discharge of the insurer from liability is automatic and is not dependant upon any decision by the insurer to treat the contract or the insurance as at an end'. Rather confusingly, however, although liability ceases automatically (as determined by *The Good Luck*) section 34(3) of the MIA entitles the insurer to 'waive' the breach and treat the policy as still existing. Subsequent decisions have clarified this difficulty by establishing that waiver can only occur by estoppel and not election by the life office. Thus, for example, continuing to accept renewal premiums after knowledge of the breach[2] could amount to a waiver if the assured was genuinely led to believe that acceptance of his premium indicated clearly an intention to treat the policy as valid. This would not be so if the life office accepted the premium whilst reserving its position.

It is possible that delay which prejudices the assured or the rights of third parties would also amount to waiver of a breach.

G Misrepresentation

2.39 A breach by the assured of the duty of disclosure may also amount to a positive misrepresentation of existing fact. This is likely to be the case where the breach consists of giving inaccurate information in answer to a material question in the proposal.

The circumstances in which a proposer supplies information to the life office may be such as to fall within the rules governing fraudulent misrepresentation.

1 *Wheelton v Hardisty* (1857) 8 E & B 232.
2 *Holdsworth v Lancashire and Yorkshire Rly* (1907) 23 TLR 521.

The office might, in such cases, pursue the proposer for fraud. Fraud renders the policy voidable at the option of the life office which may rescind the contract and recover anything paid[1]. It could also recover damages which would include all expenditure reasonably and properly incurred arising from the deceit. There is also authority for the proposition that if the policy is avoided for fraud then the office is not obliged to return the premium[2].

An innocent misrepresentation is, essentially, any misrepresentation which does not amount to fraud. Within the ambit of innocent misrepresentation two types can be distinguished. Misstatements which are a result of negligence or carelessness and those as a result of pure error made under a misapprehension not amounting to negligence. For an innocent misrepresentation to be actionable it must be a statement of fact and not of opinion or law. (It may be that statements relating to law are now actionable since *Kleinwort Benson Ltd v Lincoln City Council*); it must be untrue or inaccurate; it must be material to the life office's acceptance of the proposal; it must be a statement as to present fact and must have induced the life office to accept the proposal on the terms upon which it did so.

Innocent misrepresentation is ground for avoiding the policy and rescinding the contract provided that the office restores the consideration received (ie the premiums which have been paid) and the recission is not inequitable to the assured.

H Effect of non-disclosure or misrepresentation

2.40 As stated above, normally non-disclosure or misrepresentation by one party enables the other party to avoid the contract and this avoidance would take effect ab initio (ie from the beginning and not merely for the future). In seeking to rescind, the application must be made without undue delay after discovery of the truth[3] and the ability to rescind is lost if the person entitled to rescind has conducted himself in such a way as to give the impression that he has waived his right to rescind and intends to affirm the contract[4]. Rescission must be total, not partial[5].

In *Pan Atlantic Insurance Co Ltd v Pine Top Insurance Co Ltd*[6] the House of Lords decided that an insurer cannot rely upon the misrepresentation or non-disclosure of a material fact to avoid the contract if that misrepresentation or non-disclosure did not in fact induce the making of the contract on the terms accepted. Establishing that a fact is material does not necessarily mean that it induced the insurer to enter into the contract. The case of *St Paul Fire and Marine Co (UK) Ltd v McConnel Dowell Constructors Ltd*[7] supported the conclusions arrived at in *Pan Atlantic*.

1 *London Assurance v Clare* (1937) 57 Ll L Rep 254.
2 *Anderson v Fitzgerald* (1853) 4 HL Cas 484.
3 *Foster v Mutual Reserve Life* (1904) 20 TLR 715.
4 *Cleary v Prudential Ass Co* [1927] 1 AC Rep 29.
5 *Urquhart v Macpherson* (1897) 2 App Cas 831.
6 [1995] 1 AC 50.
7 [1995] 2 Lloyd's Rep 116 (CA).

In rare cases, the materiality and inducement may be 'obvious' but in others the insurer must prove that he was induced. Generally, the standard of the prudent underwriter will be applied to see if he would have refused cover or changed its terms. As an alternative the underwriting practice of the particular office may be considered.

Under section 2(2) of the Misrepresentation Act 1967, it is possible that the court may award damages instead of recission where there has been an innocent misrepresentation. It is understood that the FOS may also take this approach.

Damages for fraud or deliberate misrepresentation made without reasonable grounds may be recoverable under section 2(1) of the Misrepresentation Act 1967. Another alternative is that for negligent misrepresentation the insured may have a cause of action in tort[1].

I Action on discovery of misrepresentation or non-disclosure

2.41 The aggrieved party has an election whether or not to avoid the contract as it is voidable, not void. When all the facts are ascertained, the other party should be informed within a reasonable time if the intention is to avoid the contract, otherwise the other party may be led to conclude that the contract is being affirmed, for example, where premiums are received after discovery of the facts this will be evidence of waiver[2]. It is clear, however, that the aggrieved party must actually have knowledge of all the relevant facts and of his right to avoid. Constructive knowledge or being put on notice is probably not sufficient.

In *Malhi v Abbey Life Assurance Co Ltd*[3], it was argued that a life office had waived its right to avoid a contract on the basis that the information in question was in the life office's records (there had been a previous application). This was rejected. There was no duty on the underwriters dealing with this case to search the office's files for previous disclosures.

J Criminal sanctions

2.42 Under section 16 of the Theft Act 1968, a person who by any deception dishonestly obtains for himself or another any pecuniary advantage commits a criminal offence. A pecuniary advantage is to be regarded as obtained where he is allowed to take out any policy of insurance or annuity contract, or obtain an improvement of terms, as a result of his deception. 'Deception' is defined in section 15[4]. There is also a provision in the Financial Services and Markets Act 2000, which makes it a criminal offence to deliberately or recklessly make mis-

1 *Hedley Byrne v Heller and Partners Ltd* [1964] AC 465.
2 *Hemmings v Sceptre Life* [1905] 1 Ch 365.
3 3 [1996] LRLR 237.
4 See *Norwich Union Life Insurance Society v Qureshi* [1998] CLC 1605, *Aldrich v Norwich Union Life Insurance Co Ltd* [1998] CLC 1621 and *R v Manning* [1999] 2 WLR 430.

leading statements and practices or to dishonestly conceal material facts[1]. However, the wording of the section seems to be designed to regulate the behaviour of insurers (and other investment providers) and does not apply to representations made by the insured.

K Unfair contract terms

2.43 Insurance companies were exempted from the provisions of the Unfair Contract Terms Act 1977 relating to contractual exemption clauses. The reason for this exemption was the acceptance of the industry's argument about the potential detrimental effects and the standing of the London market, and the agreement to adhere to a non-statutory code of good practice. For life insurers this code was contained in the Association of British Insurers (ABI) Statements of General and Long-Term Insurance Practice (see **2.44**). This did much to redress the balance between the parties in consumer cases and the codes have effectively been given effect by the Insurance/PIA Ombudsman and now the Financial Ombudsman Service.

The Unfair Contract Terms Directive[2], which came into force in this country on 1 July 1995, does apply to insurance contracts. The directive introduced for the first time the civil law concept of good faith (not to be confused with the common law requirement of good faith in insurance contracts) and allows policyholders to challenge terms in contracts which do not describe the risk covered by the contract. It is submitted, that the ABI statement is still relevant to the question of fairness. For further discussion of the Unfair Contract Terms Directive see Chapter 1.

L Statement of Long-Term Insurance Practice

2.44 Paragraph 3(a) of the AB1 Statement of Long-Term Insurance Practice provided that insurers would not unreasonably reject claims or repudiate liability for non-disclosure of a material fact which the policyholder could not reasonably be expected to have disclosed, or for misrepresentation unless it is deliberate or negligent. In addition, proposers had to be warned on proposal forms of the requirement to disclose material facts and the consequences of failure to do so. Insurers were expected to ask clear questions about facts generally found to be material and refrain from asking questions outside of the proposer's knowledge. The ABI's statement of Long Term Insurance Practice was effectively replaced by regulatory rules (eg the FSA's Conduct of Business Rules (COB)). Although the relevant requirements are no longer set out in the current FSA COBS rules, it is submitted that they should still be used as a benchmark of what is considered to be fair. The rules for pure protection contracts are to be found in the Insurance

1 Section 397.
2 93/13/EEC.

Conduct of Business Rules (ICOBS) which still refer indirectly to the requirements (see ICOBS 8.1). This is supplemented by a January 2009 ABI Code of Practice relating to the management of claims which recommends paying claims in full if the non disclosure or misrepresentation was innocent and paying a proportionate amount if it was negligent. Firms should also consider Principle 6 of the FSA's Principles for Business, which requires them to treat their customers fairly.

SECTION 3 LAW COMMISSIONS PROPOSED CHANGES

A Law Commissions proposed changes

2.45 The Law Commissions of England and Wales and of Scotland began their review of insurance contract law in 2006. Calls for reform of the law on misrepresentation and non-disclosure in insurance contracts are not new. A law reform committee first recommended reform in 1957, followed by further calls in a 1980 report. Indeed, the 1980 English Law Commission report described reform to the law of insurance contracts as 'too long delayed'. There has been widespread support for reform in the area of consumer contracts as the existing law can have harsh consequences on a public largely oblivious of their legal obligations. Insurers, brokers, consumer groups, lawyers and the Financial Ombudsman Service (FOS) have all recommended legislative reform to clarify these obligations. For many years industry practice guidelines and the FOS's approach to resolving complaints have been out of sync with the strict letter of the law; resulting in two alternative approaches in law and in regulatory and market practice.

The Law Commissions have commented that the current law leaves the unsatisfactory situation that reforming legislation is needed to avoid what might be regarded as arbitrary decision making, and requires proposers to volunteer information about the risk. At present there is no obligation in law for the insurer to ask questions in relation to those facts he wishes to know. Thus a consumer must ask themselves what information a professional underwriter would wish to know. Very few consumers are even aware of this duty; and, if they are, do not have the means to know what information they are required to volunteer to the insurer. The current law does not take into account what a reasonable consumer might think relevant to disclose. Similarly, the rules on insurable interest limit such interest to husbands, wives and civil partners or those who can show a financial dependency or pecuniary loss.

2.46 The Law Commissions started their review of insurance law by issuing a scoping paper[1]. This was followed by a series of Issues Papers, Issue Paper 1 dealt with misrepresentation and non-disclosure and Issues Paper 4 dealt with insurable interest. The Law Commissions have defined their recommendations separately in relation to consumers and business customers. The Law Commissions also recommended making a distinction for very small (micro-

1 In January 2006.

businesses) which would treat them as consumers but this does not seem to have been taken forward in their proposed definition of consumer (see **2.48**).

B Insurable interest

2.47 Issues Paper 4 on Insurable Interest was issued in January 2008. In the paper the Law Commissions posed the question whether there should continue to be a requirement for insurable interest at all in non-indemnity insurance. Other jurisdictions, such as Australia, have abolished the requirement. The Law Commissions' preliminary view was to retain the concept of insurable interest in life assurance but to expand the categories of those who are assumed to have an interest in another's life to include dependants in the lives of their parents/guardians, cohabitants and parents in the lives of their adult children. In addition, the Commissions stated that they were considering the following relationships: parents of children under 18, fiancé(e)s, siblings, grandparents and grandchildren. The Law Commissions also propose that consent of the life assured be an alternative means of showing insurable interest (resembling the current practice of assigning life policies). They also propose that the category of insurable interest supported by pecuniary interest be relaxed to include the assured's reasonable expectation of pecuniary loss on the death of the life assured and that a requirement be imposed upon insurers to inquire whether a valid insurable interest exists at the outset of a life assurance contract. This would lessen the possibility of insurers defeating a claim by requiring the insured to establish insurable interest where the insurer has already negotiated contract terms and has accepted premiums. The Law Commissions propose that insurers should not be permitted to avoid policies only on the basis that the persons interested (other than the policyholder) are not specified in the policy as required under section 2 of the 1774 Act.

Although a draft bill has been issued in relation to mis-representation and non disclosure, it is not yet clear whether legislation can also be expected in relation to insurable interest.

C Misrepresentation and non disclosure

2.48 The Law Commissions' proposal in relation to misrepresentation and non disclosure was to abolish the duty of disclosure in consumer cases. 'Consumer' being defined in a similar way as in the FSA Rules (ie someone acting wholly or mainly outside of their trade or business or profession). This would shift the onus onto the insurer to ask appropriate questions for business cases. The duty of disclosure would be retained but the existing prudent underwriter test (see **2.29**) would be converted into a prudent assured test.

The Consumer Insurance (Disclosure and Representations) Bill had its first reading in the House of Lords on 16 May 2011. This first stage is a formality which signalled the start of the Bill's journey through the House of Lords. The second reading opens the general debate on all aspects of the Bill, which will begin its passage through Parliament in the Lords before reaching the House of Commons. Implementation is expected in 2013.

The Bill proposes to change the nature of the parties' pre-contractual negotiations so that insurers are obliged to ask those questions about the risk they want to know. In response, consumers will be under a new duty to take reasonable care to answer the questions asked by the insurer fully and accurately.

Where a consumer has made a mistake in answering the insurer's questions, the Bill makes a distinction between 'careless' and 'deliberate or reckless' misrepresentations. The remedy which an insurer will have in the event of a misrepresentation will depend upon the category of mistake. This new classification of misrepresentations will give legislative effect to the approach currently taken by the FOS.

Where the misrepresentation was deliberate or reckless, the insurer's remedy is that they can refuse the claim. A statement will be deliberate or reckless if the consumer knew that it was untrue or misleading or did not care that it was so and knew that the matter was relevant to the insurer. Following a deliberate or reckless misrepresentation the policy will be treated as if it had never existed and all claims by the insured can be refused. This approach is like that taken under the current law, although the insurer will now be able to retain any premium unless there are compelling reasons for the premium to be returned (for example in life policies containing an investment element). The retention of premium and avoidance of the policy retains the penal element currently included to dissuade consumers against deliberately or recklessly misleading insurers.

Where the misrepresentation is merely careless, the Bill provides for a proportionate remedy which will reflect the position that the insurer would have been in had the true facts been known. It is for the insurer to show that a misrepresentation was deliberate or reckless, otherwise it will be deemed merely careless. Under the current law, insurers are able to avoid the entire policy for an innocent misrepresentation with potentially severe consequences for the insured. The Bill provides the insurer with a compensatory remedy. Therefore, where the insurer would have excluded a particular type of claim, the insurer should not have to pay claims falling within this exclusion. Where a warranty or excess would have been imposed, the resulting claim should reflect the policy had such a warranty been included. Where the insurer, on knowing the true facts, would have charged a higher premium, a proportionate settlement should be given to the insured. Finally, where the insurer would have declined the risk altogether, the policy may be avoided and the premium returned.

The proposed new law retains the requirement that the insurer must have been induced by the misrepresentation (see **2.33**)[1]. Therefore, under the proposed Bill, the insurer will still have to demonstrate that without the misrepresentation, it would not have entered into the contract at all – or at least on the same terms. However, the new law no longer requires the insurer to prove that the misrepresentation would have influenced the judgement of other underwriters in the market. It will be enough for the insurer to show that they were so induced and that a reasonable consumer would not have made such a mistake.

1 As set out in *Pan Atlantic Insurance Co Ltd v Pine Top Insurance Co Ltd* [1995] 1 AC 501.

2.49 The Bill requires that insureds take reasonable care not to make a misrepresentation. The standard of care will be that of 'a reasonable consumer' but an additional element is added which demands that the insurer should take into account the actual circumstances of the individual consumer where they are aware of them. It further includes an additional specification to clarify that a dishonest misrepresentation (even if reasonable to the average consumer) will always be deemed unreasonable. This prevents the more knowledgeable person relying upon the excuse that a less well informed consumer would not have known the significance of a particular fact.

As mentioned above, consumers are required to take reasonable care not to make any misrepresentations. However, the Bill will take into account certain circumstances which will affect the degree of care that should be taken. The circumstances to be taken into account are: the type of consumer policy and its target market; any relevant explanatory material or publicity produced or authorised by the insurer; how clear and specific the insurer's questions were; and whether or not an agent was acting on the insured's behalf.

The Bill has largely followed the approach taken by the Financial Services Authority (FSA) and various EU directives in their definition of a consumer insurance contract but it may apply to certain mixed purpose contracts (eg if the main purpose of the contract is to cover non business interests).

D Other issues

2.50 Chapter 4[1] describes the current law in relation to insurance brokers and Independent Financial Advisers (IFAs) who are generally regarded as the agent of the client. This can cause issues, particularly in non-life cases where disclosures are made to such an intermediary. The Bill introduces a statutory determination of when the intermediary will be considered to be acting for the insurer rather than the insured.

In its 2007 Consultation Paper on reforming consumer insurance law, the Law Commissions proposed a single bright line test to determine whether an intermediary acted for the consumer or the insurer. The Commissions' initial view was that, unless an intermediary clearly acted for the consumer, they should be taken to act for the insurer. In response to considerable criticism of this approach, Schedule 2 of the Bill now states that an intermediary will be acting for the insurer in the following circumstances:

(1) where the intermediary is the appointed representative of the insurer;

(2) the insurer has given the intermediary express authority to collect the information as its agent; or

(3) the insurer has given the intermediary express authority to enter into the contract on the insurer's behalf.

1 See Section 7.

In other cases the intermediary is presumed to act for the consumer unless, in light of relevant circumstances, it appears that they act for the insurer. The Schedule sets out factors which will tend to show whether the agent is acting for either the insurer or the insured. It is still rare for IFAs or appointed representatives of a life office to be given power to bind or to accept the disclosure of information. Appointed representatives are likely to be considered agents for these purposes while IFAs may continue not to be.

2.51 The Bill abolishes 'basis of the contract' clauses (see **2.36**) by stating that any representation made by a consumer is not capable of being converted into a warranty by means of a provision of the contract. Basis clauses have been criticised for many years and their use was prohibited under the ABI's Statement of Long Term Insurance Practice (which also forms an annex to the 2006 ABI guidance on application form design). The FSA rules do not directly outlaw basis clauses, even though their application to consumers is likely to fall foul of the FSA's Principle 6 (which requires firms pay due regard to the interests of its customers and treat them fairly). In their research, the Law Commissions found numerous examples of the continued use of basis clauses in consumer contracts; the Bill would unequivocally remove these onerous terms from consumer policies.

2.52 Special provisions are included in the Bill for group insurance schemes. Under section 7 of the Bill, where a misrepresentation is made by a group member of a scheme there will only be consequences for that individual, rather than for the group as a whole. Group policies such as those made by businesses on behalf of their employees do not usually fall within the consumer regime. The proposals ensure that any dispute about a misrepresentation made by a person entitled under the group policy will be treated in accordance with the consumer rules.

In addition to the proposals for group policies, the Bill establishes that where a consumer takes out insurance on the life of another person, and information is provided by the person insured (but not the policyholder), any misrepresentations will be treated as though they were supplied by a party to the contract. Under the current law, should the person insured make a misrepresentation (for example about their state of health) the insurer is not entitled to any remedy as only the policyholder is under a duty not to misrepresent information. In the absence of basis of the contract clauses, the insurer is offered no protection in such circumstances. The Bill addresses this potential problem by placing both the policyholder and the insured under the duty to take reasonable care not to misrepresent information.

2.53 Another issue considered by the Law Commissions (but not included in the Consumer Insurance (Disclosure and Representations) Bill was whether changes should be made in relation to any ongoing duty of good faith. They asked whether, for example, policyholders should be under a duty not to make a fraudulent claim and what appropriate remedies for fraud might be. It is assumed that no further rules, at least in relation to consumers, are likely to be forthcoming in this area.

CHAPTER 3

FSMA and the life office

SUMMARY

SECTION 1 INTRODUCTION TO FSMA AND THE FSA HANDBOOK

3.1 This Chapter seeks to provide a high level of overview of the Financial Services and Markets Act 2000 (FSMA) regime including the Financial Services Authority (FSA)'s Handbook of rules and guidance and, to identify those provisions which are likely to be of most relevance to life assurance practitioners. Issues relating to insurance mediation (eg introductions, advice, sales and arranging insurance contracts) are considered in Chapter 4.

A Background to FSMA

3.2 The Financial Services Act 1986 governed the provision of life assurance contracts from 1988. Responsibility for the prudential aspects of life offices was, however, retained by the Department of Trade and Industry and subsequently, the Insurance Directorate of HM Treasury. However, after the 1997 election it was announced that, in the future, one authority would take on the responsibility for the regulation of the whole of the UK's financial services sector. A report was commissioned and was prepared by Sir Andrew Large. This led to the Securities and Investments Board (SIB) being renamed the FSA in October 1997. In June 1998, the FSA took over the Bank of England's responsibilities for banking supervision. The FSA also took over the regulatory and registration functions of a number of bodies, the most relevant to life assurance being the Insurance Directorate of HM Treasury and the Self Regulatory Organisation responsible for life insurance, the Personal Investment Authority (PIA). FSMA had a long and laborious journey onto the statute book. It received Royal Assent on 14 June 2000 but did not come into effect until 1 December 2001 (N2).

B Move to Tri-partite Regulation

1 Overview

3.3 At the time of writing, a significant shift in regulatory responsibility to Europe is taking place which it is expected will result in a single European rule book for insurers (see **3.7** and **3.57**). The first steps in the process have seen the establishment of new European Supervisory Authorities and the European Systemic Risk Board (ESRB). Structural changes are also being proposed to the UK Regulatory regime which would create a UK equivalent of the ESRB and two new regulatory authorities, the Prudential Regulation Authority (PRA) and the Financial Conduct Authority (FCA).

The UK equivalent of the ESRB will be called the Financial Policy Committee (FPC). It will be responsible for protecting the stability of the UK financial system as a whole (ie at the macro level). The FPC will be situated within the Bank of England and its aim will be to identify the risks which have the potential to cause instability to the UK financial system. It will have oversight, through governance arrangements, of the new regulatory bodies and will make recommendations and offer advice. Ultimately, it will also have power to intervene to ensure action is taken to guard against risks to financial stability. Management of the more day to day (micro level) risk to the financial system will be undertaken by the two new regulatory bodies. The changes will involve a fairly significant amendment of FSMA. It is anticipated that the proposed new regulatory bodies will be in place in early 2013 but work is already taking place to reorganise the FSA, (for example, the current Supervision and Risk Business units have been replaced with a Prudential Business Unit and a Conduct Business Unit) so that, in a similar way to the introduction of the FSA itself in 2001, the new regime will be operating behind the scenes prior to the formal transfer of power.

Treasury Consultation papers on the 'new approach to financial regulation' were issued in July 2010 and February 2011, with a further paper, 'the blueprint for reform' and the draft Bill issued in June 2011. On 20 June 2011 the Bank of England and the FSA published a joint paper entitled 'The Bank of England Prudential Regulation Authority – our approach to insurance supervision'. On 28 June 2011 the FSA issued a paper. 'The Financial Conduct Authority – Approach to Regulation'.

These papers together give a reasonable insight to the proposed future structure but clearly much of the detail will emerge and be discussed over the period until 2013.

2 *Prudential Regulation Authority*

3.4 In simple terms, the new regime will involve prudential regulation of banks, insurers and some investment firms that have the potential to pose a systemic risk to the UK financial system, moving to the PRA. The PRA will be part of the Bank of England Group. Unsurprising the role of the PRA will be to focus on the financial soundness of these regulated entities and their potential to pose systemic risk (see **3.10** in relation to its proposed objectives). It has already been stressed that the regime will not try to ensure that no such entity fails. In fact, it is intended that the system will allow poorly run firms to fail with the regulators seeking to insulate the rest of the financial system from such failures. As part of the Bank of England group, and as the FPC will also have an oversight role in the running of the PRA, it is anticipated that the PRA will be able to exercise a more 'judgement-based' approach to regulation. It will be interesting to see how this evolves in practice as one of the consistent complaints made about the FSA's regulation of insurance companies has always been that it does not have sufficient experience and expertise in relation to insurance. This could well present problems under the new regime, especially if the PRA is given more extensive powers than the FSA or if, as suggested, some of its decisions may not be open to appeal.

3 *Financial Conduct Authority*

3.5 Insurers will be dual regulated. Regulated by the PRA for prudential matters and also by the FCA for conduct issues. The PRA will, however, be the lead regulator. As its name suggests, the FCA will regulate the conduct of business with consumers and other businesses. As well as focussing more on wholesale conduct issues, it is intended that the FCA be more interventionist (described as having a 'lower risk appetite' than the FSA) and forward thinking in nature. It appears that the FCA intends to achieve this by focusing more on industry and sector issues (see also the FSA's Discussion Paper issued in January 2011 and FS 11/3 issued in June 2011 below). It seems that the FCA will not be an economic regulator (eg like Ofcom) although it may prohibit excessive charges. It will also not pre-approve products (or give them kite marks) but there is likely to be a much higher level of scrutiny of proposals to launch new products, and more evidence is likely to be required to show how the product is suited to the target market and the appropriateness of the means by which it will be sold. The FCA will apparently do more than the FSA has done to engage directly with retail consumers to explain what they should expect of firms (and presumably what remains their own responsibility).

Before both the Treasury's February 2011 consultation paper and the draft Bill to effect the proposed regulatory changes were issued, the FSA had already started down the path of a more interventionist strategy[1]. In January 2011, the FSA issued DP 11/1 Product Intervention which was followed by FS 11/3 on the

1 See speech Adair Turner 13 July 2010.

same subject in June 2011. These papers explain the FSA's rationale for requiring additional powers but also explain how it will use its existing powers for this purpose. What seems to have become clear to the FSA from consumer research, is that point-of-sale disclosure is not sufficient to inform consumers as to the nature and risks of a product or to enable them to understand the nature of what they are buying. The FSA's view, which it is submitted must be correct, is that a combination of fairness/targeting in product design and charges, application of unfair contract term rules/TCF, appropriate advice or sales techniques (including remuneration arrangements) together with clear point-of-sale disclosure is all required to enable the customer to avoid nasty surprises or an inappropriate product. However, in addition to this, and because a combination of all of these things has not yet proved to be sufficient to avoid customer detriment, the FSA concludes that it needs additional powers to intervene.

These powers of intervention are likely to take the form of banning certain products either entirely or mandating certain product features. The FSA describes this intervention as 'an essential part of effective regulation[1]. DP 11/1[2] sets out a table of indicators of problematic product features. These include bundling products together, cross subsidisation, and (implicitly) unduly burdensome eligibility criteria, factors leading to loss of cover and complex claims notification procedures for insurance. These areas are borne out in many of the undertakings given to the FSA under the Unfair Terms in Consumer Contracts Regulations 1999 (UTCCR). The FSA makes clear in DP11/1[3] that it intends to continue to use all the levers available to it, namely those under UTCCR, imposing a requirement on a firm's permission and more aggressive enforcement action, including the imposition of penalties where earlier FSA action (eg Dear CEO or guidance) has not had the desired effect.

FS 11/3 is interesting as, predictably, consumer organisations were broadly in agreement with the FSA whilst product providers were a bit more divided. This division represents the genuine concern that, even a product which the FSA wants to ban, will be suitable for someone and so a ban is a very blunt instrument. It is submitted that this must be true and that to be effective, such a power must be used sparingly. However, it is possible to see, taking Payment Protection Insurance (PPI) as an example, that the FSA might, as evidence of both inappropriateness and lack of competition emerged, have been able to intervene in the selling of single premium PPI at a much earlier stage and prevented both harm to consumers and the entrenchment that inevitably flows from providers having a lot at stake. The FSA acknowledges that early intervention can limit the downside of challenge to a product precisely because the product provider does not have too much at stake. The feedback in FS 11/3 broadly reiterates the points made in DP 11/1, presumably secure in the knowledge that the Treasury[4] was already convinced of the need for the FCA to have this power going forward. In FS 11/3 the FSA states that the timetable it will adopt for the introduction of new

1 Paragraph 2.14 of DP11/1.
2 Paragraph 3.39.
3 Paragraph 4.44.
4 In its February 2011 Consultation Paper.

rules and additional interventions will reflect the outcome of the UK legislative process and also similar proposals to enable product banning at EU level.

The proposed FCA power to intervene is contained in clause 137C of the draft Bill. The draft power allows the FCA to make rules prohibiting or imposing requirements in relation to authorised persons entering into what are defined as 'specified agreements' (ie of a type specified in its general rules by the FCA). The FCA can also provide for such agreements to be unenforceable, for monies paid to be recoverable or for the payment of compensation.

4 *Division of responsibilities*

3.6 The obvious question that arises in relation to the division of responsibility between the PRA and FCA is the scope for both regulatory overlap and underlap. It is intended that there will be a Memorandum of Understanding between the relevant bodies to try to set out how each will operate and co-operate with the other. The Government intends to create a number of other measures designed to facilitate the effective operation and co-operation of the PRA and FCA. These include a statutory duty to coordinate the exercise of their functions (to ensure they consult each other), cross-membership of boards and a veto mechanism for the PRA to reduce the risk of regulatory actions threatening financial stability or the disorderly failure of a firm. The chief executive of the FCA will sit on the governing body of the PRA and vice versa.

The areas of potential overlap for insurers include change of control, appointment of approved persons, Part VII schemes and passporting. It has already been announced that the PRA will have sole responsibility for regulating with-profits businesses which should include the COBS 20 rules on treating with-profits customers fairly but presumably not the general conduct rules applicable to all products. Change of control should be the responsibility of the PRA. Appointment of approved persons will depend on the nature of the underlying function, so a new actuary or significant influence function should fall to the PRA, whereas customer facing sales functions should fall to the FCA. The Bank of England/FSA June 2011 joint paper states that a full list detailing which functions will be approved by each authority will be published in due course. The PRA and the FCA will design a simple and transparent process for approving individuals to significant influence functions which minimises the administrative burden on individuals and firms.

As regards Part VII transfers, the process under the current Part VII mechanism (see Section 8), is that the courts are ultimately responsible for approving or rejecting an application for a business transfer. The FSA has the right to make representations to court and is responsible for approving the necessary documentation and issuing its report. The Treasury's February 2011 consultation paper confirmed that the Government does not intend to alter the substance of the current framework. The PRA will be primarily responsible for the process but the FCA also has an interest (eg in policyholder communications) and will need to satisfy itself that, as a minimum, the transfer will not adversely affect the customers of the firms involved in the transfer. Both authorities will be able to make representations to the court during the transfer process.

For firms passporting out of the UK, the Government has confirmed that the PRA will be responsible for issuing all relevant notices. It is clear that the PRA needs to oversee the entire financial system in the UK, including parts made up of branches passporting in from other countries. To achieve this, the PRA will need to build close working relationships with overseas regulators in relation to the Reinsurance Directive and the Consolidated Life Assurance Directive (and Solvency II when it replaces both of those directives) It will therefore also be responsible for inward passporting notices in order to mirror its responsibilities for UK firms. Notifications in relation to other directives will go to the FCA.

As regards authorisation in the dual regulator model, firms will need to apply to the PRA for authorisation if they wish to effect or carry out contracts of insurance. The PRA will administer the application and be responsible for granting authorisation. According to the joint paper, authorisation to carry out regulated activities will not be granted unless both the PRA, as prudential regulator, and the FCA, as conduct regulator, are satisfied that it should be. Before granting authorisation, the PRA will assess whether the firm satisfies relevant statutory threshold conditions. The PRA and the FCA will seek to minimise the administrative burden on firms of the new authorisation procedures. The joint paper also states that there will be a single administrative process with a single application form and timetable or decision by each authority. Essentially, the paper attempts to provide reassurance to firms that the importance of ensuring that the authorisation process is both clear to applicants and handled efficiently is fully recognised.

The joint paper also acknowledges that the PRA's policies and supervisory actions will take place within the international context and that much of the PRA's proposed approach will be achieved through the application of Solvency II. The joint paper states that the PRA will pay an active and constructive role in shaping the development of the common framework for regulation and supervision at a global level and in the EU. As many international insurers operate in the UK, the PRA will collaborate with other organisations including the new European Supervisory Authority, the European Insurance and Occupational Pensions Authority (EIOPA) and the International Association of Insurance Supervisors to ensure that it is able to address risks that non-UK insurers may pose to its statutory objectives. The PRA and the FCA will work together to ensure that the other regulator, and any other relevant authorities, are kept fully informed of any matters due to be discussed which fall within their sphere of responsibility. When another body has an interest, the PRA may bring along a non-voting representative of that national body. This is a particularly important point as conduct issues fall within the scope of EIOPA.

5 Powers of the new regulatory bodies

3.7 The PRA and FCA will have different statutory and operational objectives and slightly different powers to those currently applicable to the FSA. The PRA will have an insurance-specific objective to seek to ensure an appropriate degree of protection for policyholders (ideally to ensure that a company can meet its liabilities but if not, to ensure an orderly handover). In the short to medium term, the PRA's ability to make rules to meet this objective will be more constrained by European rules than the FCA.

It is also unclear what 'form' the rules of the PRA and FCA will take (ie will they actually have rule books, will they just use 'copy out'[1], or will they only issue guidance). Solvency II is already a good example of the move at European level towards directly applicable regulation rather than directives that have to be implemented. The insurance field has historically seen European regulation in the form of directives which need to be transposed into the law of the relevant member state. This has not produced the level of harmonisation that might otherwise have been expected. In part this is due to options negotiated by member states, inconsistency in implementation (or at the other extreme, gold plating of requirements). One of the fundamental findings of the De la Rosiere Report[2] into the global financial crisis, was that there was not sufficient harmonisation or consistency in the European regulatory framework and therefore too many gaps existed. The creation of the new European Supervisory Authorities is intended to lead to a single European rule book. The powers given to EIOPA and its intended remit in relation to much of the detail of Solvency II implementation, mean that directly enforceable rules are likely to emerge at EU level. That being the case and particularly as it seems likely Solvency II implementation will involve binding technical standards and Level 3 guidance issued by EIOPA, it is difficult, in relation to prudential regulation, to see much scope for the PRA to make rules itself.

The PRA will, however, need to give guidance as to how it intends to regulate insurers. Interestingly and consistent with its role as lead regulator, the PRA should generally be able to direct the FCA not to exercise a regulatory power in relation to a PRA authorised person. It can do this if it reasonably believes it is required in order to prevent the FCA exercising a power in a way that might threaten the stability of the UK financial system or lead to the failure, in a disorderly manner, of the PRA authorised person. Both regulators potentially have the power to issue directions to the other where they are regulating members of a group subject to consolidated supervision (see Chapter 7).

3.8 As regards the FCA, which will technically step into the shoes of the FSA, it is expected to continue the FSA's initiative on product intervention (see **3.5**) and the Retail Distribution Review (effectively banning commission for advised sales of investment products – see Chapter 4). However, it apparently intends to be more aggressive when it comes to enforcement, to continue the FSA's move towards a 'credible deterrence strategy', and it seems likely it will use its new powers to intervene and ultimately, ban products. Interestingly, as it will have a duty to have regard to competition, it could have regard to products which are problematic because of a lack of competition in the underlying market. The FCA will also have the power to direct firms to immediately withdraw or amend misleading financial promotions and to publish the fact that a warning

1 The PRA will apparently use copy out to the maximum extent.
2 February 2009.

notice in relation to the disciplinary matters has been issued. The last power should not be underestimated, as it is generally easier for firms to negotiate with the FSA whilst the matter is not in the public domain.

It seems certain that the FCA will move away, at least in part, from 'Principles based' regulation to a greater level of prescription. Until conduct of business rules appear at the European level, there will therefore be scope for the FCA to decide to intervene. However, it is interesting to note developments in relation to Packaged Retail Investment Products (PRIPS) where the Commission intends to introduce greater harmonisation in relation to sales rules and pre-contractual disclosure, irrespective of the legal forms or 'wrapper' packaging the investment (see **4.15**). It is also anticipated that the FCA will work more closely with the Financial Ombudsman Service (FOS) and having regard to information from the FOS is specifically referred to in the FCA's consumer protection objective.

One other anticipated change relates to unregulated holding companies. There is a proposal to introduce a wider power enabling the PRA to challenge UK holding companies. It is questionable the extent to which such a provision could have extra territorial effect, although European regulators in a group situation may be able to assist, by making use of similar powers, if such a holding company is in their jurisdiction. It may, however, have the unintended result of encouraging holding companies to relocate outside of the UK.

6 Financial Services Act 2010

3.9 The Financial Services Act 2010 was introduced to make a number of changes to FSMA. It received Royal Assent on 8 April 2010 but with various provisions coming into force at different dates thereafter. One of the main changes made by the 2010 Act, was the amendment of the FSA's statutory objectives to include the need to enhance the stability of the UK financial system (and to enable it to support overseas regulators exercising similar powers). The FSA's powers were increased[1] to enable it to make rules, vary permissions or use its other powers to meet any of its objectives, not just its consumer protection objective. The 2010 Act also contained powers relating to company's remuneration policies[2] and imposed a duty on the FSA to require firms to produce and maintain recovery and resolution plans (eg actions a firm would take in stressed scenarios to try to avoid (ie recover from) or mitigate a likely failure (resolution)). The 2010 Act also gave the FSA new disciplinary powers. These are considered in Section 5. The 2010 Act removes the FSA's public awareness objective, although the FSA should still have regard to the desirability of enhancing public understanding of the financial system. The 2010 Act required the FSA to set up what is now called the Money Advice Service. This is independent from the FSA and designed to improve public knowledge and understanding of financial matters and to assist in enabling members of the public to manage their own financial matters. The FCA will need to have regard to comments received from the Money Advice Service.

1 With effect from 8 June 2010.

2 Applied by the FSA to banks and investment firms.

The 2010 Act also provided for the possibility of a 'Consumer Redress Scheme' (designed to deal with industry wide compensation issues including cases where no complaint has been made). The interaction between such schemes and the FSA's existing rules was considered in the British Banker's Association (BBA) judicial review of the FSA and the FOS (see Section 6). The FSA is able to exercise its power to create such a scheme if there are widespread or regular regulatory failures and consumers have suffered loss and could bring claims. Such a scheme would impose an obligation on firms to conduct an investigation (as previous mis-selling reviews have) and to provide any appropriate redress to consumers. As highlighted in the BBA judicial review case, the regulatory failures in question cannot only be breaches of FSA Principles.

C Overview of FSMA

1 Statutory objectives of the FSA

3.10 FSMA provides a framework for detailed rules to be made by regulation. Under FSMA, the FSA is required to have regard to a set of statutory objectives set out in Part I. These are as follows: market confidence, stability of the UK financial system; the protection of consumers and the reduction of financial crime. With regard to protection of consumers, section 5 refers to 'the appropriate degree of protection' so acknowledging that different consumers require different degrees of protection[1]. Section 2(3) requires the FSA to pursue these objectives whilst having regard to the effective use of its resources; the responsibilities of senior management (which consequently places a significant onus on the management of authorised persons); the application of cost benefit analysis to the imposition of rules and regulations; the need for innovation in regulated markets; the international character of financial services markets and the desirability of maintaining the competitive position of the United Kingdom; and not distorting or impeding competition unnecessarily. The draft Bill, issued in June 2011, amends the regulatory principles to be applied by both the FCA and the PRA, to some extent. Notably, the provisions highlighting the desirability of encouraging innovation and the desirability of maintaining the competitive position of the UK have been dropped.

In its February 2011 consultation and the draft Bill, the Government confirmed that a new section will be inserted into FSMA stating the PRA's insurance objective. The objective states that the PRA will contribute to the securing of an appropriate degree of protection for those who are, or may become, policyholders. This complies with the Solvency II directive which requires regulators to have the protection of policyholders as an objective of supervision. The June 2011 joint paper from the Bank of England and FSA confirms that the PRA will have another concurrent objective, under which it will seek to minimise the adverse impact that either the failure of an insurer, or the way it carries out its business, could have on the stability of the financial system. The Treasury has

1 Sections 3 to 6.

confirmed that the PRA will employ a judgement-based supervisory approach. Practically, this means that the nature and intensity of the PRA's supervision will be commensurate with the level of risk a firm poses to policyholders and to the stability of the system. The Bank of England/FSA joint paper lists some of the factors that the PRA will consider when judging the risk posed by a firm. For example, whilst there is an acceptance that insurers are not systemic in the same way as banks, the combination of insurance and banking in a single group may give rise to a system-wide risk if the failure of the insurer threatens the financial condition of the bank. Also, the investment decisions of insurers can accentuate movements in asset prices and groups containing an insurer may undertake non-insurance activities that bring risk to the system.

The FCA will have a single strategic objective of protecting and enhancing confidence in the financial system. It will also have three operational objectives, namely: securing an appropriate degree of protection for consumers; promoting efficiency and choice in the market for financial services; and protecting and enhancing the integrity of the financial system. The FCA was originally named the Consumer Protection and Markets Authority and was branded by the Government as a 'strong consumer champion'. This label was heavily criticised by the Treasury Select Committee who considered it to be inappropriate, confusing and potentially dangerous. The crux of their argument was that the promotion of a regulator as a consumer champion would lead consumers to falsely believe that all financial products are risk free, creating moral hazard. Whilst the Government has renamed the authority, it has stressed that the term 'consumer champion' should be viewed in the context of the FCA's role as a focused and proactive conduct regulator, that is entirely independent and impartial.

The FSA's June 2011 paper on the FCA, confirms that the FCA will adopt a more issues and sector-based supervisory approach when compared to the FSA. This will build on changes proposed or already made by the FSA. According to that document, the essence of the new approach can be illustrated by considering the FSA's response to the mis-selling of payment protection insurance (PPI). Whilst the FSA intervened robustly to secure redress of consumer detriment, in the future the FCA will look to ensure that fewer such problems develop in the first place. These sentiments signal a commitment to the approach discussed in *DP11/1: Product Intervention*, which advocated a supervisory strategy involving earlier regulatory intervention and discussions with firms to ensure that new products serve the needs of the customers to whom they are marketed (see **3.5**).

2 *Other obligations of the FSA under FSMA*

3.11 Schedule 1 imposes further overarching obligations on the FSA. It is required to provide for the independent investigation of complaints[1]. It must make an annual report to the Treasury[2]. An annual public meeting is also required to enable this report to be considered[3]. The FSA is required to maintain

1 Paragraphs 7 and 8.
2 Paragraph 10.
3 Paragraph 11.

arrangements to monitor and enforce compliance with the requirements of FSMA[1]. Although the FSA may delegate the performance of these functions to a competent body or person who need not be regulated, it cannot delegate its duty in this respect. The FSA cannot fund its activities by levying fines (and this approach is also confirmed in the draft Bill to create the PRA and FCA). Fines are to be for the benefit of authorised persons but not in terms of reducing fees[2]. The FSA (including its staff) has immunity from civil actions except in the case of bad faith or where the claim arises under the Human Rights Act 1998[3].

3 Consultation

3.12 The FSA has a duty to consult practitioners and consumers on policies and practices[4] and must create a Practitioner Panel and a Consumer Panel[5]. The Treasury may appoint an independent person to conduct a review of how the FSA is carrying out its functions[6]. The Treasury can also arrange independent inquiries where there appears to be a serious risk to the financial system or significant damage (or risk thereof) to the interests of consumers. The situation must also have occurred as a result of a serious failure of the regulatory system and such an inquiry must be in the public interest. This was designed to give a statutory basis to inquiries such as Barings (1995) and Bank of Credit & Commerce International (1991)[7].

4 General prohibition

3.13 Part I of FSMA also sets out one of its core provisions namely 'the general prohibition' **that no person should carry on a regulated activity unless that person is authorised or exempt**[8]. The offences and consequences of breach are also set out[9]. Contravention of the general prohibition is a criminal offence and agreements made will generally be voidable and the customer can claim compensation for any loss[10]. There are limited exceptions when the courts may allow agreements to be upheld[11].

5 Regulated activities

3.14 Part II of the Act and Schedule 2 contain an indication of the activities which are regulated but the specific details are set out by Order. The 'Regulated

1 Paragraph 6.
2 Paragraphs 16 and 17.
3 Paragraph 19.
4 Section 8.
5 Sections 9 and 10.
6 Section 12.
7 Section 14 to 18.
8 Section 19.
9 Section 23.
10 Sections 21 to 27.
11 Section 28.

Activities Order'[1] sets out the activities and investments which are in fact regulated[2]. The activities unsurprisingly include dealing, arranging deals in, and managing investments and investment advice. They also include effecting and carrying out contracts of insurance, deposit taking, custody, establishing collective investment schemes and using computer-based systems for giving investment instructions[3]. The definition of investments includes 'contracts of insurance' amongst a long list[4]. For an activity to be regulated it must be carried on by way of business[5]. The meaning of 'by way of business' in this context is set out in the Financial Services and Markets Act 2000 (Carrying on Regulated Activities by way of Business) Order[6]. A different test applies in relation to insurance mediation activities where if the activities are carried on for remuneration, whether or not they are a sufficient to constitute a business, they will satisfy the test (see the Perimeter Guidance Manual (PERG) 5.4 for further guidance). Similarly, subject to various exemptions (including exemptions for small self administered schemes and certain insured schemes), pension scheme trustees will be carrying on activities by way of business if they do so in running the scheme (eg if they take investment decisions on behalf of the scheme members) (see PERG 10). PERG 2.3.3 provides guidance as to the test of whether an activity is being undertaken by way of business as follows: 'Whether or not an activity is carried on by way of business is ultimately a question of judgement that takes account of several factors (none of which is likely to be conclusive). These include the degree of continuity, the existence of a commercial element, the scale of the activity and the proportion which the activity bears to other activities carried on by the same person but which are not regulated. The nature of the particular regulated activity that is carried on will also be relevant to the factual analysis'.

6 *Financial promotion*

3.15 Section 21 sets out the framework of restrictions on financial promotion. One of the aims in updating the legislation in this area was to bring together the two regimes relating to advertisements and unsolicited (or solicited) calls. One of the side effects of this is to create criminal sanctions for 'real-time' communications. Previously only a breach of section 57 of the Financial Services Act 1986 relating to 'investment advertisements' created a criminal offence. Financial promotions may only be communicated by authorised persons. Alternatively, the communication may be approved by an authorised person. Where the promotion originates outside the UK, the restrictions only apply where it is capable of having an effect in the UK (unless an exemption is avail-

1 SI 2001/544.
2 SI 2001\544.
3 Paragraphs 2 to 9 of Sch 2.
4 Paragraphs 11 to 24 of Sch 2.
5 FSMA, s 22.
6 SI 2001/1177.

able). This is largely intended to apply to internet communications. (See Chapter 5 for detailed coverage of financial promotions and also **3.52**.)

7 *Authorisation and exemption*

3.16 The relevant requirements are set out in Part III. In order to obtain authorisation there would normally be an application for permission under Part IV (under the draft Bill an application for permission will be made under Part 4A). However, other methods are possible, namely 'passporting' under the single market directives (such as the Consolidated Life Assurance Directive[1]); using rights under the Treaty of Rome (where a 'passport' cannot be obtained via the single market provisions, provided the relevant Home State protections are equivalent to those of the Host State); and persons who are otherwise authorised under FSMA[2].

The persons who may be exempted are set out by Order and can include policyholder advocates in reattributions (see **6.40**). The regime for exemption of 'Appointed Representatives' is established under section 39. Banks and building societies which under the Financial Services Act 1986 operated as Appointed Representatives of other product providers now have to be regulated directly for this business (or not do it at all). This is because it is not possible for an authorised person to be exempt for some activities and authorised for others. In practice the banks or building societies involved have achieved much the same result via a subsidiary company being the Appointed Representative rather than the bank or building society itself. The provisions related to Appointed Representatives are explained further in Chapter 4.

8 *Permissions and threshold conditions*

3.17 The requirements relating to applications for permissions to carry on one or more regulated activities are set out in Part IV[3] (as stated above at **3.16**, upon implementation of the draft Bill an application will be made under Part 4A). By obtaining the appropriate permission the applicant will become an authorised person or 'firm' in the context of the FSA Handbook. Permission is only granted once, so if an authorised person wishes to carry on additional activities then they need to vary their permission[4]. This is supported by Schedule 6 which sets out the 'threshold conditions' which an applicant must meet before permission can be granted. These are: requisite legal status of applicant (insurance companies must generally be corporate bodies and not limited liability partnerships); requirement for Registered Office and Head Office to both be in the UK where constituted under the law of any part of the UK; provisions relating to the structure of the applicant's group and any 'close links' (eg parent, subsidiary,

1 Directive 2002/83/EC.
2 Section 31.
3 Sections 40 to 55.
4 Sections 42 and 44.

other group or associated company, not inhibiting regulatory supervision (eg fit and proper and not likely to enable financial crime); adequate resources including effective means to manage risks and that the applicant is 'fit and proper'. Interestingly, under section 42(7), the FSA may specify a *wider* description of regulated activity than that to which the application relates and give permission for the carrying on of a regulated activity which is not included in the relevant application. The FSA has power to place restrictions on the level of that activity[1]. Section 43 relates to the imposition of requirements by the FSA and subsection (3) is of particular interest, as it enables the FSA to extend its requirements to 'activities which are not regulated activities'. This is extended even further by subsection (4) under which requirements may be imposed by reference to the person's relationship with his group or other members of his group.

Interestingly, the draft Bill, adds a new threshold condition to Schedule 6, the so-called business model requirement. The requirement provides that in addition to satisfying the regulator that they are 'fit and proper', any applicant for Part 4A permission will also need to demonstrate that their business model (ie their strategy for doing business) is suitable, having regard to the regulated activities that they carry on or seek to carry on. The Bank of England and FSA Joint Paper stresses that the importance of scrutinising firms' business models is one of the key lessons learnt from previous episodes of insurance distress (in particular, it cites HIH Group and Independent Insurance as examples of attracting business through aggressive pricing, without setting aside sufficient reserves; and Equitable Life, where the firm's business model ran ahead of its capital-raising potential). It should also be noted that the PRA will judge whether a firm can meet the threshold conditions in current and future states of the world.

The FSA can vary or cancel permissions, in certain cases, at the request of the authorised person[2] and can restrict or vary permissions or impose limitations on its own initiative[3]. Variations of permissions can also take place where control over an authorised person changes[4]. The FSA has six months in which to determine an application[5]. Incomplete applications may be refused but if not, the FSA must decide on the application within 12 months of the initial receipt of the application[6].

9 *Approved persons*

3.18 Part V of the Act relates to the performance of regulated activities by such persons as employees and other office holders. This requires approval by the FSA for specified types of functions, known as 'controlled functions' (either significant influence functions (SIFs) or customer functions (CFs)). Such

1 Section 42(7)(a).
2 Section 44.
3 Section 45.
4 Section 46.
5 Section 52(1).
6 Section 52(2).

persons will attain 'approved person' status[1]. 'Controlled functions' are not set out in FSMA but in the Supervision Manual (SUP) 10.5.4R. SIFs are those functions which enable a person to significantly influence the conduct of an authorised person (eg a director) and the CFs are functions which involve dealing directly with customers or dealing with a customer's property (such as stockbrokers or financial advisers). The FSA has the power to prohibit an individual from performing specific function(s)[2]. The FSA has power to issue statements of principle and codes of conduct for approved persons[3] although it is made clear that breach of these will not (in themselves) give a person grounds for action[4]. Further detailed provisions are contained in the FSA Handbook mainly in the Statements of Principle and Codes of Practice for Approved Persons(APER), and the Fit and Proper Test for Approved Persons (FIT). The FSA also now has the power to impose penalties on approved persons[5].

The FSA is in the process of updating the controlled functions. The FSA issued CP 10/3 and PS 10/15 to consult and explain its view that new controlled functions were required to improve governance and reflect proposals made by the Walker review of corporate governance. The FSA is introducing various new functions and amending certain elements of the existing functions. Most notably it is introducing a separate parent entity significant function, (which will apply unless the parent entity is EEA authorised) and refining the non-executive director (NED) functions. The new NED functions include: chairman, senior independent director and the chairman of each of the risk, audit and remuneration committees.

Significant influence function	*Current function*	*New/changed/ unchanged*	*Proposed new function*
Governing functions		New	CF00 (Parent entity SIF)
	CF1 (Director)	Changed	Decreased scope
	CF2 (NED)	Changed	Decreased scope
			CF2a (Chairman)
			CF2b (Senior independent director
		New	CF2c (Chairman of risk committee)
			CF2d (Chairman of audit committee)
			CF2e (Chairman of remuneration committee)

1 Section 59.
2 Section 56.
3 Sections 64 and 65.
4 Section 64(8).
5 FSMA, s 63A (see **3.68**).

Significant influence function	*Current function*	*New/changed/ unchanged*	*Proposed new function*
Governing functions – *contd*	CF3 (Chief executive)	Unchanged	n/a
	CF4 (Partner)		
	CF5 (Director of unincorporated association)		
	CF6 (Small friendly society)		
Required functions	CF8 (Apportionment and oversight)	Unchanged	n/a
	CF10 (Compliance oversight)		
	CF11 (Money laundering reporting)		
	CF12 (Actuarial)		
	CF12a (With-profits actuary)		
	CF12B (Lloyd's actuary)		
Systems and controls functions		New	CF13 (Finance function)
			CF14 (Risk function)
			CF15 (Internal audit function)
	CF28 (Systems and controls)	Changed	Deleted
Significant management function	CF29 (Significant management)	Changed	Increased scope

To ease the administrative burden, if the individuals performing these rules are already carrying on controlled functions, the process will be more of a notification than an application for approval. It was expected that the rules would come into effect in May 2011 but the FSA has deferred them until further notice.

The FSA's stance in relation to those carrying on controlled functions has changed significantly in recent years. The FSA expects firms to be able to provide much more evidence of the due diligence and checks undertaken to ensure that the persons they nominate for such a role are both competent and fit and proper persons. The FSA has stated[1] that it will assess this by looking at; honesty integrity and reputation; competence and capability and financial sound-

1 [CP 10/3] paragraph 4.14.

ness. The FSA also expects to understand the recruitment and selection process to enable it to confirm that these factors have been taken into account. As FSA approval is required before the person undertakes the role, the FSA expects, for senior appointments (eg chairman, CEO and senior independent director), that it is advised at the time of the final shortlisting of candidates.

For SIFs the FSA expects the individual to have and presumably display, certain competencies:

Core competences for SIFs
Market knowledge – awareness and understanding of the wider business, economic and market environment in which the firm operates.
Business strategy and model – awareness and understanding of the firm's business strategy and model appropriate to the role.
Risk management and control – the ability to identify, assess, monitor, control and mitigate risks to the firm. An awareness and understanding of the main risks facing the firm and the role the individual plays in managing them.
Financial analysis and controls – the ability to interpret the firm's financial information, identify key issues based on this information and put in place appropriate controls and measures.
Governance, oversight and controls – the ability to assess the effectiveness of the firm's arrangements to deliver effective governance, oversight and controls in the business and, if necessary, oversee changes in these areas.
Regulatory framework and requirements – awareness and understanding of the regulatory framework in which the firm operates, and the regulatory requirements and expectations relevant to the SIF role.

The FSA will expect to interview candidates as a matter of course if they are being proposed as chairman, CEO, senior independent director, finance director/CEO, risk director/chief risk officer and NEDs of large, complex or high risk businesses. The FSA may also take soundings from representatives of the firm. In CP 10/3[1], the FSA explains that they use the interview both as an assessment tool and to ensure that candidates have a clear understanding of the FSA's objectives, expectations and the candidates' prospective responsibilities. The FSA may also suggest areas for further development to the candidate in order to meet the required standards.

10 Part VII transfers

3.19 Part VII relates to business transfers and its provisions replace section 49 and Schedule 2C of the Insurance Companies Act 1982. Further

1 Paragraph 4.23.

detail about the process is set out in regulations. The provisions are essentially the same as under the previous regime but there are wider powers to modify the rights of both policyholders and third parties as a result of the transfer (see further Section 7 below). As stated above at 3.6, the draft Bill has confirmed that the Government does not intend to alter the substance of the current framework.

11 Financial Services and Markets Tribunal

3.20 Part IX required the establishment of the Financial Services and Markets Tribunal[1]. This has now been replaced by the Upper Tribunal (Tax and Chancery Chamber) which is part of an Independent Tribunal Service but which for FSA purposes is still referred to as the Tribunal. Where the FSA makes a decision with which a party does not agree, he can appeal to the Tribunal. Decisions of the Tribunal can also be appealed in the courts but only on a point of law[2], the Tribunal being treated as a Court of First Instance (ie appeal is to the Court of Appeal).

12 FSA Rules and Information Gathering Powers

3.21 The power to make rules and issue guidance applicable to authorised persons in carrying out regulated activities is set out in Part X, and, in particular, section 138. In practical terms the provisions of this part of FSMA enable the FSA to issue and update its Handbook and underlying Sourcebooks. Section 141 is of specific relevance in that it enables the FSA to make rules, for example, prohibiting insurers from carrying on a specific activity which may include activities which are not regulated. This section specifically makes reference to rules concerning linked benefits (see **3.38**). Section 155 requires the FSA to consult on proposed rule changes. The FSA has the power to make rules in connection with the prevention and detection of money laundering under section 146. Section 157 enables the FSA to issue guidance where considered appropriate to do so in relation to certain specified circumstances.

In Part XI of FSMA the FSA is given wide powers to gather information and documents[3]. The FSA also has investigative powers including powers to appoint competent ('skilled') persons to conduct investigations where the FSA has reasonable grounds to do so[4]. Sections 170 to 175 deal with the powers of persons appointed by the FSA to carry out investigations and the use of information arising from such investigations. Section 176 sets out the powers which the FSA has to enter and search premises (see further Section 5 below).

1 Section 132.
2 Section 137.
3 Section 165.
4 Section 167.

13 Controllers

3.22 Part XII requires persons who propose to acquire control over certain authorised persons to notify and obtain approval from the FSA. Section 178 provides that a person who decides to acquire or increase control over a UK authorised person must give the FSA notice in writing before doing so. The notice must be in a form prescribed by the FSA. The FSA has to consult with any relevant EEA authorities. Normally the FSA has 60 working days to consider the application but it may, provided it does so by the 50th working day, ask for further information. This can add another 20 days to the process. If the Controller is outside the EEA or not regulated under one of the main EU single market directives (eg Undertakings for Collective Investment in Transferable Securities (UCITS), Insurance, Markets in Financial Instruments Directive (MiFID), Reinsurance or Banking), this period can be up to 30 days.

The thresholds for assessing control are 10%, 20%, 30% and 50% for insurers. For insurance intermediaries there is a single 20% threshold. It is also necessary to take into account holdings of parties acting 'in concert'.

14 The Financial Services and Markets Compensation Scheme

3.23 Under this scheme compensation will be payable to customers who suffer financial loss as a result of the inability of an authorised person to meet its liabilities. The Scheme derives its statutory basis from Part XV of FSMA. It replaced five pre-existing schemes and, interestingly, from a life assurance perspective, it replaced the Policyholders Protection Acts. The FSA is under a duty to establish a company to manage the new Scheme. The Board must be appointed by but be independent of the FSA. The Board is required to report at least annually to the FSA on the discharge of its functions[1]. Section 214 sets out the broad requirements of the Scheme. The detailed provisions are set out in rules[2] and are considered further in Section 6 below.

15 Financial Ombudsman Service

3.24 The relevant provisions are set out in Part XVI. The FSA is required to establish a single, compulsory ombudsman scheme for speedy and informal resolution of disputes between members of the public and authorised persons. The jurisdiction of the FOS extends to certain small businesses which, in the insurance sector, was a new feature. Section 226 provides for a compulsory jurisdiction which applies to regulated activities. The FOS will also have a voluntary jurisdiction for certain other types of dispute[3]. The FOS replaced eight existing

1 Section 218.

2 See Consultation Paper 58, Consultation Paper 86 and the policy statement 'Financial Services Compensation Scheme Funding Rules' (September 2001). Also, the Financial Services and Markets Act 2000 (Compensation Scheme: Electing Participants) Regulations 2001, SI 2001/1783, as amended by SI 2003/1476, SI 2003/2066, and modified by SI 2001/3084.

3 Section 227.

schemes including, amongst others, the PIA Ombudsman and the Insurance Ombudsman, although the Pensions Ombudsman remains as a separate statutory scheme, at least for now. A motivating factor for the creation of one single scheme was the reduced potential for confusion and overlap which existed with numerous schemes. It should also be noted that as a result of transitional arrangements, membership of these previous schemes (eg for insurers, the insurance ombudsman scheme) effectively grandfathers such activities into the FOS Scheme, so that the FOS has jurisdiction in relation to such activities.

16 Auditors and Actuaries

3.25 Part XXII concerns the appointment of auditors and actuaries by authorised persons and their responsibilities. Part XXIII requires the FSA to maintain a public record of authorised (and certain other) persons, and makes provision regarding the purpose for which confidential information may be disclosed by and to the FSA. See also SUP 4 which deals with the appointment of actuaries by life companies (see also **6.49**).

17 Action taken by the FSA

3.26 The procedures which the FSA must follow when giving notices of proposed actions under various provisions of FSMA are set out in Part XXVI. This includes such things as decisions not to give permission or to refuse applications for approvals and decisions to take regulatory action, such as imposing penalties and making public statements. The FSA must issue a warning notice in accordance with certain prescribed requirements[1]. Such a notice must be in writing and set out the reasons for the issuing of the notice. The FSA must give the person in receipt of the warning notice at least 28 days in which to make representations in respect of the notice (under the draft Bill the time period to make representations will be reduced to at least 14 days). Following a warning notice there may be a decision notice. This will set out in writing the FSA's decision and the reasons for that decision. The FSA is also required to explain any right the person receiving the decision notice has to refer the case to the Tribunal.

The disciplinary measures available to the FSA are set out in Part XIV. The FSA can publish statements about how authorised persons have contravened certain specific requirements. The FSA can also impose fines on authorised persons who have contravened the rules. The FSA is under an obligation to publish a statement of its policy in respect of the imposition and level of such fines which it has done in the Decisions Procedures and Penalties Manual (DEPP) (See Section 5).

18 Misleading Statements

3.27 Part XXVII creates certain offences, including making misleading statements and supplying false information to the FSA. This aspect of FSMA is

1 Section 387.

clearly of particular relevance in connection with financial promotions. Section 397 makes it an offence for a person to deliberately make a misleading statement with a view to influencing another person's decisions.

19 Professional firms

3.28 Under the Financial Services Act 1986, another means of obtaining authorisation was certification by a recognised professional body (RPB) such as the Law Society, the Institute of Chartered Accountants and the Institute of Actuaries. However, the position changed under FSMA, and some firms previously regulated by such bodies needed to be authorised directly by the FSA. Where the activities undertaken by the professional firm, which might otherwise necessitate authorisation, are merely 'incidental' to the firm's professional services such activities will be 'exempt regulated activities'. Provided further that certain detailed conditions are met, the professional firm will be able to carry on exempt regulated activities under the supervision and regulation of their professional bodies ('designated professional bodies') and will not need direct FSA authorisation. The FSA is under a duty to keep itself informed about the way in which designated professional bodies supervise and regulate the carrying on of exempt regulated activities by exempt professional firms and the way in which exempt professional firms carry on exempt regulated activities. The relevant statutory provisions are set out in Part XX of FSMA.

D The FSA Handbook

1 Content and interpretation

3.29 The FSA's rules are contained in its Handbook and are directed at 'firms' (eg authorised persons including those acquiring authorised person status using EU passporting rights). The FSA Handbook is made under Part X of FSMA. The Handbook runs to thousands of pages and can be difficult to navigate if you are not familiar with it. The FSA has issued a Reader's Guide which, whilst not formal guidance, is a very useful starting point in trying to get to grips with the Handbook.

The first point to make about the Handbook is that the definitive version is in the statutory instruments effecting changes, called the rule making instruments. In practice, as the FSA consolidates the web version of the Handbook on a daily basis, the web version is likely to be the most up-to date version and is the version used most in practice.

Sections of the Handbook are known as sourcebooks or manuals. The FSA's guide makes clear that all of these sourcebooks and manuals (modules) fall into seven blocks. In addition there are sector specific tailored handbooks for small firms aimed at specific industry sectors.

Block 1 of the Handbook deals with overarching requirements for all authorised persons and approved persons. This block includes the 11 FSA Principles (see **3.30**) and the rules relating to the conditions for authorisation and the systems and controls requirement.

Block 2 sets out the Prudential requirements for insurers. This is currently the Interim Prudential Sourcebook for Insurers (IPRU (INS)), the General Prudential Sourcebook (GENPRU) and the Prudential Sourcebook for Insurers (INSPRU).

Block 3 contains most of the requirements that apply to firms in conducting their day-to-day business. For insurers, predominantly the Conduct of Business Sourcebook (COBS) and the Insurance: Conduct of Business Sourcebook (ICOBS) but including Client Assets (CASS).

Block 4 consists of modules describing the operation of the FSA's authorisation, supervisory and disciplinary functions. These include the provisions on enforcement action by the FSA.

Block 5 deals with complaints and compensation.

Block 6 are specialist sourcebooks, including the one for collective investment schemes.

Block 7 provides the sourcebooks relating to the UK official list (eg including the listing rules).

In addition, in order to reduce the size of the Handbook, the FSA has removed some guidance from the Handbook and issued regulatory guides. The main one is PERG which gives guidance in relation to the need for authorisation. The Enforcement Guide (EG) is also useful to understand how the FSA exercises its disciplinary and other powers. There is also a regulatory guide which explains how the FSA regards its powers in relation to unfair contract terms.

Each module of the FSA Handbook is divided into Chapters. A Chapter is divided into sections and each section is divided into paragraphs. Generally each module, or in some cases each Chapter or section, will specify who it applies to.

The FSA Handbook contains three kinds of provisions: rules, evidential provisions and guidance. A rule clearly indicates a binding duty on the firm and is generally issued under section 138. If a firm complies with an evidential provision, it will tend to establish a firm's compliance with the rule in question[1]. However, it is still possible for the firm to show that it has achieved compliance with the rule to which it is linked by some other means. Guidance[2], although not binding, may be used to flesh out a particular rule. Sometimes a specific example will be cited. However, it does not create an expectation that a firm must follow the guidance to ensure compliance and the burden of proof is not put onto the firm. However, where a firm has followed current guidance on a particular subject, then the firm will usually have the benefit of a 'safe harbour' from disciplinary action provided this is in the circumstances contemplated by that guidance. In the text itself the three kinds of provision are referred to by the identification letters 'R', 'E' and 'G' and each has its own specific typographic design. Where certain words or phrases have particular meanings which are defined in the Glossary part of the Handbook, they are set out in italics in the text.

1 Section 149.
2 Section 157.

2 FSA Principles for business

3.30

Table 1: The Principles

1 Integrity	A firm must conduct its business with integrity.
2 Skill, care and diligence	A firm must conduct its business with due skill, care and diligence.
3 Management and control	A firm must take reasonable care to organise and control its affairs responsibly and effectively, with adequate risk management systems.
4 Financial prudence	A firm must maintain adequate financial resources.
5 Market conduct	A firm must observe proper standards of market conduct.
6 Customers' interests	A firm must pay due regard to the interests of its customers and treat them fairly.
7 Communications with clients	A firm must pay due regard to the information needs of its clients and communicate information to them in a way which is clear, fair and not misleading.
8 Conflicts of interest	A firm must manage conflicts of interest fairly, both between itself and its customers and between a customer and another client.
9 Customers: relationships of trust	A firm must take reasonable care to ensure the suitability of its advice and discretionary decisions for any customer who is entitled to rely upon its judgment.
10 Clients' assets	A firm must arrange adequate protection for clients' assets when it is responsible for them.
11 Relations with regulators	A firm must deal with its regulators in an open and cooperative way, and must disclose to the FSA appropriately anything relating to the firm of which the FSA would reasonably expect notice.

Even before plans were announced to replace the FSA with the PRA and FCA, the FSA had started to move away from Principles-based regulation. Whilst in one sense Principles-based regulation gave flexibility, in another, it provided uncertainty (or wriggle room). It will be interesting to see what happens to the FSA's treating customers fairly (TCF) initiative which was founded on its Principle 6, and developed into a broad, and changing requirement, to treat customers fairly. It has advanced a long way since the FSA's original paper on the subject and it is now clear that firms must embed the Principle of TCF into their business. TCF requires an end-to-end process or, as it is often described, looking at the complete customer journey or outcomes. In practice, it requires firms to analyse their product design against their target markets and against complaints. In relation to complaints, it also means that customers in the same situation need to be treated consistently making one-off ex gratia payments difficult.

It would appear from DP11/1 and FS11/3 that TCF will continue to be used by the FCA going forward but the precise mix of Principles and detailed rules remains to be seen.

3 Conduct of Business Sourcebook (COBS)

3.31 In practical terms, the parts of the FSA Handbook which have most impact on an ongoing basis on life companies are the Prudential rules (GENPRU and INSPRU) and the conduct of business rules (COBS and ICOBS). The most relevant sourcebook for the day-to-day business of life offices is COBS which applies to the marketing of all life contracts other than pure protection (eg term assurance) products. The sale of 'non-investment' life contracts ('pure protection contracts') is covered by ICOBS, which applies primarily to general insurance.

COBS effectively continues the regulatory regime in place since 1988 under the Financial Services Act 1986, but which since 2001 has been significantly revised to reflect the ending of polarisation, the implementation of the Distance Marketing Directive, the Insurance Mediation Directive (IMD) and more recently MiFID.

When an adviser and a potential customer first meet, COBS requires that the adviser disclose his or her status (that is, whether advice is given on the whole of the relevant market, from a limited range of providers or on the products of a single product provider). The adviser must also set out the basis upon which charges are made. The FSA has a pro forma disclosure document called the Services and Costs Disclosure Document (SCDD) but its use post 1 November 2007 is not compulsory. Only firms offering advice on a whole of market basis and offering clients the option to pay fees can refer to themselves as 'independent' advisers. This is dealt with in more detail in Chapter 4 which also explains proposed changes as part of the FSA's Retail Distribution Review.

COBS also contains the rules governing financial promotions. Different regulations apply to real time promotions (face-to-face meetings (solicited or unsolicited) and telephone calls), non-real time promotions (brochures, sales aids, emails, websites) and direct offer promotions (mailing packs or magazine and newspaper advertisements which can lead directly to a purchase). This is dealt with in more detail in Chapter 5.

Advisers must ascertain the personal and financial circumstances of their client to satisfy the 'suitability' requirements. Based on this information, the adviser must select the most suitable product from the relevant range (this being, the range available to them or the whole of the market as the case may be). When a personal recommendation is made, the adviser must issue a 'demands and needs' statement to the client unless he has issued him with a 'suitability report'.

Clients must be provided with a 'Key Features document' prior to conclusion of the contract which sets out the main features and risks of the product in question. The form and content is prescribed in COBS Chapter 13 and is considered in Chapter 5. The client must also be told the amount of commission payable to the adviser if the transaction proceeds, unless the adviser is being remunerated solely by payment of a fee from the client.

One point to note in relation to COBS (and ICOBS), is that they both contain a provision which allows third party administrators (TPAs) to provide services in the name of the product provider, even where that service provider is itself authorised or is an appointed representative and might otherwise have to disclose details about itself and its regulated status. For this exemption (which is in Annex 1 paragraph 6 of COBS and ICOBS) to apply the provider must have agreed (vis a vis the customer), to take responsibility for the TPA. There must also be an outsourcing agreement in place providing that the TPA will act on the provider's instructions in relation to such activities and will cooperate in relation to the management of complaints, even after the outsourcing arrangement has been terminated.

4 *Insurance: Conduct of Business Sourcebook (ICOBS)*

3.32 'Term' or 'temporary' life assurance with no investment element (eg surrender value) can be governed by the ICOBS sourcebook. Its provisions are mostly similar to the COBS sourcebook, although generally less prescriptive (eg there is no requirement to disclose commission to consumers). The sale of general insurance business (technically known as 'non-investment insurance contracts') became regulated with effect from 14 January 2005. ICOBS was also used to implement the IMD. To seek to provide a level playing field for the various sectors of the industry, the Treasury and the FSA also decided that it was necessary to regulate the sales activities of insurance companies carrying on insurance mediation activities even though insurers are not covered by the IMD. ICOBS only applies to insurers and intermediaries, although insurers are predominantly regulated only in relation to sales to consumers.

ICOBS sets out the information required to be given to customers when first meeting with an intermediary which can be through the issue of an 'initial disclosure document' (IDD) which details the services a firm can offer and the charges to be made. The intermediary must also prepare a 'statement of demands and needs' which analyses the customer's requirements and sets out the proposed solution together with the intermediary's reasons for selecting the particular policy. ICOBS also details the documentation to be provided to the customer before completion of the contract and the documentation to be issued upon completion of the contract. See Chapters 4 and 5 for more details.

5 *Other relevant parts of the FSA Handbook*

3.33 PERG gives guidance about the circumstances in which authorisation is required, or exempt person status is available.

SUP governs the ongoing relationship between the FSA and the authorised person. The FSA has stated that it will take a 'risk-based approach' to supervision (ie direct most attention to the greatest risk) and has emphasised, partly as a result of fears expressed by the industry, that the cost burden on firms should be proportionate to the benefits. More specifically, this manual deals with supervisory provisions relating to approved persons, auditors, waivers, individual guidance, notifications (eg of problems) and reporting. The Statements of Principle and Code of Practice for Approved Persons (APER) and the Fit and Proper Test for Approved Persons (FIT) set out standards in this area. The general reporting requirement is in SUP 15.3.

DEPP and EG describe the FSA's enforcement powers under the Act and set out its policies for using those powers, including the new basis for imposing penalties. Schedule 1 to FSMA requires the FSA to 'maintain arrangements for enforcing the provisions of, or rules made under, this Act'[1]. The governing section of FSMA is section 395. The statutory notices are warning notices[2], decision notices and further decision notices[3], notices of discontinuance[4], final notices[5] and supervisory notices[6]. In the guidance, the FSA emphasises the need for an open and cooperative relationship between the FSA and those it regulates. The FSA states that it will seek to exercise its enforcement powers in a transparent, proportionate and consistent manner and that it seeks to ensure fair treatment when exercising its enforcement powers.

Senior Management Arrangements, Systems and Controls (SYSC) provides an obligation on firms to apportion responsibility, in particular in relation to controlled functions of senior management. It also requires and gives guidance in relation to the firm's systems and controls. A firm must take reasonable care to establish systems and controls which are appropriate to its business[7]. What is appropriate will depend on the nature, scale and complexity of the business. The firm is required by SYSC to assess its systems and controls. Guidance on the areas likely to be covered is set out in SYSC 3.2 and includes delegation, financial crime, the need for a risk assessment function and the provision of management information to the governing body, suitability of employees and agents, on audit committee and internal audit. SYSC also includes much of the specific rules and guidance in relation to risk policies and risk management (SYSC 11–17).

It is recommended[8] that firms have appropriate arrangements for business continuity to ensure that they can meet their regulatory obligations in the event of a disaster or other unforeseen interruption. These arrangements should be updated regularly and tested to ensure their effectiveness. Fundamental to good systems and controls is the keeping of adequate records and adequate security arrangements in relation to them. There is a specific section of SYSC dealing with the

1 Paragraph 6(3) of Sch 1.
2 Section 387.
3 Section 388.
4 Section 389.
5 Section 390.
6 Section 395(13).
7 SYSC 3.1.1.
8 SYSC 3.2.19.

systems and controls advisable to manage operational risk[1]. This includes, in particular, requirements relating to outsourcing.

6 FSA Outsourcing Rules

3.34 Material outsourcing is defined as outsourcing services of such importance that weakness or failure of the service would cast serious doubt on the firm's compliance with the FSA's Principles or the threshold conditions. SUP 15.3.8G(i)(e) contains guidance that a firm should notify the FSA when it intends to enter into or significantly change a material outsourcing arrangement.

SYSC 13.9 contains the FSA's guidelines on outsourcing, including 'due diligence' requirements in relation to any proposed outsourcing supplier. Similar requirements will apply under Solvency II (see **7.67**). This is to ensure that the supplier is suitably solvent and has the requisite expertise. The guidance also sets out issues to be considered and covered in the contract between the parties. The areas to be covered include the following:

(1) Need to allow firm to monitor and control provision of the service (eg service levels, reporting, escalation processes, key employees) including qualitatively and by independent assessment/benchmarking.

(2) Process for making changes to the services (eg change management, volume, type, adding new services).

(3) Right to terminate or change the agreement in the event of:

 (a) a change of control of the service provider;

 (b) a significant change in service provider's, business and operations; or

 (c) inadequate services that may lead to the firm being unable to meet its regulatory obligations.

(4) Adherence to the firm's policy(ies) particularly if the supplier's staff are on the premises (eg IT security).

(5) Information ownership rights and confidentiality agreements (ie ownership rights/escrow arrangements for third party software used in provision of the services).

(6) Adequacy of guarantees and indemnities.

(7) Business continuity.

(8) Exit management.

(9) Access rights to and cooperation with internal auditors, external auditors or actuaries and the FSA.

(10) Cooperation with new service provider.

(11) PI cover (level, obligation to maintain and to evidence).

1 SYSC 3A.

A firm should notify the FSA of significant operational exposures, changes to its organisation infrastructure or the wider business environment. It should also advise the FSA if it needs to invoke its disaster recovery arrangements.

A firm cannot merely rely on the fact that the outsourced service provider is regulated or is a member of its group although this may be a mitigating factor and normally reduces the amount of due diligence required.

The Solvency II requirements for outsourcing of critical or important functions are very similar to the current UK requirements in SYSC, particularly those for MiFID firms. They require adequate due diligence in relation to the service provider and contractual terms which set out clearly the services to be provided, give the insurer the ability to direct how the services should be provided, and comply with applicable legal and confidentiality requirements (including data protection provisions). There are also additional obligations. So, for example, the service provider will be required by the outsourcing contract to answer questions from the regulator (in addition to co-operating and allowing access to records and premises) and to disclose 'developments' that may have a material impact on its ability to perform the contract. It will also be a requirement of such contracts that the service provider can only terminate on notice which is sufficient to allow the insurer time to 'find an alternative solution'. There will also be a requirement to verify that the staff of the service provider are chosen on the basis of criteria that give reasonable assurance that they are sufficiently qualified and reliable. The insurer should have the right to terminate the outsourcing contract with a reasonable period of notice if for any reason the services rendered shall prove to be inadequate. The service provider can only terminate by giving a period of notice sufficiently long to enable the undertaking to find an alternative solution.

7 *CASS*

3.35 CASS sets out requirements in relation to the holding of client money or the holding by an intermediary of money which belongs to an insurer. The rules provide that a long term insurance company is not subject to the client money rules (either the general rules in Chapter 7 of CASS or the insurance mediation rules in Chapter 5 of CASS) in carrying on any activity for which it has a permission (which will normally include some insurance mediation activities). Intermediaries conducting designated investment business may hold monies in respect of life assurance business subject to the rules in CASS 5 (rather than the CASS 7 rules which apply to other designated investment business eg MiFID business). In high level terms, and because life offices rarely permit intermediaries to hold money on the life office's behalf, the rules in CASS 5 effectively require that client money be placed in a statutory or non-statutory trust account that cannot be used to pay creditors if the firm fails. The FSA is in the process of making changes in relation to the client money rules as a result of the effect of its rules being challenged in ongoing litigation relating to the failure of Lehman Brothers.

D Misleading statements and practices

3.36 Section 397 FSMA broadly replaced section 47 of the 1986 Act. Under section 397(2) it is an offence for any person to:

(a) make a statement, promise or forecast which he knows to be misleading, false or deceptive in a material particular (or to recklessly, dishonestly or otherwise, do any of the above);

(b) dishonestly conceal any material facts for the purpose of inducing; or

(c) to be reckless as to whether it may induce, another person (whether or not the person to whom the statement, promise or forecast is made or from whom the facts are concealed) to enter or to offer to enter into, or to refrain from entering into, a 'relevant agreement' or to exercise, or refrain from exercising, any rights conferred by a 'relevant investment'.

It is a defence for the person to show that the statement, promise or forecast was made in conformity with price stabilising rules or control of information rules. It is also an offence under section 397(3) for a person to do an act or engage in a course of conduct which creates a false or misleading impression as to the market in or the price or value of any relevant investments if he does so for the purpose of creating that impression and thereby inducing another person to acquire, dispose of, subscribe for or underwrite those investments or to refrain from doing so or to exercise, or refrain from exercising, any rights conferred by those investments. It is a defence if the person 'reasonably believed' he was not creating a false or misleading impression or that the conduct was for the purpose of price stabilisation and in conformance with price stabilising rules or the conduct was in conformity with control of information rules[1].

The act complained of under section 397(2) must have been made in or from the UK and the intended recipient must be in the UK or the agreement is or would be entered into or the rights are or would be exercised in the UK. The act or the course of conduct under section 397(3) engaged in, must have been in the UK, and the false or misleading impression created there.

E Actions for damages

3.37 By virtue of section 71(1), contravention of certain sections of FSMA[2] is actionable by a person who suffers loss as a result, subject to the defences and other incidents applying to actions for breach of statutory duty. Section 71(2) potentially extends this power to a person who is not a 'private person'. A person is not guilty of a criminal offence by virtue of section 71.

In addition, contravention of rules issued under FSMA (but not per se the FSA Principles) is actionable by a private person who suffers loss as a result of the contravention, subject to the defences applying to actions for breach of statutory

1 Section 397(5).
2 Section 56(6) or 59(1) or (2).

duty[1]. In prescribed cases the provisions may be extended to non-private persons. In respect of certain rules no actions for damages will lie, such as the financial resources rules and listing rules[2].

F Permitted links

1 Linked contracts

3.38 Linked Long Term contracts are defined as 'contracts under which the benefits payable to the policyholder are wholly or partly to be determined by reference to the value of, or the income from, property of any description (whether or not specified in the contract) or by reference to fluctuations in, or in an index of, the value of property of any description (whether or not so specified).'[3] The reference to 'wholly or partly' in this definition is intended to catch contracts which are otherwise conventional (ie not linked) policies but where, for example, benefits are linked to the value of an index, such as the retail prices index.

The rules which determine the permissible investments of UK unit linked insurance funds are[4] contained in COBS 21[5]. The rules apply to linked long terms contracts and to Class VII business and are often referred to as the 'permitted links' rules. The COBS rules incorporate high level principles in relation to the operation of unit linked funds. One of the principles is that firms must look at the substance of any transaction rather than the legal form. Underlying all of the principles is the need to treat customers fairly by considering the effect of any decision on them 'first and foremost'. Although the rules begin with the high level principles they are supplemented by some fairly detailed rules, mainly incorporated into the definition of each type of 'permitted link'. The actual 'permitted links' are specified in COBS 21.3. These are divided into those linked to the values of certain defined types of property (for example, via unit trusts, open-ended investment companies or an internal linked insurance fund) and those linked to the performance of certain defined indices. The former known as 'property linked' assets and the latter as 'index linked'.

The categories of permitted assets are: approved securities; listed securities; permitted unlisted securities; permitted land and property; permitted loans; permitted deposits; permitted scheme interests; cash; permitted units; permitted stock lending; and permitted derivatives contracts. Each of these terms is defined in the FSA Handbook Glossary and they are considered further below.

The rules should allow a greater range of both listed and potentially unlisted investments than were allowed under the predecessor rules. The rules also permit investment in property in countries that were not permitted under the previous rules. It should also be noted that it is expected that the permitted links rules will

1 Section 150.
2 The Financial Services and Markets Act 2000 (Right of Action) Regulations 2001, SI 2001/2256.
3 FSA Handbook Glossary.
4 Subject to certain historical exceptions in COBS 21.1.2.
5 See also prudential requirements described in **7.39**.

need to be changed when Solvency II is implemented. This may mean they become based on the UCITS rules (see **7.76**).

The permitted links rules also apply to business effected through a UK branch even if the insurer is an EEA insurer. It is arguable, however, that these rules constitute prudential requirements and that an EEA insurer would be able to show that this is a matter reserved to its home state regulator.

2 High level principles

The high level principles in COBS 21.2 include requirements on a firm to ensure that:

(1) the value of its permitted links are determined fairly and accurately;

(2) its linked assets are capable of being realised in time for it to meet it obligations to linked policyholders and are matched to its liabilities as required by the close matching rules in INSPRU (1.1.35 and 3.1.57-59 – which in addition to requiring matching make clear that a firm is not permitted to hold different assets and to cover the mis matching by holding excess assets);

(3) there is no reasonable foreseeable risk that the aggregate value of any of its linked funds will become negative;

(4) it notifies policyholders of the risk profile and investment strategy of linked funds at the outset and before making any material changes;

(5) its systems and controls and other resources are appropriate for the risks associated with its linked assets and linked liabilities;

(6) when selecting linked assets that its systems and controls and other resources are appropriate to ensure that there is no reasonably foreseeable risk of a conflict of interest with its linked policyholders and that if such conflict does arise, the firm takes reasonable steps to ensure that the interests of policyholders are safeguarded; and

(7) in applying the rules in COBS 21, it considers the economic effect of its permitted linked and linked assets ahead of their legal form.

3 Readily realisable

3.39 There were a number of issues with the permitted links rules which the FSA inherited in 2001. One of the issues which caused most difficulty in practice, was the requirement that both listed and unlisted securities be capable of realisation at 97.5% of their value within seven days. A similar requirement applied to the underlying assets of collective investment schemes other than UCITS. A new principle (COBS 21.2.5) provides that all linked assets need to be capable of being realised in time for the firm to meet its obligations to linked policyholders. The FSA indicated in its Policy Statement 07/17 that this requirement and the need to realise assets in the short term (which is a requirement for 'permitted unlisted securities'), could be met if a firm satisfies itself that it could not reasonably foresee any circumstance in which it would need to realise the asset at a few days' notice and would not be able to do so. It is worth noting that the value of unlisted securities in a unit linked fund is no longer subject to a 10% limit.

4 Collective investment schemes and insurance funds

3.40 It should also be possible to invest in a range of collective investment schemes (*permitted scheme interests*). UK authorised funds, non UCITS retail schemes and all 'recognised schemes' (as that term is defined in FSMA, so allowing EEA UCITS, specified schemes from Jersey, Guernsey and the Isle of Man and individually recognised schemes) are permitted without any 'look through' to their underlying assets. In addition, linked funds may be invested in a Qualified Investor Scheme (or its EEA equivalent) or any other scheme, including unregulated schemes, that invest only in permitted links and publish their prices regularly, but such investment is limited to 20% of the gross assets of the linked fund. Institutional policyholders (limited to trustees of defined benefit occupational schemes) may also invest in both such schemes but without the 20% limit.

Internal funds managed by the insurance company or by someone for whose acts and omissions the insurer is responsible are also permitted (*permitted units*) provided they only invest in permitted links and the insurer effectively takes responsibility for them (see definition of *permitted units*).

5 Property

3.41 There are also rules on the type of real property a unit linked fund can invest in, whether directly or indirectly. These place greater emphasis on the insurer to satisfy itself that the underlying property market in the relevant country is appropriate and that any structures used to hold property do not pose a materially greater risk than a direct holding. Unregulated property funds will be permitted, subject to the conditions for unregulated collective investment schemes, including the 20% limit referred to above for such collective investment schemes.

6 Gearing

3.42 A number of other issues previously dealt with in guidance appended to IPRU (INS) are covered by the COBS rules. COBS 21.2.3 provides that a firm must ensure that there is no reasonably foreseeable risk that the aggregate value of any of its linked funds will become negative. There is also an explicit gearing restriction in relation to property funds, of 10% of the gross value of the linked fund (excluding UCITS, UK authorised and recognised schemes). This 10% restriction does not however apply to funds held on behalf of an individual beneficiary where they, or someone acting on their behalf, request that the firm hold such investment (eg 'member directed' investments such as Self Invested Personal Pensions (SIPPS)).

7 Derivatives and stock lending

3.43 Derivative contracts are permitted, subject to certain safeguards. Broadly, they must be approved derivatives for the purposes of INSPRU 3.2

(see Chapter 7) and be based on or used in connection with assets which are themselves permitted links. The terms for approval under INSPRU mean that derivatives must be used for efficient portfolio management or reduction of investment risk; they must be covered and be listed on a regulated market. If not listed they must be written by an approved counterparty (eg an EU authorised bank or relevant firm authorised to write derivatives) on terms which permit valuation and they must be capable of being readily closed out at their current valuation. The FSA has also responded to comments about the restrictive nature of the definition of efficient portfolio management (EPM) as part of the test of whether a derivative contract is a permitted investment for a linked fund. For the purposes of the permitted links rules, the definition of EPM is now stated to be wider than that for admissibility of non linked fund assets but it is not clear what this is intended to permit. The FSA commentary in the relevant policy statement (PS07/17) does not shed any further light on this.

3.44 One of the other issues formerly dealt with by guidance is the use of linked funds' assets for stock lending. The previous guidance is now incorporated into the rules together with an extended list of stock lending counterparties. It makes clear that where a unit linked fund bears the risk of stock lending it should receive all the profit (less expenses) and even where it does not bear the risk of loss, it should receive fair recompense for the fact that its assets have been used.

8 Reinsurance

3.45 The FSA has also introduced requirements relating to reinsurance of unit linked obligations. As a result of changes in insurance insolvency rules, direct policyholders of a reinsurer have priority over other non secured debts (eg reinsurance obligations)[1]. In practice many insurers seek to create the same effect by use of suitable legal charges, but (reinsurance) policyholders would not normally be aware of this. Policyholders must now be made aware of the implications of any credit exposure they face in relation to the insolvency of a reinsurer. The firm must also continue to discharge it responsibilities under the contract as if there was no reinsurance (see **8.5**). This will include monitoring the way the reinsurer manages the business. If the investment risk on the unit linked contract is with the policyholder, this obligation should not, however, require the firm to hold additional capital.

9 Notification of failure to comply

3.46 Firms no longer need to apply for a waiver in respect of a breach of the permitted link rules. Firms are now required to notify the FSA of any failure to comply with the rules whether or not it is material to the size of the fund. However,

1 Insurers (Reorganisation and Winding Up) Regulations 2004, SI 2004/353.

COBS 21.2.11 G makes clear that in considering whether any action is necessary, the FSA will have regard to the extent to which the cause is exceptional or temporary in nature (eg action is unlikely to be required for a short term suspension).

SECTION 2 FSMA AND THE CONDUCT OF LIFE ASSURANCE BUSINESS

A Life policies treated as investments under FSMA

3.47 Insurance contracts, including life assurance contracts, whether or not they are investment orientated, will fall within the definition of 'investments' by virtue of Schedule 2, Part II, paragraph 20 of FSMA. This refers to 'contracts of insurance'. This term is divided into 'contracts of general insurance' and 'contracts of long-term insurance' by the Regulated Activities Order[1] which sets out (in Part II of Schedule 1) the various 'contracts of long-term insurance'. This essentially replicates the previous Schedule 1 of the Insurance Companies Act 1982. For the purpose of the FSA's conduct of business rules, long term contracts are further divided into pure protection contracts and everything else, namely a qualifying contracts of insurance. The ambit of 'long-term insurance' includes life and annuity, linked long-term, permanent health insurance, capital redemption contracts and pension fund management. Life companies are also able to conduct Class I or II general insurance (accident and sickness) on a supplementary basis[2]. The categories of long-term business are as follows:

I Life and annuity	Contracts of insurance on human life or contracts to pay annuities on human life, but excluding (in each case) contracts within paragraph III.
II Marriage and birth	Contracts of insurance to provide a sum on marriage or the formation of a civil partnership or on the birth of a child, being contracts expressed to be in effect for a period of more than one year.
III Linked long term	Contracts of insurance on human life or contracts to pay annuities on human life where the benefits are wholly or party to be determined by references to the value of, or the income from, property of any description (whether or not specified in the contracts) or by reference to fluctuations in, or in an index of, the value of property of any description (whether or not so specified).
IV Permanent health	Contracts of insurance providing specified benefits against risks of persons becoming incapacitated in consequence of sustaining injury as a result of an accident or of an accident of a specified class or of sickness or infirmity, being contracts that—

1 SI 2001\544.
2 IPRU (INS) 11.6(b).

	(a)	are expressed to be in effect for a period of not less than five years, or until the normal retirement age for the persons concerned, or without limit of time; and
	(b)	either are not expressed to be terminable by the insurer, or are expressed to be so terminable only in special circumstances mentioned in the contract.
V Tontines	Tontines.	
VI Capital redemption contracts	Capital redemption contracts, where effected or carried out by a person who does not carry on a banking business, and otherwise carries on a regulated activity of the kind specified by article 10(1) or (2).	
VII Pension fund management	(a)	Pension fund management contracts; and
	(b)	pension fund management contracts which are combined with contracts of insurance covering either conservation of capital or payment of a minimum interest
	where effected or carried out by a person who does not carry on a banking business, and otherwise carries on a regulated activity of the kind specified by article 10(1) or (2). (FN of the Regulated Activities Order).	
VIII Collective insurance, etc	Contracts of a kind referred to in article 1(2)(e) of the first life insurance directive.	
IX Social insurance	Contracts of a kind referred to in article 1(3) of the first life insurance directive.	

3.48 The categories of insurance business are known by their class names so, for example, life business is generally Class I or Class III. Conventional 'whole of life' business (eg where a fixed premium is agreed for a specified benefit with or without profit) is much less common these days. More common, is business written to a term and used for protection purposes. Class III (unit linked business) is mainly used for investment contracts. The idea behind unit-linked business is that the customer pays their money into an investment fund. The charges for benefits (eg life or sickness cover) are variable and are charged to this fund. The approach was much more attractive than conventional business whilst inflation and investment growth were high and mortality and morbidity charges were lower. At the time of writing, because of the certainty and simplicity of conventional whole of life or term life and sickness contracts, they have become popular again and unit linked contracts are used less for the purposes of protection. Class II business is conversely not popular.

Class IV business includes income protection or health insurance contracts designed to provide a fixed sum when a person is incapacitated and cannot work due to injury or sickness. Class IV business is notable as it also forms part of the definition of Class 2 general business, the two being mutually exclusive. It is also the only class of long-term business which is explicitly required to be a long-term contract. Income protection or permanent health insurance (PHI), will be long-term business where it is expressed to be in place for at least five years, to retirement, or it is whole of life (ie no limit is expressed) and the contract only allows the insurer to terminate it in special circumstances set out in the contract. In practice, a life office would not therefore have a right to terminate such a contract. Conversely, where a contract contains a general right to terminate (ie one which is not just applicable in specified special circumstances), it should instead be classified as Class 2 general insurance.

Class VII business is not very common these days. It enables insurers to manage pension funds although there is some uncertainty as to whether this is limited to occupational pension funds (based on the definition in the CLD and the Solvency II directive). There is a lack of clarity as to what is covered by a pension fund management contract. It is arguably implicit that it includes management of monies with a view to providing annuities but whether it also has to provide such annuities is not so clear. In practice, this type of business is often actually conducted as Class III business or looks very similar to it. Class VII business is now subject to the same investment rules as Class III business (eg the permitted links rules) (see **3.38**)). Tontines (Class V) and Capital Redemption (Class VI) are not classes of business known to UK insurers although offshore insurance companies (eg in the Isle of Man), may be authorised to write them. These types of business are not consistent with the UK requirement for insurance interest. Tontines are basically a last man standing type contract. Capital redemption contracts provide a guaranteed amount at the end of a specified term without there being a life assured. Both concepts are used by other European insurers passporting in the UK.

As has already been stated, Class 1 and Class 2 general insurance benefits may be added to a life contract (Class I or III) on a supplementary basis. These benefits are as follows:

1 Accident	Contracts of insurance providing fixed pecuniary benefits or benefits in the nature of indemnity (or a combination of both) against risks of the person insured or, in the case of a contract made by virtue of section 140, 140A or 140B of the Local Government Act 1972 (or, in Scotland, section 86(1) of the Local Government (Scotland) Act 1973), a person for whose benefit the contract is made—	
	(a)	sustaining injury as the result of an accident or of an accident of a specified class; or
	(b)	dying as a result of an accident or of an accident of a specified class; or
	(c)	becoming incapacitated in consequence of disease or of disease of a specified class,
	including contracts relating to industrial injury and occupational disease but excluding contracts falling within paragraph 2 of Part I of, or paragraph IV of Part II of, this Schedule.	

2 Sickness	Contracts of insurance providing fixed pecuniary benefits or benefits in the nature of indemnity (or a combination of both) against risks of loss to the persons insured attributable to sickness or infirmity but excluding contracts falling within paragraph IV of Part II of this Schedule.

It should be noted that there is no equivalent provision for general insurers to write any life business other than accidental death benefit falling within Class 1 general insurance. They may write 'ancillary' risks only within other classes of general insurance.

3.49 It is notable that the classes of insurance business do not include 'pensions' business, other than in relation to Class VII pension fund management. Pension contracts, whether insured occupational schemes, personal pension contracts, or older retirement annuity products, are normally contracts to provide an annuity. Effectively their terms provide for investment (normally on a unit-linked basis) until such time as pensions benefits become payable. At that time the contract will normally provide for an annuity on the life office's then current terms and conditions.

In personal pension schemes, the policyholder will have an 'open market option' which means that, whilst the insurer is bound to offer the annuity, the policyholder is not bound to accept it. The insurance risk on the annuity may therefore never materialise but it is the trigger for treating the contract as insurance business. Reassurance in this area also normally utilises the obligation to provide reassurance of an annuity on current terms to transfer insurance risk. As tax rules change (eg removing the need to buy an annuity), and if the contract does not trigger a payment on the death of the pension scheme member, insurers may need to carry on offering annuity cover as an option to such customers. This begs the question whether insurers may instead (at least for individual contracts), seek to offer pensions contracts as life contracts, especially now that the decision in *Fuji v Aetna* (see **1.69**) appears to permit unit-linked contracts without any additional life cover. The life cover argument will not generally be available as an option in pensions reassurance unless the underlying insurance contracts contain an obligation to pay benefits on the death of individual members.

As has already been stated in Chapter 1, the FSA Glossary contains a definition of life policy which includes personal pensions contracts where the contributions are paid to the life office; the apparent purpose of this being to apply the relevant COBS rules to such contracts. Personal pension schemes offered by UK insurance companies are often incorporated into a contract of insurance to enable insurers to sell them because of the restriction to insurance business in (INSPRU 1.5.13). However, since the advent of true self-invested personal pensions (SIPPS) that do not use an insured unit linked private fund, it has also become common for personal pension schemes to be set up by creating a trust with the trustees of that scheme then buying an insurance contract (known as a trustee investment plan (TIP)).

B Ambit of investment business

3.50 Having established that a life policy is an investment within the ambit of FSMA, it is then necessary to ascertain whether the activity in question constitutes a 'regulated activity'[1]. The relevant 'regulated activities' are:

(1) effecting and carrying out contracts of insurance (Article 10);

(2) dealing in investments as agent (Article 21);

(3) arranging deals in investments (Article 25(1));

(4) arrangements with a view to bringing about an investment (Article 25(2));

(5) assisting in the administration and performance of a contract of insurance (Article 39A);

(6) managing investments (Article 37);

(7) investment advice (including basic advice in relation to a stakeholder product) (Article 53);

(8) establishing, operating and winding up a stakeholder pension scheme (Article 52) and any personal pension scheme including SIPPS.

They also include 'agreeing' to do any of the above except (8) (Article 64).

Effecting a contract of insurance broadly encompasses the negotiation and conclusion/issue of the contract whereas carrying it out means administering it and dealing with changes and claims. There is no statutory definition of these terms but the issues have been considered in case law[2] under the provisions formerly contained in the Insurance Companies Act 1982 relating to 'carrying on insurance business'. Carrying on insurance business covered both the effecting (issuing) of contracts and carrying them out (eg claims management) and it is submitted that the cases are therefore still relevant to FSMA defined activities .The cases make clear that a non-UK insurance company may be able to cover UK risks without carrying on insurance business in the UK. In order to do so it will need to ensure that no insurance activities are carried on in the UK. It is not possible to be definitive about what these encompass but broadly it is likely to mean that neither the insurance company nor any intermediary acting on its behalf in the UK should:

(1) accept risk or negotiate in relation to underwriting issues (acceptance of risk or price);

(2) issue policies or receive premiums;

(3) negotiate/manage or agree claims on the insurer's policies; or

(4) negotiate or agree terms under other insurance contracts (eg reinsurance).

1 Schedule 2, Part 1 and the RAO.

2 See *Bedford Insurance Co Ltd v Instituto de Resseguros do Brasil* [1985] QB966 and *Phoenix General Insurance Co Greece SA v Administration Asiguraliror de Stat* [1988] QB 216.

However, in practice as only life companies authorised in EEA states and a handful of non EEA states can issue or direct financial promotions at policyholders in the UK (see **3.52**), it is virtually impossible to actually market contracts of other non EEA insurers.

Although the main regulated activity for an insurance company is effecting and carrying out contracts of insurance, because of the FSA's permission regime, other activities conducted as part of an insurer's business of effecting and carrying out insurance contracts also need the requisite permission. So, for example, arrangements in connection with the effecting of a contract of insurance may require the insurer to have a permission which includes arranging deals in investments. The FSA seems to accept that an insurer managing its own investments is not doing so by way of business and does not require permission to manage investments.

Article 52 of the Regulated Activities Order requires the person establishing, operating or winding up a stakeholder pension scheme to be authorised. From April 2007, the same activities in relation to a personal pension scheme, including SIPPS require authorisation. Life companies establishing such schemes by way of incorporation into an insurance contract are the 'product provider' (eg they contract with the member to admit them to the scheme). If they outsource the administration to another company they are likely to still be the person operating the scheme. Conversely, in non-insurance and trust situations, the scheme administrator would normally be the person operating the scheme[1] and liable in relation thereto to the members.

The activity of assisting in the administration and performance of an insurance contract will by definition (ie assisting) be carried on by someone other than the insurer. In any event, exemptions exist for an insurance company's own management of claims and claims management undertaken on behalf of an insurer on a professional basis. Similarly, loss adjustment and expert appraisal of claims are not regulated activities. Intermediaries, call centres or claims managers assisting claimants in relation to the management of claims (eg completing claim forms) are likely to be considered to be carrying on this regulated activity.

The activities of life assurance salesmen or independent intermediaries in recommending a life insurance contract could clearly fall within the ambit of 'investment advice'[2] and 'arranging deals in investments'[3]. However, unless they advise on the specific choice of underlying funds available to such a product, their activities would not normally constitute the activity of managing investments. 'Managing investments' could include, for example, the management of what are generally known as 'private funds', namely unit linked funds made available by the insurer to one or a specific group of policyholders. These are a specified part of the life unit-linked life funds where independent intermediaries or investment managers manage the investments held in the insurer's funds. The investment advisory activities and those of arranging or introducing are covered by the IMD and are explained further in Chapter 4.

1 See CP 06/05 and PS 06/07.
2 Article 53 RAO.
3 Article 25 RAO.

SECTION 3 THE NEED TO BE AUTHORISED OR EXEMPT UNDER FSMA

A The general prohibition

3.51 Section 2 above and Chapter 4 explain which activities constitute regulated activities in relation to insurance contracts and in particular how effecting and carrying out such contracts can constitute regulated activities. Section 19 of FSMA prevents a person from carrying on regulated activities by way of business in the UK unless it is either authorised or exempt ('the general prohibition'). A person who contravenes this provision is guilty of a criminal offence. By virtue of section 23, it would be a defence to prove that all reasonable precautions were taken and due diligence was exercised to avoid the commission of the offence. In prescribed cases, any person who suffers loss as a result of the contravention may bring an action subject to the usual provisions applying to breaches of statutory duty[1]. Section 26 provides that an agreement made in contravention of the general prohibition is unenforceable against the other party and the investor is entitled to recover any money or other property paid or transferred together with compensation for any loss sustained as a result of having parted with it. Section 380 of FSMA enables the court to grant injunctions and make restitution orders in respect of actual or likely contravention of a 'relevant requirement' (essentially a requirement under FSMA and certain other provisions). Where a person who is authorised carries on a regulated activity otherwise than in accordance with his permission, this is not an offence. The transaction is neither void nor unenforceable nor does it give rise to an action for breach of statutory duty.

B Financial promotions

3.52 Section 21 of FSMA prevents a person from 'communicating an offer or inducement to engage in an activity specified by the FSA as a controlled activity' ('the financial promotion restriction'). This is explained further in Chapter 5 but includes marketing materials and brochures. It should also be noted that COBS 4.9.4 imposes restrictions on the ability of an authorised firm to approve a financial promotion for a non EEA long-term insurer. It provides that a financial promotion can only be approved for an authorised or exempt person or an insurer falling within this definition of an overseas long-term insurer. An overseas long-term insurer includes an EEA insurer which has not exercised a passporting right (ie it is therefore not an authorised person) and an EEA branch of an insurer. For this purpose insurers in Gibraltar are included as EEA insurers. In addition insurers in Jersey, Guernsey, the Isle of Man, the Commonwealth of Pennsylvania and the State of Iowa are included as overseas long-term insurers and can have their financial promotions approved. As it is very difficult to sell products without issuing any financial promotions, this makes it difficult for other overseas insurers to do such business with UK policyholders.

1 Section 20.

C How is authorisation obtained?

3.53 The way in which authorisation is obtained for a UK insurance company or branch of a non-EU company is mainly set out in Part IV of FSMA. Authorisation will be achieved by a successful application for a permission[1]. It is not possible to apply for a permission if there is one already in force for that person. In this case there would have to be an application for a variation. It is also necessary to satisfy the 'threshold conditions'[2] which are set out in Schedule 6. Effecting or carrying out contracts of insurance requires the authorised person to be a body corporate, a registered friendly society or a member of Lloyd's. UK insurers must have their head office and registered office in the UK. The insurer's close link (eg group and associated companies) must not prevent effective supervision by the FSA. The insurer must have adequate resources and be suitable (essentially 'fit and proper'). It is also proposed that a new threshold condition relating to suitability of a firm's business model be added by the draft Bill to reform UK financial regulation (**see 3.17**).

An insurer will need to appoint individuals to carry on the appropriate 'controlled functions'. Such functions include the Chief Executive, non executive directors, the actuarial functions, (eg known as the actuarial function holder and the with-profits actuary) the finance functions and the compliance oversight functions. It has become more common for the FSA to interview prospective approved persons (see **3.18**). A new insurer may also wish to utilise outsourcing providers and the FSA is also likely to be keen to understand such arrangements and how the risks of outsourcing are to be managed. The management of risk more generally will be assessed as part of the suitability and resource requirements and, in particular, the insurer's assessment of the amount of capital it requires.

Alternatively, a person may be 'exempted', and the statutory provisions relating to this are set out in section 38 and particularly section 39. This is considered further in Chapter 4 in relation to Appointed Representatives. Authorisation for insurance companies established in other EEA states by exercising 'passport' or 'Treaty' rights[3] is described in Section 4.

Existing insurers and friendly societies were 'grandfathered' at N2 with the appropriate permission.

SECTION 4 EU AND PASSPORTING

A Background

3.54 The EEA includes, in addition to the member states of the EU, Iceland, Liechtenstein and Norway (the EFTA countries)[4].

1 Section 31.
2 Section 41.
3 Schedules 3 and 4.
4 Separate provisions apply in relation to Switzerland.

The main sources of EU law are the EC Treaty signed in Rome (as extended by the Maastricht and Lisbon Treaties), legislation made under that Treaty (which may take the form of regulations, directives and decisions), and the case law of the European Court of Justice (ECJ). Upon their entry into force, Treaty provisions, regulations and decisions (in so far as the persons to whom they are addressed are concerned) become law and need no further enactment. Where the provisions of the Treaty are clear, precise and unconditional and intended to give individual rights, they are directly effective and may be relied upon by nationals in the courts of member states. All directly effective community law overrides conflicting national legislation.

Directives are addressed to member states and leave to member states the choice of form and method for achieving the requirements of the directive[1]. If the terms of a directive are clear, precise and unconditional, namely without discretions to be exercised by member states, and if the date for implementation has passed, then it can be used by an individual in spite of conflicting national laws (see *Becker v Finanzamt Munster-Innenstadt*[2]). EU law can also impact on national law in interpreting domestic legislation. In the *Marleasing* case[3] the ECJ held that national courts must interpret national legislation which is ambiguous in a manner which is as far as possible consistent with the relevant EC directive even where national law predated the directive.

The right to freedom of establishment and freedom to provide services within the EU are enshrined in the EC Treaty[4]. Most of the EU single passport directives were part of the European Communities' Single Market programme and latterly the Financial Services Action Plan, the aim of which was to harmonise parts of the laws of member states to achieve the main aims of the EU, namely freedom of movement of persons, services and goods and capital. The Financial Services Action Plan saw the introduction of a streamlined process for adopting EU Legislation (the Lamfalussy process,based on the recommendations of the committee chaired by Baron Lamfalussy). This involves high level (Framework) EU legislation with detail being agreed by committees with appropriate expertise. There are four levels to the process. The first stage is that any directive(s) and regulations are drafted in higher level terms. The second stage is technical implementing measures determined by reference to relevant supervisory bodies. The third stage involves interpretative documents, guidelines and standards designed to produce consistency, particularly in relation to options or discretions in the directives/regulations. The fourth stage is a check by the Commission. The directives adopted using the process to date have been implemented in a much shorter timeframe than might otherwise have been the case. The process applies in relation to securities, banking, insurance and pensions. The Solvency II Directive (on insurance company solvency) uses this process. EIOPA (see **3.57**) will have a significant role to play in the implementation of Solvency II (see **3.57**).

1 Article 249 of EC Treaty.

2 Case 8/81, *Becker and Finanzamt Munster-Innenstadt* [1982] ECR 53, [1982] 1 CMLR 499.

3 *Marleasing SA v La Comercial Internacional de Alimentacion SA* [1990] ECR I-4135, [1992] 1 CMLR 305.

4 Articles 43 and 49.

B The First, Second and Third Life Directives

3.55 Previous editions of this book charted the history and implementation of these directives in some detail. For present purposes, only a very high level summary is provided. It should also be noted that the directives have been consolidated and the relevant provisions are now contained in the Consolidated Life Directive[1]. The First Life Directive, known as the 'Establishment Directive', permitted insurance companies incorporated anywhere in the EEC (as it was then called) to establish a head office[2], branches or agencies in respect of their long-term business in other EEC countries, subject to the obtaining of a licence (or 'official authorisation')[3]. The directive also provided for a harmonised definition of long-term insurance business[4] which includes capital redemption business[5]. Companies were required to maintain specified reserves and a margin of solvency calculated in accordance with the directive. They were also required to limit their activities to the business of insurance and operations arising directly therefrom[6]. Additionally, insurers were required to manage their life and general business separately and there was a prohibition on the authorisation of new composites. It was also necessary for future EEC life operations of a UK composite to be via a subsidiary and not a branch[7].

The Second Life Directive built on the right of establishment provided by the First Life Directive by providing the right for EC insurance companies to accept business from policyholders in other member states. The limited ability the directive provided to accept such business was superseded by the implementation of the Third Life Directive. However, it should be noted that the provisions of the Second Life Directive regarding the law of the contract and cancellation continue to apply and are dealt with in other Chapters of this book[8].

What the Second Life Directive essentially did, was to allow an insurer without a licence in that country, to accept unsolicited (called 'own initiative') business from residents of other EC states. Although the directive defined own initiative business as including unsolicited intermediary business, it contained an option which allowed own initiative business to be restricted further by member states to situations where there had been no contact at all with the prospective policyholder.

3.56 The Third Life Directive[9] was implemented in the UK from 1 July 1994. It provided a single licence (or 'single passport') for insurance companies to offer their products within the EEA subject to a notification procedure. An insurance company authorised in the UK may now carry on insurance business from

1 SI 2002/83/EC.
2 See Chapter 7.
3 Article 6.
4 Article 1.
5 This was implemented in the UK by the Insurance Companies Act 1982, Sch 1.
6 Section 16, ICA 1982.
7 Article 13.
8 Chapters 1 and 5.
9 which was also known as the 'framework directive'.

a sales or full insurance branch or via brokers, in any other member state, without having to be authorised itself or to have its policy terms, conditions and premiums authorised in that other member state.

The directive introduced the concept of home state authorisation (namely the state where the insurance company is established), subject to compliance with the notification requirements. The host state still has power to require the notification of the technical basis for calculating scales of premium and technical provisions, but not prior to marketing. The directive itself provided for the co-ordination of the way technical provisions are calculated by laying down a basis of actuarial principles[1].

The single licence is, however, subject to the power of the host state to prohibit the sale of an insurance contract by an insurer if it conflicts with the host state's legal provisions protecting the 'general good'. There was also a specific requirement that overseas insurers comply with the rules of the host country regarding the form and content of advertisements adopted in the interest of the 'general good' (Article 41). The concept of 'general good' is a matter of EU law and applies throughout the EU. From existing cases of the ECJ and recital 20 of the directive, it appears that such restrictions will only be upheld if they are objectively necessary, in proportion to their objective, non-discriminatory and do not repeat any safeguards in the home (ie the insurer's in this case) state. These requirements may be in addition to the mandatory rules of law applicable if the host state's law does not govern the contract. (See Section 5 of Chapter 1.)

Other changes included changes to the assets which can be used to cover technical provisions (ie amount of future insurance liabilities), a requirement of localisation of assets anywhere in the EU and changes to the rules on valuation of assets and determination of liabilities. Specific requirements on the information to be provided to policyholders, both pre-contract and where a contract is varied, and the right for existing composites to establish life branches were also included. The directive also provided rules relating to the transfer of insurance portfolios and the obligation to monitor the suitability of anyone wishing to acquire qualifying holdings in an insurer (broadly, holdings of 10% or more of the capital or voting rights).

The directive required (in Annex II) that prior to a contract being entered into (or varied), the prospective policyholder be provided with certain details which are specified in the directive. Further, these should be provided in writing, in an official language of the member state of habitual residence, unless the policyholder requests otherwise. The matters to be included are set out in COBS 13 Annex 1. Generally they will be covered by Key Features document requirements apart from:

(1) The arrangements for handling complaints concerning contracts by policyholders, lives assured or beneficiaries under contracts including, where appropriate, the existence of a complaints body, without prejudice to the right to take legal proceedings.

1 Articles 17 to 25.

(2) The law applicable to the contract where the parties do not have a free choice or, where the parties are free to choose the law applicable, the law the assurer proposes to choose.

There is also a requirement to notify policyholders during the existence of the contract of changes in the details of the insurance company and to provide information every year on the state of bonuses.

As stated above, the First, Second and Third Life Directives were consolidated by the Consolidated Life Directive[1].

C EIOPA, and Solvency II

1 EIOPA

3.57 In addition to proposed changes to the UK regulatory framework the global financial crisis gave rise to changes to the European regulatory framework for insurers. From January 2011 the Committee of European Insurance and Occupational Pension Supervisors (CEIOPS) was replaced by EIOPA. Similar European authorities were created at the same time for banks, the European Banking Authority and for securities, the European Securities and Markets Authority. The creation of EIOPA was designed to address issues identified by the De la Rosiere Report issued in February 2009. This report identified that despite numerous single market directives, there were divergent rules and gaps in regulation at the European level. As much of the European regulation in the insurance field has taken the form of directives which needed to be implemented and enforced in each member state, this is perhaps not too surprising. However, the result of this finding is that EIOPA now has very extensive rule making and enforcement powers. Its aim is to produce a single European rule book which eradicates differences in EU law which have arisen because of exceptions, derogations, lack of uniformity in implementation and ambiguity. The FSA has already acknowledged that this will involve a power shift to Brussels, with the UK authorities having less strategic input to rules which they effectively have to enforce, becoming the supervisory arm of an EU policy setting body. To enable it to perform its role, EIOPA has been given a series of wide ranging powers. The current guidance, (ie Level 3) stage of the Lamfalussy process allows non binding guidelines to be issued in relation to technical issues. EIOPA now has power, although technically subject to endorsement by the Commission, to issue binding technical standards at Level 2 of that process. Such standards can only apply to technical and not political issues but in areas like prudential regulation, such technical issues can have an enormous effect on insurers in member states. A process whereby the Commission endorses the standards is specified so that they become

1 SI 2002/83/EC.

directly enforceable in individual member states. The process incorporates public consultation and cost benefit analysis but the Commission can only really object to such standards for reasons of Community Interest.

EIOPA has power to ensure the consistent application of community law. This power is expected to be used in the first instance against national supervisors where the national supervisors do not respond to a requirement to act or stop acting in a particular way. EIOPA may, as a last resort, adopt a binding decision which is applicable to a relevant financial institution in a member state. EIOPA also has powers to intervene in disputes between national supervisors and again, EIOPA has the power to adopt binding decisions in relation to financial institutions. It is intended that EIOPA's intervention be limited to material issues where there is expected to be a serious detrimental effect on customers because of the relevant supervisor's failure to act on a decision of EIOPA. EIOPA will also have the power to prohibit or restrict harmful activities or products in emergency situations. On a day to day basis, EIOPA has other roles in terms of provision of its technical expertise and advice (eg preparing equivalence decisions for Solvency II) and generally co-ordinating supervision across the member states. It has a supervisory board made up of the heads of each of the national supervisors. This board can act by qualified majority in relation to the adoption of binding technical standards. The PRA will be represented on the board of EIOPA when dual regulation is introduced in the UK.

2 *Omnibus II*

3.58 The Omnibus I Directive introduced the new European Supervisory bodies including EIOPA. The proposed Omnibus II Directive will make changes to Solvency II, not least to change the date for implementation to 1 January 2013. The other area where EIOPA will have a significant role is in formulating transitional provisions for Solvency II. The draft Omnibus II directive provides for maximum periods for any such transitional provisions. For Capital Instruments the maximum transitional period is ten years. Similarly, for reporting and the Solvency and Financial Condition Report, the period is up to three years and for 'equivalence' the period is up to five years (see further Chapter 7).

D Using the single passport

1 *Introduction*

3.59 The provision of financial services in the UK, or by UK companies pursuant to a passporting right, is governed by FSMA. UK regulation is undertaken in relation to 'regulated activities' which include effecting and carrying out contracts of insurance. Section 418 of FSMA extends the FSA's jurisdiction outside of the UK to allow it to regulate passported activities. The provisions of the single market directives have been incorporated into FSMA (Part III of Schedule 3, paragraphs 20 and 21); and in the Financial Services and Markets Act 2000

(EEA Passport Rights) Regulations (the 'Passporting Regulations')[1]. There are also rules in SUP 13.5 and guidance in the rest of SUP 13 and Annex 3. These provide that a UK authorised insurance firm needs to notify the FSA, as home state regulator, of its intention to use its passporting rights. The FSA then provides the appropriate certificates to the host state regulator. The process for insurers is described in more detail at **3.61**. However, in order to comply with the relevant notification requirements, it will be important to accurately identify whether the particular activities which the company wishes to pursue fall within the right of establishment or the freedom to provide services. The notification procedures for insurance business differ in terms of content and timing depending upon which passporting right is used. In the future, for firms passporting out of the UK, the Government has confirmed that the PRA will be responsible for issuing all relevant notices.

A UK insurance company will have a separate 'permission' from the FSA to conduct insurance mediation activities (eg advising on, arranging or assisting in the performance of a contract of insurance). However, if it wishes to sell its products itself in another EEA country it will do so under the Consolidated Life Directive as the IMD does not cover insurers. Insurance intermediaries would passport under the IMD.

The branch and services notification obligations are set out in more detail later in **3.61–3.63** but it is worth noting that there is a different treatment depending on whether the passport exercised is direct insurance, pure reinsurance or insurance mediation. For a UK pure reinsurer, the Reinsurance Directive provides an automatic passport but SUP 15.5.1A requires certain information to be provided to the FSA. For IMD activities, EEA states need to inform the Commission if they wish to receive passport notifications. Only if they have done so, do the time periods specified below apply. Broadly, the timeframe for IMD services is that the FSA has one month, having received the required notice from the firm, to provide the host state with a consent notice and then IMD activities can commence one month after the firm is notified that a consent notice has been given. For insurance services, the insurer should be able to provide services once the FSA notifies it that the consent notice has been given. The FSA's guidance in SUP 13.4 is a little unclear on this point as it seems to imply that the insurer is supposed to wait to be notified of any applicable host state restrictions. This appears to be at odds with paragraph 20(4)B of Schedule 3 of FSMA and the Third Life Directive which merely provided for one month's notice for services business[2]. For IMD activities, the period appears to be the same as for services business (ie two months in total if the country in question has requested to be informed). For insurance branches, the period is up to five months (three for the FSA to consider giving the consent notice and two for the host state).

The passported activities would be subject to rules applied by the host state regulator 'in the general good'. The rules of the host state applicable to marketing products would also be applied on the same basis. Similarly, the host state may specify that any contracts covering risk in their territory or with policyhold-

1 SI 2001/2511.
2 See also Article 42, CLD.

ers habitually resident in their country must be governed by a law of that country. Alternatively, if a choice of law is permitted and another law governs the contract then host state 'mandatory rules' may also be applied. This will ordinarily necessitate advice from lawyers in each EEA host country.

2 *Distinction between 'establishment' and 'services'*

3.60 In practice, it is often difficult to distinguish between what constitutes an establishment and what constitutes the provision of services, and therefore which notification procedure should apply. The distinction can have taxation implications, as an establishment in an EEA country is more likely to give rise to liability to pay corporate income taxes in that country. This distinction is especially difficult in the case of insurance intermediation type activities and it is hoped that when the IMD is revised this issue will be addressed.

The concept of provision of services is basically distinguished from that of establishment by its 'temporary character', to be assessed in the light of duration, regularity and continuity. This distinction caused problems following implementation of the Third Life Directive. The Commission therefore issued an interpretative document to provide guidance[1]. This states that a firm operating on a services basis may equip itself with necessary infrastructure, despite the temporary nature of its activities. This may cover both 'upstream and downstream support activities' (eg use of risk assessment services, receipt of notices of claim and evaluation of local damage). However, it is clear that this cannot extend to performing insurance activities which would require a branch (eg accepting new proposals/agreeing claims).

The guidance also makes clear that use of an independent intermediary should not constitute a branch of the insurer unless that intermediary is:

(1) subject to the direction and control of the insurer;

(2) able to commit the insurer; and

(3) has a permanent brief.

This means that if the insurer were to use an 'independent person' (eg independent intermediary) to sell products in another EEA country, if such intermediary has permanent authority to commit and is subject to the direction and control of the insurer, the insurer would need to passport on an 'establishment' basis in respect of that intermediary.

The guidance also states that only activities actually carried on in another member state should require use of passporting rights. This is helpful for services business generally and insurance mediation activities in particular (See also SUP Appendix 3.6.5).

1 OJ CO43 16/2/2000.

3 Procedure to establish a branch for insurance activities

3.61 An insurer (ie other than a pure reinsurer) should notify the FSA of its intention to passport its authorisation into the relevant EEA host state on an establishment basis. It would do this by completing and submitting to the FSA the FSA's pro-forma 'notice of intention'. This identifies the activities and classes of business which it seeks to carry on through that branch and includes other specified information (in relation to, for example, its authorised agents in the host state); its organisational structure; its reinsurance arrangements; and how its solvency requirements will be met (see SUP 13.5 and Annex 1 to the Passporting Regulations).

The FSA has three months from the date of receipt of the 'notice of intention' to consider the proposal. If it does not object to the 'notice of intention', the FSA will give a 'consent notice' to the host state regulator; and give notice to the insurer that it has given such consent to the host state regulator (a 'written notice').

The FSA has discretion to refuse to send a 'consent notice' to the host state regulator only if it has reason to doubt the adequacy of the insurer's resources or its administrative structure in relation to business which it is proposed be written through the branch; or to question the reputation, qualifications or experience of the directors or managers of the insurer or its proposed authorised agent in relation to the business that it intends to conduct through the branch.

Whilst it is possible that the FSA may ask the insurer for more information or require a report from a skilled person before giving its 'consent notice' to the host state regulator, provided that the 'notice of intention' is completed in sufficient detail, the consent notice should be forthcoming. In the unlikely event that the FSA were to propose to refuse its consent, it would need to issue a warning notice to the insurer. Subsequently, if the FSA decided to actually refuse to give a 'consent notice' it would need to give the insurer a 'decision notice' to that effect within three months of receipt of the 'notice of intention'. The insurer could then appeal the FSA's decision to the Tribunal (see **3.66**).

The insurer can establish its branch in the host state either when the host state regulator notifies the FSA (and the FSA notifies the insurer) of any 'applicable provisions' (ie local rules with which the insurer will be required to comply with when conducting business through a branch in the host state; (see Part III of Schedule 3 to FSMA); or two months have elapsed from the date of the written notice.

The insurer must notify the FSA and the host state regulator of any change to the relevant details of its branch (provided in the notice of intention), including, the address of the branch and the name of its authorised agent; the classes of business carried on and the nature of the risks covered; the details of the structural organisation of the branch; the guiding principles as to reinsurance of business carried on, or to be carried on; the estimated costs of installing administrative services, and for each of the first three years following the establishment of the branch, the estimate of the firms' margin of solvency, the margin of solvency required and the method of calculation (see SUP13.6 and Regulation 15 of the Passporting Regulations). Unless the change results from circumstances outside the insurer's control, the process to approve the change may take up to two months (one month for the FSA and one month's notice to the host stage regulator).

4 Insurance services

3.62 The procedure for establishing a 'services' authorisation for insurance activities is much more straightforward. The insurer provides a notice of intention in the same way but the amount of detail required and the timings are different. The information required in relation to the activities to be carried out on a services basis is limited to details of the proposed host EEA country and the nature of the risks to be covered. The FSA has one month to consider giving the consent notice .The insurer may commence the activities when it is notified by the FSA that the consent notice has been given (see paragraph 20(4)B of Schedule 3, FSMA).

Similar provisions to those for a branch apply in respect of the FSA refusing to give a consent notice and changes in the details notified in respect of services business. The FSA has a month to consider the effect of the proposed change(see SUP 13.7 and Regulation 16 of the Passporting Regulations).

5 EU providers passporting in

3.63 Under the Consolidated Life Directive[1], EU direct insurers can passport into the UK using the process specified by their host state. The Passporting Regulations impose additional notification requirements (to notify the FSA in addition to the home state regulator) in relation to changes to details of an EEA insurer's branch.

In order to be able to exercise a passporting right an EEA insurer must be an EEA firm. An insurer will be an EEA firm if it has its head office in the EEA. An EEA insurer becomes a FSMA authorised person (therefore a 'firm' for the purposes of the FSA Handbook) by satisfying the establishment conditions in Schedule 3 of FSMA, broadly by notifying its regulator and the regulator providing an appropriate certificate to the FSA. The certificate from the home state regulator should specify the activities which the EEA insurer is authorised to carry on. An EEA insurer cannot apply for permission for these activities[2], it should automatically be given the appropriate permission by the FSA. It can apply for top-up permissions in respect of activities it would not be able to carry on under its EEA right. As non-UK insurers will normally be authorised in their own state to conduct activities which in the UK would constitute insurance mediation activities, it is arguable that their permission should also include limited insurance mediation permission (ie in relation to their own business). Again, the draft Bill to reform UK financial regulation (see **3.3**) states that notifications from overseas regulators in relation to the Reinsurance Directive, the Consolidated

1 SI 2002/83/EC.
2 Section 40(3).

Life Directive and the First, Second and Third Non-Life Insurance Directives will go to the PRA, in order to mirror its responsibilities on a domestic basis.

EEA firms, once authorised, should be advised of relevant UK provisions applicable to them. The FSA provides that its rules only apply to the extent that the matters concerned are not reserved to the firm's home state (eg by the Consolidated Life Directive for prudential issues). Selling without a UK establishment still requires compliance with large sections of COBS and, where relevant, (eg for pure protection business), ICOBS. Firms writing with-profits business have to produce something similar to the Principles and Practices of Financial Management required for UK with-profits firms by COBS 20.3 (see Chapter 6). They will also need to comply with the permitted links rules for business effected by a branch in the UK (see **3.38**).

SECTION 5 SUPERVISION AND INTERVENTION

A Supervision

3.64 The FSA supervises UK authorised firms on many different levels. Because of its statutory objectives and the need to be proportionate, it aims to focus its efforts on those areas where the risk to the consumer or orderly financial markets is perceived to be greatest. In practical terms, the lifecycle of regulation starts with the application process and the need to satisfy the 'threshold conditions', including the need to be fit and proper. The appropriateness of the firm's key personnel and those dealing with customers is assessed. On an ongoing basis those people need to adhere to standards of conduct or be potentially held personally liable or ultimately disqualified. Once a firm is up and running there are the overriding obligations imposed by the FSA's Principles. The emphasis also shifts primarily to prudential risk, which now of course involves having adequate systems and arrangements, in accordance with SYSC, to manage risk. Conduct of business rules also start to feature prominently, as does the need to report annually to the FSA on the basis set out in IPRU INS Rule 9 . At this point the FSA may decide it would like to come for a visit, as part of its supervisory review process. This may involve individual interviews and the provision of information followed by a risk mitigation programme to sort out any issues arising.

Although there are many FSA requirements operating at different levels, it is probably fair to say that the emphasis on an ongoing basis is on risk management (and the effect on capital requirements). This is likely to be reflected in the PRA's insurance objective, namely to contribute to the securing of an appropriate degree of protection for those who are or may become policyholders of an insurer. The FSA's current supervisory tool ARROW was introduced as a means of adopting a risk-based approach to supervision and thereby complying with its statutory objectives (see Section 1 above). The process is based on thematic reviews and individual assessments, both desk-based reviews and on-site visits, the aim being to identify the large ticket items and the systemic or control failures in a business. The end product is a risk map which leads to a risk rating based on impact and probability of the risks concerned. This leads to a risk mitigation programme which the firm is expected to follow. The FSA has stated that the FCA is likely to move away from using ARROW and will use a tool which is easier to communicate to senior executives[1].

The FSA was also given additional powers by the Financial Services Act 2010[2]. These include powers to suspend or restrict firms' authorisation or the status of approved persons who are guilty of misconduct. The FSA can also impose a penalty on those carrying on controlled functions without approval from the FSA. These provisions came into effect on 8 June 2010. FSMA originally imposed a general prohibition preventing the FSA (and any person to whom a warning or decision notice is given) from publishing or giving details of that notice. Section 13(1) of the Financial Services Act 2010 lifted the prohibition in relation to decision notices and the FSA utilised this power for the first time in May 2011. The proposed Bill to reform UK financial regulation amends section 391(1) in order to relax the general prohibition against the publication of warning notices. Section 391(1)(c) now allows the FCA or the PRA (as the case may be) to publish information about the matter to which the notice relates, following consultation with the persons to whom the notice is given or copied. The appropriate regulator need not do this if it considers that such publication would be unfair or against the interests of consumers. This will potentially lead to publicity at an earlier stage of enforcement actions and could have a bearing on a firm's strategy for dealing with action taken by the FSA (and, in the future, the FCA and the PRA).

The FSA's policy in relation to use of its disciplinary powers is set out in DEPP and EG. The FSA introduced its new approach to enforcement and the use of penalties (see further below) with effect from 6 March 2010. It summarised the effect of these changes in PS10/4. The determination of penalties is covered by a five step penalty framework and importantly, is expected to increase penalties in line with the FSA's 'credible deterrence strategy'. The FSA has also sought to improve transparency and consistency. DEPP also sets out the FSA's approach in cases where a person claims a financial penalty will cause them serious financial hardship.

B Own initiative and powers to vary permissions

3.65 The FSA's own-initiative powers enable the FSA to vary, cancel or restrict a permission. Similar powers are also set out in Part IV[3]. In dealing with an application for permission the FSA may incorporate in the description of the regulated activity such limitations (for example, as to the circumstances in which the activity may or may not be carried on) as it considers appropriate[4]. Similarly, a permission may include such requirements as the FSA considers appropriate[5].

1 Speech, Margaret Cole, 28 June 2011.
2 Sections 9–13.
3 See sections 42 to 45.
4 Section 42.
5 Section 43.

The examples given being to require or prohibit certain specified action in relation to regulated activities. Section 45 of FSMA sets out the own-initiative power. It authorises the FSA, on its own initiative, to vary a Part IV permission to remove a regulated activity, vary a requirement applicable to the permission or to cancel it, if it appears that an authorised person is not complying with the 'threshold conditions', is not carrying on regulated activities or it is desirable to do so to meet any of its regulatory objectives. This last basis is very wide. However, EG 8.3 makes clear that the FSA will normally seek to agree with the firm those steps it must take to address the FSA's concerns. Section 53 sets out when the variation would take effect. It can take effect immediately if the FSA reasonably considers it necessary. Normally, it will be on a specified date or when the matter to which the notice relates is no longer open to review. Notice to the authorised person should specify the period for representations to the FSA about it and inform the authorised person of their right to refer the matter to the Tribunal. Section 8 of EG provides more guidance as to the FSA's approach in this area.

As a result of the 2010 Act, the FSA also now has the power to suspend, limit or otherwise restrict a firm's permission for up to 12 months where it considers that the firm has breached a requirement imposed under FSMA (or potentially for intermediaries, a directly applicable EU requirement under MiFID). The FSA will now also be able to impose a penalty in addition to withdrawing a firm's permission/authorisation.

C Enforcement related powers and the Tribunal

3.66 EG sets out the enforcement related powers of the FSA and its policy on using them. The FSA states in EG that it will seek to exercise its enforcement powers in a transparent, proportionate manner which is consistent with its publicly stated policies and will ensure 'fair treatment' when exercising its enforcement powers[1]. It is worth bearing in mind the role of the Tribunal in reviewing decisions of the FSA. The Upper Tribunal (Tax and Chancery Chamber) is part of a consolidated government tribunal service and is an independent judicial body established by the Tribunals, Courts and Enforcement Act 2007. It replaced the Financial Services and Markets Act Tribunal as a result of the Transfer of Tribunal Function Order 2010.

The FSA's powers of investigation are set out in Part XI of FSMA and include the power to require information, send in investigators and in some cases apply for a warrant to search premises[2]. Guidance in relation to these powers can be found in EG3. One important point in relation to such investigations is the effect of section 413 which enables a party to retain legally privileged documents (or documents which are enclosed with or referred to in such documents[3]). The FSA will often ask for such documents to be disclosed under Principle 11 but the firm cannot be required to do so, unless the documents are held with the intention of

1 EG 2.2.
2 Section 176.
3 Section 413(2)(c).

furthering a criminal purpose. If a firm does decide to disclose such information to the FSA, then it should seek to limit the purpose for which it can be used and make clear that privilege is not being waived.

The general power to obtain documents from a firm (or a connected party) on request applies to such information and documents as are reasonably required in connection with the exercise by the FSA of its functions under FSMA. It can be a very burdensome obligation as the FSA may specify such format as it reasonably requires. Also, if the information is historical, there may be logistical problems of retrieval. If these cause anything other than delay, then the firm will need to be careful to show that it has adequate systems in this area.

3.67 One option open to the FSA when it is investigating a firm is to require the firm to obtain a 'skilled person report' from an appropriately skilled (expert) person approved by the FSA[1]. In some of the enforcement actions to date, firms have themselves decided to commission such reports in order, it is assumed, to give themselves greater control over the scope of the report and the terms of reference.

The power to appoint investigators is set out in section 167 and may be exercised either by the FSA or the Secretary of State. The scope of the investigation can include the nature, conduct or state of the business of the firm or its Appointed Representative, a particular aspect of that business or the ownership or control of an authorised person. The investigation can also be extended to group companies[2]. Section 168 enables investigations in particular cases (eg where it appears there may have been market abuse). There are three criminal offences in section 177 relating to non-cooperation with FSA investigators. Not surprisingly these cover providing false or misleading information but they can also include destroying or otherwise disposing of documents that the person knows or suspects would be relevant to the investigation.

The draft Bill adds section 166A to FSMA, which confers a power on the regulators to appoint a skilled person to collect or update information which an authorised person was required (but failed) to collect or maintain under rules imposed by the regulator. Section 166A(6) allows the skilled person to obtain confidential information whereas section 166A(7) provides for the disclosure of such information. Section 175 is also amended to include subsections (2A) and (2B). Both concern the retention of confidential information. Essentially, they state that where a regulator or investigator has obtained documents under information-gathering powers, they may retain the originals for as long as necessary for the purpose for which they were requested or until any legal proceedings are concluded.

The FSA may also exercise certain powers at the request of an overseas regulator (eg power to investigate section 165). Conversely, the FSA's powers may be restricted in relation to EEA companies because of matters reserved to the home state regulator[3].

1 Section 166.
2 Section 167(2).
3 Section 199.

D FSA Sanctions

3.68 In DEPP 6.2.1.G the FSA sets out factors which may be relevant to its decision as to whether to actually take enforcement action against a firm. These include breaches which reveal serious or systemic weaknesses of the management systems or internal controls relating to all or part of a firm's business. Other factors include the scale of the issue (amount gained or risk of loss to customers) and whether any financial crime is involved.

Having decided to take disciplinary action, often the most powerful regulatory sanction is a public statement followed closely by a large fine. Withdrawing, cancelling or imposing a requirement on a permission can also be effective too. Under section 205, if the FSA consider that an authorised person has contravened a requirement imposed on him by or under FSMA it may publish a statement to that effect.

The FSA also has powers to sanction approved persons and to make disqualification orders. This now includes restricting or suspending their approval for a controlled function for up to two years. The FSA will take into account the statement of principles and the code for approved persons (see APER 2-4). The FSA is unlikely to take action unless the person's behaviour falls below that what would be reasonable to expect and there is an element of personal culpability. The more senior the person or significant the controlled function, the greater the likelihood of FSA action. The FSA may also now impose a penalty on someone carrying on a controlled function without being approved[1]. Again the more senior the role and the likelihood that the person should have understood that they were carrying on a controlled function without approval, the more likely the FSA is to take action In its new penalty regime the FSA specifies a sliding scale of the person's income as the basis for setting the level of the penalty (eg 0-40%). The FSA has sought to provide for situations where individuals claim that they are unable to pay such penalties but only where the value of their income or assets is relatively low[2]. The FSA has also added a new rule which prevents firms paying fines for employees, directors or partners of entities in their group[3].

The FSA's other main grounds for imposing a penalty are where an authorised person has contravened a requirement imposed on it by FSMA (or for example in relation to intermediaries carrying on mixed business) a directly applicable requirement of MiFID . Under section 206, the FSA may impose a penalty of such amount as it considers appropriate. The approach is set out in DEPP 6.5 and is based on a new 'five step framework' (see PS10/4). The new framework applies to breaches after 6 March 2010. The Steps are as follows: Step 1: Disgorgement (ie the aim is to deprive the firm of any financial benefit of the breach); Step 2: Acting proportionately (ie to reflect the nature, impact and seriousness of the breach); Step 3: Adjustment for mitigating factors; Step 4: Adjustment for deterrence; and Step 5: Discount for settled cases. The intention seems clearly to increase the level of penalties (and thereby presumably the

1 Section 63A D of FSMA.
2 See DEPP 6.5D.
3 GEN 6.1.8R.

FSA's power to influence behaviour). Step 2 includes a sliding scale of the firm's relevant income ranging from 0 to 20%. The early settlement discount is fixed and ranges from 10-30% depending on the stage at which the issue is resolved. The level of discount will be specified in each case by the FSA.

The FSA has to give the firm a warning notice that it proposes to impose a fine or make a public statement setting out the fine and/or the statement as appropriate. If the FSA decides to go ahead with the planned action it must issue a decision notice. The firm may then refer the matter to the Tribunal.

SECTION 6 FINANCIAL OMBUDSMAN SERVICE

3.69 Schedule 17 sets out the constitution and other aspects of the FOS. Central to this is the creation of a separate limited company. The board is appointed by the FSA but must be independent in its operation. Annual reports to the FSA are required. As stated, a voluntary element is also provided for whereby it may be agreed that unregulated firms be bound by the scheme rules in relation to certain activities of a financial services nature. The Ombudsman has power to require specified information and documents under section 231. The disputes it deals with include mis-selling, unsuitable advice, unfair treatment, maladministration, misleading advertising, delay and poor service in relation to products or services provided by insurers and other financial services firms. The Ombudsman is not required to decide cases on ordinary legal principles and may impose a result it considers fair and reasonable in all the circumstances. This introduces great uncertainty into the scheme, makes the scheme difficult to assess for consistency and inevitably leads to a real lack of accountability. In practice, the costs of the FOS are borne by the industry and the service is generally free to the complainant.

One of the benefits of the FOS is that it is supposed to be informal and generally does not involve a hearing to resolve disputes. The service is directed at consumers and very small businesses (eg with less than two employees and an annual turnover of less than €2 million). The amount of compensation available is £100,000 but will rise to £150,000 on 1 January 2012.

The compulsory jurisdiction applies to the regulated activities of authorised persons. The voluntary jurisdiction is effectively a contractual arrangement by which the voluntary jurisdiction participant agrees that the scheme will apply. The voluntary jurisdiction can only extend to activities which, although not regulated activities, could be or be made to be regulated activities. It is also significant that in signing up to the voluntary jurisdiction the voluntary jurisdiction participant becomes subject to the jurisdiction of the FOS in relation to acts or omissions that occurred before that date if they could have been regulated activities.

As stated in **3.24** above, the effect of the FOS transitional provisions[1] is that complaints in relation to pre N2 (ie December 2001) contracts which were subject to, for example, the insurance ombudsman scheme, form part of the com-

1 SI 2001/2326.

pulsory jurisdiction of the FOS. This means complaints in relation to such contracts (or acts or omissions taking place before the FOS was set up) can be dealt with by the FOS if they would have been covered by the predecessor scheme, provided the complainant is eligible under the FOS rules.

One potential constraint on the ability to use the FOS scheme is its territorial scope. Essentially, business not carried on from a UK establishment is excluded from the compulsory jurisdiction[1] so that the activities of an authorised person selling cross border from the EEA will not be covered by FOS. EEA firms operating on a service basis may however be able to sign up to the voluntary jurisdiction in respect of their UK services (ie directed at least in part at the UK) provided their contracts are covered by the law of the UK and they have advised their home state regulator[2]. It is not necessary for the complainants to live or be based in the UK.

The process for complaints is that the complainant has to have exhausted the firm's internal complaint procedure and received a final response or eight weeks have elapsed since the complaint was made. A complaint becomes time barred six months after the final response or, if no complaint has been made, six years after the event complained of, or if later, three years after the complainant was, or ought to have become aware, that they had cause for complaint. An interesting distinction was drawn in relation to mortgage endowment cases where a red letter and an amber letter were to be sent out to customers. On a neutral reading both made clear that there was a risk that the mortgage in question would not be repaid but only the red letter was considered to be significant enough to start the three year period running. This may mean in practice that consumers will be able to claim not to have been aware of a cause for complaint where objectively they would otherwise have been considered to be so aware. For mortgage endowment cases there was also an obligation to send a reminder to start the clock ticking.

The FOS also has discretion to extend the time limits for complaints in exceptional circumstances (eg illness of the complainant) or pursuant to the transitional provisions, or if the firm does not object.

Generally, as befits an informal dispute resolution procedure, the Ombudsman does not award costs against the party that loses (the complainant does not have to pay at all as the case fee is borne by the provider). It is, however, possible that an award of costs could be made. The Ombudsman can also award interest on top of the maximum award limit.

In practice, most cases are dealt with by an adjudicator who gives a provisional view. If the firm is unhappy with this, it can ask one of the Ombudsmen to review the decision. One of the biggest complaints in relation to the FOS is the quality of the adjudicators and the transparency of the process. However, it is very clear that firms will have little or no ability to challenge decisions of the FOS, even if they appear perverse. This is because the FOS not only decides cases on what is fair and reasonable in all the circumstances but the Ombudsman may also have a view on the evidence based on their own experience. This seems to be the case even where the area is one where there is contemporaneous expert

1 DISP 2.6.1.
2 DISP 2.6.4.

evidence to the contrary (see *R v FOS* [2008] EWHC 2142). The cases to date have set a very high bar in order to challenge a decision by the Ombudsman. The Ombudsman must effectively be acting arbitrarily or perversely in the sense that there is no justification at all for their decision. The point was effectively reiterated by the judicial review, brought by the BBA in relation to the FSA and FOS's handling of PPI cases. This case was brought to challenge the FSA's actions in issuing a Policy Statement (PS10/2), setting out how it expected firms to deal with PPI mis-selling cases. It also challenged how the FOS dealt with such PPI cases. The BBA argued that it was unlawful for the FSA to rely upon its Principles as giving rise to obligations to customers as, under section 150 of the FSMA, breach of a Principle is not actionable per se. They also argued that the Principles could not be used to augment detailed rules in a particular area and that what the FSA had required was effectively a Customer Redress Scheme (pursuant to section 404 of the FSMA). Breach of Principles is excluded from the ambit of such schemes. The issue in relation to the FOS related to the extent of the discretion it had in deciding cases based on what was 'fair and reasonable in all the circumstances' and the fact that its website had stated that the FSA Principles would be taken into account. The judgment held, just because the Principles were not actionable on their own, did not mean that they could not be taken into account in construing the FSA Rules (as was the clear intention of the FSA's regulatory regime). The judgment also confirmed that the FSA was not obliged to promote a Customer Redress Scheme to address the failures it had identified (ie it was not the exclusive remedy in all cases where it could apply). Finally, the judgement re-emphasised that the basis on which the FOS decides cases is fairness in all the circumstances.

SECTION 7 FINANCIAL SERVICES COMPENSATION SCHEME

A Structure of the scheme

3.70 The Policyholders Protection Act 1975 (PPA) initiated a compensation scheme to assist policyholders of an insurance company which had been wound up. The compensation scheme was brought into force by the Act and was administered by the Policyholders Protection Board. The scheme was designed to protect 90% of the benefits payable under life policies. The scheme was replaced from N2 (ie 1 December 2001) by the Financial Services Compensation Scheme (FSCS).

One of the objects of the FSCS was to merge all the previous compensation schemes applicable to retail investments and to provide a single point of contact for consumers in the event of a firm being unable to pay claims against it. However, that merger did not mean harmonisation of the levels of cover. For protected investment business there is a limit of £48,000 (100% of the first £30,000 and 90% of the next £20,000 up to £48,000). This limit does not apply to life insurers where the limit for eligible claimants is 90% of the amount of claim without limit (see **3.72**).

The functions under Part XV of FSMA are undertaken by the scheme manager. FSCS Limited, appointed by the FSA for this purpose, is independent of the FSA but accountable to it. FSMA sets out the required constitution and essential provisions of the scheme[1] and provides for the FSA to be able to make rules relating to the scheme and provides for the scheme manager to be able to impose levies[2]. Outline provisions for the Scheme are provided for in section 214. The rights which the compensation scheme has in the event of the insolvency of an institution covered by the scheme are covered by section 215. Of particular relevance to life insurers are sections 216 and 217 which relate to the continuity of long-term policies and the provisions relating to insurers in financial difficulties respectively.

3.71 The scheme manager is required to report to the FSA on the discharge of its functions[3] and has power to require specified information or documentation to be provided or produced[4]. The scheme manager may also inspect information held by receivers, administrators, liquidators, etc, but not where such person is the Official Receiver or certain others[5]. The requirement can be enforced by the court[6]. The scheme manager and various officials also enjoy a degree of statutory immunity[7].

The scheme rules require FSCS Limited to manage, hold and apply the funds held by the scheme in accordance with the rules. The rules set out the details relating to the annual report as required by section 218. A three-monthly report on the business conducted by the scheme and other information requested by the FSA is also required. FSCS Limited must also advise on certain other events such as the appointment of a chief executive, secretary or a change in auditors. Further, FSCS Limited must keep records of the scheme's transactions for at least six years. FSCS Limited must take steps to inform potential claimants that claims may be made for compensation where a firm is declared 'in default'. Effective procedures and service standards must be put in place for dealing with complaints about the scheme.

When an authorised insurer which provides long-term insurance cover is declared in default, FSCS Limited must try to arrange to continue cover with another insurer if this is more cost effective than paying compensation[8]. If FSCS Limited determines that an authorised insurer is in financial difficulties, it must try to arrange for the transfer of the business to another authorised person or give financial assistance to the insurer in difficulty to enable it to continue. Such action must only be taken if it is more cost effective than paying compensation. 'Financial difficulties' encompasses provisional liquidation; inability to pay debts under formal insolvency proceedings or where an application has been

1 Section 212.
2 Section 213.
3 Section 218.
4 Section 219.
5 Section 220.
6 Section 221.
7 Section 222.
8 Rule 3.4.

made to court to secure a voluntary creditors' arrangement, but the firm is not yet in liquidation or being wound up. The FSCS, like a liquidator also has the power to reduce the amounts payable if it regards them as excessive.

B Eligible claims

3.72 The FSCS may pay compensation to an 'eligible claimant' in respect of claims under a protected insurance contract where the insurer is in default. An eligible claimant is a person entitled to bring a claim under the Compensation Sourcebook (COMP) 4.2.1R. Essentially, all long-term policyholders will continue to be protected (even if they are large companies) unless they are connected with the insurance company in some way[1].

The claim must be in respect of a 'protected contract of insurance' which will exclude claims under reinsurance contracts[2]. Contracts will only be protected where the establishment of the relevant person is in the UK, another EEA state, the Channel Islands or the Isle of Man. The complainant must also be habitually resident in one of these territories at the time the policy is entered into[3]. Similarly EEA insurers issuing contracts through a UK establishment to people habitually resident in the UK are covered. This does not cover reinsurance contracts.

3.73 The FSCS will determine whether an insurer is in default based on whether it is unable or unlikely to be able to satisfy a protected claim. If compensation is offered the claimant may be required to transfer to FSCS Limited his rights to claim against other parties. The reasoning behind this is to maximise recoveries by FSCS Limited and prevent the affected consumer from taking action against the party(ies) in default[4]. COMP 8 contains provisions relating to the rejection of applications where the claimant has omitted material information or his claim contains inaccuracies (unless FSCS Limited considers the information was provided in good faith). Offers may be withdrawn if disputed or not accepted within 90 days. Offers may be reissued or varied. COMP 9 sets out time limits for the payment of compensation. Payments in respect of life policies are to be made directly to the claimant or on his instructions. Partial payments or payments on account are also permitted where there may be some uncertainty about paying the full amount. Interest may also be payable on compensation payments at the discretion of FSCS Limited. The rate of interest may be no higher than the clearing bank base rate[5].

1 COMP 4.3.2R but with exceptions for connected companies acting as pension scheme trustees.
2 See COMP 5.4.2.
3 COMP 5.5.4.4(a).
4 COMP 7.
5 COMP 11.

SECTION 8 PART VII PORTFOLIO TRANSFERS

A Transfer of insurance business between companies

3.74 Firms seeking to reorganise or sell part of their insurance business would ordinarily need the agreement of their policyholders to change the insurance provider. The Consolidated Life Directive provides for portfolio transfers in relation to all or part of an insurer's book of business[1]. Reinsurance entities have a similar right under the Reinsurance Directive[2].

The provisions governing such transfers are set out in Part VII, sections 104–117, Schedule 12 of FSMA and the Control of Business Transfer Regulations[3] and SUP 18 provides FSA guidance. Essentially the process requires an application to court. The insurance company has to put together a scheme setting out in detail how the transfer of funds is to take place and comment on the effect of the transfer on all different classes of policyholder. The firm's actuary then has to produce a report to the Board on the scheme stating that in his opinion the scheme should proceed and that no class of policyholder will be disadvantaged by the scheme. The report sets out how the scheme would work and the benefits of the transfer. An independent actuary (acting as an expert) must also produce a report. The appointment is a personal one but in order to satisfy the requirement of independence the position of any firm the actuary works for should also be considered. The independent actuary (the independent expert) must have no interest in either party to the transfer which would prejudice his status in the eyes of the court. If the independent expert's firm were, for example, the only firm used by either party recently, it would probably struggle to show the required level of independence, even if the individual actuary had not personally been involved. The FSA needs to approve the independent expert's appointment. (See also the provisions relating to reattribution schemes in Chapter 6 where the scheme involves the inherited estate of a with profits fund). As stated above at 3.6, the draft Bill to reform UK financial regulation will not alter the substance of this framework.

B The Scheme Report

3.75 The independent expert must produce a report in a form approved by the FSA. The principal purpose of the Scheme Report is to inform the court of the likely effects of the Part VII transfer on all relevant classes of policyholder. Accordingly, the independent expert producing the report is under a duty to the court and must comply with the rules on expert evidence set out in Part 35 of the Civil Procedure Rules.

1 But not a friendly society which is covered by the Friendly Societies Act 1992.
2 SI 2005/68/EC.
3 SI 2001/3625.

The Scheme Report should cover:

(1) information relating to the independent expert, including his qualifications, any circumstances which might prejudice his independence and the person or persons who appointed him;

(2) the purpose of the Part VII transfer and a summary of its terms;

(3) the documents, reports and other information considered in producing the Part VII report, including whether any requested information has not been provided;

(4) the extent to which the independent expert has relied on information provided by or the opinion of others; any steps taken to verify such information or opinion; and why he believes such reliance to be reasonable;

(5) the Independent Expert's opinion on the likely effects of the Part VII transfer on the security and reasonable expectation of:

   (a) the transferring policyholders;

   (b) the remaining policyholders of the transferor (if any); and

   (c) the transferee's existing policyholders; and

(6) any matters not taken into account that may be relevant.

C Issues

3.76 Although the consent of the FSA is not formally part of the process, the Scheme is almost certainly going to fail if it is opposed by the FSA. In practice this means that the FSA is involved (as they should be in accordance with Principle 11) in a scheme's planning from an early stage. The FSA also now produces a report to the court which is presumably very useful for the court when asked to exercise a discretion or exercise judgment (eg to grant a waiver from the notification requirements).

The practical issues likely to arise in relation to a proposed scheme are the time required when there are overseas risks, the notice requirements for different classes of policyholder and the effect of the scheme on non-UK assets or contracts not subject to a law of the United Kingdom.

Where a risk to be transferred is situated in another EEA state the FSA is required to consult with the host state regulator(s) concerned. As the regulators may take three months to respond before deemed consent will apply, the FSA may need to wait three months before it can issue the required certificate. If the transferee is not UK authorised, the FSA must also seek a certificate from the EEA home state regulator that the transferee will meet relevant solvency margin requirements after the transfer (certificate as to margin of solvency). For UK authorised insurers the FSA will provide this certificate.

The portfolio transfer process is designed to work within the EEA and will not necessarily work in other jurisdictions.

Although notice of an application to transfer an insurance should be circulated to all known policyholders of the transferor and the transferee, the FSA may waive part of this requirement if it is satisfied that the policyholders not receiving notice will not be adversely affected. This is a welcome relaxation as there are cases where it is either impractical and/or more confusing for distinct classes of policyholder who cannot be affected by the transfer. The FSA expects policyholders to be provided with a summary of the scheme, including the scheme report. This summary and the full report itself must be made available free of charge on request.

As regards non-UK assets or contracts governed by a law of a country outside the UK it is possible for the court order effecting the transfer not to have the required effect. The relevant provisions of section 112(2) of FSMA permit the UK court to transfer 'other property or liabilities' and liabilities that the transferor might not have capacity to transfer (ie under an agreement or an enactment). This provision has been held to be wide enough to enable contracts to be transferred without the consent of the other contracting party[1] (eg reinsurers whose consent was required under the reinsurance agreement). In practice companies may obtain the consent of such third parties (even where the court could make an order without consent). Significant practical issues can arise where, for example, a treaty is to be split between the transferor and transferee and ideally these should be resolved in advance so as not to prejudice the feasibility of the scheme.

D The process

3.77 The court process itself is commenced by submission of a claim form with supporting witness statements. A 'hearing for directions' will then be requested by application notice accompanied by the Scheme Report. At the hearing for directions the court will establish the timetable for the process and any waiver applications.

The court is likely to rely on the evidence of the independent expert that the respective policyholders are not likely to be prejudiced by the transfer and the report from the FSA. It is also likely to have regard to the FSA's view of the proposals. It seems inconceivable that a transfer opposed by the FSA could be approved. The FSA, and any person affected by the transfer, have the right to attend and speak at the court hearing. In the AXA Equity & Law Life Assurance Society and AXA Sun Life plc[2] reattribution scheme (under the predecessor legislation) the Consumers Association appeared on behalf of a representative policyholder.

The court must normally be satisfied that the transferee company will be able to carry on the classes of business transferred under the scheme and that the appropriate certificates (eg solvency margin and consent of overseas regulators) have been provided. The role of the court is not to be satisfied that the scheme is

1 *Carter Insurance Co Ltd v WASA International Insurance Co Ltd* EWHC 2698 (Ch).
2 [2001] All ER (Comm) 1010.

the best available. The court will assess the evidence including the FSA's view as to whether the scheme is within the range of reasonable outcomes. The court will be concerned that the scheme is being promoted for proper purposes and operates fairly between classes affected by it.

In a couple of instances there has been an issue with the Portuguese regulator not actually having consented to the transfer within three months (because it was still conducting its own consultation). In the Arriva Reattribution scheme[1], as the Portuguese regulator had not actually objected to the transfer and the court had jurisdiction because the three month time period had elapsed, it took the view that it would be disproportionate not to continue, especially given the number of Portuguese policyholders involved. The court cannot sanction any scheme until at least 21 days after the FSA is given the documents relating to the scheme. The transferee must deposit the court order with the FSA within ten days of it being made.

1 [2009] EWHC 2521 Ch.

CHAPTER 4

Intermediation and distribution of life insurance products

SUMMARY

SECTION 1 THE DISTRIBUTION LANDSCAPE

A Overview

4.1 The current UK regulatory regime applicable to insurance intermediary and other distribution businesses is to a large extent the result of historical provisions (many of which, eg polarisation, have now been removed) and the EU passport directive in this area, the Insurance Mediation Directive (IMD). The activity of arranging or introducing a client to an authorised person in relation to the potential sale of an insurance contract is now more tightly regulated than similar activities carried on in relation to other regulated products. The FSA, via its Retail Distribution Review will make further changes in this area with effect from the end of 2012.

B Depolarisation

4.2 One of the original aims of the Financial Services Act 1986 was to try to make it clear who intermediaries were acting for. The current legal position in the UK for insurance brokers (see Section 7 below) is that insurance brokers, other than Appointed Representatives ('ARs'), are generally regarded as the agent of the client. At the time of writing, following recommendations from the Law Commission, the Consumer Insurance (Disclosure and Representations) Bill, which had its first reading in the House of Lords on 16 May 2011, aims to make changes to this area of the law (see **2.48**).

The rule, known as polarisation, included in the original rules of the relevant Self Regulatory Organisation LAUTRO (rather than the 1986 Act), required brokers to be either independent (selling based on the whole of the market), or tied to only one product provider (or their group companies) and to disclose their status to potential clients[1]. For many years, it therefore provided clarity in this area. As a result of a report by the Office of Fair Trading in 1999 into the anti-competitive nature of the polarisation rule, the FSA announced its intention to remove it[2]. The FSA issued a series of consultation papers[3]. The earlier consultation papers provide a good summary of the polarisation regime and the issues involved in making changes to it. The FSA also started diluting the rule by not applying it to stakeholder pension schemes and direct offer financial promotions. Much of the focus in the latter stages of the FSA's consultation was on the precise mechanism for disclosing to clients the intermediary's status and commission levels (ie the content of the Initial Disclosure Document and the Menu which were introduced as part of depolarisation). Removal of the polarisation rule, took effect from 14 January 2005, and allowed a firm to operate on a whole of market or more limited basis, provided it disclosed its 'scope' to its customer. A firm that advises on a whole of market basis can offer customers a more limited range initially and then widen its range if that becomes appropriate. Firms can also offer different ranges to different customers and increase their range during the course of a sale to a particular customer. Controls still apply to the use of the term 'independent' by firms operating on a whole of market basis. Until the Retail Distribution Review is implemented, use of the term independent will depend on whether the customer is given the option to pay by way of fee rather than commission.

Changes were also made by removing the 'better than best' rule which effectively prevented many sales of products of connected providers.

The only extent to which the polarisation rule still applies, is in respect of ARs who may have only one principal for investment purpose. In practice, if that one principal is a distribution company (eg authorised in its own right to sell), then the limitation can create a whole of market or multi-tie situation (ie acting for a limited number of providers). ARs of insurance companies can also represent other insurance and UCITS operators in their group (subject to SUP12.5.6A).

1 In relation to packaged products.
2 July 2000.
3 CP 80, 121, and 04/03.

Retail Distribution Review

1 Background and issues

4.3 In June 2007, the FSA started a review, the Retail Distribution Review (RDR), to look into ongoing issues relating to distribution. Its proposed changes will take effect from the end of 2012. Their impact is likely to be a wide-scale and fundamental change to the way in which investment products are sold in the UK. The new regulations (in COBS 6), will apply to the distribution of 'retail investment products', which, although they have a wider remit than the current term 'packaged products', still include life contracts other than pure protection contracts.

The review was prompted by various inadequacies within the current sales regime identified by the FSA. Nearly all of the inadequacies have at their root the failure to treat customers fairly, resulting in insufficient consumer trust and confidence in the products and services being supplied by the life market. The specific failures identified related to charging structures and transparency of remuneration, product bias, inappropriate switching and the quality (in terms of knowledge and experience) of advisers. There were also issues with the fact that mis-selling invariably takes time to come to light. The FSA's initial views on the issues were as follows:

Charging structures/transparency of remuneration: FSA research indicated that many consumers believed that advice is 'free' if the adviser receives commission. Because commission is paid for by the product provider, many consumers are unaware that such commission is deducted from the value of their investment. So, whilst the regulatory requirement for disclosure of remuneration in theory provides sufficient information for consumers, it is not necessarily the case that consumers understand the information well enough to use it. The FSA particularly highlighted trail commission as an area with an especially poor transparency, it often not being clear what the payment of trail commission was for.

Product bias: The use of commission by product will incentivise advisers to recommend the products that pay them the most commission.

Inappropriate switching: The FSA believed that the current commission structure makes it worthwhile for advisers to switch at least some of their clients' investments between product providers at regular intervals. Although costs from switching are often largely borne by product providers, these costs are likely to be reflected in higher product charges of the market as a whole.

Quality of advisers: The FSA felt that the quality of advisers was such that they have a poor reputation among consumers and that there is a perceived lack of professionalism in the sector. This has contributed to low academic entry criteria, weak benchmark entry exams and a sales-led culture.

The FSA's stated objectives for the RDR were: to deliver fairer outcomes for consumers; to modernise the industry; to give consumers more confidence and trust in the industry; and to encourage more people to save for their retirement. In order to achieve these objectives, the fundamental measures the FSA is seeking to deliver with the RDR are: to provide greater clarity to the consumer about the services being offered; to modernise the way financial advice is paid for; and to raise the professional standards of all advisers.

2 *FSA consultation*

4.4 The FSA has consulted extensively in relation to the RDR issuing the following papers:

DP07/1 (June 2007), 'A Review of Retail Distribution'; 'Retail Distribution Review – Interim Report' (April 2008); **FS08/6** (November 2008), 'Retail Distribution Review'; **CP09/18** (June 2009), 'Distribution of retail investments – Delivering the RDR'; **CP09/31** (December 2009), 'Delivering the Retail Distribution Review'; **PS10/6** (March 2010), 'Delivering the RDR – Feedback to CP09/18 and final rules'; **CP 10/8** (March 2010), 'Pure Protection Sales by retail investment firms: remuneration transparency and the COBS/ICOBS election'; **DP10/2** (March 2010), 'Platforms delivering the RDR and other issues for discussion'; **CP10/12** (June 2010) 'Competence and Ethics'; **PS10/10** (June 2010) 'Delivering the Retail Distribution Review: Corporation pensions – Feedback to CP09/31 and final rules'; **CP 10/26** (November 2010). **PS11/1** (January 2011) 'Distribution of Retail Investments: Delivering the RDR Professionalism'; **PS11/9** Platforms.

In addition there have been the following papers on the prudential requirements for personal investment firms (eg advisers): **DP07/4** (July 2007), FS08/2 (April 2005), **CP08/20** (November 2008), **PS09/19** (November 2009) and **CP11/3** (February 2011) 'Product Disclosure: Retail Investments changes to reflect RDR Adviser Charging and to improve pension scheme disclosure'.

The rules which are in final form in most areas (except for Platforms, See **PS11/9**), have been made and will come into force at the end of 2012. There are, however, a number of issues where there is still some consultation to be undertaken by the FSA or where changes may be required due to EU changes (eg to the Insurance Mediation Directive (IMD), Markets in Financial Instruments Directive (MiFID), and the EU's proposals for Packaged Retail Investment Products (PRIPS) (see **4.15**). Personal Investment Firms will become subject to new prudential rules from the end of 2011 on a transitional basis.

3 *Summary of changes*

(a) Charges

4.5 The main changes proposed by the FSA involve a prohibition on the payment of commission and product provider involvement in setting charges, in relation to advised sales (ie involving a personal recommendation) of a retail investment product. It will still be possible to pay/receive commission in relation to pure protection products (whether sold under the FSA's Conduct of Business Sourcebook (COBS) or Insurance Conduct of Business Sourcebook (ICOBS)) and for retail investment products sold without advice[1]. It should also be noted that legacy business (ie business issued before implementation of RDR) can con-

1 But not for Group Personal Pensions, see below.

tinue to attract commission, even in respect of new members of existing pension schemes.

Advisers will also be divided between those who are 'independent' (giving advice based on a comprehensive analysis of the relevant market) and those giving 'restricted' advice. Somewhat confusingly, there will also continue to be basic advice in relation to stakeholder type products (with non group pensions products still being able to generate commission) and simplified advice. These are discussed further below (see **4.53**) but the rationale for simplified advice is to try to provide an advised process for products that can be sold to a mass market where it is perceived that a personal recommendation is required. Other consequential effects are that rebates from product providers (eg collective investment schemes), factoring or indemnity payments and soft commission will be banned. Allocation rates of more than 100% will also be banned. The FSA is also still discussing the full effect on stakeholder pensions with the Department of Work and Pensions and has been looking separately at Platforms.

The rules made by the FSA to implement the RDR (see PS10/6, PS10 and PS11/1) refer to the fees to be paid by customers as 'adviser charges' or in the case of group pension arrangements (collectively called GPPs), 'consultancy charges'. For adviser charges, the adviser firm can set its own charges for advice and this may include the situation where the client decides not to accept any recommendation made. The total amount of charges payable to the firm or its associates needs to be disclosed in cash terms. The charges may be deducted by product providers from the underlying product provided the provider has the client's written authority to do so. This will have implications for various products. (eg where the charges are structured to be payable at regular intervals). As regards life investment contracts, the charge can either be deducted before the premium is used to buy units or units can be cancelled to pay the charge. This could have an effect on the tax efficiency of the product in certain circumstances and this must be made clear to the client.

Consultancy charges in connection with GPPs are to be agreed with the employer, rather than the individual pension scheme member and notably cannot be charged where an employee elects not to join the pension scheme. Consultancy charges also cannot be levied in respect of the initial setting up of the underlying scheme. The employer may pay a fee in relation to GPPs instead of consultancy charges applying. If no fee is paid, then the employer and the adviser need to agree the consultancy charges in respect of advice (or services) to be provided to employees. In determining the level of charges, a firm should have regard to the best interests of the employer and the employer's employees. Such charges would not be expected to vary accordingly to the product provider or to conceal the amount or purpose of any such charges from the employer or an employee. The charges must be set out in writing in good time before advice or services are provided and the language used must be clear. Cash terms should also be used or if not, examples should be given in cash terms. As with adviser charges, a total consultancy charge payable to the firm or its associates in cash terms needs to be provided as early as practicable. It also needs to be clear what services the charges relate to.

In addition to banning commission and the rebating of charges to customers, the FSA's new rules will require that a firm's charges for similar (substitutable) products are the same. This is consistent with charges being product neutral. The FSA is also aware of the need to ensure that any ongoing charges are made in respect of services provided and that there is no product bias in favour of products with ongoing charges, unless that is in the customer's best interest. The FSA states that where a client changes adviser any trail commission that was being paid for ongoing service should be paid to the client, as the new adviser did not provide the service for which the commission was payable. As clients may not have the means to pay upfront charges, it might be possible instead to justify arranging credit to do so. It seems difficult to imagine (unless the credit is short term) how this will be in the clients' best interest as it might mean that they end up worse off than if the advice had not been sought because they are paying interest on the cost of the advice.

Adviser charging needs to be transparent to work. The FSA has specifically stated[1] that advisers recommending their own products will not be able to continue to receive other income streams for acting in connection with the product. It will be challenging in group situations, where services are provided by group companies, to ensure that additional profit is not being passed in the form of a cost for a service related to the product itself. The FSA will require a clear separation between advice charges and product charges and any cross-subsidisation should not be significant in the long term. As stated above, there will also be a requirement to show 'total adviser charges' in cash terms (based on likely charges where fund based). In addition to preventing inducements, firms will need to ensure that their remuneration of staff does not produce product bias. On incentives, the FSA will consult on changes to make clear that any incentives paid or provided to an adviser that do not explicitly enhance the service given to customers, would be unacceptable.

(b) Independence

4.6 The FSA describes the new regime for 'independent advice' as a new standard which makes a clear distinction between independent advice and restricted advice. To be independent, adviser firms need to make recommendations based on a comprehensive and fair analysis of the relevant market and to provide unbiased, unrestricted advice. To satisfy this requirement firms will need to show that they have conducted a review of the 'relevant market' and chosen products which are in their clients' best interests. In the FSA's view, it is reasonable for clients to expect an independent adviser to be able to advise on the full range of products that might be suitable for the client. It would therefore seem that to exclude products the firm would need to be able to justify a conclusion that particular products (eg unregulated collective investment schemes of Exchange Traded Funds) would not be suitable for its clients. Firms can still construct panels but against this backdrop and subject to the proviso that any panel must be reviewed regularly. Advisers also need to be careful in relation to their own or group company's products (eg Distributor Influenced Funds) to ensure that there is no bias. A 'relevant market' for these purposes is all retail invest-

1 CP/0/6 at 4.11.

ment products that are capable of meeting the investment needs and objectives of a retail client. So for example, if a firm specialises in giving advice to particular clients (eg charities), there will be products which are not appropriate to charities and do not form part of that relevant market. However, if there is a product outside the relevant market which the firm is not able to consider, it must direct the client to an adviser that is capable of doing so. The FSA does not currently intend to prevent IFAs from being financed, owned or part-owned by product providers. However, they said they will wish to keep this under review. In particular they will need to be satisfied that firms have appropriate controls to prevent ownership or financing arrangements translating into any form of restriction on the products and services that the advisers might access in making recommendations to clients.

(c) Restricted advice

4.7 The other basis on which advice can be provided is 'restricted advice', which as its name suggest is restricted in some way, either a restricted range of companies or just one company. Despite apparent concerns that 'restricted' has negative connotations, the FSA believes it to be the best term available. An important point to note about restricted advice is that it is still subject to the full suitability requirement. If, therefore, the adviser's choice of products does not include a suitable product, it should not sell any product. The adviser cannot recommend the closest match that it has available. It would need to refer the client to another adviser. Firms providing restricted advice will be required to make an oral disclosure to explain that they are providing restricted advice. They will not, however, have to also explain that independent advice is also available.

(d) Advice

4.8 The FSA has decided to restrict its new regime to retail investment products (a new defined term but which still catches qualifying life contracts). This means that non-advised sales (other than in relation to GPPs) will not be subject to the regime. This will make the distinction between situations where a personal recommendation is made, and one where it is not, much more significant. In practice this is already quite difficult in cases of telephone sales. The FSA has set out a guide to borderline issues in Annex 7 of its Feedback Statement 08/6. The FSA makes the point that advice must be specific (ie not generic), more than just information and must relate to the merits of a proposed course of action. The other point to note is in relation to simplified advice, sometimes called guided sales. It is considered desirable that, for at least some products, a new form of advice (presumably predominantly technology based and/or using decision trees), be available for products suitable to mass market customers who may not be able to afford (or wish to pay for the full advice regime). It appears that the FSA is expecting the industry to come up with proposals on this and the industry has been looking for a steer from the FSA. However, the FSA has made it clear that advisers involved in simplified advice will need to meet the same professional standard and have the same qualifications as other advisers.

(e) Further changes

4.9 The FSA has made most of the relevant rules in good time before the implementation date but it has a number of issues still to address. The FSA has said it will look at a possible early transition arrangement for firms wishing to use the new basis before implementation. Perhaps a bigger issue, is the ongoing development at EU level of the relevant 'product' based underlying directives and in particular sales and disclosure requirements (eg IMD and UCITS) and the proposed regulation of PRIPS (see **4.15**). The EU is currently reviewing these underlying directives (see **4.12** in relation to IMD) and may make rules in relation to PRIPS which are inconsistent with the FSA's rules. It appears this is something the FSA accepts it will need to manage.

(f) Advisers

4.10 The FSA proposes to increase the quality of advice given to consumers by raising minimum standards of competence, skills, knowledge and professional qualifications for advisers – these measures seem to have been broadly accepted by the industry. The FSA intends that advisers giving non-independent advice will have to meet the same professional standards as apply to independent advice. There will be an overarching Professional Standards Board to establish a common framework for professional standards across all advice channels. Initially (and for an interim period) this will be a sub-committee of the FSA Board. For all investment advisers there will be a benchmark qualification of at least QCA level 4 (from level 3) which apparently equates to first year degree level.

(g) Platforms

4.11 The one area where there are outstanding RDR issues relates to advised sales via Platforms.The FSA has made some rules (eg defining 'platform services' and 'platform service provider' and including them in the provisions relating to adviser charging) but has indicated that it intends to make further rules in two particular areas, payments from Platforms and the payment of cash rebates from Platforms.

Platforms have sprung up in recent years in two forms. First, the fund supermarket model which generally provides access to a large number of funds at no explicit added cost to the consumer. Secondly, the wrap Platforms which have a separate charge for their services, paid direct by the customer. The wrap Platforms offer cash accounts to pay charges and these also receive any rebates from product providers that the Platform has negotiated, essentially for dealing on a wholesale basis. The FSA was concerned that Platforms could be used to undermine the effect of the RDR ban on commission. The main issues identified were how adviser charging could be delivered, how the Platform itself would be remunerated and whether advisers using a Platform could deliver independent advice. The FSA issued DP 10/2 in March 2010, CP 10/29 in November 2010 and PS11/9 in August 2011. In PS11/9 the FSA indicated that it would make further rules in relation to product provider payments to Platforms and rebates but that they would not come into effect before the end of 2012, when RDR will be implemented.

On the main issue of facilitating adviser charging, the FSA accepted that Platforms could facilitate the payment of adviser charges. To do so they would need the consent of the underlying customer. In PS11/9 the FSA responded to questions about the requirement to 'obtain and validate' the client's instruction and whether that needed to be a wet signature. The FSA stated (in 2.9) that a copy of the form signed by the client could be enough if there is no reason to doubt the validity of the information.

The issue of how Platforms should be remunerated stems partly from the difficulty in categorising what they do as either distribution or administration. In many ways they have been described as the back office of the product provider and their services can save the provider administration expense. However, as the gateway to the underlying advisers, the choice of funds available on a Platform clearly influences both the investment and cost options available to the ultimate client. In the fund supermarket scenario, there was a concern that the lack of transparency over costs and issues with disclosure, meant that customers would not get an accurate picture. Conversely, with the wrap Platforms, there was concern over the way fund managers deliver a particular price (eg through charging a standard charge and paying a rebate).In PS 10/29 the FSA accepted that Platforms are not predominantly distributors and could be allowed to continue to charge a fee for their administration services. They were still concerned, however, that Platforms do not charge too high a price to allow underlying investments 'shelf space', which might thereby limit choice. The FSA also said that it intended to stop the practice of fund managers rebating money (ie cash) which is then passed back to clients. In PS11/9 the FSA retained its stance in relation to cash rebates but has changed its mind in relation to payment from providers to Platforms. It now says that it intends to make rules to ban payments by product providers to Platforms.

The issue in relation to the independence of advisers using the services of a Platform, is really one of whether they can cover the whole market and comply, in relation to MiFID type investments, with their obligation to provide best execution. The FSA accepts that an independent firm may be able to use a single Platform for the majority of its clients but this choice must be based on a comprehensive and unbiased view of the market. In doing this, the adviser firm would need to comply with the client's best interest rule (see **4.33**).

C The Insurance Mediation Directive

4.12 The IMD was adopted by the EU in 2002. Insurance mediation activities are the activities of introducing, proposing or carrying out other work preparatory to the conclusion of a contract of insurance or of concluding such contracts, or of assisting in the administration and performance of such contracts, in particular in the event of a claim[1]. The IMD also provides that these activities when undertaken by an insurance undertaking or an employee of an insurance undertaking, who is acting under the responsibility of the insurance undertaking, shall

1 Article 2, Directive 2002/92/EC.

not be considered as insurance mediation. In implementing the directive, the Treasury and the FSA decided to extend the relevant provisions to insurance companies in relation to their authorised activities (ie the permission they need) and in their dealings with retail clients (COBS/ICOBS). This has the bizarre effect of requiring UK insurers to have permission to arrange their own contracts even where they have been sold by an independent intermediary. The IMD requires member states to authorise and keep a register of authorised intermediaries carrying on insurance mediation. Only appropriately authorised individuals can be involved in the sales process. Intermediaries must be of good character, satisfy minimum training and experience requirements and maintain appropriate capital assets. Authorised intermediaries must disclose information to customers, including providing a statement of demands and needs, and a policy summary.

1 Exclusions

4.13 The IMD provides an exclusion for insurance mediation in connection with short-term[1] non-life contracts with an annual premium of 500 euros or less which are 'complementary' to a product or service ('connected contracts'). The requirements of this exclusion are that the insurance covers risk of breakdown, loss of baggage and other risks related to travel booked with the provider. This travel cover may include life and liability risk (which are otherwise excluded) provided they are ancillary to the travel-related risk. It is further a requirement of this exclusion that the principal professional activity of the intermediary is not insurance mediation and that the intermediary is not required to have knowledge of other types of insurance contract in order to provide its services in relation to the contract.

The IMD does not apply if the activity undertaken is limited to the provision of information as part of another professional activity and provided the provision of information was on an 'incidental basis'. Further exclusions apply in relation to the activity of 'assisting in the administration and performance of a contract of insurance' as part of an insurance company's own management of claims and management undertaken on its behalf on a professional basis. Similarly, loss adjusting and expert appraisal of claims do not constitute insurance mediation. However, it is worth noting that the provisions of the directive do apply to insurance mediation activities in connection with reinsurance business.

The IMD was implemented in the UK on 14 January 2005 ('NGI')[3] at the same time as the regulation of general insurance. It was implemented in the main by changes to the Regulated Activities Order[3] (RAO) and the Appointed Representatives Regulations 2001, SI 2001/1217.

2 Review of the IMD

4.14 On 26 November 2010, the European Commission invited member states and interested parties to submit comments on the current functioning of, and a number of possible changes to, the IMD. The Commission has identified

1 Five years or less.
2 Except in relation to long-term care insurance which was regulated from 31 October 2004.
3 SI 2001/544.

six main areas for consultation as follows: consistent policyholder protection and information; the scope of the regime; professional requirements; the application of the IMD to non-EEA countries; notification requirements for cross border business; and conflicts of interest, remuneration and transparency. Many of these issues are similar to those identified by the FSA as part of the RDR. In the consultation paper the Commission stated that any revision of the IMD would consist of two parts, one the introduction of MiFID inspired conduct of business and conflicts of interest rules regulating the sale of packaged products (PRIPS) and another for non-PRIPS products. The Commission has also raised the issue of whether commission disclosure should be mandated and whether 'introducing' should be excluded from the scope of the IMD. These are therefore likely to be considered in any future changes.

The Commission received 125 responses to the public consultation and has now published a document summarising these contributions. The prevailing opinion is that the level of policyholder protection embodied in EU law needs to be raised. Members of the insurance industry highlighted the need for consumer protection to be consistent across the whole of the EU and many stakeholders suggested the introduction of a European standard for 'status' information in order to harmonise the information requirements for insurance intermediaries.

The Commission reports that many respondents felt that there needed to be greater transparency in relation to administrative costs. Conversely, there is a view that increased disclosure requirements could result in a number of adverse effects, including the provision of lower quality advice and a shift to low cost non-advised sales via the internet. The bulk of respondents also supported the Commission's proposal to extend the scope of the IMD to other entities involved in insurance mediation activities, eg banking and insurance companies. Some respondents added the caveat that the expansion should not impose an excessive administrative burden on market players with a different core activity and that all requirements should be proportionate to the consumer exposure and risk entailed. A general clearing system for 'general good' requirements was also suggested. The Commission reports that there was a level of disagreement as to whether higher levels of professional requirement should be introduced for insurance intermediaries but a majority of respondents agreed that the revised IMD should contain a Chapter on the selling practices of PRIPS insurance products. Finally, there was a widely-held view that the revised IMD should contain definitions of 'advice', 'freedom of establishment' and 'freedom to provide services'. It was felt that this would enhance the IMD's effectiveness and improve its clarity.

The next step is for the Commission to prepare a formal proposal, although this may need to reflect the review of MiFID also taking place.

D PRIPS

4.15 A PRIP is likely to be defined as:

> 'a product where the amount payable to the investor is exposed to **fluctuations** in the market value of assets or payouts from assets, through a combination or **wrapping** of those assets or **other** mechanisms **than a direct holding**'.

It is also understood that personal pensions may not be categorised as PRIPS. The EU consultation on PRIPS closed in January 2011. It identified similar issues to the IMD consultation regarding conflicts of interest and investor confidence. It is believed that the way to restore consumer confidence is to provide a standardisation across wrappers available to packaged products so that consumers can make a more informed choice. It is therefore proposed that there be new rules relating to sales of such products and that this be achieved by aligning the underlying product directives, with a more MiFID based approach. However, for pre-sales disclosure, it would appear that the opposite approach of mandating a prescribed 'Key Investor Information Document', similar to that applicable to UCITS is likely. This document would be deemed to comply with the other directive requirements (eg IMD and MiFID). The timetable for this is not yet known.

SECTION 2 THE NEED FOR AUTHORISATION

A Overview

4.16 IMD activities include both the obvious advising, dealing as agent and arranging insurance contracts and the much less obvious activities in relation to insurance contracts of introducing to authorised or exempt persons, assisting in the administration of contracts or agreeing to carry on any of these regulated activities. The scheme of the Financial Services and Markets Act 2000 (FSMA) is that the Regulated Activities Order ('RAO') sets out the detail of the instruments (investments) and the activities in relation to investments which are regulated. In implementing the IMD (and to provide for the regulation of general insurance contracts) the FSA had to deal separately with ARs and their 'representative'[1] staff who are also covered by the directive[2].

B Implementation of the IMD

4.17 The FSA only needed to introduce two new regulated activities as IMD activities were, subject to existing exemptions, already covered by the RAO. Those existing exemptions may not now apply where they relate to contracts of insurance. This will affect preliminary or introductory activities which could lead to the sale of an insurance contract, particularly where the intermediary is remunerated on the basis of the number of insurance contracts sold which could formerly have been covered by Article 33 of the RAO. The FSA has included fairly detailed guidance in Chapter 5 of PERG (the Perimeter Guidance Manual) in relation to activities which constitute IMD activities.

The 'investments' covered by the RAO were extended from 31 October 2004 to long-term care insurance and from 14 January 2005 to general insurance and pure protection (mainly term assurance) life contracts. The first new 'activity' intro-

1 See FSA Glossary definition of representative and **4.27**.
2 Appointed Representatives Regulations SI 2001/1217.

duced was 'assisting in the administration and performance of a contract of insurance'[1]. Consistent with the IMD, this does not include claims management and loss adjusting on behalf of an authorised insurer or expert appraisal carried on in the course of any profession or business[2]. The second new 'activity' is in Article 25(2), making arrangements 'with a view' to a person buying an insurance contract (eg introducing them to someone else for that purpose). As stated above, the exemption in Article 33 for introducing, no longer applies in relation to introductions with a view to an insurance contract. However, there is still an exemption in Article 72C in relation to the provision of information on an 'incidental basis'. The dividing line for Article 25(2) activity and the exemption in Article 72C is, however, a fine one. PERG 5 makes clear that the exemption in Article 72C could allow a dentist to provide information about dental (but not pet insurance) but it would not permit the dentist to assist in the completion of any forms (see **4.19**).

The question of how the dentist is remunerated may also be relevant. Another important requirement emphasised in the FSA guidance is the need to carry on the activities by way of business (as required by section 22 of FSMA 2000)[3]. In relation to insurance mediation, the FSA says there are two questions. First does the person receive remuneration (in its widest sense), and second, if so, does he pursue the activities by way of business? This is obviously slightly circular but will not usually cover activities undertaken on a one-off basis. Normally an activity (eg introduction in exchange for a fee) will be a critical element. A flat fee for the provision of information on an incidental basis[4] may not be caught whereas a volume-related payment could be. PERG 5.4.8 G contains a table that summarises the main issues surrounding the business test and draws out the difference between a 'reward' for insurance mediation activities and remuneration which is not specifically identified as such by the parties involved.

It is worth looking in detail at the guidance in PERG which takes the reader through most of the issues relating to who should be authorised for IMD purposes. In PERG 5.15.2 G the FSA has included a flowchart to assist with the question of whether authorisation is required. PERG 5.2.8 summarises the regulated activities that may potentially apply in relation to a contract of insurance as follows:

(1)	Article 21	Dealing as agent.
(2)	Article 25(1)	Arranging (bringing about) deals.
(3)	Article 25(2)	Arrangements 'with a view' to bringing about (eg introducing).
(4)	Article 39A	Assisting in administration and performance of.
(5)	Article 53	Advising.
(6)	Article 64	Agreeing to carry on any such regulated activities.

Whilst the RAO relies in the main on its own categorisation of 'investments' and 'activities', whether certain exemptions will continue to apply is determined by

1 Article 39A.
2 Article 39B.
3 PERG 5.4.2 and the Business Order (SI 2001/1177).
4 Article 72C.

reference to the IMD itself. The relevant provisions of the IMD are included in Schedule 4 of the RAO[1].

1 Arranging

4.18 In relation to the other potential triggers for authorisation for insurance mediation purposes, the guidance makes clear[2] that in the FSA's view, Article 25(1) (arranging) extends to a person whose involvement in the chain of events leading to the contract of insurance is so important that without it there would be no policy. Somewhat surprisingly it then goes on to include in this category the insurance company issuing the policy. This means that in order to 'effect' a contract of insurance a UK authorised insurer must have permission to arrange it. The FSA's stance in applying the IMD provisions to insurers seems at odds with the previous nature of the authorisation given to insurers which exempts them from other requirements (eg in relation to deposits and activities undertaken as part of the investment of their assets) in carrying on insurance business and arguably with the implied scope of the Consolidated Life Directive.

2 Introducing

4.19 Arrangements 'with a view' to bringing about a potential transaction generally take the form of introductions. Article 33 provides an exemption for specified introductions which was previously relied upon in relation to insurance contracts. As a result of the IMD, this exemption may not now apply in relation to activities in respect of potential insurance contracts. Article 33 can still, however, apply where the introduction is for independent advice on investments[3]. The FSA emphasises that to require authorisation for the purposes of introducing the person must first satisfy the 'by way of business' test. Part of this test is likely to be whether the person introducing receives a pecuniary reward linked to the volume of insurance business done as a result of his introductions. The FSA guidance also makes clear that one-off introductions not part of a pre-existing arrangement between introducer and introducee will not be caught by Article 25(2). A table in PERG 5.6.21 contains examples of the application of Article 33. A further exclusion is set out in Article 32 in relation to introductions in relation to the provision of finance to fund the acquisition of the contract of insurance.

The exclusion in Article 72C is also relevant. This exclusion applies[4] to information provided to potential or actual policyholders. It must be provided by a person carrying on any profession or business which does not otherwise consist of regulated activities. The FSA emphasises that the business may involve carrying on regulated activities (eg exempt professional firms) but those activities

1 In relation to Articles 39, 66 and 67. Article 4A of the RAO.

2 PERG 5.6.2G.

3 PERG 5.6.19.

4 In relation to arranging and assisting in the administration and performance of a contract of insurance.

must not be the main focus of the business. The provision of information must also be capable of being reasonably regarded as 'incidental' (in the sense of being complementary) to that profession or business (eg the dentist providing information related to dental but not pet insurance).

Further exclusions to Article 25(2) apply in respect of communication companies[1] and where the arranger is the policyholder but not the insurer[2].

3 Advice

4.20 In relation to the regulated activity of providing advice, the FSA makes the point[3] that the advice must relate to a particular contract of insurance (eg a particular insurer or contract but not just life insurance). Generic or general advice will not therefore be caught by this. Further guidance is included in the table in PERG 5.8.5. Article 54 contains an exclusion from Article 53 in relation to advice given in periodical publications, regularly updated news and information services and broadcasts, provided the principal purpose of the publication is not to provide advice.

4 Assisting in administration and performance

4.21 Exclusions also apply to the regulated activity of assisting in the administration and performance of a contract of insurance in relation to claims management and loss adjustment on behalf of an authorised insurer. Similar activities undertaken on the policyholder's behalf, particularly where they involve the person dealing with the insurer (eg helping the policyholder to complete a claims form and agreeing claims) are likely to require authorisation[4].

5 Agreeing to carry on

4.22 In relation to Article 64 (agreeing to carry on other regulated activities), the FSA emphasises that merely making an offer to do so is not enough. A legally binding agreement is required and authorisation is required even if the activities themselves are never actually undertaken. Also exclusions applicable to the underlying regulated activity itself will also apply in relation to agreeing to carry on the activity.

6 Other exclusions

4.23 Generally available exclusions, including Article 67 (activities as part of a profession or non-investment business), Article 72B (connected contracts) and Article 72 (large risks outside the EEA) can also apply to IMD activities.

1 Article 27 providing the means of communication.
2 Article 28.
3 In PERG 5.8.4.
4 PERG 5.7.7.

Article 67 permits professional firms, such as solicitors, to continue to provide insurance mediation activities (subject to the relevant individuals' names being kept on the register of their designated professional body – eg by the Law Society). Connected contracts are the contracts referred to at **4.4** and cover breakdown of non-motor goods and travel insurance provided on an incidental basis. Other exclusions are specifically stated not to be available in connection with contracts of insurance (eg Article 29, arranging deals with or through an authorised person and Article 69, activities provided within a group or joint enterprise). These were both previously important exemptions. In relation to groups, the FSA pointed out (as part of the IMD implementation) that the group company (eg normally a service company) has to be providing the relevant service by way of business to be caught. As many intra-group service companies only provide services to the insurer they may not be providing services by way of business but they need to be careful if they are involved in other activities such as helping a policyholder to fill in an application form (eg arranging) or providing services to a third party[1].

7 *Territorial scope*

4.24 PERG 5.15.8G contains a flowchart to help answer the question of whether regulated activities are carried on in the UK. Consideration should be given to section 418 of FSMA 2000 which extends territorial scope (eg in relation to UK authorised companies using passporting rights) and the availability of the overseas person exemption (Article 72 – where there is no UK place of business). The FSA notes that the activity of arranging will usually be considered to be carried on where those activities take place[2]. In relation to advice it will generally be carried on where the advice is received. PERG 5.2.17 reminds firms that services provided by electronic means will, despite the E-Commerce Directive, be required to comply with IMD requirements (eg registration in country of origin).

8 *Appointed Representatives*

4.25 An AR can only carry on the activities specified in the Appointed Representatives Regulations[3]. These include the IMD activities set out in the table in PERG 5.3.4. For life policies they are arranging, introducing, advising and assisting in administration and performance of a contract of insurance and agreeing to carry on those activities. SUP 12.4 sets out what a firm must do when it appoints an AR. SUP 12.5 sets out detailed requirements relating to the content of the contract making the appointment. An AR will not be able to provide insurance mediation activity until he is included on the FSA register for such activities. It is worth remembering that the principal will need to be authorised for

1 PERG 5.11.G.
2 PERG 5.12.8.
3 SI 2001/1217.

insurance mediation activities and that ARs cannot approve financial promotions.

SECTION 3 APPOINTED REPRESENTATIVES

A Exempt status

4.26 Section 39 of FSMA 2000 allows an authorised person to appoint others (ARs) for specified purposes that are treated as 'exempt' for the purpose of FSMA 2000. This does not mean that their activities are not regulated; they are but normally through the authorised person, their principal. The principal will have to accept responsibility for any such activities undertaken by the AR[1]. One of the changes under FSMA from the 1986 Act is that a person can no longer be an authorised person for one regulated activity and an AR for others[2]. The activities that can be undertaken by an AR are set out in a statutory instrument (the Appointed Representatives Regulations[3]). These regulations also deal with the provisions to be covered by the contract between an AR and their principal. Even in the post-depolarisation world, ARs selling packaged products (eg life products other than pure protection) are required to sell only the products of one principal (or relevant companies in their group). It is common for ARs appointed in relation to life investment contracts to also sell mortgages and general insurance. This means that they will have other principals (in the case of general insurance there may be more than one principal for different classes of such business). The contract is required to deal with this (see **4.29**).

SUP 12 contains rules and guidance relating to ARs. SUP 10 contains provisions in relation to Approved Persons which are also relevant.

It is implicit in the rules (and the FSA states it to be the case in SUP 12.4.1A) that regulated activities covered by an AR agreement need to fall within the scope of the principal's own permission or be excluded by Article 28 (arranging transactions to which the arranger is a party). This means UK authorised insurers also need a permission to cover these activities. This approach creates some uncertainty when it is applied to EEA insurers passporting into the UK whose own home authorisation includes such activities. As there is no passporting right under the IMD for insurers, their single licence is derived from their home state under the Consolidated Life Directive which enables them to both sell into and set up branches in the UK. Also, in their home state they will normally be able to appoint agents to do what they themselves can do. It is submitted that such authorisation should apply throughout the EEA and in particular should enable them to sell through a UK agency by satisfying the branch requirements for passporting (see Chapter 3). The FSA accepts that ARs can passport under the IMD (effectively using the principal's authorisation).

1 They will have responsibilities as Approved Persons.
2 FSMA 2000, s 39(1).
3 SI 2001/1217.

4.27 Before looking at the Appointed Representatives Regulations and the provisions of SUP 12, it is worth setting out the meaning of some of the terms used in this area (eg Adviser AR, Representative, Introducer, Introducer AR Network).

Adviser: an individual who is: a representative; or an appointed representative.

Appointed Representative: (in accordance with section 39 of the Act (other than an authorised person)):

(a) is a party to a contract with an authorised person (his principal) which:

  (i) permits or requires him to carry on business of a description prescribed in the Appointed Representatives Regulations; and

  (ii) complies with such requirements as are prescribed in those Regulations; and

(b) is someone for whose activities in carrying on the whole or part of that business his principal has accepted responsibility in writing;

and who is therefore an exempt person in relation to any regulated activity comprised in the carrying on of that business for which his principal has accepted responsibility.

Introducer: an individual appointed by a firm, or by an Appointed Representative, to carry out in the course of designated investment business either or both of the following activities:

(a) effecting introductions;

(b) distributing non-real time financial promotions.

Representative: an individual who:

(a) is appointed by a firm, or by an appointed representative of a firm, to carry on any of the following activities:

  (i) advising on investments;

  (ii) providing basic advice on stakeholder products;

  (iii) arranging (bringing about) deals in investments;

  (iv) dealing in investments; or,

(b) although not appointed to do so, carries on any of the activities in (i) to (iii) on behalf of a firm or its appointed representative.

An AR may be a company, a partnership or an individual. Where the AR is an individual they may also be a 'representative' for the purposes of regulation.

B Prescribed activities and the AR contract

4.28 The prescribed activities an AR can be appointed to perform are:

(1) Article 21: Dealing in investments as agent.

(2) Article 25(1) and 25A(2): Arranging (bringing about) deals in investments or regulated mortgages.

(3) Article 25(2) and 25A(2): Arrangements 'with a view to' a transaction in investments or regulated mortgages.

(4) Article 39A: Assisting in the administration and performance of a contract of insurance.

(5) Article 40: Arranging safeguarding and administration of assets.

(6) Article 52B: Basic advice on stakeholder products.

(7) Article 53 and 53A: Advising on investments or regulated mortgages.

(8) Article 64: Agreeing to carry on any of the above regulated activities.

4.29 A firm therefore needs to satisfy itself that the terms of the AR contract enable it to ensure that the AR's activities fall within both the prescribed activities and the scope of the principal's own permission. The contract must also require the AR to co-operate with the FSA and allow it access to premises[1]. It must provide access rights for the firm's auditors specified in section 341 of the FSMA 2000[2].

The AR must be required by the contract to advise the firm when it is 'seeking' appointment as an AR of another firm[3]. It must also be required to advise the firm as soon as possible of changes to or termination of such appointments. This will only be relevant where the principal has not prohibited such appointments. The AR agreement must allow the principal to prohibit or restrict such appointments in the future[4]. Where the AR is carrying on IMD activities other than introducing, there must be a provision to the effect that he is not permitted to carry on such business unless he is included in the FSA register for IMD purposes[5]. The AR contract must also provide for compliance with relevant requirements (including the FSA Rules) by contractors or employees of an AR firm. In relation to the AR's activities on behalf of the firm, the firm must also be able to terminate the contract unless it has reasonable grounds to believe that the AR is suitable (see below), that the firm has adequate control over the activities for which it is responsible and that the firm is able to and is organised to comply with requirements of SUP 12.

Because of the way a number of insurance groups are organised the FSA has retained the ability for ARs of long term insurers (or operators of UCITS) to

1 SUP 14.5.3. See also SUP 2.3.4G and 2.3.5G(2).
2 See SUP 3.6.6.G
3 SUP 12.5.5.
4 Regulation 3(1)-(3) AR Regs SUP 12.5.6A.
5 SUP 12.5.2(3).

permit their ARs to sell the insurance and UCITS products of members of their groups (eg the same holding company) provided the scope of each appointment does not overlap as to both activities and investments (SUP 12.5.6A).

C Approved Person status

4.30 The AR, its senior management (governing functions) and any representatives dealing with customers will need to become Approved Persons (see Chapter 3). In addition to the application to the FSA for 'approval', the firm will need to comply with other rules before appointing an AR. In relation to a full AR (as opposed to an introducer AR) the firm must establish on reasonable grounds that the AR is suitable to act as its AR. This includes a requirement that the AR is solvent and has no 'close links' (eg connected parties) likely to prevent the effective supervision of the AR by the firm. In considering suitability the firm should have regard to SUP 12 Annex 2G. The process includes reviewing the character, competence and financial resources of the AR. The firm must also ensure that the appointment does not prevent it from continuing to satisfy the 'threshold conditions'[1] (see **3.17**). In particular it must have adequate control of the AR's activities and be organised and able to comply with SUP 12.

Where the AR has already been appointed as the AR of another authorised person, the firm should enter into a multiple principal agreement with the other principals before it appoints the AR. The main purpose of the multiple principal agreement is to provide clarity to consumers (eg in relation to a single principal to manage complaints)[2]. The requirements include arrangements for approving financial promotions, training and competence, co-operation and sharing of information between the principals. The firm to whom the consumer complains is known as the 'lead principal'[3].

D Introducer Appointed Representatives

4.31 The requirements are slightly different in relation to Introducer ARs. Although the firm still has to check that the person is of good repute and otherwise fit, it does not have to carry out the more extensive due diligence required for the appointment of an AR under SUP 12.4.2.R. Introducer AR contracts are also not included for the purpose of the requirement to enter into multiple principal agreements or the Approved Persons regime[4].

1 SUP 12.4.2.
2 SUP 12.4.5B and C.
3 SUP 12.4–5D.
4 SUP 10.4.1R.

E Continuing requirements

4.32 The continuing obligations of the firm in relation to ARs are set out in SUP 12.6. These require the firm to take immediate remedial action and/or terminate the AR contract if appropriate. ARs holding client money must be required to comply with CASS (the client money rules). Firms should also ensure that the AR does not overstep its authority or hold itself out as being able to do so[1] and complies with the required terms of the AR contract[2]. Notification to the FSA of the appointment of an AR and any changes are required in accordance with SUP 12.7. SUP 12.8 requires firms to make and retain records in relation to its dealings and agreements with ARs[3].

Training and competence requirements are a major part of the practical requirements in respect of ARs. Training and Competence (TC), the relevant part of the FSA Handbook, sets out requirements for advisers in relation to recruitment, training and competence including the need to be assessed and pass relevant exams before being authorised to advise customers.

SECTION 4 THE COBS REQUIREMENTS – CLIENT CLASSIFICATION, DISCLOSURE AND SUITABILITY

A Overview of COBS

4.33 The Conduct of Business (COBS) rulebook replaced COB with effect from 1 November 2007 as part of the FSA's implementation of the Markets in Financial Directive (MiFID). As with changes from ICOB to ICOBS (see Section 6), the FSA has sought, where possible, to streamline its detailed rules by referring to the provisions of relevant EU directives, which for COBS includes MiFID, the Consolidated Life Directive (CLD), the Insurance Mediation Directive (IMD) and the Distance Marketing Directive (DMD). COBS 1, Annex 1 also now includes guidance as to the territorial scope of COBS. This is done by reference to the underlying directives specified above. The general rules for EEA insurers and intermediaries are therefore specified in relation to the IMD and CLD. So, for example, an insurance intermediary passporting into the UK will be subject to the rules of its home country implementing the IMD minimum requirements and additional rules. If there are no such rules in the home state, the intermediary will be subject to the COBS rules. For EEA insurers selling to the UK policyholders, the rules on cancellation, pre-contractual disclosure and financial promotions apply.

COBS introduced the overriding concepts of the 'client's best interest rule' and the 'fair, clear and not misleading rule' which apply to designated investment business (ie including life products other than pure protection) carried on for a retail client. The client's best interests rule, in COBS 2.1.1, is that a firm

1 SUP 12.6.6.
2 SUP 12.6.11A.
3 SUP 12.9.1.

must act honestly, fairly and professionally in accordance with the best interests of the client. The fair, clear and not misleading rule, in COBS 4.2.1, provides that a firm must ensure that a communication or financial promotion is fair, clear and not misleading. Note that COBS states that not only financial promotions but all communications with customers must be fair, clear and not misleading. Also, a firm should not, in any communication relating to designated investment business, seek to exclude or restrict any duty or liability that it may have to a client under the regulatory system (eg FSMA, applicable directives, FSA 'Principles' rules and guidance (COBS 2.1.2-3).

COBS contains numerous disclosure requirements (see **4.39**).The FSA has replaced the Initial Disclosure Document and Menu formerly required by COB with the 'services and costs disclosure document'. There are still 'combined disclosure documents' (eg pure protection, regulated mortgages and a packaged product) and initial disclosure documents applicable for the purposes of ICOBS. In COBS 6.3.3G, the FSA explains that a services and costs disclosure document (SCDD) or combined disclosure document (CDD) (both of which can use the Key Facts logo) will, in its view, enable insurance intermediary to comply with the status disclosure requirement (see summary of disclosure requirement in **4.39**). However, the FSA cannot now (because of MiFID), require that its standard documents be used. This Chapter does not, unless specifically stated, seek to describe any of the requirements that apply in relation to MiFID (or equivalent third country business) as insurance is not covered by MiFID but some advisers may be subject to additional rules if they are giving independent advice or also advising in relation to collective investment schemes.

Where there is an obligation to make a disclosure, it is required to be made in a 'durable medium' or using a website which satisfies the 'website conditions'. Durable medium is defined in the FSA Handbook but basically means paper or any other means of communication that can be stored by the customer. The 'website conditions' are that the website must provide up to date information which is continuously accessible for such time as the client may reasonably need to check it. The client must have consented to the provision of information via a website. The firm must also believe it to be appropriate (eg the client has provided an email address for communications) and the client must have been notified electronically of the details of how to access the information (eg website address and location of the information).

B Classifying the customer

4.34 COBS 3.2.1 provides that, before providing a service in the course of carrying on regulated activities with or for any client, a firm must notify the client whether that client is a retail client, a professional client or an eligible counterparty. A client for this purpose is defined as someone to whom the firm may provide services in carrying on regulated activities, a person to whom a financial promotion is or is likely to be communicated or a person who is a client of a firm's Appointed Representative[1]. A client also includes a potential

1 COBS 3.2.1.

client[1]. The FSA has also specified in certain circumstances who is to be treated as the client (eg normally the underlying client if the firm deals with an agent or the trustee of a trust).

1 Retail client

4.35 Much of the protection provided by COBS relates only to retail clients but this is expanded (particularly in relation to product disclosure) to cover information provided, for example, in relation to pension schemes and life policies sold by intermediaries to other types of client. 'Retail client' is defined as a client that is not a professional client or an eligible counterparty. It will generally cover private individuals (eg acting outside the course of their ordinary business) and small businesses (eg annual turnover less than £5m) acting on a similar or mixed purpose basis[2]. The obligation on a firm to classify the client is therefore vital to establish the way an intermediary firm should deal with that client. It should also enable particularly sophisticated customers to opt out of regulatory protection, at least in part. At the other end of the investment spectrum, a range of simplified stakeholder products can be sold with very limited basic advice (see Section 4G below).

2 Professional client and eligible counterparty

4.36 A professional client may be either a 'per se professional client' or an 'elective professional client'[3]. Many FSA authorised entities will be per se professional clients and can be eligible counterparties. Elective professional clients can be a body corporate (including an LLP) whose holding companies or subsidiaries have a called up share capital of at least £5m, or who satisfy two of the following criteria: a balance sheet total of €12.5m, a net turnover of €25m or an average number of employees during the year of 250, a local or public authority, a partnership with at least £10m, a trustee of a trust with assets of £10m or a trustee of a large occupational pension scheme. An elective professional client is one who is a per se professional client or meets the criteria and elects to opt up to the higher status. Similar provisions apply for eligible counterparties who can be either per se[4] or elective eligible counterparties[5]. An elective eligible counterparty is an entity which meets the requirements for a per se professional client, is a body corporate (including an LLP) whose holding companies or subsidiaries have a called up share capital of at least £10m or meets two of the three requirements above relating to balance sheet, turnover or number of employees. Slightly different threshold tests apply for MiFID and COBS 3.1.4 requires that in

1 COBS 3.2.1(2).
2 See definition of per se professional client, COBS 3.5.2(2).
3 COBS 3.5.2 and 3.5.3.
4 COBS 3.6.2.
5 COBS 3.6.4.

relation to mixed business (ie involving potentially MiFID investment or non MiFID investment), the client should be categorised using the MiFID thresholds.

A firm must notify a client that it can request a higher level of regulatory protection[1] but it need not notify it that it can request a lower level of protection. A client who is an elective professional client may, in relation to a transaction for which they could be treated as a professional client, request that they be treated as an elective eligible counterparty. A firm may obtain confirmation of a client's agreement to be treated as an eligible counterparty in a general agreement or in an agreement for each transaction.

3 *Reclassification*

4.37 A firm may classify a client who would otherwise be a retail client as a professional client if, having taken reasonable care in its determination, it decides that the client has sufficient experience and understanding to be classified as a professional client. The firm must also give a written warning to the client of the regulatory protections he will lose, give the client sufficient time to consider the implications of that and obtain either the client's written consent or be able to demonstrate that informed consent has been given. The firm will also need to warn the client that its expertise will be taken into account in the way the firm communicates with the client if it is reclassified as a professional client.

The case of *Bank Leumi (UK) plc v Lund Joy Wachner*[2] is an interesting example of a case relating to a client who had been re-categorised as an 'intermediate costumer' (under the COB regime) and made huge trading losses. She claimed damages for breach of statutory duty under section 150 of the FSMA 2000 as the firm had failed to properly categorise her. The judge held that the requirement was for the firm to have taken reasonable steps to arrive at the correct classification, not that she must in fact possess sufficient knowledge and experience. The case also emphasises the importance of having well drafted terms of business, particularly in relation to services provided on a non advisory basis and liability for non-contractual duties (eg mis-statement).

C Terms of business

4.38 Having categorised a client as a retail client, a firm carrying on designated investment business for that client is required to provide its terms of business to the client[3]. If a firm only provides advice on investments this is not required. The agreement should be set out in writing or other durable medium (including a website if the website conditions are satisfied (see last paragraph of **4.33**)) and set out the essential rights and obligations of the firm and the client. The firm must also provide information about the firm and its services relating to that agreement or those services required by COBS 6.1.4.R, including informa-

1 COBS 3.7.1.
2 [2011] EWHC 656.
3 COBS 8.1.3 requires this to be done in good time before the business is conducted.

tion on communications, conflicts of interest and authorised status[1]. This must include the name and address of the firm and contact details necessary to enable a client to communicate effectively with the firm. The name of the firm's regulator (eg FSA or, if it is an EEA company passporting into the UK, the regulator in that EEA State). If the firm is acting through an AR a statement that that is the case and specifying the EEA State in which the AR is registered needs to be provided.

Although firms must provide the required information 'in good time' before the provision of designated investment business, exemptions apply where a transaction is executed at the request of the client and for telephone sales (see **4.41** and **4.42**).

D Disclosure

1 Summary of disclosure requirements

4.39 One of the difficulties in the practice with the approach adopted by the FSA (ie the copying out of provisions from a number of underlying directives), is that it results in a firm being subject to a number of very similar disclosure requirements (eg there are numerous obligations to 'specify the name and address of the firm, its registration details and the insurers it acts for). In its guidance relating to the SCDD and CDD (see COBS 6.3.3G) the FSA lists the various requirements applicable to insurance mediation. These stem from the IMD, DMD and the FSA's own status and other disclosures (mainly COBS 2, 6 and 8). The applicable requirements can be summarised as follows:

(1) **Cost**: Fees, commissions and non-monetary benefits under COBS 2.3.1.R(2)(b) (as qualified by COBS 2.3.2R); information about costs and charges required by COBS 6.1.9R if actual rather than indicative hourly rates are used; information about the firm and its services, costs and associated charges.

(2) **DMD**: distance marketing disclosures required by COBS 5 relating to name, business, address, details of any representative, statutory status disclosure, main characteristics of the service to be provided, details about complaints and compensation, name and address for communications required under COBS 6.1.4R.

(3) **IMD**: information: required by COBS 7.2.1, including FSA registration details, ownership of or by insurance companies, procedures for FOS complaints, scope of advice (ie tied or not) and the fact that the client can request the names of its product providers.

The COBS provisions on 'inducements' and the obligations to disclose commission are described in more detail in Section 5, Remuneration. The DMD and

1 COBS 8.1.3.

IMD disclosure requirements are considered in this section, as are disclosures relating to an intermediary's product scope and range.

2 *Distance marketing and E commerce Directive requirements*

4.40 The Distance Marketing Directive[1] requirements apply where there is a sale to a consumer using purely distance means as part of an 'organised distance selling campaign or scheme'. The requirements of the directive are to make prescribed disclosures (the distance marketing information). The directive requires a 30 day cancellation period (which has been incorporated into the requirements for long term contracts, see for example, COBS 15) and seeks to prohibit distance means being used to enforce an unsolicited transaction. There are a number of useful exceptions in the directive, notably in relation to successive transactions and voice telephony communications. The requirement to provide the distance marketing information applies in relation to a distance contract or offer in relation to a distance contract. A distance contract is a contract concerning a regulated financial service or product, concluded between a supplier and a consumer (namely someone acting outside the purposes of his trade business or profession), where there has been no face to face contract between the consumer and the product provider or the intermediary. It must be a part of an organised campaign and not a one off personal communication. The firm providing the service or product must provide the information in good time before the consumer is bound. The disclosure must be appropriate to the distance means used and to the type of consumer. It must have regard to the principles of good faith in commercial transactions and the legal principles governing the protection of those who are unable to give their consent such as minors[2].

The actual information to be disclosed is in COBS 5, Annex 1. It is very similar to other information required to be disclosed either under COBS directly or by the provisions of other relevant directives, (eg the Consolidated Life Directive). In practice, it is normally complied with by adding additional points to the Key Features document (see Chapter 5). The areas that normally need additional information to be provided are the requirement to advise of the right of either the client or the insurer to terminate unilaterally, a notice of the possibility that taxes or costs may exist that are not paid via the firm or imposed by it, a requirement to specify the jurisdiction of courts, and a statement about the language(s) that will be used in relevant product documentation and communications. A firm must also communicate to the consumer all the contractual terms and conditions applicable to the contract. As with other disclosures the information must be provided in a durable medium or using an appropriate website[3]. All information provided must be consistent with the law presumed to be applicable.

4.41 The exceptions in the DMD include one for 'successive operations'. This allows firms which perform the similar activities under an initial service

1 2002/65/EC.
2 COB 5.1.2.
3 Provided the FSA website conditions are complied with (see **4.33**).

agreement not to have to comply with the disclosure obligations every time they carry out the same transaction. The exception will also apply if there is no initial service agreement but a transaction of the same nature is performed within 12 months of the initial transaction or the last in a series (none of which had left more than a 12 month gap). The FSA usefully provides guidance by saying that an agreement will be a initial service agreement in relation to a life policy, personal pension or stakeholder pension scheme if it includes a pre-selected option for future increases or decreases in regular premiums or payments. It should also be noted that the requirements do not apply if the distance contract is a stage in the completion of another contract or provision of another service (see COBS 5.1.7).

The 'voice telephony' exception enables a contract to be sold using voice telephony communications with only an abbreviated form of disclosure (see COBS 5, Annex 2), provided the client's consent or instruction to do so is obtained. There is also an exemption to cover situations where the client requests immediate cover and the full disclosure cannot be made because of the distance means used. The abbreviated form of disclosure must be given during the course of the call. It covers the main characteristics of the contract (eg parties, price including taxes and the right to cancel or request more information). The full distance marketing information should be disclosed before the consumer is bound, unless the consumer requests that it be made available after the contract is concluded because the means of communication used does not enable the provision of the information in good time before the consumer is bound (COBS 5.1.13). This will presumably apply predominantly (if not exclusively) to sales concluded by telephone.

A consumer who has dealt by distance means always has the right to ask for paper copies of the contractual terms or to change the means of distance communication used (unless the latter would be incompatible with the nature of the service provided).

A firm cannot enforce or seek to enforce an obligation under a distance contract against a consumer resulting from an unsolicited supply of services to which the customer has not consented. The rule does not apply to the tacit renewal of the distance contract.

COBS 5.2 provides the information disclosures required by UK firms carrying an electronic commerce activity (eg providing financial services contracts by automatic means ie using electronic processing (including digital compression) and storage of data at the individual request of a service recipient[1]. Those provisions implement the E-Commerce Directive[2]. In addition to information disclosures they require promotion information and offers to be clear and the process by which the firm deals to be specified (eg process for placing and dealing of offers), see **1.31**.

1 COBS, see FSA definition of information service society.
2 2002/311/EC.

3 IMD requirements

4.42 As stated in **4.3** above, the IMD seeks to regulate the provision of insurance mediation activities. COBS 7 provides rules to implement the disclosure requirements of the IMD. COBS 7 applies to a firm carrying insurance mediation activities with policyholders habitually resident in the EEA and will supplement home country rules for incoming EEA insurers from member states which have not implemented, or not implemented all of the IMD provisions (see COBS 1, Annex 1, paragraph 4).

Prior to the conclusion of a life policy (and if necessary an amendment or renewal), a firm must provide a client with at least the information set out in COBS 7.2.1. This includes its name and address, the fact that it is registered on the FSA Register (or an identified equivalent in another EEA State), and the procedures to take complaints to the FOS or other applicable schemes. It must disclose whether it has any cross shareholdings either in an insurance company or the insurance company (or its parent) has a holding in the firm, whether directly or indirectly. The threshold for this requirement to apply is 10% of the voting rights.

In addition to information about itself, it must inform the client about its status and whether it will give advice, and if so, on what basis. The firm must either state that it gives advice on the basis of a fair analysis of the market, (eg independent if it meets the other requirements for use of that term, see **4.6** and **4.46**) or that it is required, contractually or otherwise, to give advice in relation to a limited number of insurers' products. If such a restriction is contractual, the names of the insurers must be stated. If not, the client can request the names of the insurers, which the firm must provide. Where a firm gives independent advice, it must be based on an analysis of a sufficiently large number of life policies available in the market to enable the firm to make an appropriate and professional recommendation. Where a firm does not give advice, it must set out the demands and needs of a client (COBS 7.2.4). Information to be provided must be clear and accurate and in language comprehensible to the client. It must be in the official language of the policyholder's habitual residence or another agreed language. It must be in a durable medium available and accessible to the client.

The IMD also allows for the exceptions permitted by the DMD in relation to telephone selling and clients requesting immediate cover (see **4.41**). The required information must then be provided immediately after the conclusion of the life policy. The IMD requirements will apply to policies sold to professional clients.

4 GPP disclosure

4.43 There are also rules providing for disclosure to employees where the firm makes contact with them to promote their employer's GPP or stakeholder pension scheme. This is designed to make it clear whether advice is provided, whether it is limited to the pension scheme and the amount and nature of fees and commission payable by the employee for the advice[1] (see also provisions relating to consultancy charges under the RDR in **4.5** above).

1 COBS 6.3.21.

5 Custody of client money

4.43a A firm that holds designated investments or client money for a retail client either as custodian (subject to the FSA's custody chapter in CASS 6) or as client money (subject to the client money chapter (CASS 7), must make specified disclosures[1]. These include details of any consequences for the client of money being held by a third party co-invested or subject to the provisions of another law. Where a security interest or lien or a right of set off exist, the client must be informed[2]. A more limited disclosure applies in relation to professional clients[3].

E Scope and range of advice

1 Overview

4.44 COBS 6.2 sets out rules and guidance which apply to firms which give advice on packaged products to a retail client (including UK firms giving advice to EEA resident policyholders[4]). The full advice regime does not apply to basic advice on stakeholder products for which there is a simplified but obligatory process (see Section 4G below). Firms are required to disclose their status (ie whole of market, limited number of providers or single company). The rules limit the ability of a firm providing advice to alter the range of products without further disclosure. The requirements in relation to advised sales are that firms know their customer (fact-find), only recommend suitable products and explain why a recommended product is suitable to that client (see COBS 9). Firms also need to ensure that their advisers only advise on products in relation to which they are technically competent and that they refer the client on appropriately or, if necessary, do not sell any product to that client. This could happen where the products available to a sales representative do not contain a suitable product.

2 The scope and range of products

4.45 A firm's 'scope' of advice relates to the product providers whose products it sells whereas its 'range' relates to the actual products or sub-set of products from those providers.

COBS 6.2.6 effectively reminds firms of its obligations under the 'client's best interest' rule in COB 2.1.1 and the IMD, to disclose whether it expects the scope of the advice it gives to retail clients on packaged products to be based on:

(a) the whole (or a specified sector) of the market;

(b) a limited number of product providers; or

(c) a single product provider[5].

1 COBS 6.1.7.
2 COBS 6.1.7(2).
3 COBS 6.1.7 (14).
4 COBS 6.2.3.
5 Or group if SUP 12.5.6A applies, see **4.29**.

A firm must have business processes which are designed to ensure that its representatives consider, based on adequate knowledge, products from across their scope and range, before making a recommendation. The processes should also be designed to ensure that the firm does not recommend products that are not in its scope or range.

Representatives who are not competent to sell across the entire range should be prevented from recommending the relevant product or category of product and should refer the client to a representative that is competent. The firm's processes also need to cater for the requirement not to narrow its scope and to provide new disclosures to the client if it increases its scope. However, increased commission in relation to the sale of a packaged product should only happen where the increase is due to an increase in premiums payable, as otherwise the client's best interests rule might be breached (COBS 2.3.11). A firm's representative should be able to provide a client with a copy of the appropriate range of packaged products on request[1].

In practice, the FSA accepts[2] that a firm may cover the whole of a market by the use of appropriate panels of product providers provided it reviews the panel on a regular basis. Similarly, the FSA accepts that some firms will operate only in niche markets (eg pension transfers).

Firms have fairly onerous obligations to keep records in relation to the scope and range that representatives have offered to each customer. COBS 6.2.12 provides that a firm must keep records for five years from the date a change in scope or range was made, or in relation to the client specific records, from the date of the advice. This will include details of each product provider and their products where anything less than whole of market is offered to customers.

3 *Independent financial advice*

4.46 One of the debates which ensued from the depolarisation changes (and continued under the RDR), related to whether, and in what circumstances, intermediaries would be able to call themselves 'independent'. The issue is of course complicated by the fact that intermediaries may be operating in a number of other markets (eg non-package product insurance and mortgages). An intermediary may be independent in one sector but not in another. COBS 6.2.15 specifies the basis on which a firm can hold itself out as acting independently. First, it must give advice in relation to the whole of the market and second it must offer its customer the opportunity to pay a fee for its services (rather than the firm receiving commission)[3]. If payment by fee is an option, firms may as an alternative offer a choice of fee or commission. A fee may be contingent (eg on a client purchasing a product). Where a fee is agreed, the firm must obtain the customer's agreement to the fee level before acting for the customer. Any commission then received should be used to reduce the fee, increase the investment or refunded direct to the customer. The firm may, however, retain renewal commission up to

1 COBS 6.3.17.
2 COBS 6.2.9 G.
3 COBS 6.2.15(1)(b).

an amount each year specified in the agreement and in practice which is too small to be returned or rebated[1]. A firm's selection of products also needs to be sufficiently large to satisfy the 'client's best interest' rule and the 'fair, clear and not misleading' rule (see **4.28**). A firm selling pensions products must include SIPPS (COBS 6.2.10).

4 Telephone sales

4.47 There is a FSA guidance in relation to status disclosure for telephone sales in COBS 6.3.19. This provides that before making a personal recommendation on packaged products sold by telephone there should be an equivalent disclosure of status. This should include disclosure of the firm's scope, the fact that clients can request a copy of the firm's range and the basis of charging (eg fee and/or commission). The firm should also tell the client that all of the relevant information will be confirmed in writing. Firms are required to anticipate that clients might want a list of the scope by producing a list of the insurance companies for which they act[2].

F Know your customer

4.48 Advising a client in relation to a financial product can be a very complicated business. The advice given can be completely unsuitable if relevant information is not made available to the adviser. Similarly, a client cannot realistically be expected to understand the interdependence between products and the impact of their own circumstances. COBS therefore contains a requirement on firms giving advice to a retail client in relation to packaged products to effectively 'know their customer' (see **4.49**). The requirements do not apply in relation to basic advice on stakeholder products. They are, however, applicable to arranging pension opt-outs or pension transfers from an occupational scheme and are extended, in respect of the IMD requirements to professional clients and eligible counterparties.

The precise type of information required to assess suitability and enquiries to be made (see **4.49**) varies depending on the type of customer concerned. The process is commonly referred to as 'fact-finding'. The information collected should be recorded in writing, the document often being called a fact-find.

A statement of demands and needs must be given to the customer unless a suitability report explaining a personal recommendation in accordance with COBS 9 is provided to him.

1 COBS 6.2.16(2).
2 COBS 6.2.7.

G Suitability

1 Overview

4.49 A firm which makes a personal recommendation to a retail client to buy or sell a packaged product (which will include a life policy[1]), must take reasonable steps to ensure that it is the most suitable one from the relevant range. The suitability rules expand the high level requirement set out in Principle 9 (Customers: relationships of trust) which requires firms to take reasonable care to ensure the suitability of advice and discretionary decisions. Suitability should be assessed by reference to the client's needs, priorities and attitude to risk, income and expenditure and to any likely changes in these.

The COBS requirement in relation to suitability is that before making a personal recommendation, a firm must take reasonable steps to ensure that the product is suitable for its client. The information that the firm should obtain from the client includes his knowledge and experience in the relevant investment field, his financial situation and investment objectives[2]. The firm is required to obtain such information as is necessary to understand the essential facts about the client. The firm must have a reasonable basis for believing that the client will be able to understand the risks involved, the product meets his investment objectives and those objectives including those relating to timing, are consistent with his financial resources[3]. The firm must not encourage a client not to provide information for the purposes of its suitability assessment. The firm may rely on the information provided unless it is manifestly out of date, inaccurate or incomplete[4]. If a firm does not have sufficient information to assess suitability then no recommendation should be made. Firms need to be careful if no recommendation is made but the client instructs them to arrange a policy on a non-advised basis, that carrying out the transaction is consistent with the 'client's best interest' rule in COBS 2.1.1.

One issue which has given rise to problems in this area in the past is churning. 'Churning' means entering into transactions with unnecessary frequency having regard to the customer and the agreed investment strategy. A firm needs to have regard to the client's agreed investment strategy in determining the frequency of switching between packaged products[5]. The FSA also provides guidance on factors to consider in relation to income drawdowns and short term annuities (COBS 9.3.3).

The importance of ensuring the suitability of adviser's recommendations was highlighted in April 2006 when the FSA imposed a fine of £550,000 in relation to the sale of with-profits policies[6]. Essentially the policies were sold as general savings vehicles to significant numbers of the firm's older customers who had no demonstrable need for the life cover sold.

1 Which includes pensions schemes where the contributions are paid to a life office.
2 COBS 9.2.1.
3 COBS 9.2.2.
4 COBS 9.2.5.
5 COBS 9.3.2.
6 Royal Liver Assurance.

2 Requirement for a suitability report

4.50 A firm must provide a suitability report to a retail client if the firm makes a personal recommendation to the client which the client acts on. The recommendations covered in relation to a life policy include advice to buy, sell, surrender, convert or cancel rights under or suspend contributions to a personal pension scheme or stakeholder scheme, to make income withdrawals or purchase a short term annuity or enter into a pension transfer or pension opt-out. There is no obligation to provide a suitability report if the client is not present in the UK when they agree to act on the recommendation and is habitually resident outside the EEA. A suitability report is also not required for additional regular or single premiums on existing contracts[1]. For telephone sales the suitability report should be provided immediately after the conclusion of the contract[2]. The IMD requirement (see **4.42**) also requires that the language used be both comprehensible to the client and the appropriate or agreed language for communications. The FSA has also included guidance as to the explanation of disadvantages and risks for income withdrawals (see COBS 9.4.10).

A firm must provide a 'suitability report' before the conclusion of the contract, unless immediate cover is necessary, in which case it should be provided afterwards. For other cases, it should be provided as soon as possible and, within 14 days, where a personal pension scheme or stakeholder pension scheme contract has a right to cancel. The suitability report must explain why the firm has concluded that the policy is suitable for the client, having regard to his personal and financial circumstances. It must contain any possible disadvantages of the transaction[3].

6 Content of suitability reports

4.51 The current requirements for suitability reports are to at least specify the client's demands and needs, explain why the firm thinks the product is suitable in light of the information provided by the client and any possible disadvantages[4]. This is much less detailed than the FSA's former guidance in relation to suitability letters[5] which is still worth bearing in mind. The FSA previously stated that a successful suitability letter explains simply and clearly why the recommendation is viewed as suitable having regard to the customer's personal and financial circumstances, needs and priorities, as identified in the fact-find and attitude to risk in the relevant area. The style and presentation is mainly left for firms to decide so that they can design a document which works best for their particular market. The FSA also gave certain pointers. The more personalised the suitability letter, the more effective it was likely to be. The language used should be plain English. If technical terms need to be used and the customer is unlikely

1 COBS 9.4.3(5).
2 COBS 9.4.6 (2).
3 COBS 9.4.7.
4 COBS 9.4.7.
5 In relation to COBS 5.3.19.

to understand them, they should be explained in brief terms. Ideally each suitability letter should be different, reflecting the approach of the representative, the customer's profile, subjects discussed and the considerations on which the advice was based. The FSA recommended that any standardisation of the letter be limited to the description of the most common needs and the products which would satisfy those needs. The FSA recommended that the firm should clearly link the customer's own needs, priorities and attitude to risk to the product recommended rather than just setting out stock motives that could apply to all customers. Tick box, pre-printed forms should rarely be used, and if they are, only in the simplest and most straightforward advice situations. The choice of provider and product features should also be explained.

This advice appears still to be relevant when considering the format of suitability reports.

3 Records

4.52 The rules on record keeping for suitability reports require that the records are kept indefinitely for pensions transfer, pension opt-out of Free-Standing AVCs (FSAVC) and five years for life policy, personal pension scheme or stakeholder pension scheme business, unless the client does not proceed with the transaction recommended[1].

H Basic advice on stakeholder products

4.53 In response to concerns about the cost of advice and the need to encourage saving and pension provision, the government introduced the stakeholder pension scheme in 2001. The concept is a simple product with low (initially 1% now up to 1.5%) charges. Employers not offering a pension scheme were required to offer a stakeholder scheme. The problem was that they were not required to contribute to it. It has not as yet proved to be a success. However, the concept and the idea of basic advice have been extended to other types of 'stakeholder product'.

Establishing, operating or winding up a 'stakeholder pension scheme' is a regulated activity[2] as is providing basic advice to a retail client on any stakeholder product[3]. Basic advice is a curtailed form of assessment of the client's needs in relation to a limited range of products[4]. A person provides basic advice when, with the client's agreement, he assesses whether a stakeholder product is appropriate to the client based on information provided. Stakeholder products in addition to pensions (and other deposit-based products) are Child Trust Funds and units in collective investment schemes or linked long-term contracts (other than smoothed products) which satisfy the stakeholder criteria[5]. These

1 COBS 9.5.2.
2 Article 52 RAO.
3 Someone acting outside the course of a business carried on by him.
4 Article 52B.
5 See Article 7, SI 2004/2738.

include cautious/balanced investment criteria and requirements as to costs and expenses.

COBS 9.6.5 sets out the requirement to provide the basic advice initial disclosure information set out in COBS 9 Annex 1 and to explain how the advice will be paid for and the fact that any commission will be disclosed. Basic advice cannot be given on a whole of market or independent basis. A stakeholder range can also only include one stakeholder collective investment scheme/linked life policy product, one stakeholder pension scheme and one stakeholder Child Trust Fund[1] but the firm can have more than one range available to different clients. Basic advice for a particular client must be based on one range and advice should not be given outside this range or include smoothed (ie with-profit type contracts). The advice should not extend to fund choices under the products or contribution levels needed to achieve a specific income in retirement or which could cause contributions in breach of ISA limits. The advice must be provided through a process which incorporates pre-scripted questions. The client should be given or sent a copy, in a durable medium, of the completed scripted questions and answers[2]. The adviser must describe the product to the client and make a recommendation.

The rest of the basic advice process involves the adviser explaining the 'aims', 'risks' and commitment sections of the Key Features document and providing a summary sheet specific to the client for each product recommended. This should set out the amount the client wishes to pay and the reasons (taking into account the information provided by the client) for the recommendation. Clients must also be advised that the Financial Ombudsman Service (FOS) may take the limited nature of the advice process into account in relation to complaints. Further provisions apply to conducting basic advice by telephone and require that the adviser reads the summary sheet to the client. When a firm provides basic advice it must, if requested, explain why it chose the products and providers in its relevant range and give the client a list of them[3]. The client has to indicate that they have understood the description of the product and the adviser's recommendation. The suitability test for stakeholder products is that the firm has reasonable grounds for believing that the product is suitable for the client, and that the client understands the advice, and the basis on which it has been provided. If a contract is concluded, a firm must provide a copy of the completed questions and answers to the client in a durable medium as soon as reasonably practicable afterwards.

Similar rules to those applicable to non-basic advice (eg record keeping) in relation to scope and range apply[4]. As do rules on the structure of remuneration[5]. Also, whilst basic advice should stay within the appropriate range[6], it is possible, provided the customer is advised that this is what is happening, to 'depart' from the process[7].

1 COBS 9.6.2. It can include more than one deposit arrangements.
2 COBS 9.6.16.
3 COBS 9.6.15.
4 COBS 9.6.19.
5 COBS 9.6.18.
6 COBS 9.6.10(1).
7 COBS 9.6.11.

SECTION 5 REMUNERATION – INDUCEMENTS AND CONFLICTS

A Overview

4.54 COBS 2 contains the new 'client's best interests rule' and the 'rule on inducements' which are designed to prevent allegations that intermediaries have directed business to product providers on the basis of a benefit to the intermediary rather than the best interests of the client. These provisions supplement Principles 1 (integrity), 2 (skill, care and diligence) and 6 (customers' interests). Although in a different format, the inducement provisions have a long history. One of the original aims of the regulation under the Financial Services Act 1986, was to remove product bias caused by commission, through harmonised levels of permissible commission payable to intermediaries and by limiting indirect benefits. Unfortunately this very laudable and practical aim was to be prevented by competition considerations. The current rules therefore seek to achieve the same aim but arguably in a more convoluted fashion. In practice, the LAUTRO maximum commission rules are also still in use as a means of defining commission (eg 120% LAUTRO).

At a high level, the FSA rules aim to prevent a firm or its associates giving or receiving 'inducements' in placing business (eg agreeing to channel business to a provider in return for a benefit to the firm). The main focus of the rule against inducements is that fees, commission and other benefits, holdings in intermediary companies or loans provided by a product provider should not cause product bias and should be disclosed to the client. The rules are supplemented by some permitted exceptions (mainly relating to the provision of marketing literature and training). These exceptions are known as the 'indirect benefit rules'. All of the rules are drafted widely to catch group companies carrying on the specified activity but are generally disapplied where all parties are in a group.

B COBS 2.3 inducements

1 Disclosure

4.55 Where there is a personal recommendation in relation to a packaged product, fees, commissions and other non-monetary benefits can only be accepted to the extent that they are consistent with the client's best interest rule. The basic rule is that a firm should disclose any such fee commission or benefit (or the means of calculating it). This is supplemented by a specific requirement in COBS 6.1.9 and COBS 6.4.3 to disclose the total price to be paid by the client (see **4.53**). A firm is not required to disclose the existence of certain benefits called 'reasonable non-monetary benefits' (but also known as indirect benefits). The disclosure must be in a manner that is both comprehensive and understandable as well as being accurate and must take place before a personal recommendation to buy a package product is made. The requirement does not apply to a firm giving basic advice (see **4.53**). A firm may make a disclosure in summary form provided it undertakes to provide further details, if requested by the client, and actually do so if requested. The firm must keep a record of the information disclosed pursuant to the rule on inducements and also record indirect benefits that do not need to be disclosed, in both cases for at least five years from the date the information was given.

2 *COBS 2.3: Guidance on 'inducements'*

4.56 There is a detailed evidential provision, breach of which will tend to establish a contravention of the rule on inducements. This relates to the holding of an interest (eg in the capital or voting rights) of an intermediary firm by a product provider or its associates and/or the provision of credit to such companies. These are not permitted unless the interest is acquired on commercial terms. This means that the terms should be such that an independent person, unconnected to the product provider, would be prepared, in all the circumstances, to acquire the interest or offer the credit or accommodation. This fact must be supported by 'reliable written evidence'. There are further conditions relating to the channelling of business. There must be no arrangements relating directly to the channelling of business and the product provider (and its associates) must not, because of the arrangement, actually be able to exercise any influence over the advice given in relation to packaged products. These rules so apply to arrangements between authorised intermediaries and unauthorised packaged product providers (eg insurance firms or the operator of a regulated collective investment scheme outside of the UK) or investment trusts[1].

4.57 COBS 2.3.3 provides guidance in relation to the rule on inducements which makes the point that a non-monetary benefit can be an arrangement that results in the intermediary referring business to a particular product provider. COBS 2.3.7 states that the fact that a fee commission or non monetary benefit is paid, or provided, to or by an AR, does not prevent the application of the rule on inducements. There are also evidential provisions designed to prevent volume overrides or arrangements which can offer an intermediary an additional financial benefit in the event of commission (eg indemnity commission) becoming repayable[2].

3 *Indirect benefits*

4.58 In addition to interests in and credit provided to intermediaries, indirect benefits can constitute an inducement. The most obvious being gifts and hospitality, but extending to possible business benefits like use or provision of software to help the intermediary improve their business offering. It can also limit compensatory payments made to intermediaries involved in sorting out problems caused by a life office. A list of benefits that may be provided to intermediaries without constituting an inducement are set out in a table forming part of COBS 2.3.15. Strictly, this table is guidance but it is extensively relied upon in practice.

1 COBS 2.3.12(6).
2 COBS 2.3.10.

There can be a fine line between assistance given to an intermediary which does not conflict with its duty to its clients and assistance which does.

The list of permitted indirect benefits includes joint marketing exercises but provides rules about the use of generic materials and the costs which the product provider is permitted to bear. This includes distribution costs (postage, freepost envelopes which are made available generally to intermediaries). It may also provide a generally available freephone link. Literature may include the name of the intermediary but, in line with the FSA's view on white labelling, it can only be included if it enhances the quality of the service to the client and is not primarily of promotional benefit to the intermediary[1].

There are a number of other exemptions covering financial promotions paid for at a market rate (eg adverts in the client magazine of an intermediary), participation in seminars and conferences (where the participation is for a genuine business purpose, any contribution to costs is proportionate to the active involvement of the provider's staff at the seminar or, if it is a third party seminar, access is open to other firms generally) and training provided by the product provider (if made generally available to firms which might advise on its packaged products). A product provider may also provide generic technical information in writing either generally or to niche areas of the market. A product provider may reimburse some reasonable travel and accommodation expenses of another firm in specified circumstances including to attend training provided or visits to the product provider's office to receive information about administrative systems or client meetings[2]

3 IT support

4.59 In this day and age where much business is done, at least in part online, the provision of software or contribution toward the cost of software used is an important issue. The rules state that product providers may give access to software that provides information about their packaged products or 'where appropriate' (the example given being for use in a scheme for review of past business or for producing projections or technical product information). However, this may not cover all of the software that could be of use to the Intermediary. Product providers are, however, permitted to provide access to data processing facilities or to data and to third party electronic dealing or quotation systems that relate to the product provider's business.

C Commission payments and repayments

1 Commission terms

4.60 Perhaps the easiest way in which a product provider could pass a benefit to intermediaries is in the terms on which it pays commission and ultimately that

1 COBS 2.3.15(5)(b).
2 COBS 2.3.15 (14).

is why the FSA intends to ban commission for advised sales of investment products under the RDR (see **4.3**). Commission is currently required to be disclosed to the client purchasing a packaged product (eg such as a life investment contract). A firm must not agree to pay commission other than to the firm responsible for a sale. Another firm may become entitled to current commission if it has given advice on investments to the same customer after the sale. Note, this need not be in relation to the product paying the commission. Commission may also be paid in respect of direct marketing (eg by a product provider to an intermediary's clients)[1] and to another firm in the insurer's immediate group.

To those unfamiliar with the sale of insurance products the arrangements under which commission may currently be paid are strikingly one sided. For regular premium contracts a couple of years' commission (depending on the initial period) can be paid upfront, discounted slightly to reflect early payment. If all of the customer's premiums are not paid then clawback of the 'unearned' commission is triggered. This is called 'indemnity commission'. It is not prohibited by the FSA rules but the rules provide that the terms on which indemnity commission is paid/clawed back must not permit an additional financial benefit to the intermediary in the event of the commission becoming repayable[2]. This will mean that such debts should attract interest and be pursued in a commercial manner.

2 *Amount of commission*

4.61 The main requirements in relation to actual costs to a customer are in COBS 6.1.9R and COBS 6.4.3R. COBS 6.1.9 provides that a firm must provide a retail client with information on costs and associated charges including, if applicable, the total price to be paid by the client in connection with the designated investment (ie the product) or the services provided in relation to designated investment business. This includes all related fees, commissions, charges and expenses and all taxes payable via the firm and arrangements for payment and future performance. If an exact price cannot be indicated, the basis for the calculation of the total price should be disclosed so that the client can verify it. Commission charged by the firm must be itemised separately in every case. This information should be provided in good time before the provision of the designated investment business.

Disclosure can, however, be provided after the firm has started to provide its services, if it was unable to make the disclosure because it was dealing with the client using a means of distance communication which prevented the firm from doing. This also applies where the rule on voice telephony communications (see **4.41**) would not apply because the retail customer is not a 'consumer' but the firm treats them as if they were. This last point allows for potential differences in treatment caused by the different categorisation used in underlying directives (eg retail customer in MiFID and consumer in the DMD). As with other disclosure it

1 COBS 6.4.7(3).
2 COBS 2.3.10.

must be in a durable medium or an appropriate website[1]. A firm must also let the client know if there are any material changes to the information provided in respect of the services provided and again this should be in a durable medium or via an appropriate website.

COBS 6.4.3 provides particular rules for packaged products which require disclosure of commission (or commission equivalent paid to a firm's representatives). The rule applies to UK firms and includes business carried on for a client resident in another EEA State at the time (or from a EEA branch with UK residents unless the business would have the benefit of the Overseas Person Exemption[2] if the branch were a separate legal entity (eg branch business not solicited or acquired through use of a financial promotion in the UK). The rule applies to those advising (ie as a result of a personal recommendation) and unadvised sales where a firm arranges the sale of a packaged product. Importantly, this rule requires disclosure at the time of sale but not necessarily before a personal recommendation is made. It also requires disclosure 'subsequently', if requested by the client. The obligation is to disclose in cash terms the amount of commission payable to the firm or its associates in connection with the transaction. If the firm is also the product provider, any commission or commission equivalent (eg cash plus the cash value of non-cash benefits[3] and services) calculated in accordance with COBS to Annex 6 need to be disclosed. The value of permitted indirect benefits do not need to be included. Commission equivalent is expected to be at least as high as the amount of commission payable[4]. The amount of commission equivalent may need to be estimated if not known in advance. Timing of payments and any features that would affect the value (eg an exchange of future commission for a lump sum) should also be explained. The requirements in COBS 6.4.3 will normally be complied with by providing a Key Features documents and illustration (see Chapter 5). COBS 6.4.3(4)(c) provides that the rule does not need to be complied with provided that the firm discloses to the client the actual amount of value of commission or commission equivalent within five days of effecting the transaction.

COBS 6.4.3(5) provides that if the terms of packaged product are varied and result in a material increase in commission or commission equivalent then the increased amount also needs to be disclosed to a retail client in writing.

SECTION 6 ICOBS AND PPI

A Overview

4.62 As has already been stated, the COBS rules, which replaced the COB rules, set out detailed requirements relating to the sale of packaged products. Life companies may also sell 'pure protection' contracts (eg term assurance). A pure protection contract is broadly a contract in respect of death or incapacity, which

1 Where the website conditions set out in the FSA definition apply, see **4.33**.
2 In Article 72, RAO.
3 COBS 6.4.6.
4 COBS 6.4.4.

has either no surrender value or, for single premium contracts, the surrender value is not more than the premium paid. An insurer may elect to treat a pure protection policy as covered by COBS instead of ICOBS. Such an election must be retained indefinitely. The IMD also applies to these contracts. As part of the regulation of general insurance and implementation of the IMD, the FSA introduced a new section of the Handbook, the 'Insurance Conduct of Business' section, known as ICOB. ICOB was similar to COB in high level terms but was generally much less detailed. ICOB was replaced with a more principles based version known as ICOBS[1].

This section provides a brief summary of the ICOBS provisions relevant to insurance mediation or the product provider of a life contract which is not an investment contract. The product disclosure requirements (eg policy summary) are dealt with in Chapter 5.

Like COBS, ICOBS now contain an ICOBS I Annex I which gives guidance as to its territorial scope (see **4.28**). Unlike COBS, ICOBS uses the term 'consumer' rather than 'retail client' and the term 'commercial customer' to mean everyone else. A consumer is a natural person who is acting for purposes which are outside his trade or profession. Where it is not clear whether a customer is a consumer he should be treated as a consumer. If a customer is acting for both consumer and commercial customer purposes in relation to a particular contract of insurance, he should be treated as a commercial customer.

Communications with customers and financial promotions must be fair, clear and not misleading (ICOBS 2.2). Product information may be provided in a policy summary or a Key Features document (see ICOBS to Annex 2). Unlike COBS, ICOBS contains a requirement to handle claims promptly and fairly and to assist the policyholder (ICOBS 8.1.1).

ICOBS only applies to direct insurers and intermediaries (reinsurers are not caught by ICOBS unless acting as intermediaries), but only to the extent that the party has direct contact with the customer or is the product provider. All chapters Chapters of ICOBS apply to any firm that deals with a consumer. Some Chapters, however, will only apply in part or not at all if a firm is dealing with a commercial customer (ie all other customers). The provisions of ICOBS 4 relating to advising and selling[2] apply only in relation to IMD intermediation activities (ie including those carried on by an insurer or reinsurer). Intermediaries are subject to requirements in relation to both retail and commercial customers. Insurers are not subject to the status disclosure, statement of demands and needs (unless a recommendation is made and even then the customer may consent to forgo the statement) or commission disclosure rules when dealing with a commercial customer[3]. Certain requirements do, however, apply to the insurer where there is no authorised intermediary. ICOBS 6, Annex 1 helpfully sets out a list of responsibilities of the insurer and the intermediary in certain situations.

1 With effect from 5/1/08.
2 ICOB 5.
3 ICOBS 4.4.1.

B ICOBS 2: Unfair inducements

4.63 The firm must take reasonable steps to ensure that it, and any person acting on its behalf, does not offer, give, solicit or accept an inducement. An 'inducement' is a benefit offered to a firm, or any person acting on its behalf, with a view to that firm, or that person, adopting a particular course of action. This can include but is not limited to cash equivalents, commission, goods hospitality or training programmes.

There may be circumstances where a firm is able to demonstrate that it could not reasonably have knowledge of an associate giving or receiving an inducement. It is useful to note the FSA's former guidance in relation to the ICOB which used to state that inducements that operate at a distance from the sales process may not be unfair if they do not have an effect on the sales person. The rule on inducements is therefore less detailed than the equivalent COBS provision which specifically prohibits certain shareholdings in and loans to intermediaries. Whilst some such arrangements may still in principle be capable of having the effect of an inducement, that fact would need to be proved (unlike the position in COBS).

C ICOBS 4: Advising and selling

1 Commission disclosure

4.64 The most noticeable difference between the COBS and ICOBS regimes for consumer is in relation to commission disclosure. Under ICOBS fees are disclosed but currently commission is not, unless requested by a commercial customer[1].

2 Disclosure of status and fees

4.65 An insurance intermediary (including an insurer carrying on insurance mediation activities) must make disclosure of its status to a consumer before conclusion of the insurance contract. The initial disclosure document (IDD) or combined initial disclosure document can be used to satisfy the requirements which are essentially those from the IMD (see **4.42**). The disclosure must be in a durable medium. The pro forma IDD is in ICOBS 4, Annex 1G or where relevant, the CDD pro forma is in COB 6, Annex 2. The information includes details of shareholdings by the intermediary in an insurer (if more than 10%) and similar interests held by an insurer (or its parent) in the intermediary. There is no disclosure in relation to credit provided. As with COBS the Key Facts logo can be used on IDDs and CDDs but additional requirements apply in relation to the use of the logo.

An intermediary may advise on the basis of a 'fair analysis'. It must disclose whether or not it is contractually obliged to limit its scope in this way. The inter-

1 ICOBS 4.4.1.

mediary must maintain a list to be provided to customers on request of the insurers it selects or deals with in relation to the relevant contract[1]. To provide services on the basis of 'fair analysis', a firm must consider a sufficiently large number of contracts from the relevant market and be knowledgeable enough to make the assessment. An intermediary may satisfy this requirement by operating an appropriate panel. The panel needs to be reviewed on a regular basis[2]. Selection of products should also be based on the product features, etc and not solely on the benefit that the insurer offers to the intermediary.

Where the intermediary is introducing to another person or an insurer, a more limited disclosure is required[3]. This includes details of the firm and its regulatory status, details of fees and whether the introduction is between members of the same group.

3 Demand and needs

4.66 Prior to the conclusion of a contract a firm must specify, on the basis of the information provided by the customer, the 'demands and needs' of that customer as well as the underlying reasons for any advice based on the complexity of the product. This is part of the IMD requirements (see **4.42**) and must be communicated in accordance with its rules (eg durable medium, comprehensible and in the appropriate language). The information may be provided orally where immediate cover is necessary or whether the voice telephony exception in the DMD applies (see **4.41**) (ie the customer consents and hears abbreviated information with the full information to follow). For non advised sales the FSA guidance includes example wordings[4].

Prior to the conclusion of a contract with a consumer a firm must state whether it is giving advice or just information[5].

4 Suitability

4.67 The suitability requirement in ICOBS is that the recommended product is 'suitable to the customer's demand and needs[6]. Unlike the requirements in COBS, an intermediary need only seek such information as might reasonably be expected to be relevant to the customer's current requirement. This should include existing insurances. One of the issues that both ICOB and ICOBS have had to deal with has been PPI sales. A number of rules have been specifically included to address PPI issues. ICOBS 5.1.1. provides that a firm should take reasonable steps to ensure that a customer only buys a policy under which he is eligible to claim benefits[7]. This should include checking the eligibility criteria.

1 ICOBS 4.1.6.
2 ICOBS 4.1.8
3 ICOBS 4.1.3.
4 ICOBS 5.2.4.
5 ICOBS 4.1.7.
6 ICOBS 5.3.2.
7 ICOBS 5.1.

ICOBS also reminds firms of the ability for insurers to reject claims for non disclosure and suggests explaining this to the customer and ensuring that the customer is asked clear questions about any matter material to the insurer[1].

5 *PPI cases*

4.68 One of the areas that has tested the effectiveness of the ICOB/ICOBS rules in recent years is the mis-selling of PPI. There were a number of underlying causes for complaint about PPI. First, single premium PPI was often sold to cover a loan of a different duration and without an effective ability to surrender the policy if the loan was paid off early. Second, PPI was sold to the self-employed when in many cases it did not cover them. Third, certain types of PPI were sold as renewable or reviewable contracts without necessarily making clear what the basis of the renewal or review was to be. Fourth and finally, and particularly in relation to single premium contracts, PPI was often very expensive or poor value for money when compared to other products. The FOS was deluged with PPI complaints and this effectively lead to the FSA setting out a basis on which PPI complaints and reviews were to be undertaken. The FSA's approach was challenged unsuccessfully by the British Bankers Association judicial review case (see 3.69).

There are two particularly interesting points to note in relation to the PPI complaints. The first is the changes made to the ICOBS rule to try to redress the balance in these cases, especially when sales are made over the phone. The second, is the approach of the courts to ICOB in relation to PPI sales. The ICOBS Rules[2] require that if a firm provides information orally during a sales dialogue with a customer on a main characteristic of a policy, it must do so for all the policy's main characteristics (both advantages and disadvantages – exclusion and limitations). A customer should also be told of the importance of reading the documentation. For payment protection contracts, a firm must also provide information in a way calculated to enable the customer to relate it to a regular budget. The other point to note is that it should be made clear whether or not a product is compulsory. Price information is also expected to provide a total premium so that the customer can work out the full cost. The Competition Commission has also supplemented the rules in this area. Its Payment Protection Insurance (PPI) Market Investigation Order 2011, introduced a number of changes with effect from 6 April 2011. Most notably a prohibition on selling PPI at and before the point of sale for credit and for seven days afterwards. It also introduced obligations to provide information about the cost of PPI, key messages to be delivered when marketing PPI and an obligation to provide a personal PPI quote. Interestingly, it also prohibits the sale of single premium PPI.

This leads on to the second point of note in relation to ICOB/ICOBS. Most disputes relating to ICOBS will be dealt with by the FOS but the FOS's decision is not binding on complainants and there is also always the option to sue in the courts. The effect of the ICOB rules in the context of PPI was considered by the

1 ICOBS 5.1.4.
2 ICOBS 6.4.2.

High Court in the case of *Harrison v Blackhorse Limited*[1]. The case concerned the sale to a couple of a single premium PPI policy in connection with a loan. The policy cost £10,200 in relation to a loan of £60,000. The term of the policy was five years whereas the term of the loan was 23 years. The sales process was conducted using a standard questionnaire and the sales representative was not incentivised to make the sale. The complainants argued a number of points in relation to the suitability of a product with a five year term to cover a 23 year loan and based on the level of commission payable to the bank, that there had been a breach of the rules against inducements.

The judge accepted that there had been a breach in relation to the term of the product as information had not been sought as to the desired length of the cover[2]. However, the judge did not find that as a result the PPI would not have been taken out and so the complainants had not suffered a loss. In relation to the breach of the rule on inducements[3] the judge found, that as the sales person followed a script and the commission was not paid to her, there was little or no prospect of her having a conflict in the way she dealt with the sale. In fact it was apparently common ground that there was no pressure or misrepresentation of any kind on her part towards the complainants and the documentation made clear that the product was not compulsory. The real mischief of the case appears to have been the comparative cost of the product compared to an annual policy providing the same level of cover. The judge held that there was also no breach of the suitability requirement, essentially because the sales person was not able to offer an annual policy. The bank was also only required to have regard to the cost of the contract where it was relevant to the customer's demands and needs and there was no specific information that cost was a relevant factor. The decision is also interesting from the perspective of a common law claim for negligence. The judge effectively held that as the ICOB requirements were so detailed, they would set the standard to be expected in relation to a claim in negligence.

SECTION 7 AGENCY AND LIFE ASSURANCE

A Introduction

4.69 This section seeks to deal with the legal consequences applicable (under the general law of agency) to an agency relationship and, in particular, in relation to FSA authorised intermediaries. The requirements apply in addition to any FSMA-related requirements.

As has already been stated, one of the objectives of the 1986 Act was to make clear whether an intermediary was an agent of the client or the product provider. Post-depolarisation the position has become slightly blurred. It is not clear whether a multi-tie distribution company is merely the agent for a number of providers or is the agent of the client. The law in this area predates this change,

1 [2010] EWHC 3152.
2 ICOB 4.3.2(1).
3 ICOB 2.3.

but it is submitted that it is likely the distribution company, authorised in its own right and subject in the main to the same FSA rules as a whole of market adviser (eg inducements), would be treated as the agent of the client. This can have far-reaching consequences as the law in this area is harsh (eg disclosure to such an intermediary would not satisfy the requirement to disclose to the insurer). The Law Commission issued a scoping paper in January 2006 in relation to insurance law. One of the issues it identified was the question of the difficulty of insurance brokers being remunerated by the insurer but categorised as the agent of the client. This is discussed further in **7.49** below.

B General principles

1 Nature of agent

4.70 In simple terms, an agent is any person who has authority (ie actual authority) to act on behalf of another, known as a 'principal'. In this wide sense the term may include an employee, because a company or corporation (including an insurance company) can only act through an agent. The agent, through whom the principal organisation acts, may therefore be a director, the chief executive or other employee.

Actual authority (ie within the specific terms of the agency appointment), also encompasses implied authority. Implied authority relates to those acts which an agent with actual authority needs to do in order to exercise his actual authority and those acts which are incidental to the exercise of actual authority. Ostensible or apparent authority arises from the position or office in which the agent is placed or the credentials which he has been permitted to hold. This is the authority which the law regards as having been conferred on the agent by the words or conduct of the principal. The effect may be to create an agency where none previously existed or extend the scope of existing actual authority. A person dealing with the agent is entitled to assume that the agent's actual authority is equal to his apparent/ostensible authority unless there is reason to suspect otherwise[1]. However, it is not possible for an agent to confer ostensible authority upon himself[2]. It has been said that ostensible authority is based on an estoppel such that the principal is estopped by his conduct from denying that the agent had the requisite authority to bind the principal. A third party affected in this way and

1 *Willis, Faber & Co v Joyce* (1911) 27 TLR 388; *Eagle Star Insurance Co Ltd v Spratt* [1971] 2 Lloyd's Rep 116. See, however, the case of *British Bank of the Middle East v Sun Life Assurance Co of Canada (UK)* [1983] 2 Lloyd's Rep 9, HL, in which it was held that neither the life office's salesman nor branch manager had actual or ostensible authority to give undertakings to a bank despite a statement by the branch manager that the salesman was so empowered.

2 See *Freeman & Lockyer v Buckhurst Park Properties (Mangal) Ltd* [1964] 2 QB 480, where Diplock LJ summarised the position and also considered the additional layer of complication created by a corporate body purported giving such ostensible authority. In such circumstances the official of the company must himself have actual authority. These principles were applied in *British Bank of the Middle East v Sun Life Assurance Co of Canada (UK)* [1983] 2 Lloyd's Rep 9.

claiming against the principal must show that the principal, by his words or conduct or even by silence and acquiescence,[1] held out the agent as having the alleged authority, which he relied upon and that he acted to his detriment in so doing. In some cases the agent will claim to have authority when he does not. In this case the third party who is thereby affected will have a claim for any loss suffered against the agent personally on the basis of breach of warranty of authority. In practice the third party will generally not want this result as the principal will in most cases be the party worth suing. Another possible scenario is where the third party is put on enquiry or he ought to have asked questions which would have established the true position. In such a case he will not be entitled to rely on the ostensible authority to bind the principal. Furthermore, even if the agent acted outside the scope of his authority, the principal may ratify his unauthorised act provided that it is within its own powers[2].

There are significant differences, in practice, between the positions of agents acting in relation to life insurance when compared to those of general insurers. For example, general insurance agents often have the power to conclude contracts. The position of Financial Advisers is in many respects a basic agency in that such 'agents' do not have such authority from the life office and will generally only recommend and suggest actions to the client. Only rarely will the Financial Adviser be in a position to conclude life contracts on behalf of the client.

2 *Duties of the agent*

4.71 It is the duty of the Financial Adviser, as agent, to deal honestly with his principal who will generally be a member of the public with little or no specialist knowledge[3]. One aspect of this relationship is the fiduciary duty owed by the agent to his principal. Therefore, a Financial Adviser employed by a proposer to effect an insurance contract must not secretly take a commission from the life office[4], or if he does he must account to the proposer for what he receives[5]. Under the general law of agency there is no objection to his retaining such commission where the principal is aware he is receiving it, or where he might reasonably have inferred that the agent was to have commission, even though he may not know the actual amount (although for all practical purposes, if governed by COBS disclosure of commission, disclosure will be made either in the Key Facts document or separately).

In addition to commission payments as understood, payments which may be covered by these general principles include claims by agents against life offices for additional work undertaken as a result of administrative errors and oversights by the life office. If a claim is made in connection with a particular client's business, the agent remains the agent of that client, unless he has agreed with the life

1 *Eagle Star Insurance Co Ltd v Spratt* [1971] 2 Lloyd's Rep.
2 *Re Phoenix Life Assurance Co* (1862) 2 John & H 441.
3 *Connecticut Fire Insurance Co v Kavanagh* [1892] AC 473, PC.
4 *Leete v Wallace* (1888) 58 LT 577.
5 *Re Lord Berwick, Lord Berwick v Lane* (1900) 81 LT 797, CA.

office to act as their agent and has disclosed this agency to his first principal and that principal has assented. If he fails to account to his principal (the client) for the receipt of such payments, it would appear that this amounts to a secret profit. The life office might also expose itself to a claim from the client for payment of the same amount on the basis of having facilitated such payment.

In general terms, it is the duty of the agent to carry out the transaction which he is employed to carry out, or, if it is impossible for him to do so, to inform the principal promptly in order to prevent the principal from suffering loss through relying upon the unsuccessful completion of the transaction by the agent. Financial Advisers acting for clients in connection with life assurance (and other financial products such as pensions and unit trusts) consider which contracts would best meet identified needs of the client and advise accordingly. In view of the number of broadly similar contracts available on the market, this is a potentially onerous undertaking. Assuming the client is happy to proceed with the Financial Adviser's recommendation, an application is then made for a policy. The Financial Adviser is likely to assist with the application process. He may even suggest answers to certain questions but care must be exercised by the Financial Adviser in this respect. As agent of the client, if his advice in some way disadvantages his client, for example non-disclosure of a material fact, the Financial Adviser could be liable to his client. It is quite common to find in proposal forms a statement to the effect that in signing the proposal the client confirms his agreement to anything which is not in his own handwriting, which offers a degree of protection to the life office for anything written by the Financial Adviser.

The agent has a duty to obey his instructions and to act strictly in accordance with the terms of his authority[1] or, as regards matters on which they are silent, the usual course of business. In the exercise of the authority entrusted to him, the agent must act with reasonable and proper care, skill and diligence. If he is a professional agent, such as a Financial Adviser, the standard by which the duty is measured is the standard of skill and care which is normally possessed by persons in that profession, otherwise he is to be judged by what an ordinary person might, given the particular circumstances, be expected to do. The test is not whether the Financial Adviser was correct in arriving at the advice in question but whether 'he did or did not exercise reasonable and proper care, skill and judgment'[2]. This is to be judged by the standard of other Financial Advisers.

3 Authority

4.72 An agent is responsible to his principal and can bind the principal only to the extent of his express, implied or ostensible authority. The terms of the express authority are to be found in the agreement between the agent and his principal. The implied authority arises from the further power to do all things necessary in the ordinary course of business for the efficient and proper perfor-

1 *Barron v Fitzgerald* (1840) 6 Bing NC 201.
2 *Chapman v Walton* (1833) 10 Bing 57.

mance by the agent of his duties. If a person contracts with an agent where the contract is not one usually within the scope of an agent's authority, the contracting party should ascertain that the agent has in fact express authority.

4 Payment

4.73 Unusually for the position of an agent, in most cases Financial Advisers are currently paid by the life office rather than by their principal (ie the client). The fact that Financial Advisers receive commission from life offices is one of the factors which tend to cause confusion in ascertaining whose agent the Financial Adviser is. In most other cases the agent is paid by the client. There are a growing number of Financial Advisers who are paid on a fee basis by the client and this will be required from 2013 as a result of implementation of the RDR (see **4.5**). In cases where fees are currently paid, it is normal for the Financial Adviser to rebate any commission to the client, thus enhancing the value of (or reducing the cost of) the life assurance policy (or other product) to the client. This method of remuneration of Financial Advisers has the advantage that there should be no temptation for the Financial Adviser to seek to recommend a product merely for the purpose of generating a commission in breach of his duties as an agent. As mentioned, the Financial Adviser is required to disclose the amount of commission payable to him[1] in respect of packaged products.

Commission is paid under an agreement between the Financial Adviser and the life office (often termed a 'Terms of Business letter' or, misleadingly, an 'Agency Agreement'). Amongst other things, this will set out the details relating to commission payable to the Financial Adviser and how this is to be calculated. It will also deal with other methods regarding commission such as the 'claw back' of indemnity commission on early termination of contracts before the commission has been fully earned. This certainly muddies the water as to whose agent the Financial Adviser is. However, the law indicates that he is the agent of the client. Even an agent of the Insurer acting outside his authority has been held to be the agent of the client in some circumstances.

5 Whose agent?

4.74 In *Newsholme Bros v Road Transport and General Insurance Ltd*[2] an agent of the insurance company filled in the proposal form (for motor insurance) at the request of the proposer as a result of which it was decided that for those purposes he became the agent of the proposer[3] because he was not authorised by the company to do so. The majority of the cases on this point relate to general business and Lloyd's underwriters but the principle is the same. The rule that an

1 COBS 5.7.5R.
2 [1929] 2 KB 356.
3 See also *Facer v Vehicle and General Insurance Co Ltd* [1965] 1 Lloyd's Rep 113 and *Biggar v Rock Life Assurance Co* [1902] 1 KB 516.

insurance broker is the agent of the client was upheld in *Roberts v Plaisted*[1], where it was held that full and frank disclosure by a proposer to a Financial Adviser was not effective against the insurer. However, it is worth considering part of the judgment of Purchas LJ (which has been quoted by the Insurance Ombudsman in the past):

> 'To the person unacquainted with the insurance industry it may seem a remarkable state of the law that someone who describes himself as a Lloyd's broker, who is remunerated by the insurance industry and who presents proposal forms and suggested policies on their behalf should not be the safe recipient of full disclosure but that is undoubtedly the position in law as it stands at the moment. Perhaps it is a matter which might attract the attention at an appropriate moment of the Law Commission.'[2]

As stated above this has now been reviewed by the Law Commission and changes and further clarification are proposed (see **2.48**).

More recently, in the case of *Winter v Irish Life Assurance plc*[3] it was asserted that an Independent Financial Adviser (IFA) was the agent of the life office. This was rejected and the appropriate question was stated to be: 'who has asked or authorised the intermediary to perform the particular service, is it the insurer or the assured?'. In this case the evidence was clearly that the proposers had constituted the Financial Adviser as their agent.

It is worth noting that the Insurance Ombudsman Bureau has stated that he was prepared to hold insurers liable for the default of intermediaries in what, he considered, were appropriate cases[4]. It is to be presumed that the FOS, which is not bound by the strict legal position, may do the same.

6 *Knowledge of agent*

4.75 As a general rule, the knowledge of an agent will bind the principal, so that the life office will ordinarily be bound by knowledge of its tied agents (ARs) or their employees. Conversely, a life office will not normally be bound by knowledge of Financial Advisers acting on behalf of a client.

Questions sometimes arise as to how far information given to an intermediary will bind the life office in respect of the completion of proposal forms and the various other dealings between the proposer, intermediary and life office at the time of effecting the life policy. Although there is conflicting authority on the point, it is suggested that the line taken in *Newsholme Bros v Road Transport and General Insurance Co Ltd*[5] above is supported by the later cases.

1 [1989] 2 Lloyd's Rep 341.
2 [1989] 2 Lloyd's Rep 345.
3 [1995] 2 Lloyd's Rep 274. See also *Searle v Hayes & Co* [1996] LRLR 68 for further support for the 'classical' position.
4 Insurance Ombudsman's Bureau Annual Report 1989, para 2.14. Although in his 1992 Report this view seems to have been contradicted. He referred to '...any intermediary or other person for whom the insurer has no responsibility'.
5 [1929] 2 KB 356.

The following case also illustrates the difficulties which may arise (in individual circumstances) in this area of the law[1]:

> '*Bawden v London, Edinburgh and Glasgow Assurance Co*[2]
>
> B effected a policy against accidental injury, under which total incapacity included loss of both eyes. The proposal had been obtained by an agent, Q, who saw that B had only one eye. B could neither read nor write, although he could sign his name. Q completed the proposal form at B's dictation and B signed it, but Q did not mention the previous loss of one eye. B subsequently lost the sight of his other eye in an accident. Held, that Q was the agent of the company and his tasks included putting proposals into shape. Consequently, his knowledge must be imputed to the company and therefore the company was liable.'

This case was distinguished by the Court of Appeal in the *Newsholme* case as not being applicable to a case where the agent is requested by the proposer to fill in the answers in accordance with information supplied by the proposer. *Bawden* has been followed in other cases and was approved by the Court of Appeal in *Stone v Reliance Mutual Insurance Society Ltd*[3].

4.76 Summary of other cases:

> '*Biggar v Rock Life Assurance Co*[4]
>
> B effected a policy against accident through the agency of C, who deliberately filled in the proposal form falsely. B signed the proposal without reading it. Held, that the agent may be the agent of the company with the responsibility to ensure that the form was properly completed, but he was not at liberty to invent answers. To the extent that he did so, he was agent not of the company but of the proposer and the company was not therefore liable.
>
> *Facer v Vehicles and General Insurance Co*[5]
>
> B was the agent of an insurance company and A was one of his employees. F proposed for a policy and disclosed to A that he only had one eye. A filled in the proposal form and included a statement that F did not suffer from defective vision or from physical infirmity. The form included the statement "If this proposal is written by another it shall be deemed he shall be my agent and not an agent of the [company]". F signed the proposal form and a policy was issued. Held, that F was not entitled to a declaration that the company were liable to indemnity him under the policy. A was F's agent, not the company's.

1 It should be noted that these cases were decided at a time when it was possible for an independent intermediary, given the activities that he could conduct on behalf of the life office, to be the agent of the life office. This will now only be the case in the rarest of circumstances.
2 [1892] 2 QBD 534.
3 [1972] 1 Lloyd's Rep 469.
4 [1902] 1 KB 516.
5 [1965] 1 Lloyd's Rep 113.

Stone v Reliance Mutual Insurance Society Ltd[1]

S insured his home. Following a fire the policy lapsed. The company's inspector, O (ie as agent of the company), called on S to persuade him to revive the lapsed policy and to effect new ones. He saw Mrs S, produced fire and burglary proposal forms, and filled them in himself. Mrs S signed them as "proposer" without reading them. The question as to lapsed policies and claims were both incorrectly answered with "None". The printed form contained a declaration that if any part of it was not written by the proposer, the person writing did so as the proposer's agent. The company rejected a claim for loss by burglary. It was shown that it was the company's policy that O should put the questions to the client and write down the answers and that the answers were put in by mistake, which was O's. It was his duty, owed to his employers, to take care in writing the answers. The mistake was not a misstatement by the insured which avoided the contract, but one induced by the company's employee, and the company could not rely on it to avoid the policy.'

The question of whose agent an intermediary is has been less of an issue in relation to life assurance principally because of the polarisation rule and the fact that IFAs are rarely authorised to accept insurance contracts or to hold client money. The Law Commission have recommended changes to the law in this area these are described in Chapter 2 (see **2.48**).

Lord Denning MR described the case as quite different from the *Newsholme* case (above), because there the agent was merely the amanuensis of the proposer. It was far more like *Bawden's* case (above), where the agent could see for himself that the proposer had lost an eye, and that knowledge was the company's knowledge. In *Stone* Mrs S assumed (justifiably) that the agent would have knowledge of the previous policy. The Company were not assisted by the declaration in the proposal that the answers were true and that where answers were not written by the proposers, the person who did write them did so as the proposer's agent.'

4.77 It seems, therefore, that where a proposer signs a proposal containing a statement which is untrue or incomplete, but the agent had knowledge of the true facts (which were acquired by him *as agent of the company* and in the course of the transaction) the company is liable.

This point was reaffirmed in the following case:

'*Woolcott v Excess Insurance Co Ltd*[2]

In April 1974, T, who were brokers, insured W's house with the defendant insurance company, E. In August 1974, the house was destroyed by fire. E denied liability because of W's non-disclosure of his criminal record, which W admitted but claimed that T knew about. Held, that (1) W ought to have disclosed his criminal past; (2) T, in the ordinary course of business as brokers and agents of E, had acquired some knowledge of W's past; (3) on these facts W had no duty to disclose his past to T; (4) therefore E could not avoid the policy, but was entitled to be indemnified by T, who were plainly under a duty to disclose their knowledge to E.'

1 [1972] 1 Lloyd's Rep 469.
2 [1978] 1 Lloyd's Rep 633.

Again, *Newsholme* was distinguished because in *Woolcott*, rather than acting as the proposer's amanuensis, the broker had authority to issue policies on behalf of the insurers. He knew all the material facts and in the light of that issued the policy. All the knowledge which the intermediary had was therefore rightly imputed to the insurer. In practice the *Woolcott* scenario is very unlikely to arise in the context of life assurance and it is much more likely that Financial Advisers will be held to be the agent of the client.

7 Law Commission

4.78 The question of whose agent an intermediary has been is less of an issue in relation to life assurance than general insurance, principally because of the polarisation rule and the fact that IFAs are rarely authorised to accept insurance contracts or to hold client money. The Law Commission have recommended changes to the law in this area, these are described in Chapter 2 (see **2.48**).

CHAPTER 5

Financial promotion and product disclosure

SUMMARY

SECTION 1 FINANCIAL PROMOTION

A Introduction

5.1 The promotion (or advertising) by a life office of itself or of its products, whether in writing, television, radio, the internet, telephone or text message is a substantial undertaking for the majority of life offices actively seeking new business (or of an associated marketing company). In addition, direct marketing by eg 'off the page' advertising (where it is possible to apply for a life policy by completing a short application form in a newspaper, magazine or online), is a substantial part of some life offices' business and is accompanied by its own particular issues partly at least as a result of the customer not receiving any personal advice and the target audience for such advertising.

The Financial Services and Markets Act 2000 (FSMA) contains restrictions on and provisions relating to investment advertising, or more precisely 'financial promotion', which are built on in considerable detail in Chapter 4 of the Conduct of Business Sourcebook Rules (COBS) which is part of the Financial Services Authority Handbook. Guidance in this area is provided in COBS itself and also in the 'Perimeter Guidance' (see PERG 8 in the Handbook). 'Financial promotion' is wider than what might generally be understood to be 'advertising' and also encompasses provisions relating to unsolicited calls. The COBS Rules relating to financial promotion essentially amplify the FSA Principles relating to 'customers' interests' and 'treating customers fairly' (see **5.46–5.53** for further information on 'Treating Customers Fairly' (TCF)) set out in Principle 6 and also Principle 7 which relates to 'Communications with clients'.

The FSA Discussion Paper 11/1 regarding product intervention should be borne in mind in the context of financial promotion and product disclosure as, if implemented, it would give powers to: (1) ban products; (2) require providers to include certain product features; (3) specify minimum product standards; (4) prevent the sale of a particular product to certain types of customer; and (5) restrict sales volumes. The FSA would therefore potentially be involved much earlier on in the product cycle. The benefits of the approach are broadly perceived to be greater consumer protection and confidence.

This chapter must also be considered against the backdrop of the major changes taking place in terms of regulation generally in the UK. The proposal is to replace the FSA by the Prudential Regulation Authority (PRA) and the Financial Conduct Authority (FCA) with the 'equivalent' of the product disclosure and financial promotion rules being overseen by the FCA. It is not clear at present whether the FCA's approach will in practice differ much from the current approach of the FSA.

5.2 The core provision of the FSMA in respect of financial promotions is section 21 under which a person must not, in the course of business, communicate an invitation or inducement to engage in investment activity unless the person is an authorised person or its contents have been approved by an authorised person. The purpose being that there is an authorised person involved and responsible for ensuring that the relevant rules are complied with. There are exemptions set out in the Financial Services and Markets Act 2000 (Financial Promotion Order) 2005[1] (the 'FPO') (and subsequent amending orders).

A person who contravenes section 21 is guilty of a criminal offence which is punishable with a maximum of two years' imprisonment or a fine, or both. However, it is a defence for the accused to show that he believed on reasonable grounds that the communication was prepared, or approved for the purposes of section 21, by an authorised person or that he took all reasonable precautions and exercised all due diligence to avoid committing the offence[2].

5.3 Section 21 does not itself refer to the term 'financial promotion' except in the heading and in a reference to subordinate legislation and so 'financial promotion' is in effect shorthand for the reference in section 21(1) to the communication of an invitation or inducement to engage in investment activity.

In the case of a communication originating outside the UK, section 21 only applies if the communication is capable of having an effect in the UK. This section would include internet advertisements. This appears to give a broad territorial scope to section 21 and would seem to catch all relevant communications

1 SI 2005/1529.
2 Section 25.

originating from overseas capable of having an effect in the UK. However, the exemption for communications to overseas recipients in article 12 of the FPO prevents section 21 from applying to communications which are not directed at persons in the UK (whether originating from inside or outside the UK)[1]. For communications made by persons in other EEA States account must be taken of the relevant EU directives, such as the E-Commerce Directive and the Television Without Frontiers Directive, to prevent the UK from imposing restrictions on incoming financial promotions.

COBS 4.1.8 R sets out the rules relating to the geographical application of the financial promotion.

B Firms subject to financial promotion rules

5.4 Subject to COBS 4.1.1 R and 4.1.1 A R ('who' and 'what?') and COB 4.1.8 R ('where'?) the financial promotion rules apply to every firm (with an exception not relevant to life offices) which communicates or approves a financial promotion[2]. Under section 39(3) of the FSMA a firm is also responsible for financial promotions communicated by its appointed representatives when acting as such[3]. There is an exemption in article 36 of the FPO in relation to nationals of EEA States (other than the UK) where the financial promotion is communicated by such a person in the course of a controlled activity lawfully carried on by him in that State.

C Agreements resulting from unlawful communications

5.5 A 'controlled agreement' (such as a life policy – see further Schedule 1 of the FPO) entered into pursuant to an 'unlawful communication' is not enforceable, and a policyholder would be entitled to recover any money paid or other property transferred by him under that agreement together with compensation for any loss resulting from having parted with it. The compensation would be such as the parties may agree or as the court may determine (on application by either party).

The court may allow an agreement to stand or money or property transferred to be retained, if it is satisfied that it is just and equitable in the circumstances of the case. Where a person elects not to perform an unenforceable agreement or obligation he must repay any money and return any property received by him under the agreement. If a person recovers money paid or property transferred by him he must likewise repay any money or return any other property received under the agreement or as a result of exercising the rights in question[4].

1 See PERG 8.8.3G for further details and guidance.
2 COBS 4.1.1R.
3 COBS 4.1.3G.
4 Section 30.

D Exemptions to Restrictions in Section 21

5.6 Exemptions are set out in the FPO[1], and in COBS itself and explained further in the 'Perimeter Guidance' contained in the FSA handbook[2]. In practice, UK life offices marketing to UK residents in the UK do not always seek to take advantage of exemptions for its financial promotions even where they may be available. The benefits to be gained from doing so are not usually that significant and as it usually represents an exception to most life offices systems, controls and procedures it can actually prove to be more trouble than it's worth. However, the precise circumstances should be considered in each case.

As mentioned, the term 'financial promotion' is wider than 'advertisements' and also includes personal visits and telephone calls. This part of COBS therefore combines the old regime relating to solicited and unsolicited calls with the same regime as that relating to advertisements.

E What constitutes a financial promotion?

5.7 There is no restriction on the media of communication to which COBS 4 applies. Guidance on the meaning of 'communicate', 'invitation or inducement' and 'engage in investment activity', which together make up the essential elements, is contained in PERG 8.4, PERG 8.6 and PERG 8.7.

1 'Invitation or inducement'

5.8 There is no definition of these terms in the Act or in COBS. Guidance is contained in PERG 8.4. Only communications containing a degree of 'incitement' amount to 'inducements'. Purely factual statements would not ordinarily constitute an inducement although they could be presented in such a way that they did[3]. There must be some promotional element[4]. Objectively, there must be an intention to persuade or incite the recipient to engage in investment activity and the communication must seek to persuade or incite the recipient to engage in investment activity[5]. An 'invitation' is something which directly invites a person to take a step which will result in him engaging in investment activity. An obvious example of this would be a direct offer financial promotion[6]. Merely asking a person if he wishes to enter into an agreement with no element of persuasion or incitement will not be an invitation[7].

In PERG 8.4.9G to PERG 8.4.34G the FSA set out at some length the application of the principles in PERG 8.4.1G to PERG 8.4.7G. From a life assurance perspective the following are of relevance:

1 SI 2005/1529 (see **5.42**).
2 PERG 8.
3 PERG 8.4.2G.
4 PERG 8.4.3G; *Pepper (Inspector of Taxes) v Hart* [1995] AC 593.
5 PERG 8.4.4G.
6 PERG 8.4.5G.
7 PERG 8.4.6G.

(a) *Directory listings* will not normally be inducements but could be depending on how they are presented.

(b) *'Tombstone' advertisements* (announcements of a firm's past achievements) would not be inducements unless they contained some additional promotional material.

(c) *Website links* will almost certainly be inducements but depend very much on their precise wording as to whether they are inducements to engage in investment activity.

(d) *Banner advertisements* will almost certainly be inducements but may not amount to inducements to engage in investment activity.

(e) *Publication or broadcast of investment prices* (historic or live) are probably not inducements without some additional promotional material.

(f) *Journalists* may publish inducements although they are likely to be covered by one of the exemptions in articles 17, 20 or 47 of the FPO.

(g) *Investment performance tables* would not be inducements in their own right.

(h) Decision trees or flow charts – if used as an educational tool then they will not be inducements, but they may be if specifically used for promotional purposes.

(i) *Image advertisements* are almost certainly not an inducement or invitation.

(j) Advertisements which invite contact with the advertiser are likely to be inducements.

(k) It is not clear whether 'Introductions' as described in this part of PERG is the same as the activity of introducing as described under 'introducer' or 'introducer appointed representative' in the Glossary. 'Introductions' or 'introducing' are not defined terms in the Glossary. In this context it refers to 'an offer to make an introduction or action taken in response to an unsolicited request'. Introductions in this context may be inducements, but very much depends on the particular circumstances of each case.

(l) Distributors of financial promotions which have been issued or approved by an authorised person are likely to be covered by the 'mere conduit' exemption in article 18 or article 18A of the FPO but may not be covered if they go further. 'Distributors' in this context must be distinguished from distributors under distribution agreements which constitute an agreement to sell and market the products of 'product providers', which will clearly require authorisation.

(m) *Invitations to attend meetings or to receive telephone calls* will clearly be invitations or inducements. Whether this will be to engage in investment activity will depend on their purpose and content.

(n) *Explanations of terms*, without more, will not be an invitation or inducement.

(o) *Enquiries about a person's status* (eg whether or not they are a certified high net worth individual) or intentions (eg what they intend to do in respect of a takeover offer) will not without more be inducements to engage in investment activity.

(p) *Solicited or accompanying material* which does not contain any invitation or inducement to engage in investment activity will not in itself be a financial promotion.

(q) *Telephone services* will be inducements where a person seeks to persuade or incite the prospective customer to receive investment literature or a personal call or visit from a representative. However, if the services are purely reactive and contain no element of persuasion or incitement then they will not be financial promotions.

(r) *Personal illustrations* on their own may or may not be an invitation or inducement but may be accompanied by other material which would constitute financial promotions, but even then the financial promotion rules would not usually apply.

(s) *Instructions or guidance (eg help lines) on how to invest* (ie the mechanics of investing) will not, in themselves, be inducements.

(t) *Communications by employers to their employees* arises more often in the context of personal pensions and stakeholder schemes and these are covered by specific exemptions under the FPO. In the context of life assurance the employer will have to be careful that material constituting a financial promotion produced by the authorised person is merely referred to by the employer in, for example, a covering letter which does not seek to persuade or incite employees into action. Otherwise it will need to be approved by an authorised person.

2 *'In the course of business'*

5.9 Under section 21(4) of the FSMA the Treasury has the power to specify the circumstances in which a person is viewed as 'acting in the course of business' or not as the case may be for financial promotion purposes. To date this power has not been exercised so it bears its ordinary or natural meaning[1].

'In the course of business' requires a commercial interest on the part of the communicator. The interest does not have to be direct nor does the communicator need to be carrying on regulated activities. It does not need to be part of the communicator's business. Nor does the communication need to be in the course of carrying on activities as a business in their own right. The position may not be totally clear with regard to individuals although it is designed to exclude such things as conversations in the pub, letters or emails between family members, internet chat-rooms or bulletin boards for personal reasons. Persons who carry on

1 PERG 8.5.1G.

a business which is not a regulated activity need to be particularly careful when making communications which may amount to financial promotions. Examples include financial promotions regarding employee share schemes, group-wide insurance arrangements and stakeholder pensions schemes although many will be covered by exemptions. If not so covered, approval by an authorised person is required.

3 'Communicate'

5.10 This is extended to include causing a communication to be made[1]. A person is communicating where he gives material to the recipient or where, in certain circumstances, he is responsible for transmitting the material on behalf of another person. The distinction between 'communicators' and 'causers' is not usually of great significance (both are subject to section 21). The more difficult point is whether or not a person is causing a communication to be made by another. Primary responsibility rests with the originator. This person is responsible for its overall contents. Where a person other than the originator (such as a newspaper publisher or intermediary) transmits a communication on the originator's behalf he is communicating it and the originator is causing the communication[2]. This might initially be a concern for, eg newspapers but the financial promotion would ordinarily be approved by the life office or other provider.

Certain persons are not considered to be communicating or causing the communication as follows: (1) advertising and design agencies; (2) printers or producers of material; (3) professional advisers; (4) persons responsible for securing the placing of the advertisement[3]. In order to communicate a person must take an active step to make the communication. The FPO contains an exemption for 'mere conduits' in article 18. This includes (1) postal services providers; (2) telecommunication services providers; (3) broadcasting services providers; (4) courier services providers; (5) persons employed simply to hand out or disseminate communications; (6) newsagents selling newspapers and journals containing financial promotions[4]. In other cases persons may be able to rely on the mere conduit exemption[5].Website operators providing links to other sites are not usually regarded as communicating the contents of those other sites[6]. An exemption will apply equally to a person causing a communication to be made as it does to the person communicating it[7].

Guidance on 'made to', 'directed at' and 'recipient' are set out in PERG 8.6.9 and 10G.

1 FSMA 2000, s 21(13).
2 PERG 8.6.1 & 2G.
3 PERG 8.6.3G.
4 PERG 8.6.5G.
5 PERG 8.12.18G.
6 PERG 8.6.6G.
7 PERG 8.6.7G.

4 Exemptions

5.11 There are a number of exemptions set out in the FPO and there is guidance in PERG 8.11 to 8.13. Some exemptions apply generally, other specifically to contracts of insurance albeit, in the context of life assurance only to 'pure protection' policies. Part III of the FPO sets out various interpretative provisions, and certain conditions which apply to exemptions. For example, some exemptions require that certain indications are made. Article 9 requires a certain degree of prominence. Other exemptions rely on the communicator believing on reasonable grounds that the recipient meets certain conditions. Guidance is set out at PERG 8.11.6G. Further details are set out in **5.42**.

F Medium of financial promotions

5.12 There is no restriction on what medium a financial promotion may appear in, so it can include printed advertising, personal visits, telephone calls, emails, the internet, pictures, films, radio or television programmes and other forms of electronic media such as digital and other forms of interactive television and media. Examples of financial promotions include product brochures; advertising in magazines, newspapers, radio and television programmes and websites; telemarketing activities; written correspondence, telephone calls and face-to-face discussions; sales aids; presentations, etc.

A distinction is drawn between 'real time communications' and 'non-real time communications'. The former refers to invitations or inducements made in the course of a personal visit, telephone calls or other interactive dialogue. 'Non-real time communications' is only really defined in terms of it not being a real time communication[1] so would include financial promotions made by letter, email or contained in a newspaper, journal, magazine, other periodical publication, website, television or radio programme, or teletext service.

G Obligations of firms

5.13 Before a firm communicates or approves a non-real time financial promotion it must meet the requirements of the financial promotion rules set out in COBS 4.

The position has changed significantly from the preceding COB Rules in that the COBS 4 rules do not prescribe what type of systems and controls a firm should have in place to approve or confirm compliance of a financial promotion. SYSC 3 and 4 require firms to put in place systems and controls (SYSC 3.1.1) necessary to ensure the form complies with promotion and other communication rules in COBS 4. The requirement applies equally to non-promotional as it does to promotional communications. Under COB 3 firms were used to having in

1 FPO, article 7(2).

place more prescribed processes to confirm compliance of promotional material. They are now left more to their own devices. In practice the processes established for the purposes of COB 3 have largely continued into the COBS 4 regime.

H 'Fair, clear and not misleading communications'

5.14 The essential requirement of Rule 4.2.1R is that the promotion should be fair, clear and not misleading and these are concepts which permeate the whole of the FSA Handbook in respect of any form of customer communication. The firm must have taken reasonable steps to ensure this otherwise a breach of it will give rise to a right of action under section 150 of the FSMA[1]. This overarching requirement is expanded on by some mainly high level rules (compared to COB 3) although a few rules are still necessarily detailed.

The main changes introduced by COBS 4 are:

(1) A smaller number of high level rules replaced detailed, product-specific rules and guidance in many cases. One of the effects of this is to put more responsibility on firms for determining whether a communication meets the 'fair, clear and not misleading' requirement. The 'checklist' approach under COB 3 has largely been removed.

(2) The FSA believes that firms benefit from greater flexibility in determing how best to achieve the desired outcomes. An alternative view is that firms are even less certain whether their communications are compliant.

(3) The rules cover not just financial promotions but also other communications (non-promotional communications).

(4) A lot of the changes introduced by COBS 4 are as a result of the introduction of 'MiFID' (Markets in Financial Instruments Directive) which is not directly relevant to life assurance and so these provisions are not considered in detail in this chapter. However, MiFID has had an effect on terminology, so for example client categorisation is now slightly different (it is now retail client, professional client and eligible counterparty as opposed to private customer, intermediate customer and market counterparty). Also, some MiFID principles have been applied to life assurance financial promotions for consistency.

Guidance in this area provides that this rule is to apply in a way that is 'appropriate and proportionate taking account of the means of communication and the information the communication is intended to convey'. It should be noted that this guidance applies specifically to the fair, clear and not misleading rule in COBS 4.2.1 and is not of general application. When considering the content of a communication, firms are expected to take into account the nature of the product and the target market in question. The 'proportionate' approach allows a firm, in

1 COBS 4.2.6 R.

deciding appropriate content for a client communication, to take into account matters such as the target client's understanding of the product or similar products.

More specific guidance is set out in COBS 4.2.4 G. The provisions relevant to life assurance are that: (i) it should be made clear if a product or service places a client's capital at risk; (ii) where the investment or service being promoted has a complex charging structure or where the firm will receive more than one element of remuneration the necessary information should be included to ensure it is fair, clear and not misleading and contains sufficient information taking into account the needs of the recipients; (iii) for promotions that name the FSA as the firm's regulator and also refer to non-FSA regulated matters then it must be made clear which matters are not regulated by the FSA; (iv) with regards to promotions of 'packaged products' (which includes life policies) where these are produced by someone other than the promoting firm the financial promotion must give a fair, clear and not misleading impression of the product provider.

COBS 4.5.6 R is specifically concerned with comparisons. The comparison must be meaningful and presented in a fair and balanced way. This can pose some difficulty of interpretation. Some people may, for example, use an instant access building society account for long-term savings and others may use it as a home for day-to-day income and expenditure. Generally, however, the more disparate the types of investment being compared the more difficult it probably is to justify the comparison.

If information relating to protection under an investor compensation scheme, such as the Financial Services Compensation Scheme is mentioned, this must be restricted to factual references[1].

I Financial promotions to be identifiable as such

5.15 A firm must ensure that a financial promotion addressed to a retail client is clearly identified as such. It must not disguise or misrepresent its promotional purpose (some advertisements, for example, appear to be part of the normal text of the publication in which they appear – known colloquially as 'advertorials'). It will probably be sufficient to clearly state somewhere that 'This is an advertisement'. This provision does not apply to 'image advertising'.

J Communicating with retail clients

5.16 In communications, the name of the firm must be included .This may be a trading name or shortened name provided the retail client can identify the firm communicating the information[2].

The information must be accurate and must not emphasise any potential benefits without giving a fair and prominent indication of any risks.

1 COBS 4.4.1 R.
2 COBS 4.5.2 R(1) & COBS 4.5.3 G.

Although not specifically retained in COBS, it is worth bearing in mind certain provisions of the previous rules. For example, the provision that a communication must not contain any false indication, in particular as to the firm's independence, the scarcity of any investment or service (for example, incorrectly representing that the investment is available in limited quantities or for a limited time) or the scale of activities or the resources available to the firm. For example, some firms have not always sufficiently differentiated the assets of the firm with the funds it has under management which are clearly two entirely different things.

In addition, the old COB rules provided that the content, design or format of a promotion must not in any way disguise, obscure or diminish important items statements or warnings. For example, risk warnings should not be 'counterbalanced' by text which detracts from the impact of risk warnings or be hidden in 'small print'. Generally, risk warnings must be sufficiently prominent and appropriately placed in context and in a typeface comparable with the statements which they are intended to balance. An example of counterbalancing would be a statement such as 'past performance is not a guide to the future, but it is usually the best measure you have of a fund's likelihood of achieving its objectives (or similar)'.

The question of 'balance' is a constant source of difficulty in interpretation. It can be a very subjective issue which in practice is not assisted by the commercial pressures. Where benefits or positive features of products are stated then, in general, this should be followed reasonably closely by relevant risks.

The financial promotion should also not omit matters which would result in information being insufficient, unclear, unfair or misleading.

Where information communicated refers to a particular tax treatment, there must also be a prominent statement about tax treatment. Such a statement must make it clear that the tax treatment depends on individual circumstances of each client and may be subject to change[1].

Information contained in any promotion must be consistent with any other information the firm provides to the retail client. Such other information would include the terms and conditions of a life policy and the key features document.

Financial promotions must be sufficient for and presented in a way which is likely to be understood by the average member of the group to whom it is directed or who is likely to receive it.

5.17 Guidance in this area emphasises that recipients will not necessarily have an understanding of the investment being promoted and so ambiguous terms should not be used nor should an audience be targetted which is unlikely to understand the promotion. The FSA have indicated that the following points are important when deciding on how information should be communicated to a particular target market: the nature of the product or business; the risks involved; the client's commitment; the likely information needs of the average recipient and the role of information in the sales process. The firm must make it clear if it is directing a promotion at a specific collection of individuals who are reasonably believed to have relevant specialist knowledge.

1 COBS 4.5.7R.

A useful list of examples was set out at COB 3.8.7G(3) which suggested that a financial promotion does not meet the general requirement of being fair, clear and not misleading. So as far as life assurance is concerned these were as follows:

(i) a statement such as 'no initial charges' or 'no entry or redemption charges' where, for unit-linked policies, the 'bid' and 'offer' (selling and buying) prices of units are different;

(ii) a statement of a company's assets without also stating its liabilities or a statement of its total costs, or income or turnover, without making it clear the period to which the statement relates;

(iii) an implication that the assets of the whole group can be drawn on by a subsidiary when this is not the case;

(iv) a statement of the amount of authorised share capital of a company without the amount of the issued share capital.

5.18 Some of the following examples may provide a flavour of the issues arising in deciding whether or not a financial promotion is 'fair, clear and not misleading':

(i) Use of the term 'unique'. In order to be unique the subject must be 'without a like'. This is a demanding test which on a more thorough analysis is often not found to be the case.

(ii) Sometimes the wording of promotions can be construed as advice or a 'personal recommendation'. Clearly, for an anonymous financial promotion wording of this nature should not be used.

(iii) Use of the term 'free'. Some promotions state that the first premium is 'free'. In the sense that no payment is actually made at the time then this is correct. However, it may be that the loss to the life office in offering the first premium for free is recouped by a corresponding increase to subsequent premiums in which case the original statement may not now appear so correct.

(iv) Use of term 'affordable' in relation to premiums. This can be difficult in that the financial circumstances of all recipients is not necessarily known. It may be that if the life office had conducted research into the premium level(s) in question which had revealed that the premium level was thought to be affordable then this might be acceptable evidence to support such a statement.

(v) Directive nature of promotions. Especially for more vulnerable customers language which urges action may go beyond what is reasonable especially if it appears in official sounding language.

(vi) Audience. Some promotions may be appropriate for advisers or experienced investors but would not be for less sophisticated readers.

(vii) Popularity rather than 'needs'. Some promotions focus on the fact that a product has been taken out by many other customers rather than the financial needs it meets for those customers. The fact that a product may be popular should not be a prime factor upon which it is marketed.

(viii) Use of false 'close-by' dates. Dates up to which a product is available should not be artificial (in order to encourage action) or there should at least be a warning that the offer may be repeated. There may, of course, be genuine reasons for close dates, eg, birthdays may pass (so premiums may increase) or mailing lists acquired from third parties may only be available for a certain time.

The FSA issued a report in October 2009 ('Fair, clear and not misleading – review of the quality of financial promotions in the structured investments products marketplace') which also gave further examples of issues which arose, for example, being clear where customers money is invested; counterparty and capital risk; appropriate language for the target audience and only describe a product as 'protected' or 'guaranteed' if this is accurate and not misleading.

In accordance with the Financial Promotions Guidance (Amendment) Instrument, 2011, when this is brought into force on 22 March 2012, references to 'guaranteed', 'protected' or 'secure' may only be used where such terms are capable of being 'fair, clear and not misleading'. This will requires the firm to present such information 'with sufficient clarity and prominence'.

K 'Past, simulated and future performance information'

5.19 There were indications that the FSA may ban past performance information completely around the time of the introduction of the FSMA 2000. Although this did not happen there are now considerable restrictions in the rules in this area. The FSA view of past performance information is that it is not a reliable indicator of future returns. The concern is that, despite the inclusion of stipulated risk warnings, consumers place too much reliance on it. The COBS rules therefore require firms to reduce the emphasis placed on past performance information.

The relevant rules are contained in COBS 4.6. COBS 4.6.2R (1) to (6) provide the following in relation to past performance information: (1) must not be the most prominent feature of the communication; (2) must cover the last five years or as long as possible if less than five years' information. It must only show complete twelve month periods; (3) clearly state the reference period and source of the information; (4) contain a prominent warning that the information relates to the past and that past performance is not a reliable indicator of future results; (5) clearly state the currency and that this may affect returns if different from that of the client's home state; (6) disclose the effect of commissions, fees and other charges if the past performance indication is based on gross performance.

Simulated past performance information is also permitted but must comply not only with the COBS 4.6.2R provisions but also further restrictions as set out in 4.6.6R, for example a prominent warning that the figures refer to simulated past performance and that this is not a reliable indicator of future performance.

The main difference from COB 3 is that the new rules do not prescribe how the past performance information should be presented. The FSA have adopted the MiFID approach to past performance which does not prescribe the format.

L Previous guidance on particular types of financial promotions: COB 3 Annex 4

5.20 COB 3 Annex 4 provided some additional guidance which still has relevance. So far as life assurance is concerned, it related to the following areas.

1 'High income' products

5.21 Concerns have regularly been expressed about the advertising of so-called 'high income' products. The crux of the problem is the fact that, with regard to single premium insurance bonds (or indeed any life assurance product), the 'income' in question is technically a withdrawal of capital, so that the capital sum represented by the investment is thereby eroded, the danger being that this could become worth less than the amount originally invested where investment performance does not compensate for such withdrawals.

For life assurance products (and in spite of the implications in much marketing material) it is not possible for an income to be produced in the established legal and taxation sense of the word. A life assurance policy is a non-income producing asset.

The confusion has been exacerbated by virtue of the fact that some life office investments (eg so-called 'distribution bonds') have been structured so that they pay out an amount based income earned by the underlying fund investments. Nevertheless, these would still be capital payments from the policy.

The FSA stated that if the term 'income' is used, it will be difficult for the promotion to avoid being misleading unless it is used to indicate payments which are solely interest or dividend earnings (which, as mentioned, is not possible for life assurance policies but would be for unit trusts and open-ended investment companies) or 'income' is clearly defined at an early point as having a different meaning, and in particular specifies the risk to capital necessary to achieve the payment.

If the rate of income available is at some capital risk or at the expense of growth, or the income or some of it comprises a return of capital, this must be clearly explained.

Where an 'income' is guaranteed but the capital is not there should be a clear statement where the relevant benefits are not guaranteed, or no benefits are guaranteed.

2 With-profits bonds

5.22 Concern was originally expressed by LAUTRO in several areas, including failure to emphasise the fact that such bonds were not suitable for short-term investment; unclear statements as to the factors which determine the cash-in value of the bond; reserving the right to adjust the encashment value without adequately explaining the significance or likelihood of such a procedure (the 'market value reduction' by life offices) and using a bonus rate implying that this rate will necessarily apply throughout the term of the investment.

The FSA reiterated these concerns in COB 3 Annex 4. In particular they were concerned with the quotation of values based on existing bonus rates leading customers to anticipate necessarily receiving such amounts. They also pointed to references to building society accounts in comparison to such bonds without adequately explaining the difference between the two.

Quoting high initial bonus rates has historically been a commonly used marketing tool. However, the FSA identified that such rates may only be available for customers who make a sizeable or early investment. In addition, bonus rate may be affected by a variety of charges and market value reduction factors so it should be made clear that such bonus rates may not actually be achievable.

3 'Hybrid bonds'

5.23 There are two elements to such a product and it may be better to obtain them from separate providers. Generally, hybrid bonds are lump sum life assurance arrangements which divide the investor's investment into two parts. The first is used to provide a high 'guaranteed income' for a limited period. This is achieved by means of an annuity.

The second part is invested, for example, in a unit-linked life investment bond with the objective of restoring over a similar period the total amount of capital originally invested. LAUTRO identified four interconnected problems:

(1) The use of the word 'income' with regard to the annuity part is not entirely correct as the major part of the payment comprises a return of the capital itself.

(2) Whilst 'income' may be guaranteed the original capital is not similarly guaranteed.

(3) In order to seek to replace the first part over a reasonably short time span the second part is invested in investment vehicles with a considerable risk of loss.

(4) Although most of the investor's capital is invested in the second part, the 'income' provided by the first part is given by far the greater prominence. This gives an unbalanced picture of the product and the balance of risk of the investment as a whole.

Annex 4 G I of COBS expressed concern with the description of 'income' where this is provided out of capital and so capital is vulnerable to varying degrees of risk exposure. This needs careful attention. The presentation should not over-emphasise one component part of the plan as against another where this is disproportionate to the amount of investor's capital which goes into it.

The use, size and prominence of the word 'income', together with associated graphics, figures or the word 'guaranteed' must not distract from the overall makeup of the product and the overall risks. In this context the use of a product which uses the words 'guaranteed' or 'income' should be avoided. Unless payments are generally comprised of solely interest and/or dividend earnings, the use of the word 'income' to describe such payment should be avoided altogether – unless 'income' is specifically and clearly defined elsewhere in the advertisement.

4 'Stock market products'

5.24 Generally, in the context of life assurance such products are single premium investment bonds under which the investor is offered the growth potential of a stock market or other index. The guarantee is that some, or all, of the original capital sum invested will be protected against the volatility of the relevant market by a guaranteed minimum payment at the end of the specified term. Six interconnected issues were originally identified which were reiterated and added to by COBS Annex 4G as follows:

(1) *Minimum amount payable at end of term.* The word 'guarantee' is usually used but this is at some cost to the investor and so it must be made clear what that cost is and when it is levied.

(2) *Growth potential.* Expressions such as 'stock market growth' or 'the growth of the FT-SE Index' are often used and may be misleading because the underlying investments do not wholly reflect the stocks which make up the index. Advertisements for products linked to growth in the FT-SE 100 Index should also make it clear that this index does not include an allowance for any return or reinvestment of dividend income.

(3) *Amount invested.* Advertisements which quote returns in excess of the percentage increase in the FT-SE 100 and which do not mention that there will not be a full 100% allocation of capital invested will be misleading unless there is a full explanation regarding the allocation rate (where less than 100%).

(4) *Gross returns and tax on underlying fund.* Advertisements showing guaranteed returns against the FT-SE 100 expressed in 'gross' terms are potentially misleading where the underlying funds are taxable and so a gross return is thus unavailable to the investor. Only advertisements showing the net position after tax has been levied should be shown.

(5) *Taxation of investors.* The tax treatment of the investment in the investor's hands should be made clear.

(6) *Early encashment.* The consequences need to be fully explained. Where there is a minimum return an appropriate risk warning should be included where the value of the investment can fall on early encashment.

(7) *Averaging.* Sometimes the value of the contract is based on an average level of the index over a certain time period. The FSA stated that this will reduce the investment potential of the contract. Where the averaging covers more than six months then it should not be implied that averaging is to protect

against falls at the end of the term. It should be made clear that investors only benefit from some of the performance of the index and that one effect of averaging is likely to constrain the final level of the index used to calculate benefits.

(8) *Maximum benefits*. These should not be promoted as a particular feature if the economic circumstances required to meet such benefits are in excess of the higher of the growth assumptions specified by the FSA.

Such products came to prominence from 1999 onwards when the FSA recognised the risks, in particular in 2003 when stock markets experienced a substantial downturn. The products were then referred to as 'SCARPS' (Structured Capital at Risk Products) or 'Precipice bonds'.

5 *'Guaranteed or protected products'*

5.25 For these products:

(a) Equal prominence should be given to both guaranteed and non guaranteed benefits.

(b) Guaranteed income but not capital – (a) clear statement where relevant benefits are not guaranteed, (b) name of guarantor (if any), (c) an equivalent annualised rate of return should be quoted if the cash rate is quoted.

(c) If relevant the words 'guarantee', 'protected element' or similar may be used to describe the minimum amount payable at the end of the term. If there is a cost to the investor in doing this the amount of that cost and how it is imposed must be made clear.

(d) Explanation of any risk of counterparty failure.

M Overseas insurers' advertisements

5.26 There are specific provisions in the rules relating to financial promotions of non-UK authorised insurers or of authorised or exempt persons approving such promotions. These requirements are set out in COBS 4.9 Certain statements are required depending on whether or not the insurer is named in the advertisement.

For financial promotions where the overseas insurer does not have a place of business in the UK) it is necessary to state the full name, country or countries of registration and, if different, where the head office of the insurer is situated. It is also necessary to give a prominent warning about the Financial Services Compensation Scheme not applying. Also, where any trustee, investment manager or UK agent of the overseas life office is named which is not independent of the overseas life office, there must be a prominent statement of that fact.

In addition, where the overseas life insurer is authorised in Jersey, Guernsey, the Isle of Man, the Commonwealth of Pennsylvania or the State of Iowa it is additionally necessary to give the full name, principal address and registered office, if different, of any trustee of any property held by the overseas life office in respect of the promoted contracts or, if relevant, as the above-mentioned details regarding any external investment manager used in relation to such property. It is also necessary to give details of any UK agent of the overseas life insurer.

Where the insurer is not named in the financial promotion then there is a required statement to make it clear that the advertisement relates to an insurance contract of a non-UK supervised insurer, the management and solvency of which is not subject to the supervision of the Financial Services Authority and that the policies issued will not be protected by the Financial Services Compensation Scheme and that there is no right of complaint to the Financial Ombudsman Service. The statement must be prominent[1].

N Rules which apply to direct offer financial promotions: 'off the page' advertisements[2]

5.27 A direct offer financial promotion is defined as 'a financial promotion that contains:

(a) an offer by the firm to enter into a 'controlled agreement' with anyone who responds to the communication; or

(b) an invitation to any person who responds to the communication to make an offer to the firm or another person to enter into a controlled agreement; and which specifies the manner of response or includes a form by which any response may be made.

An example of this would be providing a tear-off slip in a newspaper or magazine inviting the recipient to complete it and return it together with a cheque for the first payment. Another example would be a promotion with a phone number where the promoter is waiting to take the recipient's application details and not just to provide further details. A more modern version of this is a promotion inviting the recipient to apply via a website. An application form on its own would not constitute a direct offer financial promotion.

The provisions at COBS 4.7 are additional to the general financial promotion provisions in COBS 4. The key provision is COBS 4.7.1R(1)(b) which requires 'additional appropriate information about the relevant business and relevant investments so that the client is reasonably able to understand the nature and risks of the relevant business and relevant investments and consequently take investment decisions on an informed basis'. There is some relaxation of this requirement if, in order to respond to the an offer or invitation contained in it, the retail client must refer to other documents(s) which alone or in combination do contain that information[3]. The FSA have indicated that one way in which to show

1 COBS 4.9.7R
2 COBS 4.7.
3 COBS 4.7.1R(2).

that the client had referred to all the relevant information prior to responding would be to include a 'tick-box' in the application form to this effect. It is therefore very important to include appropriate relevant confirmatory wording to accompany that tick box.

5.28 Guidance[1] indicates that in order to make an informed assessment a firm 'may' wish to include the following (the use of 'may' being evidence of the less prescriptive regime now in place as previously these were required statements):

(1) A summary of the taxation position of the investment and for the average member of the group to whom it is directed or by whom it is likely to be received. This is likely to include a warning that taxation levels, bases and (if relevant) reliefs can change and (where taxation reliefs are mentioned) statements distinguishing between reliefs which apply directly to investors and those which apply to anyone else (for example, the underlying funds); that the reliefs are those which currently apply; that the value of the relief depends on the circumstances of the investor. For example, the fact that the proceeds on maturity of a qualifying endowment policy are tax-free for a higher rate taxpayer means that this is more valuable to him than to someone who is a non-taxpayer or who pays tax at the lower rate(s)[2].

Where the words 'free from tax liability' (or similar) are used then, if relevant, a balancing statement may be required that this only describes the benefits paid to the customer and there must also be a statement that the benefits are payable out of a fund which has already paid income tax, capital gains tax or corporation tax (as relevant).

(2) A statement that the recipient should seek a personal recommendation if he has any doubt about the suitability of the investments or services being promoted, and

(3) A key features illustration in which a generic promotion may generally be used (basically the projected performance and the effect of charges relating to the investment).

O Other provisions relating to financial promotions

5.29 Other provisions which could be relevant to life assurance are the codes issued by the Advertising Standards Authority, Office of Communications ('OFCOM') (the independent regulator and competition authority for the UK communications industries); regulations of an overseas regulator and the Privacy and Electronic Communications (EC Directive) Regulations[3]. There are, of course many others and some of the provisions are considered below.

1 COBS 4.7.4G.
2 3.9.20.
3 SI 2003/2426.

I Advertising Standards Authority ('ASA')

5.30 The ASA Codes apply to a wide range of advertising and advertising media and not just that relating to financial services or life assurance. The CAP Code relates to non-broadcast advertising, sales promotion and direct marketing. The BCAP Code relates to broadcast advertising. The Codes do not have the force of law but are designed to work within and complement the legal controls which affect advertising. All advertisements are required by the code to be 'legal, decent, honest and truthful'.

In many cases the provisions of the ASA Code will be satisfied by adherence to the financial promotion rules issued by the FSA. However, it is still important to bear in mind the ASA Code when considering advertising communications. For example, 6.1 and 6.2 of the CAP Code relates to Privacy (which is not regulated under COBS) so that advertisers should obtain written permission in advance if they refer to individuals or their identifiable possessions in any advertisement. Advertisers who have not obtained prior permission from those with a high public profile should ensure that they are not portrayed in an offensive or adverse way, and advertisements should not imply an endorsement where none exists. References to members of the royal family are not normally permitted although incidental references unconnected with the product may be acceptable.

The Committee of Advertising Practice (CAP) devises, reviews and amends the Code, gives advice and provides information. The purpose of the ASA is to provide independent scrutiny of the system, to identify and resolve problems and investigate complaints and to ensure that the system operates in the public interest. The ASA is a limited company, and independent of both the government and the advertising business. In the event of the ASA upholding a complaint it may ask that the advertisement be withdrawn or amended. Adjudications are published weekly on the ASA website.

Complaints are also investigated free of charge. They should be in writing and accompanied by a copy of the advertisement or a note of where and when it appeared. Complainants are not identified by the ASA without permission (unless required to do so by a competent court) and complainants are encouraged to resolve differences with advertisers wherever possible. Complainants will be asked to assure the ASA that they have no commercial or other interest in registering a complaint unless the complainant is prepared to be named. Complaints are not normally pursued where there is a simultaneous legal action. The Secretariat of the ASA and CAP will conduct a fact-finding investigation into those complaints which are pursued and will produce a recommendation to the ASA Council based on its findings. Such recommendations can be reviewed by the appropriate Review Panel. The final decision on complaints rests with the Council. Advertisers may be asked to take interim action. Appeals against ASA adjudications are made in writing to the Independent Reviewer and they should be accompanied by new evidence or demonstrate a substantial flaw in the conclusion reached by the ASA Council.

5.31 The principle sanctions for breach of the codes are as follows:

(1) the media may deny access to space on the advice of the ASA;

(2) adverse publicity may result;

(3) trading sanctions may be imposed or recognition revoked by the advertiser's professional association;

(4) financial incentives provided by trade, professional or media organisations may be withdrawn;

(5) pre-vetting of marketing material may be required for persistent or serious offenders; and

(6) under the Consumer Protection from Unfair Trading Regulations 2008[1], if an advertiser refuses to comply with the ASA, the ASA can refer the matter to the Office of Fair Trading. Ultimately, the OFT can seek an injunction from the Court to prevent an advertisements further appearance. Anyone not complying can be found to be in contempt of court.

Since March 2011, the ASA have also had responsibility for internet advertising.

2 Consumer Credit Act 1974 (as amended by Consumer Credit Act 2006)

5.32 The effects of this Act on marketing activities of life offices is usually very limited but may apply, for example, to advertising loans against the security of life policies.

3 Companies Acts

5.33 In connection with communications from life offices the provisions of the Companies Act, 2006 requires certain basic details on all business letters, notices and other official publications and certain other items such as invoices, receipts, promissory notes and cheques[2]. The requirement to disclose its registered name applies to a very wide range of communications. 'Limited company' may be abbreviated to 'Ltd' and 'public limited company' may be shortened to 'plc'[3]. Every company must also have the following particulars in all business letters, order forms and websites which, it could be argued, might also include proposal/application forms. These requirements are (so far as life offices are concerned): (a) company's place and number of registration; (b) the address of its registered office.

4 Forgery and Counterfeiting Act 1981

5.34 In some financial promotions the advertiser may wish to represent bank notes for marketing purposes. Section 18(1) of this Act requires the prior consent

1 SI 2008/1277.
2 Companies Act 2006, s 82; The Companies (Trading Disclosures) Regulations 2008, Articles 6 & 7.
3 Companies Act 2006, ss 58 & 59.

of the Bank of England for the reproduction of bank notes. The Bank of England also owns the copyright in its notes. If the Bank gives permission it will tend to restrict what type of images can be shown in advertising literature in terms of size and the angle from which the note is viewed. See section 19 for similar provisions regarding coinage.

5 *Intellectual property rights*

5.35 Life offices need to be aware of issues relating to 'passing off', copyright and trademarks. Regarding 'passing off' the life office must ensure that the product being advertised is sufficiently differentiated from others such that the public does not confuse the product with one issued by another provider[1]. The basis upon which a 'passing off' action is pursued is that the complainant party has lost the customer because the latter is misled by the representations of a competitor.

Copyright is the right given against the copying of defined types of productions and it is feasible that this could extend to marketing literature. Generally, life office logos and emblems would also be registered as trademarks.

With regard to comparative advertising care needs to be exercised in connection with displaying other companies' logos as this will often involve displaying another advertiser's registered trademarks, although relief may be obtained via section 10(6) of the Trade Marks Act 1994.

6 *Libel*

5.36 Whilst reasonable comparison and criticism is possible the life office must ensure that it does not go too far and unfairly criticise other product providers (or any other person mentioned in advertising literature).

7 *Gambling Act 2005*

5.37 Life offices may seek to encourage greater response to advertisements by incorporating prize draws or competitions. This area is subject to its own detailed regulation. As a general rule (and subject to certain other limited exceptions) prize draws will be illegal unless the entrant is not required to provide any consideration for the entry. What constitutes 'consideration' can be difficult to ascertain. Clearly, an entry fee would be consideration but the position regarding, for example, commercial information, such as an entrant's details, may not be so clear although Schedule 2 to the Gambling Act 2005 ('Lotteries: Definition of Payment to Enter') has clarified this to some extent. There are specific exclusions from consideration (eg cost of postage) and specific inclusions (eg payment to discover if a prize has been won) but 'transferring money's worth' still seems open to interpretation.

1 See *Reddaway v Banham* [1896] AC 199.

8 Consumer pressure

5.38 Consumer pressure can come from various sources, such as the Consumers Association (publishers of Which? magazine), newspaper campaigns, from groups of disgruntled policyholders forming themselves in to action groups, etc. Life offices may be influenced in their decisions and activities in such cases although, of course, much will depend on the life office's own interpretation of the facts and events. The issues and problems arising from endowment mis-selling in the 1990s saw a proliferation of consumer pressure groups[1]. The financial problems arising in respect of Equitable Life and substantial cuts to policy values have also witnessed the establishment of several policyholder action groups.

9 Consistency between policy and marketing literature

5.39 With the increasing complexity and volume of the literature which accompanies life policies (for example, brochures, sales aids, flyers, key features documents, etc) the chances of information in those documents being inconsistent with the policy document will invariably increase. Life offices should seek to ensure consistency. As well as being consistent with treating customers fairly and COBS requirements, this will tend to protect their own positions.

P 'Cold calls and other promotions that are not in writing'

5.40 This relates to a financial promotion made in the course of a personal visit, telephone conversation or other interactive dialogue. With a written promotion the recipient has a choice whether or not to read it but the recipient has limited control over a cold call. The additional protections for cold calls are designed to counter high pressure sales techniques.

To be a 'cold call' it must not have been initiated by the recipient of the financial promotion and must not take place in response to an 'express request' by the recipient. There is no such express invitation where the person has simply omitted to indicate that he does not wish to receive a call, visit or dialogue or by reason of agreeing to standard terms that indicate such calls, visits or dialogue unless he has clearly signified that he is willing for them to be made. If a call, visit or dialogue is initiated or requested by one person it is treated as also having been initiated or requested by any other person to whom it is made at the same time if that other recipient is a close relative or is expected to engage in any investment activity jointly with the person who inititiated or requested the call, visit or dialogue.

Guidance on what constitutes a real time financial promotion (as opposed to 'non real time') is contained in PERG 8.10.1G to 7G and guidance on what

1 See 'Restoring confidence in long-term savings: Endowment mortgages', House of Commons Treasury Committee, 25 February 2004.

constitutes 'solicited' and 'unsolicited' real time financial promotions is contained in PERG 8.10.8G to 14G.

Firms are unable to make cold calls other than in respect of a generally marketable 'packaged product' which is not, in a life assurance context, 'a life policy with a link (including a potential link) to a higher volatility fund'[1]. Cold calls may also be made where there is an existing established relationship which envisages such calls being made.

The general requirement that any communication must be clear, fair and not misleading will apply; the purpose of the communication must be made clear at the outset and the caller must identify himself and the firm he represents. He must check that the customer wishes him to communicate and terminate the communication if the customer does not wish him to proceed. The customer must be given a contact point. Communication with the customer must only be undertaken at an appropriate time of the day[2].

I Miscellaneous obligations regarding financial promotions

5.41 COBS 4 does not prescribe the systems and controls a firm should have in place to approve or confirm compliance of a financial promotion. Instead, high-level guidance points out the need to comply with the SYSC requirements. SYSC 3 and 4 require firms to put in place systems and controls (SYSC 3.1.1) necessary to ensure the firm complies with COBS 4. The requirement applies equally to non-promotional as to promotional communications. As an example of the more high level approach of COBS 4 in COB 3 this specifically required a firm to arrange for the confirmation of compliance required to be carried out by an individual with 'appropriate expertise'. COBS has no such specific requirement (although it may be thought that this is appropriate under SYSC).

COBS 4.10 contains specific provisions relating to the approval by a firm of a financial promotion for an unauthorised firm in order for that unauthorised firm not to be in breach of section 21 of the FSMA. It is not possible to approve a 'cold call' as it is not possible to be certain of the content of a verbal financial promotion prior to the communication of the promotion.

Promotions which were initially compliant may not continue to be compliant with the passage of time. In such cases the firm should withdraw its approval and notify any person it knows is relying on its approval as soon as reasonably practicable. This would not apply to financial promotions which are 'clearly only relevant at a particular date'[3]. Therefore it is important for all forms to monitor their financial promotions on an ongoing basis (whether they have produced, approved and/or communicated them) as part of their compliance monitoring procedures.

The high level record keeping requirements are contained in COBS 4.11.1R. This includes copies of scripts for telemarketing campaigns. A record of the

1 COBS 4.8.2R.
2 COBS 4.8.3R.
3 COBS 4.10.8 & 9G.

financial promotion must be retained for six years in the case of a life policy[1]. Unlike COB 3 they are not detailed so, for example, there is no specific requirement that the record must contain the name of the individual confirming the compliance or the date of such confirmation or approval. All that is stated in this respect is that a firm should consider maintaining a record of why it is satisfied a financial promotion is compliant. If the financial promotion is not in a written form there is no requirement to keep an adequate record except as mentioned with regard to telemarketing scripts. SYSC 3.2.20R (Records) requires a firm to take reasonable care regarding making and keeping records.

A firm may approve a financial promotion for an overseas person who does not have permission provided it makes it clear which firm has approved or communicated it. The financial promotion must also make clear (as appropriate) that customer protection rules do not apply, that the Financial Services Compensation Scheme may not be available or only available to an extent, although references to another protection or compensation scheme may be included. The firm must take reasonable steps to satisfy itself that the overseas person will deal with retail clients in the UK in an honest and reliable way'[2].

Q The Financial Services and Markets Act 2000 (Financial Promotion) Order 2005 ('FPO')

5.42 This statutory instrument (which has been the subject of numerous amending instruments) specifies the controlled activities and controlled investments which are exempted from the provisions of section 21 of FSMA 2000.

Schedule 1 sets out the controlled activities and controlled investments.

Part IV of the Order sets out those exemptions which apply to communication relating to all types of controlled activity. Guidance in this respect is set out in PERG 8.12. These activities are as follows:

(i) Article 12: Communications to overseas recipients, or which are directed only at persons outside the UK. This is subject to certain conditions: the communication must be accompanied by indications that it is directed only at persons outside the UK and that it must not be acted upon by persons in the UK; the financial promotion is not referred to in or directly accessible from another communication which is itself made or directed at persons in the UK by or on behalf of the overseas person and there are proper systems and procedures in place to prevent recipients in the UK from engaging in the investment activity to which the financial promotion relates.

(ii) Article 13: Communications from customers and potential customers.

(iii) Article 14: Certain follow up non-real time communications and solicited real time communications.

(iv) Article 15: Certain introductions to authorised or exempt persons.

1 COBS 4.11R(3)(b).
2 COBS 4.9.3R.

(v) Article 16: Communications from exempt persons.

(vi) Article 17: Generic promotions which do not identify (directly or indirectly) a person who provides the 'controlled investment' in question (or identify any person as a person who carries on a controlled activity in relation to that investment). An example would be 'Investment Bonds are wonderful' provided no particular investment bond is mentioned.

(vii) Articles 18 and 18A: 'Mere conduits', by which is meant such person only communicates it in respect of a course of business carried on by him the principal purpose of which is transmitting or receiving material provided to him by others, the communication is wholly devised by another person and he does not in any way edit the content of the communication (unless required to do so in certain circumstances). Examples are postal and internet service providers, courier companies and telecommunications companies.

(viii) Article 19: Communications to investment professionals, subject to certain conditions.

(ix) Article 20: Communications by journalists contained in a qualifying publication.

(x) Article 20A: Promotions broadcast by a company director, etc. The main purpose of this exemption appears to be to guard against the possibility that during a broadcast interview or a live website presentation a financial promotion is made inadvertently by a director or employee of an organisation.

(xi) Article 20B: Incoming electronic commerce communications (exemption not available to EU authorised life offices).

Part V of the Order sets out exemptions specific to communications in respect of deposits and insurance contracts which are not a 'qualifying contract of insurance' as set out in the Regulated Activities Order[1]. This exemption will only apply to certain types of life policies (essentially 'pure protection' contracts). Part VI sets out a range of exemptions which only apply to certain controlled activities.

R Distance Marketing Directive ('DMD')

5.43 The Distance Marketing Directive (DMD)[2] was implemented in the UK largely in October 2004 mainly through the Distance Marketing Directive Instrument 2004 and the Distance Marketing Directive (Amendment) Instrument 2004. The DMD has particular effects on the rules relating to direct offer financial promotions which are set out at COBS 4.7. The DMD applies to 'distance

1 SI 2001/544.
2 The Distance Marketing of Consumer Financial Services Directive 2002, (2002/65/EC).

contracts' which have a long and detailed definition in the Financial Services Authority Handbook but which are essentially contracts which are advertised, negotiated and completed without any face-to-face contact with the supplier or intermediary and which are part of an organised distance sales or service provision scheme run by the supplier. Therefore, the DMD would not apply if the customer completes the contract in a meeting with the firm's representative, even if it is as a result of responding to a promotion that could have led to a contract being completed 'at a distance'.

COBS 5.1.5R(1) requires that the consumer is provided with all the contractual terms and the information contained in COBS 5.1.1R to COBS 5.1.4R in a 'durable medium' available and accessible in good time before the consumer is bound. There are exceptions for 'successive operations', voice telephony communications (but the information must still be provided before the customer is bound) and other means of distance communication not enabling disclosure.

A firm must be able to provide a paper copy of the terms and conditions whenever requested and must change the means of the distance communication used (unless incompatible with the contract or the nature of the service provided). It is not possible for a consumer to contract out of his rights. Where no advice has been given (which is the normal position) there must be a prominent statement to this effect stating if the person has any doubts regarding suitability he should contact the firm for advice (or another appropriate firm if that firm does not offer advice). Commission and remuneration details must also be included.

As mentioned, a consumer must be provided with all the contractual terms and conditions of the service in a durable medium in good time before he is bound. The phrase 'in good time' is not defined anywhere and would depend on the nature of the contract and the target customers. So a simple plan would require less time than a more sophisticated one.

S Systems and controls in relation to financial promotions

5.44 The FSA continue to emphasise that failures in the area of non-compliant financial promotions may also be indicative of failures in a firm's systems and controls. In one case which went to Enforcement (the FSA's disciplinary division) a firm was held to be in breach of SYSC 3.2.6R as a result of a failure to establish and maintain effective systems and controls to enable it to comply with the applicable requirements relating to financial promotions as set out in COB 3. This continued emphasis is highlighted in particular by reference in COBS 4.10 to SYSC 3 and SYSC 4.

T Markets in Financial Instruments Directive ('MiFID')[1]

5.45 This 'high level' Directive (which was adopted in April 2004) affects the way certain types of investment business are sold, organised, administered

1 2004/39/EC.

and controlled. It replaced the Investment Services Directive. MiFID does not directly apply to life offices. Indeed, insurance undertakings are one of the main exemptions from the MiFID Directive. However, to ensure a level playing field and in the interests of consumers, business efficiency and competition the FSA extended some of the MiFID requirements to insurance companies and applied some of the wholesale requirements to retail firms. Therefore, as a result of having to implement MiFID, the FSA reviewed and amended much of its current regime, even for firms which are not within MiFID's scope.

The FSA also took the opportunity to take forward other initiatives which were dependent to some extent on its approach to MiFID. This included the move towards principle-based regulation, to simplify its rule book and to review the financial promotions regime, disclosure and projections. The FSA brought in all these changes at the same time. Implementation of MiFID occurred on 1 November 2007. However, in respect of financial promotions the MiFID and non-MiFID regimes are largely dealt with separately.

U Treating Customers Fairly ('TCF')

5.46 In view of its potential effects on the financial promotion regime (although its effects permeate throughout the whole of regulated financial services) it is thought appropriate to include a brief description of the FSA's TCF initiative. TCF is a major part of the FSA's emphasis on principles-based regulation as opposed to a predominantly rules-based regime. Indeed, the FSA stated that TCF will help it 'remove a significant number of detailed requirements'. The concept of TCF has met with some criticism for potentially imposing legal liability on the basis of high-level principles.

1 Origins of TCF

5.47 In September 1998, the FSA issued Consultation Paper 13: 'The FSA's Principles for Business'. This set out an expanded version of Principle 6 which included additional aspects such as paying due regard to customer's information needs, communicating information in a way which is fair and not misleading and managing conflicts of interest fairly. The subsequent Policy Statement (October 1999) split out Principle 6 so that what remained of Principle 6 was 'A firm must pay due regard to the interests of its customers and treat them fairly'.

In December 2003 Consultation Paper 207 specifically addressed issues of TCF for with-profits policyholders, which led to the introduction of the PPFM document (Principles and Practices of Financial Management). In July 2004, the FSA published a more general report 'Treating customers fairly: progress and next steps'. In May 2005, the FSA published a statement of good practice on fair contract terms, highlighting particular concern on 'variation clauses' affecting premiums under long-term insurance contracts. In July 2005, the FSA published a further general report 'Treating customers fairly: building on progress'. In July 2006 the FSA issued 'Treating Customers Fairly – Towards fair outcomes for consumers' setting out (1) an explanation of the outcomes for consumers that the

FSA are looking to achieve; (2) progress made by firms based on their own assessments and the findings of the FSA's own supervisory work; and (3) those areas where further work is required and how the FSA plan to take this forward. In November 2008 the FSA announced the acceleration of the full integration of TCF into core supervisory work. The FSA also published a TCF update reminding firms of their requirements and explaining how firms would be assessed.

2 What is TCF?

5.48 The FSA do not define TCF on the basis that it is not possible to do so in a way which is meaningful to all firms. However, the FSA have stated what they consider TCF does not mean in the 2005 paper referred to above:

(a) being 'nice' to customers or creating satisfied customers;

(b) all firms required to offer the same, or highest, levels of service;

(c) inhibiting innovation in new products;

(d) that a firm must design or market different products for individual consumers;

(e) that the FSA will be arbiter of what products consumers want;

(f) that consumers will not be expected to take responsibility for their decisions;

(g) new rules or obligations for firms;

(h) a continuous ratcheting up of standards;

(i) that the FSA will determine pricing policies;

(j) firms adopting the same or bureaucratic processes;

(k) collecting large amounts of management information[1].

'Fairness' is not a term defined by the FSA or, indeed, by English law generally. The FSA have attempted to correlate fairness with established legal principles such as equity and natural justice, although it has at the same time emphasised that its meaning is not the same.

3 Potential consequences of breaching TCF

5.49 The FSA 'Principles' Sourcebook ('PRIN') states, at paragraph 1.1.7G, that breaching a Principle makes a firm liable to various disciplinary sanctions. Paragraph 1.1.8G goes on to state that the breach of a Principle will be relevant in the FSA considering whether or not to exercise its intervention powers and in extreme cases in varying or cancelling a firm's Part IV permission.

1 FSA July 2005 Paper 'Treating Customers Fairly – building on progress'.

In an Enforcement action against Legal & General Assurance Society Limited the Financial Services and Markets Tribunal stated (January 2005) 'It may be harder to show a breach of general standards than of specific rules'. The approach of the FSA may therefore be to cite specific rule breaches, alongside general principles, such as Principle 6. PRIN 3.4.4R states that breach of a high-level Principle does not (in itself) give rise to an action for damages whereas a breach of a rule provides a private person who suffers loss as a result of a breach with a statutory cause of action[1].

4 *FSA cluster reports, case studies and management information*

5.50 Although the FSA's intention is not to be prescriptive concerning the meaning of TCF it has recognised the need to develop a common understanding of what TCF means in practice. It has developed this in two main ways, namely cluster reports and case studies. Cluster reports have focussed on product design; staff remuneration; managing the interface between producers and distributors; role of management information; complaints management and strategic change. In terms of financial promotion the issues for firms to consider (under the 'Product Design' heading) include communication of product features and risks to customers and adequacy of supporting literature in explaining product features and risks.

Useful material in this respect has been provided by the FSA in 'Treating Customers fairly: Progress update' (June 2008). This provides examples of good management information ('MI') measures. Also, the 'Treating Customers fairly: Progress update' (June 2008). This provided examples of good MI measures which senior mangers may consider utilising. Robust and appropriate MI and senior management involvement is continuously emphasised.

5 *Implementing a TCF strategy*

5.51 The FSA have emphasised that one size does not fit all and that firms will need to take into account their various activities, products and services when implementing TCF. The FSA will look for evidence of a structured approach which is likely to involve: defining what TCF means for the firm; assessing current performance to identify gaps; developing an action plan to close any gaps and embed TCF in strategy operations and culture; implementing change where necessary and monitoring effectiveness. The FSA continually emphasise the role of senior management and that they are in the frontline for developing TCF. TCF should be reflected in a firm's business strategy and embedded throughout the business.

6 *Risk mitigation and enforcement*

5.52 The main supervisory tool which the FSA will use to assess whether the firm is complying with its TCF obligations is its risk-based assessment process

1 Section 150.

known as 'ARROW' ('Advanced Risk Responsive Operating frameWork'). The FSA have stated that where its supervision work identifies failures in systems and controls it will take account of whether firms have carried out a proper TCF analysis and whether senior management have played the role it would expect. Where they have not the FSA have said that it is more likely to take enforcement action.

7 *Criticism of TCF regime*

5.53 The TCF regime, for all its undoubtedly laudable intentions and benefit to customers, has not met with universal approval. In particular, some parts of the legal profession have expressed the view that TCF may be unpredictable, retrospective and potentially falls foul of its own standards of legitimacy. Predictability must be a fundamental requirement of a principle-based regime and it is argued that TCF principles may be unacceptably vague. One of the detrimental effects of this could be a reduction in innovation due to uncertainty that certain actions could be judged not to be in line with TCF. As the concept develops it should follow that clarity also improves.

V 'Financial Promotions: taking stock and moving forward' (February 2005)

5.54 Other than the financial promotion rules themselves the FSA have issued a number of papers and updates on the subject which help provide an insight into the rules and how they are applied in practice. This paper sets out some of their major concerns about financial promotions and systems and controls. It described how the FSA will build on its work reviewing promotions, visiting firms and communicating with the industry. Of particular interest is the FSA statement that they do not wish to introduce more detailed rules and this is reflected in the subsequent (now current) COBS Rules issued on 1 November 2007.

The status of papers such as this is for information purposes and not guidance. 'General guidance' is set out in the Handbook and it is possible for firms to receive 'individual guidance' in particular circumstances.

The FSA emphasised that as part of TCF firms should, when preparing promotions, consider whether:

(a) the material is clear, fair and not misleading;

(b) it provides a balanced picture of the product;

(c) the marketing matches the product;

(d) they have identified and understood their target audience; and

(e) the promotion will be easily understood by their customers.

This paper also indicated the setting up of a new department devoted exclusively to financial promotions. This department expanded the monitoring activities, focussed on direct offer materials and resulted in visits to firms to assess their systems and controls. A hotline was also set up so that consumers and regulated firms can report purportedly misleading financial promotions. One tool the FSA use is the 'Dear CEO Letter' which highlights any issues and concerns they have in a particular area. Relevant information also appears on the FSA website. Financial promotions are monitored through a combination of proactive and reactive work. Proactive work tends to focus on areas of the highest risk to consumers.

1 Where the FSA consider that a financial promotion does not comply

5.55 Any action taken will be based on the seriousness of the breach and the likely risk to consumers. After initial communication with the firm involved there are a number of possible outcomes:

1 accept the firm's position;

2 ask the firm not to issue the promotion again;

3 ask the firm to amend the promotion or withdraw it (in the unlikely event that the firm does not agree to withdraw it then it can vary the firm's permission or seek an injunction to require it to withdraw the promotion);

4 if there has been actual customer detriment (or the customer has purchased on the basis of a non-compliant promotion) the FSA may ask the firm to offer remediation either by withdrawing from the product without penalty or by offering compensation;

5 refer the case to enforcement.

In enforcement actions concerning financial promotions the FSA have, for example, highlighted failures to provide sufficient information on how the product worked or the risks involved. Issues of balance have been raised where there was focus on the benefits (including the offer of free promotional gifts) but less prominence was given to key information about risks.

2 Systems and controls

5.56 The FSA visit firms to examine their strategies, policies and procedures for producing promotions and to establish how effective these procedures actually are. Interviews with staff and senior management and 'walk through tests' of the firm's processes may be carried out. The firm's records may also be reviewed.

Issues which have been identified in visits include the following. Where firms do have good procedures, sometimes these are not followed by staff. Monitoring of adherence to procedures can be irregular. Senior management are not always fully involved and, in particular, do not have adequate management information. Some firms do not have adequate audit trails of how financial promotions are approved.

Other aspects to look out for include:

1 Ensuring systems and controls apply equally to electronic as well as paper financial promotions.

2 Ensuring adequate controls over appropriate staff issuing financial promotions.

3 Establishing clear accountabilities for design and approval of promotions.

4 Making sure the 'shelf life' of financial promotions is managed regularly.

5 Ensuring complaints are analysed and the findings applied.

Adequate training should also be given and positive steps should be taken to ensure that the approval system is operating properly.

3 General concerns

5.57 The FSA identified five particular recurring issues:

1 *Clarity of product.* A financial promotion should clearly indicate what the product or service is. Technical descriptions may not be relevant or meaningful to intended customers. Exposure to the ups and downs of the stock market should be made clear.

2 *Risk warnings.* Financial promotions must present a balanced indication of the product but not every possible risk needs to be incorporated in a short advert. Risk warnings should have sufficient prominence and not be buried in small print and/or on the back page.

3 *Percentages and headline claims.* Unrealistic and misleading headline figures should be avoided.

4 *Misleading statements.* Statements should not mislead the customer into believing something that is not true, or highly unlikely.

5 *Charges and early redemption penalties.* Information about charges and early redemption penalties should be described appropriately with the relevant degree of prominence.

4 Issues arising from thematic work

5.58 The FSA looked at particular products, industry sectors or media in depth.

1 *Website promotions.* Specific concerns included: non-compliant past performance warnings (should be on every page mentioning past performance); use of the FSA logo on sites.

2 *Direct offer material.* Specific deficiencies identified included: balance (risk warnings should appear close to the relevant benefits and not just in, for example, the key features document); target audience (explanations

should be tailored to the audience to which they are directed); media (communications should be adjusted depending on what media they appear in).

3 *Investments for children.* The issues here mainly involved lack of balance. In particular, comparisons with bank or building society savings accounts did not refer to the relevant differences such as risks to capital, certainty about growth and access.

4 *Capital secure structured products.* Also known as 'guaranteed equity bonds' or 'secure equity bonds'. Some promotions did not indicate that there were early encashment penalties or no access to capital until the end of the period. In view of the complexity of such products there should be an adequate explanation of all important features of the product.

5.59 The paper concludes with emphasis on a principle-based approach. Senior management responsibility is reiterated.

W 'Financial Promotions: progress update and future direction' (August 2006)

5.60 This paper indicated that financial promotions continue to be a priority for the FSA as part of the TCF initiative, although the FSA did acknowledge that generally the standard of financial promotions had improved.

It provided updates on the FSA's work and outlined how the financial promotions work forms part of the wider move towards a more principles-based approach. It also detailed the specific areas on which the FSA intended to focus. The outcomes approach is highlighted rather than compliance with detailed rules. Emphasised strongly again is the role of firms' senior management in taking a lead in ensuring effective systems and controls are in place around advertising and marketing and that they receive and act where necessary on accurate management information.

The FSA did accept, however, that some important detailed rules will need to be retained, perhaps accepting that a purely principles-based regime can be difficult to police.

X 'Financial Promotion and other Communications': Consultation Paper: October 2006 (06/20)

5.61 This consultation paper was issued at the same time as another FSA consultation paper 'Reforming Conduct of Business Regulation'. Together these consultation papers represented a significant step towards more principles-based regulation. They were also intended to implement the relevant parts of MiFID.

The rules which emerged from these consultation papers are the rules set out in Conduct of Business Sourcebook ('COBS'). This replaced the old COB 3 financial promotion regime (on 1 November 2007) in its entirety (but retained substantial aspects of it at the same time).

Y FSA's COBS 4 post-implementation work

1 *May 2008 update*

5.62 The FSA published an article on its website reporting on the extent to which firms are complying with the new, simplified financial promotion regime under COBS. The article noted that firms had taken a conservative approach to the new regime and had yet to take advantage of the flexibility on offer. In terms of the financial promotion process there was still much more that firms could do to integrate compliance into the design process for financial promotions so that, from the start, the focus is on the needs of the target customers based on their knowledge and understanding. Compliance should not simply be 'bolted on' at the end of the design process.

2 *Conduct of Business Sourcebook (COBS) post-implementation review: 2008 statement on interim findings"*

5.63 This interim report was published in December 2008. It echoed many of the May 2008 findings. However, it was noted that there were some changes in the way financial promotions were being prepared with earlier engagement between marketing and compliance, increased senior management involvement and increased management information. There were some changes, or plans to change risk warnings and/or their presentation to make them more meaningful and relevant.

3 *Conduct of Business Sourcebook (COBS) post-implementation review: final statement of findings"*

5.64 The final report findings are based on a 2009 review of firms' compliance with the COBS 4 financial promotion rules. Again, this reported no radical change in behaviour and very little use by firms of the additional flexibility. However, more positive findings related to greater interaction between compliance and marketing functions, increased senior management involvement and increased management information; more appropriate information for the target market; more meaningful risk warnings and use by firms of consumer testing.

Z FSA's ongoing thematic work

5.65 Examples of issues on which the FSA has reported in the area of financial promotions relevant to life assurance include:

(1) Website financial promotions (November 2007).

(2) Online Sponsored Links (November 2007): these are text based advertisements returned from keyword searches on a search engine or associated website.

(3) Insurance Comparison websites (November 2008).

(4) Financial promotions for over 50s life plans (June 2009).

(5) Financial promotions in the Structured Investments Products Marketplace (October 2009).

In October, 2010, the FSA introduced a new process (known as 'Guidance Consultations') for issuing general guidance relating to the FSA Rules published outside the Handbook. This has included guidance relevant to financial promotions, for example prominence in July 2011, and general guidance in January 2011, which for example included guidance on the 'customer journey' and making the point that financial promotions are 'a window on the culture of a firm'.

SECTION 2 PRODUCT DISCLOSURE AND CONDUCT OF BUSINESS SOURCEBOOK ('COBS')

A General

5.66 The rules relating to 'product disclosure' are concerned with seeking to ensure that the potential investor understands all the details relating to the contract he is considering purchasing prior to actual purchase.

The disclosure requirements as set out mainly in COBS 13 and 14 underpin Principle 7 (Communications with clients) which requires a firm to pay due regard to the information needs of its customers. In the case of packaged products such as life policies there is a special need to ensure that customers are supplied with information which will highlight product features in view of the sometimes complex nature of such products and their long term nature. This needs to be achieved in a way which will optimise the customer's ability to make a comparison of different products. An additional aim of these requirements is compliance with the disclosure requirements contained in the Consolidated Life Directive (previously contained in the Third Life Directive). When a firm sells a life policy (or other type of packaged product) to a retail client then prior to the firm carrying on the relevant business (and free of charge)[1]. There are exceptions to the timing rules for distance contracts and voice telephony communications. The firm must provide the following:

(1) A 'Key features document' and a 'key features illustration' to that client relevant to the product explaining such features of which he ought to be aware above all else. Where a customer responds to a direct offer financial promotion, this must include an example 'key features'. There is no requirement to provide a further set of key features in respect of the same transaction.

1 COBS 14.2.14 R (2).

(2) The information required by the Consolidated Life Directive information to that client.

(3) In respect of a variation of a life policy or person al pension scheme the client must be provided with sufficient information about the variation to be able to understand the consequences of the variation[1].

The remainder of the provisions in this rule are not relevant to life policies:

(1) Firms must not do anything in providing such documentation to cause confusion about the identity of the product producer[2]. A firm is not required to provide the above information where another person is required to provide that information[3]. As a provider of a life policy life offices are required to provide a key features document and key features illustration anyway in good time before those documents have to be provided[4].

(2) Firms are not required to provide a key features document or key features illustration for a life policy if the firm is operating from an establishment in another EEA State and the sale is by a distance contract or where the client is habitually resident outside of the UK and the sale is not by a distance contract. Additionally a firm is not required to provide a key features document or illustration for a traded life policy[5]. The provision of such information is also not required where the client is buying in response to a direct offer financial promotion without receiving a personal recommendation to do so provided the firm provides materially the same information in some other way[6]. The information is also not required where the client is habitually resident outside the EEA and not present in the EEA when the relevant application is signed[7].

B Requirement to produce key features

5.67 COBS 13.1.1R requires a provider to produce key features which, in terms of design and content, comply with the relevant parts of COBS 13. Key features documents must be produced and presented to at least the same quality and standard as the associated marketing material. It must also display the firm's brand at least as prominently as any other and also display the 'keyfacts' logo in a prominent position at the top of the document (also required on the key features illustration if this is not an integral part of the key features document. Also required is a statement (in the Key Features Document (or Key Features Illustration which does not form an integral part of the key features document) as

1 COBS 14.2.1 R.
2 COBS 14.2.4R.
3 COBS 14.2.5R.
4 COBS 13.1.1R.
5 COBS 14.2.7 R (2) & (3).
6 COBS 14.2.8R.
7 COBS 14.2.9R.

follows: 'The Financial Services Authority is the independent financial services regulator. It requires us, [provider name] to give you this important information to help you decide whether our [product name] is right for you. You should read this document carefully so that you understand what you are buying, and then keep it safe for future reference'. The Consolidated Life Directive information may be included in the KFD, KFI or any other document. Nothing in any of the above documentation may include anything that might reasonably cause a retail client to be mistaken about the identity of the producer firm[1].

I Content of key features document

5.68 COBS 13.3 sets out the framework for production of the KFD. The core provision in COBS 13.3.1R requires the KFD to include enough information about the nature and complexity of the product, how it works, any limitations or minimunm standards that apply and the material benefits and risks of buying or investing for a retail client to be able to make an informed decision about whether to proceed. Market research initially conducted by LAUTRO (one of the self regulatory organisations established under the Financial Services Act, 1986) indicated that investors are more attracted to documents which appear on no more than four sides of A4-sized paper. The normal style of technical product particulars and marketing material was generally found to be off-putting, purely because of its length. Sometimes key features documents are frequently much longer than this and contain much more detail than was originally envisaged such that the objective of providing just 'key' features is not achieved. The purpose of key features documents is defeated where documents are of such length and detail.

A KFD must explain the complaint handling arrangements; that compensation may be available under the Financial Services Compensation Scheme; and cancellation details (whether such a right exists, its duration, conditions for exercising the right, how much a client may have to pay if he exercises the right (for example any 'shortfall' suffered on cancelling as a result of movement in investment values etc), the consequences of not exercising it and practical instructions for the exercise of the right and the address to send the cancellation notice).

C Additional requirements for packaged products (including life policies)

I General

5.69 The key features document must set out prescribed information as specified in Table 13.3.2R. Ignoring provisions which are not relevant to life assurance, the key features document should be entitled or headed 'Key Features of the [Name of the Life Policy]'.

1 COBS 13.2.4R.

The policy must be described under certain sub-headings and give certain information as appropriate: 'its aims', 'your commitment' or 'your investment' (whichever is more appropriate), 'risks' and 'Questions and Answers'.

The aim of the policy is simply what it will actually or potentially achieve for an investor. Therefore, the aim of an insurance based investment bond would be to provide capital growth. The aim of a whole of life policy is to provide a lump sum on death whenever that may happen.

The commitment for regular premium policies is that the investor must pay a certain amount as a regular monthly or yearly premium for a specified number of years. If relevant it should be pointed out that if the investor fails to maintain the commitment and, for example, stops the policy early, he will not be covered in the event of his death and, for example, any mortgage linked to his policy would not be repaid from the proceeds. For an investment bond the heading which is probably more appropriate is 'your investment'. This will simply be a lump sum single premium. The risks are those matters which may have an adverse effect on performance or are otherwise material to the decision to invest. The following are some examples which may be relevant to life policies:

(i) whether the value of capital and any income from it might fluctuate (although see **5.21** regarding 'income' from life policies);

(ii) extra degrees of risk concerned with certain types of investment, eg emerging markets funds where there may be dealing difficulties or settlement or custody issues; potential problems with investment in real property in respect of liquidity, that the property may not be readily saleable, and that property valuation is a matter of the valuer's judgement;

(iii) that certain funds carry special risks, such as high volatility;

(iv) possibility of 'market value adjustment' (or 'reduction') for with-profits policies which could reduce the benefits payable;

(v) the risk that current tax benefits may be withdrawn;

(vi) if a customer does not maintain contributions he may not meet any projected target benefits and may lose any life cover;

(vii) for new funds if assumed size is not achieved the proportion of charges and expenses may be higher and the value of the investment will consequently suffer;

(viii) the fact that there is no guarantee (where this is the case) that a life policy will provide sufficient funds at the end of its term to repay a mortgage and the investor may need to increase payments;

(ix) where there is a fixed regular payment of 'income', the customer should be informed that such payments often involve a risk to capital (where relevant);

(x) the effect or potential effect of guarantees or other liabilities, whether they relate to the product which the customer is or may be acquiring; or to any of the provider's other products or the business activities of the provider or its associates (if they have or may have a material adverse effect on returns or are otherwise material to the decision to invest).

These examples are not, however, exhaustive.

2 *Key features illustration*

5.70 Within a KFI there is a requirement to include 'appropriate charges information' and a 'standardised deterministic projection' which must be consistent with eachother. Alternative projections may also be included provided they are not more prominent than the standardised deterministic projection[1].

Within the category of 'standardised deterministic projection' are 'generic projection' and 'personal projection'. Generic projections are not normally appropriate unless there are either reasonable grounds for believing it will be sufficient to enable the retail client to make an informed decision (unlikely if personal characteristics are relevant) or it is for a direct offer financial promotion[2]. There is no requirement for a projection for single premium life policies, a product whose benefits do not depend on future investment returns or any other product, where it is reasonable to believe that it will not be needed to make an informed decision[3]. If there is no requirement to provide a projection if one is provided it must nevertheless still follow the appropriate requirements[4].

COBS 13, Annex 2 sets out the requirements relating to projections. The benefit projections must be given at the three prescribed rates of growth for the policy in question, the 'lower, intermediate and higher rates of return' which are currently 4%, 6% and 8% for taxed life products and 5%, 7% and 9% for tax exempt products. They should be rounded down and shown to no more than three significant figures. They must be calculated using lower rates of return if the rates overstate the investment potential and may be calculated using a lower rate if the client requests it. The FSA stipulated rates have been criticised as being unrealistic in the current investment climate. It is understood that they are shortly to be reviewed by the FSA.

There are assumed projection dates for whole life assurance contracts. Either the first anniversary falling after the seventy fifth birthday of the life assured or that of the oldest life assured for first death policies or that of the youngest life assured for last survivor policies. Subject in all cases to a minimum of ten years. For other contracts the projection date may be the maturity date (if there is one) or an appropriate date which highlights the features of the product in other cases or, if neither of these are relevant, then the tenth anniversary.

All contributions during the projection period must be taken into account. They must be calculated on the basis that they are accumulated net of charges at the appropriate rate of return compounded on an annual basis. Any contribution

1 COBS 13.4.1R.
2 COBS 13.4.2R.
3 COBS 13.4.4R.
4 COBS 13.4.5G.

increases in accordance with an index must be taken into account on the basis of stated assumptions.

If inflation is taken into account there are stipulated rates depending on which rates of return are used.

Charges must reflect all of the charges, expenses and deductions a client will, or may be expected to pay. In appropriate circumstances tax relief and the off-setting of charges may be reflected. However, charges must not include the firm's dealing costs incurred on the underlying portfolio. Guidance provides further details regarding writing off of development and capital costs; assumption of higher expenses in future; appropriate apportionment of charges between products; no assumption that charges will fall and any projection of surrender value, cash-in value or transfer value should take into account any current surrender value basis and penalties which may be applied. There are additional requirements for with-profits policies, in particular with regard to assumptions relating to bonus rates.

Also required are appropriate risk warnings, including those relating to volatility, the relationship between figures in real and nominal terms and the degree to which any figures can be relied upon. Additionally certain prescribed statements must be included in the document containing the projection. Essentially, these are that projection rates are standardised or, if relevant, that they are lower than the standard rates used and why. Also, that charges may vary and that certain contributions (and increases where relevant) have been assumed. Finally, the sum of any actual premiums charged for any rider benefits or increased underwriting risks if these have been charged must be stated.

5.71 COBS 13, Annex 3 sets out the provisions relating to charges which a KFD is required to include. 'Appropriate charges information' comprises a description of the nature and amount of charges a client will or may be expected to bear; an 'effect of charges' table and 'reduction in yield' information. The table and reduction in yield information are not required for a life policy without a surrender value but there must be appropriate wording that the policy does not have any such cash-in value. Furthermore, reduction in yield information is not required for a without profits life policy with guaranteed benefits (except on surrender or variation), a life policy with a term not exceeding five years or a life policy held within a child trust fund. The 'Effect of charges' table must be accompanied by, or refer to: (1) a statement that all relevant guarantees have been taken into account (if there are any); (2) a warning that one of the effects of the charges is that the client may get back less than they invest (if that is the case); and (3) the rate of return used to calculate the figues in the table. This must set out potential surrender values for each of the first five years, every subsequent fifth year and the final year of the projection period, total paid to date, total deductions to date (optional), the effect of deductions to date (may be deleted in certain circumstances, eg if a without profits life policy with guaranteed benefits) and what the customer might get back.

Effect of Charges Table

First column	This shows the years in respect of which information is disclosed. Information is given for the first five years, every subsequent fifth year and the final year. Figures may be given for every subsequent tenth year where the projection period exceeds 25 years. Where the figures would depart significantly from a steady trend, figures are also required for the intervening years. For whole life policies if the projected fund reaches zero before the end of the projection period the consequences of this must be brought to the customer's attention. Figures for a longer term may also be shown.
Second column	This shows total cumulative contributions assumed paid in to that date and should allow for automatic changes in premium where applicable.
Third column	Withdrawals – this is required to show the cumulative withdrawals taken or income paid to the end of each relevant year (if any). The column may be omitted if withdrawals or income are not anticipated or allowed.
Fourth column	An optional column which shows the cumulative total deductions at the end of each relevant year (using a prescribed method).
Fifth column	This shows the accumulated value of the fund without reference to charges and then subtracting from this the figure in the 'What you might get back' column for that year. It may be deleted in certain circumstances, eg a without profits life policy with guaranteed benefits.
Sixth column	This column must show the standardised deterministic projection of the surrender value, cash-in value or transfer value, calculated in accordance with COBS 13, Annex 2 at the appropriate intermediate rate of return to the end of each relevant year.

The above table may be amended only if and to the extent that it is necessary to properly reflect the nature and effect of the charges in a particular product.

3 Reduction in yield

5.72 This is a statement showing the reduction in investment growth. This calculation may (in accordance with the terms of the policy) include the cost of mortality/morbidity where it would produce a misleading figure not to include it. Otherwise it is not required. This requirement relates to the 'appropriate charges information' referred to in **5.70**.

A firm must present reduction in yield as a A% figure as part of a statement which explains that charges and expenses have the effect of reducing your anticipated returns from B% to C%, or in some other appropriate way, for example, 'Putting it another way, if the growth rate were to be x%, which is in no way guaranteed, this would have the effect of reducing it to y% a year.'

Reduction in yield (A) is B less C where B is the intermediate rate of return and C is determined by carrying out a standardised deterministic projection to the projection date using B and then calculating the annual rate of return (C) rounded to the nearest tenth of 1% required to achieve the same projection value if charges are left out of account.

4 Further information

5.73 Also required is the information that Annex III of the Consolidated Life Directive requires to be communicated to policyholders as specified in COBS 13, Annex 1.

5 Principles and Practices of Financial Management (PPFM)

5.74 The PPFM requirements set out in COBS 20 replaced the previous requirements relating to with-profits guides. A firm which issues with-profits policies is required to produce a PPFM guide relating to its with-profits fund or funds and also a 'customer friendly' version (CFPPFM). There are also requirements relating to the provision of such information. For example, a firm must provide a CFPPFM free of charge with the key features document for a with-profits policy[1].

These requirements are set out in more detail in Chapter 1.

6 Abolition of post sale confirmation requirement

5.75 COB 6.5.46 set out the information which had to be given to investors once the customer buys a life policy. The information given to the investor in the original key features document was confirmed (ie an example, tables and deductions summary and the commission/remuneration which has been paid). These requirements were not replicated for COBS. See FSA Consultation Paper 170 and subsequent feedback.

7 Consolidated Life Directive

5.76 The information requirements of the Consolidated Life Directive are set out in Annex 1 to COBS 13. COBS 13.1.2 requires a firm to prepare the required information in good time before that information has to be provided (usually in the key features document). The information required is as follows: (1) firm's name and legal form; (2) EEA State where the head office of the firm is situated and, if appropriate, where the agency or branch concluding the contract is situ-

1 COBS 20.4.5R(3)(c).

ated; (3) address of aforementioned head office, agency or branch; (4) definition of each benefit and option; (5) term of contract; (6) means of terminating contract; (7) means of payment of premiums and duration of payments; (8) means of calculation and distribution of bonuses; (9) indication of surrender and paid-up values and the extent to which they are guaranteed; (10) information on premiums for both main and supplementary benefits where appropriate; (11) for unit-linked policies, definition of the units to which benefits are linked; (12) indication of the nature of the underlying assets for unit-linked policies; (13) details of cancellation rights; (14) general information on tax arrangements for that type of policy; (15) complaints handling details and information regarding any complaints handling body and that this is without prejudice to the right to take legal proceedings; (15) applicable law or, if there is a free choice of law, the law the insurer proposes to choose.

Many of the requirements of the Consolidated Life Directive will be covered by other provisions in COBS.

D Commission and remuneration disclosure

5.77 The provisions and requirements in this area are likely to be substantially amended following the implementation of the Retail Distribution Review, scheduled for the beginning of 2013, which has as one of its main strands the prohibition on commission being paid by a provider such as a life office for certain of its products. The following is therefore a high level summary of the current position. A firm which sells, personally recommends or arranges the sale of a packaged product (including a life policy) to a retail client is required to disclose to that person any commission receivable by it or any associates in connection with the transaction, or, where the firm is also the product provider (eg a life office) the amount or value, in cash terms, of any commission or commission equivalent payable in connection with the transaction. This must be as close as practicable to the time of the transaction and at any time the customer subsequently requests[1].

Disclosure must be made in a durable medium or where the retail client does not make a written application then it can be made orally but must be followed up in writing within five business days[2]. Disclosure should indicate the timing of such payments[3].

Disclosure would generally be made in a 'services and costs disclosure document' or 'combined initial disclosure document'. The former will contain the keyfacts logo[4], headings and text in the order shown in COBS 6, Annex 1G, and the latter will contain the keyfacts logo, headings and text in the order shown in COBS 6, Annex 2. Guidance is set out in the table at COBS 6.4.11G regarding the content and wording of commission or equivalent disclosure statements. For example, this relates to the names of the firms involved in paying and receiving

1 COBS 6.4.3R.
2 COBS 6.4.5R.
3 COBS 6.4.8G.
4 GEN 5 Annex 1 G, 2.2.

commission or commission equivalent; a plain language description of whether the remuneration takes the form of commission or commission equivalent; timing of payments and period over which they are paid; and examples of the amounts which would be taken from funds at certain value levels.

E Calculating commission equivalent

5.78 The table at COBS 6, Annex 6 sets out the basis on which the firm should calculate the value of the commission equivalent (ie the total of the cash payments, benefits and services) to be disclosed under COBS 6.4.3R. Benefits and services only need to be included where the value is such that they could not be provided as a non monetary benefit (also known as 'indirect benefits') under 2.3.15G. The table contains a lot of detail and the following is necessarily only a brief overview.

Part A: *Cash payments.* Where representatives, etc receive a straightforward payment on each sale, the first element is relatively simple. However, the precise rate of commission equivalent may not be known in advance. In such cases the firm must reasonably estimate the likely rate applicable. This would also include other payments such as bonuses, manager's overrides and other earnings conditional on amounts of new business.

Part B: *Benefits.* Such benefits include any item considered as a benefit or expense and whether or not the representative is liable to income tax or otherwise chargeable to tax on it (eg use of a car, subsidised loans, attendance at conferences, contributions to pension schemes, value of share options, etc).

Part C: *Services.* 'Services' for these purposes include those which cannot be provided under the indirect benefits rules.

Part D: *Calculation methodology.* This covers where estimating commission equivalent is appropriate and construction of commission equivalent scales.

5.79 If the firm pays commission equivalent to another firm in the same immediate group, or an appointed representative or tied agent which is an associate of the firm, the commission equivalent may not be on a commercial basis. In such circumstances the sum disclosed will be based on the higher of: (a) all payments, benefits and services provided to the firm or its appointed representative or tied agent, from whatever source plus an additional allowance for profit of 15% unless the firm can demonstrate that this figure is inappropriate and can substitute a more realistic figure in its place; or (b) the cash payments actually paid by the firm, plus the value of services provided.

F Retail Distribution Review

5.80 The Retail Distribution Review (RDR) was launched by the FSA in 2006. Its aim is to increase trust and confidence in retail investment markets to encourage the public to use financial services and products more. Implementation is (at the time of writing) required by 31 December 2012. Its main proposals are:

(1) Improving clarity for customers about advice services: so firms will be required to clearly describe their services as either 'independent advice' or 'restricted advice'. It will be possible for an adviser to still be 'independent' but to operate within a narrower 'relevant market'.

(2) Banning Commission: the purpose is to avoid remuneration bias, in other words advisers recommending products essentially only because they pay more commission than other (potentially better) alternatives. Adviser firms will have to set their own charges which they must agree with clients. Product providers cannot pay commission, but they can facilitate adviser charging, by setting up arrangements to pay such charges on behalf of the customer. Alternatively, a customer could pay a fee directly to the adviser. Pure protection policies (eg term life assurance) are excluded from this provision.

    Product providers who do facilitate adviser charging must: (a) 'obtain and validate' the customer's instructions; (b) offer sufficient flexibility in terms of the adviser charges it facilitates; (c) not pay out adviser charges over a materially different time period or basis to that in which it recovers the adviser charges from the client.

(3) Increasing adviser's professional standards.

At the time of writing there are some criticisms of the proposals. In particular, a perceived 'advice gap' in that people may not seek advice because they are more obviously paying for it. At the time of wroting the FSA are consulting on a 'simplified advice' process which is a form of 'restricted advice' under RDR which may help meet such criticisms. Please see Chapter 4 for further information.

G Information about the firm

5.81 A firm must provide a retail client with the following general information about the firm if relevant[1]:

(1) name, address and contact details necessary to enable a client to communicate effectively with the firm;

(2) the methods of communication between firm and retail client;

(3) a statement that the firm is authorised and the name of the competent authority which has authorised it having regard to GEN 4 Annex 1R;

(4) if the firm is acting through an appointed representative or tied agent a statement of that fact specifying the EEA State in which that appointed representative or tied agent is registered;

(5) the nature, frequency and timing of the reports on the performance of the service to be provided by the firm (in accordance with COBS 16).

1 COBS 6.1.4 R.

The provisions of the Companies Acts should also be borne in mind where relevant (see **5.31**).

H Churning and switching

5.82 'Churning' means entering into transactions with unnecessary frequency having regard to the best interests of the customer and the agreed investment strategy. This includes a firm switching a private customer within or between packaged products (such as life policies) unnecessarily[1]. This is a good example of the application of Principle 6 (Customers' interests) which requires a firm to pay due regard to the interests of its customers and treat them fairly. This provision forms part of the guidance on assessing 'suitability'.

I 'Know your customer'

5.83 Now referred to by the slightly more prosaic term 'Assessing suitability: the obligations', this is a core requirement of COBS and seeks to ensure that the interest of the customer is paramount. A firm giving a personal recommendation (or when managing his investments)[2] must obtain the necessary information regarding the client's: (a) relevant knowledge and experience; (b) financial situation; and (c) investment objectives to enable the firm to make the recommendation or decision which is suitable. More details regarding the information required are set out in COBS 9.2.2 & 3R. A firm must not encourage a client not to provide information for these purpose[3]. A firm is entitled to rely on information provided by its clients unless it is obviously out of date, inaccurate or incomplete[4]. If the firm does not obtain the necessary information it must not make a personal recommendation or take a decision to trade for him[5]. There are certain relaxations where the client is a professional client or the recommendation relates to a small friendly society life policy[6].

The analysis of the customer's personal and financial circumstances should lead to a clear identification of his needs and priorities so that, combined with his attitude to risk, a suitable product can be recommended. Due regard should be had to the customer's current level of income and expenditure and to any likely changes in this.

The 'fact-find' is the colloquial name given to the process which is undertaken in order to establish the investor's current financial position and his needs and requirements for the future. It is retained and recorded pursuant to COBS 9.5.2 & 3R. Unless the personal recommendation is not proceeded with, a firm must

1 COBS 9.3.2 G
2 COBS 9.2.1R.
3 COBS 9.2.4R.
4 COBS 9.2.5R.
5 COBS 9.2.6R.
6 COBS 9.2.8 & 9 R.

make and retain a record of a customer's personal and financial circumstances that it has obtained for a minimum period after the information is obtained. For life policies this is five years.

The 'know your customer' requirements are an example of the operation of Principle 9 (Customers: relationships of trust) which requires firms to take reasonable care to ensure the suitability of its advice and discretionary decisions.

A suitability report must be given to the customer unless it falls within one of the exceptions, such as the personal recommendation being in respect of an additional single premium to a life policy[1]. In the case of a life policy the report must be provided before the contract is concluded unless the information is provided orally or immediate cover is necessary, in which case the information must be provided immediately after the conclusion of the sale. For telephone sales the suitability report must also comply with the distance marketing directive[2]. COBS 9.4.7 to 9R set out the required contents and manner of presentation for a suitability report.

J COBS

5.84 On October 31 2006 the FSA published the consultation paper which led to changes in the Conduct of Business rules. This was entitled 'Reforming Conduct of Business Regulation (06/19)'. This reflected the move towards more principles-based regulation and away from prescriptive rules although clearly many rules do remain. In addition, COBS partly implements MiFID which, whilst not directly applicable to life offices, has had a general effect on the COBS rules. COBS replaced the existing COB Sourcebook from 1 November 2007.

SECTION 3 CANCELLATION

A Background

5.85 The underlying purpose of the cancellation rules coupled with the associated disclosure requirements is to give investors the opportunity to make considered and well informed investment decisions. Therefore the rules give the consumer in appropriate circumstances a period for reflection. An ancillary purpose of these rules is to reduce the incentive to adopt 'hard sell' tactics.

The cancellation rules also give effect to requirements of the Consolidated Life Directive and are contained in COBS 15.

The rules are subject to the 'habitual residence' of the consumer. Where he is habitually resident in an EEA State other than the UK at the time of signing the application or a state which is not an EEA State and is not present in the UK at the time of signing the application the right to cancel does not apply. However

1 COBS 9.4.3R.
2 COBS 9.4.4 – 6R.

for non-UK EEA State customers firms must apply cancellation in accordance with the rules of that member state .

A right to cancel arises only for those contracts set out in the Table in COBS 15.2.1R and survives the exceptions set out in the Table at COBS 15, Annex 1. Exceptions include such contracts as life policies of six months or less, certain life policies effected by the trustees of occupational pension schemes or the employer, or the manager or trustees of a stakeholder pension scheme, traded life policies, life policies for defined benefits pension schemes, etc. The provisions of 1.5 in the Table provide for the alternative of a 'cancellation substitute' to be possible in some circumstances. These arrangements apply to pension transfers, annuities and the exercise of an option to make income withdrawals only where the right to cancel has been replaced with a pre-contract right to withdraw of at least 14 calendar days. The combined period of the right to withdraw and any residual right to cancel must be at least 30 calendar days.

B Giving the investor notice of his right to cancel

5.86 In an agreement that can be cancelled under these rules the investor must be given notice of his right to cancel[1]. The notice must be sent in good time before or, if not possible, then immediately after the consumer is bound. If a firm does not give the customer information about his cancellation rights the contract remains cancellable and the customer will not be liable for any shortfall (see **5.89** below)[2].

C Exercising the right to cancel

5.87 An investor who has the right to cancel may, without giving any reason, cancel the contract in accordance with the instructions given to him before the expiry of the relevant deadline. This will require notifying the firm[3]. Notice of cancellation is valid where it is served in accordance with the conditions of notification[4]. Where the notice is in a durable medium and served in accordance with the aforementioned conditions and accessible to the recipient it must be treated as being served on the firm on the date it is despatched by the customer[5]. Notice is not valid if given outside the relevant period provided the firm has provided information on cancellation rights in accordance with COBS 15.2.5R. (COB provided that where there were joint policyholders, cancellation by one of them (if he has a right) is as valid as cancellation by all.) There is no equivalent provision in COBS.

1 COBS 15..2.5R.
2 COBS 15.2.4G
3 COBS 15.3.1R.
4 COBS 15.3.3R.
5 COBS 15.3.1RR.

D Effect of cancellation

5.88 By exercising the right to cancel the customer withdraws from the contract which is thereby terminated. The firm must pay back to the customer any sums paid to the firm in connection with the agreement. These sums must be paid without undue delay (with a limit of 30 calendar days after having received the cancellation notice). The firm is entitled to receive back any sums paid by the firm or property which became the customer's under the agreement (within 30 days) and the firm is also generally entitled to retain any shortfall.

E Shortfall

5.89 Where the cancellation notice is sent back to the firm in the required time period and the price of the investment falls due to market movements during the cancellation period, the firm is entitled to a charge on cancellation to make up for the market loss involved in the termination[1]. In terms of life assurance it is only single premium investment policies which are subject to the shortfall provisions.

A firm cannot reclaim shortfall if the firm has not complied with its obligations to disclose cancellation rights as required.

F Record-keeping

5.90 Where notice of cancellation has been validly served on the firm, it must make and retain records for at least five years in the case of life policies[2].

SECTION 4 ANTI MONEY LAUNDERING PROVISIONS

5.91 It is necessary for persons involved in life assurance to have an understanding of money laundering issues and for life offices to implement the necessary regime in order to counter (so far as it is possible) the practice of money laundering with its links to organised crime and terrorism.

A Relevant legislation

5.92 The Money Laundering Regulations 2007 (SI 2007/2157) repealed and replaced the 2003 Regulations (SI 2003/3075). They give effect to and implement in the UK the Third Money Laundering Directive (2005/60/EC). In the UK

1 COBS 15.4.3 R.
2 COBS 15.3.4R.

the authorities responsible for their enforcement are HM Treasury, the Financial Services Authority and HM Customs & Excise.

The Proceeds of Crime Act 2002 (POCA) was enacted in July 2002 and was effective from 24 February 2003. It was amended by the Serious Organised Crime and Police Act, 2005 (SOCPA) and the Serious Crime Act, 2007.

POCA made the most significant impact on the money laundering legislation since 1994. It consolidated the previous legislation in respect of drugs (Drugs Trafficking Act 1994) and serious crime (Criminal Justice Acts 1988 and 1993). The legislation relating to drugs and crime money laundering are encapsulated in POCA and the legislation relating to terrorist funding is set out in the Terrorism Act 2000 and the Anti Terrorist Crime and Security Act 2001.

Money laundering offences were created under Part 7 of POCA. The Act focuses on knowledge of the illegitimacy of funds being dealt with by persons. It introduced an objective test of 'knowledge or suspicion' in respect of offences of 'failure to disclose' under section 330. Sections 327 to 329 of the Act relate to the laundering of money or property that is or represents a benefit from criminal conduct. The 2002 Act also extended the range of persons who are subject to money laundering provisions. In addition to firms which undertake investment business such as life offices it extends to general professional activities, such as accountancy and legal services.

I What are the obligations?

5.93 The regulations set out the obligations on 'relevant persons', one of which (in the 'Financial institution' category) is 'an insurance company duly authorised in accordance with the life assurance consolidation directive'. Relevant persons are required to maintain certain policies, systems and procedures designed to prevent money laundering (Regulation 3).

Part 2 sets out the customer due diligence requirements, such as identification procedures. Part 3 sets out the record-keeping procedures and training requirements and Part 4 sets out the supervision and registration provisions.

B FSA's Money Laundering Rules

5.94 The FSA Handbook used to contain a dedicated Money Laundering Sourcebook but its provisions have now been amended and moved to the SYSC Handbook (see SYSC 3.2.6 and 6.3). The relevant provisions in the Senior Management, Systems and Controls Sourcebook (SYSC) are a less prescriptive approach and aim to put a clear focus on senior management responsibility for anti money laundering systems and controls rather than simply treating anti money laundering as complying with detailed requirements. Firms should benefit from having more flexibility to implement relevant systems and controls in the most appropriate way for them. It should also create a better fit between FSA requirements and money laundering legislation and industry guidance, so the overlaps and potentials for confusion are less.

C Joint Money Laundering Steering Group's Guidance Notes for the financial sector

5.95 The Joint Money Laundering Steering Group ('JMLSG') is comprised of the leading UK trade associations in the financial services industry. Its aim is to promulgate good practice in countering money laundering and to give practical assistance in interpreting the UK Money Laundering Regulations. The primary tool used to achieve this is the publication of Guidance Notes.

The JMLSG has been producing Guidance Notes for the financial sector since 1990. The Guidance Notes have been regularly updated to reflect changing circumstances and developing good practice. The latest Guidance Notes were issued in December 2009, although in October 2010 a new Part III was published. This part contains 'specialist guidance' on electronic payments; equivalent jurisdictions and markets, compliance with the UK financial sanctions regime and the Counter-Terrorism Act 2008.

The Guidance Notes are issued by the trade associations and not by the regulators and so their application is not mandatory. Failure to comply with the Guidance Notes does not mean that a financial sector firm has automatically breached the Regulations or the FSA rules. They do, however, provide an indication of what is expected of financial sector firms and in assessing compliance with SYSC, the FSA will have regard to these Notes. The specific sectoral guidance relating to life assurance is set out in Section 7 of Part II of the Notes and it is specifically recognised that most of what might be described as the 'traditional' types of life assurance would not provide the functionality and flexibility to be the first choice for money launderers but others such as single premium investment bonds are more likely vehicles. Therefore, term assurance policies are generally categorised as 'reduced risk', endowment savings plans are 'intermediate risk' and single premium insurance bonds are 'increased risk'.

SECTION 5 INSURANCE: CONDUCT OF BUSINESS ('ICOBS')

5.96 'Pure protection contracts' are essentially long term insurance contracts which have no surrender value and only pay out on death or incapacity and cannot be converted or extended so as not to comply with these conditions. Life offices who provide such contracts and advisers on such contracts should therefore also be aware of the ICOBS Sourcebook. Its provisions are broadly similar to the COBS Sourcebook, although there are differences.

Prior to FSMA 2000, and the creation of the FSA, there was little regulation of the way general insurance business was conducted. Insurance companies were subject to prudential regulation, first by the Department of Trade and Industry, then by the Treasury Insurance Directorate and latterly by the FSA. Insurance brokers were regulated by the Insurance Brokers Registration Council (IBRC), which was dissolved in April 2001. Intermediaries not regulated by the IBRC were subject to a voluntary code of practice issued by the Association of British Insurers and monitored by its members in conjunction with an accountancy firm. During 2001 the regulation of the conduct of general insurance business (whether by insurers or intermediaries) passed to a self-regulating body, the General Insurance Standards Council (GISC).

Before the adoption of the EU Insurance Mediation Directive[1], which required state regulation, it had been hoped by many in the industry that the existence of the GISC would be sufficient in terms of regulatory involvement in connection with the conduct of general insurance business. However, the requirement of state regulation meant that this attempt at self-regulation by the industry was superseded on 14 January 2005. The FSA assumed responsibility from that date for regulating the conduct of general business. The rules which came into force on that date implement the Insurance Mediation Directive and also the Distance Marketing Directive[2].

General insurance business became regulated with respect to both prudential and conduct of business issues with effect from 14 January 2005 although insurance companies have been prudentially regulated since 2001. Although falling within the definition of 'Contracts of Long-term Insurance' under Schedule 1, Part II of the Regulated Activities Order[3] contracts such as 'pure protection' life insurance (for example, term assurance) are currently governed by the ICOBS as opposed to COBS Sourcebook. However, it is possible for firms to elect for COBS to apply to 'pure protection contracts' instead of ICOBS so that they will be treated as a 'life policy' instead.

The Insurance Mediation Directive is concerned with the regulation of all types of insurance intermediaries, including 'tied' insurance intermediaries. The Treasury and the FSA also decided that it was necessary to regulate the sales activities of insurance companies to seek to provide a level playing field for the various sectors of the industry. From 14 January 2005, the processes by which insurers and intermediaries alike sell policies must comply with the relevant FSA rules.

A General approach

5.97 ICOBS applies to firms in relation to certain activities in relation to 'non-investment insurance contracts' which in the context of life assurance essentially means 'pure protection contracts', which are contracts which meet the following conditions: (a) benefits only payable on death or incapacity due to injury, sickness or infirmity; or (b) no surrender value (or premium is a single premium and surrender value does not exceed that premium; and the contract makes no provision for conversion or extension in a way which would result in it ceasing to comply with the above).

In addition for ICOBS to apply it must relate to certain activities (or connected activities) which in the context of life assurance are: (1) an insurance mediation activity; (2) effecting and carrying out contracts of insurance; and (3) communicating or approving a financial promotion.

1 2002/92/EC.
2 2002/65/EC.
3 SI 2001/544.

ICOBS sets out the information required to be given to customers when first meeting with an intermediary. Using an 'initial disclosure document' (IDD) (ICOBS 4, Annex 1G) or 'combined initial disclosure document' can be used to satisfy the status disclosure, scope of service and fee disclosure requirements if used in accordance with its notes and provided to the customer at the correct time.

B Conduct of Business Rules for ICOBS

5.98 These are not examined in detail here. In many respects they are very similar to the COBS Rules for investment products. However, the general approach is more 'light touch' than the COBS Rules.

Under ICOBS (unlike COBS) there are no commission disclosure requirements applicable to retail customers, only in respect of commercial customers, although any fees for an insurance mediation activity must be disclosed. An adviser should bear in mind his potential fiduciary obligations as an agent under the general law with regard to commission payments.

If a personal recommendation is made (that is, the firm recommends a particular pure protection policy as being suitable) the firm must specify, in particular on the basis of information provided by the customer, the customer's demands and needs as well as the underlying reasons for any advice given to the customer on that policy. The details must be appropriate bearing in mind the complexity of the policy[1]. ICOBS does not prescribe a format for a demands and needs statement but it must be on paper or other durable medium accessible to the customer; be communicated in a clear and accurate manner, comprehensible to the customer, and in an official language of the State of the commitment or any language agreed with the customer. If the sale is taking place by telephone, it can be provided in accordance with the distance marketing disclosure rules in ICOBS 3.1.14R. Information may be provided orally where the customer requests it or where immediate cover is necessary. In such cases it must be provided in writing or other durable medium immediately after conclusion of the contract[2].

ICOBS 6.3 sets out the required life insurance directive (ie Consolidated Life Directive) disclosure requirements and in 6.4 the requirement to provide a policy summary in good time before the contract conclusion. Other provisions in 6.4 relate to oral sales, price information and information requirements relating to mid-term changes (ie during the term of the policy).

Whilst inducements are not prohibited a firm that offers such inducements should consider whether doing so conflicts with its obligations under Principles 1 and 6 to act with integrity and treat customers fairly[3]. ICOBS does not have specific record-keeping requirements but ICOBS firms would still be subject to the high level record keeping requirements in SYSC 3.2.20R[4].

1 ICOBS 5.2.2R.
2 ICOBS 5.2.3R.
3 ICOBS 2.3.
4 ICOBS 2.4.

C Communications to clients and financial promotions

5.99 Communications must be 'clear, fair and not misleading'[1]. If a firm becomes aware that a communication has become non compliant it must withdraw its approval and notify any person that it knows to be relying on its approval as soon as reasonably practicable (a potentially wide and onerous obligation)[2]. Guidance which is not specifically reflected in COBS is found in ICOBS 2.2.4G which relates to pricing claims, for example that a firm provides the cheapest premium. The guidance provides that the claim should be consistent with the result reasonably expected to be achieved by the majority of customers who respond unless the proportion of customers likely to achieve the pricing claims is stated prominently. It should also state the basis for any claimed benefits and any significant limitations. It should also comply with other relevant legislation – specifically mentioned in the rules are the Consumer Protection from Unfair Trading Regulations 2008 and the Business Protection from Misleading Marketing Regulations 2008.

The particular requirements for distance contracts for retail customers are set out at ICOBS 3.1 and regarding e-commerce transactions at ICOBS 3.2. Annexes 1 to 3 of ICOBS 3 set out particular requirements regarding Distance Contracts.

Firms must not exclude or restrict any duty or liability to a customer unless reasonable to do so and the duty or liability arises other than under the regulatory system. Specifically referred to are the Unfair Terms in Consumer Contracts Regulations 1999 (SI 1999/2083) (as amended) and the limits in those regulations to the firm's ability to exclude or restrict liability to a consumer[3]. This rule also contains guidance on the extent to which it is possible to rely on others to comply with the Handbook Rules. However, it is not possible to delegate ultimate responsibility under the regulatory system[4].

5.100 Unlike COBS there are provisions in ICOBS specifically relating to claims handling. This requires insurers to handle claims promptly and fairly, provide reasonable guidance to policyholders when making a claim, not unreasonably reject a claim and settle claims promptly once settlement terms are agreed, see ICOBS 8.1.1R. ICOBS 8.1.2R contain provisions relating to where non-disclosure and misrepresentation may affect claims, in many ways echoing the new Consumer Insurance (Disclosure and Representations) Bill.

SECTION 6 DATA PROTECTION ISSUES

5.101 Acquiring, retaining and using personal data is primarily governed by the Data Protection Act 1998 (DPA). The DPA imposes duties on persons who

1 ICOBS 2.2.2R.
2 ICOBS 2.2.3R.
3 ICOBS 2.5.
4 ICOBS 2.5.3G.

handle personal information to comply with certain data protection principles. It also gives individuals rights over their personal information. The DPA applies to the 'processing' of 'personal data'. This is widely defined and includes the information collected by life offices in their dealings with policyholders. Certain definitions, contained in the DPA, are relevant:

(1) 'Data controller' is defined as the person who (alone or with others) determines the purposes for which, and the manner in which, personal information is to be processed. In most cases, the life office will be the data controllers and it will therefore be their responsibility to ensure compliance with the DPA.

(2) A 'data processor' is a third party who processes personal information on a data controller's behalf. However, it is the data controller, rather than the data processor, who is required to ensure compliance with the DPA. 'Processing' is so widely defined in the DPA it is easy to fall within the category of data processor. For example, it will catch a third party who initially collects data on behalf of the data controller. In the context of a life office, it will include third party administrators and advisers. It will not, however, include employees of the data controller.

(3) The 'data subject' is the living individual who is the subject of the personal information (the data). In the case of life assurance, this will usually mean the policyholder and/or the life assured if different.

(4) The DPA only applies to 'personal data'. The definition of 'data' covers any information relating to living individuals which is held on a computer. In certain cases, the definition will also extend to manual records. 'Personal data' means information which relates to a living individual who can be identified either from that information or from that information and other information which is in, or is likely to come into, the data controller's possession. This could simply mean the name and address of an individual, although a life office is likely to possess additional detailed personal data about individuals.

(5) There are additional rules in respect of the processing of 'sensitive personal data'. In particular, information which falls into this category can only be lawfully processed if the explicit consent of the data subject has been obtained. Sensitive personal data includes information relating to health, which is likely to be the most relevant for life offices. For example, medical evidence would fall within the category of sensitive personal data. Life offices must obtain the express consent of the applicant to use such data. 'Processing' is broadly defined by the DPA to include obtaining, recording, holding, using, disclosing or erasing data. In effect, any activity by a life office involving personal data will be caught by this definition.

A Data protection Principles

5.102 Schedule 1 of the DPA sets out eight data protection Principles. The aim of the Principles is to promote high standards in handling personal information in order to protect the individual's right to privacy. In summary, the Principles state that personal data must be: fairly and lawfully processed; processed for specified purposes; adequate, relevant and not excessive; accurate and, where necessary, kept up to date; not kept for longer than is necessary; processed in line with the rights of the individual; kept secure; and not transferred outside the European Economic Area (EEA) unless the information is adequately protected.

In addition to the Principles, the DPA confers certain rights upon individuals in respect of personal data which relates to them. The most important of these rights is known as the 'right of subject access' which gives data subjects a general right to see information that is held about them[1]. Life offices must ensure that an appropriate procedure is in place to deal with such requests for information in the manner prescribed by the DPA.

Data controllers are required to comply with the Principles, unless they can claim certain exemptions, specified by the DPA. The Information Commissioner can take enforcement action to require a data controller to bring their processing into line with the Principles. Failure to comply with such an enforcement notice is a criminal offence, but may result in civil liability as well if an individual suffers damage as a result. The Commissioner also has the power to issue a monetary penalty notice imposing a fine of up to £500,000 in relation to serious breaches of the Principles that occurred on or after 6 April 2010. This is an important development in that it adds a meaningful sanction for breach of the DPA. A monetary penalty can only be issued to data controllers. It cannot be imposed on a data processor. The Commissioner may only issue a monetary penalty notice if it is satisfied that the following three conditions are met: a serious contravention of the Principles; the breach is likely to cause 'substantial damage or substantial distress'; and the breach was either deliberate or reckless (with no reasonable steps having been taken to prevent it)[2].

If the Commissioner is satisfied that these conditions are met, he may serve a notice of intent on the data controller setting out the proposed amount of the penalty. The data controller has an opportunity to make written representations to the Commissioner who will then decide whether or not to serve the monetary penalty notice or to vary it. A monetary penalty notice must be issued within six months of service of the notice of intent. The Commissioner has published guidance on monetary penalty notices setting out the circumstances in which it would consider it appropriate to issue such a notice of how the amount of the penalty will be determined (see Information Commissioner's guidance about the issue of monetary penalties prepared and issued under section 55C(1) of the Data Protection Act 1998).

B Data to which the Principles apply

5.103 The personal data to which the Principles apply may take the form of computerised records or (in some cases) paper records. Paper records (otherwise

1 DPA 1998, s 7.

2 DPA 1998, s 55A and reg 2; the Data Protection (Monetary Penalties) (Maximum Penalty and Notices) Regulations 2010 (SI 2010/31).

known as 'manual data') will be covered by the DPA if they form part of a relevant filing system. This is a set of information which is structured, either by reference to individuals or by reference to criteria relating to individuals, in such a way that specific information relating to a particular individual is readily accessible. Such information could include application forms, trust forms and other paper based records held by life offices.

In one case the Court of Appeal gave a very narrow interpretation of 'relevant filing system'[1]. The Court's decision limits the categories of manual records that might have fallen within the scope of the DPA to those 'of sufficient sophistication to provide the same or similar ready accessibility as a computerised filing system'.

A life office must notify the Commissioner that they are data controllers. The Commissioner maintains a public register of data controllers and the personal data which they process. Notification is the system by which a data controller's details are added to that register. The DPA requires every data controller to notify unless they are exempt. Failure to notify (or renew notification annually) is a criminal offence.

Data controllers must comply with the other provisions of the DPA, even if they have failed to notify or are exempt from notification.

C Life offices' dealings with data processors

5.104 Life offices will often use external administrators who will act on their behalf to administer life policies as data processors. In such cases, life offices must consider how they will deal with the following issues: security measures that they should implement; requests from data subjects (Subject access requests); notifying on the public register.

1 Security

5.105 Data controllers are required to take 'appropriate technical and organisational measures' to protect against the 'unauthorised or unlawful processing of personal data and against accidental loss or destruction of, or damage to, personal data'[2]. The DPA gives limited guidance on what security measures will be considered to be 'appropriate'. The Commissioner's view is that what is appropriate will depend on the circumstances and, in particular, the nature of the data being processed. When life offices appoint data processors to act on their behalf, they remain responsible for ensuring that personal data is kept secure. An administrator should therefore be chosen with care and a written contract must be put in place. This contract should contain the following provisions: the administrator must keep the information secure in accordance with the Principles of the DPA; the administrator must only act under the life

1 *Durant v Financial Services Authority* [2003] EWCA Civ 1746.
2 DPA 1998, Sch 1.

office's instructions when processing data; and the life office should monitor the work of the administrator closely to ensure compliance with the provisions of the DPA.

2 *Subject access requests*

5.106 In view of the statutory right of subject access, a life office must set out clear guidelines on how requests for information from policyholders and other data subjects (or their agents) should be dealt with. If the administrator is to respond directly, the life office must ensure that the request is dealt with in the manner prescribed by the DPA.

3 *Notification*

5.107 As data controllers, the trustees will be required to notify (or renew notification annually). Data processors do not have to notify on their own account.

D Dealings with policyholders

1 *Consent*

5.108 The DPA does not impose an obligation on the life office, as data controller, to obtain the consent of policyholders before processing personal data. However, obtaining consent is considered to be the simplest way for the trustees to comply with the first data protection principle. This principle states that personal data shall be processed fairly and lawfully and, in particular, shall not be processed unless certain conditions are met[1]. The most relevant conditions will be: 'processing with the consent of the data subject', in the case of normal data; and 'processing with the explicit consent of the data subject', in the case of sensitive personal data. The DPA does not specifically define 'consent'. However, to be valid, consent must be freely given. Policyholders should therefore be told clearly the nature and purpose of the personal data to be processed and give a positive indication of agreement, for example, a signature.

2 *Fair processing information*

5.109 In order to comply with the requirements of the first data principle, the life office must also ensure, 'so far as practicable', that data subjects have been provided with 'fair processing information' which includes: the identity of the data controller; the purposes for which the data is intended to be processed; and any additional information which is necessary to ensure that the processing is fair in the circumstances[2].

1 DPA 1998, Sch 1, Part 1.
2 DPA 1998, paras 2-3, Part II, Sch 1.

3 Data protection notice

5.110 In relation to new policyholders, a data protection notice should be incorporated in the explanatory literature given to policyholders on effecting the policy. This should include: the fair processing information referred to above; and a requirement that the policyholder gives explicit consent to the processing of their personal data (so as to cover the processing of both normal and sensitive data).

CHAPTER 6

With-profits funds

SUMMARY

SECTION 1 INTRODUCTION AND THE NATURE OF WITH-PROFITS

A Introduction and background

6.1 Chapter 1[1] explained the difference between a mutual insurer and a proprietary company. The traditional model for mutual long-term insurers was as providers of with-profits funds. With-profits funds have also traditionally been provided by proprietary companies. Often the provision of with-profits investment is part of the constitution of such companies with policies referring to an Act of Parliament and/or the Articles of the Company.

As its name suggests, with-profits business is a means by which 'investors' share in the profits generated by the company. One of the primary aims of with-profits investments is to provide a stable return. This is done by 'smoothing' the return, holding back in some years and supplementing in others. The advent of unit-linked policies highlighted the discretionary nature of with-profits arrangements and led to a slightly more transparent version: the unitised with-profits contract. Whilst something of a hybrid, it is not a unit-linked contract because of the discretion still exercised by the life office in setting bonus payments.

1 1.67.

With-profits business is not as straightforward a concept as it might seem. This is due to the differing nature of assets held to back different types and generations of policies and the fact that not all life offices operate their with-profits business in the same way. In addition, commercial interests, particularly of proprietary companies, have often had a bearing on the contracts offered, the bonuses payable and the source of such payments (eg from other resources of the insurer or 'inherited' estates).

Following the House of Lords judgment in *Equitable Life v Hyman*[1] in 2000, the sector attracted much criticism and ultimately, a regulatory overhaul. This regulatory overhaul involved changes to key personnel (the introduction of the new with-profits actuary role), the requirement to produce Principles and Practices of Financial Management, and a host of new rules designed to ensure policyholders were treated fairly. Each of these is described in more detail in this Chapter. At the time of writing, the FSA is also in the process of reviewing and updating various aspects of this regime. The FSA's proposals (in CP11/5) aim to make further changes to the regime and are also described below.

B The nature of with-profits contracts

6.2 With-profits as a concept has traditionally been used as an investment vehicle to provide a guaranteed level of life cover with potential investment upside. It worked well in high inflation/high growth environments but this led to a general investor expectation that the target amount desired (often as part of an endowment mortgage), would not only be achieved but would be exceeded. For a number of years in the late 1980s and 1990s, it is probably fair to say that with-profits endowments were mis-sold because it was not anticipated that the prevailing favourable economic conditions would change[2]. As a result of the stock market falls in the first few years of the new millennium and the effect of the *Equitable Life* decision, many with-profits funds had to adopt a much more cautious investment strategy. The likely level of return on a with-profits policy and the transparency likely to be required under Solvency II for the cost of guarantees do not, at the time of writing, make with-profits a very attractive proposition.

A conventional with-profits insurance contract will have a guaranteed maturity value to which bonuses can be added either annually (reversionary bonuses), when the investor surrenders (interim), or at maturity (terminal bonuses). From a strict contractual perspective, the policyholder is only entitled to the guaranteed amount on maturity or death. Entitlement to bonuses already declared also only arises at that time (there is no contractual right to any future bonuses). Whilst there are a number of commercial variants, for example only part of the insured sum attracting bonuses, the general structure is normally the same.

A unitised with-profits contract is an arrangement whereby the assets are notionally allocated to establish the value of units. However, unlike a unit-linked

1 [2000] 3 All ER 961.
2 FSA Endowment Mis-selling Review.

fund where there is a direct link to the underlying assets, the process contains discretions enabling the value of units to be increased (or reduced) to reflect any past or potential future poor performance of the underlying assets (similar to bonus setting on conventional contracts with smoothing). The bonus is generally a greater proportion of any growth on the underlying assets and is added to the value of the contract on a more regular basis. This gives the policyholder a clearer view of how much their contract is currently worth. That amount should be available on surrender unless a Market Value Adjustment or Reduction (MVR) is applied by the life office. The FSA's rules specify when an MVR can be applied (eg where the value of the underlying assets held is less than the face value of the units).

6.3 The nature of with-profits led to a number of practical issues. First, was dissatisfaction with the calculation of surrender values. Prior to 2005 there was little formal control of surrender values as contractual provisions gave huge discretion to the life office in determining the amount payable on surrender. It was therefore possible for a surrender value to be hugely discounted. Because of the difference in the surrender value and the market value of certain types of life policy, a market established in second-hand endowment contracts, predominantly in relation to with-profits contracts. The rules in COBS 20.2.11-16 relating to the calculation of surrender values, may, however, restrict this market in the future.

A second major issue for with-profits contracts was the perception that, even if policies were held to maturity, policyholders would not get their fair share of 'profits'. The *Equitable Life* decision (see **6.4**) is relevant here. Regulators have had a difficult task historically checking that policyholders are being treated fairly. In part this arose because of the vague nature of the bargain the policyholder struck (ie a share in some of the profits of the life office). Over time companies held different assets to support different groups of with-profits policies, sharing in different types of profit. This meant that different rates of bonus were awarded to such groups. This was facilitated by the creation of different bonus series', sometimes with different charges and participation in other business such as non-profit business. Unfortunately, life offices' practices in operating their funds varied quite significantly, which made the regulator's task difficult. The FSA mounted a multi-level attack on this area by imposing minimum standards and standardising some of the terminology and calculations. It significantly increased the disclosure requirement in relation to each fund by replacing the With-Profits Guide with a much more detailed Principles and Practices of Financial Management ('PPFM'). A consumer-friendly version of this document is also required. (See **6.16**). In addition to providing transparency, these requirements have the knock-on effect of requiring life offices to ensure that they have documented the processes referred to. Historically, many of the practices may not have been formally recorded even within the life office itself.

Another way in which with-profits policyholders may not get their fair share of profits, is because of smoothing. Although a with-profits fund is designed to smooth out the peaks and troughs of investment performance, it is not an exact science. A life office's assumptions about future returns may be too cautious and the life office therefore retains reserves which arguably should be distributed to policies who participated in the relevant profits. Over time significant amounts of money can be built up. If this is not distributed to the policies responsible for creating it, it can become what is known as an 'inherited estate' or 'orphan assets'. The FSA defines the inherited estate as the fair market value of the with-profits assets less the realistic liabilities. As the realistic liabilities include an element in respect of expected future bonuses, the inherited estate can be regarded as the surplus in the funds – some, but not necessarily all of which, may be needed to give investment flexibility and security. Where there is an excess amount and if that excess has been passed from generation to generation of policyholder, it can become difficult to establish who actually owns it. The FSA introduced new rules in 2005 as part of its treating with-profits customers fairly project (see COB 20.2.21), which were designed to prevent such surpluses being built up in future. These rules relate to what the FSA defines as 'excess surplus' (see **6.15**) It has also introduced new requirements in relation to the process for reattributing existing inherited estates (COBS 20.42-52).

There have also been a number of other issues which have caused the nature and use of with-profits funds assets to be called into question. These include the use of the with-profits fund to buy assets for strategic purposes (ie business reasons) and new business strategies which result in existing business being disadvantaged by the terms on which new business is accepted. The rules in COBS 20.2.28-31 and the PPFM requirements in COBS 20.3 also seek to deal with these issues.

C The *Equitable Life* decision

6.4 *Equitable Life Assurance Society v Hyman*[1] was something of a watershed in terms of the regulation of with-profits business. The fallout from it and the Penrose report into the collapse of the Equitable, played a large part in the FSA's treating with-profits customers fairly initiative which led to a more stringent form of regulation of with-profits business. The case involved an application to the court for a declaration to enable the directors to make an allocation of bonus in accordance with asset share (which was the bonus philosophy of the fund and therefore the primary driver from the Equitable's perspective of achieving fairness between its policyholders). Interestingly, as will be seen later, it (ie distribution of asset share) has subsequently become the driver of the FSA's treating with-profits customers fairly initiative, although importantly, there are now also requirements to communicate and explain this to customers.

Mr Hyman was a representative policyholder who would lose out if the declaration were approved. He was expecting to get more than his asset share because the benefits under his contract could be taken in the form of an annuity at guaranteed rates (ie he was expecting his full asset share to be applied at the guaranteed rates to determine the amount of his annuity). It is important to bear in mind that the annuity was an intrinsic part of the contract, as without the obligation on

1 [2000] 3 All ER 961, HL and [2000] 2 All ER 331, CA.

the life office to provide the annuity, it may not have been an insurance contract at all. It would arguably have been different if the annuity were a separate product to be purchased from the proceeds of the first contract.

To understand the case it is helpful to start from basics. All policyholders, whether or not their policy contained guaranteed rates on the ultimate annuity, bought a contract which guaranteed a maturity value which could be increased over-time by bonuses. These bonuses were normally allotted annually and on maturity, the amount, (if any), being allocated in accordance with the contract. The contract provided for allocation by the directors among the participating policies using 'such methods and principles as the directors may from time to time determine'. This meant that the directors had a very wide discretion.

The stated bonus policy of the Equitable was to aim for payment of asset share (broadly the amount the individual policy's premiums had earned less charges). The terms of the guarantee were an add-on to this and, it is fair to say, were something of a marketing gimmick, as when originally included, they were not necessarily of any value. However, over time they acquired value and the Equitable did not seek to impose any charges in relation to them, it would appear believing that as bonuses for individual policies should reflect asset share, the value could be dealt with in the amount allocated by way of terminal bonus. This issue arose because the contracts allowed the policyholder to decide to use the policy proceeds to buy an annuity with another provider. So as not to disadvantage people exercising this option by paying an amount reduced to reflect the cost of the guaranteed annuity rates, the directors made the adjustment by way of differential terminal bonuses. The bonus amount under the differential bonus was, however, neutral between the two options, as it always paid out the asset share amount. If the option to buy an annuity from a third party was taken, then the asset share was paid as a lump sum. If the option to take the annuity under the existing contract was taken, then the asset share was applied to purchase an annuity on terms which reflected the cost of providing the guaranteed rates. Whilst this ensured that the policyholder got their asset share (and only that) irrespective of how they took their benefits, it had the effect in practice of negating the value of the guaranteed annuity rates.

As the contractual discretions included were very wide and as stated the aim was to return asset share, it is arguable that the real mischief in such cases was the prominence given to the guaranteed rates in marketing the contracts to individuals. Such marketing should have made clear that the guaranteed rates would not increase the person's share of the amount distributed (either because a charge would be imposed to cover the costs of providing the guarantee or because a lower terminal bonus would be applied to that benefit) – not an ideal marketing message and certainly not the one conveyed. Also, marketing of these policies at that time tended to be high level relying on the policy terms (which the customer probably would not have seen until they bought the contract). Although the court case did not deal with individual sales issues, it did clearly take into account the impression that had been created (in part by the guaranteed rates added to the policy) that the guaranteed rates were somehow additional to the main with-profits bargain and could result in the person getting more than their asset share.

6.5 The original application for the declaration in the High Court was successful and it is worth quoting from the reasoning of Sir Richard Scott VC which sets out the whole issue very succinctly:

> 'He [a policyholder taking an annuity at the guaranteed rate] is being allotted a lesser final bonus because a lesser final bonus is all that is needed to bring the value of the benefits he receives up to his asset share … to allot final bonus on … a basis that used assets share as a yardstick for the value of benefits taken rather than as a yardstick for the capital sum by reference to which the amount of the annuity taken was calculated, was in my judgment a decision well within their discretion.'

It is only a pity, in view of the consequences, that the case did not stop there but the rest, as they say, is history.

The House of Lords decision, which confirmed the Court of Appeal's majority decision, was that it was necessary to imply a term into the contract to prevent the directors acting as proposed and thereby cutting across the reasonable expectations of the relevant policyholders. The fact that the Equitable was a mutual without the means to satisfy the judgment and that the result of the decision would be to cut across the reasonable expectations of the non-guaranteed annuity option holders, did not prevent such a term being implied. It was clearly a difficult situation because there was a conflict between the main terms of the contract and the way the guaranteed annuity rates had been added. In the authors' view it is clear (from the differential bonus scheme) that the Equitable did not intend to offer the guaranteed rates as a means of increasing one person's asset share at the expense of another and, had the implied term which effectively permitted that to happen, been suggested to them at the outset, they would not have agreed to it as it was inconsistent with the policy of distributing asset share.

Arguably a fairer basis for the decision, would have been to accept that the contractual provision was wide enough to allow the directors to allocate differential bonuses and to treat the additional costs of the guaranteed annuity rates as a mis-selling cost that should, as it was mutual, have been applied to all policies sharing in the profits of the society (thereby reducing relevant bonuses). This might also have permitted the potential liability to non guaranteed annuity rate policyholders for such mis-selling to be dealt with in a similar way, thereby reflecting the mutual status of the Equitable. In practice, because there were no shareholders or an estate to pick up this cost and as the FSCS would undoubtedly have reduced bonuses to better reflect asset share, this may have produced the same effect as the decision ultimately did (ie a reduction in bonus rates). It may, however, have been more orderly than the chaos that actually ensued.

6.6 There is some unclear dicta between the two appellate court decisions relating to what has been known as the 'ring-fencing' issue. Waller LJ suggested in the Court of Appeal case that the Equitable could lawfully have declared different bonuses for classes of policies with guaranteed annuity options and for those without. This would in effect have reduced the bonuses to reflect asset share. Lord Steyn makes clear in the House of Lords judgment that he believes this would have been precluded by the implied term described above. The House of Lords judgment leaves a number of questions unanswered, such as the extent to which existing policyholders can be charged for the cost of benefits such as guarantees where life offices have not charged for them before (eg because of a change in economic conditions). Some life offices have tried to deal with this issue in their PPFMs by specifying the basis on which such charges could be imposed in the future. It is difficult, in relation to existing policies, to be clear from a legal perspective whether over time such statements will be sufficient to prevent the creation of a reasonable expectation that such charges will not be imposed.

It is fair to say that the result of the House of Lords case was an unmitigated disaster. Although Equitable Life had brought most of the consequences on itself because of its own precarious financial position, as it was a mutual, those consequences were borne by its members. The result was a 746 page report, the Penrose report, which highlighted failings in the management of Equitable Life. Apart from issues with specific individuals and an apparent failure to challenge the senior management, it appears that the company was over distributing and not reserving for significant downturns, which is supposed to be one of the features of with-profits business. The practice of relying on terminal bonus adjustment rather than reserving for the guaranteed annuity options (which started in 1994) should also have been picked up by the regulator at the time but it appears it was not. The failings of the regulator lead to ten findings of maladministration in relation to the prudential regulation of Equitable Life and a recommendation from the Parliamentary Ombudsman that compensation be paid. The government has accepted that those who suffered a loss (relative to other similar products) should receive compensation. It will be interesting to see how such compensation is calculated.

D Further developments

6.7 The FSA's 'treating with-profits customers fairly' initiative resulted in new rules which were first introduced in June 2005. The first immediate effect of the rules was in relation to the requirement to produce PPFMs and subsequently, consumer friendly PPFMs (see **6.35**), but there continued to be potential issues around the operation of closed with-profits funds. The first real test of the new rules was the Aviva Reattribution in 2008/9. Some of the correspondence between the Aviva Policyholder Advocate and the FSA relating to the effect of the FSA's rules was made public by the FSA. The letter of 6 December 2007 from the FSA to the policyholder advocate dealt with a number of issues that had been raised by the policyholder advocate (see **6.39**). This resulted in a Treasury Select Committee enquiry into the operation of the UK with-profits market which focussed on a number of the issues pertinent to reattributions. The Treasury Select Committee's report was issued on 19 June 2008. It was critical of various aspects of the FSA's regime for with-profits firms. The Treasury Select Committee seems to have been particularly irritated by the FSA's evidence as to the effect of its rules operating 'in the round'. The Treasury Select Committee concluded that the current FSA regime is not sufficiently robust or balanced. The Committee identified areas of concern including: transparency of the smoothing process; the need for robust challenge of new business estimates (eg in a reattribution); charging of mis-selling costs and shareholder tax to the inherited estate; and phasing of excess surplus distributions and concerns in relation to the role, resources, remit and visibility of with-profits committees. One specific point made in relation to reattributions was that the FSA should seek to ensure that a 'fair price' rather than an 'adequate price' is paid to policyholders. Another was that the policyholder advocate's terms of reference should provide that the policyholder advocate be free to communicate with policyholders whenever they wish to. The Treasury Select Committee asked the FSA to issue a formal response, which it did on 22 October 2008. The FSA agreed to conduct a comprehensive review and to publish its results by the end of 2009.

The FSA undertook a review of its regulatory regime for with-profits and published a report in June 2010: The With-Profits Review Report. The FSA had also already introduced rules in 2009 to prevent mis-selling costs being charged to the inherited estate of proprietary companies. The main findings of the With-Profits Review Report were that the majority of firms did not satisfactorily demonstrate that all of their practices were consistent with well run with-profits businesses. The FSA's main concerns seemed to centre on governance and policyholder communication. It made clear its next steps would be further consultation papers (and some potential enforcement action). The FSA also stated that it would review the existing rules on charging shareholder tax to with-profits funds. The first consultation paper (CP11/5) was issued in February 2011. The FSA has stated that it intends to respond to the consultation responses later in 2011.

6.8 CP11/5 seems designed to make clear the FSA's position on a number of issues that have been contentious over the last few years. The overriding point seems to be that the FSA, supported by a Counsel's opinion, is of the view that a with-profit policyholder's interest in a with-profits fund is not limited to receiving its asset share. The FSA emphasises the right of with-profits policyholders to participate in distributions of existing excess surplus and, in the event of run-off or winding down of new business, in a share of the working capital (the inherited estate). The FSA states that its own rules (eg on excess surplus (see **6.15**)), make it more likely that a distribution will be made to with-profits policyholders.

The FSA's proposals seem designed to ensure that, notwithstanding the fact that such policyholders' rights are by nature contingent, they are still protected. So, for example to protect the inherited estate being used to 'buy' business, it would like to change the threshold of the test for writing new business and investing/retaining strategic assets, to a requirement that they are 'likely to have no adverse effect' on existing with-profit policyholders. The FSA is also seeking to formalise the distribution of surplus monies by requiring excess surplus that the firm cannot justify retaining, be distributed rather than reattributed and by also requiring that all firms have a fair distribution plan for their inherited estate. The FSA makes the point that to enable a fair distribution to take place, there needs to be a plan to deal with the realisation of strategic assets which are often illiquid in nature (such as a head office). The need to have a fair distribution plan over the right timeframe is particularly important for mutuals who are closed or writing very little new with-profits business. As the with-profit fund is often the owner of the whole of a mutual's business, the value of that business (including the benefit of non-profit business), needs, in the FSA's view, to be distributed to the with-profit policyholders. The FSA's approach to mutuals seems to be to suggest that they get the consent of their with-profits policyholders if they wish to make structural changes (eg to pass part of the inherited estate to non with-profits policyholders or to create a fund of mutual capital to support ongoing non profit business).

The FSA also wants to improve governance of with-profits funds, for example, by improving the status and independence of with-profits committees (see **6.51**) and to require firms to tell the FSA if its governing body has not followed the advice of the with-profits committee. The FSA intends to consult separately on changes, that will be required to implement Solvency II: one of which, it would seem, is the contentious issue of with-profits funds effectively paying tax in relation to shareholder distributions.

The FSAs proposals in CP11/5 are described in more detail in Section 2 below. It has also been announced that regulation of with-profits (including the rules described in Section 2) will be the responsibility of the Prudential Regulatory Authority (PRA) rather than the Financial Conduct Authority (FCA) and it remains to be seen whether the PRA's views on these issues will be different to the FSA's.

SECTION 2 COBS 20 – TREATING WITH-PROFITS POLICYHOLDERS FAIRLY

A An overview of TCF and COBS 20.2

6.9 The FSA needed to deal with the issues identified in **6.3** (the lack of transparency making it difficult to assess whether customers were getting a fair deal and the consequences of the *Equitable Life* decision). This coincided with the FSA's increased emphasis on the concept of treating customers fairly (TCF) which led to the issue of a number of consultation papers and a policy statement[1] directed at the fair treatment of with-profits policyholders. In high-level terms what the FSA sought to do was to require detailed disclosure in PPFMs. The required disclosures include specifying maturity and surrender value targets, and these are supported by a need to manage the fund to achieve those targets. The FSA also imposed restrictions on the calculation of surrender values and Market Value Adjustments/Reductions (MVRs). To prevent the under distribution of profits, life offices are required to assess the surplus held and, where there is an 'excess surplus', they would normally be expected to distribute it. Rules also apply to the reattribution of inherited estates. A further myriad of rules seek to prevent the life office using its funds inappropriately and to control the basis on which it enters into significant new transactions.

1 CP207, CP04 and PS05/1.

As stated in **6.7** above, the FSA's regime for with-profits funds has been subjected to the scrutiny of the Treasury Select Committee which has resulted in a review by the FSA. The FSA's proposals for change are set out in CP11/5 and these proposals are described below.

6.10 COBS 20.2 applies to all with-profits funds maintained and operated in the UK but as non-directive friendly societies (ie with premiums of less than €5 million) are not required to produce PPFMs, it applies appropriately amended to such companies. COBS 20.2 is designed to supplement the FSA Principles, in particular Principle 6 (Treating Customers Fairly), Principle 7 (Communications with Clients) and Principle 8 (Conflicts of Interest).

COBS 20.2 (in the form of COB 6.12) came into force on 30 June 2005 (apart from in relation to maturity and surrender targets, which came into force on 31 December 2006). It applies to EEA life offices carrying on with-profits business in the UK but only to the extent that a matter is not reserved to the home state regulator[1]. In broad terms it contains the following: rules requiring life offices to set target maturity (and surrender values) for their contracts and to manage the fund with a view to achieving those targets in at least 90% of cases; rules restricting a life office's ability to charge early surrender penalties or Market Value Reductions (for unitised contracts) where the amount involved is not directly related to the value of the underlying assets or (until CP11/5 is implemented), their liquidity; rules preventing distribution (other than from surplus) and requiring an annual assessment of 'excess surplus'; rules restricting the charging of expenses to a with-profits fund; rules preventing the payment of compensation or redress from a with-profits fund; rules restricting the ability to write new business or provide loans or guarantees to or for connected parties other than on commercial terms; restrictions on material transactions (eg bulk outwards or *any* inwards reinsurance or financial engineering transactions); and notification and other rules relating to closing funds and run off.

Each of these is explained in more detail below except the rules on closed funds which are described at **6.46** in Section 5.

B Target maturity and surrender values

6.11 Firms are required as an overriding principle to have good reason to believe that their payouts on individual with-profits policies are fair. One of the ways in which the FSA has sought to provide greater transparency and consistency in with-profits funds, is by introducing the concept of target maturity and surrender values. This is coupled with a requirement to manage the fund in a way which aims to achieve the target values. The obligation to specify a target range is expressed in relation to unsmoothed asset share (premiums paid plus investment return on them, net of charges). To the non-actuarial mind, it may come as something of a surprise to find that the term 'asset share' did not have a universally accepted meaning. Some life offices apparently calculated asset shares to include purely investment returns whereas others included a share of other busi-

1 COBS 20.1.3.

nesses in which a policy or group of policies (or the estate) were participating. The FSA's rules define how unsmoothed asset share should be calculated. The FSA also accepts that an unsmoothed asset share may not always be possible or appropriate in all circumstances. In such cases a life office may use a more 'appropriate' methodology to set bonus rates provided that methodology is 'consistently applied and properly reflects its representations to with-profits policyholders[1].

The definition of unsmoothed asset share is contained in COBS 20.2.5(3). The methods to be applied are specified in INSPRU 1.3.119-123 but include amounts added as a result of a distribution from an inherited estate[2]. COBS. 20.2.5(3)(c) makes clear that 'where the terms of the policy so provide', the effect of a participation in insurance business should be reflected. The reference to the terms of the policy so providing is probably a get-out in most cases to including such profits, as historically, very few (if any) policies will have detailed the particular pockets of insurance business in which groups of policies may have participated. Losses which result from a failure to comply with COBS 20.2 cannot be deducted unless they cannot realistically be met from the estate or shareholder funds[3]. A life office may calculate its unsmoothed asset share on an actual policy or on a specimen policy basis but it should normally specify in its PPFM which basis is applied to particular groups of policyholders.

COBS 20.2 imposes requirements in relation to maturity values which will affect the amount paid out unless a firm is contractually obliged to provide a higher amount. A life office must set a target range, either for all of its with-profits policyholders or for each group of with-profit policyholders. The target range is required to be expressed as a percentage of unsmoothed asset shares and must include 100% of unsmoothed asset share. This is interesting because 100% is merely required to be included somewhere within the range[4]. Once the life office has established its target range it must specify it in the PPFM and manage the fund with the aim of meeting the target range. It also has to have 'good reason' to believe that 90% of its maturity amounts are within the target range. In addition, as a long-term aim, the with-profits business should be managed to make aggregate maturity payments on its with-profits policies of 100% unsmoothed asset share[5]. This 'aggregate' target is designed to encourage life offices to treat generations of policyholders in the same way.

The *Equitable Life* decision looms large in many of the provisions in COBS 20.2. Further rules apply to the calculation of unsmoothed asset share, relating to the life office's ability to deduct the cost of guarantees and similar policy benefits. In high-level terms, life offices are required to have a plan (having regard, of course, to legal considerations), specifying the basis on which charges can be applied. This should be consistent with and disclosed in a life office's PPFM[6].

1 COBS 20.2.11.
2 COBS 20.2.5(3)(b).
3 COBS 20.2.5(3)(d)
4 COBS 20.2.5(1)(b) (ii).
5 COBS 20.2.2.10.
6 COBS 20.3.6(4).

Any deduction must be proportionate to and consistent with the costs that it is intended to offset and disclosed in Key Features and projections. The charges should also not change unless justified by a review carried out by changes in the business or economic environment or changes in the nature of the life office's liabilities as a result of policyholders exercising options in their policies.

6.12 COBS 20.2.12-16 introduces fundamental obligations in relation to surrender values. First, although a life office may use its own methods to calculate surrender values, in aggregate they must be not less than the target maturity values less an amount 'necessary, in the opinion of the life office's governing body, to protect the interests of the life office's remaining with-profits policyholders'. COBS 20.2.15G provides that this may include the life office's unrecovered costs (eg commission payments), amounts to reflect the true value of the underlying assets, the life office's costs in administering the surrender, and a fair contribution towards benefits under continuing policies which would otherwise result in higher costs falling on the continuing with-profits policies. This last point seems very broad and it remains to be seen how this will be dealt with in practice.

6.13 Similar provisions apply in relation to unitised with-profits contracts to limit reductions in unit values on surrender or switching out of a with-profits fund. Life offices may only apply MVRs where the market value of the underlying assets or liquidity problems will affect the life office's ability to realise the assets (eg when a high volume of surrenders is anticipated). The market value reduction (MVR) must also be limited to the amount necessary to reflect these risks[1]. One of the criticisms post the *Equitable Life* judgment was based on the perception that the MVRs applied were penal. This provision, by limiting reductions to the amount 'necessary' to reflect the risk to the fund, should protect policyholders from such actions in the future. However, the FSA continues to have concerns in relation to use of MVRs and in CP11/5 it has said that it will remove the ability for firms (under COBS 20.2.16R) to impose MVRs on the grounds of surrender volumes alone. The FSA wants MVRs only to be applied where the face value of the policy is higher than the value of the underlying assets. The FSA also accepts that a large number of small reductions in value may lead to application of an MVR. The FSA will remove the requirement for the difference in value to be 'significant' (eg as even a small difference in a large fund could potentially justify an MVR).

In the interests of fairness where an MVR is applied COBS 20.2.17R(3) requires shareholder distributions to be reduced to reflect 'negative distributions' to policyholders (eg amounts clawed back using an MVR). The FSA intends to amend the rule to make its effect clearer.

C Distributions

6.14 A life office must not make a distribution from a with-profits fund unless the whole of the cost of that distribution can be met without eliminating

1 COBS 20.2.16.

the regulatory surplus in that fund[1]. Realistic life offices (ie large with-profits life offices)[2] also need to ensure that there is a surplus on a realistic basis[3]. As the realistic basis of calculating liabilities includes discretionary and other non-contractual benefits, the realistic surplus should be higher than regulatory surplus and therefore potentially reduce the amount available for distribution. The life office must also ensure that the amount distributed to policyholders is not less than the 'required percentage' of the total amount distributed. The required percentage is not less than 90% unless the company's constitution or a court order specifies otherwise. A life office that has an established practice specified in its PPFM to pay a different amount may continue to do so. It is not clear how these rules fit with the rules in Rule 3.4 of IPRU INS which were designed to impose a similar restriction.

In CP11/5 the FSA has stated that it intends to clarify the definition of required percentage applicable to distributions[4] to make it clear that it should reflect the significance of a firm's established practice, whether or not that is reflected in its Principles and Practices of Financial Management. The FSA will add guidance to COBS 20.2.17R to highlight the significance of the issue of established practice in determining the required percentage and to clarify its expectations of firms in relation to their approach to the issue. The FSA will expect firms to justify any reliance on established practice by showing that it has been clearly and unambiguously communicated to their with-profits policyholders. If there is some ambiguity between a firm's behaviour and its communications, the FSA may consider that the firm's established practice is different to that suggested or that such an established practice does not exist.

The FSA's view seems to be that it is unlikely that many mutuals will be able to show that they have communicated an established practice to policyholders in relation to distributions of less than 100% to the with-profits policyholders. The FSA states that the guidance will also deal with the situation where a firm puts forward an established practice that involves allocating (but not distributing) some portion of a surplus in its with-profits fund to persons other than with-profits policyholders. It is not clear what this means, as the draft guidance attached to CP11/5 seems to say that it will pay particular attention to how clearly this practice has been communicated by the firm. It is also not really clear who would own monies allocated (but presumably not distributed) to non-profit policyholders. The FSA also intends all companies to produce distribution plans which should show how they intend to distribute relevant profits (eg from non-profits business or any part of the inherited estate) to with-profits policyholders. The plan will need to be based on existing and expected new business.

1 COBS 20.2.17.
2 With-profits liabilities of £500m or more.
3 COBS 20.2.18.
4 COBS 20.2.17R.

D Excess surplus

6.15 In order to prevent life offices building up future inherited estates (eg excess of assets over realistic liabilities – see **6.3**) they are now required[1] to perform an annual assessment[2] to see if they have an 'excess surplus' and, if so, normally to distribute it or carry out a reattribution. The FSA intends to remove the option to reattribute an excess surplus. Broadly excess surplus is the surplus held in the with-profits fund, having taken into account any additional support available to the fund, the capital it is required to hold to meet its 'risk appetite', and any planned new business. A life office will only not have to distribute or reattribute an excess surplus if it is consistent with Principle 6 and in the interest of customers to retain the surplus. The judge in the Aviva reattribution case (see **6.45**) appeared to accept that this caveat was a substantive additional requirement. The Aviva reattribution also highlighted that the excess surplus calculation can be based on the company's own risk appetite and not the ICA basis of calculating risk based capital required (see **7.6**). As the ICA basis is said to equate to a rating of BBB, any company managing its fund to a higher rating requirement will, by definition, be retaining more assets in the fund than are required to meet the benchmark risk-based solvency requirement. Retention of excess surplus is clearly a matter of judgement in individual cases but it is difficult, if the insurer is happy with its risk appetite, to see how it would justify retaining a surplus, which is by definition excess to requirements, without creating a conflict with its customer's interests. In CP11/5 the FSA gives some examples of situations which may justify not distributing a surplus in the fund. These are, to comply with prudential requirements or maintain a level of financial strength/credit rating, to support future plans, including the writing of new business. The excess surplus calculation seems to already include such factors and so the point becomes a bit circular. It could therefore be difficult in practice to justify retaining an excess surplus.

E Investment strategy

6.16 Reliance on support from shareholders or a dedicated pool of assets may allow a with-profits fund to have a more risky investment strategy. In cases where support (eg from the inherited estate, a scheme or shareholders) is made available to the fund and is properly sub-ordinated to the fair treatment of policyholders, the strategy should be to manage the funds as if that support did not have to be repaid[3]. However, where there is no such sub-ordination no reliance should be placed on the support[4]. COBS 20.2.35G also gives guidance on the factors to take into account in setting the investment strategy.

1 COBS 20.2.21.
2 Every three years for a non-directive friendly society.
3 COBS 20.2.33
4 COBS 20.2.34.

F Restrictions in relation to new business

6.17 The life office's governing body also needs to be satisfied that its plans for new business are not likely to have a material adverse effect on its existing with-profits policyholders[1]. COBS 20.2.29 sets out circumstances in which it might be appropriate to establish a new bonus series to mitigate this risk. This can be useful where the life office wishes to impose additional charges on new business or where accepting the new business may necessitate a change in investment mix. If a new bonus series cannot contain the risk then it may be necessary to establish a new fund.

The FSA has stated in CP11/5 that it will strengthen the current rules and guidance on accepting new business so that new business can only be written if the governing body is satisfied, and can demonstrate, that there is likely to be 'no adverse effect' on with-profits policyholders' interests. There is clearly a significant shift here from the current 'no material effect' to 'no adverse effect'. Firms will be required to carry out and obtain all appropriate analysis (including a profitability analysis) on the impact of the new business to support this conclusion and to provide that analysis to the firm's with-profits committee or alternative arrangement for independent assessment.

The FSA intends to give guidance as to the continuing effect of the rule, and to make it clear that they consider loss-leading business to be likely to have an adverse effect on with-profits policyholders' interests. The FSA also made clear during the Aviva reattribution that the inherited estate cannot be used to write loss-leading business as any finance/support needs to be repaid over a reasonable period of time.

G Procedure for material transactions and strategic assets

6.18 A life office must not enter into a material transaction (or a series of transactions which together are material) relating to a with-profits fund unless, in the reasonable opinion of the life office's governing body, it is unlikely to have a material adverse effect on the interests of the fund's existing policyholders[2]. Material transactions include a significant bulk outwards reinsurance, *any inwards* reinsurance, a financial engineering transaction and a significant restructuring of the fund. The governing body may need to seek professional advice to substantiate its opinion. COBS 20.2.35 G reminds firms of the need to consider both at the outset and on an ongoing basis whether the use of with-profits fund assets for strategic purposes (eg to buy another business) is appropriate. The FSA has also made clear in CP11/5 that as a fund is running off it needs to ensure a timely realisation of strategic assets (eg head office buildings) so that the benefit of the particular asset is shared by the appropriate policyholders.

1 COBS 20.2.28
2 COBS 2.2.39.

In CP11/5 the FSA has said it will introduce a new rule requiring that, where strategic investments are made or retained, the firm's governing body must be satisfied, so far as it reasonably can be, and must demonstrate, that the purchase or retention is likely to have 'no adverse effect' on the interests of with-profits policyholders. If a firm reviews its strategic investments and concludes that it is no longer in the interests of its with-profits policyholders to retain them, the FSA expects firms to put disposal plans in place enabling them to realise the best price for the assets that they are selling. The FSA has also said that it will restore the guidance on strategic investments previously contained in COB 6.12.86G which was removed in 2007. This will be amended to reflect the new rule. The guidance sets out issues firms should take into account in relation to strategic investments including the relative size of the transaction, the expected risk and return and whether the firms' actuaries and a knowledgeable policyholder would regard it as appropriate.

H Loans and guarantees to connected third parties

6.19 A life office can only make a loan to a connected person or give a guarantee in respect of them in specified circumstances. These are that the arrangement is on commercial terms and that it is believed by the firm's senior management to be beneficial to policyholders and will not expose them to undue credit or group risk[1].

I Charges and compensation

6.20 A life office should not charge a cost to a with-profits fund unless it has incurred or will incur the cost in the operation of the fund[2]. This can include a fair proportion of overheads but not profit of a group company. It is common for firms and groups to use an in-house service company which, for example, may employ all staff and may cross-charge other parts of the organisation for the work they do. In the FSA's view, the principle relating to charging costs to a with-profits fund, set down in COBS 20.2.23R, (eg actual proportionate charges and a fair share of overhead) should apply however a firm or group chooses to organise itself. This means that a group service company should not extract any profit from a with-profits fund. The FSA stated in CP11/5 that it intended to change the wording of the rule to make this clear.

6.21 One of the areas where the FSA was heavily criticised during the Aviva Reattribution and by the Treasury Select Committee, was in relation to the ability to charge compensation costs to with-profits funds (eg inherited estates). It therefore consulted during 2008/9[3] on changes to its rules to prevent with-profits

1 COBS 20.2.32.
2 COBS 20.2.23.
3 See CP08/11 and CP09/09.

firms, other than mutuals, charging the costs of compensation and redress to with-profits funds. Despite responses that made the point that sharing in profits and losses was often part of the concept of with-profits, the FSA decided to go ahead with its proposed rule change. The change took effect in relation to events happening after 30 July 2009. The rules[1] therefore currently provide that compensation and redress costs have to be borne by the shareholders' assets (eg rather than the inherited estate). Mutuals may continue to charge such costs to with-profits funds to asset shares only if the firm's governing body reasonably believes that they cannot be paid from other assets of the fund. It is, however, explicitly stated in COBS 20.2.25B, that payments to rectify errors (eg over and under payments) may continue to be made from a with-profits fund. COBS 20.2.26 provides that the costs of a skilled person's report (because of an apparent failing of the life office) should also not be borne by the fund (unless a mutual).

J Shareholder tax

6.22 One of the other issues which has been contentious for some time and for which the FSA has also been criticised, is the ability to charge an amount of tax in respect of distributions to shareholders (shareholder transfers) to with-profits funds. Again this was an area addressed during the Aviva Reattribution and by the Treasury Select Committee. When the FSA issued its original rules on treating with-profits policyholders fairly (ie COB 6.12, now COBS 20.2), it effectively prohibited future arrangements permitting such tax to be charged to the fund. However, where a firm can show an established practice of charging such tax to the with-profits fund[2], an amount up to the notional corporation tax liability in respect of shareholder transfers that would be charged if it were a standalone entity can be charged to the fund[3]. The firm's practice must be explained in its PPFM and the amount should not be charged to asset shares.

Solvency II is likely to lead to changes in the basis of taxation of life companies and HM Revenue and Customs have already consulted on this, but it is not yet clear what the new tax regime will be. Further changes to these provisions may be required upon implementation of Solvency II and the FSA therefore intends to return to the issue of shareholder tax at a later date.

K Other issues in CP11/5

6.23 One of the biggest sector-wide failings the FSA's With-Profit Review Report identified was the poor quality of communications provided to with profits policyholders, particularly surrender and transfer notices, post sales information and consumer friendly PPFMs. The FSA has reminded firms that

1 COBS 20.2.25 25A.
2 COBS 20.2.20.
3 COBS 20.2.27.

they must ensure that their literature is clear, fair and not misleading. The FSA strongly encourages firms to review all of their with-profits communications in light of its June 2010 Report and, where necessary, revise and improve them.

6.24 One of the other areas that the FSA is going to make clearer going forward is the nature of conflicts within a with-profits fund and the need to deal with them appropriately to treat policyholders fairly. In CP11/5 the FSA has said it will convert COBS 20.2.1G, relating to fairness of a firm's operating practices and conflicts of interest, into a new rule. It will also expand its guidance to make clear that potential conflicts of interest are not limited to those between shareholders and with-profits policyholders, but include conflicts between with-profits policyholders and non-profit policyholders within the same fund; the members of mutually-owned funds; management; and different classes of with-profits policyholders (eg those with and without guarantees).

The FSA has suggested improving governance arrangements of with-profits funds, for example, by improving the status and independence of with-profits committees. The FSA also intends to introduce new notification requirements obliging firms to tell the FSA if their governing body has not followed the advice of the with-profits committee (see **6.50**).

SECTION 3 PRINCIPLES AND PRACTICES OF FINANCIAL MANAGEMENT (PPFM)

6.25 COBS 20.3 sets out the requirement for life offices conducting with-profits business to produce a PPFM. The detailed requirements apply to UK authorised life offices but EEA life offices are also required to provide equivalent information[1]. The PPFM is a very detailed record of the life office's relevant procedures and practices. The idea seems to be to get insurers to disclose the information required to enable assessment of whether their funds are being operated as they should be – almost providing an external benchmark by which to judge it. Life offices (including EEA insurers) are also required to produce a consumer-friendly 'potted' version of the PPFM in language the customer would be able to understand.

If a life office has more than one with-profits fund it may need to produce a PPFM for each fund unless they are, and have in the past, been operated in a similar way, in which case the relevant differences would need to be noted. Life offices are required to provide a copy of the PPFM free of charge to their with-profits policyholders and for a reasonable cost (to cover copying) to anyone else. The FSA's guidance advises that a life office may wish to publish its PPFM on

1 COBS 20.4.4.

its website. This is in contrast to the requirement[1] to prominently signpost the availability of its consumer friendly PPFM on its website.

The required contents of the PPFM are set out in COBS 20.3.6. Guidance is provided in COBS 20.3.8 as to what should be in the principles and what should be in the practices. Each topic is split between the high level principles which are not expected to change and practices which may in certain circumstances be changed. The PPFM requirements can be categorised as follows:

A Calculation of bonuses and smoothing

B Investment strategy

C Business risk

D Charges and expenses

E Management of the inherited estate

F Controlling new business and closure to new business

G Equity between the fund and shareholders

A firm is required to maintain a record of each version of its PPFM for five years[2].

A Calculation of bonuses and smoothing

6.26 The requirements in relation to the calculation of the amount due to with-profits policyholders (eg bonuses and smoothing) focus on the need to record the methods used, the degree of approximation, how changes are made and where it is all recorded. The practices also need to specify the target ranges for maturity values (and therefore surrender values) and the factors a life office is likely to have regard to in determining excess surplus (ie relevant to policyholders' interests or security). The practices should also make clear whether expenses are borne by the inherited estate or in some other way. There is a theme in the PPFM requirements which is to make transparent the extent to which external support is provided to the fund, the idea being to commit the provider of the support, either the inherited estate or the shareholder, to provide the specified level of support (see also Section 4 below). Following the *Equitable Life* decision, life offices are also required to describe in the practices how they bring items such as the cost of guarantees into account and how the inherited estate is used[3].

The PPFM requires life offices to explain their approach to setting annual and final bonuses. The principles should specify constraints due to economic factors and indicate how the life office would determine 'the range or generations of

1 COBS 20.4.5(4).
2 COBS 20.3.1.
3 COBS 20.3.8(1)(j)and 20.3.8(5)(d).

policyholders' covered by a single bonus series[1]. In relation to final bonuses, the significance of early surrender on the maturity value or application of a MVR should be described. The practices should cover the interaction between final bonus and MVR and should also describe any limits applied in setting bonuses (eg maximum/minimum changes in bonus rates from one year to the next) and the life office's approach to setting interim bonuses.

The PPFM should also set out the life office's approach to smoothing. A life office's PPFM must include details in relation to the smoothing policy applied to each type of with-profits policy, any limits to the total cost or excess amount to be smoothed and any limits applied to year on year maturity amounts for the purposes of consistency[2]. The principles should specify whether a life office considers that the cost of smoothing will be neutral over time[3]. A life office must also state in the practices whether or not it applies a single smoothing strategy to all generations of policyholder, and in particular how it deals with new entrants or whether it has differences of approach[4].

B Investment strategy

6.27 By manipulating or simply changing its investment strategy a life office could significantly change the return on a with-profits policy. Changing the investment strategy is a particular issue for closed life funds (and life funds which are very close to closure). In the PPFM a life office must describe the significant aspects of its strategy. The firm's controls on using new assets or liability instruments and the approval required should also be included. The principles should specify the investment strategy in some detail and how the mix of assets is determined. The FSA has previously stated[5] that it should be in more detail than simply achieving the best return within the framework of the likely volatility of asset values. The principles should also set out the strategy in relation to derivatives and other instruments. Reliance on assets held outside the fund should be described.

The practices should describe whether assets are notionally allocated to policies and the approach to investment in different asset classes and assets of different credit or liquidity quality, including assets not normally traded. The period between formal reviews of the investment strategy should also be stated[6].

Details of external support available and how this affects the investment strategy should be stated in the practices. COBS 20.2.35 G makes clear that where external support provided is sub-ordinated to the fair treatment of policyholders, such support can be relied upon in setting the investment strategy. Many demutualisation and other schemes include arrangements to provide support to with-profits funds, either when policyholders' expectations will not be met, or perhaps

1 COBS 20.3.8 1(b)&(c).
2 COBS 20.3.6 1(c).
3 COBS 20.3.8(1)(d).
4 COBS 20.3.8 1(q).
5 COB 6.10.41G/1.
6 COBS 20.3.8(2)(c)-(e).

more drastically, to ensure solvency of the with-profits fund on a stand-alone basis. These schemes often provide contingent support which becomes permanent in specified circumstances. Other similar arrangements may exist more informally. Where the obligation to repay such support is sub-ordinated to the fair treatment of policyholders and where there are no provisions to the contrary in the scheme, such support may be taken into account and should be described.

In relation to strategic assets the principles should describe why the assets are of use to the fund and how that is reviewed, any limits on such assets and whether holding them will impact the policyholders' pay out.

C Business risk

6.28 It is common for different classes of with-profits policyholder to be exposed to different business risks (eg in relation to non-profit business and/or guarantees). A life office should make clear how it considers business risk exposures before accepting them and how it assesses the risk/reward position[1]. In its principles, the life office should be explicit about whether it excludes business from classes of policyholders and if so where residual risk (eg smoothing/guarantees) falls. In particular it should define where compensation costs from a business risk would be borne. The practices should describe current limits applicable to the taking on of business risk and specify the extent to which different generations or classes of with-profits policies might bear particular risks. This should include, for example, crystallised or contingent guarantees to other policyholders. Alternatively, if business risk is shared across all with-profits policyholders then that should be stated. The life office should also specify the procedures for reflecting resulting profits/losses in payouts.

D Charges and expenses

6.29 The PPFM must explain how a life office applies charges and allocates expenses between the fund, the inherited estate and shareholders assets including, if material, any interaction with connected entities (eg service companies)[2]. The risk for with-profits policyholders is that the life office extracts additional profit from the fund which, because of the lack of transparency in the fund, it is difficult to identify. Where service company arrangements exist, they may have been set up to fix the amount the fund pays for a service but with a view to the service company making a profit by providing the service more efficiently. In practice, the FSA (and the DTI as its predecessor) has often exerted a substantial amount of control over the amount such service companies can charge. For with-profits funds, the FSA rules are clear that this should be costs incurred plus a fair proportion of overheads and should not include any element of profit to group service companies (see **6.20**). The requirement in the PPFM is to disclose to the

1 COBS 20.3.6(3)(a)-(c).
2 COBS 20.3.6(4)(a)-(b).

policyholder, and anyone else reading the PPFM, how charges and expenses are borne. For conventional policies this will normally be an allocation of expenses. For unitised policies there will often be an explicit management charge but the fund will also bear expenses (eg dealing costs) so that the total cost is a mixture of charges and expenses. Where the fund invests in a collective investment scheme (either of an associated company or a third party) the way in which costs and expenses of such investment are allocated should be included. The principles should set out the factors that would drive a change in the life office's practice.

The practices should describe the current charges and expenses apportioned to major classes of with-profits policies and the 'relationship' between the actual charges and expenses and those applied to the policy. Life offices also need to state the circumstances under which they charge expenses on a basis other than at cost and the reason for doing so. Furthermore, a life office should specify how often it reviews its outsourced services and how it can terminate such arrangements[1].

E Inherited estate

6.30 The PPFM must describe the life office's management of any inherited estate (eg excess of assets over realistic liabilities) and the uses to which the life office may put that inherited estate[2]. The principles should indicate the amount of inherited estate the life office is aiming for, for example, by reference to the volume of its business or the risks borne by the life office's existing business. The principles should also describe any division of the inherited estate or restrictions applying to inherited estate by virtue of previous dealings (eg a scheme or reattribution). The practices should specify the costs the inherited estate is currently meeting. They also need to describe the investment strategy of the estate and how the life office would deal with the estate if it were to become too big or too small. The practices should also state whether the investment strategy for the inherited estate differs from the rest of the with-profits fund. It is understood that Aviva may have been able to release excess surplus prior to its reattribution by de-risking. One method of de-risking (ie reducing the capital needed to cover a with-profits fund), is to apply a different investment strategy (eg less or no equity content) to the inherited estate. There does not appear to be any additional restriction on a company choosing to change its investment strategy for the inherited estate in this way but the practices should state whether the investment strategy for the inherited estate differs from the rest of the with-profits fund.

F New business

6.31 The value of with-profits funds can be affected both by business risk undertaken by the fund and by new with-profits business. In some cases it is

1 COBS 20.3.8(4)(e).
2 COBS 20.3.6(5).

better for the fund to accept business only into a new bonus series or not to accept such business at all. COBS 20.2 contains rules to restrict the ability of a fund to enter into new arrangements. The principles should describe how the life office would limit its exposure to new business and how it would deal with closing to significant new business, in particular how it would deal with the inherited estate. A life office which is still open to new business must describe its practice for reviewing limits on the quantity and type of new with-profits business and the actions that the life office would take if it ceased to take on new with-profits business of any significant amount[1]. The practices might also describe the level of new business required to keep the fund open.

G Equity

6.32 One of the other major potential sources of concern for with-profit policyholders in a proprietary company is the inherent difficulty in situations where there might be a conflict of interests between the policyholders' interests and those of the shareholder. For this reason, rules exist to prevent life offices manipulating the amount that can be distributed to shareholders. The PPFM has to describe the basis on which the shareholders' share in profits to be divided can be changed. It also has to deal with other means of passing value to shareholders (eg by the way tax is borne on the shareholder distribution or the effect of a change in the valuation basis)[2]. The practices need to describe the current basis on which profit is divided between the shareholder and the policyholders. In CP11/5 the FSA has highlighted the need to show an established practice in relation to this profit sharing percentage, particularly where it is suggested that profit may also be shared with non-profit policyholders. It will clearly be important in such cases to be able to evidence such established practice. The practices should also state whether the pricing of any policies are being written at the expense of the inherited estate and that such amounts will be repaid to the estate.

H Changes to the PPFM

6.33 When the requirement to produce PPFMs was first introduced life offices were able to make changes to the principles on three months' notice[3], changes to practices merely having to be notified. Now COBS 20.3.1(4) provides in addition that changes must, in the opinion of the governing body, be justified by the need to: respond to changes in the business or economic environment (including changes in the law); protect the interest of the policyholders; or, in respect of a change in the practices, better achieve the principles. Other changes are permitted[4] to rectify errors, to improve clarity or presentation, or if they are immaterial (it is not clear what immaterial means for this purpose). In any event

1 COBS 20.3.6(6).
2 COBS 20.3.8(6)(a).
3 COBS 20.4.2.
4 COBS 20.3.1(5).

these requirements mean that life offices need to ensure the continued accuracy of their documents and be able to justify any changes made.

I EEA

6.34 COBS 20.4.4 and COBS 20.4.5 set out the obligations for EEA insurers. 'Equivalent information', which must not be narrower in scope or less detailed in content than the equivalent PPFM (the full version not the consumer-friendly one) has to be provided on request. The EEA insurer must also give three months' advanced notice to its UK habitually resident customers of changes to 'principle' equivalent information and give notice in relation to changes to 'practice' equivalent information. An EEA Insurer must produce a consumer friendly PPFM.

J Consumer-friendly version

6.35 COBS 20.4.5 requires life offices to produce a consumer-friendly version of the PPFM (the CFPPFM). It must describe the most important information set out under each of the headings in the PPFM in language that can be easily understood by inexperienced policyholders. Life offices need to provide a copy of the consumer-friendly PPFM with written notices proposing changes to the PPFM, with Key Features documents and with annual statements sent to with-profits policyholders (unless there has been no material change since last supplied). The consumer-friendly PPFM can be included in another document and must be provided free of charge. An EEA insurer is subject to the rules on consumer friendly PPFMs[1]. The FSA appears to have accepted (CP11/5) that the effectiveness of CFPPFM needs to be reviewed.

K Annual report

6.36 COBS 20.4.7 requires a life office to make an annual report available to its with-profits policyholders, see further **6.50**. Guidance in relation to governance arrangements is set out in COBS 20.3.2.

SECTION 4 PROCESS FOR REATTRIBUTION OF INHERITED ESTATES

A Background

6.37 The FSA Rules define the term 'inherited estate' as the 'fair market value of the with-profits assets less the realistic liabilities'. This is considered

1 COBS 20.1.3(4).

further below but the basic concept is that it is the surplus carried in the fund. The term 'estate' is also often used to refer to the inherited estate.

The COBS 20.2 rules relating to inherited estates seek to do two things: first to prevent future *new* inherited estates being built up; and second to introduce rules and specific guidance relating to the process for reattribution of existing excesses in with-profits funds. To avoid the creation of new inherited estates, life offices are now required to undertake an annual assessment of 'excess surplus'[1]. Any such excess surplus not realistically required to be retained by the fund should normally be distributed or currently reattributed (see **6.15** above). The FSA accepts that life offices need to retain some working capital to run a with-profits fund but it is clearly concerned to see that policyholders get a fair share of profits generated by their money.

COBS 20.2.42-52 specifies a process for reattribution of inherited estates. A life office that is seeking to make a reattribution (an arrangement whereby policyholders give up rights in relation to the estate in return for a current or future benefit) must appoint a policyholder advocate to act on behalf of its relevant with-profits policyholders. If the reattribution is not a Part VII scheme, in which case it is likely to be a scheme of arrangement[2], the life office must also appoint an actuary as a reattribution expert. If it is a Part VII scheme, there will be an actuary acting as independent expert. Provisions relating to the involvement of the FSA and rules relating to the costs of the reattribution are also set out in these rules (see **6.40**).

6.38 Inherited estates are often referred to as 'orphan assets' because they are surpluses that have been carried in the fund for some time and cannot really be said to belong to the fund's current policyholders. There are two diametrically opposed views as to who owns such assets. Proprietary life offices take the view that any surplus that they carry in with-profits funds from one generation to another belongs to the shareholders of the company. As many traditional life offices were formed in the 17th Century, trying to work out how the surplus arose in the first place can be difficult. In some instances a surplus can, however, be seen to have arisen as a result of particular actions (eg particular investment decisions). Shareholders would argue that as they bore the risk of such decisions, particularly where the business contained guarantees, they are entitled to any surplus that has been amassed over time. The view of consumer protection organisations is that any excess in the fund that is not realistically required to cover the existing or realistic proposed new business should be distributed in the usual way through the 90/10 or other appropriate gateway. They refer to a ministerial statement to this effect in 1995. This statement (see Annex B of FSA Issues Paper 1 (2001)) makes clear that in the absence of evidence to the contrary, the starting point for a reattribution is a 90:10 split and such contingent interests in the surplus need to be factored into any dealing with the inherited estate.

The FSA has repeatedly stated that the starting point for any discussion about ownership and distribution of the inherited estate is the 1995 Ministerial

1 COBS 20.2.21
2 Companies Act 2006, Part 26.

Statement. However, what has become clearer and has been stated explicitly, both in relation to the new rules on payment of compensation from with-profits funds and in CP11/5, is that the FSA regards with-profits policyholders as having a contingent interest in the inherited estate. In CP09/9 the FSA stated:

> 'With-profits policyholders have a contingent interest in any surplus which may exist. With-profits policyholders in a shareholder-owned firm will typically receive 90% of any surplus inherited estate that is distributed. While they have no reasonable expectation that they will share in a special distribution from a with-profits fund during the lifetime of the policies, if a distribution does take place during the term of their policies, with-profits policyholders have a reasonable expectation of participation in the distribution. Therefore, we view with-profits policyholders as having a contingent interest in any surplus'.

This is based on the fact that they may get a distribution of inherited estate because of an excess surplus (see **6.15** above). The judgment in the Aviva Reattribution case is particularly interesting in relation to the issue of excess surplus and the issues that are likely to be raised in a reattribution (see **6.45**).

6.39 In its With-Profits Regime Review Report, the FSA stated that they were concerned at the length of time the Aviva reattribution took because of the uncertainty for policyholders and the increased difficulty in effective financial planning. The FSA stated that it would like firms to do more in the way of preparation, presumably before a public announcement is made and the FSA has proposed changes in CP11/5. In CP11/5 the FSA is also proposing to remove the ability to reattribute excess surplus and the option of using a scheme of arrangement to effect a reattribution.

B The policyholder advocate

6.40 The policyholder advocate will stand in the shoes of the policyholders to negotiate with the life office and must be free from conflicts of interest. The policyholder advocate must be nominated or approved by the FSA before he or she is appointed[1]. The FSA suggests consultation with groups of policyholders or the use of recruitment consultants to ensure that the firm is able to evidence an independent element to the selection process. The FSA will nominate a policyholder advocate if the firm's choice is not approved.

The FSA rules[2] currently require a life office to start the process to appoint a policyholder advocate and include him/her at the earliest appropriate point where it is 'seeking' to make a reattribution. The FSA intends to require the firm's proposals to be at a more advance stage in future before such an appointment is made. When a firm proposes a reattribution, it should be required to discuss the issue with the FSA in advance. The firm will need to

1 COBS 20.2.44
2 COBS 20.2.42(2).

show whether it has an excess surplus and, if so, the amount of it. The FSA will also discuss the firm's capital requirements for future new business. The potential actions that a firm is obliged to take will be discussed in this process and will include the distribution of any identified excess surplus before the proposed reattribution of the remaining estate is progressed. The forecast level of new business is crucial as it drives the level of capital the firm will need to retain (rather than distribute), and the level of surplus to be reattributed. A firm must be able to set out a solid basis for its view on the excess surplus; its plan for distributing the excess surplus to policyholders; and its overall justification for removing the remaining working capital in the estate from the with-profits fund in a reattribution. Only once that is done, should the firm start the process to appoint the policyholder advocate. Firms will need to discuss governance arrangements with the regulator, including the terms of reference for the policyholder advocate. The FSA intends to amend its existing guidance to reflect its expectation that, in practice, discussions in respect of the policyholder advocate will lead to an agreement about the policyholder advocate's precise role.

The role of the policyholder advocate will vary but will include negotiation with the life office on behalf of the with-profits policyholders on the deal on offer. This should include commenting on the methodology used to allocate benefits amongst the policyholder or groups of them, the criteria for eligibility, and the views expressed by the expert and the with-profits actuary[1]. The policyholder advocate is also expected to advise policyholders whether and if so, why, the life office's proposals are in their interests and if not, why not.

The policyholder advocate's terms of appointment must define the relationship and how it can be terminated. It must stress the independent nature of the role[2]. The terms should also include the arrangements under which the policyholder advocate is to communicate with policyholders. The FSA expects the policyholder advocate to be able to communicate freely (and without the firm's approval) with policyholders. The firm is also required to ensure that policyholders get appropriate and timely information. The policyholder advocate must also have free and confidential access to the FSA.

The question of who bears the costs incurred is one for negotiation unless the reattribution does not go ahead, in which case, the life office would normally be expected to pick up the costs. Otherwise, it is intended that the costs will split in a fair manner, with shareholders paying a 'reasonable proportion'. The terms of the policyholder advocate's appointment may include an indemnity from the life office in respect of 'certain claims' provided the indemnity does not extend to acts of bad faith on the part of the policyholder advocate[3].

Once a policyholder advocate's appointment is agreed in principle he/she should be given time to organise advisers and gather the appropriate information about the life office and the proposals being made.

1 75% by value voting.
2 COBS 20.2.47.
3 COBS 20.2.46.

C Reattribution expert

6.41 The policyholder advocate will be a feature of all reattributions. Where the reattribution takes the form of a Part VII scheme (see Chapter 3), and it seems likely that in future all such schemes will[1], there will be an independent actuarial expert involved in the process. However, where there is no Part VII scheme, and policyholders are asked to agree to another arrangement or scheme, a reattribution expert must be appointed[2]. The reattribution expert must be free from conflicts of interest and the appointment must be approved by the FSA. The expert's terms of appointment must allow him/her to communicate freely, and at their discretion, in confidence with the FSA[3]. The role is very similar to that of the Part VII independent expert, as are the reporting requirements[4]. The report must be made available to the FSA, the policyholder advocate and the court (if relevant). An adequate summary of the report must be made available to all policyholders. One important difference between the reattribution expert/independent expert and the policyholder advocate is that the latter's aim is to look at the proposals from the policyholders' perspective. The experts are required to be impartial in their assessment of the effect of the arrangements proposed. The expert's costs are to be borne by the life office.

D Process for reattribution

6.42 In practice, the division of assets in a reattribution needs to be agreed with both the FSA and policyholders (although a 75% majority of policyholder voting may currently be sufficient on a scheme of arrangement[5]). The FSA appears to base its view very much on the advice of the appropriate expert (the independent, or if there is no Part VII scheme, the reattribution expert).

The current rules in COBS 20.2 are much less prescriptive about the process for reattributing inherited estates than the original rules in COB 6.13. Based on the Aviva Reattribution, which is the only reattribution to have actually taken place under the FSA's regime and to have involved a policyholder advocate, it seems likely that the policyholder advocate would seek the views of policyholders on what they would expect from the company. It is understood that the Aviva policyholder advocate undertook a series of roadshows around the country for this purpose. The Aviva policyholder advocate was critical of the FSA's regime for with-profits. She was also critical of the extent of the company's ability to effectively hold back part of the inherited estate to cover expected levels of future new business. Ultimately, however, the offer to policyholders was accepted. It is worth noting that a substantial distribution of excess surplus had also been agreed.

The life office's responsibility to policyholders also specifically includes the

1 CP11/5.
2 COBS 20.2.53.
3 SUP 4.3.12A.
4 COBS 20.4.7.
5 COBS 20.2.42(1).

obligation to keep them informed about the process[1]. This should include explaining the roles of the various parties involved, the benefits and disadvantages of the process (ie what they are likely to be asked to give up) and the policyholder advocate's views.

6.43 The life office must tell policyholders when negotiations with the policyholder advocate are complete, explain the outcome and, if appropriate, the life office's proposals. It must provide details of the effect of the proposals (including benefits the policyholder is likely to receive and what they are being asked to give up) and send the report from the policyholder advocate explaining why they consider the proposals to be in the interests of policyholders. A summary of the expert's report should also be included with details of how the report can be obtained. Policyholders must then be given the chance to either accept or reject the proposals, or if it is a scheme of arrangement, to vote on them[2]. In CP11/5 the FSA states that it would like to remove the option of a scheme under Part 26 of the Companies Act 2006 because it does not give policyholders a choice to retain their interest in the inherited estate. It therefore seems likely in future reattributions that policyholders will always have a choice whether to accept the offer being made to them or to retain their interest in the inherited estate.

6.44 The FSA's letter to Clare Spottiswoode, the Aviva policyholder advocate, of 6 December 2007, made a number of interesting points in relation to its role in a reattribution, the likelihood of excess surplus distributions and the uses to which the inherited estate can be put. The FSA sees its role in a reattribution as to test whether the firm's proposals are fair and consistent with the FSA's Principles and Rules. The FSA will also inform the court of its view where there is a court approved scheme. The FSA's position seems to be that if there are proposals for a reattribution, it is likely there will be an element of excess surplus to be distributed. The FSA is also aware that firms could avoid an excess surplus and increase the amount being attributed by changing their 'risk appetite' after the reattribution (its risk appetite being the basis of testing for excess surplus (see **6.15**). The FSA has said[3] that it will take steps to avoid firms seeking to obtain an advantage post a reattribution by changing their risk appetite. The FSA says that reattribution proposals should limit distributions to shareholders based on the pre-reattribution risk appetite and not any post-scheme amendments.

One of the areas where there has been uncertainty in the past in relation to the use of inherited estates has been in covering loss leading products or absorbing expense overruns which market conditions prevent from being passed on to policyholders. The FSA made clear in the letter to Ms Spottiswoode that the uses to which the inherited estate may be put were to permit investment flexibility or greater risk, to facilitate smoothing and cushion against unexpected adverse events; and to provide capital to support the writing or development of new products. This last point being subject to requirements that the business be expected

1 COBS 20.2.49.
2 COBS 20.2.51.
3 In a letter of 6 December 2007.

to be profitable and that the estate be reimbursed over a reasonable period of time.

6.45 The Judgment of Mr Justice Norris relating to the Aviva Reattribution[1] makes some very interesting points in relation to the FSA rules (eg on excess surplus and governance) and implicitly whether the FSA had to ensure that the deal on offer was the best available. It also very helpfully sets out issues raised before the court in relation to the reattribution and Mr Justice Norris' response. The judge had been encouraged by the Aviva policyholder advocate to comment on the conduct of with-profits business generally within the industry but declined to do so. He reiterated the point made in the AXA reattribution[2] that his role, based on the expert evidence before him, was to ascertain whether the scheme was being promoted for proper purposes and operated fairly as between the classes of person whose rights were affected by it. This did not require him to be satisfied that it was the best scheme available or likely, as a result of negotiation, to be available. The judge accepted and relied upon the FSA's opinion that the bargain struck was within the reasonable range of outcomes and he also referred to the fact that if new business assumptions turned out to be wrong, they would be subject to an appropriate 'clawback' mechanism[3]. The judge made the point that the payment made by the Aviva shareholders was not itself a distribution but an offer to buy out the policyholders' contingent interest in the estate. He accepted, based on the evidence before the court, that the inherited estate did not derive from the current generation of policyholders[4]. The judge also dealt with suggestions that a re-attribution was either a breach of the company's Articles of Association or a breach of contract[5]. One other point of a procedural nature to note, is that the court order was made despite the fact that the Portuguese regulator had not provided its consent to the scheme. The judge took the view that as the three month required period[6] had elapsed and as the Portuguese regulator had not refused its consent, the court had jurisdiction to sanction the scheme.

SECTION 5 CLOSED LONG-TERM FUNDS

6.46 Closing life funds to all or most new business has become a popular way to deal with a contracting underlying market. It is one of a number of ways of capping a life office's liabilities and historically has often been the precursor to another exit strategy or the option taken when none of the other options are available. The other options most commonly used are:

- Disposal – this is often the preferred route as it is the cleanest.

1 [2009] EWHC 252A.
2 [2000] 1 ALL ER 1010.
3 At para 74.
4 At para 64.
5 At paras 67 and 68.
6 Provided under paragraph 4(b) of Schedule 12 of FSMA.

- Portfolio transfers – many transfers have been used to prevent insurance business withering on the vine (ie being left in a closed fund) but a transfer can also be used in order to ring fence liabilities.
- Reassurance – by effectively passing some or all liability on to a reinsurer, a life office can achieve a level of certainty and release from its obligations in relation to long-term funds. It still, however, retains the underlying liability and needs to manage its relationship with the reinsurer. Reassurance of with-profits liabilities can be difficult to achieve in practice and requires the ceding insurer to maintain adequate controls[1].

Firms are also under an obligation to contact the FSA to discuss whether or not the fund should be treated as a closed fund if they are no longer writing a material volume of new business, or only do so by reinsuring of its new business to another insurer[2].

A closed fund is generally a fund which is not actively being marketed. The FSA's definition is in COBS 20.2.54.

6.47 Probably the most important thing to understand about closed funds is that they are a significant part of the long-term insurance savings market and many of them are still growing significantly year on year. This is because of increments or top-up new business. The most likely source of these increases is pension schemes business. An ongoing scheme may have new members and the existing scheme members' contributions would normally increase as their salaries increase. The FSA definition therefore makes clear that a fund can be closed even if it is accepting 'increments' on existing business. It can also be closed when the life office has not actually decided to close it but is not actively marketing it[3]. The other important point to note is that generally, such funds remain subject to the same FSA rules as funds which are not closed. They therefore need to specify target maturity values and manage the fund with the aim of achieving target maturity and surrender values in 90% of cases. Historically, funds have closed to allow a life office to concentrate on other types of business and it is fair to say that some, not all, of such companies have invested the fund in a very conservative way so as to reduce ongoing involvement by the life office. This can have a very negative impact, particularly on pensions contract customers who will remain in that fund for a long time.

In September 2004 the FSA issued an Insurance Sector Briefing on the regulation of closed with-profits funds. This was against the backdrop of its ongoing TCF proposals for with-profits. Many of the issues identified in the paper are now addressed by relevant provisions of COBS 20.2 The first requirement of COBS 20.2 in relation to funds that have closed since 2005 is for the life office to notify the FSA and its customers[4]. This should be done within 28 days of ceasing to effect new contracts, a decision to close or ceasing to

1 COBS 20.2.38.
2 COBS 20.2.55.
3 SUP 4.3.16 A R (4).
4 IPRU (INS) 9.6(6).

actively market new contracts. As stated above, life offices cannot avoid the obligation by not making a formal decision to close. Life offices are required to submit a run-off plan to the FSA as soon as reasonably practicable but within three months. The run off plan must comply with requirements set out in SUP Appendix 2.15 and have been approved by the firm's governing body. This must specify how the life office intends to ensure a 'full and fair distribution' of the fund's inherited estate. As investment of the fund's assets and its distribution are the most important issues for a closed fund, life offices are required to explain to with-profits policyholders the effect of run-off on the life office's investment strategy for the fund. A firm also needs to tell its policyholders why the fund has been closed and any reasonably foreseeable effects on policyholder payouts. It should also provide them with information in relation to options available to them and material factors. The firm may not have all of this information available before it completes its run off plan. If there is to be a delay in providing the information, firms should explain this to policyholders and let them know when they can expect the information to be provided. Firms should then adhere to this timeframe, providing the information as soon as possible.

6.48 In its Dear CEO Letter of 19 September 2007, the FSA stated that its review of closed funds had concluded that most of the firms reviewed that went into run-off before the new run-off rules were introduced in 2005, were unable to demonstrate effective management of with-profits funds. The FSA wants to move away from the binary open/closed position under the current rules, which often leads firms to avoid the actions that the FSA considers to be in their with-profits policyholders' best interests.

In CP11/5 the FSA stated that it will delete COBS 20.2.55R and replace it with a rule requiring firms to discuss their position with the FSA at an early stage, including discussing whether they should take any particular action in their with-profits policyholders' interests. Firms will be obliged to discuss their position if they experience significant and sustained falls in either the volume of new non-profit insurance contracts; or the volume of new with-profits policies, written into the with-profits fund. The FSA will add guidance confirming that if a firm is no longer writing a material volume of new contracts of insurance but can demonstrate that the business is expected to be profitable, then it is likely to be able to continue to write it, as long as it proposes to treat its with-profits policyholders fairly.

The FSA will require firms to have a fair distribution plan. This plan should be based on current and future new business prospects and have an investment strategy consistent with such prospects. Firms will also need to have a management plan which should include contingency arrangements. The management plan should cover investment, credit and operational risk plus any other risks of running the fund if existing or new business levels fall significantly. Both plans will need to be reviewed regularly and updated to reflect expected levels of business. Firms will need to ensure that their distribution and management plans are reviewed and kept up-to-date to reflect any material changes in both current and expected levels of new non-profit insurance contracts and new with-profits policies. If firms experience a significant and sustained fall in the levels of business, they should amend these plans accordingly and submit them to the FSA at least a week before the required discussion with the FSA.

The current rules requiring run-off plans affect funds that have closed to new business since 2005. The FSA now proposes to require a run-off plan for all closed firms. Firms should submit plans to the FSA within three months of the proposed rules coming into force if they have not done so already. The revised requirement to have a detailed run-off strategy will apply to all with-profits funds closed before the relevant date.

SECTION 6 GOVERNANCE

A Actuaries

6.49 As part of its review of with-profits business the FSA introduced the new and separate role of the with-profits actuary for UK with-profits insurance companies. This means that rather than just having one Appointed Actuary as previously, life offices will be advised by at least one actuary in relation to all classes of its long-term business (known as the Actuarial Function Holder or AFH) and by another in respect of its with-profits business. Both the 'actuarial' function and the 'with-profits actuary functions' are controlled functions and the people performing them (who should be at least two separate people) will need to be approved persons. This means that their appointment needs to be approved in advance by the FSA. SUP 4.3.1 requires a life office to appoint an actuary to fill any such vacancies at the time the vacancy arises or as soon as reasonably practicable after that. The FSA indicates that as it needs time to approve the person, life offices should ensure that they plan and make arrangements appropriately. Life offices also need to notify the FSA without delay when they are aware that a vacancy has or will arise. If the life office fails to make an appointment within 28 days the FSA may do so.

SUP 4.3.9 specifies the requirements in terms of qualification, skill and experience required of an actuary of a life office. The requirements include obtaining appropriate references. A life office must also take reasonable steps to ensure that an actuary appointed or to be appointed does not perform the function of chairman or chief executive and, if he is to be the with-profits actuary, he cannot be a member of the life office's governing body. He must also not perform any other function on behalf of the life office which could give rise to a significant conflict of interest[1].

The role of the actuarial function is mainly to advise the governing body appropriately in relation to material risk faced by the business, the life office's own risk assessment, and the capital needed to support the business. The actuary will also be involved in issues relating to the annual return to the FSA. SUP 4.3.15 sets out a list of areas where the FSA thinks a life office should take actuarial advice (which could be provided by the person(s) performing the actuarial

1 SUP 4.3.12A.

function). This list includes risk and capital management issues and issues such as variation of charges, discretionary surrender charges and adequacy of reinsurance protection.

The main role of the life office's with-profits actuary is to advise in relation to the life office's discretions affecting the relevant classes of business to which he has been appointed and, in relation to realistic basis companies, the calculation of the with-profits insurance capital component[1]. He must also, at least once in each calendar year, report to the life office's governing body in respect of the exercise of discretion, including, where relevant, reporting on the life office's application of its PPFM. He must also report to the with-profits policyholders, via a report to be included with the annual report[2], on whether in his opinion the life office's exercise of discretion has taken policyholders' interests into account in a reasonable and proportionate manner[3]. He should advise the life office in relation to the data and systems that he reasonably considers necessary to be kept and maintained to provide him with the information he needs. The with-profits actuary should be kept informed by the life office of relevant information and changes (eg to business plans, etc). He should also have appropriate resources and access to the governing body.

From the FSA's comments generally in relation to governance and with-profits committees, it seems clear that the FSA expects the with-profits actuary not to take too narrow a view of his remit and for the firm to involve him appropriately and in good time. The FSA also intends to add a new item to the section on conflicts of interest contained in SUP 4.3.17R. This will refer to the with-profits actuary not reporting to or having his remuneration determined in a way that would give rise to a conflict of interest over the advice he gives.

B Annual report and with-profits committees

6.50 COBS 20.3.2 provides guidance on governance arrangements relevant to a with-profits life office's compliance with SYSC. It also requires an annual report to with-profits policyholders to confirm compliance with its PPFM for each financial year.

The annual report should specify the reasons for the life office's belief that it has complied with its PPFM. It should detail the exercise of any discretion and address any competing or conflicting rights. This annual report must be annexed to the annual report of the with-profits actuary required by SUP 4.3.16 A R(4). In preparing its annual report the life office should take advice from the with-profits actuary. The life office should make the annual report available to with-profits policyholders within six months of the end of the relevant financial year. In its annual statement to policyholders the life office should notify policyholders of how copies of the report can be obtained. In any event, the life office must deposit the report with the FSA when it makes its annual return[4]. Life offices are

1 INSPRU 1.3.
2 SUP 4.3 16A.
3 SUP 4.3.16A.
4 SUP 4.3.16A.

advised to use some 'independent judgment' to assess compliance with its PPFM and the management of conflicting interests. This independent judgment may take a number of forms including a review by a with-profits committee, an independent assessment, or, for small life offices, a review by the non-executive directors. Any adverse comment resulting should, if required, be included in the annual report[1]. Life offices are not currently required to have with-profits committees but it is expected in the case of large companies. The FSA has decided to require larger funds to have a with-profits committee[2]. Smaller funds will keep the options that they have now (eg independent person or non executive director(s)).

In defining a 'small' with-profits fund, the FSA will use the size limits from the existing definition of a firm that is not subject to the realistic reporting regime as set out in GENPRU 2.1.19R (eg with with-profits liabilities that were under £500m on 31 December 2004 and which have remained below that threshold). The FSA proposes that its definition will refer to the fund size as of the date of the proposed rules coming into effect. While the limit for a 'small' fund is set at the fund level as opposed to the firm level, the FSA will require a firm with one or more funds with a with-profits committee to appoint the same with-profits committee for all of its with-profit funds. The FSA is likely to have to review governance arrangements including with-profits actuaries and committees again when Solvency II comes into force (see Section 8 of Chapter 7).

C FSA's proposals to change with-profits governance

6.51 The FSA identified a number of issues in relation to the independent judgement requirement and with-profits committees in particular, in its Dear CEO letter of 19 September 2007. The Dear CEO letter identified apparent failings in relation to the perceived independence of with-profits committees, the level and timing of their involvement (eg being told of significant decisions after they have been taken) and an overly restrictive view of their role (ie limited to ensuring compliance with the PPFM) and not looking at conflicts of interest more generally.

A key part of the role of a with-profits committee is to challenge the management. Having an element of independence is crucial to achieving this. The FSA has considered two models for the structure of the with-profits committees being, either wholly independent and external of the firm, or with an independent majority. In both options the FSA would expect a quorum of at least two members, to avoid undue influence from a single dominant figure.

The FSA appears to consider the option of an independent majority as likely to be the most practicable because of the pool of people available for the role. The FSA's expectation is that the committee's chair would normally be a senior independent non-executive or external person. In determining the independence of the members, the FSA intends to adopt the criteria listed in the Financial

1 COBS 20.4.8(2).
2 CP11/5.

Reporting Council's (FRC) UK Corporate Governance Code B.1.1. This delegates responsibility to the board to identify which non-executive directors it considers to be independent and gives examples of circumstances where independence may be compromised through certain relationships or circumstances. If a firm with a small fund appoints an independent person instead of a committee, the FSA expects the governing body to adopt the same approach.

6.52 The FSA also intends to deal with the other areas where there has been criticism of with-profits committees, namely the breadth of their terms of references and the need for them to be consulted in a meaningful way. The FSA will require the governing body to establish a proper functioning with-profits committee, which it must provide with information sufficiently comprehensive to enable the committee to discharge its functions. The information must be given far enough in advance of the decisions being made to enable the committee to give proper consideration and report back to the governing body. A firm should discuss the terms of reference of the with-profits committee with the FSA and publish them on the firm's website. The FSA will add a new requirement that the committee should satisfy itself that the way the fund is run is properly reflected in the PPFM. The terms of reference must include a requirement for the governing body to consult with the with-profits committee in a timely manner concerning *all matters the committee could reasonably expect to be consulted on.*

Issues which with-profits committees should consider include, but are not confined to: both the firm's compliance with its PPFM as currently drafted and whether the way in which the fund is run is properly reflected in the PPFM; how conflicts of interest have been identified and managed; the identification of surplus and excess surplus and the merits of its distribution versus retention; how bonus rates and MVRs (if relevant) have been set and applied and the application of smoothing; any significant changes to the risk/investment profile of the with-profits fund – including the management of material illiquid investments and strategic investments; the impact of any planned or implemented management actions; the firm's strategy for future business in the with-profits fund; the firm's customer communications; relevant management information, such as customer complaints data; drafting and adherence to the distribution, management and run-off plans and court schemes as appropriate; the costs incurred in operating the with-profits fund; and any other issues the with-profits policyholders may reasonably expect the with-profits committee to scrutinise.

The FSA will issue guidance to encourage a clearer separation between the with-profit committee's recommendations and the governing body's decisions. The FSA accepts that the ultimate decision should be taken by the governing body but with-profits committees should provide the governing body with clearly recorded independent advice. The governing body's decision or response should be minuted. The FSA will require notification in the event of the governing body departing from the with-profit committee's advice on significant issues if the with-profits committee requests the firm does so.

These requirements should also apply to the alternative arrangements used by smaller funds (ie independent persons and non-executive directors).

The FSA states that with-profits committees, the independent person or non-executive director (as applicable) should all have the right to make a reasonable request to obtain external advice, including actuarial advice if they believe that it is necessary to aid their decision making. In shareholder-owned funds they should be able to request this at the shareholder's expense.

One of the issues that has been raised in the past is whether the with-profits actuary should report to the with-profits committee. SUP 4.3.16A requires the with-profits actuary to advise the firm on its use of discretion and to make an annual report to the policyholders. The FSA has decided that the with-profits actuary should advise the firm but it proposes that a provision be included in the terms of reference for with-profits committees, stating that 'all material discretionary actions proposed in relation to the with-profits business of the Company will be discussed by the Committee with the Company's with-profits actuary'.

CHAPTER 7

Prudential regulation

SUMMARY

SECTION 1 INTRODUCTION TO UK PRUDENTIAL REGULATION

A Development of prudential rules

7.1 The main objective of prudential regulation is to try to ensure that insurers have sufficient assets to meet their insurance liabilities. The majority of the prudential regulation the FSA inherited was contained in the Insurance Companies Act 1982 and various insurance companies regulations. Some of this regulation derived directly from EU legislation (eg the First, Second and Third Life Directives now contained in the Consolidated Life Directive[1]). This regulation principally dealt with defining contracts of insurance, specifying a minimum solvency margin and restrictions on the type of business carried on by insurers. It also sought to reinforce the life/non-life divide in terms of the way insurers operate. The FSA introduced its own slightly modified version of these rules in

1 2002/83/EC.

IPRU (INS)[1]. This applied until 31 December 2004 when the FSA introduced the Integrated Prudential Handbook ('PRU'). IPRU (INS) still contains some rules which interact with the other prudential rules.

PRU provided a whole new basis for assessing an insurer's capital requirements (including an obligation to produce its own risk-based assessment) and the assets (including derivatives) that it holds to cover its liabilities and its capital requirements. In addition, much of PRU was taken up with guidance on risk management and in particular the content of risk management policies. PRU also specified capital and other requirements for intermediaries and provided regulation of insurance groups and financial conglomerates (large groups with banking or investment business combined with insurance business).

Although the FSA intended PRU to be an integrated handbook applicable to banking, investment and insurance businesses authorised by the FSA[2], it was only implemented in relation to insurers. At the end of 2006 the FSA moved away from the concept of a single integrated handbook by replacing PRU with GENPRU and INSPRU. GENPRU is applicable to insurers and banking and investment firms. Those parts of PRU which were applicable to insurers only, are now in INSPRU. For consistency the risk management provisions of PRU (other than in relation to liquidity) moved to SYSC.

At the time of writing, the prudential regulation of EU insurance companies is expected to become subject to the Solvency II Directive with effect from 1 January 2013. Solvency II will replace all of the existing EU prudential rules and, in particular, will replace the Consolidated Life Directive. Transitional provisions are anticipated in relation to a number of the key areas to be regulated by Solvency II and there is much work still to be done to establish the detail of the new regime. However, in high level terms it will provide a risk based capital requirement similar to the FSA's current rules. The FSA's current rules are described in Sections 1-7 of this Chapter. A summary of Solvency II is set out in Section 8.

B Overview

7.2 Much of the framework on which the regulation of insurers is currently undertaken is based on requirements similar to those applicable to banks and investment firms. These requirements themselves stem from the Basel Framework (applicable to international banks). The framework can be explained as follows:

Basel 'Three Pillars'

Pillar 1: Provides minimum capital requirements;

Pillar 2: Provides for supervisory review which can lead to a requirement for capital above the minimum capital requirement; and

Pillar 3: Provides for market discipline through greater public disclosure of a firm's capital position.

1 Note parts of IPRU (INS) are still in force.
2 Generally small friendly societies are excluded.

The FSA adopted this framework and introduced the concept of risk-based capital for insurers at the end of 2004. The Pillar 1 requirement for insurers (in FSA terminology, the Capital Resource Requirement) is based on the need to satisfy existing requirements (eg EU legislation). These are described in Section 3. Under Pillar 2, the insurer discusses with the FSA a 'risk'-based assessment of capital; if the FSA is unhappy with this it can provide Individual Capital Guidance (ICG) to the insurer. This process is described in Section 2. Additional transparency and reporting requirements have been introduced as part of the Pillar 3 process.

For life insurers with significant with-profits exposures, a completely new basis for specifying the minimum Pillar 1 capital required, known as the 'twin peaks' basis was introduced by PRU. It is designed to improve transparency in with-profits funds by requiring large with-profits companies to calculate their assets and liabilities on a 'realistic' basis as well as on the standard 'regulatory' basis. The realistic value of liabilities takes into account the value of discretionary benefits (in keeping with customers' reasonable expectations and treating customers fairly) and options in policies. The regulatory calculation is based on the firm's mathematical reserves (contractual and guaranteed amounts); this should in many cases result in the realistic basis of calculating liabilities being higher than the regulatory basis. The life company is obliged to hold assets in the with-profits fund itself and capital based on whichever is the higher of the realistic and regulatory calculation of liabilities, hence the phrase twin peaks.

At the Pillar 2 level, insurers produce their own assessment of the risks they face and the capital they need to cover those risks. Unlike the Pillar 1 calculations of liabilities and assets which may not be produced on a market consistent basis the intention is for the Pillar 2 basis to be a realistic one. Insurers are required to produce an Individual Capital Assessment (ICA). INSPRU 7 specifies a prescribed basis on which the risk assessment must be shown (ie it is calculated based on a 99.5% probability of being able to cover its liabilities over a one year period). This is said to equate to a risk rating of BBB. For many insurers this will also be seen as a 'minimum' capital reporting requirement, as in managing their business, they will specify a higher threshold (normally in terms of a probability over a longer period than one year or an acceptance of risk tied to a credit rating higher than BBB – see **7.6**).

The Solvency II Directive will produce a similar but different regime. It is similar in terms of its risk based approach but it is different in that it will prescribe a basis for calculating an insurer's minimum (ie Pillar 1) capital requirement using a risk based standard model. Subject to regulatory approval, insurers may be able to use their own internal models instead to calculate all or part of their solvency capital requirement under Solvency II.

SECTION 2 RISK MANAGEMENT AND LEGAL RISK ISSUES

A Risk based capital requirements

7.3 The FSA's main requirement in GENPRU 1.2.26 (the 'Overall Financial Adequacy Rule') is that a firm (eg UK insurer or branch authorised by the FSA) must at all times maintain overall adequate financial resources, including capital and liquidity resources which are adequate both as to amount and quality, to ensure there is no significant risk that its liabilities cannot be met as they fall due. A firm must maintain appropriate processes, strategies and systems to enable it to identify and assess the risks of being unable to meet its liabilities as they fall due. It must manage those risks and the amount and type of financial resources the firm should hold to cover risk. The requirement to maintain such systems and controls is the 'Overall Pillar 2 Rule' which is found in GENPRU 1.2.30. The firm's assessment of risk should be proportionate to the nature, scale and complexity of its activities.

The processes and systems used by a firm to assess the adequacy of its financial resources must enable it to identify and assess how to deal with the major sources of risk to its ability to meet its liabilities as they fall due. These will include, but are not limited to, the following major sources of prudential risk:

(1) *Credit risk*: risk of loss resulting from another party failing to perform its financial obligations or failing to perform them in a timely manner.

(2) *Market risk*: risk of loss arising from fluctuations in the values of, or income from, assets, interest rates or exchange rates.

(3) *Liquidity risk*: risk of loss resulting from the inability to convert assets into cash in a timely manner and without excessive cost.

(4) *Operational risk*: risk of loss resulting from inadequate or failed internal processes, people or systems or from external events including legal risk.

(5) *Insurance risk*: risk of loss resulting from inherent uncertainties regarding the occurrence, amount and timing of insurance liabilities.

Firms may also be exposed to group risk (eg from other entities in their group or from the group financial position), concentration risk, residual risk, securitisation risk, business risk, interest rate risk and pension obligation risk. Insurers may be subject to residual risk to the extent that any credit mitigation techniques used are not as effective as anticipated. Pensions obligation risk is also normally an issue for insurers. The explanation of pensions obligation risk in GENPRU 1.2.31 is very wide, including contractual and moral obligations to employees of related companies. This may be because of its applicability to banks and investment firms but the FSA also refers to potential obligations due to action taken by the Pensions Regulator (eg contribution notices). Because of INSPRU 1.5.13, insurers need to be very careful in their dealings with group pension schemes to make clear to the trustees that they are not, and cannot be liable for, any pensions costs of group company employees other than to the extent of services provided to the insurer. This should help to mitigate any extension of the insurer's own pension obligation risk. It is, however, possible (see further below in relation to stress and scenario testing), that life insurers could end up having to hold additional capital in respect of this risk (eg if that risk is held within its group). Another area of potential exposure for life insurers is business risk which is described as the risk of not being able to carry out its business plan because of changes in its business, including risk arising from its remuneration policy.

Concentration risk (eg the risk of holding too much of one type of asset), securitisation (eg the risk that capital held in respect of assets a firm has securitised are inadequate because there has not been sufficient risk transfer) and interest rate risk, are normally an issue for banks.

7.4 For each major source of risk identified by it, the firm must carry out appropriate stress tests and scenario analyses. Stress tests look at how the insurer's position is affected by an adverse occurrence or set of circumstances, such as falling equity values, systems problems or legal uncertainty. Scenario tests look at the effect of multiple occurrences at the same time (eg falling equity values, rising interest rates and a catastrophic external event). The idea is that the insurer builds in appropriate contingency funds for the happening of events which the insurer regards as foreseeable[1] even if unlikely. These must include a broad range of stresses and scenarios including some over a protracted period and which are sudden and severe. This should include reverse stress testing whereby the firm works out the scenarios that could cause it to fail and effectively works backwards in assessing risk and appropriate responses. Potential application of stress tests to insurers might include:

(1) *Credit risk*: firms should consider the effect of non-payment of reinsurance or other debtors such as intermediaries or policyholders (see also INSPRU 2.1).

(2) *Market risk*: firms should allow for reduced market values of investments, variations in interest rates, a lower level of investment income than planned and the possibility of counterparty default (see also INSPRU 3.1 and SYSC 16).

(3) *Liquidity risk*: firms should consider their cash-flow position and ability to withstand sharp, unexpected outflows of funds, via claims or an unexpected drop in premium (see also INSPRU 4.1).

(4) *Operational risk*: factors to consider should include reputational risk, including damage to brand, marketing and distribution risks and the impact of legal risk (see INSPRU 5.1).

(5) *Insurance risk*: firms should consider the potential for catastrophic loss, the cost of reinstatement premiums and reinsurance exhaustion. Other factors will differ depending on the business actually written (see also SYSC 17).

In its focus on risk management and the effect on capital, the FSA has effectively created a real cost for poor risk management. This is probably most novel in concept when applied to operational risks; (for example, poor systems or inadequate staff can now have a capital implication for a firm). Also, whilst firms can generally mitigate risk by holding appropriate loss-absorbing capital, this will not always be possible and the firm may need instead to rectify the underlying issue.

1 GENPRU 1.2.42 require an appropriate range of adverse circumstances.

7.5 As part of the minimum, Pillar 1 requirements, firms are required by INSPRU 3.1 to calculate a risk capital requirement ('RCR')[1]. This is an additional amount of capital held to cover specified market-related risks (such as falls in the value of equities and property). This calculation (the 'resilience reserves') was formerly part of the mathematical reserves (ie calculation of the amount held to cover its future liabilities). When carrying out its risk-based capital assessment, a firm should consider the extent to which the market risk scenarios set out in INSPRU 3.1 are appropriate to the nature of its asset portfolio. A firm may conclude that it needs to apply further stress tests and/or test other forms of assets. The RCR should therefore be a *starting point* for the firm in assessing its own risk-based capital requirement and this is consistent with it forming part of the minimum capital requirements specified by GENPRU 2.

As part of its Pillar 2 activities, the FSA will review a firm's capital against the minimum capital requirements and the firm's own risk-based assessment. The FSA will also look at the extent to which senior managers have been involved in the risk assessment process. FSA guidance[2] indicates that it will consider the results of other (ie economic capital or sophisticated modelling) techniques provided that the major risks are identified and that the model calculates the effect on a firm's financial position where they crystallise (or are assumed with a particular probability to crystallise). This could in theory (perhaps if there is significant diversification) lead to a lower capital requirement than would otherwise apply.

B ICA and reporting to the FSA

7.6 The FSA defines its rules relating to the Overall Pillar 2 Rule[3], its rules on stress and scenario testing[4] and the need to document the risk capital assessments made[5] as the 'ICAAP Rules'. Although this terminology is used in the rules in relation to insurers, the assessment for insurers is known and documented as an ICA, see **7.7**. The ICAAP Rules can apply on a solo or consolidated/group basis. GENPRU 1.2.45 provides that if an insurer is a member of an insurance group (as defined for the purposes of the IGD – see **7.44**), the ICAAP rules apply to it on a consolidated basis (ie to show the group position) and do not apply to it on a solo basis. Conversely, INSPRU 1.2.47 provides that if they do not apply on a consolidated basis, the ICAAP Rules do apply on a solo basis. As there may be more than one firm subject to the requirement to provide the risk based capital assessment on a consolidated basis, GENPRU 1.2.54 provides that a firm may adopt the assessment prepared by another member of its group. In GENPRU 1.2.55 the FSA sets out guidance in relation to this requirement. The FSA explains that the purposes of the risk capital assessment on a consolidated

1 Under INSPRU this applies only to the regulatory calculation.
2 INSPRU 7.1.93.
3 GENPRU 1.2.30-1.2.39.
4 GENPRU 1.2.42.
5 GENPRU 1.2.60-61.

basis is to enable the FSA to assess the extent to which the individual companies in the group would have a higher capital requirement if they were not part of the group. It should also be remembered that whether or not a risk capital assessment is undertaken at the group level, the Overall Financial Adequacy rule in GENPRU 1.2.26 (ie overriding requirement to maintain sufficient capital) applies on a solo basis and a consolidated basis, if appropriate.

7.7 Insurers are subject to specific requirements in relation to reporting their risk capital assessments to the FSA. These are set out in INSPRU 7 and the assessment is called the 'Individual Capital Assessment' or 'ICA'. These provisions provide the basis on which the assessment must be carried out and specify that the assessment must include the prescribed basis (ie at a confidence level of 99.5% over a one year period[1]). This is stated to be required whether or not the firm uses this confidence level in its own assessment of internal capital and it is worth noting that this is also the confidence level used in the Solvency II Directive. The FSA states that it will use the ICA assessment in its review of a firm's resources to assess whether the minimum Capital Resource Requirement (CRR) see Section 3, is appropriate. This review will include the assessment and the processes and systems by which that assessment is made[2]. The advantage of the risk-based assessment of capital held is that firms may consider forms of capital other than those complying with the capital resources table in accordance with GENPRU 2.2.17 and described in Section 4. A firm must be able to explain and justify its reliance on other forms of capital[3].

INSPRU 7 mainly provides guidance in relation to the ICA process. First, the FSA explains that the need to carry out a risk based review of capital (both required and available) is a standalone requirement to the obligation to carry out stress and scenario testing. This means that where appropriate to a company's size, or the nature of complexity of its business, a firm may choose to carry out its ICA in another way[4]. For firms which are realistic basis life firms (which are required to hold an ECR (see **7.17**)), the ECR will also be a relevant consideration. In broad terms the ICA needs to demonstrate to the FSA that the firm holds sufficient capital to make planned investments and take on new business (within an appropriate planning horizon). It also needs to ensure that if a firm had to close to new business, it would have sufficient assets to be able to meet its liabilities. The FSA states that 'the costs of writing new business, the expenses incurred in servicing all liabilities, including liabilities to new policyholders and the nature of intra-group arrangements and reinsurance arrangements, should be considered as part of the assessment as well as the costs that would be incurred in the event of closure to new business'[5]. In calculating its assets a firm should only rely on assets held outside the firm where it has a right to call on them[6].

1 INSPRU 7.1.42.
2 INSPRU 7.1.6.
3 INSPRU 7.17.
4 INSPRU 7.1.10.
5 INSPRU 7.1.16.
6 INSPRU 7.1.24.

Similarly, a firm should only rely on management actions (eg to reduce its liabilities or capital requirement) where it has considered any preconditions to taking such action, including satisfying itself that such actions are consistent with its regulatory obligations (eg the FSA's Principles for Business)[1]. They should also be consistent with its own systems and controls[2].

The FSA also explains that the value of assets used for the purposes of the ICA should be a realistic one which, where possible, should be on a mark to market basis. The valuation of liabilities should also be on a realistic basis and not contain explicit margins for risk[3].

If a firm selects a confidence level other than the prescribed one, in that it has a longer time horizon, it may, provided it can justify doing so, use a lower probability than 99.5%[4]. When it documents its ICA, the firm needs to show the basis (assumptions, methodologies and results) of the assessment at the prescribed 99.5% one year confidence level and identify the major differences between that assessment and other assessments carried out by the firm using a different confidence level[5]. Understanding this written record of the prescribed assessment and major differences between this and other assessments is key to the FSA's understanding of the firm's risk and capital management processes. Although the ICA process is described at the solo level, INSPRU 7 also applies to the capital assessment of a group at the consolidated level referred to in **7.6** above.

C Systems and controls

7.8 The risk-based capital assessment required in GENPRU 1.2 is only part of the Pillar 2 process. Firms are also required to design and maintain systems and controls to ensure that senior management can make business planning and risk management decisions based on accurate information about risks and financial resources. These systems and controls (eg including risk policies) have been a very visible result of the introduction of risk based capital requirements in the UK.

SYSC 14 is made up predominantly of guidance, much of which reinforces other FSA Handbook provisions. The main 'requirement' flowing from SYSC 14 is to maintain, document and communicate appropriately a business plan, including individual risk management policies, in relation to the prudential risks set out above (see **7.3**). These policies need to set out the firm's appetite and tolerance for the risk in question. SYSC gives specific detailed guidance as to the content of each such risk management policy and to recommend other courses of action. Certain actions underpin each of the individual risk policies. In the FSA's view these are: use of risk management committees; management information adequate to enable proper oversight of the business and which is

1 INSPRU 7.1.26.
2 INSPRU 7.1.27; INSPRU 7.1.61.
3 INSPRU 7.1.36-38.
4 INSPRU 7.1.45.
5 INSPRU 7.1.49.

provided on a timely basis[1]; creation of separate risk assessment and internal audit functions; and appropriate segregation of duties for individuals. In addition, adequate internal controls must be in place to ensure the firm's business plan and risk management systems operate as expected to mitigate risks which can reasonably be foreseen. Firms are specifically directed, when considering the adequacy of their internal controls, to look at how they manage delegated (including outsourced) activities and are reminded of the guidance in SYSC 13.9 on outsourcing.

The impact of this formalisation of risk management in insurance companies has been enormous. The FSA's guidance about what should be in each risk policy is detailed. In some areas, the guidance covers issues that might also be dealt with by specific rules or which are designed to fit in with other FSA initiatives (eg treating customers fairly). For example, the insurance risk policy is expected to cover the firm's approach to pricing long-term insurance contracts including the determination of the appropriate level of any reviewable premiums[2].

The insurance risk policy and the operational risk policy are those most likely to cut across legal issues[3] (see **7.12**). The insurance risk policy requires firms to understand and manage legal risk in its policy documentation and its claims management process. Management of reinsurance exposures is also a key part of this. Non-insurance related legal risk (such as risk inherent in the systems and personnel of the firm) is normally dealt with as part of operational risk.

D Legal risk and the legal risk policy

7.9 Legal risk can be a significant part of an insurer's business (for example, contractual issues with policies and operational risk arising from the way the company operates). Similarly, changes in the business and legal environment can affect the nature of the underlying risks a firm is seeking to manage. As a transitional measure prior to the introduction of PRU, the FSA specified[4] what it considered legal risk to be and how it expected firms to manage it. Legal risk was defined as follows:

> 'Definition of Legal Risk:
>
> the risk that the law is proved to operate in a way adverse to the interests or objectives of the insurer where the insurer: did not consider its effect; believed its effect to be different; or operated with uncertainty as to its effect'.

1 In order to be useful, management information needs to be timely. The FSA guidance implicitly accepts that a balance will sometimes need to be struck in sacrificing an appropriate degree of accuracy for timeliness. Whilst in practice getting the balance right might be tricky, the information must enable a decision to be taken in time to control or mitigate the risk.

2 Rules on setting premiums at sustainable rates are included in INSPRU 1.1.42.

3 See also PS140 and the transitional arrangements for PRU.

4 CP150/PS140 and subsequently the relevant Handbook Instrument (the interim Prudential Sourcebook Insurers (Systems and Controls) Instrument 2002).

Similarly, the FSA specified systems and controls that insurers should put in place to deal with legal risk. These were as follows:

> 'C1 Insurers should have processes for identifying which legal risks the business is exposed to, including: risks in existing products, including those where the interpretation of contracts could be challenged; the risk that a change in legislation may be overlooked or inadequately responded to; uncertainties surrounding existing or forthcoming court rulings; and risks in enforcing contracts with third parties, particularly reinsurance contracts.
>
> C2 Insurers should also have processes for controlling (where possible) the risks that have been identified.
>
> C3 There should be processes for reporting identified legal risks to the risk assessment function, risk committee, senior management and the "governing body".
>
> C4 There should be processes for raising appropriate provisions against legal risk.
>
> C5 Regular reviews of legal risk within the business units, including risk relating to new products, investment activities and reinsurance, should be undertaken.'

7.10 These requirements and related guidance are now a bit scattered around the FSA's rules. Some are specified in relation to the insurance risk policy, and others pervade a number of the other risks such as operational risk, market risk and liquidity risk. One of the aims of a legal risk policy is to identify the sources of legal risk and to ensure that they are monitored and managed appropriately.

As legal risk in products can result from general changes in the law, SYSC 17.1.12 provides that the identification of insurance risk should normally include:

(1) processes for identifying business environment changes (for example, landmark legal rulings) and for collecting internal and external data to test and modify business plans;

(2) processes at the point of sale for identifying potential claims for mis-selling;

(3) processes after the point of sale for identifying potential and emerging claims for the purposes of claims management and claims provisioning.

This could include:

(a) identifying possible judicial rulings;

(b) keeping up to date with developments in market practice; and

(c) collecting information on industry-wide initiatives and settlements.

Firms will therefore need to be able to show how they monitor existing and future changes in the law and market practice and the process for dealing with them. This would normally be included in the firm's legal risk policy.

Management of legal risk can also involve establishment of a legal risk committee or sub-committee of the risk committee. The legal risk policy may specify referral arrangements to such a committee or specify how the committee interacts with other risk committees. It is difficult to anticipate in advance the legal risk a firm may face. Legal risk policies sometimes seek to deal with this by specifying engagement arrangements (eg to help the relevant business areas to establish the types of issue which require legal advice or input). As every risk cannot be catered for in advance, it is also advisable to raise awareness of legal risk within the organisation and include the issue of raising awareness in the legal risk policy. As with other risk policies, the legal risk policy should provide for audit of the policy and for it to be reviewed periodically.

7.11 The areas where the FSA either explicitly or implicitly require legal input and which a legal risk policy would need to cover include the following:

(1) risk resulting from the business environment or changes to it; the need to review policy and other contractual wording and to have appropriate controls for new product development;

(2) the need for legal input into reinsurance arrangements and appropriate assessment of risk transfer;

(3) the need to document agency/delegation of underwriting authority and outsourcing arrangements to comply with FSA rules;

(4) the need to monitor and act on developments in the law (including judicial rulings and prospective UK and EU legislation);

(5) managing litigation and claims and ensuring remedial action is taken when appropriate in light of past experience;

(6) ensuring documents securing collateral or guarantees or mitigating credit risk are valid and enforceable on an ongoing basis;

(7) ensuring documentation or arrangements relied upon to provide liquidity (including, for example, securitisations) is adequate and fit for the purpose;

(8) ensuring appropriate categorisation of capital into the relevant regulatory tiers; and

(9) appropriate categorisation of admissible asset categories and interpretation of counterparty limits (including, in particular, the rules relating to 'approved derivative contracts').

Items 1, 2, and 3 are considered further below. 'Categorisation of assets' and 'tiers of capital' are considered in Sections 5 and 4 respectively.

1 Policy documents

7.12 As what an insurance company sells depends on what it describes in its product documentation, the FSA focuses, as part of insurance risk, on the need to review and develop policy documentation. Provisions in SYSC 17.1.30 require firms to pay close attention to the wording of their policy documentation and to consider: whether they have adequate in-house legal resources; the need for periodic independent legal review of policy documentation; the use of standardised documentation and referral procedures for variation of terms; reviewing the documentation used by other insurance companies ('peer review'); revising documentation for new policies in the light of past experience; and the operation of law in the jurisdiction of the policyholder. These requirements are similar to the transitional arrangements referred to in **7.9** above and it is worth noting both the ongoing nature of the peer review and the desirability of periodic external assessment.

In addition, SYSC 17.1.9 requires a firm as part of its insurance risk policy to consider its approach to the exercise of any discretion available in its long-term insurance contracts (eg in relation to charges or the level of benefits payable), bearing in mind applicable legal and regulatory constraints, the inclusion of options in its new long-term insurance contracts and the possible exercise by policyholders of options on existing contracts. These issues should also form part of any process for reviewing policy documentation.

2 *Reinsurance*

7.13 If firms wish to take appropriate credit for reinsurance they need to ensure that reinsurance arrangements pass risk as they should, and do not distort the apparent financial condition of the insurer[1]. In SYSC 17 the FSA emphasises the need for legal assistance in putting reinsurance in place. A firm's insurance risk policy should also therefore include:

(1) the firm's approach to the use of reinsurance or the use of some other means of risk transfer; and

(2) how the firm intends to assess the effectiveness of its risk transfer arrangements and manage the residual or transferred risks (for example, how it intends to handle disputes over contract wordings, potential payout delays and counterparty performance risks).

In addition, SYSC 17.1.34 provides that before entering into or significantly changing a reinsurance agreement, or any other form of insurance risk transfer agreement, a firm should 'ensure there are adequate legal checking procedures in respect of the draft agreement' and understand the nature and limits of the agreement. Particular attention should be given to the wording of contracts to ensure that all of the required risks are covered, that the level of available cover is appropriate, and that all the terms, conditions and warranties are unambiguous and understood.

3 *Agency, underwriting and outsourcing*

7.14 The actual management of claims falls within insurance risk and an insurer should have processes to monitor both the volume and type of claim

1 See INSPRU 1.19A.

(including fraudulent claims) and potential sources of group claim. In relation to assessment of the validity of claims, the FSA recommends 'procedures' to determine when experts such as lawyers should be used.

A firm will also, as part of its operational risk, be exposed to potential litigation from a number of sources and receive complaints from customers about actions of the firm or its staff. The FSA is keen for lessons learnt from previous disputes, claims or complaints to be reflected in future operations and documentation. It will look for a process to communicate such lessons learnt to all the appropriate areas of the business.

7.15 Another area of risk in the operation of many insurers is delegation to others. For UK insurers this often arises in relation to sales and outsourcing. There is a risk in any form of delegation or outsourcing that the delegate may either not perform as expected or may commit the firm to potential liabilities that it would not itself have been prepared to accept. In general terms, the effect of the provisions of SYSC is that such delegations should be documented in such a way as to make clear the extent of the delegation and the respective responsibilities of the parties (including details of any underwriting limits for employees). Firms must also consider the provisions of Chapter 3 of SYSC relating to operational systems and controls and the FSA's guidance on outsourcing (SYSC 13.9).

E Adequate records

7.16 A firm is required[1] to take reasonable care to make and retain records to ensure that adequate information is available regarding its financial situation and business activities. A firm must make, regularly update and retain accounting and other records for at least three years. These must be sufficient to enable the firm to demonstrate its financial position and exposure to risk and that the firm is financially sound with appropriate systems and controls. The records must be kept in the UK unless they relate to business carried on outside the UK in which case they can be kept in that country, but an adequate summary of the records must periodically be sent to the UK.

SECTION 3 PILLAR 1 CAPITAL REQUIREMENTS

7.17 GENPRU specifies a minimum level of 'capital' which a firm must hold in addition to the assets it is required to hold to cover its potential liabilities to policyholders (ie the Pillar 1 capital requirement). The absolute minimum level of capital is that required to comply with EU requirements (the 'Minimum Capital Requirement'). The FSA has modified the EU minimum capital requirements for large with-profits life insurers (the 'Enhanced Capital Requirement'). Further capital may also need to be held as a result of the firm's risk-based assessment of its capital requirements or Individual Capital Guidance from the FSA (ie the Pillar 2 requirement) (see Section 2 above.)

1 By SYSC 3.2.30.

The Minimum Capital Requirement[1] applies to all insurers including pure reinsurers unless the insurer is within stated exceptions[2]. A separate calculation is required for composite insurers in respect of their long-term and general business. A composite firm may use excess assets held in respect of its general business to cover its long-term business capital requirements but may not use long-term assets to cover its general business capital requirements.

The Pillar 1 requirement to hold a specified minimum level of capital is expressed in the FSA Rules as the Capital Resource Requirement (the 'CRR')[3]. The amount of the CRR varies depending on the type of business carried on. For life assurers other than large with-profits insurers, the minimum capital requirement is the Minimum Capital Requirement (MCR). For large with-profit insurers, which for this purpose means firms having with-profits liabilities of £500m or more[4], the CRR is the Enhanced Capital Requirement (ECR). Such firms are known as *realistic*-based or *twin peaks* life firms. Firms with lower with-profits liabilities may opt in to the requirement to maintain an Enhanced Capital Requirement[5].

The CRR requirements are set out in GENPRU 2.1.14 to 2.1.39 but may be broadly summarised as follows:

Capital Resource Requirement (CRR)	(for non-twin peaks firms) Equals MCR
	(for twin peaks firms) Higher of MCR and ECR
Minimum Capital Requirement (MCR)	Higher of:
	• base requirement; and
	• sum of LTICR and RCR[6]. The LTICR is made up of:
	• insurance death risk capital component[7]; and
	• insurance health risk capital component[8]; and
	• insurance expense risk component[9]; and
	• insurance market risk capital component[10]

1 In GENPRU 2.1.
2 In GENPRU 2.1.1.
3 In GENPRU 2.1.
4 As at 31/12/2004.
5 GENPRU 2.1.20.
6 INSPRU 3.1.10.
7 INSPRU 1.1.81.
8 INSPRU 1.1.85.
9 INSPRU 1.1.88
10 INSPRU 1.1.89.

Enhanced Capital Requirement (ECR)[1]	Sum of:
	LTICR[2]
	with-profit insurance capital component[3] (WPICC)

The 'base requirement' is the EU requirement and is set out in GENPRU 2.1.30. For a large with-profits proprietary company it is currently €3.2m.

7.18 The Risk Capital Requirement (RCR) forms part of the calculation of the minimum capital required. The purpose of the RCR is to ensure that capital is set aside to mitigate the potential effect of market risk on the insurer's asset and liability position. It works by applying a specified level of market movement (eg in relation to equities, fixed interest securities and real properties) to the insurer's assets and liabilities. Where the result is that the insurer's assets would be less than its liabilities, it is required to cover that amount by holding it as a capital reserve. The basis for calculating the RCR is specified in INSPRU 3.1.10 with the factors set out in INSPRU 3.1.16 to 3.1.26. A slightly different basis is assumed for significant interests outside the United Kingdom. It also includes provision to deal with temporary situations by including some averaging in the factors used (eg over 90 days).

A realistic basis life company will, as part of its realistic calculation, also have to calculate a Risk Capital Margin ('RCM'). This can be confusing as the RCM covers market risk in a similar way to the Risk Capital Requirement. However, the RCM also covers credit risk and persistency risk.

The With-Profit Insurance Capital Component ('WPICC') is calculated as the amount by which the regulatory surplus exceeds the realistic surplus. This can also be confusing as it is expressed in relation to 'surplus' rather than liabilities. Generally, for with-profits business, the realistic surplus should be less than the regulatory surplus because the realistic liabilities plus the RCM should be higher than the regulatory liabilities, plus the fund's share of the LTICR and RCR. The flowchart in INSPRU Annex 1G sets out the calculation clearly.

SECTION 4 TIERS OF CAPITAL

A Summary of Capital Resources

7.19 The capital an insurer can hold to cover its Capital Resource Requirement is divided into categories or 'tiers' which reflect differences in the extent to which the capital instrument meets the characteristics of permanency and loss

1 PRU also required (4.2.9) the addition of the RCR but this was removed from 31 December 2006.
2 INSPRU 1.1.80.
3 INSPRU 1.3.

absorbency. The best form of capital (Core Tier 1), which includes permanent share capital, can be used without limit. Other capital instruments which are either not perpetual or which contain cumulative obligations fall into other tiers.

There are two tiers of capital applicable to insurers, Tier 1 and Tier 2. There will be three tiers of capital, known as 'Own Funds' under Solvency II. The current Tier 1 capital is divided into three types (Core, Perpetual non-cumulative preference shares and Innovative Tier 1). Tier 2 capital is divided into two types (Upper and Lower Tier 2 capital). Other forms of capital may be used with the FSA's consent in the form of a waiver. This may include implicit items (See GENPRU 2 Annex 8). A firm's total capital resources are broadly calculated as the Tier 1 and 2 capital[1] less specified deductions. The deductions include inadmissible assets and assets in excess of counterparty or asset limits set out in GENPRU 2.1.22.

The characteristics for Tier 1 and Tier 2 capital are set out in GENPRU 2.2.9 to 11. The following table is a guide to the basic types of capital and their limits.

Tier of capital	**Examples**	**Limit**
Tier 1		
Core Tier 1	Permanent share capital (ordinary shares, paid-up contribution by a member to a mutual, part of a mutual's initial fund) Reserves Share premium account Verified interim net profits Positive valuation differences Fund for future appropriations	Unlimited
Perpetual non-cumulative preference shares	Perpetual non-cumulative preference shares	50% of MCR
Innovative Tier 1	Capital instruments Innovative tier 1 instruments	15% of total tier
Tier 2		
Upper Tier 2	Perpetual cumulative preference shares Perpetual subordinated debt Perpetual subordinated securities	50% of total capital resources
Lower Tier 2	Fixed term preference shares Fixed term subordinated debt Fixed term subordinated securities	50% of total capital resources
Other capital – waiver required	Unpaid share capital	25% of total capital resources
	Unpaid initial funds and calls for supplementary contributions Implicit terms	50% of total resources

1 Plus specified positive adjustments.

GENPRU 2.2.24 to 41 set out additional restrictions as follows:

(1) at least 50% of a firm's MCR must be made up of Core Tier 1 capital and perpetual non-cumulative preference shares (less deductions from Tier 1 capital);

(2) life companies are required to meet the higher of 1/3 of the LTICR and the base requirement (see GENPRU 2.2.34 and 2.2.41) with Core Tier 1 capital and Upper and Lower Tier 2 capital (less deductions from Tier 1 capital); and

(3) a firm's Tier 2 capital resources must not exceed its Tier 1 capital resources.

B Tier I Capital

7.20 Tier 1 capital instruments must satisfy the requirements in GENPRU 2.2.64. These include rules on coupons, redeemability and connected transactions. The purpose of these rules is to ensure that the instrument is adequately sub-ordinated (ie to rank no higher than an ordinary share) and that it cannot except in specified circumstances, be redeemed. Insurers also have access to a form of Core Tier 1 capital which results from positive valuation differences. If positive, 'valuation differences' are added to capital resources but, if negative, they must be deducted[1]. A valuation difference will occur when the FSA's regulatory treatment produces a different effect to the accounting basis used for financial reporting. A good example of this is securitisations of future profit where, the FSA allows insurers not to include as liabilities, payments to be made by the insurer which are dependent on the actual emergence of profit[2]. Insurers also benefit from amounts needed, pursuant to the insurance accounts rules, in the fund for future appropriations. This will cover amounts which have not been allocated to either shareholders or policyholders by the year end.

C Innovative Tier I capital

7.21 The concept of 'Innovative Tier 1' capital is intended to cover instruments which are likely (for example, because of their terms), to be redeemed and therefore not provide the desired permanency required for Core Tier 1 capital. For this reason, Innovative Tier 1 capital is limited to 15% of the total Tier 1 capital and it is important to recognise instruments which are likely to be redeemed. One indication that an instrument is innovative is when the instrument includes what the FSA refer to as a 'step up', such as an instrument marketed as a perpetual instrument which allows the issuer to increase the coupon (step-up is also relevant to the characteristics of Tier 2 instruments, see GENPRU 2.2.151). The table below reproduces the FSA's guidance in CP190 comparing typical characteristics of a Tier 1 innovative instrument with an ordinary share (which is

1 GENPRU 2.2.105 and 2.2 Annex 1.
2 See INSPRU 1.2.79.

Core Tier 1 capital). This comparative analysis gives a good indication of the likely characteristics of Innovative Tier 1 capital.

Characteristic	**Ordinary share**	**Innovative instrument**
Accounting treatment	Equity	Liability
Coupon payments	At the sole discretion of directors	May be deferred with any deferred coupons payable only in shares
Maturity	Cannot be redeemed	No specific redemption date but terms may include an issuer call which may coincide with an increase in the coupon
Subordination	Junior to all other claims	Normally ranks pari passu with preference shares
Ability to extinguish losses	Fully absorbs losses	Loss absorbency could be achieved by means of conversion into shares at predetermined trigger event

A Tier 1 instrument can only include a 'step-up' if it is moderate[1]. The FSA explains this requirement in GENPRU 2.2.148. Use of an Innovative Tier 1 instrument requires a legal opinion from an appropriately qualified individual.

D Tier 2 Capital

7.22 The characteristics that identify Tier 2 instruments are either a requirement to make a payment (eg coupon) or a fixed duration. Tier 2 is split into Upper Tier 2 and Lower Tier 2. Only perpetual instruments are Upper Tier 2 instruments, with all dated instruments being Lower Tier 2. GENPRU 2.2.159 sets out the conditions that need to be satisfied for Tier 2 capital instruments. These include the rules on sub-ordination, redeemability, and connected transactions. Additional requirements apply separately to each category of Tier 2 capital[2]. In addition the rules on steps-ups in GENPRU 2.2.175 also apply to Tier 2 capital. As with the rules for Tier 1 capital, these rules seek to ensure that the instrument will be available to absorb losses (ie controlling the basis on which it can be redeemed or amended and requiring it to be appropriately sub-ordinated). Insurers carrying a with-profits business also need to ensure sub-ordination to the fair treatment of with-profits policyholders in order to protect their expectation in relation to future discretionary benefits[3]. An independent legal opinion

1 GENPRU 2.2.147.
2 See GENPRU 2.2.177-184 and GENPRU 2.2.194.
3 GENPRU 2.2.271.

from an appropriately qualified individual is also required (other than in relation to perpetual cumulative preference shares).

E Other capital

7.23 Other forms of capital require a waiver from the FSA.

SECTION 5 VALUATION AND ADMISSIBLE ASSETS

A Valuation

7.24 One of the FSA's stated aims in the consultation process for PRU was to simplify the asset valuation rules for insurers and to create a more explicit link to relevant credit or market risk. Formerly the IPRU (INS) rules set out in detail how to value particular assets. The current rules mainly defer to accounting rules/practices and standards or market prices which will apply unless otherwise stated[1]. This means that the insurance accounts rules and accounting treatment will normally determine the value a company can place on its assets. Shares in and debts due from related undertakings are treated differently. GENPRU 1.3.3 provides specific adjustments and GENPRU 1.3.6 provides for the possibility of a waiver to permit positive valuation differences for UK ISPVs.

7.25 Unless GENPRU or INSPRU provide another method of valuation, 'marking to market', 'marking to model', 'independent price verification', or 'adjustment or reserves' apply. Marking to market must generally be used to value investments and derivatives[2]. This can cause problems when markets are spiralling downwards. GENPRU 1.3.15-16 provide the basis for marking to market. When marking to market is not possible, a firm must use 'mark to model' which means it uses a model and market data to calculate what the price should be[3]. Independent price verification involves market prices or model inputs being verified for accuracy and independence. A firm may need to consider adjustments or reserves in relation to, for example, early termination costs, future funding or administrative costs. Unless the basis for doing so is set out elsewhere in the FSA's rules, this must be done in accordance with GENPRU 1.3.33. If such an adjustment is made it needs to be disclosed to the FSA in the firm's prudential returns.

Solvency II will change the basis on which insurers value their liabilities. It will also change the rules on asset admissibility and counterparty limits. These will be replaced by the 'prudent person principle' which places the emphasis for managing asset quality and counterparty risk on the insurer. Such risk should

1 GENPRU 1.3.
2 GENPRU 1.3.14.
3 GENPRU 1.3.17-25.

then be reflected in the Solvency Capital Requirement (SCR). Where a firm uses the standard formula to calculate SCR. Solvency II may include some quantitative limits on counterparty exposures.

B Admissible assets

7.26 Once an asset (other than one held to cover property linked liabilities[1]) has been valued appropriately, it needs to satisfy the requirement to be admissible. GENPRU 2.2.17 and GENPRU 2 Annex 1R require a deduction from a firm's capital resources in respect of inadmissible assets. INSPRU 1.1.20 requires a firm to ensure that its technical provisions are covered by admissible assets. Technical provisions are a firm's on-balance sheet provisions for liabilities under its insurance contracts. For life business, technical provisions will be the mathematical reserves which are actuarial estimates of a firm's liabilities in respect of future benefits due to policyholders.

Life companies carrying on with-profits business must cover the technical provisions in each of their with-profits funds with admissible assets. The requirement that assets be admissible therefore applies to cover the firm's liabilities and its Pillar 1 obligations (other than the realistic calculation for twin peak firms). A realistic basis life firm[2] must also ensure that the realistic value of assets in each of its with-profits funds is at least equal to the realistic value of liabilities in that fund but the assets need not be admissible or comply with the counterparty limits[3].

To be admissible the asset must appear on the list of admissible assets which is set out in GENPRU 2 Annex 7R and reproduced below:

(1) Investments that are, or amounts owed arising from the disposal of:

- (a) *debt securities*, bonds and other money and capital market instruments;
- (b) loans;
- (c) *shares* and other variable yield participations;
- (d) *units* in *UCITS schemes, non-UCITS retail schemes, recognised schemes* and any other *collective investment scheme* where the insurer's investment is sufficiently small to be consistent with a prudent overall investment strategy)[4];
- (e) land, buildings and immovable property rights;
- (f) an *approved derivative* or *quasi-derivative* transaction that satisfies the conditions in INSPRU 3.2.5R or an approved stock lending transaction that satisfies the conditions INSPRU 3.2.36.

1 GENPRU 2.2.251.
2 One with with-profits liabilities of £500m as at 31/12/04.
3 INSPRU 1.1.28 and 1.1.29.
4 Having regard to the investment policy of the scheme and the information available to the insurer to enable it to monitor the investment risk being taken by the scheme (Annex 7 1(d)(iv)).

(2) Debts and claims:

(a) debt owed by *reinsurers*, including *reinsurers'* shares of technical provisions[1];

(b) deposits with and debt owned by ceding *undertakings*;

(c) debts owed by *policyholders* and *intermediaries* arising out of direct and *reinsurance* operations (except where overdue for more than three months and other than *commission* prepaid to agents or intermediaries);

(d) for *general insurance business* only, claims arising out of salvage and subrogation;

(e) for *long-term insurance business* only, advances secured on, and not exceeding the *surrender value* of, *long-term insurance contracts* issued by the insurer;

(f) tax recoveries;

(g) claims against *compensation* funds.

(3) Other assets:

(a) tangible fixed assets, other than land and buildings;

(b) cash at *bank* and in hand, *deposits* with *credit institutions* and any other bodies authorised to receive deposits;

(c) for *general insurance business* only, *deferred acquisition costs*;

(d) accrued interest and rent, other accrued income and prepayments;

(e) for *long-term insurance business* only, reversionary interests.

Certain admissible assets are not defined (eg bonds, capital market instruments and variable yield participations) leaving scope for interpretation. In relation to variable yield participations, it is understood that the FSA has stated that this could cover interests in limited partnerships. In practice, as the list of assets is fairly generic (eg shares), admissibility may not be too problematic except perhaps in relation to derivative contracts and collective investment schemes. It should be noted in relation to each of the categories, that even if the asset satisfies the requirements of any other category of admissible asset, it must (if it could also be categorised as such), be treated as a derivative or, provided it is not a derivative or quasi derivative, as a collective investment scheme (eg shares in a collective investment scheme entity must not be treated as shares).

The FSA explains in INSPRU 3.2.5A(2) that where a quasi derivative is embedded in another asset (eg debt with return linked to performance of another asset) that element should be subject to the rules relating to derivatives. So for

1 But from 31 December 2006 excluding amounts recoverable from an ISPV unless an FSA waiver is obtained.

example, a UCITS fund, a bond or debt whose return is linked to performance of another asset should normally be treated as a derivative if units in that scheme or the return are expected to mirror the value of a derivative.

In relation to collective investment schemes, the FSA gave some useful guidance on unauthorised schemes permitted under (1)(d) above in CP06/13. The FSA explained that the rules permit a small amount of exposure to inadmissible assets to be obtained through this type of collective investment scheme provided derivatives are covered and the exposure to inadmissible assets, using a principles based test, is suitably small.

INSPRU 1.130 requires a UK firm to hold its admissible assets in any EEA State or (where admissible assets cover technical provisions in a currency other than pounds sterling) in any EEA State or the country of that currency.

In addition to the rules on admissibility there are overriding requirements on insurers to match their assets and liabilities. The rules are in INSPRU 1.1.34.

B Counterparty and concentration risk

7.27 The IPRU (INS) rules on admissibility also contained counterparty and asset limits. These limits now apply separately[1]. They apply in addition to the general requirement[2] on a firm to restrict its exposure to counterparties and assets to prudent levels and to ensure that those exposures are adequately diversified. A deduction to a firm's capital is required in respect of assets in excess of the market risk and counterparty limits.

Counterparty exposure is the amount a firm would lose from its capital resources (calculated in accordance with GENPRU) if the counterparty were to fail to meet its obligations or if assets were to become worthless. In making this determination a firm must take into account exposures held by a subsidiary undertaking and synthetic exposures arising from derivatives or quasi-derivatives. Obtaining exposures using derivatives or quasi derivatives can in fact increase the overall counterparty exposure. A firm may take credit for collateral provided it is in the form of admissible assets and the exposure created by the collateral does not exceed the counterparty and asset limits set out in INSPRU 2.1.22. Exposures which do not decrease the amount of a firm's capital are not taken into account, so, for example, holdings in relation to which the firm has not attributed any value will not form part of the counterparty exposure.

The limits are expressed in relation to types of counterparty (or similar counterparties within their group) and are calculated as a percentage of the firm's business amount. This is broadly its gross technical provisions plus other liabilities plus total capital (see INSPRU 2.1.22(4)). Technical provisions in this case do not include those in respect of pure unit-linked liabilities.

1 INSPRU 2.1.22.
2 SYSC 1.5.1.

The limits set out in INSPRU 2.1.22 can be very broadly summarised as:

Total counterparty/group	
approved credit institutions	5–10% (plus 10% for short-term deposits so 20% in total*)
approved counterparty	5% (increased to 10% in certain cases*)
corporate body	5%
regulated institution	5% non-hybrid debt securities and 2.5% for unsecured debt
individual(s) or partnership	1% (or 0.25% for unsecured debt)
There are also **asset limits** as follows:	
UCITS	Unlimited (unless a quasi derivative)
approved securities	Unlimited
listed securities	5%
unlisted investments (including securities and 'other collective investment schemes')	1% (plus 10% all counterparties limit)[1]
unsecured loans (other than with an approved counterparty)	5% (all counterparties limit)
non UCITS retail scheme or recognised scheme	5% (any single scheme but may include the 'issuer')
other collective investment schemes	1% (any single scheme but may include the 'issuer')
cash in hand	3%
one piece of land	10%

*This additional exposure is only available where such exposures (ie to all approved counterparties that are more than 5%) amount in total to less than 40%. There is a separate limit for Covered Bonds (eg a regulated bond issue by a credit institution which satisfies the covered bond requirements). This limit is 40% but it affects the limit for approved counterparties including credit institutions. It appears that if all of the 40% limit for Covered Bonds is used then the approved counterparties limit is limited to 5%.

7.28 Where a counterparty could fall into more than one category the highest limit normally applies.

Approved counterparty means an approved credit institution or a firm authorised to write derivatives off market.

Approved credit institution means an EEA authorised/permitted banking institution.

Approved securities means a security issued or guaranteed by Zone A country or a loan/deposit with an Approved Financial Institution or specified financial entities.

1 Under INSPRU there is a 1% limit for individual collective investment schemes unless they are non-UCITS retail schemes or recognised schemes, in which case there is a 5% limit.

Corporate bodies means an entity which is not an individual or unincorporated association or closely related group of individuals or an approved counterparty. It covers regulated institutions except in relation to the assets for which there are specific rules for regulated institutions.

Hybrid securities means a debt security (other than an approved security) where the creditor cannot demand capital and interest to be fully repaid within 75 years.

Listed/unlisted means dealt in/not dealt in on a regulated market.

Regulated institution means an EEA insurer, bank or firm authorised to write derivatives off market.

The counterparty limits do not apply to:

(1) premium debt and loans covered by security in a long-term policy;

(2) rights of salvage or subrogation;

(3) deferred acquisition costs (as defined in the insurance accounts rules);

(4) assets held to cover pure unit-linked liabilities (eg without guarantees, etc);

(5) debts from or guaranteed by a Zone A country; or

(6) holdings in a UCITS.

The limits also include closely related counterparties exposures. The meaning of closely related[1] is broadly determined by control and the existence of a parent and subsidiary undertaking or consolidation relationship. It also includes any similar relationship between a natural or legal person and an undertaking. It is a very wide provision and will catch most of the scenarios which a firm could envisage. In relation to collective investment schemes (other than UCITS for which there is no limit), there may be a counterparty exposure to the 'issuer' or another company in its group (eg either the authorised corporate director of an ICVC (UK authorised open-ended investment company), or the ICVC itself, or the manager (of a unit trust)). INSPRU 2.1.39 provides that if the relevant parties are so interconnected that a failure of the issuer would be likely to affect the value of the units, those units should be aggregated with exposures to the manager or authorised corporate director. In other cases, they will just be subject to the asset limits in INSPRU 2.1.22 3(i) or (j) (i.e. 5% or 1%).

Although the counterparty limits do not apply to exposures to reinsurers, firms are required to notify the FSA as soon as they first become aware that a reinsurance exposure is reasonably likely to exceed 100% of their capital resources (excluding capital resources held to cover property-linked liabilities) and to demonstrate that they can either explain the arrangements or have a plan to manage them appropriately. In each financial year a firm should restrict its gross

1 INSPRU 2.1.39 and 2.1.40.

earned premiums paid to a reinsurer (or group of related reinsurers), to the higher of 20% of its gross earned premiums for that financial year and £4 million[1].

C Derivatives and stock lending in insurance funds

7.29 To be an admissible asset, derivatives and quasi-derivatives (assets having the effect of a derivative contract) must be approved derivatives and stock lent by a firm must be under an approved stock lending transaction, which includes repos.

INSPRU 3.2 sets out the applicable rules and guidance. The former extensive example-based guidance and 'Dear CEO' letters have been replaced by high-level guidance in INSPRU 3.2. In the authors' view it still worth looking at the former guidance as some of the examples can help the reader to understand how the rules are applied in practice.

INSPRU 3.2 provides that a derivative or quasi-derivative is approved if:

(1) it is held for the purpose of efficient portfolio management ('EPM') or reduction of investment risk ('RIR');

(2) it is covered; and

(3) it is effected or issued on or under the rules of a regulated market or off market with an approved counterparty and (except for a forward transaction) on approved terms and is capable of valuation.

D EPM/RIR

7.30 Efficient portfolio management is defined in relation to:

(1) generation of additional capital or income by taking advantage of *pricing imperfections* in assets which are equivalent to admissible assets or receiving a premium for selling a covered call option based on an admissible asset (even if in doing so the firm gives up the chance of greater capital or income);

(2) *reducing tax or investment costs* in relation to admissible assets; or

(3) acquiring or disposing of rights in relation to admissible assets or their equivalent *more efficiently or more effectively*.

The first limb of this definition is likely to give rise to most issues in practice. In particular, it is not clear what assets are 'equivalent' to admissible assets (ie whether they should actually exist or can merely reproduce the same economic effect). It is also not clear to what extent the additional risk inherent in the pricing imperfection is acceptable.

1 Evidential provision in INSPRU 2.1.28. Compliance with this provision may be relied upon in relation to the obligation of prudence and diversification.

Investment risk is defined for this purpose in INSPRU 3.2.12 as the risk that the asset may not be equal to liabilities, be of appropriate safety, yield, marketability or in the appropriate currency. Additionally, where assets are held to cover unit-linked liabilities, the risk is that they may not be appropriate cover for those liabilities.

Reduction of investment risk broadly replicates the previous requirement that it must reduce an aspect of investment risk without significantly increasing another aspect of that risk (ie any such increase in risk is small and reasonable or the risk is remote). The guidance specifically still contemplates that some adverse consequences (eg loss of premium) may arise through the use of derivatives.

E Cover

7.31 The FSA requires cover for three reasons: to protect against loss; to protect against the risk of a firm not being able to deliver 'appropriate' (ie the right type of) assets; and to prevent excessive gearing in the investment portfolio. The requirement for cover arises in relation to a firm's obligation to transfer assets or pay a monetary amount under a contract (other than a contract of insurance), for the purchase, sale or exchange of assets or under a derivative or quasi-derivative. Cover must be in the form of assets, a liability, provision or an offsetting transaction. If a firm covers a liability with assets they must be admissible assets and it must reasonably believe that those assets will be sufficient to pay the amount of the obligation when it falls due. An obligation can be covered by a liability where the amount of that obligation would be offset by a decrease in the amount of liability. Similarly, a provision recognised by GENPRU 1.3 at least equal to the value of the asset can be used as cover. The guidance makes clear that a derivative may be split to the extent it is covered, with the not covered portion treated as not being an approved derivative.

Cover from one transaction cannot be used for cover in respect of another and an offsetting transaction must provide the firm with the relevant assets *before* the obligation it is offsetting falls due. The guidance includes examples of the cover requirement and specifically states that borrowings may not be used to gear an investment portfolio[1]. The FSA now also requires firms to cover options by holding the exercise price even though they may never actually exercise the option.

F Over the counter transactions

7.32 INSPRU provides that a derivative is on approved terms only if the firm reasonably believes that it could, in all reasonably foreseeable circumstances and under normal market conditions, readily enter into a further transaction with the

1 INSPRU 3.2.30 and 3.2.31.

counterparty or a third party to close out at the value attributed to the derivative by the firm (taking into account any valuation adjustments or reserves established by the firm)[1]. The FSA makes clear that the firm needs to be able to satisfy itself that the contract could be realised at the appropriate value. INSPRU also provides that a contract is only 'capable of valuation' if the firm reasonably believes it will be able to value it with reasonable accuracy on a reliable basis throughout the life of the transaction[2].

G Stock lending

7.33 INSPRU also provides rules in relation to the basis on which an insurer can lend stock or enter into repo transactions but still treat[3] the stock as its asset. There are no specific rules relating to the borrowing of stock by an insurer.

A *stock lending transaction* will be approved and therefore the assets lent will continue to constitute admissible assets if:

(1) the assets lent are admissible assets;

(2) the counterparty is an authorised person or an approved counterparty (eg a bank or firm authorised to write OTC derivatives or as specified in INSPRU 3.2.36 (including certain US authorised broker/dealers)); and

(3) adequate and sufficient immediate collateral is obtained to secure the obligation of the counterparty.

The rules specify the type of collateral which can be used for these purposes. Assets must be adequate in quality, be admissible assets and be transferred to the firm or its agent at or before the time of the transaction in question (by end of the business day on which the loan is made). Collateral also continues to be adequate only if its value is at all times equal to the value of securities transferred to the firm.

SECTION 6 INTERNAL CONTAGION RISK

7.34 The provisions of INSPRU 1.5 are concerned with prudential risk which the FSA describes as 'internal contagion risk' and apply to insurers other than small friendly societies[4]. They are intended to protect a firm against different types of activity or business carried on within the firm.

1 INSPRU 3.2.34.
2 INSPRU 3.2.35.
3 INSPRU 3.2.36.
4 £5m premium income but see INSPRU 1.5 and 1.5.2 respectively.

A The section 16 restriction

7.35 The First Life Directive required member states to restrict an insurer's ability to carry on non-insurance related activities. This control was for many years to be found in section 16 of the Insurance Companies Act 1982. This required insurance companies to limit their activities to insurance business and activities in connection with it. When IPRU (INS) was implemented, the FSA (in Rule 1.3) rewrote the restriction to reflect more closely the provisions of the First Life Directive that had introduced the requirement in the first place. There were two perceived areas of concern. First, the 'in connection with' wording in section 16 was too vague and regarded as a 'gloss' on the directive's requirement. Second, the restrictions only applied to activities being carried on by way of business. The substance of Rule 1.3 is now set out in INSPRU 1.5.13, which states that a firm 'must not carry on any commercial business other than insurance business and activities directly arising from that business'. FSA guidance indicates that activities directly arising from insurance business could include investing the firm's assets and employing staff. There is little other guidance in relation to the meaning of directly arising.

There is however a judgment of the European Court of Justice in relation to the underlying directive requirements in the context of the 'commercial business' point. The BASCO[1] case related to whether a not for profit joint venture of two insurers, providing the services of an optician, constituted the carrying on of 'commercial activities'. The court held that the nature of the activities determined whether or not they were a commercial business rather than whether or not the activities were carried on for profit. In the past insurers operating without a service company may have provided services to a group company on a not for profit basis. Based on this decision, it will be difficult to sustain an argument that activities which are commercial in nature can be carried on by an insurer, unless they 'directly arise' from its insurance business. Another interesting point to note from the Judgment is that it reiterates the 'mischief' of this rule which is to ensure that the insurer's assets are available to pay its insurance liabilities and that other activities do not expose the insurer to a risk of having to use those assets for other purposes.

Any non-insurance business which is permitted within this restriction (ie which 'directly arises' from its insurance business) should be limited, controlled and managed so that it does not lead to any significant risk that the firm might be unable to meet its liabilities as they fall due, and in quantifying this risk, a firm should consider how likely it is that financial risk from this type of business could diverge from expectations.

1 *Association Basco-Béarnaise des Opticien Independants v Préfet des Pyrenees-Atlantique* (ECJC 109/99).

B Separation of life funds and use of their assets

7.36 The FSA will not grant a firm a permission which incorporates both general and long-term insurance business[1]. Also, although firms authorised to effect or carry out life and annuity business are permitted to carry out accident and sickness general insurance contracts on an ancillary or supplementary basis, there is no equivalent right for non life offices to carry on long term business.

INSPRU[2] requires firms carrying on long-term insurance business to identify those assets which relate to their long-term insurance business, and to only apply such assets for the purpose of the long-term business. A firm must also not agree to, or allow, any mortgage or charge on its long-term insurance assets other than in respect of a long-term insurance liability.

Long-term insurance business includes payment of long-term insurance claims, expenses and liabilities, and also loans (provided that the loan was incurred for the purpose of the long-term insurance business). Long-term insurance assets include premiums, income and capital receipts and receivables in respect of long-term insurance business, and any other assets available to meet its long-term insurance liabilities (including assets to which these assets have been converted).

Separate accounting records must be maintained in respect of each long-term insurance fund. The question sometimes arises as to whether a firm has just one long-term fund or a number of funds[3]. INSPRU provides that all long-term insurance assets constitute a firm's long-term insurance fund, unless a firm can identify particular life assets in connection with different parts of its life business, in which case the assets identified in relation to each such part constitute separate long-term insurance funds of the firm.

Further, the maintenance of separate funds may be necessary to ensure policyholders are treated fairly where any surplus is shared between policyholders and shareholders in different ways for different blocks of business[4]. The most obvious example is where a proprietary life office writes some with-profits business. IPRU (INS) rule 3.5 also requires an insurer to avoid unfairness between its long-term funds or between a long-term fund and other assets of the insurer.

Firms may merge separate funds for different types of business[5] provided the merger will not result in policyholders being treated unfairly.

C Established surplus

7.37 Assets may not be transferred out of a long-term insurance fund unless the assets represent an established surplus, established no more than three

1 INSPRU 1.5.17. This does not prevent historic composites from continuing to carry on both types of insurance business, but the various systems and controls are designed to ensure that policyholders are adequately protected from the resulting risks.
2 INSPRU 1.5.30 and 1.5.31.
3 In practice this often seems to be determined based on historic and/or accounting practice.
4 INSPRU 1.5.25.
5 INSPRU 1.5.26.

months previously[1]. The established surplus can only be determined by actuarial investigation. Even where the investigation is still less than three months old, a firm cannot make the transfer unless there are sufficient funds at the time of transfer to enable it to be made without a firm breaching the requirements to cover its liabilities[2].

These provisions are reinforced by regulations made under section 378 of the Financial Services and Markets Act 2000 ('FSMA'). The regulations provide that when an insurer is being wound up, the assets maintained in a long-term fund are to be available only to meet the liabilities of that fund unless on winding up there are surplus assets in the fund. It is therefore important for third parties dealing with UK long-term insurers to be clear whether the insurer is contracting on behalf of a long-term insurance fund and, if so, which one. This is particularly the case where they enter into a netting arrangement or where a charge over assets is proposed.

Firms are permitted to transfer non-life assets (eg assets referable to the general business) into the long-term insurance fund. However, once transferred, such assets may not be transferred out of the long-term insurance fund save where they represent an 'established surplus'. Assets may be transferred for value or an arm's length basis (eg by way of sale).

D Appropriate assets, adequate premiums and fairness

7.38 INSPRU 1.1.34 provides that save in relation to assets held to cover property-linked or index-linked liabilities, the assets held by firms to cover technical provisions must:

(1) have characteristics of safety, yield and marketability appropriate to the type of business carried on by the firm;

(2) be diversified and adequately spread;

(3) be of sufficient amount, and of appropriate currency and term, to ensure the cash inflows from those assets will meet expected cash outflows from the firm's insurance liabilities as they become due.

INSPRU 1.1.41 provides that a firm must not enter into a long-term insurance contract unless it is satisfied on reasonable actuarial assumptions that the premiums are sufficient to enable it to establish adequate technical provisions covered by admissible assets and to maintain adequate overall financial resources. Guidance makes clear that adequacy may be assessed on a firm's total portfolio of business. It may therefore loss lead on individual products but it should be noted that a firm's ability to do so for with-profits contracts is more constrained (see **6.17**).

Note that if the FSA imposes a financial penalty on a life office, the firm is not permitted to pay such penalty from a long-term insurance fund. This rule does

1 INSPRU 1.5.27.
2 INSPRU 1.1.27 and 1.1.28.

not apply to mutuals but is one of the few which does apply to EEA and Treaty Firms (ie firms relying on a single market home state authorisation or rights under the Treaty of Rome).

IPRU (INS) rule 3.2(b) continues to restrict a long-term insurer's ability to pay dividends where its long-term insurance assets are less than its long-term insurance liabilities (ie technical provisions and current liabilities).

E Unit-linked contracts

7.39 Much of the detail of GENPRU and INSPRU does not apply to unit-linked funds, particularly admissibility and counterparty limits in relation to property-linked and index-linked benefits. Certain provisions do, however, apply to property-linked funds.

INSPRU 1.5.35 applies identification and maintenance provisions to property-linked funds and states that a life office should not apply those assets (as long as they are needed to cover property-linked benefits) for any other purpose. There is no equivalent provision on insolvency and typically unit-linked funds do not form separate long-term funds because the link to the underlying assets is notional. This means that on insolvency unit-linked assets, which while the company is solvent are required to be ring fenced, are potentially available to satisfy other liabilities of the same long-term fund.

INSPRU 1.5.36 provides for property-linked funds to cover their liabilities as closely as possible with the property to which those liabilities are linked taking into account both contractual and regulatory duties (eg treating customers fairly). INSPRU 3.1.57 also requires a firm to cover its property-linked liabilities with assets which as closely as possible match those liabilities and/or a property-linked insurance contract.

Similarly, a firm must cover its indexed-linked liabilities with assets of appropriate marketability and security which correspond as closely as possible to the assets which form the index[1]. Alternatively, an insurer should hold a portfolio of assets whose value or yield is reasonably expected to correspond closely with index-linked liabilities and indexed-linked to the insurance contract or an indexed-linked approved derivative or quasi-derivative contract. Unlike the situation with currency matching, a firm is not permitted to hold different assets and to cover the mis-matching by holding an excess of assets. Firms are also directed in particular to consider credit risk in accordance with INSPRU 2.1.

F Reinsurance

7.40 INSPRU 1.1.19 includes specific requirements in relation to reinsurance (and other forms of risk transfer). It imposes a general obligation to notify the FSA of changes to existing reinsurance arrangements or any new arrangements.

Additional provisions relating to reinsurance now apply to with-profits funds.

1 INSPRU 3.1.58.

These are set out in COBS 20.2. COBS 20.2.39 provides that a with-profits fund should not enter into a material transaction unless the firm's governing body reasonably believes it is unlikely to have a material adverse effect on the interests of the fund's with-profits policyholders. Material transactions include significant bulk outwards reinsurance, *any* inwards with-profits reinsurance and any financial engineering that would materially change the emergence of surplus on existing business.

Prior to entering into or significantly changing a reinsurance agreement, or any other form of insurance risk transfer agreement, a firm should conduct appropriate due diligence on the reinsurer, the contractual terms offered and the effect on the insurer's own regulatory position. In managing its reinsurance agreements, a firm should have in place appropriate systems that allow it to maintain its desired level of cover including conducting regular stress and scenario testing.

SECTION 7 INSURANCE GROUPS AND FINANCIAL CONGLOMERATES

A Group risk

7.41 INSPRU 6[1] deals with group risk management and capital requirements which form the 'insurance sector rules' for the purposes of the Financial Groups Directive[2]. The directive applies to Financial Conglomerates (groups with significant interests in both the banking/investment sector and the insurance sector). These provisions mean that FSA regulated insurers now potentially face three types of supervision (see INSPRU 6.1.6):

(a) prudential supervision on a stand-alone basis (which will be an 'adjusted' calculation where the insurer has significant interests in other insurers);

(b) consolidated or supplementary supervision on a sectoral basis (ie for insurance groups or subgroups);

(c) supervision on a mixed-group-wide basis if they are a member of a financial conglomerate.

The rationale for the prudential supervision of corporate groups in the banking, investment and insurance sectors, is the risk that weaknesses (such as inadequate capital or poor systems and controls) at group level could threaten the position of individual regulated firms within the group.

7.42 SYSC 12 sets out prudential requirements applicable to all groups (including FSA-regulated Financial Conglomerates)[3] and requires group-wide

1 See SYSC 12, GENPRU 3.1 and 3.2 and INSPRU 6.1.
2 GENPRU 3.
3 Broadly, where the ultimate EU parent company is established in the UK.

systems and controls to manage risks. All authorised firms within groups that are in the insurance, banking or investment sectors must have 'adequate, sound and appropriate risk management processes and internal control mechanisms for the purpose of assessing and managing their *own exposure to group risk*, including sound administrative and accounting procedures'[1]. Group risk also includes risk arising from non-regulated entities which are part of a group.

A similar requirement[2] applies *at group level*. The group level requirement is of more limited application. It applies in respect of Financial Conglomerates and groups only if regulated by the FSA. It also excludes the conglomerate's or its group's interest in any firms in which it (they) holds only a 'participation' (broadly a 20% holding but see below).

As with other areas of risk management, the FSA guidance states that what will constitute 'adequate, sound and appropriate' controls should be judged in light of the nature, scale and complexity of the group's business. Also, whilst appropriate systems and controls may be organised on a 'group-wide basis', with functions delegated to specific group members, each firm within the group retains individual responsibility for complying with its own obligations. A firm may rely upon its parent's systems and controls (where the parent is also subject to the group level requirement), provided it has made an appropriate assessment of such systems and controls. This is important in practice, as many companies rely upon group functions and controls.

An FSA-regulated EEA Financial Conglomerate's internal control mechanisms must include sound reporting and accounting procedures for the purpose of identifying, measuring, monitoring and controlling intra-group transactions and risk concentrations.

B Insurance groups

7.43 The Insurance Groups Directive ('IGD') (as amended) provides supplementary supervision for EU insurance groups (the sectoral supervision referred to above). The IGD requires that group level capital adequacy calculations (in the UK the 'Group Capital Resources Requirement' (GCRR) and 'Group Capital Resources' (GCR)) must be reported to the group's supervisor (normally the supervisor of the ultimate EEA parent). Authorised firms may therefore find that group supervision is conducted from another member state. As stated in Section 2, the FSA's risk based assessment of capital will also apply to an insurance group and the FSA may provide capital guidance at the group level[3]. The IGD also imposes additional reporting and system and control requirements.

The main aim of the IGD group supervision is to prevent double counting of capital within an insurance group. The IGD used to only apply to group interests in insurance companies but was extended by the Financial Groups Directive ('FGD') to include other financial 'regulated' entities. It works by requiring a

1 INSPRU 12.1.8(1).
2 SYSC 12.1.8(2).
3 INSPRU 6.1.16G.

parent undertaking which has a significant interest in an insurance company to value its interest on a 'look-through' basis (ie it must look through to the capital of the insurance company and deduct the book value of the group's interest as shareholder). To allow limits on capital to be applied consistently at group level, group capital is aggregated and then the total deduction for total book values for each type of capital (Tier 1, Tier 2, etc) is made, producing a net total group figure for each type of capital.

The IGD does not require groups actually to hold capital calculated on a group basis. The FSA decided that with effect from 31 December 2006, group capital must be held in respect of any insurance group of an EEA parent company (which may be an insurance holding company or an insurer) which is supervised by the FSA.

Where the FSA is not the group supervisor for a group which includes a UK firm, that firm may calculate its group requirements (GCR and GCRR) in relation to its ultimate EEA insurance parent undertaking, using the rules of that other EEA State.

C Application of the group requirements

7.44 INSPRU 6.1 applies to insurers that are either 'participating insurance undertakings' (ie holding a significant interest (at least 20%) in other insurance undertakings) or are themselves members of an 'insurance group'. A firm may also be a participating insurer in relation to firms connected by an 'Article 12 Consolidation Relationship' (eg if they are managed on a unified basis or the administration, management or supervisory bodies of the undertaking consist of the same people)[1].

A firm is part of an insurance group if there is either sufficient cross shareholder control to amount to at least a participation (eg 20%) or control through the exercise of voting rights, rights to appoint directors or to exert a dominant influence. A group will normally include a company, its holding company and subsidiaries of the holding company but in each case extended to include companies in which another company in the group has a participation.

As the group capital calculation may be conducted in relation to an unauthorised parent company (for example, an insurance holding company), the FSA has made all insurers in the group subject to the requirement to ensure the group is adequately capitalised[2]. For insurers holding participations, this requirement is in INSPRU 6.1.9. Such insurers are required[3], on a regular basis, to calculate the Group Capital Resources (in accordance with INSPRU 6.1.36-70[4]) and Group Capital Resources Requirement (in accordance with INSPRU 6.1.33-35). These

1 Article 12 of the Seventh Company Law Directive 83/349/EEC.
2 Other than pure reinsurers INSPRU 6.1.15.
3 INSPRU 6.1.8.
4 INSPRU 6.1.70A-78 provide rules for pure reinsurance.

calculations must be made in relation to the following entities, known as the 'Relevant Calculating Entities':

(a) the insurer itself, if it qualifies as a 'participating insurance undertaking' (ie if it holds at least a participation in another insurer);

(b) the 'ultimate insurance parent undertaking' (ie the ultimate parent of the insurance group which is either an insurer with at least a participation in another insurer, or qualifies as an insurance holding company (ie its main business is to acquire and hold participations in subsidiaries which are either exclusively or mainly insurance undertakings, at least one of which is EEA based)); and

(c) the 'ultimate EEA insurance parent undertaking' (if different).

An insurance holding company ceases to be an insurance holding company if it is a mixed financial holding company (ie a holding company with participations across the insurance and banking/investment sectors). This then means that supervision at the level of that company's group is under the FGD. Sub-groups will continue to be regulated as insurance groups. This distinction may have more significance under Solvency II where accounting consolidation is used as the basis for calculating group requirements and there is no solo adjusted calculation (eg for insurers holding a participation) (see **7.48** and Article 215 of the Solvency II Directive).

Under both the IGD and FGD there are issues if the ultimate parent of the group is outside of the EEA. The FSA requirement to hold group capital does not apply in relation to the ultimate parent of an insurance undertaking who is outside of the EEA. It is, however, still necessary to calculate the Group Capital Resources Requirement and the Group Capital Resources at that level and report it to the FSA. INSPRU 6.1.25 provides that such calculations be undertaken in accordance with accounting practices applicable for the purposes of the regulation of insurers where the parent has its head office 'adapted as necessary to apply the general principles set out in Annex I paragraphs B C and D' of the IGD and that such a firm may elect to carry out such calculation in accordance with the 'accounting consolidation' method set out in Annex I(3) of the IGD.

D Calculation of group capital adequacy

1 GCRR

7.45 Calculation of GCR and GCRR involve looking at the individual Capital Resource Requirements of each 'regulated related undertaking' in the group of a Relevant Calculating Entity. This includes firms in the investment, banking and asset management sectors, as well as insurance undertakings, and the holding companies of the same (excluding holding companies of asset management companies). It also includes Financial Institutions which are very widely defined by reference to the Banking Consolidation Directive (see FSA definition).

Under Article 3(3) of the IGD[1], an undertaking within an insurance group may be excluded from supplementary supervision (and therefore the requirement that its capital adequacy forms part of the GCR and GCRR), if it is not based in the EEA and there are legal impediments to the transfer of the necessary information, *or*, if in the opinion of the regulator responsible for supplementary supervision, its inclusion would be inappropriate/misleading or of negligible interest. For a UK group to take advantage of this (eg in relation to intermediate insurance holding companies), it is necessary to get a waiver from the FSA. Similar provisions will apply in relation to groups under Solvency II.

Normally, the GCRR of a Relevant Calculating Entity is calculated as the sum of the individual Capital Resources Requirements of itself and each of its regulated related undertakings. One of the issues which needs to be calculated as part of the GCRR is the capital requirement of non insurance companies. Typically this can include an insurance holding company, a non EEA subsidiary or a Financial Institution (see FSA definition of regulated 'related undertaking'). It may also include an EEA authorised ISPV. INSPRU 6.1.34 sets out the relevant Capital Resource Requirements. For insurance holding companies it is zero. For non EEA subsidiaries (not in designated territories where local rules may be used), it is a proxy capital resources requirement. For Financial Institutions that are not regulated, it is the requirement that would apply if it were treated as being in the banking sector. For ancillary insurance services undertakings the requirement is zero whereas other ancillary services undertakings need to apply the relevant sectoral rules as if they were regulated[2].

The GCR is calculated as the proportional share (being the proportion of the total number of shares in the regulated related undertaking held by the Relevant Calculating Entity or where an Article 12(1) Consolidation Relationship exists, such proportion as the FSA decides), of the sum of the Tier 1 and Tier 2 Capital Resources of the individual members of the group who qualify as regulated related undertakings, less the book value of investments in such group undertakings held by all other group members.

As with the calculation of the Group Capital Resource Requirement, it is sometimes necessary, in calculating a group's capital, to know how to treat non insurance entities. INSPRU 6.1.37 provides that entities not subject to the Capital Resources Table[3] calculate their resources as if they were subject to that table subject to adjustment in accordance with relevant 'sectoral rules'. INSPRU 6.1.38 provides that insurance holding companies be treated as within the sectoral rules for insurers or pure reinsurers depending on the main businesses they acquire. The rules for a Financial Institution that is not a regulated entity are those of the banking sector. However, where such a Financial Institution has invested in a parent undertaking's Tier 1 or Tier 2 capital and the parent is an

1 INSPRU 6.1.18.
2 INSPRU 6.1.64.
3 GENPRU 2.2.17 and Annex 1R.

insurer or an insurance holding company, the sector rules for the insurance sector apply instead. INSPRU 6.1.40 sets out how much of such capital resources of the Financial Institution can be included in the GCR.

2 *GCR and deductions*

7.46 Capital which a firm is itself required to hold cannot be assumed to be transferable intra-group. Capital which is not transferable for other reasons (for example surplus capital in the long-term fund) is also excluded from group capital calculations[1].

The group capital calculation involves deductions for inadmissible assets[2] and investments in 'ancillary services undertakings'[3] (ie undertakings whose principal activity consists of owning/managing property, managing data-processing services, or any similar activity which is ancillary to the principal activity of insurance, banking or investment firms). Changes to the rules were introduced by the Reinsurance Directive. Pure reinsurers are not subject to the admissibility and counterparty limits applicable to other insurers. The rules in INSPRU 6.1 make allowances for this change. INSPRU 6.1.60(2) treats assets of a pure reinsurer as inadmissible for these purposes if they breach the prudent person principle (see INSPRU 3.1.61A). There are also additional rules in INSPRU 6.1.70A-78 for pure reinsurers that are Relevant Calculating Entities because they are participating insurance undertakings.

One of the main purposes of group supervision is to eliminate double counting of assets within a group and give an accurate view of capital at the group level across business units and lines of business, making appropriate allowance for the correlation between risks[4]. This also means that 'recipricol financial' arrangements with third parties should be excluded. INSPRU 6.1.42A provides that a firm must exclude:

(1) the book value of any investment by a regulated related undertaking of the Relevant Calculating Entity (ie an entity included in the group calculations) in shares of or loans to persons outside that group calculation (ie a non related undertaking) which has itself invested in the capital resources of an entity included in the group calculation; and

(2) any other item of capital to the extent that it is the result of, or otherwise attributable to, reciprocal financing arrangements entered into by the Relevant Calculating Entity or an entity included in its group calculations.

1 INSPRU 6.1.62.
2 INSPRU 6.1.59.
3 INSPRU 6.1.62.
4 GENPRU 1.2.37.

3 *Limits on group capital resources*

7.47 These limits are complicated not least because they are expressed by means of formulae but there are some areas of common ground with the individual limits in GENPRU 2, for example:

(1) Innovative Tier 1 is limited to 15% of total Tier 1;

(2) Core Tier 1 must be at least 50% of total group Tier 1;

(3) total group Tier 2 must be no more than total group Tier 1; and

(4) total group lower Tier 2 must be no more than 25% of total group Tier 1.

4 *Adjusted solo calculation*

7.48 A participating insurer will also have an adjusted solo calculation. This is because when calculating its own capital requirements, it must value interests in other insurers amounting to a participation on a look through basis. It must also make deductions in respect of assets in excess of market risk and counterparty limits as applied by INSPRU 6.1.70 to 6.1.78 and ineligible surplus capital (eg capital which is not transferable – INSPRU 6.1.65).

E Financial Conglomerates

7.49 The Financial Groups Directive[1] came into effect for financial years beginning on or after 1 January 2005. The Directive introduced rules to regulate Financial Conglomerates (groups with significant interests in both the insurance and banking/investment sector). The FGD rules are now in GENPRU 3. The rules provide for calculation and holding of adequate capital and a single EU supervisor at the financial conglomerate level. Financial conglomerates are also subject to risk concentration and intra-group transaction requirements (the mixed group-wide basis of supervision referred to above). The FGD rules will continue to apply post Solvency II but there are proposals to amend the FGD in the near future.

F What is a Financial Conglomerate?

7.50 A group will be a Financial Conglomerate if:

(1) at least 40% of its business is financial; and

(2) at least 10% or €6 billion of its financial business is in each of the insurance and the combined banking/investment sectors.

1 2002/87/EC.

Whether a firm is a Financial Conglomerate is determined by applying the decision tree in (GENPRU3 Annex 4R):

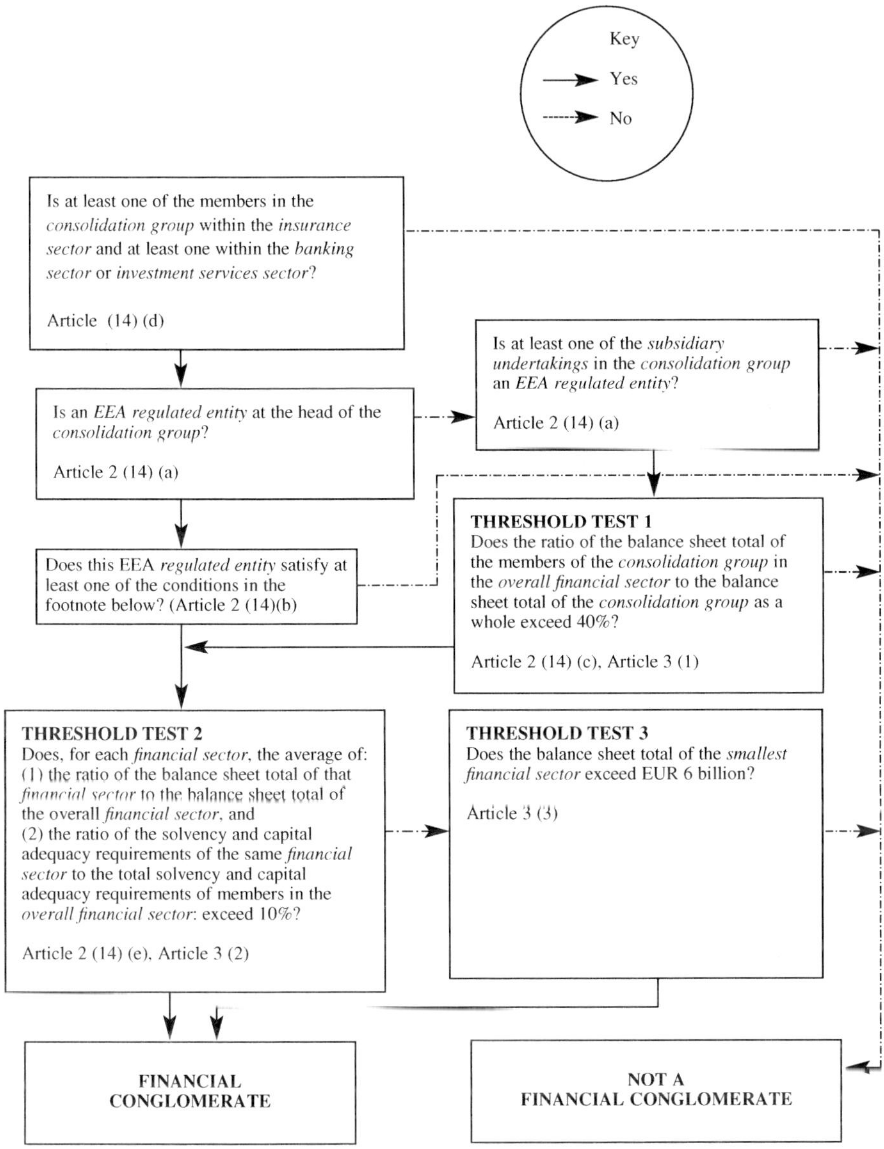

Once identified as a Financial Conglomerate, the threshold limits to be included in the decision tree are reduced if/when the Financial Conglomerate would cease to qualify as a Financial Conglomerate based on the original figures and for three years following that date. This is to avoid sudden changes in status and the uncertainty that would bring. The reduction means that only 30% of its business needs to be in the overall financial sector and only €5 billion is required to be in each of the insurance and banking/investment sector.

However, under the FGD, relevant EEA regulatory authorities ('competent authorities') are permitted to change the definition of 'Financial Conglomerate' and the obligations applying to them, on a case-by-case basis. Competent authorities will identify (through a consultation process with other EEA regulators and the relevant groups as necessary), if any Financial Conglomerate exists. The FSA has also confirmed that firms have an ongoing responsibility to check whether they consider they are (or have ceased to be) part of a Financial Conglomerate and to notify the FSA accordingly (see SUP 15.9).

Where the ultimate parent company of a Financial Conglomerate is in the EEA, a single EU co-ordinator is appointed. The co-ordinator will exchange information and co-operate with other relevant competent authorities to take a cross-sectoral overview of the group and whether it meets the prescribed requirements. One of the co-ordinator's tasks is to decide which of the methods for determining capital adequacy specified in the directive is to be applied to a particular Financial Conglomerate (in consultation with other competent authorities and the conglomerate itself).

Although Article 10 of the FGD sets out the criteria to be used to establish which authority should be the co-ordinator, the competent authorities may, if they think it more appropriate, waive the criteria and appoint a different co-ordinator. It is anticipated this could happen where there are significant holdings in one state but the ultimate holding company is in another state.

G Third country groups

7.51 EEA Financial Conglomerates whose ultimate parent is not in the EEA are referred to in the FGD as a 'third country group'. Where there is a third country group, the regulator which would be the co-ordinator if the identification criteria set out in the FGD were to apply, verifies whether the EEA regulated entities in that group are subject to equivalent supervision by a third country regulator. If it does not meet the equivalence standards, relevant regulators may:

(a) effect worldwide supervision by an EU co-ordinator applying the requirements for an EU group by analogy to the wider group; or

(b) apply other methods to ensure appropriate supervision of the EEA-regulated entities in that third country group in accordance with the aims of supplementary supervision.

It is not clear how realistic worldwide supervision is. The FSA stated in consultation that where it would be the coordinator, unless the group is essentially an EEA group (eg only a holding company outside of the EEA), it is unlikely to seek to use worldwide supervision. UK authorised firms within a third country Financial Conglomerate may, as part of their Part IV Permission, be required to comply with GENPRU. This would require them to comply with additional systems and controls and capital adequacy requirements and perhaps to have to provide ring-fencing of capital held at the EEA level.

H The Financial Conglomerates' capital requirements

7.52 A regulated firm that is a member of a Financial Conglomerate must at all times maintain capital resources of such an amount and type that results in the capital resources of the Financial Conglomerate taken as a whole being adequate.

Under the FGD there are four potential methods for calculating capital adequacy (both the capital requirements and the amount of capital):

Method 1	using accounting consolidation
Method 2	using a deduction and aggregation approach
Method 3	using book values and the deduction of capital requirements
Method 4	a combination of methods 1, 2 and 3, or any two of them

The relevant co-ordinator decides which method is to be applied. Where the FSA is co-ordinator, it has effectively chosen method 4. This should require the least amount of change as broadly each sector uses the method applied to it on a sectoral basis. For insurance companies within the group, INSPRU 6.1 applies whereas for other sectors their existing methods are used.

The rules work in a circular manner by requiring firms to hold capital to ensure that the conglomerate has the resources required under Part 4 of GENPRU 8 Annex 1R, which in turn refers to the sectoral rules in para 4.2 of the Annex. Where the FSA is either not the co-ordinator or there are no capital ties within a group, the rules provide for more bespoke arrangements. These can be agreed with other supervisors and imposed as a requirement on a firm's Part IV Permission. The requirement will specify the appropriate method to be used or any share of deficit to be included.

I Risk concentration and intra-group transactions

7.53 A firm must ensure that it complies with the sectoral rules regarding risk concentration (large exposure) and intra-group transactions of the most important financial sector in the conglomerate, in respect to that financial sector as a whole (including the mixed financial holding company). The effect of this is summarised in the table set out in GENPRU 3.1.36.

For the insurance sector, there are no risk concentration requirements. The intra-group transaction requirements are specified in rule 9.39 of IPRU (INS) (unlike Solvency II where these are not yet defined). These require notification on specified forms of details of transactions that have taken place during the financial year in question. The idea is to give sufficient information on the financial impact of material connected party transactions (eg transactions with a connected party the value of which exceeds 5% of the insurer's liabilities from long-term business (other than unit-linked and net of reinsurance) or insurer's general insurance liabilities (net of reinsurance)).

SECTION 8 SOLVENCY II

A Overview

7.54 Solvency II will radically change the supervision of insurers and reinsurers across Europe[1]. The Consolidated Life (CLD)[2] will disappear and will be completely replaced by the Solvency II Directive. Unlike the existing CLD directive regime (known as Solvency I) which is formulaic, the new regime aims to introduce a consistent, risk-based, regime which better reflects modern valuation, solvency and reporting requirements.

The Solvency II Framework Directive[3], which was adopted on 25th November 2009, required the provisions of the new regime to be in force by the end of October 2012. It is currently anticipated that the Omnibus II Directive (see **7.59**) will delay implementation of Solvency II until at least 1 January 2013 and will provide for transitional provisions to delay certain of the Solvency II provisions even further. It therefore seems likely that there will, in practice, be a staggered implementation of the new regime.

1 Background to Solvency II

7.55 During 2004 and 2005 the European Commission undertook a review of EU insurance law in order to improve consumer protection, modernise supervision, deepen market integration and increase the international competitiveness of European insurers and reinsurers. This resulted in the proposal for a new Insurance solvency regime.

Although the current Solvency I regime has been amended, it is over 30 years old. Financial markets have developed significantly since then, leading to a large discrepancy between the reality of an insurance business today and the basis on which its liabilities and solvency margin/capital requirements are calculated. The reforms have been driven forward as a consequence of the European Commission concluding that there are widespread divergences in the implementation of the existing insurance directives and with the aim of ensuring that the insurance sector has a comparable regulatory and prudential regime to that of the banking and securities sectors in the EU. EIOPA, the new European Supervisory Authority for insurers (see **3.57**) will have a very significant role to play in the implementation of Solvency II.

Under Solvency II, insurers will be required to take account of all types of risk to which they are exposed and to manage those risks more effectively. Solvency II rules stipulate the minimum amounts of financial resources that insurers and reinsurers must have in order to cover the risks to which they are exposed, known as 'Own Funds' which are divided into three Tiers to reflect their ability to absorb losses. The rules also lay down principles that should guide insurers'

1 In a similar way to the current exemption for non-directive firms it will not apply to small firms meeting the requirements in Article 2 of the directive.

2 2002/83/EC.

3 2009/138/EC.

overall risk management so that they can anticipate and manage the risk of any adverse events. The new solvency requirements have been designed to ensure that insurers have sufficient capital to withstand adverse events, both in terms of insurance risk (as under the previous regime), and now also in terms of economic, market and operational risk.

2 *Lamfalussy process*

7.56 Solvency II is being adopted in accordance with the 'Lamfalussy' process as amended by the Treaty of Lisbon . The Lamfalussy process takes a four-stage approach to the introduction of financial services regulation. In the first stage a framework directive is proposed (after a full consultation process). At stage two currently (Level 2), technical implementing measures known as 'delegated acts' or 'implementing technical standards' are introduced; (eg in places where the Level 1 text states that implementing measures will be adopted by the Commission). Much of the detail is added at this stage. The third stage (Level 3) involves work on recommended guidance and non-binding standards which are not included in the legislation. Finally, the fourth stage of the process requires the Commission to monitor compliance by member states.

B How is Solvency II structured?

7.57 Solvency II will be based on a 'three pillar' framework. The pillar system originates from the approach taken in the Capital Requirements Directive, which followed the international Basel II Accord for banks and investment firms. This also forms the basis of the FSA's current risk based system (see **7.2**).

I *Pillar I – minimum capital requirements*

7.58 Under the first pillar, insurers are required to maintain reserves against insurance liabilities (technical provisions). A consistent market-based system is applied for assessing liabilities as well as ensuring a greater matching of assets to liabilities. Insurers and reinsurers must adhere to a Minimum Capital Requirement (MCR), which is the fundamental level of solvency required of any insurer. This has been set at an absolute floor of €3.2m for both reinsurance and life insurance undertakings. It will be a calculated based on technical provisions, written premiums, capital-at-risk, deferred tax and administrative expenses (see **7.60**). If the MCR is breached the insurer must notify its supervisor immediately and submit a realistic recovery plan. The plan will need to resolve the situation within three months[1] or supervisory action will be taken which could ultimately lead to the insurer losing its authorisation.

1 Article 139(2).

The Solvency Capital Requirement (SCR) represents the target level of solvency which an insurer or reinsurer needs to maintain. It is a risk-based calculation and it can be determined either through a 'standard formula' or by using an 'internal model' (or a combination of both). Basically the SCR is the amount of capital needed to leave a less than 1 in 200 chance of capital being inadequate to pay liabilities as they fall due over the forthcoming year. This is the same basis as the benchmark for the FSA's current ICA test. Breach of the SCR should trigger regulatory intervention but with a view to rectifying the problem, rather than a loss of the insurer's authorisation.

Unlike the Solvency I regime for direct insurers, which requires technical provisions and solvency margin requirements to be covered by admissible assets and to comply with specified counterparty limits, Solvency II requires that insurers and reinsurers invest their assets in accordance with the 'prudent person' principle and that they invest in such a manner as to 'ensure the security, quality, liquidity and profitability of the portfolio as a whole'.

2 *Pillar 2 – supervision of risk*

7.59 Insurers will be required to submit their own assessment of risk and solvency capital adequacy (known as the Own Risk and Solvency Assessment or ORSA) which may reflect areas where, for example, the standard formula is not appropriate to the insurer. In addition, they must submit details of their internal systems and controls. The internal risk and capital review process is subject to a regulatory supervision process akin to the FSA's 'ICA' regime.

Should it be seen to be necessary, supervisors may add a 'capital add-on' (eg the supervisor may request that further capital be injected following the review process). This should only occur when the supervisory authority concludes that the risk-profile of the insurer 'deviates significantly' from the assumptions underlying the SCR. Capital add-ons are expected to be used only in exceptional circumstances.

Pillar 2 also contains, for the first time in European insurance regulation, extensive requirements relating to governance (see **7.64** et seq).

3 *Pillar 3 – public disclosure*

7.60 The third pillar harmonises disclosure requirements. Insurers are required to report publicly on their financial condition, providing information on capital in a document called the Solvency and Financial Condition Report (SFCR).

Much of the detail in relation to Solvency II has yet to emerge but there are expected to be differences between Solvency II and the current FSA regime in a number of areas. These include the more formalised nature and supervisory approach of internal models; the need to show the model is 'used' in business decisions; use of a different basis for calculating group capital adequacy and eligible capital instruments; changes to the rules relating to investment of assets and to the rules relating to reinsurance and risk mitigation.

The other point to note about Solvency II is that it relies in numerous areas on the principle of proportionality (eg risk assessment and reporting). Level 3 guidance will be needed to improve our understanding of what this means in practice.

C Timeline for Solvency II

7.61 CEIOPS, now the European Insurance and Occupational Pension Authority (EIOPA), has delivered advice to the European Commission on all Level 2 measures. It has also delievered the report of its Liquidity Premium Task Force (see **7.63**). CEIOPS arranged a series of quantitative impact studies (QIS) to gain insight into how the proposals under the Solvency II regime will impact insurers' balance sheets. These QIS studies help to guide the Commission on the best possible approaches for implementation and to assess the financial impact and practicality of the Level 2 proposals. The latest QIS study QIS 5 was completed in 2010. The key findings from QIS 5 were that although Solvency II would lead to higher capital requirements for the industry, it is thought to be broadly on track. In the UK 70% of insurers participated in QIS 5 and 80% of insurers met their SCR.

The European Commission is currently considering draft Level 2 implementing measures, following the advice from CEIOPS. These are expected to take the form of directly enforceable regulations. The Commission is in discussion with various stakeholders including the various Ministries of Finance of member states, in addition to members of the insurance industry. There will be no public consultation on the Level 2 measures but the measures will be discussed between the European Insurance and Occupational Pensions Committee, the European Council and the European Parliament. Final adoption of the Level 2 measures was expected late in October 2011 but may be delayed. EIOPA is also working on the Level 3 guidance, which the European Commission has requested by December 2011. CEIOPS published its first Level 3 guidance on 31 March 2010 on the pre-application process for firms' internal models.

There is still significant uncertainty as to whether the directive will be implemented on time, even in the timeframe currently proposed. EIOPA has a significant amount of work to do in order to enable the finalisation of Level 2 legislation, Level 3 guidance and any binding technical standards to be issued. As stated in **3.58**, it is the draft Omnibus II Directive which will give EIOPA the power to make binding technical standards and which will amend the underlying Solvency II Framework Directive to reflect the delayed implementation date. Omnibus II may not now be agreed during 2011. There is still also a significant amount of work to do to determine the nature and duration of any transitional provisions. The power to permit such transitional provisions is also contained in the draft Omnibus II Directive. This currently includes maximum transitional periods as follows:

Own Funds, transitional SCR	Up to 10 years
Third country equivalence	Up to 5 years
Reporting including group SFCR	Up to 3 years

D The MCR and SCR

7.62 One of the fundamental changes to be made by Solvency II is the move to a market consistent valuation of liabilities (on the basis that your capital will never be assessed properly if you do not have a realistic view of your liabilities). In broad terms this means that insurers should value their liabilities based on expected future cash flows (the 'best estimate'), discounted appropriately to bring it back to a current value and, unless they can find a hedge for their liabilities, they must hold a 'risk margin' to reflect the cost of capital that would be required to transfer the liabilities to a third party. As part of this process there will also be new rules on how to treat reinsurance and other risk mitigation techniques. Capital should be calculated on an annual basis and monitored. Changes in the underlying risks or the firm's risk profile could necessitate a recalculation.

The MCR is a capital requirement which approximates to a confidence level of 85% over a one year period. It is subject to an absolute floor of €3.2m for life insurers. The calculation is made as a linear function of a set or sub-set of specified variables, net of reinsurance (ie technical provisions, written premiums, capital at risk, deferred tax and administrative expenses). It is required to be maintained within what is known as a 'corridor', namely 25-45% of SCR, including any capital add-ons.

The SCR will be calculated using either a standard formula or a bespoke 'internal' model, or in some circumstances, a partial internal model together with the other components of the standard formula. The risks to be covered by 'modules' of the model include underwriting risk, market risk, credit risk and operational risk. Internal models will need to be 'used' to manage the business and approved by the relevant supervisor. This is likely to require documentation to be of a sufficiently high standard that the model can be properly understood. Internal models will not, however, be subject to a separate external audit.

E Technical provisions and liquidity premium

7.63 As stated above, under Solvency II insurers should value their liabilities based on expected future cash flows (the 'best estimate'), discounted appropriately to bring it back to a current value. One of the areas where there has been debate in relation to Solvency II relates to the calculation of technical provisions and how to determine the risk free rate used for discounting purposes – as this is supposed to reflect the type of rate available for government debt. This seems to have been resolved but one area where assuming a risk free rate causes problems for UK insurers, is in relation to annuities. The nature of annuities is such that the liabilities are by definition illiquid. Except in relation to guarantees on death, the payments only become due if a person is alive at a future scheduled payment date. Because of this, and to maximise assets, insurers often hold assets to cover such liabilities which are themselves less liquid than government securities (eg corporate debt). Under the Solvency II regime, the estimate of future required cashflows is discounted back to a present value using the risk free rate. This rate would be lower than a rate that reflected an element of illiquidity in the underlying debt. Using a lower rate increases the face value of the liability and requires more capital. This presents a problem for UK annuity writers. CEIOPS set up a Task Force to look at how this issue, known as the 'liquidity premium' issue, should be dealt with under Solvency II. The Task Force concluded that where assets with an element of liquidity are held to back illiquid liabilities, a liquidity premium could be used.

It is currently understood that the Level 2 measures will provide that the risk-free rate used in calculation of insurance liabilities (ie applied to the best estimate) will include, where applicable, a liquidity premium corresponding to relevant insurance or reinsurance obligations. EIOPA will calculate the liquidity premium and it may be applied in periods of stressed liquidity if the following conditions are met:

(a) a material part of the spread between the rates of credit risk-free liquid assets and the rates of assets that insurance and reinsurance undertakings are invested in cannot be attributed to the credit risk of the issuer and is unlikely to be due to any other reason than the liquidity of those assets; and

(b) the liquidity of the assets in which undertakings are invested is more likely than not to result in undertakings selling a large part of those assets unless a liquidity premium is taken into account in discounting technical provisions.

The work on the liquidity premium issue is a good example of an area where the original Solvency II Directive was thought to take an overly cautious approach. Much of the detail emerging from EIOPA in relation to the calculation of liabilities, the requirements for Own Funds and calibration of the SCR standard formula have been criticised as overly cautious. The Commission has also stated[1] that parts of the Solvency II framework are too complicated. It may well be that further changes will need to be agreed during any relevant transitional periods.

F Governance

7.64 Insurers will be subject to requirements to have adequate governance arrangements in place, including risk management, actuarial and compliance functions. The risk management function will be responsible for the design, implementation and validation of any internal model. The internal audit function also needs to be independent of the business (ie free to comment and with access to the governing body), whilst the compliance function must have 'appropriate standing' in the organisation. It is hoped that UK life insurers with documented risk and other policies will be relatively well placed in relation to the Solvency II governance requirements. The greatest change is expected to come in relation to the way businesses are managed. The high level aim of Solvency II is to require insurers to take a realistic and market-consistent view of their assets and liabilities. Insurers using an internal model will need to show that the model is used in the management of the business. One obvious area of potential change is in

1 Letter to EIOPA, 4 April 2011.

relation to the cost of guarantees which, if fully reflected in the costs of products (eg with-profits and unit-linked pensions), might make them unattractive. An expected consequence of being able to evidence use of an internal model is that Board minutes could need to be more detailed (eg to specifically refer to the outputs from the model and to capture the nature of any related discussions). This is something the FSA is also keen on. It will be a significant task to educate and provide information to Board members who will need to understand and have sufficient comfort in relation to both the reliability of the data going into any model, and the limitations of the model. Board members may need their own actuarial advice.

7.65 The FSA's process for approval of internal models (IMAP) was set out in DP05/4. In April 2010, the FSA announced that it required those companies who wanted to have an internal model approved in time for Solvency II implementation to submit a pre-application qualifying criteria document by 28 February 2011. The FSA has accepted 77 firms into the pre-application process. These firms can submit the application now but the FSA does not intend to start to review them until 30 March 2012. The FSA has announced that the review process will be more detailed for the top 10 firms and subsidiaries of major EU groups ('top tier' firms). However, this should not result in such firms gaining an advantage. All firms subject to the pre-application process must have completed all the required information and must have contingency plans in place in case their internal model is not approved or not approved in time. The FSA has also stated that it will try to tell firms as early as possible in the process if it looks likely that their model will not be approved. For firms which are not included in the pre-application process, they should be able to apply for approval once the directive is implemented. The FSA would then have six months to consider their application.

7.66 Insurers may need to undertake internal re-organisations to reflect the 'ownership' and 'independence' requirements for certain internal functions (eg the risk management function effectively owning any internal model and the required independence of internal audit functions). Firms will be expected to set their own limits on the type of assets and counterparties they are exposed to. There is also a requirement in the Solvency and Financial Condition Reports (see further below) to certify that assets have been invested in accordance with the 'prudent person principle'. Insurers are likely to have to undertake additional work to substantiate the level of control they have over their investment managers (see **7.73**).

Another area where additional effort may be required to formalise existing practices is in relation to management actions, particularly for life companies where the proposed action (eg to sell equities) could have an impact on the amount of technical provisions or mitigate the effect of some stressed scenarios – at least going forward. The CEIOPS guidance (in CP32) and the subsequent advice to the European Commission, says management actions must be 'objective, realistic and verifiable'. It seems clear that supervisors will scrutinise management actions more closely in the future. This could mean that lawyers may also be asked to review and help formalise them.

7.67 The Solvency II requirements for outsourcing of critical or important functions are very similar to the current UK requirements in SYSC, particularly those for MiFID firms. They require adequate due diligence in relation to the service provider and contractual terms which set out clearly the services to be provided, give the insurer the ability to direct how the services should be provided, and comply with applicable legal and confidentiality requirements (including data protection provisions). There are also additional obligations. So, for example, the service provider will be required by the outsourcing contract to answer questions from the regulator (in addition to co-operating and allowing access to records and premises) and to disclose 'developments' that may have a material impact on its ability to perform the contract. It will also be a requirement of such contracts that the service provider can only terminate on notice which is sufficient to allow the insurer time to 'find an alternative solution'. There is also a requirement to verify that the staff of the service provider are chosen on the basis of criteria that give reasonable assurance that they are sufficiently qualified and reliable. This will presumably result in a warranty in the agreement to this effect.

One of the potential issues with Level 2 requirements being in the form of directly enforceable regulation, is that the requirements are not written in the same way as UK regulations and require interpretation. Some insurers are trying to anticipate the Solvency II requirements on outsourcing, based on the CEIOPS guidance to the Commission which it is understood has been accepted and will form the basis of the Level 2 requirements. In that guidance CEIOPS stated that critical or important functions are functions fundamental to the carrying on of the insurer's core business eg design and pricing of products, investment of assets, portfolio management or claims handling[1]. As stated above, the insurer should have the right to terminate the outsourcing contract with a reasonable period of notice if, for any reason, the services rendered shall prove to be inadequate whereas, the service provider can only terminate by giving a period of notice sufficiently long to enable the undertaking to find an alternative solution. In practice, it is not clear whether the contract must use these terms or whether the parties are free to interpret them (eg to specify that they regard a particular period of notice to be sufficient to enable an orderly transition to a new provider). It is also not clear what will happen in practice in relation to the obligation on the service provider to disclose any developments that may have a material impact on its ability to carry out the outsourcing (including changes in law or regulation) and any material change to its financial resources or its risk profile.

7.68 Remuneration is also an area where there should be changes under Solvency II. The FSA's remuneration code does not currently apply to insurers. Under Solvency II, the fixed component of remuneration should be 'sufficiently high enough to allow a fully flexible bonus policy' and payment of the major part of bonus should contain a deferred component which reflects the 'nature and time horizon of the business'[2]. Any bonus should also be made up of both individual and collective performance objectives.

1 See Article 49 and CP[33].
2 See CEIOPS CP59 Remuneration.

G Groups

7.69 Groups will also need to calculate a group solvency capital requirement (Group SCR). This could produce a lower group requirement than the aggregate of the individual members' own requirements. Individual members of the group must still comply with their own 'solo' requirements but any surplus arising only at the group level (eg because of any diversification benefits) may be treated as additional capital for the individual group members. There are capital instruments (eg hybrid capital and subordinated liabilities) which will count towards the solo SCR but not the Group SCR. The group capital adequacy calculations must be carried out at least annually[1] but the position needs to be monitored and where there is a significant change in the risk profile previously used, the calculations need to be redone.

The impact on groups is one of the main areas where change is expected as a result of Solvency II, primarily because the standard basis of calculating group capital requirements and resources will be the Accounting Consolidation basis (rather than the FSA's current aggregation of the underlying individual calculations). The original proposals for group support, which would have allowed groups to hold a minimum level of capital at the solo level, with the balance being held at the group level, were not included in the final text of the Solvency II Directive. Group Support may be introduced at some stage in the future (eg following the review three years after implementation)[2]. For now, Solvency II issues relating to groups include determining whether all or part of a group is subject to Solvency II or local rules, determining the group supervisor and, if applicable, obtaining supervisory consent for a group model and considering issues of equivalence in relation to group companies located outside of the EEA. The directive also introduces, for insurance groups at least, the concept of colleges of supervisors. The idea is to foster co-operation between supervisors involved in supervising parts of a group. Ultimately, responsibility for the group is with the group supervisor, but they are required to consult other relevant supervisors. In the event of dispute, EIOPA has power to intervene (see **3.57**). The group regime is also intended to be reviewed after two years, including in relation to the co-operation of the supervisory authorities[3].

In a similar way to the current Insurance Groups' Directive regime (see **7.43**), supervision at group level is applied by reference to a parent undertaking, being either a participating insurer (eg one holding an interest of at least 20% in another insurer) or an insurance holding company (which is not a mixed financial holding company subject to the Financial Groups Directive – see **7.49**). Supervision is effectively exercised in relation to related undertakings[4] (being a group company[5] or other undertaking in which a participation is held or an undertaking which is linked by an Article 12(1) Consolidation Relationship[6] (eg

1 Article 219.
2 Article 242.
3 Article 242.
4 Article 212.
5 For accounting consolidation see Article I of Seventh Company Law Directive 1983/349/EC.
6 Seventh Company Law Directive 83/349/EEC.

if they are managed on a unified basis or the administration, management or supervisory bodies of the undertaking consist of the same people)). Alternatively, the group could be based on arrangements that provide for centralised co-ordination, decision-making or control to be exercised by one entity over other entities where the establishment or dissolution of such arrangements are subject to supervisory control. This is understood to be intended to cover mutual associations. The provisions on group supervision vary depending on whether or not the parent undertaking (eg the equivalent of Relevant Calculating Entities under the IGD) or any subsidiaries are established outside the EEA. Where the parent has its head office in the EEA, Articles 218 to 258 apply. Where the parent has its head office outside the EEA, Articles 260 to 263 apply.

The group supervisor will normally be the supervisor in the member state where the parent insurance undertaking (eg the equivalent of Relevant Calculating Entities under the IGD) has its head office. Where there is an unauthorised insurance holding company and an insurer in the group with its head office in the same member state, it should be that member state. If not, the member state where the largest (ie balance sheet total) insurer has its head office will be the relevant member state. It can be seen from this, that the concept of 'head office' is used to determine location (as it has been in the previous insurance directives). The term head office is not defined in the directive. It is understood to be the place where management of significant group functions takes place and is not necessarily the country of residence for tax purposes. It is worth looking at the FSA's guidance in COND 2.2.3 in relation to the threshold conditions for authorisation in the UK. This gives a sense of the requirement as follows:

> 'This is not necessarily the *firm*'s place of incorporation or the place where its business is wholly or mainly carried on. Although the *FSA* will judge each application on a case-by-case basis, the key issue in identifying the head office of a *firm* is the location of its central management and control, that is, the location of:
>
> (1) the *directors* and other senior management, who make decisions relating to the *firm*'s central direction, and the material management decisions of the *firm* on a day to day basis; and
>
> (2) the central administrative functions of the *firm* (for example, central compliance, internal audit).'

Once it is established whether the parent of the group is located inside or outside of the EEA, it is necessary to also consider the location of subsidiaries of that parent. In a similar way to the scope under the IGD to ignore certain entities in a group (see **7.45**), it may be possible for the group supervisor to exclude entities (eg undertakings outside the EEA) due to size or difficulty in obtaining appropriate information).

7.70 The regime for groups with an EEA parent is that the Accounting Consolidation Basis is used to calculate the Group SCR and Own Funds. This is the Solvency II 'Default Method' and it treats the group as if it were one entity although restrictions still apply to reflect the fact that in some entities, their contribution will be limited to assets covering their own SCR, eg life insurers. It therefore produces group diversification (if there is any). This can be advantageous when compared to calculating each undertaking on a solo basis (which would not consider diversification benefits of related group companies). By necessity (as you treat the group as subject to the requirements of the member state where group supervision is taking place), this treats third country entities as if they were subject to Solvency II. It will, therefore, create a calculation in respect of such entities which is different to their own solo calculation based on the local rules in their home country. Where exclusive application of the Accounting Consolidation Basis 'would not be appropriate', the group supervisor, following consultation, may apply the aggregation and deduction method or a mixture of both methods[1]. The aggregation and deduction, called the Alternative Method, is similar to the FSA's current basis for IGD. It is basically the sum of all the parts calculated in a prescribed way. This does not have the benefit of allowing for diversification. Where this alternative basis applies, if the third country in which the entity is located is assessed as equivalent, its calculations would not need to be redone on the Solvency II basis. An equivalence assessment can be made by the Commission or in the absence of a finding that a country is not equivalent, the group supervisor may assess it to be equivalent. Where it has been assessed as not equivalent or there is no assessment of equivalence, its own calculations, based on its local rules, cannot be used and a Solvency II calculation would be required.

Where the parent undertaking is not located in the EEA, there is a similar issue of equivalence. If the parent is in a country assessed to be equivalent, then its local basis of calculating group solvency can be relied upon. Where the parent is not located in a country assessed to be equivalent, it is not yet clear how the group supervision will be undertaken. The options for the EEA subsidiaries in the group are that the group supervisor will require this group to be treated as if there were an EEA level insurance holding company, applying the requirements just to the EEA subsidiaries. The supervisor could instead require the parent company to apply the Solvency II basis of calculation (ie Accounting Consolidation) for the group. This would be the most drastic option as it would subject the whole group to a Solvency II based calculation. It is assumed that this would only be done if the rest of the group created significant group risk for the EEA sub-group (eg through cross-shareholding, loans, guarantees, or other transactions) or if the group was, in substance, an EEA group with a non-EEA holding company. As stated above, the concept of equivalence is used in both group scenarios (ie EEA parent with third country subsidiary, and third country group). It is also relevant to reinsurance (see **8.23** which sets out the proposed criteria for assessing equivalence). For the purposes of the group supervision scenarios, the countries currently being assessed at EU level and likely to benefit from a finding of equivalence in this area, are Switzerland and Bermuda. However, whilst there is no finding of non-equivalence by the European Commission, subject to any guidance from EIOPA, it should also be open to group supervisors to come to their own view on equivalence in particular cases. The draft Omnibus II Directive also introduces the concept of 'transitional

1 Article 220.

equivalence' where the third country is in the process of introducing an equivalent regime. Only the European Commission can make a finding of transitional equivalence.

7.71 Group supervision under Solvency II applies only to the ultimate EEA parent and not to intermediate insurance sub-groups within such group[1]. However, where there is a sub-group headed by a participating insurer or insurance holding company in a different member state to the parent entity, Article 216 enables member states to permit the parent entity to be subjected to group supervision at national level in accordance with the terms of that Article. It is expected that Level 2 measures will set out when this power could be used.

One of the purposes of group supervision is to give a view of the group's financial position that eliminates the effect of two members of a group owning shares or holding debt or having guaranteed each other's liabilities. Solvency II provides explicitly that the double use of eligible Own Funds shall not be allowed[2]. It builds on this by further provisions relating to intra-group or reciprocal financing. Article 222(1) discounts the value of assets which represent the financing of eligible Own Funds of the insurers in the group. Article 223 provides that no account should be taken of reciprocal financing between the insurer and a related undertaking, a participating undertaking and/or any other related undertaking of any of the insurer's participating undertakings. Similarly, no account should be taken in relation to reciprocal financing of any other related undertaking of the parent entity. Reciprocal financing is deemed by Article 223(3) to include the situation where the parent entity or any of its related undertakings 'holds shares in, or makes loans to, another undertaking which directly or indirectly holds Own Funds eligible for the Solvency Capital Requirement of the first undertaking'.

7.72 In addition to the group capital requirement, Solvency II also deals with management of group risk, group systems of control, risk concentration and intra-group transactions[3]. The group supervisor specifies the risks on which the group parent entity needs to report at least annually in relation to risk concentration at the group level. This provision is disapplied in certain circumstances[4]. The requirement to report is in relation to significant intra-group transactions including those undertaken by controllers or others with close links to the group. Intra-group transactions are not yet defined. Where an entity which would be the parent for group supervision purposes is part of a Financial Conglomerate (see **7.50**), the group supervisor (having consulted with other supervisors of group companies) may decide not to apply the directive's provisions on risk concentration[5] and/or intra-group transactions[6].

1 Article 215.
2 Article 222.
3 Article 244.
4 Article 245.
5 Article 244.
6 Article 245.

H Capital instruments and assets

7.73 The directive also includes rules on how insurers' capital requirements can be satisfied. Capital held, known as '**Own Funds**', is either Basic Own Funds (what an insurer has on the balance sheet, eg the excess of assets over liabilities plus subordinated liabilities) or Ancillary Own Funds (what an insurer may be able to call upon if needed, eg unpaid capital, letters of credit, guarantees and other legally binding commitments). Ancillary Own Funds can only be used as capital with the approval of the supervisor. In addition, Own Funds are divided into three tiers to reflect their permanence and ability to absorb losses. The MCR cannot be covered by Tier 3 Own Funds or Ancillary Own Funds. It is currently proposed that at least 50% of capital held to cover the SCR needs to be Tier 1 (with the highest level of permanence and loss absorbency) and that no more than 15% can be held as Tier 3.

The rules which provide how capital instruments will be classified under Solvency II are different to the current FSA rules. Own Funds will be divided into three Tiers (rather than two) to reflect their permanence and ability to absorb losses. There will be minimum duration requirements in relation to each 'Tier' of capital. Broadly, Tier 1 must have a minimum term of 10 years, Tier 2 of 5 years and Tier 3 of 3 years (although this last is arguably contrary to the Framework Directive which provides that any excess of assets over liabilities that is neither Tier 1 nor Tier 2 shall be Tier 3). This is subject to the very important caveat of the 'sufficient duration principle' which means that the term must reflect the insurer's underlying liabilities. CEIOPS has suggested that 'the average duration of capital instruments should not be significantly lower than the average duration of the undertaking's liabilities'. Also, Tier 1 instruments must rank pari passu to absorb losses on a going concern or winding up basis.

Although the vast majority of reserves (ie representing the excess of assets over liabilities) will be categorised as Tier 1 Basic Own Funds, some assets will not be able to count as Tier 1 (eg where their use is restricted or they cannot be freely realised).

Solvency II contains requirements, similar to the current FSA rules in GENPRU (see 2.2.64 and 2.2.159) relating to particular terms to be included in such instruments. These include requirements to: obtain regulatory consent prior to repayment of the instrument (or for Tiers 2 and 3 any coupon or dividend payable); to prohibit encumbrances in connection with such an instrument; and, to ensure that the instrument cannot cause or accelerate the insurer's insolvency. In addition, there may be requirements to get external legal opinions in relation to the enforceability of certain instruments.

The current rules on admissible assets (ie a list of qualifying asset types) will be replaced by the 'prudent person principle'[1]. The regime will also encourage firms to better match their assets to their liabilities. In high level terms, this requires the insurer covering its capital requirements to invest so as to ensure the security, quality, liquidity and profitability of the portfolio as a whole and to invest assets covering technical provisions in 'the best interests' of policyholders

1 Article 132.

in a way which is appropriate to the nature and duration of its liabilities. It is not really clear what investment in the best interests of policyholders means but it could cause issues for intra group or strategic investments or where there are potential group conflicts. It should be noted that there is an additional requirement in Article 132, that in the case of a conflict of interest, insurers or their asset managers need to ensure that investment is made in the best interest of policyholders. The prudent person principle also requires that assets not traded on a regulated market be kept to prudent levels and that derivative instruments be used if they contribute to a reduction of risks or facilitate efficient portfolio management. It is not yet clear whether there will be Level 3 guidance in relation to this permitted use of derivatives. It is understood that there are currently different views on the meaning of the same terms in the Consolidated Life Directive, and if there is to be a harmonised approach under Solvency II, guidance is likely to be required.

The prudent person principle (which essentially already applies to pure reinsurers), effectively places responsibility on the insurer to decide whether the nature of any investment is appropriate and to be able to show that it has appropriate systems and controls to hold and manage any such investments. In practice, this may mean insurers having to give their investment managers more detail about the type of investments permitted (particularly where a greater use of derivatives is to be made post Solvency II). Insurers also have to ensure that the location of assets is such as to 'ensure their availability'.

Similarly, the formal counterparty and asset limits currently in INSPRU 2.1.22 will disappear but quantitative limits may be built in to the Standard Formula calculation. Omnibus II contains a provision permitting quantitative counterparty limits to be set as part of the standard formula SCR. There is also a specific requirement in Article 132 that assets be diversified and that excessive counterparty exposures be avoided. Calculation of the market risk will involve a 'look through' to underlying investments of derivatives and collective investment schemes which, unlike current counterparty rules, will also extend to UCITS (although UCITS will benefit from a specified formula to simplify the calculation). Also, as part of their own governance requirements, insurers will be expected to adopt their own internal limits on counterparty and group exposures. It will be interesting to see how these compare to the existing maximum regulatory limits.

I Treatment of reinsurance and ISPVs

7.74 The detailed Solvency II rules or, if the reinsurer is outside the EEA (and does not have the minimum rating of BBB suggested by CEIOPS), the requirement for 'equivalence' of supervision, will need to be met before credit is given for reinsurance under the new regime. Additional requirements will also apply in relation to risk mitigation techniques. From a lawyer's perspective there will be increased emphasis on risk transfer and the terms and enforceability of agreements passing insurance risk. The guidance in relation to risk transfer set out in the relevant CEIOPS paper mirrors the current FSA INSPRU guidance (see INSPRU 1.1.19A-F and Chapter 8). It stresses that although the economic effect takes precedence over legal form, there needs to be legal certainty in relation to the effectiveness and enforceability of the relevant arrangements. This could involve getting legal opinions both in the UK and other jurisdictions. It should also be noted that as with the Reinsurance Directive, supervisory authorities cannot insist on collateralised reinsurance obligations being represented by assets held in the EEA if the reinsurer is authorised in the EEA or a third country deemed to be equivalent in accordance with Article 172.

In addition, the Solvency II regime for Special Purpose Vehicles (see Article 211) is likely to be different to the current UK ISPV regime. It seems that there will need to be a fixed limit on the SPV's liability (rather than, as currently, one that is linked to the value of the assets held) . There will also be a requirement for an alignment of interests which could lead to the cedant needing to retain part of the risk (as for assets which are securitised where the issuer will need to retain 5%). It will also not be possible to obtain a group SCR benefit using an SPV for a purely internal reinsurance (ie if there is no external financing). The directive does, however, provide that existing ISPVs can continue post Solvency II in respect of their existing activities but 'any new activities commenced' after the date of implementation will be subject to the Solvency II regime[1].

Solvency II provides[2] that member states shall ensure that insurers involved in finite reinsurance activities are able to properly identify, measure, monitor, manage, control and report the risks arising from those contracts or activities. Level 2 measures are expected in relation to risk mitigation techniques.

J Public disclosure and audit

7.75 Under Solvency II, insurers will be required to produce and publish an annual Solvency and Financial Condition Report (SFCR) which, in addition to setting out its financial position, provides details of its business, its internal controls and its risk management. The SFCR has to contain a summary written for the benefit of policyholders and in terms that they can understand. In addition, the insurer will have to make an annual Report to its Supervisor (RTS) on a private basis which will include a section on 'legal and regulatory issues'. There should also be a quarterly RTS, at least on a solo basis.

H Unit-linked and non-profit life business

7.76 There will be changes to the financial position for unit-linked and non-profit life business due to the move to a more realistic market based valuation of liabilities. It is anticipated that this could take out some of the margins currently included in the current reserves for non-profit products. It seems there may also continue to be separate investment rules (ie, not the 'prudent person principle') for unit-linked contracts, provided that the policyholder is a natural person who

1 Article 211(3).
2 Article 210.

bears the investment risk and the rules are not more restrictive than those for UCITS. This could involve a significant change in the UK, as the current permitted links rules are more restrictive than the UCITS rules, particularly in relation to the use of derivatives. It may also mean that unit-linked investment contracts could be sold to corporate bodies subject only to the prudent person principle, which would be a significant derogation from the UK permitted links rules (eg for corporate trustees of pension schemes). The directive also continues the existing requirement that linked funds adhere to the closing matching principle (eg liabilities being represented by assets of appropriate security and marketability which correspond as closely as possible with those on which the value of liabilities is based)[1].

1 Article 132.

CHAPTER 8

Life reassurance

SUMMARY

SECTION 1 WHAT IS REASSURANCE?

A Introduction

8.1 This Chapter aims to give the life assurance practitioner an overview of reassurance of long-term insurance obligations (for a more detailed review of reassurance the reader is referred to standard texts on the subject). Reassurance occurs when an insurer ('the primary insurer' or 'cedant') passes some or all of the risk it has accepted from an insured person to another insurer ('the reassurer'). The term 'reassurance' is used in this Chapter in relation to underlying risks which are long-term in nature. However, in practice the terms 'reassurance' and 'reinsurance' are often used interchangeably to cover long-term business and of course life assurers often buy reinsurance to cover other (eg operational) risks of their businesses.

The importance and purpose of reassurance lies in the ability of primary insurers to spread risk and so contribute to the function of the insurance market in distributing risk in a sustainable and economically efficient way. A reassurer can reassure its liability by way of 'retrocession', the reassurer being termed the 'retrocessionaire' and the reassured the 'retrocedant'. Multiple levels of reassurance can cause confusion and, more importantly, serious practical complications. Occasionally, the same insurer appears at different levels of the reassurance with the result that an insurer is effectively reassuring itself.

B Legal definition and nature of reassurance contracts

8.2 A precise legal definition of reinsurance or reassurance has proved to be elusive. In *Forsikringaktieselskapet Vesta v JNE Butcher* [1989] 1 AC 852, 908 Lord Lowry stated that 'reinsurance is prima facie a contract of indemnity...under which the reinsurer indemnifies the original insurer against the whole or against a specified amount or proportion...of the risk which the latter has himself insured'. Because of the underlying concept of indemnity (acknowledged by the Law Commissions Issues Paper No 4, page 3) there has been uncertainty as to whether reinsurance should be categorised as liability insurance (eg an insurance of the original insurer's liability) or a reinsurance of the risk covered by the underlying contract. This issue was considered in the House of Lords' decision in *Wasa v Lexington*[1] which is considered further in **8.12** below. In that decision Lord Collins[2] refers to a statement of Lord Hoffmann in *Charter Reinsurance Co Ltd v Fagan* [1997] AC 313 at 392 as follows:

> '[a] contract[s] of reinsurance .. is not an insurance of the primary insurer's potential liability or disbursement. It is an independent contract between reinsured and reinsurer in which the subject matter of the insurance is the same as that of the primary insurance, that is to say, the risk to the ship or goods or whatever might be insured. The difference lies in the nature of the insurable interest which in the case of the primary insurer, arises from his liability under the original policy.'

The House of Lords in the *Wasa* case, especially Lord Phillips, was of the view that the reinsurance in that case was an independent contract under which the reinsurer insured the property that was the subject of the primary insurance. In that case the effect of a different governing law between the primary contract and the reinsurance contract meant that the reinsurer was not liable to indemnify the reinsured in respect of amounts held to be payable to the primary insured. The primary insurer had been ordered to pay damages in respect of losses occurring over a period of about 44 years even though it was only on risk for three years. It was therefore not able to pass this to its reinsurers under a contract which also only covered losses occurring during a three year period. The decision also still leaves doubts as to whether some types of contract (eg stop loss) are reinsurance.

As a reinsurance contract is an independent contract, it is generally of no help to the primary insured if the primary insurer is insolvent or the primary insurance contract is defective, as the reassurance contract cannot be called upon by the primary insured. One way to seek to deal with the potential problems this could cause is to insert 'cut-through' clauses under which the reassurer makes payment direct to the primary insured. These clauses are not commonly used in long term reassurance and not dealt with any further here, although it should be noted that they have encountered difficulty in many respects, for example, in terms of privity of contract, the Insolvency Act 1986 and whether this requires the reas-

1 *Lexington Insurance Co v AGF Insurance Ltd, Lexington Insurance Co v Wasa International Insurance Co Ltd* [2009] UKHL 40.

2 At paragraph 113.

surer to obtain the relevant regulatory status as a primary insurer. Section 9(2) of the Third Parties (Rights Against Insurers) Act 1930 provides that it does not apply to rights against reinsurers.

C Types of reassurance

8.3 One fundamental distinction in reassurance is between optional or facultative reassurance on the one hand, and treaty reassurance (which is usually obligatory) on the other. In the former case the primary insurer approaches the reassurer to seek cover for a particular risk or category of risks. The contract is then negotiated in broadly the same way as a primary insurance contract. In the latter case, the agreement, in the form of a 'treaty' is made between primary insurer and reassurer, is that the reassurer will accept, subject to agreed limits and conditions, specified risks written or to be written by the primary insurer. In the case of an obligatory treaty, as soon as the primary risk is undertaken, it is automatically added to the risks reassured without the need for any further action from either party. The advantage of this type of reassurance is that it provides certainty, relative ease and cheapness of administration. The possible disadvantage for the reassurer is that he must accept the primary insurer's judgement of what risks should be accepted, although in many cases the treaty will provide for the primary insurer to follow the reassurer's underwriting criteria which are often set out in a dedicated handbook or online tool. The primary insurer may retain a proportion of the risk.

A 'halfway house' is a type of reassurance rather confusingly referred to as 'facultative/obligatory reassurance' (or colloquially as 'fac/oblig' reassurance). In this case the primary insurer can choose which risks he will reassure, but the reassurer is obliged to accept those risks which the primary insurer passes onto him. From the reassurer's perspective this may be less satisfactory as the primary insurer can pick and choose which risks he wants to retain and those he does not, potentially passing on poor quality business to the reassurer. The practical value in this type of reassurance is that it enables the insurer to redistribute the risks which are particularly large compared to the general level of the business it transacts.

8.4 Reassurance treaties may be further distinguished into two main types, proportional and non-proportional. Proportional reinsurance may be 'quota share' or 'surplus'. Under quota share a proportion of the risks written by the primary insurer is automatically ceded to the reassurer. This is quite a simple concept in that the reassurer reinsures a stated percentage of a given book of business. Possibly, different portions of the risk will be reassured in different places, and the primary insurer will generally (and may be required by the treaty to) retain at least some part of the risk himself.

For 'surplus' reassurance the insurer retains the risk up to a certain amount with the reassurer accepting the surplus of risk over and above that retention. The retention will be expressed either in relation to individual risks or in relation to the total of risks of a certain class.

With both quota share and surplus reassurance a proportion of the risk is 'ceded' and for this reason this type of reassurance is referred to as 'proportional'. Other types of reassurance are referred to as 'non-proportional', the most common examples of which are 'excess of loss' and 'stop loss'. Stop loss policies provide cover against losses incurred on particular primary policies over and above a specified amount. This amount is usually fairly high. Excess of loss cover is usually arranged in a series of layers. The premium for the higher layers will be less than for the lower layers (reflecting the lower risk that the higher layers will be reached). It is often a feature of this type of reassurance (particularly so-called 'catastrophe cover') that it covers claims arising from a single event or occurrence. Issues tend to arise on what constitutes a 'single event'[1] (see **8.12**). Stop loss insurance covers total losses on particular types or classes of policy during the period of insurance (see **8.14**).

One other issue which arises in relation to reinsurance contracts relates to coverage and duration of the contract. Reinsurance contracts are often annual contracts or expressed to cover a specified period. There are a number of different coverage options used in different lines of reinsurance business. In broad terms these options are:

(1) Claims made. In this case cover is provided in respect of claims made during the stated period of the insurance irrespective of when the cause of loss started.

(2) Losses occurring. In this case the loss must occur during the stated period of insurance.

(3) Risks attaching/policies issued cover, in this case cover is provided in respect of relevant risks that the cedant accepts during the stated period of the insurance (see **8.14**).

D Fronting

8.5 Having reinsurance available enables smaller insurers to accept risks which are beyond their capacity and possibly also their expertise by 'fronting' the insurance whilst reinsuring all, or the major part of, the risk to a reinsurer who specialises in that type of business. Fronting is also used, perhaps more controversially, where the reinsurer is not permitted to conduct direct insurance business in a particular jurisdiction and therefore has to find a local reinsurer to insure the risk initially.

E Financial reassurance/alternative risk transfer

8.6 In addition to the traditional reinsurance market there is now a range of financial reinsurance and alternative risk transfer arrangements that enable life

1 *Mann v Lexington Insurance Co* [2000] 2 All ER (Comm) 163.

assurance companies to mitigate risks that they face or to optimise aspects of their capital management. These are described in Section 4C below.

SECTION 2 ANALYSIS OF REASSURANCE CONTRACTS

A Recent developments

8.7 Reassurance contracts have tended to lag behind the standards of most modern commercial agreements although it is probably true to say, that in recent years, following the intervention of the FSA and as a result of the London Market Group's work, the standard has improved significantly. However, unless a fully bespoke contract is agreed between the parties, the contract can often still be quite difficult to follow. The FSA has placed a lot of emphasis on the need for insurers to have properly documented reinsurance arrangements in place in order to rely upon such reinsurance in calculating their own solvency position. This has required insurers to demonstrate a genuine transfer of risk and the continued availability of such cover at the point at which it is likely to be required (INSPRU 1.1.19A), both of which mean that the agreement needs to be clear and should not contain terms likely to negate the benefit of the cover provided. Adequate legal checking procedures to confirm this are required by SYSC 17.1.34 (see **8.2** below).

B Issues in connection with reassurance contracts

1 Clarity and security

8.8 Historically, reassurance arrangements have lacked clarity, leading to costly litigation. Problems with such arrangements have included contracts which are not fully documented, contracts giving the reinsurer very wide powers to make changes or withdraw cover and a lack of consistency in market or contract wordings as a result of using wordings from a variety of sources.

In reality often the biggest concern for a ceding life assurer will be the solvency of the reassurer and many long term reassurance agreements (eg in relation to longevity risk) will have collateral or security obligations.

There are also cases such as unit linked reassurance where the amount due to the primary insured is linked to the performance of an internal fund of the reassurer and/or the amount recovered from the reassurer. The FSA's conduct of business rules[1] effectively require the ceding insurer to consider taking a charge over the reinsurer's assets in such cases (see **8.25**). However, one additional point to note in relation to reassurance, is that amounts due under reassurance contracts are not covered by the Financial Services Compensation Scheme (FSCS). This may be an issue for unit linked reassurance (see **8.25**).

1 COBS 21.3.3.

2 Utmost good faith

8.9 One of the paradoxes for life assurers in relation to reassurance and other reinsurance that they might have the benefit of, is that the onus of the duty of utmost good faith falls upon the reassured. This means that a ceding life assurer may be subject to the duty to make full disclosure of all material facts. The common law duty of utmost good faith is codified in relation to both marine and non marine reinsurance by sections 17-20 of the Marine Insurance Act 1906. The duty to disclose material facts can be modified by the contract. It is also possible to consider the duty waived by election or estoppel.

Section 17 of the Marine Insurance Act 1906 states that a contract of insurance is a contract of utmost good faith. Section 18(1) provides that '... the assured must disclose to the insurer, before the contract is concluded, every material circumstance which is known to the assured ...'. Section 18(2) provides that: 'Every circumstance is material which would influence the judgment of a prudent insurer in fixing the premium, or determining whether he will take the risk.' Section 18(3) provides, however, that in the absence of enquiry, certain circumstances need not be disclosed; namely those; which diminish the risk; which are known or presumed to be known by the reinsurer; as to which information is waived by the reinsurer; and which are superfluous by reason of express or implied warranty.

The reader is referred to Chapter 2 above in relation to cases on non disclosure and the Law Commissions' recommendations for changes. In practice, this duty means that life assurance practitioners need to ensure that their reassurance agreements do not allow the reassurer to avoid the contract for an unintentional non disclosure or misrepresentation. In recent years it has become more common for the duty of utmost good faith to be waived and replaced with proportionate remedies for innocent and negligent non disclosure/mis-statement with fraud remaining a ground for avoidance of the contract. However, a ceding reassured should still expect to have to negotiate the consequences of a breach of the duty of good faith with the reassurer. It should also be noted that the duration of the duty to disclose ceases when the treaty is concluded after which the treaty attaches to a risk automatically if it meets the requirements specified in the treaty.

3 Insurable interest

8.10 In relation to insurable interest for reassurance contracts, it is important to note that the risk which is insured under the reassurance contract is the same as that which is covered by the primary insurance. The insurer will have a reinsurable interest in the risk if the original insured has insurable interest under the primary policy. The leading recent case on insurable interest in this context of life risk is *Feasey v Sun Life Assurance Company of Canada*[1]. This case is discussed in more detail in Chapter 2 above, but it is interesting to consider it in the context of reinsurance. Broadly the case concerned a reinsurer covering a

1 2003 EWCA 885.

potential liability on the life of employees of an assured (a member of its P&I club). It appears that the reassurance should have been written as liability insurance but for administrative reasons the parties were trying to avoid this categorisation. The issue centred on whether the contract was made on the life or lives of any person and whether the reinsured had an insurable interest because of its potential obligation to pay out if one of the assured's employees died or was injured. The reason insurable interest seems to have been in doubt was that the contract covered an agreed amount based on an estimated liability rather than the actual loss that the underlying insured could suffer. Lord Justice Waller opined that where a pecuniary liability will arise on death there will be sufficient insurable interest. From a life assurance perspective this case does not add much to existing case law as there are in fact numerous other accepted cases of third parties taking out contingent life cover for fixed amounts (eg debtor/creditor type arrangements and group life assurance (see Chapter 2).

4 Regulatory permissions

8.11 The Financial Services and Markets Act regulates the activities of effecting and carrying out contracts of insurance but FSMA does not make a distinction between insurance and reinsurance when specifying the activities which require authorisation. As a matter of practice, the FSA allow insurers (other than pure reinsurers) to reinsure only the risks that they could insure directly. This is consistent with the Consolidated Life Directive requirement for non-composite insurers, that they limit their direct business to either life or non life. Pure reinsurers can hold permission to insure all types of risk.

5 Aggregation

8.12 One of the more reinsurance-specific issues that may arise is the applicability of aggregation clauses. Aggregation clauses enable two or more separate losses to be treated as a single loss for certain purposes where they are linked in some way. This can be to the advantage of the reinsurer, for example, the reinsurer may not be liable where separate losses are held not to be capable of aggregation, or his loss will be limited where the aggregate total loss arising from an occurrence or event is over a certain monetary amount. Conversely, where there is a deductible, it can be to the advantage of the ceding insurer to aggregate issues that arise from the same cause. Aggregation can also benefit a life office which has obtained insurance (such a professional indemnity) in relation to the operation of its business (eg mis-selling, but see further below). Clearly, there will be occasions where what constitutes a single event or cause will be unclear yet could have considerable implications for the reinsurer's liability.

The choice of language by which the parties describe the unifying factor in an aggregation clause is clearly of great importance and careful consideration of previous cases is required. The more general the description of the unifying factor the wider the scope of the aggregation clause. Examples of unifying factors commonly used are an 'event' or 'occurrence', 'originating cause' and 'one source or original cause'. So for example: 'An 'event' is something which happens at a particular time, at a particular place and in a particular way ... a cause ... is something altogether less constricted. It can be a continuing state of affairs; it can be the absence of something happening'[1]. 'Occurrence' usually has the same meaning as event but can be wider. A state of affairs or an omission cannot constitute an event. The 'unities' test was developed in relation to the question of what constitutes an event by Mr Michael Kerr QC sitting as an arbitrator in Dawson's Field Arbitration Award in 1972[2]. This arose out of the hijacking of four aircraft in 1970 by the Popular Front for Liberation of Palestine. Three of the aircraft were destroyed at Dawson's Field and the question was whether this arose out of 'one event'. As the hijackings occurred at different locations and by different perpetrators they could not be regarded as one event. However, their destruction on the ground in close proximity, more or less simultaneously, within a few minutes and as the result of a single decision was, the arbitrator decided, one event. In the absence of unity in time or place, unity of intent or central orchestration is probably not sufficient to constitute a single event or occurrence. A similar issue arose in relation to whether the 11 September 2001 attacks constituted one or more events.

In relation to whether claims for pensions mis-selling could amount to a series of related acts or omissions, the House of Lords in *Lloyds TSB General Insurance Holdings Ltd v Lloyds Bank Group Insurance Co. Ltd*[3] held that they could not. In that case a provision in an Errors and Omissions policy provided that 'a single act or omission or a related series of acts or omissions' be treated as a single claim and therefore subject to a single deductible. The House of Lords considered that the fact that claims might have arisen from the same underlying cause (eg failure to adequately train and manage sales staff) or because they were similar in nature was not enough to bring them within the aggregation clause and the deductible therefore applied to each claim.

6 'Follow the settlements' clause

8.13 In order to make a recovery from its reinsurer, a primary insurer must, unless otherwise agreed, be able to establish both its liability under the primary insurance contract and its right to an indemnity under the reinsurance contract. The House of Lords has confirmed that the parties are free to agree how these requirements are proved[4]. Many reinsurance contracts contain a 'follow the settlements clause'. These are designed to oblige the reinsurer to accept bona fide settlements made between the primary insurer and the primary insured. Such a clause was considered in the Court of Appeal decision in *Insurance Co of Africa*

1 *AXA Reinsurance (UK) plc v Field* [1996] 1 WLR 1026, 1035G, Lord Mustill.
2 Although arbitral awards are usually confidential, this one has, by consent of the parties, come into the public domain.
3 [2002] 1 All ER 42.
4 *Hill v Mercantile & General Reinsurance Company Ltd* [1996] 1 WLR 1239.

v Scor (UK) Reinsurance Co Ltd[1]. The Court held that provided the claim falls within the risks covered by the policy as a matter of law, the reassurer must follow and honour any settlement entered into by the ceding company unless the reinsurers can show lack of good faith, collusion or failure on the part of the ceding company to take all proper businesslike steps to have the amount of the loss fairly and carefully ascertained. The more recent House of Lords case of *WASA v Lexington* referred to above,[2] is an example of case where the risks did not fall within the risks covered by the reinsurance contract even though there was a judgment of a foreign court establishing liability under the underlying insurance contract. In that case the reinsured was found liable, under the laws of Pennsylvania, in respect of all property damage that had occurred during a period of about 44 years even though the underlying insurance contract had only provided cover for three years. The reinsured then sought recovery from its reinsurer even though the period of insurance under the reinsurance contract was also only three years. The reinsurance contract was governed by English law and contained a follow the settlements clause. The House of Lords held that it was a requirement of English law that temporal limits (ie the period of cover) be strictly adhered to and that on its terms, the reinsurance contract did not provide cover for the full period during which the loss had been sustained. It only covered damage caused during the period of cover. The judgment reiterates, although not actually in dispute in *Wasa*, the point that a reinsurance contract under English law is not simply a contract under which the reinsurer agrees to indemnify the primary insurer in relation to any liability the latter may incur under the primary contract. The judgments tread a very careful line between previous cases where different underlying laws were not held to cause problems in relation to less significant terms because of the 'back to back' nature of the arrangements. It might also be significant that at the time the reinsurance contract was entered into (1977), the basis on which the losses were actually awarded could not have been anticipated. Following *Wasa*, in order to provide absolute certainty under English law that a follow the settlements clause will work, both the primary and the reinsurance contract would need to have the same governing law.

Follow the settlements clauses, where enforceable, can impose quite a heavy burden on the reassurer and modern reassurance contracts generally impose certain restrictions and responsibilities on the primary insurer which are designed to protect the reassurer. It is commonplace for the reinsurer to require that certain claims data should be produced periodically. Also, where the claims approval limit has been exceeded, reference may need to be made to the reassurer for approval. These are generally known as 'claims control and co-operation' clauses. Where a reinsurance contract contains both a follow the settlements and a claims co-operation or control clause. it has been established[3] that in the event of conflict, the claims co-operation or control clause will prevail.

1 [1985] 1 Lloyd's Rep 312, CA.
2 [2009] UK HL40.
3 *ICA v Scor* [1985] 1 Lloyd's Rep 312 CA.

7 Termination and commutation

8.14 One aspect of reassurance which is different from underlying life assurance, is the terms on which the agreement is terminated either partially or completely. An agreement may expire, be cancelled or terminated in accordance with its terms or pursuant to another legal right (eg breach of warranty). However, normally termination would not affect existing obligations reassured under the contract. In order for the insurer to reassume the risks that have already been reassured, the parties need to agree a commutation. To provide the cedant with greater control where a reassurer defaults it has become more common for the reinsurance contract to provide a basis for commutation. This will involve triggers for commutation, calculation of a commutation payment and terms providing for the reassurer to be released from its obligations. Having said that, terms relating to the basis on which commutation will be effected can appear vague, often specifying a process which involves at least some input by an appropriate expert (eg an actuary). Commutation might also be subject to agreed dispute resolution procedures. However, any such terms need to be clear about when the reassurer will be released from its reassurance obligations (eg on receipt of the agreed or determined commutation payment).

It is important to consider the effect of INSPRU 1.1.19 in relation to termination and commutation of reinsurance. This rule requires there to be proper risk transfer in order that an issuer may take credit for reinsurance. In INSPRU 1.1.19E the FSA provides examples of factors which the firm should take into account in assessing whether the transaction effectively transfers risk and the extent of that transfer. This includes:

(3) whether the transaction contains any terms or conditions the fulfilment of which is outside the direct control of the firm. Such terms and conditions may include those which:

  (a) would allow the third party unilaterally to cancel the transaction, except for the non-payment of monies due from the firm to the third party under the contract;

  (d) would allow for the termination of the transaction due to an increased likelihood of the third party experiencing losses under the transaction; or

  (e) could prevent the third party from being obliged to pay out in a timely manner any monies due under the transaction.

This wording is intended to prevent unilateral termination/commutation without cause (eg because business is unprofitable). However, it has been interpreted by some cedants very rigidly as meaning that a reinsurer can never terminate a contract or pass risk back to the cedant because the reinsured has failed to perform or become insolvent unless the cedant has not paid monies due under the contract. This may be reasonable in cases where all of the financial obligations fall on the reinsurer but in cases (such as longevity reassurance referred to below) this may not be the case. Also, 'cancel the transaction' in this context presumably means that the risk is passed back to the cedant. As the cedant can negotiate the basis of commutation, if any, it seems unreasonable to expect an unconnected third party reassurer to forego the usual right to terminate to new business in the event of the cedant's insolvency or unremedied breach. It would certainly not make sense for such a reinsurer to continue to accept new risk (with or without the required premium) from a cedant which is, or is close to, insolvency. It is therefore submitted, that in some cases, it may still be reasonable and in accordance with the risk transfer principle, for the reinsurer to protect itself by being able to terminate on insolvency (even if the insurer has not yet failed to make a payment). This argument should be strongest where the effect of that termination is only to protect the reinsurer from being obliged to accept new business (ie if existing business would continue). Ultimately of course, this is a decision for the cedant who is seeking to rely on the reassurance.

8 Foreign judgments, jurisdiction and law

8.15 Subject to situations where the reassurer is bound to follow the settlements of the reassured (see above), in order to recover under a reassurance policy, insurers have to establish that they are liable under the primary insurance policy. English courts should treat a foreign judgment as binding in respect of a reassured's liability under the original insurance contract, provided: (1) the foreign court was of competent jurisdiction; (2) the judgment had not been given in breach of any exclusive jurisdiction clause; (3) the reinsured had taken all proper defences; and (4) the judgment was not manifestly perverse. However, this may not be the case to the extent that the foreign judgment covers losses which are not properly covered under a reinsurance contract governed by English Law (see *Wasa v Lexington* in **8.13** above where the foreign judgment was not thought to be perverse but it created circumstances where the claim was not covered by the reinsurance contract).

The special rules relating to insurance in the Rome I Regulation (which applies to choice of law) and the Brussels Regulation (which applies to choice of jurisdiction) and which must be applied by courts in the EU do not apply to reinsurance contracts.

C Arbitration

8.16 Arbitration is the most common method of dispute resolution used in reassurance contracts. From the parties' perspective it has the advantage of privacy and confidentiality and the ability to have the dispute resolved by arbitrators with expert knowledge of reassurance with a binding decision at the end of proceedings. Reassurance is a highly specialised field with its own complexities, customs and practices. However, it should be borne in mind that arbitration can be as costly and time consuming as court proceedings and some very large insurers will use mediation and expert determination instead.

Where arbitration is applicable it is sometimes necessary to have first exhausted contractual dispute resolution procedures. Arbitration is likely to follow an agreed set of rules, for example the ARIAS Arbitration Rules[1]. An arbitrator is likely to be selected from both sides with a third arbitrator selected by the two party appointees. Arbitrators are likely to be required to be persons with life/reassurance experience of at least ten years and to be lawyers or other professional advisers serving the industry. If the two arbitrators fail to appoint the third arbitrator then ARIAS themselves would do so. The place of arbitration will be stipulated and there is likely to be a time limit by which the decision of the arbitration must be issued together with any award. The usual rule is that the costs of the arbitration (including legal costs) are in the discretion of the tribunal, although the parties may make an agreement in this regard (eg to share the costs except for their legal fees, which will remain the responsibility of the side incurring them) provided that they do so after the dispute has arisen; any antecedent agreement relating to costs is rendered invalid by section 60 of the Arbitration Act 1996. Importantly, the arbitration clause would normally survive any termination of the reassurance agreement. Arbitration has the attraction of providing privacy in relation to a dispute unless there is an appeal to the courts in respect of lack of jurisdiction, serious irregularity in the proceedings award or a mistake of law.

SECTION 3 REINSURANCE DIRECTIVE AND PRUDENTIAL STANDARDS RELATING TO REINSURERS

A Introduction to the Reinsurance Directive

8.17 The EU Life and Non-Life Directives apply to direct insurers. As many EU countries did not regulate reinsurance, it was necessary for a separate directive to be agreed to apply similar provisions to reinsurers. The Directive therefore provides for: harmonisation of the basis of authorisation/regulation, portfolio transfers, the right to exercise a single market passport subject to home country supervision and for reinsurers to be included in insurance group and financial conglomerate group calculations. The Reinsurance Directive also prevents reinsurers in a financial conglomerate from holding captives. The Reinsurance Directive[2] was implemented in the UK mainly by changes introduced in INSPRU with effect from 31 December 2006. The main aim of the directive was to bring prudential regulation of pure reinsurers in Europe into line with the standards applying to direct insurers with a view to giving them increased credibility in the world market. For this reason, the directive also prevents member states from requiring reinsurers to pledge assets to cover the liabilities reinsured. The Reinsurance Directive is an interim measure and will be replaced by the Solvency II Directive. The Reinsurance Directive applies to all firms exclusively conducting reinsurance business, including captive reinsurance undertakings. The existing EU Life and Non-Life insurance

1 'ARIAS' stands for 'AIDA Reinsurance and Insurance Society of the UK', 'AIDA' stands for 'Assocation Internationale de Droit des Assurance'.

2 Directive 2005/68/EC on Reinsurance.

Directives are also amended so that where direct insurance firms accept a significant amount of reinsurance business, the Reinsurance Directive's solvency requirements can be used.

The Reinsurance Directive is largely based on the EU's Non-Life insurance Directives. In the UK most of the EU's insurance requirements were already applied to reinsurance business. The effect of implementation was therefore limited for most UK firms although there were some advantages for 'pure reinsurers' over mixed (ie direct and reinsurance) insurers. The position was less straightforward for certain other EU countries which had not generally regulated reinsurers in the same way as primary insurers.

B Special purpose vehicles and finite reinsurance

8.18 The Reinsurance Directive sets out special provisions relating to finite reinsurance and insurance special purpose vehicles (ISPVs).

ISPVs are special reinsurance vehicles which must be fully funded, usually by debt raised from third parties. The Reinsurance Directive defines an insurance special purpose vehicle as:

> 'any undertaking whether incorporated or not, other than an existing insurance or reinsurance undertaking, which assumes risks from insurance or reinsurance undertakings and which fully funds its exposure to such risks through the proceeds of a debt issuance or some other financial mechanism where the repayments rights of the providers of such debt or other financing mechanism are subordinated to the reinsurance obligation of such a vehicle'.

Traditionally, insurance structured finance products have been difficult to establish within Europe due to the lack of simple structures that combine tax efficiency, flexible regulatory and prudential requirements. The Reinsurance Directive provided member states with the framework to allow ISPVs to be used to provide additional reinsurance capacity. By definition such entities need to fund their reinsurance liabilities fully through the issue of an appropriate financial instrument (eg debt). Once that funding is in place they need to maintain sufficient assets to cover their liabilities (eg by capping their maximum liability at the level of their assets). They should not need to hold capital or meet any other solvency margin. The ceding insurance company should be protected by the fact that the ISPVs liabilities are fully funded and that the return of this funding (or other payments to investors) is sub-ordinated to the need to cover the insurance liabilities. However, the Reinsurance Directive left the discretion to apply additional solvency requirements with the home state.

8.19 Finite reinsurance has been described as a means of limiting underwriting risk to a finite amount. Its purpose is to smooth the effect of losses or provide financing. Finite reinsurance became controversial as a result of the collapse of various entities (eg Enron and HIH), where side letters and other arrangements were apparently used to change the substance of a transaction that otherwise appeared to pass risk. The Reinsurance Directive definition of finite reinsurance, which is also used in Solvency II is:

> 'reinsurance under which the explicit maximum loss potential expressed as the maximum economic risk transferred, providing both a significant underwriting risk and time risk transfer, exceeds the premium over the lifetime of the contract by a limited but significant amount together with at least one of the two features, namely:
>
> (i) explicit and material consideration of the time value of money; and
>
> (ii) contractual provisions to moderate the balance of economic experience between the parties over time to achieve the target risk transfer'.

The Reinsurance Directive provides that home states may lay down specific provisions concerning finite reinsurance activities including mandatory conditions for inclusion in all contracts; sound administrative and accounting procedures; adequate internal control mechanisms and accounting and essential information requirements; the establishment of technical provisions; investment of assets and rules relating to solvency margin.

I *Implementation in the UK*

8.20 There are four main areas where the Reinsurance Directive introduced changes for UK reinsurers. It:

(a) introduced a principles-based (prudent person) approach to asset admissibility for the reinsurance business of pure reinsurers and mixed firms;

(b) allowed the reinsurance solvency requirements for life reinsurance 'protection' business to be reduced;

(c) enabled the FSA to authorise and supervise insurance special purpose vehicles and (subject in the UK to receipt of a waiver) to allow amounts outstanding or recoverable from them to be counted as regulatory capital or as reinsurance/retrocession; and

(c) required that an assessment of the risk transferred by finite reinsurance be made and that the credit for the liabilities reinsured be limited to the risk transferred.

The 'prudent person' test requires that assets held must take into account the type of business carried out, in particular, nature, amount and duration of the expected claims payments in order to secure the efficiency, liquidity, security, quality, profitability and matching of investment. The reinsurer must ensure that: assets are diversified and adequately spread; that derivatives contribute to a reduction of investment risk or facilitate efficient portfolio management; and that it avoids excessive risk exposure to a single counterparty and other derivative operations.

As regards ISPVs, although this was an optional part of the Reinsurance Directive (unlike Solvency II), the FSA chose to implement it. The FSA's implementation consisted of rules (INSPRU 1.6) that provide that an insurer may only take credit for reinsurance to the extent that there is risk transfer (the risk transfer principle in INSPRU 1.1.19A). INSPRU 1.1.19.D also provides that the amount of credit be determined by applying standard methods for determining the regulatory balance sheet. For this purpose the FSA defines reinsurance widely as including arrangements with an ISPV and 'analogous non reinsurance financing agreements' which potentially include other securitisations, arrangements that provide finance and transfer risk and contingent loans (see also Section 4C below).

One of the points of note is that a UK ISPV will be 'fully funded' if its funding has been provided (eg through debt issuance) that is not contingent and if its liabilities are limited to the amount of its assets. This means that the residual risk falls on the ceding reinsurer. The ceding insurer also has to obtain a waiver before it can take credit for amounts recoverable or outstanding from an ISPV. Such waivers (granted under section 148 of the Financial Services and Markets Act 2000), are subject to rigorous vetting procedures by reference to, for example, the 'risk transfer principle' and the impact of the ISPV transaction on the ceding firm's individual capital assessment. One specific example of a situation where the FSA would not expect full credit to be taken for reinsurance using an ISPV is where the insurer invests in the debt securities issued by the ISPV. In such a case the insurer would clearly still be bearing risk in relation to the value of the securities held (INSPRU 1.1.19 F G). It should be noted that Solvency II provides (Article 211(3)) that Reinsurance Directive ISPVs (ie authorised before Solvency II is implemented) can continue to operate but 'new activities' will be subject to the Solvency II regime.

C Restriction of business to reinsurance

8.21 Ever since the first generation of EU directives relating to direct insurance, there has been a requirement in broad terms that insurers should not carry on any commercial business other than insurance and other activities directly arising from that business (although the precise provisions have varied over time). Section 16 of the Insurance Companies Act 1982 contained the first version of this rule in the UK, which was subsequently contained in the Interim Prudential Sourcebook for Insurers (IPRU(INS)). The provision has now moved to INSPRU 1.5.13R. It has often been difficult to determine precisely what is covered by this restriction (see **7.35** above). The corresponding provision for reinsurers is in slightly different terms[1]. It allows pure reinsurers to carry out reinsurance and related operations such as the provision of statistical or actuarial advice, risk analysis or research other related financial sector activities. Currently, this 'relaxation' will only apply to pure reinsurers but the position of mixed insurers and pure direct insurers may need to be considered in the context of Solvency II.

1 INSPRU 1.5.13A.

D Prudential requirements

8.22 The Prudential standards relating to reinsurance are to be found in the general Prudential Sourcebook ('GENPRU'), the Insurance Prudential Sourcebook ('INSPRU') and the Senior Management Arrangements, and Systems and Controls ('SYSC') . These requirements set out the non-customer facing requirements for insurers in running their businesses. So, for example, they include provisions relating to adequacy of financial resources, valuation of assets, risk management and associated systems and controls. As stated above, INSPRU requires reinsurers to cover their technical provisions with appropriate assets and to hold appropriate capital (see also Chapter 7). INSPRU also sets out the terms on which insurers can take credit for reinsurance including the risk transfer principle (see INSPRU 1.1.19A). SYSC 17 sets out the rules and guidance relating to 'insurance risk' and, for the purposes of this Chapter, this contains several references to reinsurance.

SYSC 14.1.19R(2) requires a firm to document its policy for insurance risk, including its risk appetite and how it identifies, measures, monitors and controls that risk and SYSC 14.1.27R requires adequate internal controls to be established in order to maintain effective risk management systems. Part of that 'insurance risk policy' should be 'the firm's approach to the use of reinsurance or the use of some other means of risk transfer' (SYSC 17.1.9G(12)). In terms of monitoring risk, SYSC 17.1.22G indicates that a firm should have appropriate procedures in place to allow managers to monitor the application and the effect of its reinsurance programme.

SYSC 17.1.34G gives specific guidance on 'reinsurance and other forms of risk transfer'. Therefore, prior to entering into or significantly changing a reinsurance agreement, or any other form of insurance risk transfer agreement, a firm should analyse how the proposed agreement will affect its exposure to insurance risk, its underwriting strategy and its ability to meet its regulatory obligations. The insurer should carry out appropriate due diligence of the reinsurer's financial stability (solvency) and expertise. It should also ensure there are adequate legal checking procedures in respect of the draft agreement. This seems to echo concerns that contractual documentation for reassurance contracts has often historically been deficient. A firm should also understand the nature and limits of the agreement. Particular attention should be given to the wording of contracts to ensure that all the required risks are covered, that the level of available cover is appropriate, and that all the terms, conditions and warranties are unambiguous and understood. This should involve obtaining appropriate legal expertise as necessary.

When managing reinsurance agreements, or other insurance risk transfer agreements, a firm should have appropriate systems in place to enable it to maintain required cover levels. This could involve systems for: (1) monitoring the scope of risks covered by these agreements and the level of available cover; (2) keeping underwriting staff up to date regarding any changes in the scope or level of cover; (3) properly coordinating all reinsurance/risk transfer activities so that the aggregate required level and scope of cover is maintained; (4) ensuring the firm does not become overly reliant on any one reinsurer or other risk transfer provider; and (5) conducting regular stress testing and scenario analyses to assess the resilience of its reinsurance and risk transfer programmes to catastrophic events that may give rise to large and/or numerous claims (SYSC 17.1.35G).

When claiming under a reinsurance contract (known as 'reinsurance recoveries'), or some other risk transfer contract, a firm should ensure that it can identify and recover any money due in good time. Firms should also make adequate financial provision for the risk that they are unable to recover any money expected to be due, as a result of either a dispute with or a default by the reinsurer/risk transfer provider. Additional guidance on credit risk in reinsurance/risk transfer contracts is provided in INSPRU 2.1.

E Solvency II

8.23 At the time of writing, Solvency II is still something of a moveable feast. The directive has been adopted and provides a framework for the more detailed rules. CEIOPS (now EIOPA) has consulted on the Level 2 issues (eg areas where the directive text required further detailed input to be provided). It is expected that the Level 2 legislation will take the form of a directly applicable EU regulation. Consultation in relation to Level 3 guidance is expected to start in 2011. However, there is also considerable remaining uncertainty because of changes proposed in numerous areas including valuation, technical provisions and reporting by the Omnibus II Directive. It is anticipated that this could lead to transitional arrangements for capital instruments, liquidity premiums and equivalence status. Chapter 7 contains a more detailed summary of the directive and its current status.

As regards reinsurance, the main point to note in relation to Solvency II, is that the Solvency II requirements will apply to both direct insurers and reinsurers, replacing the Consolidated Life Directive and the Reinsurance Directive. This is likely to impact the treatment of reinsurance for ceding companies (including ISPVs and other risk mitigation techniques). It is also likely to require improved governance arrangements.

The treatment of reinsurance from the cedant's perspective will depend upon the nationality or status of the reinsurer (ie where it has its head office). Reinsurers in EU countries (and therefore subject to the Solvency II regime) or non EU reinsurers with a credit rating of at least BBB, will be recognised under the new regime. Other reinsurers will need to be in a country that has been assessed by the EU as equivalent. In its advice to the Commission in March 2010, CEIOPS recommended that the assessment of equivalence for the purposes of recognition of reinsurance cover be based on the following principles:

(1) Powers and responsibilities of the supervisory authority

This is designed to ensure that the reinsurer is and can be properly supervised and that the supervisor has the necessary powers and supervisory tools.

(2) Authorisation requirements

This is also designed to ensure adequate supervisory structure, limitation of operations to insurance and tests similar to the 'threshold conditions' in the UK.

(3) Systems of governance

This is designed to ensure sound and prudent management and compliance similar to requirements in SYSC in the UK.

(4) Business change assessment

This is designed to ensure ongoing supervision of management/ shareholders (eg similar to Approved Person and Controller regimes) and certain business changes.

(5) Solvency assessment

This is designed to produce a solvency requirement (ie reinsurer with adequate resources and capital) similar to that of Solvency II (eg risk based/realistic).

(6) Supervisor co-operation, exchange of informant and professional secrecy

The draft Ominibus II Directive currently contemplates a transitional period for equivalence of up to five years in cases where specified conditions have been satisfied. These conditions relate to commitments given by relevant supervisory authorities, their convergence to an equivalent regime over a set period of time, the existing or intended content of the regime and matters of co-operation, exchange of information and professional secrecy obligations having been satisfied. At the time of writing it is anticipated that this transitional provision will be applied to Switzerland, Bermuda and Japan.

For risk mitigation techniques (including securitisations and ISPVs), it is expected that the Level 2 legislation will impose a requirement that the issuer retain at least 5% of the issued securities and that there be no material basis risk (eg if an index is the trigger for the instrument whether its composition is sufficiently close to the insurer's underlying risk). It should also be noted that existing UK ISPVs will no longer work under Solvency II as they cannot claim to be 'fully funded' by limiting their liability to their assets. Existing ISPVs will be able to continue to operate in relation to existing arrangements but 'new activities' will be subject to the Solvency II ISPV regime (Article 211(3)).

For captives (ie companies set up to retain risk within a non insurance group), the most important point to note is that they are likely to be subject to the full Solvency II regime unless they are very small. There are some simplifications that can be applied to the Solvency II standard formula for the Solvency Capital Requirement in relation to captives but these are expected to produce a higher capital requirement and may not be attractive to captives. Because of increased governance requirements and the fact that captives are unlikely to be able to obtain diversification benefits, it seems likely that the implementation of Solvency II will have a significant effect on captives.

F Conduct of business requirements

Ceding reinsureds are normally treated as professional customers for the purposes of the FSA's Conduct of Business Rules (COBS) unless they elect to be treated as eligible counterparties. This means that (unless they do elect to be treated as eligible counterparties) reinsurers will benefit from FSA Principles (eg Principle 6, Treating Customers Fairly). In practice, as regulated insurance companies who are experts in their own field TCF is unlikely to have any real impact. Also the specific rules in COBS only apply in relation to 'Life Policies' a term which is defined to exclude reinsurance.

SECTION 4 SPECIFIC USES OF REASSURANCE

A Unit linked funds

8.24 One of the uses of reassurance that has grown significantly, as companies have started to offer a broader range of investment options, is the ability to invest via one insurer in the linked funds of another insurer. By its nature any such contract needs to be one of reassurance. This will often be a 100% reassurance of the insurer's liability to pay out on death (eg for investment bonds) and/or to provide an annuity on standard rates (eg for pensions contracts). As such contracts are an insurance of the subject matter of the underlying insurance contract, it should be categorised as reassurance. Conceptually, reassurance of linked liabilities can sometimes cause difficulties because it relies upon the fact that the underlying contract is an insurance contract. So for example, with an investment bond which pays 100 or 101% of the unit value on death, it would be usual to categorise this as insurance contract, based on *Fuji Finance v Aetna Insurance Co*[1] because the insurer has to pay out if the relevant life assured dies. The reinsurer would be under an obligation to pay out on death in the same way and it is submitted that it is that obligation which makes it a reassurance contract.

In practice, the terms of such reassurance will generally centre on the terms on which units are made available and the arrangements for buying, selling and pricing such units. There will be additional terms for pensions business which may include warranties that the underlying business constitutes pensions business for the purposes of section 431 of the Income and Corporation Taxes Act 1988 and appropriate indemnities if such status were to be lost.

One of the issues that sometimes arises and unsurprisingly is often an issue of interpretation of the primary insurance documentation – is exactly what the 'link' is for the purposes of establishing linked liabilities and who bears credit risk in relation to the reassurer. Normally such a reassurance contract will make it clear that the reassurance debt is calculated by reference to the performance of 'notional' units in a fund maintained by the reinsurer. The contract will allow the reinsurer to manage the fund in a specified way and to make appropriate deductions and charges to the fund and those terms should be reflected in the primary

1 [1997] Ch 173.

insurance contract. If, for any reason, the reinsurer were unable to fulfil its obligations under the reassurance, if the assets of the reassurer's funds can still be identified (as they should be because of the ringfencing requirement in INSPRU 1.5.35), it is arguable that the value of the primary policy can still be calculated by reference to such fund (even if the insurer cannot realise that amount from the reinsurer). It would then be up to the insurer to recover that amount from the reinsurer. However, in many primary contracts, the insurer operates a 'mirror fund' which holds the reinsurance debt. In such cases the value of the policy is normally linked to the value of that mirror fund. The amount due from the insurer to the underlying insured is therefore limited, either implicitly or explicitly, to the amount available to, or recoverable by, the insurer from the reassurer. This means that the underlying insured usually bears the credit risk in relation to the reassurer in the same way as it does for other investment counterparties of a notional linked fund.

8.25 The FSA's Conduct of Business Rules require insurers to make policyholders aware of any credit risk they bear in relation to such reassurance. COBS 21.3.3 also requires insurers to continue to manage such obligations. The wording of this rule is not as clear as it could be and it is worth bearing in mind paras 2.29 and 2.30 of the FSA consultation response (PS 07/17) which explain the purpose of the rules as follows:

> 'Firms widely use reinsurance treaties to offer policyholders access to linked funds run by other firms. Where this is the case we believe firms have a duty to ensure all the obligations due to the policyholder are discharged in relation to the reinsured business.
>
> Q14: Do you agree with our approach on reinsurance?
>
> This proposal attracted support, although qualified in a number of cases, from most respondents. The main objection results from reading the rule as requiring firms to hold capital against the possible default of the reinsurer.
>
> **Our response:** Our rule on reinsurance has two policy objectives. The first is that the policyholders must be made aware of the implications of any credit risk exposure they may face in relation to the solvency of the reinsurer. The second is that the firm has a continuing responsibility to its policyholders over the way the reinsurer manages the business and must take appropriate steps to be able to discharge the responsibility.
>
> We have amended the wording of the rule to make these two policy objectives clear. There is no requirement for a firm to hold capital against the possibility that a reinsurer may default, **unless the terms of the policy are that the firm, and not the policyholders, is exposed to that risk (emphasis added).'**

This wording makes it clear that policyholders can bear credit risk but they must be informed of the risk (eg in Key Features and policy documentation). Where the insurer has assumed such risk in the policy documentation, the insurer would need to hold capital to cover the risk of any such default taking into account any applicable credit mitigation in place. It is rare in practice for the insurer to bear the credit or investment risk in relation to unit linked contracts.

As stated above, COBS 21.3.3 requires the ceding insurer to manage the exposure including the credit exposure to any such reassurer. It is worth noting that reinsurance debts are not direct policyholder debts for the purposes of the Insurers (Reorganisation and Winding Up) Regulations 2004, SI 2004/353 which means that they do not have the same priority on insolvency as the reinsurer's direct policyholders. In practice, this normally results in a floating charge being put in place to protect amounts due under such contracts. Such charges seek to ensure that reinsurance debts rank at least equal to the reinsurer's direct policyholders and therefore before most other unsecured creditors. Such charges are often in a fairly standard form attaching to the long term fund of the reinsurer but allowing the reinsurer to create other security interests in the normal course of carrying on their business.

As noted above (see **8.8**) amounts due under 'reinsurance contracts' are not covered by the FSCS. Reinsurance contracts are defined as 'contracts of insurance covering all or part of a risk to which a person is exposed under a contract of insurance'. It would therefore appear, although in view of the fact that a consumer often bears the credit risk it is perhaps not intended, that amounts due under reassured fund arrangements would constitute amounts due under reinsurance contracts as they are technically reinsurance debts. Insurers offering such funds need to be careful not to state or imply that FSCS compensation could mitigate reassurer credit risk borne by policyholders. It should also be noted that although the insurer may not bear credit risk in relation to such a reassurer, it will be required to bear operational risk because of the definition of permitted units in the Permitted Links Rules in COBS 21. These require the insurer to take responsibility for the reassurer's actions in managing a reassured fund.

B Longevity risk

8.26 Another type of reassurance that seems to have become more popular, and to have evolved in recent years, is reassurance of longevity risk. At the time of writing many UK final salary pension schemes have deficits which are problematic for their sponsoring employers. This has lead to some such schemes buying cover for all or part of the longevity risk in the scheme. At the same time, many traditional carriers of longevity risk have been passing on longevity risk on annuity contracts by way of reassurance either to other insurers or using securitisation structures. Reassurance of longevity risk was traditionally undertaken by a full reassurance of the business in question that included passing investment risk to the reassurer. More recently such transactions have often just passed longevity risk on its own. This is often referred to as a longevity swap as the ceding company or pension scheme swaps the current expected cashflows for the actual amounts that will be payable for the full life of the annuity. These are complicated transactions and involve obligations to provide collateral in the event of significant changes in the expected cashflows. These contracts are contracts of insurance because the company, or the pension scheme, is passing on their actual liability to make pension payments. This can only be established by reference to their actual liability and by the counterparty assuming such risk. It would be possible instead to buy a capital markets swap, perhaps linked to a relevant mortality index with the insurer or scheme bearing the risk of mis-match between the two.

C Financial reassurance and alternative risk transfer

8.27 The traditional purpose of reassurance has been to protect the life office against the adverse mortality and morbidity experience. However, reassurance is often employed with alternative or additional purposes in mind. Whilst the risk element must always remain, (see Section 3 above in relation to finite reinsurance), the primary purpose of financial reassurance is normally either tax planning or financing.

If a company is expanding rapidly, it may find that it does not have enough capital available to finance its rate of growth. In such cases the reassurer is able to provide financing of the costs of acquiring new business (often known as 'new business strain'). Probably of more concern to most life offices is the need to meet its explicit solvency margin requirement and financial reassurance can be used to help a company optimise its capital position.

The non-life market has seen an increased use of securitisation structures to pass insurance type risks (eg natural disasters) to the capital markets. These normally involve a Special Purpose Vehicle (SPV) authorised outside the EU being established to package such risk and pass it to the capital markets in the form of a debt instrument, often with a guarantee from a third party insurer. The diagram below illustrates a simple securitisation structure. The basic structure would be the same for an EU authorised Insurance Special Purpose Vehicle (ISPV). An insurer (or reinsurer) transfers some risks to a special purpose vehicle (SPV) in return for premium or assets. In return, the SPV issues a cover (usually a reinsurance contract) to the cedent, triggered upon the occurrence of a determined event. The SPV sells contingent securities to investors paying regular interest.

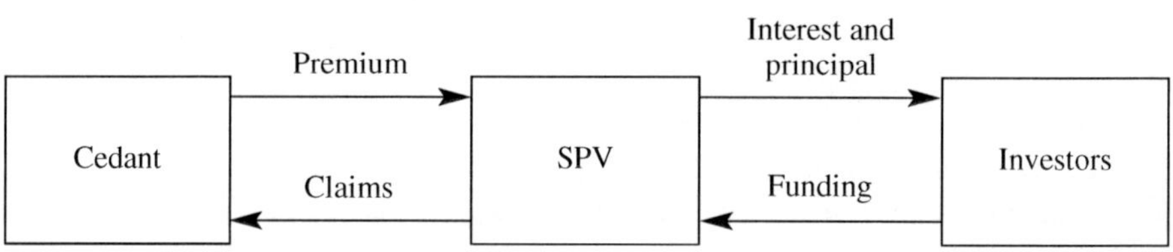

Upon the occurrence of the event (such as, the occurrence of a catastrophe), the loss is paid to the cedent under the reinsurance contract and the repayment rights (interest or the principal amount of the notes, as appropriate) are reduced accordingly. As a result, exposure to the triggering event will be transferred from the cedent to the investors, through the SPV. This form of securitisation has been much criticised in relation to sub-prime mortgage debt because of the lack of transparency and ongoing management of the underlying risk. It is also generally considered that undue reliance was placed on the insurer providing a guarantee to such issuer and any related ratings given to such debt. The Solvency II rules on credit mitigation techniques will seek to address some of these issues and, as stated in Chapter 7, may require the issuer of such securities to retain an interest in the issue of debt securities.

To date, securitisation has only really been used by life companies to pass longevity/mortality risk or as part of an embedded value securitisation. As stated in Section 3C above in relation to the FSA's implementation of the provisions on finite reinsurance under the Reinsurance Directive, to be effective financial reassurance must pass risk (INSPRU 1.1.19A). Provided an arrangement passes risk, a life company may be able to reflect the reduction in risk when calculating its own liabilities and/or solvency requirement. Alternatively, it may be able to bring into account an additional capital item (eg created by a positive valuation difference in accordance with GENPRU 2.2.105R). A positive valuation difference can arise as a result of INSPRU 1.2.79 where contingent cash flows related to the emergence of surplus are effectively ignored in calculating liabilities. This is the basis of embedded value securitisations. An embedded value securitisation can therefore be used to effectively bring forward the benefit of profits locked in a life company. The structure is similar to other securitisations involving the use of a SPV with the underlying debt being linked to emergence of surplus on the particular book of business rather than contingent on losses not occurring. Because of INSPRU 1.2.79, it is not necessary to include expected payments out as reinsurance cashflows when calculating the company's liabilities. This can create a positive valuation difference and therefore additional tier one capital. Such structures can only be used for non profits funds or in relation to charges or shareholder transfers from with-profit funds. At the time of writing economic conditions are such that it is thought difficult to make such securitisations financially viable.

SECTION 5 OVERVIEW OF A REASSURANCE CONTRACT

A Structure of a reassurance contract

8.28 The following is a high level description of a possible structure which has been broadly adopted by certain leading reassurers and reassurance brokers.

Schedule. This will set out the specific basic details of the contract (eg limits) and may also include the signing provisions.

Special Conditions. These will tend to amend or add to the 'General Terms and Conditions' so are likely to vary most from treaty to treaty.

General Terms and Conditions ('GTCs'). In crude terms this is similar to the 'policy booklet' which a policyholder would receive in that it contains all of the standard terms and conditions which, as mentioned above, may be derogated from by the Special Conditions, etc.

The GTCs are likely to include: underwriting and claims processes (eg generally, it is a term of the contract that the ceding insurer must use the reassurer's underwriting/claims manual). Similarly, there would usually be provisions relating to claims management (eg limits on the reassured's ability to agree claims and terms setting out the process to be followed). As stated above (see **8.14**) there may also be provisions related to termination and commutation.

8.29 The original policy may be incorporated by reference into the reassurance contract. The presumption in proportional reassurance is that the scope of cover is 'back-to-back' with the original policy. However, it is not likely to apply to ancillary or procedural provisions such as arbitration or choice of law clauses. The purpose of the incorporation is not always totally clear and specific clauses should be included to clarify whether and in what way the underlying provisions are incorporated.

CHAPTER 9

Claims and title to life policies

The slightly archaic term 'title' in this respect means the right to the policy or evidence of such a right or even more simply ownership of the policy.

SUMMARY

SECTION 1 DISCHARGE OF CONTRACT

A General principles

9.1 When a contractual obligation is released and the contract (such as a life policy) brought to an end it is said to be 'discharged'. Discharge of a contract usually takes place in one of the following ways:

(1) agreement;

(2) novation;

(3) breach; or

(4) performance.

The obligations under a life assurance policy may be terminated in any one of such ways.

1 Agreement

9.2 As the parties form their contract by agreement, so it can also be ended by agreement. An agreement by the parties to an existing contract to extinguish the rights and obligations that have been created is itself a binding contract provided that it is either made by deed or supported by consideration.

In the case of a life policy, the policyholder and the life office may agree that on surrender of the policy for a cash payment the policy will cease. The consideration for the policyholder is the surrender value and for the life office it is the release from having to provide any further benefits under the policy. In many life policies there will be specific terms relating to the surrender of the policy and the calculation of any surrender value (assuming the policy has accumulated a surrender value). Of course many life policies are structured so that they would never provide a surrender value, for example term or temporary assurance policies.

The policyholder and the life office may similarly agree to vary the terms of a life policy. They may, for example, alter a whole life assurance so that premiums are reduced with a corresponding reduction in the sum assured. Evidence of such a variation may be provided by what is known as an 'endorsement' set out in a separate document which may be attached to the original policy document. Alternatively, it may possibly just be evidenced by written correspondence between the life office and the policyholder. The terms of the policy may contain terms providing the ability to amend its own terms. In some circumstances a new contract may arise as a result. Care should be taken when varying the terms of a life policy because if this constituted a 'significant variation' this could have an adverse effect on qualification and potentially result in a chargeable event for income tax purposes (see further Chapter 13).

2 Novation

9.3 Where the original obligations of one party are released by the other in consideration of obligations being undertaken by a third person the effect of this is a new contract and the original contract is said to have been discharged by novation[1].

The transfer of obligations under a life assurance contract from one insurance company to another will now generally be effected under the provisions of Part VII of the Financial Services and Markets Act 2000 (which replaced section 49 and Schedule 2C of the Insurance Companies Act 1982), without the consent of the policyholder necessarily being obtained.

1 *Re European Assurance Society* (1876) 3Ch D 391.

3 Breach

9.4 A breach of contract by one party, no matter what form the breach takes, always entitles the other to commence an action for damages. However, only nominal damages will be awarded where no loss has been suffered as a result of the breach and, in practice, it would not be worth pursuing an action.

The common law rule is that the right of a party to treat a contract as discharged by a breach arises where the party in default has repudiated the contract before performance is due or before it has been fully performed. He is deemed to have repudiated the contract where he has totally or partially failed to perform his obligations under the contract. However, if the said failure is only partial then it will be a repudiation of the contract only if the party in default has committed what is known as a fundamental breach, ie if, having regard to the contract as a whole, the promise that has been broken is of major importance. As stated by Chitty: 'Any breach of contract gives rise to a cause of action; not every breach gives a discharge from liability'.(See cases such *as Suisse Atlantique Societe v NVR Kolen Centrale*[1], *Hong Kong Fir Shipping Co Ltd v Kawasaki Kisen Kaisha Ltd*[2] and *Dalkia Utilities Services plc v Celtech International Limited*[3]).

A written contract usually contains within its own terms the circumstances in which it may be terminated as a result of breach; and that is normally the case for life policies. For example, the payment of the premium is always made a condition precedent. Payment of the premium is not ordinarily enforceable by the life office, and failure to pay it within the conditions defined by the policy or agreed by the parties is likely to result in the lapse of the policy or the reduction of the benefits covered on a basis defined in the policy. This latter consequence is known as the policy being made 'paid up'. Temporary non-payment may be catered for by 'payment holiday' provisions within the policy terms or possibly by 'days of grace' provisions giving a specified number of days for the premium to be paid before, for example, the policy is lapsed.

The contract may similarly be discharged if the life assured breaks one of the conditions of the assurance, eg if he engages in some hazardous pursuit, participation in which is a ground on which the policy is expressed to become void. In practice it is unlikely to come to the attention of the life office during the existence of the policy but what is more likely is for a policy to be avoided at the claim stage on the basis that the policyholder has not disclosed a material fact, for example the policyholder dies whilst flying a private plane which crashes when he had not disclosed that he undertook such an activity (see further Chapter 2).

4 Performance

9.5 A contract is discharged by performance, ie by carrying out the obligations under the contract. Where the contract is to pay money, performance may

1 [1966] 2 All ER 61.
2 [1962] 2 QB 26; [1962] 1 All ER 474.
3 [2006] EWHC 63 Comm.

be by payment or by tender. When a cheque is given in payment of the debt it is usually accepted merely as a conditional payment[1]. The taking of the cheque suspends the right of action on the contract but does not extinguish the contract until the cheque is paid. If the cheque is not met, the right to payment in the original contract revives. The payee may refuse to accept the cheque and insist on cash; payment must then be made in legal tender, although the precise terms of the contract, where relevant, need to be considered to ascertain the precise position.

Tender other than legal tender does not discharge the debt but is a good defence to an action claiming the amount already paid. Legal tender is a tender of money which is in legal currency.

The policy terms relating to payment of claims are the first place to look. There is likely to be a requirement to execute the life office's standard claim form, which is likely to incorporate a formal discharge to the life office. It may also contain an indemnity against further or third party claims. The Financial Services Authority have indicated that they do not consider the word 'indemnity' to be 'plain and intelligible language' and so it should be replaced by appropriate language as well as otherwise being fair[2]. Historically, it was usual to provide that the claim under a life policy shall be paid at the principal office of the assurance company. This is not so common or relevant in modern times although if the question relates to the place of performance of the contract (for example, in relation to a conflict of laws query) then there is generally a choice of law clause indicating the law of England and Wales.

It is not thought that the debtor office must go to disproportionate lengths to seek out its creditor and pay him on the basis that the policyholder (or his successors in title) is in possession of all relevant facts (or should be).

As a result of the Second Life Directive[3] the law of the contract may be the law of the country in which the policyholder is habitually resident where there is no express or effective choice of law, in which case the question of mode of performance/discharge would be governed by the law of that country which could cause difficult practical problems. The policy should ideally also specify the currency in which payment is to be made.

B Payment and discharge of life policies

9.6 Much will depend on the type of life policy in question. Endowment life policies will be payable to the policyholder on survival of the life assured to the end of the term or to his executors or administrators (personal representatives) on proof of his death during the term of the policy. Whole of life policies will also be payable on death to the personal representatives on proof of title (by the grant of representation) or to the policyholder himself on surrender or encashment. Payment to the policyholder is more likely for investment orientated whole of life policies such as 'Investment Bonds'. Term or temporary policies will only

1 *Marreco v Richardson* [1908] 2 KB 584.

2 See 'Undertaking: Abbey Life Assurance Company Limited terms and conditions', November, 2008.

3 Council Directive 90/619, art 4; now see consolidating directive 'Directive Concerning Life Assurance' 2002/83/EC.

ever be payable to the personal representatives (or the policy will expire where the life assured survives until the end of the term). In all the above cases payment will be subject to proof of title, and of age where that is required. The above examples assume that the policyholder and life assured are the same person. Of course the policyholder may be some other 'successor in title' such as assignees or trustees of a trust which the policy was subject to. So for policies subject to trust or which have been assigned, payment on death of the life assured (or on surrender) would be made to the trustees or assignees and not to the personal representatives..

By making payment to the person entitled , the life office is discharged or released from its obligations under the contract. If the life office pays to the wrong person it will not have discharged its liability under the contract. The term 'discharge' is often used loosely to refer to what is in fact a receipt which is merely evidence of payment of money. However, a formal receipt may be combined in one document with a discharge of all claims under the policy.

The policy terms are likely to contain provisions on how notice of a claim is to be given to the life office. Usually this must be given in writing[1]. The notice is likely to have to be given to the life office at a specified address. Generally, with life assurance the time at which a claim is made is not normally as important as under, for example, general insurance or indemnity-based insurance and so a specific time limit for a claim is not common. However, it is possible to envisage situations where making a claim within a certain time period could be important, for example non-disclosure of a known medical condition where the passing of time may mean that vital evidence is no longer available. On receipt of notice, the life office will normally require the completion of a standard claim form or discharge form. This will usually provide for an acknowledgement by the claimant that he will have no further claims against the life office in respect of that benefit. It may go further and contain an indemnity in favour of the life office regarding any subsequent claims by third parties (although see **9.5** above). Clearly, the life office will not be protected where it can be shown that it was aware that it was not paying to the correct person.

The position of partial surrenders or withdrawals must also be considered as the remainder of the policy will continue in force. Some types of contracts expressly provide for the policyholder to take partial surrenders or withdrawals (usually investment bonds). There are likely to be terms relating to the method of withdrawal, level of withdrawals and the residual value of the policy and other matters so it is important to have regard to the precise contractual terms. It is also important to consider the taxation consequences of partial withdrawals (see further Chapter 13).

9.7 A life office may only safely pay policy moneys to the person or persons entitled to them. The life office should always obtain its discharge by paying the person entitled to sue at law for the policy moneys, or some person properly authorised by him to receive them. If the office accepts anything less than the discharge of the person entitled to sue at law, then it stands the risk of having to pay out twice on the policy. The person entitled to suewill either be the original

1 *Brook v Trafalgar Insurance Co Ltd* (1946) 79 LIL Rep 365 (CA).

policyholder (ie the person with whom the contract was made by the life office, known also as the 'grantee' or 'assured'), or his personal representatives; but may be his trustee in bankruptcy, or the trustees under a Married Women's Property Act policy[1], or the trustees of a trust declared in respect of the life policy, or a legal assignee of whose assignment the office has received notice, or a mortgagee. An appropriate payee may also be an attorney under a general or lasting power of attorney or a deputy under a Court of Protection Order. The life office should not pay an equitable assignee without the agreement of the person entitled at law to sue. Where the office has notice of an equitable interest (other than a beneficiary's interest under a trust, will or on intestacy and other than the equity of redemption under a mortgage) the person entitled to such interest should be required to join in with the legal owner before the life office makes payment.

If the policy is expressed to be payable to a third party (ie some person other than the policyholder), such a person may not have the right to sue and the policyholder (or his successors in title) alone may have the right to enforce the contract[2]. This is subject to the Contracts (Rights of Third Parties) Act 1999, depending on whether the provisions of the Act have been expressly excluded. Assuming it has not been excluded the policy may be worded so that payment to the third party is an essential term of the contract, in which case the company can carry out the contract by paying him, and the carrying out of the contract will discharge it by performance[3]. Although such a payment may be a good discharge to the life office, the person to whom the payment is made may have to account to the personal representatives of the policyholder. A person will not normally be able to sue on the policy unless it is executed by deed or the Contracts (Rights of Third Parties) Act 1999 has not been excluded and the contract gives benefits to the third party or expressly provides that he may enforce it. If the payee is merely an agent of the policyholder, his mandate may be withdrawn, and is normally withdrawn automatically by the policyholder's death. Therefore, if the policy is payable to a third party and payment to him is not expressed to be an essential part of the contract, the office should only pay to, or on the express authority of, the policyholder or those deriving title through him.

9.8 Formal discharges or authorities for payment by individuals are normally given under hand, ie signed by the said individuals and they need not be in the form of a deed.

Section 43 of the Companies Act 2006 provides that a company may contract by writing either under its common seal, or by any person acting under its express or implied authority. This section also provides that the same formalities required by law in the case of a contract made by an individual also apply, unless a contrary intention appears, to a contract made by or on behalf of a company.

Therefore, where a company wishes to deal with a life office, for example if it wishes to insure an employee's life, the proposal form can simply be signed by an authorised signatory. The life office can always rely on section 40 of the

1 Made under the provisions of the Married Women's Property Act 1882, s 11.
2 See *Re Engelbach's Estate, Tibbetts v Engelbach* [1924] 2 Ch 348.
3 *O'Reilly v Prudential Assurance Co Ltd* [1934] Ch 519.

Companies Act 2006, whereby a third party acting in good faith with a director or a person authorised to act on behalf of the company will bind the company even if the action in question is ultra vires (beyond the powers of) the company.

Since 1989[1], if a company wishes to execute a deed, it need not affix its common seal. Indeed, it need not even have such a seal. A deed signed by two authorised signatories (directors and/or, for a private company, the company secretary) or by one director in the presence of a witness and expressed to be executed by the company will have the same effect as if it had been executed under seal.

Where there is any doubt about the persons authorised to sign discharges on behalf of a company or corporation, the life office may either obtain a discharge under the company's seal, duly attested, or require evidence that the person signing is authorised to do so.

The Limited Liability Partnerships Act 2000 provided for the creation of limited liability partnerships (LLPs). The Limited Liability Partnerships (Application of Companies Act 2006) Regulations 2009[2] apply the execution provisions applicable to companies to LLPs.

9.9 Regarding payment of claims by cheque, the Cheques Act 1992 provides that a cheque crossed and marked with the words 'account payee' or 'a/c payee', either with or without the word 'only', will not be transferable. Payment of a claim, whether by one sum or by instalments, may be made by cheque although it is becoming increasingly common for the policy moneys to be paid directly into the claimant's bank account.

In many cases the sum assured will be a fixed amount and so there is no question regarding the amount to be paid out. However, in other cases, for example with investment bonds, a calculation of benefits is required. With investment bonds, the death benefit may be expressed as, for example, 101% of the value of the units allocated to the contract, with the relevant value being taken as at the first valuation after notification of the death, but in all cases the precise terms of the policy would need to be examined.

It is unusual for the policy to provide for payment to be made at any particular time. Payment of benefits should normally be made within a reasonable time of the claim. If there is a need to investigate matters concerning the death and title to the policy this would obviously tend to extend the time between claim and payment.

When payment is made, any outstanding premiums will normally be deducted from the proceeds payable. Interest is likely to be payable on the policy proceeds either as the result of any relevant policy term or, if there is not one, life offices which are members of the Association of British Insurers would still ordinarily pay interest in accordance with the 'Long-Term Insurance: Statement of Normal Practice'. Essentially, this provided that the insurer will pay interest on claims delayed more than two months from the happening of the insured event (or for unit-linked policies from the cessation of the unit linking if later) unless the

1 Companies Act 1985, s 36A, as inserted by the Companies Act 1989, s 130(2). Now see s 44 of the Companies Act 2006.

2 SI 2009/1804.

amount of such interest would be trivial. Interest is calculated at a relevant market rate from the end of the two-month period until the date of actual payment. For example, where there is a delay between death and the personal representatives obtaining a grant of probate, interest will be payable on the proceeds less any overdue premiums. A statement of account will be sent to the claimant explaining how the amount paid has been calculated.

In an Issues Paper published on 23 March, 2010, the English and Scottish Law Commissions expressed the view that insurers who delay paying valid claims should be liable to policyholders for any foreseeable losses they cause. Currently, even if payment of an insurance claim is delayed for years, the insured cannot claim compensation for any additional losses caused by that delay. However, this was stated to be unfair, biased and ignores commercial reality. The tentative solution is to amend the law so that policyholders would be able to claim damages in cases where an insurer acts in bad faith and to make insurers liable if they fail to pay a valid claim within a reasonable time. Although not a life assurance case the Court of Appeal in *Sprung v Royal Insurance (UK) Ltd*[1] highlighted the perceived injustices in this area of the law. In this case it was decided that there can be no claim for consequential loss by an insured for breach of a contract of insurance.

I Treating Customers Fairly ('TCF')

9.10 More detail on TCF is contained in Chapter 5. The spectrum of TCF is wide ranging as it increasingly permeates the financial services industry as a result of the FSA making it clear that it will be a central part of their move towards a more principle-based regulatory regime. Clearly, in dealing with customers at the claims stage the organisation's approach to TCF will be brought sharply into focus.

In July 2006 the FSA issued a paper entitled 'Treating Customers Fairly – towards fair outcomes for consumers'. The desired 'Outcome 6' is that 'consumers do not face unreasonable post-sale barriers imposed by firms to change product, switch provider, submit a claim or make a complaint'. The FSA explain that post-sale barriers to fair treatment can be cultural, contractual or competitive. The consumer should be able to change products or switch providers without incurring excessive penalty. The reference to 'penalty' is probably not used in a strictly legal sense as penalty clauses in contracts are not generally upheld anyway. Firms should also not make it unnecessarily difficult for consumers to make claims or to complain when something goes wrong.

In March 2011the ABI issued the 'Good Practice Guide: Handling Customer Claims' which was partly intended to help companies meet TCF objectives. Much of the guidance reflects what now happens (or is intended to happen) in practice although some aspects of it possibly go a step further for some providers. For example, specifically drawing attention to exit charges or 'penalties' which may reduce benefits; sending 'warm-up' communications to

1 [1999] 1 Lloyd's Rep IR 111.

customers ahead of maturity dates so that they can start planning and developing a flexible approach to claims documentation.

2. ICOBS

9.11 Any life assurance policies which are within the ICOBS regime ('pure protection contracts') will, in relation to claims, be subject to the Insurance Conduct of Business Sourcebook and, in particular, ICOBS 8.1.1 and 8.1.2. These rules require an insurer to handle claims promptly and fairly; provide reasonable guidance to help a policyholder make a claim and provide appropriate information on its progress; not unreasonably to reject a claim and to settle claims promptly once agreed[1].

9.12 In the absence of fraud it will be unreasonable to reject a claim even if there is non-disclosure of a material fact if the policyholder could not reasonably have been expected to disclose it. It would also be unreasonable to reject a claim even if it is a material fact if the misrepresentation is not negligent. It would be reasonable to reject a claim where, for breach of warranty or condition, the claim is connected to the breach and either: (a) if a 'life of another' case, if the life assured had made the statement in respect of a policy which he had effected, the insurer could have rejected the claim; or (b) the warranty is material to the risk and was drawn to the customer's attention prior to the conclusion of the contract[2].

3 Payment by mistake

9.13 Prior to the case of *Kleinwort Benson Ltd v Lincoln City Council*[3] it was not possible to recover any amounts paid by mistake if the mistake was one of law. With regard to the long-standing rule concerning mistake of law, it was held (Lords Browne-Wilkinson and Lloyd dissenting) that this should no longer be maintained as part of English law.

With regard to mistake of fact it is clear that where the mistake is one of fact material to the mistake[4], it may be able to recover the money in an action for money had and received. The mistake need not be mutual, nor need there be any fraud or misrepresentation by the payee. By way of example, in *Admiralty Comrs v National Provincial and Union Bank of England Ltd*[5] recovery was made of money paid into the current account of a deceased customer of the bank in the

1 ICOBS 8.1.1.
2 ICOBS 8.1.2.
3 TLR 30/10/98; ILR 4/11/98; (1998) 4 All ER 513; (1998) 3 WLR 1095; (1998) Lloyd's Bank Rep 387; (1999) LGR 1. (See also *Deutsche Morgan Grenfell Group plc v Inland Revenue Commissioners* [2006] All ER (D) 298 (Oct).)
4 *Bize v Dickinson* (1786) 1 Term Rep 285, ie which if true would have rendered the party under the mistake liable to pay the money in question or which is otherwise fundamental to the transaction.
5 (1922) 127 LT 452.

belief that he was alive. A person who accepts and keeps money to which he knows he is not entitled because of a mistake by the payer may furthermore be guilty of theft.

> *R v Gilks*[1]
>
> G kept £106 of £117 paid to him by a bookmaker which he knew he was not entitled to because of a mistake on the bookmaker's part. He admitted he knew of the mistake, but said it was 'hard lines' on the bookmaker and 'there is nothing dishonest about keeping the money'. Held, by the Court of Appeal that he was properly convicted of theft under section 1(1) of the Theft Act 1968, since he was guilty of theft at the moment he accepted the money. But the refusal to restore the money was not theft as he was under no obligation to restore a sum which arose out of a betting transaction.

9.14 Where a life office pays moneys under a mistake of fact, not realising the true position, it will still be entitled to recover even if it had been careless in its investigation of the facts. The general rule is that carelessness is irrelevant. Having the means to obtain the knowledge is not regarded as synonymous with knowledge for these purposes.

> *Kelly v Solari*[2]
>
> The plaintiff was the director of a life assurance company. The defendant's husband had been insured, but had not paid the last premium. The insurance therefore had lapsed, and the lapse had been noted by the company. The defendant claimed the policy moneys, on her husband's death, and the plaintiff, forgetting the lapse, paid them to her. It was held, that the moneys could be recovered by the plaintiff.

In *Kelly*, Parke B laid down the principle that money can be recovered if paid:

> 'upon the supposition that a specific fact is true, which could entitle the payee to the money, but which fact is untrue, and the money would not have been paid if it had been known to the payer that the fact was untrue…'

This principle was cited with approval in the case of:

> *Barclays Bank Ltd v WJ Simms Son & Cook (Southern) Ltd*[3]
>
> A housing association, a customer of the plaintiff bank, drew a cheque in favour of a builder to cover an interim payment under a building contract. When the builder went into receivership the association immediately stopped the cheque. The defendant receiver, however, in good faith, had it specially cleared and, owing to an oversight by the plaintiff, paid. The bank sued the liquidator for money paid by mistake, relying on *Kelly v Solari*. They said that they had paid the cheque in the mistaken belief that it had not been stopped. It was held that they could recover.

1 [1972] 3 All ER 280.
2 (1841) 9 M & W 54.
3 [1980] QB 677.

For such cases of unilateral mistake it should be noted that in order to be entitled to rescind the contract the mistake must relate to a term of the contract[1].

In addition, the case of *Hartog v Colin & Shields*[2] emphasised the state of mind of the party seeking to enforce the contract against the mistaken party. So, for example, if that party either knew or must be taken to know that a term of a contract is incorrect then he cannot enforce the contract.

9.15 It may be inequitable to require that the money be repaid, where there has been some representation by the life office which has misled the person to whom the money was mistakenly paid and caused that person to alter his or her position. This is the rule known as 'estoppel'. However, the fact that such a person cannot be put into the same position he was in before the money was paid will not necessarily prevent the money being recovered. If it can be shown that the payee would not have spent the money if he had not been influenced by the payer's mistake, the payer will not be able to recover.

Avon County Council v Howlett[3]

The defendant was injured in the course of employment with the plaintiffs and as a result was absent from work for nearly two years. The plaintiffs discovered that during that period they had overpaid the defendant to the extent of £1,007. They brought an action against the defendant claiming repayment of that sum on the ground that it had been paid by mistake. It was held that the plaintiffs were estopped from asserting their right to repayment. This was due to the fact that the plaintiffs made representations to the defendant which led him to believe that he was entitled to treat the overpaid moneys as his own. The misrepresentations were not caused by incorrect information given to them by the defendant and the overpayments were not brought about by the defendant's own fault. The defendant changed his position in reliance on the representations, by losing the claim for £86.11 social security benefit and expending the sum of £460.50 which he would not have incurred if he had not been paid the moneys in dispute. Therefore, the plaintiffs should be estopped from recovering the overpaid moneys at least to the extent of £546.61. However, Slade LJ held that estoppel was incapable of operating pro tanto, ie in respect of part only of the overpaid moneys, on the basis that it was contrary to principle and authority. He did add, however, that there may be exceptional circumstances where estoppel could operate to prevent the payer from recovering part but not all the overpaid moneys. However, such circumstances did not exist in the particular circumstances of the case.

9.16 The cases of *Kelly v Solari* and *Avon County Council* were considered in *Scottish Equitable plc v Gordon Derby*[4].

Scottish Equitable plc v Gordon Derby

Scottish Equitable (SE) claimed restitution of £162,000 paid to GD under a mistake of fact as to the amount of the final retirement benefits to which he was

1 *Statoil v Louis Dreyfus Energy Services LP* [2008] EWHC 2257 (Comm).
2 [1939] 3 All ER 566.
3 [1983] 1 All ER 1073.
4 [2001] 3 All ER 818.

> properly entitled. In calculating and paying out these benefits, SE failed to take into account certain benefits that GD had taken early. The total overpayment was £172,451. This was applied by GD in reducing his mortgage, on ordinary living expenses and the balance in a new pension fund with Norwich Union (NU). GD relied upon change of position and/or estoppel, contending also that carelessness was a bar to the recovery of money paid under a mistake. In the circumstances NU were prepared to unwind the policy and return him to the position he would have been in if SE's mistake had not been made. At first instance, Harrison J held that mere carelessness did not preclude the recovery of money paid under a mistake of fact, and GD could not rely on either change of position (there was no causal link) or estoppel by way of defence to SE's claim for the balance of the overpayment. The Court of Appeal held that the judge correctly applied the test set out in *Kelly v Solari*. The defence of change of position was not available to GD as the changes made by GD to his lifestyle were modest and not irreversible. The Court of Appeal also agreed with the judge that the defence of estoppel was precluded by the decision in *Avon County Council v Howlett* mainly because it is incapable of operating 'pro tanto'. It can only ever be a complete defence which would have been inequitable in this case. However, with regard to the pro tanto operation of the rule signposted in *Avon County Council v Howlett* for a case where the decision was that a partial retention of money was appropriate see *National Westminster Bank plc v Somer International (UK) Ltd*[1].

The Pensions Ombudsman case of *Kenny*[2] emphasised a pragmatic approach to estoppel and the Ombudsman introduced an additional requirement of good faith. In this case the pension was 64% larger than it should have been and so the complainant 'should have been aware that something was amiss'.

C Statute of Limitation

9.17 Section 5 of the Limitation Act 1980 provides that all actions founded on a simple contract must be commenced within six years from the date when the cause of action arises. Therefore, any action to recover the sum assured under a life policy which has not been issued under seal should be brought within six years of the happening of the event upon which the benefits under the policy are expressed to be payable. Normally, the sum assured under a life policy is payable only after proof, satisfactory to the life office, of the death of the life assured and title to the policy (or simply title to the policy on maturity of an endowment assurance or surrender of a life policy) has been provided. As the proof required by the life office relating to death and title are wholly within the power of the claimant the operation of the Limitation Act 1980 is not suspended in the meantime. However, where an action is based on fraud or mistake the period of limitation only begins to run when the fraud, concealment or mistake is discovered, or could with reasonable diligence have been discovered[3].

1 [2001] EWCA Civ 970.
2 *Kenny* (28034/5). See also *Smith* (Q00734).
3 Limitation Act, 1980, s 32.

The relevant period during which an action must be brought is 12 years in the case of policies issued under seal[1].

D Payment into court

9.18 If, in the opinion of the board of directors of a life office, no sufficient discharge can be obtained in any other way, the life office may pay the policy moneys into court under the Life Assurance Companies (Payment into Court) Act 1896[2]. The procedure for doing this is set out in Part 37 of the Civil Procedure Rules 1998 (Practice Direction – Miscellaneous Provisions about Payment into Court, paras 4 and 5). An office wishing to make payment into court must file an affidavit or witness statement made by its secretary or other authorised officer[3]. The receipt or certificate of the proper officer of the court is a sufficient discharge to the life office for the moneys paid into court. Payment may not be made into court under the Act if any other action is pending in England in relation to the policy unless the court gives leave to do so. The office is required to give immediate notice of a payment into court to every person appearing to be entitled to the moneys or to have an interest in them. The life office cannot deduct from the policy moneys any costs of or incidental to the payment into court and must bear the costs of payment in.

By proceeding under the 1896 Act the life office obtains an absolute discharge against all claims present and future and not only, as in the case of interpleader proceedings, in respect of an existing conflict between rival claimants. Payment into court therefore offers a remedy when the office faces the problem that the person legally entitled or the person who has given notice of his equitable claim cannot be ascertained or traced or where, perhaps, the title is unclear or unsatisfactory. For example, the identity of an assignee is not clear from a deed of assignment. Where the office claims a charge or other interest in the policy moneys it should deduct the amount it claims, paying only the balance into court. Payment in of the whole amount may be taken as an admission by the office that it has no claim on the moneys in court.

The life office must bear the costs of payment in, unless it has agreed with the claimants that they will bear the costs. The office will not normally have to bear the costs of a subsequent application for payment out unless the original payment into court was not reasonable. The advantage to the life office is that it will avoid the cost of deciding the issue of entitlement as between competing claimants. Although possible, it should rarely be necessary to pay into court solely on the ground of the loss of policy documents unless conflicting claims to the policy are also being made and cannot be reconciled.

9.19 Where the life office could be sued in different countries (eg England and Scotland) payment into court in one action is not an absolute bar to proceed-

1 Limitation Act 1980, s 8.
2 As amended by the Administration of Justice Act 1965, s 17 and the Courts Act 1971, s 56.
3 Para 4.1 (See Appendix 7).

ings in the other country. However, generally, if payment into court is made in the country in which the claim is payable, the court in the other country would not allow proceedings to continue until there had been an adjudication on the claim against the moneys paid in.

The Life Assurance Companies (Payment into Court) Act 1896 applies to Northern Ireland but does not apply to Scotland. The office faced there with competing claims on the policy may be able to raise an action of multiplepoinding in the Court of Session. This process is similar to interpleader proceedings in England. It is only available when the policy money has become payable and the office admits liability to pay to the person or persons entitled. The only interest of the life office must be that of obtaining a discharge and there must be conflicting claims to the proceeds (the 'fund in medio'). The procedure of multiplepoinding is not available where the inability to obtain a discharge arises from the inability to find a claimant or from some doubt as to the validity of the title produced by a sole claimant.

SECTION 2 PROOF

A Proof of death

9.20 Policy proceeds arising on death are usually made payable when proof satisfactory to the life office has been submitted of the death of the life assured and of the title of the claimant. Death must be proved by such evidence as the life office requires but its demands for proof must not be unreasonable – which will be a question of fact in the circumstances of the particular case[1]. It should be borne in mind that the life office is often being asked to pay out considerable sums of money hence it not being unreasonable to require a commensurate level of proof.

Death must be proved by:

(1) direct evidence, ie by the oath of some person present at the death (eg a doctor);

(2) death certificate, ie by production of a certified copy entry in the Register of Deaths or in some other public record which is admissible in evidence; or

(3) evidence of prolonged absence or other facts from which the fact of death may be properly inferred.

In practice proof is usually provided in accordance with (2) above.

Generally, where a death claim arises under a life policy, an official certificate of death (ie a certified copy of the entry of death in an official register) should be produced to the life office. A certified copy of an entry, made in the General

1 *Braunstein v Accidental Death Insurance Company* (1861) 1 B&S 782.

Register Office and bearing the seal or stamp of that office is, under section 34(6) of the Births and Deaths Registration Act 1953, sufficient evidence of death without any other proof of entry. In Scotland the relevant provisions are contained in the Registration of Births, Deaths and Marriages (Scotland) Act 1965. In Northern Ireland the provisions of the Births and Deaths Registration (Northern Ireland) Order 1976 are the governing provisions.

9.21 In practice an official copy death certificate issued by a local Registrar is normally accepted. Because of the ease with which it is possible to produce falsified reproductions of death certificates by photographic or similar means, copy death certificates should not be accepted. Furthermore, from January 2001 the position with regard to copy certificates (whether for death, marriage or birth) was clarified so that the Crown now assert copyright over such documents so that only originals can be used unless a licence is obtained. Where the age of the life assured has not been admitted and the age in the death certificate does not correspond with the life office's records, proof of age should be called for. This may be established by:

(1) direct evidence as to the date of birth;

(2) birth certificate, ie by production of a certified copy entry in the Registry of Births, or in some other public record of the birth which is admissible in evidence; or

(3) baptismal certificate (albeit that this is only evidence of the date and fact of baptism).

For certain policies, such as investment bonds with very little additional life cover, the age of the life assured is not important in terms of, for example, setting premium levels and so verifying age is likewise not so important.

In the case of jurisdictions outside of the United Kingdom, evidence may be provided by a certified entry in a foreign public register, the use of which is provided for by the Evidence (Foreign, Dominion and Colonial Documents) Act 1933 and the Oaths and Evidence (Overseas Authorities and Countries) Act 1963.

9.22 Where the life assured has disappeared and there is no direct evidence as to whether he is alive or dead then his death may be proved by either:

(1) circumstantial evidence, ie proof of facts from which a jury might reasonably infer the fact of death; or

(2) a presumption of common law arising from the life assured's disappearance and absence for seven years.

Where the life assured was also the policyholder, in order to obtain a Grant of Representation, it will be necessary for someone to apply to the district judge or registrar for leave (permission) to swear the death.

Leave to swear the death does not find as a matter of fact that the individual has died but is required in order to obtain a grant of representation where there is no direct evidence of death. The application to the High Court for leave to swear the death in these circumstances must be made only after the best possible enquiries and searches have been made amongst those who would be likely to hear of or from him if he were alive[1]. The application must be accompanied by an affidavit which should include particulars of all policies on his life. Notice should be given to the life office. No order will be made until the life offices in question have been notified of the application. If the life office opposes the application and is successful it will get its costs, but the life office may find it difficult to argue against the declaration if it does not take part in the proceedings. In a court action it may well be sufficient if the party who alleges death simply calls the missing person's nearest relatives in the United Kingdom to give evidence that he was living here and disappeared more than seven years ago and that they have not heard from him or of him since he disappeared. The party alleging death must, however, show that reasonable enquiry has been made abroad if it was known that the missing person went or intended to go to a foreign country.

Where enquiries are made in respect of a missing person, rumours and reports may be heard from people who think they have seen him and due enquiries appropriate to the circumstances should be made. If, however, such rumours and reports are in fact without foundation, the fact that they have been received within the seven years does not prevent the presumption of death arising. Sometimes, a person disappears in circumstances which suggest that even if he were alive it would be unlikely that his relatives or friends would hear of or from him. There may be good reason why he would wish to disappear from the circles in which he moved previously. In such circumstances the presumption of death does not arise from the mere fact of seven years' absence without being heard of. The court will want further evidence[2].

9.23 Although death may be presumed after seven years' absence, there is no presumption of law as to the exact time of death within the seven-year period[3]. So if there is a need to establish death at or before any particular time during the seven years (eg where a temporary assurance expired during that period) this must be proved as a fact by suitable evidence, eg by evidence of ill-health when he was last heard of. The position where the individual is in a 'persistent vegetative state' and would die but for a life support system can raise extremely difficult issues where, for example, such a state may persist persists beyond the termination date of a temporary insurance.

As mentioned in (1) above, if the life assured has disappeared, it is not always necessary to wait for seven years before his death can be proved. The circumstances surrounding his disappearance (eg if he was a passenger on a ship that went missing) may be such that a court may reasonably find as a matter of fact that the life assured is dead, and so an application for leave to swear the death may be made within the seven years[4]. For example, in *National Trust*

1 *Prudential Assurance Co v Edmonds* (1877) 2 App Cas 487.
2 *Watson v England* (1844) 14 Sim 28.
3 *Re Phené's Trusts* [1870] 5 Ch App 139 and *Chard v Chard* [1956] P 259, [1955] 3 All ER 721.
4 *Re Norris's Goods* (1858) 1 Sw & Tr 6.

v Sterling[1] a person was lost at sea who had been on the SS Titanic. In this case it was enough for an affidavit to be produced that the insured had been lost on board at the time of sinking and had not been seen among the survivors. In *Bayes-Walker and another v Bayes-Walker and others*[2] the High Court declared that a missing person was to be presumed dead for the purposes of rights to a life insurance policy amongst other assets. The court applied the rebuttable presumption that a person is dead if those who would be likely to have heard news of him had not heard anything of him for at least seven years.

A case in this area which caught the public imagination was that of John Darwin who faked his own death in a supposed canoe accident in 2002. A death certificate was issued following leave to swear his death had been granted. This enabled his wife to claim under his life assurance policies.

No action can be brought against the life office where the life assured has disappeared until the personal representatives have completed their title by obtaining probate or letters of administration. The personal representatives are unable to do this until they have obtained leave to swear the death.

9.24 In cases of common disaster where it is likely that more than one application for leave to swear the death will emerge the Principal Registry will keep a record of all evidence accepted when the first application is granted for guidance in respect of subsequent applications, so that in such a case, enquiry should first be made to the Principal Registry. If passenger lists and evidence of death have been supplied to the Principal Registry by, for example, the shipping company or airline concerned then a circular may be issued listing the names of those who have died and no further evidence of death will be necessary and there will be no need for leave to swear the death. However, for disasters such as the World Trade Centre in New York destruction on 11 September 2001 and the tsunami in South East Asia on 26 December 2004, leave to swear the death in each case (in the absence of a death certificate) would be required in view of the difficulties in ascertaining the victims with complete accuracy.

If the courts of a foreign country where the presumed deceased was domiciled have made orders presuming his death and vesting his estate in the persons entitled, his death may (depending on the circumstances) be presumed without further evidence, but if there is only an order by the foreign court presuming the death but not vesting the estate, further evidence will certainly be required to show that the presumed deceased is in fact dead[3].

A life office will not necessarily be bound by an order for presumption of death made for some purpose other than that of obtaining a grant of representation, or even by an order of the Family Division giving leave to swear the death. It is still open to the office to defend proceedings against it either on the ground that there is no evidence of death or that there is no evidence of death before the date when the policy expired. But once the will has been proved or an administrator appointed, the office will then become liable to an action to enforce payment and may have to pay the costs of all subsequent proceedings. The life

1 [1916] QR 51.
2 [2010] EWHC 3142.
3 *Re Schulhof, Re Wolf* [1948] p 66, [1947] 2 All ER 841; *Re Dowds' Goods* [1948] P 256.

office may decide to pay the claim and if it emerges that the life assured is still alive it can seek to reclaim the money paid out on the basis of a mistake of fact although once payment has been made retrieving the funds may prove difficult.

In Scotland the Presumption of Death (Scotland) Act 1977, which repealed the Presumption of Life Limitation (Scotland) Act 1891, governs the position for presuming the death of a person who is thought to have died or has not been heard of for seven years in Scotland. The earlier statute did not apply to claims under life policies and the claimant had to prove the death as best he could. Under the 1977 Act, where a person, domiciled in Scotland (or resident there for a year prior to the action), is missing and is thought to have died or has not been known to be alive for a period of at least seven years then any person having an interest may raise an 'action of declarator' of the death of the missing person.

9.25 If two persons die in circumstances where it is uncertain which of them died first, the deaths are, for all purposes affecting the title to property, presumed to have occurred in order of seniority, and so the younger is deemed by section 184 of the Law of Property Act 1925 to have survived the elder. Therefore, if the elder has by will left his property to the younger, the bequest will not lapse. Conversely, a bequest in a will from younger to elder will lapse. These provisions are subject to the Law Reform (Succession) Act 1995[1], under which the intestate's spouse must survive the intestate by 28 days in order to be entitled. This statutory presumption in section 184 can be excluded by an express contrary provision in a will. This was the case in *Re Guggenheim*[2] where the deceased had made a declaration to the effect that in the event of he and his wife dying simultaneously, or in circumstances where there was no evidence as to who died first, his wife should be deemed to have predeceased him.

The statutory presumption does not apply for the purpose of incidence of inheritance tax. In this case the persons are treated as having died at the same instant and their property as having devolved accordingly[3].

9.26 The seniority rule applies even though the circumstances suggest that the victims probably died at the same time.

> *Hickman v Peacey*[4]
>
> Four persons were killed when a bomb exploded in a small air raid shelter. There was no evidence to show whether any of them had survived the others. It was held that in the absence of such evidence it was uncertain which of them survived the other or others within the meaning of section 184 and the section applied. The fact that it appeared they had died simultaneously did not make the section inapplicable.

Section 31 of the Succession (Scotland) Act 1964 provides that where two persons have died in circumstances indicating that they died simultaneously, or

1 Section 1(1), (3).
2 (1941) *Times*, 20 June.
3 Inheritance Tax Act 1984, s 4(2).
4 [1945] AC 304.

rendering it uncertain which survived the other (known in Scotland as 'common calamity'), then for all purposes affecting the title to property or claims to legal rights or the prior rights of a surviving spouse[1], (a) where the persons are husband and wife it shall be presumed that neither survived the other, and (b) in any other case it shall be presumed that the younger survived the elder, unless the elder has left a testamentary disposition containing a provision in favour of the younger if he survives the elder and failing the younger in favour of a third person, and the younger person has died intestate, in which case it shall be presumed for the purposes of that provision that the elder survived the younger. In *Lamb v Lord Advocate etc*[2] it was held that no presumption arises for consideration if there is proof that one person survived the other and such proof is on a balance of probabilities.

B Proof of survival

9.27 With a life annuity, payment by a life office depends on survival. Evidence of continued existence may be requested to be certified by a responsible independent person, or the annuitant himself.

Normally life annuity payments are made directly to the bank account of the annuitant. Evidence of survival may then be waived, on the understanding that the bank will inform the life office when it receives notice of the death of the customer. This obviously relies on the bank informing the life office appropriately and the bank would ordinarily exclude or seek to refuse liability for failure to do so. Although not ideal, it may be the most practical way to proceed given the administrative inconvenience to the life office in verifying the annuitant's continued existence.

This practice involves certain risks (eg that both husband and wife might be entitled to draw on the same account), but in practice the risk may be thought worth taking in the circumstances. Also, the life office should be able to recover amounts paid out in the mistaken belief that the annuitant is still alive[3].

C Proof of title

9.28 A life office may need to examine title to a policy in many different circumstances, but most cases will fall under one of the following heads:

(1) Claim on death.

(2) Claim on maturity (ie survival of term of endowment assurance).

(3) Surrender.

1 See **9.62–9.64**.
2 1976 SLT 151.
3 See Section 1B, 'Payment by mistake', **9.13–9.16**.

(4) Part surrender or surrender of bonus.

(5) Conversion, eg to paid-up policy.

(6) Exercise of option.

(7) Loan.

1 Where no notice has been received

9.29 Where the claimant is the person who effected the policy, and the life office has received no notice (formal or informal, legal or equitable) of a trust, assignment, insolvency or incapacity, the claimant should in general be required to produce the policy, and to sign a suitable form of request, discharge or authority for payment.

2 Where notice has been received

9.30 Where the life office has received notice of a trust, assignment or charge, it would normally call for production of the original deeds or documents relating to the title to the policy and examine them before it pays the proceeds to the claimant(s) or permits any other dealings with the policy. It would not normally be concerned with documents which evidence dealings with beneficial or equitable interests protected by trustees (but should concern itself with trustee dealings such as deeds of appointment and retirement of trustees), or with second or subsequent mortgages, but the proper course is to call for all documents of which notice has been received. Until it has examined them the office cannot be certain that they affect only the beneficial interests. In addition, the life office is not able to ignore equitable interests where, for example, it has actual or constructive knowledge that actions in connection with a policy will prejudice such an interest.

D Loss of policy documents

9.31 Life offices frequently have to decide what course of action to take where a claim is made (or other dealings are proposed) where the policy is stated to be lost or destroyed. In some cases, where the amount of money involved is modest the life office may take a pragmatic approach and simply make payment on request especially if payment is to be made to the account from which premiums were paid (although care needs to be exercised for joint accounts, trust policies, etc). Assuming the life office is not prepared to do this the following sets out the general position.

There are no statutory provisions relevant to the loss of life policies. The inability of the claimant to produce it or to account for it may amount to constructive notice to the life office of an equitable assignment or other dealings.

The loss of a life policy is not in itself normally a sufficient ground for payment into court under the Life Assurance Companies (Payment into Court)

Act 1896, although the particular facts may sometimes justify this course[1]. The life office can require proof of the loss and of the searches that have been made in order to rebut constructive notice of any other interest. The claimant may be asked to make a statutory declaration (under the Statutory Declarations Act 1835) before a commissioner of oaths as to the facts surrounding the loss. This should include a statement that there have been no dealings with the policy, if appropriate, or if not, the statement should give particulars of all such dealings. If the loss is reported after the death of the policyholder, his executors are unlikely to be aware of the circumstances of the loss and can usually do little more than assert that they cannot find the policy.

All potential searches for the lost policy should be made and it is sometimes possible for the life office from its records to indicate suitable directions for enquiries. For example, it can give the names of any firm of solicitors who have served a notice of assignment.

If all searches and enquiries fail, payment under a statutory declaration and/or an indemnity by the claimant may be appropriate. Executors and trustees may hesitate to give an indemnity, and in such cases the indemnity of one or more of the principal beneficiaries may be thought sufficient. Even more problematical is the situation where the claimants allege that it is the life office (or an adviser) which has lost the policy document or that the document has never been received. A claimant may legitimately question why he is being required to indemnify the life office in such cases.

With regard to indemnities the undertaking given by Abbey Life Assurance Company Ltd to the Financial Services Authority should be borne in mind (see **9.5** above)

9.32 Life offices tend to have standard forms for the purpose of statutory declarations and indemnities and they may require a full history of the policy, details of any dealings and the circumstances surrounding the disappearance and details of the searches for the policy.

It is unlikely that a life office can insist on an indemnity[2]. If the matter went to court it is likely that the life office would be ordered to pay out, and the court order would be sufficient indemnity, but in view of the costs involved this must be viewed as an extreme measure for a life office to take in order to obtain a discharge.

If the policy was assigned as security for the repayment of a loan, there should be a reassignment on the loan being repaid in which case production of the reassignment will be sufficient evidence for the life office to be able to pay to the policyholder in the absence of any other indication that the policy has been assigned or otherwise dealt with. Failing this, a letter of disclaimer by the mortgagee or his personal representatives may be required.

1 *Harrison v Alliance Assurance Co* [1903] 1 KB 184.
2 *Crockett v Ford* (1855) 25 LJ Ch 552.

SECTION 3 SUICIDE AND UNLAWFUL ACTS

A Suicide

9.33 In order to avoid claims under policies effected with a view to suicide, some life offices exclude death by suicide occurring within a specified period (usually 12 or 13 months). A few exclude suicide whilst sane at any time.

Suicide was (until 3 August 1961) a crime if committed voluntarily by a person of sound mind. It is contrary to public policy that a man should derive an advantage from his own criminal act and it followed that, until the law was altered, no benefit could have been taken by the personal representatives of a person who committed the crime of suicide.

The Suicide Act 1961 abolished the rule that suicide was a crime. The position now is that the policy moneys will often become payable on the life assured's death by suicide. However, payment may still be excluded expressly or impliedly by the terms of the policy or under general insurance law principles as described below.

If there is no express reference to suicide in the policy then two results follow:

(1) It appears from the remarks of Lord Atkin and Lord Macmillan in *Beresford v Royal Insurance Co Ltd*[1] that the life assured's personal representatives cannot recover if he commits suicide whilst of sound mind. This was on the ordinary principle of insurance law that a man cannot by his own deliberate act cause the event upon which the insurance money is payable. This is not the result of any rule of public policy but of a rule of construction of the contract, by which it is presumed that the insurers have not agreed to pay on that happening. In *Beresford*, Lord Atkin believed the life office could have resisted payment on the basis of public policy. Since the decriminalisation of suicide the public policy factor would no longer be relevant. Beresford's case would therefore now be decided differently as, in that case, the clause relating to suicide only prohibited payment on suicide during the first year of the policy and suicide occurred after the expiration of one year[2]. So, if public policy was not a factor, the terms of the policy only excused payment in the first year. The general principle regarding payment not being made as the insured had brought about the event insured against was negated by the specific policy terms.

(2) This principle does not apply to suicide whilst insane and in that event the personal representatives can recover the sum assured[3].

Therefore, if the policy expressly deals with suicide (as in *Beresford*) one must look to the words of the policy to ascertain whether the sum assured is payable in that event. It may provide that suicide, sane or insane, is not covered at any time, or that it is not covered if it takes place within a limited period. If the life assured

1 [1938] AC 586.

2 *Gray v Barr* [1971] 2 QB 554 CA at 582A, per Salmon LJ.

3 *Horn v Anglo-Australian and Universal Family Life Assurance Co* (1861) 30 LJ Ch 511.

commits suicide after that period has expired, the life office would, on the construction of the policy, be liable even if he was then of sound mind because the express protection is limited to that period and the implication is therefore that the life office has accepted the risk after that time[1]. The Court will, of course, normally give effect to a term wholly excluding suicide even if the life assured is insane at the time[2].

9.34 Where the life assured commits suicide and the sum assured is not payable either because of an exception in the policy or on general principles, the premium is not returnable, because there has not been a total failure of consideration. The life office has been on risk throughout to pay the sum assured on death from other causes.

The claimant is not normally required to disprove suicide[3]. Unless there is evidence suggesting otherwise (the death certificate may or may not indicate that suicide was the cause), there is a presumption that death was accidental or natural. In seeking to resist a claim the burden of proof is on the insurer to prove suicide on the balance of probabilities.

Exclusion from payment on suicide potentially affects the value of a policy. This is of particular concern to an assignee or mortgagee. It is usual, therefore, to provide that in the event of suicide, whilst sane or insane, within the specified period (if any) the policy shall be valid to the extent of any interest acquired by a third party for consideration in money or money's worth. Such a clause has been upheld on the basis that it did not tend towards encouraging suicide and meant that the life policy was a safe security in the hands of the assignee. (See *Moore v Woolsey*[4] and *White v British Empire Mutual Life Assurance Co*[5].) The life office itself will not usually be considered a third party although the precise wording of the clause must be considered. *White v British Empire Mutual Life Assurance Co* was distinguished in:

> *Royal London Mutual Insurance Society v Barrett*[6]
>
> D borrowed from the life office on the security of a policy and leasehold property. The policy contained a suicide clause, but with the usual saving for 'the pecuniary interest of third parties bona fide acquired for valuable consideration'. D committed suicide. It was held that the life office was not a third party; that the policy was void; and that the life office could recover its debt against the leasehold property.

It would appear that a trustee in bankruptcy of the life assured would not be viewed as someone who had acquired an interest for value. Such interest arises solely through operation of law[7].

1 *Beresford v Royal Insurance Co Ltd* [1938] AC 586 at 596, per Lord Atkin.
2 *Ellinger v Mutual Life of New York* [1905] KB 31.
3 *Boyd v Refuge Assurance Co Ltd* 1890 17 R 955.
4 (1854) 4 E & B 243.
5 (1868) LR 7 Eq 394.
6 [1928] Ch 411.
7 *Jackson and others v Forster* (1859 and 1860) I El & El 463 and 470.

B Unlawful killing

9.35 A person who has insured the life of another cannot benefit under the life policy if he murders the person whose life he has insured[1]. Nor can he benefit in any other manner (ie other than as the assured under the policy). This is an application of the principle of 'ex turpi causa non oritur actio' (a right of action will not arise from a base cause) which was reaffirmed in the following case in the context of the Social Security Act 1975.

> *R v Chief National Insurance Comr, ex p Connor*[2]
>
> The applicant had stabbed her husband with a knife and was convicted of manslaughter. The court, affirming the Chief National Insurance Commissioner, held that it was contrary to public policy to admit her claim to a widow's allowance under the Social Security Act 1975.

This rule (known as the 'forfeiture rule') does not, however, apply where the murderer is insane[3]. The public policy which prevents a sane murderer recovering was held by the Industrial Assurance Commissioner to have no application when the perpetrator was insane[4].

The rule generally applies to manslaughter but its effect has been softened by case law and by statute. In *Gray v Barr*[5] the rule which appeared to emerge was that if the person responsible for the death was guilty of deliberate, intentional and unlawful violence, or threats of violence then the rule of public policy applied. However, if the case in question fell outside of this ambit then the public policy provisions will not apply. But the precise extent of *Gray v Barr* is not entirely clear. An application of this principle can be seen in *Re H (deceased)*[6] where it was found that the plaintiff could benefit under his wife's will where he had killed his wife but was found guilty of manslaughter on the ground of diminished responsibility.

Where the forfeiture rule applies it also bars all persons claiming through or under him such as his children. This was criticised by the Law Commission in Consultation Paper 172, 'The Forfeiture Rule and the Law of Succession', published on 16 September 2003. This resulted in a Law Commission report in 2005, 'The Forfeiture Rule and the Law of Succession' (Law Com No 295) which concluded that 'under our proposed reforms, the property will devolve in exactly the same way as if the killer had predeceased the victim'. In March 2011 a Bill was published ('Estates of Deceased Persons (Forfeiture Rule and Law of Succession) Bill') which would largely implement the Law Commission Report.

1 *Prince of Wales Assurance v Palmer* (1858) 25 Beav 605; *Davitt v Titcumb* [1989] 3 All ER 417.
2 [1981] QB 758.
3 *Re Batten's Will Trusts* (1961) 105 Sol Jo 529.
4 *Chaplin v Royal London Mutual* [1958] IAC Rep 2.
5 [1971] 2 QB 554.
6 [1990] 1 FLR 441.

9.36 Statutory relief from the severity of the forfeiture rule was introduced in the Forfeiture Act 1982. In appropriate circumstances, this Act relieves persons guilty of unlawful killing from forfeiture of various rights such as inheritance, pensions and social security benefits. The Act does not apply to murder or suicide but could still apply to someone who assisted the deceased to commit suicide or to someone guilty of manslaughter. The Act gives the court a wide discretion to modify the effect and application of the forfeiture rule, but the court must take into account:

(1) the conduct of the offender;

(2) conduct of the deceased; and

(3) other material circumstances.

In the light of these the justice of the case must require the effect of the rule to be modified (section 2(2)). Proceedings under the Act must be commenced within three months of the conviction.

In *S (deceased)*[1], the plaintiff and his wife effected a joint lives first death endowment policy. He subsequently killed her but although charged with murder was ultimately convicted of manslaughter on the grounds of diminished responsibility. In the application under the Forfeiture Act the plaintiff sought an order that the policy proceeds should be paid into a trust for the sole benefit of the son. In agreeing to the application the following factors were emphasised:

(1) the plaintiff's responsibility was substantially impaired;

(2) the order was for the benefit of the son, not the plaintiff;

(3) no one else was interested in the policy proceeds.

The case of *Dunbar v Plant*[2] involved a suicide pact in which only one of the participants died. The Court of Appeal held that the survivor was guilty of aiding and abetting the suicide and the forfeiture rule applied. In applying the test set out in section 2(2) of the Forfeiture Act 1982 the court decided that, whilst there would be exceptions, the normal approach would be to grant full relief against forfeiture in the case of suicide pacts.

In *Dalton v Latham*[3] the claimant was convicted of the manslaughter of the deceased and his sentence was six years' imprisonment. He applied to modify the forfeiture rule to enable him to benefit under the will on the basis that he had cared for the deceased. His application was refused as the court decided he had taken advantage of the deceased and the conviction for manslaughter rather than murder merely reduced his responsibility for the crime.

1 [1996] 1 WLR 235.
2 [1997] 3 WLR 1261.
3 [2003] EWHC 796 (Ch), (2003) 147 Sol Jo LB 537.

C Repudiation of claims

9.37 Where the life office may repudiate a claim on the grounds that the policyholder caused the loss by his own wrongdoing, then his personal representatives and all who claim a share of his estate as a beneficiary under his will or on intestacy, as a creditor, as a trustee in bankruptcy, or as an assignee[1], are equally barred from claiming. This extends also to the trustees of a trust declared by the policyholder of a policy effected on his life[2]. However, the position is different where the rights in question are 'alternative or independent'. So, for example, enforcement of the policy by a mortgagee of the policy would be possible. In *Davitt v Titcumb*[3] the right of a building society as mortgagee was in issue. A joint life policy was assigned to the building society and it was held that where one of the lives assured murdered the other the building society could still recover. However, the defendant was not to benefit, even indirectly.

To repudiate a claim on the basis of suicide or other wrongdoing, the life office must prove that the death was indeed caused by suicide or such other wrongdoing as appropriate[4].

SECTION 4 DEVOLUTION AND GRANTS

A Devolution of property on death

9.38 The broad rule is that on death *immovable property* (ie all interests in land or 'real property') will pass to the person or persons who become entitled under the law of the country where the property lies (the 'lex situs'). Where property is abroad, consideration should be given to drawing up a separate will dealing solely with this property with the help of a local lawyer.

Conversely, for *moveable property* (ie 'personal property' (including life policies)) the general rule is that property will pass to the person or persons who become entitled under the law of the country in which the deceased died domiciled (the 'lex domicilii').

The question whether or not property is moveable or immoveable is decided by the lex situs[5].

Where the deceased dies domiciled in England, his real property in England and his personal property wherever situated therefore vest in the first instance in his personal representatives:

(1) where he has made a will and has appointed executors who accept office, this will be the executor or executors; and

1 *Cleaver v Mutual Reserve Fund Life Association* [1892] 1 QB 147; referred to in *Davitt v Titcumb* above.
2 See *Cleaver v Mutual Reserve Fund Life Association* [1892] 1 QB 147.
3 [1989] 3 All ER 417.
4 *Walsh v Legal and General Assurance Society Ltd* (1935, unreported).
5 *Drummond v Drummond* (1799) 6 Bro Parl Cas 601.

(2) where he has died intestate, or where he has made a will but has not appointed executors or has appointed executors who do not accept office, this will be the administrator or administrators.

An interest in a life policy which the deceased held jointly with another person as joint tenant who survives him will pass not to the personal representatives of the deceased but by survivorship to the other person. It will pass to the survivor who will hold it either as absolute beneficial owner or as trustee for himself and the deceased's personal representatives. This will depend on whether the legal joint tenants beneficially owned the interest in question as joint tenants or tenants in common.

The above analysis regarding joint tenancies of life policies now needs to be considered in the light of the decision in *Murphy v Murphy*[1] which surprised the authors and is not universally accepted. In particular, the judge at first instance and one of the judges in the Court of Appeal (Chadwick LJ) did not agree with the majority decision of the Court of Appeal. The position which appears to emerge from this case is that the death benefit under a jointly held temporary assurance policy constituted two separate interests rather than a joint tenancy capable of severance (which would have meant that half of the joint interest was potentially available for redistribution under the Inheritance (Provisions for Family and Dependants) Act 1975). It does seem clear that the decision was not intended to apply to non-temporary policies especially as the policy in question also contained an additional terminal illness benefit which was specifically stated not to be subject to separate interests.

I Executors and administrators

9.39 An executor derives his title from the will and may act as such before obtaining probate (although a life office would naturally be reluctant to deal with an executor until probate had been obtained as they have no proof of his ability to act). Title will relate back (doctrine of 'relation back') to the testator's death once probate is granted. However, an administrator derives his title entirely from the grant of representation and has no power to do anything as administrator before letters of administration are granted to him[2]. The title of the administrator usually relates back to the date of death of the deceased. However, this will only be the case if this would be beneficial to the estate from an objective point of view. Accordingly, relation back will not be allowed for the purpose of validating acts which were done before the grant with the subjective aim of benefiting the estate but which have not in fact benefited the estate at all[3].

No one is obliged to be an executor, but if a person shows an intention to act as executor, he must prove the will and act until the court releases him. A purported renunciation, before a grant of probate has been obtained, in order to pur-

1 [2004] 1 FCR 1.
2 *Wankford v Wankford* (1704) 1 Salk 299, 309.
3 *Mills v Anderson* [1984] 2 All ER 538.

chase part of the estate may be void if the executor has already acted as executor (ie joined in some act of administration of the estate). In the case of *Holder v Holder*[1] the plaintiff sought to have the sale to the defendant of certain farms rescinded on the ground that the defendant had acted as executor. Before probate was granted, the defendant had with the other executors opened an executors' bank account, paid money into it, signed cheques for sums totalling £600 drawn on and paid out of the account, endorsed insurance policies and instructed solicitors to act for the estate. He had then decided not to accept the executorship because he wanted to purchase two farms which were part of the estate to be administered. It was held that though technically the defendant had joined in acts of administration which meant that his renunciation of executorship was invalid, the sale should not be rescinded in view of the special circumstances of the case which included the fact that the defendant had not interfered in the administration of the estate and that the beneficiaries knew that the defendant was a potential purchaser and did not look to him to protect their interests.

Where a will appoints a minor to be an executor, the appointment does not operate to vest in the minor the estate of the testator, or to constitute him a personal representative for any purpose, unless and until probate is granted to him in accordance with the probate rules[2] after he attains the age of 18.

If an executor has been appointed merely for a limited period, his powers will cease upon the expiration of such period.

2 *Wills*

9.40 Some fundamental provisions affecting English wills are as follows:

(1) The testator (ie the person making the will) must be of full age and mental capacity.

(2) It must appear that the testator intended by his signature to give effect to the will (the old requirement for the testator to sign at the end of the will is no longer applicable) or by some other person in his presence and at his direction[3]. The signature must be made or acknowledged by the testator in the presence of two or more witnesses, present at the same time, each of whom must sign or acknowledge their signature in the presence of the testator, but not necessarily in the presence of each other (although in practice it will be easier if they are all in each others presence throughout the signing and witnessing process).

(3) Any additional testamentary document, known as a codicil, must be similarly signed and witnessed.

1 [1968] 1 All ER 665, CA. This case provides the potential for relief from the rigid position as set out by Lord Eldon in *Ex Parte James* (1803) 32 ER 385 and *Ex Parte Lacey* (1802) 6 Ves 625.
2 Supreme Court Act 1981, s 118.
3 *Barrett v Bem and others* [2011] EWHC 1247.

A will may be revoked:

(a) by another will or codicil or a document signed and witnessed in the same way as a will, with the intention to revoke the earlier will;

(b) by destruction with the intention to revoke[1]; or

(c) by marriage.

However, a will expressed to be made in contemplation of a particular marriage is not revoked by the occurrence of that contemplated marriage[2]. In the case of *Re Coleman, Coleman v Coleman*[3], a will made in September 1970 gave gifts and devised the testator's freehold house 'unto my fiancée' and disposed of the residue for the benefit of others. In November 1970 the testator married his fiancée and died in November 1972. It was held that the construction of the document as required by section 177 of the Law of Property Act 1925 failed to show that the whole of the will was made in contemplation of marriage (although certain clauses had been) and accordingly the will was revoked on the testator's marriage by virtue of section 18 of the Wills Act 1837. However, doubts were expressed about this decision, perhaps most notably by the Law Reform Committee[4]. Following the Administration of Justice Act 1982[5], the position now is that where it appears from a will that at the time it was made the testator was expecting to be married to a particular person and that he intended that a specific disposition in the will should not be revoked by that marriage, that disposition takes effect despite the marriage. Furthermore, any other disposition takes effect also, unless it appears from the will that he intended it to be revoked by the marriage. Effectively, this extends the concept to individual dispositions and not necessarily the will as a whole so the result in *Coleman* would be different if decided today.

Section 18A of the Wills Act 1837 (inserted by the Administration of Justice Act 1982, section 18(2)) dealt with the effect of divorce on wills. It provided that any appointment of the former spouse as executor be deleted and that any gift to that spouse be treated as having lapsed. The unfortunate effect of providing that the gift 'lapsed' was evident in the case of *Re Sinclair*[6] with the ultimate result being that Mr Sinclair's brother benefitted at the expense of the Imperial Cancer Research Fund whereas if the wife was treated as having predeceased the gift over to the charity would have survived. Subsequently, the Law Commission presented a report in September 1983[7] which was eventually enacted as sections 3 and 4 of the Law Reform (Succession) Act 1995. Essentially, this provides for

1 *Re Adams* [1990] 2 All ER 97 (obliteration of signature with ball point pen).

2 Law of Property Act 1925, s 177 (repealed and replaced by the Administration of Justice Act 1982, s 18 which has the same effect for wills made after January 1983).

3 [1976] Ch 1.

4 22nd Report, pp 14–16.

5 Section 18(1).

6 [1985] Ch 446.

7 Family Law: The Effect of Divorce on Wills (Law Com No 217).

the former spouse to be treated, in most cases, as having predeceased the testator. In particular, the substituted section 18A(1)(b) negates the effect of *Sinclair*.

A soldier, sailor or airman (such terms being given a wide meaning) on active service or a mariner or seaman at sea may, whether or not of full age, make a valid will; and such a will need not be witnessed with the formalities required in the case of a civilian. It may even be made by word of mouth[1].

3 Property vested in trustees

9.41 Property vested in trustees is held by them in joint tenancy and on the death of one of them vests in the survivor or survivors but, of course, still subject to the trusts. If there is a sole trustee or a sole surviving trustee, then on his death where the trust property is real property it vests in his personal representatives despite any provision in the trustee's will or in the instrument creating the trust[2]. The position with personal property is not specified although it is clear that the personal representatives may either carry on the trust[3] or appoint new trustees in their place[4]; but, if there is a person nominated by the trust instrument to appoint new trustees, then he has priority in making an appointment ahead of the personal representatives.

Where there has been a change of trusteeship by, for example, appointment or retirement then the trustees would normally be required to produce evidence of this by production of the relevant deeds, etc.

B English grants of representation

9.42 A grant of representation will be issued by the Principal Registry of the Family Division, or by a District Probate Registry or a sub-registry, to evidence the title of the personal representatives to administer the estate of a deceased person where that person is domiciled in England and Wales at the time of his death.

Such grants are essentially of two kinds (although either may be limited in some way):

(1) probate;

(2) administration.

If the claimant does not wish to employ a solicitor, he can apply personally for a grant at any registry or sub-registry. He will have to produce a death certificate or such other evidence of the death of the deceased as the registrar may approve[1],

1 Wills Act 1837, s 11; and Wills (Soldiers and Sailors) Act, 1918; *Ayling v Summers and others* [2009] EWHC 3168 (Ch).
2 Administration of Estates Act 1925, s 1(2) and (3).
3 Trustee Act 1925, s 18(2).
4 Section 36.

and supply all information necessary to enable the papers leading to the grant to be prepared in the registry[2].

Every application must be supported by an oath made by the applicant (and such other person as the registrar may require) which must state certain information, for example, that the document of which probate is to be granted is the true and original last will of the deceased and must prove the marking of the will (ie the signatures of the applicant and the person before whom the oath is sworn)[3], the name and last address of the deceased and the date of death.

In addition the personal representatives must deliver to the Commissioners for Her Majesty's Revenue and Customs an account specifying to the best of their knowledge and belief all appropriate property for inheritance tax purposes and the value of the said property[4]. A grant of representation will not be made until such an account has been produced and any inheritance tax payable has been paid. There are exceptions from having to provide a return for 'excepted' estates which, in this context, essentially means estates below the inheritance tax threshold (or 'nil-rate band').

1 Probate

9.43 The executors derive their title from the will and not from probate, and acts done by them before probate are binding on the estate. However, although they can begin an action as executors before probate they cannot proceed beyond the stage at which it becomes necessary to prove their title until probate is granted.

Probate is prima facie evidence that the will is valid, that it is the last will and also that any inheritance tax payable has been paid.

Where more than one executor is appointed, probate is sometimes granted to one or more of them, power being reserved to the others to come forward later and obtain a grant. Until that occurrence persons may safely deal with the executor(s) to whom probate has been granted. If a later grant is obtained it is called 'double probate'.

Any executor may decline to act if he so wishes. In such a case he is said to renounce probate.

The High Court has confirmed that the balance of probabilities is the standard of proof required to admit a lost will to probate[5].

2 Letters of administration

9.44 If the deceased has: (i) appointed executors who have predeceased him or who are unable or unwilling to act, or (ii) has appointed no executors, or (iii)

1 Non-Contentious Probate Rules 1987, SI 1987/2024, r 5(5).
2 Rule 5(6).
3 Rule 10(1).
4 Inheritance Tax Act 1984, s 216.
5 *Ferneley v Napier and others* [2010] EWHC 3345 (Ch).

has died without leaving a will, then letters of administration may be granted. There is a recognised order of priority in which persons may apply for a grant in such cases[1]. The person entitled to the grant has no title to act before the grant is made (except for matters of humanity and necessity) but when the grant has been made his title usually 'relates back' to the death.

The following are examples of types of letters of administration:

(a) *Administration with the will annexed ('cum testamento annexo').* Where there is a will but no available and willing executor. The court cannot appoint an executor and so it must grant letters of administration with the will annexed.

(b) *Administration pending suit (pendente lite).* Where legal proceedings are pending as to the validity of a will or obtaining or revoking any grant of representation. Often the grant is made to someone who is considered to be indifferent to the contesting parties.

(c) *Administration during mental incapacity.* Where the only executor is incapable of managing his affairs by reason of mental incapacity the district judge or registrar may grant a limited administration to specified persons. Or where there are other executors a grant may be made to them with power reserved to the mentally incapable executor.

(d) *Administration de bonis non administratis.* Where a sole or last surviving executor has died intestate, or without executors (so that the 'chain of representation' is broken) or where a sole or last surviving administrator has died; in both cases before the estate is fully administered. The courts grant administration to a new representative for the purpose of completing the administration.

(e) *Administration for the use and benefit of a minor ('administration durante minore aetate').* This is a grant, limited as to time, which is made to an adult when (1) the person, or all the persons, entitled to administration is, or are, under age; or (2) the person appointed sole executor is a minor.

(f) *Administration ad colligenda bona.* Where there is delay in obtaining a grant with the result that the preservation of the estate is put at risk, an application may be made for an order for a grant of letters of administration ad colligenda bona. Unlike an ordinary executor or administrator, someone with such a grant cannot make any distribution of the assets. His role is to protect the assets until a proper grant can be made.

3 Cessate grant

9.45 A cessate grant is granted when a testator has directed that on the happening of a certain event, some other person is to be substituted for the original

1 Non-Contentious Probate Rules 1987, r 22 and Administration of Estates Act 1925, s 46.

executor and that particular event occurs. A cessate grant will also be granted for a person who has taken a grant for the use and benefit of a person under disability (eg a mentally disordered person or a minor) until removal of the said disability.

4 Probate in solemn form

9.46 Probate may be granted in common form or solemn form. Proof of a will in solemn form follows a court action, and is granted in cases where the validity of the will is open to question, or where there is a likelihood that it may be opposed.

5 Receipt by one personal representative

9.47 One of several personal representatives can give a life office a good discharge, but it is usual to ask for the signatures of all the executors who have proved the will, or all the administrators, as appropriate. Moreover, if the administration of the estate is complete and the executors have become trustees under a trust in the will, the receipt of all the trustees would generally be required[1].

6 Executor de son tort

9.48 Any 'intermeddling' with the deceased's assets by a person who is not an executor or administrator makes him accountable and he could potentially be sued by the rightful executors, administrators, beneficiaries or creditors. 'Intermeddling' essentially means an action carried out in relation to an estate which a personal representative would carry out but where that person is not entitled to that role and does not wish to act as such. He is called an executor de son tort ('de son tort' means 'of his own wrong').

7 Payment without a grant

9.49 A life office is sometimes asked to pay without a grant but unless it has special power to do so, either in the policy or through its constitution, such a request should generally be treated with great caution, as it might later be found, for example:

(1) that if an unproved will is produced to the office, it is invalid, or even a forgery, or is not the last will;

(2) that the deceased left a will though the claimant is not aware of it;

1 *Luke v South Kensington Hotel Ltd* (1879) 11 Ch D 121, 125; Trustee Act, 1925, s 14.

(3) that the claimant has not paid the debts and funeral expenses, in which case a creditor can obtain a grant and compel payment;

(4) that the life office (or others who 'intermeddle' with the estate assets) is liable for inheritance tax as though it was an executor[1].

An exception may sometimes be made for pragmatic purposes where the value of the policy and the estate are small and where there is little or no risk of insolvency, or of liability to tax or of dispute between rival claimants. The decision for the life office may be easier where there is an unproven will and/or the deceased left a widow(er). Sometimes life offices adhere voluntarily to certain unrelated statutory provisions[2] which permit other types of assets such as national savings up to a limit of currently £5,000 to be paid without a grant of representation. The life office may impose its own requirements, for example, a maximum amount in excess of which it will not pay out. It should bear in mind its 'Treating Customers Fairly' obligations and not put in place unreasonable requirements. For example, the FSA defined consumer 'Outcome 6' that: 'Consumers do not face unreasonable post-sales barriers imposed by firms to change product, switch provider, submit a claim or make a complaint', although as the life office may be faced with the possibility of having to pay out twice it is not unreasonable to put in place proportionate requirements. Where the policyholder dies intestate and does not leave a widow(er), the life office might have particular difficulty in determining who to pay the money to, for example, as yet unknown children from other relationships would be entitled to share in the estate. A grant of representation may be advisable in this case.

8 *Deaths of executors*

9.50 Where one of two or more executors dies, whether before or after obtaining probate, the survivor(s) can act or continue to act, and so can the last survivor of them. The executors of the last survivor represent the original testator (on the basis that the last survivor proved the will) and so on, in what is known as the 'chain of representation'.

The effect of section 7 of the Administration of Estates Act 1925 is as follows:

(1) An executor of a sole or last surviving executor of a testator is the executor of that testator.

The provision does not apply to an executor nominated as such in the will who does not actually prove the will of his testator. Also, in the case of an executor who on his death has not proved the will, the rights of that executor cease and the representation to the testator and the administration of his

1 Inheritance Tax Act 1984, s 199(4) and s 200(4).

2 Administration of Estates (Small Payments) Act 1965 and Administration of Estates (Small Payments) (Increase of Limit) Order 1984, SI 1984/539.

estate devolve in the same way as if the executor had never been appointed as such[1].

(2) So long as the chain of representation is unbroken, the last executor in the chain is the executor of every preceding testator.

(3) The chain of representation is broken by:

   (a) an intestacy;

   (b) the failure of a testator to appoint an executor; or

   (c) the failure to obtain probate of a will;

   but is not broken by a temporary grant of administration if probate is subsequently granted[2].

(4) Every person in the chain of representation to a testator effectively stands in the shoes of the original executor.

In any case where the chain of representation is broken before the administration is complete, it will be necessary to obtain letters of administration *de bonis non administratis* in order to complete the title.

C Scottish grants

1 Scotland

9.51 There are two types of grant, the *confirmation nominate* and the *confirmation dative*. The confirmation nominate is granted where there is a will. Where there is no executor nominate appointed by the will, the Executors (Scotland) Act 1900 provides that the following persons will be deemed to be the executors nominate: the testamentary trustees failing whom, those legatees to whom the whole or the residue of the estate has been bequeathed. The confirmation dative is granted where there is no will. The court will appoint an executor dative in accordance with a recognised order of priority.

A Scottish grant gives power to collect only the property specified in a schedule (the inventory) attached to the grant; and if the executors subsequently discover additional assets, they have to obtain a further grant known as an *eik*. Where one of two or more executors dies, the survivor or survivors can act, but not the executors of the last survivor. There is no chain of representation as there is in England.

2 Resealing

9.52 The Administration of Estates Act 1971 abolished the necessity for a grant made in Scotland or Northern Ireland to be resealed in England before

1 Administration of Estates Act 1925, s 5(i).
2 Administration of Estates Act 1925, s 7(3).

English assets could be collected. The Act provides that where a person dies domiciled in Scotland or Northern Ireland, the local grant of representation (provided it notes his Scottish or Northern Irish domicile) is treated as a valid grant in England, without any need for resealing. There are reciprocal provisions validating English grants in the other parts of the UK.

D Grants made outside the United Kingdom

1 Section 19 of the Revenue Act 1889

9.53 Where a person dies domiciled abroad, the persons entitled must, as a general rule, obtain an English grant before they can collect his English assets; but there is an exception in the case of life policies, under section 19 of the Revenue Act 1889, which amends section 11 of the Revenue Act 1884, as follows:

> 'Provided that where a policy of life assurance has been effected with any insurance company by a person who shall die domiciled elsewhere than in the United Kingdom, the production of a grant of representation from a court in the United Kingdom shall not be necessary to establish the right to receive the money payable in respect of such policy.'

The United Kingdom does not include the Isle of Man or the Channel Islands.

Where section 19 applies, payment can be made on evidence of domicile and production of the appropriate documents identifying the person entitled to collect the policy moneys under the law of the country of domicile. If required by the life office, the claim should be supported by evidence of the validity of the grant and, where necessary, by evidence of the law of the country of domicile.

> *Haas v Atlas Assurance Co Ltd*[1]
>
> H was the testamentary executor by Swiss law of a man who had effected policies on his life with an English life office and died domiciled in Switzerland. H H was entitled to claim payment without an English grant.

Section 19 of the Revenue Act 1889 concerns the requirements to establish title to the proceeds of a policy rather than liability for duty or tax on policies. Therefore, where the policy is a United Kingdom asset of the foreign domiciled policyholder, the life office should satisfy itself that any inheritance tax liability in respect of the policy has been discharged before payment of the proceeds otherwise the office may become accountable for the tax. Therefore, in practice the life office may well still seek the production of a grant of representation.

1 [1913] 2 KB 209.

2 The Potential Liability of the Life Office to Inheritance Tax

9.53a Section 200(1)(c) of the Inheritance Tax Act 1984 makes any person in whom the relevant property is vested at any time after the death liable for any inheritance tax payable, and this is so whether or not that person is beneficially entitled to the property. For this purpose, the meaning of the word 'property' is extended by section 200(4) of the 1984 Act to include any property directly or indirectly representing the original property. It may be argued that the 'property' of a life policy is the right to sue the office in respect of its obligation to pay a sum of money and that this 'property' is never vested in the life office but it would clearly apply to the proceeds of such a policy. The life office may also be liable for inheritance tax if it has received notice that the policy in question is subject to a statutory charge for tax under section 237 of the 1984 Act.

9.54 A life office may also be liable for inheritance tax where it has made a payment without the production of an English grant of representation or not in accordance with the provisions of section 19 of the Revenue Act 1889[1]. The life office may be held to have intermeddled with the policy proceeds so as to become liable as though it was an executor. The policy proceeds are then deemed to have vested in the life office[2] so that it becomes liable for the inheritance tax payable.

The following case may assist in understanding the meaning of intermeddling:

> *IRC v Stype Investments (Jersey) Ltd*[3]
>
> In February 1979, Sir Charles Clore made a Jersey settlement of the shares in Stype Investments (Jersey) Ltd. In May 1979 he conveyed to that company an estate in Hertfordshire on terms that it should be held by the company as bare nominee for him. Shortly afterwards, he directed the company to sell the estate and completion was fixed for September 1979. Sir Charles died in July 1979. The sale proceeds were subsequently received by the company and transferred to its account in Jersey. The Inland Revenue sought to serve process on the company in Jersey, alleging that it had 'intermeddled' with Sir Charles' property so as to become liable for capital transfer tax (the forerunner of inheritance tax) under section 25 of the Finance Act 1975[4]. It was held by the Court of Appeal that the conduct of the company in relation to receipt of the proceeds of sale of the estate constituted an intermeddling with the estate and so the company was an executor de son tort and therefore within section 25.

3 Domicile

9.55 A person's domicile is a different legal concept to residence or nationality (although a person may be domiciled and resident in, and a national of, the same country). Domicile is a matter of fact. A person's domicile is the country

1 See *New York Breweries Co Ltd v A-G* [1899] AC 62.
2 Inheritance Tax Act 1984, ss 199(4)(a), 200(4).
3 [1982] Ch 456.
4 Now replaced by the Inheritance Tax Act 1984, s 200(4).

where he either has (or is deemed by law to have) his permanent home, although he may be resident in some other country for other purposes.

Formerly, a woman acquired the domicile of her husband on marriage, and it changed with his throughout the marriage. Section 1 of the Domicile and Matrimonial Proceedings Act 1973 provided that the domicile of married women, after 1 January 1974, is ascertained in the same way as for men . But a woman married before 1974 retains her husband's domicile until she acquires another.

A woman married before the 1973 Act and acquiring her husband's English domicile by dependence, has to retain it as her domicile of choice while she continues to live with him, even though she intends ultimately to return to her domicile of origin. Although the purpose of the 1973 Act was the abolition of the wife's dependent domicile, a woman married before 1974 wishing to revive her domicile of origin has not only to have an intention to cease living permanently in England but has also to take up residence permanently in another country, leaving her husband if necessary. See *IRC v The Duchess of Portland*[1].

A person's domicile of origin is that of his father, except that a child posthumous to the father or a child born to unmarried parents takes the domicile of his mother. His domicile may change to that of his mother if his parents are separated and he lives with her; and unless he goes back to live with his father, her domicile will in effect then become the child's domicile[2]. After age 16, a person may acquire an independent domicile of choice, but his domicile of origin will be restored if the domicile of choice is abandoned and a new domicile of choice is not immediately required. The domicile of origin is never therefore entirely lost[3]. To acquire a domicile of choice it is necessary to reside in the country of choice, but residence alone is not sufficient, however long continued – there must also be the intention to remain permanently. It is necessary to show a clear unequivocal intention to remain in the country of choice permanently. There must be convincing evidence before a court will hold that a new domicile has been acquired[4].

For inheritance tax purposes a person will be deemed to be domiciled in the UK at the time of the transfer/death if:

(1) he was domiciled in the UK within the three years immediately preceding the transfer/death; or

(2) he was resident in the UK in not less than 17 of the 20 years previous to the date of transfer/death[5].

1 [1982] Ch 314.

2 Domicile and Matrimonial Proceedings Act 1973, s 4(1).

3 *IRC v Bullock* [1976] 1 WLR 1178, CA.

4 *Buswell v IRC* [1974] 1 WLR 1631, CA; *Re Clore (No 2), Official Solicitor v Clore* [1984] STC 609; *Plummer v IRC* [1988] 1 All ER 97, [1988] 1 WLR 292.

5 Inheritance Tax Act 1984, s 267.

4 Resealing of grants made abroad

9.56 Under the Colonial Probates Act 1892, extended by the Colonial Probates (Protected States and Mandated Territories) Act 1927, and various Orders in Council, grants may be resealed in England if made by courts in certain countries which have generally been at some time British possessions, protected and trust territories.

When a grant of representation is obtained in a country to which the Act applies, and is then subsequently resealed in England, it will have the same effect as if it had been granted in England. The person who obtained the grant will have the same powers and duties as any person to whom a grant of representation was granted in England.

Section 109(1) and (2) of the Supreme Court Act 1981 (now renamed the Senior Courts Act), as amended by the Finance Act 1984 (s 294(1)(b)(4)), provides that an applicant for a grant or the resealing of a grant issued outside the UK is required to deliver an account for inheritance tax and pay any inheritance tax.

SECTION 5 DISTRIBUTION

9.57 The executor or administrator must first ascertain the assets and liabilities of the deceased. On his application for probate or letters of administration he must generally first pay inheritance tax on the net value of the deceased's estate after deduction of the liabilities payable out of it, and must swear that he will administer the estate according to law and render a true account whenever required by law to do so.

When the executor or administrator has obtained probate or letters of administration, he can collect, or establish his title to, the assets and pay the funeral expenses (where appropriate), debts, and any further inheritance tax. (The personal representatives may discover during the course of the administration that the deceased owns other assets which were not initially taken into account when calculating the inheritance tax payable.) The executor or administrator must then deal with the remainder of the property in accordance with the will or the law of intestate succession as appropriate. The rules relating to intestate succession also apply to any property which is not disposed of by the testator's will. This would be a 'partial intestacy'.

A Distribution in England and Wales

1 Deaths on or after 1 December 1993

9.58 Where, on or after 1 December 1993, a person dies intestate, the law governing the succession to his property is to be found in Schedule 1 to the Intestates' Estates Act 1952 which conveniently sets out the appropriate sections of the Administration of Estates Act 1925 (as amended) but has itself been amended by section 1 of the Family Provision Act 1966 and by orders made under that Act, the latest being the Family Provision (Intestate Succession) Order 2009[1]. The position is summarised in the table below. These rules only apply where the deceased dies domiciled in England. For the Scottish law of intestate succession reference should be made to the Succession (Scotland) Act 1964 (as amended) summarised later in this section, and for Northern Irish law, to the Administration of Estates Act (Northern Ireland) 1955 and orders made under that Act, such as the Administration of Estates (Rights of Surviving Spouse or Civil Partner) Order (Northern Ireland) 2007[2].

While a decree of judicial separation is in force, the separated spouses are not entitled to any rights of intestate succession in each other's estates – by section 18(2) of the Matrimonial Causes Act 1973 the property will devolve as if the other party to the marriage had then been dead.

If the intestate and the spouse of the intestate die in circumstances where it is uncertain which of them survived the other then section 184 of the Law of Property Act 1925 (under which the younger is deemed to have survived the older) does not apply and so the younger does not take on the intestate's death (see section 46(3) of the Administration of Estates Act 1925).

Where the intestate dies on or after 1 January 1996, then in order to take any beneficial interest on his intestacy, his spouse must survive by 28 days (see section 1(1) of the Law Reform (Succession) Act 1995, which inserts a new sub-section (2A) into section 46 of the Administration of Estates Act 1925).

9.59 England

Where the intestate leaves	*Interest or share of estate taken*
(1) a husband or wife, but (a) no issue (ie children, grandchildren and other lineal descendants), and (b) no parent or brother or sister of the whole blood, or issue of a brother or sister of the whole blood	The surviving husband or wife takes the whole estate absolutely
(2) a husband or wife and issue (whether or not persons mentioned in (1)(b) above also survive)	The surviving husband or wife takes: (i) the personal chattels (ie personal property) (ii) the remainder up to £250,000 free of inheritance tax and costs with interest up to payment or appropriation. The residue (if any) is held: (a) one half upon trust for the surviving husband or wife for life and thereafter on statutory trusts (see below) for the issue (b) the other half on statutory trusts for the issue

1 SI 2009/135.
2 SR (NI) 2007/452.

Where the intestate leaves	*Interest or share of estate taken*
(3) a husband or wife and one or more of the following, ie parent, brother or sister of the whole blood or issue of brother or sister of the whole blood but no issue	The surviving husband or wife takes: (i) the personal chattels (ii) the remainder up to £450,000 free of costs and inheritance tax with interest up to payment or appropriation (iii) one half of the residue (if any). The other half is taken by the parents and if more than one in equal shares or if no parent survives then it is held on statutory trusts for brothers and sisters of the whole blood or their issue (that is, nephews and nieces).
(4) issue but no husband or wife	The whole estate is held on statutory trusts for the issue

Where the intestate leaves no husband or wife and no issue, the distribution is as follows. (If any member of one class survive, those in a subsequent class cannot benefit):

Relatives surviving at death of intestate	*Interest or share of estate taken*
Parents	The whole and if more than one in equal shares (not on statutory trusts)
Brothers and sisters of the whole blood (or their issue)	The whole on the statutory trusts
Brothers and sisters of the half blood (or their issue (where deceased and beneficiary had one common parent))	The whole on the statutory trusts
Grandparents	The whole and if more than one then equally (not on statutory trusts)
Uncles and aunts of the whole blood (or their issue)	The whole on the statutory trust
Uncles and aunts of the half blood (or their issue)	The whole on the statutory trusts
and if no relative takes an absolute interest	The Crown, Duchy of Lancaster, or Duke of Cornwall takes the whole as bona vacantia

9.60 Where a surviving husband or wife takes a life interest in part of the intestate's estate and elects to do so (within 12 months of the grant of representation unless the court extends this period), he or she is entitled to have it purchased or redeemed by the personal representatives for a capital sum. The capital sum is calculated by reference to article 3 of the Intestate Succession (Interest and Capitalisation) Order 1977[1].

In addition, where the estate includes an interest in the matrimonial home , he or she may require (again within 12 months of the grant of representation unless the court extends this period) the personal representatives to appropriate that interest in or towards satisfaction of any absolute interest taken by the survivor, including the redemption value of a life interest.

Where there is a partial intestacy, the statutory legacy to be taken by the surviving spouse is reduced by the value at the death of any beneficial interests (other than personal chattels specifically bequeathed) acquired under the will of the deceased.

An adopted child is treated as the child of the adopter (and not the child of any other person) for purposes of distribution on the death of an intestate after the date of the adoption order. Under the Family Law Reform Act 1987, illegitimate children have the same right to share in their relatives' estates as if they were legitimate. However, where an illegitimate child dies intestate, it will be presumed that he was not survived by his natural father, or any person related to him only through his natural father, unless the contrary is shown[2].

2 *The statutory trusts*

9.61 The statutory trusts mentioned above are briefly as follows:

(a) *For issue.* In equal shares for the children who attain the age of 18 or marry. If any of those children predecease their parent(s), the children of that deceased child will take the deceased child's share per stirpes (ie they take in equal shares the share to which the deceased child would have been entitled).

(b) *For persons other than issue.* In equal shares for members of the class who attain the age of 18 or marry. If any of these members predecease the deceased, the children of the deceased member will take the deceased member's share per stirpes.

B Scotland – legal and other prior rights – intestate succession

1 *Legal and prior rights*

9.62 In Scotland the surviving spouse and issue of the deceased have legal claims against that person's estate, which take precedence over other claims on intestacy and which, with certain qualifications, cannot be defeated by testamentary disposition. These claims are known as 'legal rights'. They are not strictly rights of succession, but are more in the nature of debts, arising and being fixed

1 SI 1977 / 1491 (and subsequent amending orders, eg SI 2008/3162.
2 Family Law Reform Act 1987, s 18(2).

at the moment of death, vesting on death and requiring to be satisfied out of the net moveable estate before any other part of the estate can be distributed.

The common law entitlement to 'legal rights' was modified to some extent by the Succession (Scotland) Act 1964 and by subsequent legislation. Where a person has died after 10 September 1964, either totally or partially intestate, the 'legal rights' rank after statutory 'prior rights' as extended by that Act. However, prior rights do not have the characteristic of legal rights in that legal rights prevail against a contrary testamentary disposition[1]. A beneficiary must elect whether or not to claim his or her legal rights and cannot claim both legal rights and entitlement under the will.

The rules of intestate succession operate only on the residual part of the deceased's estate which is not required to satisfy prior rights and legal rights. The legal rights are as follows:

(1) *Jus relictae*: the right of a widow to one-third of her husband's moveable estate (essentially anything other than land) if he leaves any issue entitled to legitim (see below for definition); or to one-half if he leaves no such issue, or if all claims to legitim were discharged in his lifetime. The fund subject to the widow's claim consists of the free moveables net of debts, expenses and any deduction for prior rights.

(2) *Jus relicti*: the equivalent right of a widower in his deceased wife's estate.

The same provisions now apply for civil partners.

(3) *Legitim*: the right of children (including illegitimate and adopted children and the surviving issue of deceased children who would have had a claim had they survived) to one-third of the net moveable estate if there is a surviving spouse claiming legal rights; or to one-half if there is no surviving spouse or if his or her claim has been discharged.

Where all the persons entitled to claim legitim are in the same degree of relationship to the deceased (eg if they are all children of the deceased), the division is on a per capita basis (ie they all receive an equal share). Where the persons claiming legitim are in differing degrees (eg if some are children and some are issue of a deceased child) then the division is per stirpes at the level of the nearest degree of relationship to the deceased in which there are surviving members (so a sole grandchild would be entitled to the share his parent would have received and if there are two or more grandchildren of the same parent then they are entitled to an equal share of what their parent's share would have been).

9.63 In calculating the shares of legitim, any advances of moveable property made by the deceased during his lifetime to claimants on the fund must be *collated*. This is similar to the old hotchpot rule under English law. The amount of such advances must be added back to the legitim fund which is then divided with the amount of the advances being deducted from the share falling to the person to whom they were made.

1 Succession (Scotland) Act 1964, s 36(1).

Legal rights of spouses may be discharged in their lifetime by marriage contract. However, nothing in such a contract executed after the commencement of the Succession (Scotland) Act 1964 may exclude rights to legitim unless the child or issue entitled, being sui juris, consents. A spouse or child may also renounce legal rights.

Formerly, any bequest or other testamentary provision for a surviving spouse or child was additional to any legal rights, unless declared to be given in satisfaction of legal rights and so accepted. But testamentary dispositions executed after the commencement of the Succession (Scotland) Act 1964 which do not contain such a declaration have effect as if they did contain such a declaration, in the absence of express provision to the contrary[1].

2 *Statutory prior rights*

9.64 As from 1 June 2005 the statutory prior rights of an intestate's surviving spouse are as follows[2]:

(1) If the intestate's estate includes an interest as owner or tenant in a dwelling house in which the surviving spouse was ordinarily resident at the intestate's death:

   (a) where the value of the interest does not exceed £300,000 to the interest itself or in certain circumstances to its value instead; or

   (b) in any other circumstances, to the sum of £300,000.

(2) If the intestate's estate includes the 'furniture and plenishings' of a dwelling house to which paragraph (1) above applies the surviving spouse is entitled to the whole of them if the value does not exceed £24,000, or in any other case to such part not exceeding £24,000 as the surviving spouse may choose.

(3) The surviving spouse is entitled to a sum of money – £42,000 if the intestate is survived by issue and £75,000 if not; in either case with interest at a specified rate from the date of death to the date of payment. However, if the surviving spouse, in the case of a partial intestacy, is entitled to a legacy (other than of property to which (1) or (2) above applies) then he or she is entitled only to the excess of the £42,000 or £75,000 over the legacy. This monetary amount is borne proportionately by heritable (essentially land) and moveable property.

9.65 Under the 1964 Act[3], an intestate's estate, net of prior rights and legal rights, devolves as follows. If there is any person in one group then no-one in a subsequent group may benefit:

1 Succession (Scotland) Act 1964, s 13.
2 Prior Rights of Surviving Spouse (Scotland) Order 2005, SI 2005/252.
3 Section 2.

(1) children (includes adopted children and the issue of predeceasing children);

(2) a parent or parents and brothers and sisters; half to the parents, half to the brothers and sisters;

(3) brothers and sisters (or their issue) (brothers and sisters of the whole blood exclude those of the half blood);

(4) a parent or both parents;

(5) the surviving spouse;

(6) uncles or aunts, irrespective of whether they are on the paternal or maternal side;

(7) grandparent or grandparents;

(8) brothers and sisters of any of the grandparents; or

(9) ancestors of the intestate, generation by generation successively, without distinction between paternal and maternal lines, the brothers and sisters of any ancestors having right before ancestors of the next more remote generation;

(10) The Crown.

References above to brothers and sisters include those of the half blood only if none of the whole blood are entitled.

If any person (other than a parent or spouse of the intestate), who would have been entitled had he survived, predeceases the intestate leaving issue who survive the intestate, then those issue take the whole or part to which the deceased person would have been entitled. If any person, who would have been entitled had he survived, predeceases the intestate leaving no issue who survive the intestate, then any other person who is also entitled takes his share and if there are more than one then the intestate's share will be divided equally between them if they are all related in the same degree to the intestate (for example, brothers and sisters) and per stirpes (for example, children of a deceased child taking in equal shares the share that the child would have taken had he survived) in other cases.

C Northern Ireland – distribution on Intestacy

9.66 The law governing intestate succession is to be found in the Administration of Estates Act (Northern Ireland) 1955 and in various orders made under that Act, the latest being the Administration of Estates (Rights of Surviving Spouse or Civil Partner) Order (Northern Ireland) 2007[1].

1 SR (NI) 2007/452.

The following table sets out the position in Northern Ireland:

Northern Ireland

Where the intestate leaves	*Interest or share of estate taken*
(1) a husband or wife, but (a) no issue, and (b) no parent or brother or sister or issue of a brother or sister	The surviving husband or wife takes the residuary estate absolutely
(2) a husband or wife and issue (whether or not parents, brothers or sisters survive)	The surviving husband or wife takes: (a) the personal chattels (b) the remainder up to £250,000 free of costs, with interest at the specified rate up to payment. The residue is distributed as follows: (i) Where only one child of the intestate survives, as to one half to the surviving husband or wife and as to the other half amongst the issue equally per stirpes. (ii) Where more than one child survives, as to one third to the surviving husband or wife, and as to the residue amongst the issue equally per stripes. If a child of the intestate predeceased him leaving issue who survive him, the surviving spouse of the intestate takes the same share as if the child had survived.
(3) a husband or wife and one or more of the following, namely parent, brother or sister or issue of brother or sister but no issue	The surviving husband or wife takes: (a) the personal chattels (b) the remainder up to £450,000 free of costs with interest at the specified rate up to payment (c) one half of the residue. The other half of the residue is taken by the parents and if more than one in equal shares, or if no parent survives, by brothers and sisters or their issue equally per stirpes.
(4) issue but no husband or wife	The whole estate is distributed amongst the issue equally per stirpes

Where the intestate leaves no husband or wife and no issue, the distribution is:

Relatives surviving at death of intestate	*Interest or share of residue taken*
Both parents	The whole in equal shares
One parent	The whole
Brothers or sisters or issue of deceased brothers or sisters	The whole estate in equal shares per stirpes

If the intestate leaves no husband or wife, issue, parent, brother, sister or issue of a deceased brother or sister, his estate is distributed to grandparents or if none are living then to uncles and aunts (the surviving issue of deceased uncles and aunts taking their parents' share per stirpes). If no person takes under the foregoing provisions, the estate passes to the Crown as bona vacantia.

Unlike the position in England, brothers and sisters and other relatives of the half blood are treated in the same way as and inherit equally with relatives of the whole blood in the same degree.

The references to 'spouse' in the above intestacy provisions now includes references to registered civil partners under the Civil Partnership Act 2004.

SECTION 6 RELEVANT STATUTORY PROVISIONS

A Children

1 Illegitimacy

9.67 The Family Law Reform Act 1987 provides, subject to any contrary intention, certain rules of construction. No reference needs to be made to the terms 'legitimate' and 'illegitimate' as the term 'children' will encompass both legitimate and illegitimate children. Sections 1, 18 and 19 have the effect of providing that illegitimacy will not be taken into consideration when determining an illegitimate person's rights of succession on intestacy or under a will or inter vivos disposition. It is, however, open to a testator or donor to specifically exclude illegitimate children if he so wishes. The term 'illegitimate' and its derivations are no longer used in statutory references. Section 21 of the Family Law Scotland Act 2006 abolished the status of illegitimacy in Scotland.

2 Adoption

9.68 The Children Act 1975 changed a lot of provisions concerning succession (and other) rights relating to adopted children. The provisions relating to adoption were re-enacted in the Adoption Act 1976, and the Children Act 1975 was then repealed by virtue of Schedule 4 to the Children Act 1989. The Children Act 1989 made certain amendments to the Adoption Act 1976.

The Children Act 1975 (now repealed but the relevant provisions have been effectively re-enacted) provided that the adopted child qualified as a child of his adoptive parents' marriage[1].

An adopted child was therefore brought more fully into the adoptive family so far as property rights are concerned. But, as a corollary, he lost any succession rights as a member of his natural family.

Where a child is adopted and a natural parent of such child has effected an insurance policy with a friendly society or an industrial assurance company for the payment on the child's death of money for funeral expenses, the rights and liabilities under the policy are transferred to the adoptive parents who will be treated as the person who took out the policy[2].

If a disposition depends on the date of birth of a child then, by section 42(2) of the Adoption Act 1976, it is to be construed as if: (1) the adopted child had been born on the date of the adoption; and (2) two or more children adopted on the same date had been born on that date in the order of their actual birth. This rule regulates, for example, the relative seniority of children where there is a provision in a will or trust 'to the eldest son of A' and A adopts a child or children.

Where it is necessary to determine for the purposes of a disposition of property effected by a trust, etc whether a woman can have a child, it is presumed (rather curiously) that, following execution of the trust, once a woman has attained the age of 55 she will not adopt a child. If she does, the child will not be treated as her child for the purposes of the instrument[3].

3 Trustees and personal representatives

9.69 Both the Adoption Act 1976 and the Legitimacy Act 1976 contain useful protections for trustees and personal representatives in distributing property. A trustee or personal representative is not under a duty to enquire, before distributing any property, whether any adoption has been effected or revoked[4], or whether any person is illegitimate[5] if that fact could affect entitlement to the property.

However, trustees and personal representatives have to enquire whether an illegitimate person exists who has or may have an interest in the property before they distribute it[6].

However, there is protection for trustees and personal representatives in section 27 of the Trustee Act 1925. Provided they advertise for claims to the property and the conditions of that section are satisfied, they will be exempt from liability to all claimants except those of whom they had notice. Another means by which personal representatives can safely make a distribution in circumstances where it is not clear if a beneficiary is alive is by obtaining a 'Benjamin Order' which gives personal representatives leave to distribute assets on the

1 Now Adoption Act 1976, s 39(1)(a)
2 Adoption Act, 1976, s 49.
3 Adoption Act, 1976, s 42(5).
4 Adoption Act, 1976, s 45.
5 Legitimacy Act 1976, s 7(1).
6 Section 20 of the Family Law Reform Act 1987.

basis set out in the order[1]. A Benjamin Order does not require advertising or searches to have been made.

B Family provision

9.70 The Inheritance (Provision for Family and Dependants) Act 1975 implemented the recommendation of the Law Commission in their second report on family property[2]. It gives the courts wide powers to order financial provision out of the estate of the deceased for his family and dependants if the court believes that under the will (or intestacy), the deceased failed to make reasonable financial provision for them.

The persons who may apply to the court are set out in section 1(1) of the 1975 Act, and are as follows:

(1) the wife or husband of the deceased;

(2) a former wife or former husband who has not remarried;

(3) a child of the deceased;

(4) any person (not a child of the deceased) who was treated by the deceased as a child of the family;

(5) any other person who immediately before the death was being maintained wholly or partly by the deceased;

(6) a cohabitee of the deceased for at least two years immediately before the death of the deceased (provided the deceased died after 1 January 1996). This last provision was added by section 2 of the Law Reform (Succession) Act 1995.

References to wife, husband and former wife or husband include references to same-sex civil partners and former civil partners[3].

The 1975 Act lists the types of order in section 2(1) which the court may make when it decides that reasonable financial provision has not been made for the applicant and in particular specifies methods by which periodical payments may be provided out of the estate, which is explained in section 2(2). The Act also sets out (in section 3) the matters which the court must have regard to when deciding whether reasonable financial provision has been made for an applicant.

The property which is available for financial provision is extended by the 1975 Act to include in the estate any property or money comprised in a nomination or donatio mortis causa and, if the court so decides, the deceased's severable share of property jointly owned with others. In *Powell v Osborne*[4] the court ordered

1 *Re Benjamin* [1902] 1 Ch 723.
2 Family Provision on Death (Law Com no 61) (1971).
3 Civil Partnership Act 2004.
4 [1993] 1 FLR 797, CA.

that half the proceeds of a life policy that the deceased held as a joint tenant should be paid to his wife. The deceased had left his wife to live with another woman with whom he had purchased a property on mortgage supported by the policy on their joint lives. The case effectively turned on the value of the policy immediately before the husband's death[1]. The policy had no surrender value immediately before death. However, it was held that as the value of the policy depended on death, its value was for these purposes the same immediately before death as on death.

9.71 The courts also have the power to review certain transactions effected by the deceased within six years before his death other than for full valuable consideration, which were made with the intention of defeating claims for family provision. The courts may require that the property comprised in those transactions be made available for financial provision[2]. Therefore inter vivos gifts or part-gifts may be vulnerable in the hands of any person for the prescribed length of time.

By section 146 of the Inheritance Tax Act 1984, any inheritance tax paid on property, which is required to be made available for family provision, may be reclaimed from Her Majesty's Revenue and Customs if the revised provisions would result in less (or no) Inheritance Tax being payable. Effectively, the property is added back into the deceased's estate, the order by the court is treated as a disposition by the deceased on his death, and a new calculation of the inheritance tax, if any, is made. For example, the court order may provide for property to be redistributed to the deceased's spouse in which case the new calculation will provide that no inheritance tax will be payable in respect of that property due to the spouse exemption.

'Maintenance' for which an applicant might receive financial provision under section 1 of the Inheritance (Provision for Family and Dependants) Act 1975 cannot include provision for liability for inheritance tax[3].

Failure by the deceased to discharge his responsibilities to the applicant, during his minority, did not in itself entitle the applicant to receive financial provision from the deceased's estate under the Act[4]. In *Ilott v Mitson and others*[5] the Court of Appeal overturned the High Court's decision that a mother could reasonably make no financial provision for her estranged adult daughter, instead leaving her entire estate to charity.

An application to the court cannot normally be made, without the permission of the court, after six months from the date on which representation to the estate is first taken out. Personal representatives are protected from liability for distributing any part of the deceased's estate after this six-month period notwithstanding the fact that the court might make further orders or vary an existing order.

1 Inheritance (Provision for Family and Dependants) Act 1975, s 9.
2 Inheritance (Provision for Family and Dependants) Act 1975, s 10.
3 *Re Dennis, Dennis v Lloyd's Bank Ltd* [1981] 2 All ER 140.
4 *Harlow v National Westminster Bank plc* (1994) 138 Sol Jo LB 31, CA.
5 [2011] EWCA Civ 346.

The 1975 Act does not apply in Scotland where provision for dependants is secured by the legal rights and statutory prior rights mentioned in the previous section[1]. It was, however, effectively extended to Northern Ireland by the Inheritance (Provision for Family and Dependants) (Northern Ireland) Order 1979[2].

C Income support and other state benefits

9.72 Section 134(1) of the Social Security Contributions and Benefits Act 1992 and associated regulations provide that a person is not entitled to income support if his capital exceeds £16,000[3]. This limit has come in for criticism on the basis that it does not encourage persons to save or to take measures to put in place funds for periods when they are unemployed etc. Also, a claimant is treated as possessing income and capital of which he has deprived himself for the purpose of securing entitlement to income support or increasing the amount of that benefit[4]. This question may arise in relation to the holding of single premium or other life assurance policies where the policyholder requires nursing home care and fees are payable.

The surrender value of a policy is treated as capital, however, the Income Support (General) Regulations 1987[5] provide that the surrender value can be disregarded in assessing the claimant's eligibility for income support[6]. Interesting questions arise when a claimant invests (deliberately or not) in a single premium life policy which would appear to have the effect of reducing his capital. It is not obviously a disposal of capital as the claimant would still retain ownership of the asset (ie the policy). In a case before the Social Security and Child Support Commissioners[7] the claimant had invested £10,000 into a single premium insurance based investment bond. The Commissioner decided that the surrender value was to be disregarded. However, he also decided that where a significant amount was invested then this operated as a 'deprivation' and an adjudication officer should always consider whether the investment was made for the purpose of securing income support. However, the general position seems to be that such insurance bonds will not be taken into account. See further the Charging for Residential Accommodation Guide (2003) 22, October 2003 (known as 'CRAG') for further details.

1 See **9.60–9.62**.
2 SI 1979/924.
3 Income Support (General) Regulations 1987, SI 1987/1967 and the Social Security (Miscellaneous Amendments) (No 2) Regulations 2005, SI 2005/2465
4 Income Support (General) Regulations 1987, SI 1987/1967, regs 42, 51, 51A; For care home fees see the National Assistance (Assessment of Resources) Regulations 1992, reg 25.
5 Income Support (General) Regulations 1987, SI 1987/1967.
6 Income Support (General) Regulations 1987, SI 1987/1967, Sch 10, para 15 and Sch 4, para 13, National Assistance (Assessment of Resources) Regulations 1992, for the position regarding ability to pay local authority care home fees.
7 R(IS) 7/98.

SECTION 7 ASSENT AND APPROPRIATION

A Assent

9.73 Where a policy on the life of the testator is, by his will, made the subject of a specific legacy, the policy (or the sum assured if the testator was the sole or last surviving life assured) will pass in the first instance to his executors. If, however, the policy is on the life of another person or the policy money is payable by instalments it will have a continuing existence and where the executors do not need it for purposes of administration they may vest it in the legatee.

An assent is some action which activates the gift of the property to the beneficiary concerned (even if further formalities are required to transfer the subject matter to the person entitled) and show that the executors do not require the property for administration. The beneficiary derives his title from the will; the assent merely makes the gift operative. Once the personal representatives have effectively assented, they hold the property on trust to carry out the further requirements. Some form of documentation is often needed in order to vest the legal title to the property in the beneficiary. An assent, by itself, is often of little practical use except in relation to tangible moveable property such as jewellery, furnishings, etc. For a life policy an assignment would be required.

Assents to the vesting of personal estate such as a life policy need not be in writing or in any particular form. This is different to the vesting of a legal estate in land which is required to be in writing. Stamp duty is no longer payable on a written assent relating to non-land transactions (except for some documents relating to stocks, shares and marketable securities)[1].

B Appropriation

9.74 Appropriation is the transfer by the personal representatives of a particular asset in satisfaction of a legacy or a share of the estate.

An appropriation of a policy may be made under section 41 of the Administration of Estates Act 1925 or under an express power in the will. For a life policy continuing beyond the death of the testator, for example, a policy he had purchased on the life of another person, this would therefore require an assignment (see further Chapter 10).

SECTION 8 MISCELLANEOUS MATTERS

A Legacy of policy subject to a loan

9.75 Property subject to a charge passes under the will subject to the charge. If, for example, a testator makes a specific bequest of a policy on which there is

1 Finance Act 2003, s 125.

a policy loan, the legatee will, unless a contrary intention appears from the will, take the policy subject to the loan. He cannot require the executor to pay off the loan out of other property of the testator[1]. It should be noted that the ambit of 'charge' is wide and includes, for example, an equitable charge.

B Donatio mortis causa

9.76 When a document which represents, or is evidence of, a chose in action (such as a life policy) is delivered by a person in contemplation of death on condition that it shall be the property of the donee only in the event of the death of the donor in the circumstances threatening him, there is a donatio mortis causa of the chose in action. The court will uphold this against the personal representatives. It is a question of fact whether the delivery of a document was made as a gift inter vivos or mortis causa, and to establish the latter there must be evidence that the donor made the gift in contemplation of death.

A life policy can be the subject of a donatio mortis causa[2]. If it is delivered by a person in contemplation of death in circumstances which indicate an intention to give, the court will presume that it was given to be retained only in the event of death and to be returned if the donor should recover. An essential part of the validity of a donatio mortis causa is that the donor should part with dominion over the property so as to prevent it being dealt with by him in the interval between the gift and his death or recovery. It is possible to pass most types of property by donatio mortis causa, such as chattels, but with land the position was not clear until the case of *Sen v Headley*[3] which decided that the personal representative held the land on trust for the beneficiary of the gift.

C Mentally disordered persons

9.77 The affairs of mentally disordered persons in England are administered by the Court of Protection mainly in accordance with the Mental Health Acts of 1983 and 2007, the Mental Capacity Act 2005 and various Court of Protection Rules. The Court of Protection may make orders affecting the property of a person who lacks capacity and may appoint a deputy who must act in accordance with the Code of Practice under the Mental Capacity Act, 2005 and the court's directions. The Office of the Public Guardian will supervise the deputy and has an administrative and complaint handling role. A person who lacks capacity cannot deal with his own property whilst the appointment is in force. Before making a payment to the deputy, the life office must be satisfied that the court has made an order authorising the deputy to give a discharge. If the person

1 Administration of Estates Act 1925, s 35. See *Ross v Perrin-Hughes* [2004] EWHC 2559 (Ch), [2004] All ER (D) 159 (Nov), where a 'contrary intention' was found. This case examined the construction of a gift in a will of a property subject to a mortgage together with surrounding evidence. In this case it was held that the lease should be taken free of the mortgage.

2 *Amis v Witt* (1863) 33 Beav 619.

3 [1991] Ch 425.

lacking mental capacity recovers and becomes capable of dealing with his own affairs, the deputy is discharged by a further order of the Court of Protection; the deputy's powers cease automatically on the death of the person lacking capacity.

It should be noted that a person lacking capacity cannot grant a valid power of attorney (see **9.79** below), and any ordinary power he may have given before his incapacity arose will cease to be effective. However, if he gave an enduring or lasting power of attorney before his incapacity, and provided the said power is registered, it will not cease to be effective[1]. It is not possible to effect new Enduring Powers of Attorney but existing Powers signed before 1 October, 2007, may remain in force.

The Court of Protection may execute a will or codicil or effect a settlement for a person lacking capacity. This is known as a 'statutory will'. A patient may make a valid will for himself in a lucid interval even if there is a deputyship order is in force but the person propounding the validity of the will would have to show that it was made during such an interval[2].

9.78 Where a policyholder domiciled abroad becomes mentally disordered, the person able to deal with his affairs is the officer appointed by the proper court of the country of domicile. Therefore, a a person properly appointed by a foreign court to look after the affairs of a mentally disordered person domiciled and resident abroad may sue for that person's personal estate in England.

> *Didisheim v London and Westminster Bank*[3]
>
> G was entitled to securities deposited with the bank. She was domiciled and resident in Belgium. She became mentally disordered and D was appointed by the Belgian court as her curator. It was held that D could give the bank a good discharge and that on general principles of private international law the English court was bound to recognise the order of the Belgian court.
>
> *Pelegrin v Coutts and Co*[4]
>
> A domiciled Frenchman resident in Paris deposited securities with Coutts and Co. He became of unsound mind and an administrator was appointed by the Civil Tribunal of the Seine with express power to receive the securities. Coutts and Co refused to act without an order of the English court. Held, that in refusing to act on the order of the French court, Coutts and Co had shown undue and unreasonable excess of caution and must bear their own costs.

9.79 The Mental Capacity Act 2005 received a lot of media attention for its 'living wills' provisions but it also replaced Enduring Powers of Attorney with 'Lasting Powers of Attorney' ('LPAs') on 1 October, 2007. These are wider than EPAs in that there are two types of LPA. One type relates to property and affairs and the other to personal welfare issues.

1 Enduring Powers of Attorney Act 1985, s 1; Mental Capacity Act, 2007, Section 9.

2 *Cartwright v Cartwright* (1793) 1 Phill 90. (See *Banks v Goodfellow* (1870) LR 5 QB 549 for the test of testamentary capacity.)

3 [1900] 2 Ch 15.

4 [1915] 1 Ch 696.

9.80 Unlike EPAs, LPAs only take effect upon registration with the public guardian. Therefore, donors who wish their attorneys to act on their behalf, even though they retain capacity, will either have to register the LPA or complete a separate ordinary power of attorney. This seems a backward step in that some donors found it helpful to rely on their unregistered EPAs. For example, a donor may be in hospital or nursing home, unable for practical reasons (as opposed to mental incapacity) to attend to their affairs or simply disinclined to get involved with certain issues. EPAs could be used to ease the burden in these circumstances. However, EPAs were open to abuse and the new system requiring registration of LPAs has the advantage of requiring a greater degree of supervision by the Public Guardianship Office. Another safeguard is that a 'prescribed person' must certify that the donor understands the effect of the LPA and that no undue pressure has been placed upon him to sign it. This would appear to be quite an onerous obligation upon the doctor or other prescribed person. Another safeguard is that attorneys and deputies are legally required to have regard to the Mental Capacity Act, 2005, Code of Practice.

9.81 For life offices dealing with attorneys they will obviously need to ensure that the LPA is registered and still in force. The Public Guardian maintains a register of LPAs which can be checked. A life office can also rely on the office copy of the LPA with regard to the content of the LPA which it should check in particular to ensure there are no restrictions or conditions.

CHAPTER 10

Assignments

SUMMARY

SECTION 1 ASSIGNMENTS GENERALLY

10.1 An assignment of a life policy is the transfer of ownership of a policy by a document or other action from one person or persons to another or others. Assignments may be made for a variety of reasons, including:

(1) sale or exchange;

(2) gift or voluntary transfer;

(3) trust or settlement, transferring the policy to trustees;

(4) transfer to beneficiaries in pursuance of the trusts;

(5) mortgage; transfer of mortgage; or reassignment on repayment;

(6) assignment to a trustee for the benefit of creditors; or

(7) assignments by operation of law (eg on insolvency).

Before the Policies of Assurance Act 1867 (see Appendix 2), assignments of life policies were not recognised at law. The power to discharge the life office on payment or to sue on it in default was vested in the original policyholder. He had made the contract and could give a good discharge even if he had later made an assignment. But in the early part of the seventeenth century the courts of equity began to recognise assignments and would assist an assignee by permitting him to join the assignor as plaintiff or, if he refused, as defendant in an action brought by the assignee. Policies of assurance were accordingly said to be assignable in equity, with the effect that the assignee could acquire the *beneficial* interest but not the *right to sue without joining the assignor*. Additionally, all choses in action (including but not limited to life policies[1]) became assignable at law in 1873, by virtue of section 25(6) of the Judicature Act 1873 (re-enacted as section 136 of the Law of Property Act 1925). So this section provided an additional means of legally assigning a life policy.

To constitute a legal assignment under the Policies of Assurance Act 1867 or the Law of Property Act 1925, certain conditions laid down by those statutes need to be complied with. Where such conditions are not satisfied, it is still possible that there will be an equitable assignment.

Although a life office may get a legal discharge from an assignee following a legal assignment under the 1925 Act, the assignee will still be subject to any equities (which is a shorthand expression for any equitable rights or claims) which have priority. However, an assignment under the 1867 Act is, unlike the 1925 Act, subject to that person also being the person entitled in equity to the proceeds of the policy.

As a general rule where there are competing claims, either equitable or legal, the person entitled will be the first assignee, without knowledge (constructive or actual) of prior equitable interests, to serve notice on the life office[2].

The main benefit of a legal assignment is therefore the procedural and practical advantages of not having to join the assignor into the proceedings or involve him in any dealings with the life office.

SECTION 2 LEGAL ASSIGNMENTS

A The Policies of Assurance Act 1867

10.2 The Policies of Assurance Act 1867 (set out at Appendix 2) provides that an assignee can sue in his own name if:

(1) as a result of assignment or other derivative title he becomes entitled to a policy of life assurance and possesses at the time the action is brought the right in equity to receive[3] and the right to give a valid discharge to the assurance company for the policy moneys (ie it is a pre-condition that he be beneficially entitled to them at the time of the claim, the purpose being to

1 *Re Moore* (1878) 8 Ch D 519.

2 See **10.37**.

3 *Scottish Amicable Life Assurance Society v Fuller* (1867) IR 2 Eq 53.

ensure that the assignee under this Act does not obtain a better title than he would have done as an equitable assignee before the Act);

(2) he has obtained an assignment, either by endorsement on the policy or by separate instrument, in the words or to the effect as set out in the Schedule to the Act[1]; and

(3) written notice of the assignment has been given to the assurance company.

Notice must be given to the life office's principal place of business, or if more than one, at any one of them in England, Scotland or Ireland. Life offices must state in every policy their principal place or places of business at which notices of assignment may be given.

Under the 1867 Act, a policy of life assurance is defined as 'any instrument by which the payment of monies, by or out of the funds of an assurance company, on the happening of any contingency depending on the duration of human life, is assured or secured'. This wording is sufficiently wide to include individual pension policies.

Assignments under the 1867 Act must be in, or to the effect of, the prescribed wording so it is not necessary to follow that wording precisely. It is not necessary for the assignment to be by deed (although it usually is). They need not be for consideration and the assignee cannot get priority over a prior assignee who has given notice to the life office. This can cause difficulties for the life office in making payment out as the life office cannot get a legal discharge if there is a prior equitable assignee. For this reason assignment under the Law of Property Act 1925 may be preferable since, although such assignments are 'subject to equities…', this is not a precondition of it being a legal assignment[2].

In addition, the person giving notice may require the assurance company to deliver a written acknowledgement of receipt of notice (on payment of a fee not exceeding 25p)[3].

See Chapter 12 for taxation effects of assignments for consideration.

B The Law of Property Act 1925

10.3 Section 136 of the Law of Property Act 1925, re-enacting section 25(6) of the Judicature Act 1873, provides a method for assigning the legal title to 'any debt or other legal thing in action'. A policy of life assurance (or, more correctly, the right to receive payment under a policy) is a chose or 'thing' in action. The provisions of section 136 are as follows:

> '(1) Any absolute assignment by writing under the hand of the assignor (not purporting to be by way of charge only) of any debt or other legal thing in action of which express notice in writing has been given to the debtor, trustee or other person from whom the assignor would have been entitled to claim such debt or

1 Section 4A, **10.7**.
2 See, Priority, **10.37**.
3 Section 6.

thing in action, is effectual in law (subject to equities having priority over the right of the assignee) to pass and transfer from the date of such notice:

(a) the legal right to such debt or thing in action;

(b) all legal and other remedies for the same; and

(c) the power to give a good discharge for the same without the concurrence of the assignor.

Provided that, if the debtor, trustee or other person liable in respect of such debt or thing in action has notice:

(a) that the assignment is disputed by the assignor or any person claiming under him; or

(b) of any other opposing or conflicting claims to such debt or thing in action;

he may, if he thinks fit, either call upon the persons making claim thereto to interplead concerning the same, or pay the debt or other thing in action into court under the provisions of the Trustee Act 1925.'

Effect of the section compared to the Policies of Assurance Act 1867.

Under both Acts the assignee takes subject to any existing equities. But unlike the 1867 Act, the operation of section 136 is not dependent on the assignee having the right in equity, at the time an action is brought, to receive the policy money. All that is necessary is an absolute assignment and express notice in writing. Once an absolute written assignment under the Law of Property Act 1925 has been obtained by an assignee and he has given notice then, provided he is the first assignee so to do, he obtains the right to sue at law (even if there is a prior equitable assignment). The life office can obtain a legal discharge from the legal assignee in these circumstances even if it has notice of the previous equitable assignment. This is not the case with an assignment under the 1867 Act. Under section 136 the life office can require any person who has provided notice of a conflicting claim or dispute to interplead or the life office may pay the policy proceeds into court.

Is it possible to have a legal assignment of a life policy under both Acts at the same time? The answer is thought to be yes but the matter is not entirely free from doubt. The problem stems from the fact that the Law of Property Act 1925 provides that section 136 'does not affect the provisions of the Policies of Assurance Act 1867'[1]. It is at least arguable, therefore, that section 136 was only intended to cover choses in action other than life policies. Although in practice the substance of an assignee's interest in the policy will rarely depend on whether or not the assignment is under the 1867 Act or the 1925 Act, it does mean that the life office may not get a good legal discharge under the 1867 Act without joining the assignor as a party in any civil proceedings. An alternative view is that section 136(2) is making it clear that the 1867 Act continues in force providing another remedy for the assignee and that it was not impliedly repealed by the 1925 Act. From the life office's point of view, the safest course in such

1 Section 136(2).

circumstances is not to pay out on the policy unless the assignee can make out a good title under the Policies of Assurance Act 1867 (ie he must have the right in equity to receive the policy moneys). If the assignment is (unusually) expressly subject only to section 136 of the Law of Property Act 1925 then this would not be necessary.

In practice assignments documents do not tend to distinguish whether they are being made under the 1867 Act or under the 1925 Act.

SECTION 3 EQUITABLE ASSIGNMENTS

A General

10.4 The 1867 and 1925 Acts did not affect the validity of equitable assignments and 'whether or not what has been done in any particular transaction amounts to an equitable assignment is a matter of inference from the facts and documents concerned'[1]. So an oral assignment would be possible but may have evidential problems[2]. An assignment or agreement to assign is binding as between the parties without notice to the life office but as mentioned notice to the life office can be crucial for priority purposes[3]. A direction by the policyholder to the life office to pay the policy moneys to a third party is (without more) merely a revocable mandate, at any rate until the policyholder's intention to give that third party the benefit of the policy has been established[4]. The mere delivery (or deposit) of a policy for valuable consideration is an equitable assignment, even without a memorandum of deposit or notice to the life office[5]. An example of this is the deposit of the policy with a bank or building society as security.

There is also authority for mere delivery (without consideration) being sufficient but the position is not entirely clear[6]. The precise circumstances surrounding the delivery would therefore be important[7]. Mere physical possession of the policy document would not in itself give the holder any rights as the holder (eg a bank or building society) may be holding it for a variety of reasons other than as security.

Unlike a legal assignment it is possible to assign part of a life policy or some interest under it, for example bonuses under a with-profits policy, by an equitable assignment.

The essential requirement is that the intention of the assignor to assign the rights in question should be clear. If the assignment is in writing, no particular form of words is necessary[8].

1 Per Cohen LJ in *IRC v EMI Ltd* [1949] 1 All ER 120, CA; affd sub nom *EMI v IRC Ltd* [1950] 2 All ER 261, HL.
2 *Brandt's Sons & Co v Dunlop Rubber Co Ltd* [1905] AC 454.
3 See **10.37**.
4 *Re Williams, Williams v Ball* [1917] 1 Ch 1.
5 *Maughan v Ridley* (1868) 8 LT 309.
6 *Cook v Black* (1842) 1 Hare 390 cf *Howes v Prudential Assurance Co* (1883) 49 LT 133.
7 *Chapman v Chapman* (1851) 13 Beav 308.
8 *Brandt's Sons & Co v Dunlop Rubber Co Ltd* [1905] AC 454.

Where there has not been a legal assignment but the assignee has given *consideration*, equity will (subject to the rules on priority)[1] assist him to perfect his title against third parties, even though he may not have obtained a formal assignment.

If, however, a *voluntary* assignee seeks the support of equity, he will succeed only where:

(1) the assignment is complete as between assignor and assignee, ie everything necessary has been done by the assignor to make a present transfer and render the assignment binding (even if there remains something to be done by the assignee (for example, give notice))[2]; or

(2) the assignor has constituted himself as trustee for the assignee.

10.5 The assignee will not, however, succeed if there is only an agreement or intention to assign in the future as opposed to a present unconditional intention to transfer the policy, unless there is consideration for the promise to assign.

> *Re Williams, Williams v Ball*[3]
>
> The policyholder gave his housekeeper a policy with the following signed endorsement: 'I authorise X to draw this insurance in the event of my predeceasing her'. It was held that the assignment was inoperative as it contained no present words of gift and was without consideration and conditions; and it did not take effect as a testamentary disposition because it was not executed in accordance with the rules relating to the execution of wills or codicils.
>
> *Re Westerton, Public Trustee v Gray*[4]
>
> A man handed to his landlady an envelope in which were enclosed a bank deposit receipt, a signed order directing the bank to pay to her, and a letter addressed to her stating that in view of her kindness he desired to make some return by giving her the amount on deposit. In this case it was held that there was a valid and complete gift by way of assignment.

In relation to (1) above a possible interpretation is that everything necessary to transfer title to a life policy requires a valid legal assignment which is presumably not the case otherwise this category of equitable assignment would effectively be non-existent. A parallel may be drawn with cases dealing with the transfer of company shares and the distinction between tasks to be completed by the assignor and those which are outside his control (eg directors of the company actually registering the shares subject to the transfer, in the name of the transferee)[5]. Failure to serve notice (and therefore no valid legal assignment) does not prevent the assignment being a valid equitable assignment[6].

1 See further Section 6, **10.37**.
2 *Milroy v Lord* (1862) 4 De G F & J 264 at p 274, per Turner LJ.
3 [1917] 1 Ch 1.
4 [1919] 2 Ch 104.
5 See *Re Rose* [1952] Ch 499.
6 *Holt v Heatherfield Trust Ltd* [1942] 2 KB 1.

The principle has been developed further in *Pennington v Waine*[1] where it was held that for an equitable assignment of shares by way of gift, although delivery of the share transfer form was generally thought to be required, it could be dispensed with in some circumstances. In this case there was a clear finding that the donor intended to make an immediate gift. The intended recipient had been informed of it and it would have been unconscionable for the donor to have recalled the gift once the recipient had signed the prescribed form of consent to act as a director. In the circumstances delivery of the share transfer form before the donor's death was unnecessary so far as perfection of the gift was concerned. In any event applying the principle that a benevolent construction should be placed upon words of gift in order to give effect to the donor's clear wishes, the words used by the company's auditor in a letter to the recipient should be construed as meaning that the donor (and the company's auditor through her) had become agents for the purpose of submitting the share transfer to the company.

In the absence of a better right in equity a debtor (such as a life office) cannot refuse to pay an assignee who is a volunteer merely on the grounds of lack of consideration[2]. If the debtor does pay to such an assignee, the assignor will be unable to sue the debtor as the assignment as between the assignor and assignee was complete.

Express notice of the equitable assignment should be given to the life office so that it is in no doubt as to the situation. Otherwise the life office is entitled to pay the assignor and thereby obtain a discharge[3]. Whether or not notice is given to the life office does not affect the position between the assignee and assignor[4]

The effect of an equitable assignment is that the assignee acquires the beneficial interest in the insurance policy but not the right to sue. He will have to sue with the assignor as co-claimant with his consent or join him as a co-defendant if he does not consent.

B Scotland

10.6 There was never a separate equity jurisdiction in Scotland, law and equity having always been administered together by the same courts. Although the Policies of Assurance Act 1867 (but not the Law of Property Act 1925) applies to Scotland, it was not required there to give recognition at law to assignments of life policies. The Transmission of Moveable Property (Scotland) Act 1862 (specifically section 4) already applied to assignments of policies issued by Scottish companies whether the policyholder was resident in Scotland or not. The provisions of the Policies of Assurance Act 1867 provide an alternative form of assignment.

1 [2002] EWCA Civ 227.
2 *Walker v Bradford Old Bank* (1884) 12 QBD 511.
3 See **10.37**.
4 *Fortescue v Barnett* (1834) 3 My & K 36.

SECTION 4 FORM OF ASSIGNMENT

A Form of legal assignments

10.7 An assignment may be under hand (by just writing) or made by deed. The use of the word 'assign' is not necessary. Any words indicating assignment, for example, 'transfer', 'convey', or 'make over', will suffice. As mentioned above, it can be important to distinguish between a legal assignment and an equitable assignment and indeed, it will usually be the form of the assignment which determines its nature.

The requirement in the Policies of Assurance Act 1867 is that there be a written assignment either endorsed on the policy or by separate instrument in the words or to the effect set out in the Schedule to the Act[1]. Stamping is no longer required[2].

The prescribed wording is as follows:

> 'I, AB of, &c in consideration of, &c do hereby assign unto CD of, &c, his Executors, Administrators and Assigns, the [within] Policy of Assurance granted, &c [here describe the Policy]. In witness, &c.'

Despite the brevity of this form, the wording of an assignment of a policy is usually expanded and, for example, expressed to assign not just the policy but all sums assured by or to become payable under or by virtue of it and all benefits and advantages of the policy as well. Any benefit by way of bonus or otherwise will in any event pass under the assignment unless express terms are used to exclude it[3]. This would include policies effected in substitution for the assigned policy under an option in the original policy[4].Also, where the policyholder assigned as a gift a policy on his life for a one-year term, and later extended the policy and died during the extended term, it is presumed that the extension was effected for the benefit of the assignee who was entitled to claim the whole of the policy moneys[5].

Although section 136 of the Law of Property Act 1925 does not provide a prescribed wording, it states that the assignment must be under the hand of the assignor and notice must be given to the life office. It need not be in the form of a deed (although in practice normally would be). It also states that it must be an absolute assignment of the chose in action and not merely an assignment by way of charge only. It is submitted that due to the nature of the right under the Policies of Assurance Act 1867 (ie the requirement of being beneficially entitled to receive the policy moneys), an absolute assignment is also implicitly required by that Act as well[6].

1 Policies of Assurance Act 1867, s 5.
2 Finance Act 2003, s 125.
3 *Gilly v Burley* (1856) 22 Beav 619.
4 *Nesbitt v Berridge* (1864) 10 Jur (NS) 53.
5 *Royal Exchange Assurance v Hope* [1928] Ch 179.
6 *Re Williams, Williams v Ball* [1917] 1 Ch 1 at p 4, per Astbury J.

To constitute an absolute assignment, the instrument must express a clear and final intention to make an immediate and outright transfer of the whole policy[1]. An assignment subject to a condition for defeasance and revesting in the assignor upon the happening of a future event, and an assignment subject to a condition precedent, or an agreement to assign at a future date (even if supported by consideration)[2] do not therefore constitute valid legal assignments. An assignment expressed to be as security does not necessarily prevent the assignment being absolute. However, if it is combined with conditions as to defeasance, it will not be absolute. An assignment by way of charge would not be an absolute assignment as it does not transfer any property[3]. By way of contrast an assignment by way of mortgage may, however, be absolute if there is a provision, express or implied, for reassignment on repayment of all outstanding moneys[4]. An assignment of a policy as collateral security until it is reassigned is absolute[5]. The governing principle is that the life office must not be placed in a position of uncertainty as to the person to whom it should pay the money[6]. Therefore, with a mortgage the proviso as to reassignment is important because it enables the life office to know where the title to the policy is, without knowing the state of the borrowings on which the policy is secured.

It is generally considered that part of a policy cannot be the subject of a valid *legal* assignment.

> *Re Steel Wing Co Ltd*[7]
>
> A creditor purported to assign part of a debt. Held, that the assignment would not pass the right to sue for that portion of the debt under the Judicature Act 1873, but that it would operate in equity.

Life policies with some investment element are often issued as a group of identical 'sub–policies' or 'Segments' so that, for example, a policy may be subdivided into a hundred such constituent policies. Sometimes this is referred to as a 'cluster policy'.

An assignment of one segment or sub-policy under such a contract would not be treated as an assignment of part of a policy, even where the policy is subject to certain conditions which apply across all the segments (for example, the investment funds in which the segments are invested). In such cases the assignee is free to encash the segment(s) assigned to him and there is no uncertainty from the life office's point of view as to the person entitled to payment.

1 *Williams v Atlantic Assurance Co Ltd* [1933] 1 KB 81.
2 *Spencer v Clarke* (1878) 9 Ch D 137.
3 *Tancred v Delagoa Bay Railway Co* (1889) 23 QBD 239.
4 See *Tancred v Delagoa Bay Railway Co* (1889) 23 QBD 239 and *Durham Bros v Robertson* [1898] 1 QB 765.
5 *Comfort v Betts* [1891] 1 QB 737 (CA).
6 *Durham Bros v Robertson* [1898] 1 QB 765.
7 [1921] 1 Ch 349.

1 *Joint tenancy and tenancy in common*

10.8 Personal property (such as a life policy) can be held subject to a 'joint tenancy' or a 'tenancy in common' in equity. Much will depend on the precise wording of the life policy (or other relevant document). For real property, at law, the property must be held as joint tenants but may be held in equity as either joint tenants or tenants in common. On the death of one joint tenant the beneficial interest passes to the survivors or survivor of the joint tenants and on the death of the last survivor to his personal representatives. On the death of a tenant in common his share passes to his personal representatives and not to the surviving tenants. In certain cases equity will presume a tenancy in common of the beneficial interest, eg where property is purchased by two persons with money provided in unequal shares, mortgages made to two persons jointly[1] and where the property is acquired by business partners.

There is some authority for the proposition that, at law, personal property cannot be held as tenants in common. In the case of *McKerrell, McKerrell v Gowans*[2] which related to an assignment of a policy held jointly by a husband and wife, it was said 'whatever else the assignment by the husband may have been it did not affect the right of the wife as survivor to sue at law on the policy'. Accordingly, there was no legal assignment under the Judicature Act 1873 (the predecessor of section 136 of the Law of Property Act 1925). The logic behind this reasoning is that as a chose in action is merely a right of action then the common law was concerned only with the proper persons to bring the action and regarding them as one person in law recognised only joint tenants and not tenants in common.

Similarly, it has been submitted[3] that section 136(1) of the Law of Property Act 1925 (which requires an absolute assignment of the whole chose in action) does not permit one joint owner to effect a severance of the legal title by assigning his interest to the other joint tenant. To enable the life office to obtain a legal discharge, the assignment would have to be from both joint owners to the sole future owner. In practice, an assignment by one joint owner to the other of the former's interest in the policy should create a valid equitable assignment. Provided there are no existing or prior interests of which the assignee has knowledge, or which have been notified to the life office, then the assignee's interest is well established. However, in order to get around the inability of a person without the legal title to give a good discharge and in the absence of the legal owner, a life office may ask for an indemnity before it pays out to a person with only the equitable title to the policy.

2 *Equity*

10.9 No special form of words or writing is necessary to pass equitable rights to the proceeds of a policy so long as the intention of the parties that those rights should pass is clear.

1 *Morley v Bird* (1798) 3 Ves 629, 631 per Arden, MR.
2 *McKerrell, McKerrell v Gowans* [1912] 2 Ch 648 at 653.
3 See 35 *Halsbury's Laws* (4th edn Reissue) para 1245, n 5.

B Assignments by way of sale

1 Assignments on sale[1]

10.10 Where a policy is sold, the consideration is usually the payment of money. The vendor should be required to prove his title to the purchaser.

The purchaser should ask the life office what notices have been received and whether all premiums due have been paid. If he cannot obtain possession of all the earlier documents he should require an acknowledgement of his right to production, which may be incorporated in the assignment itself or in a separate form. The vendor may assign with full title guarantee, with limited title guarantee or with no title guarantee although often the assignment is silent in this respect[2]. An assignment on sale, which in practice is usually made by deed, should contain a receipt for the purchase money. The purchaser should serve notice on the life office.

Ideally, the purchaser should make arrangements to be kept in touch with the life assured, so that if the life assured dies he can claim under the policy. In practice this may not be easy or practical.

An assignment of a policy made for an *illegal* consideration is not enforceable against the assignor. Also, where an assignment is made otherwise than for full consideration in the five years preceding the petition for an assignor's bankruptcy or commencement of winding up, it may be capable of being reversed by the trustee in bankruptcy or liquidator[3].

The traded endowment policy (TEP) market witnessed substantial growth in the 1990s with the result that there are numerous companies who have established themselves as intermediaries for sellers and buyers . Generally speaking, the prices obtained by the sale of life policies exceed the surrender values offered by the life office. There are also companies who conduct auctions of life policies.

3 Void and voidable assignments

10.11 The assignment of a policy, or an agreement to assign, where without the knowledge of the contracting parties the life assured is already dead, is void "ab initio" (from the beginning).

> *Scott v Coulson*[4]
>
> C purchased from S a policy on the life of D, and it was assigned to him. It was subsequently discovered that at the date of the contract and unknown to both parties, D had already died. It was held the contract was void on the ground of mutual mistake and must be set aside.

1 This can be more advantageous than surrendering the policy particularly for with-profits endowments where a large amount of the return would normally be derived from terminal bonuses.
2 See Chapter 1 for implied covenants under the to Law of Property (Miscellaneous Provisions) Act 1994.
3 Section 339, Insolvency Act 1986.
4 [1903] 2 Ch 249.

A sale or gift of a life policy is voidable and may be set aside by the court on the ground of misrepresentation, even if innocent[1], duress, or undue influence, and this should be borne in mind, for example, if on examination of an assignment on sale, the consideration recited appears to be grossly inadequate.

There are certain cases of fiduciary relationship where, unless the contrary is shown, the court will *presume* an undue influence. For example, the relationship between trustee and beneficiary; solicitor and client; doctor and patient; parent and child; guardian and ward; and also husband and wife. In the context of this type of relationship there is no need to produce evidence to show that actual undue influence was exerted. This is presumed unless the contrary is shown.

C Assignments for nominal consideration

10.12 Sometimes the assignment may be expressed to be for nominal consideration even though it does not represent the true consideration. No consideration may actually pass hands but there is a concern that if the assignment is not in the form of a deed, and is expressed to be for nil consideration, it would not be binding on the parties. However, no consideration need be mentioned in the assignment, nor indeed is consideration necessary where the assignment is purely a gift[2].

D Assignments by way of gift

10.13 A gift of a policy should be described as such on the face of the instrument, so that no doubt can arise that the assignor intends to pass the beneficial interest. Unless the intention to make a gift is clear, there may be a presumption that the donee holds the policy on a resulting trust for the donor.

Where the donee is the wife or a near relative of the donor, the assignment is sometimes expressed to be in consideration of natural love and affection, although this practice largely seems to have died out and is, in any event, unnecessary.

If the policy is subject to a mortgage the deed should, unless the contrary be intended, provide that, as between the assignor and the assignee, the assignee shall be liable for the repayment of the mortgage debt, ie so the gift in effect is only of the amount in excess of the mortgage debt. This is advisable in the light of the decision in the following case:

> *Re Best, Parker v Best*[3]
>
> B mortgaged a policy to the life office, entering into the usual covenant to repay the mortgage. He later assigned the policy as a gift to his wife, but the deed did not refer to the mortgage. The life office deducted the mortgage debt from the claim. Held, that the widow must be reimbursed by the executors of the husband.

1 Misrepresentation Act 1967.
2 *Re Westerton, Public Trustee v Gray* [1919] 2 Ch 104.
3 [1924] 1 Ch 42.

E Assignments made abroad

10.14 Where there is a foreign element to an assignment the question as to which country's law (the 'proper law') governs the assignment between assignor and assignee, or between two assignees with conflicting claims, will be determined by the Contracts (Applicable Law) Act 1990 which gives statutory force in the UK to certain international conventions on Conflicts of Laws. The position is, however, similar to the common law rules of private international law which it replaced.

A distinction must be drawn between the law which governs the assignment and the law of the life policy itself. Where the question is the liability of the life office to be sued in the name of the assignee, or whether the latter can give a discharge to the life office, the rights of the assignee will be determined according to the proper law of the original contract, ie the life policy. For a UK insurer (for pre-18 December 2009 contracts), where the policyholder is habitually resident in a member state of the EU, the proper law is determined in accordance with the Financial Services and Markets Act 2000 (Law Applicable to Contracts of Insurance) Regulations 2001[1], implementing the relevant parts of the Second and Third Life Directives (now the Consolidated Life Directive)[2]. Subject to any choice of law the proper law would normally be the law of the country in which the policyholder has his habitual residence. The term 'habitual residence' is defined in the Glossary to the FSA Handbook as (where the policyholder is an individual) 'the address given by the policyholder as his residence if it reasonably appears to be a residential address and there is no evidence to the contrary'. For contracts entered into after 17 December 2009, the applicable law provisions will be governed by the 'Rome Regulation on the law applicable to contractual obligations' ('Rome I'). In practice, there are unlikely to be any practical differences, although interestingly Article 7.3(b) specifically provides that the parties may choose the law of the member state of which the policyholder is a 'national', with which the individual and life office may have no connection with. Rome I also has specific rules which apply where there is no choice of law.

In relation to non-EU policyholders the provisions of the Contracts (Applicable Law) Act 1990 would apply in the absence of a choice of law. In relation to the law of the assignment, the 1990 Act essentially provides that the law applicable to the assignment is the law chosen by the parties. This choice may either be expressly specified in the assignment (which is not common) or implied by the circumstances of the case. It also provides that the parties may agree to change the law governing the assignment. Where no choice has been made, the law applicable to the assignment is the law of the country with which the assignment has the closest connection. There is a presumption that the assignment is most closely connected with the country where the assignor has his habitual residence.

Voluntary assignment is specifically provided for by Schedule 1 to the 1990 Act (Article 12 of the Rome Convention). The law governing the right to which

1 SI 2001/2635
2 Second Life Directive; Council Directive 90/619; Third Life Directive; Council Directive 92/96; Consolidating Life Directive of 5 November 2002 (No 2002/83/EC).

the assignment relates shall determine its assignability, the relationship between the assignee and debtor (eg the life office) and any question whether the debtor's obligations have been discharged[1]. Essentially, 'the right to which the assignment relates' will therefore mean English law for a policy with a life office with its registered office in England.

10.15 The following cases illustrate the operation of the application of the proper law of the assignment:

> *Lee v Abdy*[2]
>
> A policy with an English life office was effected by a man domiciled in the Cape of Good Hope and was subsequently assigned by him to his wife. Under the law of the Cape, a husband could not assign a policy to his wife. It was held that the assignment was a nullity.
>
> *Pender v Commercial Bank of Scotland Ltd*[3]
>
> A man domiciled in Scotland effected with an English life office a policy on his life under the Married Women's Property Act 1882 for the benefit of his wife. The wife mortgaged her interest in it to a Scottish bank. Under English law she could validly do this but she could not do so under the law of Scotland. Held, that her capacity to mortgage her beneficial interest in the policy (which requires an assignment to the lender) must be determined by the law of Scotland and so the mortgage was invalid.
>
> *Scottish Provident Institution v Cohen & Co*[4]
>
> A Scottish life office issued a life policy in Scotland to a domiciled Scotsman. Afterwards, then being resident in England, he deposited the policy with a domiciled Englishman as security for an advance, notice being given to the office. The policyholder was made bankrupt in Scotland. The trustee questioned whether the policy should vest in him. It was held that, although under the law of Scotland the deposit would not have been a good assignment, in view of the fact that the transaction was completed in England the law of England would apply, and the deposit was good (as an equitable assignment) against the trustee acting for the general creditors in Scotland[5].

An assignee whose assignment is valid by foreign law, but does not entitle him to give a discharge in England, may nevertheless have an equitable right which will be recognised by English law.

1 See *Raiffeisen Zentralbank osterreich AG v Five Star General Trading LLC and others* [2001] EWCA Civ 68, CA.

2 (1886) 17 QBD 309.

3 1940 SLT 306.

4 (1888) 16 R (Ct of Sess) 112.

5 It would appear that a mere deposit of the policy is not sufficient in England without a memorandum in writing to effect an assignment in England. See *United Bank of Kuwait plc v Sahib* (1994) Times, 7 July; [1997] Ch 107, [1996] 3 All ER 215, CA.

F Miscellaneous

1 Examination of title

10.16 Before making any payment under a policy, or agreeing to any variation in the terms of a policy or the exercise of an option under the policy (or any other dealings with the policy), the life office should ascertain the person or persons entitled to deal with the policy or give a discharge if relevant. This may be the grantee(s) (the original contracting party or parties), or persons deriving title from the grantee(s) either by assignment or by operation of law (eg his personal representatives, trustees or trustee in bankruptcy).

2 Payment to nominee

10.17 It is possible that a good discharge can be given by persons other than the original policyholder or person deriving title under him. If it is an essential term of the policy that payment shall be made to a specified third party, then the life office is entitled to carry out the precise terms of the contract. It follows that a good discharge can be obtained by paying the third party although the right to sue may remain with the policyholder or his personal representatives. However, the payment to the third party cannot be intercepted by the policyholder[1]. Furthermore, as the principle of 'privity of contract' was fundamentally affected by the Contracts (Rights of Third Parties) Act 1999 a specified third party may have an enforceable right of his own if the policy is worded appropriately and the effect of this Act is not excluded.

The correct interpretation of the contract may be that payment is to be made to the named person. However, the life office may also seek to obtain authority from the policyholder or his personal representatives for the payment to be made to the named person and an acknowledgement that such a payment will discharge the contract.

Where a policy contained a proviso that the receipt of the husband or wife or certain relatives of the policyholder was a good discharge, it was held that the proviso was an integral part of the contract and was not repugnant to the usual obligation to pay to the executors or administrators of the policyholder. The payment by the life office to a relative without knowledge that a grant of representation had been taken out must be accepted in satisfaction of their obligation in view of the express provision in the policy that such payment was conclusive evidence that all demands against the life office had been fully satisfied. However, this did not mean that any person other than the executors could actually enforce the contract[2]. Although it should be noted that the case referred to was decided prior to the 1999 Act.

Life offices are sometimes placed in a difficult position when the policyholder purports to make a 'nomination' of a policy and this is not a term of the contract

1 *Re Schebsman, ex p Official Receiver, Trustee v Cargo Superintendents (London) Ltd* [1944] Ch 83.

2 *O'Reilly v Prudential Assurance Co Ltd* [1934] All ER Rep 672.

as in the example above. A nomination as such of a life policy is not recognised under English law (although it is under certain continental and other systems of law). It is possible that the nomination may amount to a declaration of trust under section 11 of the Married Women's Property Act 1882 or otherwise (see Chapter 12 for the interpretation of wordings which have been held to create a trust). Also, as mentioned above, it could be a contractual term in that A may have agreed with B to make payment to C (potentially for C's own benefit in view of the Contracts (Rights of Third Parties) Act 1999 where the Act has not been expressly excluded). The case of *Gold v Hill*[1] generated considerable interest in view of the references to 'nominations' in connection with a life policy. However, it was held that the 'nomination' had the effect of establishing a secret trust at the time of death rather than establishing that a nomination, as such, was an effective means of transferring the benefits of a life policy.

The sum payable under certain Friendly Society policies may be transferred by nomination under section 66 of the Friendly Societies Act 1974 provided the sum in question does not exceed £5,000.

3 *Enjoyment of benefit*

10.18 The person or persons entitled to sue and to receive the policy moneys will not, of course, necessarily be entitled to enjoy them beneficially. The claim may, for example, be made by executors, whose duty it is to collect the policy moneys and to deal with it in accordance with the will of the testator, or by trustees who will deal with it in accordance with the instrument constituting the trusts and general trust law.

4 *Equitable interests*

10.19 The right to sue and to receive the policy moneys is not affected by equitable interests under wills, trusts and mortgages which are protected by executors, trustees or mortgagees. Such interests concern the life office only if it has notice that the executors, trustees or mortgagees have exceeded or propose to exceed their powers or have committed or propose to commit a breach of trust. In such cases the life office may be affected by having notice of equitable interests not otherwise protected and it cannot disregard them otherwise it may be fixed with constructive trusteeship. In such circumstances the life office may well seek a discharge from all interested (or potentially interested) parties. In more extreme cases it may pay the proceeds into court.

5 *Policy provision that policy cannot be assigned*

10.20 It is possible for the policyholder and the life office to agree that the policy is to be non-assignable with the result that any purported assignment is not

1 TLR 24/8/98: (1999) 1 FLR 54; [1998] Fam Law 664, 142 Sol Jo LB 226. Applied in *Beddar and others v Prestidge* [2001] All ER (D) 254.

binding. However, it may still be possible for an equitable assignment or declaration of trust to be effected[1].

SECTION 5 NOTICE

A Summary of reasons for service of notice

10.21 Service of notice is required for four main reasons:

(1) In the case of a legal assignment to give the assignee the right to sue at law in his own name under the Policies of Assurance Act 1867, or under the Law of Property Act 1925.

(2) To bind the life office and to prevent it from paying to the assignor.

(3) To acquire, in the case of an assignee for value, priority over earlier equities of which notice has not been served on the life office and which are unknown to the assignee.

(4) To preserve priority against interests subsequently acquired.

B Notice to agents

10.22 If notice is given to an agent authorised by the life office it is as good as notice to the life office itself. However, policy documents often contain a condition that agents of the company are not permitted to accept notice of any assignment and that assignment can only be given at the company's head office. In including such a provision the life office predominantly has in mind the representatives (or 'tied agents') of the life office. As a result of such a provision the notice given to such an agent would not constitute a formal notice and priority (where relevant) would not be acquired as a result.

C Notice under the Policies of Assurance Act 1867

1 *Effect of the Act*

10.23 The Policies of Assurance Act 1867 enables an assignee to sue in his own name. The 1867 Act is concerned only with the determination of the person to whom the life office may pay. It does *not* affect the *priorities* of equitable interests in the policy money although it requires the assignee to have 'the right in equity to receive' the policy moneys.

1 *Re Turcan*(1889) 40 Ch D.

The Act gives the assignee the right to sue in his own name, provided that:

(1) He has the right in equity to receive the policy money and to give an effectual discharge.

(2) He has a written assignment in the appropriate form.

(3) A written notice of the date and 'purport' of the assignment has been given to the life office[1].

2 *Notice*

10.24 The provisions of the 1867 Act with regard to notice are as follows:

(1) A written notice of the date and purport of the assignment must be given to the assurance company at its principal place of business, for the time being, or, if it has two or more principal places of business, then at one of those principal places.

(2) The assurance company must on every policy specify the place or principal places of business at which notices may be given.

(3) The assurance company must, upon payment of a fee not exceeding 25p, give in writing, under the hand of its manager, secretary, treasurer or other principal officer, an acknowledgment of the receipt of the notice.

The Act does not indicate whether more than one fee of 25p can be charged if the notice affects more than one policy or deed. In practice, life offices do not generally make any charges for acknowledgment of receipt of notice.

The Policies of Assurance Act 1867 provides that a bona fide payment made by a life office before receipt of notice shall be as valid against the assignee giving notice as if the Act had not been passed. Therefore, notice and consequently legal title to the policy will only be complete on receipt by the life office of the notice.

D Notice under the Law of Property Act 1925

1 *Debts and choses in action*

10.25 Section 136[2] of the Law of Property Act 1925 provides that express notice in writing must be given, but there are no provisions on the subject of acknowledgement of notice. Without notice there can be no assignment under section 136 although it may still amount to an equitable assignment.

1 Policies of Assurance Act 1867, ss 1, 3 and 5.
2 See Section 2B concerning legal assignments.

2 Content of notice

10.26 The production of the assignment instrument itself is service of notice, as the document is in writing (and for the purposes of the 1867 Act its date and purport are shown). In one case[1] the Court of Appeal held that a letter referring to an assignment of a debt but without giving any date and wrongly stating that notice had previously been given was, nevertheless, itself a sufficient notice of assignment. However, if a notice identifies a document by its date, and the date is wrong, the notice is bad. Denning LJ in *W F Harrison & Co v Burke*[2] (approving an earlier case of *Stanley v English Fibres Industries Ltd*[3]) declared that it was clear from section 136(1) of the Law of Property Act 1925 that notice in writing was 'an essential part of the transfer of title to the debt and, as such, the requirements of the Act must be strictly complied with, and notice itself … must be strictly accurate – accurate in particular in regard to the date which is given for the assignment'. It is possible that this may have amounted to an equitable assignment.

3 Provisions as to notice

10.27 Section 196 of the 1925 Act provides that:

(1) Any notice required to be served or given shall be in writing.

(2) That it shall be sufficient to leave the notice at the last known business address (of the insurance company) in the UK.

(3) That notice may be served by registered post and if the letter is not returned undelivered, it is deemed served when the letter would in the ordinary course be delivered. Under the provisions of the Recorded Delivery Service Act 1962 the notice may be sent by recorded delivery instead of by registered post.

There are no provisions as to the time within which notice must be given, but it must be given before an action to enforce the assigned rights[4]. Indeed, valid notice may even be given after the death of the life assured[5]. No mention is made in section 136 (or section 196) as to any requirement of communication to the assignee.

E Constructive notice

10.28 The concept of constructive notice can be very important in establishing priority of assignments. Section 199 of the Law of Property Act 1925 provides

1 *Van Lynn Developments Ltd v Pelias Construction* [1969] 1 QB 607.
2 [1956] 1 WLR 419 at 421.
3 (1899) 68 LJQB 839.
4 *Bateman v Hunt* [1904] 2 KB 530 at p 538.
5 *Walker v Bradford Old Bank* (1884) 12 QBD 511.

that: 'A purchaser shall not be prejudicially affected by notice of any instrument or matter or any fact or thing unless:

(1) it is within his own knowledge, or would have come to his knowledge if such enquiries and inspections had been made as ought reasonably to have been made by him; or

(2) in the same transaction with respect to which a question of notice to the purchaser arises, it has come to the knowledge of his counsel, as such, or of his solicitors or other agent, as such, or would have come to the knowledge of his solicitor or other agent, as such, if such enquiries and inspections had been made as ought reasonably to have been made by the solicitor or other agent'[1].

'Purchaser' in the section means a person acquiring an interest in good faith for valuable consideration and includes a mortgagee; while valuable consideration includes marriage and formation of a civil partnership it does not include nominal consideration in money.

Section 199 of the 1925 Act is consistent with the established equitable rule of constructive notice, namely that a person who is aware of such facts as would have put a reasonable man on inquiry is deemed to be aware of facts which a reasonable inquiry would have revealed. Failure to produce the policy may fix the purchaser with implied or constructive notice of an earlier charge[2].

1 *Production of policy*

10.29 A technical case may be made for the life office requiring production of the policy for every transaction with it, even though the transaction does not bring the policy to an end. For example:

(1) Partial surrenders and surrenders of bonuses.

(2) Payments of sums assured by instalments (as in family income policies).

(3) Payments of annuities.

(4) Exercise of options or variations to the policy.

In practice, however, where small or regular and frequent payments are to be made, the production of the policy on each occasion is waived in the interests of convenience. Usually this may be done without serious risk.

2 *Production of deeds relating to more than one policy*

10.30 Where a deed which affects two or more policies with the same life office is produced in connection with a transaction under one of them, it is

1 Conversely, notice by the assignee to a broker does not generally constitute valid notice. See *Amalgamated General Finance Co Ltd v C E Golding & Co Ltd* [1964] 2 Lloyd's Rep 163.
2 *Spencer v Clarke* (1878) 9 Ch D 137. See **10.38** for a summary of the facts of the case.

thought that this amounts to notice of any dealing with the other policy or policies. However, it would presumably need to be clear on the face of the deed that it affected the other policies.

F Withdrawal of notice

10.31 The Policies of Assurance Act 1867 does not contain any provisions about withdrawal or amendment of notice.

A person who serves notice sometimes wishes to amend it on the ground that it contains some error and may serve a second notice to that effect. He may, on the other hand, desire to withdraw his notice altogether because:

(1) it was served in error;

(2) the deed to which it relates is no longer operative (eg a mortgage that has been paid off);

(3) the deed to which it relates has been superseded by a fresh deed;

(4) no deed or document was in fact executed.

The rules for payment into court under the Life Assurance Companies (Payment into Court) Act 1896[1] (see Appendix 7) contain a reference to withdrawal of notice albeit in the context of the life office seeking to obtain a discharge rather than a policyholder looking to protect his interests.

It seems obvious that notice can be withdrawn only by the person who served it or by the person on whose behalf it was served. In any event, withdrawal of notice should be treated with great caution for the following reasons:

(1) The deed in question may contain recitals or references to other interests of which notice of withdrawal has not been served.

(2) The deed said to be superseded may contain an assignment of the policy which does not become a nullity merely because another deed (perhaps in the same form) is subsequently executed by the assignor.

If notice is withdrawn, it is desirable, in practice, to examine the title immediately and to have sight or access to any cancelled or superseded documents.

G Recording receipt of notices

10.32 The Policies of Assurance Act 1867 did not forbid equitable assignments or impair their efficiency, and a life office should still record an equitable interest of which it has received notice.

1 CPR Pt 37 Practice Direction – Miscellaneous Provisions about Payment into Court (paras 7 and 8).

It is important, therefore, for a life office to record, as well as the dates of receipt of notice, the following:

(1) The date and effect of every assignment of which it receives notice (statutory or otherwise).

(2) The date and effect of any event whereby the title passes by operation of law (eg on appointment of a trustee in bankruptcy).

(3) The date of death of any assignee, etc and the date and details of the grant of representation to his estate.

(4) The date and particulars of any equitable interest (eg charge by memorandum of deposit) of which it receives notice.

Policy records are generally now held on the life office's computer systems. Original written notices may not be retained, but are instead scanned in and retained on the life office's systems in that way.

I Information as to notices

10.33 The Policies of Assurance Act 1867 does not state whether the life office must give an enquirer information about notices received but the general practice is to do so and this would usually be in the best interests of the life office. Generally, it is accepted that information should be given on receiving a written request from a known interested party. It will also normally be given where the enquirer is a solicitor, banker or accountant as the life office would normally accept the enquirer's statement that he is making the enquiry with the consent or on behalf of some person known by the life office to be interested in the policy.

In *Re Weniger's Policy*[1], it was assumed that the life office would on request give such information, as it was stated that if a first mortgagee makes a further advance on a fresh bargain he must, to preserve priority, enquire whether notice of another charge has been received. When giving information, the life office should seek to disclaim responsibility for any error or omission in the information given especially in view of the fact that to a substantial extent the life office is relying on others for the accuracy of that information and can only relay such information as has been communicated to it.

SECTION 6 PRIORITY

10.34 This Section deals with the effect of notice on priorities of equitable interests. As far as *priorities* are concerned, a legal assignee is in the same position as an equitable assignee. In this context it is also worth noting the following statement regarding section 136 of the Law of Property Act 1925[2]:

1 [1910] 2 Ch 291.

2 Per Phillips J in *E Pfeiffer Weinkellerei-Weineinkauf GmbH & Co v Arbuthnot Factors Ltd* [1988] 1 WLR 150.

'[S]ection [136] enables the assignee to acquire a title that has all the procedural advantages of legal title but as far as priorities are concerned his position is no better than if the assignment had been effected prior to that Act. It follows that even if the assignment is effected for value without notice of a prior equity, priorities fall to be determined as if the assignment had been effected in equity, not in law.'

A Effect of notice on priorities of equitable interests

1 The Policies of Assurance Act 1867

10.35 As indicated, this Act gives a simpler remedy against a life office by avoiding the need for the assignee to join the assignor of the policy in actions against the life office; and to make it easier for a life office to settle a claim.

Newman v Newman[1]

A had a policy assigned to her and served notice on the life office but which was not in accordance with section 3 of the 1867 Act. Later B, with notice of that interest, received an assignment of the policy and served notice which did comply with the Act. It was held that B did not take priority. The 1867 Act was not intended to affect the priorities of interested parties between themselves where the subsequent assignee had notice of the prior interest.

The 1867 Act was *not* intended, for example, to provide that a person who has advanced money on a second charge with notice of a first charge (and subject to it) should, by giving statutory notice to the life office, take priority over the first charge – nor does it have this effect. If, when taking an assignment, the assignee has notice of some existing equitable interest, he cannot take priority over that interest merely by giving notice to the life office, and that is so whether or not the life office has notice of the equitable interest. The 1867 Act does not affect the position as between the assignee and the person with the equitable interest. In these circumstances, if the assignee has actual or constructive notice of the existing equitable interest, the person with that interest is entitled to the policy proceeds. An example of constructive notice is the case of *Spencer v Clarke*[2] (see **10.28**). In simple terms, constructive notice is where the assignee fails to make a reasonable investigation with the consequence that he will be presumed to have notice of what would have been discovered had he made reasonable enquiries.

The priority in point here is priority in the right to sue. The 1867 Act does not determine the priority of conflicting interests in the policy money. This follows the ordinary rules of priority of equitable interests (see **10.37**).

1 (1885) 28 Ch D 674.
2 (1878) 9 Ch D 137.

2 *The Law of Property Act 1925, section 136*

10.36 'The statute does not forbid or destroy equitable assignments or impair their efficiency in the slightest degree'[1]. This point, although in some respects fairly well established ever since the Judicature Act 1873, has been doubted in some cases, for example, by Robert Goff J in *Ellerman Lines Ltd v Lancaster Maritime Co Ltd*[2]. There is dicta in that case that there is a distinction between the priority of legal and equitable assignments although the case did not turn on that point. The apparent discrepancy has, however, been addressed by Mummery J in the case of *Compaq Computer Ltd v Abercorn Group Ltd*[3], Mummery J preferring the view expressed in *E Pfeiffer Weinkellerei-Weinenkauf GmbH & Co v Arbuthnot Factors Ltd*[4]. He stated the following in relation to section 136:

> 'Section 136(1) provides that the assignment is subject to equities having priority over the right of the assignee. The effect of those words is to create, in the case of a statutory assignment of a chose in action, an exception to the general rule that equity will not prevail against a bona fide purchaser of a legal estate for value without notice of the prior equity.'

Thus it would appear that the priority of assignments, whether legal or equitable, is determined by the rules for equitable encumbrances.

B Priorities of equitable interests

10.37 The priorities of equitable encumbrances of choses in action such as life policies are, apart from the doctrine of notice, determined by the date of the encumbrances. Where, however, there is a life office, trustee or other person to whom notice can be given to restrain the holder of the fund from parting with it, priority is prima facie determined by the date of giving notice. This is known as the rule in *Dearle v Hall*[5]. It is worth noting the statement of Phillips J in *Pfeiffer*[6]:

> 'The rule in *Dearle v Hall* is an exception to the general principle that equitable interests take priority in the order in which they are created. The rule applies to dealings with equitable interests in any property and in particular to equitable assignments of legal choses in action. Under the rule priority depends upon the order in which notice of the interest created by the dealing is given to the person affected by it, ie in the case of assignments of a debt, the debtor.'

No assignee can, however, by giving notice obtain priority over a prior assignment if he had actual or constructive notice of it at the time. He will have to show

1 *William Brandt's Sons & Co v Dunlop Rubber Co* [1905] AC 454 at 462.
2 *The Lancaster* [1980] 2 Lloyd's Rep 497 at 503.
3 [1993] BCLC 602.
4 *E Pfeiffer Weinkellerei-Weineinkauf GmbH & Co v Arbuthnot Factors Ltd* [1988] 1 WLR 150.
5 (1828) 3 Russ 1.
6 *E Pfeiffer Weinkellerrei-Weineinkauf Gmbh & Co v Arbuthnot Factors Ltd* [1988] 1 WLR 150.

that he has given value and he must have acted in good faith, without notice, actual or constructive, of any earlier assignment. For example, if a person lends money on the security of a life policy which is not delivered to him and is in the hands of an earlier mortgagee, he has constructive notice of the earlier mortgage.

Spencer v Clarke[1]

The borrower deposited his policy with A as an equitable security for a loan. A retained it but gave no notice to the life office. Later B, in ignorance of the deposit with A, agreed to lend on the policy and when the borrower alleged he had left the policy at home by mistake, B completed his loan by means of a memorandum of charge under which the borrower undertook to execute a mortgage upon request. B served notice on the life office. It was held that B was put on enquiry by the conduct of the borrower and was fixed with constructive notice of A's security; and that the title of A, who held the policy, must prevail.

Re Lake, ex p Cavendish[2]

A solicitor misappropriated his client's money but later executed a mortgage of his life policies in favour of the client to secure part of the appropriated money. He did not inform the client or give notice to the life office. Later, he executed a second mortgage to another client without disclosing the first mortgage and the second client gave notice to the life office. It was held that the second mortgage had priority.

10.38 The case of *Re Weniger's Policy* may help to illustrate the above mentioned rules.

Re Weniger's Policy[3]

W charged a life policy as follows:

Date	*Action*
20 Dec 1897	
13 Dec 1899	Memoranda of deposit with the life office for £250.
14 July 1905	Memorandum of charge to Kapp for £146, subject to the above life office charge.
1 Sept 1905	Charge to Metropolitan Credit Co for £115.
27 Nov 1905	Charge to Telegraph Co for £600, out of which the life office was repaid. Telegraph Co accordingly then held the policy. It paid premiums of £115.
30 April 1906	Charge to Kapp for £73.
9 May 1906	Charge to Cohen.
25 May 1906	Charge to Ramsay

1 (1878) 9 Ch D 137.
2 [1903] 1 KB 151. This case followed *Foster v Blackstone* (1833) 1 My & K 297, 2 LJ Ch 84.
3 [1910] 2 Ch 291.

No notice had at this stage been given by any encumbrancer.

Notices were then given in the following order:

(1) Metropolitan Credit Co.

(2) Ramsay.

(3) Kapp (both charges).

(4) Cohen.

(5) Telegraph Co.

The life office is deemed to have notice of its own charge.

The court determined the priorities as follows and for the reasons shown:

(1) Telegraph Co for £250 (ie transfer of the life office charge) and the premiums paid to preserve the security.

(2) Metropolitan Credit Co, being first to give notice, but having constructive notice of the life office charge by reason of the fact that it had been deposited with the life office. They had no notice of Kapp's interest and therefore took priority over it.

(3) Kapp, as to his original charge, which was subject to the life office charge. He had no constructive notice at that time affecting his position, for had he enquired for the policy he would have found it to be with the life office, as he would have expected his interest being subject to the life office charge. (Ramsay, although second to give notice, was postponed because if when making his advance he had enquired for the policy he would have found that Telegraph Co had it.) He would, however, have lost priority had they not all been fixed with constructive knowledge.

(4) Telegraph Co for remainder of its charge (Kapp's second charge and Cohen are postponed for the same reason as Ramsay's ie constructive notice of potential prior interests).

(5) Ramsay

(6) Kapp's second charge.

(7) Cohen.

With regard to (5) to (6) in order of notice as all had constructive notice of potential prior interests.

An important practical point to emerge from the above is that an assignee should therefore always insist on the production of the policy or a satisfactory explanation for its non-production. Otherwise he will be unable to gain priority over any prior equity of which he had no actual notice because he will be fixed with constructive notice of previous assignments.

I *Position of voluntary assignees and trustees in bankruptcy*

10.39 While a person who takes an equitable interest bona fide and for valuable consideration can by service of notice obtain priority over an earlier equitable interest of which he had no notice, a voluntary assignee cannot obtain priority in that way[1]. However, giving notice still has the advantage for the voluntary assignee that this will prevent subsequent assignments for value gaining priority by giving notice.

A trustee in bankruptcy as statutory assignee takes the assets of the bankrupt subject to all equities affecting the property in the hands of the debtor, and as he is not an assignee for value he cannot, therefore, by giving notice obtain priority over an earlier equitable interest of which no notice has been given[2] (except that if any assignment is for less than full consideration it may be impeached in certain circumstances by the trustee in bankruptcy as a transaction at an undervalue or preference)[3].

He should nevertheless give notice of his appointment to the life office so that the possibility of subsequent assignees (who took their assignment without notice of the bankruptcy) from gaining priority over him by giving prior notice is eliminated. From a purely practical point of view as well it prevents the life office from innocently paying out the policy moneys to the bankrupt with the resulting difficulties which could arise (see *Rooney v Cardona*[4], see further Chapter 12).

C Summary

10.40 In summary, therefore:

(1) The priority of equitable and legal assignments are determined primarily in accordance with the date on which notice is served on the life office.

(2) However, the question of knowledge or constructive knowledge at the time of giving notice can affect priority.

(3) Failure to produce the policy documents without a valid explanation will normally be constructive knowledge of prior interests except (eg in cases such as Kapp's in *Re Weniger's Policy*[5] above), where an interest is expressed to be subject to a prior assignment, in which case the second assignee would not expect the assignor to have the policy. If there were two such subsequent interests with notice of the earlier interest but not of each other then priority will be in order of service of notice (eg Metropolitan Credit in the example above).

1 *Justice v Wynne* (1860) 12 Ir Ch R 289.
2 *Re Wallis, ex p Jenks* [1902] 1 KB 719 and *Re Russell's Policy Trusts* (1872) LR 15 Eq 26.
3 See Chapter 9.
4 [1999] 1 WLR 1388, [1999] 2 FLR 1148, [1999] Fam Law 542, [1999] All ER (D) 124.
5 [1910] 2 Ch 291.

SECTION 7 STAMP DUTY

10.41 From 1 May 1987, assignments of policies, where there was no consideration, were exempt from stamp duty provided they contained the relevant certificate. As a result of section 125 of the Finance Act 2003, stamp duty was abolished on all instruments (except those relating to stock or marketable securities) so that the requirement for a stamp duty certificate has similarly disappeared (although certificates are occasionally still seen on assignment documents).

SECTION 8 MORTGAGES

A Nature of mortgage

1 General principles

10.42 Life assurance policies are sometimes used as security for loans either on their own or as collateral security in house purchase. This practice used to be much more common than it is now, essentially because lenders increasingly view their security in the property as sufficient in itself. Life offices may themselves grant loans on the security of policies issued by them although again this is less prevalent than it used to be, partly as a result of the cost and complexity of complying with the Consumer Credit Act.

A mortgage is a transfer of property (real or personal) from one person (*the mortgagor*) to another (*the mortgagee*), as security for a debt. In section 205(1)(xvi) of the Law of Property Act 1925 its meaning is stated to include 'any charge or lien on any property for securing money or money's worth'.

Where an individual has borrowed money, to purchase his home, the lender may require the borrower to effect a policy (with the sum assured equal to the value of the outstanding loan) to ensure that on the death of the borrower, there is sufficient money to cover the outstanding loan. Historically, such a policy was generally an endowment policy which also acted as an investment vehicle so that the borrower may be able to repay the sum borrowed before his death from the policy proceeds on maturity, which generally coincided with the end of the mortgage term. The use of endowment policies has declined, not helped by mis-selling issues, and it is more common for a term or temporary assurance policy to be effected with a view to repaying the mortgage if death occurs before the end of the mortgage term. The lender may require the borrower to mortgage the policy as security to the lender but again this has become much less common.

A lender is technically able to effect a policy on the life of the borrower to protect its position in the event of the borrower's death before the mortgage has been repaid. It can do this as it has an insurable interest in the life of the borrower to the extent that it would incur a pecuniary loss if the borrower died before repaying the debt. This is not a common occurrence.

More generally, an existing policyholder may wish to raise money and he may use a life assurance policy on his own life as security for a loan.

(a) Background to mortgages

10.43 Historically, a mortgage (usually of land) took the form of a conveyance by the mortgagor to the mortgagee on condition that the mortgagee reconveyed it to the mortgagor if the loan was repaid on a date mentioned in the conveyance (usually fixed at six months from the date of the loan). Such a conveyance or transfer was strictly construed, so that if the mortgagor failed to repay the loan on the fixed date, there was no obligation on the mortgagee to reconvey the land. The mortgagee could retain the land for his own benefit.

(b) Equity of redemption

10.44 Eventually, equity intervened and gave relief to the mortgagor under the maxim 'once a mortgage always a mortgage'. As a result, where a mortgagor intended a conveyance to be by way of security, he can now compel the mortgagee to reconvey the property on repayment of the loan, not only on the day fixed for its repayment (customarily six months) but also any time thereafter. This right is called the equity of redemption. The equity of redemption is what essentially distinguishes a mortgage from an absolute assignment.

The mortgagor will always have this right, unless he defaults on his interest payments and the mortgagee sells the mortgaged property or obtains a court order of foreclosure which vests the property in the mortgagee free from the mortgage.

(c) Clog on the equity of redemption

10.45 An agreement between the mortgagor and mortgagee which prejudicially affects or acts as a fetter on the equity of redemption (ie the mortgagor's right to redeem the mortgage) is known as a 'clog on the equity' and is unenforceable by the mortgagee.

(d) Legal mortgages

10.46 A legal mortgage transfers the legal interest in the mortgaged property. For life policies it must be by written assignment and comply with the Policies of Assurance Act 1867 or section 136 of the Law of Property Act 1925. A mortgage deed which transfers the property, with a proviso for redemption and reconveyance, satisfies the requirements of this section.

(e) Equitable mortgage

10.47 An equitable mortgage transfers the equitable but not the legal interest in the property. This can be by way of an oral agreement between the parties, where the intention to create a mortgage is clear, or by a deposit of the policy document with a memorandum of deposit, a method sometimes used by life offices to secure policy loans on policies issued by them. Where deposit of the policy occurs without any accompanying memorandum this may still constitute an equitable mortgage provided this is the intention of the parties[1]. Possession of the policy in itself is not enough to establish the existence of a mortgage as the policy may have been deposited for other reasons. However, on the face of it if the deposit is made as security for a debt it will be presumed (unless there is a contrary intention) that he intended to mortgage the policy[2].

(f) Differences between legal and equitable mortgages

10.48 Where the mortgagor defaults, a mortgagee who has only an equitable mortgage cannot, without further action, exercise the power of sale under the Law of Property Act 1925[3] because he has not acquired the legal title. He will have to apply to the court for an order to enable him to sell.

With an equitable mortgage, the mortgagor has a right to the return of any title deeds in the possession of the mortgagee on repayment of the loan. There need be no reassignment of the mortgaged property as, under an equitable mortgage, there has been no assignment of the legal interest. For legal mortgages, there will need to be a formal reassignment of the mortgaged property.

(g) Liens

10.49 Although there is no transfer of property liens provide a third party with an interest in the property in question. A precise definition is elusive although many definitions assume actual possession of the property. These would be 'possessory' liens but it is also possible to have an equitable lien where there is no actual possession. A voluntary payment of premiums under a policy does not, as a general rule, give any lien or interest in the policy to the payer. The circumstances under which an equitable charge or lien can be asserted on a policy by reason of payment of a premium were discussed in *Re Leslie, Leslie v French*[4] where a husband voluntarily paid premiums on a policy on the life of his wife and it was held that he had no lien.

A lien may be acquired if a person pays a premium or premiums in the following circumstances (the first four of which were set out by Fry LJ in *Re Leslie, Leslie v French)*:

(1) By contract with the beneficial owner of the policy.

(2) By reason of the right of trustees to an indemnity out of the trust property for money expended by them to preserve it. For example, where the trustee has paid premiums out of his own funds in order to maintain the policy. Where, however, the relationship of parent and child or husband and wife exists as between the trustee and beneficiary, the payment of premiums is presumed to be for the benefit of the beneficiary and so cannot be recovered (unless the presumption is rebutted). In addition, in many cases the pro-

1 *Shaw v Foster* (1872) LR5 HL 321, 340.
2 *Norris v Wilkinson* (1806) 12 Ves 192.
3 Law of Property Act 1925, s 101(1)(i).
4 (1883) 23 Ch D 552.

poser and the settlor will be the same person and he will also be a trustee so the normal right of indemnity would be negated by the presumption that, as settlor, he intended to benefit the beneficiaries (but see *Clack v Holland*[1]).

(3) By subrogation to the right of trustees where some person, at their request, advances money to preserve the trust property.

(4) By reason of the right of mortgagees to add to their security with money paid by them to preserve the mortgaged property. Therefore, where the lender pays the premiums to prevent the policy from lapsing or being made paid up.

(5) Where a married woman has paid premiums on a policy taken out at her husband's request in their joint names. (In a case where the trustee in bankruptcy had knowledge that the premiums were being paid by the wife the court ordered that the trustee repay her out of the policy moneys (*Re Tyler*[2])).

(6) Where the person paying the premiums did so under the mistaken belief that the policy benefits belonged to him, and the true owner allows this to be done[3].

(7) Where an assignee has paid premiums although a prior interest in the policy had been created.

10.50 In *Foskett v McKeown*[4] the House of Lords disagreed with the Court of Appeal that the purchasers were entitled to a lien on the proceeds of a life policy to secure repayment of premiums paid with their money. Lord Millett (House of Lords) explained that an equitable lien is a '...proprietary interest by way of security. It is enforceable against the trust property and its traceable proceeds. The finding of the majority that the purchasers had no proprietary interest in the policy or its proceeds should have been fatal to their claim to a lien'. The Court of Appeal reasoning was that the purchasers were entitled (by subrogation to Mr Murphy's lien) to be repaid the premiums. They believed he was 'entitled to the Trustee's ordinary lien to indemnify him for expenditure laid out in the preservation of the trust property'. This was in accordance with cases (2) and (3) in *Re Leslie, Leslie v French.* This was rejected by Lord Millett as although he was a trustee of the policy he did not pay premiums in this capacity. He paid them as a settlor. In any event, Lord Millett went on to state that the main reason for rejecting the Court of Appeal's argument was that '...it makes the purchaser's rights depend on the circumstance that Mr Murphy happened to be one of the trustees of his children's settlement'. Lord Millett concluded this part of his judgment by stating 'The purchaser's rights cannot turn on such chances as this'.

This raised the question how the purchaser's rights were to be protected. In summary, Mr Murphy effected a policy on his own life and declared a trust of it

1 (1854) 19 Beav 262.
2 [1907] KB 865.
3 *Re Foster, Hudson v Foster (No 2)* [1938] 3 All ER 610.
4 (2000) WLR 1299; (2000) 3 All ER 97; ILR 3/7/2000.

for his children. He paid the first two premiums out of his own funds but subsequent premiums were paid from funds held under express trust for purchasers of plots of land to be developed in Portugal. These funds had become mixed up with Mr Murphy's own funds via various bank accounts. Mr Murphy committed suicide and the sum assured of £1 million was paid out. The purchasers claimed at least a 40% share of the proceeds, a share proportionate to their contribution to the premium paid. The Court of Appeal held that the purchasers were only entitled to a lien equal to the premiums they had paid. The House of Lords reversed this (albeit only by a majority of 3-2). Where a trustee wrongfully used trust money to provide part of the cost of acquiring an asset, the beneficiary was able to claim a proportionate share of the asset. In every case, the value inherent in the trust property had become located within the value inherent in the new asset. A conclusion that the beneficiary could only assert a lien over the new asset would result in any appreciation in value going to the trustee. The process of tracing involved the purchasers tracing the premiums through mixed substitutions not into the insurance money directly but firstly into the policy. That policy represented the traceable proceeds of the premiums and so the purchasers were entitled to a proportionate share of the policy and this was the case whether it was immediately before or after death. The fact that the policy had increased in value was not relevant. Lord Millett described this case as '...a textbook example of tracing through mixed substitutions'.

2 *Form of mortgage of life policies*

(a) Creation of a mortgage of a life policy

10.51 Mortgage deeds of life policies contain all the usual provisions of a mortgage deed and also provisions which relate specifically to life policies.

(I) USUAL PROVISIONS

10.52 The usual provisions include date; parties; details of the property mortgaged; amount borrowed; various covenants (eg to repay the loan on a fixed date, and to pay interest) and the required notice periods.

(II) SPECIFIC PROVISIONS TO BE INCLUDED IN MORTGAGES OF LIFE POLICIES

10.53 Specific provisions which are likely to be included:

(1) A covenant by the mortgagor to pay the premiums as they fall due and any other moneys required to keep the policy in force and that he will restore the policy if it is made paid up or lapses.

(2) A covenant by the mortgagor that the policy is valid (and that it will not become void) and that if it does become void he will effect a new policy for an equivalent amount and assign it to the mortgagee and will effect and assign a further policy in the same way if any such substituted policy becomes void.

(3) A power to the mortgagee to pay any premium in arrears and add the amount to the principal (ie the outstanding loan).

(4) A power in the case of default for the mortgagee to pay premiums and for any such payments to be a charge on the policy (although there will be a right to do this even without express provision)[1].

(5) A power to the mortgagee to exercise his power of sale by surrender to the life office[2].

(6) A power to the mortgagee, if his power of sale has arisen, to convert the policy to a fully paid-up policy.

(b) Use of policies in connection with loans and mortgages

(I) LIFE OFFICE LOAN

10.54 Life offices may make loans to policyholders, on the security of their policies. A policyholder may wish to raise money for general purposes or he may wish to finance his premium payments. If a policyholder would otherwise have no option but to let his policy lapse it may be better for the life office to grant a loan within the policy's surrender value, rather than for the policyholder to completely surrender his policy. In this way, the life office will continue to receive the premiums and would also receive interest payments on the loan. The advantages for the policyholder are: he is able to maintain his life cover; for with-profits policies, he does not lose any terminal bonus on maturity of the policy (generally the right to a terminal bonus is forfeited on complete surrender of a policy before maturity); and, assuming the surrender value increases over time, the policy may be used as security for future loans[3].

Life offices will not normally loan more than a certain percentage (eg 90%) of the surrender value of a policy. They may limit themselves to a lower amount on unit-linked policies as opposed to with-profits policies, due to the volatility of the price of units.

Such loans are increasing less common as life offices tend to view this as an increasingly peripheral activity with disproportionate costs and resource requirements. The complexity of the Consumer Credit Act can require significant resources in order to ensure ongoing compliance.

(II) POLICIES USED IN CONNECTION WITH MORTGAGES OF REAL PROPERTY

10.55 As mentioned at **10.43**, policies are sometimes used in connection with mortgages of real property (eg home purchase), as collateral security for the loan used to purchase the property. Where the lender requires a policy to be taken out, it may also require it to be mortgaged to it (either legally or equitably by the

1 *Gill v Downing* (1874) LR 17 Eq 316.

2 See **10.65–10.66**.

3 However, a loan on a life policy may cause a chargeable event in certain circumstances giving rise to a liability to higher rate tax. See Chapter 12.

deposit of the policy document). However, this is an increasingly rare requirement.

The type of policy used will depend upon the type of mortgage which has been chosen:

(1) *Repayment mortgage.* The capital element of the loan is repaid in regular instalments, together with the interest payable. Over time the capital sum reduces and so if the mortgagor is making a fixed payment then more of that sum goes to pay off capital as less is required to pay interest. A lender may require that a policy be taken out to ensure that if the borrower dies before the loan is repaid, the balance outstanding on the loan can be repaid with the policy proceeds. It is generally a wise precaution for the borrower to effect such a policy irrespective of the borrower's requirements. The sum assured under such a policy should, at the outset, equal the value of the outstanding loan. The policy may be a whole life, a level term or a decreasing term and may or may not be mortgaged to the lender.

(2) *Endowment mortgage.* During the term of the mortgage, the borrower repays the lender only the interest accruing on the outstanding capital sum, whilst also paying premiums towards an endowment policy with the same term as the mortgage so that the proceeds from the endowment policy will be used to repay (or partially repay if investment returns have not been as favourable as hoped) the principal on maturity or on death before then (on death the policy would pay out the full sum assured irrespective of investment performance).

(3) *Pension mortgage.* As with an endowment mortgage during the mortgage term, the borrower repays only the interest accruing on the outstanding capital sum. The borrower may use any cash lump sum he is entitled to on retirement to repay the principal. However, the lender would not have any right against the pension provider to the cash lump sum.

(c) Assignments absolute in form

10.56 Where a policy is effected by the debtor on his own life and assigned to a creditor in order to give security to that creditor, the question may arise whether the creditor is entitled to the policy absolutely or only as mortgagee. The maxim 'once a mortgage always a mortgage' applies[1].

If a person is entitled only as mortgagee he must account to the debtor for the balance of the policy moneys after satisfaction of his debt. The court will look at the substance of the transaction and not merely the form[2]. An apparent absolute assignment may, in fact, be a mortgage. As a general rule the policy belongs to whichever of the mortgagee or debtor is (as between themselves) liable to pay for it. If the debtor has agreed to pay the premiums, or that they should be debited to

1 *Salt v The Marquess of Northampton* [1892] AC 1.
2 *Re Watson* (1890) 25 QBD 27.

his account, he is entitled to an equity of redemption even though the policy is in the name of the creditor or has been assigned to him[1]. Therefore, the creditor is deemed to be a mortgagee and is only entitled to have the debt repaid. On repayment of the debt, the debtor is entitled to have the policy reassigned to him, or, if he is dead, his personal representatives are entitled to the balance of the policy moneys.

But if (unusually) the creditor has effected and paid for the policy, the debtor has no right to any part of the policy money purely on the basis that he has repaid the debt.

3 Capacity

(a) Capacity to borrow

(I) MINORS

10.57 The general rule is that contracts to create a mortgage or charge, for the repayment of money lent or a charge over his equitable interest[2] are voidable at the minor's option until a reasonable time after reaching the age of majority, although they are binding on the lender. In practice, life offices would rarely lend to minors.

(II) COMPANIES

10.58 The capacity of a company or other corporation to borrow depends primarily on its constitution although any company engaged in commerce has for a long time had an implied power to borrow for the purposes of its business. In effect this has been extended even further by the Companies Act 2006 under which all companies have unlimited objects unless they choose to restrict them.

A life office can, in any event, rely on section 40 of the Companies Act 2006 which means that if it has no notice of any restriction on the company's power to borrow and is acting 'in good faith', any loan agreement with the company will be binding.

Every limited company must keep a register of charges affecting the company's property 100.

(III) TRUSTEES

10.59 Where trustees hold a policy on trust, they can borrow on the security of the policy if there is express provision for that purpose in the trust instrument, or if they need money to pay premiums to preserve the policy, or under section 16

1 *Courtenay v Wright* (1869) Giff 337, 351.

2 Goods and services which are necessary to the minor such as food, drink, clothing, lodging, medicine and medical and legal services.

of the Trustee Act 1925 which gives the trustees statutory power to do so[1], or if all the beneficiaries, being legally capable and between them entitled to the whole beneficial interest, authorise them to do so.

(b) Capacity to release security

10.60 Where a mortgagee considers that he holds ample security, he may be prepared to release a part of it. If, for example, he holds a life policy, he may allow the mortgagor to surrender the reversionary bonus for his own benefit.

B Rights and remedies of the mortgagor

1 Rights of the mortgagor

10.61 The mortgagor retains an interest in the mortgaged property in the form of the equity of redemption.

Therefore, he can:

(1) give the mortgagee a further charge on the property;

(2) mortgage the property (subject to the first mortgage and any further charges) to a second, third or subsequent mortgagee (subject to prior mortgages).

If the mortgagor later wishes to give a first mortgage to a second mortgagee, he may be able to arrange with the first mortgagee that the second mortgagee shall have priority. In such a case the first mortgagee must either be a party to the second mortgage in order to postpone his interest or must execute a separate document to that effect.

If, for example, a policyholder has mortgaged his policy to X and later wishes to borrow on it from the life office, he will probably find the life office unwilling to lend unless X is prepared to postpone his mortgage and rank his security after that of the life office.

2 Remedies of the mortgagor

(a) Legal mortgage

10.62 The mortgagor has the following remedies:

(1) The right *at law* to have the property reassigned if, *on* the day fixed in the mortgage, he pays the principal, interest and costs.

1 The trustees will have the power to mortgage a life policy under s 16 if they are authorised by the instrument, if any, creating the trust or by law to pay or apply capital money subject to the trust for any purpose or in any manner. However, this section does not apply to trustees of property held for charitable purposes, or to trustees of a settlement for the purposes of the Settled Land Act 1925, not being also the statutory owners.

(2) The right *in equity* to have the property reassigned if, *after* the day fixed in the mortgage, he pays the principal, interest and costs. He must, however, normally give notice of his intention to repay or pay interest in lieu of notice[1]. (A common period was six months but modern mortgage deeds tend to provide for much shorter notice periods.)

(3) The right on repayment to require the mortgagee to transfer the mortgage to a third party as the mortgagor may direct. Such a right is useful if the mortgagee calls in the loan and the mortgagor has to arrange another loan to repay it.

(4) The right at his own expense to inspect and make copies of or extracts from the documents of title to the mortgaged property in the custody or power of the mortgagee. This right cannot be excluded by contract[2].

(b) Equitable mortgage

10.63 The mortgagor of an equitable mortgage has the right to the return of the documents of title of the mortgaged property on payment of principal, interest and costs[3].

C Remedies of the mortgagee

1 General

10.64 At any time after the date for repayment mentioned in the mortgage has passed, the mortgagee can give the mortgagor notice requiring him to repay the mortgage money. If the mortgagor fails to repay, the mortgagee has various remedies which are summarised below:

(1) The right to sue the mortgagor on his personal covenant to repay the loan. This right is very rarely exercised as at this stage, the mortgagor is unlikely to have sufficient funds to perform the covenant.

(2) The right to sell the mortgaged property. The mortgage may contain an express power of sale but otherwise the mortgagee can rely on the statutory power.

(3) The right to appoint a receiver. The receiver is deemed to be the agent of the mortgagor under the statutory power and collects the income from the property. He pays out of it the outgoings, interest, premiums and other disbursements. The appointment of a receiver may be a convenient remedy for a mortgagee on the security of real property or of a life interest, but is not used in connection with life policies.

1 See *Smith v Smith* [1891] 3 Ch 550.
2 Law of Property Act 1925, s 96(1).
3 The mortgagor should give reasonable notice.

(4) The right to transfer the mortgage to another person.

(5) The right to tack further advances on to the original mortgage to rank in priority to subsequent loans.

(6) The right to marshall against another mortgagee's security subject to the security of that other mortgagee.

(7) The right to apply to the court for an order of foreclosure. On an order of foreclosure absolute, the mortgaged property is vested in the mortgagee absolutely, free from the mortgage, and the right of the mortgagor to redeem is gone. This is a drastic measure and it is more usual for a sale to be ordered.

(8) The right to consolidate two or more mortgages from the same mortgagor if that power is expressly reserved in the mortgage deed or one of them. On consolidation, the mortgagee can refuse repayment under any of the consolidated mortgages unless he is repaid under all. The power is of considerable value where one of the mortgages is well secured and another only partially secured.

If the mortgagor does not pay the premiums on a policy which he has mortgaged there is authority that the mortgagee has an implied power to pay the premiums and add the amount which it has paid out (with interest) to the security[1]. There may, of course, be an express power to this effect[2].

A mortgagee is also entitled to all reasonable costs charges and expenses incurred by him in relation to the mortgage, and in particular his legal costs

(a) Relevance of the statutory power of sale for life policies

(I) MORTGAGES MADE BY DEED

10.65 Where a policy is mortgaged by deed, its surrender to the life office is, in effect, equivalent to the exercise of the power of sale and can, it is generally considered, be made under the statutory power of sale but the position is not entirely clear as there is no specific reference to surrender as an alternative to sale and so to remove any doubt a specific power to this effect should be inserted in the deed .

In addition, the surrender of a policy may not be a permissible exercise of the statutory power of sale if the surrender value is not equal to the sort of price the mortgagor could reasonably expect to obtain on the market. This is particularly pertinent in the case of endowment policies. The market in 'second-hand' or 'traded' policies has grown considerably. It is quite likely, therefore, that the open market value of endowment policies will be more than the surrender value. It is questionable, therefore, whether the mortgagee should exercise his power of sale by surrendering the policy or whether he should, instead, sell the policy on the open market. The mortgagor will clearly want the mortgagee to get the best

1 *Hodgson v Hodgson* (1837) 2 Keen 704.

2 *Browne v Price* (1858) 4 CB (NS) 598.

price for the policy as he will benefit from any balance of the sale or surrender proceeds after the loan has been repaid. However, the mortgagee is under no duty to obtain the best possible price for the mortgagor although the mortgagor owes a duty in equity to take reasonable care to secure a proper price[1].

(II) MORTGAGES NOT MADE BY DEED

10.66 In such cases the statutory power does not apply, even if the document contains an assignment of the policy. However, there may be an express power of sale in the mortgage instrument or even an implied power of sale.

A life office will not be concerned to see whether the power of sale is properly exercised where:

(1) the mortgage is by deed and the deed gives power to the mortgagee to surrender and the office accepts a surrender from a mortgagee in exercise of the power; or

(2) the office acts on a title derived by a purchaser from a mortgagee exercising the power.

The life office must not, however, accept a title from a purchaser where it is clear that the power of sale has been improperly exercised[2].

If the mortgagor and the mortgagee join in surrendering the policy the life office is not, of course, concerned whether the power of sale has arisen or not.

(b) Conditions affecting exercise of the mortgagee's rights

(I) OVERRIDING INTERESTS IN THE MATRIMONIAL HOME

10.67 A mortgagee will not be able to exercise his power of sale if a third party has a beneficial interest in the property and the mortgagee has made no enquiry as to that third party's rights, if any[3].

The decision in *Williams & Glyn's Bank Ltd v Boland*[4] caused great concern to conveyancers and lenders. The difficulty the case creates is that a mortgagee or purchaser, despite having searched the Land Register, cannot be certain whether or not a third party has an equitable right to occupation of the property which binds the mortgagee or purchaser. And there is no procedure which can provide a complete safeguard.

The perceived problems do not appear to be as great as initially feared (including by the Law Commission). Mortgagees now normally adhere to a code of practice which ensures that the necessary enquiries are made. These enquiries enable them to ascertain whether persons other than the mortgage applicant are

1 *Downsview Nominees Ltd v First City Corporation Ltd* [1993] AC 295, [1993] 3 All ER 626, PC.
2 *Selwyn v Garfit* (1888) 38 Ch D 273.
3 *Williams and Glyn's Bank Ltd v Boland* [1981] AC 487.
4 [1981] AC 487, [1980] 2 All ER 408, [1980] 3 WLR 138.

or will be occupying the property and if there are or will be other occupants, whether any of them claim an overriding interest.

If an overriding interest is claimed, the mortgagee will have to ensure that the persons with such an interest relinquish their rights before it advances the moneys the mortgagor wishes to borrow. Although inquiry need not be made of the children of the vendor as their occupation is only through their parents[1]. Subsequent cases such as *Bristol & West BS v Henning*[2] which concerned a cohabitee may have limited the effect of the *Boland* case (albeit that *Boland* was not cited in this case). The case *of Link Lending Ltd v Hussein*[3] suggested a wide definition of 'occupation' and *HSBC Bank plc v Dyche*[4] provided a timely reminder to lenders to make adequate enquiries regarding other occupiers of the property – in this case the defendants' parents.

(c) Undue influence

10.68

> *Barclays Bank plc v O'Brien*[5]
>
> The defendant O'Brien was a shareholder in a company which had a substantial unsecured overdraft. He arranged with the company's bank an overdraft facility for the company on the security of his guarantee of the company's indebtedness. O'Brien's liability was secured by a second charge over the matrimonial home he jointly owned with his wife. The wife signed the legal charge without reading it. The company's indebtedness increased beyond the agreed limit and the bank brought possession proceedings to enforce payment under the guarantee. In her defence, the wife contended that she had signed the charge under undue pressure from her husband who had also misrepresented to her the effect of the legal charge.
>
> It was held in the House of Lords, that because the bank knew that the transaction was not to Mrs O'Brien's advantage and because there is a substantial risk in transactions of this kind that there has been undue influence the bank should have been put on inquiry as to the circumstances in which Mrs O'Brien had agreed to act as surety. It should, therefore, have taken reasonable steps to ensure her agreement was properly obtained. The bank could have asked her to attend a private meeting to warn her of the amount of the potential liability under the charge and the risks involved and also advised her to take independent legal advice. Having failed to do this, it was fixed with constructive notice of the undue influence and wrongful misrepresentation made by the husband. On this basis, it was held that the legal charge should be set aside.

Subsequent cases have built upon the principles established in *Barclays Bank plc v O'Brien*. In *RBS v Ettridge (No 2)*[6], for example, the mortgagee would be put

1 *Hypo-Mortgage Services Ltd v Robinson* [1997] 2 FLR 71.
2 [1985] 2 All ER 606.
3 [2010] EWCA Civ 424.
4 [2009] EWHC 2954 (Ch).
5 [1993] 4 All ER 983.
6 [1998] 4 All ER 705. See also *First National Bank plc v Achampong* [2003] EWCA Civ 487, [2004] 1 FCR 18.

on enquiry if the relationship between the surety and the debtor is known to the mortgagee and raises a legal presumption of undue influence. In *Bank of Scotland v Bennett*[1] it was emphasised that the risk must be sufficiently real and substantial in order to conclude that the mortgagee ought reasonably to have made further enquiries to satisfy himself that the surety's consent was not obtained improperly. The mortgagee is not put on enquiry simply because the surety has no control or involvement in the business whose liabilities are secured or because the loan exceeds the value of the mortgaged property[2]. A mortgagee is not required to inquire as to the relationship between debtor and surety or as to the personal motives of the surety for wanting to help the debtor[3]. Where the transaction was so improvident that it is inexplicable on any other basis the mortgagee was put on inquiry[4]. Although not concerned with undue influence the case of *Investec Bank (UK) Ltd v Zulman*[5] emphasised the importance of seeking independent legal advice and recommending this course of action but failing to follow it through.

To avoid constructive notice of the surety's rights the mortgagee should take reasonable steps to allay his suspicions. Therefore, for example, the mortgagee should insist that the surety attend a private meeting on their own with the mortgagee's representative at which she is told of the extent of her liability, alerted to the risk and advised to take independent legal advice.

(d) Jointly mortgaged policies

10.69 Many couples, whether married or not, effect policies where the death benefit is payable on the failure of their joint existence, in order to cover the amount borrowed under a mortgage. The policy may be assigned to the mortgagee (although as indicated increasingly lenders do not take a mortgage of the policy). Where the policy is mortgaged the normal intention is that the maturity value or the death benefits are used to repay the mortgage and the mortgage is thereby discharged. If the mortgage is satisfied out of other funds then on the first death the surviving assured will be generally entitled to the policy proceeds and not the estate of the deceased assured[6]. Much can depend on the proven intention of the parties.

D Discharge of mortgage

1 Repayment and reassignment

10.70 The mortgagor or any person entitled to any interest in the equity of redemption, may redeem the mortgage. As mentioned above the money secured

1 [1999] 1 FCR 641.
2 *Britannia Building Society v Pugh* [1997] 2 FLR 7, 29 HLR 423, CA.
3 *Banco Exterior Internacional SA v Thomas* [1997] 1 All ER 46.
4 *Credit Lyonnais Bank Nederland NV v Burch* [1997] 1 All ER 144.
5 *Smith v Clerical Medical and General Life Assurance Society* [1993] 1 FLR 47. See also *Ross v Perrin-Hughes* [2004] EWHC 2559 (Ch), [2004] All ER (D) 159 (Nov).
6 *Bovill v Endle* [1896] 1 Ch 648.

is usually made payable on a fixed day, usually six months from the date of the mortgage. The mortgagor cannot redeem before then unless the mortgagee has taken steps to procure repayment by taking possession of the property or otherwise (for example, by surrendering a mortgaged policy[1]); but he has a legal right to redeem on the fixed day. Thereafter he has a right in equity to redeem on giving the prescribed notice or on paying interest for that period instead. Clearly, the specific terms of the mortgage deed must be consulted and currently the trend is towards shorter, or even non-existent, notice periods.

On repayment, the mortgagor must at his own expense take whatever steps are necessary to restore his title to the property free from the mortgage. He may perhaps ask for a re-assignment of the policy by the mortgagee. A receipt is, however, usually sufficient to show that all money secured by the mortgage has been repaid and that the mortgagee has no further interest in the property (see **10.71** below).

Many life office standard mortgage deeds have pre-printed reassignments contained within or on the reverse of them. These simply require dating and signing by the mortgagee at the appropriate time.

(a) Statutory receipt

10.71 Section 115(1) of the Law of Property Act 1925 provides that, on repayment, a receipt endorsed on (or written at the foot of, or annexed to) the mortgage operates to discharge the mortgage and reconvey the mortgaged property to the person entitled to the equity of redemption. A form of the statutory receipt is given in Schedule 3 to the Law of Property Act 1925.

(b) Delivery of documents of title

10.72 On repayment, the mortgagee should return the policy document to the mortgagor. The mortgagee is not liable if he delivers the document to a person not having the best right to them unless he has notice of such a right[2].

2 *Claims under mortgaged policies*

10.73 When a claim is made by a mortgagee, the life office may, subject to satisfactory proof of title, pay the policy proceeds to the mortgagee relying on section 107(1) of the Law of Property Act 1925:

> 'The receipt in writing of a mortgagee shall be a sufficient discharge for any money arising under the power of sale conferred by this Act, or for any money or securities comprised in his mortgage, or arising thereunder; and a person paying or transferring the same to the mortgagee shall not be concerned to inquire whether any money remains due under the mortgage.'

1 [2010] EWCA Civ 536

2 Law of Property Act 1925, s 96(2).

In view of this section, it is considered that a mortgagee can give a good discharge for the policy moneys payable on the life assured's death, or on his survival until the maturity of an endowment assurance, whether his mortgage is by deed or not, and whether or not it contains an assignment.

The life office is not concerned with the state of account between the mortgagor and the mortgagee or with equitable interests in a legal mortgage where it is dealing in good faith (see section 113 of the Law of Property Act 1925). However, it can, if desired, examine the accounts and pay to the mortgagee only the amount due to him, and the balance of the policy moneys to the person with the equity of redemption.

If a life office has notice that no money is owing under a mortgage, it cannot properly pay to the mortgagee without the concurrence of the mortgagor or persons deriving title under him. In such a case the mortgagee has no right in equity to receive the policy money.

In the same way, where a mortgagee makes a claim and the life office has notice of another mortgagee who has priority over the mortgagee making the claim, the life office should notify the mortgagee with priority and only pay out if the latter has given its consent.

(a) Simple receipt

10.74 Discharge of a mortgage is usually evidenced by a statutory receipt (which also has the advantage of operating as a reconveyance), but a simple receipt would suffice and the receipted mortgage might be returned to the mortgagor to evidence his title to the policy[1].

In practice, most life offices, when investigating title to a policy for the purpose of payment of a claim or on surrender, will accept a simple receipt as sufficient evidence of the discharge of a mortgage. A formal reassignment or a statutory receipt may be required, however, if the office is proposing to grant a loan on the security of the policy or to carry out any other transaction which does not involve the encashment of the policy.

(b) Equitable interests

10.75 When investigating title to a mortgaged policy, the life office need not be concerned with any trust affecting the mortgage money.

Section 113 of the Law of Property Act 1925 provides:

> '(1) A person dealing in good faith with a mortgagee, or with the mortgagor if the mortgage has been discharged, released or postponed as to the whole or any part of the mortgage property, shall not be concerned with any trust at any time affecting the mortgage money or the income thereof whether or not he has notice of the trust, and may assume unless the contrary is expressly stated in the instruments relating to the mortgage:
>
> (a) that the mortgagees (if more than one) are or were entitled to the mortgage money on a joint account; and

1 *Edwards v Marshall-Lee* (1975) 119 Sol Jo 506.

(b) that the mortgagee has or had power to give valid receipts for the purchase money or mortgage money and the income thereof (including any arrears of interest) and to release or postpone the priority of the mortgage debt or any part thereof or to deal with the same or the mortgaged property or any part thereof;

without investigating the equitable title to the mortgage debt or the appointment or discharge of trustees in reference thereto.'

The life office can get a good discharge from the trustees to whom the property was mortgaged who have not died unless it has been notified of the appointment of additional trustees or the discharge of existing trustees, in which case the life office will only get a good discharge from the current trustees.

Where property has been mortgaged to more than one person jointly or to secure a sum advanced from money belonging to them on a joint account, then, unless a contrary intention is expressed, a good discharge may be obtained from the survivor or survivors alone in the event of one or more having died (or from the personal representatives of the last survivor)[1].

In view of the wide meaning given to 'mortgage' in section 205(xvi) of the Law of Property Act 1925, section 113 enables an equitable mortgagee by deposit to give a valid receipt.

1 Law of Property Act 1925, s 111.

CHAPTER 11

Trusts and life assurance[1]

SUMMARY

SECTION 1 INTRODUCTION

11.1 The common practice of declaring trusts of life assurance policies, and of including policies as part, or all, of the property in a trust means that those involved in life assurance should understand at least the nature and basic principles of the law relating to trusts. Trusts play a large part in the mitigation of inheritance tax and in estate planning and so a knowledge of trusts is also of great benefit to advisers and their customers. Readers are recommended to consult more specialist texts for more detailed coverage[2].

A The nature of trusts

1 Definitions and uses

11.2 There is no universally accepted definition of a trust. Perhaps one of the most satisfactory definitions is set out in *Underhill and Hayton*[3]:

1 See generally, Underhill and Hayton *Law of Trusts and Trustees* (18th edn, 2010).
2 See also Chapter 14.
3 Article 1, Underhill and Hayton *Law of Trusts and Trustees* (18th edn, 2010) p 2.

> 'an equitable obligation, binding a person (called the trustee) to deal with property (called trust property) owned by him as a separate fund, distinct from his own private property, for the benefit of persons (called beneficiaries or, in old cases, cestuis que trust), of whom he may himself be one, and any of whom may enforce the obligation'

Likewise, there is no universally accepted definition of the term 'settlement' which is often used as an alternative term for a trust but is generally wider. Parliament has from time to time defined the word for the purposes of particular tax statutes. For example, the Income Tax (Trading and Other Income) Act 2005 (ITTOIA 2005)[1] defines the word for the purposes of income tax, to include 'any disposition, trust, covenant, agreement, arrangement or transfer of assets'.

Trusts are created for many reasons and may take a variety of forms. Their origins lie in medieval times with the object of preserving landed estates intact for as long as possible. Trusts today are used for a variety of purposes, for example, to enable property to be held for persons (eg minors) unable to hold it themselves; to tie up property for the enjoyment of persons in succession; to protect family property from creditors and from particular members of the family with reckless or extravagant tastes; to enable provision to be made for dependants or others privately; to provide a framework for charitable giving, for causes or non-human beneficiaries; to enable investment to be made through unit trusts; to provide a framework for pension schemes; and for estate planning and to minimise the incidence of various taxes.

11.3 The practical uses of trusts in connection with life policies are explained more fully in Chapter 14 but it is useful to bear in mind that the main uses centre around:

(1) speed of payment (no need to wait for a Grant of Representation provided there is a surviving trustee);

(2) taxation mitigation (the reader is referred to Chapter 13 in particular for a commentary on the provisions in the Finance Act 2006, which drastically affected the inheritance tax treatment of trusts);

(3) the ability to benefit a certain beneficiary outside of the will (which is ultimately a publicly available document); and

(4) in some cases, protection against the effects of bankruptcy (see further Chapter 12).

Modern trusts tend to be flexible rather than fixed or absolute and are usually designed so that the interests in the trust property may be altered in the light of changes in taxation legislation or practice or in family or personal circumstances.

Trusts are classified in a variety of ways. One of these is by the degree of instruction given to the trustees. If the trustee is given no active duties to perform in relation to the trust property, eg S assigns a life policy to T1 and T2 to hold on

1 Section 620(1).

trust for B, the trust may be described as a *simple* trust (or an absolute, fixed or bare trust). In such a trust, the beneficiaries are absolutely entitled as against the trustees (subject to any incapacity, for example, being under 18 years of age). If, however, duties are declared, eg S transfers £10,000 to T on trust to pay the income and/or capital to A, B and C at T's discretion, it may be classified as a *special* trust (or discretionary or flexible trust).

Trusts are further categorised by how they come into existence: express; resulting or implied; and constructive, but reference should be made to more specific works for a detailed explanation of this[1]. Trusts are further classified for the purposes of taxation and a more detailed examination of this can be found in Chapter 13.

A common question which arises in relation to trusts in general and very often with regard to life policy trusts is where a person is both a beneficiary and a trustee. It is sometimes thought that the two are incompatible. However, this is very often the case with a life policy trust and, in practice, it is rarely an issue. Presumably, the settlor is happy with this state of affairs in view of the fact that he will have selected both trustees and beneficiaries and provided that the trustee-beneficiary acts in accordance with the terms of the trust and the rules of common law, equity and statute there should not be a problem. However, to put the matter beyond doubt the settlor may wish to insert a provision in the trust instrument that the trustee is able to benefit himself personally or a provision to the effect that at least one other trustee must be involved in such decisions. The settlor may also be a beneficiary but this may have adverse tax consequences (see Chapter 14).

B Trusts distinguished from powers

11.4 A power is an authority vested in a person to deal with or dispose of property which is not his own. It may take effect at law, as with a power of attorney; or it may be equitable only, as in the case of a power of appointment, which enables the donee to declare in whom and in what manner property is to vest without giving him any right of ownership over the property.

The main distinction, however, is that a trust is mandatory, a power is discretionary; a trustee is bound to carry out the terms of a trust and if he does not, the court will do so for him, but the donee of a power cannot be compelled to exercise it, and if he does not, the property will pass to the persons entitled in default of its exercise.

The distinction between trusts and powers is not always entirely clear. The question depends on what the intention of the donor was: if he intended that in any event the objects of the power should benefit, it is a power in the nature of a trust, a 'trust power'. Otherwise it will be a mere power. In *Burrough v Philcox*[2] a testator gave property to his two children for their lives, with power to the

1 See Underhill and Hayton *Law of Trust and Trustees* (18th edn, 2010).
2 (1840) 5 My & Cr 72. See also *Schmidt v Rosewood Trust Ltd* [2003] All ER (D) 442 (Mar).

survivor of the children to dispose of the property by will amongst the testator's nephews and nieces or their children 'either all to one of them or to as many of them as my surviving child shall think proper'. It was held that a trust was created in favour of the testator's nephews and nieces, subject, however, to a power of selection by the surviving child. As this power had not been exercised, the property had to be divided equally amongst the members of the class in accordance with the equitable maxim 'equality is equity'.

C Creation of trusts

1 Requirements of a valid trust

11.5 An express trust may be created by will, deed or some other form of written instrument. For a trust of personal property such as a life policy (also known as 'personalty'), writing is not essential and a trust may be created orally or even by conduct. It should be borne in mind that section 53 of the Law of Property Act 1925 requires a trust of an equitable interest in either real or personal property to be in writing. So, for example, if a beneficiary under a trust wishes to declare a trust of his interest then that trust must be in writing.

11.6 For the creation of a trust the following conditions, known as 'the three certainties'[1], must be present:

(1) the words used must be construed as imperative. There must be an intention to create a trust and 'precatory' words are not sufficient;

(2) the subject matter (the property) of the trust must be certain; and

(3) the objects, ie the beneficiaries, must be certain.

Where a life assurance policy is effected with the intention that it should benefit someone other than the grantee (the person to whom the policy is 'granted' by the life office), a trust should be created by the use of language which clearly indicates such an intention, rather than language which infers a general intention to benefit a third party. Where a policy is effected and expressed to be for the benefit of a third party, then, except in the case of trusts created under the Married Women's Property Act 1882 (see Chapter 12), the policy moneys will belong to the policyholder's estate, unless he has effectively constituted himself a trustee for that third party. Numerous cases have demonstrated this requirement, both for trusts generally and for trusts specifically of life assurance policies[2]. Some examples are given below[3].

1 *Knight v Knight* [1840] 3 Beav 148.

2 See *Re Engelbach's Estate, Tibbetts v Engelbach* [1924] 2 Ch 348; *Re Foster, Hudson v Foster* [1938] 3 All ER 357; *Re Sinclair's Life Policy* [1938] 3 All ER 124; *Re Webb, Barclays Bank Ltd v Webb* [1941] 1 All ER 321 and *Re Foster's Policy, Menneer v Foster* [1966] 1 All ER 432.

3 See also *Swain v Law Society* [1982] 2 All ER 827.

In *Re Foster, Hudson v Foster*[1], a father effected a policy on the life of his son, expressed *to be payable* to the representatives or assigns of the son at death on or after the age of 21. The father paid the premiums during his life and after his death the premiums were paid by or on behalf of the son until he died. It was held that (1) the father had not constituted himself a trustee for his son and that the policy moneys were payable to the personal representatives of the father; and (2) that, as all parties had acted under the mistaken belief that the policy belonged to the son, his personal representative was entitled to a lien on the policy for the premiums paid by the son or on his behalf.

In *Re Engelbach's Estate, Tibbetts v Engelbach*[2], a father effected an endowment policy to provide for the payment of the sum assured on 3 February 1923, if his daughter should be alive at that time. In the proposal form, opposite the words 'full name and description of the proposer', he had written 'Edward Coryton Engelbach for his daughter Mary Noel, aged one month'. The father died on 7 March 1916, and the daughter survived to the fixed date when the policy moneys were paid to her. She was, however, persuaded to pay them to a stakeholder pending a decision as to the legal rights of the parties. The question for the court was whether the policy was for the benefit of the daughter, or whether the policy moneys belonged to the father's estate. It was held that as the daughter could not sue on the contract nor did her father constitute himself a trustee for his daughter, the policy moneys belonged to the father's estate and must be paid to his executors.

In *Re Sinclair's Life Policy*[3], S effected an endowment policy under which the benefit was expressed *to be payable* at the end of 17 years to his godson, H. S had handed the policy to H's father and told him to retain it so that he could collect the money. S died in 1924 and the policy matured in 1936 when the life office paid the money into court. Farwell J held that the evidence was insufficient to establish a trust in favour of H. There was no doubt that A's intention was to make provision for his godson, but he did not constitute himself a trustee of the moneys payable.

11.7 Where a policy is effected by an adult *as trustee* for a child, however, it would create a trust and give the child an enforceable right. Such a trust is usually created by express words and this is the safest course, but it seems that in some circumstances a trust may be implied, eg by provisions which indicate that after a certain period the beneficial interest will pass to the child and the adult will cease to have a beneficial interest.

In *Re Webb, Barclays Bank Ltd v Webb*[4] a father effected a policy 'on behalf and for the benefit of' his child. The policy money was expressed to be payable to the personal representatives or assigns of the child, provided that he survived to his 21st birthday. Under the policy the father could exercise various options,

1 [1938] 3 All ER 357.
2 [1924] 2 Ch 348.
3 [1938] 3 All ER 124.
4 [1941] 1 All ER 321.

including to borrow or surrender, modify, vary, assign or charge the policy *on behalf of the child*, until the child attained 21, at which time, all the rights and powers of the father or his personal representatives were to cease and the child was to become entitled, subject to any assignment or charge, to the policy absolutely. It was held that the form of the policy *established a trust* in favour of the child, as the intention to create a trust was sufficiently clear. Farwell J stated:

> 'The whole matter rests entirely upon the true construction of the policy in question. I think that one must take it that unless there is in the policy something which does establish reasonably clearly that the assured was in fact constituting, and intending to constitute, himself a trustee for the third party of the assurance moneys, the third party is not and the personal representatives of the assured are, entitled to the money payable.'

Further:

> 'It is for a person to make clear by the language used that he is constituting himself a trustee and the absence of any clear words to that effect makes it difficult to establish a trust.'

In *Vandepitte v Preferred Accident Insurance Co of New York*[1], Lord Wright stated:

> 'The intention to constitute the trust must be affirmatively proved.'

11.8 In *Re Foster's Policy, Menneer v Foster*[2] a father effected a policy on the life of his daughter for his own benefit until the 'option anniversary' and thereafter all rights shall then be vested in his daughter or her personal representatives or assigns. The policy was on similar lines to that in the *Webb* case, except that there was no specific provision that the father should cease at the end of the deferred period to have any beneficial interest in the policy. It was held that on the true construction of the policy, the father's interest ceased at the end of the deferred period and a trust was therefore *implied* for the child, for whose benefit the policy was expressed to have been effected. The fact that from the 'option anniversary' the right to surrender the policy, etc became vested in the child for her own benefit was inconsistent with the father retaining any beneficial interest thereafter.

In *Davis v Davis*[3] the court was required to construe the intentions of the deceased. On the evidence available it was held that the deceased's sister held a property as nominee for the deceased and that a life policy which had been assigned to her was not for her own benefit but for the purpose of discharging a mortgage over the property. It was established that a secret trust in favour of the deceased's step-daughters existed. This was on the basis of wholly oral statements.

1 [1933] AC 70 at 79–80.
2 [1966] 1 All ER 432.
3 [2001] All ER (D) 352.

The difficulties created by not clearly evidencing certainty of intention can be seen from the case of *Simpson v Simpson and another*[1] where the existence of a trust created orally was eventually established but not without the great inconvenience and expense of court proceedings.

Where premiums are paid by a father in respect of a policy taken out by him on his child's life and for the benefit of that child, the premiums may be rebuttably presumed to be made by way of 'advancement' (a type of gift intended for a specific purpose), in which case the child's estate will (subject to any rebuttal) be entitled to the policy moneys.

Where two parties have demonstrated a clear joint intention and have acted in pursuance of an agreement, equity will protect their beneficial rights under such an agreement. In *Smith v Clerical Medical and General Life Assurance Society*[2], D and E bought a house together with a 100% mortgage and effected an endowment policy, which was designed to pay off the full amount of the mortgage if either of them died within 25 years. When E died, D sold the house and paid off the mortgage from the sale proceeds. There was then a dispute as to whether the policy monies should be paid to E's personal representatives or to D. The Court of Appeal held that D was beneficially entitled to the money in pursuance of the joint intention of the deceased and D.

In *Hyett v Stanley*[3] the Smith case was quoted with approval and it was decided that a joint policy effected with the intention of repaying a mortgage must initially be used for that purpose with the surviving joint tenant entitled to the surplus only above that required to repay the mortgage.

The terms of jointly owned policies should be examined closely as these tend to vary between life offices. For example, whilst such policies generally tend to be worded so as to establish a beneficial joint tenancy they may actually be structured as a tenancy in common.

11.9 Certainty of the subject matter of the trust can cause difficulties (see, for example, *Boyce v Boyce*[4]) although it will almost invariably be clear that a particular policy is the subject matter of the trust, although difficult questions can arise when settlors attempt to declare trusts of only part of a policy or of certain sums payable under the policy or where only one of two joint policyholders attempts to declare a trust of the policy or part of the policy. The precise wording of the purported trust must be analysed in each case. It may be that the settlor has successfully created a trust of an equitable interest but not of the policy itself. This can create complications surrounding payment out of benefits under the policy.

11.10 The test for certainty of objects will differ depending on the type of trust. For a fixed trust to be valid, it must be possible to ascertain each and every beneficiary: it must be possible for the trustee to compile a complete list of those

1 [2005] EWHC 2098 (Ch).
2 [1992] 1 FCR 262, CA.
3 [2003] EWCA Civ 942 [2004] 1 FLR 394.
4 (1849) 16 Sim 476.

entitled[1]. For other trusts (and for powers) the test is whether it can be said with certainty that any given individual is or is not a member of the class[2].

Unless the trust gives the trustees a discretion or a power of appointment, the precise share which each beneficiary is to take must also be certain.

Another essential to the establishment of a trust is that of 'complete constitution'. When this has been achieved the beneficiary will be able to enforce the trust and this will be the case whether or not he is a 'volunteer' (ie whether or not he has given consideration). A leading case in this area is *Milroy v Lord*[3] where Turner LJ stated that this was achieved by the settlor having 'done everything which, according to the nature of the property comprised in the settlement, was necessary to be done in order to transfer the property and render the settlement binding upon him'. Essentially, there are two methods of achieving this. One is by the settlor declaring himself as a trustee. As has been seen by **11.7–11.8** clarity is required and so establishing certainty of intention is important. The other is by the effective transfer of the property to trustees. The transfer must be appropriate to the nature of the property being transferred so in the case of a life policy this would be by assignment in accordance with the Policies of Assurance Act 1867, or under section 136 of the Law of Property Act 1925. Some uncertainty has more recently crept into this area of the law with the case of *Pennington and another v Waine and others*[4] where the donor did not do all she was able to do to divest herself of the property (shares), but Arden LJ stated that the donor clearly intended to make an immediate gift and the stage had been reached where it would have been unconscionable to have recalled the gift. The possibility of this third method was considered in *T Choithram International SA v Pagarani*[5] and *Pennington v Crampton*[6]. Essentially, this relies on the fact that it would have been unconscionable (and hence contrary to equitable principles) for the donor to recall a gift after a certain length of time.

It is also usually possible for a corporate body to create a trust provided this is not in conflict with its memorandum and articles of association. A minor cannot create a trust although if he purports to do so then at his majority it will become binding unless he repudiates it within a reasonable time of attaining the age of 18[7].

Trusts may be created in the ways set out below.

2 Statutory trusts

11.11 Some trusts are expressly created or implied by the operation of statute. For example, a policy effected by a man or a woman on his or her own life and

1 *IRC v Broadway Cottages Trust* [1955] Ch 20.
2 *McPhail v Doulton* [1970] 2 All ER 228 and *Re Baden's Deed Trust (No 2)* [1972] 2 All ER 1304.
3 (1862) 4 De GF & J 264 at pp 274–275.
4 [2002] 1 WLR 2075.
5 [2001] WTLR 277.
6 [2002] WTLR 387.
7 *Edwards v Carter* [1893] AC 360.

expressed to be for the benefit of his or her spouse and children or any of them will create a trust under section 11 of the Married Women's Property Act 1882 (see Chapter 12).

Another common form of statutory trust arises where two or more people co-own a legal estate (one of the two ways of legally holding real property under the Law of Property Act, 1925)[1]. The co-owners will hold the property on trust for themselves. Also, where an individual dies intestate, the Administration of Estates Act 1925 (as amended) provides that the estate shall be distributed in a specified manner, which in certain circumstances includes the creation of a trust.

3 *Express trusts*

11.12 An express trust is one which has been intentionally and deliberately created. This expression covers all trusts created in this manner irrespective of what other descriptions they may have. For example, 'fixed trusts', 'power of appointment trusts', 'inheritance trusts', or whether by reference to its taxation status, for example, 'interest in possession', 'discretionary' or 'accumulation and maintenance'.

4 *Implied trusts*

11.13 An implied trust is not expressed in any form but is to be implied from the actions or relationship of the parties. Where, for example, business partners purchase property and direct the vendor to convey it to one partner, he may hold it upon implied trust for all the partners.

A 'species' of implied trust is the 'resulting trust', which may arise on the failure of an express trust, either wholly or partially, in which event the beneficial interest may 'result' back to the settlor or his estate. Where, accordingly, a man effected a policy for the benefit of his wife and she had murdered him, she was barred from receiving any benefit and there was a resulting trust to his estate and thus for the beneficiaries of his estate[2].

5 *Constructive trusts*

11.14 These are a species of implied trust imposed by equity, irrespective of the intention of the owner of the property, in order to satisfy the demands of justice and good conscience. The concept of constructive trusteeship can be elusive and can arise from different sets of circumstances. For example, if a third party knowingly receives trust property and also knows that it is transferred to him in breach of trust, equity will deem him to hold it upon a constructive trust for the beneficiaries[3]. Actual receipt of trust property is not essential for a third

1 Law of Property Act 1925, s 36.

2 *Cleaver v Mutual Reserve Fund Life Assurance* [1892] 1 QB 147. See also *Davitt v Titcumb* [1989] 3 All ER 417.

3 See *BCCI (Overseas) Ltd v Akindele* [2000] 4 All ER 221.

party to be deemed to be a constructive trustee. A person can still become a constructive trustee on the basis of 'intermedelling', ie if he knowingly enables a fraudulent purpose to be effected. The question of the requisite state of mind was considered in *Royal Brunei Airlines v Tan*[1]. Lord Nicholls referred to 'a person who dishonestly procures or assists in a breach of trust or fiduciary obligation'. This would seem to suggest that a finding of constructive trusteeship would be difficult to achieve, although Lord Nicholls went on to indicate that the meaning of dishonesty in this context is not the same as would apply in a criminal matter. He went on to say that '… for the most part dishonesty is to be equated with conscious impropriety'. So, for example, a life office who was aware that a trustee of a policy who had applied to surrender the policy intended to use the proceeds for his own benefit must refuse to pay to him otherwise it could be held to be a constructive trustee of those moneys.

The test relating to dishonesty was also explored more recently in *Barlow Clowes International Ltd (In liquidation) v Eurotrust International Ltd*[2] where, in broad terms, an objective approach to dishonesty was stated to be required.

The knowledge need not be actual, it may be constructive. Constructive knowledge for these purposes can be very difficult to define. It obviously falls short of actual knowledge but must be sufficiently obvious so as to put the third party on notice that something is amiss. It may require that he should investigate further, as he is not entitled to 'shut his eyes' to the obvious.

Constructive trusteeship can arise in other scenarios. One of the oldest cases involved a fiduciary using his position to obtain an unauthorised profit (renewal of a lease held as trust property by a trustee in his own favour)[3].

In another case, where one of two joint tenants murdered the other, the Ontario High Court held that although the normal rule of survivorship applied and the full interest accrued to the survivor, the court would impose a constructive trust so that he held the property as to an undivided one half interest for the benefit of the deceased joint tenant's next of kin[4].

In a more recent case, a Crown employee purchased property with the proceeds of bribes accepted during the course of his employment. It was held that the property was held on constructive trust for his employer[5].

Constructive trusts have also been found to exist where a common intention between the parties can be inferred. A constructive trust was not held to exist in the case of *Pratt v Medwin*[6]. O and M, who were business partners, purchased a house as tenants in common with a mortgage. They were required to have a supporting life insurance policy which, amongst other benefits, guaranteed to pay off the mortgage if O died. The premiums were paid from their partnership account but equivalent amounts were deducted from O's personal drawings

1 [1995] 2 AC 378; [1995] 3 WLR 64.

2 [2006] 1 All ER 333.

3 *Keech v Sandford* (1726) Sel Cas Ch 61.

4 *Schobelt v Barber* (1966) 60 DLR (2d) 519.

5 *A-G for Hong Kong v Reid* [1994] 1 All ER 1, PC. See *Rockbrook Ltd v (1) Khan (2) Miracles by Design Limited* [2006] EWHC 101 Ch for an example of the difficulties which can be encountered in seeking to establish a constructive trust.

6 [2003] EWCA Civ 906.

account in the partnership. M, however, was unaware that the accountant was deducting these sums from O's personal drawings account and was under the impression that the purpose of the policy was to guarantee the mortgage debt and hence was intended to be shared beneficially. It was held in dismissing the appeal that a party was not bound by any inference which the other party drew to his attention unless that inference was one that could reasonably be drawn from his own words and conduct. The policy was separate from the property and was in the name of O and the payments were made by O. There was no evidence, apart from M's 'impression' that there was a common intention that the proceeds of the policy be shared. The case was differentiated from *Smith v Clerical Medical* (see **11.8** above) where it was stated that 'Each case in this field must turn on its individual facts'. This can also be contrasted with the case of *Oxley v Hiscock*[1] where a common intention was found and a constructive trust held to exist.

6 *Creation of a trust of a life policy*

11.15 There are a number of ways in which a life assurance policy can become the subject of a trust:

(1) A policy may be effected for the benefit of the grantee's spouse and/or children and create a trust by reason of the Married Women's Property Act 1882 (see Chapter 12).

(2) The grantee may assign the policy to trustees to hold for the beneficiaries.

(3) The grantee may declare an express trust of the policy. This may be on the basis of a 'trust request' (submitted with the proposal/application form to form part of the contract between the grantee and the life office) for use prior to the policy being effected, or a declaration of trust of the policy any time after the policy is effected.

(4) Trustees may effect a policy possibly for investment purposes or perhaps to cover an inheritance tax liability.

An interesting case on the subject of declaring trusts of life assurance policies and which concerns certainty of words is *Pappadakis v Pappadakis*[2]. A document provided by the life office, described as a 'Declaration of Trust', was used purportedly to create a trust of a policy in favour of the proposer's wife and children. This was subsequent to an initial trust document (about which there was no dispute) under which the proposer himself was a potential beneficiary along with family members.

Following the birth of his son the proposer effected three further documents. The first appointed an additional trustee. Under the second the trustees irrevocably appointed the policy benefits to the proposer and assigned the policy to the proposer free of trust. The third document (which was the 'Declaration of Trust' referred to above under consideration by the court) provided that the Declaration

1 [2004] 3 All ER 703.
2 TLR 19/1/2000.

was made by the person whose name appeared in a blank space and was expressed to take effect as an assignment of the policy by the settlor to named persons who were described as trustees, to be held by them as trustees for the persons whose names appeared in the space provided for the names of the beneficiaries. The space for the trustees was left blank. This form was signed by the proposer alone.

Before he died the proposer and his wife executed a deed of gift which recited that there were doubts about the validity of the Declaration of Trust and that it was believed that the proposer was absolutely entitled (at both law and in equity) to the policy, and by which the proposer assigned the policy to his wife absolutely. It was held that the Declaration of Trust was invalid and the widow was entitled to the whole proceeds of the policy. Although headed a Declaration of Trust it was in fact worded and structured as an assignment of the policy to trustees. It could not be effective because the trustees (the assignees) were not named and it was not possible to assign something to nobody. As the assignment was voluntary and gratuitous, but failed to take effect as such, it could not be saved by equity holding it to be a declaration of trust. The proposer had not intended it to be a declaration of trust and as a matter of construction it was clearly not a declaration of trust. It was not possible to overrule this by an inference to be drawn from the absence of certain manuscript words which should have been added to the document. Nor could the document be rectified as there was no clear and convincing evidence as to what it was intended that the Declaration should have said.

Justice Park concentrated on the effect of the document rather than what it was called. Presumably, if the additional trustees had been appointed then the assignment in the document would have been operative and the document effective as a result.

In view of the confusion and issues which arose, *Pappadakis* might be taken as support for the view that policyholders/settlors should not rely on trust documentation supplied by life offices, which is necessarily of a standard and non-specific nature and should instead obtain a bespoke trust document from their own legal advisers. However, the vast majority of life policies which are made subject to a trust document provided by the life office fully achieve the settlor's objectives at little or no cost. Another possible course of action is for the settlor to refer the life office's specimen trust (where available) to his own legal advisers, preferably those with knowledge and experience in this area. Hopefully, this will involve less expense than a bespoke trust instrument. Indeed, this is the approach suggested by most life offices when providing specimen documentation. Realistically, for policies with relatively low sums assured the cost of independent legal advice to the settlor will often be prohibitively expensive.

A further example of the confusion surrounding specimen life office trust documentation arose in the case of *Strover v Strover*[1] where partnership protection trusts (which involved individual policies on the lives of each partner in trust for their co-partners) were entered into with what appeared to be the understanding on the part of the deceased that if he left the firm the beneficial interest would

1 [2005] EWHC 860 (Ch).

revert to him. Hart J stated that the partners had not '...collectively or individually...directed their minds to what was to happen in the event of a retirement'. The actual wording of the trust provided for the benefits to continue to be payable to the surviving partners. However, the court decided that there was a 'proprietary estoppel' so that the deceased's estate was the ultimate beneficiary.

The Pensions Ombudsman case of *Andrews*[1] provides a warning for life offices. It involved the provider of a retirement annuity contract (a forerunner of personal pension policies). The provider gave the policyholder the incorrect form for writing the death benefits in trust and compounded the error by subsequently treating the form as valid. It was decided that the provider was liable for the resulting loss which amounted to £137,000 in inheritance tax which could otherwise have been avoided. The complaint came from the sons of the deceased policyholder as the intended beneficiaries of the failed trust. The Pensions Ombudsman decided that they could bring the complaint as 'actual or potential beneficiaries' within the Pension Schemes Act 1993. It is not entirely clear what the result would have been had the provider not subsequently treated the form as valid as the trust document would generally be provided on the basis that it was a draft for the consideration of the parties and their legal advisers.

7 *Scotland*

11.16 There are important differences between English and Scots law as to what is required to create a valid trust. Also, the trust terminology differs. To create a valid trust, 'delivery', or some other overt act signifying irrevocability, is necessary if the trust is not to be revocable by the *truster* (settlor). Delivery is the requirement that the subject matter of the trust is delivered to the trustees, or to some person on their behalf, with the intention of transferring the rights in such subject matter so that they are held against the *truster* for *behoof* (on behalf of) the beneficiaries. (Delivery need not be physical delivery and, in fact, this would only occur in rare cases.) If there is no delivery there must be one of the permitted equivalents, such as intimation[2] or possibly registration of the trust deed in the Books of Council and Session.

In *Allan's Trustees v IRC*[3] it was held by the House of Lords that a person could create a valid trust by declaring himself a trustee of the policy and giving intimation to one of several beneficiaries. Intimation of the deceased life assured's intentions prior to the policy coming into force does not constitute delivery; and a parent is not an appropriate person to whom intimation, on behalf of an adult beneficiary, may be given[4]. If a Scottish trust is not properly constituted because the requirements as to delivery or its equivalent have not been fulfilled, there is likely to be a resulting trust for the truster. In the case of policies under the Married Women's Policies of Assurance (Scotland) Act 1880, the pro-

1 19 March 2010 (76528/1).
2 Intimation is accepted as being the equivalent of delivery: *Clark's Trustees v Inland Revenue* 1972 SLT 189.
3 1971 SLT 62.
4 *Kerr's Trustees v Inland Revenue* [1974] SLC 193.

visions of the Act create an irrevocable trust, without any need for delivery or intimation of the policy, since the Act provides that the policy vests immediately on its being effected in the life assured and his legal representatives in trust for the beneficiaries expressed, or in any trustee nominated in the policy or appointed by separate writing duly intimated to the life office.

The Married Women's Policies of Assurance (Scotland) Act 1880 can therefore operate to create a trust where one would not otherwise exist. In the case of *Re A Policy No 6402 of the Scottish Equitable*[1] a policy was effected by A on his own life 'for behoof of' his wife's sister. Additionally, the policy document was never handed to her. It was held that such words did not create a trust. There was a resulting trust in favour of A. Had the words been in favour of his wife then a trust under the Act would have arisen.

8 *Online trusts*

11.17 A more recent process introduced by some life offices is the ability to set up trusts of life policies online where a written trust document may not be executed by the settlor. It is possible to effect a trust of a life policy (or any chose in action) without the need for writing. However, there may be issues where evidence of the settlor's intention is required. Without the settlor's signature there will be more room for argument as to the existence of the trust and its terms. There are certain measures which can be taken to reduce the risk of such a trust being challenged by, for example, beneficiaries under the settlor's estate or by Her Majesty's Revenue and Customs, perhaps claiming that inheritance tax should be payable on the proceeds as they form part of the deceased's estate. For example, correspondence between the life office and the settlor regarding the trust, perhaps including a copy of the purported trust and a covering letter from the life office to the effect that this is the trust applying to the policy (and nothing subsequent from the settlor inconsistent with this). Additional measures could include confirmation from the policyholder's adviser regarding his understanding that the policy is subject to the trust in question. It should be noted that in Scotland as a result of the Requirements of Writing Act, 1995, it is not possible for a settlor to declare a trust without writing unless he appoints an additional trustee.

D Variation of trusts made in contemplation of or during marriage[2]

11.18 On granting a decree of divorce, nullity or judicial separation, the court may, under the 'property adjustment orders' powers contained in the Matrimonial Causes Act 1973, make an order varying, for the benefit of the parties to the marriage and/or the children of the family, any ante-nuptial or

1 [1902] 1 Ch 282.

2 See also *Bown v Bown and Weston* [1948] 2 All ER 778; *Gunner v Gunner and Stirling* [1948] 2 All ER 771; *Lort-Williams v Lort-Williams* [1951] 2 All ER 241, CA.

post-nuptial settlement made on the parties to the marriage, or an order extinguishing or reducing the interest of either of the parties to the marriage under any such settlement. In this context, 'settlement' is given a wide interpretation. Divorce in itself will notdestroy the interest of a named spouse, but the interest may be varied as a result of any order the court makes. The Civil Partnership Act 2004[1] introduces the same provisions for same sex couples relating to, for example, property adjustment as apply under the Matrimonial Causes Act 1973.

In *Gulbenkian v Gulbenkian*[2], a husband effected two endowment assurances on his life; one payable to him at maturity if he was living, or if he died during the term, to his wife; and the other payable to him at maturity if he was living, or if he died during the term, to his wife if she was living, and if she was not, to the personal representatives of the husband. The husband divorced the wife and asked for an order varying the trusts. It was held that the name of the wife should be struck out.

SECTION 2 TRUST PROVISIONS

A The trust property

11.19 All types of property, real or personal (eg a chose in action such as a life policy), legal or equitable, in possession, remainder or reversion and whether vested or contingent may be the subject matter of a trust.

The following paragraphs consider some of the common provisions, trusts and powers which will be encountered in trust documentation.

B Life interests

11.20 A person who has a life interest (a 'life tenant') has an interest in the property of the trust only during his lifetime. If the trust property is land, he would only be entitled to the use and enjoyment of it, or the rents and income from it and if the trust property is personal property, he would only be entitled to the income from the trust property. Life tenants (who have no other interest in the trust property) cannot therefore (unless there is a specific power to advance or appoint capital to the life tenant or it is possible to vary the trust) receive any capital from the trust, nor can a capital investment be made on their behalf. A life tenant will have an 'interest in possession' in the property to which his income entitlement refers[3]. It is not common to solely create a life interest in a trust of a life policy as it is a non-income producing asset. However, a life interest is often created in conjunction with some sort of capital interest.

1 Section 72 and Schedules 5, 6 and 7.
2 [1927] P 237.
3 Inheritance Tax Act 1984, s 49: see further Chapter 13.

C Protected life interest

11.21 The life interest may be framed in such a way that it will come to an end if the life tenant attempts to dispose of it, or becomes bankrupt. Although a life interest can be given to a person *until* bankruptcy, an individual cannot settle his own property on *himself* with an interest determinable on bankruptcy, as this would be an attempt to defeat his creditors[1] (see further Chapter 12).

D Protective trusts

11.22 A protective trust combines a determinable interest with a discretionary trust. Under a protective trust, the interest of the beneficiary is determinable upon bankruptcy or attempted alienation, upon which a discretionary trust arises in favour of himself and other beneficiaries (usually family members). The original beneficiary may then receive such income as is necessary for his maintenance with the surplus directed to any spouse and/or issue. These trusts may be created by using express terms, but such settlements became so popular that section 33 of the Trustee Act 1925 enables creation of such a trust by merely directing that property is to be held 'on protective trusts' (see further Chapter 12).

E Powers of appointment

11.23 Settlors often prefer to retain flexibility over future interests under the trust and so confer upon the trustees (one of which will usually be the settlor), or themselves, a power of appointment. This is a power to declare at some future date the persons in whom the benefits of the trust are to vest, the extent of their interests, and the time at which they are to vest. Such appointments may be authorised to be made by deed, will, or simply in writing, and may be revocable or irrevocable. The appointor, if he appoints at all, can do so only in favour of one or more persons of the specified class or classes set out in the original trust instrument, which may include the settlor (where the trust is not designed to mitigate inheritance tax)[2].

Where the power of appointment is being exercised, the appointors must take care to specify that they are appointing revocably if they do want to retain the ability to make further appointments. Otherwise, it would appear that the appointment will be irrevocable and cannot therefore be further altered[3].

1 See the cases collected in *Mackintosh v Pogose* [1895] 1 Ch 505.

2 See, generally, *In Re Baden's Deed Trusts (No 2)* [1972] 2 All ER 1304; *In Re Manisty's Settlement Manisty v Manisty* [1973] 2 All ER 1203 and *In Re Hay's Settlement Trusts* [1981] 3 All ER 786. Refer also to *Turner v Turner* [1983] 2 All ER 745 in which it was held that where trustees exercised a power of appointment but without exercising their discretion – simply acting at the behest of the settlor – they would be in breach of their duty and the purported appointments would be set aside.

3 *Worrall v Jacob* (1817) 3 Mer 256.

The case of *Sieff and others v Fox and others*[1] analyses the rules relating to what trustees should take into account (and what they should not take into account) when exercising their powers. In this case the trustees exercised a power of appointment without regard to the correct capital gains tax consequences. It was held that if they had the correct information they would not have exercised the appointment in question and, as a result, it was held that the appointment should be set aside. However, in *Pitt v Holt*[2] and *Futter v Futter*[3] the actions of, in the former case, the receiver and in the latter case, the trustees had followed professional advice but this had resulted in the latter case in adverse tax consequences. The correct principle was that acts outside the scope of the trustees' powers were void, but acts within their powers were at most voidable depending on whether there was a breach of fiduciary duty. Trustees who followed professional tax advice would not generally be in breach of their duties. This decision therefore limits the rule in Hastings-Bass. This rule allowed a court to overturn an action where the effect of exercising a power is different to that intended and the trustees would not have acted as they did because they had either failed to take into account relevant considerations or had taken into account considerations they ought not to have taken into account.

The flexible power of appointment trust is commonly used in relation to trusts of life policies. This is discussed further in Chapter 14.

11.24 Normally, an appointor is under no duty to exercise the power of appointment, but if he chooses to exercise it, he must do so honestly[4]. It must be exercised for the purposes intended by the trust and not for corrupt or extraneous reasons, for otherwise the exercise of the power will in equity be regarded as a 'fraud on the power' and be void[5]. The word *fraud* in this connection does not imply or require any intention of fraud in the criminal legal sense. The appointment may be void, not only where the appointer is seeking a benefit for himself but also in some cases where he is arranging a disposition of the trust fund for some purpose foreign to the power or as a result of a bargain with the appointee to benefit persons who are not objects of the power[6].

It is not, however, in itself a fraud on the power to *release* the power so that it cannot be exercised, even though the person who releases the power does so in order to obtain some benefit for himself under the trusts in default of appointment or otherwise[7].

1 [2005] 3 All ER 693. See also *Re Hastings-Bass [1975] Ch 25.*
2 [2010] EWHC 15 (Ch).
3 [2010] EWHC 449 (Ch).
4 *Cloutte v Storey* [1911] 1 Ch 18.
5 *Re Brook's Settlements, Brook v Brook* [1968] 3 All ER 416.
6 *Vatcher v Paull* [1915] AC 372. See *Re the X Trust* 5 ITELR 119 (Judgment date 13 June 2002 – Jersey) for an example of a case where a non-beneficiary benefited but where the exercise of the power was nevertheless upheld.
7 See *Re Radcliffe, Radcliffe v Bewes* [1892] 1 Ch 227.

F Hotchpot clause

11.25 A hotchpot clause is intended to ensure that the shares of all the children who are beneficiaries in the trust fund shall be equal. The clause provides that if a power to advance or appoint part of the fund is exercised in favour of one child, the amount advanced or appointed is to be taken into account when the shares of the children in the remaining part of the fund fall to be determined, unless the person exercising the power has a power to direct otherwise.

G Care of children

1 Maintenance, education and benefit

11.26 It is clearly desirable in a trust providing for minor children that the trustees should have power to apply the income of the trust fund for their maintenance and education. Trusts normally contain express powers for this, but if they do not (unless excluded expressly or by implication), the statutory power will apply.

The statutory power of maintenance is set out in section 31 of the Trustee Act 1925.

(1) Before the beneficiary attains the age of 18 the trustees *may*, subject to contrary direction in the trust instrument, express or implied, pay to his parent or guardian, or otherwise apply, the whole or part of the income of the trust property for his maintenance, benefit or education.

(2) This power is discretionary, and is exercisable irrespective of any other fund available for the same purpose, or the existence of some person bound by law to provide for such maintenance or education[1]. In considering whether to exercise this power, the trustees should, however, have regard to the beneficiary's age, requirements, the general circumstances of the case, and of what other income, if any, is applicable for the same purposes.

(3) Any income which is not so applied for maintenance or education *must* be accumulated at compound interest. The trustees may, during the beneficiary's minority, apply the accumulations or any part thereof as if they were income of the current year[2].

(4) On reaching age 18, if the beneficiary does not have a vested interest, then the trustees *must* pay the whole of the income and any accumulations of income to the beneficiary until he either attains a vested interest or dies, or until failure of his interest[3]. This would also give the beneficiary in question

1 Section 31(1)(ii).
2 Section 31(2).
3 Section 31(1)(ii). The beneficiary's right to income creates an interest in possession: *Swales v IRC* [1984] 3 All ER 16 at 24. See Chapter 13.

an interest in possession for inheritance tax purposes in the relevant share of the trust fund. This is explained further in Chapter 13. Although it is more common for an interest in possession to be expressly provided under the terms of the trust rather than to rely on section 31.

2 *Application of section 31 of the Trustee Act 1925*

11.27 The section only applies if the trust property carries the intermediate income and if there is no express contrary indication in the trust instrument, ie a direction to accumulate. (Essentially, for these purposes 'carrying the intermediate income' means that the income or interest produced by the trust property is to be applied for the benefit of the relevant beneficiary).

Where section 31 is applicable, the trustees must apply their discretion, rather than simply paying out the income automatically to the parent or guardian of the beneficiary[1]. The circumstances of the beneficiary should be reviewed regularly.

Since the power is discretionary, the court will not interfere with the trustees' discretion, so long as they exercised it bona fide[2].

Sums of income paid by trustees in the exercise of this discretionary power form part of the income of the beneficiary for tax purposes. An exception to this rule is in section 629 of the Income Tax (Trading and Other Income) Act 2005 where, if any income (or accumulated income) in excess of £100 is distributed to a minor and unmarried child of the settlor, during the settlor's lifetime, it will be taxed as the income of the settlor in the tax year in which the income is distributed.

The court has an inherent jurisdiction to allow a minor's trust property to be used for his maintenance. Usually the court will only apply income for this purpose, but it can also use capital from the trust. The court also has a statutory power to sell or otherwise deal with a minor's property to provide funds for his maintenance[3].

3 *Advancement – section 32 of the Trustee Act, 1925*

11.28 Older trusts often contained an express power for the trustees to raise and apply capital for the 'advancement' of any of the remaindermen (the persons entitled to the capital of the trust after the expiry of a life interest). In every post-1925 trust of, in effect, personal property, the statutory power of advancement applies by virtue of section 32 of the Trustee Act 1925, unless excluded by express words or necessary implication.

Modern trusts usually rely on the statutory power, making minor alterations, often with power to advance the whole instead of one half (as provided for in section 32) of the beneficiary's presumptive or vested share or interest.

1 *Wilson v Turner* (1883) 22 Ch D 521.
2 *Re Senior, Senior v Wood* [1936] 3 All ER 196.
3 Section 53.

An 'advancement' is strictly a payment out of capital, historically intended for the purpose of advancing a child in life, by for instance, enabling him to study for some profession or occupation, or to set him up in business. In view of the quite restricted meaning of 'advancement' it became more common in trusts to add the words 'or benefit' and this was adopted in section 32. More modern uses therefore include paying school fees, paying tax on behalf of the beneficiary, or in any other way using the capital to 'benefit' the beneficiary. A payment under section 32 is an advance distribution to the beneficiary of part of his expectant share. The power applies even if there is a possibility that the beneficiary's interest may be defeated but does not apply to a beneficiary who does not have an interest in capital, eg the life tenant.

In *Re Pauling's Settlement Trusts, Younghusband v Coutts & Co*[1], the Court of Appeal held that a power of advancement can be exercised only if there is some good reason for it – and the good reason must be beneficial to the person to be advanced. The power cannot be exercised capriciously or with some other benefit in view.

The other limitations of the statutory power of advancement are:

(1) the capital advanced must not exceed half the beneficiary's vested or presumptive share (unless expressly altered);

(2) when the beneficiary's interest vests, any advances must be brought into account in calculating his share ('hotchpot'); and

(3) the advance must not prejudice the prior life, or other, interest of any person (eg a life tenant) unless he is sui juris and gives his consent.

In *CD v O*[2] the court varied a trust of two life policies by extending the statutory power of advancement to the whole of a beneficiary's share in a fund.

I Other clauses

11.29 A trust may also contain some or all of the following clauses. Following the coming into force of the Trustee Act 2000, certain provisions (for example, regarding extending investment powers) are now automatically incorporated into trusts unless specifically excluded. Nevertheless, it is still common to see express provisions dealing with such matters:

(1) Trustees' indemnity clause. There have been several cases addressing the effectiveness of such clauses. *Armitage v Nurse*[3] and *Bogg v Raper*[4] indicated that such clauses were, surprisingly to many observers, firmly established in terms of their effectiveness unless the trustee had been 'dishonest'. Although in cases of doubt such clauses would be construed against a

1 [1963] 3 All ER 1.
2 [2004] EWHC 1036 (Ch).
3 [1998] Ch 241, [1997] 2 All ER 7095, CA.
4 (1998) Times, 22 April, CA

trustee seeking to rely on such a clause. See for example, *Wight v Olswang*[1]. However, this view was modified in *Walker v Stones*[2] where it was held that, at least in the case of a solicitor-trustee, it was necessary to take into account the fact that where the trustee's 'honest belief', though actually held, is so unreasonable that no reasonable solicitor-trustee could have thought that an action was for the benefit of the beneficiaries. Further, in *Twinsectra v Yardley and others*[3] a combined test was introduced. Here it was held that a solicitor would be liable as an accessory to a breach of trust if he acts dishonestly. This required that (a) his conduct was dishonest by the standards of ordinary and reasonable people, and (b) he himself realised by their standards this conduct was dishonest. In this case the solicitor was not also a trustee. In any event *Barlow Clowes International Limited v Eurotrust*[4] clarified that it was a purely objective test for the liability of accessories such as solicitors (as opposed to the liability of the trustee himself).

In *Fattal v Walbrook Trustees (Jersey) Ltd*[5] the test of dishonesty for professional trustees in relation to trustee exemption clause was confirmed. It was held that a subjective belief that a deliberate breach of trust was in the best interests of the beneficiaries was not enough to protect a professional trustee from a claim of dishonesty if that belief was not also objectively reasonable.

In December 2002 the Law Commission consulted on trustee exemption clauses. Their favoured proposal seemed to be that trust corporations and other 'professional' trustees[6] should not be able to exclude liability arising from 'negligence'. The final report was published on 19 July 2006. The report recommended that the trust industry adopt a non-statutory rule of practice which should be enforced (so far as this is possible) by the regulatory and professional bodies who govern and influence trustees and the drafters of trusts. The Law Society and the Institute of Chartered Accountants in England and Wales introduced regulation for their members. The Society of Trust and Estate Practitioners ('STEP') launched a version of the rule that will bind its members in England and Wales.

The recommended rule of practice governs the disclosure and explanation of clauses in trust instruments which have the effect of limiting or excluding liability for negligence. The rule requires paid trustees to take reasonable steps to ensure that settlors understand the meaning and effect of such clauses before including them in trust instruments. The Report recommended that trust drafters should also be subject to the rule. The Government announced in September 2010 that it accepted these recommendations.

1 (1998) Times, 17 September.
2 [2001] 2 WLR 623.
3 [2002] 2 AC 164.
4 [2005] UKPC 37.
5 [2010] EWHC 2767 (Ch).
6 Trustee Act 2000, s 28.

(2) Charging clause. Without an express clause trustees were historically not able to charge more than their out of pocket expenses[1]. Under the Trustee Act 2000, trust corporations and professional trustees are entitled to reasonable remuneration for their services to the trust, provided, in the case of professional trustees, that he is not a sole trustee and that each other trustee has agreed in writing to the remuneration[2]. This is the case even if the services are capable of being provided by a lay trustee. Clearly, an express charging clause could provide even greater flexibility.

(3) A clause specifying who has the power of appointing additional trustees.

(4) An investment clause. Until the Trustee Act 2000 such a clause was very important as the statutory investment provisions were comparatively limited (see below). It is still common to see a specific detailed investment clause set out in modern trusts.

(5) A specific power to effect insurance and to effect life assurance policies as investments. Again, the Trustee Act 2000 means that a specific provision to this effect is no longer necessary in trusts[3], although in practice they are often included.

J Society of Trust and Estate Practitioners ('STEP') Standard Provisions

11.30 A trust document can be extremely lengthy – there are many more administrative provisions which may be used in addition to those mentioned above. It is now possible to avoid this by incorporating a standard set of administrative provisions.

STEP have produced a standard form which may be incorporated by the words 'the standard provisions of the Society of Trusts and Estate Practitioners (1st edition) shall apply'. The standard form shortens the length of a document and reduces the risk of accidental omissions. However, many settlors and trustees prefer to have all the relevant provisions set out in full in the trust document and there may be additional clauses required by settlors (or not required as appropriate). Independent legal advice should be taken on this. A second edition of the Standard Provisions is under consideration.

SECTION 3 THE DUTIES AND POWERS OF TRUSTEES

11.31 The duties of a trustee are onerous, and must be strictly complied with if the trustee is not to commit a breach of trust and potentially be personally liable for any resulting loss to the trust. Both statute and case law impose many duties and powers which may be expressly amended by the terms of the trust.

1 Trustee Act 1925, s 30(2).
2 Sections 28 and 29.
3 Sections 3 and 34.

A Standard of care

11.32 The common law duty of care has largely been codified by the Trustee Act 2000, although the precise extent to which this codification extends is not entirely clear and is examined further below. The position at common law (which is not necessarily replaced) is that an unpaid and non-professional trustee must perform his duties and exercise his discretionary powers in accordance with certain standards of care. In discharging his *duties* the duty on the trustee is to take the same care as an ordinary prudent man of business would use in the management of his own private affairs[1]. When performing his *duties of investment*, however, the trustee has a slightly higher duty of care, that of a prudent man of business investing for persons for whom he felt morally obliged to provide[2].

If trustees are professional trustees, eg a solicitor or bank, and are paid for performing their duties, it is generally thought that an even higher standard is expected, that of the degree of care and skill which could reasonably be expected of persons with the same professional attributes as the trustees. A professional trustee is liable for loss through neglect to exercise the special care and skill it professes to have.

> *Bartlett v Barclays Bank Trust Co*[3]
>
> A settlement created in 1920 for the benefit of the settlor's wife and issue consisted of 99.8% of the debenture stock and shares in a private company. The bank was the trustee of the settlement. By 1960, following the death of the settlor and his wife, no beneficiary or member of the family was on the company's board, which comprised two surveyors, an accountant and a solicitor. No director regarded himself as the bank's representative. The bank did not attend the board's monthly meetings, and without the bank's knowledge the board embarked on two very hazardous property deals, one at Guildford and one at Old Bailey. The Guildford project succeeded, and the proceeds were used to invest in the Old Bailey project. It failed and the company suffered a large loss. As the board did not provide regular information to the bank and the bank was content to receive only that information it gleaned at annual general meetings, the bank was unaware of the hazardous nature of the property deals. The beneficiaries took proceedings against the bank for breach of trust. It was held that a prudent businessman would not have been content only with information from annual general meetings in the conduct of his own affairs. Moreover, the bank, as a professional corporate trustee owed a higher duty of care, and was liable for loss caused by failure to exercise the special care and skill which it professed to have. The bank was therefore held to be in breach of trust and was liable for the loss that had arisen. However, other cases have displayed a more lenient attitude towards professional trustees.

1 *Speight v Gaunt* (1883) 9 App Cas 1. See also *Bartlett v Barclays Bank Trust Co Ltd* [1980] 1 All ER 139.

2 *Learoyd v Whiteley* (1887) 12 App Cas 727.

3 [1980] 1 All ER 139.

> *Nestle v National Westminster Bank plc*[1]
>
> This case has been heavily criticised. The bank was sole trustee of a trust fund which achieved very little real growth over the investment period. The bank had not understood the clause in the trust instrument relating to the scope of its investment powers and had not taken steps at any time to obtain legal advice on the matter. The Court of Appeal held that the bank had failed in its duty to review the investments regularly and should have taken legal advice about the scope of its powers under the will which created the trust. Although it had failed in its duties, the bank was not liable to the plaintiff who failed to prove loss as a result of the bank's breaches of duty.

11.33 The statutory duty of care as set out in section 1 of the Trustee Act 2000, applies in the circumstances specified in Schedule 1. These are quite limited and include the exercise of investment powers, powers in relation to land, powers to compound liabilities, power to insure trust property and powers in relation to reversionary interests, valuations and audit. It also applies when trustees enter into arrangements for the appointment of agents, custodians or nominees and when reviewing their activities. It would appear from the way in which it is drafted that the duty only applies to acts and not to omissions, so for omissions the only action possible is for a breach of the common law duty of care (which does not seem to be wholly replaced by the new statutory provisions). Another feature of section 1 of the Trustee Act 2000 (in sub-section (1)) is that whilst the common law duty looks at objective standards of care, the statutory duty takes account of subjective factors[2] so differences could arise depending on whether a beneficiary's complaint relates to an act or omission.

The statutory duty of care does not apply to the extent that the trust instrument itself excludes its application[3].

Whenever the duty does apply the trustee must exercise such care and skill as is reasonable in the circumstances, having regard in particular to any special knowledge or experience that he has or holds himself out as having, and if he acts in the course of a business or profession he must have regard to any special knowledge or experience that it is reasonable to expect of a person acting in that kind of business or profession[4].

B Summary of main duties of the trustee

1 On acceptance of the trust

11.34 Assuming a person named as trustee accepts trusteeship then on accepting the trust, the trustee should immediately:

1 [1994] 1 All ER 118, CA.
2 Section 1(1)(a).
3 Schedule 1, para 7.
4 Section 1(1).

(1) make himself familiar with the terms of the trust, the contents of any document handed to him as trustee (including the trust instrument) and any relevant deeds or title papers and, generally make himself aware of the assets of the trust;

(2) (if this has not already happened) arrange for all of the trust property to be transferred into the joint names of himself and his co-trustees[1];

(3) investigate any circumstances indicating a possible prior breach of trust and, if necessary, seek to recover the trust fund if such a breach has occurred (for if he does not do this, he may be personally jointly liable);

(4) consider the investments.

2 *Possession and control of trust property*

11.35 The trustees (whether original or appointed subsequently) must immediately, on their appointment, obtain possession and control of the trust property by the appropriate legal method in relation to the particular property of the trust. For example, if the trust property is cash, the trustees should jointly open a bank account and pay in the cash; if it is land, they should obtain a conveyance; if it is stocks and shares, they should obtain the appropriate certificates or registration in the names of the trustees (in particular CREST is an electronic system which records share transactions and provides details of who owns shares without the need for a share certificate) and deposit bearer bonds with a bank where it will be held in their joint names; if it is a life assurance policy, they should obtain the policy and (where necessary) an assignment of it. They should serve notice on the life office and enquire from the life office about notice of any earlier assignments.

The trustees should retain control of the trust property separately from any of their own property. Where the money is paid into a personal bank account (whether intentional or not), the trustee will be deemed to have spent his own money before that of the trust[2].

(a) Vesting declarations

11.36 Section 40 of the Trustee Act 1925 removes the need in certain circumstances for a formal conveyance or other appropriate means of transferring the property of the trust from the old trustees to the new, or to the remaining trustees upon a retirement of other trustees. The section provides that, with some exceptions, and subject to any express provision to the contrary, if the appointment or retirement is by deed, it operates as if it contained a vesting declaration. It does not apply where the property is held by personal representatives, rather than trustees[3].

1 See 'Vesting declarations' at **11.35**.

2 *Re Hallett's Estate* [1880] 13 Ch D 696.

3 *Re Cockburn's Will Trusts* [1957] Ch 438, [1957] 2 All ER 522.

One of the exceptions set out in section 40(4) is that the automatic vesting declaration cannot extend to 'property which is only transferable…in a manner directed by or under Act of Parliament'. One view is that as life policies are assignable *at law* only as directed by the Policies of Assurance Act 1867, or section 136 of the Law of Property Act 1925, they are excluded from the automatic vesting provisions of section 40. However, a life policy is not *only* transferable in this way so it is thought that the exception would not apply to life policies. To avoid any doubt at all it is suggested that the deed contains a specific assignment of life policies.

3 *Duty not to profit from the trust*

11.37 'Equity prohibits a trustee from making any profit by his management, directly or indirectly'[1]. A trustee who acquires a benefit in his position as a trustee must surrender that benefit to the beneficiaries. This rule does not apply where the person who created the trust and appointed the trustee also grants the conflicting interest to that trustee[2].

4 *Duty against a conflict of interest or self-dealing*

11.38 A trustee must not put himself in the position where his duty to the trust and his own personal interest may conflict. This, in the view of the authors (unless the trust instrument expressly provides to the contrary), should require that independent intermediaries, representatives and appointed representatives refuse trusteeship of life policy trusts if investments are to be made upon their recommendations. They would, from the outset, be in a position of conflict and, in particular, ought properly to return any commission earned as a result of any trust investments made on their recommendation, although the precise terms of the trust instrument should be considered.

A trustee cannot generally purchase trust property for himself, even if he pays a fair price for it[3].

5 *Duty to maintain an even hand between the classes of beneficiaries*

11.39 The trustees must administer the trust honestly and impartially for the benefit of all the beneficiaries. Where the trust has life tenants (entitled to income) and remaindermen (entitled to capital), the trustee must keep an even balance between the respective interests, and in particular, ensure that their investment strategy does not favour one at the expense of the other. Where the life tenant and the remaindermen are the same then issues in this respect are less likely to arise. The position is of particular relevance to life assurance policies as they are not income producing assets so there may be concerns about balancing

1 *Regal Hastings Ltd v Gulliver* [1942] 1 All ER 378.
2 *Sargeant v National Westminster Bank plc* (1990) 61 P & CR 518, CA.
3 *Tito v Waddell (No 2)* [1977] 3 All ER 129.

the interests of beneficiaries under such trusts[1]. However, it is rare to specifically create a trust of a life policy with a life interest for one beneficiary with capital payable to a different beneficiary as the life tenant would not have any tangible benefit during his lifetime and is entitled to complain to the trustees that his interests are not being considered. For such trusts which hold a variety of assets the fact that a life policy is one of those assets will be a consideration for trustees when considering trust investments as it would need to be balanced with income producing assets.

6 *Duty to account*

11.40 Trustees must keep accounts[2] and produce them when requested by the beneficiaries. They must also give the beneficiaries all reasonable information as to the running of the trust and must allow inspection of any title deeds or other documents relating to the trust, if so requested.

7 *Duty to act unanimously*

11.41 Unless the trust instrument provides for a majority decision, the trustees must act unanimously; their decisions and actions must be undertaken by all the trustees, as one body[3].

8 *Duty to act personally and not delegate*

11.42 Each trustee must act in his personal capacity except to the extent that delegation is authorised, either by law or specifically by the trust instrument (or by the beneficiaries where they are all mentally capable and over the age of 18). For example, the trustees may wish to delegate investment management functions to an investment manager. There may be a specific power in the trust instrument, or the trustees can rely on the statutory powers to delegate set out in the Trustee Act 2000. The Trustee Act 2000 contains specific provisions regarding the appointment of asset managers by trustees (see further **11.44**).

Regarding appointment of an agent for other purposes, section 3(3) of the Enduring Powers of Attorney Act 1985 allowed a trustee to delegate his functions by using an enduring power of attorney. This was criticised on the basis that it did not involve as many of the safeguards for beneficiaries as a power of attorney under section 25 of the Trustee Act 1925. For example, under section 25, delegation is not permitted to a sole co-trustee and notice of the power of attorney must be given to the co-trustees. Under section 3(3), however, an appointment could be made to a sole co-trustee and notice was not required to be given to any party. Also, a section 3(3) delegation was indefinite. Further, a power of

1 *Re Fisher, Harris v Fisher* [1943] Ch 377.
2 *Springett v Dashwood* (1860) 2 Giff 521.
3 *Re Butlin's W.T* [1976] Ch 251; Law Reform Committee, 23rd Report, 'The Powers and Duties of Trustees' (1982, cmnd 8733) paras 3.60–3.65 – which recommended the retention of this rule.

attorney under section 25 will be extinguished upon the mental incapacity of the donor, whereas under section 3(3), the grant of the power can survive[1]. These unintended effects in the law were the subject of a Law Commission report, 'The Law of Trusts, Delegation by Individual Trustees'[2]. It examined the circumstances and manner in which an individual trustee should be authorised to delegate and made recommendations for change, contained in a draft Bill.

11.43 The Trustee Delegation Act 1999 implemented, with minor modifications, the changes recommended by the Law Commission in their report. It should be noted, however, that sections 1 and 2 only apply in respect of attorneys of trustees with beneficial interests in land. Section 4 of the Trustee Delegation Act 1999 repealed section 3(3) of the Enduring Powers of Attorney Act 1985 subject to various transitional provisions. The repeal implemented the policy that trustees should only be able to delegate their trustee functions by statute subject to the safeguards under section 25 of the Trustee Act 1925. This repeal ended the existence of the inconsistent but overlapping regimes for delegation by individual trustees and applies to all enduring powers of attorney (EPAs) created after the 1999 Act came into force[3].

A new section 25 of the Trustee Act 1925 was introduced by section 5 of the 1999 Act. Both the current and previous sections require that notice of appointment be given to specified persons and provide that the trustee remains liable for the acts and omissions of the attorney. The powers conferred under both current and previous sections can be excluded or restricted by specific provisions to that effect in the trust document. Section 5(1) of the 1999 Act sets out the new section 25. The power of attorney can define the period for which it is to be effective (subject to a 12-month maximum) but if nothing is stated then the default period is 12 months.

The new section 25(3) no longer prohibits a sole co-trustee being the donor of a section 25 power but this scenario is subject to the practical difficulties which would arise as a result of the application of the 'two-trustee' rules. Section 7 specifies the various 'two-trustee' rules (generally that moneys accruing to a trust should always be dealt with by two trustees) and that these cannot be satisfied by one person acting in two capacities.

A new prescribed form of power of attorney which may be used by a *single* trustee wishing to delegate all of his or her trustee functions in relation to a single trust to a single attorney is provided by section 25(6).

The Enduring Powers of Attorney Act was repealed and replaced by the Mental Capacity Act 2005 which provided for two types of Lasting Powers of Attorney and so no new EPAs can be created although those existing prior to the repeal of the Act and not yet registered may still be registered (see further Chapter 9).

11.44 The trustees' powers to *collectively* delegate under the 2000 Act are wide ranging. Trustees may delegate any of the defined 'delegable functions'.

1 For a discussion on powers of attorney generally, see Thurston *A Practitioners' Guide to Powers of Attorney* (7th edn, 2010).
2 Law Com No 220, January 1994.
3 Section 4(1).

With regard to non-charitable trusts these are any function other than (a) any function relating to whether or in what way trust assets should be distributed; (b) any power to decide whether fees or payments should be paid from capital or income; (c) power to appoint trustees; (d) any power to delegate or to appoint a nominee or custodian. For trustees of charitable trusts the definition is much narrower[1].

Almost anyone may be appointed as an agent except a beneficiary[2]. Where 'asset management functions' are delegated to an agent additional requirements are imposed. The appointment must be made in an agreement made or evidenced in writing. Furthermore, trustees must prepare a policy statement providing guidance to their agent as to how the delegated investment powers should be used. This must be done with a view to ensuring the powers are exercised 'in the best interests of the trust'. In addition, any agreement with an investment manager must have a confirmation that the investment manager will secure compliance with the Policy Statement and the trustees must assess whether the Policy Statement is being complied with. The trustees must also review the Policy Statement from time to time.

The trustee can specify the terms of the delegation including reasonable remuneration for services provided and reimbursement for expenses properly incurred. Certain terms can only be agreed so far as 'reasonably necessary'. These are sub-delegation, limitation of liability of the agent and acting despite conflicts of interest[3].

9 Duty to invest

11.45 The trustees must seek to safeguard the value of the trust property by investing it in accordance with the terms of the trust instrument or (if the trust is silent on this point) in accordance with the Trustee Act 2000. Until this this Act came into force on 1 February 2001 the relevant statutory provision was the Trustee Investments Act 1961. Unless the trust instrument contained wide investment powers, the trustees did not have power to invest in a life assurance policy under the 1961 Act. The provisions of the 2000 Act relating to investment are far-reaching and the 1961 Act has been repealed. There is a 'general power of investment' which enables them to make any investment they could make if they were absolutely entitled to the trust assets except land other than in loans secured on land[4]. It is sometimes stated that this empowers the trustees to invest in anything they like. However, this is not quite the case as this is subject to the 'standard investment criteria', the need to obtain and consider 'proper advice', and the imposition of the statutory duty of care on trustees exercising those duties. Trustees must have regard to the suitability of the investments and the need for diversification[5]. Trustees must further review the

1 Trustee Act, 2000, s 11.
2 Section 12(3).
3 Section 14(1) to (3).
4 Section 3(1).
5 Section 4.

trust instrument from time to time to consider any possible variations[1]. In considering suitability the trustees must firstly look at the type of investment to see if it is a good investment for the trust and then look at the specific investment of that type, taking into account such things as performance. Trustees must also obtain and consider proper advice[2] when reviewing the investments of the trust[3]. However, a trustee need not obtain such advice if he reasonably believes that in all the circumstances it is unnecessary or inappropriate to do so[4].

The general power of investment is in addition to powers otherwise conferred on trustees[5], but is also subject to any restriction or exclusion imposed by the trust instrument, or by any enactment or any subordinate legislation[6].

10 Nominees and custodians

11.46 The 2000 Act also contains provisions regarding nominees and custodians. Previously, there was no existing general power to use custodians and nominees so, for example, it was technically impossible to use CREST (an electronic settlement system for shares – see **11.35**), etc without an express power (although many trustees were prepared to accept the risk where the status of the nominee or custodian was such as to give them reasonable comfort). Sections 16–20 contain express powers in this respect. Writing is required and the statutory duty of care applies to the trustees in making such an appointment. Sections 16 and 17 (power to appoint custodians or nominees) do not apply where there is a 'custodian trustee'. There are restrictions on who can be a nominee or custodian. Only those who carry on such a business or a body corporate controlled by trustees can be nominees or custodians. As with a standard delegation certain aspects can only be agreed if reasonably necessary (sub-delegation, limitation of liability and conflicts of interest)[7].

With both the appointment of agents and the appointment of nominees and custodians there is a duty to review such arrangements[8]. Intervention must be considered if necessary and where relevant the 'policy statement' must be kept under review[9]. There is no general liability for the acts of agents etc appointed under the 2000 Act provided the duty of care is complied with[10]. Third parties have no need to check compliance with the terms of the 2000 Act[11].

1 Section 4(2).
2 Section 5(1).
3 Section 5(2).
4 Section 5(3).
5 Section 6(1)(a).
6 Section 6(1)(b).
7 Section 20.
8 Section 22.
9 Section 22(2).
10 Section 23(1).
11 Section 24.

11.47 Trustees must seek to obtain the best rate of return available irrespective of their own, or the beneficiaries', political, social or moral views[1].

11 Duty to consider powers

11.48 Whilst under a discretion as to whether or not to actually exercise their powers and under no duty to actually exercise them, the trustees are under a duty to actively consider whether or not to use them[2].

C Breach of trust

11.49 Failing to comply with any of their duties will constitute a breach of trust, for which the trustees will be personally, jointly and severally liable. A defence may be available under section 61 of the Trustee Act 1925, which provides that the court may relieve, in whole or in part, a trustee's potential liability if he has acted honestly and reasonably and ought fairly, in all the circumstances, to be excused.

1 Indemnity

11.50 An indemnity may be available under section 62 of the Trustee Act 1925 if the breach of trust is at the instigation, request, or with the consent in writing of a beneficiary. In this case, the court may impound all or any part of the particular beneficiary's interest in the trust property by way of indemnity to the trustee. This provision, however, will not be allowed to benefit a trustee who is also a beneficiary.

2 Participation, consent, release or acquiescence by the beneficiaries

11.51 If they are sui juris (having full legal capacity), such consensus will prevent the beneficiaries from bringing a claim against the trustees[3].

D Powers

11.52 Various powers are conferred upon trustees by statute and the trust instrument may (and often will) extend or alter these. Apart from the powers of maintenance and advancement already considered, the Trustee Act 1925 gives, for example, powers of sale; power to give receipts; power to insure; power to partition property; powers of compromise, etc. The Trustee Delegation Act 1999 and the Trustee Act 2000 have also expanded the trustee's statutory powers.

1 See *Cowan v Scargill* [1985] Ch 270 and *Harries v Church Comrs for England* [1993] 2 All ER 300.
2 *Re Hay's Settlement Trust* [1981] 3 All ER 786.
3 *Fletcher v Collis* [1905] 2 Ch 24.

The full range of powers may be detailed in the trust instrument or the settler may simply rely on the general law although this would be unusual in an express trust. As mentioned, a set of standard powers may be incorporated by using STEP's short form.

E Position of the beneficiaries

11.53 The beneficiaries cannot, generally, control the trustees while the trust remains in being. The trustees are guided by the trust instrument, the rules of equity and statutory provisions, and in the exercise of their functions they are entitled to use their own judgment and are not ordinarily obliged to consult the beneficiaries[1].

The beneficiaries do have a right to compel proper administration of the trust either by insisting on an audit of the accounts by a solicitor or accountant acceptable to the trustees[2], or by making an application to the court for the determination of a specific question[3] or for the general administration of the trust[4].

If the beneficiaries are sui juris and together entitled to the whole beneficial interest they can put an end to the trust and direct the trustees to hand over the trust property[5].

SECTION 4 DEALINGS WITH LIFE POLICIES IN TRUST

A Introduction

11.54 Dealings with the trust property by the trustees should only be effected:

(1) under a direction or authority in the trust itself, which may be express or implied;

(2) by direction of the beneficiaries, being sui juris and between them entitled to the whole beneficial interest;

(3) under the authority of statute; or

(4) by order of the court.

1 Authorisation in the trust instrument

11.55 In many cases it will be clear from the trust instrument that the trustees can authorise or enter into the proposed transaction. Where a trust of a life policy

1 *Re Brockbank, Ward v Bates* [1948] 1 All ER 287.
2 Public Trustee Act 1906, s 13.
3 CPR Part 64, para 1.
4 CPR Part 64, rule 2(1).
5 *Saunders v Vautier* (1841) 4 Beav 115.

has been created using one of the life office's standard trust forms, the life office should ideally still check the terms of that trust, as the settlor may have altered the standard terms to suit his particular circumstances. Pragmatically, time and resource issues may make this unrealistic and unless the proposed transaction is unusual or the life office has notice that the trustees are clearly acting in breach of trust the risks to the life office will usually be small.

If the trust instrument specifically authorises the trustees to carry out the transaction, the life office may safely accept the trustees' discharge or request, subject however to any notice of the purpose of the transaction being inconsistent with the purposes of the trust.

B Trustees' powers to deal with life policies

1 Power to sell or mortgage

11.56 In modern times trustees will almost always be given express power to sell or mortgage by the trust instrument and, in any event, this may be possible under statute for property 'in possession'[1]. (However, see **11.58** below.)

2 Power to surrender

11.57 A modern trust instrument will usually give the trustees a power (either specific or general) to sell or surrender the policy and hold the proceeds as part of the trust property or to exercise any options under the policy (although sometimes the power to exercise options, make investment switches, etc is reserved by the settlor to himself). From *Re Steen Trusts, Steen v Peebles*[2] it would seem that a trustee may, without a specific power, surrender a life policy in exchange for a fully paid up policy of less value in cases where the party liable to pay the premiums is unable to do so.

Where a trustee has an express power of sale, but not expressly a power to surrender, it is thought that the power of sale is sufficient to authorise the trustees to surrender the policy as a surrender is in substance a sale of the policy to the life office but the matter is not entirely free from doubt.

3 Power to raise money by sale, mortgage, etc

11.58 Section 16 of the Trustee Act 1925 provides:

> 'Where trustees are authorised by the instrument, if any, creating the trust or by law to pay or apply capital money subject to the trust for any purpose or in any manner, they shall have and shall be deemed always to have had power to raise the money required by sale, conversion, calling in or mortgage of all or any part of the property for the time being in possession.'

1 Eg Trustee Act 1925, s 16.
2 (1890) 25 LR Ir 544.

This section applies notwithstanding anything contrary contained in the trust instrument (but does not apply to certain types of trust such as charitable trusts).

A policy is, however, unlikely to be treated as 'property in possession' within the meaning of section 16 of the Trustee Act 1925: 'All personal things are either in possession or in action. The law knows no *tertium quid* between the two'. (A 'tertium quid' essentially being a third possibility[1].) A policy is a chose in action, ie a thing of which the owner does not have the possession, but only a right to recover it by a suit or action at law. Cash in a person's pocket is an example of a thing in possession.

'Property' is defined by section 68 of the Trustee Act 1925 as including real and personal property, any thing in action, and any other right or interest, whether in possession or not. 'Possession' is defined as including receipt of rents or profits, or the right to receive the same, if any. A life policy does not produce an income[2], although it is clear that there can be an interest in possession in a policy even though it produces no income[3].

In view of the provisions of section 16 it cannot be relied on as conferring a power to sell, surrender or mortgage a policy and so a settlor should expressly provide for this in the trust document although section 3 of the Trustee Act may assist (see **11.59** below).

4 *Power of sale implied in order to invest*

11.59 Section 3 of the Trustee Act 2000 enables any kind of investment to be made by a trustee as if he were absolutely entitled. It is probably reasonable to conclude that he would have an implied power to sell the current trust assets in order to make an investment.

5 *Powers to raise money to pay tax*

11.60 Under section 212 of the Inheritance Tax Act 1984, where a trustee is liable for inheritance tax, he has the power to sell or mortgage or create a terminable charge on the property to which the inheritance tax is attributable in order to raise the amount of the tax and any interest and expenses properly incurred by him in respect of the tax. Section 212(3) further enables any money held on the trusts of a settlement to be expended in paying the inheritance tax attributable to the value of any property comprised in the settlement and held on the same trusts.

6 *Protection to purchasers and mortgagees dealing with trustees*

11.61 Section 17 of the Trustee Act 1925 provides that a purchaser or mortgagee paying or advancing money on a sale or mortgage purporting to be made

1 *Colonial Bank v Whinney* (1885) 30 Ch D 261, per Fry LJ.
2 *Re Fisher, Harris v Fisher* [1943] 2 All ER 615.
3 See Chapter 14.

under a trust or power vested in trustees shall not be concerned to see that the money is necessary, or that no more than is necessary is raised, or otherwise as to its application. It may be arguable that a life office would be a 'purchaser' when, for example, making payment out on a surrender or claim.

7 Power to borrow

11.62 The trust instrument will often confer on the trustees a specific power to borrow to pay the premiums in respect of a life policy. Such a power is in any case implied if the trustees have no funds to keep up a policy which is in danger of lapse[1]. If a trustee pays a premium with his own funds, he will have a lien on the policy for the amount of the premium[2]. A voluntary payment by a third party is not, however, sufficient to give a lien[3].

8 Liens on premiums

11.63 In *Re Smith's Estate, Bilham v Smith*[4], B effected an endowment assurance on his life under the Married Women's Property Act 1882 for the absolute benefit of his wife (W). W died, but B maintained the policy until maturity. He died shortly after maturity and his second wife, as his executrix, claimed a lien on the policy money for premiums paid by B after W's death. It was held that the claim of the executrix on behalf of B's estate was enforceable. It was for money expended by B as a trustee to preserve the property of a beneficiary[5].

It is thought that no lien would be acquired if B had continued paying premiums after the death of W with the intention of benefiting the persons entitled through her. If, therefore, a husband (or other person in such circumstances) does not wish to acquire a lien, he should take steps to see that there is evidence available as to his intention. Some life offices incorporate in their forms of proposal and request for trust policies, a declaration by the proposer that no premiums he may pay shall give rise to a lien, it being his intention in paying them to make a gift to the persons beneficially entitled to the policy.

9 Power to raise a loan on the security of a policy

11.64 Assuming there is the right (or facility) to raise a loan on the security of the policy from the life office in the policy terms this is sometimes restricted to the 'absolute owners' of policies. This may not include trustees, even if the trust instrument provides that they shall have the investment power of an absolute owner on the basis that they hold the legal, but not the beneficial, interest. The trust instrument may, however, specifically authorise the trustees to raise money

1 *Clack v Holland* (1854) 19 Beav 262, 24 LJ Ch 13.
2 *Re Smith's Estate, Bilham v Smith* [1937] 3 All ER 472.
3 See *Re Leslie, Leslie v French* (1883) 23 Ch D 552 and *Re Jones' Settlement, Stunt v Jones* [1915] 1 Ch 373.
4 [1937] 3 All ER 472.
5 See also *Re Roberts* [1946] Ch 1.

in this fashion. The trust instrument and the policy terms should therefore be examined closely.

10 Power to exercise options

11.65 Where the policy contains options they will also form part of the trust property and the trustees must exercise them for the benefit of the beneficiaries under the trust, and not so as to defeat their interests. The rights conferred by the options are part of the assets of the trust, unless specifically excluded (sometimes the settlor reserves the right in the trust to exercise these). In *Re Fleetwood's Policy*[1] the settlor exercised an option to surrender the policy and it was held that the trusts continued to attach to the resulting surrender value, which consequently had to remain in court until it was clear who was entitled to it.

In *Re Policy of Equitable Life Assurance Society of the United States and Mitchell*[2] a policy had been effected in favour of a named wife, if living, at the life assured's death, or if she was not living then for his children, and if none survived him, for his executors, administrators or assigns. The named wife and one child died. The assured remarried and assigned all his property to a trustee for his creditors. The trustee proposed to exercise the option of taking the cash value of the policy for the benefit of the creditors. The court decided that the options could be exercised by the assured only as trustee for the beneficiaries under the policy, and that the proper course was to issue a paid-up policy for the benefit of the children who survived the life assured, but if none survived, then for his estate.

11 Power of trustees to exercise contractual rights

11.66 If, under the policy, the assured has a right to surrender, convert to a paid-up assurance, raise a loan or exercise an option, it seems that his right to do any of those things will pass to the trustees of a trust to which the policy is subject. It seems, therefore, that, unless they are expressly prohibited, the trustees are entitled to exercise any such right in the policy in whatever manner they think is most beneficial to the beneficiaries, unless the exercise of the option would be inconsistent with the purposes of the trust. It is also possible for the settlor to specifically retain for himself in the trust the right to exercise certain options.

Most trusts give the trustees specific power or powers to deal generally with the policy or other trust assets and so in practice there is unlikely to be an issue. Assuming the trustees have the necessary powers it is for the trustees to decide how they shall exercise their powers and the life office is not concerned with their reasons unless it has notice that a breach of trust is intended, or that the proposed transaction is inconsistent with the trust purposes, in which case it should be concerned as a potential constructive trustee.

1 [1926] Ch 48.
2 (1911) 27 TLR 213.

An alternative (but not generally held) view, however, is that trustees can only exercise a contractual right under a policy if they are specifically authorised to do so by their trust instrument or otherwise (see **11.56–11.65** above).

12 Power to compound liabilities

11.67 Under section 15 of the Trustee Act 1925, a personal representative, two or more trustees acting together or (where authorised by the trust instrument or by statute) a sole trustee, are given a wide discretion to settle claims (and ancillary matters) which may be made by third parties against the trust or vice versa. Section 15 of the Act is not concerned with disputes arising within the trust.

Without such a wide power the trustees might be obliged to litigate every possible claim in order not to be in breach of trust. Section 15 only protects trustees who have acted or at least exercised an active discretion and will not relieve them where they have ignored the claim[1]. The trustees may apply to the court for directions or to sanction a compromise where the court will consider the most desirable compromise as is fair between all the beneficiaries[2].

There are differences of opinion as to whether section 15 allows the trustees, in exercise of their wide powers of compromise, to surrender a policy. In the absence of authority, it seems unsafe to rely on this section alone (albeit that in the authors' opinion the section appears wide enough to permit this). In *Wrightson v IRC*[3], it seems to have been accepted that because there was no power in the settlement to surrender the policies, the trustees could not do so; it was not suggested in argument that there might be power under section 15 of the Trustee Act 1925, or any other statutory provision.

13 Maintaining the policy

11.68 The trust instrument may include any of the following provisions:

(1) A covenant by the settlor to pay the premiums; if the policy should become voidable, to restore it; and, if it should lapse, to effect a further policy for the amount which would have been payable at death under the lapsed policy. This is a rare provision for a settlor to impose upon himself in view of the fact that he would be subjecting himself to an onerous obligation and is more likely to arise in commercial or dispute settlement situations.

(2) A power to the trustees to pay the premiums out of the income or capital of the trust fund if the settlor fails to pay them.

(3) A proviso that the trustees shall not be responsible for seeing that the policy is kept up and that it shall not be a breach of trust for them to allow it to lapse or become void.

1 *Re Greenwood* (1911) 105 LT 509.
2 *Re Earl of Stafford, Royal Bank of Scotland v Byng* [1979] 1 All ER 513, CA.
3 *Wrightson v IRC* [1957] 2 All ER 745.

Trustees are not bound to pay the premiums under a settled policy where they have no funds available to enable them to do so but, if they have funds available, they have power to use them to pay premiums if the policy would otherwise lapse. If they pay them out of their own funds they will usually be entitled to be indemnified out of the trust property for the amount they have paid out[1]. If the assured does not pay the premiums and the trustees cannot do so, they must take whatever course is likely to be in the best interest of the beneficiaries. It might be in their interest that the policy be converted into a paid-up assurance. If the policy can be fully maintained, this is likely to be more advantageous to the beneficiaries than conversion to a paid-up assurance, for example if the life assured were to die whilst the policy was in force.

14 Dealings with the policy at the direction of beneficiaries

11.69 Even if not authorised by the trust instrument, or by statute, surrenders and other dealings with policies are possible provided that the persons entitled to the beneficial interest are all ascertained, and are of full age and capacity, and all of them concur in the transaction[2].

In *Re Smith, Public Trustee v Aspinall*[3], the trustees held property upon trust at their discretion to pay or apply income or capital for the maintenance or support of a wife, with trusts over for the children. All the beneficiaries were ascertained and of full capacity. It was held that the trustees must give effect to a mortgage of the trust assets executed by the beneficiaries, who were able if they wished to require the trustees to hand over the trust fund to them.

It has also been accepted by the Court of Appeal that this principle is capable of applying in the case of a pension trust (but in the case in question did not apply because it could not be said to own the whole of the beneficial interest in the pension fund)[4].

15 Powers of the court

11.70 Under section 57 of the Trustee Act 1925, where a sale, mortgage, surrender or other disposition of the policy, or other transaction, is, in the opinion of the court, expedient but the trustees have no power to effect it, the court may by order confer upon the trustees the necessary power for the purpose.

16 Settlor's powers of revocation

11.71 It is a common misconception that the trust (and its assets) is in some way 'owned' by the settlor and so he can therefore do what he wants with it.

1 *Re Smith's Estate, Bilham v Smith* [1937] 3 All ER 472 (but see *Clack v Holland* (1854) 19 Beav 262, 273, 277).

2 *Saunders v Vautier* (1841) 4 Beav 115.

3 [1928] Ch 915.

4 *Thorpe v Her Majesty's Revenue & Customs* [2010] EWCA Civ 339.

However, once the settlor has constituted a valid trust of the policy he has given up control of the policy which is then owned by the trustees to deal with in accordance with the terms of the trust. It is open to the settlor to reserve the right to withdraw the policy from the trust or otherwise benefit from the policy by including appropriate provisions in the trust. This is subject to the trust not being held to be a 'sham'[1]. In most trusts of life policies the settlor is also usually a trustee and so may exercise a degree of control in that capacity even where he does not wish to retain any beneficial interest.

17 The extent of the trust property

11.72 It is a question of construction as to the extent of the trust property. In most cases there is little doubt that the whole of the policy and anything deriving from it or accruing to it is the subject of the trust. However, doubt can arise, for example, where the trust is not clearly worded as to whether bonus payments are subject to the trust or are retained by the settlor[2]. It may also be the case that the settlor only intended to declare a trust of something less that the whole policy benefits.

18 Summary

11.73 Policies held by trustees may be surrendered or otherwise dealt with by the trustees alone if power to do so is conferred on them by the trust instrument or by statute. Probably, a right to surrender set out in the policy can be exercised by trustees, even in the absence of specific power in the trust instrument provided that its exercise is not inconsistent with the trust purposes. In the case of policies specifically settled, however, it may be inconsistent with the purposes of the trust for the trustees to surrender the policy in the absence of an express power to this effect. Any transaction may, however, be carried out if the beneficiaries are all ascertained and sui juris and they all join with the trustees in effecting it; or the transaction may be carried out if authorised by the court under section 57 of the Trustee Act 1925.

C Dealings with the beneficial interest in trust policies

1 Assignments

11.74 A beneficiary may deal with his interest in the policy in the same way and under the same conditions as he could deal with any interest under a trust. The assignee or mortgagee of such an interest should serve notice on the trustees of the policy.

1 See, for example, *Rahman v Chase Bank (CI) Trust Co Ltd* [1991] JLR 103.
2 *Gilly v Burley* (1856) 22 Beav 619; *Roberts v Edwards* (1863) 9 Jur (NS) 1219.

D Claims by trustees: examination of title[1]

11.75 When a claim under a life policy is made by trustees at death or maturity or on surrender, the trust document and all deeds of appointment or retirement of trustees should be produced to the life office. If they are in order, the life office may safely pay the policy moneys to the trustees, unless it has knowledge of an intended breach of trust. If the life office has such knowledge, it should not pay out, as it may subsequently find itself liable as a constructive trustee for any loss suffered by the beneficiaries.

Where any appointment of new trustees has been made by the survivors or survivor of two or more persons in whom the power to appoint new trustees was vested, evidence of death of the deceased appointor or appointors should be produced.

If a trustee dies, the surviving trustee(s) will continue. When the last remaining trustee, or sole trustee, dies, the trust property will devolve upon his personal representatives[2]. The person on whom the deceased trustee's estate devolves cannot be compelled to act in the trusts which have devolved upon him[3], nor can he insist upon doing so against the wishes of a donee of a power of appointing new trustees in place of the deceased trustee(s)[4].

If the claim is made by the personal representatives of a last surviving trustee, evidence of the deaths of trustees should be produced, together with the grant of representation to the estate of the last survivor.

Where the trustees apply to surrender a policy, to convert it to a paid-up assurance, to borrow on its security or to exercise any option, the life office should satisfy itself: (1) as to the title of the trustees, (2) that they have the power to carry out the desired transactions, and (3) that the office has no notice that the power is being exercised for a purpose not permitted by the trust instrument or otherwise.

1 Notice of breach of trust

11.76 If the life office is satisfied that the trustees have power to effect a proposed transaction, it is entitled, in the absence of notice to the contrary, to assume this is consistent with the general purposes of the trust. But where it is apparent from the trust instrument itself that the trustees' actions are inconsistent with the trust purposes, or where the office is aware that a breach of trust is intended, it should not agree to the trustees' request. If the life office agreed, it could be liable as a constructive trustee if it had actual or constructive knowledge of the breach.

In most cases, however, it is probable that there would be some trust purpose that could be served by the particular transaction. So long as there is some such purpose which could be served, the life office is under no obligation to enquire what that particular purpose is, and still less to satisfy itself that the proposed

1 For a general discussion on this subject see Chapter 9.
2 Trustee Act 1925, s 18(2).
3 *Re Benett* [1906] 1 Ch 216; see also *Re Ridley* [1904] 2 Ch 774 and the cases cited therein.
4 *Re Routledge's Trusts* [1909] 1 Ch 280.

course of action is the best one in the circumstances. In some cases, the life office may require the beneficiaries to join in the transaction. In seeking to protect its own position and in looking to provide a service to its customers the life office cannot of course act as a legal adviser to the trustees and must confine itself to remarking upon its own position although this may have the associated effect of assisting the trustees in understanding their own position. If the life office knows the purpose for which the money or the transaction is required, it should satisfy itself that it is within the terms of the trust. A life office paying money to the trustees with knowledge that it will be applied in breach of trust will not get a good discharge. In practice, the life office will rarely know any information beyond the identity of the trustees.

The life office will wish to seek to avoid any questions being raised regarding its conduct. So where it has notice of dispute it should proceed with caution, perhaps delaying payment until all parties have reached agreement.

2 *Method of payment*

11.77 Normally, payment should be made to *all* the trustees (or on the instructions of all the trustees). Although a sole trustee would appear to have a statutory power to give a complete discharge to the life office conferred by section 14 of the Trustee Act 1925 provided land is not included. It provides that the receipt in writing of *a* trustee for any money, securities or other personal property or effects payable, transferable or deliverable to him under any trust or power shall be a sufficient discharge to the person paying, transferring, or delivering the same and shall effectually exonerate him for any loss or misapplication thereof. Section 14 applies, notwithstanding anything to the contrary in the instrument (if any) creating the trust[1].

Where there is more than one trustee, it is not entirely certain whether it is sufficient for one trustee to give a receipt, or whether all trustees must join in the receipt. The section clearly refers to *a* trustee. However, this does conflict with the fundamental principle that trustees must act unanimously. Further, certain texts[2] also state that only a receipt by *all* the trustees will give a good discharge to a purchaser. The texts which support this view cite cases in support[3] which were decided prior to the passing of the Trustee Act 1925. The safest course to take where there is more than one trustee is for the life office to insist on the receipt of all of them, unless the trust instrument allows a majority of trustees to give a good receipt and discharge or possibly even one of their number.

Instead of acting personally, the trustees may[4] employ and pay an agent to exercise any or all of their 'delegable functions'. This does not include, for example, deciding whether or in what way any assets of the trust should be distributed. There may, of course, be an express power relating to delegation.

1 Section 14(3).
2 See *MacGillivray and Parkington on Insurance Law* (11th edn, 2010).
3 *Lee v San key* (1872) LR 15 Eq 204, *Re Flower and Metropolitan Board of Works* (1884) 27 Ch D 592.
4 Trustee Act 2000, s 11.

A life office must accordingly pay, for example, an agent or solicitor who, by producing the policy and the receipt, gives evidence of his appointment as agent to receive the money.

A personal representative is a trustee within the meaning of the Trustee Act 2000[1]. It is clear that, on express direction in writing from the trustees, the life office can pay a solicitor, banker, stockbroker or similar professional person. It should not ordinarily, however, pay to:

(1) just one of the trustees, who is not a solicitor, banker or stockbroker or similar professional person;

(2) a bank, if the account to be credited is not the account of the trustees or of their appropriate professional agent; or

(3) a beneficiary

unless, perhaps, the life office is satisfied that the payment is being made in the due course of the performance of the trusts, or the terms of the policy[2] and that there have been no dealings with the beneficial interest of which the trustees or the life office have notice and which is inconsistent with such payment. It is, of course, possible that the life office may take a pragmatic view regarding payment where the sum of money at stake is not large and there is nothing which otherwise arouses suspicion.

Where the trustees receive money as a result of any transaction, eg on surrender, they must pay or apply it in accordance with the provisions of the trust instrument or their statutory powers (eg of maintenance or advancement), or invest it as part of the trust fund, unless the beneficiaries being sui juris and between them entitled to the whole beneficial interest, direct otherwise.

E Trust policies and cancellation

11.78 The requirements for an insurer to issue a cancellation notice are explained in Chapter 5. There is nothing in statute or the regulations or rules (in particular COBS 15) which explain the consequences of a cancellation by the proposer of a policy which has been written under trust from the outset. The following is therefore only one possible view. The right to cancel would appear to be vested in the proposer as the cancellation rights vest in the 'consumer' under the COBS Rules. It is difficult to see how the trustees could be viewed as the 'consumer' in this context. The trust is properly and completely constituted prior to the expiration of the cancellation period (as the trust property is in existence). The proposer's (consumer's) right to cancel does not affect the validity of the trust (albeit that the trust could subsequently have no trust property if cancellation rights were exercised and so would cease as a result).

Assuming that the proposer is under no contractual liability to maintain the policy (which might arise in the case, for example, of cross partnership or share-

1 Section 35.

2 See *O'Reilly v Prudential Assurance Co Ltd* [1934] All ER Rep 672.

holder policies) there will be no breach of duty if the proposer serves a notice of cancellation in respect of a trust policy. The beneficiary of the trust takes the beneficial interest in the trust property subject to all the restrictions and provisions attaching to it, including the power vested in the proposer to cancel the policy during the cancellation period.

Where the insurer returns sums to the proposer from cancellation of a trust policy, the question arises as to the capacity in which the proposer holds the returned sums. Much here depends upon a proper construction of the trust instrument. No general statement can be given in view of the variety of trust wordings in use. One view is that the returned sums would not normally constitute trust property because the settlor intended to declare a trust of a life policy at the outset, so that intention is not fulfilled with the result that the trust fails. However, it can also be argued that a policy was in existence and the proceeds are therefore trust assets. The life office discharges its legal duties on returning the premiums and any other appropriate sums to the 'consumer'[1], who will be the proposer. The cancellation rules would benefit from clarification in this respect as they do not sit happily with established principles of trust law.

It is considered that the right of cancellation expires on the proposer's death as there is no one who would be a 'consumer' and the COBS rules do not specifically provide for the right to cancel to survive the consumer's death. It is also thought that the power to cancel vested in the proposer is personal to him and is not capable of assignment.

SECTION 5 THE APPOINTMENT, RETIREMENT AND REMOVAL OF TRUSTEES

A Who can be a trustee?

11.79 In general, any individual, limited company or other body able to hold property may be appointed a trustee. Apart from persons under 18 there is no statutory prohibition upon the appointment of any person as a trustee. However, there are some persons who, whilst they have the legal capacity, are undesirable as trustees and a court may, upon application by a beneficiary or co-trustee, remove them if they are appointed, eg:

(1) if there is financial irresponsibility leading to bankruptcy[2],

(2) if there is conviction of crimes involving dishonesty[3];

(3) where the business of the trustee would conflict with the interests of the beneficiaries (but this does not mean that a trustee cannot be a beneficiary)[4].

1 COBS 15.4.4 R
2 *Re Barker's Trusts* (1875) 1 Ch D 43.
3 *Coombes v Brookes* (1871) LR 12 Eq 61.
4 *Re Parsons, Barnsdale and Smallman v Parsons* [1940] 4 All ER 65.

It is common for banks, insurers, solicitors, accountants and other financial services organisations to establish 'in house' trust companies for either their own internal purposes or for commercial reasons.

B Number of trustees

1 Maximum

11.80 For trusts of property such as life policies (there are different provisions for land, etc), there is no legal restriction on the number which may be appointed and also hold legal title to the particular property except as provided by section 36(6) of the Trustee Act 1925 relating to the appointment of additional trustees (which restricts the number of trustees to four). The application of this subsection can be disapplied by the express terms of the trust instrument.

2 Minimum

11.81 One trustee is sufficient except where it is necessary to give a good receipt for the purchase money of land in England or Wales (unless that sole trustee is a trust corporation). At least two trustees must remain after the retirement of a trustee under section 39 of the Trustee Act 1925 or after the discharge of a trustee under section 37(1)(c) (except where only one trustee was originally appointed).

C Appointment of first and new trustees

1 First (or additional) trustees

11.82 When an inter vivos (ie set up during lifetime) trust is created, the settlor will usually appoint the first trustees which is usually himself and such additional trustees as the settlor selects at the outset. The settlor will almost certainly give someone the power to appoint further trustees or he may reserve the power himself. But if he makes any future appointment under that power he will do so because he is the person named or specified in the trust instrument as having that power, and not simply because he is the settlor.

2 Effective vesting of policy in first trustees of life policy trusts

11.83 It is common practice to appoint additional trustees from the outset, in the same document used to declare the trust perhaps with a direction to issue the policy to the trustees (usually the settlor and the additional trustees). In the case of new policies the question arises whether or not such an appointment will result in the legally effective vesting of title to the policy in the trustees.

Where an existing policy is assigned to an existing trust, there will be existing trustees, in whom the policy will vest so long as it is properly assigned. Where an existing life policy is to be subject to a new declaration of trust, the settlor may assign the policy to the trustees (one of which may be the settlor himself). Often, even without any conveyance or assignment, the declaration of trust and appointment of trustees will be by way of deed and so the title to the policy will automatically vest in the trustees by reason of section 40 of the Trustee Act 1925.

Where, however, the trust is created by using what has been termed a 'trust request', whereby the proposer requests the life office to effect and issue the policy to him and the additional trustees, on trust, there is a school of thought that there will be no effective vesting of title of the policy in the additional trustees as, at the time of the appointment, the policy is 'future property', which is not, in law, capable of being assigned. This might, it is argued, require a subsequent, formal assignment of the policy (once it is in existence) to the trustees in order for the life office to recognise their status as trustees. The question would seem to concern the precise legal position of the trustees in relation to the life office and the beneficiaries. Even if legal title to the policy may not be technically vested in the trustees this does not affect the fact that they have been validly appointed as trustees by the settlor. The terms of the policy would require payment to be made to the trustees so the life office is doing no more than complying with its contractual duties in making payment to them[1]. Once payment has been made to the trustees they would be required to account to the beneficiaries (in the same way as they would be if the policy had been properly vested in them) at the very least on the basis that they were trustees de son tort.

11.84 The effect of the Contracts (Rights of Third Parties) Act 1999 could also be of relevance here in that where a contract expressly provides that a third party is able to enforce a term of the contract or the term in question purports to confer a benefit on him then such third party may enforce such a term. However, it is open to the parties to exclude the effects of the Act and so would very much depend on the policy wording..

Another possible route which could be used to deal with the possible non-vesting issues is for the settlor (who is clearly a trustee) to appoint the additional trustees as his agents under the trust. Whilst the policy is not vested in such additional trustees in their capacity as such they would nevertheless be in a position to deal with the trust property in their capacity as agents of the settlor.

In practice, the authors are not aware of the technical issues surrounding vesting of life policies in additional trustees ever having been a contentious issue and the question currently appears to be a purely academic one.

Where a new policy is effected in accordance with the Married Women's Property Act 1882, the statutory provisions provide for the effective vesting of property in the trustees (see Chapter 12).

3 Appointment of new trustees

11.85 A will or trust instrument will usually name the persons entitled to appoint new trustees. If the document is silent on this point, the statutory

1 *Re Schebsman decd* [1944] 1 Ch 83.

provisions apply. Section 36(1)(b) of the Trustee Act 1925 provides that 'the surviving or continuing trustees or trustee for the time being, or the personal representatives of the last surviving or continuing trustee' may, in writing, appoint a new trustee or trustees in place of an outgoing trustee.

A common approach in trusts of life policies is to expressly give the power of appointing additional trustees to the settlor during his lifetime and to the trustees for the time being thereafter.

Unless there is a contrary provision in the trust instrument, the section 36 power provides that a *replacement* trustee may be appointed where the trustee:

(1) is dead;

(2) remains outside the UK for a continuous period exceeding 12 months (this ground is often expressly excluded);

(3) wants to retire;

(4) refuses to act or disclaims before accepting office;

(5) is unfit to act;

(6) is incapable of acting (this includes physical and mental illness, old age and in the case of a corporation, dissolution);

(7) is an infant; or

(8) is removed under a power in the trust instrument.

A common issue facing life offices when being asked to make payment under a life policy under trust is that not all of the trustees are available to give a discharge to the life office. This may be for a variety of reasons, for example, they are refusing to act or they simply cannot be found. The latter presents a particular difficulty if there is no express power of removal as this does not fit neatly into any of the above categories. It may be that the sum of money at stake is relatively small or the beneficiaries are clearly established in which case the life office may take a pragmatic view in making payment out at the direction of the available trustees. However, a 'missing' trustee may also raise the suspicions of the life office (for example he may not actually be untraceable but simply disagrees with the other trustees). In appropriate circumstances the life office may seek an indemnity from the acting trustees or possibly seek the directions of the court.

Under section 36(6) of the Trustee Act, 1925, an appointment may be made without replacement provided there are no more than three current trustees. This may be amended by the specific terms of the trust.

4 Method of appointment under section 36

11.86 An appointment under section 36 of the Trustee Act 1925 is merely required to be in writing, although it is common practice to appoint by deed which also has the benefit of the automatic vesting provisions contained in section 40 of the Trustee Act 1925.

5 Appointment by the court

11.87 Where it is inexpedient, difficult or impracticable to appoint a new trustee, the court has wide power to appoint new trustees 'either in substitution for or in addition to any existing trustee or trustees, or although there is no existing trustee'[1]. An order can be made on the application of a trustee or a beneficiary[2].

6 Delegation of trustee functions[3]

11.88 A trustee who, for example, goes abroad for a limited period, or is about to undergo a serious operation, will not necessarily wish to retire from the trusts. Under section 25 of the Trustee Act 1925 as substituted by section 5(1) of the Trustee Delegation Act 1999, he may appoint an attorney to act for him in his absence. The power itself need not state the reason why it is given (and the reasons are not confined to those mentioned, or limited in any way); but the notice referred to in (3) below must specify the reason why it is given. The period of delegation must not exceed 12 months[4]. The power of attorney may define a shorter period but, if nothing is stated, the default period is 12 months from the date of execution of the power by the donor. The following points should also be noted (and see also **11.42–11.44**):

(1) The previous rule that a trustee cannot appoint as attorney his only other co-trustee unless that co-trustee is a trust corporation was removed . Protections were better secured by other means[5].

(2) The appointor is liable for the acts and defaults of the attorney as if they were his own[6].

(3) Before, or within seven days after, giving the power the donor must give written notice of it to each of the other trustees and to the persons having power to appoint new trustees. The notice must specify the date on which the power came into operation, its duration, the name of the donee, the reason it is given and what trusts and powers are delegated, where they are not all delegated. Failure to comply with these requirements will not (in favour of a person dealing with the attorney) invalidate any act the attorney may do or instrument he may execute.

(4) The section applies to, amongst others, a personal representative in the same way as it does to a trustee[7].

1 Trustee Act 1925, s 41.
2 Trustee Act 1925, s 58.
3 See **11.42**.
4 Section 25(2).
5 Section 7.
6 Section 25(7).
7 Section 25(10).

(5) The 1999 Act introduced a prescribed form which can be used by a single trustee wishing to delegate his trustee functions under a trust to a single attorney. This is similar to the prescribed form in section 10 of the Power of Attorney Act 1971, which cannot be used by trustees but which is used by individuals[1]. As with the 1971 Act it must be executed as a deed.

D Ending trusteeship

1 Disclaimer

11.89 An individual is not bound to accept the onerous duties of a trustee. If he desires, a 'trustee' may disclaim before he does any act indicating acceptance of his office.

2 Retirement

11.90 A trustee may retire by deed, provided that:

(1) either a trust corporation or two trustees will remain after his retirement; and

(2) his co-trustees and the person, if any, entitled to appoint new trustees, consent by deed[2].

The deed of retirement will normally contain a declaration by the retiring and continuing trustees vesting the property in the continuing trustees and, except in certain cases, one will be implied anyway unless there is a contrary intention in the trust instrument[3].

3 Replacement

11.91 A trustee may be replaced under the provisions of section 36(1) of the Trustee Act 1925 (see **11.85** above).

4 Removal

11.92 A trustee may be removed from his office in four situations. The first is under an express power contained in the trust instrument; the second is under the replacement powers of section 36 of the Trustee Act 1925; the third is by the court appointing a new trustee in his place under section 41 of the Trustee Act 1925; and the fourth is under the court's inherent jurisdiction (eg if there is a permanent condition of hostility with his co-trustees and the beneficiaries)[4].

1 Section 25(5) and (6).
2 Trustee Act 1925, s 39(1).
3 Trustee Act 1925, s 40(2), (3).
4 *Letterstedt v Broers* (1884) 9 App Cas 371 at 386.

5 Death of trustee

11.93 The trustees hold property as joint tenants so that by the jus accrescendi (the 'right of survivorship'), on the death of one trustee, the property passes automatically to the surviving trustees. If a sole or last surviving trustee dies the office of trusteeship, by operation of law, passes to his personal representatives[1]. They can, if they wish, act as trustees, until the person entitled to appoint new trustees makes an appointment. This provision does not impose any obligation upon the personal representative to act and 'such a personal representative of a deceased trustee has an absolute right to decline to accept the position and duties of trustee if he chooses to do so'[2]. If they do not wish to act and the trust instrument is silent as to who may appoint additional trustees, they may make an appointment themselves.

SECTION 6 PERPETUITIES AND ACCUMULATIONS

A Perpetuities

11.94 It is against public policy that property should be settled on trusts which may last for an indefinite period. The rule against perpetuities (or perhaps more accurately the law against remoteness of vesting) prevents the settlor 'ruling from the grave'. Following the Perpetuities and Accumulations Act 1964 (the 1964 Act), there were two 'systems' in operation: the common law system applying to those trusts effected prior to the commencement of the 1964 Act and the system applying to trusts created thereafter. The law in this area has now been overhauled again as a result of the Perpetuities and Accumulations Act, 2009 (The 2009 Act).

1 The common law rule

11.95 The rule laid down that unless it is certain, at the date of the settlement, or in the case of a will, at the date of death of the testator, that the interest under a settlement *will* vest within the perpetuity period, the trust is void. The common law perpetuity period was a maximum of 21 years after the death of an expressly or impliedly relevant 'life in being' at the creation of the trust (with a further period for gestation).

2 The 'wait and see' rule

11.96 The 1964 Act was not retrospective and only applied to instruments coming into operation after 15 July 1964. Where an interest would have been void under common law, the 1964 Act introduced a 'wait and see' rule. The

1 Trustee Act 1925, s 18.
2 *Re Bennett* [1906] 1 Ch 216 at 225, CA, per Vaughan Williams LJ.

interest was valid until it became absolutely clear that the interest could not vest within the perpetuity period. The 1964 Act set out a list of statutory lives in being[1]. The 'wait and see' rule is preserved by section 7 of the 2009 Act.

11.97 The 1964 Act allowed a settlor or testator, if he wished, to provide for a perpetuity period of any fixed period not exceeding 80 years.

The fundamental rule (which is not changed by the 2009 Act) is that the property need not vest *in possession* during the period so long as every benefit under the settlement will vest *in interest*. It must be possible during the period for the beneficiaries to act together to put an end to the trusts. While, therefore, every valid life interest under the settlement must *commence* during the period, it need not *end* during the period.

The 1964 Act provided that so far as the rule is concerned, there is a presumption that a female can have a child only between the ages of 12 and 55 and that a male under the age of 14 years cannot father a child. Again, this is not altered by the 2009 Act.

3 The 2009 Act – how the law has changed

11.98 The 2009 Act specifically now only applies to trust interests. The previous acts and common law applied to a variety of other interests such as easements, restrictive covenants, options and pre-emption rights. All new trusts and wills have a 125 year perpetuity period, even if the document specifies a different period[2]. It should be noted that the 125 year period begins on the date the trust takes effect but, for wills the date the will was executed determines whether the new perpetuity period applies. Interests created by exercising special powers of appointment continue to be subject to the perpetuity period that applies to the instrument containing the power[3].

For some trusts starting before the 2009 Act came into force a 100 year perpetuity period is available. However, essentially this only applies to trusts documents specifying a perpetuity period by reference to a life in being. This requires the trustees to make an irrevocable deed to this effect[4].

As with the 1964 Act the rule against perpetuities does not apply to transfers of assets passing between charities, including charitable trusts[5].

4 Pension schemes

11.99 The 2009 Act excludes almost all pension schemes from the rule against perpetuities, provided they are 'relevant pension schemes' (this would include personal pension schemes)[6] but the exclusion does not extend to interests created

1 Section 3(5).
2 Section 5.
3 Sections 6(2) and 15 (1)(b).
4 Section 12.
5 Sections 2(2) and (3).
6 Section 2(4).

by nominating benefits or exercising powers of advancement under pension schemes.

B Accumulations

11.100 A further consequence of the general principle that property and wealth should be free to circulate has been the statutory control of accumulations of income from property in trust.

Section 164 of the Law of Property Act 1925 and section 13 of the Perpetuities and Accumulations Act 1964 provided that income may not be accumulated for longer than one of six specified alternative periods.

If there is a direction in the trust instrument to accumulate for a period longer than one of these periods then: (1) if the period is also longer than the perpetuity period then the direction to accumulate is totally void[1], and (2) if the period is not longer than the perpetuity period then only the excess over the nearest of the six authorised periods is invalid. The income released as a result of (1) or (2) passes to the person who would have been entitled had no accumulation been directed[2].

The rules against accumulations do not apply where the settlor is a corporation provided the company is not acting merely as a nominee for an individual, as a company is not a 'person' for the purposes of section 164(1) of the Law of Property Act 1925[3].

11.101 The changes made to the accumulation rules by the 2009 Act are fundamental in that the statutory provisions restricting accumulations are abolished for post-commencement non-charitable trusts[4]. This abolition does not prevent settlors from restricting accumulation if they want to. A knowledge of the pre-2009 rules is still required as restrictions on accumulation continue to apply to appointments made by exercising special powers of appointment under pre-commencement trusts. The pre-2009 restrictions on accumulation remain for charitable trusts.

SECTION 7 STAMP DUTY

A Background

11.102 Stamp duty was first imposed by the Stamp Act 1694 and is a tax on documents rather than transacations. There have been various consolidating and amending acts, for example the Stamp Act 1891 and the Stamp Duties Management Act 1891 which were in turn amended by various Finance Acts. Section 125 of the Finance Act 2003 introduced a major reform of stamp duty.

1 Law of Property Act 1925, s 164(1).
2 Law of Property Act 1925, s 164(1).
3 *In Re Dodwell & Co Ltd's Trust* [1978] 3 All ER 738.
4 Section 13.

With regard to transactions in land, stamp duty was replaced by stamp duty land tax. In other respects stamp duty was abolished in respect of all documents and in respect of transfer of most assets, the exceptions being shares and securities and certain partnership assets.

B Stamp duty on life assurance policies

11.103 The liability to pay stamp duty on policies of life insurance or assurance was abolished for instruments with effect from 31 December 1989[1].

C Stamp duty on assignments of life assurance policies

11.104 The assignment of a policy used to attract 'ad valorem' duty under the head 'conveyance or transfer' on a sale but this could be avoided by certification that the instrument fell within the Category L exemption where there was no consideration for the assignment[2]. There is, of course no need to include such a certificate now.

D Stamp duty on trusts of life assurance policies

11.105 From September 1999, the categories of exempt instruments under the 1987 Regulations was extended to include declarations of trust of life policies as defined[3]. These added a new Category N provision. From 2003 stamp duty on trusts has been abolished and so there is no requirement for such a certificate.

1 Finance Act 1989, s 173.

2 Stamp Duty (Exempt Instruments) Regulations 1987, SI 1987/516.

3 Stamp Duty (Exempt Instruments) (Amendment) Regulations 1999, SI 1999/2539.

CHAPTER 12

Insolvency and MWPA trusts

SUMMARY

SECTION 1 LIFE POLICIES AND BANKRUPTCY AND INSOLVENCY

12.1 Bankruptcy of an individual or insolvency of a company can be relevant to both ownership and any dealings with a life policy. A life office needs to understand the various types of arrangement that can affect ownership or prevent dealings in relation to a policy. This Chapter gives a brief overview of the types of insolvency and other proceedings, arrangements and personnel with whom a life office may have to deal. For a fuller understanding of a particular process readers are referred to specialist works on insolvency.

In practice life offices have more issues with individual bankruptcy than the insolvency of companies. In part this is because of the 'statutory assignment' of an individual's policy into the name of the trustee in bankruptcy. This necessitates a proactive reassignment of the policy by the trustee when the bankrupt is discharged as there is no automatic reassignment back to the original policyholder on discharge. Other issues tend to arise in relation to policies that the bankrupt either forgot about or asked someone else to pay premiums on, particularly where the policy had no surrender value and would otherwise have been worthless to the trustee.

There is also a preliminary issue around the effect of the statutory assignment to the trustee in bankruptcy. The traditionally accepted view is that an assignment may not be completed without notice to the life office. This is because even if a policy is transferred beneficially by an assignment, notice is still required to perfect that assignment (under both the Policies of Assurance Act 1867 and section 136 of the Law of Property Act 1925). Section 311 of the Insolvency Act 1986 provides that notice should be served where it is required to protect the priority of the trustee. In practice trustees in bankruptcy do normally serve notice. However, the case of *Rooney v Cardona*[1] seems to indicate that such notice is not necessarily required in order to protect their interests.

In this case the life office paid the policy moneys to Mr Cardona at a time when he was an undischarged bankrupt. Mr and Mrs Cardona had effected a policy in 1992 with themselves as grantees and lives assured. The policy was not subject to any express declaration of trust and did not contain any reference to it being for the benefit of anyone else or to it being subject to the Married Women's Property Act 1882 (MWPA) (the Court of Appeal did not agree with the parties' agreed premise that the policy was subject to the MWPA but were obliged to accept the position – see **12.43** below). In 1995 Mr Cardona was adjudicated bankrupt and notice of this bankruptcy was published in the London Gazette. The decision of the Court of Appeal assumes that as the policy was beneficially owned by the trustee in bankruptcy and there were no conflicting priorities (ie no third parties had registered an interest) no notice was required to protect the trustee's position as against the life office.

This case is interesting in that the life office was partly at fault because the policy document was stated to have been lost and it relied upon an indemnity for the lost policy without doing a bankruptcy search. It is not clear whether the case would have been decided differently if the policy had been produced to the life office.

A Non-payment of premiums

12.2 Where a trustee in bankruptcy refused to pay premiums on the bankrupt's policies and disclaimed all interest in them, and the bankrupt died, his legal personal representatives were held entitled to the policy moneys as against the trustee[2]. Where, however, during the bankruptcy, a policy lapsed through non-payment of premiums and the life office voluntarily endorsed it as a paid-up policy for a reduced amount, it was held that the trustee in bankruptcy was entitled to the benefit of the policy so endorsed[3].

B Undisclosed policy

12.3 Difficulties sometimes arise, either because the bankrupt considers the policy valueless and does not disclose it in his statement of affairs, or because the trustee does not take any action. The bankrupt or anyone who pays the premiums for the policy may be unaware that the policy remains the property of the trustee and so an asset of considerable value may be built up for the benefit of the creditors. Two cases illustrate the point:

1 [1991] WLR 1388.
2 *Re Learmouth* (1866) 14 WR 628.
3 *Re Shrager* (1913) 108 LT 346.

Tapster v Ward[1]

T effected a policy and his affairs were liquidated when only one premium had been paid and the policy had no surrender value. The policy was not disclosed to the trustee but was kept up by T until his death. It was held that the trustee in bankruptcy was entitled and was under no obligation to repay any part of the premiums to the bankrupt's personal representative.

Similar difficulties arise where a policy is effected by an undischarged bankrupt who does not realise that it may be vested in the trustee or appreciate the consequence.

Re Phillips[2]

An undischarged bankrupt effected a policy. He was later discharged, but again became bankrupt. The policy was disclosed in the second bankruptcy, but not in the first. It was held that the trustee in the first bankruptcy was entitled.

Re Stokes, ex p Mellish[3]

S effected a policy while his affairs were in liquidation by arrangement under the Debtors Act 1869. Unknown to the trustee he paid the premiums out of his salary and continued to do so after his discharge. It was held that the trustee was entitled to the policy. The principle of *Re Tyler* (see **12.4**) did not apply as the trustee was ignorant of the existence of the policy.

The position is now largely covered by section 307 of the Insolvency Act which deals with the issue of 'After-acquired property'. This allows the trustee in bankruptcy, on service of notice, to augment the bankrupt's estate to include property acquired after the commencement of the bankruptcy (subject to prior interests of third parties acquired without notice of the bankruptcy in good faith, and for value). This is supplemented by a duty on the bankrupt[4] to give the trustee notice of the relevant facts within 21 days of becoming aware of them and not to dispose of the property within 42 days commencing on the date of the notice unless the trustee consents in writing[5]. Where the bankrupt does dispose of the property there are provisions enabling the trustee to serve notice on the recipient of the property to vest it in the trustee[6]. In practice, life offices should require the trustee's written consent before they issue a new policy to an undischarged bankrupt.

C Knowledge of the trustee

12.4 The trustee in bankruptcy is neither bound to pay the premiums nor disclaim the policy. However, if the policy is disclosed and the trustee knows that

1 (1909) 101 LT 503.
2 [1914] 2 KB 689.
3 [1919] 2 KB 256; see also *Re Bennett, ex parte Official Receiver* [1907] 1 KB 149.
4 Section 333(2).
5 Rule 6.200(2).
6 Section 307(3) and r 6.201.

premiums are being paid by a third party, he may have to allow a lien for the premiums, even though such payment of premiums would not in other cases afford any claim for a lien. This essentially arises out of his position as an officer of the court.

> *Re Tyler, ex p Official Receiver*[1]
>
> A husband had effected a policy and, being in difficulty, requested his wife to pay the premium and the interest on a loan on it. She continued to do so after the adjudication in bankruptcy of the husband. The trustee claimed the policy free from any lien by the wife. He was aware that payments were being made by her. It was held that the lien must be allowed. The trustee as an officer of the court must be even more straightforward and honest than an ordinary person in the affairs of everyday life.

D Reassignment

12.5 It must be emphasised that discharge of the bankrupt does not operate to automatically re-vest in the bankrupt any life policy owned by him at the time of the bankruptcy or acquired by him before discharge. If he wishes to maintain such a policy, he should ask the trustee in bankruptcy either to disclaim the policy or to agree to assign it to him after his discharge.

SECTION 2 BANKRUPTCY

12.6 When people think of insolvency in relation to individuals, most people think automatically of bankruptcy. However, over the years other methods have evolved (which have significantly increased in number in recent years) of dealing with situations where a person is in financial difficulty and, therefore, technically insolvent. The aim of many of these procedures is to avoid bankruptcy. In this Section references to the act or to sections are references to the Insolvency Act 1986 and to the Insolvency Rules 1986[2]. Section 3 looks at individual voluntary arrangements, and briefly at county court administration orders, debt relief orders and deeds of arrangement under the Deeds of Arrangement Act 1914.

A Obtaining a bankruptcy order

12.7 The aim of the law of bankruptcy is to take the property of a debtor and distribute it among his creditors, and then, subject to certain safeguards and with certain exceptions and after the expiry of a certain time period, to grant the

1 [1907] 1KB 865.
2 SI 1986/1925, as amended by SI 1987/397, SI 1991/495 and SI 1993/602.

debtor himself a discharge so that he can start afresh. The bankruptcy proceedings will therefore (with certain exceptions) divest the bankrupt of all property he owned at the time of the bankruptcy and (on service of notice), property acquired subsequently but before discharge. At the same time it will, on the whole, release him from his obligations at the time of bankruptcy. A bankruptcy action is commenced by a petition to the court for a bankruptcy order. It is a prerequisite that there be a debtor and that he is personally amenable to the jurisdiction of the courts in England and Wales[1]. The essential determinant of the ability to present a petition is the debtor's domicile in England and Wales or his presence there on the day the petition is presented or where he has been ordinarily resident or carried on business during the three years before the presentation of the petition. The petition may be brought by creditor(s), the debtor himself, the supervisor of (or a person bound by) a voluntary arrangement or by the Financial Services Authority where the debt relates to a regulated activity[2]. Except in cases where the debtor petitions for his own bankruptcy on the grounds that he is unable to pay his debts, the debt in question must be for £750 or more, it must be a liquidated sum payable immediately or at some certain future time and it must be unsecured. In order to be successful in obtaining a bankruptcy order, it is necessary to show either: (i) that the debtor is unable, or (ii) it appears that there is no reasonable prospect of him being able to pay the debt and that this is not affected by any application to set aside a statutory demand.

The grounds on which inability to pay are to be shown, are exclusively those in section 268:

(1) that the debtor has not complied with a creditor's statutory demand; or

(2) there is an unsatisfied execution in favour of the creditor on a judgment debt against the debtor.

Similarly, no reasonable prospect of being able to pay can also be established where the debt is not immediately payable by non-compliance with a statutory demand, provided certain conditions are fulfilled[3]. A statutory demand is not a document issued by the court. However, it must be in the prescribed form[4] and served upon the debtor, although there are provisions for advertising it in a newspaper in the case of a judgement debt where the debtor has absconded or is keeping out of the way with a view to avoiding service. After three weeks and on production of an affidavit proving service of the demand, the petitioner will be entitled to the bankruptcy order (assuming the debtor has not succeeded in having the statutory demand set aside). Similarly, in relation to an unsatisfied execution, it needs to be shown that this has not been satisfied in whole, or in part.

If there is a serious possibility that the property will be significantly diminished during that period it is possible for a bankruptcy petition to be presented

1 Section 265 and see *Zvonko Stojevic* (1) *Komercni Bank SA* (2) *Yvonne Venvil (the Trustee in Bankruptcy of Zvonko Stojevic* (3) the Official Receiver (2006).
2 See under voluntary arrangement, **12.28**; see Financial Services and Markets Act, 2000, s 372
3 Section 268(2).
4 See Insolvency Rules 1986, r 6.1.

before the end of the three-week period, this being known as an expedited petition[1].

1 Secured debts

12.8 Section 285[2] provides that a secured creditor is free to enforce his security in the event of the debtor's bankruptcy, but he may equally petition for bankruptcy if he is either willing to give up his security, which would normally only happen if the value of the security was small, or if his petition is expressed to not be made in respect of the secured part of the debt and it contains a statement of the estimated value of the security at the date of the petition. In this event the debts are treated as two separate debts, one secured, and one unsecured as to the balance.

2 Set-off

12.9 Section 323 provides that amounts owed by a creditor may be set off against amounts owed by the bankrupt at the date of the bankruptcy order if they arise out of mutual credits, mutual debts or other mutual dealings. This right is wider than the general right of set-off but is subject to a number of limitations, for example:

(1) The parties must owe each other money in the same right[3], not in any representative or fiduciary situation.

(2) The right will not apply where the creditor had notice that a bankruptcy petition was pending at the time the debt became due.

(3) The mutual dealings must be such as would lead to a money claim and not to any other remedy.

(4) It had been thought that mutual credits may not be set off where the creditor's right is contingent and that contingency has not yet occurred, however, Hoffman LJ held[4] that the requirement for dealings to be mutual is unreasonable and that all that is required for mutuality is that the obligations the subject of set-off are incurred by the same parties in the same right or capacity.

It is also worth noting that where there is sufficient mutuality (eg where the debts arise out of the same contract) it is impossible by contract to exclude the statutory right of set-off. Further, in relation to debtor companies, there is a similar provision in the Insolvency Rules[5].

1 Section 270.
2 Subsections 4 and 5.
3 See *National Westminster Bank Ltd v Halesowen Presswork and Assemblies Ltd* [1972] AC 785 at 821.
4 *Secretary of State for Trade and Industry v Frid* [2004] UKHL 24.
5 Rule 4.90 and rule 2.85.

3 Interim receiver and the Official Receiver

12.10 An application may also be made in extreme cases for the Official Receiver to be appointed as an interim receiver to prevent dissipation of the potential bankrupt's property[1]. Normally, the Official Receiver will become receiver and manager of the bankrupt's property from the date the bankruptcy order is made. In either event, if the bankruptcy order is made, either the Official Receiver or an insolvency practitioner will be appointed as trustee in bankruptcy. An insolvency practitioner is essentially someone who holds a valid authorisation, either by membership of a recognised professional body, or by virtue of a licence granted directly by the Secretary of State for Trade & Industry or the Insolvency Practitioners Association. The bankrupt is required to prepare a statement of affairs and submit it to the Official Receiver. The Official Receiver may require further disclosure[2] and may decide to apply for the holding of a public examination of the bankrupt at a duly convened sitting of the court (see section 290). The Official Receiver's other main responsibility is to decide whether the assets are sufficient to justify the summoning of a meeting of creditors to appoint a trustee in bankruptcy.

4 Bankruptcy order and provable debts

12.11 The order made by the court is required to state the date of presentation of the petition and the date of the making of the order (see Insolvency Rules 6.33 & 6.34). The order takes effect on the beginning of the day on which it is granted and, although the property of the bankrupt remains in his name until the trustee is appointed, he has no ability to deal with it. That power is with the Official Receiver. By virtue of section 284, any disposition of property by the bankrupt between the dates of the presentation of the petition and the making of the order is void, except to the extent that it either has the consent of, or is subsequently ratified by, the court. However, subsection 4 provides that where a person has received any property or payment from the bankrupt before the bankruptcy order and has done so in good faith, for value without notice that the petition has been presented, or where another person obtains an interest in such a property from someone who satisfies those criteria, then those dispositions will not be void.

The effect of the bankruptcy order is that, subject to limited exceptions, the bankrupt may not be sued in respect of debts which are provable in the bankruptcy, namely debts or liabilities to which he is subject at the time of the bankruptcy order[3].

1 Section 286(2).
2 Insolvency Rules 1986, r 6.66(1).
3 Section 285.

B Appointment of trustee

12.12 The Official Receiver must decide as soon as possible, within 12 weeks from the date of the bankruptcy order, whether or not to appoint a trustee in bankruptcy. Otherwise the trustee in bankruptcy would be appointed at the first creditors' meeting, or the Official Receiver could refer the matter of appointing the trustee in bankruptcy to the Secretary of State, who would then appoint a trustee. If no reference is made by the Official Receiver, then the Official Receiver will become the trustee in bankruptcy from the date on which he notifies the court of his decision not to refer the matter to the Secretary of State. The appointment of a trustee in bankruptcy will take effect only if the person accepts the appointment in accordance with the Insolvency Rules. On appointment of the trustee in bankruptcy, the bankrupt's property ('his estate'), including any life policies, vests in the trustee in bankruptcy without conveyance, assignment or transfer[1]. However, this is subject to the rule that the trustee in bankruptcy takes subject to the equities. He is not considered to be an assignee for value and cannot therefore gain priority over existing equities by giving notice. This is often explained as the trustee merely stepping into the shoes of the bankrupt.

> *Re Wallis, ex p Jenks*[2]
>
> A husband deposited a policy with his wife to secure advances made by her to him. He was adjudged bankrupt. The trustee gave notice to the life office and claimed the policy free from any charge on the ground that he first gave notice. It was held that the trustee takes subject to equities and cannot obtain priority by notice.

Section 311(4) provides that notice of assignment need not be given 'except in so far as it is necessary' in a case where the deemed assignment is from the bankrupt himself, for protecting the priority of the trustee. It is submitted that because of the Policies of Assurance Act 1867 notice of an assignment is necessary to protect the assignee from a purchaser for value without notice of the bankruptcy. It is not clear how this fits with the case of *Rooney v Cardona* where the Court of Appeal held that as against the life office itself notice was not required. If that case were followed to its logical conclusion it could mean that section 311(4) would be redundant as priority could never be obtained over the trustees' interests. This could cause a major problem in markets like the second-hand endowment market which relies upon the life office's title records. Also, it is worth noting that *Rooney v Cardona* did not deal with this issue in these terms and there is dicta in the judgment re-enforcing the effect of section 311(4) and emphasising that notice in the London Gazette is not constructive notice to the whole world of the bankruptcy. It may be that the only person who is at risk in not receiving notice is the life office which does not have a competing claim. Much will also depend on the circumstances as it may be possible (eg where the trustee leaves the policy with the bankrupt) or the life office completes reasonable

1 Section 306(1) and (2).
2 [1902] 1KB 719.

searches to rely upon some of the other authorities in this area. Also, in practice, if trustees need to register their interests as against third parties[1] notice is likely to continue to be served.

C Property subject to a bankruptcy order

12.13 The bankrupt's estate is defined for these purposes primarily in section 283 as all property belonging to the bankrupt at the commencement of a bankruptcy and all property which, by virtue of provisions in that part of the Insolvency Act, is to be comprised or treated as falling into the estate[2]. Property is given a very wide definition in section 436, including all present and future property and specifically including 'things in action' (such as life policies).

Section 307 provides the framework and power for the trustee to vest 'after-acquired property' into the estate by service of notice on the bankrupt. This power does not, however, apply where such property is disposed of to a person for value, or if a banker enters into a transaction, in both cases in good faith without knowledge of the bankruptcy[3]. However, there is authority for the proposition[4] that money received and paid away by the bankrupt, even to a person with notice, may be treated as valid against the trustee if the trustee has not intervened. In relation to income, the bankrupt is allowed to retain the amount of income deemed necessary to maintain him and his family in reasonable circumstances and subject to that the trustee may apply for an income payments order under section 310. It is also worth noting the effect of protective and MWPA trusts (see Section 6).

D Power to avoid prior transactions

12.14 Additionally, there are powers in the Insolvency Act for the trustee to apply to the court effectively to retrieve property or restore a previous situation, in relation to the estate of the bankrupt. There are three grounds on which this can be done:

(1) where there is a transaction at an undervalue (ie for less than full consideration) in the five years before presentation of the petition;

(2) where there is a preference (ie one creditor is put in a better position than another);

(3) where there is a transaction effectively delaying or defrauding creditors at any time.

1 *Re Russell's Policy* (1872) LR 15 Eq 26 and s 311.
2 See **12.20–12.22** for excluded property.
3 This maintains and clarifies the position formerly contained in the Bankruptcy Act 1914, s 47.
4 *Re Vanlohe* (1871) 7 Ch App 1985.

1 *A transaction at an undervalue*

12.15 A transaction at an undervalue is defined[1] as either a gift for no consideration or a transaction in consideration of marriage (or formation of a civil partnership), or a transaction, the consideration for which in money's worth is significantly less than the value in money or money's worth of what is provided. However, in order to be impeached the transaction must have been entered into at a "relevant time", which is defined in section 341. The basic rule is that any transaction at an undervalue within *two years* of the presentation of the petition can be attacked. Transactions which occurred *between two and five years* before presentation of the petition can only be set aside if, at the time of the transaction, the bankrupt was already, or became, insolvent in consequence of it. Insolvent for this purpose means unable to pay debts as they fall due, or the value of a person's assets are less than the amount of his liabilities, taking into account contingent and prospective liabilities. In respect of a transaction which is not to an associate[2] of the bankrupt, the burden of proof to show that the person was or became insolvent is on the trustee. However, if the other party to the transaction was an associate then the burden of proof is reversed and is, therefore, placed on the associate. Thus, if a bankrupt gratuitously or for much less than full consideration had assigned or declared a trust of property (eg a life policy) then, unless it is an MWPA trust (essentially in favour of wife or children)[3], it will be a transaction at an undervalue for these purposes. It may, therefore, be attacked by the trustee in bankruptcy if it took place less than five years before presentation of the petition, unless the beneficiaries can show that the settlor was not and did not became insolvent because of the gift.

The court may make such order as it thinks fit for restoring the position to what it would have been if the bankrupt had not entered into the transaction. Additionally, the court has wide general powers to order restitution and trace the proceeds of transactions. Protection is afforded[4] to third parties acquiring an interest in property or a benefit from a transaction in good faith for value without knowledge of the relevant circumstances, that would render the transaction voidable.

2 *Preferences*

12.16 Preferences are essentially advantages being given to one creditor over another. To be capable of being attacked by the trustee in bankruptcy a preference has to take place at the 'relevant time' and the court has power to put the parties back into the position they would have been if the preference had not taken place. The term 'preference' is defined[5] in relation to a person who is a

1 Section 339.
2 See **12.18**.
3 Section 6, **12.48** et seq.
4 Section 342(2).
5 Section 340(3).

creditor, a surety or a guarantor of debts or liabilities of the bankrupt, as the bankrupt doing something or suffering something to be done which has the effect of putting that person in a better position, in the event of the debtor's bankruptcy, than he would have otherwise been in. There is also a requirement that the bankrupt 'desired' to produce this effect, although this need not be his dominant motive in acting in any particular way. This can be a difficult concept to ascertain. Guidance was set out by Millett J in *Re MC Bacon*[1]. The court is required to presume that the motive is satisfied where a preference is given to an associate of the debtor (otherwise than by reason of his being an employee), although this presumption is rebuttable. The relevant time is two years in the case of a preference to an associate, or six months in any other case. However, it is worth noting that unlike the situation with transactions at an undervalue, it is necessary for the trustee in every case of preference to establish that the bankrupt was insolvent[2] at the time the preference was given.

The term 'associate' is defined very widely in the Insolvency Act[3] and covers most forms of blood or marital relationship (including civil partnership), including a former spouse or a reputed spouse. It also extends to business associates and partners, and employment relationships. A company can also be an associate of an individual if it is controlled by that individual or if that individual and his associates together control the company, either by securing that the company acts in accordance with their instructions or by exercising control of more than one-third of the voting rights of the company. Trustees and beneficiaries can also be associates if the bankrupt or his associates are beneficiaries, or if the settlor is a potential beneficiary.

3 Transactions defrauding or delaying creditors

12.17 Sections 423 to 425 (which together form Part XVI of the Insolvency Act) relate to 'Transactions defrauding creditors', although there is no actual condition of fraud in the criminal sense. These sections, unlike those relating to transactions at an undervalue and preferences, do not apply only on insolvency. They apply at any time where it can be shown that a transaction at an undervalue was entered into for the purpose either of putting assets beyond the reach of a person who is making or may at some time make a claim against a person, or otherwise prejudicing the interest of such a person in relation to the claim which he is making, or may make. Because of the presumptions available in respect of transactions at an undervalue, particularly where associates are involved, it is likely that the Part XVI provisions will only be used in an insolvency situation when the transaction took place more than five years before the bankruptcy. It is worth remembering that transaction is defined as including a gift, agreement or arrangement. The motive of defeating or delaying claims of creditors is essential

1 [1990] BCLC 324.
2 See **12.17** in relation to transactions at an undervalue.
3 Section 435.

and has to be proved in each case. When it is not an insolvency situation the claim can be brought by the person who would be defeated or delayed, but it is provided that in the specified cases only the person acting in the insolvency or the supervisor in a voluntary arrangement have the right to bring such a claim. There are wide powers to order restitution and protection for innocent third parties for value without notice of the circumstances giving rise to the impeachability of the original transaction.

E Excluded property

12.18 There are various exceptions to the assets which would otherwise be included in the bankrupt's estate. First, there are two categories of exempt assets provided by section 283(2), as follows:

> '(a) such tools, books, vehicles and other items of equipment as are necessary to the bankrupt for use personally by him in his employment, business or vocation; and
>
> (b) such clothing, bedding, furniture, household equipment and provisions as are necessary for satisfying the basic domestic needs of the bankrupt and his family.'

Neither of these would extend to life policies.

The second exclusion is set out in section 283(3)(a) which provides that property held on trust for any other person will not form part of a bankrupt's estate. There is no requirement that the trust be a formal written trust. In relation to powers of appointment[1], the property subject to the power will not be included where it is not for the time being included in the bankrupt's estate and where either it is exercisable at a time after the bankrupt's discharge or the bankrupt is not a potential beneficiary, provided, of course, in both cases that the bankrupt is not the settlor and that the trust, assignment or other transaction is not capable of being avoided under the powers discussed in Section D above.

Further, it is specifically provided[2] that the ambit of a bankrupt's estate is subject to the provisions of any enactment not contained in the Insolvency Act 1986 under which any property is to be excluded from a bankrupt's estate. In this respect it is worth noting section 159(5) of the Pension Schemes Act 1993 which excludes protected rights under a personal pension scheme from being passed from the bankrupt's estate to a trustee in bankruptcy. Also, section 159A of that Act (inserted by section 14 of the Welfare Reform and Pensions Act, 1999), provides that there shall be no forfeiture on bankruptcy of rights under personal pension schemes. Further, section 11 of the Welfare Reform and Pensions Act, 1999 provides that in respect of bankruptcies taking place on or after the coming into force of this section all pension rights are excluded from the bankrupt's estate.

1 See s 283(4).
2 Section 283(6).

F Forfeiture

12.19 It is also possible for property to fall out of the bankrupt's estate by virtue of a forfeiture clause[1] in a settlement to which the property belongs. In order to be valid, such a clause must be expressed to operate upon the *presentation* of a bankruptcy petition, the settlement should contain a gift over of the interest to be forfeited[2] and the settlor cannot be the bankrupt[3]. Where the settlement comprises property from other sources, such a clause in favour of the partial settlor may be effective to the extent of that other property not provided by the bankrupt. Where the settlement contains a power of appointment to appoint away from the settlor prior to commencement of the bankruptcy, namely between the date of the petition and the order, the trustees should exercise such power to appoint away from the settlor. This effectively takes such property out of the settlor's estate[4], as it would not be a disposition by the bankrupt in that period. On the other hand, amounts receivable by the bankrupt from a discretionary trust may be treated like income, with the trustee in bankruptcy being entitled to the balance over the amount required for the deemed needs of the bankrupt and his family.

Forfeiture wordings are still included in occupational pension schemes and personal pension schemes to cater for pre-29 May 2000 bankruptcies. Since they contain a gift over and since the settlor is not (usually) a settlor of the scheme, they are generally considered to be effective. However, in respect of pensions which are already in payment at the time of bankruptcy, pension payments may be treated as income for the purposes of income payments orders under section 310, even though the pension could not itself vest in the trustee in bankruptcy because of a forfeiture or non-assignment clause in the pension scheme[5].

G Discharge of the bankrupt

12.20 When the bankrupt is discharged from bankruptcy, the effect is to release him from all of the debts which were provable in the bankruptcy, such that creditors no longer have the right to claim for any outstanding amounts. A bankrupt will be automatically discharged after one year unless an order is made by the court, on the application of the Official Receiver or trustee in bankruptcy, to suspend discharge due to the bankrupt's failure to fulfil his obligation under the Insolvency Act[6] or the Official Receiver has agreed an earlier discharge if appropriate (section 279(2)). By virtue of section 281, discharge of the bankrupt will not extend to secured debts and will have no effect on the remaining functions, duties and powers of the trustee in bankruptcy.

1 See also Section 5, **12.45**.
2 *Brandon v Robinson* (1811) 18 Ves 429; 34 ER 379.
3 *Re Johnson* [1904] 1KB 134.
4 *Re Balfour's Settlement* [1938] Ch 928.
5 *Re Garrett* [1930] 2 Ch 137.
6 Section 279.

As distinct from a discharge, the bankrupt may also apply for the bankruptcy order to be annulled on the grounds either of facts existing at the time of the order, such that the order should not have been made (for example, the debtor's lack of capacity[1], or if all of his debts have been paid or secured[2] or the bankrupt has agreed an individual voluntary arrangement with his creditors (section 261).

H Death of an insolvent person

12.21 The Administration of Insolvent Estates of Deceased Persons Order (as amended)[3] provides a slightly modified but analogous system to deal with situations where a person dies insolvent, both where proceedings in bankruptcy have and where they have not already been commenced. Where proceedings have not been commenced, creditors may petition for an order for the administration of the deceased person's estate according to the laws of bankruptcy. Equally, the personal representative may petition for this purpose. Where proceedings in administration have already begun, it is necessary to apply to have them transferred. The court may transfer them to the bankruptcy court, although this power is discretionary. Where the modified provisions apply the powers to make adjustments to prior transactions, namely, at an undervalue, or preferences and the ability to disclaim onerous property, all still apply.

I Insolvent partners or partnerships

12.22 Section 420 made provision for the position of insolvent partnerships to be dealt with by statutory instrument[4]. As a result of the original order made in 1986, the position with regard to partnerships is that there are effectively three ways of dealing with an insolvency situation:

(1) individual members of the partnership could be the subject of proceedings in bankruptcy without the partnership being involved;

(2) the partnership could be wound up under the provisions in the Act dealing with unregistered companies[5]; or

(3) there could be a winding up of the partnership together with the bankruptcy of two or more of its members. The same insolvency practitioner would act in both matters.

The original order was revoked and replaced by the Insolvent Partnerships Order 1994[6] with effect from 1 December 1994. The subsequent order maintains the

1 *Haworth v Cartmel* [2011] EWHC 36 (Ch).
2 Section 282(1) and Insolvency Rules 1986, r 6.206.
3 SI 1986/1999.
4 See the Insolvent Partnerships Order 1994, SI 1994/2421; Insolvent Partnerships (Amendment) Order 1996, SI 1996/1308.
5 See the Insolvency Act 1986, Pt V.
6 SI 1994/2421, subject to transitional provisions in art 19.

basic premise of the original order but makes separate provision, depending on who has presented the petition for winding up. Notably, it provides for the availability of voluntary arrangements and administration orders (suitably modified) for insolvent partnerships[1]. Other changes to the provisions of the 1986 order include a change to (3) above, so that on a creditor's petition, at least one partner (not two) now needs to be made insolvent, together with the partnership. Specified provisions of the Company Directors Disqualification Act 1986 will apply in certain circumstances to an insolvent partnership[2].

It is also possible that one partner may be bankrupt but that the partnership itself is solvent. In that case the individual could be made bankrupt without the partnership being involved although it is possible, depending on the partnership deed, that such a bankruptcy would cause a dissolution of the partnership.

J Undischarged bankrupts and subsequent debts

12.23 Debts arising after the commencement of an individual's bankruptcy which are not in respect of obligations incurred before the bankruptcy commenced are not provable in the bankruptcy. This means that unless the bankrupt subsequently enters into a voluntary arrangement, it will be necessary to seek a second bankruptcy order to try to protect the interests of those creditors. There is unfortunately no means of consolidating successive bankruptcies. The rules relating to second bankruptcies whilst still undischarged from the effects of a previous bankruptcy are set out in sections 334 and 335 of the Insolvency Act.

K bankruptcy searches

12.24 Bankruptcy searches may be made on-line through the Individual Insolvency Register and through the local official receiver's office.

SECTION 3 OTHER INDIVIDUAL ARRANGEMENTS

A Voluntary arrangements

12.25 Sections 252 to 263G inclusive in Part VIII of the Insolvency Act govern the making of voluntary arrangements by individuals. Essentially, a voluntary arrangement either enables a person who is insolvent to avoid bankruptcy, or enables a bankrupt to bring the bankruptcy to an end in a shorter period of time, by making arrangements which are acceptable to the required majority of his creditors. The arrangement operates such that once the requisite majority is obtained, then all creditors who were entitled to receive notice of the creditors'

1 SI 1994/2421, arts 4–6.
2 See arts 16 and 18 and the Insolvent Partnerships (Amendment) Order 2001.

meeting, even those who did not agree to the arrangement, are bound by it and are normally bound to accept a lesser amount than that to which they were originally entitled.

Given the ability to lessen the amount that creditors receive, certain safeguards have been built into the arrangement, namely the debtor's statement of affairs and proposal must undergo preliminary scrutiny by a qualified insolvency practitioner (called the 'nominee') who must report to the court stating whether, in his opinion, the proposal should be carried forward and submitted to a meeting of the debtor's creditors for possible approval. Then, only if the court is satisfied, will the meeting of creditors be convened. The meeting will be chaired by the nominee or his delegate and a majority of three-quarters in value of the creditors present in person or by proxy and voting on the resolution must be obtained. If the consent is obtained then the nominee (thereafter called the 'supervisor') supervises the arrangement. Both the nominee and anybody bound by the arrangement have the right under section 276 to petition for bankruptcy if a debtor fails in his obligation under the arrangement or they can show that the information in his statement of affairs, as presented to the meeting, was false or misleading[1].

I Interim order

12.26 In order to enable a debtor to make the necessary arrangements, an interim order may be made under section 252 (save where a 'fast-track' IVA is proposed in the case of an undischarged bankrupt). This provision prevents any petition being presented or proceeded with, and no other proceedings, execution or other legal process may be commenced or continued without leave of the court during the period of the order. Once the voluntary arrangement has been approved, the interim order ceases to have effect and any pending petitions for bankruptcy are normally automatically discharged, although there is a 28-day challenge period for such an arrangement. As mentioned, a voluntary arrangement may be used to bring a bankruptcy to an end and the court then has power, at its discretion, to annul the bankruptcy under section 261, on which happening (subject to the arrangements and supervision of the supervisor) the property reverts to the individual under the voluntary arrangement subject to any terms the court may direct or may vest in such other person as the court may appoint.

B County court administration order

12.27 Under Part VI of the County Courts Act 1984, if a debtor is unable to pay a judgment debt and his whole indebtedness is less than the 'county court limit' he may apply to the county court for a county court administration order. The order will make provision for the payment of debts by instalment or

1 *Cadbury Schweppes plc v Alimudin Amiraly Somji* (2001) WLR 615.

otherwise. While such an order is in force no creditor included in the list of creditors may petition or join in a bankruptcy petition unless certain criteria are satisfied.

C Deeds of arrangement

12.28 Deeds of arrangement made under the Deeds of Arrangement Act 1914 are little used today. They operate by a debtor giving up his property to a trustee in return for a release from his creditors' claims. The deed has to be registered with the Insolvency Service within seven days of execution otherwise it is void. A disadvantage of these deeds of arrangement is that, unlike the procedure under the Insolvency Act 1986, they cannot be used to bind dissenting creditors. There is no equivalent of an interim order to prevent such creditors petitioning for bankruptcy.

D Debt Relief Orders

12.29 The relevant statutory provisions relating to Debt Relief Orders are mainly set out in section 251 A to X of the Insolvency Act 1986. They were introduced by the Tribunals, Courts and Enforcement Act 2007. They are a way for a debtor with assets of limited value and limited income to obtain release from his debts provided such debts do not exceed £15,000. They provide the debtor with a year's protection from his creditors taking steps to enforce their debts against him unless given leave by the court. At the end of a year, he is discharged from liability for those debts. They do not lead to the realisation of assets or distribution of assets to creditors.

SECTION 4 CORPORATE ARRANGEMENTS

12.30 This section deals briefly with the variety of methods of dealing with the insolvency of a company, the relevant personnel in each case and their powers. Briefly, these are an administrator, an administrative receiver, a liquidator, provisional liquidator or a supervisor of a voluntary arrangement, all of whom must be qualified insolvency practitioners.

A Administrative receiver

12.31 A receiver is normally appointed by a debenture holder and the court is not usually involved. The Insolvency Act 1986 gave statutory effect to much of the existing common law relating to receivership and introduced the concept of an administrative receiver who may be appointed in respect of the whole or substantially the whole of a company's property, and who holds a charge which when created was a floating charge over part (or all) of the company's property.

This basically excludes receivers appointed under a charge of a specific asset (ie a fixed charge) only. Whereas the powers of a receiver are set out in the instrument or court order appointing the receiver, the powers of an administrative receiver are deemed to include the powers set out in Schedule 1 of the Insolvency Act 1986, unless they are otherwise inconsistent with the instrument under which he was appointed. Moreover, section 42(3) of that Act provides that a person dealing with an administrative receiver in good faith and for value is not concerned to enquire whether he is acting within his powers. A receiver is deemed to be the agent of the company until the company goes into liquidation.

Under the Enterprise Act 2002 administrative receivership was effectively abolished as a remedy for all floating charges created after the Act, subject to some important but limited exceptions.

B Administration

12.32 Administration is a procedure introduced by the Insolvency Act 1986 to provide the benefits of receivership where no floating charge exists. A company is put into administration and an administrator is appointed. Before the Enterprise Act 2002 came into force on 15 September 2003, the powers of an administrator were set out in Part II of the Insolvency Act 1986. These powers have now been replaced by those inserted by the Enterprise Act 2002 at Schedule B1 of the Insolvency Act 1986. The administrator's powers are wide and allow him to effectively manage the business of the company.

Since the Enterprise Act 2002, the administrator's objectives are three-fold. Primarily the objective is to rescue the company as a going concern. If this is unachievable, the administrator must try to achieve a better result for the company's creditors than would have been possible if the company had been wound up. Finally, if it is not reasonably practicable to achieve the first two objectives, the administrator has a third objective which is to realise the property of the company so that a distribution may be made to one or more secured or preferential creditors. The administrator is obliged to perform these functions in the interests of all the company's creditors and to do so as quickly and efficiently as possible. The administrator acts as the company's agent and cannot be held liable on the contracts made as agent of the company.

Prior to the Enterprise Act 2002, administration could only be effected by the granting of a court order. However, it is now possible for the shareholders of the company, its directors or holders of qualifying floating charges to appoint an administrator out of court too. This route is seen as being cheaper and more flexible for companies in financial difficulties. Before the 'out of court' route was established, a floating charge holder was able to block the making of an administration order as floating charge holders had to be given notice of any petition to seek an administration order. One of the main advantages of the current administration procedure is the protection the company receives from a statutory moratorium, which prevents creditors from taking action against the company's assets (including the enforcement of security), therefore allowing the administrator to carry on the running of the business of the company. An exception to the moratorium exists for financial collateral arrangements in the Financial Collateral

Arrangements (No 2) Regulations 2003 (as amended). It should also be noted though, that for floating charges created before 15 September 2003 the right to veto an administration order and put in place an administrative receiver still exists.

The effect of a company going into administration is that on the making of an administration order, any petition for winding up of the company is dismissed. If a qualifying floating charge holder appoints an administrator, any petition for winding up is suspended.

In a similar manner to liquidators[1], an administrator has powers to set aside transactions at an undervalue, transactions defrauding creditors and preferences. However, unlike liquidators, administrators do not have powers to disclaim onerous contracts nor to seek an order of the court against directors for a contribution to the company's assets for wrongful or fraudulent trading.

C Arrangements with creditors

12.33 There are two types of statutory arrangement available to a company. First, like an individual, a company may enter into a voluntary arrangement under section 1 of the Insolvency Act, and secondly, the company may enter into a scheme of arrangement under Part 26 of the Companies Act 2006. Although both mechanisms may be used where a company is in financial difficulty and wishes to come to an arrangement with creditors, they are rarely used in such circumstances because they provide no protection against persons seeking to wind up the company, nor do they allow the company to continue trading without the threat of the directors being subsequently made personally liable for any losses occurring during that period[2]. In this way they are similar to the deed of arrangement for individuals.

A compromise or arrangement under Part 26 is often used for company reorganisations where the company is solvent. This scheme takes effect only after it has been approved by meetings of the relevant classes of creditors and members, by the requisite majority, by the company and by the court. Once approved the scheme will bind all the members and creditors of the relevant classes. A voluntary arrangement, on the other hand, allows a company to enter into a binding composition with its creditors, and was mainly intended to be used following an administration order (which would itself include the 'moratorium' on actions) or during a liquidation (either by its administrator or liquidator as appropriate – the directors cannot propose a composition or scheme if the company is in liquidation or under administration). It is very similar to an individual voluntary arrangement in that an insolvency practitioner supervises the arrangement and every creditor with notice of the meeting is bound by the voluntary arrangement once the requisite majority has been obtained. However, as has been previously noted, unlike an individual arrangement there is no protection against creditors before the proposal is approved unless there is an administration order in place.

1 See further Section 4D, **12.37**.

2 ie for wrongful or fraudulent trading: ss 213 and 214.

D Liquidation

12.34 Liquidation is a means by which a company's affairs are wound up, leading to the dissolution of the company as a legal entity. There are effectively three types of liquidation, one compulsory and two voluntary: a members' voluntary liquidation and a creditors' voluntary liquidation and a compulsory liquidation. A members' voluntary liquidation is slightly at odds with the rest of this Chapter, in that in such a liquidation the directors declare that the company is solvent. A creditors' voluntary liquidation takes place where such a declaration has not been made. It should be noted that a winding-up petition may be presented and an order for compulsory liquidation made in respect of a company which is already in voluntary liquidation.

A voluntary liquidation commences at the time when the resolution to wind up the company is passed[1]. Whereas a compulsory liquidation commences on the date of presentation of the winding-up petition, unless a resolution for voluntary liquidation has previously been passed, in which case it commences at the time of the passing of that resolution[2].

The situation is similar to that found in bankruptcy cases in that, after the commencement of a winding up, any disposition of the company's property and any transfer of shares or alteration in the status of the company's members is void, unless the court orders otherwise[3].

1 Provisional liquidator

12.35 At any time after the petition for a compulsory liquidation is presented to the court and before the court makes an order, an application may be made to appoint a provisional liquidator to maintain the status quo. The order appointing a provisional liquidator will specify the functions he is to carry out and may limit his powers. The appointment will terminate when the court so orders and will normally terminate if the petition for winding up is dismissed or granted.

2 Powers of directors and liquidators

12.36 In a voluntary winding up where no liquidator has been appointed or nominated, a provision exists[4] similar in effect to section 284 relating to individual bankruptcy (which prevents individuals from dissipating assets prior to the bankruptcy order). This prevents the directors from exercising powers other than those necessary to preserve the assets of the company, or in a creditors' winding up, relating to their statement of affairs or the convening of the creditors' meeting. In a compulsory liquidation, on the making of the court order the Official Receiver becomes the liquidator until another person is appointed,

1 Section 86.
2 Section 129.
3 Section 127.
4 Section 114.

unless the company was, prior to the winding-up order, subject to an administration order or a voluntary arrangement, in which case the court may appoint the administrator or supervisor[1].

In both voluntary and compulsory winding up, the powers of the directors cease on appointment of a liquidator. In the case of voluntary arrangements, this cessation is provided by the Act but in the case of compulsory liquidation it is established by the case of *Re Farrows Bank*[2]. The company cannot deny the apparent authority of its directors until notification has officially been made[3].

The powers of the liquidator are set out in sections 165 to 167 and in Schedule 4. The powers are divided into those that require a sanction and those that do not. Generally, the liquidator acts as the company's agent and will not be personally liable on contracts made expressly as liquidator on behalf of the company.

3 Avoiding prior transactions

12.37 A liquidator may apply to the court to restore the company's position in relation to transactions at an undervalue[4] and preferences[5]. The relevant time for this purpose in relation to both a transaction at an undervalue and a preference given to a connected person (other than a mere employee) is two years before the date of commencement of the winding up[6], unless the recipient can show that the company was not insolvent[7] or becomes unable to pay its debts in consequence of the transaction or preference. In the case of any other preference, the time period is six months before the date of the winding-up order[8]. In either case it is a relevant time during the period between the presentation of the petition for, and the making of, an administration order. In relation to preferences it is also necessary to show that the company was influenced in deciding to give the preference by a desire to put that person in a better position in the event of the company's insolvent liquidation[9]. However, this will be presumed if the preference is given to a person connected with the company (otherwise than by reason only of his being an employee). A 'connected person' for these purposes is defined in sections 249 and 435 as a director, shadow director or an associate of either of them or the company.

Additionally, floating charges may be invalid if created in the period of 12 months (or two years in the case of a connected person) before the date of the presentation of the petition or commencement of the winding up, except to the extent of the value of any new consideration given at the time of execution of the charge.

1 Section 140(1) and (2).
2 [1921] 2 Ch 164.
3 Companies Act 2006, s 1079(1) to (3).
4 Section 238; *Knights (Liquidator of Taylor Sinclair (Capital) Ltd) v Seymour Pierce Ellis Ltd* LTL 27 July 2001.
5 Section 239.
6 Or in relation to an administration order the date of presentation of the petition.
7 Section 123.
8 Or in relation to an administration order the date of presentation of the petition.
9 Section 239.

A liquidator, like a trustee in bankruptcy, will realise assets, pay debts (there are provisions relating to expenses and preferential debts similar to those for bankruptcy) and distribute any surplus to shareholders. Once the company's affairs are fully wound up, the liquidator in a voluntary liquidation will prepare an account of the winding up and lay it before a shareholders' meeting, which is advertised in the London Gazette, at least one month prior to it taking place. Any remaining property of the company on dissolution will be treated as bona vacantia (essentially ownerless property). In the case of a compulsory liquidation a final meeting of creditors is called. Following such meetings the Registrar of Companies is informed and the company is normally dissolved three months later.

SECTION 5 PROTECTIVE TRUSTS

12.38 As has already been seen above[1] it is not possible for a person to create a trust which contains a forfeiture clause relating to their own interest under the trust. It is equally not possible to declare a trust with a condition subsequent that the trust will terminate if the beneficiary in question is made bankrupt. However, it is possible to include a forfeiture clause in a trust which operates in cases of an alienation by, or bankruptcy of, the beneficiary or which can operate on an alienation prior to bankruptcy of the settlor. For example, in *Re Detmold*[2] the settlor created a trust which contained a life interest for himself subject to a gift over to his wife and children in the event of alienation of his interest either voluntarily or involuntarily by process of law. The condition as to alienation was breached and the settlor subsequently became bankrupt. It was held that the forfeiture having taken place prior to the bankruptcy, it was valid to defeat the interest of the trustee in bankruptcy. The distinction here is that the trust created a determinable interest for a person until he attempted to alienate rather than attempting to alienate property which has already been given absolutely.

A type of such a trust is the protective trust. Such trusts can be useful to provide an income for life for a spendthrift or financially naive beneficiary and his dependants. A protective trust is essentially a trust of income to a beneficiary for his lifetime provided that if he alienates the interest or is made bankrupt, his life interest will cease and be replaced by a discretionary trust for the benefit of himself and/or his family[3]. Before the Trustee Act 1925, it was necessary to include a clause to this effect in the settlement[4]. However, section 33 of that Act provides a 'shorthand arrangement' so that a reference to protective trusts will bring the protective trust set out in that section into effect. This provides that where any income, including an annuity or other periodical income payment, is directed to be held on protective trusts for the benefit of any person ('the principal beneficiary') for the period of his life or for any lesser period, then during

1 See forfeiture clauses Section 2F, **12.19**.

2 [1889] 40 Ch D 585.

3 In this respect it is similar to the forfeiture clauses found in occupational pension schemes.

4 *Re Walker* [1939] Ch 974.

that period ('the trust period') the income shall without prejudice to any prior interest be held on the following trusts:

(1) upon trust for the principal beneficiary during the trust period or until he does or attempts to do any *act or thing* or until any event happens (other than an advance under any statutory or express power) whereby if the income was payable during the trust period to the *principal beneficiary* absolutely during that period, he *would be deprived of the right to receive the same or any part thereof in any of which cases the said trust of the income* shall fail or determine;

(2) if the *trust fails or determines* during the trust period then for the rest of that period the income is to be held upon trust to be applied as *the trustees in their* absolute *discretion* (without being liable to account for the exercise of such discretion) think fit, for the maintenance or support or otherwise *for the benefit* of all or any of the following persons:

   (a) the principal beneficiary and his or her wife or husband if any and his or her children or more remote issue if any; or

   (b) where there is no wife or husband or issue in existence the principal beneficiary and the persons who would, if he were dead, be entitled to the trust property or the income.

In addition to the statutory trust provided by section 33, it is still possible to have an express protective trust. It is also provided that nothing in that section operates to validate any trust which, if contained in the trust instrument, would be liable to be set aside. This has the effect of preserving the pre-existing law so if the settlor himself is to take the income until the happening of the event then if that event is bankruptcy the income will go to his creditors.

A Conditions causing forfeiture

12.39 The condition that will cause forfeiture under section 33 is any act or event whereby the principal beneficiary would be deprived of the right to receive the income during the trust period. This has a very wide meaning and extends to bankruptcy or assignment by the principal beneficiary.

One problematic area with forfeiture under protective trusts is the effect of court orders on divorce. There is authority in *General Accident Fire and Life Assurance Corpn Ltd v IRC*[1] that an order of the divorce court to pay a sum of money to the principal beneficiary's wife during her life did not bring about a forfeiture of her husband's protective interest. This was not an event contemplated by section 33(1). In *Re Richardson's Will Trust*[2], however, an unsatisfied court order that the principal beneficiary charge his interest to create an annual

1 [1963] 1 WLR 1207.
2 [1958] Ch 504, [1958] 1 All ER 538.

payment for his wife created an equitable charge, which therefore caused a forfeiture. Similarly, in *Edmonds v Edmonds*[1] an attachment of earnings order to secure a former wife's maintenance was held to cause a forfeiture of a pension held on protective trust.

Conversely, acts which have been held not to cause a forfeiture include appointment of an attorney to receive income[2] or appointment of a receiver where the principal beneficiary was a person of unsound mind[3]. Also, an order of the court under section 57 of the Trustee Act 1925 giving power to trustees to raise capital moneys for the benefit of a life tenant has been held not to cause a forfeiture since all settlements are subject to this overriding section[4].

Although provisions to create a protective trust can be included in a settlement from the outset, it has been held that, in a trust containing a power of appointment, the donee of the power is unlikely to be able to make an appointment on a protective trust basis because of the discretionary nature of the trust following forfeiture of the principal beneficiary's interest. This would, in effect, be a delegation of that person's power which would not be possible unless the settlement itself made provision for it[5].

The case law[6] is not clear regarding payment by the trustees (once the forfeiture has occurred) of the income to the principal beneficiary even though this accords with the express wording of the section. The reasoning appears to be that the principal beneficiary would be bound to hand over to the creditor/assignee whose interest caused the forfeiture any part of the income paid to him and that the trustees having notice of such interest are equally bound not to pay the income to him. The cases, however, rather strangely establish that the trustees may expend such income for the principal beneficiary's benefit[7].

SECTION 6 MARRIED WOMEN'S PROPERTY ACT 1882 (MWPA)

A Protection against creditors

12.40 A transaction at an undervalue[8] to an associate, which includes wife and children, can be overturned for up to five years if a petition in bankruptcy is presented within the period, unless it can be shown by the wife and/or children (as appropriate) that the donor was not and did not thereby become insolvent. In view of the fact that 'insolvent' for this purpose means unable to pay debts as they fall due it can be quite difficult to establish. Section 11 of the Married Women's Property Act 1882 (MWPA) provides protection in such circum-

1 [1965] 1 All ER 379n.
2 *Re Tancred's Settlement* [1903] 1 Ch 715.
3 *Re Oppenheimer's Will Trust* [1950] Ch 633.
4 *Re Mair* [1935] Ch 562.
5 *Re Boulton's Settlement Trust* [1928] Ch 703.
6 See eg Stirling LJ in *Re Fitzgerald* [1904] 1 Ch 573 at 593.
7 *Re Bullock* (1891) 64 LT 736.
8 See Section 1D, **12.17**.

stances in relation to life policies. It provides (in part) in respect of an MWPA trust that:

> '… the moneys payable under any such a policy shall not, so long as any object of the trust remains unperformed, form part of the estate of the insured or be subject to his or her debts: Provided, that if it shall be proved that the policy was effected and the premiums paid with intent to defraud the creditors of the insured, they shall be entitled to receive, out of the moneys payable under the policy, a sum equal to the premiums so paid.'

It would appear from cases decided under the Bankruptcy Act 1914[1] and section 172 of the Law of Property Act 1925 (now repealed), that the wording in section 11 will be effective to prevent the trustee in bankruptcy seeking to avoid such trusts as prior transactions.

There appears to be some uncertainty as to the extent of a creditor's right to recover premiums where it can be shown that there was an intention to avoid creditors. The wording in section 11 of the MWPA is that the creditors are entitled 'to receive out of the *moneys payable under the policy*, a sum equal to the premiums so paid'. There is some authority on the point. First, in *Holt v Everall*[2] it was held that the surrender value of an earlier policy used to pay premiums on a second policy could be recovered by the creditors. In relation to when the amount can be recovered (ie on bankruptcy or death), there is a Scottish case[3], which indicates that under similar wording in the Scottish Act of 1880, the creditors claim their interest when the 'policy comes to be realised'. In that particular case, it was when the policy came to pay out on death. However, in relation to policies with a surrender value or unit-linked policies with a potential investment value, there appears to be no authority on the question of whether the creditors would be entitled to the moneys earlier than on death.

B Conditions and benefits of an MWPA trust

12.41 The relevant part of section 11[4], which defines what an MWPA trust is, provides as follows:

> 'A policy of assurance effected by any man on his own life, and expressed to be for the benefit of his wife, or of his children, or of his wife and children, or any of them, or by any woman on her own life, and expressed to be for the benefit of her husband, or of her children, or of her husband and children, or any of them, shall create a trust in favour of the objects therein named … The insured may by the policy or by any memorandum under his or her hand, appoint a trustee or trustees of the moneys payable under the policy, and from time to time appoint a new trustee or new trustees thereof, and may make provision for the appointment of a

1 *Re Harrison and Ingram, ex p Whinney* [1900] 2 QB 710.
2 [1876] 2 Ch D 266.
3 *Stewart v Hodge* 1901 SLT 436.
4 As amended by the Law Reform (Married Women and Tortfeasors) Act 1935 and the Statute Law (Repeals) Act 1969.

> new trustee or new trustees thereof, and for the investment of the moneys payable under any such policy. In default of any such appointment of a trustee, such policy, immediately on its being effected, shall vest in the insured and his or her legal personal representatives, in trust for the purposes aforesaid. [...] [repealed by Statute Law (Repeals) Act 1969 Schedule Part III] The receipt of a trustee or trustees duly appointed, or, in default of any such appointment, or in default of notice to the insurance office, the receipt of the legal personal representative of the insured shall be a discharge to the office for the sum secured by the policy, or for the value thereof, in whole or in part.'[1]

From this it can be seen that in addition to the protection afforded to creditors, the effect of section 11 of the MWPA 1882, is to enable:

(1) the creation of a trust of life policies without the formalities otherwise required[2];

(2) the appointment of trustees and vesting of the policy in those trustees from the outset[3].

C Trustees of MWPA policies

1 Method of appointment

12.42 The assured may by the policy or by a memorandum under his hand appoint a trustee or trustees, and may from time to time appoint new trustees and he may vest the power to appoint new trustees in himself or some other person or persons. If he makes no appointment, or until he makes an appointment, he will himself be the trustee and if he dies his executors or administrators will be the trustees.

The assured does not under modern practice execute the policy himself, but he may be said to have made the appointment by the policy if he accepts a policy naming trustees. An appointment by memorandum under hand may be incorporated in the proposal (which may itself be incorporated in the policy by reference), or may be a separate document. It is customary to record such an appointment in the policy if made at the time the policy is effected. If the policy is for the benefit of the wife, the husband may think it suitable to appoint her as trustee jointly with himself. He can then retain some control of the policy during his life and at his death the wife can as surviving trustee collect the policy money without any formality other than proof of his death and production of the policy.

Section 11 refers to the appointment of a new trustee and there is some doubt

1 The section replaced the Married Women's Property Act 1870, s 10, the terms of which were somewhat similar, though there are important differences; namely, under the 1870 Act, the trust was created only where a policy was effected by a *married man.*

2 As mere use of the words 'on behalf of' would not be sufficient to satisfy the certainty of words requirement.

3 See Chapter 11 on the issues relating to the appointment of trustees and associated vesting issues.

as to whether this includes an additional, as opposed to replacement, trustee. In practice there will rarely be an issue as there will either be express provision to this effect in the trust or section 36(6) of the Trustee Act 1925, will apply.

D Requirements for an MWPA trust

12.43 In order that a policy may create a trust under the section, it must fulfil the following requirements:

(1) *It must be a policy effected by a man on his own life or by a woman on her own life.* The Act mentions any man or any woman. A bachelor or spinster, widower or widow may effect a policy under the Act. It does not therefore include a life of another contract.

In *Re Oakes' Settlement*[1] it was held that a policy is effected by the person who signs the proposal form and the fact that some other person is generous enough to pay the first or subsequent premiums is not relevant. This decision was, however, made for the purpose of interpreting a provision regarding estate duty (a forerunner of inheritance tax) on policies which has since been repealed and should not therefore be taken as necessarily having general application.

The decision in *Griffiths v Fleming*[2] is sometimes cited as authority for the proposition that a husband and wife can effect a joint lives policy under the MWPA for the benefit of, say, a child. But the judges, although they were prepared to treat the policy as effected in trust under the MWPA, preferred not to do so and in any case expressly based their opinions on the fact that there were two proposals and two contracts and that the life office had issued the wrong policy. Vaughan Williams LJ said that the joint policy was not within the MWPA. It is therefore submitted that, if any view at all can be formed regarding joint lives policies as a result of this case, it is that such policies are not within the provisions of the Act.

Griffiths v Fleming[3]

Husband and wife each signed a proposal form for a policy on his or her own life, and each paid a proportion of the first premium corresponding to their representative ages. The company issued a policy for a joint lives assurance payable, on the death of the first of them to die, to the survivor. The wife committed suicide. The insurance company refused to pay on the ground that the husband had no insurable interest in her life. The plaintiff pleaded that he had such an interest and alternatively that each of the lives had effected an insurance in favour of the other. It was held by the Court of Appeal that a wife has an insurable interest in her husband's life without need of proof. Two of the judges said that separate proposals to insure the respective lives were accepted by the insurance company and there was nothing to show any intention to have one joint life policy. The

1 [1951] Ch 156.
2 [1909] 1 KB 805, CA.
3 [1909] 1 KB 805.

> company could not set up a form of policy which was not in accordance with the proposals so as to defeat their liability. The policy should therefore be read as two assurance contracts, and the court preferred to treat them as two assurances effected by one spouse on the life of the other. Therefore, each policy fell within the terms of section 11 of the MWPA (although not that part of section 11 which automatically creates a trust).

In *Rooney v Cardona*[1] the Court of Appeal took the view that an ordinary joint life endowment contract on the lives of a married couple was not within section 11 despite the conclusions reached at first instance. In this case the parties had not referred to section 11 and the policy was not expressed to be for the benefit of the lives assured. Also, unlike *Griffiths v Fleming*, there were not separate proposal forms.

12.44

(2) *The policy must be a policy of assurance on life.* The MWPA does not contain a definition of 'policy of assurance' but a policy is nevertheless on life because it covers death only from a particular cause (such as a personal accident policy) or provides benefits payable on other events than death.

> *Re Gladitz, Guaranty Executor and Trustee Co Ltd v Gladitz*[2]
>
> G effected a Lloyd's policy covering payments to be made in the event of death by accident and of disablement. The policy contained the following memorandum: 'It is understood and agreed that all claims under this policy shall be payable to Winifred Gladitz, wife of the assured, if she is living at the happening of the event upon which the claim becomes payable'. Held, (1) that a policy which, besides including provision for payment upon the happening of a man's death by a particular cause, also provides for payment upon other events is nevertheless a policy of assurance effected by a man on his own life within the MWPA, even though that Act is not mentioned in the policy, and (2) that the memorandum printed at the foot of the policy sufficiently expressed it to be for the benefit of the wife.

The MWPA accordingly extends to whole life, temporary and endowment assurances, family income and other life assurance policies including whole of life policies with dread disease or critical illness cover.

(3) *The policy must be expressed to be for the benefit of husband, wife and/or children only.* It is not necessary to mention the MWPA in the policy but it is preferable to do so in order that, in any case of conflict of law owing to differences in domicile of the proposer, the beneficiaries and place of establishment of the life office, there shall be no doubt that the policy is intended to create a trust under the MWPA and is not subject to the law of some other country. It is not necessary to use words expressly declar-

1 [1999] 1 WLR 1388.
2 [1937] Ch 588.

ing a trust, nor indeed does it seem that there need be a positive intention to effect the policy under the Act, so long as it is expressed in such a way as to bring it within the MWPA. However, a policy not 'effected' in trust for any object within the MWPA cannot later be the subject of a declaration of trust under the MWPA (although it can be subject to a trust outside of the Act).

E Beneficiaries under MWPA trusts and the nature of their interests

1 Objects (beneficiaries) of the trusts

12.45 Reference must in every case be made to the policy to ascertain the objects of the trust, and the nature and extent of the interests which the beneficiaries are to take[1].

2 Class of beneficiaries

12.46 The class of beneficiaries comprises wife or husband, and children, including illegitimate[2], and adopted children. It does not, however, extend to stepchildren or grandchildren whether legitimate or not.

If a policy is expressed to be for the benefit of any person other than the wife or child of the life assured, it may not be protected by section 11 of the Married Women's Property Act 1882 except possibly to the extent that it benefits the wife or children[3]. The life assured may, however, have constituted an effective trust outside the MWPA for the other beneficiaries, though the mere statement in the policy that it is effected for the benefit of those persons would not be sufficient in itself to create such a trust. Where there is no effective trust for those other beneficiaries there will be, to that extent at least, a resulting trust for the life assured.

Re *Parker's Policies*[4] has been cited as authority for the proposition that a policy expressed to be for the benefit of any person other than the wife or child of the life assured is not protected by section 11 even to the extent of the interests of wife or child named as beneficiaries. However, no such decision was made in that case and it does not appear that the judge's obiter remarks support this view. However, the question is clearly not free from doubt and the proposer would be well advised to be specific about both the Act and the beneficiaries where it is desired that such a policy is to be subject to the MWPA.

1 *Cousins v Sun Life Assurance Society* [1933] Ch 126.
2 With effect from 1 January 1970, Family Law Reform Act 1969, s 19.
3 *Re Clay's Policy of Assurance; Clay v Earnshaw* [1937] 2 All ER 548.
4 [1906] 1 Ch 526.

3 Named and unnamed beneficiaries

12.47 Where a policy is effected for the benefit of a named wife or child the identity of the beneficiary is clear, but in a case where there is a reference to relationship only, it is necessary to construe the policy in order to ascertain who the beneficiaries are to be. Where, for example, a policy is effected by a man, and expressed to be for the benefit of his wife (without naming her), the policy will have to be construed to determine whether the beneficiary is the wife living at the date of the inception of the policy or whether a second or subsequent wife living at the life assured's death is to take. In *Re Browne's Policy, Browne v Browne*[1] the proposer's first wife died and he remarried. It was held that his second wife took an interest on his death where the policy was expressed to be 'for the benefit of his wife and children'.

4 Named wife

12.48 A policy expressed to be for the benefit of or to be payable to a named wife, husband or child without further words will give the beneficiary an immediate vested interest in the whole policy. The following expressions all have the same construction:

(1) For the benefit of Lilian, wife of the life assured.

(2) For the benefit of Lilian, wife of the life assured, absolutely.

(3) For the benefit of Lilian, wife of the life assured, her executors, administrators or assignees.

The last of these expressions is not perhaps ideal since it is clearly not the intention of the husband to personally *benefit* his wife's executors or administrators although it would normally be assumed that it was held in their capacity as executor etc. Prior to the following case there were some cases which expressed a contrary opinion.

> *Cousins v Sun Life Assurance Society*[2]
>
> A husband effected a policy on his life under the MWPA, for the benefit of his wife, Lilian. She died in his lifetime and he applied to surrender the policy. Held, that the wife took an immediate vested interest from the commencement of the policy, which passed, on her death in the husband's lifetime, to her personal representatives as part of her estate.

5 Limited interests

12.49 The interest of the beneficiary need not be the whole extent of the policy money but may be *limited* in various ways by the use of appropriate words.

1 [1903] 1 Ch 188.
2 [1933] Ch 126.

Re Fleetwood's Policy[1]

A husband effected a policy whereby the life office agreed to pay to his wife if she should be living at his death but otherwise to his executors. The policy reserved to the husband various options, one of which he exercised. This was the option to receive cash with its share of accrued profits and to discontinue the policy. Held, that he had exercised the option as trustee, and that the trusts attached to the resulting benefit. Moreover, the policy was expressed to be for the benefit of the wife in a certain event only, but the fact that her interest was of a limited or contingent character did not prevent the policy from being a policy within the MWPA. Unless the husband and wife came to an agreement the fund must be accumulated in court until it could be ascertained, by the death of either party, who was entitled to it.

Re Ioakimidis' Policy Trusts, Ioakimidis v Hartcup[2]

A husband effected an endowment assurance expressed to be for the benefit of his wife only in the event of his death before 28 May 1938, leaving her surviving him. The assured died in 1924 and his creditors claimed the policy money. Held that the policy was within the MWPA and created, in the event which happened, a valid trust for the wife.

The interest of a named wife under an endowment assurance may accordingly be:

(1) for her absolutely;

(2) for her if she is living on survival of the husband to the end of the term or on his previous death;

(3) for her only if the husband dies before maturity leaving her surviving.

If the proposer wishes, he may give the wife or other beneficiary a life interest only or, it is submitted, reserve a power of appointment among his wife and children.

6 *Interests of children*

12.50 The interests of children may be made contingent on attaining majority or surviving the assured, or may be limited in such other manner as the proposer may think fit.

Before effecting any policy which is to be for the benefit of children, it is important to determine:

(1) whether the children are to be named, so that any further children born will be excluded;

1 [1926] Ch 48.
2 [1925] Ch 403.

(2) whether, if not named, the class of children is to be limited to the children of the existing marriage or to any children of the life assured. Since 1969 a provision for children without further description will include any illegitimate children of the life assured; and

(3) whether any child's interest is to continue for the benefit of his or her estate:

   (a) if he or she predeceases the assured, or dies before the event upon which the sum assured becomes payable; or

   (b) if he or she dies before attaining majority or marrying.

7 *Maintenance, education, and advancement of children*

12.51 The trustees will have the statutory powers to use income for maintenance, education or benefit, and capital for advancement or benefit. If further powers are required, eg to use the whole of the capital for education (the statutory power[1] only allows one half), they must be specifically given in the trust provisions.

8 *Policy effected by an unmarried person*

12.52 A policy under the MWPA can be effected by an *unmarried* man or woman for the benefit of his or her legitimate or illegitimate child or children; or for any person the life assured may marry. If the proposer is already engaged to be married, it may be suitable to express the interest of his fiancée as contingent on her marriage to the proposer and to be effected in consideration of marriage.

9 *Divorce*

12.53 Divorce will not *of itself* destroy the interest of a named wife; but she may lose her interest if the husband applies to the court for an order to vary the settlement of the policy.

On granting a decree of divorce, nullity or judicial separation the court may make an order varying, for the benefit of the parties to the marriage and of the children of the family, or either or any of them, any ante-nuptial or post-nuptial settlement made on the parties to the marriage[2]. The court also has power to make an order extinguishing or reducing the interest of either of the parties to the marriage under any such settlement[3]. 'Settlement' is given a wide interpretation and would include trusts of life assurance policies.

The following are cases under previous enactments which gave the court powers similar to, but not as wide as, those under the Matrimonial Causes Act 1973.

1 Trustee Act, 1925, s 31.
2 Matrimonial Causes Act 1973, s 24.
3 Matrimonial Causes Act 1973, s 24(1)(d).

Gulbenkian v Gulbenkian[1]

A husband effected two endowment assurances on his life as follows:

(1) A policy payable to him at maturity if then living, or, on his death during the term, to his wife.

(2) A policy payable to him at maturity if then living, or, on his death during the term, to his wife if living, and otherwise to his personal representatives.

The husband divorced his wife and asked for an order varying the trusts. Held, that the name of the wife should be struck out.

Gunner v Gunner and Stirling[2]

A husband effected, under the MWPA, a whole life policy for the benefit of a named wife absolutely. He divorced her and applied to the court to vary the policy as a settlement. Held, that the settlement of the policy could be varied.

Lort-Williams v Lort-Williams[3]

A husband took out a policy on his life under the MWPA 'for the benefit of the widow or children or any of them of the assured in such shares and proportions and interests and generally in such manner as the assured shall by will or deed revocable or irrevocable appoint or may have so appointed'. The wife divorced him and applied to the court to vary the terms of the policy, the husband having in the meantime married again. The Court of Appeal held that the policy could be varied notwithstanding that the wife's interest was contingent on her surviving the husband and uncertain, and even though the use of the word 'widow' contemplated that a second wife might benefit.

F Notes on MWPA policies construed by the court

12.54

Wording	*Construction*
Policies issued under section 10 of the Married Women's Property Act 1870 (very similar predecessor to 1882 Act).	
For the benefit of his wife, Susan, and of the children of their marriage[4].	(1) The children who take are those living when the fund comes into existence. (2) The wife and surviving children take as joint tenants.
For the benefit of his wife and children[5].	The wife and children take as joint tenants.

1 [1927] P 237.
2 [1949] P 77.
3 [1951] P 395.
4 *Re Seyton, Seyton v Satterthwaite* (1887) 34 Ch D 511.
5 *Re Davies' Policy Trusts* [1892] 1 Ch 90.

Wording	*Construction*
For the benefit of his wife or if she be dead between his children in equal proportions[1].	The widow (who was a second wife and not the wife living at the date of the policy) was not entitled. The children of both marriages take in equal shares. The words 'if she be dead' pointed to the wife living at the date of the policy.
For the benefit of his widow or widow and children or some or one of them in such shares and proportions and interest and generally in such manner as the assured shall by any will or codicil or by deed revocable or otherwise appoint[2]. Note – the assured by deed appointed to his second wife if she should survive him.	The second wife survived the assured. The appointment was good and the second wife took absolutely.
For the benefit of his wife[3].	The wife living at the date of the policy died in the lifetime of the husband. She was not named in the policy. The words 'for the benefit of his wife' mean in these circumstances 'for the benefit of her who by surviving the assured shall become his widow'.
Policies issued under section 11 of the Married Women's Property Act 1882.	
For the benefit of L the wife of the assured.	The specifically named wife takes an immediate absolute vested interest in the policy, which passes on her death in the husband's lifetime to her personal representatives[4].
For the benefit of his wife and children[5].	The wife living at the date of the policy died. The assured was survived by a second wife and children of both marriages. The second wife and all the children take as joint tenants. Note – had the policy been effected after 1969 any illegitimate children would have been entitled to share equally with the second wife and lawful children.

1 *Re Griffiths' Policy* [1903] 1 Ch 739.
2 *Re Parker's Policies* [1906] 1 Ch 526.
3 *Re Collier* [1930] 2 Ch 37.
4 *Cousins v Sun Life Assurance Society* [1933] Ch 126.
5 *Re Browne's Policy, Browne v Browne* [1903] 1 Ch 188.

G Scotland

1 The MWPA (Scotland) Act

12.55 The corresponding Scottish Act is the Married Women's Policies of Assurance (Scotland) Act 1880, which extended to Scotland facilities already available in England under the English Act of 1870. It was amended in 1980 by the Married Women's Policies of Assurance (Scotland) (Amendment) Act 1980 to extend to men and women whether married or not.

Section 2 of the MWPA (Scotland) Act, as amended, makes provisions which in general are similar to those in the English MWPA with regard to trustees, protection against creditors, and receipts for sums secured by the policy or for the value thereof, in whole or in part. The provision entitling the creditors to claim a return of premiums applies if the life assured is made bankrupt within *two years* of the date of the policy, as well as if it is proved that the policy was effected and premiums paid with intent to defraud creditors.

A man or woman can therefore now effect a policy in trust under the MWPA (Scotland) Act and any one or more members of the classes known as 'spouse and children' can be beneficiaries. 'Children' includes children which the person effecting the policy has, or may have in the future, including illegitimate children and adopted children. It does not, however, extend to children of a spouse and another person unless the person effecting the policy has adopted them.

The MWPA (Scotland) Act, as amended, further provides that where a policy vests in trust by virtue of section 2 of the 1880 Act then:

(1) that trust constitutes a trust within the meaning of the Trusts (Scotland) Act 1921; and

(2) any person in whom such a policy vests is a trustee within the meaning of that Act. The sometimes onerous requirement for delivery is not essential for MWPA (Scotland) Act trusts.

Moreover, a policy is not prevented from vesting in a trustee merely because it contains a provision that a trustee may in his professional capacity charge a reasonable remuneration for his services. The powers of trustees are clarified by the 1980 amendment act. Trustees under such trusts will therefore have all the powers of trustees within the meaning of the Trusts (Scotland) Act 1921. One notable amendment introduced by the 1980 Act was that a beneficiary under such a trust may now assign or renounce his interest[1]. This is the case whether or not the policy was dated before or after 29 October 1980.

This Act extends to Scotland only and although the effect of this is not clear it seems wise to use the 1880 Act only for policies payable in Scotland effected by people resident and domiciled in Scotland.

1 Section 3(1) and (3).

CHAPTER 13

Income tax and capital gains tax

SUMMARY

SECTION 1 INTRODUCTION

13.1 The effect of the Finance Act 1984 was to remove income tax relief for premiums payable in respect of life policies effected after 13 March 1984. In addition, any policy effected prior to 14 March 1984 loses relief if it is varied after 13 March 1984 so as to increase the benefits or extend the term of the policy.

This introduction gives a brief outline of the subject to be dealt with in more detail in later Sections.

A person who paid the premium on a life policy on his or her own life, or the life of his or her spouse, could, subject to certain conditions, have obtained a reduction in income tax liability. This relief applied only to basic rate, not to tax at the higher rate.

For premiums under a policy effected after 19 March 1968 to have been eligible for income tax relief, the policy, besides satisfying the other rules prescribed in the Income and Corporation Taxes Act 1970 (ICTA 1970), had to satisfy (or be exempt from) a number of qualifying conditions: ie it must have been a 'qualifying policy' within the meaning of Schedule 1 to that Act. These conditions, which were intended primarily to prevent tax avoidance, were first introduced by the Finance Act 1968 but were later consolidated in ICTA 1970. However, because it was believed that the rules under the 1968 Act were deficient in some respects, further qualifying conditions were imposed by Schedule 2 to the Finance Act 1975 with effect from 1 April 1976. The 1975 Act also provided for the taking over by the Inland Revenue (HMRC) from the life offices of the function of testing and certifying policies as 'qualifying' under the statutory requirements.

The status of a policy as 'qualifying' continues to be important subsequent to the Finance Act 1984. If a policy is non-qualifying, a potential liability to higher rate tax will arise under sections 461–546 of the Income Tax (Trading and Other Income) Act 2005 (ITTOIA 2005) – (formerly sections 539–554 of the Income and Corporation Taxes Act 1988 (ICTA 1988)) – on the profit (or gain) derived from the contract. Even if the contract is a qualifying policy, such a tax charge may arise in the event, for example, of termination of premium payments within ten years of commencement or within three-quarters of the term, if less.

SECTION 2 TAX RELIEF ON LIFE PREMIUMS – POSITION PRIOR TO THE FINANCE ACT 1984

13.2 In view of the fact that this is now mainly only of historical interest it is dealt with only briefly in this edition. For a fuller treatment the reader is referred to the tenth edition of this book.

A Premiums ranking for relief – conditions applicable to all policies[1]

13.3

(1) The premium must have been one payable on a policy effected with an insurance company legally established in the UK or any branch in the UK of an insurance company lawfully carrying on life assurance business in the UK, or on a policy effected with a registered friendly society, or on a policy issued by underwriting members of Lloyd's or any other approved association of underwriters.

HMRC previously interpreted the old section 19(2)(i) of ICTA 1970 as meaning that relief was not due unless the management of a policy issued overseas had been transferred to the UK branch. They ultimately concluded, however, that the legislation did not impose such a condition and so if the premium on such a policy is paid to the UK branch and the conditions for relief were otherwise satisfied, relief would have been due[2].

1 See now ICTA 1988, s 266.
2 Inland Revenue Press Release, 4 February 1981.

(2) The policy must have been a policy of insurance made by a man on his own life or on that of his wife; or a woman on her own life or the life of her husband.

A premium on a joint life policy would not normally have ranked for relief, unless the lives were husband and wife.

Wilson v Simpson[1]

Two directors, W and M, effected a policy on their joint lives and paid the premium in equal shares. One director claimed relief on his half-share of the premium. Held, that as the assurance had been made jointly with another person, it was not a contract made by him only, nor was the assurance made on his life, but on their joint lives. The payments he had made were his contribution towards the joint payment. Relief, was, therefore, not available.

(3) The policy must have secured a capital sum on death.

Gould v Curtis[2]

G effected a double endowment assurance, the benefit being £100 if death should occur during a term of years or £200 on survival to the end of the term. Held, that the whole of the premium was available for relief and not only that part charged to provide the capital sum on death.

B The extent of relief

13.4 After 5 April 1979 a fixed percentage of each premium is deducted from the life assurance premium on payment and retained by the taxpayer. The premium limit from 6 April 1990 is the larger of one-sixth of total income (after charges) and £1,500 for each spouse. Different rules applied prior to 6 April 1990. There is no actual limit on the deduction from premiums as life offices never know if the one-sixth limit is being exceeded. Tax relief may therefore be deducted irrespective of the size of the premium and so it is up to HMRC to ensure that the limit is not exceeded. In the event that the limits are exceeded, HMRC are able to recover the excess tax relief by issuing an assessment to the policyholder. It can also issue a 'Paragraph 4' notice. This is a notice to the policyholder and the life office specifying that premiums must henceforth be paid gross[3].

If such a notice is received from HMRC, the life office must make arrangements to collect premiums without deduction of tax relief from the date specified in the notice.

From 6 April 1989 the rate of relief is 12.5%.

1 [1926] 2 KB 500.
2 [1913] 3 KB 84.
3 ICTA 1988, Sch 14, para 4.

C Conditions and limits of relief

13.5

(1) The policy, if effected after 19 March 1968, must be either a qualifying or exempt policy within the provisions laid down in what is now Schedule 15 to ICTA 1988 (see Section 3). A policy effected on or before that date is treated as one made after that date if varied after that date so as to increase the benefits secured, or to extend the term of the assurance.

(2) The total maximum relief in any year is relief in respect of one-sixth of the 'total income' of the taxpayer. 'Total income' for this purpose is the aggregate of the income from all sources reduced by all charges and other deductions but before deducting personal allowances[1]. The capital element of a purchased life annuity is not included in total income for this purpose.

(3) The premium must have been *paid* by the claimant. The relief is not lost if the assured raises the money by borrowing from his bank or elsewhere on another or even the same policy. A premium is not, however, regarded as *paid* if it is charged against the benefits under the express terms of the policy. Thus, where the premiums are only partly paid in cash and the balance is advanced by way of loan by the life office, then relief is only available on the part of the premium paid in cash.

> *Hunter v R*[2]
>
> A policy provided for a sum assured of £1,500 payable on death and the premium was £66 per annum. Of this, £33 was paid in cash and the remaining £33 plus interest thereon was to be deducted from the proceeds. The taxpayer contended that the £33 was paid by an advance from the life office. Held, that relief was available only on the £33 actually *paid* by the taxpayer. Payments can be made net of relief via a third party, such as a broker or employer, but must come ultimately from the assured or his spouse.

There is no requirement that premiums should be paid out of income; relief can be obtained even if they are paid out of capital.

(4) The relief for any year of assessment should be based on the premiums paid in that year. The renewal date is not material. If accordingly the premiums fall into arrears and several premiums are subsequently paid in one year, all the payments rank for that year. Where an advance of the premium is made by the life office and is subsequently paid off, the payment will be treated as a payment of premium on which relief can be claimed but relief will be allowed only if such an advance of premium is actually repaid. Cancellation of the debt by way of set-off is not sufficient.

1 ITA 2007, s.23.
2 [1904] AC 161.

R v Income Tax Special Commrs, ex p Horner[1]

H effected an endowment assurance and on maturity the portions of premium advanced by the life office were deducted from the policy money. Held, that no relief could be made in respect of amounts so deducted.

Watkins (Inspector of Taxes) v Hugh-Jones[2]

H-J effected a policy entitled to share in profits in the form of reduction of premium. He claimed that he had paid the full premium and received a set-off of the reduction. Held, that the reduced premium only was available for relief.

(5) The policy must not have been varied after 13 March 1984 so as to increase the benefits or extend its term[3].

The following are not regarded as increasing the benefits or extending the term:

(a) reduction of term of endowment assurance if premiums remain unchanged but sum assured is reduced;

(b) change in premium frequency (eg annual to monthly);

(c) conversion from without to with-profits if premiums are not increased but sum assured is reduced;

(d) removal of a debt premium loading or exclusion imposed because of an exceptional risk of death, even if premiums consequently increase;

(e) commutation of future premiums (although this is still a 'significant variation' for qualification purposes, and hence may disqualify the policy anyway).

(f) the reinstatement on original terms of a pre-14 March policy which has lapsed or become paid up through non-payment of premiums, provided it occurs within 13 months of the due date of the first unpaid premium and all arrears, including interest, are paid;

(g) switching funds under a unit-linked policy;

(h) variation in sum assured under a unit-linked policy where no increase in premium;

(i) automatic increases in premiums at set intervals in accordance with the original terms of the policy;

(j) increases in premiums, sums assured or extension of premium paying period as a result of a 'review clause' in a unit-linked policy in line with the performance of the underlying investments or mortality experience;

1 [1932] 17 TC 362.
2 [1928] 14 TC 94.
3 ICTA 1988, Sch 14, para 8(4).

(k) variation in premiums within defined limits specified in the policy;

(l) changes to premiums or sum assured, or extension of term, to correct bona fide misstatement of age.

The following (although not intended to be exhaustive) are, however, regarded as removing eligibility:

(a) alteration from one class of assurance to another;

(b) conversion from an endowment assurance to a low cost endowment assurance and vice versa;

(c) reduction of term of endowment type assurance, if premiums are simultaneously increased;

(d) conversion from without-profits to with-profits (or to unit-linked) for same sum assured;

(e) addition of disability or accidental death benefits or the addition of any new option;

(f) extension of term of an endowment policy whether or not for an increased premium;

(g) extension of premium paying term of whole life assurance where premiums were payable for a limited period;

(h) the rewriting of a pre-14 March policy from 'non-Married Women's Property Act 1882 (MWPA 1882)'[1] to 'MWPA 1882'.

If an alteration does remove eligibility, it is the whole premium which is disallowed, not just that part attributable to the increased benefits or extended term.

D Title

13.6 The relief is normally independent of any question of title. If a father effected a policy and, having assigned it to his daughter, continued to pay the premiums, he may claim relief notwithstanding that he has no longer any title to the policy. If he effected the policy subject to the MWPA 1882, or under any form of trust, relief may similarly be claimed.

SECTION 3 TAX RELIEF BY DEDUCTION FROM PREMIUMS

13.7 The Finance Act 1976 contained provisions for the introduction of the system of allowing tax relief on life assurance premiums by deduction at source (commencing with the year of assessment 1979–80). The system is commonly known as Life Assurance Premium Relief (LAPR).

1 Married Women's Property Act 1882, s 11.

The central feature of the system is that relief for eligible premiums is normally allowed without the intervention of a tax office. Any person who pays an eligible premium is entitled to deduct and retain an appropriate sum for relief (12.5% since 6 April 1989) from the amount of the premium, and the life office receives, under a system of bulk repayments, reimbursements from HMRC for the 'deficiencies' in its premium receipts. Tax offices are involved only when, in particular cases, it becomes necessary to make an adjustment at the end of the year of assessment because circumstances have led to over or under allowance of relief under the deduction system. Prior to 6 April 1989 the relief was 15% of premiums and had been more.

The legislation which implemented the system was contained in Schedule 4 to the Finance Act 1976 and is now contained in section 266(5) of ICTA 1988. The legislation comprised basic provisions establishing the system and a number of supporting provisions making changes in the rules and conditions for premium relief. There was also a series of regulations and HMRC practice notes for the guidance of life offices and individual policyholders.

Under this system relief is not dependent on a claim being made and, somewhat strangely, is available although the policyholder has no income against which to set relief. Thus, individuals with income below the tax threshold receive relief under the system which previously was not available to them. The policyholder is authorised to deduct the tax relief from his premiums and the life office is obliged to accept the reduced amount in full satisfaction of the policyholder's liability.

A Limits

13.8 The overall limit on relief as previously set out under section 19 of ICTA 1970 was amended for this system so as to allow tax relief on life premiums up to a maximum of £1,500 or one-sixth of the policyholder's total income whichever is higher.

The Finance Act 1976 provided that the aggregate amount of the premiums on which relief is available *by deduction* would be restricted to £1,500 in any one year (being any period of 12 months beginning with an anniversary of the effecting of the policy). This was achieved by reducing the amount of each premium eligible for relief by the proportion that £1,500 bears to the aggregate of premiums for that year. However, as the operation of this *deduction* limit would have proved an administrative burden, amending legislation was introduced in the Finance Act 1978 to remove the restriction. This meant that offices can accept premiums net of income tax relief whatever the amount of premium, provided they are within the *overall* limit mentioned above.

Where the correct relief has not been given under the deduction system, an adjustment is made. This may occur, for example, where a person is paying premiums under more than one policy and there is an over-allowance of relief. In cases of over-allowance the Inspector of Taxes has power to make any necessary assessments to recover the difference. HMRC is empowered also, in cases where it appears that the relief to which a person is entitled has been or might be exceeded, to issue a notice to both policyholder and life office requiring future premiums to be paid gross.

B Husband and wife

13.9 Under the system of premium relief by deduction, once premiums are established as eligible for relief they will broadly continue to be eligible throughout subsequent changes in marital status. The legislation ensures, therefore, that, in the case of policies on the life of a spouse, relief is preserved on divorce provided that the marriage was subsisting on 6 April 1979, when the new rules came into force.

Relief is also available for policies effected prior to 14 March 1984 if marriage (or a registered civil partnership) takes place after that date.

C Residence

13.10 The policyholder must be resident in the UK to be able to pay premiums net of tax relief[1]. Residence has been explained by HMRC in the following terms[2]:

> 'An individual can be regarded as resident in the United Kingdom if his "home" in the ordinary sense is here, who if he goes abroad on business or pleasure goes for short periods only. For taxation purposes the United Kingdom comprises England, Scotland, Wales and Northern Ireland only, and does not include the Channel Islands or the Isle of Man.'

This definition is provided as a simple test which will apply to the vast majority of cases. Residence for this purpose is not necessarily the same as for other taxation purposes.

Residence under the Income and Corporation Taxes Act 1988 is normally determined for the whole of an income tax year. A person who is in the UK for part only of a tax year will be treated as resident or not, as the case may be for the whole of the year.

Members of the armed forces and their spouses are counted as UK residents. Other persons resident abroad but taxed as UK residents, such as diplomatic staff are, however, not eligible to pay premiums net of relief. Policyholders resident abroad may be able to claim tax relief direct from HMRC under section 278 of ICTA 1988. This includes British subjects, Crown Servants and Isle of Man or Channel Islands residents.

D Industrial assurance

13.11 Generally speaking, the system of relief by deduction applies to industrial assurance policies and policies issued by friendly societies. Under previous rules the premiums on certain categories of industrial assurance policies were not

1 ICTA 1988, s 266(5).

2 Notes on Statements Prescribed under the Income Tax (Life Assurance Premium Relief) Regulations 1978, SI 1978/1159, reg 2.

eligible for relief. Paragraph 11 of Schedule 4 to ICTA 1970 (now Schedule 14 to ICTA 1988), provided that virtually all such policies issued before the passing of the Act would be eligible for relief under the new system. Two categories of policy, viz 'statutory' policies (effected by a child on the life of a parent or grandparent), or 'juvenile' policies (effected by a parent or grandparent on the life of a child) became eligible for relief, subject to certain restrictions.

E Temporary assurances

13.12 The Finance Act 1976 excluded from the category of qualifying policies temporary life policies where the term is less than one year. Thus no relief was available in respect of premiums paid under short-term policies such as holiday or travel insurance.

F The future of LAPR

13.13 In March 2011, the Office of Tax Simplification produced a report looking into the continued viability of various tax reliefs, one of which was LAPR. The report recommended that LAPR should be abolished and this recommendation was subsequently endorsed in the 2011 Budget. However, a precise date for abolition has not yet been set and it is understood that there will be discussions with the life assurance industry as to precisely how the abolition will take place. In any event, abolition is not likely to take place until some time after 2012.

SECTION 4 QUALIFYING POLICIES

A Policies effected after 19 March 1968

13.14 For premiums under a policy effected (or in some cases varied – see below) after 19 March 1968, but before 13 March 1984, to be eligible for income tax relief and for any gains arising under such a policy to avoid any possible liability to the higher rate of income tax, the policy must be a 'qualifying policy' as defined in Schedule 15 to ICTA 1988, or be exempt from the provisions of that Act. For the premiums to be eligible for income tax relief, it must also of course satisfy the rules set out in Section 2[1] of this Chapter and the amount of relief may be limited as mentioned in that Section. Qualifying status is also one of the factors relevant to a possible charge to the higher or additional rate of income tax on the profit (or gain) under the policy (see Section 6). But the two aspects (ie premium relief and qualification) must not be confused. Thus a life of another

1 See **13.2–13.6**.

policy may be a qualifying policy for this purpose, and be free from the charges to tax on policy gains, although it will not normally have been eligible for life assurance premium relief.

These provisions do not apply at all to life policies issued in connection with schemes approved under Chapter I of Part XIV of ICTA 1988, and its forerunner, the Finance Act 1970 (ie 'new code' schemes). So far as life assurance premium relief from income tax is concerned, exemption is irrelevant for policies effected under pension schemes which are 'exempt approved', as employees' contributions will be treated as a deduction from earned income. HMRC has indicated that policies effected under schemes approved by it will be treated as exempt, irrespective of how much of the cost is borne by the employer[1]. 'Salary sacrifice' arrangements (ie where an employee agrees to forgo part of his salary on inclusion in a scheme) are treated as paid for by the employer.

Schedule 15 to ICTA 1988 does not apply to a policy effected on or before 19 March 1968 unless it has been 'varied after that date so as to increase the benefits secured or to extend the term of the insurance', in which case it will be treated in the same way as a policy effected after 19 March 1968. The expression 'increase the benefits secured' is not defined. The allocation of a reversionary bonus to a policy would not be within the meaning of the term; but the conversion of a without-profits policy to a with-profits or a conversion from whole life to endowment assurance for the same sum assured would be regarded as increasing the benefits secured by the policy; so would the introduction of disability benefits not previously included.

I *Conditions for eligibility as a qualifying policy*

13.15 The conditions for eligibility as a qualifying policy vary according to the class of assurance. They are set out in Part I of Schedule 15 to ICTA 1988 and are summarised below together with a note of any special HMRC treatment or concession, where relevant.

(a) Whole life assurances

13.16

(1) The policy must secure a capital sum or series of capital sums payable only on death (or on death or earlier disability), and must not secure any other benefits. It is not regarded as securing other benefits by reason only that it:

- (a) participates in profits;
- (b) has a guaranteed surrender value;
- (c) contains an annuity option;
- (d) provides for waiver of premiums during disability, or secures disability benefits of a capital nature;

1 Inland Revenue Press Release, 6 March 1980.

(e) provides for effecting further policies without evidence of insurability.

HMRC has issued guidance in respect of variations of qualifying policies. Certain policies which may be converted or restructured in certain ways will no longer be certified as qualifying policies[1].

(2) The premiums must be payable at annual or shorter intervals, over a period of at least ten years or until the earlier death (or disability) of the life assured.

(3) The total premiums payable in any period of 12 months must not exceed twice the total premiums payable in any other such period (medical and occupational loadings being disregarded).

(4) The total premiums payable in any period of 12 months must not exceed one-eighth of the total premiums payable over the premium paying term (or where premiums are payable throughout life, over the first ten years). Again, medical and occupational loadings are disregarded.

The following further points should be noted:

(1) The words in paragraph 1(1) of Schedule 15 to ICTA 1988 'if a policy secures a capital sum which is payable only on death' do not mean that the capital sum must be of the same amount whenever death occurs. It may vary not only according to the date of death but also according to the manner of death (eg natural causes or accident).

(2) No objection will be raised in cases such as whole life limited premium payment policies where, for example, the first premium is a half-yearly premium with annual premiums thereafter and there is a final half-yearly premium. This would not be treated as an infringement of the 'two times' or 'one-eighth' rules, and the policy will be regarded as qualifying.

(b) Temporary assurances – term exceeding ten years

13.17

(1) The policy must secure a capital sum or series of capital sums payable only on death (or on death or earlier disability), and must not secure any other benefits. It is not regarded as securing other benefits by reason only that it:

(a) participates in profits;

(b) has a guaranteed surrender value;

(c) contains an annuity option;

(d) provides for waiver of premiums during disability, or secures disability benefits of a capital nature;

1 Inland Revenue Press Release, 22 January 1988.

(e) provides for effecting further policies without evidence of insurability.

HMRC has issued guidance in respect of variations of qualifying policies. Certain policies which may be converted or restructured in certain ways will no longer be certified as qualifying policies[1].

(2) The premiums must be payable at annual or shorter intervals, over at least ten years, or for at least three-quarters of the term, whichever is the shorter period. Therefore, the ten-year term will apply for terms over 13 years and four months.

(3) The total premiums payable in any period of 12 months must not exceed twice the total premiums payable in any other such period (medical and occupational loadings being disregarded).

(4) The total premiums payable in any period of 12 months must not exceed one eighth of the total premiums payable over the whole term (medical and occupational loadings being disregarded).

(c) Temporary assurances – term ten years or less

13.18

(1) The policy must secure a capital sum or series of capital sums payable only on death (or on death or earlier disability), and must not secure any other benefits. It is not regarded as securing other benefits by reason only that it:

(a) participates in profits;

(b) has a guaranteed surrender value;

(c) contains an annuity option;

(d) provides for waiver of premiums during disability, or secures disability benefits of a capital nature;

(e) provides for effecting further policies without evidence of insurability.

HMRC has issued guidance in respect of variations of qualifying policies. Certain policies which may be converted or restructured in certain ways will no longer be certified as qualifying policies[1].

(2) The policy must provide that any payment made by reason of surrender shall not exceed the premiums paid.

(d) Endowment assurances

13.19

(1) The policy must secure a capital sum payable either on survival to end of term or on earlier death (or disability). This includes a sum payable on

1 Inland Revenue Press Release, 22 January 1988.

death only if it occurs after the attainment of an age not exceeding 16, in which case the benefit on earlier death must not exceed the total premiums paid before the death. In applying this rule any loading for premiums payable more frequently than annually is ignored. Unlike whole life and temporary assurances, other benefits may be included, except benefits of a capital nature payable before death, disability or survival (except by surrender or cashing bonuses).

(2) The term of assurance must be at least ten years and premiums must be payable at annual or shorter intervals over at least ten years.

(3) The total premiums payable in any period of 12 months must not exceed twice the total premiums payable in any other such period (medical and occupational loadings being disregarded).

(4) The total premiums payable in any period of 12 months must not exceed one-eighth of the total premiums payable over the whole term. Medical and occupational loadings are disregarded.

In the case of policies where the sum assured is payable by instalments, the capital sum is taken as the total of the instalments and not the cash sum for which they could be commuted when the sum assured becomes payable.

Again, the words 'a policy which secures a capital sum payable either on survival for a specified term or an earlier death' do not mean that the capital sum must be of the same amount whenever death occurs or that the capital sum on maturity must be the same amount as the capital sum on death. The capital sum payable on maturity can in fact be different from that payable on death and the capital sum on death may also vary according to the date and manner of death.

(e) Other types of policy

13.20

(1) *Mortgage protection policies.* Policies effected solely to cover a mortgage of the taxpayer's residence or his own business premises are exempt from the provisions relating to qualifying policies provided the sum assured is substantially the same as the amount outstanding under the mortgage. The principal amount secured must be repayable by instalments payable annually or at shorter intervals. The policy should thus be purely a decreasing term assurance to which no permanent benefit is attached[1].

(2) *Family income policies.* The same conditions apply to family income policies as to temporary assurances. If a whole life or endowment assurance policy includes income benefits the policy will be a qualifying policy either:

1 ICTA 1988, Sch 15, para 9.

(i) if both the basic assurance and the income benefits would have qualified separately; or

(ii) if the policy fulfils the conditions for a whole life or endowment assurance as the case may be.

(3) *Pure endowments.* Pure endowments (ie policies securing a capital sum payable only on survival for a fixed period, with or without a provision for return of premiums on death) if issued after 19 March 1968 are non-qualifying policies.

(4) *Contingent assurances.* Contingent assurances (ie policies payable on the death of the life assured, provided another person (the 'counter-life') is still alive) are treated in the same way as if payment on the death of the life assured did not depend on the continued existence of the counter life.

(5) *Industrial life policies.* Industrial life policies are specially dealt with in paragraph 7 of Schedule 15 to ICTA 1988.

(6) *Policies with increasing premiums.* If there is provision for an increase of the premium to more than twice its original amount, the policy will be non-qualifying.

(7) *Last survivor policies.* Premiums ceasing on first death. Where a last survivor policy is written with the premium paying period ceasing on the first death, HMRC takes the view that this will not be a qualifying policy as it will not comply with paragraph 1(2)(a) of Schedule 15 to ICTA 1988, in as much as the premium paying period may not be for ten years. If premiums are expressed to be payable until the first death but subject to a minimum premium paying period of ten years the policy will qualify.

(8) *Children's assurances.* Policies on the lives of young children often have life cover deferred to, for example, age 16. In order to qualify, the policy must provide that if life cover is deferred until 16 or some lower age, any payment made on death during the deferred period must not exceed the total premiums paid.

2 *Dating back*

13.21 For the purpose of the conditions for qualification, in particular the 'one-eighth' rule, policies may be dated back for a period of up to three months without causing an otherwise qualifying policy to become non-qualifying. This is because in such circumstances the assurance will be regarded as having been made on the effective date of assurance, ie the date to which the policy is back-dated. But if the assurance is dated back more than three months it will be regarded as having been made on the actual date of assurance and this may mean that an otherwise qualifying policy is non-qualifying.

3 Variations and substitutions

13.22 The rules relating to variations in the terms of policies and substitutions are to be found in paragraphs 17 to 20 of Schedule 15 of ICTA 1988 and are summarised below.

(a) Assurances effected after 19 March 1968

13.23 In applying the following rules 'old policy' means the policy as it stood immediately prior to the alteration, and 'new policy' includes the converted policy viewed as if it were a new policy commencing at the date of the conversion, ie ignoring previous premiums and benefits.

If the old policy did not qualify the revised policy does not qualify. An exception to this is where the person making the insurance was an infant when the old policy was effected and the policy secured a capital sum payable not later than one month after his 25th birthday or on the anniversary of the policy immediately following that birthday. If the old policy was a qualifying one and the new policy is also a qualifying one then the policy as converted will normally also qualify. The only exception to this rule is where the old policy has been in force less than ten years at the time of variation, in which case the revised policy will qualify only if the highest revised premium payable in any period of 12 months during the remainder of the ten years is not less than one half of the highest total paid over any period of 12 months under the old policy (or any related policy).

It follows that conversions from whole life to endowment assurance or from a longer to shorter term endowment assurance will usually result in the revised policy continuing to qualify provided the new unexpired term after conversion is ten years or more.

Variations which do not affect the terms of the existing policy in any significant respect are disregarded. These include changes in the intervals at which premiums are payable within one year and most changes due to misstatement of age.

It is not possible to define precisely what variations would be regarded as significant. Prima facie, however, variations in the following would all be significant and would require a policy issued after 19 March 1968 to be retested:

(1) sum assured;

(2) type of benefit which alters the premium or benefit paid (historically HMRC stated that a change from without-profits to with-profits or vice versa would be significant but changes between without-profits, with-profits, unit-linked and unitised with-profits are only significant if the premium and/or benefit also change. This change is effective from 5 November 2005);

(3) policy term;

(4) premium paying term;

(5) change in premium payment, including payment in commutation of future premiums. A mere change in frequency of premium payments is not a significant variation.

13.24 In section 485(2)(a) of ITTOIA 2005 (formerly section 540(1)(b)(i) of ICTA 1988), reference is made to surrender, assignments or conversion into a paid-up policy 'before the expiry of ten years from the making of the insurance or, if sooner, of three-quarters of the term for which the policy is to run' ('the chargeable event period'). In the case of varied policies which are subsequently surrendered or made paid-up, if the premiums did not increase as a result of the variation then the chargeable event period runs from the date of the original policy. If the premiums payable were increased as a result of the variation then the chargeable event period runs from the date of the variation. HMRC has confirmed that in deciding whether or not the premiums payable have been increased the rate of premium payable before and after the variation should be compared. For this purpose it ignores any increase due solely to a change in the frequency of payment.

Where the existing policy was qualifying, and was effected more than ten years before the conversion, but the revised policy would on the face of it be non-qualifying (eg, an endowment assurance maturity within the next ten years or an infringement of the spread of premium rules ie 'twice the premium' and 'one-eighth' rules) then the revised policy will nevertheless be a qualifying policy if:

(1) the premiums payable in any period of 12 months under the revised policy are not greater than the smallest total paid over any period of 12 months before the conversion; or

(2) the old policy was issued outside the UK and the conversion is in the following special circumstances as set out in paragraph 17(3) of Schedule 15 to the 1988 Act.

(b) Offshore policies effected before 17 November 1983

13.25 The new policy satisfies the normal rules relating to substitutions referred to above (the offshore policy will also need certification by HMRC) and:

(1) the policyholder became resident in the UK in the 12 months before the issue of the new policy;

(2) the issuing company certifies that the new policy is in substitution for the offshore policy and that it has arrangements with the offshore company to issue such substituted policies; and

(3) the new policy confers benefits which are substantially equivalent to those under the old policy.

(c) Offshore policies effected after 17 November 1983

13.26 The offshore policy must have been capable of being certified as a qualifying policy under the pre-18 November 1983 rules, and the new policy must satisfy the normal substitution rules, and the conditions laid down in (1), (2) and (3) above.

An offshore policy effected on or before 17 November 1983 will be deemed to have been effected after the said date if it is varied after that date (whether by exercise of an option or otherwise) so as to increase the benefits secured or to extend its term.

When a policy is varied more than once, on each occasion the 'old policy' dates from the last preceding variation.

(d) Assurances effected before 20 March 1968

13.27 Such policies will remain exempt from the provisions of Schedule 15 unless the alteration increases the benefit secured or extends the term of the assurance, in which cases the same rules apply as where the existing assurance was effected after 19 March 1968, the existing policy being treated as a qualifying policy if it would have been a qualifying one had it been effected after 19 March 1968.

(e) Variation of term assurance policies

13.28 If under a term assurance of ten years or less, the original sum assured is reduced to less than half or the term is extended to cover an additional period (but the total term is still more than ten years), any resulting reduction in premium to less than half is not treated as disqualifying the policy under paragraph 17(2)(b) of Schedule 15 to ICTA 1988.

4 Certification of qualifying policies

13.29 Under paragraph 22 of Schedule 15, the life office must issue a Qualifying Life Assurance Policy Certificate when requested by the policy holder. The certificate must show the name of the life assured, the policy number, the sum assured, the amount and due dates of the premiums. For policies issued on or after 1 April 1976 it must also show the HMRC certification reference. This will state that in the life office's opinion the policy does qualify.

B Policies effected on or after 1 April 1976: additional requirements

13.30 The practical operation of the 1968 qualifying rules had given rise to some difficulties. Moreover, the rules had proved inadequate in some circumstances to prevent what was regarded as an abuse of the tax relief. In particular, it was believed that the life assurance element of some contracts was too low and that a minimum requirement ought to apply.

Accordingly, further qualifying conditions were introduced by the Finance Act 1975 to supplement those already in operation from 1968. In consequence, for life policies taken out on or after 1 April 1976, life assurance relief was given in respect of premiums, and any gains arising under a policy avoided any possible liability to the higher rate of income tax, only if the policy was a qualifying policy within the provisions of what was Part I of Schedule 1 to ICTA 1970, as amended by Part II of Schedule 2 to the Finance Act 1975[1]. All such provisions are now contained in Schedule 15 to ICTA 1988.

The changes introduced by the Finance Act 1975 applied to 'insurances made' on or after 1 April 1976. Thus, for example, a whole life assurance or a term assurance policy which does not comply with the 75% rule (see below), but which was effected before that date, continues to qualify. However, such a policy which is 'significantly' varied on or after 1 April 1976 has to comply with the 75% rule in respect of premiums payable from the date of variation.

1 Whole life and temporary assurances

13.31 The qualification rules relating to whole life and term assurances were therefore amended by the imposition of a condition *additional* to the 1968 provisions.

To be a qualifying policy, a whole life or temporary assurance must assure a capital sum on death of not less than 75% of the premiums which would be payable under the policy if death were to occur at age 75. If a capital sum is payable under a joint life policy (ie on the first death), the period taken is to the seventy-fifth birthday of the older of them. In the case of a last survivor policy it is the age of the younger of the lives assured which is relevant. In the case of a policy which does not secure the payment of a capital sum if death occurs before age 16 or lower, the policy must not provide for any payment which exceeds the total premiums previously paid on the policy.

A temporary assurance policy which makes no provision for any payment on total or partial surrender, and where the term of the policy does not run beyond age 75 of the life assured, is excluded from the application of the 75% rule.

If the capital sum on death may be payable as a single sum, or a series of sums, the 75% calculation is to be made applying the smallest total sum payable. This rule prevents avoidance of the qualification rules by giving an option to take a series of payments where in reality this option is unlikely to be taken up.

Any addition to a premium made where the payment is otherwise than annually is to be disregarded.

2 Endowment assurances

13.32 The qualification rules relating to endowment assurances were added to by Part II of Schedule 2 to the Finance Act 1975.

To be a qualifying policy, an endowment assurance must secure a capital sum in the event of death of at least 75% of the premiums payable during its prospective term. But as this rule might operate harshly in the case of policies on older lives (where the premiums are likely to be high in relation to the capital sum assured), the 75% standard is reduced by 2% for each year by which the age of the life assured exceeds 55 years.

1 Note that not all of the changes introduced by the Finance Act 1975, Sch 2 were consolidated into ICTA 1970, Sch 1 and so the Finance Act 1975 should be referred to separately.

3 Options

13.33 Paragraph 3 of Schedule 2 to the Finance Act 1975 introduced changes in the rules for determining whether a policy which includes one or more options is a qualifying policy.

It was previously the practice, when a policy was tested for qualification at its inception, to test it initially without regard to options and to retest it if and when an option was exercised. This basis of testing continues in respect of policies issued before 1 April 1976 and, if an option is exercised, any change in the terms is treated as a variation to which the substitution and variation rules of paragraph 17 of Schedule 15 to ICTA 1988 apply.

For policies issued on or after 1 April 1976 the policy is tested taking into account at the outset the existence of the options, but with no retesting on the subsequent exercising of any option. This is achieved by testing at the outset all the hypothetical policies which would result from exercising all or any of the options to see whether all of them would be qualifying policies. Only if this is so is the policy a qualifying policy.

In practice, rather than spell out only the options which can be allowed, the policy can contain a clause limiting the options available, which require to be tested as 'significant' variations, to those which would allow the policy to remain a qualifying one when tested under the variation rules. HMRC have indicated that the following would be acceptable as a modification to options to convert, to meet the qualifying rules:

> 'The right of conversion under this option is limited to making such changes in the terms of the policy (and/or substituting a new policy) as would be compatible with the requirements of paragraph 19(3) of Schedule 15 to ICTA 1988 for this to be a qualifying policy.'

When the option is actually exercised in a particular case, the test has to be carried out but the alteration does not constitute a variation (the option having been provided in the policy from the outset) and no new ten-year period, which could affect a subsequent variation, has started.

4 Maturity or surrender value as first premium

13.34 Under the 1968 rules a new policy sometimes failed to qualify solely because the initial premium was inflated by the inclusion in it of the maturity or surrender value of an old policy – thereby infringing the provisions requiring an even spread of premiums. For policies issued on or after 1 April 1976 in appropriate circumstances this value is left out of account of the first premium for the purpose of testing the new policy for qualification. The maturity or surrender value of the previous policy must have been retained by the life office in the following circumstances:

(1) where the previous policy was a qualifying policy and has been in force for at least ten years and the person or persons effecting the new policy are the

same as under the previous policy and are acting in the same capacity (ignoring any change in trustees) although the life assured may be changed; or

(2) whether or not the previous policy was qualifying it was issued when the person effecting the new policy was an infant and the capital sum secured under the previous policy was payable not later than one month after the child's 25th birthday or on the policy anniversary following that age.

5 *Certification of qualifying policies*

13.35 With effect from 1 April 1976, the certification of qualifying policies was taken over from the life offices by HMRC[1]. Thus, a policy issued or varied on or after that day must, if it is to be a qualifying policy, be so certified by HMRC, or must conform to a standard form which is certified by it.

In 2005 HMRC introduced new legislation to assist life companies who restructured as part of an insurance business transfer scheme[2]. While re-certification of the company name was still required, any variation, which alters the basis on which the benefits secured by the policy are to be determined, did not require to be tested as a significant variation. This part of the legislation was retrospective.

In addition, the legislation also adopted the same rule for all variations of that nature as from 7 October 2005. This is particularly useful for policies which allow switches between unit-linked funds and unitised with-profit funds without affecting the premium or sum assured. If such a policy is nearing maturity customers will no longer need to defer the maturity date so there would still be ten years to maturity. Whether it is wise to switch into a unitised with-profit fund close to maturity is another matter.

Strictly this legislation also means that a change from non-profit to with-profit or to unit-linked (and vice versa) no longer needs to be tested as a variation for qualification. However, such variations usually occur simultaneously with variations to the premium and sum assured which still have to be tested as significant variations.

6 *Industrial life policies*

13.36 In general terms, paragraph 7 of Schedule 15 to ICTA 1988 provides that certain types of industrial assurance policies which would not qualify under the normal rules are none the less qualifying policies, provided that the total capital sums involved on all such policies held by one policyholder do not exceed stipulated monetary limits.

1 ICTA 1988, Sch 15, para 21.
2 Schemes falling within section 105 of FSMA 2000, sanctioned by a court under Part 1 of Schedule 2C to the Insurance Companies Act 1982 or by a court under section 49 of that Act with regard to certification.

7 Reinstatement

13.37 HMRC have agreed that non-forfeiture provisions of a qualifying policy may allow premiums to remain outstanding for a period of up to 13 months from the date of the first unpaid premium during which application may be made by the policyholder to reinstate the policy. Reinstatement of a policy within 13 months will not, therefore, affect its status and this applies regardless of whether in the meantime the policy has lapsed, been paid up or converted into a term assurance.

A provision in the policy allowing reinstatement (or simply deferment of premiums) during a longer period than 13 months disqualifies the policy ab initio. Similarly, if regardless of policy conditions, the policy is allowed to be reinstated outside the 13-month period it would be deemed to be varied.

For policies effected before 20 March 1968 the 13-month period referred to is extended to five years provided neither the benefits nor the term of the policy are increased.

8 Combination of policies

13.38 Section 30 of the Finance Act 1980 was introduced in order to put an end to the exploitation of LAPR by the issue of certain contracts, known generally as 'short-term bonds'. In the typical case these consisted of a combination of policies under which one policy attracted a very high rate of return which depended on the availability of premium relief on another policy. Section 30 denied the premium relief, that made possible the high return on these bonds, by disqualifying any policy forming part of such an arrangement which would otherwise be a qualifying policy. The section provides that a policy will not be treated as qualifying if it is connected with another policy, the terms of which provide benefits which are greater than would reasonably be expected if any policy connected with it were disregarded. The section operates therefore if two or more policies are connected and one or more of them is uncommercial. A policy is regarded as connected with another policy if they are at any time simultaneously in force and either of them is issued with reference to the other or with a view to the issue of the other policy on particular terms. These provisions now appear in paragraph 14 of Schedule 15 to ICTA 1988[1].

The following features where they occur in relation to a policy are not in themselves regarded as bringing the policy concerned within the scope of the section:

(1) the policy fee is reduced or a higher unit allocation allowed where a policyholder is taking out more than one insurance, providing the reduction or increase (as the case may be) reflects only the saving in the life office expenses;

(2) an insurance is split into a cluster of separate policies (known as 'segmentation') each of which is a qualifying policy and provides identical benefits for an identical premium;

1 The Finance Act 1984 introduced adjustments to cover 'capital and income bonds'.

(3) owing to the existence of other policies:

   (a) a policy is issued on terms not taking into account an exceptional risk of death; or

   (b) less than normal underwriting information is sought;

(4) a policy is issued simultaneously with a temporary purchased life annuity which is intended to fund the premiums payable under the policy (a 'back-to-back arrangement');

(5) a policy is issued in exercise of an option contained in a convertible term assurance where the latter policy remains wholly or partly in force.

9 Restructuring of qualifying policies issued on or after 25 February 1988

13.39 As a result of taking legal advice, HMRC issued a Press Release on 22 January 1988. This announced a change in their interpretation of the qualifying provisions. Certain policy alterations, whether by exercise of an option or by agreement, are viewed as sufficiently fundamental as to create a new contract, even though they do not give rise to the issue of new policies. Consequently, the new contract may not satisfy the qualifying rules.

Changes which give rise to new contracts are, for example, conversions changing the event upon which benefits under policies become payable, for example, whole life to endowment policy. One common example was the 'peppercorn option' under which a qualifying endowment policy is converted at maturity to a whole life policy. All or part of the policy proceeds are reinvested and premiums of, eg £1 a year, are paid. Such changes almost invariably result in the rescission of the existing contract thus giving rise to a new non-qualifying policy and so any gains may give rise to a tax charge.

However, the following changes are not affected by the new interpretation:

(1) those resulting from policy reviews under unit-linked whole life assurance policies;

(2) variations of sums assured/premiums within the qualifying rules.

   In 2005, HMRC introduced new legislation to assist life companies who restructured as part of:

(3) changes between with-profits and without-profits and unit-linked switches (these changes are to be treated as 'insignificant' with effect from 7 October 2005);

(4) cessation of premiums (within qualifying rules);

(5) extension of term;

(6) change of life or lives assured;

(7) reduction of term of endowment assurance; and

(8) conversion to paid up, commutation, part surrender or partial conversion to paid up, provided there is no simultaneous change in the nature of the event on which the benefits are payable[1].

10 Free gifts

13.40 Insurance companies frequently offer incentives in connection with policies of life insurance, contracts for life annuities and capital redemption policies. These are often described as 'free gifts' and may take a variety of forms, such as small consumer goods, store vouchers, or discounts offered by hotels or travel agents.

So long as the aggregate cost to the insurer of all 'gifts' provided in connection with an insurance does not exceed £30, no account will be taken of the gifts in assessing whether policies are qualifying life insurance policies nor in computing any gain under the chargeable event legislation[2].

SECTION 5 'CLAW-BACK' OF TAX RELIEF

13.41 HMRC became concerned at the number of qualifying policies which were effected with the deliberate intention of being surrendered in the first ten years. The surrender value paid out would result in a profit, the essential source of which was the tax relief rather than investment by the life office.

The Finance Act 1975 therefore introduced provisions, effective from their introduction in the Budget of 26 March 1974, designed to recover part or all of the tax relief allowed on premiums for qualifying policies, on the happening of certain events.

A Surrender, etc within first four years

13.42 The relevant rules were originally set out in section 7 of the Finance Act 1975 and apply to qualifying policies effected after 26 March 1974. They are now set out in section 268 of ICTA 1988. However, these provisions are now of no practical importance in view of the fact that more than four years have passed since the withdrawal of life assurance premium relief on 13 March 1984.

B Surrender, etc after four years

13.43 There are further rules in section 269 of ICTA 1988 which provide for tax relief to be recovered if certain events occur in the fifth or any later year from the inception of the policy. These rules which apply to qualifying policies

1 See IPTM8210 and IPTM8215 regarding HMRC's views on paid-up policies.
2 Inland Revenue Extra Statutory Concession B42.

effected after 26 March 1974 were introduced to counter an avoidance device whereby tax relief was obtained for premiums paid out of periodic partial surrenders or cashing of bonus. Their effect is to ensure that tax relief on an established policy is only granted to the extent that the current year's premium, in effect, remains invested.

Thus, where, during the fifth or any later year from inception of a policy, there is:

(1) a total or partial surrender;

(2) bonus encashment; or

(3) a policy loan at a non-commercial interest rate, except for a loan to a full-time employee of the issuing company for house purchase or improvement[1], *and any of these events has happened before* in connection with the policy, then the life office by whom the policy was issued is required to deduct from the proceeds becoming available an appropriate amount by way of recovery of tax relief which must be paid over to HMRC. It will be noted that the claw-back under section 269 of ICTA 1988 does not apply in the case of the first surrender, etc (even total surrender) since the start of a policy. Nor does the recovery apply to conversion of a policy into a paid-up or partly paid-up policy.

The recovery under these rules is at a rate equal to the rate allowed on premiums for the year of assessment in which the event giving rise to the recovery occurs. This rate is applied to the lower of:

(1) the total premiums *payable* during the year; or

(2) the sums *payable* on surrender or otherwise falling due.

If, during the course of a year, more than one surrender, etc takes place, the sums payable on each occasion are aggregated for the purpose of calculating the amount of claw-back. The deduction from proceeds, made by the life office, is to take account of the amounts of claw-back already retained during the same year. The total amount recovered is not to exceed one half of the basic rate of tax on the premiums for the year on the policy concerned.

The calculation is modified if the policy concerned is one which, by reason of an increase in annual premiums by more than 25% of their former amount, is deemed to have given rise to a new and separate policy to the extent of any additional rights attributable to the increase. In such cases a new four-year period is deemed to commence.

C Collection procedure

13.44 Any office which deducts and retains from proceeds arising on surrender, etc any amount by way of recovery under section 269 of ICTA 1988, must

1 See ICTA 1988, s 271.

make a return to HMRC of all such sums falling due during each return period. The return is made annually.

A life office which has accounted for any such recoveries must within 30 days thereof provide the policyholder with a statement specifying the amount recovered and indicating how it has been calculated[1]. Although claw-back is potentially payable under qualifying policies the policyholder may not have received the tax relief on the premiums because, for example, the policy was written on a life of another basis or he was non-resident. The life office must still deduct claw-back but if the policyholder has not had any, or full, tax relief on the premiums, he can reclaim the excess claw-back from HMRC using his claw-back certificate.

SECTION 6 TAXATION OF GAINS ON POLICIES

13.45 A gain realised on a life policy, life annuity contract or capital redemption policy effected after 19 March 1968, which does not satisfy certain conditions, is subject to income tax at the higher rate. The statutory provisions are to be found in Chapter 9 of Part 4 of ITTOIA 2005 (formerly sections 539–554 of ICTA 1988). It should be borne in mind that capital gains tax is not relevant in this context[2]. This can be quite confusing. The correct terminology in this context is 'gains chargeable to income tax'.

The charge to higher rate or additional rate tax on gains arising on the realisation of policies extends to:

(1) all life policies effected after 19 March 1968 which are non-qualifying, including of course single premium bonds – although there are different rules for policies effected by companies where gains arise in accounting periods ending after 1 April 2008;

(2) qualifying life policies in certain circumstances;

(3) all capital redemption policies and annuity contracts effected after 19 March 1968 in most circumstances – although from 9 February 2005 separate rules for capital redemption bonds effected by UK companies were introduced.

A policy will be classed as a qualifying or non-qualifying policy as the case may be and the question of whether a charge to tax arises on the realisation of the policy will be dealt with accordingly. Exempt policies do not come within the charge. Policies effected before 20 March 1968 are not subject to the charge unless varied on or after that date so as to increase the benefits or extend the term and therefore the policy has been 'retested'.

1 ICTA 1988, s 272.
2 See **13.72** and **13.73**.

A Chargeable events and computation of gains under policies in years falling wholly after 13 March 1975

1 Life policies

13.46 The gain arises and tax becomes chargeable only upon the occurrence of a 'chargeable event' defined, in relation to a life policy, in section 484 of ITTOIA 2005 and subject to the exclusions in relation to qualifying policies set out in section 485 of ITTOIA 2005.

In the case of single premium bonds and other non-qualifying policies, this means:

(1) death giving rise to benefits under the policy;

(2) maturity;

(3) total surrender;

(4) assignment for money or money's worth;

(5) part surrender (including bonus encashment) or part assignment where the amount payable by way of surrender or an assignment exceeds the total of the 5% annual allowable credits.

In the case of qualifying life policies it means:

(1) death;

(2) maturity;

(but in either event, only if the policy is made paid up within ten years of inception or, if sooner, three-quarters of the term of the policy)

(3) surrender of the policy;

(4) assignment for money or money's worth;

(5) part surrender or part assignment (see (5) above);

(but for each of the latter three events, only if it occurs within the above mentioned period or the policy has been converted into a paid-up policy within that date).

These time limits run from any variation to a policy by which the premiums are increased. The maturity of a policy is not a chargeable event if a new policy is issued under an option conferred by the maturing policy and the whole maturity value is transferred to the new policy.

No event is a chargeable event once the rights under the policy have been assigned for money or money's worth, unless the contract has been reassigned so that at the time of the event the contract is held by the original beneficial owner. This is a change which was introduced by the Finance Act 1975, with effect from 10 December 1974, designed to prevent the avoidance of the tax charge by the device of assigning the policy to a second person who then reassigns it to the original beneficial owner.

13.47 A further change was introduced by section 18 of the Finance Act 1983 to counter the tax avoidance device known, generally, as 'second-hand bonds'. These contracts were single-premium life policies which were sold by the original purchaser (often a broker or other agent) to the person who was intended to hold the policy ultimately. As a result of this transaction, the policy was taken out of the income tax charge to gains on non-qualifying life policies and became an asset subject to the then lower rate of capital gains tax. Section 18 provided that after 26 June 1982 (when the Chancellor's announcement was made) an income tax charge is imposed on gains arising from non-qualifying policies and annuities which are assigned for money or money's worth and not held by the original beneficial owner.

No account is taken of assignments of policies on mortgages or discharges thereof, and assignments between spouses or registered civil partners living together are similarly ignored. The insurer can assume that spouses and civil partners are living together unless it knows otherwise.

HMRC has been told by another government department that there would be a court order for almost every divorce involving property. Therefore it has agreed that a life office can assume that an assignment as part of a divorce settlement is under a court order, and because of that is not a chargeable event, unless the life office definitely knows otherwise. The life office does not have to make enquiries into the circumstances of the assignment. An assignment as part of a separation settlement under a court order is likewise not a chargeable event.

13.48 The amount to be treated as a gain on a policy depends on the nature of the chargeable event giving rise to it. The amounts are as follows:

(1) On death, the excess of the surrender value immediately before death, plus the amount of any relevant capital payments *over* the sum of the total premiums paid under the policy, plus the total gains on previous chargeable events.

(2) On maturity or full surrender, the excess of the amount payable, plus the amount of any relevant capital payments *over* the sum of the total premiums paid, plus the total of gains on previous chargeable events (where there is a right to receive periodical payments the amount taken as payable is the capital value of those payments).

(3) On assignment, the excess of the consideration, plus the amount of any relevant capital payments or previous assignments *over* the sum of the total premiums paid, plus the total of gains on previous chargeable events (where a policy is assigned as a gift, surrenders or assignments taken up to the time of the assignment are charged on the assignor and not on the person beneficially interested in the policy at the end of the relevant year).

(4) On part surrender (including bonus encashments) or part assignments, the amount payable by way of surrender or assignment over the 5% allowable credits (see **13.52** under 'partial surrenders').

'Relevant capital payments' means any sums or other benefits of a capital nature paid or conferred under the policy before the chargeable event, eg previous part surrenders. Surrender of bonus is treated as though it were a surrender of rights conferred by the policy.

2 *Life annuity contracts*

13.49 A chargeable event in relation to a life annuity contract is defined in section 484 of ITTOIA 2005 and means:

(1) total surrender (the taking of a cash option instead of the annuity payments is treated as a surrender and from 10 December 1974 so too is the payment of a capital sum on death);

(2) assignment for money or money's worth;

(3) certain part surrenders or part assignments (see (5) at **13.46** in relation to non-qualifying life policies).

The amount to be treated as a gain depends on the nature of the chargeable event giving rise to it. The amounts are as follows:

(1) on surrender, the excess of the amount payable plus the amount of any relevant capital payments over the sum previously paid under the contract by way of premium or as a lump sum (reduced by the capital element of any annuity instalments which have been paid), plus the total gains on previous chargeable events;

(2) on assignment, the excess of the consideration plus the amount of any relevant capital payments or of any previously assigned share *over* the sum previously paid by way of premium or as a lump sum (reduced by the capital element of any annuity instalments which have been paid), plus the total of gains on previous chargeable events (where a contract is assigned as a gift, surrenders or assignments taken up to the time of the assignment are charged on the assignor and not on the person beneficially interested in the policy at the end of the relevant year).

(3) (See (4) at **13.46**, in relation to life policies.)

The definition of the term 'relevant capital payments' is broadly similar to that applying in respect of life policies. Surrender of a bonus or other sum is, again, treated as a surrender of rights conferred by the contract.

3 *Capital redemption (or sinking fund) policies*

13.50 A chargeable event in relation to a capital redemption policy is defined in section 484 of ITTOIA 2005, subject to the exclusions contained in section 486 of ITTOIA 2005, and means:

(1) maturity (except where the sums payable on maturity are annual payments already subject to tax under Schedule D);

(2) total surrender;

(3) assignment for money or money's worth; or

(4) certain part surrenders or part assignments (see (5) at **13.46** in relation to non-qualifying life policies).

The computation of the taxable gain under capital redemption policies is broadly similar to that under life policies.

4 Policy loans

13.51 As it would otherwise be possible to avoid the charges to tax on gains by withdrawing funds from policies and annuity contracts in the form of loans rather than by surrender, the Finance Act 1975 provided that such loans are treated as equivalent to surrender for this purpose. This only applies where the loan is made by, or by arrangement with, the company issuing the policy. These provisions do not apply in respect of a qualifying policy if either interest is payable at a commercial rate or money is lent to a full-time employee of the company issuing the policy for the purpose of purchase or improvement of his only or main residence.

5 Partial surrenders

13.52 Many modern policies allow partial surrenders at frequent intervals and so, in order to reduce the work involved in what could be a complex calculation both for life offices and HMRC, the previous system for charging higher-rate tax on partial surrenders was replaced by a new system[1] involving fewer and simpler calculations and freedom from the tax charge so long as the amount withdrawn by partial surrenders does not exceed certain limits. Thus, for policy years falling wholly after 13 March 1975, a chargeable event occurs only if the value of surrenders and assignments not brought into account on previous chargeable events exceeds the allowable credits (the annual twentieths referred to below) of all premiums paid.

The main elements of the system can be summarised as follows:

(1) Action is related to policy years (ie years running from the start of the policy or its anniversary) instead of to individual partial surrenders.

(2) Each year there is an allowance of:

- (a) one-twentieth of any premium paid during the year, and
- (b) one-twentieth of any premium on which an allowance has been due in previous years, up to a maximum of 20 twentieths.

1 ITTOIA 2005, s 507.

In other words, the policyholder is able to withdraw 5% per annum of a single premium for a maximum of 20 years or, in the case of an annual premium policy, 5% per annum of the premiums paid in that year. Allowances, so far as not used in any one year, will be carried forward cumulatively.

(3) At the end of each policy year the cumulative figure of partial surrenders is compared with that of the aggregate of the allowable credits (the annual 5% allowances). If the former exceeds the latter a chargeable event arises and the amount of the excess will be the chargeable sum. Where this happens the allowances up to that point will be deemed to be used up and the process of accumulation of allowances and annual comparison with surrenders taken will start afresh.

(4) These rules are applied in relation to policy years and a period from an end of a policy year to final termination of the policy is treated as a policy year. If the period to final termination begins and ends in the same year of assessment, both the final period and the year preceding it are together treated as one year.

(5) On final termination of the policy there will be a charge on the total profit on the policy (final proceeds plus any previous partial surrenders less total premiums paid and any chargeable gains arising on previous chargeable events). Withdrawals under the 5% limit are thus technically tax-deferred rather than fully tax free.

6 *Assignments of jointly owned policies*

13.53 The assignment of the whole of a policy for no consideration does not constitute a chargeable event. The life insurance industry has, for many years, held the view that where a policy is owned jointly by one or more persons and one of those persons assigns their share in the policy to the other or others, that action constituted an assignment of the whole policy and thus no tax would be payable. However, during the course of 1996/97 it emerged that HMRC did not share this view and considered such a transaction to be a part-assignment which could give rise to a chargeable event under the 'reckonable excess' rules even if no consideration is involved. Furthermore, they considered that the person who should suffer the tax charge should be the assignor although the legislation appeared to indicate that any tax charge should be assessed on the assignee.

Following long correspondence between HMRC and the Association of British Insurers (ABI) on this subject, section 83 and Schedule 28 of the Finance Act 2001 clarify the position in these circumstances. This legislation took effect for ownership changes occurring in policy years on or after 6 April 2001. The changes are broadly as follows:

(1) All ownership changes where joint owners transfer ownership of the policy to one of the previous joint owners will be deemed to be part-assignments for tax purposes. This will also apply where an individual who was previously the sole owner of a policy assigns ownership to himself and another person or persons.

(2) Although these part-assignments will continue to give rise to chargeable events in accordance with the 'reckonable excess' rules, an exception will be made for transactions by way of gift. Thus the treatment of part-assignments will be aligned with that of assignments of the whole policy.

(3) It will be the person assigning their share in the policy who will be liable to any tax charge arising on the transaction, not the assignee.

B Assessment to tax

1 Method of charging tax (sections 465–467 of ITTOIA 2005 – formerly section 547 of ICTA 1988)

13.54 The gain computed in accordance with the principles set out above will form part of an individual's income if, immediately before the chargeable event, the rights under the policy or contract were held:

(1) by the individual as beneficial owner;

(2) as security for a debt owed by the individual; or

(3) on trusts created by the individual, including trusts under the Married Women's Property Act 1882, or the corresponding Scottish or Northern Irish Acts (although he can recover the tax from the trustees: section 551 of ICTA 1988).

If the policy is vested in personal representatives, the gain is deemed for this purpose to be part of the deceased's aggregate income.

The gain will be chargeable only to higher-rate or additional rate tax in the tax year in which the chargeable event took place and at the rate applying in that tax year, assuming the policy is effected with a UK-based life company. If the person chargeable is not liable to such tax for that year, after the gain calculated as above has been added to his income, no assessment will arise.

13.55 The effect of the application of the old section 547 ICTA 1988 gave rise to what became known by tax planners as the 'dead settlor' provisions. If the chargeable event could be postponed until a tax year beyond that in which the settlor under a trust died (eg by a joint lives (last survivor) policy on the lives of two spouses effected by, typically, the older of the couple or where a single premium bond or similar policy was effected by trustees under a trust where the settlor had already died) then there would be no one on whom HMRC could assess the gain and thus on any subsequent chargeable event (eg death or surrender) no tax liability should arise.

As a result of advantage being taken of this very generous tax treatment, the legislation was changed in the Finance Act 1998. The previous rules relating to the tax treatment of policies effected subject to trust will only continue to apply where the policy was already in force before 17 March 1998, provided that the policy had not been varied on or after that date so as to increase the benefits payable or extend the term and that the person who had created the trust had died before that date.

If any of these criteria cannot be met, the current legislation[1] states that if, immediately before the happening of a chargeable event, the policy was held on trust and the person who created the trust was either non-UK resident or had died in a tax year prior to the occurrence of the chargeable event, or the policy was held as security for a debt owed by the trustees, the amount of the gain shall be deemed to form part of the income of the trustees for the year of assessment in which the chargeable event occurred and shall be charged at the rate applicable to trusts for that year. The rate for 2011/12 is 50% but credit is available for basic rate tax deemed to be paid within the fund (assuming again that the policy is effected with a UK life company) and thus the actual rate of tax will be 30%.

If it is not possible to assess the trustees to tax as would be the case if they were offshore, HMRC can take advantage of sections 714–751 ITA 2007 (formerly section 740 of ICTA 1988) to assess the gain to tax on any UK resident beneficiaries who derive benefit from the policy proceeds.

2 *'Top-slicing'*

13.56 The relevant provisions are now set out in section 535 of ITTOIA 2005 (formerly section 550 of ICTA 1988). The rate of tax to be charged on the gain following a chargeable event is assessed on the 'top-slicing' basis as follows:

(1) The gain is divided by the number of complete relevant years between the effecting (or variation) of the policy and the chargeable event. This sum is the 'top-sliced' gain.

(2) The top-sliced gain is added to the total income for tax purposes in the appropriate year and tax is calculated on the total thus arrived at.

(3) The total tax liability without the top-sliced gain is then calculated, and deducted from (2).

(4) From this difference is deducted tax at the basic rate (20% for 2011/12) on the top-sliced gain included in (2).

(5) The result is multiplied by the number of complete years in (1) to determine the tax liability on the whole gain.

When adding in the top-sliced gain, it is important that the computation is made in the correct order. Earned income is taxed first, then rental income, then savings income, then dividend income, then the gain.

For gains arising in policy years falling wholly after 13 March 1975 the period of 'spread' (referred to in (1) above) for calculating the 'top-slicing' relief is:

1 ITTOIA 2005, s 467.

(1) on the first chargeable event – back to the start of the policy;

(2) on any later chargeable event other than final termination – back to the previous chargeable event;

(3) on final termination – the number of whole years from the start of the policy.

It is stressed that top-slicing relief can only be used to obtain relief from the higher rate of income tax. It cannot be used to mitigate starting or basic rate tax, nor can it be used to ascertain the availability of the age-related allowances. It should also be noted that, for offshore policies, on the occurrence of a chargeable event, the top-slice divisor is always calculated back to the start of the policy even if there had been previous chargeable events subsequently.

3 *Certificates of chargeable events*

13.57 By virtue of section 552 of ICTA 1988, a UK life office was required in cases where a chargeable event occurs to give a certificate to its Inspector of Taxes. The certificate, in addition to specifying the name and address of the policyholder and the nature and date of the event, had to set out the surrender value or the sum payable by reason of the event, the amount or value of any relevant capital payments, the premiums (or other consideration) paid and the number of full years for the top-slicing procedure. The certificate had to be given within three months of the event or its written notification to the life office.

A certificate did not have to be issued automatically if no gain has arisen by virtue of the event or if the amount paid out (except on a part surrender, bonus encashment or surrender) does not exceed £500. However, an Inspector of Taxes can still request a certificate in these cases. If so requested it must be delivered within 30 days of receipt of the notice.

On the introduction of self-assessment for income tax purposes from the tax year 1996/97, HMRC felt that section 552 should be amended to fit better with the needs of policyholders in having to self-assess chargeable gains under life policies. New legislation was therefore included in the Finance Act 2001 which applies to chargeable events occurring on or after 6 April 2002.

Insurers now have a statutory duty to report all chargeable event gains of which they are aware to policyholders. The existing de minimis limit of £500 mentioned above no longer applies although there is a threshold figure (half the higher rate tax threshold) below which it is not necessary to send copies of the notification of potential chargeable event certificate gain to HMRC.

In place of the information formerly required, the new notification of potential chargeable event certificate gains will need only to state information needed to complete tax returns, namely:

(1) the amount of the gain;

(2) the date of the event giving rise to the gain;

(3) the number of years for top-slicing relief purposes;

(4) whether credit for savings rate tax is available in respect of the gain.

Insurers will, of course, be able to provide additional information if they wish to do so.

13.58 As far as offshore life offices are concerned, section 552A of ICTA 1988 provides for the appointment of UK-based fiscal representatives by offshore insurers to provide details of chargeable gains made by UK resident policyholders to HMRC. However, regulations which supplement section 552A came into force from 6 April 1999 and exempt offshore insurers from the requirement to appoint fiscal representatives in certain circumstances such as where the insurer is resident in a state in the European Economic Area in which it is a criminal offence to disclose information to HMRC (Luxembourg and Switzerland for example), where the amount of premiums from relevant insurances is nil or negligible, or where the insurer enters into an agreement to supply information relating to chargeable events to HMRC. Insurers must agree to issue chargeable event certificates to UK-based policyholders in the following circumstances:

(1) For policies written prior to 6 April 2000, when the amount paid out is greater than twice the higher rate income tax threshold in the tax year when the chargeable event occurs, ie from 6 April 2011, £35,000 × 2 = £70,000.

(2) For policies written on or after 6 April 2000, details of the amounts of all chargeable gains. Copies of the chargeable event information must be sent to HMRC where the gain is greater than half the higher rate income tax threshold in the year the gain is made, ie from 6 April 2011, 50% of £35,000 = £17,500.

4 Non-resident policies and offshore capital redemption policies

13.59 Section 528 of ITTOIA 2005 (formerly section 553 of ICTA 1988) has the effect of modifying the rules for computation of tax on gains in respect of offshore policies effected after 17 November 1983 which are not substituted by a qualifying policy effected by a UK life office and offshore capital redemption policies effected after 22 February 1984. On the happening of a chargeable event under such policies, any gain arising thereunder will be subject to the starting rate for savings income, if applicable, the basic, higher and additional rate of income tax. 'Top-slicing' relief will, however, be allowable in determining the higher or additional rate tax liability and for a part surrender or part assignment the number of complete relevant years can be computed from the start of the policy rather then back to the previous chargeable event. Where the policyholder was resident in the UK for only part of the period since the policy was effected, chargeable gains will be reduced to:

$$\frac{\text{Total gains under the policy} \times \text{Period of residence in the UK}}{\text{Total period the policy has been in force}}$$

For the purposes of top-slicing relief, the reduced gains as computed above will be spread over a period equal to the complete number of years the policy has been in force less the complete number of years during which the policyholder was not resident in the UK.

There is an anti-avoidance provision which prevents a deduction being claimed for a period of non-residence in respect of policies issued after 19 March 1985 held by non-resident trustees. This provision also applies to policies issued before 19 March 1985 where the trustees subsequently become non-resident.

5 Personal Portfolio Bonds (PPBs)

13.60 Where an offshore bond is of a highly personalised nature, HMRC, in the past, attempted to assess all the investment income of the bond on the policyholder, using section 739 of ICTA 1988. However, this approach was deemed incorrect by the House of Lords in the case of *IRC v Willoughby*[1].

As a result of this, in March 1999, new regulations were laid before Parliament under section 553C of ICTA 1988 concerning the tax treatment of PPBs. A PPB is defined as a policy which allows the policyholder to choose the investments that determine the benefits under the policy. Personalised investments include stocks and shares quoted on recognised stock exchanges including the Alternative Investment Market, shares in family companies and also more unusual assets such as fine wines, vintage cars, etc. There is still, however, a wide range of permissible investments including unit trusts and other collective investment funds.

For PPBs, a taxable gain will arise each year from 6 April 2000. This gain is calculated as 15% of the sum of the total amount of premiums paid under the bond and the aggregate total of similarly calculated 15% amounts for earlier years since the bond was first taken out. Tax is charged at the individual's marginal rate on the gains each year. The legislation concerning personal portfolio bonds is now contained in sections 515–526 of ITTOIA 2005.

PPBs taken out prior to 17 March 1998 can continue to hold stocks, shares, warrants and options listed on a recognised stock exchange or the AIM. However, pre-17 March PPBs must not be enhanced in any way.

C Companies effecting life policies

13.61 The tax treatment of gains under life assurance and capital redemption policies effected by companies is different from that applicable to individuals and trustees.

1 Policies effected before 14 March 1989

13.62 Prior to 14 March 1989, gains arising under life policies were generally assessed to tax only if the company was a close company and the policy was a non-qualifying policy. Gains under qualifying policies were not normally subject

1 [1997] STC 995.

to tax unless a chargeable event arose – this would occur generally only if such a policy was surrendered or made paid-up within the first ten years or three-quarters of its term if sooner.

Any gains made were computed as laid down in section 6, and in general were apportioned to shareholders who were potentially liable to higher rate tax thereon.

These rules continue to apply to pre-14 March 1989 policies even following the changes to the tax treatment of company-owned policies introduced by the Finance Act 2008. Policies varied on or after 14 March 1989 so as to increase the benefits or extend the term are treated as policies effected on or after 14 March 1989 and so are subject to the rules applying to such policies.

2 *Policies effected on or after 14 March 1989*

13.63 Major changes to the taxation of gains under life assurance policies effected by companies were contained in section 90 and Schedule 9 of the Finance Act 1989.

Following the Finance Act 1989, the method of computation of gains remained the same as before, but:

(1) the legislation covered all companies, whether close or not;

(2) qualifying as well as non-qualifying policies were chargeable to tax on their gains;

(3) instead of apportionment of the gains to shareholders, these were treated as income gains of the company (ie chargeable to corporation tax). Withdrawals within the 5% entitlements could still be taken tax free at the time of withdrawal for up to 20 years by companies but any withdrawal in excess of 5% was potentially liable to corporation tax. However, top-slicing relief was not available on a policy effected by a company. Furthermore, companies did not receive the benefit of a credit for any tax paid within the fund – ie the entire gain was be taxable. Thus where a company effected a policy with a UK-based insurer, there was an element of double taxation, making such a course of action very unattractive from a taxation perspective.

Clearly these rules were much harsher than those that applied before 14 March 1989. Policies issued on or before this date were not affected unless they were varied after that date so as to increase the benefits secured or extend the term of the assurance (any exercise of rights conferred by the policy would be treated as a variation for this purpose). Where a policy was effected prior to 14 March 1989 and is not varied thereafter, any gains arising under qualifying policies can still be taken tax free.

3 *Changes introduced by the Finance Act 2008*

13.64 Changes introduced in the Finance Act 2008 mean that, for company accounting periods starting on or after 1 April 2008, gains under life assurance policies that have a surrender value will be taxable under the 'loan relationship' rules contained in Parts 5 and 6 of the Corporation Tax Act 2009 rather than the chargeable event legislation contained in ITTOIA 2005. Term assurances with no surrender value are not affected by the new rules. The new rules will apply to all policies effected by companies no matter when they commenced, except that they will not apply to pre-14 March 1989 policies unless they are subsequently altered so as to increase the benefits payable or extend the term.

Capital redemption bonds effected by companies have been subject to the loan relationship rules since 10 February 2005.

Broadly speaking, the fundamental rules taxing loan relationships provide that income, gains and losses of a company arising from loan relationships are subject to corporation tax as income.

A company has a loan relationship if

(a) it is either a creditor or debtor for a money debt; and

(b) that debt arises from the lending of money.

Examples of loan relationships are overdrafts, bank loans, building society loans, bank deposits, building society deposits and mortgages.

Income and gains are treated as trading income where the company holds the loan relationship for the purpose of its trade, and non-trading income otherwise. Relief is available for expenses or losses whether or not a loan relationship is held for the purpose of its trade.

Where a company is investing funds surplus to its immediate requirements then income and gains would be treated as non-trading income which gives rise to a non-trading credit. A loss would rank as a non-trading debit. Credits and debits on non-trading loan relationships are aggregated to arrive at an overall profit or loss on non-trading loan relationships in an accounting period.

Net profits from non-trading loan relationships are taxed under Case III, Schedule D. Net losses, known as a non-trading deficit, can be relieved as follows:

(i) by offset against the company's profits (which includes capital gains) chargeable to corporation tax in the accounting period; or

(ii) by carry back against, broadly, earlier profits from non-trading loan relationships; or

(iii) by carry forward against future non-trading profits (ie profits exclusive of trading income).

Loan relationship debits and credits are based on the profits of company accounts prepared in accordance with UK generally accepted accounting practice or international accounting standards.

The application of the loan relationship rules to all investment-based products broadly means that gains or losses made under UK and offshore insurance policies (whether such gains are realised or not) will be taxed as non-trading income. The important thing to note is that the tax treatment arising from the loan relationship rules should follow the accounting treatment adopted by the company, provided that the accounting treatment follows 'generally accepted accounting practices'.

Whether tax deferral is available under a single premium bond will be determined by the accounting practice adopted. If a current cost basis is being used, no deferral will be available. However, if the company is accounting on an historic cost basis – typically this would apply to companies applying the Financial Reporting Standard for Smaller Entities (FRSSE), it should still be possible to obtain tax deferral until money is actually withdrawn from the policy or it is fully surrendered. The FRSSE are accounting standards that apply for small enterprises which satisfy two of the following three criteria: a turnover of less than £6.5 million; a balance sheet of no more than £3.26 million; and no more than 50 employees.

Listed companies have a requirement to account on a fair value basis, and so there is no opportunity at all for tax deferral in these circumstances.

When a policy is already owned by the company before the start of its first accounting period beginning after 31 March 2008, the company will be treated as surrendering the policy as at the date of the commencement of that accounting period. Any chargeable event gains arising on this deemed surrender will be brought into account as a non-trading credit in the accounting period in which the company actually disposes of its interest in the policy. In those circumstances, the gains made under the policy prior to the commencement of its first accounting period beginning after 31 March 2008 will be taxed under the chargeable events regime and all subsequent gains will be taxed under the loan relationship rules.

A further change brought about by the Finance Act 2008 is that credit is now given for the UK (or equivalent) tax suffered at life fund level in arriving at the yearly charge under the loan relationship rules. This credit will be taken into account when the policy is finally surrendered, not on a year by year basis for those companies not accounting an the historic cost basis.

D Group life assurance policies: application of section 541(1)(a) and 541(5)(a)

13.65 Prior to 9 April 2003 an anomaly arose from HMRC's interpretation of the chargeable event legislation with regard to group life assurance policies which were not exempt under the provisions of Chapter I of Part XIV of ICTA 1988. Where one policy was effected on the lives of more than one person so that more than one death benefit could be paid under the policy, in the event of the second and subsequent deaths, previous death benefits were treated as 'relevant capital payments' when calculating chargeable gains.

This lead to very harsh results. For example, where an employer had effected a group life policy on the lives of, say, 50 employees, on each death (other than the first), chargeable gains would be computed by taking into account all the previous payments of death benefits.

This can be compared with the position of the employer effecting separate policies for each employee. No gains as described in the previous paragraph would have arisen as there would have been no relevant capital payments.

The position altered following the Finance Act 2003 with effect from 9 April 2003. Group life policies which only provide death benefits are now excluded from the chargeable event rules provided that they meet certain conditions which are set out in sections 480-483 of ITTOIA 2005. If these conditions are not met, policies will continue to be taxed in accordance with the above rules.

The conditions are, broadly, as follows;

(a) The policy must pay out the death benefits on the death of an individual before age 75 although the age limit need not be the same for all the individuals insured under the policy. It is possible for the policy to contain an exclusion stating that the benefit will not be payable in the event of the individual committing suicide or dying as a result of a terrorist act.

(b) The terms of the policy must specify that the same method is to be used for calculating the benefits payable or arising on each death of an individual in the group insured by the policy. This condition may stretch quite widely so long as the method is pre-determined and consistently applied.

(c) A limitation in the policy on the death benefits payable is permitted provided that the limitation is the same in the case of any death.

(d) The policy must not have a surrender value (other than an amount which equates to a proportion of unused premiums if the policy is cancelled).

(e) The policy must not allow for payments to be made under any circumstances other than death, for example, disability.

(f) Generally, the beneficiaries must only be the families, dependants and nominated charities of the deceased.

(g) No individual whose life is insured under the policy, or any individual connected with such an individual, may directly or indirectly receive benefits on the death of another insured person merely because he or she is also one of the persons insured under the policy. This effectively means that share or partnership protection policies are not included.

Where a group life policy was effected before 9 April 2003 and did not meet the criteria set out above, transitional provisions allowed it to be varied so the conditions could be met. Provided the terms of the policy were varied before 6 April 2004 so that it met the conditions for excepted policies above, the policy is treated as having met the conditions throughout the transitional period from 9 April 2003 until 5 April 2004 and no chargeable events will have arisen providing that no sums were paid from the policy other than on death or disability before the variation was made.

Furthermore, where an event which would have been a chargeable event, such as death, arose on a 'pure protection' group life policy before 9 April 2003, that event is retrospectively deemed not to have been a chargeable event ensuring that no taxable gain can have arisen. For this purpose, a 'pure protection policy' means one whose terms do not provide for sums or other benefits to be paid other than on death or disability.

SECTION 7 ANNUITIES AND INCOME TAX

A Deduction of tax from annuities

13.66 Income tax is deductible from annual payments and annuities[1]. The deduction is made by the person or company that makes the payment, and the payee is bound to allow the deduction[2]. The person making the payment must, however, notify the payee that the deduction is being made[3].

Where an annuity payment is made by a life office under an annuity contract, the life office must, therefore, (except where a special arrangement has been made) deduct income tax at the basic rate from the payment, and account to HMRC for the amount deducted. In the case of a payment made under a purchased life annuity (see later), the life office must deduct income tax at the basic rate (20% for 2011/12) from the taxable portion of the annuity.

B Annuities payable without deduction

13.67 As a matter of convenience for annuitants of modest means and to reduce the number and amount of claims for repayment of income tax, HMRC has made special arrangements under which life offices may, in certain circumstances, pay life annuities without deduction of income tax.

I Residence in the United Kingdom

13.68 The limits within which the arrangement operates vary from time to time and are amended where rates of tax and personal and other allowances are varied by Finance Acts, but by way of illustration, the following table shows the limits of income for the year 2011/12.

Age of annuitant	*For payment without deduction of income tax*
	Single
Under age 65	£7,475
Age 65–74	£9,940
Age 75 and over	£10,090

These limits may be higher in the case of married couples or registered civil partners where one or other of the couple was aged 65 or over as at 6 April 2000.

The annuitant has to make, on the appropriate official form, a declaration that his income falls below the appropriate limit, and changes in his circumstances must be notified to HMRC. He must, if required, renew his declaration.

1 ITA 2007, ss.898 and 899.
2 ITA 2007, s.901.
3 ITA 2007, s.975.

If the annuity is one which is regarded, for income tax purposes, as containing a capital element, the capital element is excluded in assessing the annuitant's total income.

13.69 The arrangements do *not* extend to any proportionate payment to the date of death.

> *Bryan v Cassin*[1]
>
> S was entitled to an annuity payable quarterly. On his death his executor claimed repayment of income tax deducted from the proportionate payment to the date of death. If the payment had been made during the lifetime of S, he would, because his income was small, have been entitled to repayment of the amount of tax deducted. Held, that the proportionate payment formed no part of the income of the deceased, and that the executors were not entitled to any repayment of the tax deducted.

In practice, however, where during life an annuity is being paid without deduction of income tax, the same arrangement can concessionally be applied to the proportionate payment.

In applying the arrangements, the life office should be satisfied that the title to the *beneficial* interest is vested in the annuitant in the following cases:

(1) where an annuity is purchased by executors or trustees;

(2) where a joint life annuity is purchased by two or more persons jointly;

and in the latter case the life office may have to sever each instalment of annuity into appropriate parts if, during the joint life, it is enjoyed in shares to each of which a different tax treatment is to be applied.

The arrangements do not affect the income tax liability of the life office, for, in the computation of its liability or claim for repayment, the treatment of annuities paid under the arrangements is taken into account.

2 *Residence abroad*

13.70 Similar arrangements can sometimes be made in the case of certain persons resident abroad.

The Taxation (International and Other Provisions) Act 2010 provides for relief from double taxation in the case of residents in territories outside the UK which make conventions with the UK. These provisions were previously contained in Part XVIII of ICTA 1988.

Conventions have been made with many countries under which annuities purchased in the UK or in respect of pensions arising in the UK are, where taxable abroad, exempt from UK income tax; and such annuities and pensions can be

1 [1942] 2 All ER 262.

paid without deduction of income tax under the procedure laid down by the Double Taxation Relief (Taxes on Income) (General) Regulations 1970[1].

C Annuities containing a capital element

1 Purchased life annuities

13.71 Prior to 1956, all purchased life annuities were treated, for taxation purposes, as consisting wholly of income but the Finance Act of that year provided that such annuities, with certain exceptions, should be regarded as containing a 'capital element' not subject to tax. The balance of the annuity payment is taxable as investment income. The relevant provisions are now contained in sections 717–723 of ITTOIA 2005 (formerly sections 656–658 of ICTA 1988). They apply, subject to the exceptions mentioned, whether or not the life on which the annuity depends is that of the purchaser and whether or not it is for his own benefit.

The capital element is a fixed amount of the purchase price, and is determined on the basis of rules laid down in ITTOIA 2005 and in regulations made in pursuance of that Act. The effect of the rules is that if the annuitant survives for precisely the period of his expectation of life according to the prescribed mortality table, he will have received in the form of tax-free payments exactly the amount paid by way of premiums.

The capital element is a function of mortality and the younger the age the lower the capital element of any given type of annuity. In the case of a temporary annuity the effect of mortality is smaller and the capital element represents a greater percentage of the annuity than in the case of a whole life annuity commencing at the same age.

The practice is for the office granting the annuity to provide the annuitant with the official claim form which the annuitant completes and returns to the office, which forwards it to its own Inspector of Taxes. In due course the annuitant and the office are officially advised by HMRC whether or not the annuity qualifies as one which contains a capital element and, if it does, what the amount of capital element is.

As a result of the *Test-Achats* case heard by the European Court of Human Rights in March 2011, with effect from 20 December 2012 it will be a breach of human rights law for insurers to use gender-related factors in determining benefits payable under insurance and annuity contracts.

SECTION 8 CAPITAL GAINS TAX AND LIFE POLICIES

A Life policies and deferred annuity contracts

13.72 Section 210 of the Taxation of Chargeable Gains Act 1992 provides that no chargeable gain accrues on the disposal of rights under a policy of assurance

1 SI 1970/488.

or contract of deferred annuity, except where the person making the disposal has acquired the rights for actual consideration. Where a gain does arise, the payment of the sum assured under a life policy (including the transfer of investments or assets to the policyholder where applicable)[1], or the first instalment of a deferred annuity or the surrender of either contract will be a chargeable disposal of rights under the contract.

It follows, therefore, that where the beneficial ownership of a life policy or a deferred annuity contract remains vested in the same person throughout its duration, there will be no charge to capital gains tax on its becoming payable or being surrendered. Where beneficial ownership changes, no liability will arise at any time provided the new beneficial owner acquires his interest as a result of a gift inter vivos, a bequest, or under the law of intestate succession. Only if he acquires his interest for actual consideration does a liability arise when the policy is subsequently disposed of; there will be no liability on the original beneficial owner when he sells the policy.

Where there is a chargeable gain on the disposal of a contract for a deferred annuity, the amount of the consideration for the disposal will be the market value at the time of the right to the first and further instalments of the annuity.

Where the gain on a non-qualifying policy which has been assigned for money or money's worth is charged also to income tax under ITTOIA 2005 then the income tax charge takes precedence and by section 37 of the Taxation of Chargeable Gains Act 1992 a double liability is avoided.

B Calculation of tax

13.73 It will be seen that it will not often be necessary to calculate the chargeable gain on an assurance policy, but where this is necessary the computation must be made according to the provisions of Schedule 2 to the Taxation of Chargeable Gains Act 1992.

The chargeable gain is computed by deducting from the proceeds of 'disposal' (which term includes payment of the policy moneys) the total cost of acquisition. This includes all premiums paid by the person making the disposal, and, in the case of a purchased policy, the purchase price. A deduction may be claimed for incidental costs of acquisition and disposal, eg legal fees.

Premiums which have been allowed as a deduction in computing profits for income tax or corporation tax purposes must be excluded from the computation of gain.

C Annuities and pensions

13.74 A chargeable gain does not accrue to any person on the disposal of a right to or to any part of:

1 Taxation of Chargeable Gains Act 1992, s 210(3)(b).

(1) any allowance, annuity or capital sum payable out of any superannuation fund or under any superannuation scheme established solely or mainly for persons employed in a profession, trade, undertaking or employment and their dependants;

(2) an immediate annuity granted by a life office, whether or not including instalments of capital; or

(3) annual payments under a covenant not secured on any property[1].

1 Taxation of Chargeable Gains Act 1992, s 237.

CHAPTER 14

Inheritance tax

SUMMARY

SECTION 1 INTRODUCTION

14.1 From 1894 transfers of capital on death were subject to estate duty. The Finance Act 1975 replaced estate duty with capital transfer tax (CTT) from 26 March 1974. This taxed not only transfers of capital on death but also lifetime gifts and was codified by the Capital Transfer Tax Act 1984. The Finance Act 1986 replaced CTT with inheritance tax (IHT) which applies to all transfers made on or after 18 March 1986 and renamed the codifying act the Inheritance Tax Act 1984 (IHTA 1984).

A Nature of IHT

14.2 The general principle is that transfers of capital out of an individual's estate are liable to IHT. The essential features of IHT are that:

(1) it applies (subject to certain exceptions) to transfers by way of gift during lifetime, as well as to the value of an individual's estate on death;

(2) it is generally charged on the donor, not the donee, ie, the tax is applied by measuring the loss suffered by the transferor, not the benefit received by the transferee;

(3) it is cumulative, ie, it is chargeable on the cumulative total of chargeable transfers made by an individual during a seven-year period (on transfers in excess of the 'nil rate band', a threshold of £325,000 from 6 April 2011 which will stay at that level up to and including tax year 2014/15), and any transfers made more than seven years before the transfer in question will not be taken into account; and

(4) it is levied separately from any other tax, so that it is possible for a transfer to be liable to both IHT and capital gains tax (CGT), without any allowance in one for the other.

IHT is not restricted to cases where an individual actually makes a gift during lifetime or the value of his estate on death. It also applies to cases which are treated as if a transfer had occurred, eg in connection with settled property and the failure to exercise a right. IHT applies to individuals. However, special rules exist to charge individuals in respect of dispositions made by close companies and to bring trustees within the scope of the tax.

The tax applies to the whole of the United Kingdom (UK), including Northern Ireland.

B Relationship to life assurance

14.3 Life assurance itself is linked with IHT because it plays a large part in mitigating and providing for the tax. Life assurance practitioners should, therefore, be aware of at least the basic principles of IHT for this reason and also to be able to appreciate fully the IHT consequences of movements of certain assets within the client's estate. This Chapter sketches the general scheme of the tax[1] and looks more closely at the relevant IHT provisions relating to life assurance contracts. Chapter 15 will then examine the effect of IHT on various types of life policy trust wordings and consider the role and use of life assurance in estate planning.

SECTION 2 LIFETIME TRANSFERS

A The charge

14.4 IHT is charged on the *value transferred* by a *chargeable transfer*[2] which, in the case of a lifetime gift, means any *transfer of value* made by an indi-

1 For a detailed treatment of IHT see one of the major works on the subject, eg Foster *Inheritance Tax*.

2 IHTA 1984, s 1.

vidual which is not exempt[1] and which is in excess of the nil rate band (£325,000 for transfers made on or after 6 April 2011). For IHT purposes, certain lifetime transfers are potentially exempt transfers (PETs)[2] which are assumed to be exempt at the time of transfer and do not enter the cumulative total until death[3]. A *transfer of value* is a *disposition* made by a person (the transferor) as a result of which the value of his *estate* immediately after the disposition is less than it would be but for the disposition and the amount by which it is less is the 'value transferred' by the transfer[4].

IHT is levied, therefore, by reference to the *reduction* in the transferor's estate, as a result of making the gift, not by reference to the increase in the transferee's estate. This means that if tax on the gift is paid by the transferor, the reduction in his estate includes the amount of the tax, as this forms part of his loss. To calculate the total tax payable in these circumstances it is necessary to 'gross up' the value transferred at the appropriate rate[5].

On a transfer for partial consideration, only the balance, ie the element of gift, is chargeable. Similarly, if the transferee assumes responsibility for a liability of the transferor (eg where he pays CGT arising on the gift) the value of the transfer is reduced accordingly.

B Transfers which are not transfers of value

14.5 There is no transfer of value, and thus no IHT, if the transfer was not intended to confer any gratuitous benefit on any person and either the transaction was at arm's length between unconnected persons, or was such as might be expected to be made in a transaction at arm's length between unconnected persons[6]. 'Connected persons' means, essentially, a spouse, registered civil partner, or relative (including uncle, aunt, nephew and niece)[7].

If the transfer was of a sale of shares or debentures in an unquoted company it is also necessary to show that the price was freely negotiated at the time of the sale or that the price was that which would have been expected had it been freely negotiated at the time[8]. (This is to avoid the possibility of avoiding IHT by imposing a fetter on the disposition of shares in the company's articles of association.)

Certain other 'transfers' are also deemed not to be transfers of value, including dispositions for the maintenance of one's family[9] and transfers of property by a close company to trustees to hold on trust for the benefit of employees (excluding any shareholder with 5% or more of the shares[10]).

1 Section 2(1).
2 Section 3A.
3 See Section 4C, 14.32.
4 IHTA 1984, s 3(1).
5 See Section 5A, 14.41.
6 IHTA 1984, s 10(1).
7 IHTA 1984, s 270 and Taxation of Chargeable Gains Act 1992, s 286.
8 IHTA 1984, s 10(2).
9 Section 11.
10 Section 13. (See also ss 12, 14, 15, 16.)

C Disposition

14.6 This term is not defined and carries its ordinary wide meaning which includes, inter alia, the payment of money, the conveyance, transfer or assignment of property (by sale or gift), and the creation of a settlement[1], ie any transaction by which a person disposes of an interest in an asset or creates a new interest in another person in an asset. Where an individual deliberately omits to exercise a right, which as a result reduces his estate and increases another's, the omission is treated as a disposition[2]. This could, for example, cover the failure to collect a debt or to vote in respect of shares in a company. In relation to settled property a surrender of a life interest has been held to be a disposition[3].

D Associated operations

14.7 A disposition includes one made by 'associated operation', which is where a transfer of value is made by any two or more operations of any kind by the same or different persons and whether simultaneous or not affecting the same property, or where one operation affects a further operation[4]. Note that 'operation' includes an omission.

The 'same property' means property which represents directly or indirectly the property or income (including accumulations) arising from it. Similarly, operations which in any way provide for, or facilitate, the performance of other operations will be associated with them.

Where the associated operations provision applies, the composite transfer (ie the value of the overall loss to the estate) will be treated as being made at the time of the last of the operations.

This provision is designed to counter avoidance measures whereby an individual's estate is reduced through a series of transactions or where property is transferred in stages, the aggregate value of the constituent transfers being less than the value of the property as a whole; or where a gift is made of property worth little at the time but which subsequently increases in value by reason of some other act of the donor. This matter will be raised again in connection with 'back-to-back' arrangements and certain other arrangements referred to in Chapter 15.

HMRC does not view the sharing of one spouse's or registered civil partner's estate with another, where that other makes gifts out of the money received as an associated operation, unless it is a blatant case of a gift conditional upon using it to make gifts to others[5].

1 *Ward v IRC* [1956] 1 All ER 571 (an estate duty case).
2 IHTA 1984, s 3(3).
3 *IRC v Buchanan* [1958] Ch 289 at 296 (an income tax case). See also *Grey v IRC* [1959] 3 All ER 603.
4 IHTA 1984, s 268(1), see *IRC v Macpherson* [1988] STC 362, HL.
5 See HC Official Report, SC A, 13 February 1975, Col 1596.

E Estate

14.8 IHT only arises if a disposition reduces the value of the transferor's estate[1]. Broadly, an individual's estate comprises the aggregate of all property to which he is beneficially entitled (not including excluded property)[2], less his liabilities. In addition to tangible property, equitable rights, debts and other choses in action, an individual is treated as beneficially entitled to all property, other than settled property, over which he has (or would if he were sui juris) a general power to appoint or dispose as he thinks fit or on which he can charge money. An individual beneficially entitled to an interest in possession in settled property (such as a life interest) was treated as entitled to the property in which the interest subsists[3]. However, this position was altered by the Finance Act 2006. This will only remain the case for settlements created before 22 March 2006 provided the existing beneficiaries at that date have not been changed, unless that change occurred before 6 October 2008 in which case the new beneficiaries will be treated as having been the beneficiaries in existence at 22 March 2006. For new settlements created on or after 22 March 2006, the former treatment will continue to apply only if the settlement is made for the benefit of disabled persons as defined in section 89 of the IHTA 1984 or if the trust used is an absolute or bare trust. If this is not the case, such settlements will be treated for IHT purposes as trusts without an interest in possession and will be taxed accordingly.

SECTION 3 TRANSFERS ON DEATH

A The charge

14.9 On the death of an individual, IHT is chargeable as if immediately before his death, the deceased had made a transfer of value equal to the value of his estate at that date[4]. In valuing the estate, any changes brought about by the death (eg the cessation of a life annuity, or the proceeds payable on a claim under a single life policy owned solely by the deceased) are to be taken into account[5]. This provision does not apply, however, to the termination on the death of any interest or the passing of any interest by survivorship[6] (eg the interest under a jointly owned, joint lives, last survivor contract) which would, therefore, be valued at the full open market value at death[7]. No grossing up is required in determining the value transferred, since the tax is payable from the estate by the personal representatives.

Any PETs within seven years prior to death become chargeable at the value of the property at the time of the PET, subject to any claim for a fall in the

1 IHTA 1984, s 5.
2 Section 6, see Section 4A, 14.22.
3 Section 49(1).
4 Section 4(1).
5 Section 171.
6 Section 171(2).
7 Sections 160 and 167(2)(a).

value of the property from the date of the gift to the date of the transferor's death or earlier sale by the transferee[1] and taper relief. If there are any available annual exemptions, they may be applied retrospectively. If a PET does become chargeable by virtue of the donor dying within seven years, it will be necessary to look back over the seven years before the PET to see whether any chargeable lifetime transfers have been made. If this is the case, account needs to be taken of such transfers in determining the amount of tax, if any, due on the failed PET.

If an individual dies within seven years of making a chargeable transfer, the IHT death rates will retrospectively apply with credit for any lifetime tax already paid and taper relief as appropriate[2]. The donee is liable for the extra IHT and so no grossing up is required.

B Estate

14.10 The meaning of estate is similar to that for lifetime transfers, and is the aggregate of property to which, immediately before his death, the deceased was beneficially entitled, other than excluded property. Certain property is left out of account, however, for the purpose of the IHT charge on death. Thus, where the deceased had an interest in possession in property settled before 22 March 2006, and on his death: (1) the property reverts to the settlor during the settlor's lifetime, or (2) the settlor's spouse or registered civil partner becomes beneficially entitled to the property, then its value is excluded from the deceased's estate – unless the settlor or the settlor's spouse or registered civil partner acquired the reversionary interest for money or money's worth[3]. (Spouse includes widow or widower in cases where the settlor died less than two years before the deceased.) Also left out of account are interests in certain superannuation schemes and certain overseas pensions. The value transferred is the value representing the sum which the estate might reasonably be expected to raise if sold in the open market (less liabilities)[4].

C Gifts with reservation of benefit

14.11 The Finance Act 1986[5] introduced the concept of 'gifts with reservation of benefit' (a similar concept existed under the estate duty regime). Where property is disposed of by way of gift (on or after 18 March 1986) but either:

(1) possession and enjoyment of the property is not bona fide assumed by the donee at least seven years before the donor's death; or

1 Section 131.
2 See 14.40.
3 Section 53.
4 Sections 5(3) and 160. For a discussion on 'excluded property', see Section 4A, 14.22.
5 Finance Act 1986, s 102, Sch 20.

(2) at any time within seven years of the donor's death ,the property is not enjoyed to the entire exclusion, or virtually[1] to the entire exclusion, of the donor and of any benefit to him by contract or otherwise,

the property is deemed to be 'property subject to a reservation', ie property to which the donor was beneficially entitled immediately before his death, and it will be added to and form part of his taxable estate for IHT purposes. Furthermore, no CGT uplift will be available on the donor's death.

If the reservation ceases before the donor's death, he will be treated as having made a PET at that time. If the cessation was more than seven years before the death, the PET will have fallen out of account, but if not, IHT will be assessed on normal principles[2]. Note that the value of the PET cannot be reduced by any of the available annual exemptions.

The rules relating to gifts with reservation involving land were tightened with effect from 9 March 1999 in response to the House of Lords ruling in *Ingram and another v IRC*[3]. Section 102A of the Finance Act 1986, as inserted by the Finance Act 1999, extends the existing provisions to prevent the avoidance of IHT on death by way of a lifetime gift where the donor or his spouse enjoy a significant right or interest or is a party to a significant arrangement in respect of land. Where this happens, the interest disposed of will be treated as a gift with reservation. A right, interest or arrangement is significant if it entitles or enables the donor or his spouse to occupy all or part of the land (or enjoy some other right) otherwise than for full consideration in money or money's worth. The right, etc is not significant if it:

(1) cannot prevent another person or persons enjoying the land virtually or entirely to the exclusion of the donor;

(2) does not enable the donor to occupy the land immediately after the disposal but would have done so were it not for the disposal; or

(3) was granted or acquired more than seven years before the gift.

Similar provisions also apply to gifts of undivided shares in land under section 102B.

14.12 The gift with reservation of benefit rules do not apply to any disposals which are exempt within any of the provisions of the IHTA 1984 (see below), except for the £3,000 per annum and normal expenditure exemptions[4].

Thus any property enjoyed by or benefiting the donor's spouse did not automatically fall within these provisions but this situation came to an end with effect from 19 June 2003[5]. Prior to that date, the opportunity existed for a settlor to

1 For the Inland Revenue's interpretation on gifts with reservation of benefit and their interpretation of the de minimis rule see FRPI/80 and Tax Bulletin Issue 9 (November 1993).
2 See Section 5, 14.40.
3 [1999] STC 37.
4 Finance Act 1986, s 102(5).
5 Sections 102(5A) and 102(5B).

create a trust for the benefit of his or her spouse. The settlor could be a potential beneficiary under the trust without infringing the gift with reservation rules. Some months after the creation of the settlement, the trustees made an appointment away from the settlor's spouse in favour of the children or grandchildren. This course of action constituted a PET by the spouse but a situation had been created whereby a trust had been set up for the benefit of the settlor's children or grandchildren, but under which both the settlor and his spouse were potential beneficiaries and the gift with reservation rules had not been breached. From 19 June 2003 onwards, however, this is only the case whilst the settlor's spouse actually has the interest in possession. Once this is appointed away, if the original settlor is still a potential beneficiary, the gift with reservation rules would apply.

Where the disposal by way of gift was made in connection with an insurance policy (issued before 18 March 1986), the gift with reservation provisions will not apply unless the policy is varied on or after that date so as to increase the benefits secured or extend the term of insurance. Any change made in the policy terms in pursuance of an option or other power conferred is deemed to be a variation, apart from the exercise of an indexation option with respect to benefits or premiums before 1 August 1986 if the option or power could only be exercised before that date[1].

The following are examples of changes which will be regarded as increasing the benefits or extending the term[2]:

(1) altering from one class of assurance to another;

(2) converting from an endowment assurance to a low cost endowment assurance or vice versa;

(3) reducing the term of an endowment assurance if premiums are being simultaneously increased;

(4) converting from a without- to a with-profits policy for the same sum assured;

(5) adding premium waiver benefit or double accident benefit or the addition of an option not previously included in the policy.

D Pre-owned assets tax

14.13 Historically, HMRC have sought to litigate in situations where they feel that the gift with reservation rules have been infringed. Where they have lost

1 Sections 102(6) and 102(7).

2 See Life Insurance Council Circular 139/86 in a letter dated 21 November 1986 from the Life Insurance Council of the Association of British Insurers to LIC members following clarification from the Inland Revenue confirming that in deciding whether a policy is varied as mentioned in the Finance Act 1986, s 102(6), account would generally be taken of the Inland Revenue's interpretation of the corresponding wording used in the provisions relating to life assurance premium relief (see Chapter 13).

cases (*Ingram and another v IRC*[1] and *IRC v Greenstock*[2]) they have amended the legislation to render planning of that nature ineffective. However, HMRC were becoming increasingly frustrated that tax advisers were finding ever more complex ways to circumvent the gift with reservation legislation.

It was therefore decided to introduce a completely new tax, pre-owned assets tax which, from 6 April 2005, has the effect of imposing an income tax charge each year on the benefit people enjoy when they have arranged free continuing use of major capital assets that they once enjoyed.

The legislation concerning the tax is contained in Schedule 15 of the Finance Act 2004. Three classes of assets are covered by the new rules: land, chattels and intangible property which includes policies of life assurance.

Each class of assets has its own rules, but for life assurance policies, a pre-owned assets income tax charge can arise where any income arising under a settlement would be treated by virtue of sections 624 and 625 of the Income Tax (Trading and Other Income) Act 2005 (income arising under a settlement where the settlor retains an interest) as income of the settlor.

The life assurance policy would be valued at the time that it first falls within the charge and thereafter HMRC has stated in correspondence with the ABI that it should be sufficient for policies to be revalued every five years. This would hold good for regular premium policies too assuming the chargeable person remains in normal health throughout the five-year period. Once valuation has taken place, a rate of interest equal to the official rate of interest (5% at the time of writing) would be applied. There is a de minimis limit of £5,000 on the value of the benefit assessable so if the amount calculated as above was below this figure, no tax would be payable. Note that where the same settler has made a number of gifts all of which are potentially liable to pre-owned assets tax, the taxable benefits of each gift must be added up to see whether the overall £5,000 limit has been breached. If the benefit is in excess of £5,000, pre-owned assets tax will be payable on the whole benefit at the settlor's marginal rate of tax.

It should be noted that it is not possible to make a gift with reservation and also to pay pre-owned assets tax on the same gift. It must be either one or the other. The combination of the two taxes does, however, mean that it is now very difficult to make a gift, retain a benefit under it and avoid being liable for one of the taxes.

E Variation of dispositions taking effect on death

14.14 When an individual has been left property by will, under the intestacy rules, or under the right of survivorship, any transfer of that property would, prima facie, be a transfer of value, and potentially liable to IHT. Provisions exist[3] to mitigate this where the original donee is simply redirecting (or disclaiming) the deceased's dispositions. In certain circumstances, such a variation (or dis-

1 [1999] STC 37.
2 [2003] STC 825.
3 IHTA 1984, ss 17(a), 142.

claimer) will not be treated as a transfer of value and will be treated as if the deceased had effected the variation (or the disclaimed benefit had never been conferred).

A variation occurs when the individual who benefits or would benefit under the deceased's will (or intestacy or otherwise) redirects property to another party of his choosing; a disclaimer occurs when the property is merely refused by the individual and the property falls into residue. The provisions apply equally to variations and disclaimers (referred to hereafter as variations), but do not apply to settled property in which the deceased had an interest in possession[1] or to property which is deemed to be included by virtue of the gift with reservation of benefit provisions[2].

To be within these provisions, the following conditions must be satisfied:

(1) The variation must be made within two years after the death of the testator or intestate.

(2) The variation must be made by an instrument in writing made by the individual(s) who benefit or would benefit under the dispositions. Any such individual must be aged 18 or over and must be of sound mind. A deed is usually used[3], although any instrument in writing will be effective. In *Crowden v Aldridge*[4], a unanimous direction by residuary legatees by memoranda (even though it was executed in contemplation of executing a formal deed which never in fact was executed) was held to be an effective variation of the estate.

(3) An election in writing must be submitted to HMRC that the provisions should apply. This election can be contained within the deed itself. The election must be made by the individual(s) who effected the instrument (and also by the personal representatives, if the variation causes more IHT to be payable) within six months of the date of the instrument (or such longer period as the board may allow).

(4) The variation must not be made for a consideration in money or money's worth unless the consideration is itself a qualifying variation or disclaimer relating to another of the deceased's dispositions.

A deed of variation may be rectified[5] and there may be more than one deed of variation in respect of the same estate, but each deed can only vary property that has not already been varied.

A deed of variation can be used to set up what would otherwise be a gift with reservation. For example, if a grandfather leaves property on trust to his son in his will, the son could redirect that property onto trust for himself and his own

1 See ss 142(5), 49(1).
2 See s 142(5), (6), Finance Act 1986, s 102, Sch 19, para 24.
3 See *Law Society Gazette* 18 December 1991.
4 [1993] 3 All ER 603.
5 *Russell v IRC* [1988] STC 195, *Matthews v Martin* [1991] STI 418, *Schneider v Mills* [1993] 3 All ER 377.

children as the beneficiaries. For IHT purposes, this variation will be treated as being made by the testator, not by the son and thus would not be a gift with reservation of benefit.

F Redirection of severable share of joint property

14.15 Under the provisions set out in Section E, it is possible to sever the beneficial interest in a joint tenancy with, for IHT purposes at least, retrospective effect. It would normally be used where property is owned jointly by husband and wife or by two registered civil partners and one party dies without making use of the nil rate band, and with insufficient assets in the free estate for the surviving spouse or registered civil partner to redirect other property. It would then be appropriate to sever the beneficial joint tenancy to pass the deceased's share of the property to other beneficiaries to use up the nil rate band, whilst utilising the remaining free assets for the benefit of the surviving spouse or registered civil partner.

G Inheritance (Provision for Family and Dependants) Act 1975

14.16 A court may order financial provision for family and/or dependants of a deceased person out of his net estate. Property so redirected is treated for IHT purposes as having devolved on death subject to the provisions of the court's order[1].

H Surviving spouse election

14.17 Where a surviving spouse or registered civil partner elects under section 47A of the Administration of Estates Act 1925 to take the capital value of his or her life interest in the residuary estate in lieu of the income for life, the election is not a transfer of value. The surviving spouse or registered civil partner is treated as having been entitled not to the life interest, but to a sum equal to the capital value of the interest[2].

I Commorientes[3]

14.18 When two individuals die in such circumstances that it is impossible to know which died first, the general law, and the law of succession to property, presumes that the older was the first to die[4]. For transfers on death, this rule is

1 IHTA 1984, s 146(1).
2 Sections 17(c) and 145.
3 See Chapter 4.
4 Law of Property Act 1925, s 184.

excluded, and it is presumed instead that the deaths occurred at the same instant[1], thus avoiding a double charge.

Example

If mother and daughter die in a road traffic accident, the general law would treat any property bequeathed by the mother to the daughter as passing to the daughter's estate and then to the beneficiaries under the daughter's will (or intestacy). However, because of section 4(2), IHT is charged only on the transfer to the daughter's estate and not again on the transfer to the daughter's ultimate beneficiaries.

J Survivorship clauses

14.19 Where under the terms of a will, or otherwise, property is held for a person if he survives another for a specified period of not more than six months, the dispositions at the end of the specified period (or that person's earlier death) are treated as having had effect from the beginning of that period[2].

K Quick succession relief

14.20 Relief is available from the IHT charge on death where the value of the deceased's estate has been increased by a chargeable transfer to him within the preceding five years.

For property not comprised in a settlement, the tax charged on the death is reduced by a percentage of part of the tax paid on the earlier chargeable transfer[3]. The percentage varies according to the period between the transfer and the death as follows:

Not more than 1 year	100%
1 to 2 years	80%
2 to 3 years	60%
3 to 4 years	40%
4 to 5 years	20%

1 IHTA 1984, s 4(2).
2 Section 92.
3 Section 141.

SECTION 4 EXEMPTIONS AND RELIEFS

14.21 It was stated earlier that IHT is charged on the *value transferred* by a *chargeable transfer* which, in the case of a lifetime gift, means any *transfer of value* made by an individual which is not exempt. The IHTA 1984 provides for fully exempt transfers[1]. The Finance Act 1986 introduced PETs[2]. Further, there will be no IHT if the property transferred is excluded property.

A Excluded property

14.22 In measuring the loss to an individual's estate following a transfer (or the value of the estate upon death), no account is to be taken of 'excluded property'. The main categories of excluded property are:

(1) property situated abroad belonging to an individual not domiciled or treated as not domiciled in the UK[3], and

(2) reversionary interests, eg interests following life interests (other than those acquired for money or money's worth), or those, for settlements made after 15 April 1976, where either the settlor or his spouse are beneficially entitled[4].

B Exempt transfers

14.23 An exempt transfer is the most efficient transfer for IHT purposes as, following the transfer, the property is immediately treated as being out of the estate of the transferor. The exemptions are not mutually exclusive and a transfer may fall within one or more of the exemptions and be freed from IHT partly by one exemption and partly by another. If a transfer is exempt, no IHT is ever payable. Some exemptions apply to a transfer whether made during lifetime or on death. Others apply either only to lifetime transfers or only to transfers on death. The following is not an exhaustive list, but does contain the principal exemptions for most practical purposes.

1 Spouse exemption

14.24 Transfers between spouses or registered civil partners from 5 December 2005 (whether living together or not) during lifetime and on death are exempt[5] The exemption does not apply where the transfer:

1 IHTA 1984, Part II, Ch I.
2 Section 3A.
3 Sections 6(1), 48(3).
4 Section 48(2).
5 Section 18(1).

(1) depends on a condition which is not satisfied within 12 months after the transfer; or

(2) 'takes effect' on the termination after the transfer of any interest or period[1].

The exemption is not excluded merely because the gift is dependent on the recipient surviving the other spouse for a specified period. It is therefore quite common for a will to be drawn so that the surviving spouse or registered civil partner is not to benefit unless surviving for, say, 28 days (but the period must not be any longer than six months) and the exemption will apply[2].

If, immediately before the transfer, the transferor is domiciled in the UK, but the spouse or registered civil partner is not, the exemption is limited to a cumulative total of transfers of £55,000[3] (which is in addition to the nil rate band). After 17 March 1986 gifts in excess of £55,000 may qualify as PETs.

The separate taxation of spouses or registered civil partners is important for a number of reasons. They are each entitled to the benefit of the reliefs and exemptions and in calculating the rate of tax on a chargeable transfer by one spouse, gifts made by the other are not taken into account. These principles obviously have great significance for estate planning as will be considered in Chapter 15. The relationship between them is not overlooked entirely, however, and for certain valuation purposes[4], spouses or registered civil partners are treated as one.

For the purposes of the remainder of this Chapter, apart from the next paragraph, references to spouse also apply to registered civil partner.

2 *Surviving spouse exemption*

14.25 Where an individual's spouse died before 13 November 1974, leaving an interest in possession in property to the surviving spouse, estate duty would have been payable on that first death. To avoid a double charge to tax, there is no charge to IHT on either the subsequent death of the surviving spouse, or on the lifetime termination of that interest, provided that there would have been no charge on death[5].

3 *Annual exemption of £3,000*

14.26 Transfers of value made by a transferor during lifetime in any one tax year[6] are exempt up to £3,000 in total[7]. For this purpose, transfers are not required to be grossed up. If the exemption is not utilised, or not fully utilised in

1 IHTA 1984, s 18(3).
2 See 'Survivorship clauses', 14.19.
3 Section 18(2).
4 See s 161 (ie related property).
5 Schedule 6, para 2.
6 6 April–5 April.
7 IHTA 1984, s 19(1).

any one tax year, it may be carried forward to the following year and used to relieve transfers in that year only. If the exemption is unused by year three, it cannot be carried forward into that year.

Subject to two exceptions, the £3,000 annual exemption is available in addition to the other exemptions and reliefs, ie it applies to the residue of value remaining after applying any other reliefs or exemptions. It is not cumulative with the 'small gifts' exemption (see below), nor is it applicable to PETs arising as a consequence of a donor releasing his interest in property subject to a reservation[1].

4 *Small gifts not exceeding £250*

14.27 Transfers of value made by a transferor during lifetime in any one tax year by outright gifts to any one person are exempt up to £250 (without grossing up) per transferee[2].

Gifts to the trustees of a settlement are not 'outright' and so fall outside the exemption. This exemption is available only if the total of all gifts made by the transferor to the transferee in any tax year does not exceed £250. (It should be remembered that this actually refers not to the value received but the loss to the transferor's estate.) There is no carry forward facility for this exemption.

5 *Normal expenditure out of income*

14.28 A transfer of value is exempt if or to the extent that it fulfils, during lifetime, the following conditions:

(1) it was made as part of the transferor's normal expenditure;

(2) it was made out of his income (taking one year with another); and

(3) after allowing for all transfers of value forming part of his normal expenditure, the transferor was left with sufficient income to maintain his usual standard of living[3].

A gift is regarded as part of the transferor's 'normal' expenditure if its amount and type are consistent with his usual pattern of gifts. 'Normal' is regarded as broadly equivalent to regular or habitual[4]. The first gift in a series can qualify as 'normal' provided there is evidence that further gifts are intended, for example, a contract with a life office. This would cover the payment of the first premium under a regular premium life assurance policy written in trust. If there is no such evidence, but in fact further normal payments are made, the first premium may, retrospectively, qualify for this exemption.

1 Section 19(3A)(a).
2 Section 20.
3 Section 21(1).
4 *Bennett and others v IRC* 1995 STC 54.

'Income' for this purpose means net income and is determined with normal accountancy (rather than income tax) rules. The exemption is not lost merely because of fluctuations of income from one year to another; nor if the transferor makes a gift from income and, having met some exceptional expense, is obliged to resort temporarily to capital to meet ordinary living expenses.

The capital element of a purchased life annuity bought after 12 November 1974 is not regarded as part of the transferor's income for this purpose in relation to transfers of value made after 5 April 1975[1]. Furthermore, where an individual has effected a life policy as part of a 'back-to-back' arrangement[2], the premiums payable would not automatically qualify for the normal expenditure exemption. Similarly, withdrawals taken from single premium bonds would not qualify.

6 *Gifts in consideration of marriage*

14.29 Certain gifts in consideration of marriage are exempt up to various limits (without grossing up). The limits are as follows:

(1) £5,000 if the transferor is a parent of a party to the marriage;

(2) £2,500 if the transferor is a remoter ancestor of a party to the marriage;

(3) £2,500 if the transferor is a party to the marriage;

(4) £1,000 if the transferor is any other person[3].

The exemption applies to gifts made at the time of, or shortly before, the marriage. Strict proof is required when a gift made after the marriage is alleged to be in consideration of it.

7 *Gifts for maintenance of family*

14.30 A disposition is not a transfer of value if it is made by one party to a marriage in favour of the other party or of a child of either party and is for the maintenance of the other party or for the maintenance, education or training of the child in any period up to the year in which he attains the age of 18 or, if later, when he ceases to undergo full-time education or training[4]. 'Marriage' in relation to a disposition made on the occasion of the dissolution or annulment of a marriage, and in relation to a disposition varying a disposition so made, includes a former marriage[5]. A disposition in favour of a dependent relative is exempt if it constitutes reasonable provision for the relative's care and maintenance[6]. Note that 'child' includes illegitimate, legitimated and adopted children.

1 Section 21(3), (4).
2 See Section 7C, 14.71.
3 IHTA 1984, s 22.
4 Section 11.
5 Section 11(6).
6 Section 11(3). See Inland Revenue Pamphlet IR 1 (1992) F12 for the considerations applying as to whether a disposition is exempt if made by a child in favour of his unmarried mother.

8 Miscellaneous

14.31 There are some other exemptions, including: gifts to charities[1], gifts to qualifying political parties[2], gifts to registered housing associations[3], gifts for national purposes[4] and gifts for the public benefit provided they were made before 17 March 1998[5]. Further, there is no charge to IHT where a member of the armed forces dies from a wound inflicted, accident occurring or disease contracted on active service[6]. Exemptions which have particular reference to life assurance are dealt with in Section 7A, **14.67**.

C Potentially exempt transfers

14.32 A PET is a transfer of value made by an individual (on or after 18 March 1986) which would otherwise be a chargeable transfer to:

(1) another individual or property which becomes comprised in his estate or increases the value of his estate;

(2) an absolute or bare trust (although it should be borne in mind that, at the time of writing, HMRC take the view that the creation of an absolute trust for the benefit of a minor beneficiary would constitute a chargeable lifetime transfer rather than a potentially exempt transfer);

(3) an accumulation and maintenance trust provided the transfer was made before 22 March 2006[7];

(4) a disabled person's trust[8];

(5) an interest in possession trust on or after 17 March 1987 but before 22 March 2006.

A transfer out of an interest in possession trust is also a PET (since 17 March 1987) if the transferee is an individual, an interest in possession trust, an accumulation and maintenance trust, or a disabled person's trust provided that the trust was created before 22 March 2006 and that the beneficiaries with the interest in possession have not been varied since that date (or, if they have, such variation took place before 6 April 2008).

If the transferor survives for seven years after the date of the PET, it becomes fully exempt and is never taxed, but if the transferor dies within seven years, the

1 Section 23.
2 Section 24.
3 Section 24A.
4 Section 25.
5 Section 26, but subsequently repealed by Finance Act 1998, s 143(1).
6 Section 154.
7 Section 71.
8 Section 89.

PET becomes a chargeable transfer and there will be an IHT computation[1] based on the value of the property at the time of the gift, the transferor's seven-year cumulation at the time of the gift and the death rates in force at the time of death or the rates in force at the time of the gift if this results in a lower amount of tax being payable. (Note that unless and until a PET becomes chargeable, it is regarded as exempt for all purposes, so that it would not be aggregated with a later chargeable transfer (eg a transfer to a discretionary trust) for the purposes of establishing the appropriate rate of tax for the chargeable transfer.)

D Reliefs

14.33 There are a number of reliefs available from the charge to IHT. This Section deals with two main areas of relief, namely agricultural property relief and business property relief.

1 Agricultural property relief[2]

14.34 Agricultural property relief is available for transfers of the 'agricultural value' of agricultural property, during lifetime, on death and on transfers into and out of settlements. The relief also extends to certain transfers of shares in companies which own or occupy farms[3].

For the purposes of this relief, 'agricultural value' is the value the property would have if it were subject to a perpetual covenant not to use it otherwise than for agricultural purposes. 'Agricultural property' is agricultural land or pasture in the UK, the Channel Islands and the Isle of Man and includes woodland and any building used in connection with the intensive rearing of livestock or fish if the woodland or building is occupied with agricultural land or pasture and the occupation is ancillary to that of the agricultural land or pasture; and also includes such cottages, farm buildings and farmhouses, together with the land occupied with them, as are of a character appropriate to the property[4].

The relief operates before deduction of the annual exemption and other exempt transfers and before grossing up (if applicable) by reducing the value transferred (automatically, without claim) by the following percentages[5]:

(1) 100% if immediately before the transfer the transferor had the right to vacant possession of the property or the right to obtain it within 12 months;

(2) 100% subject to the old limits (£250,000 or 1,000 acres per transferor) where the transferor would have been entitled to 50% relief under the old rules and had been entitled to his interest since before 10 March 1981 and satisfies certain conditions;

1 In accordance with IHTA 1984, s 7. See Section 5.
2 Sections 115–124.
3 Section 122.
4 Section 115.
5 Section 116.

(3) 100% if the property is let subject to an agricultural tenancy commencing after 31 August 1995;

(4) 50% in all other cases.

14.35 To qualify for relief, the transferor must, immediately before the transfer, either:

(1) have occupied the agricultural property for agricultural purposes for at least two years; or

(2) have owned the agricultural property for the last seven years and throughout the period the property must have been occupied for agricultural purposes (whether by him or another)[1].

For this purpose:

(1) If the transferor inherited the property on the death of another, his period of ownership is regarded as beginning on the date of that death. Where the transferor was a spouse, the spouse's period of occupation may be added[2].

(2) Occupation by a company controlled by the transferor is treated as occupation by the transferor[3].

(3) If at the time of the transfer, the transferor had occupied the property for agricultural purposes for less than two years but it replaced property he had previously occupied for agricultural purposes, the occupation condition is treated as satisfied if he had occupied one or other of the properties for a combined period of at least two out of the five years preceding the transfer[4].

(4) In similar circumstances to (3) the ownership condition is treated as satisfied if the transferor had owned one or other property for a combined period of at least seven years out of the ten preceding the transfer and, throughout, they had been occupied for agricultural purposes[5].

14.36 Agricultural relief at the rate of 100% also apples where shares or securities in a company are transferred[6], if:

(1) agricultural property forms part of the company's assets and part of the value of the shares and securities can be attributed to it;

(2) the company was controlled by the transferor immediately before the transfer;

1 Section 117.
2 Section 120.
3 Section 119.
4 Section 118.
5 Section 118.
6 Section 122.

(3) the agricultural property had been occupied for agricultural purposes by the company or the transferor for the two years immediately before the transfer or owned by the company and occupied for agricultural purposes for seven years immediately before the transfer; and

(4) the shares or securities had been owned by the transferor for a corresponding period.

The relief in these circumstances extends to that part of the value of the shares or securities transferred which is attributable to the agricultural value of qualifying agricultural property.

Relief is not available if at the time of the transfer, the agricultural property or the shares or securities are under a binding contract for sale[1].

Where the transfer falls within seven years of the transferor's death, relief is given only if the property was owned by the transferee throughout the period from the date of the transfer to the date of death and throughout that period the property was agricultural property occupied either by the transferee or another for the purposes of agriculture[2].

2 *Business property relief*[3]

14.37 Relief is available for transfers of 'relevant business property' at a reduction (before any grossing up) of 100% or 50%, according to the category in which it falls. The relief is available for transfers during life, on death and also for transfers of settled business property.

Subject to certain conditions, relief is available on transfers of the following categories of 'relevant business property' at the rates shown:

(1) 100% relief for:

  (a) a sole proprietor's business or an interest in a partnership; or

  (b) a holding of unquoted shares or shares in a company quoted on the Alternative Investment Market (AIM).

(2) 50% relief for:

  (c) land, buildings, plant or machinery owned by a partner or controlling shareholder and used wholly or mainly in the business of the partnership or company immediately before the transfer, provided that the partnership interest or shareholding would itself, if it were transferred, qualify for business relief;

  (d) settled business property used by a life tenant in his own business; or

  (e) a holding of shares giving control of a public company either by itself or in conjunction with the related property rules.

1 Section 124.
2 Sections 124A and 124B.
3 Sections 103–114. For specific reference to Lloyd's underwriting interests, see Section 7C, 14.72.

The relief takes the form of a percentage reduction in any value transferred which is attributable to relevant business property, and any exemptions or other reliefs applying are given after the business relief has been given.

14.38 Relief is given only if:

(1) the transferor owned the business property for the two years immediately before the transfer[1]; or

(2) it replaced other relevant business property and one or other property had been held for a combined period of at least two years out of the five immediately prior to the transfer[2].

A holding of shares is treated as giving an individual control of a company if he has voting control on all questions affecting the company as a whole[3]. Shares which form 'related property'[4] (eg owned by the spouse) are taken into account for this purpose.

Relief is not available where the business is engaged wholly or mainly in dealing in securities, stocks or shares, land or buildings or holding investments[5] – unless it is the holding company of a trading group. Relief is also denied if the business or shares are subject to a binding contract for sale[6].

In addition, the value attributable to an excepted asset within a business does not qualify for relief. The main excepted assets are property rented to third parties, investments (for example unit trusts, single premium bonds) and large cash balances which are in excess of future business requirements — see *Barclays Bank Trust Co Ltd v IRC*[7].

The relief also applies to PETs[8] in a way similar to that for agricultural property, covering situations where the transfer was within seven years of the transferor's death. The relief will only be available where the transferee has retained ownership of the original property from the date of the transfer to the date of death and the property must qualify as relevant business property at the latter date (apart from the minimum two-year ownership requirement).

3 Miscellaneous

14.39 In addition to the above reliefs, there are provisions which relieve, inter alia, woodlands[9] from a charge to IHT on death and also relieve voidable

1 Section 106.
2 Section 107.
3 Section 269.
4 Section 161.
5 Section 105(3).
6 Section 113.
7 1998 (STC 125).
8 Sections 113A and 113B.
9 Sections 125–130.

transfers[1] (eg those set aside as a result of an order under the Inheritance (Provision for Family and Dependants) Act 1975).

SECTION 5 RATES AND CALCULATION OF TAX

14.40 IHT is levied by reference to the transfers of value made in the previous seven years[2] (the principle of cumulation) as well as by reference to the value (in terms of loss to the transferor's estate) of the particular transfer. The rates at which IHT is charged are set out in Schedule 1 to IHTA 1984. There is currently a 'nil rate band' within which chargeable transfers do not attract tax. The value of the nil rate band for transfers made on or after 6 April 2006 is £285,000. Chargeable lifetime transfers in excess of the nil rate band are charged at the lifetime rate which is half the death rate[3] (currently, therefore, 20%). However, where the transferor dies within seven years of that transfer, subject to the availability of taper relief, additional tax may be payable. Transfers on death are charged at the death rate in force (currently 40%), although PETs which prove chargeable may be charged at the death rate in force at the date of the gift if this results in less tax. Many transfers of value during lifetime are not immediately chargeable transfers, but PETs, upon which IHT will not be payable unless the transferor dies within seven years of effecting the transfer. If death so occurs, the PET becomes chargeable and tax is levied on a tapering scale[4] as shown below:

number of years before death	*% of applicable death rate*
less than 3	100%
more than 3 but less than 4	80%
more than 4 but less than 5	60%
more than 5 but less than 6	40%
more than 6 but less than 7	20%

When computing the tax, the value of each transfer is the amount of the original transfer (not the current value of the property representing it) and the taper relief applies to the figure of IHT due, not to the value of the property.

PETs made within three years of death are charged at the full death rate. Chargeable transfers made more than five years before death on which the lifetime rate was charged will not bear any further IHT, but transfers made more than three years but less than five years before death, will. The extra tax is effectively the difference between the relevant percentage of taper relief and the percentage of the property on which tax has already been paid (ie 50%). For

1 Section 150.
2 From 27 July 1981 to 17 March 1986, a ten-year period applied.
3 IHTA 1984, s 7(2).
4 Section 7(4).

example, after four years, but less than five, the extra tax would be 60%, less 50%, namely 10%.

14.41 Transfers of assets between UK domiciled spouses have always been exempt from IHT as described earlier. Thus, if a husband died and left all his estate to his spouse, there would be no IHT to pay at that time. However, the problem with this course of action had always been that this effectively wasted the husband's nil rate band. This situation was altered by legislation[1] enabling the personal representatives of a surviving spouse who died on or after 9 October 2007 to claim any unused nil rate band that existed on the death of the first spouse. The claim is based on the proportion of the unused nil rate band available on the death of the first spouse, not the cash amount, therefore effectively 'index linking' the nil rate band.

It is also possible for any unused nil rate band to be transferred from more than one deceased spouse up to a limit of one additional nil rate band. So, if someone has survived more than one spouse, then on their death it may be possible to claim unused nil rate bands from more than one estate. However, the unused nil rate band accumulated for this purpose is limited to a maximum of the nil rate band in force at the relevant time (ie the survivor's death).

A Grossing up

14.42 As IHT is charged on the loss to the transferor's estate resulting from the chargeable transfer, if the transferor pays the IHT, this will increase the loss and must be taken into account by 'grossing up' the net transfer to find the sum that, after the deduction of the IHT, leaves the net value transferred. (Tax is paid on the grossed-up value, which must be added to the transferor's cumulative total.)

The IHTA 1984 does not provide a specific method of grossing up. One example is by using fractions. On a chargeable lifetime transfer (eg transfer to a discretionary trust) the tax due (on the current rates) is 20% of the total, therefore the value actually transferred is 80% of the total. The fraction to find the tax due is therefore: (value actually transferred × 20/80).

If the transferee pays the IHT there is no need to gross up. (Even when the transferee pays the IHT, the amount of tax is calculated by reference to the transferor's cumulative total.)

PETs are not grossed up because no tax is chargeable at the time of the PET and should the PET prove chargeable upon the transferor's death, the primary liability will fall upon the transferee.

B Liability[2]

14.43 The primary liability to pay IHT on a chargeable lifetime transfer always lies with the transferor, with secondary liabilities on any person whose

1 Section 8A

2 Sections 199–210.

estate is increased in value by the transfer, any person in whom the property becomes vested or who has an interest in possession in it and, where the property becomes settled, any person for whose benefit the property or income from it is applied[1].

As to transfers on death, (other than property comprised in a settlement), the deceased's personal representatives have the primary (personal) liability. If, as a result of death, a PET proves chargeable or additional tax is due on lifetime transfers, the liability rests with the transferee, although if this is not paid within 12 months, the liability rests with the deceased's personal representatives[2].

For the liability arising under settlements, the primary liability lies with the trustees[3], although it may be paid, by agreement, by the beneficiaries, and where tax is payable on the death of an individual with an interest in possession, there is a secondary liability on the deceased individual's personal representatives.

C Limitation of liability

14.44 The liability of the persons above is not without limit. A person acting in a representative capacity is only liable to the extent of the value of the assets which they hold or have control over[4].

SECTION 6 SETTLEMENTS

14.45 It was stated in Section 2A, **14.4** that IHT is charged on transfers of value made by individuals[5]. However, special provisions exist to bring into charge dispositions in respect of settled property[6]. For IHT purposes, settlements are divided into two types, and two entirely different methods of taxation exist, depending on whether or not there exists a person(s) beneficially entitled to an interest in possession in the settled property. The following is a broad outline of the position.

It should be noted that the IHT treatment of gifts into settlements changed fundamentally from 22 March 2006 when all gifts into settlements (unless for the benefit of disabled persons as defined in section 89 of IHTA 1984) became chargeable transfers.

1 Section 199(1).
2 Section 200.
3 Section 201.
4 Section 204.
5 Section 2(1).
6 See Part III of the 1984 Act.

A Settlement

14.46 For the purposes of IHT, a settlement is defined as any disposition whereby property is:

(1) held in trust for persons in succession or for any person subject to a contingency;

(2) held by trustees on trust to accumulate income or under discretionary powers; or

(3) charged with the payment of any annuity or periodic payment otherwise than for full consideration[1].

It will not, therefore, include a bare trust although, at the time of writing, HMRC was of the opinion that the creation of a bare trust for a minor beneficiary would be a settlement.

B Settlements with an interest in possession

14.47 Although the IHTA 1984 contains specific rules in relation to interests in possession[2], it does not define it. HMRC's understanding of the term, however, is as follows:

> 'An interest in possession in settled property exists where the person having the interest has the immediate entitlement (subject to any prior claim by the trustees for expenses or other outgoings properly payable out of income) to any income produced by that property as the income arises – but that a discretion or power, in whatever form, which can be exercised after income arises so as to withhold it from that person negatives the existence of an interest in possession. For this purpose a power to accumulate income is regarded as a power to withhold it, unless any accumulations must be held solely for the person having the interest or his personal representatives.'[3]

The term was the subject of an important House of Lords case:

> *Pearson v IRC*[4]
>
> Three beneficiaries were absolutely entitled to a trust fund, subject to powers in the trustees of appointment and accumulation. The trustees exercised their powers of appointment by deed dated 20 March 1976 to appoint irrevocably to one of the beneficiaries a capital sum to be held on trust to pay the income to that beneficiary during her lifetime or the trust period, whichever was the shorter. HMRC sought to collect tax on what they considered to be the creation of an

1 Section 43.
2 Sections 49–54.
3 Inland Revenue Press Release, 12 February 1976.
4 [1980] 2 All ER 479.

interest in possession. The question was therefore whether or not an interest in possession existed prior to the appointment (as if it did, there would be no charge to tax when the power of appointment was exercised). The Chancery Division and the Court of Appeal found in favour of the trustees, holding that an interest in possession did so exist. The House of Lords, however, (by a bare majority) agreed with HMRC's approach. It was stated that the term 'interest in possession' must be given its ordinary meaning which implies that there must be a present right to present enjoyment. As the trustees had a discretionary power to accumulate, there was no such present right in this case, merely a right to later payment of such income as the trustees, either by deliberate decision or by inaction for more than a reasonable time, did not cause to be accumulated.

14.48 In short, it can be said that a beneficiary has an interest in possession if he has a present right to present enjoyment of the *net income* of the settled property without any requirement for any further decisions of the trustees.

The test is not whether the beneficiary is entitled to all the income, but whether he is entitled to the net income as it arises. To determine what constitutes *net income*, a distinction must be drawn (and was in *Pearson*) between two types of powers exercisable by the trustees: *dispositive* and *administrative*. Net income refers to the income arising after the payment of trust expenses (which are payable out of trust income in accordance with general trust law principles). These expenses will be met by the trustees exercising their administrative powers. Where, however, the trustees have a dispositive power, ie the power to appropriate the income in favour of any person other than the beneficiary in question, that beneficiary cannot have an interest in possession[1]. It should be noted that an overriding power of appointment does not prevent the existence of an interest in possession.

Where the property does not actually produce any income (eg a life assurance policy), it is still possible to have an interest in possession (life office specimen trust forms have generally contained a deeming provision to this effect). The relevant question is whether the beneficiary would be entitled to the income as it arose if the property were income-producing[2].

However, it is felt that the practice of life offices may change following the Finance Act 2006 which stated that, from 22 March 2006, all gifts into interest in possession trusts and accumulation and maintenance trusts would be taxed for IHT purposes, in the same way as gifts into a settlement without an interest in possession.

I Scotland

14.49 The legislation provides[3] for Scotland that an interest in possession is a right under a settlement to enjoy property. Thus, the term has the same meaning as it has, albeit undefined, in England and Wales.

1 See also *Miller v IRC* [1987] STC 108.
2 See *Westminster Bank Ltd v IRC* [1957] 2 All ER 745.
3 IHTA 1984, s 46.

2 The charging provisions

14.50 There are three parties to consider: the settlor, the primary beneficiaries (the life tenant(s)) and the remaindermen.

(a) The settlor

14.51 A transfer into an interest in possession settlement made before 22 March 2006 was a PET, which will only become chargeable if the settlor dies within seven years of the transfer. A transfer into such a settlement from 22 March 2006 onwards will be a chargeable lifetime transfer.

(b) The primary beneficiaries

14.52 A fundamental rule for property settled before 22 March 2006 is that a beneficiary with an interest in possession is treated as beneficially entitled to the whole of the property in which the interest subsists[1]. Where there is more than one beneficiary with an interest in possession, beneficial entitlement of the property for IHT purposes is apportioned according to their shares of the income[2]. When that interest ceases, a transfer of value for IHT purposes takes place[3].

If the cessation occurs during lifetime (whether by selling, surrendering or assigning), and the primary beneficiaries are those either that were actually in place as at 22 March 2006 or if there was a variation of the primary beneficiaries subsequent to that date and such variation took place before 6 April 2008, the transfer may be a PET (if it satisfies the conditions of section 3A of IHTA 1984, see Section 4C, **14.32**), eg a transfer to another individual. If the beneficiary whose interest in possession remains as a potential beneficiary under the trust, HMRC's current view is that he would be treated as having made a gift with reservation of benefit in these circumstances. If the cessation occurs during lifetime and after 6 April 2008, and the primary beneficiaries have been varied since that date, the transfer will be a chargeable transfer, assuming the trust continues in force – see **14.56** – again subject to the comments above regarding gifts with reservation.

If there is a depreciation in the value of the trust property as a result of the trustees entering into certain transactions, the beneficiary's interest will be treated as having come to an end to the extent of the depreciation[4]. It may be possible, however, to claim the exemption of 'no intention to confer any gratuitous benefit'[5].

If the cessation occurs on the death of a beneficiary, the capital value of the trust fund representing his income entitlement will be treated as part of his estate. If the death of the primary beneficiary occurs on or after 6 April 2008 and the trust continues in force, the trust will become a 'relevant property' trust and the principal charge and exit charge as described at **14.58** and **14.59** will apply.

1 Section 49(1).
2 Section 50(1).
3 Section 52(1).
4 Section 52(3).
5 Section 10.

There is no charge to IHT on a cessation of an interest in possession in the following instances[1]:

(1) where the beneficiary becomes absolutely entitled to the property;

(2) where the property reverts to the settlor or the settlor's spouse (or within two years of the settlor's death, the widow or widower), provided that the interest was not acquired for consideration in money or money's worth and the spouse or widow or widower is domiciled in the UK. This applies to trusts created before 22 March 2006 only;

(3) if the transfer is a PET.

If the interest is disposed of for a consideration in money or money's worth, the amount of the consideration will reduce the value transferred.

(c) The remaindermen

14.53 The interest of the remaindermen comes into effect only when a prior interest (that of the primary beneficiary, or life tenant) ends and is a reversionary interest and is thus excluded property[2].

3 Rate of tax and liability

14.54 The liability for any IHT falls on the trustees of the settlement[3] and the rate of tax will be determined by the beneficiary's cumulative total of chargeable transfers within the preceding seven years.

4 Quick succession relief

14.55 There is a relief for IHT where a second charge arises within five years of the first charge. The conditions for the relief are that the transferor must be entitled to an interest in possession, the first transfer was of the same property and the property became, or it was already, settled property on the first transfer[4]. The relief is calculated as a percentage reduction in tax payable on the first transfer and is allowed as a deduction against tax due on the second transfer.

C Settlements with no interest in possession[5]

14.56 Prior to 22 March 2006, the settlements within this class were primarily discretionary trusts. However, with effect from that date, gifts into interest in

1 Section 53.
2 See ss 53(1) and 48(3).
3 Section 201.
4 Section 141.
5 See generally ss 58–85.

possession trusts and accumulation and maintenance trusts are now treated in the same way for inheritance tax purposes and hereafter the term 'discretionary trusts' will be used to cover any trust which is not an absolute or bare trust. It will be useful to state some basic points and define some relevant terms in relation to the taxing of discretionary trusts for IHT purposes:

(1) Once property is the subject of a discretionary trust, only half the normal IHT rates are relevant.

(2) The IHT charges apply to relevant property, which is settled property in which there is no *qualifying interest in possession*[1].

(3) A *qualifying interest in possession* is an interest to which an individual or a company is beneficially entitled[2]. (As stated earlier, there is no statutory definition of the term and so the principles established in *Pearson v IRC*[3] are equally relevant here – but the new rules applicable to trusts created on or after 22 March 2006 mean that for settlements created on or after that date, even where an interest in possession exists, this will still be a relevant property trust – that is subject to possible entry, ten yearly and exit charges.)

(4) The *ten-year anniversary* is the tenth anniversary of the date on which the settlement commenced and each subsequent tenth anniversary (although no ten-year anniversary could fall before 1 April 1983)[4].

(5) A *related settlement* is one made by the same settlor which commenced on the same day as the settlement in consideration (unless one or both of them are charitable)[5].

An IHT charge for a discretionary trust can arise in any of the following situations:

(1) on its creation, as a chargeable transfer;

(2) on every tenth anniversary (the 'principal charge', known formerly as the 'periodic charge');

(3) on distribution of capital by the trustees or on its termination ('exit charges').

I Creation

14.57 A transfer into a discretionary trust is always a chargeable transfer. If the settlor has utilised his nil rate band, IHT will be due and may be paid by the

1 Section 58.
2 Section 59.
3 2 All ER 479.
4 Section 61.
5 Section 62.

settlor (after grossing up) or by the trustees. Thereafter, the tax treatment of the trust varies depending on whether the trust was created before 27 March 1974 (ie pre-CTT) or after 26 March 1974. The discussion below refers primarily to settlements created after 26 March 1974.

2 *The principal charge*

14.58 The principal charge is levied where, immediately before a *ten-year anniversary*, a settlement contains *relevant property*. The rate of IHT is three-tenths of the *effective rate* applied to the *relevant property* in the settlement at the date of the charge.

The *effective rate* is the average rate of tax that would be charged by applying half the IHT rates on a *notional transfer* made by an individual with a *hypothetical cumulative total of transfers*. The *notional transfer* is the sum of (a) relevant property in the settlement, (b) the value of any property in the settlement which has never been relevant property and (c) the value of any property in a related settlement. The *hypothetical cumulative total of transfers* is the sum of (a) the cumulative total of transfers, if any, made by the settlor in the seven years before the settlement commenced (ten years for transfers before 18 March 1986) and (b) the amount which was subject to the 'exit charge' (see below) in the previous ten years, ie the value of the property which has left the settlement in the preceding ten years and on which an exit charge was payable.

To calculate the *effective rate*, one must calculate the tax payable on a transfer of the notional transfer by a person with the hypothetical cumulative total as stated above. The *effective rate* is then the tax payable divided by the value of the notional transfer, expressed as a percentage.

Example

On 1 May 2001, S effects a whole life assurance policy subject to a discretionary trust with a sum assured of £250,000 and an annual premium of £3,000. There are no related settlements and S has made previous chargeable transfers of £325,000 during the preceding seven years.

The first ten-year anniversary is 1 May 2011. On that day, the amount of relevant property (ie the policy) in the settlement is £30,000 (ie the premiums paid).

The effective rate of tax would be calculated as follows:

(1) *Calculate the value of the notional transfer*

There is no non-relevant property, nor any related settlement, so the value of the notional transfer is equal to the value of the relevant property: £30,000.

(2) *Calculate the transferor's previous chargeable transfers plus any values which have been the subject of exit charges*

There are previous chargeable transfers of £325,000 and no amounts subject to exit charges.

(3) *Calculate the tax on such a notional transfer*

	Cumulative total	Tax
Previous transfers £325,000	325,000	Nil
Notional transfer £30,000	355,000	4,000
Total tax		4,000
Tax on the notional transfer		4,000

The effective rate is therefore (4,000/30,000) × 100% = 13.33%.

(4) *Calculate the actual rate*

Three-tenths of the effective rate is 4.0%.

(5) *Calculate the actual IHT payable on the ten-year anniversary*

4.0% of the relevant property (£30,000) is £1,200.

There are further provisions, and necessary calculations in situations where the *relevant property* was either not relevant property or not comprised in the settlement for the whole of the ten-year period[1]. Basically, the rate at which tax is charged is reduced by one-fortieth for every complete quarter in which it was not relevant property or not comprised in the settlement.

Further, if there were additions to the settled property after the commencement date, in calculating the hypothetical cumulative total, one can take the values of the chargeable transfers made by the settlor in the seven years prior to the commencement date of the settlement, or prior to the date of the addition, whichever is the higher[2].

It should be noted that on the current rates, the maximum possible rate is 6%.

3 The exit charge

14.59 A charge to IHT arises where property in a discretionary settlement ceases to be *relevant property*[3]. This may occur due to the settlement coming to an end, when the property is distributed to the beneficiaries, when an individual becomes beneficially entitled to an interest in possession in the settled property, when the property is held on an accumulation and maintenance trust or when the property becomes *excluded property*.

A charge to tax will also arise when the trustees make a disposition, ie do some act or deliberately fail to exercise a right that results in a reduction in the value of the settled property (although it may be possible to claim the exemption that the disposition was not intended to confer any gratuitous benefit)[4].

1 Section 66(2).
2 Section 67.
3 Section 65(1).
4 Section 10.

The rate of the exit charge is a fraction of the rate which was applied at the ten-year anniversary. The fraction is calculated as one-fortieth for each complete period of three months that has elapsed since the last ten-year anniversary[1]. The tax is charged on the amount by which the value of the relevant property in the settlement is diminished as a result of the event giving rise to the charge. Note that no tax is payable if the event in question occurs in the first quarter of a ten-year period.

> *Example*
>
> Using the figures from the previous example, the last ten-year anniversary IHT charge was £1,200 in respect of the £30,000 relevant property in the settlement. Five years (ie twenty-quarters) later, the life assured dies and the sum assured of £250,000 is paid out by the trustees. Assuming no changes in the general rates of tax since the last ten-yearly charge, the £250,000 will be taxed at the fraction of 20/40 of the rate of 4.0% (ie 2.0%) so that £5,000 will be payable.
>
> Again, special rules apply if any property has been added to the settlement or any property in the settlement has become relevant property since the last ten-year anniversary.

(a) Rate before first ten-year anniversary[2]

14.60 Where an exit charge falls due before the first ten-year anniversary, the rate of tax is a fraction of the 'effective rate' calculated in much the same way as the *effective rate* for the ten-yearly charge. The value of all the property in the settlement at the time of creation is taken together with all the property in any related settlement. The hypothetical cumulative total of the settlor's chargeable transfers in the seven years (ten years for transfers before 10 March 1986) prior to the creation of the settlement is also brought into the calculation. The actual rate is three-tenths of the 'effective rate' so calculated. The fraction is again calculated as one-fortieth for each complete period of three months which has elapsed since the creation of the settlement. The actual rate is, therefore, the sum of the 'effective rate' × (3/10) × (number of complete quarters since the trust was set up/40).

(b) Pre-27 March 1974 settlements

14.61 The calculation of the rate of tax is modified if the settlement was created before 27 March 1974.

In calculating the ten-yearly charge, the settlor's cumulative total of chargeable transfers, the value of other non-relevant property and the value of property in related settlements are all disregarded.

In calculating the exit charge arising before the first ten-year anniversary, the rules were modified[3], in particular as to the calculation of the notional transfer.

1 Section 69.
2 Section 68.
3 Section 68.

Further, the rate was simply three-tenths of the 'effective rate' (as modified), there was no account of the number of quarters elapsing between commencement and the time of the disposition.

(c) Exemptions

14.62 Although no qualifying interest in possession subsists in them, the property in the following types of trust is not to be treated as *relevant property*[1]:

(1) charitable purpose trusts[2];

(2) accumulation and maintenance trusts[3];

(3) protective trusts[4];

(4) employee and newspaper trusts[5];

(5) maintenance funds for historic buildings, etc[6]; and

(6) temporary charitable trusts[7].

D Accumulation and maintenance trusts

14.63 The life assurance practitioner should be aware of these trusts, which are basically settlements with no interest in possession which were introduced on 15 April 1976. Prior to 22 March 2006, to come within the definition of an accumulation and maintenance trust and thereby avoid the principal charge or any exit charges, certain conditions had to be satisfied[8]:

(1) There must be no interest in possession in the settled property and income not applied for the maintenance, benefit or education of the beneficiaries must be accumulated.

(2) One or more beneficiaries had to become entitled to the settled property, or to an interest in possession in it, by the age of 25 at the latest. This was an absolute requirement and means that a beneficiary must not be able to be disentitled from acquiring the necessary interest under the terms of the settlement[9]. By concession[10], HMRC regarded the age requirement as being satisfied if it is clear that a beneficiary would in fact become entitled by the age of 25, even if it was not specified in the trust instrument.

1 Section 58.
2 Section 76.
3 Sections 71 and 58.
4 Section 73.
5 Section 72.
6 Section 77.
7 Section 70.
8 Section 71.
9 See *Lord Inglewood v IRC* [1983] STC 133.
10 Extra Statutory Concession F8(1992).

(3) Either not more than 25 years have elapsed since the commencement of the settlement, or, at such later time as the conditions in (1) and (2) have become satisfied, all the beneficiaries must be or were grandchildren of a common grandparent, or children, widows or widowers of such grandchildren who were themselves beneficiaries but died before they became entitled. If this criteria is satisfied, the trust could continue indefinitely (subject to the trust rules on perpetuity).

If the trust has been for the benefit of children who do not have a common grandparent, then it can only last for 25 years. After 25 years, it will revert to being a regular discretionary trust and would incur the usual ten-year anniversary and exit charges to inheritance tax. In addition, the trust fund would incur an inheritance tax charge of 21% of the value of the property in the trust fund on losing its accumulation and maintenance status.

If the trust is caught by this, the trustees will have to consider the implications of paying the charge, which will reduce the cash held in the trust and may result in having to sell investments with a possible CGT charge.

It may be possible to avoid the charge by appointing or advancing the capital of the fund onto fixed interest trusts, bare trusts or absolutely for the benefit of any beneficiaries or to re-settle the funds on new accumulation and maintenance trusts. It should be noted that if the settlor was non-UK domiciled when the property was settled on trust, the charge would only apply to the extent that the trust holds UK assets.

If the trust was created on 15 April 1976, the 25-year period ended on 15 April 2001 and thus, this was the earliest time when the 21% tax charge could apply.

I A&M trusts created on or after 22 March 2006

14.64 Following the Finance Act 2006, all transfers into A&M trusts on or after 22 March 2006 are treated as chargeable transfers and are thus taxed in the same way as discretionary trusts as described above, that is that there may be an immediate charge to IHT to the extent that the value transferred, after deducting any available exemptions and taking account of any existing chargeable transfers made by the same settlor within the previous seven years, exceeds the current nil rate band.

Ten yearly charges and exit charges may also be payable.

However, an exception to this general rule is a trust created in a will or on intestacy in favour of a minor child of a deceased parent which can vest the benefit absolutely in the child between the ages of 18 and 25 (a so called '18 to 25 trust'). If the benefit vests absolutely at age 18, then no charge to tax will arise at that time. If the trust continues after age 18, then at age 18 the trust will become subject to the 'relevant property' trust regime but there will be no entry charge.

This means that, if the child becomes absolutely entitled at the last possible time for 18 to 25 trusts – ie at the age of age 25 – then the discretionary trust regime will apply, but the trust will be treated as having started when the beneficiary attained age 18 for the purpose of determining the appropriate fraction of the effective rate to charge.

The maximum exit charge that can therefore arise when the beneficiary becomes absolutely entitled at age 25 is 4.2% which is 28 quarters into the first ten yearly charge period. If the beneficiary became absolutely entitled, say at age 21, then the maximum exit charge would be 1.8%, that is, three-tenths of 6%.

If the value of the gift to the trust on death plus the cumulative total of chargeable transfers made by the deceased in the seven years prior to death is less than the nil rate band applicable when the beneficiary becomes absolutely entitled, there will be no tax charge.

2 A&M trusts created prior to 22 March 2006

14.65 Transfers to A&M trusts before 22 March 2006 were classed as PETs and consequently fell outside the regime for 'relevant property' trusts.

The original proposals in the Finance Bill 2006 stated that if such a trust was not amended before 6 April 2008 to give the beneficiary an absolute right to the trust capital on attaining age 18, then it would automatically become a 'relevant property' trust from that date with the ten yearly charges starting on the first ten yearly anniversary of the creation of the trust after 6 April 2008 (albeit on a proportionate basis in view of the fact that the trust property had not been 'relevant property' for the whole of the ten-year period).

However, these proposals were amended by the Finance Act 2006 so that the tax treatment outlined above in connection with '18 to 25 trusts' is also generally available for pre-22 March 2006 A&M trusts irrespective of the identity of the settlor where the beneficiary is currently under 18, provided that the trust is amended to meet the '18 to 25 trust' rules as above.

SECTION 7 LIFE ASSURANCE

14.66 Although the IHTA 1984 contains certain provisions specifically relating to life assurance, one is left, generally, to apply the basic charging principles of IHT to situations involving life assurance contracts and policy trusts.

A Lifetime transfers

1 Premiums

14.67 Premiums paid by the life assured on an own-life, own-benefit policy, or by the grantee on a life-of-another policy for the grantee's benefit, are not liable for IHT as there is no transfer of value.

Premiums paid on trust policies are transfers of value because they reduce the payer's estate. Where life assurance premium relief is available, the amount of the transfer is the net premium paid.

From 22 March 2006, gifts into new interest in possession trusts become chargeable lifetime transfers. However, in most cases, premiums will fall within one of the available exemptions, eg the £3,000 annual exemption[1] or the normal expenditure out of income exemption[2]. Any premiums in excess of the available exemptions will be chargeable lifetime transfers and will need to be taken into account in computing the settlor's IHT liability if he should die within seven years.

Prior to 22 March 2006, where the trust in question was an interest in possession trust, the first premium over and above any available annual exemptions constituted a PET[3] since the value transferred was attributable to property (the policy) which by virtue of the transfer (the payment of the first premium) became comprised in the estate of another individual. Subsequent premiums were treated as PETs[4] only to the extent that the value of the estate of the beneficiary(ies) was increased, ie to the extent that the value of the policy is increased[5]. Premium payments in the early years of a policy may not have increased the value of the policy, eg where there is no surrender value and the payments are taken up by charges. It was advisable, therefore, to gift cash to trustees (the cash then becoming settled property, which was comprised in the estate of an individual). The trustees then used this cash to pay the premiums directly to the life office. In this instance, the transfers will prove chargeable only if the payer dies within seven years of effecting the transfer.

For regular premium policies written subject to interest in possession trusts which were in force on 22 March 2006, HMRC have confirmed that they view the payment of ongoing premiums as merely maintaining the policy in force rather than adding to the trust property and thus the existing IHT treatment will remain and the trust will not become a 'relevant property' trust. It should, however, be noted that if the practice of the settlor gifting cash to the trustees to enable them to pay any premiums over and above the exemptions is continued, this will have the effect of placing the trust within the new relevant property regime as each payment to the trust will be viewed as a new gift.

HMRC have also confirmed in guidance notes issued to the ABI that where there are increases in premiums due to ten-yearly plan reviews or the exercise of cost of living or indexation options or where the policy provides for premiums to automatically increase over the term of the policy then provided such increases occur as a result of options contained within the policy or of specific policy terms, the exercise of these options would not be sufficient to place the policy in the relevant property regime. This is also true of paying further single premiums under an existing pre-22 March 2006 single premium bond provided there is an option in the original policy to do this.

1 Section 19.
2 Section 21.
3 IHTA 1984, s 3A.
4 Section 3A(2)(b).
5 See letter dated 28 October 1987 from the Life Insurance Council (LIC) of the Association of British Insurers to LIC members following clarification from the Inland Revenue.

2 Transfer of existing policy into trust

14.68 Where an existing policy is put into trust, the transfer of value is measured by the special rules of valuation in relation to life assurance policies (see **14.71**).

3 Transfer of interest

14.69 If the individual beneficially entitled to an interest in a life policy (eg the life assured under an own-benefit policy or a beneficiary with an interest in possession in a trust policy) transfers his interest during his lifetime then, unless the transfer is for full consideration, there is a transfer of value for IHT purposes. The transfer will be a PET if the usual conditions apply[1] (but will be subject to **14.52** if the trust was created prior to 22 March 2006). One of the available exemptions may apply to the transfer, eg the spouse exemption[2], however, the small gifts and normal expenditure out of income exemptions do not apply. The same principles apply to the transfer during lifetime of an interest in an annuity.

Where the trust was created on or after 22 March 2006, the trust will be treated for IHT purposes as one without an interest in possession and thus, the alteration of a beneficiary will have no IHT implications.

B Transfers on death

14.70 On the death of the life assured under an own-benefit policy, or a policy written under a trust in which the settlor reserved a benefit (unless effected before 18 March 1986 and not subsequently varied so as to increase the reserved benefits or to extend its terms), the value of the policy (ie the proceeds payable on death) will form part of his estate for the charge to IHT on the transfer on death[3]. Note that where the settlor's spouse is a beneficiary, there is no reservation of benefit provided that there is no intention that benefits accruing to the spouse will be used or are in fact used for the benefit of the settlor.

The death of the grantee under a life-of-another policy and the death of a beneficiary with an interest in possession in a settled policy (provided that the settlement had been created prior to 22 March 2006) (or a beneficiary under a simple trust policy) will constitute transfers and form part of the deceased's estate for IHT purposes.

The death of the life assured, other than the settlor under a trust policy, will not be a chargeable transfer unless the beneficiaries have predeceased him and he has acquired an interest in possession through the will or intestacy of the last of them to die.

The spouse exemption may apply to any of the transfers on death mentioned above.

1 Section 3A.
2 Section 18.
3 Section 171.

C Special provisions

1 Valuations

14.71 If there is a transfer of value of the interest in a life policy or reversionary annuity *during lifetime* then special rules apply for determining the value transferred[1]. The value is taken to be not less than the total of the premiums or other consideration paid under the policy or contract less any sums previously paid to the policyholder by way of partial surrender. The market value (either the surrender value or the second-hand value) will apply if it is higher.

The special valuation rule does not apply to term assurances of three years or less or where, if the term exceeds three years, premiums payable in any one year are not more than twice those in any other years. There is a relaxation of the rule for unit-linked assurances[2], in that any drop in the value of units allocated is allowed as a deduction from the total premiums. In both these cases the value taken is broadly the market value which, in the case of term assurances, will depend upon the state of health of the life assured and the remaining length of the term.

2 'Back-to-back' arrangements (annuity purchased in connection with a life policy)

14.72 These arrangements involve the purchase by A of an immediate purchased life annuity and a whole life policy on A's life written in trust for B. In this way, A reduces the value of his estate by purchasing the annuity (which ceases on his death and therefore does not fall back into his estate) and also creates a source of income for his life which enables him to pay premiums under the policy. The policy proceeds should normally be free of IHT as they are in trust for B and thus are not part of A's estate. Thus A's dutiable capital is replaced by non-dutiable assets in the form of a policy belonging beneficially to B.

However, great care should be taken to avoid the potential impact of section 263 of IHTA 1984 which concerns 'associated operations' as defined by section 268 of that Act. Where a life assurance policy is taken out on or after 27 March 1974 and, at the time the insurance is made, or at any earlier or later date, an annuity on the life of the insured person is purchased and the benefit of that policy is vested in another person, then unless it can be shown that the effecting of the contracts is not an associated operation, the purchaser of the annuity shall be treated as making a transfer of value at the time the policy became so vested, of the lesser of:

(1) the purchase price of the annuity plus the premium under the policy; or

(2) the value of the greatest benefit capable of being conferred by the policy at any time.

1 Section 167.
2 Section 167(4).

HMRC have stated that the purchase of an annuity and the effecting of a life assurance policy will not be treated as an associated operation if it can be shown that the policy was issued after full medical evidence of the assured's health had been obtained and that it would have been issued on the same terms had the annuity not been purchased – see HMRC Statement of Practice E4. With effect from 31 December 1987, HMRC have regarded a policy as being issued on full medical evidence if it can be shown that the life office has, as a minimum, obtained a private medical attendant's report and has used it as the basis of its normal underwriting procedures in the same way as it would have done had the annuity not also been purchased. HMRC can ask for the medical evidence to be produced in any case.

Perhaps the best way to establish that the two contracts do not constitute an associated operation is to use different life offices for each contract. This will also be beneficial in that the best rates can be obtained in both cases.

The normal expenditure from income exemption may not be available to exempt the premiums from tax because the capital element of the annuity would not be regarded as income for this purpose. If, however, the investor has enough other income which could have been utilised, this exemption may be available provided the investor does not have to resort to capital to maintain his standard of living.

3 *Lloyd's underwriting interest*[1]

14.73 A Lloyd's underwriter is entitled to business property relief at 100% on the value of his underwriting interest.

Business property relief is available on the value of the whole underwriting interest, which includes investments and cash held in the Lloyd's deposit (which underwriters are required to deposit up to a stated amount); underwriting reserves (the member's personal reserves and his special reserve), and profits on the open years' accounts at death.

If, however, the underwriting interest is thought to be excessive in comparison to the level of business written, the excess will not attract relief, as it cannot be categorised as 'relevant business property'.

Where an underwriter has funded his deposit or underwriting reserves by a letter of credit or guarantee from a bank or a life office, assets held by the bank or life office as security for those arrangements (eg a charge on a life policy) will also qualify for 100% relief up to the value of the guarantee or the letter of credit[2]. In this way, the proceeds of any life policy may qualify for business property relief.

Note. The impact of IHT on life assurance is greater than it has been possible to consider in this Section, which has dealt only with the direct effect of the tax on life assurance contracts. Accordingly, Chapter 15 looks more closely at matters such as the role and use of life assurance in estate planning for IHT, the

1 See Tolley's *Taxation of Lloyds Underwriters* (9th edn 2000). Note that this section does not refer to corporate membership of Lloyd's, which has been possible since 1 January 1994.

2 See *IRC v Mallender* [2001] STC 514.

considerations which should be applied to an assured's existing policies, and the effect of IHT on various policy trust wordings.

SECTION 8 ANNUITIES

A Single life annuities

14.74 An annuity involves the payment of a capital sum to an insurance company in return for an (immediate or deferred) payment of income, commonly for the rest of the annuitant's life. A single life annuity (unless there is a guaranteed capital return element) will cease on death and thus there will be nothing in the estate on which to charge IHT.

Where the annuity provides a capital return upon death of the annuitant, if that capital benefit is paid to the deceased's personal representatives, it will form part of his estate for IHT purposes and be taxable accordingly. It is possible, however, to place the capital return element in trust, in which case the value of the gift will need to be determined for IHT purposes. The CTO drew attention to this point[1], and stated that the value of the gift for IHT purposes will generally be substantially more than the value of the death benefit the right to which has been gifted. This is because the value is determined in accordance with the loss to the transferor's estate principle, under which the value would be the difference between the purchase price of the annuity and the open market value of the right to receive the unprotected annuity payments during the annuitant's lifetime. The CTO have pointed out that the open market value is likely to be less than the amount for which the insurance company would have sold an unprotected annuity on the same individual's life. The main reason for this difference is due to the fact that a purchaser in the open market (unlike an insurance company) would need to buy life cover to protect his investment, the cost of which would vary in accordance with the usual underwriting considerations.

B Joint lives annuities

14.75 Most joint annuities are on the lives of husband and wife, either purchased by one of them or by both jointly. Because of the spouse exemption, no IHT charges will arise on the purchase of the annuity or on the death of one annuitant leaving the other surviving, and this will be so whether the contract is (1) a joint annuity payable to them jointly and thereafter to the survivor or (2) a single life annuity for one followed by a reversionary annuity for the other.

Where a proposer purchases an annuity in joint names, to be payable during the joint lifetime of himself and his wife and then during the life of the survivor and the policy provides for payments after the first death to be made to the

1 See Life Assurance Council Circular 160/1994 in a letter dated 26 July 1994 from the Association of British Insurers to all LIC members and the Taxation (Life Policies) Panel.

survivor, it may be that the law will presume, in the absence of evidence to the contrary, that the husband intended to provide for the wife. But in view of the opinions expressed in *Pettitt v Pettitt*[1] to the effect that the former presumption of advancement in favour of a wife is now of little force, it is perhaps desirable on the comparatively rare occasions when the annuitants are not both contributing to the purchase price that the purchaser should make clear, at the time of making the proposal, that he intends his wife to take beneficially any annuity payable after his death.

Where the wife is the purchaser or in any case where the purchaser is not the husband or parent of the other life, there will not be any presumption that the purchaser intended the other to enjoy the annuity beneficially, and if that is indeed the intention the annuity policy should express a trust for that person.

SECTION 9 REGISTERED PENSION SCHEMES

14.76 This book covers the law of life assurance and not the law of pensions. However, it would not be complete without some mention of the subject, as the life assurance practitioner will invariably need to consider benefits under registered pension schemes and the IHT implications for individuals whose assets are large enough to bring them within the IHT net.

Details of registered pension schemes are given in Chapter 16.

A Impact of the IHT legislation

14.77 It can be seen from Chapter 16 that there are a wide range of structures for registered pension schemes, and a wide range of benefits that might be provided. In addition, the individual often has a good deal of flexibility in tailoring the form of the benefits for his or her personal circumstances, and deciding when to start drawing the benefits. This makes the interaction with the IHT legislation somewhat complex. However, over the years, there have been a number of exemptions from the IHT legislation for scenarios where the value of benefits under registered pension schemes would otherwise have been caught. These exemptions have been significantly extended with effect from 6 April 2011, which means that most scenarios are now outside the IHT net, but not all. So, for most cases, the value of the benefits will not form part of the estate for assessing IHT. Particular issues for each type of registered pension scheme are considered later, but first a few general observations can be made.

1 Contributions paid by an individual

14.78 Any contribution made by an individual to his or her registered pension scheme will not normally be classified as a transfer of value (section 12 of IHTA

1 [1970] AC 777.

1984). However, a transfer of value may occur where the individual was in ill health when the contributions were paid and dies within two years. But if the contributions were a continuation of an established pattern of contributions over several years there will not be a problem.

It should be borne in mind that it is possible for an individual to make contributions to another individual's pension arrangement (for example, a grandparent paying contributions into a stakeholder pension scheme for a grandchild). Looking at the situation from the perspective of the contributing individual's estate, HMRC has advised that, where such contributions do not fall within either the £3,000 annual exemption or normal expenditure out of income exemption, the contributions will constitute potentially exempt transfers.

2 *Lump sums payable on the death of an individual before retirement benefits are taken*

14.79 Any lump sum payable as of right to the legal personal representatives on the individual's death will clearly form part of the estate for IHT purposes. This situation would normally be encountered where the individual has legal ownership of the policy and all the terms governing the pension arrangement are contained in the policy. Retirement annuity policies and 'left scheme' policies would come within that category.

A retirement annuity policy, or 'left scheme' policy, can be made subject to a discretionary trust (whether at the outset or by a later declaration of trust and assignment). The whole of the policy must be made subject to the trust, but the terms of the trust will specify that the retirement benefits will be retained for the benefit of the individual. The trustees will only have power to dispose of the moneys that become available on the individual's death. The normal IHT exit charge will not arise so long as distribution takes place within two years of the date of death. If the moneys remain in the environment of a discretionary trust for more than two years, the normal rules for periodic and exit charges will apply. Making the policy subject to a discretionary trust would constitute prima facie a transfer of value for IHT purposes – but the value of the death benefit transferred is regarded as nominal provided the individual was not in serious ill-health when the transfer was made. HMRC would only investigate further if the individual died within two years of the date of setting up the trust (see Section 9A6).

14.80 Occupational pension schemes normally contain provisions such that the lump sum is distributed at the discretion of the scheme trustees to beneficiaries selected from a specified range, such distribution to take place within two years of the date of death. In these circumstances, the value of the benefit will not normally be included in the estate for IHT purposes. The legal personal representatives can be included in the range of potential beneficiaries. If the trustees decide to make payment to the legal personal representatives through the exercise of the discretionary powers, the benefit will not normally form part of the estate for IHT purposes – the only exception is where no other potential beneficiary can be traced, in which case the trustees would not actually be exercising any discretion.

14.81 Personal pension schemes (including stakeholder pension schemes) established by deed poll fall between the retirement annuity policy and occupational pension scheme structures. The individual has legal ownership of the policy, but the provisions for the payment of benefits are contained in the scheme rules. For a lump sum death benefit, the scheme rules will usually provide that the lump sum would be paid to a discretionary trust set up for the policy by the individual, or, if there is no trust, the lump sum would be paid by the scheme administrator through the discretionary provisions.

Personal pension schemes set up by trust deed have similar death benefit provisions to those set up by deed poll. The only difference is that the discretionary trust would relate to the lump sum death benefit under the scheme rather than the policy (because any insurance policy would be held by the trustees of the scheme, and there would be assets other than just an insurance policy if the scheme is a self-invested personal pension scheme).

The terms of a discretionary trust will specify that the retirement benefits will be retained for the benefit of the individual. The trustees will only have power to deal with the moneys that become available on the individual's death. The normal IHT exit charge will not arise so long as distribution takes place within two years of the date of death. If the moneys remain in the environment of a discretionary trust for more than two years, the normal rules for periodic and exit charges will apply. Making the policy subject to a discretionary trust would constitute prima facie a transfer of value for IHT purposes – but the value of the death benefit transferred is regarded as nominal provided the individual was not in serious ill-health when the transfer was made. HMRC would only investigate further if the individual died within two years of the date of setting up the trust (see Section 9A6).

Where there is no trust, the lump sum will be distributed at the discretion of the scheme administrator to beneficiaries selected from a specified range, such distribution to take place within two years of the date of death. In these circumstances, the value of the benefit will not normally be included in the estate for IHT purposes. The legal personal representatives can be included in the range of potential beneficiaries. If the scheme administrator decides to make payment to the legal personal representatives through the exercise of the discretionary powers, the benefit will not normally form part of the estate for IHT purposes – the only exception is where no other potential beneficiary can be traced, in which case the scheme administrator would not actually be exercising any discretion.

3 *Individual dies whilst in receipt of a pension on the 'secured pension' basis*

14.82 Section 151 of IHTA 1984 applies to pensions being paid on the 'secured pension' basis (ie by means of an annuity or 'scheme pension'). It provides that an interest in a pension or annuity, that comes to an end on the death of a member, shall not be taken into account in determining the value of the estate for IHT purposes. This means that any capital value that could otherwise have been placed on the pension at the time of death will be left out of account.

Where there are remaining pension payments due under a guaranteed period (which can be up to ten years from the date the 'secured pension' commenced):

(1) if the remaining payments are payable as of right to the legal personal representatives, a capital value will be ascribed to those payments and included in the value of the estate for IHT purposes;

(2) if the remaining payments are payable at the discretion of the trustees or scheme administrator of the 'registered pension scheme', no IHT charge will arise.

4 *Individual dies whilst in receipt of a pension on the 'drawdown pension' basis*

14.83 Where the member dies and the remaining fund is paid as a lump sum (less 55% tax), the process for dealing with the lump sum will be the same as described in Section 9A2. In particular it should be noted that an IHT charge could arise if the lump sum is payable to the member's estate as of right, or if a trust is set up whilst in ill health and death occurs within two years. The IHT charge would be in addition to the 55% charge, giving a total tax charge of 73%. If there are no dependants, the lump sum could be paid to a charity, in which case there would be no 55% charge nor IHT charge.

Where the remaining fund is used to provide pension benefits for a dependant, there will not be a value to include in the member's estate for IHT purposes.

Where the remaining fund is used to provide pension benefits for a dependant, the following situations could arise:

(a) The pension for the dependant could be provided on the 'secured pension' basis (by means of an annuity). On the dependant's death, the pension would simply come to an end and there would be no further value to consider. So, no IHT charge would arise in respect of the dependant's estate.

(b) The pension for the dependant could be provided on the 'drawdown pension' basis. On the dependant's death, the remaining fund will normally be paid as a lump sum (less 55% tax). The process for dealing with the lump sum will be the same as described in Section 9A2. In particular it should be noted that an IHT charge could arise if the lump sum is payable to the dependant's estate as of right, or if a trust is set up whilst in ill health and death occurs within two years. The IHT charge would be in addition to the 55% charge, giving a total tax charge of 73%. If there are no other dependants of the member, the lump sum could be paid to a charity, in which case there would be no 55% charge nor IHT charge.

5 *Individual dies whilst in receipt of a pension on the 'unsecured pension' basis (applicable where the individual died before 6 April 2011, but the benefits arising as a result of the death were not finalised until after that date)*

14.84 Where the member died and the remaining fund is paid as a lump sum (less 35% tax), the process for dealing with the lump sum will be as described in Section 9A2. In particular it should be noted that an IHT charge could arise if the lump sum is payable to the member's estate as of right, or if a trust is set up whilst in ill health and death occurs within two years. The IHT charge would be in addition to the 35% charge, giving a total tax charge of 61%.

Where the member died and the remaining fund is used to provide pension benefits for a dependant, there will not normally be a value to include in the member's estate for IHT purposes although there is a possibility that the situation described in Section 9A6 could arise.

14.85 Where the remaining fund is used to provide pension benefits for a dependant, the following situations could arise:

(a) The pension for the dependant could be provided on the 'secured pension' basis (by means of an annuity). On the dependant's death, the pension would simply come to an end and there would be no further value to consider. So, no IHT charge would arise in respect of the dependant's estate.

(b) The pension for the dependant could be provided on the 'drawdown pension' basis. On the dependant's death, the remaining fund will normally be paid as a lump sum (less 55% tax). The process for dealing with the lump sum will be as described in Section 9A2. In particular it should be noted that an IHT charge could arise if the lump sum is payable to the dependant's estate as of right, or if a trust is set up whilst in ill health and death occurs within two years. The IHT charge would be in addition to the 55% charge, giving a total tax charge of 73%. If there are no other dependants of the member, the lump sum could be paid to a charity, in which case there would be no 55% charge nor IHT charge.

6 Individual dies whilst in receipt of a pension on an 'alternatively secured pension' basis (applicable where the individual died before 6 April 2011, but the benefits arising as a result of the death were not finalised until after that date)

14.86 Where there is no 'dependant' the following situations could arise:

(a) Where the remaining fund is to be paid as a lump sum to a charity, or charities, there will be no charge to IHT in respect of the member's estate.

(b) Where the fund is disposed of by means of an unauthorised payment (ie paid out of the scheme to a recipient other than a charity, or transferred to another arrangement within the scheme for the benefit of another individual), there will be a charge to IHT in respect of the member's estate based on the value of the remaining fund (section 151A of IHTA 1984). The IHT due will be paid by the scheme administrator from the fund. The balance will then be paid as an unauthorised payment subject to the relevant tax charges.

 The amount of IHT due will be notified to the scheme administrator by HMRC Inheritance Tax. It will be calculated based on the aggregate value of the member's personal estate and the remaining fund in the pension scheme, and then apportioned between the two. So, the personal estate and the pension scheme will each benefit from a share of the nil-rate threshold.

14.87 Where there is a 'dependant' the situation is quite complex. The pensions tax legislation in the Finance Act 2004 requires the remaining fund to be used to provide pension benefits for the 'dependant'. But the inheritance tax legislation in IHTA 1984 has different provisions depending on the relationship between the dependant and the member. Accordingly it is necessary to split the range of possible 'dependants' into two categories:

A The member's wife, husband, civil partner, or any other individual financially dependent on the member (defined as a 'relevant dependant' in IHTA 1984).

B Any individual who would fit into the definition of 'dependant' but who is not a 'relevant dependant', for example, a child of the member under the age of 23 who is not financially dependent on the member.

Where the remaining fund is used to provide a pension for a dependant in category A, there is not an immediate IHT charge on the member's estate. However, the charge is only treated as deferred until the dependant's death, at which time a charge is levied against any fund remaining – the charge still being in relation to the member's estate (section 151B of IHTA 1984).

The following situations could arise on the death of the category A dependant:

(a) Where the pension for the dependant is being provided on the 'secured pension' basis (by means of an annuity), the pension would simply come to an end and there would be no further value to consider. So, no IHT charge would arise.

(b) Where the pension for the dependant is being provided on a 'drawdown pension' basis, there will be a charge to IHT based on the value of the remaining fund (section 151B of IHTA 1984). The IHT due will be paid by the scheme administrator from the fund in the pension scheme.

    The amount of IHT due will be notified to the scheme administrator by HMRC Inheritance Tax. The tax is charged as if the remaining fund was the top slice of the member's estate. The rate of tax and the nil-rate threshold will be those applicable as at the date of the dependant's death.

    The remaining fund after the IHT charge will then be paid as a lump sum, subject to a 55% tax charge, as described in Section 9A2. So, potentially the fund could be hit with a total tax charge of 73%.

    It appears that an IHT charge could also arise in relation to the dependant's estate if the lump sum is payable to the dependant's estate as of right, or if a trust is set up whilst in ill health and death occurs within two years. This IHT charge would be in addition to the charges described above.

    If there are no other dependants of the member, the lump sum could be paid to a charity, in which case there would be no 55% charge, nor IHT charges.

Where the remaining fund is used to provide a pension for a dependant in category B, there will be an immediate charge to IHT on the member's estate based on the value of the remaining fund (section 151A of IHTA 1984). The IHT due will be paid by the scheme administrator from the fund. The balance will then be used for the benefit of the dependant.

The amount of IHT due will be notified to the scheme administrator by HMRC Inheritance Tax. It will be calculated based on the aggregate value of the member's personal estate and the remaining fund, and then apportioned between the two. So, the personal estate and the pension scheme will each benefit from a share of the nil-rate threshold.

The following situations could arise on the death of the category B dependant:

(a) Where the pension for the dependant is being provided on the 'secured pension' basis (by means of an annuity), the pension would simply come to an end and there would be no further value to consider. So, no IHT charge would arise in respect of the dependant's estate.

(b) Where the pension for the dependant is being provided on the 'drawdown pension' basis, the remaining fund will be paid as a lump sum, subject to a 55% tax charge, as described in Section 9A2. In particular it should be noted that an IHT charge could arise if the lump sum is payable to the dependant's estate as of right, or if a trust is set up whilst in ill health and death occurs within two years. The IHT charge would be in addition to the 55% charge, giving a total tax charge of 73%. If there are no other dependants of the member, the lump sum could be paid to a charity, in which case there would be no 55% charge, nor IHT charge.

7 *Failure to exercise an option in connection with pension rights under a registered pension scheme (sections 3(3) and 12(2A)–(2D) of IHTA 1984 – omission to exercise a right) (applicable where the individual died before 6 April 2011, but the benefits arising as a result of the death were not finalised until after that date)*

14.88 An IHT charge might be considered under section 3(3) of IHTA 1984 where decisions have been made by the individual prima facie with the aim of benefiting others on death, rather than to make provision for the individual's own retirement. Sections 12(2A)–(2D) provide that, in certain circumstances, the failure to exercise an option in connection with the pension rights, which was available before death, can give rise to a lifetime charge to IHT under section 3(3). The circumstances where a claim might arise are where there is evidence to indicate that the individual had become aware he or she was in ill-health and was likely to die within two years, and at or after that time took some action which affected the value that could otherwise have formed part of the estate.

HMRC has stated that, in practice, they expect to see very few cases where a claim would even be considered. HMRC would not pursue a claim where the death benefit was paid to the individual's dependant (ie spouse, civil partner or any other individual financially dependent on the individual) or to a charity. In addition, a claim would not be made where the individual survived for two years or more after making the relevant decision.

Examples of the scenarios where a claim might arise are as follows:

(a) An individual reaches the age at which retirement benefits become due under the terms of the pension arrangement (eg the vesting date under a retirement annuity or personal pension scheme). He decides to defer drawing the benefits because he is in ill-health and wishes the fund to be available as a lump sum death benefit for the benefit of his family.

    Where the death benefit would automatically go to the estate anyway (eg under a retirement annuity where there is no trust), the act of deferring the benefit would not have any significance in itself. But if the individual set up a trust for the policy after the vesting date, or paid extra contributions to a policy already under trust, HMRC might raise a claim.

    Where the death benefit would not automatically go to the estate (eg under a personal pension scheme where the benefit would be payable through the discretionary provisions), the act of deferring the benefit would be sufficient in itself for HMRC to consider raising a claim. But no claim would be made if the lump sum was paid to a dependant or to a charity.

(b) An individual is in ill-health and decides to take pension on the 'unsecured pension' basis rather than purchasing an annuity – the reason being that there will be a fund available on his death for the benefit of his family.

(c) An individual becomes ill whilst taking pension on the 'unsecured pension' basis and decides to reduce the amount of income being taken so that the fund on death is higher than it otherwise would have been.

The value for a section 3(3) claim is determined from the loss to the estate at the instant before death. At that point the individual had the right to use the whole remaining fund for the purchase of an annuity. The section 3(3) claim is therefore determined as follows:

(a) The provider of the pension scheme will determine the annuity that could have been purchased, using its current annuity rates, on the basis of single life only, guaranteed ten years, non-escalating, payable monthly in advance. (If the provider does not write annuity business, HMRC will determine the annuity.)

(b) HMRC will then determine a value for the ten years' guaranteed payments that would have been made.

NOTE: The effect of sections 3(3) and 12(2A)-(2D) was removed where the 'failure to exercise an option' arose on or after 6 April 2011. The 'failure to exercise an option' is considered as continuing right up to the moment before death. So, even though the original point at which the 'failure to exercise an option' arose may have been before 6 April 2011 (for example, the benefits were not taken under a retirement annuity policy which had a vesting date of 15 January 2011), the fact that death occurred on or after 6 April 2011 will mean that there will be no charge to IHT.

8 Transfer of value in connection with pension rights under a registered pension scheme (section 3(1) of IHTA 1984)

14.89 An IHT charge might arise under section 3(1) of IHTA 1984 where a transfer of value arises which has the effect of benefiting others on death, rather than to make provision for the individual's own retirement. The circumstances where a claim might arise are where there is evidence to indicate that the individual had become aware he or she was in ill-health and was likely to die within two years, and at or after that time took some action which affected the value that could otherwise have formed part of the estate.

The scenarios where a claim might arise are as follows:

(a) An individual sets up a trust for the lump sum death benefit that would be payable under a policy of which the individual is the legal owner – ie a retirement annuity policy or a 'left scheme' policy. The individual was in ill health at the time and dies within two years. The lump sum would have been paid to the estate had the trust not been set up, so HMRC would take the view that a transfer of value had taken place for the purposes of section 3(1).

The same situation would arise where an individual sets up a trust in respect of a lump sum death benefit that could arise under a personal pension scheme (whether established by a deed poll or trust deed). Under a personal pension scheme, the rules may provide for the lump sum to be paid to the individual's estate if there is no trust, which would be analogous to the situation above. But, more likely, the rules of the personal pension scheme will provide for the lump sum to be paid to a beneficiary selected at the scheme administrator's discretion from a range of specified potential beneficiaries. In that scenario the lump sum would not normally be assessable to IHT anyway. So, HMRC's practice of bringing the lump sum into account where a trust has been set up, in relation to a scheme where the lump sum would have otherwise been paid through discretionary provisions, seems unduly harsh.

(b) An individual transfers the value of his or her benefits from one registered pension scheme to another. The individual was in ill health at the time and dies within two years. Here HMRC takes the view that:

(i) by taking a transfer, the individual has the opportunity to transfer to a scheme where the lump sum death benefit would be paid to the estate;

(ii) if the transfer ends up in a scheme where that does not happen there has been a 'transfer of value' for the purposes of section 3(1).

There is some logic to this stance in the context of the situation where the transfer is being made from a retirement annuity policy or a 'left scheme' policy (where the lump sum on death would have gone to the estate and become subject to IHT) to a personal pension scheme (where the lump sum on death would be paid through the discretionary provisions and hence would not have been subject to IHT). But where the transfer is being made from, for example, a personal pension scheme, where the lump sum on death would be paid through the discretionary provisions and hence would not have been subject to IHT anyway, HMRC's practice seems unduly harsh.

B Retirement annuities

1 Death of member before drawing benefits – lump sum

14.90 The lump sum can derive from:

(1) the retirement fund;

(2) any separately insured lump sum death benefit.

Where the member dies after reaching age 75, there will be a 55% tax charge on the lump sum.

The insurer will deal with payment of the lump sum as follows:

(a) where the policy is subject to an individual discretionary trust, payment will be made to the trustees of that trust;

(b) where (a) does not apply, payment will be made to the legal personal representatives.

Where the lump sum is payable as of right to the legal personal representatives, as in (b), then it will clearly form part of the estate for IHT purposes.

Where payment is made to an individual discretionary trust, no IHT liability will normally arise if the money is distributed within two years of the date of the individual's death. If distribution does not take place within two years, the normal rules for discretionary trusts will apply from that time, and periodic and exit charges will arise. Many policy trusts become fixed trusts in favour of the default beneficiary(ies) if distribution does not take place within the two-year period. In these circumstances, the relevant value would form part of the beneficiary's estate.

Where the individual sets up the policy trust whilst in ill-health, and dies within two years, HMRC might raise a section 3(1) claim as explained in Section 9A7.

Prior to 6 April 2006 it was possible to formally assign a separately insured lump sum to a lender in connection with a mortgage (although that practice had become largely defunct in the latter years). The legislation from 6 April 2006 prohibits all assignments of benefits, apart from assignment to a trust for the purpose of holding lump sum death benefits. Where an assignment to a lender was made before 6 April 2006, it appears that payment to the assignee can be made without infringing the new legislation, and no IHT charge will arise.

2 Death of member in annuity guaranteed period

14.91 The annuity can be set up with a guaranteed period of up to ten years. On death in the guaranteed period, the remaining guaranteed payments will be payable as of right to the legal personal representatives. A capital value will be determined for the remaining payments which will be added to the value of the estate for IHT purposes as described in Section 9A2.

HMRC has expressed the opinion that it is not possible to create a trust for such an annuity.

3 'Drawdown pension'

14.92 Retirement annuity policies were all established before the drawdown option became available. In theory, an insurer could add the option, but most likely it would be necessary to transfer the fund, before vesting, to the insurer's personal pension scheme to gain access to the option. If, exceptionally, an insurer does add the option then the same principles would apply as described for personal pension schemes in Section 9C3.

C Personal pension schemes (including stakeholder pension schemes)

1 Death of member before drawing benefits – lump sum

14.93 The lump sum can derive from:

(1) the Non-Protected Rights Fund; and

(2) any separately insured lump sum death benefit.

Where the member dies after reaching age 75, there will be a 55% tax charge on the lump sum.

The rules for most schemes will provide for the scheme administrator to deal with payment of the lump sum as follows:

(a) in accordance with any specific provision regarding payment of such sums under the contract;

(b) if (a) is not applicable, and the contract is subject to an individual trust (under which no beneficial interest in a benefit can be paid to the member, the member's estate or the member's legal personal representatives), payment will be made to the trustees of the trust; or

(c) if (a) and (b) are not applicable, payment will be made at the discretion of the scheme administrator to beneficiaries determined from a specified range of potential beneficiaries.

In scenario (a) (which is now rare), it is likely that the specific provision under the contract will mean that the lump sum is payable as of right to the legal personal representatives. In those circumstances, the lump sum will clearly form part of the estate for IHT purposes.

In scenario (b), where payment is made to an individual discretionary trust, no IHT liability will normally arise if the trust distributes the money within two years of the date of the member's death. If distribution does not take place within two years, the normal rules for discretionary trusts will apply from that time, and periodic and exit charges will arise.

Many policy trusts become fixed trusts in favour of the default beneficiary(ies) if distribution does not take place within the two-year period. In those circumstances, the relevant value would form part of the beneficiary's estate.

Where the member sets up the policy trust whilst in ill-health, and dies within two years, HMRC might raise a section 3(1) claim as described in Section 9A7.

In scenario (c), the lump sum will be distributed at the discretion of the scheme administrator to beneficiaries selected from a specified range, such distribution to take place within two years of the date of death. In those circumstances, the value of the benefit will not normally be included in the estate for IHT purposes. The member can give the scheme administrator an 'expression of wish' form, indicating who he would like the scheme administrator to consider paying the lump sum to. But this form will not be binding on the scheme administrator (otherwise the IHT exemption would not apply). The legal personal representatives can be included in the range of potential beneficiaries, and if the trustees decide to make payment to the legal personal representatives through the exercise of the discretionary powers, then the benefit will not normally form part of the estate for IHT purposes.

Prior to 6 April 2006 it was possible to formally assign a separately insured lump sum to a lender in connection with a mortgage (although that practice had become largely defunct in the latter years). The legislation from 6 April 2006 prohibits all assignments of benefits, apart from assignment to a trust for the purpose of holding lump sum death benefits. Where an assignment to a lender was made before 6 April 2006, it appears that payment to the assignee can be made without infringing the new legislation, and no IHT charge will arise.

14.94 If there is a Protected Rights Fund under the scheme, and the member leaves a widow(er) or civil partner, then the Protected Rights Fund must be used to provide a pension for that individual. However, if there is no widow(er) or civil partner, the Protected Rights Fund will be paid as a lump sum in accordance with the following rules:

(a) in accordance with any direction given by the member to the scheme administrator in writing; or

(b) if (a) is not applicable, to the member's estate.

If no directions have been left for the payment of the Protected Rights Fund as a lump sum, it will be payable as of right to the legal personal representatives, and will clearly form part of the estate for IHT purposes.

Where the member has given a written direction, the IHT situation depends on whether the direction is 'revocable' or 'irrevocable'. 'Revocable' means that the member is able to change the direction at any time during his or her lifetime. A direction will be 'revocable' unless it is specifically stated to be 'irrevocable', in which case it cannot subsequently be changed. Where the direction is 'revocable', the value of the lump sum will be added to the estate for IHT purposes. This is on the basis that the member could have revoked the direction right up to the point of death, in which case it would have been paid to the estate. If the direction is 'irrevocable', the value of the lump sum will only be included in the estate for IHT purposes if death occurs within two years and the member was in ill health when the irrevocable direction was made.

2 *Death of member in annuity guaranteed period*

14.95 The annuity can be set up with a guaranteed period of up to ten years. On death in the guaranteed period, the remaining guaranteed payments may, or may not, be payable as of right to the estate. Usually the annuity policy will be bought in the name of the member and will cease to be covered by the terms of the scheme. In that situation, the remaining guaranteed payments will be payable to the estate, and will clearly be subject to IHT.

Exceptionally, the annuity may remain subject to the terms of the scheme. The rules of most personal pension schemes will provide for the scheme administrator to decide who should receive the payments. Hence the payments will not be due as of right to the estate and no IHT liability should arise.

Where the remaining guaranteed payments are payable as of right to the estate, a capital value will be determined for the remaining payments which will be added to the value of the estate for IHT purposes as explained in Section 9A3.

HMRC has expressed the opinion that it is not possible to create a trust for such an annuity.

3 *Death of member whilst taking income on the 'drawdown pension' basis*

14.96 The member can make various arrangements for the disposal of the remaining fund on his or her death.

The member can leave written instructions that the remaining fund is to be used for the benefit of a named dependant (ie the widow(er), civil partner or other individual who is financially dependent on the member). In those circumstances, the fund would not form part of the member's estate for IHT purposes.

The dependant would normally have the following options:

(a) take the fund as a lump sum (less the 55% tax charge);

(b) use the fund to provide income on the 'drawdown pension' basis; or

(c) use the fund to purchase an annuity.

Where the member does not specify that the remaining fund is to be used for the benefit of a dependant, or the dependant has predeceased the member, the fund will be paid as a lump sum. Normally, the lump sum (less the 55% tax charge) will be paid in accordance with the process set out in Section 9C1, with the possibility of an IHT charge as described. But there is an additional option – if there are no dependants, the lump sum could be paid to a charity, with no 55% tax charge, nor IHT charge.

4 Death of dependant whilst in receipt of a pension

14.97 The various scenarios, and the IHT charges that could arise, are as follows:

(a) Where the dependant's pension was being paid from an annuity, no further benefit would arise. Hence there would be no IHT charge.

(b) Where the dependant's pension was being paid on the 'drawdown pension' basis, having been derived from the member's 'drawdown pension' fund (or the member's 'unsecured pension' fund where the member's death occurred before 6 April 2011), the remaining fund will be paid as a lump sum. Normally, the lump sum (less the 55% tax charge) will be paid in accordance with the process set out in Section 9C1, with the possibility of an IHT charge as described. But there is an additional option – if there are no other dependants of the member, the lump sum could be paid to a charity, with no 55% tax charge, nor IHT charge.

(c) Where the dependant's pension was being paid on the 'drawdown pension' basis, having been derived from the member's 'alternatively secured pension' fund (where the member's death occurred before 6 April 2011), the remaining fund will be paid as a lump sum. Normally, the lump sum (less the 55% tax charge) will be paid in accordance with the process set out in Section 9C1, with the possibility of an IHT charge as described. There may also be an IHT charge triggered in respect of the member's estate as explained in Section 9A5. But there is an additional option – if there are no other dependants of the member, the lump sum could be paid to a charity, with no 55% tax charge, nor IHT charge.

D Occupational pension schemes

1 Death of member before drawing benefits – lump sum

14.98 Under a defined benefits scheme, the benefits payable would be specified in the rules of the scheme. The benefit would typically be:

(1) a lump sum based on a defined multiple of salary (up to four times), the liability for which would usually be insured under a group life assurance contract;

(2) a return of the individual's own contributions, with or without interest;

(3) a pension payable to a dependant.

Under a money purchase scheme, the benefits are not specifically defined. What will normally happen is that moneys will become available to the trustees which will derive from:

(1) the retirement fund;

(2) any separately insured lump sum death benefit.

Where the member dies after reaching age 75, there will be a 55% tax charge on the lump sum.

The rules of the scheme will normally give the trustees power to pay the lump sum to beneficiaries determined from a specified range of potential beneficiaries, such distribution to take place within two years of the date of the individual's death. In these circumstances, no IHT liability will arise. The individual can give the trustees an 'expression of wish' form indicating who he would like the trustees to consider paying the lump sum to. This form will not be binding on the trustees (otherwise the IHT exemption would not apply). The legal personal representatives can be one of the potential beneficiaries considered by the trustees, and an exercise of discretion in favour of the legal personal representatives will not give rise to an IHT liability.

2 *Death of member in pension guaranteed period*

14.99 The pension can be set up with a guaranteed period of up to ten years. On death in the guaranteed period, the remaining guaranteed payments may, or may not, be payable as of right to the legal personal representatives. That depends on the provisions in the scheme rules.

The rules of most occupational pension schemes will provide for the trustees to decide who should receive the payments. Hence the payments will not be due as of right to the legal personal representatives and no IHT liability should arise.

Where, exceptionally, the rules of the particular occupational pension scheme provide for the remaining guaranteed payments to be payable as of right to the legal personal representatives, a capital value will be determined for the remaining payments which will be added to the value of the estate for IHT purposes as described in Section 9A3.

3 *Death of member whilst taking income on the 'drawdown pension' basis*

14.100 An option to take income on the 'drawdown pension' basis can only be provided under money purchase schemes. It is likely to be encountered mainly under executive pension plans and SSASs.

The issues to be aware of will be the same as those described for personal pension schemes in Section 9C3.

4 *Death of dependant whilst in receipt of a pension*

14.101 The various scenarios, and the issues to be aware of, will be the same as those described for personal pension schemes in Section 9C4.

E Free-standing additional voluntary contribution schemes

14.102 Since 6 April 2006, these schemes have effectively become personal pension schemes. The provisions outlined in Section 9C for personal pension schemes will apply.

F 'Left scheme' policies

1 Death of member before drawing benefits – lump sum

14.103 The lump sum can derive from:

(1) the retirement fund;

(2) any separately insured lump sum death benefit.

The insurer will deal with payment of the lump sum as follows:

(a) where the policy is subject to an individual discretionary trust, payment will be made to the trustees of that trust;

(b) where (a) does not apply, payment will be made to the legal personal representatives.

Where the member dies after reaching age 75, there will be a 55% tax charge on the lump sum.

Where the lump sum is payable as of right to the legal personal representatives, as in (b), then it will clearly form part of the estate for IHT purposes.

Where payment is made to an individual discretionary trust, no IHT liability will normally arise if the money is distributed within two years of the date of the individual's death. If distribution does not take place within two years, the normal rules for discretionary trusts will apply from that time, and periodic and exit charges will arise. Many policy trusts become fixed trusts in favour of the default beneficiary(ies) if distribution does not take place within the two-year period. In these circumstances, the relevant value would form part of the beneficiary's estate.

Where the individual sets up the policy trust whilst in ill-health, and dies within two years, HMRC might raise a section 3(1) claim as explained in Section 9A7.

2 Death of member in annuity guaranteed period

14.104 The annuity can be set up with a guaranteed period of up to ten years. On death in the guaranteed period, the remaining guaranteed payments will be payable as of right to the legal personal representatives. A capital value will be determined for the remaining payments which will be added to the value of the estate for IHT purposes as described in Section 9A2.

HMRC has expressed the opinion that it is not possible to create a trust for such an annuity.

3 'Drawdown pension'

14.105 The extent to which the 'drawdown pension' option will be available under a 'left scheme' policy will depend on whether the particular insurer is prepared to allow the option. It may be necessary to transfer the fund, before vesting, to the insurer's personal pension scheme to gain access to the option. (Care is needed when considering a transfer as there may be protected tax-free lump sum rights.)

If an insurer does provide a 'drawdown pension' option, the issues to be aware of are the same as for personal pension schemes as described in Section 9C4–C6.

SECTION 10 EMPLOYER-FINANCED RETIREMENT BENEFIT SCHEMES

14.106 'Employer-financed retirement benefit schemes' (EFRB schemes) is the term used for schemes which are not registered with HMRC and therefore do not obtain the various tax reliefs available to registered pension schemes.

Many of these schemes were set up before 6 April 2006 as 'unapproved schemes'. They became important since the introduction of the 'earnings cap' in 1989 and had their own tax treatment which was broadly set out in the Inland Revenue Guide entitled 'The Tax Treatment of Top-up Pension Schemes'. The benefits can be funded in advance by the employer (in which case the scheme will usually be established under a trust), or the benefits can be unfunded (in which case the arrangement will usually be contractual between the employer and the individual). The terms 'funded unapproved retirement benefit schemes' (FURBS) and 'unfunded retirement benefit schemes' (UURBS) became established.

From 6 April 2006 there will be no tax-advantages to EFRB schemes. HMRC will treat them in the same way as any other arrangement operated by an employer to provide benefits for employees.

Despite the fact that lump sum death benefits may be payable through discretionary provisions in scheme rules, there will be no IHT exemption.

However, the pre-6 April 2006 IHT treatment will continue to apply to the portion of the fund accrued up to 6 April 2006, as described below:

(1) Where the documentation governing the arrangement provides for the lump sum to be paid at the discretion of the trustees (in the case of a scheme set up under trust), or the employer (in the case of a contractual arrangement), an IHT liability will not normally arise, so long as the range of potential beneficiaries does not include the legal personal representatives. (If the legal personal representatives are included, there may be an IHT 'gifts with reservation' charge.)

(2) It has been confirmed by HMRC that if an individual reaches the age of 75 and decides not to take his benefits at that time, the benefits can remain subject to the trust and can be paid free of IHT on his subsequent death. However, having taken that decision at the age of 75, it will never subsequently be possible for the individual to buy an annuity at some stage in the future should his circumstances change.

SECTION 11 MISCELLANEOUS

A 'Buy and sell' agreement

14.107 It is sometimes the practice for partners or shareholder directors of companies to enter into an agreement (known as a 'buy and sell' agreement) whereby, in the event of the death before retirement of one of them, the deceased's personal representatives are obliged to sell and the survivors are obliged to purchase the deceased's business interest or shares, with funds for the purchase frequently being provided by means of appropriate life assurance policies.

This arrangement, and its variants, are considered in more detail in Chapter 17. However, it is appropriate to state in this Chapter that, in HMRC's view, such an agreement, requiring as it does a sale and purchase and not merely conferring an option to sell or buy, is a binding contract for sale within section 113 of IHTA 1984[1]. As a result, IHT business property relief will not be available on the business interest or shares.

B Valuation

14.108 There are a number of special rules applying to certain kinds of property, eg life policies, debts, options[2], but the general principle of valuation for IHT is that the value at any time of any property is taken to be the open market value[3], with no reduction on the grounds that the whole property is hypothetically to be placed on the market at one time.

In determining the open-market price of unquoted shares or securities[4] it is assumed that a prudent prospective purchaser has all the information he might reasonably require if he were proposing to purchase them from a willing vendor by private treaty and at arm's length.

In valuing property, no account is taken of the value of property owned by others unless it is 'related property'[5]. Property is related to the property comprised in a person's estate if either (1) it is comprised in the estate of his spouse;

1 See Section 4D2, 13.44–13.46.
2 See generally IHTA 1984, ss 160–170.
3 Section 160.
4 Section 168.
5 Section 161.

or (2) it is, or has been within the preceding five years, the property of a charity, charitable trust or one of the political national or public bodies to which exempt transfers may be made. Where a person transfers related property, he is regarded as transferring the value of his proportion of the total value of all the related property. Thus, for example, where husband and wife own 40% each of shares in a company and husband transfers all his shares to his son by gift, he is treated as having transferred property equal in value to one-half of an 80% holding and not a single 40% holding.

C Domicile and residence

14.109 For persons domiciled in the UK, IHT applies to all of their property wherever it is situated; whilst for persons domiciled outside the UK, it applies to any property situated in the UK. Domicile has its usual meaning, ie the country of permanent home, birth, dependency or choice. However, a person who would not under the general law be regarded as domiciled in the UK may nevertheless, for IHT purposes, be deemed to be domiciled at the time of a transfer if:

(1) he was domiciled in the UK on or after 10 December 1974 within the three years immediately preceding the transfer (ie three years' domicile outside the UK is needed to acquire a foreign domicile); or

(2) he was resident in the UK on or after 10 December 1974, in not less than 17 of the 20 years of assessment ending with the year of assessment in which the transfer was made[1].

For the purposes of (2), 'resident' has the same meaning as for income tax purposes.

1 Policies under seal

14.110 The general rule is that a chose in action, such as a life policy, is situated in the country where it is properly recoverable or can be enforced[2]. Thus, if an individual who is not domiciled in the UK owns a policy issued by a life office in the UK, the policy moneys would, in the normal course of events, be regarded as situated in the UK and be liable to IHT. However, if the person beneficially entitled to the chose in action is domiciled outside the UK and the property is situated outside the UK, the property is 'excluded property' for the purposes of IHT[3], as stated above. The general rule stated above does not apply to specialty debts (which will include a life policy effected under seal), in that a debt due on a specialty is treated as situated in the country where the specialty itself is

1 Section 267.
2 See Dicey and Morris *The Conflict of Laws* (11th edn) vol 2, p 907.
3 IHTA 1984, s 6(1).

situated. It is possible therefore for a non-UK domiciliary to avoid IHT by ensuring that the policy is effected under seal.

D Payment of tax[1]

14.111 Generally, IHT is due six months after the end of the month in which the chargeable transfer is made or, in the case of a transfer made after 5 April and before 1 October in any year otherwise than on death, at the end of April in the next year[2].

As previously stated, the primary liability to pay the tax lies on the transferor for lifetime gifts, the personal representatives of the deceased for transfers on death, the trustees where the transfer is of settled property and the donee when a PET or a chargeable transfer become liable for IHT or for additional IHT upon the death of the transferor. If tax is not paid by the due date it can be recovered from the donee or other persons who come into possession of the property transferred[3]. A right of recovery of tax from a transferor's spouse is provided but the sum recoverable is limited to the market value of the transfer when it was made to the spouse[4].

There are provisions for the optional payment of IHT in ten annual instalments[5] on certain property passing on death, notably land of any description, shares or securities giving control (as defined) of a company and other shares or securities not quoted on a recognised stock exchange in respect of which certain conditions are satisfied. The provisions apply also to (1) lifetime transfers where the IHT is paid by the transferee; and (2) settled property, where the property is retained by the trustees. Interest is chargeable on the whole of the unpaid tax at each instalment date; the rate with effect from 29 September 2009 is 3%[6].

Instalments of IHT are to be free of interest, however, where the value transferred represents land which qualifies for agricultural relief, a business or shares or securities in a company (including land and buildings if held as business assets).

Where any tax or interest is unpaid, an 'HMRC charge' may be imposed for the due amount on any property to which the tax is attributable by its transfer; and any property comprised in a settlement where the charge arises in connection with the settlement[7].

1 Sections 226–232.
2 Section 226.
3 Section 199.
4 Section 203.
5 Section 227.
6 See Inland Revenue Press Release, 24 April 2001.
7 IHTA 1984, s 237.

CHAPTER 15

Estate planning and life assurance

SUMMARY

Chapter 9 dealt with the general principles and fundamentals of settlements and trusts; Chapter 14 dealt with the general principles and structure of inheritance tax (IHT). This Chapter considers IHT mitigation, the relationship between IHT and estate planning using life assurance, the appropriate policies, and the appropriate trusts to consider in each case. Reference is made to the rationale behind the common specimen trust forms of life offices and also to specific trust wordings which may be required.

Individuals (and their advisers) should consider estate planning in order to minimise the IHT liability on their estates[1] and to create certainty as to the devolution of their personal assets upon death. Further, a grant of representation will not normally be issued (unless the estate is '*excepted*')[2] until the HMRC account giving full details of the deceased's estate is lodged and any IHT due has been paid[3]. This can often cause financial difficulties and may require, for example, a loan to be taken for this purpose. There is an agreement between HMRC and the British Bankers' and Building Societies' Association that participating institutions will accept instructions from personal representatives to transfer sums standing to the credit of the deceased direct to HMRC in payment of inheritance tax before the issue of the grant. This is of considerable practical help where the personal representatives do not have ready access to other funds outside the estate, such as life policy proceeds written in trust. However, despite this, the use

1 'Estate' is defined by IHTA 1984, s 5 as the aggregate of all property to which an individual is beneficially entitled (not including excluded property), less liabilities. See Chapter 14.

2 Capital Transfer Tax (Delivery of Accounts) Regulations 1981, SI 1981/880 (as amended). See Inland Revenue Press Release 14 February 2000.

3 Supreme Court Act 1981, s 109(1).

of life assurance policies effected to cover the IHT liability is still very important. It does not in itself ensure that the right sum of money is in the right hands at the right time, because (if the policy is subject to a trust) the policy proceeds will be paid to the trustees (for the benefit of the beneficiaries) whereas the IHT liability must be met by the deceased's personal representatives, out of the estate. Quite often, however, the policy proceeds will subsequently be paid by the trustees to the beneficiaries which will effectively replace the tax which has been paid out of the estate.

This Chapter looks at some wider aspects of the role and use of life assurance in estate planning. It considers various methods of reducing an individual's estate for IHT purposes, of ensuring that capital growth is outside the estate and of allowing retention of, control over and access to some of the investments made. Central to many of these methods is the use of trusts and the final Section considers the specimen trust forms provided by life offices, some of the more common trust wordings which may be appropriate, and their effect.

SECTION 1 PLANNING FOR IHT WITH LIFE ASSURANCE

A Importance of life assurance

15.1 Before considering particular plans, it is appropriate to summarise some of the reasons why life assurance policies are so important in estate planning:

(1) A policy can provide funds on the death of the life assured to meet tax or other liabilities which may arise at that time.

(2) The proceeds are payable in cash and if the policy is qualifying and written under trust, payment can be made free of income tax and capital gains tax to the recipient (note that the underlying funds may have been subject to corporation tax) and may be paid free of IHT. (There may be IHT to pay as a result of a potentially exempt transfer (PET) proving chargeable or on death within seven years of a chargeable lifetime transfer: see further Chapter 14.)

(3) A life policy effected on a with-profits or unit-linked basis can provide capital appreciation which may not be taxed in the assured's hands (but note the possible taxation of the underlying funds).

(4) A person wishing to divest himself of capital over a number of years may do so very effectively by paying premiums, for example, within the £3,000 annual exemption or the normal expenditure out of income exemption to effect a life policy under trust.

(5) Trusts of life policies may be created quite simply at the outset of the assurance, and the trustees may prevent minor beneficiaries from having control of gifted funds until later in their lifetime.

(6) Payment of the proceeds on the death of the life assured under a trust policy can generally be made without waiting for grant of representation and may,

in the case of Married Women's Property Act (MWPA) 1882 trusts, provide protection from creditors generally.

(7) A life policy is a flexible investment which, generally, can be surrendered, sold, used as security for a loan, gifted, charged, made paid up or varied.

(8) Finally, and most importantly of all, life assurance can provide protection for an estate owner's dependants in the event of his premature death.

B Estate planning

15.2 There are several things which an individual may do, both during his lifetime and by making provisions in his will, to mitigate IHT. Since the introduction of capital transfer tax (CTT) (the predecessor to IHT), various schemes designed to reduce the value of an individual's estate or transfer assets without an IHT charge have been promulgated. Many of these schemes have been artificial, and others of such an esoteric nature that many an individual (hereafter referred to as an 'investor') has been reluctant to commit himself to the convoluted and often circular transactions necessary to achieve the desired aims.

It is important to bear in mind the result of a series of decisions by the courts, notably *W T Ramsay Ltd v IRC*[1] and *Furniss v Dawson*[2]. The essential principle emerging from these (and other) cases is that where there is a preordained series of transactions or a single composite transaction, which includes steps which have no commercial (business) purpose apart from the avoidance of a liability to tax, the steps inserted for no commercial purpose may be ignored. More will be mentioned of this principle later.

Life assurance can play a vital part in conserving estates by ensuring that funds are available to replace the capital that would otherwise have been lost as a result of paying the tax. Where no, or only restricted business property relief is available (see **14.37** and **14.38**), life assurance may be the only means of helping small firms and private companies to stay in business. Similarly, where agricultural property relief is restricted or is not available at all, a life assurance policy could be the only way of making certain that funds are available to ensure that the agricultural assets pass intact to the desired beneficiaries (see **14.34, 14.35** and **14.36**).

Before deciding on the appropriate type of policy or policies, sums assured and other arrangements to minimise the charge to IHT and meet the IHT liability, it is necessary to know the investor's intentions for disposing of his estate upon his death, of any substantial lifetime transfers he may wish to make and his current (and likely future) requirements for income and capital. It is also necessary to consider the beneficiaries whom the investor wishes to benefit at these times and to consider the most suitable assets, in terms of tax efficiency and personal preference, to use for estate planning purposes. A balance will usually have

1 [1979] 3 All ER 213; affd [1981] 1 All ER 865, HL.

2 [1982] STC 267; affd [1984] STC 153, HL. See also *Craven v White* [1988] STC 476, HL and *Fitzwilliam v IRC* [1993] STC 502, HL, *IRC v McGuckian* [1998] STC 908, HL and *MacNiven v Westmoreland Investments Ltd* [2001] STC 237, HL.

to be found between the competing interests of the desire to pass property as tax efficiently as possible to an investor's children (or other desired beneficiaries) and the need to provide income for the investor and his spouse or registered civil partner for the remainder of their lives. For the remainder of this Chapter, spouse includes registered civil partner.

Prior to 9 October 2007, if a married couple were considering the mitigation of IHT, one of the standard planning techniques was to try to equalise their estates during their lifetimes so that each could pass up to the amount of the nil rate band on death by means of his or her will in favour of the children (or other potential beneficiaries), rather than leaving the whole estate on death to the surviving spouse thereby effectively wasting the nil rate band of the first to die. If this strategy could be adopted, any tax on the second death would therefore be reduced and could be provided for by means of a joint lives last survivor policy.

Of course, depending on the nature of the assets owned, it might not have been possible to do this in individual cases, for example, if there was a property owned as joined tenants or if adopting this course of action would have resulted in insufficient assets remaining for the surviving spouse to be able to afford to maintain his or her required lifestyle.

However, the position above was altered by proposals originally set out in the Pre-Budget Report 2007 and then contained in the Finance Act 2008[1], enabling the personal representatives of a surviving spouse who died on or after 9 October 2007 to claim any of the first spouse's unused nil rate band. The claim is based on the proportion of the unused nil rate band available on the death of the first spouse, effectively 'index linking' the nil rate band. In this way, leaving assets direct to a surviving spouse no longer wastes the nil rate band of the first spouse to die.

If someone marries a widow or widower, and survives them, it is possible to transfer the widow/widower's first spouse's unused nil rate band, up to a limit of one additional nil rate band. The same applies to someone widowed twice. For example, if someone has survived more than one spouse, on their death it may be possible to claim unused nil rate bands from more than one estate. However, the unused nil rate band accumulated for this purpose is limited to a maximum of the nil rate band in force at the relevant time (ie the last survivor's death).

I Planning on death

15.3 Prior to 9 October 2007, if the position of the surviving spouse was a concern, a popular planning technique on the first death was to leave an amount up to the value of the nil rate band subject to a discretionary trust for the benefit of a wide class of beneficiaries which could include the spouse, children and grandchildren. As the surviving spouse would be a beneficiary he or she could therefore receive income or capital at the discretion of the trustees. (In practice, many testators left a non-binding expression of wishes to the trustees expressing their desire that the trust should provide primarily for the spouse as his or her

1 IHTA 1984, ss 8A – 8C

needs require during his or her lifetime.) As the trust was discretionary, the value of the trust would not pass into the surviving spouse's estate. Income would only form part of the surviving spouse's total income to the extent that it was actually distributed and the distribution of capital within ten years would not give rise to an IHT charge[1]. If the survivor was likely to survive the tenth anniversary of the discretionary trust, consideration would have to be given as to whether it would be better to pay the principal charge[2] at the ten-year anniversary or to break the trust before that time. The decision may well depend upon the likely value of the property within the trust at the time of the ten-yearly charge (as the rate of IHT charge will depend, in part, upon the value of the property). It should be noted, however, that, on current rates, the maximum charge is 6% of the value.

Since 9 October 2007 and the introduction of the transferable nil rate band on death as described above, planning of this sort is no longer necessary purely from an IHT perspective. However, many couples have already included a NRB discretionary trust in their wills and there will generally be no need to make any changes to this as there are still many valid non-tax reasons why planning of this nature on the first death remains useful. It is therefore envisaged that the use of NRB discretionary will trusts will continue to be popular in the future, especially with wealthier clients who have more complex estates. Some of the advantages to planning of this sort are given below;

(a) Use of a discretionary trust avoids the spouse having total access and control of the assets. After the first death, it is possible that the surviving spouse could remarry. If he or she then predeceases the new spouse and leaves everything to him or her, it is conceivable that any children from the first marriage could effectively be disinherited. This could be avoided by the use of a discretionary trust on the first death.

(b) An alternative to using a discretionary trust in these circumstances would be for couples to make provision in their wills for a life interest trust in their estates to be given to the surviving spouse. If this is done, the capital supporting such a life interest will continue to form part of the estate of the survivor and will be covered by the spousal exemption. No liability to IHT will arise on the first death and the NRB remains fully transferable. This means that assets are not left outright to the surviving spouse and allows for control over the eventual destination of these assets.

(c) It is important to bear in mind that if a NRB discretionary will trust is used, any growth in the value of the assets will be kept outside the surviving spouse's estate, and if it is felt that the potential growth on the assets will outstrip the increases in the NRB, this will produce an IHT saving. This is particularly relevant now that the nil rate band has been frozen at its

1 This is because the exit charges before the ten-year anniversary are calculated by reference to the initial value of the trust fund, together with any chargeable transfers made by the settlor in the preceding seven years. If that total does not exceed the nil rate band, no tax is payable. See Chapter 14, Section 6C.

2 See Chapter 14, Section 6C.

2009/10 level and will remain so up to and including the tax year 2014/15, because it means that an IHT saving will be produced by any asset growth within the discretionary trust.

(d) Another advantage of the continued use of NRB discretionary trusts is the fact that, should it be necessary to place capital into the surviving spouse's hands at some stage, this can be done very effectively by the trustees making loans to the survivor. On the survivor's death, any such loans should form debts against the survivor's estate, further reducing the IHT bill at that time.

(e) Use of a discretionary trust also gives potential for keeping the assets out of the local authority's hands, if care fees become an issue for the surviving spouse.

(f) Leaving assets direct to children may not be desirable as should the child subsequently divorce or become bankrupt such assets would form part of his or her estate and would need to be taken into account. Use of a discretionary trust will mean that the assets will not form part of the child's estate and will not therefore be taken into account in these circumstances.

15.4 From 22 March 2006, all gifts into trusts created under a will are treated as gifts into a discretionary trust for inheritance tax purposes unless the trust falls within any of the following three criteria:

(1) it was created for the benefit of a minor child who will become absolutely entitled to the trust property on attaining age 18;

(2) it constitutes an Immediate Post Death Interest (IPDI) as set out in section 49A of the Inheritance Tax Act 1984. Briefly, to qualify as an IPDI, the settlement must have been created by the will of the deceased or under the intestacy rules, the life tenant must have become beneficially entitled to the interest in possession on the death of the testator or the intestate and the 'bereaved minor' rules as set out in section 71A of the Inheritance Tax Act 1984 do not apply, nor is the trust for the benefit of a disabled person. These latter two conditions have to apply for the whole of the period that the individual in question had the interest in possession; or

(3) it was created for the benefit of a disabled person as described in section 89 of the Inheritance Tax Act 1984.

Thus, any settlement not falling within these three criteria will be liable to the principal and exit charges in the same way as a discretionary trust.

2 *The family home*

15.5 As mentioned above, a significant practical problem when considering IHT planning is often that the principal asset is the family home, which is owned jointly by husband and wife or by registered civil partners. This was a particularly difficult problem before the introduction of the transferable nil rate band on death where the house formed a very significant part of the overall wealth of the couple. The ability to transfer any unused nil rate band of the first spouse to die to the survivor has negated this problem for many people but planning using the private residence is still useful in some cases. Where a husband and wife own the home as joint tenants, before any planning can be undertaken it will be necessary to sever the joint tenancy to create a tenancy in common. Once this has been achieved, each spouse may then leave their interest in the home to, for example, the children. This strategy may work perfectly well but it also could cause problems of a very practical nature. Assume a husband dies first and leaves his share of the home to his married son. In the event of the son subsequently getting divorced, the value of his interest in the home would be taken into account in the divorce settlement. He would also be entitled to move back into the home and, presumably, move in any new partner and/or children which might well not be to the liking of his mother. In the worst scenario it may even be possible for the son to subsequently force a sale of the home, leaving his mother looking for a new place to live.

There are, of course, other planning possibilities available involving the private residence such as transferring the half share of the deceased to a discretionary trust or gifting the house to the children and then paying them a fair market rent to continue to live there but these should not be considered without taking specialist legal advice. The gifts with reservation of benefit legislation (see **14.11** and **14.12**) is a major problem in this area and this legislation was significantly tightened in the Finance Act 1999 following the decision in *Ingram v IRC*[1] and in the Finance Act 2004 following the decision in *IRC v Greenstock*[2].

In addition, since 6 April 2005, not only is there the gifts with reservation of benefit legislation to be aware of but there is also the pre-owned assets tax legislation to take into account – see **14.13**.

3 *Business assets*

15.6 The planning of estates will need different consideration when the estates comprise business assets such as shares in a private trading company, a professional or trading partnership or a farm (any of which may attract either business property relief or agricultural property relief – see **14.34–14.38**). In those circumstances, children, other relations and non-family members might well have contributed considerably to the wealth which has been accumulated and may feel quite strongly that part of that wealth should find its way into their hands – especially if the principal estate owner is the first of the parents to die. With such estates it might be wise for more assets to be passed to the children on the first death, or a planned programme of lifetime transfers considered, although the capital gains tax (CGT) implications of lifetime gifting should be borne in mind. Life assurance can assist in such planning by providing funds to enable the surviving spouse to have an adequate income. In any event, assets qualifying for 100% business or agricultural property relief should ideally not be left to exempt

1 [1999] STC 37.
2 [2003] STC 822.

persons, such as the surviving spouse, as this course of action effectively wastes the relief. Such assets should be left to non-exempt persons such as children, grandchildren or perhaps to a discretionary trust under which the surviving spouse could be a potential beneficiary. Another provision to consider is to effect a registered pension plan (depending on the business situation) which could provide dependant's income benefits after death. The contributions are tax effective as tax relief should be available subject to HMRC's normal requirements (ie the 'wholly and exclusively' test[1] see Chapter 14, Section 3). If the death benefits payable from a registered pension arrangement are held subject to a discretionary trust, in general there will not be a charge to IHT in respect of the death benefits[2].

If the premiums paid towards the trust policies mentioned in the various situations above are not exempt, under the normal expenditure out of income exemption or the £3,000 annual exemption, the tax treatment of the premiums will be as set out at **14.67**.

C Other uses of life assurance

1 Estate planning – lifetime transfers

15.7 In addition to providing funds to meet IHT liabilities when they arise, another role for life assurance in estate planning is to mitigate the IHT ultimately payable through a reduction of the individual's estate. This is achieved by creating a medium for the tax-effective transfer to others of funds which will achieve capital growth in the estate of the recipient, not that of the transferor. A common additional objective of the transferor is to retain control over, and have access to, the investment. A common misconception is that this type of planning will provide the transferor with an income in the true sense of the word – it will not. Life assurance policies are non-income producing investments. The marketing material of many policies, notably the single premium bond, states that they provide an 'income' for the policyholder. This is not actually income, but a return of capital, (hence, the term 'income' often being presented in inverted commas in the marketing material). Some of the range of available options are described below.

(a) Gift and loan or loan only schemes

15.8 There are a wide variety of these arrangements which are sometimes known generically as 'inheritance trusts', but more commonly as 'gift and loan' or loan only shemes. The basic principle of a gift and loan scheme is that the investor establishes a settlement with a nominal sum, generally in favour of his children, and appoints additional trustees. The investor then lends a lump sum to the trustees of the settlement, expressed to be free of interest and repayable on demand (usually evidenced by a deed of loan agreement). The trustees invest the

1 Corporation Tax Act 2009, s 54(1)(a).
2 IHTA 1984, ss 151, 210; SP10/86 (9 July 1986) set out in Appendix 10.

lump sum as a single premium in a unit-linked life assurance policy, typically a single premium bond, on the life of the investor (or the beneficiaries). By part surrender, the trustees withdraw from the single premium bond each year (for up to 20 years) a sum usually within the 5% pa tax deferred allowance[1] of the original investment to repay the loan. Any amount withdrawn in excess of the 5% allowance may result in a higher or additional rate tax charge on the investor (as settlor of the trust) or possibly on the trustees if the withdrawal occurs in a tax year subsequent to the death of the settlor.

The investor thus receives an 'income' whilst the capital sum and any growth upon it (less the amount of the outstanding loan) is held as part of the trust fund for the beneficiaries outside the investor's estate and therefore free of IHT. On the death of the investor/settlor, the outstanding loan will be paid to the personal representatives and will form part of the deceased's estate for IHT purposes. The initial gift is a transfer of value which will usually be covered by the £3,000 annual exemption. If it is not, it will be a PET if made before 22 March 2006, or if made to a bare or absolute trust on or after that date which will only prove chargeable if the investor dies within seven years of the declaration of trust[2]. If the gift was made to a discretionary or power of appointment interest in possession trust on or after 22 March 2006, the gift will be a chargeable transfer if not covered by any available exemption.

There has been some concern about the efficacy of gift and loan arrangements due to section 102 of the Finance Act 1986 which provides that where an individual 'disposes of any property by way of gift' and either it is not bona fide assumed by the donee or not enjoyed to the entire exclusion or virtually to the entire exclusion of the donor, then it constitutes a gift with reservation of benefit and will be treated as property to which the donor was beneficially entitled immediately before his death.

It may be argued that such an arrangement does not constitute a 'gift' as it is not given freely (in as much as the loan is repayable), although HMRC has expressed the view[3] that an interest-free loan is not a transfer of value for IHT purposes, but may be a gift, the gifted element being the interest forgone. They have stated further that an interest-free loan in itself is not a gift with a reservation of benefit but it may be if, for example: (1) there is a statutory provision to this effect, or (2) there is some other arrangement between the lender and the borrower related to the interest-free loan which has the effect of making the loan into a gift with reservation of benefit. Such an arrangement might include the use and enjoyment of other property or arrangements which were in some way *collateral* to the interest-free loan.

15.9 The IHT regime clearly contemplates the situation whereby a donor lends money to the trustees of a settlement. Schedule 20[4] to the Finance Act

1 ITTOIA 2005, s 507 and Chapter 13.

2 See Chapter 14.

3 See letter dated 6 April 1987 from the Life Insurance Council (LIC) of the ABI to all members of the LIC following clarification from the Inland Revenue, LIC Circular no 60/87.

4 FA 1986.

1986, which supplements section 102, contains a provision relating to settled gifts[1]. It provides that where there is a gift into settlement, the property comprised in the settlement shall be treated as the property comprised in the gift and where property comprised in the settlement is directly or indirectly derived from a loan made by the donor to the trustees of the settlement, it shall be treated as property originally comprised in the gift.

The effect of this could be that everything in the settlement at the material date (the donor's death) is treated as derived from property originally comprised in the gift and could, therefore, bring the loan and the entire growth on any policy into the gift with reservation of benefit provisions.

However, having said that, such arrangements have been quite commonly entered into since the advent of IHT and, as far as the authors are aware, the Capital Taxes Office has yet to mount a successful challenge to them using the above legislation.

There is a variant of the gift and loan scheme which has become increasingly popular in recent years which is a loan only arrangement. The rationale behind this variant is that section 102 refers to a 'disposal of property by way of gift' and that if there is no gift, the gift with reservation of benefit provisions have nothing to bite on. The settlor merely makes a loan to the trustees who then use the loan monies in order to purchase a single premium bond from which they then take withdrawals to repay the loan.

Prior to 22 March 2006 these schemes traditionally used power of appointment interest in possession trusts and since that date either this type of trust or a full discretionary trust continue to be the most popular. Although gifts to this type of trust are chargeable transfers for IHT purposes as there is no gift involved in the loan only scheme and the gift involved in a gift and loan scheme would generally be within the annual exemption, this should not be a problem at outset. The main issue would therefore appear to be the principal charge at the ten-yearly anniversary. This would be calculated by reference to the value of the trust property at that time less the outstanding loan and may be an issue where very large loans are made.

This problem can be countered however, by effecting, say, two separate trusts on separate days, each involving half the amount of the loan. Each trust would have its own nil rate band and the chances of a periodic charge would therefore be halved. Planning of this type relies on the decision in *Rysaffe Trustee Co (CI) Ltd v Inland Revenue Commissioners* (2003).

(b) Discounted gift plans

15.10 Discounted gift plans aim to provide an immediate reduction in the investor's estate for IHT purposes; a regular tax-efficient income for the investor and death benefits for nominated beneficiaries which are free of IHT.

Under plans of this type the settlor puts a sum of money into a trust which carves out two separate interests. The settlor retains the right to receive a fixed sum each year for the rest of his or her life and all other benefits under the policy

1 Schedule 20, para 5(4).

are for the benefit of the selected beneficiaries who do not include the settlor. The trustees subsequently purchase a single premium bond as an investment of the trust, the lives assured under which are not the settlor or his/her spouse and use the withdrawal facility (often at 5% for income tax reasons) to pay the settlor the specified sum each year.

This is a transfer at outset of a discounted value being the total amount being put into the trust less the present value of the settlor's right to the specified sum every year for the rest of their life. This is an actuarial calculation depending on the settlor's age, sex and state of health at the time. Underwriting will be necessary to back up the discounted value, although HMRC will always reserve the right not to agree with the life office's valuation. The transfer is a PET if an absolute trust is used or it is a chargeable lifetime transfer for any other sort of trust. The chargeable lifetime transfer has to be reported to HMRC at outset if it exceeds the appropriate reporting limits.

Payments to the settlor do not generate an exit charge. The periodic charge is based on the value of the bond less the value of the settlor's interest based on age, sex and state of health at that time, ie an updated discounted value. For this purpose, if the trustees are not aware of any significant health problems of the donor they can use the office's normal tabular discounted value updated for the current age. However, if they are aware of any health problems they must incorporate these into the valuation, thereby increasing it.

One office has a discounted gift scheme based on an offshore unit-linked capital redemption bond which matures after 99 years. The plan works in the same way as already described, but the carve-out is over the policy rather than the trust. The policy and the trust are therefore put into force simultaneously. The bond provides a fixed annual withdrawal which cannot be altered and will continue for the life of the investor as long as there are sufficient units in the bond. The bond cannot be surrendered during the lifetime of the settlor. The bond is written in trust so that the investor retains the right to the withdrawals but all other benefits are held for the beneficiaries of either an absolute trust or a discretionary trust under which the settlor is not a potential beneficiary although his or her spouse could be. On the settlor's death, the policy will continue as, under a capital redemption bond, death does not produce a chargeable event. Once the settlor has died, the policy acquires a surrender value so the trustees can decide either to surrender it or keep it going for the benefit of the beneficiaries.

This is not a gift with reservation as, although the benefits which accrue to the donees vary by reference to the benefits accruing to the donor, this provision (Finance Act 1986, Sch 20, para 7) does not apply because the underlying investment vehicle is a capital redemption bond not a life policy.

These plans are not subject to the POAT rules as they are carve-out schemes whereby the settlor's interest is held on a bare trust for him or her and the settlor cannot benefit from the policy in any other way.

(l) HMRC's attitude to discounted gift schemes

15.11 In May 2007, HMRC published a Technical Note on how they expect discounted gift schemes to be operated by the various providers. The Note took effect for all cases completed on or after 1 June 2007. It is emphasised that this Note sets out HMRC's practice and does not seek to prescribe the approach that must be taken to establish the chargeable value for IHT. Alternative approaches may be used to arrive at broadly similar results and HMRC continues to be open to considering and agreeing alternative valuation bases that achieve that aim.

(2) Underwriting approach

15.12 Following the changes to the IHT treatment of trusts from 22 March 2006, it became clear to HMRC that insurance companies were adopting differing practices with regard to underwriting the settlor's life, ranging from no underwriting at all through the so-called 'sealed-envelope' method whereby medical evidence was collected but was not used in the calculation of the discount advised to the client, to full underwriting. This approach would obviously affect the discount quoted and thus, the potential tax liability at outset. HMRC's preference was that full underwriting should be carried out prior to the discounted gift scheme being effected.

The open market-based valuation method requires that evidence of the settlor's health exists at the transfer date that is sufficient for the settlor's life to be underwritten to the standards required for whole of life assurance. If no evidence of health has been obtained at the outset, HMRC takes the view that a discount is not justified unless medical evidence sufficient to underwrite the settlor's life to the standards required for whole of life assurance was already in existence and can be produced should it be necessary to quantify the gift at a later date.

HMRC adopts this stance because problems can and do arise if no evidence of health was obtained at the outset and therefore is not reflected in the estimate of the value of the gift. On the death of a settlor, for example, where no evidence has been obtained, HMRC will often need to ask the settlor's personal representatives to obtain evidence about the settlor's health at the time the gift was made. This is undesirable as the surviving family may face intrusive and upsetting enquiries at a difficult time. This can be avoided if the information is obtained in advance. Problems can also arise where medical evidence is not collected until after the transfer occurs and it then becomes apparent that up-to-date medical details are not held. This would be insufficient evidence on which to underwrite to the standards required for whole of life assurance and would therefore result in no discount. Additionally, survivors may not have been party to the transaction entered into by the settlor. They may feel entitled to particular treatment based on expectations given by financial advisors and then feel aggrieved when HMRC begins investigating.

(3) Valuation issues

15.13 A discounted gift scheme involves a gift of a bond from which a set of rights is retained, typically withdrawals or a set of successively maturing reversions. The retained rights are sufficiently well defined to preclude the gift being regarded as a gift with reservation for IHT purposes.

The gift is a transfer of value for IHT purposes, whose value is determined by the loss to the estate principle. This is set out in IHTA 1984, s3(1), and quantified by the difference between the amount invested by the settlor and the open market value (OMV) – IHTA, s160 refers – of the retained rights.

The OMV of the retained rights will depend on, among other things, the settlor's sex, age, health and thereby insurability, as at the date of the gift. If the settlor were to be uninsurable, for any reason, as at the gift date, the OMV of the retained rights would be nominal and the gift would be close to the whole amount invested by the settlor. This is because IHTA 1984, s160 provides that, in valuing the retained rights, it is necessary to assume that a sale of them takes place.

In investing in the retained rights, the open market purchaser (OMP) will need to take account of the rate of return he or she requires and the cost of insuring the settlor(s) life.

As mentioned previously, the aim of the Technical Note is to set out HMRC's practice, not to prescribe the approach that must be taken to establish the chargeable value for IHT. HMRC's current mortality and interest rate basis is:

(a) Mortality: 70% of AM/AF 80 Mortality (reflecting the improvement over the table for assured lives for males and females published by the Continuous Mortality Investigation Bureau in 1990 reference CMIR 10).

(b) Interest rate: 5.25% a year.

Open market purchaser's costs: 3% (as a deduction from the present value of the retained rights).

HMRC reviews its interest rate assumptions on a regular basis. When the Technical Note was originally published to take effect from 1 June 2007, a valuation rate of interest of 6% a year was used. This was subsequently increased to 6.75% from 1 September 2007 as HMRC analysis indicated that such a rise in the rate was warranted. The increase reintroduced the differential over base rate and corresponded to a 1% differential over short-term gilts. The interest rate was reduced from 1 February 2009 to 5.25%. It is not clear how HMRC arrived at this figure as a 1% differential over short-term gilts at that time would have meant an interest rate of approximately 3.50%.

The valuation basis is kept under regular review to ensure that it continues to reflect open market conditions and it is HMRC's intention to publish future changes to the valuation basis on their website.

(4) The position for settlors aged 90 and over

15.14 As stated previously, IHTA 1984, s160 provides that, in valuing the retained rights, it is necessary to assume that a sale of them takes place. HMRC has looked for evidence of sales of assets similar in nature to the retained rights, for example, life interests or contingent reversions which are dependent upon the survival of the relevant life to a series of predetermined dates. Its evidence indicates that such rights are not saleable unless life assurance can be effected on that life by the open market purchaser (OMP) or it comes as part of the sale. If it cannot be effected, market evidence shows that those assets will not sell. Without life cover being in place, the OMP is at risk of anything up to the total loss of his or her investment should an early death of the settlor occur. HMRC considers it to be fundamental that the open market valuation of the retained rights should be carried out having regard to what market evidence is available. Additionally, it has been unable to find any evidence that it is possible to effect cover on lives older than 90 next birthday. HMRC therefore regards lives aged 90 and over, or mortality rated to be aged 90 or over, as being uninsurable with the result that only a nominal discount will apply in these circumstances.

This approach was challenged in *Bower v IRC* (2007) (SpC). In this case, the settlor was aged over 90 when the policy was effected and died within seven years of the gift. HMRC contended that the discount should only be a nominal £250 but the Special Commissioner disagreed and valued the discount at £4,200. HMRC appealed this decision and their appeal was upheld in the High Court in November 2008 when the £250 figure was confirmed as the valuation. The current position for settlors aged 90 or over or rated as being 90 and over is as was originally set out in the Technical Note, namely that only a nominal discount will be given.

(5) Position where there are joint settlors

15.15 Prior to 1 June 2007, HMRC took a pragmatic approach to calculating the value transferred where there were joint settlors, such as a husband and wife or registered civil partners. This approach was to value the retained rights in their entirety and deduct this amount from the total sum invested. The value of the transfer was then apportioned between the settlors in the proportions in which they provided the sum invested.

In practice, where the joint settlors are of similar ages and in similar states of health, the results of this pragmatic approach do not differ dramatically from the results of considering the value of each settlor's retained rights individually.

Following the changes brought about by the Finance Act 2006, it is understood that HMRC saw a number of cases where discounted gift schemes were taken out where there was a significant age difference between the joint settlors, or where one of the joint settlors was in very poor health or even uninsurable. In such cases, the pragmatic approach did not achieve a reasonable result. HMRC had also been asked to clarify the correct method of valuation in these circumstances as different providers were calculating the gift values using different methods, resulting in a lack of consistency. This also meant that taxpayers and their advisers were unclear as to which approach was correct. In the light of this uncertainty, HMRC set out in the Technical Note what they consider to be the correct valuation approach. They intend to follow this approach for all discounted gift schemes where the transfer takes place after 1 June 2007. They will also use this method where a transfer has taken place before that date and the pragmatic approach would rovide an unreasonable valuation of the settlor's retained rights and substantial sums are involved.

In HMRC's view, the correct approach is to value the retained rights in their entirety and to apportion this value between the joint settlors by reference to the

OMV of each settlor's retained rights. In the case of joint settlors who are married or in a civil partnership, the related property provisions of the IHTA, s161 are to be taken into account in this valuation.

It is recognised that where there are significant differences in the ages of the settlors (whether their actual ages or their effective ages for insurance purposes), it is technically possible for the value of the retained rights to be calculated as a negative amount using the above approach. It is also technically possible to calculate the value of the retained rights as exceeding the contribution of the settlor. The value of the lifetime transfer is calculated, in accordance with IHTA, s3(1), as the loss to the transferor's estate. If the value of the retained rights is negative, the loss to the transferor's estate cannot exceed the amount contributed, ie there cannot be a negative 'discount'. If the value of the retained rights exceeds the settlor's contribution, there would be no loss to the estate and therefore no transfer of value.

It is understood that HMRC does not propose to re-open cases where the values transferred have been accepted in accordance with their previously adopted pragmatic approach.

(6) *Summary of the current discounted gift scheme position*

15.16 As stated previously, the Technical Note is simply HMRC's view on how they expect discounted gift schemes to be administered. Individual aspects of the guidance contained within the Note are, of course, open to challenge through the courts in the normal way as has been seen in the Bower case. Nevertheless, the Technical Note will be a comfort to all those offering advice in this area as it does set out precisely how HMRC views arrangements of this type.

(c) Retained interest trust

15.17 The purpose of this arrangement is to take advantage of the investor being able to take the full 5% annual allowance as 'income', until his interest is exhausted, whilst being able to gift away a percentage of the capital sum. The investor effects a single premium bond and carves out two separate interests in trust under it: an interest for himself absolutely (the retained or the donor's part) and the donee's part which is held on flexible trusts for his chosen beneficiaries. The investor is excluded from the donee's part and so there is no gift with reservation in relation to that part.

The 5% tax deferred withdrawal provisions refer to the initial investment in the single premium bond, not to the proportional part of the policy which the investor retains under his part of the trust. Therefore, at any time, the investor can ask the trustees to pay part of his entitlement. To be tax efficient, they would normally do this from the 5% annual entitlement, and such trusts often contain a provision to this effect. All the withdrawals must be deducted from the donor's part, which may, therefore, if the donor's part grows at a lesser rate than the total withdrawal, erode. In this way, the donor's part may be progressively reduced, or even eventually extinguished, leaving an increasing proportion of the bond in the gifted part. Once the donor's part has been completely exhausted, there can be no further payments to the investor, by way of withdrawal or otherwise, as this would constitute a gift with reservation and therefore not be IHT effective.

Prior to 22 March 2006, assuming the trust was an interest in possession trust, the transfer would have been a PET and if the death of the donor occurred within seven years, the PET would prove chargeable and the usual provisions would apply (see Chapter 14, Section 3). The balance, if any, of the donor's part, would be paid to the investor's estate and would be aggregated with his estate for IHT purposes. From 22 March 2006 onwards, gifts into such trusts are chargeable lifetime transfers unless the trust used was an absolute trust.

It can thus be seen that the true value of this type of arrangement lies with the ability to take withdrawals from the total original investment thus enabling a greater 'income' to be enjoyed. The IHT benefits are no different from the settlor simply effecting two bonds, one for his own benefit and the other in trust for the selected beneficiaries.

(d) Reverter to settlor trusts

15.18 Under these plans, a series of endowment assurances are effected which are set to mature at yearly intervals. These policies cannot be surrendered. The policies are all written subject to trusts under which the right to the maturity proceeds of the policies is retained by the investor for his own benefit but should the investor die before the maturity date of a policy, the death benefits are held for the remaining beneficiaries. Each year, a policy will mature and the proceeds will be paid to the investor which he can use as 'income'. These plans involve a discount which is calculated by reference to the actuarial value of the policy proceeds which the investor is likely to receive back by way of maturing policies.

There is a variant of these plans which does not provide for an immediate discount. Under this variant, it is possible, when a policy is approaching a maturity date, for the trustees to extend the policy if the settlor does not require the policy proceeds as income. Furthermore, this course of action does not involve a further transfer of value by the settlor.

Traditionally, the above plans have used interest in possession trusts to take advantage of the fact that the initial gift involved in creating the trust was a PET. However, with effect from 22 March 2006, all transfers into such trusts will be chargeable transfers and thus there may be inheritance tax to pay at the outset if the amount of the gift (together with any previous lifetime transfers made within the last seven years) is more than the nil rate band in force at the date of the gift. In addition, the trust may also be liable to the principal charge on the ten-year anniversary, depending on the value of the trust property at that date, and the exit charge when capital leaves the settlement.

Generally, from 22 March 2006, gifts into these arrangements will be restricted so that the amount of the initial transfer is within the nil rate band. Care will also be needed regarding the ten-yearly charges.

(e) Back to back arrangements

15.19 These plans are a combination of a whole life policy and a life annuity running 'back-to-back'. A lump sum is paid at outset, most of which buys an annuity for the life of the individual. The balance is used to pay the first premium under a whole life policy, effected under trust for the individual's beneficiaries. This is a gift for IHT purposes, but will normally be exempt under the annual exemption. The annuity is paid out, say, annually, part funding the whole life premium and the rest being available for the individual to spend as income. The annuity is a purchased life annuity and so only the interest content is taxable, the rest being the tax-free capital content.

On death, the annuity ceases and is worth nothing for IHT purposes. The life policy pays out free of IHT to the beneficiaries. There is no income tax charge because the whole life assurance is a qualifying policy. These plans are very effective for getting large amounts of capital out of the estate, whilst still giving the individual an income. They are available on a single or joint life second death basis for married couples and registered civil partners.

The individuals have to be in reasonable health because they have to be underwritten for the whole life policy. If both contracts are written by the same life office, it will not be concerned when death occurs because the 'loss' on an early death under the whole life policy is matched by the 'gain' on the annuity contract. However, section 263 of IHTA applies to back-to-back policies, unless it can be shown that the contracts were not associated operations. If the section applies, the transfer of value is the lesser of the total initial lump sum and the whole life sum assured – which would render the plan totally ineffective. The case of *Smith v HMRC* (2007) (SpC) confirmed the potential associated operations treatment of back-to-back policies. In order to show that the contracts are not associated, the whole life policy must be underwritten without reference to the annuity. The best way to establish that the two contracts are not associated is to use different life offices, which will also be beneficial in that the best rates for each type of contract can be obtained; it would be unlikely that one office would offer both the best whole life rates and the best annuity rates on the market. If the same office is used for both parts of the plan, it is essential that full medical evidence is obtained to underwrite the life policy.

A variant on this back-to-back theme is the combination of a purchased life annuity, and a term assurance which pays out on death before age 110 (or after 50 years if earlier). The effect is very similar to a whole life back-to-back plan, although the term assurance rates and sums assured are guaranteed, so it does not rely on any with-profits return or unit-linked growth rate.

(f) Peta plans

15.20 Before the introduction of inheritance tax these types of plans were well known. The investor purchased two plans: a pure endowment (ie without death benefit, the benefit only being payable on survival) under which a fixed 'income' (usually within the 5% tax-deferred entitlements so as not to attract a charge to higher rate tax)[1] was taken, and a term assurance which was written under a flexible power of appointment trust to ensure that the sum assured (which was equal

1 ITTOIA 2005, s 465 and Chapter 13.

to the bid value of the units under the pure endowment) was out of the investor's estate. For IHT purposes, the transfer of value, which would, under the legislation in force before 22 March 2006, have been a PET, would be the sum of the total investment into the plan less the value of the investor's retained interest under the pure endowment policy, at the time of effecting the arrangement. (This will be calculated on actuarial principles, depending on age, sex and health at the time the trust is declared.)

Following the tax avoidance line of cases referred to above and the Finance Act 1986, these plans were thought to have been rendered wholly ineffective for IHT purposes. The effect of the Finance Act 1986[1] is that such an arrangement (where the benefits accruing to the donee under a life assurance policy are measured by reference to benefits accruing to the donor under that or another policy) is thought to be treated as a gift with reservation of benefit.

However, similar plans are now once again available in the market. The companies which offer these plans have tried to avoid the effect of the Finance Act 1986 by having a *fixed* sum assured under the term assurance (which would be the value of the original investment of capital in the endowment policy) rather than one which varies with reference to the value of the endowment policy.

I Life policies as trustee investments

15.21 Traditionally most trusts have invested in portfolios of quoted securities although this has perhaps always been a slightly questionable policy, particularly in the case of smaller trusts where a collective investment scheme or a single premium bond could offer all the advantages of diversification and professional fund management at a reasonable cost. However, since the passing of the Trustee Act 2000 which imposed on trustees the duty to ensure the suitability of any investments they make, the arguments in favour of this type of investment have increased. Furthermore, the above Act now gives wide investment powers to virtually all trustees and thus there should no longer be a question about whether or not trustees have the power to make investments in life assurance policies.

In considering insurance policies five factors need to be taken into account:

(1) *Insurable interest.* The trustees will need to exhibit an insurable interest in the life of a beneficiary on whose life the policy is to be effected.

(2) *Investment powers.* This should no longer be a problem as modern trusts will generally have sufficiently wide investment powers to invest in such policies and the Trustee Act 2000 now confers wide investment powers on all trustees unless their powers are specifically restricted by the terms of the trust.

(3) *Power of advancement.* It is advisable (as most modern trusts do) to extend the statutory power of advancement under section 32 of the Trustee Act 1925 to apply to the whole of the trust fund (the statutory power only extends to one half of the trust fund). The trustees may then exercise this

1 Finance Act 1986, s 102 and Sch 20, para 7.

power either from time to time or on a more regular basis to make capital payments to a beneficiary.

(4) *Other taxation consequences.* As a single premium bond is a non-qualifying policy a chargeable event could arise on its encashment or if withdrawals in excess of the 5% annual entitlements are taken. If this happens then any gains arising are assessable to tax in the manner described later in this Section, and in more detail in Chapter 13.

(5) *Life tenant.* If there is a life tenant such an investment may not be appropriate as no income would be produced and capital could not normally be advanced to him. Even if a power exists to advance capital to a life tenant, care should be exercised – see later in this Section.

A single premium bond as a trustee investment has the advantage of much simplified administration from the trustees' viewpoint. As a life assurance policy, it is outside the scope of capital gains tax and thus there is no need for the trustees to concern themselves with the trustees' annual CGT exemption or with the complexities of taper relief. Furthermore, as a non-income producing asset, completion of the trust tax return is again simplified.

15.22 The ability for trustees to utilise the 5% tax deferred annual entitlement as a means of making tax-efficient payments to beneficiaries is also a big advantage, especially when one bears in mind the changes to the system of dividend tax credits from 6 April 1999 which affect discretionary and accumulation and maintenance trusts and may result in a serious reduction in net income for beneficiaries where the original source of that income is dividends.

The tax treatment of any such capital payments in the hands of beneficiaries should also be considered. In certain situations, capital payments out of a trust (eg 5% withdrawals from a single premium bond) may be treated by HMRC as adopting the nature of income for income tax purposes, in the hands of the recipient beneficiary, based on the decision in *Brodie's Trustees v IRC*[1]. In this case, the trustees of a will held property upon trust to pay the income to the testator's widow for life with a provision that if, in any year, the income did not amount to £4,000, the trustees were to use capital to ensure that no less than £4,000 was paid to the widow. On the occasions when this happened, HMRC contended that these capital payments were made to satisfy an income entitlement and should thus be taxed as income in the widow's hands. This view was subsequently supported by the court. However, this should be contrasted with the later case of *Stevenson (Inspector of Taxes) v Wishart*[2].

This case concerned regular monthly capital payments made from a discretionary trust to the beneficiary who was in a private nursing home. In making them, the aim of the trustees was to meet the cost of maintaining the patient, including medical and other expenses. HMRC maintained that such recurrent payments were paid for an income purpose and were therefore income in the

1 [1933] 17 TC 432.
2 [1987] STC 266.

hands of the beneficiary and thus liable to income tax and they raised assessments accordingly. In disagreeing with this stance the court distinguished its ruling from the precedent set in the *Brodie case*. In *Stevenson v Wishart*, the payments were deemed to be wholly of a capital nature and, apart from their recurrence, there was nothing to indicate that the payments were to be seen as income. It was suggested at the time that the case was only of limited application although experience does not seem to have borne this suggestion out. The decision in this case appears to indicate that where trustees are not specifically required to augment income out of trust capital, regular payments of capital to a beneficiary from a discretionary trust or an accumulation and maintenance trust should present no income tax problems, provided they have powers of advancement and exercise their discretion in making any such payments.

15.23 When considering interest in possession trusts it should be borne in mind that under such trusts there is an individual or individuals who are entitled to the income produced by the trust. If the trustees select a single premium bond as their investment, this is a non-income producing asset and thus any trustees contemplating this course of action should ensure that the trust confers powers on the trustees to make advancements of capital to the person or persons with the interest in possession.

For interest in possession trusts, however, the possibility of an attack by HMRC using the *Brodie* decision remains if regular capital payments are made to the life tenant of the trust. If a single premium bond is contemplated as a trustee investment in these circumstances it is recommended that the trustees take irregular withdrawals of income at irregular intervals in order to reduce the chances of such an attack.

The final point to consider is the tax treatment of the bond when it is encashed. Prior to 18 March 1998 where a policy was held in trust, any gains arising on the occurrence of a chargeable event were assessed on the creator of the trust. Thus, if the chargeable event occurred in a tax year following the death of the creator, provided there was no one beneficiary who was absolutely entitled to the trust fund at that time, there would be no charge to higher rate tax, as there would not be anybody living on whom it would be possible to raise an assessment[1] – this was referred to as 'the dead settlor' rule. This created some useful estate planning opportunities. Any bond that was effected by trustees of a trust created under a will could obviously benefit from this legislation. During lifetime, to take advantage of the dead settlor rule, an investor (normally the older spouse) could effect a joint lives last survivor single premium bond, of which he had sole ownership. The bond had to be subject to a trust to take advantage of this rule (although the trust could have been created during lifetime or under the terms of the investor's will).

The aim of the arrangement was to avoid any liability to higher rate tax by encashing the bond in a tax year following the death of the creator of the trust. This obviously relied on the sole owner actually being the first of the lives assured to die. In order to be certain that any such liability was minimised, it was

1 ITTOIA 2005, s 465.

often preferable to split the investment, so that the investors each effected a joint lives last survivor single premium bond and put it in trust (either during lifetime, or in the terms of their wills).

Another way of taking advantage of this rule was for the investor to purchase a capital redemption bond. Under this type of policy, the death of the investor (who would have been the creator of the trust) is not a chargeable event, and so, provided the 'term' is long enough, use could always be made of the 'dead settlor rule'. It was preferable for a trust of a capital redemption bond to remain 'flexible' for 80 years (to be consistent with the perpetuity period that existed as at 17 March 1998 thereby retaining flexibility for a longer period than in the standard specimen trust forms (see below) provided by life offices which commonly provide for the flexibility to cease two years after the death of the investor.

These rules still apply in situations where the creator of the trust died before 18 March 1998 and the policy was already in force at that date provided that the policy is not enhanced in any way after that date. In all other situations new rules contained in what was a revised section 547(1) of ICTA 1988, and is now sections 465 and 467 of ITTOIA 2005, apply. These new rules also state that when a chargeable event occurs in respect of a bond written subject to a trust the tax charge will still be based on the income of the settlor of the trust provided he is alive and resident in the UK. However, if the settlor is dead or non-UK resident, any chargeable event occurring in a tax year after the death of the settlor would be assessed on the trustees. The gain would be chargeable on the trustees at the rate of 50% in respect of an offshore bond but if the policy was effected with a UK life office, the trustees would get credit for basic rate tax deemed to have been paid within the fund and thus would only have to pay tax at 30% on the gain.

It may be possible to avoid this charge if the bond, or segments thereof, were to be assigned by the trustees to the beneficiaries assuming that they have attained the age of 18. Such an assignment would not trigger a chargeable event and any gain arising on a chargeable event after the assignment would then be assessed on the beneficiaries.

2 *Miscellaneous uses*

15.24 Life assurance can help in minimising the effect of IHT by providing a medium for taking advantage of the annual exemption. For example, where an estate is to pass to children and consists mainly of readily realisable assets, bank or building society deposits, the individual might use capital to pay premiums, within the limits of the available exemptions, for a life policy written under trust. The policy proceeds would provide a tax-free 'legacy' on the life assured's death and, moreover, the IHT liability on the estate would be reduced by the withdrawal of capital

Similarly, if an individual wishes to make a lifetime transfer of cash (ie income) to his children, he may make use of the annual exemption to build up a tax-free lump sum by paying premiums towards an endowment assurance written in trust for the children's benefit.

Furthermore, in some instances, IHT will be payable as a consequence of the donor dying within seven years of making a gift. This applies to gifts which are not fully exempt but which are either PETs or CLTs. Upon a donor dying within the seven-year period, a tax liability may arise in respect of the gift. The tax liability decreases over the seven years (after the third year) due to taper relief which could, if appropriate, be planned for by a seven-year decreasing term assurance.

It would not be appropriate to use a seven-year decreasing term assurance where, at the date of the particular PET or CLT, there are no relevant previous transfers and the amount of the PET or CLT falls within the nil rate band. The nil rate band is applied first of all against lifetime transfers and so in the event of the PET or CLT proving chargeable, it could be covered by the nil rate band and no IHT would be payable. The appropriate policy in this instance may be a seven-year level term assurance, in trust for the residuary beneficiaries of the investor's estate in order to cover the increased amount of IHT which would be payable by the personal representatives as a result of the nil rate band being used (in whole or in part) by lifetime transfers of value, thereby reducing the amount of the IHT-free estate upon death.

SECTION 2 DECLARING TRUSTS OF POLICIES

15.25 The proceeds of a whole life policy effected by a person on his own life and for his own benefit will be aggregated with his estate on his death and will be chargeable to IHT. For estate planning purposes, therefore, it is better to assign the policy or declare a trust of it in order to remove the value of the policy at the time of the gift (and any sum assured which becomes payable) from his estate. Further advantages are that the sums assured will be paid to the trustees (the policyholders) upon proof of death of the life assured and proof of their title to the policy, without having to wait until a grant of representation is obtained.

In the case of an endowment assurance, it may be desirable for the policy to remain for the assured's own benefit if he survives, where, for example, it is to provide for retirement. HMRC have confirmed that the retention by the settlor of a reversionary interest under an interest in possession trust effected before 22 March 2006 is not considered to constitute a gift with reservation of benefit[1].

SECTION 3 LIFE OFFICE SPECIMEN TRUST FORMS

15.26 Many life offices (and financial advisers) have specimen trust forms which a proposer or policyholder may use to place a policy in trust. In all cases, these trust forms are provided as specimens. Due to the nature of trusts and of the relevant surrounding personal circumstances of the investor, it is strongly advisable that the investor takes independent legal advice to ensure that the particular

1 Inland Revenue letter, 18 May 1987.

specimen trust form meets his requirements in the particular case and does not conflict with any existing arrangements.

Commonly, life offices have two categories of trust form, a trust request form and a declaration of trust form. These are designed to be used in two different sets of circumstances. The trust request form is designed for use by the investor at the time of proposing for a policy (or any time *before* the date of assurance), whilst the declaration of trust is designed for use at any time *after* the date of assurance. It is important that these forms are used correctly.

If an investor wishes a policy to be written in trust from the outset[1], the trust request must be submitted to the life office before the date of assurance, and preferably at the same time as the proposal form is submitted. In this way, the policy is placed in trust as a matter of contract between the investor and the life office. A common form of wording in the trust request form is as follows:

> 'I hereby declare that I make the proposal dated [ ] on the terms that the policy of assurance effected and issued as a result of that proposal on my life should be issued to me as trustee and all moneys payable and benefits under the policy (the Trust Fund) shall be subject to the following trusts: …'

If the trust request form is not received by the life office before the date of assurance, there is some doubt as to whether, legally, a valid trust will be created (ie whether the trust will be completely constituted). If the trust is not completely constituted, it cannot be enforced, the settlor could revoke the trust and there could potentially be problems as between any competing beneficiaries or potential beneficiaries of the investor's estate.

The standard trust forms should also contain suitable clauses giving the trustees power to surrender, mortgage, charge or otherwise deal with the policy, together with wide powers of investment, power to delegate investment decisions, power for the investments to be held by nominees, an extended power to advance capital to a beneficiary up to the full amount of his or her vested or prospective share, and clauses providing for the remuneration of corporate or professional trustees and for the appointment of new trustees.

A standard trust form for a Scottish trust should also contain express powers of delegation, as the common law and the Scottish statutes do not allow any form of delegation.

A Power of appointment interest in possession trust

15.27 Prior to 22 March 2006, the most popular type of trust for life policies was the power of appointment trust which gave an interest in possession to named or identified beneficiaries.

The power of appointment trust is usually in two parts, giving an immediate interest in possession to named or identified beneficiaries, known as the default

1 Note that this is particularly important for trusts for business assurance purposes, in order to avoid with certainty the possibility of a charge to capital gains tax. See further Chapter 17, Section 1A.

beneficiaries, with an overriding power in the hands of the trustees to change the beneficial interest, either revocably or irrevocably, to any of a class of 'potential beneficiaries' listed on the trust form. For trusts created prior to 22 March 2006 this gave all the advantages of placing a policy in trust already referred to (eg proceeds free of IHT), whilst retaining the ability to change the beneficiaries and being able to cater for unforeseen circumstances at the time the trust was created, eg by way of changes in the needs or structure of the investor's family and dependants.

The specimen trust forms will often provide a choice for the investor as to whether he wishes the default beneficiaries to hold their interest *in equal shares absolutely* or *absolutely*. Subject to the trustees' power to appoint the beneficial interest to another, *in equal shares absolutely* means that on the death of a beneficiary, his beneficial interest would pass according to his will (or the Intestacy Rules), whilst *absolutely* (without more) could mean that his beneficial interest passes to the remaining beneficiaries.

Life office trust forms are often drafted in such a way that the power of appointment exists until two years after the date of the death of the settlor. This is to be consistent with the IHTA provisions[1] relating to the variation of dispositions comprised in the settlor's estate and the reverter to settlor or settlor's spouse exemption within two years of death (see Chapter 14). Therefore, unless the trustees make an irrevocable appointment, the power of appointment does not cease until the expiry of that period.

If a new power of appointment interest in possession trust is effected on or after 22 March 2006 such a trust would fall within the relevant property regime. So whereas some companies continue to use trusts of this type, most providers tend to offer discretionary trusts where some element of flexibility in deciding who the beneficiaries should be is required. As an alternative to this type of trust, providers will also offer bare or absolute trusts.

Of course, many interest in possession trusts which were effected before 22 March 2006 still remain in force and it should be noted that if the power of appointment is exercised after 5 October 2008 under such a trust, and the trust remains in existence, this will have the effect of turning the trust (or at least the beneficial share in it that was altered) into a relevant property trust and thus causing it to be potentially liable to the ten-yearly and exit charges (see Chapter 14, Section 6B).

15.28 It is important, however, if a trust policy is to fulfil the purpose for which it is effected, that the provisions of the trust should clearly and correctly set out the grantee's intentions regarding the persons he wishes to benefit and the nature of their interests. The following Section considers the various dispositions of the policy benefits most frequently required by proposers, draft forms of trust wording for incorporating those dispositions in the trust policy, and discusses the tax and legal implications of doing so although some of these wordings are now of historical interest only owing to the fact that all new policies effected on or after 22 March 2006, unless written subject to absolute or bare trusts, will be

1 IHTA 1984, ss 53, 142.

treated as discretionary trusts in which no individual will have an interest in possession and all benefits will be payable at the trustees' discretion.

Before considering these draft trust wordings, it is necessary to mention a number of preliminary matters.

If not exempt as normal expenditure out of income, or by use of the £3,000 annual exemption, the premiums paid towards trust policies (if the trust is an interest in possession or accumulation and maintenance trust created before 22 March 2006)[1] will be lifetime transfers for IHT purposes and may be treated as PETs. Prior to 22 March 2006, in order for such transfers to be PETs, the property transferred must become settled property[2]. This presented no problems in relation to the first premium paid, but was obviously an issue where a premium is paid by an investor on a life policy *already* held on trust. The second or subsequent premiums therefore were only PETs to the extent that the value of the estate of the beneficiary(ies) was increased. This meant that only the part of the second or subsequent premiums which actually increased the market value of the policy will be a PET. The investor could ensure that these payments constituted PETs by making gifts of cash to the trustees who would then pay the premiums, rather than paying the premiums to the life office directly. However, since 22 March 2006, the position is now that any premiums payable in respect of policies issued under such trusts in excess of the available exemptions will be PETs. Since that date, cash gifts to the trustees to enable them to pay the premiums would no longer be necessary or desirable. For policies effected on or after 22 March 2006, if an absolute trust is used, the position will be as set out above. If this is not the case, any premiums in excess of the annual exemptions will be chargeable lifetime transfers.

15.29 Although a policy is written under trust, it will not automatically constitute a settlement for IHT purposes (and in most cases, in trusts with an absolute adult beneficiary it will not, as this will not satisfy the definition of a settlement for IHT purposes)[3]. This is important because if there is no settlement then the legal personal representatives are primarily accountable for the tax on the death of a beneficiary whereas, if there is a settlement, the trustees are primarily accountable to the extent of the property which they hold.

The wordings given here may be used for policies issued under the Married Women's Property Act 1882 (where the beneficiaries are those included in the Act), or for policies issued in trust outside the Act. The comments are, however, restricted to the positions in England and Wales. Special mention is then made in relation to the position in Scotland.

The IHT effect on the various trust wordings which follow may be better understood if the nature of the beneficiary's interest is first considered. The following comments are of general application to any fixed trust. The position would be different if the trust was a flexible power of appointment trust created pre-22 March 2006. Generally, an adult beneficiary with a vested or contingent

1 Within the terms of IHTA 1984, s 71; see Chapter 14, Sections 6B and 6D.
2 IHTA 1984, s 3A(3).
3 IHTA 1984, s 43.

interest in the policy trust will have an interest in possession. This is because section 31(1)(ii) of the Trustee Act 1925 operates, subject to any prior interests, to entitle a beneficiary to the intermediate income arising from his interest once he has attained the age of 18 — unless there is a contrary intention shown in the trust instrument (eg, where a direction is made for income to be accumulated or for it to be paid somewhere else, such as to a charity) or if section 31 is expressly excluded. The income from a minor's interest in a settlement must be accumulated during his minority in so far as it is not used for his maintenance, education or benefit.

Where the beneficiary under the trust is a minor, one of three situations may exist:

(1) The beneficiary may have an interest in possession. This will be the case where, for example, there is a deeming provision which gives the minor immediate entitlement to any income.

(2) The beneficiary may not have an interest in possession but the trust is one which is protected as an accumulation and maintenance settlement within section 71 of the IHTA 1984 (ie broadly a settlement in which no interest in possession subsists but where one or more persons will become entitled to an interest in possession on or before attaining age 25). Thus, the policy trust would be exempt from the lifetime, exit and principal (ten-yearly) tax charges normally applying to settlements without an interest in possession (see Chapter 14, Section 6C). (Note that the income tax consequences of creating an accumulation and maintenance settlement for parental settlors should be considered carefully. If capital or income is generated in excess of £100 it is all treated as the settlor's income[1]. Clearly this taxation consequence will not arise where a life policy is subject to an accumulation and maintenance trust as it is a non-income producing asset).

(3) The beneficiary may not have an interest in possession and the trust is *not* within the provisions of section 71 of the IHTA 1984 so that the policy trust is subject to the original chargeable transfer, the principal (ten-yearly) charge and the exit charges to IHT.

B Interests of children

15.30 The interests of children may be made contingent on attaining a specified age, or on surviving the grantee, or may be limited in such other manner as the settlor desires. Before drafting any trust of a policy which is to be for the benefit of children it is important to determine:

(1) Whether the children are to be named, so that any further children born will be excluded.

1 ITTOIA 2005, s 629.

(2) Whether, if not named, the class of children is to be limited to the children of the existing marriage or to the legitimate children of the life assured. (A provision for children without further description will include any illegitimate, legitimated or adopted children of the grantee and the children of any marriage.)

(3) Whether any child's interest is to continue for the benefit of his or her estate:

   (a) if he or she predeceases the grantee, or dies before the event upon which the sum assured becomes payable;

   (b) if he or she dies before attaining the specified age.

C Interests of spouse or registered civil partner

15.31 Where an own life policy is effected by a husband or wife for the benefit of the other *named* spouse, or by one civil partner for the benefit of the other, which is not conditional upon the named spouse/civil partner surviving the grantee, that spouse/civil partner takes an immediate vested interest in the trust of the policy, which on death before the grantee will pass to his or her personal representatives[1] and is unaffected by the grantee remarrying.

If there is no named spouse/civil partner and the trust wording refers to eg '*my wife*' or '*my wife immediately before my death*' and the wife dies before the husband (who does not remarry), the general view is that the policy moneys would form part of the estate of the husband for IHT purposes[2]. This is so, even if the wife's interest is unconditional upon surviving the husband. If the husband had remarried, and the second wife was alive at the death of the husband, she would be entitled to the policy moneys[3], unless there is an indication to the contrary in the trust instrument[4]. Similarly, if the trust is expressed to be for the benefit of eg '*my widow*', the second wife would be entitled to benefit[5].

Where the trust is declared to be for the benefit of a spouse and children, their interest is presumed to be a joint tenancy, unless there appears to be a contrary intention[6].

To avoid repetition in the following comments, no detailed reference is made to the intestacy or succession rules nor to the valuation of a beneficiary's interest in a policy, as both have been dealt with earlier. Similarly, the question of the exemptions available to free a transfer from an IHT charge has already been considered in Chapter 14, Section 4.

1 *Cousins v Sun Life Assurance Society* [1933] Ch 126, CA.
2 *Re Collier* [1930] 2 Ch 37.
3 *Re Browne's Policy, Browne v Browne* [1903] 1 Ch 188.
4 *Re Griffith's Policy* [1903] 1 Ch 739.
5 *Re Parker's Policies* [1906] 1 Ch 526.
6 *Re Seyton, Seyton v Satterthwaite* (1887) 34 Ch D 511; *Re Davies' Policy Trusts* [1892] 1 Ch 90; *Re Browne's Policy, Browne v Browne* [1903] 1 Ch 188.

SECTION 4 POLICY TRUST WORDINGS

15.32 Trust wordings can cater for virtually any scenario desired by the settlor. Some common provisions include:

(1) making the beneficial interest in the capital contingent upon attaining a specified age;

(2) making the beneficial interest contingent upon living at the time the policy moneys becomes payable; and

(3) a per stirpes clause.

Examples of appropriate trust wordings for the above are as follows:

(1) *Upon trust for [my son] A absolutely upon attaining the age of [21].*

(2) *Upon trust for [my son] A absolutely provided that if he should not be living at the occurrence of the event upon which the policy moneys become payable then for [my daughter] B absolutely.*

(3) *Upon trust for [the Beneficiaries] provided that if any of the Beneficiaries shall die before the occurrence of the event upon which the policy moneys become payable leaving children then such children living on the occurrence of the said event shall take by substitution and if more than one then in equal shares the share which their deceased parent would have taken had he or she been living on the occurrence of the said event.*

The trust wordings and their IHT impact are considered in more detail in the following scenarios where the policy is effected in trust for:

(1) named person absolutely;

(2) named persons in equal shares absolutely (their interests to pass to their estates if they predecease the settlor);

(3) such of the grantee's children as survive him or if none survive then for the last to die;

(4) A failing whom B (neither being the grantee);

(5) a person should he survive the grantee otherwise for the grantee;

(6) a person if living at the death of the grantee before maturity of an endowment policy, otherwise for the grantee;

(7) such of A, B, C, and D (none of whom are the grantee) as the grantee shall appoint and failing appointment for D absolutely;

(8) the survivor if any (of husband and wife on a joint lives first death policy), failing whom, the children.

The inheritance tax position of trusts will depend on whether they were effected on or after 22 March 2006 or before that date. If the trust is an absolute trust, in both cases the trust property should be outside the 'relevant property' regime as described in Chapter 14, Section 6C (subject to the comments below about minor beneficiaries). If the trust is a settlement which confers an interest in possession then if effected prior to 22 March it should be outside the relevant property regime but if effected on or after that date it would fall within that regime.

A Policy effected in trust for named person absolutely

15.33 Draft wording: *'Upon trust for [my son] A absolutely.'*

If A is over 18 then the policy trust does not constitute a settlement for IHT (as it does not satisfy the definition of a settlement)[1]. HMRC had previously contested this view if the beneficiary was a minor but they now agree that this does not make any difference. On the death of the grantee, no IHT charge arises unless the grantee was beneficially entitled to the policy at his death, eg if A had predeceased him and the policy had devolved upon the grantee under the will or upon the intestacy of A.

If A predeceased the life assured, there would be a transfer of value on A's death of the open market value[2] of his interest in the policy at that time, which would form part of his taxable estate on death. A's interest in the policy would pass in accordance with his will or the intestacy rules.

B Policy effected in trust for named persons in equal shares absolutely (their interests to pass to their estates if they predecease the settlor)

15.34 Draft wording: *'Upon trust for [my son] A and [my daughter] B in equal shares absolutely.'*

Similar principles as in **15.33** apply. In itself, this wording creates a tenancy in common which means that if A and/or B predecease(s) the life assured then his or her interest in the policy will pass in accordance with their will(s) or the intestacy provisions and, assuming it is an interest in possession trust, a transfer of value occurs of the deceased beneficiary's half-share in the value of the policy at that time.

This form of wording is used, for example, where the grantee wishes to benefit his existing children and there will be no further children (or separate provision is to be made for them). There could be a disadvantage with this wording in that, on the death of a minor beneficiary, his interest in the policy trust passes to the parents, not to the surviving beneficiary. Thus the wording is, perhaps, not wholly suitable for a policy to provide the children with funds to cover the IHT on other assets passing to them under the grantee's will for, in the event of a

1 IHTA 1984, s 43.
2 IHTA 1984, ss 160 and 167(2)(a).

minor beneficiary's death before the life assured, the parents must transfer to the surviving child (eg by assignment) the interest in the policy which passes to them on the minor beneficiary's death. On the other hand, this form of wording does mean that if a beneficiary who predeceased the life assured is married and has a family then they, and not the surviving beneficiary, could take his interest in the policy. However, this could be covered expressly by a per stirpes clause.

C Policy effected in trust for such of the grantee's children (unnamed) as survive him or if none survive then for the last to die

15.35 Draft wording: *'Upon trust for such of my children whenever born [of my marriage to X] as shall be living on the occurrence of the event upon which the policy moneys become payable and if more than one then equally between them Provided that if none of my said children shall be living on the occurrence of the said event then in trust for the last of them to die.'*

In view of the changes to the taxation of trusts created by the Finance Act 2006 the concept of the accumulation and maintenance trust for new trusts created on or after 22 March 2006 no longer exists. This wording and comments that follow are therefore included for historical interest only.

This form of trust wording constitutes a settlement for IHT. Furthermore, unless one or more of the children is aged 18 or over, it is a settlement in which, unless the trust instrument expressly provides for it by a deeming provision, there is no interest in possession. However, provided section 31 of the Trustee Act 1925 has not been excluded (either expressly, or by necessary implication) then, as each child attains the age of 18 he or she will become entitled to the income from his or her presumptive share in the settled fund and will, accordingly, then have an interest in possession in a corresponding share of the settlement[1]. Thus, the policy trust constitutes an 'accumulation and maintenance' settlement within section 71 of the IHTA 1984 because one or more of the beneficiaries will become entitled to an interest in possession on or before attaining a specified age (in this case 18) not exceeding 25[2]. It is therefore protected from the harsher IHT treatment for settlements in which there is no interest in possession.

There will be no IHT charge on the death of the grantee unless all the beneficiaries have predeceased him and he has acquired an interest through the will or intestacy of the last of them to die.

If an *adult* beneficiary predeceases the life assured then a transfer of value occurs because the beneficiary's interest in possession is terminated. IHT will be charged on the proportion of the value of the policy represented by the deceased beneficiary's presumptive share in the settled fund at the time of his death. As a consequence of his death, the presumptive shares of the remaining beneficiaries in the settled policy are increased. If a *minor* beneficiary predeceases the life assured then, as the beneficiary has no interest in possession, there will be no

1 *Re Jones Will Trusts, Soames v A-G* [1946] 2 All ER 281.
2 See Statutory Concession F8.

transfer of value on his death and no IHT will be chargeable. This will be so even if there is an adult beneficiary in existence whose presumptive share is increased as a result of the death of the minor. The death of the *last surviving* beneficiary will give rise to a transfer of value whether the beneficiary is an adult or a minor at the time.

On the birth of a child to the grantee each existing beneficiary will suffer a reduction in his or her presumptive share, and this will constitute a transfer of value by an adult beneficiary who has an interest in possession which is thereby reduced.

This form of wording (which should be used only if there is at least one child in existence or en ventre sa mere) is suitable where the grantee wishes to benefit by means of life assurance children, including those born after the commencement of the policy, who survive him. The wording is useful, therefore, for policies effected to provide funds for those children who benefit under the grantee's will, to cover the IHT liability.

D Policy effected in trust for A failing whom B (neither being the grantee)

15.36 Draft wording: *'Upon trust for [my son] A Provided that if he shall not be living on the occurrence of the event upon which the policy moneys become payable then in trust for [my daughter] B absolutely.'*

This form of trust wording also constitutes a settlement for IHT.The death of the grantee will not be a transfer of value unless he was beneficially entitled to the policy at the date of his death (see the discussion at **15.28**).

On the death of A, during the lifetime of the life assured, B will become entitled absolutely. The termination of his interest in possession will be a transfer of value and IHT will be chargeable on the open market value[1] of the policy at that time.

B's death before A and the life assured will not give rise to a transfer of value as B has only a reversionary interest, which is 'excluded property'[2]. B's death after A but before the life assured's gives rise to a transfer of the open market value of the policy at that time.

This form of wording is principally employed where the grantee wishes to benefit, for example, his children, but with a 'long stop' provision in favour of another (in order to prevent it reverting to himself).

E Policy effected in trust for a person should he survive the grantee otherwise for the grantee

15.37 Draft wording: *'Upon trust for [my son] A Provided that if A shall not be living on the occurrence of the event upon which the policy moneys become payable for me absolutely.'*

1 IHTA 1984, ss 160, 167(2)(a).
2 IHTA 1984, s 48.

As stated earlier, such a provision, where a gift is made into trust, and the settlor retains a reversionary interest under the trust does not constitute a gift with reservation of benefit[1].

F Endowment policy effected in trust for a person if living at the death of the grantee before maturity, otherwise for the grantee

15.38 Draft wording: *'Upon trust for [my son] A Provided that if I am living at the time the policy moneys become payable or if A shall not be living at my death before the time the policy moneys become payable then in trust for me absolutely.'*

The comments in relation to **15.37** apply equally hereto[2].

G Policy effected in trust for such of A, B, C and D (none of whom are the grantee) as the grantee shall appoint and failing appointment for D absolutely

15.39 Draft wording: *'Upon the following trusts:*

(i) *for such of A, B, C and D and in such shares (or wholly to one) as I may by deed or deeds revocable or irrevocable or by will or codicil appoint;*

(ii) *subject to and in default of any appointment and insofar as any appointment shall not extend or shall fail for any reason then in trust for D absolutely.'*

This is a 'flexible', power of appointment trust and constitutes a settlement for IHT purposes. For trusts effected on or after 22 March, see **15.38**. For trusts effected before that date, if D is an adult then, unless section 31 of the Trustee Act 1925 is excluded (expressly or impliedly), it is a settlement with an interest in possession because D has a vested defeasible interest and is entitled to the intermediate income arising from the settled property. On the other hand, if D is a minor then, unless there is a deeming provision, there is no interest in possession; moreover, the settlement would not be protected by section 71 of the IHTA 1984 as an accumulation and maintenance settlement, because it cannot be said that a beneficiary will become entitled to an interest in possession on or before attaining a specified age not exceeding 25 (eg an appointment may be made away from D before he was 18 in favour of someone already over 25). It is not sufficient that the power of appointment is not exercised, the terms of the trust must be restricted so they cannot be exercised to prevent at least one beneficiary becoming so entitled.

1 Inland Revenue letter, 18 May 1987.

2 See also Inland Revenue letter from the Life Insurance Council of the Association of British Insurers to members of the LIC after seeking clarification from the Inland Revenue, 21 November 1986.

In practice, most trusts providing for this arrangement contain an income direction, directing that D would be entitled to the intermediate income, thus making it an interest in possession trust. If not, unless D is an adult the policy trust would face the potentially harsher IHT treatment of trusts without interests in possession. (See further, Chapter 14, Section 6C.)

15.40 Assuming this to be the case, then on D's death, or an appointment away from him, there will be a transfer of the value of the policy at that time by D. On the death of A, B or C, before an appointment has been made in their favour, there will be no transfer of value, as they had no interest in possession in the settled policy. On the death of the grantee there will be no transfer of value unless at his death he was beneficially entitled to the policy (eg if it had devolved upon him under the will or intestacy of a beneficiary in whose favour an irrevocable appointment had been made).

The exercise of the power of appointment will give rise to a transfer of value every time an appointment is made to someone who immediately prior to the appointment had no interest in possession. (Thus, in this example, an irrevocable or revocable appointment in favour of A is a transfer of value, but an appointment in favour of D is not[1].)

If an appointment of the whole beneficial interest is made by the grantee in his will then a transfer of value based on the *policy proceeds* occurs, the rate of tax being determined by reference to the cumulative transfers of the person having the beneficial interest prior to the appointment. For this reason, careful consideration should be given before making an appointment by will.

Despite the problems of possible IHT charges on the exercise of the power of appointment, this form of policy trust prior to 22 March 2006 was often favoured by the grantee who wished to have some flexibility in his choice of ultimate beneficiary, without suffering the potentially higher tax charges of a discretionary trust.

H Joint lives first death policy (jointly owned by husband and wife) effected in trust for the survivor (if any), failing whom, the children

15.41 Draft wording: '*Upon trust for [the children] as shall be living 28 days after the occurrence of the event upon which the policy moneys become payable. Provided that if none of [the children] shall be living 28 days after the occurrence of the said event then for the last of them to die. Provided always if the survivor of us shall be alive on the said event then in trust for the survivor of us absolutely.*'

This type of wording is not thought in itself to constitute a gift with reservation of benefit for the same reasoning as expressed at **15.32**, namely that the retention of a reversionary interest under the trust is not, in itself, considered to constitute a gift with reservation of benefit.

1 IHTA 1984, s 53(2).

I The position from 22 March 2006

15.42 Power of appointment interest in possession trusts created before 22 March 2006 will continue to be outside the scope of the regime for 'relevant property' trusts (ie the ten-yearly and exit charges) assuming no appointments are made away from the persons who were default beneficiaries as at 22 March 2006. However, if trustees made appointments away to new beneficiaries before 6 October 2008, those new beneficiaries will be treated as though they were the beneficiaries in existence at 22 March 2006 and the existing IHT treatment will continue. If appointments are made on or after 6 October 2008 and the trust continues, if the appointment away is as a result of the death of the original beneficiary, the value of his or her interest in the trust property will form part of their estate as now, but the trust will then become a 'relevant property' trust. If the appointment was made whilst the original beneficiary was still alive, this would constitute a chargeable lifetime transfer by him or her. Again, the trust would then become a 'relevant property' trust.

Accumulation and maintenance trusts created before 22 March 2006 will continue to be outside the scope of the regime for 'relevant property' trusts only until 6 April 2008 at which point they will become 'relevant property' settlements and the first principal charge will be at the next ten-yearly anniversary from the creation of the settlement (although this will be proportioned as the trust had not contained 'relevant property' for the whole of the ten-year period). The only way of avoiding this is either if the trust provides for the beneficiaries to become absolutely entitled to the trust property at the age of 18 or if the trust could be amended before 6 April 2008 to provide for this to happen.

All trusts created on or after 22 March 2006 which would, in the old regime, have been power of appointment interest in possession trusts or accumulation and maintenance trusts are now treated for inheritance tax purposes as though they were 'relevant property' (ie discretionary) trusts. Thus, gifts into such trusts to the extent that they are in excess of the available exemptions will be chargeable lifetime transfers and the trustees may be liable for the ten-yearly and exit charges in addition, depending on the value of the trust property.

J Scottish trust policies

15.43 The rules relating to property rights in Scotland are different from those under English law, as too are the principles of vesting (ie those rules which govern the moment at which the interest in trust property can be said to be acquired). Section 31 of the Trustee Act 1925 does not apply in Scotland, nor is there an equivalent provision in any Scottish statute. Moreover, in the absence of an express direction to the contrary, the general presumption under Scottish law is that any intermediate income arising will not be paid to a beneficiary under a settlement (unless he has an absolute interest), but will be accumulated and form part of the capital.

As a consequence of these differences in trust law, many policy trust wordings which could have been used safely under English law to create settlements with an interest in possession, or accumulation and maintenance settlements within section 71 of the IHTA 1984 would be treated in Scotland as creating settlements without interests in possession and not protected by the section. Such policy trusts would, as a result, be subject to initial, principal (ten-yearly) and exit charges.

It was important, therefore, prior to 22 March 2006, to take care when drafting policy trust wordings for policy trusts subject to Scottish law, so that interests in possession were created at the outset or, alternatively, in the case of trusts for minors, that they were brought within the protection of section 71 as accumulation and maintenance settlements. This was, perhaps, best done by express directions that beneficiaries who were to have interests in possession were given the right to the income arising from the settled property. There should have been clear statements as to when the right to income was to commence, the duration of that right, and what was to happen to the income on the death of a beneficiary under a settlement in which there were successive interests (eg A failing whom B). If an accumulation and maintenance settlement was to be created, then there should have been explicit directions as to when interests were to vest and as to entitlements to income arising thereafter, with clear provisions, for the use or accumulation, of income arising beforehand.

In that way, with care in drafting the appropriate amendments and additions, the policy trust wordings used in England could also have been employed in establishing policy trusts under Scottish law, resulting in similar IHT treatment.

As a result of the changes to the IHT treatment of trusts contained in the Finance Act 2006 and effective from 22 March 2006, the comments contained above are now of only historic interest due to the fact that from that date, all new trusts (except absolute or bare trusts or trusts for the benefit of disabled persons) will effectively be treated as though they were discretionary trusts.

CHAPTER 16

The tax framework for registered pension schemes

SUMMARY

SECTION 1 INTRODUCTION

16.1 Registered Pension Schemes involving insurance policies can take various forms and can provide various benefits. This Chapter looks at the tax framework which governs the tax reliefs available to these schemes. The entire tax framework of private pension provision was radically changed with effect from 6 April 2006 (commonly referred to as A-Day). The previous jumble of different tax regimes and rules was replaced with a single universal set of rules.

Within the context of this publication, the authors have sought to give only a general view of the pensions tax rules from 6 April 2006. Full details can be found in HMRC's 'Registered Pension Schemes Manual'. This manual is available on the internet, and can be found at: www.hmrc.gov.uk/manuals/rpsmmanual/index.htm

A The legislative framework for pensions tax legislation

16.2 It has been government policy for many years to provide tax privileges to pension schemes. The aim is to encourage saving (by individuals and/or their employers) for the purpose of providing an income in old age, to reduce dependency on the state. HMRC has the task of controlling those tax privileges. This control is implemented by a framework of prescribed requirements that pension schemes must adhere to if their tax privileged status is to be maintained. Prior to 6 April 2006, these requirements were imposed in two ways – directly through detailed legislation, and indirectly through decisions taken by HMRC under their discretionary powers which were provided by legislation.

Many different types of pension schemes developed over the years, either as a result of legislation to reflect government policy or because of fresh ideas within the pensions industry. Each development resulted in a different raft of HMRC requirements to fit the circumstances. This layering approach resulted in a profusion of different rules for different types of pension arrangements.

Prior to 6 April 2006, the legislation governing tax-approved pension arrangements was contained in Part XIV of the Income and Corporation Taxes Act 1988. Because of the way the legislation had been developed and modified over many years (starting with the Finance Act 1970), a total of eight different tax regimes had emerged. Each regime had its own complex rules limiting the amount an individual could contribute to a pension scheme and the benefits a scheme could pay out.

Following a lengthy period of consultation and development, which started in 2002, the government swept away all the existing pensions tax legislation and introduced a single set of rules. The new rules are contained principally in Part 4 of the Finance Act 2004, and came into effect from 6 April 2006. Subsequent Finance Acts have modified various aspects of the original legislation.

Because the pensions tax legislation lays down a single set of rules, it does not need to distinguish between the different types of pension arrangements. The legislation uses the general term 'registered pension scheme'. This means a pension scheme that has been registered with HMRC as being a scheme that meets all the requirements of Part 4 of the Finance Act 2004. But it must be borne in mind that simply because every pension arrangement is called a 'registered pension scheme' for the purposes of the tax legislation, there are still many different types of 'registered pension schemes', each with their own characteristics. It does not matter whether the arrangement is a multi-member scheme (such as an occupational pension scheme) or a single contract (such as a retirement annuity), each will be classified as a 'registered pension scheme'.

B The structure of pension arrangements

16.3 Pension arrangements that are categorised as 'registered pension schemes', and involve insurance contracts, can take various forms:

(1) Retirement annuities

- This type of arrangement takes the form of a contract between the insurer and the individual – ie the policy is written in the name of the individual, and the individual has both beneficial and legal ownership. All the terms governing the operation of arrangement are laid down in the policy.

(2) Provider-sponsored personal pension schemes (including stakeholder pension schemes)

- This type of arrangement normally takes the form of a contract between the insurer and the individual – ie the policy is written in the name of the individual, and the individual has both beneficial and legal ownership. Unlike retirement annuities, the contract is held within a 'scheme' structure. The terms governing the operation of the arrangement are contained in the scheme rules, as well as the policy. The scheme itself would have been established by the insurer executing a deed poll, which adopts the rules and appoints the scheme administrator (usually the insurer itself).

- It is possible for the insurer to establish the scheme under trust, but this creates a more complex structure and is a method rarely used for fully insured arrangements. Trust-based schemes will be encountered where the scheme is operated as a self-invested personal pension scheme.

(3) Employer-sponsored occupational pension schemes

- This type of arrangement is established by the employer executing the trust instrument which adopts the rules and appoints the trustees. The terms governing the operation of the arrangement are set out in the scheme rules. The contract will be between the insurer and the trustees, and the policies will be written in the name of the trustees.

- Occupational pension schemes can take many forms:

  (i) defined benefit schemes;

  (ii) group money purchase schemes (fully insured or self-administered);

  (iii) insured money purchase schemes tailored for individuals (executive pension plans);

  (iv) small self-administered schemes (SSASs).

(4) Provider-sponsored free-standing additional voluntary contribution schemes

- This type of arrangement effectively became defunct with effect from 6 April 2006, and transformed into personal pension schemes. The arrangement was established by the provider executing the trust instrument which adopted the rules and appointed the trustees. The terms governing the operation of the arrangement are set out in the scheme rules. The contract is between the insurer and the trustees, and the policies are written in the name of the trustees.

(5) 'Left scheme' policies – to secure benefits outside the terms of occupational pension schemes

- Such policies are effected by the scheme trustees in the name of the individual, for the purpose of providing deferred benefits for an individual who has left service (a 'section 32' buy-out policy), or where the scheme has wound-up (a 'trustees' buy-out policy), or for providing a pension in the form of an annuity (a 'compulsory purchase annuity' policy), or for providing a pension in the form of income withdrawals (an 'income withdrawal' policy).
- Similar 'left scheme' policies can also arise from policies originally effected in the name of the trustees being assigned to the individual on leaving service or on the scheme winding up. The benefits cease to be covered by the rules of the scheme, and all the terms governing the operation of the arrangement are laid down in the policy. The individual has both beneficial and legal ownership.

C Summary of the pensions tax framework

16.4 The following table provides a summary of the way the tax privileges were controlled for the different types of pension arrangements before 6 April 2006.

The pensions tax framework before 6 April 2006	
Type of pension arrangement	Method of controlling the tax privileges
Employer-sponsored Occupational Pension Schemes (OPS) in their various forms, ie: • Defined Benefit OPS • Money Purchase OPS on a group 'defined contribution' basis • Money Purchase OPS on an individual 'mutually determined' basis (eg Executive Pension Plans and Small Self-Administered Scheme)	These schemes had to be approved by HMRC under the provisions of Chapter I of Part XIV of ICTA 1988. Chapter I laid down some basic rules, but mainly it gave HMRC discretionary powers, and hence flexibility, to specify the details. The level of tax relief was controlled by: Limiting the maximum benefits that could be provided, by reference to earnings at the time of retirement and length of service. The criteria for those limits had been varied over the years – ie the pre-87, 87–89 and post-89 regimes. Limiting the way the maximum benefits could be funded in advance.

The pensions tax framework before 6 April 2006	
Type of pension arrangement	Method of controlling the tax privileges
'Left scheme' policies in their various forms, ie: • section 32 buy-out policies • assigned policies • trustees buy-out policies • (secured on an OPS winding-up)	These policies derived from Chapter I schemes and were regulated by the same rules.
Provider-sponsored Free-Standing AVC Schemes	These schemes had to be approved by HMRC under the provisions of Chapter I.
Provider-sponsored Personal Pension Schemes (PPS) in their various forms, ie: • Fully insured PP Scheme • Self-Invested PP Schemes	These schemes had to be approved by HMRC under the provisions of Chapter IV of Part XIV of ICTA 1988. Chapter IV defined everything in detail (and left little to HMRC's discretion). The level of tax relief was controlled by: Limiting the maximum contribution that could be paid each tax year.
Provider-sponsored Stakeholder Pension Schemes (SHPS)	These schemes are just a special form of Personal Pension Schemes and were subject to the same HMRC requirements.
Retirement Annuity policies	These policies were approved by HMRC under the provisions of Chapter III of Part XIV of ICTA 1988. Chapter III defined everything in detail (and left little to HMRC's discretion). The level of tax relief was controlled by: Limiting the maximum contribution that could be paid each tax year. (The limits were different to those for PP Schemes.)

16.5 The following table provides a summary of the way things have changed from 6 April 2006.

The pensions tax framework from 6 April 2006	
Type of pension arrangement	Regulatory controls
Employer-sponsored OPSs in their various forms 'Left scheme' policies in their various forms Provider-sponsored Free-Standing AVC Schemes (effectively became PPSs with effect from 6 April 2006) Provider-sponsored PPSs in their various forms Provider-sponsored SHPSs Retirement Annuity policies	The benefits under all these types of pension arrangements are covered by a single set of tax rules. The tax privileges are controlled by: Monitoring the amount of input each tax year into pension arrangements for the individual against a maximum value which is defined in legislation – the 'annual allowance'. The input for an individual will be made up of all contributions to money purchase arrangements, and/or the increase in the capital value of benefits accruing under any Defined Benefit OPS. Monitoring the total capital value of an individual's pension benefits from all arrangements against a maximum value which is defined in legislation – the 'standard lifetime allowance'. If the total capital value exceeds the standard lifetime allowance, a special tax charge (the 'lifetime allowance charge') will be levied on the excess. The initial standard lifetime allowance set for the tax year 2006/07 was £1,5m. Transitional arrangements were introduced for individuals where the capital value of their benefits accrued before A-Day already exceeded, or were likely to exceed, that initial maximum value.

SECTION 2 CONTRIBUTIONS AND TAX RELIEF

16.6 There is no limit on the amount of contributions that can be paid to a registered pension scheme. But there is a limit on the amount that will be eligible for tax relief. (In addition, if the annual allowance limit is breached a tax charge will arise on the member – see **16.7**.)

Tax relief on member contributions is limited to 100% of the earnings in the particular tax year (subject to the annual allowance). For a member with low earnings, or no earnings, a contribution can be made up to £3,600 and be eligible for tax relief.

Tax relief on member contributions will normally be given on the 'relief at source' basis – ie each contribution will be treated as though it was paid net of basic rate tax. The scheme administrator will then claim the tax direct from HMRC to apply to the pension arrangement. The member will claim any higher rate relief direct from HMRC through the tax return.

For occupational pension schemes only, it is possible to operate the 'net pay' method. Here member contributions are deducted from salary before tax is applied, and the gross contribution paid to the scheme. This gives immediate tax relief at the highest rate.

Contributions by a member's employer are always gross.

The question of whether an employer's contribution will be allowable as a deduction from the taxable profits of the business will depend on whether the contributions can be considered as being paid 'wholly and exclusively for the purposes of the trade' as described in section 74(1)(a) of the Income and Corporation Taxes Act 1988. This will be a matter for the Tax Office dealing with the employer's affairs to decide. Where contributions are allowed as a deduction, companies will obtain corporation tax relief and partnerships/sole-traders will obtain income tax relief.

Allowance as a deduction will not normally be a problem where the contribution is for an ordinary employee. But a contribution may not be allowed where it is for a controlling director, or for a person connected with a controlling director (such as the director's spouse or registered civil partner). HMRC has indicated that a contribution will not be allowed if there is a non-trade purpose. An example given is where the level of the remuneration package, including the pension scheme contribution, is excessive for the value of the work undertaken by that individual for the employer.

Where the remuneration package paid in respect of a director, who is also a controlling shareholder, or in respect of an employee who is a close relative or friend of the business proprietor or controlling director, is comparable with that paid to unconnected employees, employer contributions will normally be accepted as being paid wholly and exclusively for the purposes of the trade. When there are no employees whose duties are generally comparable with the proprietor or relative, an assessment will be made by the Tax Office of whether the amount is a genuine payment for services rendered in the business. Evidence that the amount may not be a genuine business expense may be that it exceeds a reasonable rate of remuneration on a commercial basis.

SECTION 3 THE ANNUAL ALLOWANCE

16.7 The annual allowance imposes an upper limit on the amount of tax privilege that is available during a tax year.

Where the total contributions paid in a tax year to a money purchase arrangement, plus the increase in the value of any benefits under a defined benefits arrangement, exceeds the annual allowance, a tax charge will arise. This tax charge is known as the 'annual allowance charge', and is payable by the individual. The rate is 40% of the excess over the annual allowance.

Monitoring against the annual allowance, and the imposition of any charge, is dealt with through the self-assessment tax return.

The annual allowance has been set at the following levels:

Tax Year	Annual Allowance
2006/07	£215,000
2007/08	£225,000
2008/09	£235,000
2009/10	£245,000*
2010/11	£255,000*
2011/12	£50,000 (plus the ability to carry forward up to £50,000 of unused relief from each of the previous three tax years where the value of tax-relieved pension savings in each of those years was less than £50,000)
2012/13	As for 2011/12 (assumed)
2013/14	As for 2011/12 (assumed)

* In the budget on 22 April 2009, the government announced its intention to limit the tax relief for individuals with taxable income of £150,000 or over. The change was scheduled to come into force for 2011/12 onwards. As an interim measure, anti-forestalling measures were introduced for the tax years 2009/10 and 2010/11. Under these measures, a tax charge (called the 'special annual allowance' tax charge) was applied where:

(1) an individual had taxable income of £150,000 or over (changed to £130,000 or over from 9 December 2009) in any of the tax years 2007/08, 2008/09 & 2009/10;

(2) contributions were paid in excess of the higher of:

- £20,000;
- the average of single contributions paid 2006/07, 2007/08 & 2008/09, up to a ceiling of £30,000;
- (the normal regular pension savings being paid prior to 22 April.

The 'special annual allowance' tax charge was:

(1) for 2009/10, 20% of the excess;

(2) for 2010/11, 20% of the excess which relates to the 40% tax band, 30% of the excess which relates to the 50% tax band.

The proposed changes for the 2011/12 tax year had been heavily criticised by the pensions industry as being very difficult to operate. Following the change of government in 2010, the original proposals were scrapped and replaced with a reduction in the annual allowance from 2011/12 as shown above.

The following is an example of how the normal annual allowance works.

(1) An individual has earnings of £120,000 in the tax year 2010/11. He has no other taxable income, so is not caught by the anti-forestalling measures. He makes contributions to a money purchase arrangement of £100,000. In addition, the employer also makes contributions of £200,000.

(2) The individual will receive tax relief on the £100,000 contributions.

(3) However, the individual will have to report on the self-assessment tax return that the total input for the 2010/11 tax year has been £300,000. This will lead to a tax charge of 40% × (300,000 – 255,000) = £18,000.

(4) Note that it makes no difference whether or not the employer's contribution has been allowed as a deduction under the 'wholly and exclusively' rule.

SECTION 4 THE LIFETIME ALLOWANCE

16.8 There is no limit on the amount of the benefits that may be provided for an individual under registered pension schemes. But if the value of the benefits being paid under a particular scheme, when accumulated with benefits previously paid under that scheme or any other scheme, exceeds a ceiling called the 'lifetime allowance', a tax charge will arise. This tax charge is known as the 'lifetime allowance charge'.

This charge is 25% of the excess where the excess benefits are taken in pension form, and 55% where the excess benefits are taken as cash.

The standard lifetime allowance has been set at the following levels:

Tax Year	Standard Lifetime Allowance
2006/07	£1.5m
2007/08	£1.6m
2008/09	£1.65m
2009/10 2010/11	£1.75 £1.8m
2011/12	£1.8m
2012/13	£1.5m
2013/14	£1.5m (assumed)

The freezing of the lifetime allowance in 2011/12, and the reduction starting in 2012/13, stems from the government's view that the level of the tax advantages under registered pension schemes, that could be attained by the most wealthy individuals, was too generous and needed to be cut back. This was linked to the reduction in the changes in the annual allowance starting in 2010/11.

The legislation specifies the various occasions when an individual will use up part of their lifetime allowance. These occasions are referred to as 'benefit crystallisation events' (BCEs). A BCE arises when benefits under a registered pension scheme become payable, such as when a pension commences or on death.

The way benefits are valued for the purpose of monitoring against the lifetime allowance is as follows:

(1) Under a money purchase scheme, the accumulated fund value is used.

(2) Under a defined benefit scheme, the value is determined as 20 times the pension. If part of the pension is commuted for a lump sum, the value is the lump sum plus 20 times the balance pension.

16.9 The following is an example of how the lifetime allowance works.

An individual takes benefits under a defined benefits occupational pension scheme in the tax year 2007/08. The benefits comprise a tax-free lump sum of £300,000 and a pension of £45,000. This benefits package has the following value for monitoring against the lifetime allowance: £300,000 + 20 × 45,000 = £1,200,000.

Hence at this stage the lifetime allowance has not been exceeded. The individual is treated as using up 75% of the lifetime allowance – ie (1,200,000 ÷ 1,600,000) × 100.

In the tax year 2010/11 the individual takes benefits under a personal pension scheme. The fund stands at £500,000. The individual has already used up 75% of the lifetime allowance, so the available portion of the lifetime allowance in 2010/11 is 25% × £1,800,000 = £450,000. Hence there is an excess of £500,000 – £450,000 = £50,000. The individual takes the benefits in the following form:

- A tax-free lump sum of 25% × £450,000 = £112,500.
- A pension secured by the balance of £450,000 – £112,500 = £337,500.
- A lump sum from the excess. There will be a lifetime allowance charge of 55% × £50,000 = £27,500. The scheme administrator will withhold this tax and account for it to HMRC. The individual will receive the balance of £22,500.

16.10 The introduction of the lifetime allowance charge could have had a retrospective effect by catching large pension benefits that had already accrued before 6 April 2006. The government accepted that it would be unfair to penalise individuals who had accrued large benefits quite legitimately in accordance with the rules that existed before 6 April 2006. So, special provisions were introduced to enable those individuals to protect the value of their pre-6 April 2006 benefits against the lifetime allowance charge that could otherwise arise. (But it should be noted that the government had still effectively placed a cap on the benefits that might have been expected under the old rules as accrual had effectively been frozen at 5 April 2006.)

There are two types of protection – 'primary protection' and 'enhanced protection'. To take advantage of this facility, individuals had to register for protection with HMRC before 6 April 2009. It was possible to register for either type of protection or for both.

The way primary protection works is that the total value of the individual's pension benefits is determined as at 5 April 2006. That is compared to the value of the maximum benefits that would have been approvable by HMRC under the pre-6 April 2006 rules. The lower of the two values is then compared to the standard lifetime allowance. If it is higher than the standard lifetime allowance, the individual can register for primary protection. The higher value will then form the individual's 'personal lifetime allowance' going forward. The 'personal lifetime allowance' will increase each tax year in line with the rate of increase in the standard lifetime allowance. The individual can accrue further benefits from 6 April 2006, but any excess over the personal lifetime allowance will be subject to the lifetime allowance charge. The reduction in the standard lifetime allowance from 2012/13, will not result in a reduction for primary protection purposes – the increase factor for the 'personal lifetime allowance' will be frozen at $^{1.8}/_{1.5} = 1.2$.

Enhanced protection works in a different way. The total value of the individual's benefits has to be determined as at 5 April 2006. If that exceeds the value of the maximum benefits that would have been approvable by HMRC under the pre-6 April 2006 rules, the individual has to give up the rights to the excess. The individual will not then incur any lifetime allowance charge in the future, no matter how much the fund grows. But, there must be no benefit accrual from 6 April 2006. Any sort of accrual will result in the loss of enhanced protection.

16.11 As a result of the reduction in the standard lifetime allowance from £1.8m to £1.5m from 2012/13, a further type of protection has had to be devised to cater for those individuals who were expecting their pension savings to be in excess of £1.5m when they come to take their benefits on or after 6 April 2012. This has been called 'fixed protection'. Fixed protection would mean that an individual would not incur a lifetime allowance charge where the value of their benefits goes above £1.5m, up to a ceiling of £1.8m.

A condition of fixed protection is that the individual would need to stop building up benefits under registered pensions schemes by 5 April 2012. Benefit accrual after that date would result in fixed protection being lost.

SECTION 5 RETIREMENT BENEFITS

16.12 The legislation allows registered pension schemes to provide retirement benefits in various forms. It should be noted, however, that the forms of benefits available under a particular registered pension scheme will depend on what is allowed by the rules governing the scheme. This Section just provides a general description of the possibilities.

It should also be noted that the rules that have been in place since 6 April 2006 around 'unsecured pension' and 'alternatively secured pension', and taking retirement benefits by age 75, have been altered significantly with effect from 6 April 2011. In particular:

(1) the requirement to take retirement benefits by age 75 has been withdrawn;

(2) the rules around taking income on the 'unsecured pension' basis (where the individual is aged less than 75, or less than 77 for those individuals who had not reached age 75 on 22 June 2010), and on the 'alternatively secured pension' basis (where the individual is aged 75 or over), have been replaced by a single set of rules called 'drawdown pension' (all members and dependants who were taking income on the 'unsecured pension' or 'alternatively secured pension' basis were automatically moved to the 'drawdown' pension' basis with effect from 6 April 2011, although there are some transitional rules around income limits);

(3) more flexibility has been built into the rules for 'drawdown pension', which has two variants:

- 'capped' drawdown, where the maximum income is determined on a similar basis to 'unsecured pension';
- 'flexible' drawdown, where any amount can be taken as income (including the whole fund in one go if required) providing the individual can satisfy the 'minimum income requirement' (ie. the individual has total guaranteed income for life of at least £20,000 pa – which can be made up of, for example, a pension from the state, a pension from a defined benefits scheme, a pension from a lifetime annuity).

(4) the tax charge on a lump sum paid on the individual's death on or after 6 April 2011, after taking retirement benefits, has been increased from 35% to 55% (but if there are no dependants the lump sum can be paid to a charity with no tax charge);

(5) where an individual aged 75 or over dies, having deferred drawing the retirement benefits, any lump sum paid is subject to a tax charge of 55% (but if there are no dependants the lump sum can be paid to a charity with no tax charge);

(6) a number of changes have been made to the way the Inheritance Tax legislation impacts on benefits (see Chapter 16, Section 9).

A The concept of 'retirement'

16.13 The term 'retirement benefits' is still commonly used. But the concept of 'retirement' in the sense of being in full-time employment one day then ceasing all employment the next is becoming increasingly blurred. It is being gradually replaced by the concept of 'phased retirement', which allows a gradual transition from full-time employment, into part-time employment, and then eventually full retirement. Indeed, the legislation has been deliberately constructed to ensure that the rules on benefit provision from tax-approved pension arrangements can support phased retirement.

The rules of any registered pension scheme (occupational as well as personal) can allow some or all of the benefits to come into payment at any time from the 55th birthday. Benefits can be drawn before the 55th birthday in the event of incapacity or ill-health.

Prior to 6 April 2010, the benefits could be taken at any time from age 50, but had to be taken by the 75th birthday. The minimum age of 50 was increased to 55 with effect from 6 April 2010. The requirement to take benefits by the 75th birthday was removed with effect from 6 April 2011.

The legislation that applied before 6 April 2006 prevented benefits under an employer's occupational pension scheme from coming into payment before the individual had actually left the employment. The removal of this restriction has enabled a more flexible approach to be taken to the provision of retirement benefits. The opportunity is there for those employers who can see advantages in retaining access to the expertise of their experienced staff, whilst at the same time allowing them to move gradually into retirement.

The concept of 'phased retirement' is generally operated under occupational pension schemes by allowing an employee to take the whole of their retirement benefits on reaching a certain age and then continuing in employment on a part-time basis. Phased retirement in the form of the phased provision of benefits as working hours reduce in stages over a period of time is not so common under occupational pension schemes as it could increase the costs of the administration of the scheme. That form of 'phased retirement' is widely available under personal pension schemes, where it is most likely to appeal to self-employed individuals who wish to gradually reduce their workload.

B Tax-free lump sum

16.14 The rules of a registered pension scheme can allow the members to take part of their benefits in the form of a tax-free lump sum. The lump sum must not exceed 25% of the value of the benefit package coming into payment at that time (except where the member has a protected lump sum entitlement deriving from benefits accrued before 6 April 2006). This lump sum is referred to as a 'pension commencement lump sum'. It can be paid in the period starting 6 months before the date on which the entitlement to the pension arises and ending 12 months after that date.

In the case of benefits under a money purchase arrangement, the maximum pension commencement lump sum is simply 25% of the fund available to secure benefits.

In the case of a defined benefit arrangement, the maximum pension commencement lump sum is more difficult to determine. The maximum lump sum is 25% of the value of the benefit package. The value of the benefit package is made up of the lump sum plus 20 times the reduced pension that is left after commuting part of the full pension for the lump sum. A formula has to be applied which works out how much of the full pension has to be commuted to produce the requisite lump sum, using the scheme's own commutation factors.

C Pension income

16.15 The pension income can be provided in various ways, depending on the type of pension arrangement:

(1) on the 'secured pension' basis by the purchase of an annuity, which may include a guaranteed period of up to ten years and/or a reversionary annuity payable to a dependant;

(2) on the 'secured pension' basis by means of a 'scheme pension', which may include a guaranteed period of up to ten years and/or a reversionary pension payable to a dependant; or

(3) on the 'drawdown pension' basis.

All pensions from registered pension schemes are taxed under the PAYE system.

SECTION 6 DEATH BENEFITS

16.16 The legislation allows registered pension schemes to provide death benefits in various forms. It should be noted, however, that the forms of benefits available under a particular registered pension scheme will depend on what is allowed by the rules governing the scheme. This Section just provides a general description of the possibilities.

Benefits can be provided for a 'dependant'. This term is defined in the legislation and covers:

(1) the member's wife, husband, civil partner, or any other individual who is financially dependent on the member;

(2) a child of the member who has not reached the age of 23 (please note any income withdrawals would cease on the child's 23rd birthday);

(3) a child of the member who has reached age 23 and is dependent on the member because of physical or mental impairment; or

(4) any other individual who is dependent on the member because of physical or mental impairment.

A On a member's death before drawing retirement benefits

16.17 Benefits can be provided in the following forms:

(1) a lump sum, which could derive from the retirement fund and/or a separately defined lump sum death benefit (a tax charge of 55% will apply if death occurs after reaching age 75, unless the lump sum is to be paid to a charity);

(2) a pension to a dependant – which can be provided in various ways:

- on the 'secured pension' basis by the purchase of an annuity;
- on the 'secured pension' basis by the provision of a 'scheme pension'; or
- on the 'drawdown pension' basis.

Where the member dies before age 75, there is no tax charge on the lump sum (unless the lump sum results in the lifetime allowance being exceeded).

If the member dies after attaining age 75, the lump sum is subject to a tax charge of 55%. In addition, in some cases the lump sum could be treated as forming part of the estate for inheritance tax purposes (see Chapter 14, Section 9). If there are no dependants, the lump sum can be paid to a charity, in which case there would be no 55% tax charge, nor IHT charge.

All pensions from registered pension schemes are taxed under the PAYE system.

B On a member's death whilst drawing a pension

16.18 Benefits can be provided in the following forms:

(1) where the member's pension was being paid on the 'secured pension' basis (ie by means of an annuity or on the 'scheme pension' basis):

- continuation of pension payments for any remaining guaranteed period; and/or
- payment of a lump sum associated with the pension (under 'annuity protection' or 'pension protection'); and/or
- commencement of any associated pension to a dependant.

(2) where the member's pension was being paid on the 'drawdown pension' basis, the remaining fund would be disposed of by:

- payment of a lump sum; or
- provision of a pension for a dependant on the 'secured pension' basis by the purchase of an annuity, or on the 'drawdown pension' basis.

Any lump sum is subject to a tax charge of 55%. In addition, in some cases the lump sum could be treated as forming part of the estate for inheritance tax purposes (see Chapter 14, Section 9). If there are no dependants, the lump sum can be paid to a charity, in which case there would be no 55% tax charge, nor IHT charge.

All pensions from registered pension schemes are taxed under the PAYE system.

C On a dependant's death whilst drawing a pension

16.19 There are various scenarios, as follows:

(1) Where the dependant's pension was being paid on the 'secured pension' basis (ie by means of an annuity or on the 'scheme pension' basis), no further benefit would arise.

(2) Where the dependant's pension was being paid on the 'drawdown pension' basis, having been derived from the member's 'drawdown pension' fund (or the member's 'unsecured pension' fund where the member's death occurred before 6 April 2011), the remaining fund will be paid as a lump sum. The lump sum will be subject to a 55% tax charge. In addition, in some cases the lump sum could be treated as forming part of the dependant's estate for inheritance tax purposes (see Chapter 14, Section 9). If there are no other dependants of the member, the lump sum could be paid to a charity, in which case there would be no 55% tax charge, nor IHT charge.

(3) Where the dependant's pension was being paid on the 'drawdown pension' basis, having been derived from the member's 'alternatively secured pension' fund (where the member's death occurred before 6 April 2011), the remaining fund will be paid as a lump sum. As for (b), there will be a 55% tax charge, and possibility of the lump sum being treated as forming part of the dependant's estate for inheritance tax purposes (see Chapter 14, Section 9). But there may also be an IHT charge triggered in respect of the member's estate as explained in Section 9A5. If there are no other dependants of the member, the lump sum could be paid to a charity, with no 55% tax charge, nor IHT charge.

D On a member's or dependant's death before 6 April 2011 where benefits are not finalised until after that date

16.20 Where a member or dependant dies before 6 April 2011, but the benefits arising as a result of the death could not be finalised until after that date, some aspects of the pre-6 April 2011 rules will continue to apply. For example:

(1) Where the member's pension or dependant's pension was being paid on the 'unsecured pension' basis, any lump sum will be subject to a tax charge of 35% (rather than 55%).

(2) Where the member's pension was being paid on the 'alternatively secured pension' basis, the remaining fund would be disposed of as follows:

- If there is a dependant, the fund must be used to provide a pension for that dependant. The pension could be provided on the 'secured pension' basis by the purchase of an annuity, or on the 'drawdown pension' basis.

- If there is no surviving dependant, the fund can be paid as a lump sum to a charity, or transferred to another arrangement within the scheme for the benefit of another individual. (This would normally be in accordance with directions given by the member to the scheme administrator.)

(3) Where the dependant's pension was being paid on the 'alternatively secured pension' basis, the remaining fund would be disposed of as follows:

- If, exceptionally, there is another surviving dependant of the member, the fund must be used to provide a pension for that dependant. The pension could be provided on the 'secured pension' basis by the purchase of an annuity, or on the 'drawdown pension' basis.
- If there is no other surviving dependant, the fund can be paid as a lump sum to a charity, or transferred to another arrangement within the scheme for the benefit of another individual. (This would normally be in accordance with directions given by the member, or the dependant, to the scheme administrator.)

SECTION 7 UNAUTHORISED PAYMENTS

16.21 If a scheme makes a payment to a member that is not authorised by the legislation, various tax charges will arise. Examples of unauthorised payments would be:

(1) a lump sum is paid to the member on retirement which is in excess of the permitted maximum;

(2) a lump sum is paid to the member on retirement more than 12 months after the date on which the entitlement to the pension arises;

(3) the member receives retirement benefits before the minimum permissible age;

(4) the scheme sells an asset to the member for less than it is worth.

Whenever an unauthorised member payment is made, the following tax charges will arise:

(1) an unauthorised payments charge of 40% of the unauthorised payment;

(2) if the unauthorised payment is 25% or more of the total value of the rights under the arrangement, an unauthorised payments surcharge of 15% of the unauthorised payment.

The member is liable for these tax charges and accounts for them through the self-assessment tax return. They are free-standing tax charges which means that any losses a taxpayer may have cannot be set against the charges.

In addition, the scheme could be liable to a scheme sanction charge of 15% of the unauthorised payment (or higher if the member has not paid the other charges). The scheme can withhold this charge from the payment made to the member.

Overall, there is potential for a tax charge of 70%.

SECTION 8 RECYCLING TAX-FREE LUMP SUMS

16.22 The process of recycling involves drawing the benefits from an existing pension fund, then using the tax-free lump sum (pension commencement lump sum) as a direct or indirect means of paying additional contributions to a registered pension scheme on which tax relief will be generated. Higher rate relief could be used to pay further contributions. Benefits would then be drawn from the further pension fund created, and the tax-free lump sum used to repeat the cycle. So, effectively, the same money is going round in a circle, and picking up extra tax relief on the way.

Not surprisingly, the government considers the recycling concept to be an abuse of the tax reliefs made available to encourage saving for retirement.

The recycling concept is not new. It had always been possible under the pre-6 April 2006 legislation governing personal pensions and retirement annuities. However, the advantage to be gained under that legislation was fairly minimal because of the restrictions placed on the amounts that could be paid as contributions which were eligible for tax relief (ie based on a percentage of earnings, starting at 17.5%, and with the earnings being capped for personal pensions). Those restrictions were removed with effect from 6 April 2006. Individuals can now get tax relief on contributions up to 100% of their uncapped earnings (subject to the annual allowance). So, whilst the government did not think it was worth doing anything about recycling under the pre-6 April 2006 legislation, the tax advantage to be gained by recycling is now too great to be ignored.

The legislation counters recycling by deeming an unauthorised payment to have been made when a tax-free lump sum is recycled. An unauthorised payment will trigger the various tax charges outlined above.

The recycling rule will be triggered if:

- the recycling was pre-planned;
- the amount of the lump sum, aggregated with any other lump sums taken in the previous 12-month period, exceeds 1% of the standard lifetime allowance; and
- as a consequence of the lump sum being taken, the amount of contributions paid into a registered pension scheme is significantly greater than it otherwise would have been. The measure here is that the cumulative amount of the additional contributions exceeds 30% of the lump sum received.

The recycling rule is only intended to catch the relatively small number of larger potential recyclers. The government feels that the legislation strikes a balance between deterring recycling activity, catching the more blatant and artificial cases, and leaving unaffected those smaller pensions savers and those undertaking normal retirement planning.

However, the mere existence of the recycling rule could have a widespread effect on administration. Scheme administrators might feel that they need to make the appropriate warning noises to all cases. Whilst a member might only have a small fund under the particular scheme, the scheme administrator will have no way of knowing what funds are available under other schemes, nor what the individual's intentions might be.

SECTION 9 INVESTMENTS

A General

16.23 The legislation that existed before 6 April 2006 imposed specific restrictions on the investments that could be held by schemes such as small self-administered schemes and self-invested personal pension schemes, where the members were able to direct the way the funds were invested. Those restrictions have been removed in the new legislation from 6 April 2006, and there is now a single set of investment rules for tax purposes applying to all types of registered pension schemes. However, as explained later, certain investments held by certain types of registered pension schemes will attract tax charges.

Schemes will still be subject to any relevant restrictions arising from DWP legislation, or other general restrictions outside tax law. The scheme trustees have a duty under general trust law to act prudently, conscientiously and honestly when making decisions in respect of the scheme. Trustees must always act in the best interests of the scheme members.

The tax legislation does not impose any restrictions on the investments that may be made by registered pension schemes. Instead, everything is regulated by the imposition of unauthorised payment tax charges if certain conditions are breached. The conditions which may be breached are:

- Any loan made by a scheme to an employer who is connected with the member will give rise to a tax charge on the member. But a registered pension scheme in the form of an occupational pension scheme can make a loan to the sponsoring employer without incurring any tax charges providing the loan does not exceed 50% of the fund value and it is done on specified terms.
- Any loan to a scheme member will give rise to a tax charge.
- Schemes can borrow funds for any purpose – for example, to assist with the purchase of an asset, or to meet a short-term liquidity problem. But the borrowing must not exceed 50% of the fund value (less any amounts previously borrowed), otherwise tax charges will arise.
- There is a limit on the amount which a registered pension scheme in the form of an occupational pension scheme can invest in the shares of the

sponsoring employer, without giving rise to tax charges. The market value of the shares must be less than 5% of the fund value.

- Certain types of registered pension schemes are categorised as 'investment-regulated pension schemes'. Under these schemes tax charges will arise when the scheme holds assets, either directly or indirectly, that are classed as 'taxable property' (see **16.25**).

B Tax exemptions

16.24 The following tax exemptions apply to registered pension schemes:

(a) income derived from investments or deposits held for the purposes of a registered pension scheme is exempt from income tax (section 186 of the Finance Act 2004);

(b) underwriting commissions applied for the purposes of a registered pension scheme are exempt from income tax if they would otherwise be chargeable to tax under Case VI of Schedule D (section 186(1)(b));

(c) income from futures contracts and options contracts are deemed to all be from investments as is any income derived from transactions relating to futures contracts or options contracts (section 186(3));

(d) profits or gains arising from transactions in certificates of deposit are exempt from income tax (section 56 of the Income and Corporation Taxes Act 1988);

(e) profits from sale and repurchase agreements (repos) and 'manufactured payments' are exempt from income tax (SI 1995/3036, as amended by SI 2006/745));

(f) a gain arising from the disposal of investments (including (c) above) held for the purposes of the scheme is exempt from capital gains tax (section 271 of the Taxation of Chargeable Gains Act 1992).

The exemptions above do not apply to income derived from investments or deposits held as a member of a property investment limited liability partnership.

There is nothing to prevent a registered pension scheme entering into trading activities. But as income derived from trading is not investment income or income from deposits, the tax exemptions (including those relating to capital gains on assets used by a scheme for trading purposes) do not apply. So, a registered pension scheme would be liable to pay tax on any income derived from a trading activity.

C Investment-regulated pension schemes

16.25 Because the legislation does not impose any restrictions on the investments that may be made by registered pension schemes, there is potential for schemes to invest in assets which may provide the opportunity for private use by the members. The government is keen to prevent tax-advantaged pension funds being used in that way, So, the legislation contains special provisions for certain types of registered pension schemes (referred to as 'investment-regulated pension schemes') which remove the tax advantages where the investments may create an opportunity for private use.

The term 'investment-regulated pension scheme' is used in the legislation to describe a registered pension scheme where the member, or a person related to the member, can self-direct the investments held by the scheme.

A registered pension scheme that is not an occupational pension scheme will be classified as an 'investment-regulated pension scheme' where a member (or person related to the member) is able (whether directly or indirectly) to direct, influence or advise on the manner of investments held for the purposes of the member's arrangement under the scheme. This encompasses registered pension schemes in the form of self-invested personal pension schemes, and fully insured personal pension schemes where a personal managed fund facility is made available.

A registered pension scheme that is an occupational pension scheme will be classified as an 'investment-regulated pension scheme' where the scheme has fewer than 50 members and has at least one member who meets the 'self-direction' condition, or the scheme has 50 or more members and has at least 10% of members who meet the 'self-direction' condition. The 'self-direction' condition is met if the member (or person related to the member) is able (whether directly or indirectly) to direct, influence or advise on the manner of investments held for the purposes of the scheme. This will encompass registered pension schemes in the form of small self-administered pension schemes and possibly some large self-administered pension schemes.

Whenever an 'investment-regulated pension scheme' holds assets, either directly or indirectly, that are classed as 'taxable property' there will be tax charges.

'Taxable property' consists of residential property and most types of 'tangible moveable' property.

Residential property can be in the UK or elsewhere and is:

(1) a building or structure that is used or suitable to be used as a dwelling;

(2) any related land that is wholly or partly the garden for the building or structure;

(3) any related land that is wholly or partly grounds for the residential property and which is used or intended for use for a purpose connected with the enjoyment of the building;

(4) any building or structure on any such related land;

(5) ground rents (long leaseholds) held in respect of residential property;

(6) hotel or similar accommodation where ownership is conferred via timeshare rights.

Tangible movable property comprises things that can be touched or moved such as art, antiques, jewellery, fine wine, boats, classic cars, stamp collections, rare books.

16.26 It is important to note that the legislation refers to 'taxable property' that is held 'directly or indirectly'. The reference to 'indirectly' ensures that 'taxable property' held by companies and other vehicles owned by pension schemes is also caught. That acts as a deterrent to the pension scheme owning, for example:

(1) 100% of the shares in a company that owns a flat in a desirable holiday resort which could be used by a member;

(2) 100% of the shares in a trading company that deals with, for example, fine wines or antiques, that could be available for the private use of a member.

Unfortunately, the scope of this part of the legislation also catches investments in companies involved in trading activities for which there is no possibility of private use. This could have the effect of stopping schemes holding unquoted company shares, which has traditionally been a popular form of investment for small self-administered schemes.

Where an 'investment-regulated pension scheme' holds an interest in 'taxable property', whether directly or indirectly, the value of the interest will be treated as an unauthorised payment, and the following tax charges will arise. The value of the interest would be 100% of the value of the property if held directly by the scheme. If held indirectly, the value would be based on a percentage, to take into account the fact that only a part of the interest in the taxable property is held by the investment-regulated pension scheme.

(1) The member will be subject to the unauthorised payments charge at 40% of the value placed on the interest.

(2) If certain limits are exceeded, the member will also be subject to the unauthorised payments surcharge at 15% of the value placed on the interest.

(3) The scheme administrator will be subject to the scheme sanction charge, normally at 15% of the value placed on the interest.

(4) Income or deemed income received in relation to the 'taxable property' will be subject to the scheme sanction charge at 40% of the value placed on the income.

(5) Any capital gain on the disposal of the 'taxable property' will be subject to the scheme sanction charge at 40% of the value placed on the capital gain.

CHAPTER 17

Life assurance for special purposes

SUMMARY

This Chapter considers some taxation, legal and practical aspects of contracts issued by life assurance companies or long-term insurance contracts, effected for a number of special purposes, which could not appropriately be dealt with, or are referred to only briefly, elsewhere in this book.

SECTION 1 BUSINESS ASSURANCE

17.1 It is important for the members of professional partnerships and small companies to give consideration to the consequences of the death of a partner, director or shareholder. Under English law, aside from a limited liability partnership, created in accordance with the Limited Liability Partnership Act 2000 effective from 6 April 2001, a partnership is not recognised as a legal entity (although it is in Scotland). Unless there is a partnership agreement which provides otherwise, a partnership will automatically dissolve on the death of a partner[1] and any capital belonging to the deceased partner will form part of his estate for inheritance tax (IHT) purposes. The loss of this capital may cause financial and practical difficulties for the surviving partners and it may also leave the deceased partner's spouse with a business interest for which he or she may have little use or wish to hold.

Similar considerations apply in the case of private companies, with a relatively small number of people owning the company as shareholders and running it as

1 Partnership Act 1890, s 33.

directors. A company is recognised as a distinct legal entity so it will not dissolve upon the death of a director or shareholder, but the deceased director/shareholder's shares may pass in accordance with his will or the intestacy rules, to someone with no interest in the company.

In both types of organisation, therefore, it is normally far better for all parties if there is a pre-planned arrangement to cater for the parties' aims, needs and desires as appropriate. A vital part of partnership planning is to have a written partnership agreement, setting out what is to occur upon death or retirement. It must be noted, however, that if the relevant part of the partnership agreement contains what amounts to a binding buy and sell agreement, the business interest will not be treated as 'relevant business property' for IHT business property relief purposes[1].

A vital part of the planning for either organisation is the means of funding the purchase of the deceased's business interest. Similar considerations apply to both types of organisation, and reference will generally be made below to partnerships, with specific comments in relation to private companies where it is appropriate. The main aims of business assurance planning are:

(1) to provide cash in the right hands at the right time;

(2) to avoid liability to capital gains tax (CGT);

(3) to avoid liability to IHT;

(4) to ensure an equitable division of the cost of funding the planning; and

(5) to ensure the arrangements are flexible enough to cater for changes in the organisation's constitution.

Life assurance can assist in providing sufficient funds in the right hands at the right time.

A Method of effecting the policies

17.2 There are a number of ways of trying to attain the above aims. The following text refers to partners but the same issues will generally apply to shareholding directors in private companies.

1 Own life policies cross-assigned

17.3 At one time this was a popular method of arranging partners' policies. Each partner takes out a policy on his own life for the amount required, pays the premium himself and assigns the policy in favour of his partners.

The main disadvantages of this arrangement are that it may become an administrative burden (requiring a fresh assignment each time there is a change in the

1 IHTA 1984, s 113; see Chapter 14.

constitution of the organisation) and the fact that any gain under the policy (ie the profit element) could be subject to CGT[1]. (The reasoning for such a charge is fully explained at **17.14** and **17.15**.) For these reasons, this method is not, in general, to be recommended.

2 *Life of another policy*

17.4 Each partner effects, as grantee, a policy on the lives of each of his other partners, with a sum assured in each case to provide for his interest in the particular partner's business interest. As each policy would be the property of the grantee, who pays the premium, there would be no element of gift, and no IHT liability on receipt of the policy moneys, which would be received by the grantee, at the death of the other partner(s) to enable him to purchase the interest. The policies owned by a deceased partner (on the lives of the surviving partners) would be part of the deceased partner's estate for IHT purposes – the value being the market value, or premiums paid, if greater, at the date of death.

One disadvantage of this method is that if there is a wide disparity of ages it may be difficult for a young partner to afford the premiums required under policies on the lives of older partners. In addition, if there are several partners, it will result in many policies being effected and it will be inflexible in situations where new partners join a firm or existing partners leave.

3 *Joint lives (first death) policies*

17.5 Under this arrangement, the partners effect one policy on all their lives for the capital sum required on the death of any one of them, and each partner pays an appropriate proportion of the premium. On the first death the proceeds are payable to the surviving partner or partners. The benefit payable is the same whichever partner dies first and the arrangement is not suitable, therefore, where the partners' interests in the business are unequal. Furthermore, changes in the organisation's constitution cannot easily be accommodated; and a new policy would be required each time a partner dies. For these reasons, this arrangement is virtually never used, except for a two-person partnership, where the partners have equal business interests. In such a partnership, an assurance on this basis may be the most suitable. The premium is usually less than the combined premiums would be under two single life assurances for the same combined sum assured. Provided the premiums are split on an actuarial basis, there should be no IHT liability on death.

Following the changes to the taxation of trusts from 22 March 2006 as described in Chapter 14, all trusts effected on or after that date will be treated as discretionary trusts (unless they are absolute or bare trusts or trusts for disabled persons). However, it is felt that provided that any arrangements entered into are part of normal commercial arrangements and there is no intention to confer a gratuitous benefit, premiums under such trusts should not be treated as gifts at the outset.

1 Taxation of Chargeable Gains Act (TCGA) 1992, s 210.

4 Automatic accrual and own life policies

17.6 Another method, sometimes recommended for its apparent simplicity, where the business interests are equal, is that known as automatic accrual. This involves a special provision in the partnership agreement concerning the retirement or death of a partner, viz that the retired or deceased partner's interest in the goodwill and his capital account, subject sometimes to an upper limit, passes automatically to the remaining or surviving partners on his death or retirement. Coupled with this, each partner effects a whole life policy on his own life, to compensate his estate for the value of his interest passing to the co-partners. However, if automatic accrual is to operate on retirement where there is a fixed retirement age, an endowment policy might be more appropriate than a whole life policy.

The policy proceeds, if written under trust, would normally be free of IHT subject to the comments contained in Chapter 14, unless the trust used was of the absolute variety. There are no difficulties with changes in the partnership as each partner has his own policy and no one else has an interest in that policy.

5 Individual trust policies for other partners/directors

17.7 Traditionally, this has been the most popular way of writing business assurance. Each partner effects only one policy on his own life written subject to a trust for the others in whatever interests they hold in the business at a stated point at some time after the life assured's death. Prior to 22 March 2006, the trusts used were invariably interest in possession trusts. Many policies effected on or after that date are still interest in possession trusts but such policies now fall within the relevant property regime for IHT purposes as described in Chapter 14 Section 6C. As far as the premiums are concerned, provided that the arrangements are treated as commercial transactions by HMRC then payment of premiums would not involve any gifts – see **17.11** and **17.12**. Post 21 March 2006 trusts will potentially be liable to the ten-yearly charge and exit charges but HMRC have confirmed that they will be looking at the market value of the policy at each ten-yearly anniversary rather than the premiums paid and so this may not be a significant issue unless the sum assured under the policy is substantial or the life assured is in ill-health at the ten-yearly anniversary.

Even for very large sums assured, any problems at the ten-yearly anniversary can be largely avoided by the settlor effecting several policies on different days. This would have the effect of giving each policy its own nil rate band and thus dramatically reducing the chances of any future ten-yearly charge.

Many settlors wish to include themselves as potential beneficiaries under arrangements of this type so that, should circumstances change, the benefits can revert back to them. Provided that the arrangements are viewed as commercial as described in **17.11** and **17.12**, this should not have any implications from a gift with reservation point of view.

An example of a typical interest in possession trust wording is as follows:

> 'UPON trust for the benefit of such of the person or persons (other than myself) who shall be partners in the firm known as [XYZ] or its successors in business

("the Firm"') provided that such persons were partners in the Firm immediately before the occurrence of the event upon which the policy money becomes payable ("the Event") and in the like shares in which they are then entitled to share in the profits of the business of the Firm as if I had retired from the Firm on the happening of the Event.

Provided always that if I should cease to be a partner in the Firm otherwise than by reason of my death then for the benefit of myself absolutely.

I direct that the trusts hereof shall carry any intermediate income and the right to such income shall be vested in the partners in the Firm (other than myself) in existence at the time such income arises and he or they shall be entitled to receive such income in the same proportions as they would be entitled to the trust property from which such income arises as if it was seven days after my death and the said partners had satisfied any and all contingencies set out above.'

This form of wording is flexible in catering for changes in the partnership as new partners are automatically included and outgoing ones automatically excluded, although incoming partners will need to effect a policy on their own lives under a similar trust in order to retain the commerciality of the arrangement (see below).

17.8 Under the Capital Transfer Tax regime, the trusts used were often flexible, power of appointment trusts (see Chapter 15). The use of the flexible trust is not viable, however, under the IHT regime, as, due to the potential lack of commerciality (see below) it could fall within the gift with reservation of benefit (GWR) provisions of section 102 of the Finance Act 1986[1] and thus the policy proceeds would be treated as being in the estate of the person declaring the flexible trust.

The GWR provisions apply where, on or after 18 March 1986, an individual disposes of property by way of *gift* and, inter alia, the property and any benefit to him by contract or otherwise'[2] is not enjoyed to the entire exclusion or virtually to the entire exclusion of the donor. The inclusion of each partner as a beneficiary or potential beneficiary under the other partners' trusts may amount to 'a benefit to him by contract or otherwise', which may bring the arrangement within the GWR provisions, with the result that the policy would continue to form part of the estate for IHT purposes.

Further, where the beneficiaries and potential beneficiaries include individuals other than the partners (eg, where a partner's spouse and children are included), the arrangement would not appear to be commercial. It would contain an element of bounty and would constitute a gift, bringing the arrangement within the GWR provisions.

Sometimes, flexible power of appointment trusts are used, with the beneficiaries being limited to the partners for the time being, or limited to specified partners, rather than all the partners at a particular time. There is a considerable risk of such trusts not being viewed as 'commercial' as the power of appointment

1 See Chapter 14.
2 FA 1986, s 102(1)(b).

may be exercised to give a greater share of the trust fund to a particular partner than his share of the business actually warrants. There is thus, potentially, an element of gift and such a trust wording may bring the GWR provisions into operation.

17.9 To avoid the application of the GWR provisions, therefore, it is necessary to ensure that the arrangement is fully commercial, without any element of gift. HMRC have said that what is 'commercial' will depend on the individual facts of each case.

(a) Commerciality of the trust arrangement

17.10 The policies must be effected subject to reciprocal trusts by each partner in trust for all the other partners (excluding himself). HMRC have confirmed that it is acceptable, however, for the benefits to revert back to the settlor if he ceases to be a partner for any reason such as the business ceasing to exist or the individual partner leaving the firm or retiring.

(b) Commerciality of the premiums

17.11 HMRC have confirmed that arrangements can be 'commercial' even if, for example, the partners are of different ages and as a result one partner will appear to be spending more for the benefit of his partners than the other partners are spending for him, or if two partners have respectively a 20% and 80% share of the business and the 80% partner writes a larger policy in trust for the 20% partner than that partner writes for him[1]. However, if there is a disparity in the amounts of the premiums paid by each partner, it could be argued that the arrangement is not commercial. Consideration should therefore be given to equalising the premiums between the parties. This could be achieved by, for example, each person's policy being limited to the amount of cover available for the cheapest premium (probably for the youngest) and by the parties topping-up the cover required by 'life of another' policies to provide for the required deficiency in the cover resulting from the equalisation. This method does have disadvantages in that, for example, younger partners would have to pay higher premiums on the lives of senior partners and, unless it is a small partnership, with relatively few changes, the number of policies required can become high and can become an administrative burden. This method is the most appropriate for company directors, but partners may use a method which is simpler and where equalisation of the premiums is not necessary.

Under this method, the premiums could become the first charge on the profits of the partnership, charged to the relevant partners' capital accounts. In this way, the arrangement will be treated as commercial, and the GWR provisions should not apply.

1 See letter dated 6 April 1987 from the Life Insurance Council (LIC) to members of the LIC following clarification from the Inland Revenue Circular No LIC 60/87.

A further method of trying to ensure that the arrangements are commercial with regard to the premium payments for directors of companies is the undertaking and cost adjustment method.

17.12 A company is likely to consist of owners of different ages owning unequal shares in the company. For example, the policy effected by an elderly major shareholder director will probably have the highest sum assured and premiums. Yet, conversely, because of his age, he has the lowest expectation of benefiting from the arrangement. The owners, could therefore, equalise the cost of the arrangement to endeavour to exclude any element of bounty. Therefore, suitable cost adjustments between the owners ensures that each owner contributes to the total cost in proportion to the extent he expects to benefit from the arrangement. A suitable formula for calculating the necessary 'should pay premiums' for a number of owners is illustrated below. The formula can be extended to cater for any number of owners and assumes the surviving owners will purchase the deceased's shares rateably according to their existing shares in the company.

$$\text{A's should pay premium} = \frac{\text{A's share of business X B's premium}}{\text{(Total value of business – B's share)}} + \frac{\text{A's share of business X C's premium}}{\text{(Total value of business – C's share)}}$$

$$\text{B's should pay premium} = \frac{\text{B's share of business X A's premium}}{\text{(Total value of business – A's share)}} + \frac{\text{B's share of business X C's premium}}{\text{(Total value of business – C's share)}}$$

$$\text{C's should pay premium} = \frac{\text{C's share of business X A's premium}}{\text{(Total value of business – A's share)}} + \frac{\text{C's share of business X B's premium}}{\text{(Total value of business – B's share)}}$$

To endeavour to show the arrangement has been set up on a commercial basis, in other words there is no element of bounty in favour of any of the owners, an undertaking should be completed. In simple terms, the undertaking states the owners have effected and will keep in force the policies as part of a business arrangement. It also details the necessary 'should pay premiums' which should remove any element of bounty.

In addition to effecting the trust policy, each shareholder should address a letter or memorandum to his co-shareholders, which clearly states that he is undertaking to effect a policy on his own life in trust for them *in consideration* for them doing the same and that the arrangement is a business transaction between them and is *not intended to confer any gratuitous benefit* on his co-shareholders. A new, incoming shareholder should execute a similar letter or memorandum when completing his proposal.

A specimen undertaking to be addressed by each shareholder to the other shareholders is as follows:

> 'TO: [all of the shareholders] in [XYZ]
>
> I hereby undertake to effect a [ ] policy on my life in trust for you and to maintain the said policy in full force by payment of the premiums when due, in full consideration of you each severally undertaking to effect a policy on your own life in trust for me proportionate to my share of the business and to maintain the said policy in full force by payment of the premiums when due. I hereby declare that

the above mentioned life assurance arrangements are made between us at arm's length we having arranged for any appropriate financial adjustments to be made, and the said arrangements are not intended to confer any gratuitous benefit on any person.

Signed..............................

Dated...............................'

The introduction of a new shareholder into the business would, unless the new shareholder entered into mutual commercial arrangements, before 22 March 2006 have caused a PET to be made, as there would be, in effect, a transfer from the existing shareholders to the new shareholder, of a slice of their interests in possession under the existing trust policies. This would normally be measured by reference to a proportion (depending on the number of shareholders) of the total premiums paid up to the time of introducing the new partner or the market value of the policy if higher[1]. For existing pre 22 March policies varied in this way on or after 6 October 2008, this course of action would give rise to a chargeable lifetime transfer. For policies effected on or after 22 March 2006, this would not be an issue as such trusts are within the relevant property regime and thus do not form part of anyone's estate.

The death of the life assured under a policy written in trust in the way described above should not give rise to any IHT liability. The death of a shareholder/beneficiary under a pre 21 March 2006 trust could, however, be a transfer of value as there is a termination of the deceased's interest in possession, which would increase the value of the survivors' estates[2]. The value of the transfer would not be based on the sum assured, but only on the deceased beneficiary's share in the value of the trust interest at the time of his death, which would normally be calculated by reference to the open market value of the policy[3]. However, in the majority of cases, it is hoped that the arrangement would be 'commercial' (see above) and so any transfer of value would fall within the section 10 exemption, of no intention to confer any gratuitous benefit on anyone, and thus, there would be no charge to IHT.

(c) Appointment of additional trustees

17.13 If the trust is declared using a letter of request, forming part of the contract between the proposer and the life office, so that the trust is constituted from the outset (fully explained in Chapter 15, Section 3), the assured will be sole trustee of the policy from the outset. It is recommended that other persons (eg other partners) should be appointed as additional trustees by a separate deed of appointment, once the policy has been effected, so that they can act as trustees immediately on the death of the life assured.

1 IHTA 1984, ss 160, 167.
2 IHTA 1984, s 3A(2)(b).
3 IHTA 1984, ss 50, 160, 167(2)(a).

(d) Declaring trusts of existing policies for business assurance purposes

17.14 Careful consideration should be given to the possible CGT ramifications of using existing policies to declare trusts for the surviving partners on the basis expressed above, rather than effecting the contracts in trust from the outset. The relevant sections in this regard are sections 210 and 60 of TCGA 1992.

The original section 210 stated that disposals under life assurance contracts are exempt from CGT unless

(1) the person making the disposal is not the original beneficial owner; and

(2) he acquired his rights or interest for a consideration in money or money's worth.

Section 60 of TCGA 1992 states that where the trust is a bare trust (where the beneficiaries are absolutely entitled as against the trustees) the acts of the trustees are to be treated as if they were the acts of the beneficiaries.

Where a contract is effected free from trust, the original beneficial owner is clearly the grantee of the policy. If a bare trust of the contract is subsequently declared, there is obviously a change in the beneficial ownership to the beneficiaries. The relevant question is then, whether the beneficiaries acquired their rights or interest under the policy for a consideration in money or money's worth. If so and they then make a disposal, eg a claim on the policy, then a chargeable gain may accrue. In the example above, the policy moneys would be paid on death to the trustees. If the trust is a bare trust, section 60 will treat the disposal as being effected by the beneficiaries – the surviving partners (who will not be the original beneficial owners). The surviving partners would have acquired their interests for consideration, by way of the mutual declaration of trust of policies on commercial terms. Thus, the feeling was that there could be a charge to CGT on any gains to the extent that the amount received on the disposal exceeded the allowable expenditure (in effect, the premiums) and the annual exemption in the year of the disposal.

17.15 Section 157 of the Finance Act 2003 changed the wording of section 210(3) of TCGA 1992. The new wording states that disposals under life assurance contracts are exempt from CGT unless:

(a) the rights or any interest in the rights, or

(b) the rights, the interest or any interest from which the interest directly or indirectly derives (in whole or in part)

have or has at any time been acquired for any person for actual consideration.

Applying this new definition to the placing of existing policies in trust for business assurance purposes, there can be little argument that there would have been, in the circumstances envisaged, a disposal of the rights under the policy by virtue of the payment of the sum assured and, at that time, it could be said that an interest in the rights under the policy (namely the beneficial interest) had been acquired for consideration given the fact that, in a typical case, each business owner would have assigned his policy into a business trust only in return for his co-owners doing the same. This 'reciprocal' assignment will clearly amount to consideration. The question is then, does this constitute 'actual' consideration? It seems reasonable to believe that it does, since the only 'deemed' consideration that is referred to in the legislation is consideration deemed to be such for the purposes of the capital gains tax legislation. Clearly, even though the consideration for an assignment of a policy into trust in the circumstances envisaged is not a consideration in money, it is consideration nevertheless and 'actual consideration' at that.

So it would seem that far from enabling policies to more readily avoid being brought into the CGT net by virtue of an assignment between business owners after the day the policy was originally effected as was originally hoped by some advisers active in this area, the new provisions in section 210(3) seem to make it even clearer that such an assignment would be 'caught' referring, as they do, to the interest in rights under the policy being acquired by 'any person' in the policy´s history for actual consideration.

17.16 Since 6 April 2005, there may also be a problem for business assurance policies in respect of pre-owned assets tax. As far as this is concerned, the authors can do no better than quote verbatim from the HMRC Guidance Notes on Pre-owned Assets Tax as follows:

> 'In some cases, policies are taken out on each partner's life solely for the purposes of providing funds to enable their fellow partners to purchase his/her share from the partner's beneficiaries on their death. The partner is not a potential beneficiary of his/her "own" policy. In such circumstances, a charge to tax under Schedule 15 paragraph 8 Finance Act 2004 will not arise.
>
> However, in many cases, the partner retains a benefit for themselves, for example, they can cash in the policy during their lifetime for their own benefit. In such cases, even if the arrangement is on commercial terms so that it is not a gift with reservation for inheritance tax, the trust is a settlement for inheritance tax purposes and a charge to tax under paragraph 8 will arise.
>
> The valuation of a partner's, or settlor's, interest in a policy for the purposes of paragraph 8 of Schedule 15 should be his share of its open market value as at 6 April each year. That valuation will be relevant for determining the amount of charge for that year of assessment.
>
> Where the policies are term assurances, in the vast majority of cases the policyholder will be in normal health, and therefore it is likely that the chargeable amount, as calculated under paragraph 9 of Schedule 15, will have little marketable value and will fall below the de minimis exemption in paragraph 13. Therefore, a policyholder in normal health at the valuation date may assume that he will survive beyond the term of the assurance, and complete his tax return accordingly. However, in circumstances where the policyholder has been advised that their state of health is such that it casts doubt on their survival to the end of the term of assurance (ie there becomes a realistic prospect of the policy paying out and therefore having a material market value), then consideration should be given to obtaining actuarial advice about the value of the policy.'

It has to be said that there is some doubt within the industry as to whether HMRC's views in this area are correct but, at the time of writing, the views expressed above remain the official HMRC line.

(e) Types of assurance

17.17 To cover the situation on death, unit-linked whole life assurances are suitable although sometimes renewable term policies are used. If the intention is to buy out a partner's interest upon his retirement, endowment assurances, written to the anticipated date of retirement, should also be considered, although equalisation of premiums is not generally possible under these contracts.

When discussing planning for the death of a partner, consideration may also be given to the inclusion of critical illness cover. If a partner contracts a critical illness and wishes to retire early from the business, the remaining partners may therefore have the necessary funds to purchase his share of the business. However, including critical illness cover can lead to possible problems and these should be fully considered at the outset:

(1) The partner suffering the critical illness may not wish to sell at that time; he may wish to return to work, for example, after a mild heart attack.

(2) A partner disposing of a business interest following a critical illness claim must give consideration to the taxation consequences. The sale to the remaining partners will be treated as a disposal for CGT purposes and therefore a liability to tax may arise. It should be noted that in some cases CGT retirement relief and/or taper relief may be available. On subsequent death, the cash that had been received from the sale of the interest in the business could be liable to IHT in full. However, if the partner retained his business interest until death, his estate should be entitled to business property relief for IHT purposes as described in Chapter 14.

The first potential problem can be resolved by the partners having a properly drawn up agreement that includes a single option clause to cover critical illness benefits. In simple terms, the single option clause states that in the event of a critical illness claim, the partner suffering the critical illness will have the option to sell his interest in the business to the remaining partners. The other partners cannot, however, force the partner with the critical illness to sell his share. If the option is exercised it is binding on the remaining partners. Using this type of agreement enables the partner suffering the critical illness to carefully consider his future working circumstances and personal taxation position before deciding to sell his business interest.

It must, however, be emphasised that this action does not overcome the taxation problems outlined above.

The situation may arise whereby a critical illness claim arises but the partner does not wish to exercise his option to sell his interest in the business to the remaining partners. In these circumstances a claim will still be made and the proceeds paid to the trustees. The trustees should reinvest the policy proceeds for the benefit of the other partners until such time as the partner suffering the critical illness dies. At that time the trustees can irrevocably appoint the trust proceeds to the surviving partners, who can then exercise their option to purchase the deceased partner's interest in the business.

If critical illness cover is included in an arrangement, the terms of any option agreement should be such that the critical illness benefit will be 100% of the sum assured. This would ensure that the remaining partners will have the necessary funds to fully purchase the critically ill partner's interest in the business.

In view of these potential problems, it may be more appropriate for each partner to have separate critical illness cover, if required, aside from any 'business assurance' arrangement.

6 *Pension term assurance written in trust*

17.18 As an alternative to the above arrangements, it was possible for each partner to effect a pension term assurance and obtain income tax relief at their marginal rate on the contributions. Each partner would effect such a policy in trust for the other partners to ensure that they would be able to purchase the deceased's interest in the event of his death before a predetermined date, eg retirement age.

The premiums payable under such arrangements would need to be set off against the individual's annual allowance (see Chapter 16, Section 4). Furthermore, should lump sum benefits become payable as a result of the individual's death, these will also count against his or her lifetime allowance (see Chapter 16, Section 5). Thus, where the sums assured are substantial, this may make pension term assurance unattractive to some individuals.

The pre-Budget report of 6 December 2006 announced the Government's intention to abolish tax relief for stand alone pension term assurance policies. Policies effected before 6 December 2006 are unaffected. Applications fully completed on or before 6 December 2006 are also entitled to tax relief, provided that the policy was issued by 31 July 2007 and so long as the completed application was submitted to the insurance company and receipt recorded by midnight on 13 December 2006.

7 *Company effecting life of another policies*

17.19 A final alternative arrangement is for the company to effect life of another policies on the lives of the relevant shareholders.

Until 1981, it was not possible for a private limited company to purchase its own shares. However, provisions were introduced in the Companies Act 1981 to allow this. The legal requirements were then set out in the Companies Act 1985 and the Companies Act 2006 subsequently relaxed some of the requirements that have to be met before a buy-out can take place. These provisions enable company share purchase to be used as the basis of a share protection arrangement. The company effects policies on the lives of each of its shareholders with a sum assured to cover the value of each shareholding. On death, the policy proceeds are paid to the company and this gives it the necessary funds to purchase the deceased's shares and cancel them. This process effectively increases the proportionate shareholding of the remaining shareholders. Whilst this type of arrangement achieves the same effect as the surviving owners purchasing a deceased shareholder's shares the following points must also be considered:

(1) The policies are effected by the company and would not need to be written under trust. Premiums would be paid by the company but corporation tax relief would not be available, because the policy is not to meet loss of profits on death (see section 2 of this Chapter. For company accounting periods starting on or after 1 April 2008, all gains made under policies owned by companies fall within the 'loan relationship' rules as set out in Section 6C of Chapter 13. However, this is unlikely to be a significant problem with protection policies with very low cash values as, in practice, chargeable gains should not arise. However, it will be a disadvantage if savings policies are being used to provide funds on retirement as well as death.

(2) Prior to the 2006 Companies Act coming into force the company's Articles of Association had to authorise the company to purchase its own shares and for companies incorporated prior to 1982 it was unlikely that this power would have been included in the company's Articles and therefore these would have had to be changed. Following the 2006 Act, however, this requirement is no longer relevant.

(3) The directors of a private company must give a simple statement about the solvency of the company before it can effect a purchase of its own shares out of capital. It must state that, having made full inquiry into the affairs and prospects of the company, the directors have formed the opinion:

   - as regards its initial situation immediately following the date on which the payment out of capital is proposed to be made, that there will be no grounds on which the company could then be found unable to pay its debts; and
   - as regards its prospects for the year immediately following that date, that having regard to:

     (i) how the company's business is intended to be managed during that year; and

     (ii) the amount and character of the financial resources that will, in the view of the directors, be available to the company during that year,

   the company will be able to continue to carry on business as a going concern (and will accordingly be able to pay its debts as they fall due) throughout that year.

   Attached to the statement must be a note from the company's auditor stating that the company's affairs have been scrutinised and there is nothing to indicate that the directors' opinion is unreasonable.

(4) The shares purchased must be cancelled (unless it is a listed company), thereby becoming un-issued share capital.

(5) If the purchase is on a recognised stock exchange, or on the Alternative Investment Market (AIM), it must be approved by an ordinary resolution of shareholders. The resolution must specify the maximum number of shares to be purchased, the maximum and minimum prices to be paid and the period of execution (not more than 18 months).

Most purchases will be off-market and therefore not subject to the above requirement, but instead any contract (or option) to purchase shares must be authorised by a 75% majority of shareholders at a company general meeting.

17.20 In the absence of any change in tax law, the excess of the price the company paid for the shares over the capital originally subscribed would be treated as a distribution by the company. The outgoing director (or their representatives) would be liable for income tax. However, the Corporation Tax Act 2010 (CTA 2010) allows the payment to be treated as capital if the conditions in section 1033 are met (see below). CGT would be the only tax the outgoing shareholder would have to pay on the difference between what they paid for the shares and what they received for them. Since death is not a taxable disposal for CGT purposes, this would only apply on retirement and would be based on the gain after taking into account any available annual CGT exemption. Entrepreneurs' relief should be available in many cases, meaning that the tax on the first £10 million of any gains would be taxable at an effective rate of only 10%.

The conditions are as follows:

(1) The company must be either an unquoted trading company or the holding company of a trading group. Investment companies, or those dealing in shares or land, are excluded.

(2) The purchase must be for the benefit of the company's trade. It appears that HM Revenue & Customs (HMRC) interprets this fairly broadly. Press Release SP2/1982 states that this would normally include the total buy-out of a deceased or retiring shareholder. It does not matter that the outgoing shareholder (or their estate) will also benefit.

(3) The purchase must not be part of an arrangement, the main purpose of which is tax avoidance.

(4) The outgoing shareholder must be resident in the UK and have held the shares for at least five years. This period includes the ownership of a spouse or civil partner and is reduced to three years where the shares were acquired on the death of an earlier shareholder.

(5) If the company only buys part of the outgoing director's holding, and/or his or her associates (broadly, spouse/civil partner and minor children) also hold shares, then the percentage of all shares held after the purchase by the director and their associates must not exceed 75% of what it was before, or 30% of the reduced share capital. This will not usually be a problem on a complete buy-out.

(6) If the purchase is to enable a deceased director's estate to pay IHT which could not otherwise be met without undue hardship, then if substantially all the cash paid out is actually used to pay the tax within two years of the death, conditions (b) to (e) inclusive do not apply.

A procedure exists under section 1044 of CTA 2010 for advance clearance to be obtained from HMRC that the purchase is one to which section 1033 applies and HMRC has 30 days to decide. As capital will usually be leaving the company, clearance must also be obtained under section 748 ofCTA 2010. In addition, once the shares have been purchased, the company will have to notify the Registrar of Companies.

It should be borne in mind that the proceeds of a life assurance policy effected by the company to facilitate the purchase of the shares of a shareholder director will increase the value of the company. The deceased's personal representatives may wish this to be taken into account when selling the shares to the company and this could result in the policy moneys being insufficient to actually purchase the shares. A further factor to be taken into account, however, is that the death of the shareholder director has probably deprived the company of one of its principal assets and also, any loans he may have made to the company will have to be repaid. This may have a balancing effect of reducing the value of the company.

The complexity of the company share purchase arrangement means it is a method of share protection assurance which should not be considered without the assistance of legal advisers, as it needs to comply with both Company and Revenue law.

B The agreement

17.21 The arrangements described above may ensure that sufficient funds are in the hands of the surviving partners to enable them to purchase the deceased's interest in the business. This in itself, however, is not sufficient, as, for example, the deceased's spouse may not wish to sell, or the personal representatives may decide to take an interest in the running of the business. It is therefore highly desirable to have an agreement in place. The agreement may take several forms.

1 Automatic accrual

17.22 This has already been mentioned (see **17.6**).

2 Buy and sell agreement

17.23 This agreement may be contained in the partnership agreement or in the Articles of Association, or may be entered into separately. It binds the surviving partners to buy a deceased partner's share from the personal representatives and equally binds the personal representatives to sell the share to the surviving partners. Where this is enforceable (ie binding from the outset), it is HMRC's view that it amounts to a binding contract for sale[1] and business property relief for IHT purposes as described in Chapter 14 will not be available.

3 Double option agreement

17.24 This is by far the most common type of agreement, as it does not prejudice the availability of business property relief. Such an agreement would provide that:

(1) on the death of a partner, the surviving partners have the option to buy his interest from his personal representatives within a fixed time period of his death; and

(2) the personal representatives have the option to require the surviving partners to purchase the deceased's interest, also within a fixed period (not necessarily of the same time length).

If either of the parties exercise their option, the agreement would then become binding on the other party. As it is not a binding agreement from the outset, it does not fall within section 113 of IHTA 1984 and business property relief should be available on all 'relevant business property'.

Care should be taken to ensure that the double option agreement is worded to mirror the terms of the trust. For example, taking the wording of the trust example above, the double option agreement should give the options from a time period beginning seven days after the death of a partner. If the agreement does not mirror the trust and if, for example, there was a new partner in between the dates of death and seven days after death, this could result in the new partners being able to exercise the option even though they are not beneficiaries under the trust and so would not have the funds to purchase the deceased's share. Similarly, the personal representatives could bind the new partners, even though they have no funds. An example of a double option agreement is given in Appendix 11.

C Premiums paid by the organisation

17.25 The organisation may of course wish to pay the premiums in respect of the arrangements described above. In relation to a company, it is straightforward to consider its paying the premiums as a 'paying agent' on behalf of the director/shareholders, out of post tax and National Insurance income. It would normally be the case that the premiums would have been equalised and the value of the premium payment in respect of each director/shareholder would then be debited from the director's post-tax salary. If the premiums are not paid in this way, they will be treated as additional remuneration of the directors and will be

1 See Statement of Practice SP 12/80 (13 October 1980) and Press Release Memorandum TR 557 (19 September 1984) Institute of Chartered Accountants of England and Wales.

added to their taxable income, giving rise to additional tax and National Insurance charges. As a partnership is not a legal entity, any payment out of the partnership account in respect of premiums will have to be debited from the post-tax profits of the partners. It can be seen that there are no significant taxation advantages for the business paying the premiums, although there may be advantages from an administrative and certainty point of view.

SECTION 2 KEY MAN POLICIES

17.26 In many companies it is often the case that a few employees (both male and female) are most important or valuable to the business. There are many reasons why this might occur, eg:

(1) they may have a special knowledge or skill;

(2) they may be expert salesmen; or

(3) they may control a project.

Each in his own way makes a major contribution to his company's profit and profitability and in consequence each may be considered a key member of personnel. The death of such a person might result in a serious setback to the company's prosperity and progress. There may be no ready successor and the period of readjustment required after death might lead to a loss of confidence, a reversal in company fortunes and, in the worst instances, the collapse of the company.

For these reasons companies often consider it a wise precaution to assure the life of a key director or employee so that in the event of premature death the proceeds of the policy will be available to offset the financial strain of the loss.

Although it is possible that a key man will continue to be of essential importance until retirement, it is even more likely that within a much shorter time a replacement will have to be trained, or the key man's role in the company may have changed. For many reasons, therefore, the vital period for a key man may extend over five to ten years. This being so, temporary assurance should provide adequate cover.

Although an employer may have an insurable interest in the life of his employee (see Chapter 1) it is sometimes difficult to determine the extent of that interest in respect of a policy on the life of a key man. In practice, a good estimate may be made if consideration is given to certain factors such as the following:

(1) How much would it cost to find and train a suitable replacement if the key man were to die?

(2) How much company profit can be traced to the key man, ie how much would be lost in turnover and profitability if the key man were to die? (This is usually easiest to answer in the case of a salesman.)

(3) How much investment would be wasted if the key man died? (He might, for example, be responsible for the development of a specialised department.)

(4) What is the key man's salary? Cover will amount to some convenient multiple of this figure, perhaps, in most cases between five and ten times. This formula is based on the broad assumption that a salary tends to reflect an individual's contribution to the organisation. This might be a better approach where it is impossible to measure the loss accurately.

A Taxation

1 Corporation tax

(a) Premium payments

17.27 The circumstances in which premiums in respect of key man policies may be treated as an allowable business expense deductible against profits for corporation tax purposes were clearly laid down by the then Chancellor of the Exchequer, Sir John Anderson, in answer to a question in the House of Commons on 27 July 1944[1]. He stated that the general practice in dealing with insurances by employers on the lives of employees is to treat the premiums as admissible deductions, and any sums received under a policy as trading receipts, if:

(1) the sole relationship is that of employer and employee;

(2) the insurance is intended to meet loss of profits resulting from the loss of services of the employee; and

(3) it is an annual or short-term [temporary] insurance.

The sum assured must also be reasonable (considering the matters raised above). HMRC appears to hold the view that most employees can be effectively replaced within five years and so the sum assured should not reflect loss of profits for more than that time.

The general rules as to allowable deductions are to be found in section 54(1)(a) of the Corporation Tax Act 2009 , which provide that the expense must have been incurred wholly and exclusively for business purposes and it must be a revenue, not a capital, expense.

If the key man has a significant proprietary interest in the company (the rule of thumb at the time of writing is broadly 5%, although each case will be looked at on its own merits), HMRC may not allow relief as it could be argued that the policy has been effected for the life assured's own advantage and has thus not been incurred wholly and exclusively for business purposes.

1 402 HC Official Rep (6th series) col 890 (27 July 1944).

Where a parent company effects the policy and pays the premium for a key man of a subsidiary company, this is not an allowable expense as the payment has not been incurred wholly and exclusively for the parent company's own business[1].

(b) Policy proceeds

17.28 If premiums are allowed as an expense deductible against profits for corporation tax purposes, the policy proceeds will be taxed as a trading receipt (ie income) of the company and will be brought into the computation of profits in the year in which the proceeds are payable. This may result in an abnormally high tax charge, for example, where a company usually pays corporation tax at the small companies' rate, but the proceeds cause the company to have to pay at the full rate. The policy could be arranged so that the proceeds are due in instalments, so as not to cause the profits to exceed the small companies' rate[2]. However, if the death of the key man results, as expected, in a fall in a company's profits, such taxation of the proceeds may not be severe.

However, each case is considered on its own merits and in order to avoid, so far as is possible, any future dispute the company should explain the purpose of the policy to its local Inspector of Taxes and establish the tax position in advance. It should be noted, however, that in certain circumstances an advance clearing given by a local Inspector of Taxes may be subsequently withdrawn by HMRC[3].

2 *Inheritance tax*

17.29 Payment of the sum assured to the company in the event of a key man's death will not, in itself, be liable to IHT.

If, however, the key man is himself a major shareholder of the company, HMRC could argue that the payment of the sum assured has inflated the value of his shareholding for the purposes of IHT, although a counter argument could be that the death of the key man has deprived the company of one of its principal assets and may thus have a balancing effect of reducing the value of the company. Furthermore, it is possible that the payment of the sum assured may create a large cash balance in the company which is in excess of future business requirements. If this is the case, such excess cash may be treated as an excepted asset for IHT purposes and, as such, will not attract business property relief, see Chapter 14, Section 4D). It may be prudent, therefore, to arrange for the policy proceeds to be paid as a series of instalments which should minimise any possible increase in the value of the shares (and may also minimise the company's corporation tax liability, see above).

1 *Samuel Dracup & Sons Ltd v Dakin* (1957) 37 TC 377. See also FRP5/A6.

2 With effect from 1 April 1994, the small companies' rate can be claimed by UK resident companies whose profits are below £300,000: ICTA 1988, s 13.

3 See *Matrix Securities Ltd v IRC* [1994] STC 272.

B Type of policy

17.30 Taking into account considerations such as the view that a key man should be replaced within about five years and the taxation position, temporary assurances are the most usual types of policy to be recommended, which would normally expire at the key man's expected retirement age. In certain situations, however, a whole life or endowment policy may be more appropriate.

The policy could be assigned to the employee when he leaves service prior to retirement or at retirement if the policy is a whole life, endowment or continuing term policy.

The assignment is likely to be treated as an assignment for money or money's worth being in recognition of past service given by the employee. This would give rise to a chargeable event with the usual tax implications. The gain would be based on the difference between the market value (ie usually the surrender value) of the policy at the time of assignment and the premiums paid. For term assurance policies this is likely to be nil unless the life assured is in serious ill-health. There is an argument that as past consideration is no consideration, the assignment would not even constitute a chargeable event. This may well be the case but, in the absence of any known case or view being expressed by HMRC, the safer view may be to assume that the assignment is for consideration. It is reiterated, though, that with term assurance this is unlikely to be a significant problem.

However, an assignment of a qualifying policy which remains qualifying at the time of assignment and has run for ten years or three-quarters of its term if less at the time of assignment would not give rise to a chargeable event regardless of the money's worth point.

The value of the payment, ie the surrender value, is likely to be a deductible expense for the company and will therefore counterbalance any tax charge on the chargeable gain if it arises in the same tax year.

The surrender value of the policy at assignment would be assessed on the employee under Schedule E as a reward for past service. It would be usual for a payment made as a reward for services to be treated as an emolument. If the payment can be seen to be a termination payment not an emolument then it should be taxable under section 148 of ICTA 1988, and it could be that the first £30,000 will be tax free.

If actual consideration is given, which seems likely, then following the assignment (a disposal of rights within section 210 of TCGA 1992) the policy would be a chargeable asset within section 210 TCGA 1992. In these circumstances any subsequent full or part encashment under the policy will be treated as a disposal or part disposal for capital gains tax purposes if the policy is a qualifying policy. The annual gains exemption (£10,600 for 2011/12) should may, of course, be available to ensure that any chargeable capital gains are exempt or minimised.

With a non-qualifying policy, death, maturity and full or partial encashment after the assignment will give rise to a chargeable event with the tax charge falling on the employee, or his legal personal representatives, in the event of death. Where income tax and capital gains tax are both relevant, as here, the income tax charge takes precedence. Credit for any chargeable gains that may be subject to income tax is given against any capital gain. In practice, this means that a capital gains tax liability is unlikely to occur. If subsequent to assignment the individual transfers the policy into a trust (say for the benefit of his family), the policy will be outside any potential capital gains tax charge since the new owners (trustees) will not have acquired it for consideration.

If the policy remains in the ownership of the individual until his death, no capital gains tax charge will arise since no disposal will occur on death by virtue of section 62 of TCGA 1992.

Similarly, if the individual (assignee) subsequently assigns his interest gratuitously into trust, the 'chain' will have been broken and there will be no capital gains tax on subsequent death.

The above comments have all concerned the situation where a key man dies, but the position where such a person contracts a critical illness should also be considered and the company should certainly consider the inclusion of critical illness cover to cater for this situation.

SECTION 3 POLICIES FOR CHILDREN

A School fees

17.31 The cost of privately educating children needs, at the very least, careful financial consideration, and ideally, careful financial planning. School fees have increased enormously over the last few years and, at the time of writing, inflation is running in excess of Government targets. The cost of funding higher education has also risen in real terms, and the student loan scheme is now an important feature of the higher education regime.

Parents or other relatives can make advance provision for the payment of private school fees and the earlier any scheme is started the better the results will be. Provision can be made out of income, by investment of a capital sum, by borrowing (as a last resort) or a combination of these. The choice of provision is invariably determined by practical personal considerations, but consideration should be given to the following:

(1) the number of children for whom funding is required;

(2) the extent of the child's education which it is desired to fund privately;

(3) the imminence of the requirement to pay school fees;

(4) the likely cost of the fees;

(5) the likely extent and cost of sundry and miscellaneous expenses, eg uniforms, books, sports equipment, school trips;

(6) the available funds, of an income and capital nature with which it will be possible to pay the school fees, or to plan for them at as early a stage as possible;

(7) who may be providing the funds;

(8) whether the choice of school may change;

(9) the most tax-efficient method of providing the funding.

When deciding on the most appropriate type of investment vehicle, consideration should be afforded to the following:

(1) the safety of the investment, both in terms of the investment strategy (ie risk averse or not) and any available minimum guarantees;

(2) the flexibility of the investment, including the penalties for terminating the plan or changing the school attended;

(3) the relevant tax positions.

Provision for school fees can be made by individuals utilising banks, building societies, national savings certificates, or any other investment vehicle. The following discussion considers some of the mainly life assurance related options, and their taxation consequences.

1 Endowment assurance

17.32 One method of funding fees from income would be to consider endowment assurance policies (with-profit or unit-linked) for terms of at least ten years. The proceeds from such policies can be taken tax free after ten years, or, if sooner, three-quarters of the policy term, and are therefore suitable plans in situations where the fees are required at some time in the future. One option would be to invest in a series of endowment assurances, the maturity dates of which are designed to coincide with the dates at which fees will need to be paid.

Endowment assurances will provide a sum assured in the event of the premature death of the life assured, and so there is certainty that funds will be available for the payment of fees.

2 Child Trust Funds

17.33 Child Trust Funds (CTFs) have been available since April 2005 for eligible children – broadly any child who was born after 31 August 2002 and for whom child benefit is payable or the child is in care.

Initially the Government contributed a £250 voucher for each child or £500 for a child in care which could only be invested in CTF accounts in the beneficial ownership of the child. Slightly increased amounts were payable initially for children born between 1 September 2002 and 5 April 2005 to compensate for the fact that the funds for such children had a lesser time to grow before they reached age 18.

The Government made a further payment of £250 when the child attained age seven and additionally, the initial payment and the age seven payment were increased by a further £250 if the child was part of a family whose household income level was below a certain threshold.

However, on 24 May 2010 the Government announced that they would cease funding the CTF and that all children born after 2 January 2011 would not be eligible for such an account. Accounts already in force could, of course, remain.

Annual contributions can be made to CTFs by family, friends and any other persons up to an annual limit of £1,200. No withdrawals can be made until the child is aged 18 at which point he or she becomes entitled to the full value of the Fund.

CTF accounts can only be provided by approved providers and the permitted investments are similar to those for Individual Savings Accounts (ISAs) ie bank and building society deposits and stocks and shares. When a CTF matures, it will be possible to roll the maturity value over into an ISA.

3 Individual Savings Accounts (ISAs)

17.34 In a non-life insurance context, the use of Individual Savings Accounts (ISAs) as a tax efficient investment vehicle has been possible since 6 April 1999. Under current legislation, there is no liability to income tax or CGT on investments within an ISA although where ISA investments are held in shares, dividend tax credits cannot be reclaimed since 5 April 2004. The proceeds from an ISA are tax free and they may be effected on a lump sum or a regular saving basis. The maximum contribution in any tax year is £10,680 so husband and wife could invest up to £21,360 per tax year. The annual investment may be split into two components: a cash component (bank and building society accounts and designated national savings products), and a stocks and shares component. Not more than £5,340 can be invested in cash. The whole amount may be invested in stocks and shares if the saver wishes.

4 Junior ISAs

17.35 On 26 October 2010, the Government announced that it would introduce a new tax advantaged account for saving for children to be known as a Junior ISA. Junior ISAs are expected to be available in the autumn of 2011 and, at the time of writing, draft regulations have been issued for consultation.

The intention is that the Junior ISA will be available to UK resident children aged under 18 who do not have an existing Child Trust Fund. A Junior ISA will retain many of the features of a standard ISA in that investments can be in either cash or stocks and shares. The maximum annual investment that can be made will be £3,000 but this could be all into cash, all stocks and shares or any combination of the two. The account can be opened by the parent or guardian of the child or the child in a personal capacity if he or she is aged 16 or over.

Any person may contribute into the Junior ISA on the child's behalf and, if the contribution comes from a parent, the parental settlement rules which normally seek to access the parent to tax once the income generated exceeds £100, will not apply.

Just as with the CTF, children will not be able to access the Junior ISA until they attain age 18.

5 Single premium bonds

17.36 It is often the case that grandparents, for example, wish to invest money for the benefit of their grandchildren. A popular choice of investment is the single premium bond, with a desire to have the grandchildren as the lives assured. In this scenario, there is no automatic and very rarely any insurable interest as between the grandparents and the grandchildren. Some life offices will contract on this basis if the bond is effected in absolute trust for the grandchild whose life is assured. This is in order to ensure that the 'mischief' which the insurable interest provision in the Life Assurance Act 1774 was designed to prevent is not possible, ie that whatever occurs, the entire beneficial interest in the policy will lie with the life assured.

Historically, HMRC practice, where a gain arose in respect of a chargeable event on a life assurance policy (eg on a partial surrender in excess of the 5% per annum tax-deferred entitlements, or on full surrender) held under a bare trust for a minor beneficiary, was to assess the gains to income tax based on the income of the settlor of the trust, where the settlor was alive and resident in the UK. Where the settlor was not alive, or not resident in the UK, gains were assessed on the trustees if they were UK resident.

This practice was at odds with the treatment of other income arising under a bare trust, where the income belongs to, and is taxed on, the beneficiary, even if the beneficiary is a minor.

HMRC took legal advice to clarify the position for gains arising from life assurance policies and the advice suggested that the long-standing HMRC practice was incorrect. Their revised view, as announced in their Brief 51/2008, is that '…regardless of the need for trustees to perform active duties on behalf of beneficiaries who are minors, those minors with an absolute entitlement to the trust income and capital have unimpaired beneficial ownership of life insurance policies held under a bare trust. In line with the general treatment of trust income for such beneficiaries, they are the persons liable to income tax on gains arising on the insurance policies held in trust on their behalf.'

It is, however, important to recognise that HMRC's revised view does not extend to those cases where the so-called 'parental settlement' provisions of section 629 of the Income Tax (Trading & Other Income) Act 2005 will apply.

Broadly, this means that where the settlor is the parent of the beneficiary, who is a minor and who is unmarried and not in a civil partnership, and where the chargeable event gains exceed £100 in the tax year, all such gains (ie not just the excess over £100) that arise during the settlor's lifetime will be taxed on the parental settlor.

However, where a grandparent or other relative is the settlor of the bare trust, the change will provide the scope for a minor beneficiary's personal income tax allowance to be utilised by chargeable event gains that can arise when full or partial surrenders take place. This change may therefore create an opportunity for effective school fees planning by a grandparent for a grandchild based on a life assurance investment bond (particularly an offshore bond) used in conjunction with a bare trust.

Another approach that is becoming increasingly popular is for parents or grandparents to utilise offshore bonds in planning for university fees. The settlors effect the policies in trust for the benefit of the children/grandchildren and then the policies are assigned to the beneficiaries to assist with university funding as and when they attain the age of 18. Any gains under the policies can thus be set off against the personal allowances and starting rate bands of the beneficiaries.

6 Other possibilities

17.37 These could include unit trust or investment trust savings schemes under which a tax efficient 'income' may be taken each year by making encashments of units or shares within the annual exemption for CGT purposes. Furthermore, there will be some individuals with existing Personal Equity Plans (PEPs) or Tax Exempt Special Savings Accounts (TESSAs) and these investments can still be used as a tax efficient way of funding school fees. National Savings products such as Children's Bonus Bonds could also be considered.

7 Deferred annuities

17.38 A parent may purchase a deferred annuity, to commence when the fees are required. It is also possible to purchase a deferred annuity with regular premiums, paid until the end of the child's school life. At the time of writing, it should be noted that the rates offered on deferred annuities are not thought to be particularly attractive and thus this method of funding might not be so appropriate.

(a) Income tax

17.39 For tax purposes, such annuities are treated as part capital and part income and are actuarially apportioned at inception[1]. The capital element is exempt from income tax, whilst the income element will normally be subject to deduction of the basic rate of income tax (20% for the tax year 2011/12) at source.

(b) IHT

17.40 If the annuity ends on the death of the purchaser, there will be no IHT liability. If there is a guaranteed element, or a return of capital upon death, its value will form part of the deceased's estate for IHT purposes.

8 Borrowing

17.41 As a last resort, parents may have to borrow to fund the school fees. Life assurance policies may play a part in this method, for example, by a loan back facility on the surrender value of a policy or as collateral security under a property-based scheme. A loan on a policy should mean that the life office continues to receive the regular premiums and interest payments on the loan, actuarial calculations are not upset and the policyholder need not surrender his contract[2]. If the policyholder dies, the loan is repaid from the proceeds of the policy, thus, in many cases, providing a surplus which will normally be paid to the

1 ITTOIA 2005, ss717-723.
2 But see ITTOIA 2005, s 501 and Chapter 13.

policyholder's estate (which will therefore be potentially liable to IHT), and which will be available to fund school fees.

B Children's policies

1 Contractual capacity and insurable interest

17.42 The contractual capacity of children was discussed in Chapter 1. Essentially, under English law, life assurance contracts with minors are likely to be treated as voidable, whilst under Scottish law, although contractual capacity applies from the age of 16, in some circumstances, contracts may be repudiated up to the age of 18. Because of the difficulties of contractual capacity and the general lack of need for children to have life cover, the volume of 'children's policies' has never been significant.

A further consideration is that of insurable interest. In England, there is no automatic insurable interest between parent and child (unlike Scotland) thus parents cannot effect a contract on the lives of their children and vice versa, unless insurable interest can be established in some other way.

2 *Taxation of children*

17.43 For tax purposes, children are not treated any differently to adults.

3 *Parental settlements*

17.44 Section 629 of ITTOIA 2005 contains an exception to the general rule that a child's income is taxed on the child. It provides that where any income from a parental settlement, subject to a de minimis provision of £100 per year, is paid to or for the benefit of a minor and unmarried child, of the settlor, during the life of the settlor it will be treated for income tax purposes, as the income of the settlor parent for the particular tax year.

Prior to 9 March 1999, this anti-avoidance provision could be avoided by the use of an irrevocable bare trust, in which the income was not distributed. Thus, so long as any income arising was not applied for the benefit of the child, it was treated as the child's income, and not that of the parents. It was, however, necessary to take care as if any accumulated income was applied for the benefit of a child of the settlor, it too was treated as the income of the settlor for income tax purposes[1]. The effect of this provision could not be avoided by making distributions out of capital. If such a distribution was made at a time when there was accumulated income within the trust, the amount of the distribution, to the extent that there was accumulated income, was taxed as income of the settlor[2].

From 9 March 1999, such trust arrangements ceased to be effective, and all income arising is now taxed as that of the parent, subject to the £100 limit. This

1 ITTOIA 2005, ss 629 and 631.
2 See *Postlethwaite v IRC* (1963) 41 TC 224.

change does not apply to trusts in force as at 9 March 1999 unless the trust fund is added subsequent to that date.

In this sense, a life assurance policy may be an ideal investment, as it is non-income producing, so there is no income upon which the settlor may be taxed.

4 *Child's policy*

17.45 Irrespective of the difficulties occasioned by the general position in relation to contractual capacity of children, some life offices, Friendly Societies and Industrial Provident Societies are in a position where, due to a specific Act of Parliament, they are able to issue policies on the life of a child and obtain a valid legal discharge from the child. Some other life offices have devised a policy which has many different product names but which, for convenience, may be described as a child's policy.

These are designed to provide either a cash sum for the child at, say, age 18, 21 or 25 or, alternatively, to enable the child, on the attainment of the selected age, to effect a whole life or endowment assurance on his or her own life at a low rate of premium, irrespective of the state of health, residence or occupation of the child at that time.

The policy will normally be a regular premium endowment assurance (on a with-profit or unit-linked basis) effected by the parent on his or her own life for the selected term and put in trust for the child.

5 *Friendly Societies*

17.46 Most friendly societies offer a scheme whereby a lump sum can be used to purchase a 'baby bond', which will usually cover investment for a period of at least ten years through a guaranteed income bond, a temporary annuity or insurance bond. The bond can only be taken out for someone under 18 and there are maximum limits of contributions to such policies, which are currently £25 per month or £270 per annum. The advantage of Friendly Society investments is that their investments accumulate tax free.

SECTION 4 LONG-TERM CARE

17.47 With an aging population, care of the elderly is becoming an increasingly important issue. It is outside the scope of this book to go into great detail regarding legislative provision for those in need of health care, but a brief overview is given below together with details of possible insurance-based methods of assisting with the problem.

A The State and long term care

17.48 The National Health Service (NHS) has responsibility to pay all the costs of a person's care when they meet the 'eligibility criteria' for Continuing

Care. These criteria have to comply with the NHS national guidance, although, in practice, there are wide differences throughout the country in their interpretation. Eligibility for fully-funded continuing care will be determined by factors such as whether or not the patient's condition has stabilised and how complex their needs are. Reference is also made to whether the patient has a primary need for nursing care in which case the NHS pays or whether their primary need is for personal (or social care) in which case the patient has to pay.

The boundaries between these distinctions are grey and subjective yet they carry an enormous financial consequence.

If the patient meets the criteria then this is all paid for by the NHS. If not, then the most that can be hoped for by way of contribution is a payment under the rules governing Free Nursing Care. Here too, the amount received will depend upon an assessment of the 'nursing' needs of the person concerned as set out below:

The Registered Nursing Care Contribution (RNCC), paid by the Primary Care Trust (PCT), is determined by a nursing assessment of which around 130,000 a year are carried out. Until October 2007, in England, this nursing care payment ranged between £40, £87 and £139 a week, depending upon the level of nursing need. PCTs had discretion to pay a rate between the low and medium band, based on need. Since October 2007, a new single rate has applied (except for existing claimants). This single rate for 2011/12 is £108.70, although those still on the old 'higher rate' now get £149.60 a week. Around 123,000 people in England currently receive the benefit.

Different payment levels apply in Northern Ireland, Wales and in Scotland. In the case of Scotland, for 2011/12 up to £159 a week is paid by the individual's local council towards personal care and an additional £72 a week for nursing care. In Wales, the local health boards can set their own limits, but, as a guide, in 2010/11 they agreed a flat rate of £120.55 a week. In Northern Ireland the individual's local health and social care trust will pay up to £100 a week.

Financial help is also available in the form of a non-means-tested Attendance Allowance, paid by the DWP. However, this Attendance Allowance and the care component of Disability Living Allowance are not payable to Scottish care home residents in receipt of the Personal Care Allowance.

I Local-authority-funded care

17.49 Local authorities have a statutory obligation under section 47 of the National Health and Community Care Act 1990 (which took effect from 1 April 1993) to both assess a person's care needs and then to go on to meet those needs. However, they are also required under the National Assistance Act 1948 to require the applicant for care to contribute to the cost of that care if they have over a certain level of assets.

The provision is slightly different between the four countries that make up the UK. An individual's income is always taken into account. In England and Northern Ireland, a sliding scale applies where the individual's assets are (for 2011/12) between £14,250 and £23,250. Broadly speaking, between these figures, for each £250 of assets above £14,250, individuals have to pay another

£1 a week themselves (in effect, capital is assumed to produce a nominal or 'tariff' income).

Example

Mrs Smith has assets valued at £20,000. She has income of £165 per week net of tax.

Her care fees are £390 per week. Her tariff income will be £23 per week (£20,000 – £14,250 = £5,750 divided by £250 = £23).

Her total assessable income is therefore £165 + £23 = £188 less Personal Expenses Allowance of £22.60 = £165.40.

The Local Authority contribution for care costs will therefore be £390 – £165.40 = £224.60.

Assets for these purposes may include the individual's home, if they own it, unless they are receiving care at home or a partner or spouse or a dependent relative is living there – see separate section on the private residence. In any case, the value of the home is ignored for the first 12 weeks of needing care. Care home residents are also entitled to keep £22.60 a week as a Personal Expenses Allowance (in England, Northern Ireland and Scotland) and £23.00 a week in Wales. The capital disregard figure is updated from time to time.

In Scotland, the lower and upper limits for 2011/12 are £14,500 and £23,500 and in Wales there is just one limit of £22,500.

In all these situations, where the value of an individual's assets is less than the lower means-tested limit, income less the relevant Personal Expense Allowance will be assessed and topped up to the local authority fee scale. All the above figures are subject to periodic, generally annual, review.

2 Care at home

17.50 If the individual has been assessed as needing care in his or her own home, the means-testing guidelines are broadly similar to those mentioned above. Clearly the value of his or her house will be disregarded but all other assets will be included. Therefore in England if he or she have a house and more than £23,250 in other assets, he or she will be assessed as a 'self funder' paying his or her own care costs. If he or she has less than the house and the threshold, then the local authority will contribute. His or her income will be assessed to calculate their ability to contribute but the Local Authority must leave them with at least the basic amount of Pension Credit + 25%.

3 Pension credit

For individuals aged 60 or over, Pension Credit may be payable. This is in addition to Attendance Allowance and has two elements. *Guarantee Credit* ensures a minimum weekly income and is means-tested. *Savings Credit* is payable to individuals aged 65 or over who have a 'private income' on top of their state pension and is also means-tested. However, Pension Credit does count toward income in the local authority assessment for someone requiring care in a care home and is therefore unlikely to improve the overall funding situation of somebody supported by the local authority.

C Assessment of applicant's resources

17.51 Local authorities must use National Guidance in making these assessments. These are contained in the Charging for Residential Accommodation Guide (CRAG) the most recent version of which was published in April 2011.

1 Income

17.52 The income taken fully into account includes:

(1) Most Social Security benefits.

(2) Pension income

(3) Trust Income.

(4) Income from letting (or subletting part of a property which is not part of the living accommodation).

(5) Attendance Allowance.

Some income is fully disregarded and this includes Council Tax benefit.

Some income may be partly disregarded, eg 50% of an occupational or personal pension if the partner or spouse relies on that income to continue living at home.

2 Capital

17.53 The capital test includes potentially taking into account the value of the home (see below). Other items include buildings, land, building society and bank accounts, cash, stocks and shares, National Savings Certificates. (This list is not exhaustive).

Items that are disregarded include surrender value of any life insurance policy.

For some time there was discussion as to whether the definition of life assurance for the purpose of the local authority means test included an investment bond. Indeed, some local authorities had sought to take investment bonds into account as assessable assets despite the fact that, strictly speaking, most investment bonds (other than capital redemption policies) are policies of life assurance.

The CRAG makes it clear that such practice is not acceptable and has always been an unlawful practice. Any capital assessments which took account of such assets should be brought to the attention of the relevant local authority with a view to obtaining a refund of homecare fees incorrectly paid as a result.

It is useful to specifically quote some of the statements from CRAG on this point.

Paragraph 6.003 of CRAG states:

> 'The treatment of investment bonds in the financial assessment for residential accommodation is complex because, in part, of the differing products that are on offer. For this reason councils should seek the advice of their legal departments when they arise. However it is possible to offer some general advice and councils are referred to the Social Security Commissioners decision R (IS) 7/98 which rules that an investment bond falls within the disregard by virtue of its intrinsic nature as a policy of life assurane.'

Paragraph 6.004 of CRAG states:

> 'Councils are advised that if an investment bond is written as one or more life insurance policies that contain cashing-in rights by way of options for total or partial surrender, then the value of those rights has to be disregarded as a capital asset in the financial assessment for residential accommodation… In contrast, the surrender value of an investment bond without life assurance is taken into account.'

Paragraph 6.005 of CRAG states:

> 'Income from investment bonds, with or without life assurance, is taken into account in the financial assessment for residential accommodation. Actual payments of capital by periodic instalments from investment bonds, with or without life insurance, are treated as income and taken into account provided that such payments are outstanding on the first day that the resident becomes liable to pay for his accommodation and the aggregate of the outstanding instalment, and any other capital sum not disregarded, exceed £16,000.'

With regard to the treatment of withdrawals from investment bonds the position is clear cut.

Paragraph 8.016 of CRAG states:

> 'Income from investment bonds, with or without life assurance, is taken into account in the financial assessment for residential accommodation.'

17.54 Of course, the 'deliberate deprivation' rules as set out at **17.56** also need to be taken into account when considering the use of investment bonds. In addition to the surrender value of life assurance policies, the following are also disregarded:

(1) Payments in kind from charities.

(2) Social funds payments.

(3) Reversionary interests.

Further to this, some assets are disregarded for 26 weeks or longer, eg capital received from the sale of the former home where the capital is to be used by the resident to buy another home.

A resident may be treated as possessing a capital asset even where he does not actually possess it. The test is whether or not the capital would be available to him if he applied for it.

Married couples will be assessed individually. The value of jointly held assets will be divided equally amongst all the owners irrespective of how much each has individually contributed. The jointly held assets of married couples will be halved to determine the value of each one's share.

If, however, the assets of a married couple are held in the name of one of the parties alone, the full value of this asset will be attributed to that party in determining their liability to contribute to any long-term care costs. (The Guidelines do not take into account the other spouse's potential inheritance claims, nor indeed the possibility of the assets being shared if the parties divorce.)

3 The family home

17.55 The local authority will disregard the value of an applicant's home if he goes into care and his partner is still living in the property. Certain other situations may also cause the value of the property to be disregarded. These include where:

(1) A dependent child of the resident aged under eighteen is resident in the property.

(2) A relative is living in the property who is either:

  (a) elderly (defined as 60 years or over); or

  (b) incapacitated (defined as being eligible to claim one of the range of social security disability related benefits).

Note, since 9 April 2001, the value of the applicant's home will be disregarded for 12 weeks from the date that the applicant enters a residential setting for care. This means that if, but for the value of the home, the applicant would have been eligible for local authority funding, then the local authority will contribute towards the cost of their care during this period.

D Deliberate deprivation

17.56 Local authorities are empowered to take effective action against residents who *deliberately* attempt to avoid paying charges. The burden of proof in these cases is on the local authority who have to establish that the motivation of the donor was to diminish their assets in order to preclude payment due to the local authority.

Local authorities only have to prove that deliberate deprivation was a significant motive for the transfer of assets, not the only motive.

The CRAG does not specify what constitutes deliberate deprivation, however, it does indicate policy.

A guideline which is frequently used is that it would not be reasonable for a local authority to infer that the motivation for the passing of a lifetime gift was deliberate deprivation if 'the gift was made at a time and in circumstances in which the donor was in good health and did not anticipate care'.

Various decisions in the courts have emphasised that there is no time limit which constrains the right of local authorities to 'look back' at disposals of assets in terms of the donor's motivation. This is a very difficult area and practice varies from authority to authority which can make any planning process very problematic.

Generally speaking, it is accepted that when planned well ahead, there is nothing wrong with conversion of non-disregarded assets, such as cash/shares, into a disregarded form such as a non-qualifying life policy. This, of course, must always be subject to the personal circumstances and any investment objectives of the individual concerned. The emphasis must also be on the words 'planning' and 'well ahead', as a last minute avoidance measure, such as transferring assets into a life assurance bond shortly before making an application for assistance, is likely to be caught by the provisions dealing with deliberate deprivation. This is also specifically dealt with by CRAG.

Paragraph 6.067 of CRAG states that a deprivation of capital may occur if:

> 'capital has been used to purchase an investment bond with life insurance. Councils will wish to give consideration, in respect of each case, to whether deprivation of assets has occurred, ie did the individual place his capital in such an investment bond so that it would be disregarded for the purpose of the Assessment of Resources Regulations.'

It is important that in considering whether deprivation has occurred, the most important aspect is the motive or the intention of the investor. It may therefore be all the more important that good financial planning reasons are given for investment bond purchases and recorded in suitability letters.

E Use of insurance products in the long-term care market

17.57 There are basically two options when considering the use of insurance products in conjunction with long-term care planning, pre-funded plans and immediate needs annuities.

1 Pre-funded plans

17.58 Claims under these plans are based upon failing a specific number of activities of daily living, which are generally, washing, dressing, feeding, continence, mobility and transferring. Payment can also be triggered by mental impairment such as Alzheimer's disease or dementia. These plans pay out whether the care is delivered in a care home or in the client's own home. Advance funding will help the client to overcome the problem of potentially needing long-term care at some stage in the future.

The 'traditional' LTCI plan is a pure insurance contract with underwriting at outset, a premium guaranteed for five or ten years, an unlimited benefit period, but a maximum annual benefit (eg £30,000 a year). Payments are tax-free and can be made to a care provider direct or to the policyholder or their legal representative. Policies do not have surrender values and premiums can rise on review after any guaranteed period if, for example, the claims experience of the insurer is poor. Policies may include escalation options and waiver of premium. Most policies have exclusions such as alcohol and drug abuse, self-inflicted injuries and HIV/AIDS.

These contracts have never proved popular with the public and, at the time of writing, it is understood that there are no providers currently offering contracts of this type.

2 Immediate needs annuities

17.59 This product is designed to make regular monthly payments for an individual's care for the rest of their life in return for a single premium. In order to take a policy out the care recipient needs to be failing an activity of daily living or suffering a cognitive impairment and will typically be in receipt of formal care either at home or in a care home. The payments can be made totally free of tax providing they are paid directly to a registered care provider, whether that be a care home or care agency. Some companies offer the option to have the benefits paid directly to the policyholder, although in these circumstances the payments will be taxed at source in the same way as a purchase life annuity and could give rise to further taxation for higher rate taxpayers. However, any tax liability is, of course, based only on the interest element of the payments and not on that part which is considered to be a return of capital. The life expectancies involved with these cases are generally short so the payments tend to include only a small amount of interest.

Another option that is available is the ability to have the payments increase by an amount of indexation each year – either RPI or a fixed amount. A more important option for many is the option to protect a proportion of the premium against early death. None of the provider companies offer 100% protection although, obviously, a stand-alone whole of life policy could be effected. The availability of this option may be limited or the cost of it may be prohibitive bearing in mind the age and state of health of the client.

SECTION 5 MISCELLANEOUS

A Family income benefit policies

17.60 Policies called family income benefit policies or something similar usually provide on death within a specified period (normally 20 years commencing at the issue of the policy) fixed monthly or quarterly sums payable until the expiry of that period.

The policy is basically a temporary decreasing assurance payable by instalments. The instalments, although termed income, are in the nature of capital, and, under long-standing HMRC practice, are not subject to income tax.

It would be normal to write such a policy subject to trust in order to prevent the benefits forming part of the deceased's estate on his or her death.

B Home income plans

17.61 Home income plans became very popular in the mid to late 1980s. In a situation where, invariably elderly persons, owned a property in which they had considerable equity, and wanted more income, they could effect a Home Income Plan to provide them with income, and enable them to retain their home. A reversion scheme was offered, although this was not very popular, as it involved selling the reversionary interest in the property. The more popular scheme was a mortgage scheme. Under this scheme, the property was mortgaged on an interest-only basis and an annuity or a single premium bond was purchased to repay the interest and to provide 'income' for the mortgagors. The capital would be repaid on subsequent sale of the property, usually on the death of the homeowner.

The taxation treatment of purchased life annuities and single premium bonds have been discussed elsewhere[1].

From 9 March 1999 interest relief on loans to purchase life annuities has no longer been available. However, borrowers with existing qualifying loans at that date will continue to benefit up to a £30,000 limit for the remaining period of the loan. Furthermore, existing Home Income Plan owners will be able to remortgage or move home without losing the relief. Despite the lack of availability of relief on the loan, it appears that there is still a demand for this type of product and that lenders are still prepared to lend on this basis.

C Structured settlements

17.62 Structured settlements have an unusual tax history because they existed for some time before the introduction of any rules dealing with their tax treatment. There was a substantial delay between the implementation of the first structured settlement in the late 1980s (*Kelly and another v Dawes* Times Law Reports 27 September 1990) and the introduction of legislation in the Finance Act 1995.

Following the recommendations of the Law Commission on the tax treatment of structured settlements, the taxation of structured settlements was considerably simplified in 1995 and 1996. However, it may be relevant, by way of background, to outline the previous tax treatment, particularly as it had a considerable bearing on the development of structures in the UK.

In a structured settlement three parties would be involved: the general (liability) insurer, the life office and the plaintiff (the injured party). As far as the general insurer was concerned, the insurer would normally treat the premium for the annuity as reinsurance of the liability to make the payments and such

1 See Chapter 13.

treatment would be approved by the ABI and DTI for regulatory purposes (model agreements having been agreed by the ABI with HMRC). The reinsurance premium would be a trading expense for tax purposes. Although the general insurer would have been liable to tax on the receipt of the annuity, it would also be able to deduct an amount equal to the cost of the instalment payment and therefore the two payments would be tax neutral. The general insurer therefore suffered no tax costs.

17.63 As far as the life office underwriting the annuity was concerned, an argument would generally be put forward that since the payment was not pure income profit in the hands of the payee (general insurer) then there was no need for the life office to deduct tax on paying the annuity to the general insurer. Even where it was argued that the annuity should have been paid net, the general insurer could reclaim the tax at the end of the financial year, although this clearly would have created a cash flow problem for the general insurer. Also it would only allow for a tax reclaim where the general insurer had a tax liability in the first place. As far as the payment to the plaintiff was concerned, although strictly any payment should have been made from the life assurer to the defendant's insurers and then to the plaintiff, in order to reduce administration the general insurer would normally arrange for the life office to act as his paying agent although a problem could arise where the general insurer and the life assurer were both separate departments of the same company on the basis that it is impossible for a person to contract with himself. In short, the administration of structured settlements provided a considerable burden on both insurance companies.

The payments received by the plaintiff were not subject to tax on the basis they were capital payments.

In 1995 the government acted to remove tax on annuities received for injury damages. The Finance Act 1995 inserted additional section 329A in the Taxes Act 1988 headed 'Annuities purchased for certain persons'. This was replaced by sections 329AA 'Personal injury damages in the form of periodical payments' and 329AB 'Compensation for personal injury under statutory or other schemes' ICTA 1988 (now incorporated into sections 731–734 of ITTIOA 2005) which provide that in a case where an agreement is made settling a claim or action for damages for personal injury and on agreement the damages are to consist wholly or partly of periodical payments and the person entitled to the payments is to receive them as the annuitant under one or more annuities purchased for him by the person against whom the claim was brought, or that person's insurer, such agreement would be a qualifying agreement and where payments are made under such a qualifying agreement then they will not be treated as the annuitant's income for any purposes of income tax and will be paid without deduction of tax.

17.64 In 1996 the scope of the exemption was widened to include damages in the form of regular payments awarded by the court (now section 731 of ITTIOA 2005). While the 1995 changes allowed for damages in the form of an annuity payable to the victim to be exempted from tax if the annuity was purchased by the person responsible for the injury or that person's insurers, where a personal injury claim was settled by an agreement there was a need to extend the same treatment to situations in which a third party may step in to discharge the damages, for instance the Motor Insurers' Bureau in the case of a claim against an uninsured driver. The Damages Act 1996 affirms the power of a court to award, by way of consent order, damages for personal injury not as a lump sum but as regular amounts over the life of the victim of the injury. Such payments will also be exempt from tax. The exemptions also apply where the damages are handled by trustees which will be necessary in some cases of injury or a child plaintiff (the trustees holding absolutely for the plaintiff during his lifetime).

Where an annuity continues after the death of the injured party the HMRC make it clear that 'the exemption from tax is personal to the victim of the injury and does not continue beyond his death. An annuity purchased as part of a structured settlement will often be payable for a guaranteed period even if the victim should die prematurely. Payments made after the death of the victim are chargeable to tax in the normal way and can be expected to represent a purchased life annuity with an exempt capital element'.

It should also be noted that the Criminal Injuries Compensation Act 1995 similarly provided that a structured settlement of compensation payable by the Criminal Injuries Compensation Board should receive the same taxation treatment, ie such payments are also exempt from tax.

Initially, however, the conversion of a lump sum award into a Structured Settlement depended upon the agreement of both parties to the legal action and the court had no power to impose this form of award. Interest in structured settlements remained relatively low and the market for writing such annuities contracted.

Eventually the Government decided that the way forward was to allow the courts greater influence and sections 100 and 101 of the Courts Act 2003 introduced some important changes such as:

(1) Enabling the court to impose a periodical payments order in cases involving future loss.

(2) Precluding the court from ordering periodical payments unless it is satisfied that the payments are 'reasonably secure'.

(3) Enabling the court to order variable periodical payments which could be tailored much more closely to the claimant's actual requirements.

(4) Transferring the burden of funding periodical payments from the claimant to the defendant, that is to say that the claimant no longer had to buy an annuity, the defendant became responsible for funding the periodical payments, although however it chose to do this, the arrangement had to ensure that the payments were 'reasonably secure'.

In conclusion, at present all periodic payments made in respect of personal injuries are exempt from tax.

APPENDIX 1

Life Assurance Act 1774

(14 Geo 3 c 48)

An Act for regulating Insurances upon Lives, and for prohibiting all such insurances, except in cases where the persons insuring shall have an interest in the life or death of the persons insured

WHEREAS it hath been found by experience, that the making insurances on lives or other events wherein the assured shall have no interest, hath introduced a mischievous kind of gaming:

1. No insurance to be made on lives, etc, by persons having no interest. From and after the passing of this Act no insurance shall be made by any person or persons, bodies politick or corporate, on the life or lives of any person or persons, or on any other event or events whatsoever, wherein the person or persons for whose use, benefit, or on whose account such policy or policies shall be made, shall have no interest, or by way of gaming or wagering; and that every assurance made contrary to the true intent and meaning hereof shall be null and void to all intents and purpose whatsoever.

2. No policies on lives without inserting the names of persons interested etc. And . . . it shall not be lawful to make any policy or policies on the life or lives of any person or persons, or other event or events, without inserting in such policy or policies the person or persons name or names interested therein, or for whose use, benefit, or on whose account such policy is so made or underwrote.

3. How much may be recovered where the insured hath interest in lives. And . . . in all cases where the insured hath interest in such life or lives, event or events, no greater sum shall be recovered or received from the insurer or insurers than the amount or value of the interest of the insured in such life or lives, or other event or events.

4. Not to extend to insurances on ships, goods etc. Provided, always, that nothing herein contained shall extend or be construed to extend to insurances bona fide made by any person or persons, on ships, goods, or merchandises; but every such insurance shall be as valid and effectual in the law as if this Act had not been made.

NOTE

Words omitted in sections 2 and 3 were repealed by the Statute Law Revision Act 1888.

APPENDIX 2

The Policies of Assurance Act 1867

(30 & 31 Vict c 144)

An Act to enable Assignees of Policies of Life Assurance to sue thereon in their own names, 20th August 1867.

1. Assignees of life policies empowered to sue. Any person or corporation now being or hereafter becoming entitled, by assignment or other derivative title, to a policy of life assurance, and possessing at the time of action brought the right in equity to receive and the right to give an effectual discharge to the assurance company liable under such policy for monies thereby assured or secured, shall be at liberty to sue at law in the name of such person or corporation to recover such monies.

2. Defence or reply on equitable grounds. In any action on a policy of life assurance, a defence on equitable grounds, or a reply to such defence on similar grounds, may be respectively pleaded and relied upon in the same manner and to the same extent as in any other personal action.

3. Notice of assignment. No assignment made after the passing of this Act of a policy of life assurance shall confer on the assignee therein named, his executors, administrators, or assigns, any right to sue for the amount of such policy, or the monies assured or secured thereby, until a written notice of the date and purport of such assignment shall have been given to the assurance company liable under such policy at their principal place of business, then at some one of such principal places of business, either in England or Scotland or Ireland, and the date on which such notice shall be received shall regulate the priority of all claims under any assignment; and a payment bona fide made in respect of any policy by any assurance company before the date on which such notice shall have been received shall be as valid against the assignee giving such notice as if this Act had not been passed.

4. Principal place of business to be specified on policies. Every assurance company shall, on every policy issued by them after the thirtieth day of September, one thousand eight hundred and sixty-seven, specify their principal place or principal places of business at which notices of assignment may be given in pursuance of this Act.

5. Mode of assignment. Any such assignment may be made either by endorsement on the policy or by a separate Instrument in the words or to the effect set forth in the schedule hereto, such endorsement or separate Instrument being duly stamped.

6. Receipt of notice of assignment. Every assurance company to whom notice shall have been duly given of the assignment of any policy under which they are liable shall, upon the request in writing of any person by whom any such notice was given or signed, or of his executors or administrators, and upon payment in each case of a fee not exceeding [25p] deliver an acknowledgment in writing, under the hand of the manager, secretary, treasurer, or other principal officer of the assurance company of their receipt of such notice; and every such written acknowledgment, if signed by a person being de jure or de facto the manager, secretary, treasurer, or other principal officer of the assurance company whose acknowledgment the same purports to be, shall be conclusive evidence as against such assurance company of their having duly received the notice to which such acknowledgment relates.

7. Interpretation. In the construction and for the purposes of this Act the expression 'policy of life assurance,' or 'policy' shall mean any instrument by which the payment of monies, by or out of the funds of an assurance company, on the happening of any contingency depending on the duration of human life, is assured or secured; and the expression 'assurance company' shall mean and include every corporation, association, society, or company now or hereafter carrying on the business of assuring lives or survivorships, either alone or in conjunction with any other object or objects.

8. Saving of Contracts under 16 & 17 Vict c 45 or 27 & 28 Vict c 43, and of engagement by friendly societies. Provided always, That this Act shall not apply to any policy of assurance granted or to be granted or to any contract for a payment on death entered into or to be entered into in pursuance of the provisions of the Government Annuities Act 1853 and the Government Annuities Act 1864, or either of those Acts, or to any engagement for Payment on Death by any Friendly Society.

NOTE

Government Annuities Act 1853; Government Annuities Act 1864. These Acts were repealed with savings by the Government Annuities Act 1929, s 66, Sch 2, Pt II. See now Part II of that Act.

9. Short title. For all Purposes this Act may be cited as 'The Policies of Assurance Act 1867'.

Schedule

I *A.B.* of, *&c.*, in consideration of, *&c.*, do hereby assign unto *C.D.* of, *&c.*, his Executors, Administrators, and Assigns, the [within] Policy of Assurance granted, *&c.*, [*here describe the Policy*]. In witness, *&c.*

APPENDIX 3

(Bold sections move to ICOB 7.3.6 from 2005 with some small amendments to the wording. The rest of the Statement remains ABI guidance)

Association of British Insurers – statement of long-term insurance practice[1]

The following Statement of normal insurance practice applies to policies of long-term insurance effected in the UK in a private capacity by individuals resident in the UK. Nothing in this statement should be interpreted as conflicting with or overriding the rules of LAUTRO in respect of long-term insurance policies which are treated as investments for the purposes of the Financial Services Act 1986.

1. Proposal forms

(a) If the proposal form calls for the disclosure of material facts a statement should be included in the declaration, or prominently displayed elsewhere on the form or in the document of which it forms part:

(i) drawing attention to the consequences of failure to disclose all material facts and explaining that these are facts that an insurer would regard as likely to influence the assessment and acceptance of a proposal;

(ii) warning that if the signatory is in any doubt about whether certain facts are material, these facts should be disclosed.

(b) Neither the proposal nor the policy shall contain any provision converting the statements as to past or present fact in the proposal form into warranties except where the warranty relates to a statement of fact concerning the life to be assured under a life of another policy. Insurers, may, however, require specific warranties about matters which are material to the risk.

1 Much of the statement was superseded by FSA regulations in 2005. To all intents and purposes, however, it does continue to apply, as certain aspects are not covered by regulation. It also applies to any policies bought before 2005 which are still live today. The bold sections are the sections that have been taken over by regulation. For further information please contact the ABI 020 7600 3333 or visit www.abi.org.uk

(c) Those matters which insurers have commonly found to be material should be the subject to clear questions in proposal forms.

(d) Insurers should avoid asking questions which would require knowledge beyond that which the signatory could reasonably be expected to possess.

(e) The proposal form or a supporting document should include a statement that a copy of the policy form or of the policy conditions is available on request.

2. Policies and accompanying documents

(a) Insurers will continue to develop clearer and more explicit proposal forms and policy documents whilst bearing in mind the legal nature of insurance contracts.

(b) Life assurance policies or accompanying documents should indicate:

   (i) the circumstances in which interest would accrue after the assurance has matured; and

   (ii) whether or not there are rights to surrender values in the contract and, if so, what those rights are.

(Note: The appropriate sales literature should endeavour to impress on proposers that a whole life or endowment assurance is intended to be a longterm contract and that surrender values, especially in the early years, are frequently less than the total premiums paid.)

3. Claims

(a) An insurer will not unreasonably reject a claim. In particular, an insurer will not reject a claim or invalidate a policy on grounds of nondisclosure or misrepresentation of a fact unless:

   (i) it is a material fact; and

   (ii) it is a fact within the knowledge of the proposer; and

   (iii) it is a fact which the proposer could reasonably be expected to disclose.

   (It should be noted that fraud or deception will, and reckless or negligent nondisclosure or misrepresentation of a material fact may, constitute grounds for rejection of a claim.)

(b) Except where fraud is involved, an insurer will not reject a claim or invalidate a policy on grounds of a breach of warranty unless the circumstances of the claim are connected with the breach and unless:

   (i) the warranty relates to a statement of fact concerning the life to be assured under a life of another policy and that statement would have constituted grounds for rejection of a claim by the insurer under 3(a) above if it had been made by the life to be assured under an own life policy; or

(ii) **the warranty was created in relation to specific matters material to the risk and it was drawn to the proposer's attention at or before the making of the contract.**

(c) Under any conditions regarding a time limit for notification of a claim, the claimant will not be asked to do more than report a claim and subsequent developments as soon as reasonably possible.

(d) Payment of claims will be made without avoidable delay once the insured event has been proved and the entitlement of the claimant to receive payment has been established.

(e) When the payment of a claim is delayed more than two months, the insurer will pay interest on the cash sum due, or make an equivalent adjustment to the sum, unless the amount of such interest would be trivial. The two month period will run from the date of the happening of the insured event (ie death or maturity) or, in the case of a unit linked policy, from the date on which the unit linking ceased, if later. Interest will be calculated at a relevant market rate from the end of the two month period until the actual date of payment.

4. Disputes

The provisions of the Statement shall be taken into account in arbitration and any other referral procedures which may apply in the event of disputes between policyholders and insurers relating to matters dealt with in the Statement.

5. Commencement

Any changes to insurance documents will be made as and when they need to be reprinted, but the Statement will apply in the meantime.

Note Regarding Industrial Assurance Policyholders

Policies effected by industrial assurance policyholders are included amongst the policies to which the above Statement of Long-Term Insurance Practice applies. Those policyholders also enjoy the additional protection conferred upon them by the Industrial Assurance Acts 1923 to 1969 and Regulations issued thereunder. These Acts give the Industrial Assurance Commissioner wide powers to cover inter alia the following aspects:

(a) Completion of proposal forms.

(b) Issue and maintenance of Premium Receipt Books.

(c) Notification in Premium Receipt Books of certain statutory rights of a policyholder including rights to:

(i) an arrears notice before forfeiture;

(ii) free policies and surrender values for certain categories of policies;

(iii) relief from forfeiture of benefit under a policy on health grounds unless the proposer has made an untrue statement of knowledge and belief as to the assured's health;

(iv) reference to the Commissioner as arbitrator in disputes between the policyholder and the company or society.

The offices transacting industrial assurance business have further agreed that any premium (or deposit) paid on completion of the proposal form will be returned to the proposer if, on issue, the policy document is rejected by him or her.

APPENDIX 4

Specimen 'Power of Appointment' or 'Flexible' or Discretionary Trust (without an interest in possession for Inheritance Tax purposes)

NOTE: This document is provided as a specimen for the consideration of the parties and their legal advisers. Whilst every care has been taken in the preparation of this document, no responsibility can be accepted for the legal and/or taxation consequences of its use. The parties must consider their own personal circumstances in this respect.

TRUST DETAILS (Please use Block Capitals)

Section A – Settlor

Full Name of first settlor	Full name of second settlor *(if any)*

Section B – Policy

New Policies Date of Proposal	/ /20	**Existing Policies** Policy Number	
Type of Policy		Date of policy	/ /20

Life/lives assured (1) .... (2) ....

Section C – Intended Beneficiaries

Full names *(this box must not be left blank)*	Share
	100%

Section D – Potential Beneficiaries

Any of the following persons:

(i) any child or descendant of the Settlor whenever born

(ii) any spouse/Civil Partner or former spouse/Civil Partner of the Settlor (except where such person is also a Settlor)

(iii) any spouse/Civil Partner or former spouse/Civil Partner of any child or descendant of the Settlor whenever born

(iv) any person or charity (other than the Settlor) nominated in writing by the Settlor to the Trustees to be a Potential Beneficiary

(v) any person (other than the Settlor) who has an interest in the estate of the Settlor by will or codicil, under the intestacy rules, by right of survivorship or otherwise

(vi) any Intended Beneficiary

(vii) any of the following named persons

PROVIDED ALWAYS THAT THE SETTLOR MAY NOT BE A BENEFICIARY IN ANY CAPACITY WHATSOEVER

Section E – Additional Trustees

Full name of first Additional Trustee	
First Additional Trustee's address	
Full name of second Additional Trustee	
Second Additional Trustee's address	
Full name of third Additional Trustee	
Third Additional Trustee's address	

THIS TRUST is made on 20 **BETWEEN** the Settlor and the Trustees

NOW THIS DEED WITNESSES as follows:

1 IN this Trust the following definitions apply:

Expression	Meaning
'Accumulation Period'	The trust period
'Additional Trustees'	The persons mentioned in Section E
'Beneficiary'	Any Potential Beneficiary or any Intended Beneficiary but not the Settlor
'Civil Partner'	A person who is a registered civil partner in accordance with the Civil Partnership Act 2004
'Intended Beneficiaries'	The persons mentioned in Section C
'Policy'	The policy or policies mentioned in Section B
'Potential Beneficiaries'	The persons mentioned in Section D
'Settlor'	The person mentioned in Section A or where there are two settlors then 'Settlor' shall where appropriate mean either or both of them
'Trust Fund'	The Policy and all property representing it and any income thereof

'Trust Period'	The period of 125 years beginning with the date of this Trust or such longer period as allowed under statutory provisions applying to England and Wales at any time whilst this Deed is in existence
'Trustees'	The Settlor and the Additional Trustees or the trustees for the time being

2 (1) In the case of a new Policy the Settlor

(a) appoints the Additional Trustees to act with him as trustees of this Trust

(b) directs that the Policy shall be issued to the Trustees to be held by them on the terms of this Trust and declares that he holds all rights and obligations under the Policy on behalf of the Trustees

or

(2) In the case of an existing Policy the Settlor

(a) assigns the Policy to the Trustees

(b) directs the Trustees to hold the Policy on the terms of this Trust and

3 (1) (a) THE Trustees shall hold the Trust Fund for such of the Potential Beneficiaries on such terms and in such shares and for such interests (including creating any further trusts) as they may by deed or deeds revocable or irrevocable appoint in writing at any time or times during the Trust Period

(b) No exercise of this power of appointment shall invalidate any prior payment or application of all or any part of the Trust Fund

(2) Subject to any appointment the Trustees may accumulate the whole or part of the Trust income during the Accumulation Period. That income shall be added to the Trust Fund. The Trustees shall but only whilst the said power of appointment subsists apply the remainder of the income to or for the benefit of such one or more of any persons named or specified in Section D above in such shares (or wholly to one) as the Trustees may in their absolute discretion think fit.

4 THE Trustees shall have the following further powers:

(1) A Trustee who is or may be a Beneficiary may exercise the power of appointment under the Trust for his own benefit provided he is not a sole Trustee.

(2) The Trustees may deal with the Policy as if they were beneficial owners.

(3) The Trustees may

(a) apply or invest the Trust Fund as if they were the absolute beneficial owners whether or not such application or investment produces income

(b) vary such applications or investment

(c) effect any life policy

(d) make loans with or without security and/or with or without interest.

(e) borrow with or without the security of the Policy or other trust assets.

5 Any trustee (other than the Settlor) being a solicitor or other person engaged in any profession or business shall be entitled to charge and be paid all normal professional or other charges for business done and all time spent by him or his firm or company in the execution or exercise of the trusts and powers whether in the ordinary course of his profession or business or not and although not of a nature requiring the employment of a solicitor or other professional person.

6 (1) The Settlor (or where the Settlor is more than one person the settlors jointly or the survivor of them) shall have the power to appoint trustees and may by deed remove or replace Trustees.

(2) UPON the death of the Settlor the power of appointing a new or additional Trustee shall vest in the trustees.

(3) The Trustees may remove or replace a Trustee who cannot be found provided that:

(a) Reasonable efforts have been made to find the Trustee being removed; and

(b) The removal is made by deed executed by all the other Trustees.

(4) In relation to any persons dealing in good faith with the Settlor or Trustees or any other persons claiming through them a deed removing a trustee will be conclusive evidence that the trustee was properly removed.

7 No power conferred on the Trustees shall be exercised and no provisions of this Trust shall operate so as to allow any part of the Trust Fund to become in any way payable to or applicable for the benefit of the Settlor.

8 (1) The receipt of any parent or guardian of any minor Beneficiary shall be sufficient discharge to the Trustees for any moneys payable to such Beneficiary.

(2) If the company liable to pay the benefits from any policy does so in accordance with the instructions of those appearing to it to be the Trustees this will (in the absence of actual fraud of the company) be a full discharge for the company. The Trustees not the company are responsible for passing benefits on to beneficiaries.

9 Notwithstanding the trusts declared by this Trust and the provisions of the Policy the power to exercise any option in the Policy rests solely with the Settlor unless the exercise of the Option gives rise to payment of any benefit in part or in full under the Policy when the agreement of all Trustees is also required to exercise the Option.

10 This Trust is governed by English Law.

IN WITNESS WHEREOF the parties hereto have executed this Deed the day and year first before written

SIGNED and **DELIVERED** as a Deed by the said

Print name of Settlor	
Signature of Settlor	

IN THE PRESENCE OF:

Full name of Witness	
Signature of Witness	
Address and occupation of Witness	

SIGNED and **DELIVERED** as a Deed by the said

Print name of second Settlor/ Additional Trustee	
Signature of second settlor/ Additional Trustee*	

* delete as appropriate

IN THE PRESENCE OF:

Full name of Witness	
Signature of Witness	
Address and occupation of Witness	

SIGNED and **DELIVERED** as a Deed by the said

Print name of Additional Trustee	
Signature of Additional Trustee	

IN THE PRESENCE OF:

Full name of Witness	
Signature of Witness	
Address and occupation of Witness	

SIGNED and **DELIVERED** as a Deed by the said

Print name of Additional Trustee	
Signature of Additional Trustee	

IN THE PRESENCE OF:

Full name of Witness	
Signature of Witness	
Address and occupation of Witness	

APPENDIX 5

Statutory Declaration

Type of policy:

Policy Number:

Insurance Company:

Grantee:

(hereinafter called 'the Policy')

I the undersigned of

do solemnly and sincerely declare:

1. That I am legally entitled to the Policy and to the moneys assured thereby, and to give an effectual discharge for the same by virtue of [having myself effected the Policy . . .].
2. That the Policy was to the best of my knowledge and belief last in my possession in . . . 19 . . .; that it has since been lost, mislaid or destroyed; and that I have made diligent search for it but without success.
3. That the Policy has not, to the best of my knowledge and belief been pledged, assigned or otherwise parted with for value or otherwise to any person or persons whomsoever who has or could have any right, title or claim thereto as against or paramount to my title and I have not received notice of and am not aware of any such claim.

And I make this solemn declaration conscientiously believing the same to be true and by virtue of the provisions of the Statutory Declarations Act 1835.

Declared this day

of..at

before me

A Commissioner for Oaths

APPENDIX 6

Specimen Deed of Indemnity

THIS DEED OF INDEMNITY is made the day of 20

in relation to a policy of assurance, details of which are set out in the Schedule hereto

(hereinafter called **'the Policy'**)

BY

(hereinafter called the **'Policyholder'**)

WHEREAS

(i) The original policy documents relating to the Policy have been lost or destroyed.

(ii) No dealings have taken place with the Policy by way of assignment, charge or deposit. Nor has any other form of encumbrance or Interest in the Policy been created by me to my knowledge.

THIS DEED HEREBY WITNESSETH

In consideration of [the Company] agreeing to issue a duplicate policy document(s) for the Policy, the Policyholder undertakes [jointly and severally]* to indemnify [the Company] and any of its officers against any and all losses, claims, demands (and any expense thereof) which may be made by or against [the Company] or its officers in consequence whether directly or indirectly, of [the Company] agreeing to issue the said documents including but not limited to anything arising from or in connection with payment being made under the Policy without the production of the said original policy documents or any interest created thereunder.

Schedule

Type of Policy:

Policy Number:

Insurance Company:

Grantee:

SIGNED AND DELIVERED as a Deed by ....

in the presence of: ....

NAME: ....

ADDRESS: ....

....

OCCUPATION: ....

SIGNED: ....

APPENDIX 7

Payment into Court by Life Assurance Company (Ord 92, r 1)

1.(1) A company wishing to make a payment into court under the Life Assurance Companies (Payment into Court) Act 1896 (hereinafter referred to as 'the Act of 1896') must file an affidavit, made by its secretary or other authorised officer, setting out:

(a) a short description of the policy in question and a statement of the persons entitled thereunder with their names and addresses so far as known to the company,

(b) a short statement of the notices received by the company claiming an interest in or title to the money assured, or withdrawing any such claim, with the dates of receipt thereof and the names and addresses of the persons by whom they were given,

(c) a statement that, in the opinion of the board of directors of the company, no sufficient discharge can be obtained otherwise than by payment into court under the Act of 1896,

(d) the submission by the company to pay into court such further sum, if any, as the Court may direct and to pay any costs ordered by the Court to be paid by the company,

(e) an undertaking by the company forthwith to send to the Accountant General any notice of claim received by the company after the making of the affidavit with a letter referring to the title of the affidavit, and

(f) an address where the company may be served with any summons or order, or notice of any proceeding, relating to the money paid into court.

(2) The company shall not deduct from the money payable by them under the policy any costs of or incidental to the payment into court.

(3) No payment shall be made into court under the Act of 1896 where any action to which the company is a party is pending in relation to the policy or moneys thereby assured except with the leave of the Court to be obtained by summons in the action.

(4) Unless the Court otherwise directs, a summons by which a claim with respect to money paid into court under the Act of 1896 is made shall not, except where the summons includes an application for payment of a further sum of costs by the company who made the payment, be served on that company, but it must be served on every person who appears by the affidavit on which the payment into court was made to be entitled to, or interested in, the money in court or to have a claim upon it or who has given a notice of claim which has been sent to the Accountant General in accordance with the undertaking referred to in rule 1(1)*(e)*.

APPENDIX 8

Deed of Assignment

THIS DEED OF ASSIGNMENT is made the day of 20

BETWEEN

(1)

(2)

(hereinafter called the Assignor(s)) of the one part and

(hereinafter called the Assignee(s)) of the other part

WITNESSES as follows:—

The Assignors as Settlors hereby give and assign to the Assignee(s) ALL THAT Policy of Assurance with

on the life/lives of

effected on

numbered

and all moneys assured by or to become payable under the said Policy and the full benefit thereof

TO HOLD unto the Assignee(s) absolutely

It is hereby certified that this instrument falls within Category L in the Schedule to the Stamp Duty (Exempt Instruments) Regulations 1987

IN WITNESS whereof the parties hereto have hereunto set their hands the date first above written

APPENDIX 9

Notice of Assignment

To: [the Company]

I hereby give you notice that by a deed dated 20 and made between [A of] (hereinafter called 'the Assignor') of the one part and [B of] (hereinafter called 'the Assignee') of the other part, the Assignor assigned unto the Assignee all that policy issued by your company on the life of numbered and dated 20 and all sums assured or thereby payable or to become payable thereunder.

And I request you to deliver to me a written acknowledgement of the receipt of this notice.

Dated 20 Signed

Acknowledgement by Company

The [Company] hereby acknowledges the receipt of the notice of which this is a photocopy/the notice dated

Signed (for and on behalf of the Company)

NOTE

It is desirable for the Company to add a memorandum that in acknowledging the receipt of the notice, it is in no way admitting the title of the assignee, and that production of the original document will be required before payment is made.

APPENDIX 10

Draft 'Double Option' Agreement

DRAFT: FOR APPROVAL OF LEGAL ADVISERS

'DOUBLE OPTION' AGREEMENT

N.B. THIS DOCUMENT SHOULD NOT BE SIGNED. IT IS A SUGGESTED VERSION ONLY. YOUR LEGAL ADVISER SHOULD BE CONSULTED.

THIS AGREEMENT is made the day of 20

BETWEEN

(1) (Director)/(Partner)

(2) (Director)/(Partner)

(3) (Director)/(Partner)

etc.

WHEREAS:—

1. The parties hereto are shareholders and directors/partners in the Company/Firm known as (Name of Company)(Name of Partnership)

2. The parties hereto desire that 7 days after the death of any party hereto his personal representatives shall have the option to sell and the surviving parties hereto shall have the option to purchase the deceased party's shares on the terms hereinafter appearing

WHEREBY IT IS AGREED as follows:—

1. In consideration of the provisions of Clause 2 hereof 7 days after the death of any party hereto the surviving parties shall have the option to purchase the deceased's shares interest in the said Company/Firm from the deceased's personal representatives such option to be exercised by notice in writing served within three months from the date upon which a grant of representation is issued and on the exercise of such option the deceased's personal representatives shall sell the shares to the survivors on the terms hereinafter appearing

2. In consideration of the provisions of Clause 1 hereof 7 days after the death of any party hereto the deceased's personal representatives shall have the option to sell the deceased's shares interest in the said Company/Firm to the surviving parties such option to be exercised by notice in writing served within six months from the date upon which a grant of representation is issued and on the exercise of such option the surviving parties shall purchase the shares from the deceased's personal representatives on the terms hereinafter appearing

3. The price shall be such price as may be determined as the fair value thereof by the Company's/Firm's Auditor in accordance with the Company's Articles of Association/Firm's Partnership Agreement

4. If either option is exercised then the surviving parties hereto shall purchase the deceased's shares interest in the following proportions: equally/rateably according to their existing shareholdings

5. This Agreement shall:

   (a) bind the personal representatives of all the parties hereto

   (b) cease to bind any party hereto when he shall have ceased to be a shareholder of more than (nominal amount:) shares

   (c) cease to have effect on the winding up/dissolution of the Company/Firm

   (d) take effect only in compliance with and subject to the Articles of Association of the Company/Partnership Agreement of the Firm which shall take precedence over the terms hereof should there be any conflict between the two

AS WITNESS etc.

Index

[all references are to paragraph number]

S